THE RENAISSANCE WORLD

The Routledge Worlds

THE GREEK WORLD
Edited by Anton Powell

THE ROMAN WORLD
Edited by John Wacher

THE BIBLICAL WORLD
Edited by John Barton

THE EARLY CHRISTIAN WORLD
Edited by Philip F. Esler

THE CELTIC WORLD
Edited by Miranda Green

THE MEDIEVAL WORLD
Edited by Peter Linehan and Janet L. Nelson

THE REFORMATION WORLD
Edited by Andrew Pettegree

THE ENLIGHTENMENT WORLD
Edited by Martin Fitzpatrick, Peter Jones,
Christa Knellwolf and Iain McCalman

THE RENAISSANCE WORLD
Edited by John Jeffries Martin

THE HINDU WORLD
Edited by Sushil Mittal and Gene Thursby

THE WORLD OF POMPEII
Edited by Pedar Foss and John J. Dobbins

THE EGYPTIAN WORLD
Edited by Toby Wilkinson

THE BABYLONIAN WORLD
Edited by Gwendolyn Leick

Forthcoming:

THE VIKING WORLD
Edited by Stefan Brink and Neil Price

THE ELIZABETHAN WORLD
Edited by Susan Doran and Norman Jones

THE BYZANTINE WORLD
Edited by Paul Stephenson

THE RENAISSANCE WORLD

Edited by
John Jeffries Martin

Routledge
Taylor & Francis Group
NEW YORK AND LONDON

First published 2007
by Routledge
711 Third Avenue, New York, NY 10017, USA

Simultaneously published in the UK
by Routledge
2 Park Square, Milton Park, Abingdon, Oxon OX14 4RN

Routledge is an imprint of the Taylor & Francis Group, an informa business

© 2007 Selection and editorial matter, John Jeffries Martin;
individual chapters, the contributors

Typeset in Garamond by
Keystroke, 28 High Street, Tettenhall, Wolverhampton

All rights reserved. No part of this book may be reprinted or reproduced
or utilised in any form or by any electronic, mechanical, or other means,
now known or hereafter invented, including photocopying and recording,
or in any information storage or retrieval system, without permission
in writing from the publishers.

British Library Cataloguing in Publication Data
A catalogue record for this book is available from the British Library

Library of Congress Cataloging in Publication Data
The Renaissance world / edited by John Jeffries Martin.
p. cm. — (The Routledge worlds)
Includes bibliographical references and index.
1. Renaissance. 2. Europe—Civilization. 3. Europe—History—476–1492.
4. Europe—History—1492–1648. I. Martin, John Jeffries, 1951–
CB361.R476 2007
940.2′1—dc22
2006039061

ISBN10: 0–415–33259–1
ISBN13: 978–0–415–33259–0
ISBN13: 978-0-415-45511-4 (pbk)

CONTENTS

List of illustrations	ix
List of contributors	xiii
Acknowledgements	xix
Credits for illustrations	xxi

INTRODUCTION

The Renaissance: a world in motion *John Jeffries Martin*	3

I THREE PRELUDES

1 Rome at the center of a civilization *Ingrid Rowland*	31
2 Framing and mirroring the world *Lyle Massey*	51
3 The Black Death, tragedy, and transformation *Samuel K. Cohn, Jr.*	69

II A WORLD IN MOTION

4 The manufacture and movement of goods *Joanne M. Ferraro*	87
5 Cities, towns, and new forms of culture *Alexander Cowan*	101
6 European expansion and the new order of knowledge *Francisco Bethencourt*	118

— *Contents* —

7   The invention of Europe   140
    John A. Marino

8   José de Acosta: Renaissance historiography and New World humanity   166
    Anthony Grafton

III   THE MOVEMENT OF IDEAS

9   The circulation of knowledge   191
    Peter Burke

10   Virgil and Homer in Poland   208
    Michael Tworek

11   Montaigne in Italy   225
    François Rigolot

12   "Shared studies foster friendship": humanism and history in Spain   242
    Katherine Elliot van Liere

13   Niccolò Machiavelli and Thomas More: parallel lives   262
    David Harris Sacks

IV   THE CIRCULATION OF POWER

14   Courts, art, and power   287
    Malcolm Vale

15   The imperial Renaissance   307
    Thomas James Dandelet

16   Renaissance triumphalism in art   326
    Randolph Starn

17   The Ottoman Empire   347
    Daniel Goffman

18   Religious authority and ecclesiastical governance   364
    Constantin Fasolt

19   Mothers and children   381
    Caroline Castiglione

20   The Renaissance goes up in smoke   398
    Robert C. Davis

– Contents –

V MAKING IDENTITIES

21	Human exceptionalism *Kenneth Gouwens*	415
22	Worthy of faith? Authors and readers in early modernity *Albert Russell Ascoli*	435
23	The Renaissance portrait: from resemblance to representation *Bronwen Wilson*	452
24	Objects and identity: Antonio de' Medici and the Casino at San Marco in Florence *Jacqueline Marie Musacchio*	481
25	Food: Pietro Aretino and the art of conspicuous consumption *Douglas Biow*	501
26	Shakespeare's dream of retirement *David Bevington*	517

VI BELIEFS AND REFORMS

27	Speaking books, moving images *Meredith J. Gill*	535
28	Religious minorities *N. S. Davidson*	555
29	Humanism and the dream of Christian unity *Susan R. Boettcher*	572
30	Christian reform and its discontents *Brad S. Gregory*	589
31	A tale of two tribunals *David Gentilcore*	605
32	Christianity in sixteenth-century Brazil *Alida C. Metcalf*	621
33	Toward a sacramental poetics *Regina Mara Schwartz*	637

VII A NEW ORDER OF KNOWLEDGE

34 The sun at the center of the world　　655
    Paula Findlen

Index　　678

ILLUSTRATIONS

I.1	Carpaccio, *The Leavetaking of the Betrothed Pair*, 1498	4
I.2	Carpaccio, *Arrival in Cologne*, 1490	9
I.3	Carpaccio, *Departure of the Ambassadors* (detail), c. 1500	12
I.4	Carpaccio, *Departure of the Ambassadors*, c. 1500	15
I.5	Renaissance Europe	16
I.6	Carpaccio, *Martyrdom of the Pilgrims and the Funeral of Saint Ursula* (detail), 1493	17
I.7	Carpaccio, *Arrival of the English Ambassadors* (detail), 1498	18
I.8	Carpaccio, *Apotheosis of Saint Ursula*, 1491	25
1.1	Antonio Filarete, bronze doors, St Peter's Basilica	34
1.2	Bernardo Rossellino, cathedral, Pienza	37
1.3	Melozzo da Forlì, fresco in Vatican Library	40
1.4	Pinturicchio, fresco, Borgia apartments	41
1.5	Perugino, *Giving of the Keys to St Peter*	42
1.6	Raphael, *The School of Athens*	46
2.1	Albrecht Dürer, *Draughtsmen with Lute*, 1525	53
2.2	Albrecht Dürer, *Melencholia I*, 1514	60
2.3	Hans Holbein the Younger, *The Ambassadors*, 1533	62
3.1	The Black Death in Europe, 1347–52	71
6.1	Domingos Teixeira, *Planisphere*, 1573	121
6.2	Luis Teixeira, *The Atlantic Chart*, c. 1600	125
7.1	The Four Continents, *Roma triumphans*	142
7.2	Ptolemaic map of the world	146
7.3	Martin Waldseemüller, *Universalis cosmographia*	148
7.4	Martin Waldseemüller, *Carta Itineraria Europae*	149
7.5	Abraham Ortelius, *Europae* in *Theatrum Orbis Terrarum*	151
7.6	*Europa Virgo Crowned*, Johann Putsch, 1537	152
7.7	*Het Spaens Europa*, anonymous Flemish print, 1598	153
7.8	Michael Eitzinger, *De Europae virginis, tauro insidentis*	156
9.1	Map of Europe, showing centers of humanist activity	201
10.1	Jan Kochanowski, first page of the *Treny*, 1580	215
12.1	Portrait of Ambrosio de Morales	243

— *Illustrations* —

12.2	Portrait of Antonio Agustín	245
13.1	Hans Holbein the Younger, *Sir Thomas More*, 1527	266
13.2	Ridolfo del Ghirlandaio, *Portrait of Machiavelli*	267
14.1	Map of Burgundy in the late Middle Ages	289
14.2	Albrecht Dürer, *Kaiser Maximilian I*, 1519	292
14.3	*Reichenau Gospels*, c. 997–1000, Emperor Otto III enthroned	294
14.4	Rogier van der Weyden (attributed), *Philip the Good of Burgundy and his Court*, 1448	295
14.5	Portrait panels of the counts and countesses of Flanders, 1480.	297
14.6	Philip the Good, tomb of Emperor Maximilian I, begun 1502	300
14.7	Charles the Bold, tomb of Emperor Maximilian I	301
14.8	Rogier van der Weyden, *Portrait of Francesco d'Este of Ferrara*, c. 1460	302
15.1	Egnazio Danti, map of "Nuova Spagna," 1564	313
15.2	Map of Europe in the age of Charles V	314
15.3	Andrea Mantegna, *Triumph of Caesar*	317
16.1	Albrecht Dürer, *Great Triumphal Chariot* (detail), 1518–22	329
16.2	Raphael, *Pope Julius II*, 1511–12	332
16.3	Piero della Francesca, *Battle of Heraclius*, c. 1454–65	334
16.4	Urs Graf, *Battlescene*, 1521	335
16.5	Michelangelo, *David*, 1501–4	337
16.6	Raphael's workshop, *Donation of Constantine*, 1523–4	339
17.1	Nicolay, portrayal of a Greek resident of Galatea	354
19.1	Artemesia Gentileschi, *Madonna Feeding the Christ Child*, 1610–11	388
21.1	"Integrae naturae speculum" from Robert Fludd, *Utriusque cosmi historia*, 1617	425
21.2	Carpaccio, *Return of the Ambassadors* (detail), 1490–4	426
21.3	Niccolò Boldrini, parody of *The Laocoön*	427
21.4	Albert Clouet, "Imitatio Sapiens," 1672	428
23.1	Agostino Carracci, *Portrait of Giovanni Gabrielli*	453
23.2	Jan Van Eyck, *Leal Sovvenir*, 1432	456
23.3	Death mask of Lorenzo de' Medici	458
23.4	*Portrait of Matthias Schwarz*, 1526	461
23.5	Albrecht Dürer, *Portrait of Hieronymus Holzschuher*, 1526	464
23.6	Albrecht Dürer, *Self-portrait*, c. 1491	465
23.7	Pietro Bertelli, *Portrait of Mahometto II*, 1599	469
23.8	Giovanni Battista Moroni, *Portrait of a Lady*, c. 1555–60	472
23.9	Carracci, *Portrait of a Blind Woman*, c. 1490	473
24.1	Workshop of Alessandro Allori, *Portrait of Bianco Cappello and Antonio de' Medici*, c. 1587	493
25.1	Titian, *Portrait of Pietro Aretino*, 1545	513
27.1	Carpaccio, *St Augustine in His Study*, 1502–8	536
27.2	Augustine, *De civitate Dei*, Cesena, Biblioteca Malatestiana, 1450	539
27.3	Detail of *arca* of St Augustine (front), 1350s	540
27.4	Guariento di Arpo, *Conversion of Augustine*, c. 1350s	541

27.5	Ottaviano Nelli, *Augustine Receiving Instruction from Simplicianus and His Conversion*, c. 1420s	542
27.6	Benozzo Gozzoli, *Conversion of St Augustine* ("Tolle, lege"), mid-1460s	543
29.1	Hans Holbein the Younger, *Erasmus*, 1523	573
32.1	The martyrdom of Pedro Correia and João de Sousa, 1554	622
34.1	Copernicus, heliocentric universe, *De revolutionibus orbium coelestium*, 1543	656
34.2	G. B. Riccioli, "Weighing of the systems", 1651	667
34.3	Galileo, *Dialogo sopra i due massimi sistemi del mondo*, 1632	672

CONTRIBUTORS

Albert Russell Ascoli is the Gladys Arata Terrill Distinguished Professor in the Department of Italian Studies at the University of California, Berkeley. He is the author of *Ariosto's Bitter Harmony: Crisis and Evasion in the Italian Renaissance* (1987) and of a forthcoming volume entitled *Dante and the Making of a Modern Author*. He is now working on a book on faith and fidelity, credit and credibility, in the Renaissance.

Francisco Bethencourt is the Charles Boxer Professor at King's College, London. He has served as director of the National Library of Portugal (1996–8) and of the Gulbenkian Foundation Cultural Centre in Paris (1999–2004). He is the author of *L'Inquisition à l'époque moderne. Espagne, Portugal et Italie, XVe–XIXe siècles* (Paris, 1995) and co-editor of *História da Expansão Portuguesa*, 5 vols (1998–9). He is currently working on the history of racism in the Atlantic world.

David Bevington is the Phyllis Fay Horton Distinguished Service Professor in the Humanities at the University of Chicago, where he has taught since 1967. His studies include *From "Mankind" to Marlowe* (1962), *Tudor Drama and Politics* (1968), and *Action is Eloquence: Shakespeare's Language of Gesture* (1985). He is also the editor of *The Complete Works of Shakespeare* (2003), as well as of the *Oxford 1 Henry IV* (1987), the *Cambridge Antony and Cleopatra* (1990), and the *Arden 3 Troilus and Cressida* (1998). His latest books, intended for general readers, are *Shakespeare*, 2nd edition (2005), and *This Wide and Universal Theater: Shakespeare in Performance Then and Now* (2007).

Douglas Biow is Professor of Italian and Comparative Literature at the University of Texas at Austin, and the author of three books, *Mirabile Dictu: Representations of the Marvelous in Medieval and Renaissance Epic* (1996), *Doctors, Ambassadors, Secretaries: Humanism and Professions in Renaissance Italy* (2002), and *The Culture of Cleanliness in Renaissance Italy* (2006). Currently the recipient of a Guggenheim Fellowship, he is working on a book on anti-conformist authors and artists in sixteenth-century Italy.

Susan R. Boettcher is Assistant Professor of History at the University of Texas at Austin. She is the author of several articles on the contemporary historiography of the Reformation, as well as on Lutheran preaching and historical conceptions in later sixteenth-century Germany. She is completing a book on the memory and commemoration of Martin Luther after his death until the Book of Concord.

Peter Burke recently retired from his chair in cultural history at Cambridge but remains a Fellow of Emmanuel College. His 23 books include *The Italian Renaissance* (1972) and *The European Renaissance* (1998).

Caroline Castiglione, Assistant Professor of Italian Studies and History at Brown University, is the author of *Patrons and Adversaries: Nobles and Villagers in Italian Politics, 1640–1760* (2005).

Samuel K. Cohn, Jr., Professor of Medieval History, University of Glasgow, is the author, most recently, of *The Black Death Transformed: Disease and Culture in Early Renaissance Europe* (2002), *Popular Protest in Late Medieval Europe: Italy, France, and Flanders* (2004), and *Lust for Liberty: The Politics of Social Rebellion in Late Medieval Europe* (2006).

Alexander Cowan is Reader in History at Northumbria University. He is the author of *The Urban Patriciate: Lubeck and Venice 1580–1700* (1986) and *Urban Europe 1500–1700* (1998), and the editor of *Mediterranean Urban Culture 1400–1700* (2000) and co-editor of *The City and the Senses: European Urban Culture from 1500* (2006).

Thomas James Dandelet is Associate Professor at the University of California, Berkeley. He specializes in the history of the early modern Mediterranean world with a focus on the relationship between Renaissance and Baroque Italy and the Spanish Empire. He is the author of *Spanish Rome, 1500–1700* (2001), and the co-editor with John Marino of *Spain in Italy: Politics, Society, and Religion, 1500–1700* (2007). His present research is leading to a new book on the Colonna family of Rome in the sixteenth and seventeenth centuries.

N. S. Davidson, Lecturer in the History of the Renaissance and Reformation at the University of Oxford, has published widely on the social, cultural, and religious history of Renaissance and early modern Italy.

Robert C. Davis, Professor of History at Ohio State University, has written on shipbuilders, pugilists, bullfighters, slaves, the police, wine drinking, tourists, Jews, and gender relations in early modern and present-day Venice. His current research focuses on baroque Lazio and Umbria.

Constantin Fasolt, Professor of History at the University of Chicago, is the author of *Council and Hierarchy: The Political Thought of William Durant the Younger* (1991) and *The Limits of History* (2004). He is also General Editor of *New Perspectives on the Past*, published by Blackwell, Oxford.

Joanne M. Ferraro, Professor and Chair of the History Department at San Diego State University, is the author of *Family and Public Life in Brescia, 1580–1650: The Foundations of Power in the Venetian State* (1993) and *Marriage Wars in Late Renaissance Venice* (2001).

Paula Findlen is Ubaldo Pierotti Professor of Italian History at Stanford University.

– *Contributors* –

She is the author of *Possessing Nature: Museums, Collecting, and Scientific Culture in Early Modern Italy* (1994) and the editor of several volumes on science and culture in the early modern period, including *Athanasius Kircher: The Last Man Who Knew Everything* (2004). Forthcoming books include *A Fragmentary Past: The Making of Museums in Late Renaissance Italy* and *In the Shadow of Newton: Laura Bassi and Her World*.

David Gentilcore teaches early modern history and the history of medicine at the University of Leicester. His most recent book is *Medical Charlatanism in Early Modern Italy* (2006). His current project explores the reception and eventual assimilation of New World plants in early modern and modern Italy.

Meredith J. Gill is Associate Professor of Italian Renaissance Art at the University of Maryland, College Park. Most recently, she is the author of *Augustine in the Italian Renaissance: Art and Philosophy from Petrarch to Michelangelo* (2005). She also contributed the chapter on artistic life in the fourteenth and fifteenth centuries to *Rome: Artistic Centers of the Italian Renaissance*, ed. Marcia B. Hall (2005).

Daniel Goffman is Professor and Chair of History at Depaul University. His many publications include *Izmir and the Levantine World, 1550–1650* (1990), *Britons in the Ottoman Empire, 1642–1660* (1998), and *The Ottoman Empire and Early Modern Europe* (2002).

Kenneth Gouwens teaches History at the University of Connecticut. His research interests include Italian Humanism, 1494–1534; the pontificate of Clement VII (Giulio de' Medici); and comparisons drawn between humans and simians, both in the Renaissance and in our own era.

Anthony Grafton teaches the history of Renaissance Europe at Princeton. His books include *Joseph Scaliger* (1983) and *Defenders of the Text* (1991).

Brad S. Gregory is Associate Professor of History at the University of Notre Dame, where he specializes in the history of Christianity in late medieval and early modern Europe. He is the author of *Salvation at Stake: Christian Martyrdom in Early Modern Europe* (1999) and is the editor of *The Forgotten Writings of the Mennonite Martyrs* (2002).

John A. Marino, University of California, San Diego, is the author of *Pastoral Economics in the Kingdom of Naples* (1988) and the editor or co-editor of *Good Government in Spanish Naples* (1990), *Early Modern History and the Social Sciences: Testing the Limits of Braudel's Mediterranean* (2002), *Early Modern Italy 1550–1796* (2002), *A Renaissance of Conflicts: Visions and Revisions of Law and Society in Italy and Spain* (2004), and *Spain in Italy: Politics, Society, and Religion, 1500–1700* (2007).

John Jeffries Martin is Professor and Chair in the Department of History at Trinity University. His books include *Venice's Hidden Enemies: Italian Heretics in a Renaissance City* (1993), *Myths of Renaissance Individualism* (2004), and, forthcoming, *The Making of Europe: The Early Modern Experience*.

Lyle Massey is Assistant Professor of Art History at McGill University, Montreal.

Her work explores the intersection of art and science in the Renaissance. She has published on various aspects of linear and anamorphic perspective and on anatomical illustrations and gender. She is the author of *Picturing Space, Displacing Bodies: Anamorphosis in Early Modern Theories of Perspective* (2007).

Alida C. Metcalf is Professor of History at Trinity University. She is the author of *Go-betweens and the Colonization of Brazil, 1500–1600* (2005) and *Family and Frontier in Colonial Brazil: Santana de Parnaíba, 1580–1822* (1992). She is currently researching early modern maps.

Jacqueline Marie Musacchio is Associate Professor of Art at Wellesley College. Her publications include *The Art and Ritual of Childbirth in Renaissance Italy* (1999) and *Art, Marriage, and Family in the Florentine Renaissance Palazzo* (forthcoming); her current project is a study of the cultural patronage and historiography of Bianca Cappello.

François Rigolot, the Meredith Howland Pyne Professor of French Literature at Princeton, is the author of *Les Langages de Rabelais* (1972, 1996), *Poétique et onomastique* (1977), *Le Texte de la Renaissance* (1984), *Les Métamorphoses de Montaigne* (1986), *Poésie et Renaissance* (2000) and *L'Erreur de la Renaissance* (2003). He is the editor of Louise Labé's complete works and Montaigne's *Journal de voyage*.

Ingrid Rowland lives in Rome, where she is a professor at the School of Architecture of the University of Notre Dame. Her books include *The Culture of the High Renaissance* (1998), *The Scarith of Scornello: A Tale of Renaissance Forgery* (2004), *From Heaven to Arcadia* (2004), and a biography of Giordano Bruno (2008).

David Harris Sacks, the Richard F. Scholz Professor of History and Humanities at Reed College, is the author of *The Widening Gate: Bristol and Atlantic Economy 1450–1700*, an edition Thomas More's *Utopia*, and numerous essays on the history of political discourse and the relations between history and literary culture.

Regina Mara Schwartz is Professor of Religion and Literature at Northwestern University. She is the author of *The Curse of Cain: The Violent Legacy of Monotheism* (1997), *Remembering and Repeating* (1988), and *When God Left the World: Sacramentality at the Dawn of Secularism* (forthcoming)

Randolph Starn is Professor Emeritus of History and Italian studies, former director of the Townsend Center for the Humanities, and Marion E. Koshland Distinguished Professor of the Humanities Emeritus at the University of California, Berkeley. His scholarly work ranges from Renaissance studies and early modern history to art history and the history of historiography.

Michael Tworek, who has recently held a Fulbright for study in Poland, is a doctoral candidate in European history at Harvard University.

Malcolm Vale, Fellow and Tutor in History, St John's College, Oxford, is the author of *English Gascony, 1399–1453* (1970), *Charles VII of France* (1974), *War and Chivalry: Warfare and Aristocratic Culture in England, France and Burgundy at the End of the Middle Ages* (1981), *The Origins of the Hundred Years War: The Angevin Legacy, 1250–1340* (1996), and *The Princely Court: Medieval Courts and Culture in North-west Europe,*

— *Contributors* —

1270–1380 (2001). He is currently working on a book entitled *The Ancient Enemy. England, France and Europe, 1154–1558.*

Katherine Elliot van Liere is Associate Professor of History at Calvin College in Grand Rapids, Michigan. She is the author of numerous articles and book chapters on sixteenth-century universities, humanist scholarship, historiography, and religion. She is currently working on the history of the Saint James legend in medieval and early modern Spain.

Bronwen Wilson is Associate Professor in the Department of Art History, Visual Art and Theory, University of British Columbia. Recent publications include a book, *The World in Venice: Print, the City, and Early Modern Identity* (2005), and articles on portraits, costume, space, and representational technologies. Her current book, *Facing the End of the Renaissance: Portraits, Physiognomy and Naturalism in Northern Italy*, explores the visual culture of the human face, *c.* 1550–1620.

ACKNOWLEDGEMENTS

The making of this book has been a pleasure. Above all, it has been a privilege to work collaboratively with many of the leading scholars in the field of Renaissance studies – not only with historians but also with art historians and students of literature. I am grateful first and foremost to Victoria Peters, who, over lunch in Oxford just four years ago, invited me to serve as editor of this volume. What endowed her with the confidence that I would be able to do this remains a mystery to me, and there were certainly more than a few moments when I believed the undertaking would prove impossible. But my colleagues both here and abroad have been steadfast in their commitments to this anthology. I am appreciative to each and every one of them.

My children have, as always, been a loving source of support. Without their willingness to let me immerse myself in this project, I simply could not have done this work. To my daughter Margaret I am thankful for her help in preparing the illustrations, to my son Junius I am grateful for his keeping my mind on other, equally interesting things. But I would not have got anywhere without the gracious assistance of Eunice Herrington. She has not only faithfully helped me keep track of the many contributions – an organizational challenge in itself – but also proof-read each essay, offered useful suggestions about individual contributions, shared ideas about the volume as a whole, and been as much a scholarly colleague as a superb editorial assistant. I am forever grateful to her for her hard work, friendship, and professionalism. In addition, Christopher Cornell, one of our most remarkable students, also proof-read many of the essays, while Michael Fischer, Vice-President of Academic Affairs and Dean of the Faculty, offered financial support to help me bring the indefatigable Nancy Diehl on board to assist me with the editing. At Routledge, Philippa Grand, Anna Hines, Emma Langley, and Alan Fidler have all been patient and encouraging.

Finally, I must express my appreciation to my students. They have played and continue to play a critical role in my scholarship. Ever since I arrived at Trinity, I have had the privilege of teaching students who show a lively interest not only in history but also in the ways in which scholars are continually rethinking and rewriting the past. All of us who teach recognize that we learn more from our students than we are able to teach them. I am especially proud that three of my former students

— *Acknowledgements* —

are contributors to this anthology. These three – along with hundreds of others – have put up with my ramblings, incoherencies, and enthusiasms more than I deserve. It is only fitting, therefore, in a collaborative undertaking that so explicitly stands at the intersection of teaching and scholarship, that I dedicate this work to my students – past, present, and future. I hope that they – like the explorers, artists, humanists, and engineers of the Renaissance – will discover new worlds and new ways of seeing and doing things. In this sense, above all, it is important that the young pay close attention to the Renaissance and the abundant evidence it provides that art, science, literature, and ideas can change the world, at times even for the better.

John Jeffries Martin
February 2007

CREDITS FOR ILLUSTRATIONS

Illustrations are reproduced with grateful thanks to: A.C.L. Brussels; AICT/ Allen T. Kohl; The Art Archive at The Picture Desk; Art Resource NY; ltomani & Sons, Milan; Biblioteca Nazionale Firenze; Biblioteca Malatestiana; Bibliothèque nationale de France; The Bodleian Library, Oxford; Bridgeman Art Library; The British Library; Church of Sant'Agostino, Gubbio; Dallas Museum of Fine Arts; Davison Art Center at Wesleyan University; Direzione Dei Musei, Citta del Vaticano; The Frick Collection; Herzog Anton Ulrich Museum, Brunswig; Irpa-Kik; The James Ford Bell Library, University of Minnesota; John Carter Brown Library at Brown University; The Library of Congress, Washington DC; Mandeville Special Collections Library, University of California, San Diego; Metropolitan Museum of Art, New York; The National Gallery, London; National Gallery of Art, Washington; The Newberry Library, Chicago; Öffentliche Kunstsammlung, Basel; Österreichische Nationalbibliothek, Vienna; Scala Archives; Polo Museale, Fiorentino; Spada Gallery, Rome; Stewart Museum, Montreal; Tiroler Landesmuseum Ferdinandeum, Innsbruck, Austria; Universitätsbibliothek, Erlangen.

The Publishers also wish to thank the following for providing images: Bronwen Wilson, Randolph Starn, John Marino, Meredith Gill and Caroline Castiglione.

While every effort has been made to trace and acknowledge ownership of copyright material used in this volume, the Publishers will be glad to make suitable arrangements with any copyright holders whom it has not been possible to contact.

INTRODUCTION

THE RENAISSANCE
A world in motion

—•—

John Jeffries Martin

The Renaissance – a world in movement – emerges in vivid colors in Vittore Carpaccio's *The Legend of St Ursula*. Carpaccio completed this stunning narrative, displayed in a cycle of nine panels, in the 1490s. This was a watershed moment in European history. Ottoman power was expanding in the eastern Mediterranean, with the Turks overrunning many of Venice's strongholds. To Venetians, developments in the west were no less unsettling. The Portuguese had sailed around the Cape of Good Hope in the late 1480s, a feat that would soon open up a direct sea route to the lucrative spice markets of the Indies, and news of Columbus's voyages and his discovery of yet another new route to the Indies (or so it was widely believed at the time) first reached Venice while Carpaccio was working on the Ursula cycle.

In the same decade the maritime republic of Venice, long the greatest sea power in Europe, was threatened not only by the emergence of the Ottoman, Portuguese, and Spanish empires but also by France, at last recovered from the ravages of the Hundred Years War. In 1494 the French king Charles VIII, with 30,000 troops, invaded Italy, a move that made it clear that the Italian duchies and republics – for the previous 200 years the most dynamic and powerful states in Europe – were no longer a match, at least militarily, for the emerging monarchies of the Renaissance. This was also a moment of heightened religious tensions. In 1492 the Spanish monarchs Ferdinand and Isabella defeated Granada, the last Muslim emirate in Iberia, and expelled the Jews, some of whom eventually settled in Venice. In this very same period, the prophet and political firebrand Girolamo Savonarola was preaching the Apocalypse in Florence. How conscious Carpaccio was of these events is uncertain, but his Ursula cycle is filled with energies and tensions that suggest the larger forces at work in European culture and society played some role in shaping his artistic vision.

The story of St Ursula was one of many saints' lives that circulated in Renaissance Europe. Carpaccio would have read the life of this saint in the *Golden Legend*, a late medieval work, printed for the first time in an Italian translation in Venice in 1475. He had also studied an earlier narrative cycle depicting the saint's life in Treviso, a city on the Venetian mainland, and no doubt he would have heard the story told by priests and people alike. Ursula's legend was extremely popular,

Figure I.1 Vittore Carpaccio (c. 1460–1526). *Scenes from the Life of Saint Ursula: The Leavetaking of the Betrothed Pair*, from the St Ursula Cycle, originally in the Scuola di Sant'Orsola, Venice, 1498 (oil on canvas). Galleria dell' Accademia, Venice, Italy/

blending traditional hagiography with late medieval themes of romance. A confraternity had been established in Venice in her honor in the early fourteenth century, and it was this *scuola*, whose members appear to have been primarily artisans, that commissioned the narrative cycle from Carpaccio in 1488. Yet it was a story that Carpaccio, through his art, made his own. Carpaccio's work takes on a magical quality, as he blends the real and the imagined, the particular and the universal so effectively that, in the late eighteenth century Anton Maria Zanetti, a connoisseur of Venetian art, referred to Carpaccio's cycle as "un'invenzione fondata sulla verità" – "an invention founded upon truth." Finally, Carpaccio's *istoria* – his moral tale in

– *A world in motion* –

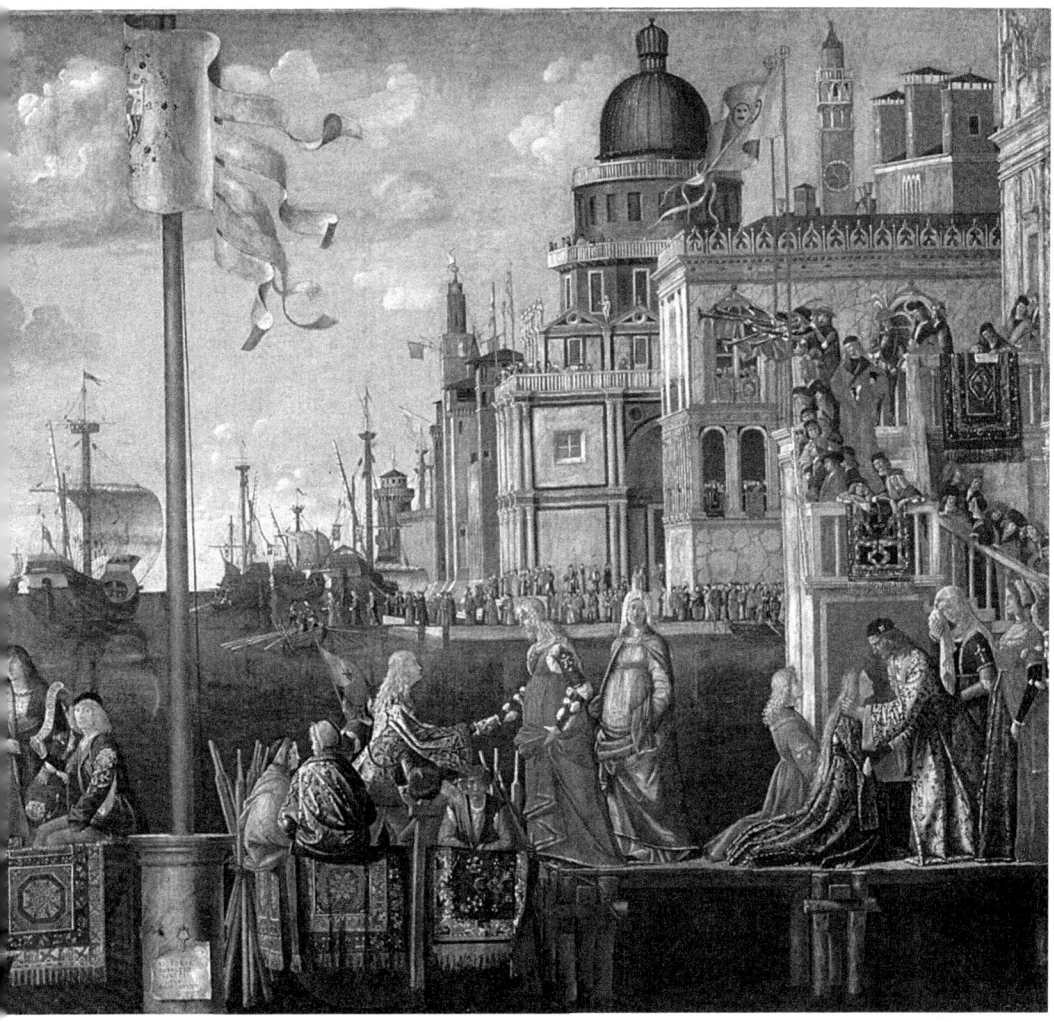

© Bridgeman Art Library. The English world, shown on the left, is evocative of the Middle Ages; Brittany, on the right, displays a Renaissance cityscape, an imaginary Venice.

pictures – told one particular story that, simultaneously, seemed to embody all human stories: civilization is a veneer that can only go so far in holding back the naked brutality of humanity.

Of all the panels, it is *The Leavetaking of the Betrothed Pair* (shown here), the largest and the most beautifully choreographed, that arrests the viewer's attention. A sort of centerpiece within the cycle, it follows the earlier paintings depicting the arrangements between the English ambassadors to Brittany who came, on behalf of their king, to seek the princess Ursula in marriage to his son – a proposal she accepted only on the condition that the groom convert to Christianity and permit her to undertake a pilgrimage along with her retinue of 11,000 virgins; it precedes the depiction of her pilgrimage, dream, martyrdom, and apotheosis. Moreover, it is this panel, above all, that depicts a world in transition. Carpaccio portrays English architecture as Gothic, but the architecture of Brittany is evocative of some of the most sophisticated Italian Renaissance buildings of his day. "England" here is a world of castles, cities fortified by walls and towers, and a ship that has run aground. "Brittany," by contrast, is a world of exquisitely proportioned buildings, of a dignified cityscape, with its ships confidently sailing out to sea. Carpaccio portrayed a changing world.

This book views the Renaissance largely as a movement in intellectual, artistic, and scientific practices that, beginning in the mid-fourteenth century, were to prove enormously consequential not only in Europe but, eventually, throughout the world. The essays gathered here include studies not only of elite culture – of art and humanism – but also of European society more broadly. The goal of this volume, in short, is to offer a series of portraits of the Renaissance both as a movement and *in movement*, dynamically connected to upheavals as well as to more gradual transformations in the economic, social, political, and religious realms – in short, to convey some sense of the Renaissance world.

By design, this collection of essays opens with three preludes – three developments that had much to do with setting the Renaissance in motion – and then quickly moves on to sections that explore, through the lenses of several disciplines, the period's economic, intellectual, political, and religious history. Even in a volume as compendious as this one, the chapters cannot possibly offer a comprehensive overview either of the causes of the Renaissance or of its multifaceted ramifications, but they do offer a starting point for readers interested both in the Renaissance itself and in some of the ways contemporary scholars approach its history, whether they are concerned with high culture or the harsh realities of poverty and disease; or interested in places we have long associated with the Renaissance such as Rome, Florence, or Venice; or engrossed with places that are somewhat less often encountered in a study of this kind: Portugal, Poland, the Ottoman Empire, and even Brazil, India, and Japan.

THREE PRELUDES

At the heart of the Renaissance was a fascination with antiquity. The memory of Rome haunted the medieval world, and the monks, scholars, monarchs, and emperors of that era had often drawn on ancient texts and images in their pursuits of power, intellectual and political. Yet in the fourteenth century, especially in Italy, new, more historically self-conscious views of the ancient world emerged. Scholars began to view their own culture not so much as continuous with Roman civilization but as something new. Even the city of Rome itself, reduced to fragments and the shells of ancient monuments, had become a relic; but it was a relic with talismanic qualities. It was when Petrarch made his first visit to this city in the late 1330s that he discerned a *coupure*, a break – a period he described as a *medium aevum*: the Middle Ages – between the ancient world and his own age. From this vantage point, which represented a new historical sensibility, the recreation of Rome required physically and intellectually exhausting efforts to recover the ideas of the Greeks and Romans. Renaissance popes may have dressed as generals and led troops into war; they may have fathered bastard children; and they may have commissioned cultural projects more out of egomania than a genuine personal concern with culture. Nonetheless, beneath papal *Realpolitik* lay also a sense that the rhetoric of architecture could do more to inculcate Christian values than could all the papal legions combined. Moreover, the Vatican Library, established in the mid-fifteenth century, made it abundantly clear that one of the most important aspects of reassembling the fragments of the ancient world involved the recovery and editing of lost manuscripts from the great writers of antiquity, both Roman and Greek. The popes, that is, recognized the power of art and ideas in shaping a new culture – and this pattern of patronage, soon widespread among the elites of other Italian and European courts and cities as well – would emerge as one of the defining features of Renaissance culture.

Although the foundations for the Renaissance were laid in the fourteenth century, it was in the early fifteenth century that the movement gained momentum. Ingrid Rowland, in her chapter on the transformation of Rome into a great Renaissance city, locates the impetus for this project in a multitude of factors: the palpable presence of ancient monuments; the ambition of the popes, and their patronage of artists, intellectuals, and humanists; social mobility within the papal court, which increasingly tapped talent over wealth; a competitive spirit among painters, sculptors, and architects; the constant movement into the city of pilgrims, refugees, scholars, and merchants; and a conscious use of art to respond to local as well as international anxieties and ambitions. The result was not so much, Rowland reminds us, a revival of antiquity as a creative adaptation, a constant recycling of earlier fragments of ancient monuments, an openness to make something new.

Yet, alongside a fascination with antiquity were new ways of seeing the world, and here none was more influential than the development of theories of perspective that enabled artists to represent with increasing precision a three-dimensional world on a two-dimensional space (a painting, for example, or a drawing). First developed in early fifteenth-century Florence by the architect Filippo Brunelleschi, then elaborated by Leon Battista Alberti in his *On Painting* (1435), perspective derived both from late medieval optical geometry and the workshop practices of Renaissance artists and architects. The results of this innovation are best known to art historians. Carpaccio's *Legend of St Ursula*, for example, stands in striking contrast to Tomaso da Modena's fourteenth-century rendering of the same theme in Treviso. Tomaso's figures are largely two-dimensional, while Carpaccio's are fully rounded; it is in his depiction of buildings though that Carpaccio is a master of perspective. And Italian theories of perspective quickly found a favorable reception in northern Renaissance art as well, most notably in the work of Albrecht Dürer in the early sixteenth century. But, as Lyle Massey's chapter makes clear, perspective was immediately recognized as central to other disciplines. It played decisive roles in breakthroughs in other fields: astronomy, cartography, engineering, and mathematics. *Perspectiva* constituted, therefore, a prelude to the Renaissance as an age of artistic creativity, scientific inventiveness, and overseas discoveries. Perspective proved a way not only of representing but also of knowing, even conquering the world.

While historians of art and culture have often emphasized the important role of artists and humanists and their patrons in the making of the Renaissance, social and economic historians have emphasized broader structural transformations in European society and culture, viewing these changes as underlying causes for intellectual and cultural developments and, at the same time, as outgrowths of the new humanist and artistic practices of the era. The growth of commerce, urbanization, changing patterns in family life and the workplace were all important – we can, in fact, imagine many "preludes" – but one event in particular stands out as especially decisive: the Black Death.

For five years, from 1348 to 1352, the Black Death spread like a slow-moving fire over the continent, mysteriously skipping some places but devastating others. This epidemic killed as many as one out of every two Europeans. As paradoxical as it might at first seem, since the Black Death was in the short term so catastrophic and disruptive, in the longer run, as Samuel Cohn argues in his chapter, the Black Death led to fundamental shifts in *mentalités*: to a new, more confident sense that humans could exercise some control over nature; to a heightened concern not only among the elites but also among peasants and urban workers with the memorialization of their families; and to the expression of new political demands by these same popular groups, increasingly hopeful as the first ravages of the plague receded, that they could change the world. The Black Death, in short, was a prelude to intellectual developments (most clearly in medicine), to a growing desire on the part of commoners to use art to preserve the memory of their families, and to the demands for greater political liberties. As Cohn makes clear, the plague precipitated many of the defining traits of the Renaissance.

A WORLD IN MOTION

However we might envision the interrelationships among the broad, far-reaching shifts in attitudes that developed in the wake of the Black Death, the simultaneous emergence of a new posture towards ancient civilization itself, and, finally, the new windows onto the world that Alberti and Dürer opened up with their theories of perspective, these three "preludes" would not have been nearly as consequential had they not developed in a world that was increasingly interconnected by trade, by the movements of mariners, merchants, diplomats, humanists, artists, mendicants, pilgrims, itinerant artisans, and other travelers – if the world itself had not been in motion. This is not to imply that the medieval world was static; from the eleventh century on Europe had witnessed the rebirth of towns and cities that would serve as centers of new cultural forms. Rather, what we see in the centuries following the Black Death is a period in which, after a season of stagnation, trade would again accelerate. And, indeed, many of the contributions to this anthology underscore the importance of the movement of goods, peoples, and ideas in the making of Renaissance culture. The mobility was simultaneously social and economic, and it provided much of the energy and a sustaining environment for the creativity of this period.

We can have a bird's-eye view of this dynamism if we imagine the Renaissance world as a series of concentric circles, growing larger and larger as we move away from Rome. Rome constitutes the first, inner circle; there, as Rowland's chapter demonstrates, mobility was a defining factor, not only in the constant influx of newcomers into the city but also in the relative ease with which people moved up and down the social hierarchy. Within a second circle (this one embracing most of the continent) Alexander Cowan's chapter on urban life, like Joanne M. Ferraro's chapter on consumption, underscores the importance of towns and cities as places in which Renaissance ideas were generated and in which many of the material goods we associate with the Renaissance (tapestries, paintings, ornaments) were in constant circulation, at least among the elites.

Figure I.2 Vittore Carpaccio (c. 1460–1526). *Scenes from the Life of Saint Ursula: Arrival of the Pilgrims in Cologne*, The Art Archive/Accademia Venice/Dagli Orti (A). This panel shows a Europe knit together by trade. The building looming in the background is suggestive of the Venetian Arsenal.

The third circle was global. The expansion of Europe, as both Francisco Bethencourt and John A. Marino demonstrate in their chapters, played a defining role in the Renaissance. The Portuguese were among the first to exploit lands beyond the European continent itself as they established forts and trading posts along the coast of West Africa from which, as early as 1441, they brought back the first large shipment of African slaves to Europe. The history of the horrors inflicted on Africans and the native populations of the Americas is well known. What is less well known – and what is emphasized here – are the vast intellectual transformations that took place in the wake of the expansion of Europe. Bethencourt traces the cultural interaction and exchanges of knowledge that took place from the fifteenth to the late sixteenth century in many areas, as Europeans traveled the globe from West Africa and then to India, China, and Japan in the east and to the Americas in the west. Throughout the sixteenth century Portuguese and Spanish settlers carried with them some of the most recent Renaissance technologies: fortress architecture, urban design, painting; but, as go-betweens, they also brought back to Europe a wide array of ornamental art from the cultures they encountered, added vast numbers of newly discovered plants and animals to the lists maintained by botanists, zoologists, and other naturalists, and gained an immense knowledge of the customs, economies, and political systems of non-European societies.

One of the most compelling examples in the transformation of Europeans' understandings of themselves lay in the development of cartography. The idea of Europe, as it had developed in the Middle Ages, had been based, above all, on the notion of Christendom, with the result that Europeans defined themselves primarily in religious terms. Towards the end of the Renaissance, by contrast, the practice of map-making – which drew on the science of perspective, the humanist interest in the works of ancient cartographers such as Ptolemy, and above all upon the practical experience of mariners who charted their routes in detailed portolans and portolan maps – made it possible for the first time, as John Marino shows in his chapter, for Europeans to define themselves in geographical terms, as inhabitants of an increasingly clearly delineated continent and to envision the world as a potential possession, the maps providing not only practical knowledge for trade but also instrumental knowledge for domination and the projection of power.

Finally, in the age of discoveries, Renaissance humanists had also to grapple with the encounter with new peoples – with the question of their humanity. In general Europeans found intellectual foundations for the subjection of Africans and the indigenous peoples of the New World in the assumptions they made about the barbarism of the peoples they encountered. Bartolomé de las Casas, in his defense of the "Indians," constituted an important exception to this trend. But the Jesuit José de Acosta, as Anthony Grafton demonstrates in his chapter on this historian-anthropologist, also offered a new perspective on the Aztecs and the Mexicas – one that did much to assimilate them to a common humanity. Acosta's acceptance of this common humanity was less, Grafton suggests, an act of compassion or genuine cultural understanding than the outgrowth of the new historical methods that were capturing the imagination of many writers in the mid- and late sixteenth century. The historiography of this period had come to place a greater emphasis on the study of non-European peoples, on comparative history, and on the natural world as decisive in the shaping of a people's development. From such a vantage point – above all in his careful analysis of the writing systems of the New World and in his elaborate descriptions of its architecture and religious customs – Acosta came to find similarities between the indigenous peoples of the Americas and Europeans. Nor was this knowledge merely theoretical. Climbing high in the Andes, Acosta was stricken with altitude sickness and recognized that his physiological response to the elevation and his eventual adaptation to the heights were identical to the ways in which the Indians also reacted and adapted to the high altitudes. In observing the interplay of the human body with the environment at a very visceral moment of violent illness, Acosta discerned, in a way that he could not learn from books alone, a common humanity.

To be sure, none of these insights led Acosta to respect the civilization he encountered and studied in the New World. To the contrary, good Jesuit that he was, he used this knowledge as the basis for evangelization. Nonetheless, Acosta's story shows in its intricacies something of the process by which Europeans mapped their experience of the New World onto their earlier studies of antiquity as well as their examinations of other cultures from Turkey to China. By the end of the sixteenth century making sense of the other had begun to require a comparative method, considerable anthropological fieldwork, and a willingness to travel to places about which the ancients had merely speculated. Such breakthroughs in the intellectual sphere did little to slow the conquest and destruction of the indigenous peoples of the New World. These breakthroughs nonetheless revealed certain latent possibilities for a new understanding of humanity that developed not merely out of the encounter with new peoples but quite explicitly out of new intellectual tools, new technologies, and new methods within humanistic practices of the period.

THE MOVEMENT OF IDEAS

We often think of the Renaissance scholar as alone, a solitary figure in his study, surrounded by ancient texts that, through arduous labor, he has learned to read in Greek or Latin or even Hebrew. Carpaccio's celebrated *St Augustine in His Study* (see p. 536) evokes precisely such a stereotype. Yet the Renaissance, as Peter Burke emphasizes in the opening section of his chapter, was to large degree the outgrowth of an unprecedented increase in knowledge (of antiquity and of new cultures) and of an equally unprecedented increase in the speed at which ideas and practices spread. Burke offers an analysis of *how*, within such a mobile culture, ideas circulated, and he focuses on the influential role of the new technology of printing, on the ongoing circulation of manuscripts and drawings, on the exchanges of letters among humanists, on the movement of artists and works of art, on acts of espionage, and on the attraction of courts, port cities, and university towns to scholars, artists, and humanists who found fresh venues in which to exchange and debate new ideas with one another. The Renaissance, in short, must be seen as a period not only of the rapid circulation of goods but also of the rapid transmission of information and misinformation – ideas that were not merely imitated but became the seeds of new ideas, of adaptations, of transformations, of misrepresentations, and, therefore, of

Figure I.3 Vittore Carpaccio (*c.* 1460–1526). *Scenes from the Life of Saint Ursula: Departure of the Ambassadors* (detail: scribe). The Art Archive/Accademia Venice/Dagli Orti (A). Writing played a central role in the movement of ideas in diplomatic as well as other circles.

new, highly creative representations in literature, art, humanism, history, travel literature, and such sciences as astronomy, cartography, and mathematics.

At least until the end of the sixteenth century, Italy constituted the intellectual and artistic epicenter of the Renaissance throughout Europe. Michael Tworek's chapter on the Renaissance in Poland, especially when read alongside Paula Findlen's discussion of Copernicus, makes it clear that both the teaching by Italian humanists in Cracow and the opportunity for young Poles to study in Italy created fertile ground for the growth of intellectual exchanges in this period. Katherine Elliot van Liere finds a similar pattern in the Spanish Renaissance. Michel de Montaigne – the subject of François Rigolot's chapter – explicitly recognized the value of travel and what he called the "commerce des hommes" or the "mixing of men from different cultures." And his travels in Italy in 1580 and 1581, when he visited, among other places, Rome, Florence, and Venice, gave him an opportunity to form his own opinions about a world that, until then, he had known only indirectly through his readings and his conversations.

Political transformations also provided an important context for the development of humanism; this is especially clear in David Harris Sack's essay on Niccolò Machiavelli and Sir Thomas More. These two humanists were deeply involved in public affairs and both struggled with the question of how best to forge a polity that would be of benefit to its citizens or subjects. In many respects, these two well-known Renaissance figures could not have been more different: More is remembered as a saint, while Machiavelli is frequently vilified. And yet both Machiavelli and More approached the major political challenges of their day largely through the lenses of the writings of the ancients. For both, in short, humanism connected them to ancient texts that enhanced their ability, however limited it might be, not only to navigate the treacherous waters of power in the early sixteenth century but also to offer new visions of society and politics.

THE CIRCULATION OF POWER

The court and other forms of political organization played major roles in the circulation of power in Renaissance Europe. Power is never static. By definition it must be projected, either through military force or through art and ideas. In his chapter on the Burgundian court at the end of the Middle Ages, for example, Malcolm Vale underscores several salient aspects of the circulation of power: the court itself was not stationary but rather "constantly moved around"; nobles, too, circulated in and out of the duke's household (as guests or representatives of other powers); and rulers became increasingly self-conscious in disseminating likenesses of themselves that served to legitimate and often exaggerate their power. Power, like trade, begat both art and intellectual activity and was, in turn, bolstered by both.

By the sixteenth century, the Burgundian model was itself one of the seeds for the far more ambitious political systems that developed in western Europe, perhaps most conspicuously in the Spain of Charles V. Charles, who was the grandson of the Holy Roman Emperor Maximilian I and of Mary of Burgundy, was the heir not only to the Habsburg Empire in Austria but also, as the grandson of Ferdinand and Isabella, of the Spanish kingdoms of Aragon, Castile, and their dependencies in Europe and the New World. Power in such a far-reaching, virtually global empire required not only constant movement by the royal court and the patronage of works of art and architecture that would serve to legitimate the emperor's authority but also a new emphasis on Roman imperial models. To be sure, the fascination with Rome's imperial rulers had a long history. But a key element in the circulation of power in the Renaissance, as Thomas Dandelet demonstrates in his chapter on the imperial Renaissance, was the recovery and circulation of Roman texts that offered models for new imperial histories, new administrative structures, and new military strategies.

Empire also depended on the production and circulation of images that magnified the power of rulers. In his ambitious chapter on triumphalism, Randolph Starn unpacks the visual vocabulary of power as it was expressed in woodcuts, portraits, statues, paintings, commemorative medals, and tapestries. Italy was in the lead in the appropriation of the triumph from ancient models, but by the sixteenth century rulers throughout Europe, drawing not only on Italian but also late medieval practices (such as those found in Burgundy), were able to deploy an ancient repertoire of images, statues, and coins to bolster their own standing in the competitive world of Renaissance politics. While indebted to patronage studies, Starn makes a forceful case that the Renaissance imaginary had roots as well in a deeply visual culture that made much of works of art in the circulation of power.

Yet power did not only flow from the center to the periphery; rulers were inevitably compelled to negotiate with those they ruled. Daniel Goffman makes this point with clarity in his chapter on the Ottoman Empire. From the outside, especially in times of intense military and religious conflict, the Ottoman Empire may have appeared monolithic. But the reality was far more complex. Goffman's chapter focuses in particular on the large number of foreigners who lived in Istanbul and other Ottoman towns and cities, the negotiations they undertook with state authorities to regulate their conditions of residency, and on the relatively tolerant attitude of the Muslim elites (in striking contrast to their Christian counterparts) towards religious minorities: in this case towards the Greek Orthodox, Roman Catholics, and Jews.

As the Ottoman example suggests, the Renaissance state may have well made claims to being unified, but it was almost always something heterogeneous, hybrid, negotiated. Throughout Europe, from Istanbul to Ireland, the state – whether an empire, a monarchy, or a republic – was less a unified system than a congeries of overlapping jurisdictions in which local lordships, bishoprics, towns, and village communities continued to have a certain degree of independence even when they were nominally under the rule of a dominant city or prince. Thus we might not only think of Europe in this period as a complex mosaic of states, as many as 1,500, but also of each state itself as a patchwork of feudal principalities, free communes, ecclesiastical lordships, and so on. Undoubtedly, one of the reasons underlying the Renaissance fascination with antiquity was a search for models of political unity in a world marked by extreme political diversity and fragmentation.

Yet the very technologies that served rulers often undermined their authority. As Constantin Fasolt observes in his chapter on ecclesiastical authority, the development of printing and the growth of literacy fundamentally transformed the understanding of the Church from a body whose authority had been seen as legitimate when writing was a technology monopolized by the clergy to an institution that came to have to compete with multiple interpretations of the truth – though the challenge to medieval conceptions of the Church's power had emerged earlier in, for example, Petrarch's appropriation of the classical virtues as the property of all, a proposition

Figure I.4 Vittore Carpaccio (c. 1460–1526). *Scenes from the Life of Saint Ursula: Departure of the Ambassadors*. The Art Archive/Accademia Venice/Dagli Orti (A). Courts played a major role in the organization of power in the Renaissance. Here, Carpaccio places particular importance on diplomatic etiquette and a culture of civility.

that ultimately eroded the clergy's claim to serve as privileged arbiters of morality. Literacy was also a critical element in the expression of power by women, as Caroline Castiglione demonstrates in her chapter on motherhood in the late Renaissance. Mothers, who often faced virtual exile from their own children if widowed, made brilliant use of both secular and ecclesiastical courts to establish a more central role for themselves in the raising of their own offspring and fashioned a more affective and eventually a central role for the mother in the shaping of her family. But

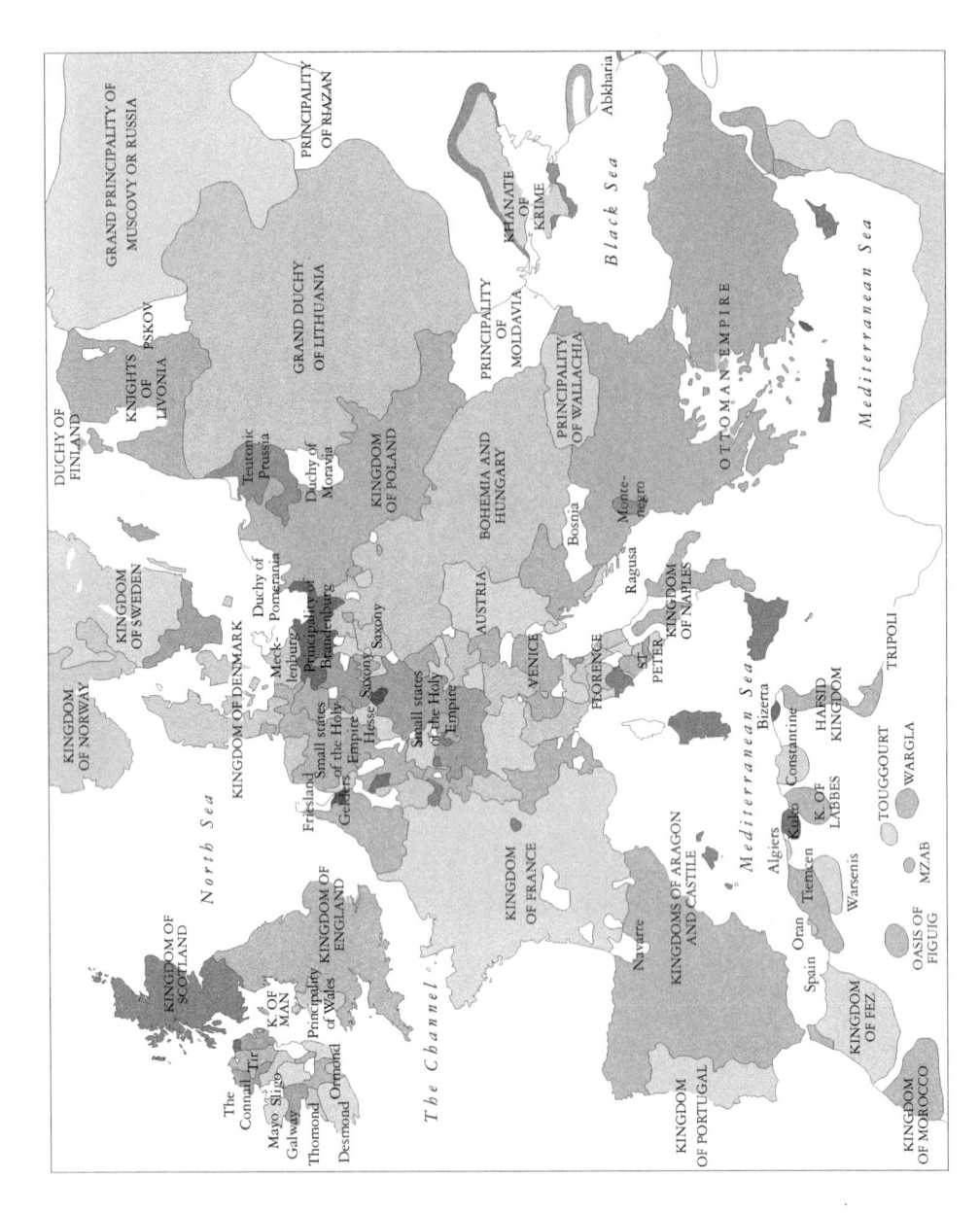

Figure I.5 Renaissance Europe.

— *A world in motion* —

Figure I.6 Vittore Carpaccio (*c.* 1460–1526). *Scenes from the Life of Saint Ursula: Martyrdom of the Pilgrims and the Funeral of Saint Ursula* (detail). The Art Archive/Accademia Venice/Dagli Orti (A). The brutality of this panel, showing the massacre of Ursula and the 11,000 virgins, stands in startling contrast to the civility of the court portrayed in Carpaccio's *Departure of the Ambassadors* on p. 15. Together, these representations show the two sides of power in the Renaissance.

power came not only from the pen but also from much noisier modern devices: the wheel-lock and then the flintlock arquebus. Focusing his attention on the endemic, low-level violence that percolated throughout Italian society in the late sixteenth century, Robert Davis offers a fascinating glimpse into the world of bandits and highwaymen, now armed with handguns, and capable, therefore, not only of eluding but also of intimidating state authorities. Thus in early modern Europe no one monopolized power. The patriarchs of the great aristocratic families were limited by the growing autonomy of women who learned to use a complex legal system to their advantage; and powerful princes were alarmed by the endemic violence of increasingly well-armed *banditi*.

MAKING IDENTITIES

Some art historians believe that the figure, dressed in red and standing outside the frame of the panel *The Arrival of the English Ambassadors*, is likely a self-portrait of Carpaccio. While this is not certain, what is certain is that questions of identity,

Figure I.7 Vittore Carpaccio (*c.* 1460–1526). *Scenes from the Life of Saint Ursula: The Arrival of the English Ambassadors*, detail, from the St Ursula cycle, 1498 (oil on canvas) (detail of 119435). The figure in the left foreground is a likely self-portrait of the artist. © Galleria dell' Accademia, Venice, Italy/The Bridgeman Art Library.

whether collective or individual, were central matters in Renaissance culture. Artists in this period, as Carpaccio appears to have done in his painting, increasingly called attention to their own individual contribution to the works they created. Yet the ways in which such claims of artistic creativity were made were themselves the result of fundamental shifts in certain intellectual currents, theories of authorship, workshop practices, and acts of self-fashioning that continually reshaped notions of identity in this period.

Without question humanist thought placed a new emphasis in the Renaissance on the dignity of man – the belief that humans had the capacity to transform themselves and their world, above all, through their use of language and, in particular, through the persuasive power of reasoned argument and rhetoric. In his imaginative chapter on what he calls "human exceptionalism," Kenneth Gouwens explores the ways in which humanists from Petrarch on engaged the question of what renders us human through an examination of Renaissance discussions of the relation of humans to apes. While, in general, humanists in this period, following Cicero, called attention to human speech as the faculty that most clearly distinguishes humans from simians, Gouwens makes it clear that the import of this claim drew its significance from the struggle of humanists to imitate the ancients while nonetheless expressing themselves rather than merely "aping" the great writers of antiquity. This tension – inextricably woven into the humanist project in which the imitation of classical models was a defining characteristic – proved profoundly consequential, inculcating a sense among many humanists from Petrarch to Angelo Poliziano and Erasmus of Rotterdam that the faculty of speech was not merely imitative but also generative, capable of transforming one's understanding of self, serving as the mirror of the mind, and providing a foundation both for the education of the individual and the creation of a human polity in which both reason and eloquence had the possibility of exercising a civilizing influence. Not all humanists, of course, believed that language was as successful in separating us from the beasts as Petrarch did. In the late sixteenth century, writing in the midst of the wars of religion in France, Montaigne wondered in his *Essays* if we humans are much different from the beasts we often disparage.

Yet the representation of the self was another, far more complex matter. Albert Ascoli explores this question in his chapter on authorship, underscoring the anxieties that underlay a seemingly endless array of strategies to establish the reader's faith in the writer as an authority. There could also be a technology of the self, as Bronwen Wilson makes clear in her engaging study of portraiture, a chapter that explores the ways in which various practices (the casting of death masks, the use of wax *ex votos*, the use of mirrors, theories of physiognomy, the artifice of clothing) served to create the representation of a self – not on the basis of the self's internal qualities but rather as a product of painterly conventions that had developed in late medieval and Renaissance culture.

Identities were made in other ways as well, often through the act of consumption, whether through the purchase of objects or through indulgence in sex and food. In her study of Antonio de' Medici, Jacqueline Marie Musacchio explores how Antonio's precarious status within the Medici family goes some way in explaining his mania for collecting objects – scientific and musical instruments, rarities from

Europe and the Americas, and paintings by major Renaissance artists – that would constitute an affirmation, at least in the private sphere, of his importance and, in particular, assert his Medicean identity. Douglas Biow examines a similar strategy of self-fashioning – though one carried out through a far more Rabelaisian, gluttonous mode – in the Venetian world of the writer Pietro Aretino. A noted satirist and critic of the court, Aretino, both in his comedies and in his life, indulged in pleasures, especially the pleasures of the table: figs, pears, melons, herring, carp, turkey, chicken, spiced bread, and wine. Many of these delights came to him as gifts from his friends and served, therefore, as markers, in a kind of culinary potlatch, for Aretino's status, as did the many banquets Aretino himself staged to call attention to his standing.

Yet the Renaissance "individual" likely also drew on his or her own experience, at the most fundamental and emotional level, in the process of self-fashioning. This appears to have been the case with Shakespeare, whose play *The Tempest* was deeply personal, not only in its presumed role as Shakespeare's adieu to the theater but also, so David Bevington argues, in Shakespeare's exploration of the relation of fathers to their children – a relation generally portrayed as broken not only in his tragedies but also in his romances. For *The Tempest* constitutes the play in which Shakespeare was finally able to resolve the family conflicts that had haunted, even shaped, his earlier plays. In *The Tempest* Prospero does not block his daughter Miranda's marriage; rather, he encourages it and thereby gains a son-in-law, while Alonso's son, presumed drowned, is restored. Perhaps Shakespeare's farewell to the theater also enabled him at last, as he entered his retirement, to welcome back, at least in his imagination, his own son whose death at the age of 11 must have been a crushing blow – beyond words. Shakespeare, for whom language flowed so easily, never comments directly on this loss. In the Renaissance world, therefore, identities were not so much a given as made, created both by larger external forces and by internal anxieties and even haunting memories of unspeakable loss – the self always negotiated as a relation between internal experience and the external world.

BELIEFS AND REFORMS

Renaissance thinkers and artists also looked back to antiquity for a deeper understanding of the human experience of the individual's relation to God. This emphasis on a return to the texts of early Christianity would lead to far-reaching reinterpretations of Scripture, eventually laying the foundations for both the Reformation and the Counter-Reformation. However, Renaissance humanists and artists also turned to other early Christian writings, and here the works of St Augustine of Hippo (354–430) would prove especially influential. From Petrarch's self-exploratory engagement with Augustine in his *Secretum* to Carpaccio's celebrated painting of the saint at the end of the fifteenth century, the Renaissance, as Meredith Gill shows, found Augustine an especially compelling figure around which to organize its notions of conversion, interiority, and divine illumination. In particular, the Renaissance saw in Augustine evidence of the transformative power of texts and of language in leading the individual to a deeper understanding of self.

Renaissance Christians also encountered saints in their everyday lives: in sermons and stories, in relics and icons, in church altars and crypts, on street corners and highways, on pilgrimages, and even at times in life itself when a compelling religious figure came to be perceived as a saint by his or her contemporaries. The cult of saints was, therefore, a major feature of late medieval and early modern Christianity. While it would become a target of the Protestant reformers, who abolished the practice of appealing to a saint rather than to God himself, in early modern Catholicism the cult remained as vibrant as ever, perhaps, in the end, because of the ways in which it facilitated adapting a "universal" faith to local traditions and circumstances. The cult of saints — especially in its extreme "localism" — is also evidence that European Christianity was, even as late as the end of the fifteenth century, far from uniform. This should not surprise us. As N. S. Davidson makes clear in his chapter, the religious landscape of Renaissance Europe was highly variegated. It encompassed not only Christians but also Muslims and Jews. And even prior to the Reformation, Christianity itself was profoundly diverse with dissident groups such as the Waldensians, the Hussites, and the Lollards following teachings that were at odds with those of Rome. The Reformation, therefore, did not represent the emergence of religious diversity in Europe, but rather, as Davidson succinctly puts it, "added to this mix."

Paradoxically, the diversity within late medieval religion forms the backdrop to a late Renaissance dream of catholicity, of unity in belief, at least about the most important matters of faith. In the early sixteenth century Erasmus gave a particularly powerful expression to this dream in his writings, as Susan Boettcher shows in her chapter. Humanist practices, as they had developed earlier, especially in Italy, appeared to offer a promise of religious unity. The return to the original sources through new, more accurate editions of the New Testament — so Erasmus and many other early sixteenth-century humanists believed — would focus the hearts and minds of Christians on the essential messages of the faith and foster a sense of unity. Yet the result was, paradoxically, a new form of diversity, as different humanists discovered that, especially within the framework of ecclesiastical and secular institutions, unity could only be achieved in smaller confessions or denominations, each one of which believed it had a monopoly on the right way to restore Christianity to its original beliefs and practices. Brad Gregory's chapter develops similar themes, though he gives greater attention to the cultural and intellectual forces that led to the growing divisions within Christianity. Gregory then offers a survey of the various confessions — magisterial and radical — that redefined the political and cultural boundaries within early modern Europe. In the religious realm as in so many others, humanism proved to be a revolutionary practice, overthrowing earlier traditions, assumptions, and even deeply held beliefs.

It was within this increasingly fragmented and confessionalized context that the theological debates and divides precipitated a greater desire on the part of elites to bring the beliefs and practices within the bounds of the official teachings of a particular "confession." Both David Gentilcore, who focuses on efforts to impose religious uniformity on ordinary Christians in Italy, and Alida Metcalf, who examines a similar, though far more contested process in Brazil, make it clear that the diversity of beliefs that existed after the Reformation and Counter-Reformation remained extremely broad and that a gulf often existed between elite and popular interpretations of Christianity. In such an environment, church elites often took repressive measures. Finally, from a historical perspective, it might be more meaningful to speak of "christianities" than of Christianity.

Religion was not only a matter of concern to humanists, theologians, and inquisitors. Renaissance poets from Dante on had immersed themselves in the central themes of Christianity. As Regina Schwartz demonstrates in her chapter on John Milton, John Donne, and George Herbert, the English poets – despite the Reformation – continued to find in the Catholic mystery of transubstantiation a sustaining metaphor for their own hope for communion. The Eucharist became a symbol of the possibility of overcoming religious differences and conflicts that, tragically, were central to the Renaissance age. Milton invested the cosmos with this *mysterium*; Donne the bedroom; Herbert the banquet table – all images that expressed a longing for spiritual union in a world that seemed increasingly broken, with God pushed further and further to the margins.

A NEW ORDER OF KNOWLEDGE

Throughout the Renaissance most men and women believed that the earth stood at the center of the universe. Looking up at the skies, they saw a cosmos in which the sun and the planets orbited a stationary world. The authority of the ancients, Aristotle and Ptolemy in particular, backed up this world-view; it was a cosmology that corresponded well with many of the most fundamental ideas of Christianity. If God had created man in his image and likeness, would he not have placed him at the very center of things?

Yet perhaps it was inevitable in a world in motion that Renaissance astronomers would come to see that even the earth itself – the very planet they inhabited – was moving, simultaneously rotating on its own axis and orbiting the sun. Nicolaus Copernicus proposed such a view of the heavens in the early sixteenth century. Like hundreds of other young scholars, the Polish Copernicus had come to Italy for his education, and his curriculum involved the study not only of the sciences but also of Greek. Copernicus, moreover, belonged to an international community of scholars. And his ideas, though put forward tentatively at first, eventually gathered a following, as other astronomers, most famously Kepler and Galileo, came to accept his radical new interpretation of the cosmos. Not surprisingly, both Kepler and Galileo drew on Renaissance practices to carry out and communicate their investigations. Even Galileo's choice of the dialogue as the literary form in which he presented his most forceful endorsement of Copernicanism reflected the popularity of this genre in the Renaissance world, a world open to debate and interested in conversation, animated by what Montaigne called the *commerce des hommes*.

Yet, in other respects, Galileo's *Dialogue of the Two Chief World Systems* – along with many other events and trends – marked a transition, bringing into existence a world that we can no longer, at least comfortably, call the Renaissance. This was not only a matter of displacing the earth from the center of Creation, it was also the matter that, as indebted as Galileo was to the study of classical texts, astronomy would now increasingly, like so many other fields of inquiry, depend upon the direct observation of natural phenomena. To be sure, scholars in the seventeenth century continued to read and find inspiration in the writings of the Greeks and the Romans, but what is most striking – even charming – about Galileo's dialogue is its appeal to experience, as his text invites the reader to partake of experiments and observations along with his imaginary interlocutors. Certainly by the mid-seventeenth century the ancient world no longer had the allure or the hermeneutical power with which Petrarch had invested it some three centuries earlier. This was true not only in astronomy but in other disciplines (botany, chemistry, medicine, mathematics, physics, geology) as well. A new order of knowledge came to reign in the seventeenth century, and, as it did so, the Renaissance faded, eventually – at first in the Enlightenment, but more decisively in the nineteenth century – slipping into the past and then becoming a field of *historical* inquiry in its own right.

THE RENAISSANCE

The Renaissance was, as a movement – or, perhaps better, a cluster of interrelated movements in architecture, astronomy, botany, cartography, engineering, historical writing, painting, poetry, and so on – the cultural expression both of an expanding and increasingly commercially dynamic continent and of new patterns of consumption and competition for prestige in the courts (from the papacy to the households of dukes and cardinals) and other centers of power (republican governments, guild halls, and churches) whose patronage elevated artists, architects, and astronomers to loftier, more influential perches within society than they had held before.

As they gained influence, artists and humanists discovered new ways to communicate with one another to exchange ideas, practices, and new modes of representation. They did so, often, in dialogue with ancient texts and models. Humanists in the Renaissance drew, in part, on medieval traditions, since in both the Carolingian "Renaissance" of the ninth century and the "Renaissance" of the twelfth century, medieval monks and teachers had demonstrated an intense interest in the writings of ancient Roman authors. But it was in the wake of Petrarch and other fourteenth-century humanists and the enthusiasms they unleashed that Renaissance practices developed. The dialogue between the ancients and the moderns was now based on a hunger for knowledge of antiquity on all levels – from architecture and epigraphy to the interpretation of works of science and literature. We can sense some of the intensity of this dialogue between ancients and moderns in the chapters assembled here. Dante's reading of Virgil, like Petrarch's reading of St Augustine and Ficino's reading of Plato, was largely a search for wisdom. Yet we sense a new form of reading from the early sixteenth century on: in Machiavelli's reading of Livy, Sir Thomas More's reading of Plato, Erasmus's reading of Scripture, Vesalius's reading of Galen, and Galileo's reading of Ptolemy – readings that sought not wisdom so much as ways of understanding the natural and the social worlds. The chronology is not absolute. Alberti's readings of Euclid and Vitruvius in the first half of the fifteenth century demonstrated an early interest in praxis, while in the sixteenth century Jan Kochanowski's engagement with Cicero and Sallust, like Montaigne's wide-ranging interest in ancient authors, provides evidence of an enduring conviction that we have the chance of gaining wisdom, perhaps above all the wisdom of the limits of our knowledge, through the reading of the classics. Nonetheless, it is clear that, in general, the Renaissance fascination with the ancient world transcended ethical concerns and embraced questions of practice, science, and method. Natural philosophers trained in the scholastic tradition also contributed to new understandings of science and culture in this period, but – by the sixteenth century – the great breakthroughs in such disciplines as astronomy, cartography, and historiography grew primarily out of humanist methods for making sense of the world.

Finally, while it is important to recognize the limits of the idea of the Renaissance – its elitist bias, its emphasis on high culture, its function as a foundation myth for modern western democracies and the secular, capitalist state – it is equally important to recognize the world-historical significance of the Renaissance as a movement. Here Zanetti's characterization of Carpaccio's art as "un'invenzione fondata sulla verità" seems applicable as well to the ways in which scholars write about the Renaissance. For the idea of the Renaissance is, without question, an invention. At the same time, the phenomena this idea highlights involved nothing short of real and far-reaching shifts in perspective, in the organization of knowledge, in the practices of intellectuals and artists in the centuries that fell between the Black Death and Galileo's trial for heresy. Bound together above all by a fascination with antiquity, Renaissance princes and popes, humanists and artists, poets and playwrights, cartographers and engineers, merchants and mariners re-imagined their world in ways that we still recognize: in our maps of our planet, in our charts of our solar system, in our knowledge of the interconnectedness of the continents, in our interest in architecture and urban design, in our love of literature, and in our sense that the humanities have the potential (too rarely realized) of enlarging our understanding of ourselves, our world, and others.

As a movement, therefore, the Renaissance was not an ethereal superstructure of consequence only to the privileged. To the contrary, ideas and images are as consequential as commerce and warfare. I can think of no clearer example of this from the Renaissance era than cartography, a practical science indebted to humanism, which played a decisive role not only in changing the perceptions Europeans had of their place in the world but also in enabling trans-oceanic trade and the construction of empires. Art and literature also touched the lives of ordinary men and women. Carpaccio's *Legend of St Ursula* must have been reassuring to the artisans who gathered in the hall it decorated. In it, and perhaps especially in the panel depicting the apotheosis of the saint, they could catch a glimpse of hope in a world that was deeply fractured. And how could the London groundlings pushed up against one another in front of the stage in the Globe Theater not have come – through laughter, cajoling, tears, and catcalls – to understand themselves in new ways?

Thus, even if we can posit a motionless history for the poor in these centuries – for the illiterate who eked out an existence in the vast rural expanses of Europe – *we still don't know how many things or how many people were transformed by Renaissance ideas, paintings, plays, and poems*. What we do know is that the Renaissance set in motion a series of de-centerings. Petrarch saw Rome as the center of a world that itself was at the center of the cosmos; Columbus's voyages eventually made it clear that the

Figure I.8 Vittore Carpaccio (c. 1460–1526). *Scenes from the Life of Saint Ursula: Apotheosis of Saint Ursula.* © Galleria dell' Accademia, Venice, Italy/The Bridgeman Art Library. Perhaps the greatest distance between our own culture and that of the Renaissance is represented in this portrayal of the ascension of St Ursula. Her cult is an important example of the roles of saints in the Renaissance. Despite civilization's failure and barbarism's triumphs, Renaissance men and women could look to an afterlife, a transcendence of the difficulties one faced in this world.

ancients had known of only a portion of the world, with a result that the order of knowledge itself was transformed; and Galileo made it clear, in a famous dialogue, that the earth itself was not at the center of the cosmos but a planet in orbit around the sun.

In an era in which ideas were subject to such rapid, even jarring transformations, how could Hamlet not have remarked to his friend that "there are more things in heaven and earth, Horatio, than are dreamt of in your philosophy"? For at the end of the Renaissance, as at the beginning, the only thing of which men and women could be certain was their own ignorance, a subject that Petrarch had made his own in one of his wisest works. He called it *On His Own Ignorance and That of Many Others*.

SUGGESTIONS FOR FURTHER READING

Barkan, Leonard. *Unearthing the Past: Archaeology and Aesthetics in the Making of Renaissance Culture.* London and New Haven: Yale University Press, 1999.
Baron, Hans. *The Crisis of the Early Italian Renaissance: Civic Humanism and Republican Liberty in an Age of Classicism and Tyranny*, 2 vols. Princeton: Princeton University Press, 1955.
Baxandall, Michael. *Painting and Experience in Fifteenth-century Italy: A Primer in the Social History of Pictorial Style.* Oxford: Oxford University Press, 1988.
Bossy, John. *Christianity in the West, 1400–1700.* Oxford: Oxford University Press, 1985.
Braudel, Fernand. *The Mediterranean and the Mediterranean World in the Age of Philip II*, trans. Siân Reynolds, 2 vols. New York: Harper and Row, 1972–3.
Brown, Patricia Fortini. *Venetian Narrative Painting in the Age of Carpaccio.* New Haven: Yale University Press, 1988.
Burckhardt, Jacob. *The Civilization of the Renaissance in Italy: An Essay*, 3rd edn, trans. S. G. C. Middlemore. London: Phaidon, 1950.
Burke, Peter. *The European Renaissance: Centres and Peripheries.* Oxford: Blackwell, 1998.
Cameron, Euan. *The European Reformation.* Oxford: Oxford University Press, 1991.
Cassirer, Ernst, Paul Oskar Kristeller and John Hermann Randall, eds. *The Renaissance Philosophy of Man.* Chicago: University of Chicago Press, 1948.
Davis, Natalie Zemon. *Society and Culture in Early Modern France.* Stanford: Stanford University Press, 1975.
Eisenstein, Elizabeth L. *The Printing Press as an Agent of Change: Communications and Cultural Transformations in Early-modern Europe.* Cambridge: Cambridge University Press, 1980.
Gilbert, Felix. *Machiavelli and Guicciardini: Politics and History in Sixteenth Century Florence.* Princeton: Princeton University Press, 1965.
Goldthwaite, Richard A. *Wealth and the Demand for Art in Italy, 1300–1600.* Baltimore: Johns Hopkins University Press, 1985.
Grafton, Anthony. *Leon Battista Alberti: Master Builder of the Italian Renaissance.* Cambridge, Mass.: Harvard University Press, 2000.
Greenblatt, Stephen. *Renaissance Self-fashioning: More to Shakespeare.* Chicago: University of Chicago Press, 1980.
Hale, John R. *The Civilization of Europe in the Renaissance.* New York: Atheneum, 1994.
Herlihy, David. *The Black Death and the Transformation of the West*, edited, with an introduction, by Samuel K. Cohn, Jun. Cambridge, Mass: Harvard University Press, 1997.
Jardine, Lisa. *Worldly Goods: A New History of the Renaissance.* London: Macmillan, 1996.
King, Margaret. *Women in the Renaissance.* Chicago: University of Chicago Press, 1991.

Koerner, Joseph Leo. *The Moment of Self-portraiture in German Renaissance Art*. Chicago: University of Chicago Press, 1993.

Kraye, Jill. *The Cambridge Companion to Renaissance Humanism*. Cambridge: Cambridge University Press, 1996.

Kristeller, Paul Oskar. *Renaissance Thought: The Classic, Scholastic, and Humanist Strains*. New York: Harper, 1961.

Martin, John Jeffries. *Myths of Renaissance Individualism*. New York: Palgrave, 2004.

Martines, Lauro. *Power and the Imagination: City States in Renaissance Italy*. New York: Knopf, 1975.

Miskimin, Harry A. *The Economy of Early Renaissance Europe, 1300–1460*. Cambridge: Cambridge University Press, 1975.

────── *The Economy of Later Renaissance Europe, 1460–1600*. Cambridge: Cambridge University Press, 1977.

Nauert, Charles G. *Humanism and the Culture of Renaissance Europe*. Cambridge: Cambridge University Press, 1995.

Parry, J. H. *The Age of Reconnaissance: Discovery, Exploration, and Settlement*. Berkeley: University of California Press, 1963.

Ruggiero, Guido, ed. *A Companion to the Worlds of the Renaissance*. Oxford: Blackwell, 2002.

Sacks, David Harris. *The Widening Gate: Bristol and the Atlantic Economy, 1450–1700*. Berkeley: University of California Press, 1991.

Skinner, Quentin. *Foundations of Modern Political Thought*, 2 vols. Cambridge: Cambridge University Press, 1978.

Spitz, Lewis W. *The Religious Renaissance of the German Humanists*. Cambridge, Mass.: Harvard University Press, 1963.

Tracy, James, ed. *The Rise of the Merchant Empires: Long Distance Travel in the Early Modern World, 1350–1750*. Cambridge: Cambridge University Press, 1990.

Trinkaus, Charles. *In Our Image and Likeness: Humanity and Divinity in Italian Humanist Thought*, 2 vols. Chicago: University of Chicago Press, 1970.

Wackernagel, Michael. *The World of the Florentine Renaissance Artist*, trans. A. Luchs. Princeton: Princeton University Press, 1981.

PART I

THREE PRELUDES

CHAPTER ONE

ROME AT THE CENTER OF A CIVILIZATION

Ingrid Rowland

The capital of an ancient empire and the center of the Roman Catholic Church, Rome, the Eternal City, now seems as durable as the Colosseum. In the fourteenth century, however, that Eternal City seemed to tell a far different tale. The ancient monuments designed for a population of one million looked out over huge tracts of deserted land. The 50,000 inhabitants of fourteenth-century Rome huddled together in an area their ancient ancestors had shunned for centuries: the flat flood plain of the Campus Martius, enclosed within a bend of the river Tiber and subject to the river's devastating surges. Fourteenth-century Rome told a tale of pagan pride brought low, of *imperium*, the divinely ordained right of command, "translated" to French and German kings under the auspices of a Holy Roman Empire that was proverbially neither holy, nor Roman, nor an empire. Under pressure from powerful French cardinals, the papacy itself had moved from Rome to Avignon, leaving Rome a depressed provincial capital, dwarfed by its thriving maritime neighbors, Naples, Pisa, Venice, and Genoa.

But the ruins survived, the concrete vaults of baths, palaces and temples and the marble statues that formed Rome's second population, consisting not only of gods and goddesses but also the real people of Rome: stern old senators, majestic matrons, their children and their animals, exotic and domestic. With a little imagination, the world of these people and these gods could still be brought to life from the words of ancient authors, carefully (or not so carefully) copied from manuscript to manuscript for over a millennium. Rome's connection with Christianity was equally physical, and that physical reality exerted an equally powerful pull on the imagination. The apostles had walked the same streets as Caesar, followed by legions of saints: Augustine in the fourth century, Benedict (as a student) in the late fifth, Francis in 1206, Bridget of Sweden in 1349. When a fourteenth-century saint in the making, Catherine of Siena (1347–80), began to plead for the popes' return to Rome, she ascribed to the city an unending mission, and her eloquence was more intoxicating to her hearers than Avignon's superb red wine.

Catherine had a powerful ally in a creature of the Avignonese papacy, Francesco Petrarca (1304–74), the son of an Italian official in the papal curia and himself destined to become a curial employee, at least until his achievements as a writer enabled him to work when and where he wished. Those wishes took him to Rome at mid-century, and then again in 1367–68. On his second visit, he lamented that the city was well and truly dead: "Although when I first . . . went to Rome, almost nothing was left of that old Rome but an outline or an image, and only the ruins bore witness to its bygone greatness, nonetheless, among those ashes there were still some noble sparks; but now the ash is long extinguished and grown cold."[1]

Significantly, neither Catherine nor Petrarch pined for an outright revival of ancient Rome. Catherine knew of the city's history only by hearsay; the last of 26 children, and a girl at that, she was illiterate. For all her influence, she knew Latin only from the liturgy and expressed herself exclusively in pungent Sienese vernacular – which she did masterfully (and so indefatigably that her faithful scribe, Raymond of Capua (1330–99), confessed to napping occasionally when she held forth for hours on end). Petrarch, on the other hand, had been trained from the outset in the scholastic Latin of the papal bureaucracy as well as the lyrical Latin of the ancient authors. A born rebel, he harbored no doubts about which Latin he preferred, and saw no reason to write documents that were not also beautiful to read. At the same time, however, his pioneering efforts to conform his own Latin to ancient style paralleled an equally meticulous attention to vernacular; he contributed fundamentally to the formation of both languages. Thus if Catherine of Siena and Petrarch, these two dominating figures, saw Rome as a relic of her ancient past, it was a relic in a strictly Christian meaning of the word, an ancient object still efficacious in the here and now.

Furthermore, they saw Rome from the outside, their longing for the city all the more extraordinary because it was not patriotic in any conventional sense. Longing was not enough, however; they both virtually demanded that their contemporaries reshape the Eternal City, not as an imaginary ideal but also as a physical, political, and religious reality, a capital as ancient as Jerusalem and as worldly as Constantinople. In their two profoundly different but complementary visions, Rome provided the essential center for a whole culture.

But it took some real Roman patriotism to return the papacy from Avignon. Martin V (reigned 1417–31) had been born in Rome (in 1366) to one of the city's oldest and most powerful families, the Colonna, whose sprawling palazzo beneath the Quirinal Hill bristled with towers (one still stands on the Via XXIV Maggio) and enclosed the Early Christian basilica of the Holy Apostles. In a sense Martin's election harked back to a time-honored pattern: for centuries the Colonna and the Orsini, their rival clan, had controlled the papacy, wresting it back and forth from one another (this violent rivalry had been a major reason for moving the popes to Avignon in the first place). Despite his ancient ancestry, however, Martin belonged to a new age; when he began planning to move the Curia back to Rome, he linked the city's renewed religious mission with a cultural revival along the lines imagined by Petrarch, hoping to infuse Christian piety with classical grace. Born into a medieval barony, he ushered Rome into the Renaissance.

The process of moving the Curia was not a simple one; Martin succeeded only partially in convincing the cardinals that they belonged in Rome, not southern France. Neither was Rome itself a hospitable place. Gangs sponsored by the city's baronial families still fought in the streets. Malaria still ravaged the countryside, undercutting a productivity that had never been outstanding in the first place.

Martin's successor, Eugenius IV (1383–1447; reigned 1431–47), spent much of his papacy in Florence, where a thriving merchant economy and a republican government supported a population of 100,000. Life in Florence was better and safer than life in Rome, and its system of communications was better – no small matter for the men charged with running the universal Church. At the same time, Eugenius understood the symbolic importance of Rome and always planned to arrive there someday. As a pledge of his intent, he outfitted Saint Peter's basilica with a set of marvelous bronze doors, designed by the Florentine artist Antonio Averlino (*c.* 1400–*c.* 1469), whose Greek nickname, Filarete ("lover of virtue"), declared his own passion for a new Christian classicism. Filarete's doors (Figure 1.1) make an illustrated declaration of Rome's religious and cultural mission: they focus on the moment of Saint Peter's crucifixion, placing it clearly among the surviving monuments of the Roman cityscape: Castel Sant'Angelo (the mausoleum of the Emperor Hadrian made over into a papal fortress) and two ancient Roman funeral monuments in the shape of Egyptian pyramids, identified as the tombs of Romulus and Remus (despite the clear inscription declaring that the "tomb of Romulus" was in fact commissioned by the Roman official Gaius Cestius). Filarete portrays the Roman emperor who oversees Peter's execution clearly and accurately as Nero, taking the emperor's characteristic double chin and Greek-boy hair directly from ancient Roman coins and his pose from ancient historical reliefs. The geographic importance of Rome to the papacy – and of the classical heritage to Christianity – could not be more emphatically stated; Filarete's doors are a stirring sermon in bronze, the most tangible reminder of what Pope Eugenius aspired to achieve.

This reemergence of Rome as a Christian capital, although the reemergence was still largely symbolic, coincided with increasing danger to another Christian capital, Constantinople. As the fifteenth century progressed, the growing power and superb military organization of the Ottoman Turks posed an ever-greater threat to the weak Byzantine dynasty that held onto Constantinople. To avert that threat, the Byzantine emperor John VIII Palaiologos (reigned 1421–49) called on Eugenius in Florence in 1438, hoping to reconcile the Eastern and Western Churches (and thereby to recruit troops for his impending battle against the Turks). Eugenius called a Church Council, whose two years of sessions in Florence and Ferrara had little effect – except for the conversion of two influential members of John's entourage to Catholicism. The implications of the Council's failure were lost on no one: a steady stream of Greek refugees began trickling into Italy, bringing icons, manuscripts, and hopes that Christian Rome, like ancient Rome, would embrace Greek culture as an essential part of the classical heritage.

The cataclysm came in 1453, in a terrible siege that earned Sultan Mehmet II his epithet "the Conqueror" and changed the city's dominant religion from Christianity to Islam. With the fall of Constantinople to the Ottomans, Rome became, by default, the New Athens in papal rhetoric. This New Athens served above all as a cultural and religious capital, whose educated citizens, like the ancient Romans before them, studied both Greek and Latin. The papal library set the example; first established in the Vatican Palace by Pope Nicholas V (1397–1455; reigned 1447–55), it contained collections in both classical languages, ancient pagan authors alongside Christian writers, and also Hebrew texts and the works of Arab writers, mostly in Latin

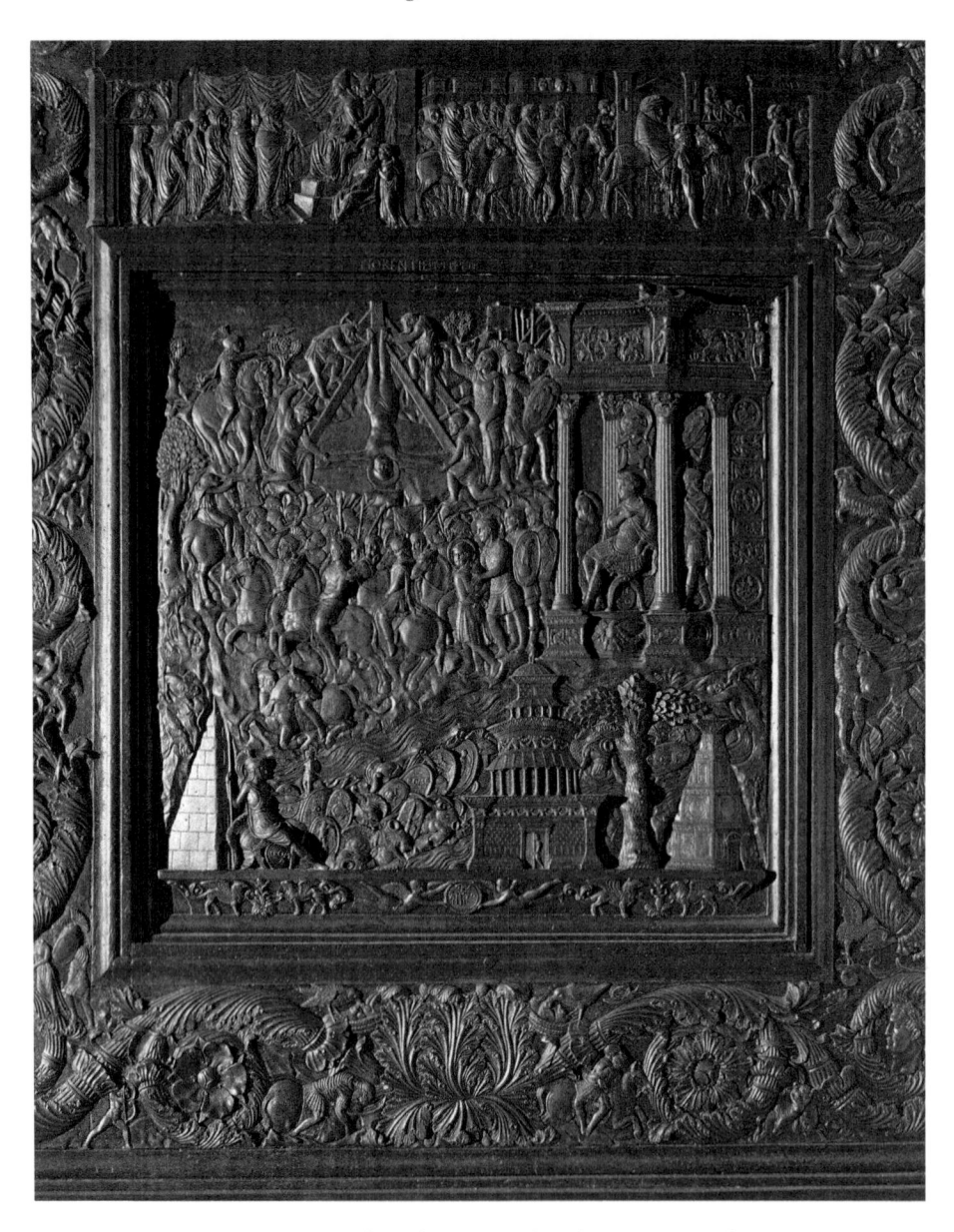

Figure 1.1 Antonio Filarete (*c.* 1400–69). *Martyrdom of St Peter*, detail from the central door of the basilica, decorated 1439–45 (bronze) (see also 247330–247337). © St Peter's, Vatican, Rome, Italy/The Bridgeman Art Library.

translation. Whatever Europe's political and religious divisions, classical culture provided a single shared tradition, modeled on the cosmopolitan society of Imperial Rome. In many ways the classical heritage may have been a fiction, but it was a story that bound widely differing people together in common projects and common ideals: churchmen, lords, scholars, merchants, and artisans.

Nicholas was the first fifteenth-century pope to reside permanently in Rome – and the first who did not have to compete with an anti-pope in Avignon or Pisa. He staffed the Curia with classically educated scholars who drafted his bulls and correspondence in a Latin that did its best to equal the example of the ancients, and set to work at transforming Rome into a city renewed in reality as well as rhetoric. The most influential of his advisors was the high-strung, versatile Leon Battista Alberti (1404–72): writer, painter, sculptor, athlete, archaeologist, and, significantly, a self-made man. Rome's renewal may have been sparked initially by the baronial pope Martin V, but most of the popes who oversaw the transformation of the ancient capital into the Eternal City came from much more humble stock, and so did the people around them. To avoid reviving the old rivalries between baronial families, the College of Cardinals, once returned to Rome, went out of its way to pick popes from obscure families. Because this arrangement also tended to favor men who had distinguished themselves by their own achievements, it ultimately worked to everyone's advantage. The popes' own social mobility in turn served as a pattern for the social mobility of the Curia around them, so that Rome and the Church more than ever became a magnet for talent, for the Italian peninsula and for the larger Christian world.

Still, passion and rhetoric were not enough on their own to sustain a project as ambitious as the revival of Rome; like any grand enterprise, the Eternal City was built on money. The Roman countryside, the Campagna, was neither outstandingly fertile nor outstandingly healthy. The city, therefore, pegged its revival on the Church as its chief source of revenue. The pilgrims who came to worship at the tombs of saints and to follow in the steps of the Apostles met with increasingly organized hospitality: the pallet-sellers who hawked straw beds under the porticoes of St Peter's competed now with the city's first real hotels, like the "Sun" near the Pantheon, attracting more elegant, and wealthier, clients. Cardinals brought in their own incomes: the staff of the Church, from Curial officials to bankers and tax collectors, paid for their positions, buying and selling them in an early version of the stock market. Musicians, artists, architects, and city planners followed the cardinals and their "families": so did tailors, shoemakers, laundrywomen, and prostitutes (the largest single group of professional women in the city). The Church's strictures on priestly celibacy skewed Roman society drastically toward single males, and to a certain extent the culture of papal Rome followed suit. Like ancient Rome, however, Renaissance Rome also knew its share of powerful women, like Lucrezia Borgia (1480–1519), Caterina Sforza (1463?–1509), and Vittoria Colonna (c. 1490–1547), who made their way despite narrowing limits on their social and legal rights over the course of the fifteenth and sixteenth centuries.

The projects initiated by Nicholas V set the pattern for subsequent Renaissance popes: he put a new lead roof on the dome of the Pantheon, put a new porch on the Early Christian church of Santo Stefano Rotondo, straightened the streets leading to the Vatican from the bankers' quarter, put a basin under the Trevi fountain, established a papal library, reinforced the Vatican's fortification walls and the bastion at Castel Sant'Angelo, and thought about remodeling Saint Peter's Basilica, by then a building with more than a thousand years behind it. In 1450, as popes had done every 50 years since 1300, Nicholas focused special energy on the Jubilee, a year-long festival when pilgrims to the city could earn indulgences – reprieves from penitential time in Purgatory after their deaths – by visiting a set group of the city's most ancient churches in a single day. For Nicholas, reviving Rome meant restoring the city's ancient monuments and preserving the written heritage of Greece and Rome, combined with encouraging acts of Christian piety, improving the city's physical conditions, and commissioning new bastions, churches, streets, and buildings – including improvements to his own palace in the Vatican. For the next 400 years, Roman popes, from Nicholas to his nineteenth-century successor Pius IX, would see all of these activities as essential duties of their pontificate, an office that assumed temporal responsibilities as well as a sacred priesthood.

Conceived as an expensive, impressive work in unending progress, papal Rome could not exist without the rest of Christendom and its contributions of faith, skill, and, not least, revenue. Taxes, tithes, and pilgrims poured into the Vatican from the whole Christian world, from churches in Ireland, Sweden, Poland, and Germany; Franciscan missions in Alexandria; Venetian colonists on Crete; Franciscans in China. Money could buy Masses, indulgences, and Curial positions, spiritual goods and services whose marketing observed the same economic principles as gold, grain, or cloth. The fifteenth century, in Italy especially, was an age of burgeoning capitalism, and Rome was not the only place where religion mixed candidly with finance. Tuscan merchants like Francesco di Marco Datini (1335–1410) headed their ledgers with the motto "in the name of God and of profit"; another Tuscan, the papal banker Agostino Chigi (1466–1520), more simply began his letters "in the name of God." From the Vatican's point of view, saying a Mass or granting an indulgence was priestly work, work no less meritorious than making a shoe or painting a Madonna, and as work it exacted its proper price. In return, Rome repaid its visitors and benefactors with spiritual as well as monetary rewards. Renaissance popes strove to make the city as beautiful as possible to attract pilgrims, but also to give them a foretaste of Heaven. As much as they talked about a crusade to win back terrain from the Turk, they trusted still more in the arts of sublime persuasion.

Only one Renaissance pope took the rhetoric of crusade further than fiery speeches. Pius II, Aeneas Silvius Piccolomini (1405–64; reigned 1458–64), had emerged from a tiny border town on the wild southern edge of Tuscany to prominence in a cardinal's entourage at the Council of Constance. Clever, cynical, and sophisticated, he must have seemed the least likely person in the world to mount an expedition against the sultan. But he was also a seasoned diplomat, a natural negotiator who took the loss of Constantinople by war uncommonly hard. Elected only five years after the siege, he heard the horrific tales of eyewitnesses to its climax, when the sultan on his white horse waded through streets washed in the blood of Byzantine Greeks. As pope, the elegant sophisticate turned into a tough old warrior, and not only against Mehmet the Conqueror. Pius is the only pope to have consigned a living person to Hell. Ironically, the object of this spectacular curse, the warlord Sigismondo Pandolfo Malatesta of Rimini (1417–68), was also the single Italian to have answered John VIII Palaiologos' call for crusade in 1438. And it was the idea of crusade that brought Sigismondo and the pope back together in 1463, as Pius prepared to set sail for Constantinople. Whatever Sigismondo's sins, real and alleged, Pius was willing to overlook them for a higher purpose.

As an urban planner, Pius devoted most of his efforts to Tuscany, transforming his birthplace, Corsignano, into a tiny jewel of a Renaissance town and rechristening it Pienza. He also built an imposing palazzo in Siena, flanked by a public loggia, both inspired by Florentine rather than Roman models. A remote backwater even after its refurbishing, Pienza did set one remarkable precedent for subsequent popes: in the tiny city's main piazza, and especially in its cathedral (Figure 1.2), Pius and his architect, Bernardo Rossellino (1409–64), strove to create a truly European style of architecture, combining Florentine, German, and Roman elements as if they belonged naturally together. Clearly, Pienza provided a miniature model for what Rome might become, but Pius would not live to see his model worked out on a larger scale. He fell ill as his crusaders gathered in Ancona, and died in 1464 before the expedition could ever set sail. His successors would use the word "crusade" to describe their belligerence against the sultan, but they carefully kept their military adventures close to home.

The first of those successors, Paul II (1417–71; reigned 1464–71), struck an uneasy balance between personal ambition and ambitions for Rome as a Christian capital. His greatest contribution to the cityscape was the huge palazzo he built beneath the Capitoline Hill (named "Palazzo Venezia" after the pontiff's native city). He hoped to make a more lasting mark on the Vatican by reforming the way it worked. In his view, the sale of Curial positions had bloated the size of his staff and removed most of the usual incentives to perform real work in office. He also seems to have harbored doubts about how Christian some of these ardent antiquarians could

Figure 1.2 Bernardo Rossellino (1409–64). Palazzo Piccolomini with the cathedral, Pienza. Scala Archives.

really be, as they dressed up in laurel wreaths and declaimed Latin poetry beneath the ruins. When some of his fired employees began to write scurrilous poems about Paul II and his reforms, he arrested them. The charges he leveled included sodomy and paganism; in his eyes, the humanist scholars who drafted his correspondence and composed his bulls had taken Rome's revival of pagan antiquity and Platonic eros much too literally. He imprisoned some in Castel Sant'Angelo for as long as a year, subjecting several of them to torture. The investigations revealed nothing, and eventually Paul was forced to release all his prisoners without pressing charges. Like a certain number of northern Italians, this Venetian pope never quite grasped the culture of Renaissance Rome, in which veneration for the ancients lived in uncomplicated coexistence with Christianity. Rather than competing with each other, the city's monuments, classical and Christian, stood as a constant reminder that the Roman Empire and the Church had come into being at virtually the same time. Inseparable in the past, they remained inseparable in the present. The city was built of layer upon layer of history, culture upon culture, with nothing ever entirely destroyed and nothing ever left quite as it was. Romans, ancient, medieval, and Renaissance, felt free to transform even their most venerable monuments; preservation meant adapting old buildings to new uses. Roman builders, architects, and sculptors also mined the ruins for building stone, statues, or colored marbles.

The first Renaissance pope to effect a visible transformation of Rome was the eminent Franciscan theologian who succeeded Paul II to the papacy, Sixtus IV della Rovere (1418–84; reigned 1471–84). Unlike his predecessor, Sixtus understood exactly what the Christian classical culture of Renaissance Rome was about, and made the most of it. He began by restoring the system of venal offices that had sustained the Curia before Pope Paul's failed attempt to reform it; in this way he won the immediate loyalty of a staff that had always included the city's best writers and speakers. The humanists, for their part, turned their voices and pens toward praising the pope rather than continuing the bitter vituperation they had unleashed on the unfortunate Paul (who, more than 500 years later, has yet to recover his reputation). Sixtus honored one of the ringleaders of the rebellion, Bartolommeo Platina (1421–81), by making him librarian of a refurbished and greatly expanded Vatican Library, throwing the collection open to scholars and commissioning an extensive series of new manuscripts to round out its holdings. He opened the world's first public museum on the Capitoline Hill, seat of Rome's city council and what remained of the Roman Senate (most of the Senate's power and pageantry had been transferred a thousand years before to the "Sacred Senate," the College of Cardinals).

At the same time, Sixtus paid close attention to the city's infrastructure, repairing walls, roads, and aqueducts and constructing a new bridge across the Tiber, the gracefully arcaded Ponte Sisto. Within the Vatican itself, he moved the library to new quarters and constructed the spacious new Sistine Chapel to house papal ceremonies. The chapel's decorative scheme shows how Sixtus worked as a sponsor. He personally chose the subjects to be shown on the walls: parallel events from the lives of Moses and Jesus, each carefully labeled in Latin; Sixtus worked out the mottoes as well. To execute the frescoes, he invited a whole team of painters from Florence: Botticelli, Ghirlandaio, Signorelli, Perugino, and Cosimo Rosselli, assigning them each different episodes. He trusted that the competitive pressures of painting side by side would challenge the artists to do their best work, and as quickly as possible. The shrewd old pope was perfectly right: the Sistine Chapel was built and painted in record time.

Although Renaissance popes tended to come from relatively undistinguished families, when elected they invariably used their office to advance the family's position in the Church and in the secular world. Sixtus had a particularly large complement of nephews to place in strategic positions; this he did with ruthless alacrity. Several of them appear in the remarkable fresco he commissioned to honor the reorganization of the Vatican Library in 1475 (Figure 1.3). Its painter, Melozzo da Forlì (1438–94), was a favorite of the pope, spared the trials of competitive painting in the Sistine Chapel to work independently on other projects, including this frescoed monument to the pope's achievements. There is no question which of the papal nephews most impressed Melozzo; he strides across the center of the painting, stealing the scene from everyone else, including his uncle the pope, who sits off to the right. At the time, Cardinal Giuliano della Rovere (1443–1513) was 34, and no one knew quite what to make of him or his evident ambition. Melozzo avoids showing the man head-on, but even from the side we can still feel the intensity of Cardinal Giuliano's gimlet gaze; his cousin Raffaele Riario visibly shrinks back from its force. No one studied the meaning of Sixtus and his papacy as carefully as this cardinal nephew. He was not Sixtus' favorite, but his central position in Melozzo's important fresco shows how much the pope respected him.

Sixtus' immediate successor, Innocent VIII, cut a much less active figure, especially by comparison with the pope who was elected in 1492, Rodrigo Borgia (1431?–1503), who took the name Alexander VI. A Spaniard like his uncle, Calixtus III (1378–1458; reigned 1455–58), Alexander had spent 30 years in the office of vice-chancellor of the Apostolic Chamber, the chief financial office of the Curia (the office of chancellor had disappeared sometime in the Middle Ages). The College elected Cardinal Borgia because he was a proven administrator (a talent he shared with his former mistress, Vannozza Cattanei (1442–1518), the mother of his four children, Juan, Cesare, Lucrezia, and Jofré; during their years together, Vannozza invested wisely in real estate, and married well, long before Borgia finally left her for a younger woman).

Alexander's papacy was the first to contend with the entry of the New World into European trading networks. Gold from one of the early Spanish expeditions covers the coffered ceiling of the Basilica of Santa Maria Maggiore, countless pre-Columbian artefacts melted down into gold leaf applied to wooden rosettes and a wooden relief of the Borgia coat of arms. Although Franciscan missions had been operating in Asia and North Africa since the Middle Ages, the intensification of travel along traditional trade routes at the end of the fifteenth century took on increasing political significance for the Church. As the Augustinian prelate Giles of Viterbo would note in about 1506, every nation in the world acknowledged God. Over the next two centuries, Christian missionaries would try to ensure that the nations acknowledged Rome as well. The most enterprising of these global missionaries belonged to an order founded in the sixteenth century (1540), the Society of Jesus; a century after the order's foundation, its members could boast that somewhere in the world the sun was always shining on a Jesuit house.

Figure 1.3 Melozzo da Forlì (1438–94). *Pope Sixtus IV (1414–84) (Francesco della Rovere) installs Bartolommeo Platina as Director of the Vatican Library*, c. 1477 (fresco transferred to canvas). © Vatican Museums and Galleries, Vatican City, Italy/The Bridgeman Art Library.

For Alexander VI, however, political problems closer to home ensured that his reign was fraught with trouble, a good deal of it caused by his own son Cesare (1475–1507), whose ruthless political ambitions wrought havoc for a few years in central Italy. When he was not reining in his son or marrying off his thrice-married daughter Lucrezia, the pope made some significant changes to Rome's cityscape, notably by tearing down an ancient pyramidal tomb near the Vatican to make way for a new street, the Via Alessandrina. Thanks to his patronage, gold glittered not only from

Figure 1.4 Bernardino Pinturicchio. *Disputation of Saint Catherine*. Borgia Apartments, Vatican, Vatican City/Scala Archives.

the ceiling of Santa Maria Maggiore but also from the frescoes he commissioned for his apartments in the Apostolic Palace, executed by Bernardino Pinturicchio (*c.* 1454–1513), whose explorations of ancient Roman ruins infused his artistic style with daring perspectives, stucco frames, and stately figures. The Borgia apartments are especially distinctive for the way that they focus on Egypt; on their walls, Rome becomes a new Alexandria, with Lucrezia Borgia taking the part of the Alexandrian princess Saint Catherine disputing with the city's famous sages (Figure 1.4) and Isis presiding over the Liberal Arts.

This emphasis on Egypt may not have been entirely fanciful (although there was also a good deal of fancy involved – the Spanish pope traced the bull on his coat of arms back to the Apis bull that represented Osiris); at the turn of the sixteenth century, the Ottoman Turks were on the move again, and this time their objective was Cairo. Just as Rome had served Byzantine refugees as the New Athens, reports from North Africa suggested that the Eternal City might soon have to take on the role of New Alexandria.

The most emphatic expression of Rome as a universal cultural capital came, however, with Alexander's successor and bitter adversary: Cardinal Giuliano della Rovere, the nephew of Sixtus IV, elected in 1503 as Julius II. Cardinal Giuliano had left nothing to chance with his election; as the cardinals gathered in the Sistine Chapel for the conclave, he managed to install his cubicle beneath Perugino's fresco of Christ handing over the keys to Saint Peter (Figure 1.5), the position that was believed to bring the best luck because it played out the founding moment of the

Figure 1.5 Pietro Perugino (c. 1445–1523). *Giving of the Keys to St Peter*, from the Sistine Chapel, 1481 (fresco). © Vatican Museums and Galleries, Vatican City, Italy/The Bridgeman Art Library.

Roman papacy. He let his bribes do the rest, drawing his example from another famous Julius who bribed his way into Rome's most important priesthood, the office of Pontifex Maximus: Julius Caesar. At his election to the papacy, Pope Julius took on both Caesar's ancient title and his name. And like Caesar before him, he knew what he wanted to do with Rome.

The image of Renaissance Rome as we see it now is essentially the vision of Julius II. His actions in office show how carefully he had studied his uncle's pontificate, and many of his interventions follow the lead of Sixtus IV. They do so, however, on a scale that Sixtus could never have imagined, and with a series of collaborators whose talents forever changed Rome's painting, sculpture, architecture, and city planning. In the first place, Julius could call upon vast reserves of money for his projects, evidence that his predecessor Alexander VI must have continued to ensure an efficient administration for the Church and its temporal state. (In fact, the Borgias' notorious reputation is another lasting legacy of Julius II.) Julius also made bold use of the papal bankers, above all the Sienese magnate Agostino Chigi. A Tuscan banker who had come into prominence under the Borgia, Chigi approached banking with the same kind of comprehensive vision that Julius applied to the Church. He became the pope's financial advisor and, on occasion, a diplomat in the papal service. He also became inordinately rich, so renowned that Sultan Bajazet II (1447–1512) called him "the great merchant of Christendom" and sent him the gift of a splendid Arabian horse – for Chigi, commerce was better than any crusade. Julius seems to have understood instinctively what an economic mind like Chigi's could do for the papacy, and what the papacy could do for Chigi; soon Agostino and his associates would routinely use excommunication as a means of coercing their debtors, creditors, and business rivals. Chigi participated in – and on occasion guided – the pope's political plans, and paid close attention to developments in art, music, and literature; he would become Raphael's most important private patron and the first publisher of an ancient Greek text in Rome.

Julius entrusted the sale of indulgences in Germany to another of his bankers, Johann Jakob Fugger of Augsburg (1459–1525), who quickly acquired his own nickname: "Der Reiche" – "the Rich." Revenue from German indulgences enabled Julius to initiate a project that Nicholas V had only considered 50 years before: the wholesale reconstruction of Saint Peter's Basilica. Julius had no intention of repairing the existing basilica: he planned to raze the early Christian monument and put a new one in its place, a building so beautiful that it would either reinforce pilgrims in their faith or convert skeptics on the spot. As architect, he chose a new arrival in Rome who had already designed a stunningly innovative classical building called the "Tempietto" or "Little Temple" – Donato Bramante of Urbino (1444–1514). The pope and Bramante became friends as well as collaborators; when Julius wanted to relax, Bramante recited Dante, or sang the popular songs called *strambotti* to his lute. A megalomaniac no less than Julius, he kept close control over most of the pope's commissions for architecture and city planning, and introduced Julius to a young relative of his, the painter Raphael, when the pope decided to redecorate his apartments.

By destroying the old Saint Peter's and replacing it with an entirely new building, Julius meant to send a signal to the newly expanded Christian world: sixteenth-century Rome was a new Rome, not just revived or remodeled but recreated, the modern capital of a truly universal Church. He ordered a team of artists to repeat the same themes on the walls of his apartments, but quickly decided to entrust the entire project to Raphael (1483–1520). To redecorate the ceiling of his uncle's Sistine Chapel, he compelled Michelangelo (1475–1564), over the artist's loud protests, to become a painter, and, as usual, his instincts proved flawless.

Julius applied the same combination of bold insight and relentless bullying to improving the rest of Rome. To set off the Vatican and impose order on Rome's labyrinthine streets, he and Bramante decided to cut two parallel thoroughfares through the city, running straight along either side of the Tiber from the Ponte Sisto of Sixtus IV to the gates of Vatican City. The river itself acted as a third corridor in between, for in those days it carried a dense traffic of cargo ships and ferries. Because ancient Roman roads also ran famously straight, their project restored an element of ancient Roman planning to a cityscape where only one ancient Roman road had continued to obey this rule: the Via del Corso that led from the city's northern gate, the Porta del Popolo, to the roots of the Capitoline Hill.

The new street that Bramante cut on the side of the bankers' quarter, the Via Giulia (obviously named for the pope), was to be anchored halfway along its trajectory by a huge palazzo, designed, of course, by himself. Here he would house the offices of the Curial bureaucracy and the papal tribunal in a single location, and in a public building rather than a cardinal's palazzo (as had been the case so far). The rest of the street would be lined by sumptuous palazzi, those on the southern side of the street with gardens reaching down to the river's edge. On the opposite side of the river, the Via della Lungara had always connected the Vatican with the densely populated area of Trastevere, passing through an area sprinkled with convents and the small garden plots called *vigne*, grape arbors, where Romans withdrew to escape the crowds and smells of the city and to produce their own personal supplies of vegetables and wine. The pope's new plan called for villas on large plots to replace the more humble retreats.

Renaissance popes had long used competition as a way of ensuring that large projects were completed quickly; Julius' uncle, Pope Sixtus IV, had engaged a whole series of prominent artists to fresco the walls of his new Sistine Chapel in 1481, confident that their eagerness to outdo one another would make them work as fast and well as they could. They finished within two years. Now Julius II and Bramante hoped that the same kinds of rivalry would speed Rome's transformation into a glorious garden city.

For a pope who reigned for only ten years, the list of Julius' interventions in Rome is astounding. Like any attentive student of ancient Roman ruins, he tried to emulate the triumphs of ancient engineering as well as ancient art, installing sewers, paving streets and squares, repairing aqueducts, and outfitting his own apartments with facilities for bathing. His eye for ancient art equaled his eye for modern talent – it was, after all, Julius who saw a great painter in the sculptor Michelangelo, not Michelangelo himself. Julius installed his personal collection of antique statues in the Vatican Palace, and asked Bramante (as always) to provide an appropriate setting, thereby creating the first version of the Vatican museums. Furthermore, although he famously declared that he was no scholar, Julius had a virtual mania for libraries, as one contemporary biographer reported:[2]

> Julius also erected many palaces, buildings, and churches from the ground up, or restored them, or remodeled them for the better . . . [In the Vatican] he built a new private upstairs library, called the Biblioteca Julia, decorating it with images of the stars and planets . . . He also decorated the library of Saint Peter's, and built still other libraries at the church of Santissimi Dodici Apostoli and San Pietro in Vincoli. He restored the Mausoleum of Hadrian, which had been fortified by Alexander VI. In the place called the Belvedere he constructed a permanent building with sumptuous stone inlay, bronze and marble statues, and pictures of the cities of Italy . . . He widened the Via Pontificalis beyond what Sixtus and Innocent had done and began the new Via Giulia all the way to the Ponte Sisto . . . In his time the Piazza Sant'Eustachio and Piazza Campo Marzio, Piazza in Piscinula and Piazza San Lorenzo in Damaso, Piazza di San Marcello and Piazza Santissimi Dodici Apostoli were paved with brick and sewers were installed . . . He installed the fountain and well at the Belvedere, with its underground aqueduct that came into the city from the second milestone. He added other aqueducts to the Aqua Virgo, restored at great expense. He cleared the old sewers and installed new ones. In the year 1506 he commanded that the Basilica of St. Peter in the Vatican be renewed and expanded, and on April 15 of that year he laid the cornerstone on the site with his own hands . . . with 25 cardinals attending, the whole Curia, and the people of Rome. He also restored the Apostolic Palace in several places, and established a public university at

the church of the Apostle James . . . He was famous to north, south, east and west, both feared and venerated.

Julius was fearsome, not only for his ferocious temper but also for the accuracy of his instincts. Projects that looked reckless proved not to be so once they had been driven to completion. And the pope was willing to do nearly anything to see his visions brought into being. Twice Julius climbed into a suit of armor to lead military expeditions against the cities of Perugia and Bologna, expelling their ruling families and installing his own governors: their status as vassal states had become more a matter of loose symbolism than real subordination. In a similar spirit, he resolved to drive the French from Italy at a time when they were firmly ensconced in Milan and Genoa, and by sponsoring a series of military campaigns and diplomatic missions (including a remarkable mission to Venice in 1511, on which his fantastically wealthy banker friend, Agostino Chigi, offered the Venetians a "loan" in exchange for political loyalty), he succeeded in driving out the last French army by 1512. He engaged a troop of Swiss mercenaries as the papal guard, an office their descendants still perform today. Not all the pope's actions were so aggressive; he also called an ecumenical council, the Fifth Lateran Council, to address charges of corruption within the Church. By the time it convened in 1512, however, his health, never good, had begun to collapse. By March of 1513, Julius was dead. In a dialogue penned for the occasion, Erasmus (1466–1536) caricatured him stomping up to Heaven in a clanking suit of armor to berate Saint Peter at the Pearly Gates. The title "Julius Excluded from Heaven" gives away the outcome of this bitingly funny pamphlet. The sight of a pope in arms had shocked many of Julius' contemporaries, too overwhelmed by his personality to notice how many of his achievements were quietly constructive and pointedly intellectual.

The real force of Julius' papacy emerges in an oration delivered before the pope on January 1, 1508: on that occasion, the Roman professor Battista Casali declared that Christendom's most powerful weapon against Ottoman aggression was not another crusade, but the Vatican Library. Shortly thereafter, as if to echo Casali's thoughts, Raphael would paint his *School of Athens* (Figure 1.6) on a wall of Julius' private apartments, a soaring temple where Greek philosophers from Athens, Syracuse, and Alexandria (and at least one Arab commentator) engage in a conversation that transcends the boundaries of place, time, language, and religion. Significantly, the books that Plato and Aristotle carry in Raphael's fresco are labeled in Italian: "Timeo" for Plato's dialogue *Timaeus* and "Etica" for Aristotle's *Ethics* – this *School of Athens* represents not so much an ideal past in classical Greece as an ideal present in papal Rome. Neither is it any accident that Raphael's great temple of wisdom looks so much like Bramante's design for St Peter's Basilica; in a painted idyll and a monumental building, each aimed to embody a new architecture in which classical style radiated spiritual conviction. As a political entity, the Rome of Julius II was as precarious as the pope's indifferent health, but as an idea, his Eternal City was as lively, as fierce, and as creative as his famously implacable will.

Julius II was the last pope to preside over an undivided western Church. His successor, Leo X, the former Giovanni de' Medici (1475–1521; reigned 1513–21), may have been the son of the charismatic Florentine magnate Lorenzo il Magnifico,

Figure 1.6 Raphael. *The School of Athens*. The Art Archive/Vatican Museum, Rome.

but he lacked Lorenzo's ruthless awareness of power; he found himself ineffectually caught between the machinations of France, Spain, and the Holy Roman Emperor. Leo's fiscal sense was if anything worse than his sense for politics; the treasury that Alexander VI and Julius II had carefully built up had been squandered early in the new pope's reign, mostly on hunting expeditions and lavish parties. Although the Lateran Council continued under Leo, its initiatives for reforming the Church were too ineffectual, and too late: in 1517, an Augustinian friar from Wittenberg in northern Germany, Martin Luther (1483–1546), posted his 95 theses disputing papal authority, and it fell to Leo to excommunicate the German renegade in 1521. Rome's stature as cultural capital would have to contend ever afterward with its northern European counter-image as a new Babylon, mired in corruption.

Ironically, Luther had visited Rome in the winter of 1510–11, when the enterprising spirit of Julius II was at its peak. His delayed reaction to the experience, like Erasmus' caricature of the same pope "Excluded from Heaven," shows that Roman culture, despite its vigorous search for universal forms of expression and universal authority, struck many outsiders as strange, artificial, and dangerously pagan. Another Erasmian dialogue, *The Ciceronian* (*Ciceronianus*) of 1528, mocks the extravagant lengths to which Roman rhetoric would go in order to preserve an antique flavor, calling the pope "Jupiter the Thunderer," nuns "Vestal Virgins," and the College of Cardinals the "Sacred Senate." The taste for collecting ancient statues and commissioning allegorical paintings had become truly international by the early sixteenth century, but the cultivation of classical style also bred opponents on both sides of the divide between Catholic and Protestant.

The Protestant Reformation quickly became a political as well as a religious question. When Holy Roman Emperor Charles V (1500–58) released a troop of German mercenaries from service in central Italy in the spring of 1527, they descended on Rome, sacking the city repeatedly over the course of six months. To classically minded contemporaries, the Sack of 1527 seemed to recall the disaster of AD 410 when Alaric and the Visigoths ravaged Imperial Rome, inspiring St Augustine to write his monumental *City of God* as an attempt to explain how the Lord could permit such tragedies and ushering in the real decline and fall of the Roman Empire. Despite its high symbolic value, the Sack of 1527 was far less cataclysmic in its real effects; both the physical city and its image as an eternal capital rebounded fairly quickly from the brief, terrifying setback. Next to the Church, construction provided the chief source of economic activity for sixteenth-century Rome, a trend that would continue throughout the seventeenth century, and one on which the Sack of 1527 had little effect.

Protestant pressures did convince the Roman Church that it should undertake its own internal reforms. In 1539, Pope Paul III (1468–1549; reigned 1534–49) called a general council of the Church, which convened in the northern Italian city of Trent in order to make at least a physical approach toward the German reformers. Contentious and politicized, the Council of Trent issued its final decrees only in 1563, generally opting for aggressive rather than conciliatory stances. Although some popes took the Council's reforms to mean that the Vatican should sell off its collection of classical statues – like the saintly Pius V (1504–72; reigned 1566–72) – in general the papacy understood its mission in the same terms as Julius II: Rome was the eternal capital of a confluence of cultures that transcended every difference of time, place, and language, and a pope's responsibilities to the city ranged from spiritual guidance to city planning, construction, and attention to infrastructure. Hence an intellectual pope like Gregory XIII (1502–85; reigned 1572–85) established colleges for the study of Greek and Hebrew, sponsored a new building for the Jesuits' Roman College, appointed the Jesuit mathematician Christoph Clavius (1538–1612) to oversee reformation of the calendar, and put that revised Gregorian calendar into effect in 1582. A militant pope like Sixtus V (1521–90; reigned 1585–90), Gregory's successor, created long, straight streets to accommodate the new fashion of transportation by carriage, and re-erected three Egyptian obelisks – after duly exorcizing them, baptizing them, and topping them with bronze crosses – to guide pilgrims on their way through Rome. But Sixtus also installed a new aqueduct to bring water to the heights of the Quirinal Hill and set up a silk factory inside the Colosseum. Every move these popes made was marked by statues, inscriptions, pamphlets, and parades, in which classical allegories continued to provide the chief means of expression. The buildings and urban schemes they commissioned, and their relationships with their architects, continued to follow the example set by Julius II and Bramante, from Sixtus V with Domenico Fontana (1543–1607) (a brilliantly ingenious engineer but a thoroughly conventional architect) to the great papal patrons of the seventeenth century, Urban VIII, Innocent X, and Alexander VII, who oversaw, and often sparked, the rivalries of the great Baroque architects Gianlorenzo Bernini, Francesco Borromini, and Pietro da Cortona, and created much of the Rome that we see today – at least the part not irrevocably altered by Benito Mussolini, who in his own way became yet another emulator of Julius II.

It took many decades for the popes to grasp how firmly Renaissance rhetoric was rooted in practical reality: Rome's most powerful asset as a Christian capital was, in fact, its beauty. Set against a background of imposing ruins, the glory of the city's modern monuments made a more powerful argument for Rome's state of economic and spiritual health than words, armies, or intimidation. The repressive popes, like Clement VIII, whose activities for the Jubilee Year of 1600 included burning the philosopher Giordano Bruno at the stake, or Saint Pius V, who contemplated selling off the "pagan" Vatican Museum, have never been able to compete with the popes who took the New Testament's insistent architectural metaphors as a guide to their own activities, building up Rome as the Gospel writers and Saint Paul exhorted Christians to build up their Church. For the Jubilee of 1650, rather than immolate dissenters, Pope Innocent X adorned the walls of St Peter's and the Lateran Basilica with panels of colored marble and commissioned a glorious fountain for Piazza Navona, conveniently set halfway along the pilgrim route from Capitoline to Vatican. Ever since its unveiling in 1651 – the designer missed his Jubilee deadline – Gianlorenzo Bernini's *Fountain of the Four Rivers* has become one of Rome's most beloved monuments. As Innocent X well realized, for sheer persuasive force the momentary shock of a burning heretic can never equal the reliable if subtle solace of a fountain. Neither have the papal armies ever obtained anywhere near the success of the papal artists, architects, and city planners. Long after the Ferrara Salt War of 1510, the War of Castro of 1640, and the siege of Rome in 1849 have become distant memories and the papacy itself musters only its colorful troop of Swiss Guards, the Eternal City draws more visitors than ever, pilgrims now of every faith, and from every region of the globe. Still a capital, Rome, in all its complexity and its resilient beauty, shows how durably ideas can shape an entity as concrete as a city, and how, in the face of constant change, fallible human minds and hands can still create works of lasting value.

NOTES

1   Francesco Petrarca, Letter to Guido Sette, *c.* 1367–68: "Inde autem . . . primum Roman adii; que, etsi iam tunc multoque prius nichil aliud quasi quam illius Rome veteris argumentum aut imago quedam esset, ruinisque presentibus preteritam magnitudinem testaretur, erant tamen adhuc cinieres in illo generose alique faville: nunc extinctus et iam gelidus cinis est." Cited from Emilio Bigi, ed., *Opere di Francesco Petrarca* (Milan: Ugo Mursia, 1979), p. 952.

2   This text is taken from the *History of Siena* (*Historia Senensium*) composed in the sixteenth century by the Tuscan cleric Sigismondo Ticci (1458–1528), whose name is usually given, inaccurately, as "Sigismondo Tizio" (not least because there is an Italian pun involved; "Tizio" is slang for "guy"). The original manuscript of the *Historia Senensium* is preserved in the Vatican Library in ten volumes; these are gradually being edited and published by the Istituto di Storia Moderna in Florence. The present text is condensed from Vatican MS Chigi G.II.37, fols. 231r.–232v.; my edition of that entire manuscript will be published in 2007.

SUGGESTIONS FOR FURTHER READING

Primary sources

Erasmus, Desiderius. *Ciceronianus*, trans. Margaret Mann Phillips, *Collected Works of Erasmus*, Vol. 28, A. H. T. Levi, ed. Toronto: University of Toronto Press, 1978.

—— *The Julius Exclusus of Erasmus*, trans. Paul Pascal, with an introduction and notes by J. Kelley Sowards. Bloomington: Indiana University Press, 1980.

Secondary sources

Ackerman, James. "The Planning of Renaissance Rome, 1450–1580," in P. A. Ramsey, ed., *Rome in the Renaissance. The City and the Myth*. Binghamton, N.Y.: Center for Medieval and Early Renaissance Studies, 1982, 3–17.

Barkan, Leonard. *Unearthing the Past: Archaeology and Aesthetics in the Making of Renaissance Culture*. New Haven and London: Yale University Press, 2000.

Cole, Bruce, *Michelangelo, Bramante and Raphael: The High Renaissance in Rome*. New York: Westview Press, 2006.

D'Amico, John F. *Renaissance Humanism in Papal Rome: Humanists and Churchmen on the Eve of the Reformation*. Baltimore: Johns Hopkins University Press, 1983.

Frommel, Christoph Luitpold. "Papal Policy: The Planning of Rome During the Renaissance," in Robert I. Rotberg and Theodore K. Rabb, eds, *Art and History: Images and their Meaning*. Cambridge: Cambridge University Press, 1988, 39–66.

Gilbert, Felix. *The Pope, His Banker, and Venice*. Cambridge, Mass.: Harvard University Press, 1980.

Grafton, Anthony, ed., *Rome Reborn: The Vatican Library and Renaissance Culture*. New Haven and London: Yale University Press, 1993.

Günther, Hubertus, "Urban Planning in Rome under the Medici Popes," in Henry A. Millon and Vittorio Magnago Lampugnani, *From Brunelleschi to Michelangelo. The Representation of Architecture*. Milan: Bompiani, 1994, 545–49.

Hall, Marcia B., ed. *Rome (Artistic Centers of the Italian Renaissance)*. Cambridge and New York: Cambridge University Press, 2005.

Jacks, Philip. *The Antiquarian and the Myth of Antiquity: The Origins of Rome in Renaissance Thought*. Cambridge and London: Cambridge University Press, 1993.

Lanciani, Rodolfo. *Ruins and Excavations of Ancient Rome*. London: Macmillan, 1897 (reprint, Boston: Elibron Classics, 2000).

McGregor, James H. *Rome from the Ground Up*. Cambridge, Mass.: Belknap Press, 2006.

Magnuson, Torgil. *Rome in the Age of Bernini*. Vol. I: *From the Election of Sixtus V to the Death of Urban VIII*. Stockholm: Amqvist and Wiksell, 1982.

Masson, Giorgina. *The Companion Guide to Rome*, revised by John Fort. Woodbridge, Suffolk: Boydell & Brewer, 2006.

Mitchell, Bonner. *Rome in the High Renaissance: The Age of Leo X*. Norman: University of Oklahoma Press, 1973.

Partner, Peter. *Renaissance Rome, 1500–1559: A Portrait of a Society*. Berkeley: University of California Press, 1977.

Partridge, Loren. *The Art of Renaissance Rome, 1400–1600*. New York: Prentice-Hall, 2003.

Pellecchia, Linda. "The Contested City: Urban Form in Early Sixteenth-century Rome," in Marcia B. Hall, ed., *The Cambridge Companion to Raphael*. Cambridge and New York: Cambridge University Press, 2005, 59–94.

Rowland, Ingrid D. *The Culture of the High Renaissance: Ancients and Moderns in Sixteenth-century Rome*. Cambridge and New York: Cambridge University Press, 1998.
Shaw, Christine. *Julius II: The Warrior Pope*. Oxford: Blackwell, 1993.
Stinger, Charles L. *The Renaissance in Rome*. Bloomington: University of Indiana Press, revised edition 1998.
Von Pastor, Ludwig. *History of the Popes*, trans. Ignatius Antrobus. London: Kegan Paul, 1923–53.
Westfall, Carroll William. *In This Most Perfect Paradise: Alberti, Nicholas V, and the Invention of Conscious Urban Planning in Rome, 1447–1455*. University Park: Pennsylvania State University Press, 1974.

CHAPTER TWO

FRAMING AND MIRRORING THE WORLD

Lyle Massey

There is perhaps no invention more closely associated with the Renaissance than that of linear or pictorial perspective. Voicing the most advanced ideas of his time, Leonardo da Vinci (1452–1519) said that perspective is "the signpost and gateway" without which nothing "can be done well in the matter of painting."[1] For Leonardo, rather than merely mirroring the seen world, perspectival pictures that are based on optical principles convey a fundamental understanding of nature. In the 500 years since Leonardo's death, this geometric technique has become indelibly associated with notions of epistemological progress and representational realism. Essentially the application of medieval optical geometry to painting, sculpture, and architecture, perspective has been credited with inaugurating a new way of seeing the world, creating a rational framework on which scientific empiricism would come to depend, and erecting an analytic scaffolding for representation itself.

While many have celebrated perspective as one of the crowning achievements of the Renaissance, this technical invention has also had its detractors. Most fifteenth-century artists and thinkers, for example, believed that painters' geometry was directly analogous to optical vision as it was then understood. But cognitive and perceptual theorists long ago rejected this comparison, arguing that sight is a far more complex and multifaceted phenomenon than perspective's reliance on a single point of view would suggest. Social theorists have also criticized one-point perspective, albeit for different reasons. They point out that while it has been hailed for having created a universal, humanist point of view, in actuality perspective posited an elite and literate viewer whose class, gender, and intellectual background were always already encoded in the technique's geometry and application. Some post-Cartesian philosophers have also rejected perspective's apparent reduction of the body to a visual apparatus. They question the mind/body distinctions and epistemological over-valuations of sight to which perspective has contributed. Some art historians have argued that the focus on perspective has created an Italian-centric bias in the discipline that overlooks many other contemporaneous theories of optics and representation, such as those exhibited in northern Renaissance art, for instance, or in non-European cultures. Others have pointed out that perspective became the arid foundation of a banal academic practice that was first challenged by modernist avant-garde movements and then irrevocably deconstructed by post-modernist theoretical practice. Perspective is therefore a conundrum. On the one hand it is associated with the lasting ingenuity and sagacity of the Renaissance and on the other with false ideologies, pre-modern philosophical complacencies, and a legacy of rigid representational formalism.

However, from its inception perspective has been a contested and heterogeneous set of theories, practices, and expectations. After centuries of debate we still do not know precisely what perspective signified in the minds of those who invented and used it. Perspective became a powerful medium for experimentation precisely because it encompassed contrasting modes of inquiry. On the one hand, it advanced theories of both optics and geometry. On the other, it was used in the service of increasingly more sophisticated illusions intended to deceive and delight the senses. Perspective thus has always embodied antithetical statements about the nature of optics, reality, and human knowledge.

In many respects, the study of perspective was merely one segment of a broader concern with vision and opticality that spread through Europe in the sixteenth century. Understanding how we see was thought to be paramount to understanding what we see. As speculations about the relationship between the senses and perception increased, artists, engineers, and natural philosophers constructed drawing machines, lens-based apparatuses, and other optical instruments that could demonstrate various theories and advance knowledge about vision. Perspective, as it was promulgated in various treatises and in practice, constituted a discourse on vision that intersected with but did not necessarily dominate these others types of investigation. However, because it was an expression of both geometric and representational ideals, perspective also stood apart from other forms of inquiry. As a technique employed to render illusions, perspective was always a paradox: that is, it was partly an experimental science, but also partly a hallucinatory aid.

In a famous illustration (Figure 2.1) that appears at the end of his treatise on proportion, *Underweysung der Messung* (Nuremberg, 1525), the German artist Albrecht Dürer (1471–1528) depicts a drawing machine used to trace the points of convergence between a lute, an intersecting plane, and a hypothetical, ideal viewpoint. This one condensed image asserts that by applying the rational principles of Euclidean optical theory and geometry to painting, artists could recreate a rationalized three-dimensional world on a two-dimensional surface. The machine's end product would have been illusionistic: e.g., the resulting image would have engaged the viewer in a visual game of *trompe l'oeil*. But in the sixteenth century, this kind of machine was also understood to demonstrate certain truths about vision and geometry and to connect representation to nature in an unprecedented way.

It is noteworthy, however, that Dürer's image also indicates how even the most rational applications of perspective reveal basic epistemological inconsistencies between theory and practice. Two men are shown manipulating Dürer's machine. One man holds a string that is fixed by a pin to a back wall, and he uses it to mark various points on the lute. The other squeezes into the small space between the pin and the apparatus in order to mark where the string crosses through the hinged window. This picture shows us that while the construction of illusions depends on the embodied view of both the artist and the viewer, the ideal projected viewpoint

Figure 2.1 From Albrecht Dürer, *Draughtsmen with Lute*, in his *Underweysung der Messung mit dem Zirkel und Richtscheyt*. Nuremberg, 1525.

of perspective is abstract, disembodied, and mathematical. Dürer's technicians give form to an ideal scenario, but they also stand outside that scenario's projection. The image presents us with a conflict between two kinds of viewpoint. One is archetypal and transcendent, and the other is heterogeneous and corporeal. One constitutes a generic, universal paradigm, and the other a complex, contingent variable.

A HISTORY OF PERSPECTIVE AS A PRACTICE

While Dürer's was the first printed treatise to depict artists actually using perspective, it was the Italian humanist Leon Battista Alberti (1404–72) who initially described the principles on which Dürer's ideas and pictures were based. In his work *On Painting* (the first version was written in Latin in 1435, and the second in Italian in 1436), Alberti linked medieval optical geometry directly to the new practices of representation that he saw emerging before him in Florence. Like many other fifteenth-century Florentines such as the artists Donatello (1386–1466), Masaccio (1401–28) and Filippo Brunelleschi (1377–1446), Alberti drew on optical geometry as it had been developed in Greek and Arabic thought. In the Renaissance, medieval optical geometry was known as *perspectiva*. Fifteenth-century artists redefined this word, fashioning it as a modern technique for viewing, measuring, and, above all, *representing* the world. Eventually artists and theorists such as Leonardo would come to distinguish between *perspectiva naturalis* (the optics of natural vision) and *perspectiva artificialis* (artificial or painterly perspective), but the two fields were understood to constitute interrelated branches of knowledge.

While the painter Masaccio produced the earliest true painted perspective (*The Holy Trinity* in Santa Maria Novella, 1426–27), it was Brunelleschi, the Florentine architect and sculptor, who is credited with having produced the methodological foundations for this new artistic technique. Around 1413, Brunelleschi used a combination of architectural surveying techniques and workshop practices to produce a small, foreshortened painting of the Florentine baptistery as if seen from the Duomo, the city's cathedral. He then set up a now-famous experiment in which he attached the painting to an apparatus with a mirror. The viewer was invited to look through a small hole in the back of the painting from which he (the viewer of a public spectacle in Florence at this time would invariably have been male) would then see reflected both the picture of the baptistery and his own eye peeping out. With this experiment, Brunelleschi sought to prove that the image achieved a convincing illusion because it was organized around a central visual ray, a concept that probably derived from the work of Alhazen (965–*c*. 1039), an Arabic natural philosopher who wrote extensively on optics. In his biography of Brunelleschi written before 1489, Antonio Manetti (1423–97) described Brunelleschi's approach. His account provides an insight into what fifteenth-century artists and theorists expected from perspective:

> [Brunelleschi] propounded and realized what painters today call perspective, since it forms part of that science which, in effect, consists of setting down properly and rationally the reductions and enlargements of near and distant objects as perceived by the eye of man: buildings, plains, mountains, places of every sort and location, with figures and objects in correct proportion to the distance in which they are shown. He originated the rule that is essential to whatever has been accomplished since his time in that area.[2]

But the details of Brunelleschi's experiment remain murky: the painting itself has never been found and most of what is known about it comes only from Manetti's description. While informative, Manetti's account lacks the necessary precision to recreate the panel experiment exactly as it was or to determine the precise technique or even epistemological framework used to obtain the image. Did Brunelleschi set out to prove a correlation between optics and painting? Or did he produce a convincing illusion of the baptistery using mechanical methods that themselves were not based on theoretical ideas about vision? Was it only later that he had an epiphany that caused him to connect his method to the theory of the central ray?

The principles of perspective were not clarified until Alberti expressed them in written form. Beginning his treatise on painting with a long description of mathematical entities such as lines and points, Alberti defined vision as a double pyramid intersected by a plane. This "visual pyramid," he observes, is anchored by a central ray (the "prince of rays") that provides the clearest focus of sight. Within the pyramid, angles of vision diminish proportionally and thus "quantities" in the visual field can be measured by triangulation. Alberti probably drew this notion from Euclid's *Optics*, which was widely circulated in fifteenth-century Italy.[3]

Establishing a base in optical geometry, Alberti then describes how to begin a composition. Stating that a painting is "the intersection of a visual pyramid at a given distance, with a fixed centre and certain position of lights, represented artistically with lines and colours on a given surface,"[4] Alberti instructs the reader to draw a rectangle and imagine it as the intersection. The visual pyramid would then pass hypothetically through this two-dimensional plane. He then directs the reader to draw a single horizontal line within this rectangle (the picture's assumed horizon) and mark a point in the middle. This point represents the prince of rays piercing the center. To determine the proportional quantities of vision, Alberti creates a *costruzione d'aiuto*, a diagram designed to help the artist establish the proper diminution of receding planes. This additional diagram appears to be directly based on Euclid's eleventh proposition in the *Optics*, which states that those intersections representing the horizontal segments that are farthest away will appear both higher in the visual field and progressively shorter in length. Transferred to the picture plane, this means that those planes that are intended to be perceived as further from the viewer should be higher on the two-dimensional surface and shorter in width. Thus Alberti invents a mechanism known as the "distance point," transposing Euclid's proposition into a formula for rationalizing the spatial relationship between the viewpoint and the pictorial field. This peripheral point mathematically determines the proportional distance between the viewer and the receding planes of the picture.

Throughout his treatise, Alberti deliberately places optical geometry and painting on equal footing (although he is also careful to maintain a distinction between them). The two dedications to the Italian version of the book reveal a great deal about Alberti's motives for making this comparison. The first dedication is in the form of a letter to Brunelleschi, and in it Alberti favorably contrasts the achievements of Brunelleschi and other Florentine artists with those of the ancient artists of Greece and Rome who were known through Pliny's *Natural History* and other sources. He concludes by asking Brunelleschi to review the manuscript and offer corrections. As Anthony Grafton points out, in doing this, Alberti identifies Brunelleschi "as a man of learning" and intimates that the relationship between the two men is "one of scholar and scholar."[5] Alberti therefore represents Brunelleschi as an equal and as someone whose success as an engineer and architect was due in great part to his intellect. The second dedication is to Gian Francesco Gonzaga (1395–1444), the Marquis of Mantua. In it, Alberti alludes to the prince's pleasure in the liberal arts and he offers *De pictura* as fodder for the prince's "customary pursuit of letters." Representing painting in this light, Alberti suggests that it be considered the result of intellect rather than learned skill. Alberti's treatise is one of the first works of literature to draw a correlation between the visual arts and the seven liberal arts (grammar, logic, rhetoric, arithmetic, geometry, music, and astronomy), thereby distinguishing painting from the artisanal practices or mechanical arts with which it customarily had been associated. In addition, Alberti uses rhetorical devices and narratives drawn from ancient sources, emulating the Greco-Roman body of literature and philosophy that had increasingly become the hallmark of a classical education and a demonstration of erudition in fifteenth-century Florence. Thus, by employing various strategies, Alberti allies painting to other intellectual pursuits and makes a persuasive case for elevating the status of visual art.

What was the historical impact of Alberti's strategy? In promoting perspective as evidence of the artist's intellect, Alberti made the remarkable and highly original claim that a certain kind of naturalistic representation should be seen as a form of inquiry about the world on a par with other forms of natural philosophy. In *De pictura*, the science of optics was transformed into a theory of painting, but painting in turn became a theory of optics or rather a proposition about how and what we see. As Leonardo had made clear, the invention of perspective heralded a new era in which painting could be seen as a proposition about vision and the order of nature. With its perfected, geometric understructure and its idealized viewpoint, perspective was thus ultimate evidence of the human ability to command knowledge of the world.

This characterization of painting informed Renaissance debates concerning the relative merits of the different arts. Enthralled by Horace's simile from the *Ars poetica*, "Ut pictura poesis" ("as is painting, so is poetry"), Renaissance artists and humanists argued over the meaning of imitation and the power of painting versus poetry to invoke the presence of what was absent. Leonardo, for instance, insisted that painting had more power than poetry to make nature present to the mind of man and this was due in part to the sheer force of vision. In the notes for his incomplete treatise on painting, he observes that the eye is the window of the soul and "is the primary means by which the *sensus communis* of the brain may most fully and magnificently contemplate the infinite works of nature . . ."[6] For Leonardo, the eye is the most rational of senses, the "prince of mathematics," and paintings that employ the principles of *perspectiva* are a direct reflection of the eye's singular reflective power.[7] Painting is exceptionally adept at rendering visible the most elemental truths of nature precisely because of its connection to the eye.

After Alberti, scholars and artists incorporated perspective into various mathematical fields: the technique figured prominently in discussions of conics, the Platonic solids, and cartographic and astronomical projections. But most texts dealing with perspective were also concerned with issues of visual representation and the ordering of space. Alberti's text was neither illustrated with diagrams (a fact that has caused no end of consternation and speculation among art historians), nor printed until much later (the Latin version was first printed in Basle in 1540 and the Italian version was not published until 1847). But there were two other important fifteenth-century treatises on painting – one by Piero della Francesca (*c.* 1420–92) and the other by Leonardo, both of which were illustrated. Piero completed *De prospectiva pingendi* sometime in the early 1480s. He extended and clarified much of Alberti's text, but also added substantial portions on mathematics and geometry and provided a series of original, detailed diagrams.[8] Although finished in the late fifteenth century, Piero's manuscript did not appear in printed form until much later. Leonardo left his treatise unfinished and it did not appear in print until more than a century after his death, although even then in an abridged and dubiously organized form. Leonardo's speculations were particularly formative for the epistemological claims that were eventually made on behalf of perspective, and his diagrams were among the most useful for explaining the new technique (for instance, his diagrams of the distance point illuminate Alberti's otherwise somewhat confusing explanations). Nevertheless, his ideas, buried as they were in his notebooks, only filtered out through the comments, observations, and plagiarisms of later authors.

The first printed treatise devoted entirely to perspective, *De artificialis perspectiva*, did not appear until 1505. It was the work of the Canon of Toul, Jean Pélerin (*c.* 1435–1524), who published under his Latin name, Viator ("voyager"). While most of the treatise's illustrations depict stage-like settings that are proffered as templates for artists and scene designers, there are also a few geometric diagrams. Unfortunately, these are accompanied by only a short and uninformative text. In contrast to Alberti, Piero, and Leonardo, Viator provides only a rudimentary rationalization of his method, barely correlating it to optics or geometry. In short, he does not offer anything like Alberti's mathematical and philosophical justification, nor does he make a plea to elevate the status of art.

Instead Viator's diagrams reflect common workshop methods that are often referred to as dual or bifocal constructions. A famous example of bifocalism appears in the Sienese artist Pietro Lorenzetti's *Birth of the Virgin* (1335–42). In this painting there are incised lines from two lateral points on either side of the frame. An intersecting grid created by these two sets of lines was used to construct the *pavimenti* (tiles) that appear on the floor. Using a method called *tiers points* (three point), Viator expanded on this bifocal technique. In his treatise he employs a centric and two lateral points to construct tiled floors and obliquely angled buildings. His method thus has far more in common with late medieval workshop practices than it does with the more intellectualized theory of Alberti. In fact, most artists and even many of the great theorists of perspective employed similar techniques. In his 1536 edition of Vitruvius, Giovan Battista Caporali (*c.* 1476–*c.* 1560) states that Leonardo once said that he preferred to construct perspectives "with two centers, or rather vanishing points."[9] Although not based on any suppositions about vision or geometry, bifocal practices may have evolved into the theory of the distance point elaborated by later commentators. Thus perspective may have been the result of a complex interweaving of workshop practices and theoretical musings.

Following Viator, a number of treatises on painting and related subjects such as proportion, architecture, geometry, and scene design were published in increasing numbers; between 1500 and 1700 roughly 90 books on these topics (many with multiple editions) were printed throughout Europe.[10] All dealt with perspective in one form or another. The proliferation of printed texts – written in many different voices and often to very different ends – reveals how the topic became a voluble and suggestive avenue for thinking about a host of problems.

As mentioned, Dürer published one of the earliest treatments of perspective in a book devoted to proportion. Dürer made two visits to Venice, where he absorbed Italian approaches, and it is clear that perspective held a particular attraction for him. During his second stay in Italy (1505–10/11) he traveled to Bologna. His reason for this trip is recorded in a letter he wrote to his close friend, the Nuremburg humanist Willibald Pirckheimer: "I shall be finished here in another ten days. Then I shall ride to Bologna in order to learn more about the secret art of perspective, which someone there is willing to teach me."[11] His contact in Bologna was most likely Luca Pacioli (1445–1517), the celebrated mathematician and Franciscan friar who lectured at various universities throughout Italy and then was invited to the

Sforza court in Milan. Pacioli knew and plagiarized the work of Piero della Francesca, and he also met Leonardo in Milan. In fact, Leonardo provided illustrations of the Platonic solids for Pacioli's *De divina proportione* (Venice, 1494), a treatise on solid geometry and proportion. Dürer was therefore apprenticing himself to a well-known mathematician who was in turn connected to some of the great Renaissance masters of perspective. Pacioli's treatise underscored the "divine" and mystical nature of proportion and mathematics, and similar associations may have at times adhered to perspective geometry. It also seemed to be an esoteric and even slightly occult kind of knowledge, which may be why Dürer deemed it "secret."

Nevertheless, it was not too secret to be published in manuals for painters. Dürer's reasons for producing a treatise on proportion and for embracing the art of perspective were similar to those of Alberti. He claimed that painting required the highest of human faculties and that it was based on unequivocal intellectual foundations. Following the publication of Dürer's manual, Nuremberg became one of the major printing sites for treatises devoted to problems of proportion and representing complex bodies. From 1543 to 1571 Nuremberg produced works by Augustin Hirschvogel (1503–53), Lorenz Stoer (*c.* 1540–1620), Wenzel Jamnitzer (1508–85), and Hans Lencker (1523–85). Conceived along Dürer's model, these treatises focused on the varied articulation of regular and semi-regular solids and firmly correlated perspective with geometry. At the same time, they were filled with increasingly intricate and beautiful illustrations that made the books expensive objects intended for literate, humanist audiences and book collectors.

In sixteenth-century Italy the study of perspective evolved in a slightly different direction. From early on, Italian writers forged a link between painting, architecture, and mathematics. One of the earliest Italian works on perspective was devoted to architecture and scene design. This was Sebastiano Serlio's *Il primo libro d'architettura* (Paris, 1545). Serlio's text was the Renaissance answer to Vitruvius' *Ten Books on Architecture* in that he established a set of surveying and representational techniques that would come to define architectural practice for ensuing centuries. But it was two other works printed in this period that established perspective as a distinct discourse with its own language and paradigms. These were *La pratica della perspettiva* (Venice, 1569) by the Venetian patrician Daniele Barbaro (1513–70) and *Le due regole della prospettiva pratica* (Rome, 1583) by the architect Jacopo Barozzi da Vignola (1507–73), which was edited, annotated, and printed posthumously by the mathematician Egnazio Danti (1536–86).

One of Barbaro's most important contributions was to show the relation between Ptolemy's astronomical projection and perspective. As with many mathematicians of his period, Barbaro was fascinated with Ptolemy's system of projection for the night sky or planisphere. According to Barbaro, the Ptolemaic planisphere "appears to me to be founded on perspective, [and thus] it seems reasonable to devote a part of my work to the practice of such a beautiful invention."[12] In fact, it has been argued that Ptolemy's geographic system for depicting the *mappa mundi* (map of the earth), which was based on a single point of visual projection, may have even provided a model for early theorists of perspective such as Brunelleschi.[13] But Barbaro's treatise also marries contemporary solid geometry to painterly perspective. Like Dürer he provides techniques for measuring and foreshortening complex, multi-sided objects, but he also connects his constructions to Euclidean principles. According to Barbaro, sight is the sense that allows for judgment, and Euclid's theorems make this clear. Vision arbitrates the proportions that appear in nature. Barbaro compares sight to the *camera obscura* (an enclosed darkened box with a pinhole that projects a reverse and upside-down image of what is outside) but only in so far as it demonstrates how the eye determines proportion and diminution. As Martin Kemp has pointed out, in equating vision and proportion Barbaro espouses the idea that works of art are best when they "mirror the geometrical structure behind natural forms."[14] Barbaro thus furnishes the reader with a full-fledged justification for certain types of representation based on geometrical projection.

On the other hand, Vignola's *Le due regole* tied together all previous speculations and was addressed equally to painters, architects, and mathematicians. Expanding greatly on projective theories of perspective, Vignola provided vividly illustrated explanations of the relation between the viewer's space, the picture plane, and the vanishing point. His remarkable diagrams of two alternative "rules" for perspective demonstrate how to correlate an architectural ground plan to a distance point construction. Danti, his editor, also provided a running commentary on Vignola's text, updating the mathematics, interjecting new discoveries, and illustrating new drawing machines and techniques. In short, Vignola and Danti identified and defined a new area of inquiry that was neither solely mathematics, nor architecture, nor painting, but a hybrid of all three: namely, perspective.

Later in the century, however, perspective fell increasingly into the domain of professional and amateur mathematicians such as Federigo Commandino (1509–75) and Guidobaldo del Monte (1545–1607). In *Ptolomaei planisphaerium* (Venice, 1558) and *Claudii Ptolomaei liber de analemmate* (Rome, 1563), Commandino used perspective as the basis for exploring Ptolemaic astronomical, conical, and orthographic projections. Guidobaldo's *Perspectivae libri sex* (Pesaro, 1600) moved perspective toward projective geometry, a field that would be fully realized by the French mathematician Girard Desargues in the 1630s. At this point, perspective became subject to a difficult and abstruse mathematics that went far beyond the demands of painted or built illusions. In fact, by the end of the sixteenth century the study of perspective had begun to split into two areas of inquiry. On the one hand it served as the basis for a more and more sophisticated and abstracted geometry of projection, and on the other it became incorporated into a series of formulaic representational and projective techniques for artists and architects.

THE SELF-CRITIQUING ART

Even before it began to split into differing areas of inquiry, perspective was a catalyst for analytic reappraisals and self-reflexive critiques. As early as the beginning of the sixteenth century, perspective was associated with the vainglorious presumptiveness of both Renaissance science and art. Dürer's famous print *Melencholia I* (1514) represents a nascent expression of these sentiments (Figure 2.2). As an embodiment of the saturnine artistic temperament, Dürer's winged female figure sits glumly, chin in hand, contemplating the ineffective instruments of inspiration that surround her.

Figure 2.2 Albrecht Dürer. *Melencholia I* (1514). Davison Art Center, Wesleyan University.

One of these is a shaded polyhedron, of the sort that appeared regularly in perspective treatises. But Dürer purposefully rendered this complex object incorrectly. Thus it can be interpreted as a symbol of geometry and proportion that nevertheless attests to a disjunction between divine and human creativity. Along with the mysterious panel of numbers, the compass, and other symbols, the polyhedron imbues the entire engraving with a sense of misapprehension and inadequacy. This image testifies to the contradictions, doubts, and insecurities of Renaissance natural philosophy and artistic ingenuity.

But perspectivists also came to incorporate these doubts into the very fabric of their practice. For instance, from the late fifteenth century on, artists were aware of a form of perspective that was initially used to produce "secret" images that only became recognizable from sidelong or hidden viewpoints. Virtually from the moment it was first invented, artists recognized that perspective could be used to create highly skewed views. Precipitously foreshortened works such as Andrea Mantegna's (1431–1506) *Dead Christ* of 1480–90 fell just shy of a disorienting distortion. While Mantegna's painting underscores the doctrine of transubstantiation by making it seem as though Christ's severely raked body is being offered to the viewer on an altar, other artists, including Leonardo, used similar raked perspectives to produce trick images of less gravity. Since the seventeenth century, these have been labeled "anamorphic."[15] Before this, other labels were used to identify this type of distortion. Gian Paolo Lomazzo (1538–1600), for example, used the term *"prospettiva inversa"* (reverse perspective), while Jean-François Niceron (1613–46) coined the phrase *"la perspective curieuse."*

A typical use of anamorphosis can be found in engravings produced by the German printer Erhard Schön (1491–1542), who was a student of Dürer's. These inexpensive prints, called *Vexierbilder* or "puzzle pictures," concealed portraits and, in some cases, erotic and scatological images. But anamorphosis also found an outlet in at least one "high art" example: *The French Ambassadors* by Hans Holbein the Younger (1497/8–1543) painted in 1533 (Figure 2.3). This double portrait of Jean de Dinteville and Georges de Selve, two French ambassadors to the court of Henry VIII, places them in the interior of Westminster Abbey (the elaborate inlaid pavement alludes to the location). They flank a table with two shelves that hold musical and scientific instruments. Among the objects we see a lute, a case of flutes, a German hymnal, terrestrial and celestial globes, quadrants, sundials, a torquetum (used to determine the motions of celestial bodies), and a mathematics textbook. Attesting to the two Frenchmen's varied intellectual pastimes, this array of objects represents the mathematical interests that would have been characteristic of the educated upper classes: geometry, astronomy, arithmetic, and music.[16] In front of this solemn portrait is a strange, floating object that seems suspended in mid-air. Neither fully part of the painting, nor of the viewer's space, the image becomes recognizable only when seen from the right side of the painting and from very close to the painted surface. At a viewpoint along the picture's edge, this amorphous shape resolves into a leering skull.

In northern Renaissance painting, particularly in the developing genre of still life, the skull was a conventional symbol of *vanitas* or *memento mori*. It is probably included in Holbein's painting as an intentional contrast to the highly detailed instruments between the two men. The point is underscored by the presence of a small crucifix on the upper left of the painting that is only partially concealed by the rich green fabric of a curtain. Scientific knowledge is juxtaposed against the truth of divine revelation, and the skull tips the scales against the former as it reminds the viewer of the vanity and hubris of human endeavors.

Figure 2.3 Hans Holbein the Younger (1497–1543). *The Ambassadors*, 1533. The Art Archive/The National Gallery, London/Eileen Tweedy.

But the skull is not simply another iconographic symbol. Through its distortion, it subverts the portrait's seemingly linear, rational organization. It contradicts the technically virtuosic, foreshortened pavement and the table's perfect diminution. At the same time it challenges the two men's capacity to measure and rationalize space through mathematics. But, of course, all this is done on purpose. In anamorphosis, perspective is turned on itself in a prevaricating game of contravention. Holbein's painting intentionally reveals perspective's paradoxical nature: the world is available to us geometrically and mathematically, but only in so far as we embrace the illusions through which this reality is conveyed.

THE LEGACY OF PERSPECTIVE

In a lecture given in 1938, the German philosopher Martin Heidegger (1889–1976) asserted that "the fundamental event of the modern age is the conquest of the world as picture."[17] The image that epitomizes Heidegger's "world picture" is the window, a metaphor first employed by Alberti in *On Painting*: "First of all, on the surface on which I am going to paint, I draw a rectangle of whatever size I want, which I regard as an open window through which the subject to be painted is seen . . ."[18] While we might assume that the idea of a world-picture or world-view is universal – a foundational characteristic of any historical age or place – Heidegger argued against this notion. He insisted that rather than simply shifting in kind from one age to another (for example, the often-repeated trope that a medieval "world picture" gave way to a "modern" one), it was the very idea of a "world picture" that distinguished the modern age from all those that preceded it.[19] For Heidegger, the "world picture" did not carry positive connotations. Instead, he saw it as the erroneous legacy of the European Enlightenment, particularly as demonstrated in Cartesian thought.

René Descartes had postulated that our understanding of the world is constituted by and in our mental pictures of it and we, as self-understanding human beings, consume these pictures from a singular and irreducible vantage point (that of the Cartesian *cogito* or subject). Because of its inherent relation to the mind, sight is the sense that connects our inner being with the world outside. It sorts out and makes clear all of our other perceptions. Fifteenth- and sixteenth-century painting and artistic theory provided a model for how this idea of mind and sight might work. The perspective picture seems to posit a homogeneous, infinite, and occurrent space with a rationalized, central point of view. It reduces the world to extended matter and represents sight as the locus of knowledge. One might say that the "perspective" picture's convergence with Cartesianism produced a "way of seeing" that united vision to enlightenment.[20] The problem for Heidegger was that this "way of seeing" ignored other (phenomenological) aspects of what he called "being-in-the-world" and thus it sustained an inherently fallacious association between seeing and knowing.[21]

Heidegger's is one of the most powerful philosophical critiques of the perspective "window" as a world-picture. But as art historian James Elkins has pointed out, while Renaissance notions of *perspectiva naturalis* were metaphorically unified around the image of the window, in practice, the *geometry* of perspective was disassociated almost completely from any type of optical framing.[22] Over time, the idea of the "window" has been consistently misconstrued as a technical image intended to imply the transparency of the picture plane itself. And yet for Alberti, the enclosure of the painting was a stage set intended to serve as an appropriate backdrop to the imaginative *istoria* or narrative constructed by the artist. A painting did not need to reflect the outside world; rather it needed to create a whole new world within the frame.[23] But if the goal of perspective in painting was not necessarily to provide an exact similitude of nature in an empirical sense, then how do we explain the persistent historical interpretation of perspective as an objective portrait of reality and human vision?

Grappling with twentieth-century perceptual psychology, the art historian E. H. Gombrich (1909–2001) argued in *Art and Illusion* (1960) that perspective was the result of a series of experiments in perception: what he called "schema-matching." Fifteenth-century artists and viewers employed a form of visual testing of reality. That is, they consistently matched what they saw to what they represented, replacing old visual schemas with newer and more salient versions. Perspective, he observes, was a result of this comparative testing. Of course, there are a number of problems with this idea, not the least of which is that the "realism" attributed to perspective was contested even in the fifteenth century (one of the most famous examples is the "curvilinear" debate concerning whether perspective should reflect the lateral distortions that occur in regular vision). Testing perceived reality against our representations of it may be a human physiological and psychological trait, but it cannot account for why a given picture of reality is acceptable in some instances or at a given moment in time, but not at others. To be fair, Gombrich took some pains to argue that while some might view the tendency to test as universal, the resulting pictures are not. Thus, one society or culture's version of a match between reality and representation does not necessarily have to be the same as another's, even if schema-matching is the underlying mechanism at work. Gombrich opened up an important debate about the contingent and contextual nature of what is perceived as "real" or "natural" in any given culture or time period. Nevertheless, the notion of schema-matching could never account for why certain versions of pictorial reality took hold over others at any given place in any given time.

In contrast, in *Painting and Experience in Fifteenth Century Italy*, the art historian Michael Baxandall offers one of the most impressive attempts to explain why perspective took hold as the preferred method of representing reality in Renaissance Florence. Rather than focus on the reception of medieval optics, Baxandall explores how a given group of people with similar economic and social interests could and did develop a shared visual language that combined elements of geometry and mathematics with certain conventions of representation. In a chapter famously titled "The Period Eye," Baxandall outlined a series of skills and expectations that were shared by the literate and political classes in fifteenth-century Florence. Given that the city's economy was based on banking and mercantile interests, arithmetic and geometry were fundamental rather than extraneous adaptive skills. Counting, measuring, weighing, and gauging were all necessary to an economy based on cloth production, trade, monetary lending, and the calculation of interest. Baxandall suggests that one reason perspective melded with these interests is precisely because it was a representational practice built on the evocation of geometric and volumetric solids and numerically determinable relationships of distance. He does not argue that the one defined or caused the other, but rather that Florentine art developed concurrently with a set of skills that themselves were deemed necessary to the smooth ordering and management of Florence's fortunes. The talent for visual judgment was highly prized in Florentine culture (the ability to gauge or assess a volume or weight by "eye"), and perspective relied on this and other conventional skills for reading and recognizing particular patterns. As Baxandall points out, the successful evaluation of an image during any historical period depends on the "interpreting skills one happens to possess, the categories, the model patterns and the habits of inference and analogy."²⁴ Thus in Renaissance Florence the new visual language of diagrams and geometric figures fulfilled a particular demand for a certain type of transparency in transactions. Florentines adapted a set of interpretive skills that relied on visual acuity to ascertain what was "true" or "honest." Perspective seemed not only to meet this requirement but also demonstrated that this acuity could be given pictorial form – that a particular style of seeing could itself be made visible.

Baxandall explains the social and economic conditions that made it possible for perspective to be accepted as an expression of pictorial reality at a given moment of time in a particular place. But his analysis does not account for how and why perspective continued to be a primary trope for human understanding and empirical inquiry even after its central axioms had long been abandoned and its connection to some version of visual "reality" dismantled. That Heidegger would feel compelled to critique the perspectival "world picture" as late as 1938 is testament to the tenacious power of the geometric view. The art historian Erwin Panofsky contended with this problem in his seminal essay of 1927, "Perspective as Symbolic Form."²⁵ Indebted to the philosophy of Ernst Cassirer, Panofsky argued that perspective must be seen as a peculiar form of symbolic thinking about human interpretations of the world. Cassirer endorsed the notion that art, literature, geometric proofs, and other forms of representation are symbolic forms through which humans mediate their encounters with the given world. Symbolic forms are not imitations of reality. Rather they are imaginative representations of human encounters with reality. As Michael Ann Holly puts it, for Cassirer a "symbolic form is neither the world nor the source of thinking about the world but is, instead, a representation of the process of human creativity."²⁶ For Panofsky, perspective operates along these lines. It is not an exercise in verisimilitude: it isn't isomorphic with either the world as it exists or as it is seen. Nor can it be said to be a "correct" evocation, in pictorial terms, of space. Humans experience space as a lived phenomenon, but the space posited by perspective is artificial: it is geometric, static, and ideal. For Panofsky, perspective must instead be understood as a mythical and conventional structure, one that symbolizes a particular way of thinking about space. Perspective does not show us how we already see but rather shows us how to see. And in this case, what we see is an expression of space that evokes mathematically consistent continuities and extensions. In short, perspective allows humans to conceive of infinity in mathematical and geometric terms. Herein lies its claim on our imagination. Perspective engendered one of the most powerfully consistent ways of seeing the world, one that still exerts a pull on human imaginative faculties. As Patrick Heelan argues, the perspective grid, once it was granted authority, implied "the notion that reality itself is pictorial."²⁷

Of course, it is precisely this view of perspective that Heidegger rejected. And yet, questions about the nature and meaning of perspective were present at its birth and were debated throughout the Renaissance by artists themselves. Because of its historical complexity and its many philosophical and cultural associations, perspective has never neatly fitted with any particular model of interpretation nor with any attempts to correlate it strictly with objectivity, naturalism, or even with the operations of vision itself. Perspective was expected to tread a fine line between science and convention, holding together unstable and often incommensurable ideas about illusion, geometry, and vision. That it repeatedly failed to do so only made it more fascinating to a Renaissance audience.

NOTES

1 Leonardo da Vinci, *Leonardo on Painting*, ed. Martin Kemp and trans. Martin Kemp and Margaret Walker (New Haven: Yale University Press, 1989), p. 52.
2 Antonio di Tucci Manetti, *The Life of Brunelleschi*, ed. and trans. Howard Saalman and Catherine Enggass (University Park: Penn State University Press, 1970), p. 42.
3 David Lindberg suggests that Alberti would have been familiar with Euclid through a Latin version of the *Optics* that was widely circulated in the early fifteenth century. David Lindberg, *Theories of Vision from Al-Kindi to Kepler* (Chicago and London: University of Chicago Press, 1976), p. 152, n. 23.
4 Leon Battista Alberti, *On Painting and On Sculpture. The Latin Texts of De Pictura and De Statua*, edited with translation, introduction and notes by Cecil Grayson (London, Penguin Press, 1972), p. 49.
5 Anthony Grafton, *Leon Battista Alberti: Master Builder of the Renaissance* (New York: Hill & Wang, 2000), p. 76.
6 Leonardo da Vinci, *Leonardo on Painting*, p. 20.
7 On the other hand, Leonardo rejected the monocular model of vision posited by one-point perspective, and also argued at times in favor of curvilinear perspective on the basis that a curved surface more closely approximated the conditions of actual vision. For a discussion of the problems and myths surrounding the issue of curvilinear perspective in the Renaissance, see chapter 5, "Curved Foundations," in James Elkins, *The Poetics of Perspective* (Ithaca: Cornell University Press, 1994).
8 Piero is an interesting case precisely because not only was he a painter of great note, but he was also a highly accomplished mathematician who wrote two textbooks on mathematics; the *Trattao d'abaco* (a treatise on calculation) and the *Libellus de quinque corporibus regularibus* (a treatise on the five regular bodies of geometry). See J. V. Field, *The Invention of Infinity: Mathematics and Art in the Renaissance* (Oxford: Oxford University Press, 1997).
9 "[I] in our time Leonardo da Vinci of Florence, with whom we have spoken about this perspective, . . . affirms that he does it, more than the others with two centres, or rather vanishing points." Presumably this is a reference to bifocal construction. Caporali as quoted in Carlo Pedretti, "Leonardo on Curvilinear Perspective," *Bibliothèque d'Humanisme et Renaissance* 25 (1963), p. 70.
10 For a comprehensive bibliography of these books and their respective editions, see Luigi Vanetti, *De naturali et artificiali perspective – bibliografia ragionata delle fonti teoriche e delle recherché de storia della prospettva; contributo all fomazione della conoscenza de un'idea razionale, nei suoi sviluppi da Euclide a Gaspard Monge*, Studi e documenti de architettura 9–10 (Florence, 1979). Although interest in perspective was born in fifteenth-century Italy, the sixteenth century witnessed its spread throughout Europe, with German, French, and Dutch authors contributing to the discourse.
11 The letter itself is dated to October 13, 1506. Citation of the letter with translation is provided in Albrecht Dürer, *The Painter's Manual*, trans. and with commentary by Walter L. Strauss (New York: Abaris Books, 1977), p. 7.
12 Daniele Barbaro, *La Pratica della perspettiva* (Venice, 1569), p. 163, as trans. by Martin Kemp, *The Science of Art* (New Haven: Yale University Press, 1990), p. 76.

13 Samuel Edgerton, *The Heritage of Giotto's Geometry: Art and Science on the Eve of the Scientific Revolution* (Ithaca: Cornell University Press, 1991). See especially chapter 5.
14 Kemp, *The Science of Art*, p. 78.
15 The term "anamorphosis" was derived from the Greek *ana* meaning "again" or "back" and *morphe* meaning "form," and was coined by the Jesuit Gaspar Schott (1608–1666) in 1657, more than a century after it was initially illustrated in perspective treatises (both Barbaro and Danti discuss it). See Book III "Magia anamorphotica" of Gaspar Schott's *Magia universalis* (Wurzburg, 1657), pp. 101–69.
16 J. V. Field and F. A. J. L. James, *Science in Art: Works in the National Gallery that Illustrate the History of Science and Technology*, British Society for the History of Science Monograph, no. 11 (Stanford in the Vale, 1997).
17 Heidegger, "The Age of the World Picture," in *The Question Concerning Technology and Other Essays*, trans. William Lovitt (New York: Harper & Row, 1977), p. 134. The lecture was first delivered on June 9, 1938, at Freibrug im Breisgau and then published in German in *Holzwege* (Frankfurt: Vittorio Klostermann, 1952).
18 The Latin text is as follows: "Principio in superficie pingenda quam amplum lebeat quadrangulum recorem angulorum inscribo, quod quidem mihi pro aperta finestra est ex qua historia contueatur . . .", in Alberti, *On Painting and On Sculpture*, p. 55.
19 Heidgger, "The Age of the World Picture," p. 130.
20 This phrase "ways of seeing" was coined by the British cultural theorist John Berger in a television series presented by the BBC in 1972. See John Berger, *Ways of Seeing* (London: BBC and Penguin Books, 1972).
21 According to Heidegger, "We call it the 'perspective,' the track of foresight. Thus we shall see not only that being is not understood in an indeterminate way, but that the determinate understanding of being moves in a certain pre-determined perspective . . . We have become immersed (not to say lost) in this perspective, this line of sight which sustains and guides our understanding of being." Heidegger, *An Introduction to Metaphysics*, trans. R. Manheim (New York: Doubleday, 1961), p. 99. In Heidegger's view, Descartes and those who followed him avoided the most important question of how or in what way we come to be in the world. Knowledge, for Descartes, preceded being, and for Heidegger this constituted a perversion of the correct order of interrogation. Thus, the perspectival picture with its Cartesian "point of view" would be an entirely inadequate metaphor for either being or understanding precisely because it posits an epistemological solution to an ontological question (it tells us how we see without asking why we see).
22 Elkins, *The Poetics of Perspective*, pp. 46–52. Elkins distinguishes between, on the one hand, what he calls "optical" metaphors associated with the classical rhetorical tradition adopted by Renaissance writers like Alberti and, on the other hand, the geometric training necessary to construct perspective. While the window was an adept metaphor, it in no way conveyed the actual practices of perspective.
23 According to Joseph Masheck, the window had only ever been intended by Alberti as "a trope, and a signal of the essentially fictive poetics of painting." See Mascheck, "Alberti's 'Window': Art-historiographic Notes on an Antimodernist Misprision," *Art Journal*, spring 1991, p. 35.
24 Michael Baxandall, *Painting and Experience in Fifteenth Century Italy* (Oxford: Oxford University Press, 1972), pp. 29–30.
25 Erwin Panofsky, *Perspective as Symbolic Form*, trans. and introduction by Christopher Wood (New York: Zone Books, 1991). Panofsky's text was originally published as "Die Perspektive als symbolische Form," in the *Vorträge der Bibliothek Warburg 1924–25* (Leipzig and Berlin: Teubner, 1927).

26 Michael Ann Holly, *Panofsky and the Foundations of Art History* (Ithaca: Cornell University Press, 1984), pp. 121–2.
27 Patrick A. Heelan, *Space-perception and the Philosophy of Science* (Berkeley: University of California Press, 1983), p. 102.

SUGGESTIONS FOR FURTHER READING

Primary sources

Alberti, Leon Battista. *On Painting and On Sculpture. The Latin Texts of De Pictura and De Statua*, edited with translation, introduction, and notes by Cecil Grayson. London: Phaidon, 1972.

Dürer, Albrecht. *The Painter's Manual*, trans. and with commentary by Walter L. Strauss. New York: Abaris Books, 1977.

Secondary sources

Alpers, Svetlana. *The Art of Describing: Dutch Art in the Seventeenth Century*. Chicago: University of Chicago Press, 1983.

Berger, John. *Ways of Seeing*. London: BBC and Penguin Books, 1972.

Baltrusaitis, Jurgis. *Anamorphosis*, trans. W. J. Strachan. New York: Harry N. Abrams, 1977.

Baxandall, Michael. *Painting and Experience in Fifteenth-century Italy*, 2nd edn. Oxford: Oxford University Press, 1988.

Damisch, Hubert. *The Origin of Perspective*, trans. John Goodman. Cambridge, Mass.: MIT Press, 1994.

Edgerton, Samuel Y. *The Heritage of Giotto's Geometry: Art and Science on the Eve of the Scientific Revolution*. Ithaca and London: Cornell University Press, 1991.

Elkins, James. *The Poetics of Perspective*. Ithaca: Cornell University Press, 1994.

Field, Judith V. *The Invention of Infinity: Mathematics and Art in the Renaissance*. Oxford and New York: Oxford University Press, 1997.

Foister, Susan, Ashok Roy, and Martin Wyld. *Making and Meaning: Holbein's Ambassadors*. London: National Gallery Publications, Ltd, 1997.

Frangenberg, Thomas. "The Image and the Moving Eye: Jean Pélerin (Viator) to Guidobaldo del Monte." *Journal of the Warburg and Courtauld Institutes* 49 (1986): 150–71.

Gombrich, E. H. *Art and Illusion: A Study in the Psychology of Pictorial Representation*. Princeton: Princeton University Press, 1960.

Grafton, Anthony. *Leon Battista Alberti: Master Builder of the Italian Renaissance*. New York: Hill & Wang, 2000.

Grootenboer, Hanneke. *The Rhetoric of Perspective: Realism and Illusionism in Seventeenth-century Dutch Still-life Painting*. Chicago: University of Chicago Press, 2005.

Heidegger, Martin. "The Age of the World Picture," in *The Question Concerning Technology and Other Essays*, trans. and introduction William Lovitt. New York: Harper & Row, 1977.

Kemp, Martin. *The Science of Art: Optical Themes in Western Art from Brunelleschi to Seurat*. New Haven: Yale University Press, 1989.

Kemp, Martin and Margaret Walker, eds. *Leonardo on Painting: An Anthology of Writings by Leonardo da Vinci with a Selection of Documents Relating to his Career as an Artist*. New Haven: Yale University Press, 1989.

Lindbergh, David. *Theories of Vision from Al-Kindi to Kepler*. Chicago: University of Chicago Press, 1976.

Panofsky, Erwin. *Perspective as Symbolic Form*, trans. Christopher Wood. New York: Zone Books, 1991.

CHAPTER THREE

THE BLACK DEATH, TRAGEDY, AND TRANSFORMATION

Samuel K. Cohn, Jr.

The Black Death – which circumnavigated Europe, from the Crimea to Messina, through western Europe to Scandinavia, and eventually to Moscow, in less than five years – was Europe's worst demographic calamity. Horrors such as the famine of 1315 to 1317, Europe's most severe, claimed no more than 10 percent of certain populations but struck only northern Europe. Even the world wars of the twentieth century were minor in comparison, scything little more than 3 percent of Europe's population. Estimates of the Black Death's toll in the period 1348 to 1352 have, of late, moved upward to half or more of Europe's population. Such estimates derive from places where the statistics are reliable and not just from reports of horrified chroniclers, monks, and merchants. The records of vacant benefices for priests in England hovered just under 50 percent; for Barcelona, they were even higher at over 60 percent. Manorial records for Cambridgeshire and similar ones for Saint-Flour in the Massif Central of France show some villages losing as many as 80 percent of their inhabitants. The death-toll in Florence may have been as high, with the population sinking from 120,000 to as low as 25,000, and other places without tax or manorial records may have suffered still greater devastation. Chroniclers claimed that the Black Death left Trapani, a Sicilian port, completely uninhabited.[1]

It is more difficult, however, to assess how much of Europe was only grazed or may not have been hit at all during the first wave of plague. As the Florentine merchant chronicler Matteo Villani described, the plague struck villages and towns like the rays of the sun on fields, shining on some, missing others entirely. In villages owned by the Bishop of Worcester population losses varied from as high as 80 to as low as 17 percent. Chroniclers reported that only one household in Milan was infected; the authorities walled it up, burnt it, and supposedly stopped the disease in its tracks. Other important centers of trade and industry, such as Douai, mysteriously appear to have escaped the Black Death in 1348–9. Here, the evidence does not depend simply on the absence of evidence. Not only do no sources mention it arriving at this cloth center, but the city's large numbers of surviving wills do not suddenly soar as they do in other places where last testaments survive, nor did any of the city's aldermen die in the plague months as happened elsewhere, such as in nearby Tournai.

Other larger tracts of territory in parts of Spain, northern Germany, Bohemia, and areas of Poland also appear to have escaped the Black Death's assault. The fact that later plagues easily reached and devastated these areas does not lend credence to claims that the Black Death of 1348–9 skipped them because of surrounding forests, mountains, or commercial isolation. In describing the second wave of plague in 1357 to 1358, Matteo Villani emphasized that it afflicted most severely those very regions of Europe skipped over or only grazed in 1348–51.[2] Some areas and cities, even along important trade routes and in densely populated areas without significant natural boundaries such as Douai, may have escaped the major brunt of plague until 1400. Such hits and misses remain mysterious.[3]

On the other hand, for most of the twentieth century, the disease itself (or at least its agent) has been seen as a mystery solved. When the Swiss-born Alexandre Yersin first cultured the bacillus of the subtropical disease principally of rodents, which took 40 years to creep across the Yunnan peninsula before infecting Hong Kong in 1894, he declared that the agent of this nineteenth-century epidemic was "bubonic plague." He also believed that this same pathogen had ravaged Europe in the sixth and seventh centuries (the Justinian Plague), caused the Black Death of 1348, and had struck regions of Europe periodically and with deadly consequences down to the plague of Marseilles in 1720. His proclamation still holds: before engaging in finer details of DNA or current geographical reservoirs of the disease, medical books invariably begin by describing these three well-known historical pandemics – the Justinian Plague, the Black Death, and the late-nineteenth-century outbreak of bubonic plague in India and China – as though they are unquestionably the same disease.

Why was Yersin, along with historians and scientists ever since, so convinced that the Black Death was the same as the bubonic plague of the modern period, especially since this disease has failed in the twentieth century to penetrate much beyond local harbors or inflict serious mortalities in temperate zones? The assumptions have rested on the supposed similarities of the signs and symptoms between the two diseases. For the late medieval diagnosis, they have relied on a handful of chroniclers and contemporary writers, especially Giovanni Boccaccio, who in the *Decameron* described swellings the size of an apple or egg in the groin and armpits.[4] To cite a prominent medievalist with a medical background: "If the bubo predominated as a sign, we can be reasonably comfortable after five centuries that there was not much error in the ascription of a death to plague."[5] But were these signs so unmistakable? Boccaccio, along with numerous other eyewitness chroniclers – the author of a necrology in Friuli, the Byzantine emperor John IV Cantacuzenos, Michele da Piazza of Messina, a Dominican chronicler of Florence's Santa Maria Novella, Giovanni of Parma, a chronicler of southern Austria, Geoffrey le Baker, the Welsh poet Llywelyn Fychan, and others – not only described the buboes or boils but other skin disorders that preceded, accompanied, or followed the formation of swellings in the lymph nodes. These were smaller pustules, spots, and carbuncles of various colors that spread onto breasts, thighs, arms, the throat, even up the nose, and often covered the entire body. According to Boccaccio, they were "sometimes large and few in number, at other times tiny and closely spaced."[6] Geoffrey le Baker and others, such as the early fifteenth-century Florentine diarist Giovanni Morelli, found the smaller pustules to have been more deadly than the buboes; once they began to spread, all hope was lost.

Figure 3.1 The Black Death in Europe, 1347–52.

By contrast, clinical reports from bubonic plagues of the late nineteenth and twentieth centuries show no such matching signs. The largest published repository of clinical cases of plague comes from hospitals in the Presidency of Bombay, collected in 1896–7 by Brigadier-General Gatacre, head of the Indian Plague Commission. Of 3,752 plague patients, 2,883 (or 77 percent) developed plague boils, but in no case did these buboes or any other rashes, bruises, or spots spread over the body. Instead, in over 94 percent of the cases, the plague victims developed one boil alone.[7]

Even if the signs and symptoms of the Black Death and the subtropical bubonic plague had been similar, it would not constitute grounds for concluding that the two diseases were the same. As the imminent immunologist Sir Macfarlane Burnet warned in his *Natural History of Infectious Diseases*, historians of disease need to look beyond signs and symptoms. The symptoms of disease can change rapidly beyond all recognition as the disease moves from a virgin-soil population to becoming endemic and domesticated. Burnet advised historians to concentrate on epidemiological patterns. On these grounds, the two diseases – the Black Death and the subtropical bubonic plague – could hardly be more dissimilar. First, the bubonic plague (*Yersinia pestis*) is a rodent disease "in which humans only occasionally participate," to use the definition coined by the great microbiologist Robert Koch in 1900. In contrast to India or China in the early nineteenth century, where natives, chroniclers, and doctors reported rat-falls preceding an outbreak of bubonic plague in these subtropical climes, no contemporary report in Europe between 1348 and at least to the plague of Marseilles in 1720 points to rats or describes an epizootic of any rodents preceding or accompanying their plagues. Moreover, because the rat is a homebound creature, this subtropical plague is a slow mover, creeping overland at a pace as slow as four miles and no further than twelve miles a year. By contrast, the Black Death can be clocked spreading over similar distances in almost a single day – that is, close to 360 times faster than the subtropical rat disease and without the benefit of the railcar, steamboat, or automobile.

Secondly, late medieval doctors and chroniclers were astonished by their plague's remarkable contagion. Some, such as a fifteenth-century doctor from southern Germany, began by defining plague as "a contagious disease."[8] Others such as the mid-fifteenth-century Saladino da Ascoli, Jacobus de Manderano (Monterone) and Johann Vinck of southern Germany saw contagion, more than the formation of buboes or other skin disorders, as the plague's distinguishing feature. To them the plague was the most contagious disease ever known.[9] By contrast, doctors and hospital workers during the bubonic outbreaks in India, Australia, and elsewhere at the turn of the twentieth century were astonished by the opposite: to their surprise their bubonic plague was hardly contagious at all; early on, they found that the safest place to be in plague time was the plague ward, despite relatives crowding around patients and, in India, passing the sputum of the inflicted from one relative to another. Yet such close familiarity brought no ill consequences. Instead, except in a small percentage of pneumonic cases (which also proved not to be terribly contagious), this plague depended on a much more complex process than person-to-person transmission. Not only did infection depend on rat-fleas leaving their preferred host, the rat, and then biting a human, the rat-flea also had to have ingested sufficient concentrations of the bacillus to block its proventriculus. Even then only 14 percent of infected fleas would successfully regurgitate the bacillus into the human bloodstream.

Thirdly, in keeping with its slow and inefficient mode of transmission, *Yersinia pestis*, despite its high lethality, has never scored high mortalities, even in India, where 95 percent of cases have been recorded in the twentieth century. During the worst decade of the so-called "Third Pandemic," and with this subcontinent hit the worst by far, plague was only its tenth most deadly killer, ranking far behind malaria, influenza, and tuberculosis.[10] The highest mortality from plague for any city in any single year occurred in Bombay in 1903, with less than 3 percent of the population killed: compare this to Florence, when in four or five months as much as 80 percent of the urban population was leveled.

Fourthly, the seasonal patterns and cycles of the two diseases varied widely. Before any plague-infected flea had been dissected, Paul-Louis Simond surmised correctly that the rat-flea was the vector of their plague. He and others of the Indian Plague Commission came to this conclusion by plotting the curves of rat and human plague cases and mortalities, observing a close fit between these seasonal patterns and the fertility cycle of the flea: both rose with warm – but not hot – average temperatures between 50 and 78 degrees and relatively high humidity. By contrast, the late medieval plague, even in its bubonic form, could continue through cold winters in places as inhospitable to the subtropical bubonic plague as Norway or Britain. And astoundingly, the plague of the later Middle Ages recurred in the Mediterranean with remarkable consistency in June and July, the hottest and driest months for Florence, Rome, and Barcelona, when the flea cycle is at its lowest ebb, even lower than in January. In the twentieth century, when rare instances of bubonic plague (*Yersinia pestis*) have hit these areas, they peaked in the autumn as late as the end of October.[11]

Finally, the subtropical bubonic plague possesses a trait more distinctive than boils (which are not unique to it):[12] humans have no natural immunity to it, nor can they acquire it. As a result, unlike the patterns of most infectious diseases, which after a number of strikes on a population become killers principally of children, the mortality and age structure of the victims of *Yersinia pestis* show no signs of adaptation between hosts and pathogen over time. In India, the number of cases and the mortality from plague mounted over the first decade of its appearance, peaking in 1907; then its annual mortalities jumped, more or less randomly, depending largely on rainfall, until around 1920 when mortalities began to decline, not because of humans acquiring immunity but because of rats acquiring it. In a similar vein, the ages of victims have remained much the same over the twentieth century, clustering between 20 and 40 as with most diseases that strike virgin-soil populations. Unlike measles, whooping cough, scarlet fever, chickenpox, diphtheria, and other killers of the nineteenth and twentieth centuries, bubonic plague has never become a childhood disease.

The Black Death, on the other hand, charts a strikingly different course over its first hundred years: adaptation between host and pathogen was remarkably swift. With the strike of the fourth plague in 1382 at Avignon, the pope's doctor, Raymundus Chalmelli, looked back over the plague experience: "In 1348, two-thirds of the population were afflicted, and almost all died; in 1361, half contracted the disease, and very few survived; in 1371, only one-tenth were sick, and many survived; in 1382, only one-twentieth became sick, and almost all survived."[13] While Raymundus's retrospective view may have been overly optimistic, surviving last wills and testaments, Dominican necrologies, and burial records chart similar trajectories across various regions of Europe; by the fourth plague at Florence in 1383, for example, the death-tolls had dipped to one-twentieth of those taken in 1348. Moreover, across Europe, chroniclers described plagues from the second one on as plagues of children. Some, such as the chronicler of Pisa, Ranieri di Sardo, maintained that by the third plague in 1374, 80 percent of the deaths were children aged under twelve: that is, those who had been born since the last outbreak of plague at Pisa in 1362 and thus were unexposed to the disease.[14] The Dominican parish cemetery in Siena – the only one I know of to distinguish between children and adults and to reach back to the first plague – shows a steady increase in the proportion of children as the plague's victims: from less than a quarter in 1348, it edged upwards to a third in 1363, to over half in 1374, and then to a staggering 88 percent with Siena's fourth plague in 1383.

Medieval doctors were the first to reflect on these trends and boldly claimed credit for the body's rapid adaptation. It is difficult to think of a more abrupt about-face in the history of ideas and attitudes than that conveyed by the doctors in their plague tracts from 1348 to the early fifteenth century. With the initial shock of 1348–50 physicians such as Jacme d'Agramont, author of perhaps the earliest Black Death tract (April 24, 1348), ultimately concluded that the best remedy was "to repent and confess our sins before the holy Roman Church and its representatives, as well as to do penance."[15] In a plague poem of around 1350 the Montpellier doctor Simon de Couvin claimed along with many others that the Black Death was new to history, that whereas with previous plagues something could be done, with this one all hope was lost; it had "miffed all doctors; the art of Hippocrates was lost." The most famous plague report, that of the Medical Faculty of Paris commissioned in the year of the plague, pinned its analysis on "remote causes" – the configuration of the planets.

These plague tracts and their doctors' opinions and explanation were not static over the *longue durée*, extending into the seventeenth century as Carlo Cipolla and several others have claimed. From the mid-1360s on doctors drew less attention to the "remote causes" of plague and pushed God into the background, if they mentioned Him at all. Instead, they observed "the immediate causes" and saw connections between recurrences of the disease and famine, war, overcrowding, and consequential disruptions in sanitary conditions. They recommended avoiding crowds and covering mouths and noses in times of plague. To priests listening to last confessions, doctors advised keeping a safe distance from plague victims with doors and windows open or even hearing confessions from the street. Further, instead of despairing over the absence of any cures for plague, they began to trumpet their own recipes and preventive measures, boasted of their experience and claimed to have saved numerous patients from plague because of their surgical interventions and pharmaceutical concoctions. Because of their experience and experimentation, physicians saw the plague as enabling their generation of practitioners to go beyond the ancients in the art of healing, Hippocrates and Galen included. Medical doctors were the first group of intellectuals I know of to have advanced such claims in any secular branch of knowledge.

Chroniclers reflect the same trajectory as the doctors, from desperation to a new sense of confidence. From 1348 to 1350 writers across Europe, such as the Irish Franciscan John Clyn of Kilkenny, thought they were nearing the world's end and that their chronicles might not find anyone left to read them. Others such as John of Reading saw the plague as God's wrath over man's immorality; still others, like the doctors of Paris, turned to the configurations of planets, earthquakes, and strange happenings in distant lands – rains of frogs and scorpions, black snows that melted mountains, and eight-legged worms that killed by their stench – to explain this disease without precedent in history. As remarkable as these apocalyptic stories were, even more remarkable is how quickly they disappeared. Far from being the gripping preoccupations through the late medieval and early modern period as historians such as Jean Delumeau have asserted, I do not know of a single chronicler returning to such tales to explain any subsequent plague, at least through the fifteenth century where my analysis ends. Like doctors, the chroniclers turned to immediate human causes – most prominently war – to analyze the spread of the disease. Further, they observed the plague's progress over its first hundred years or more, noting not only its signs and symptoms and numbers killed but elementary epidemiological traits – that it became a childhood disease, and because of its contagion, it was household specific (if one caught it, the others in the household soon died). They even had some notion of immunity, seeing, for example, successive generations of gravediggers becoming increasingly immune to plague from their exposure to it, or, as with Matteo Villani, seeing the second plague striking hardest those regions the first plague had skipped over.

The chroniclers' attitudes towards doctors and the medical profession changed as well. In 1348, the Sienese Agnolo di Tura del Grasso and Matteo Villani saw doctors during the plague as cowardly, greedy, and dishonest; they only brought their patients more speedily to the grave. Such vitriolic complaints, however, soon disappeared. By the beginning of the fifteenth century, chroniclers even copied doctors' plague recipes into their histories and recommended that their friends and progeny seek out "valiant doctors." While medical cures could not ensure survival against plague, they could provide a "shield," making the citizen far better prepared. The sharp rise in doctors' salaries both absolutely and relative to other professions suggests that others in society had followed the chroniclers' change of heart.[16]

To probe lower down the social ladder for attitudes in late medieval Europe is difficult. Last wills and testaments constitute one conduit. By the early fourteenth century, thousands of wills can be found redacted by shopkeepers, artisans, and even propertied peasants and workers in the wool industry. These sources, too, show an about-face in sentiment from the Black Death's first onslaught to its second and successive strikes to the late fourteenth century. In Tuscany and Umbria, along with northern cities such as Douai and Tournai, commoners turned from mendicant ideals to new obsessions with earthly glory and remembrance as they concentrated their last earthly sums to assure honorable burials in tombs and commissioned frescoes, sculpture, bas-reliefs, and chapels with perpetual masses to preserve their memories in this world as well as in the next. In these artistic commissions they often demanded that the executors of their estates ensure that they, their children, or parents had been sculpted or painted in their "very likeness." Before the Black Death, such preoccupations had been almost exclusively the desires or prerogatives of the rich and powerful; by the end of the fourteenth century they flooded the wills of artisans and even peasants. Further, commoners used their testaments to specify concrete means by which they could direct, in effect from the grave, the lives of spouses, progeny, and future heirs, orchestrating mundane matters as to who was to marry whom, rights of passage to communal wells, and household space to be shared by widows and sons.[17]

Popular movements, violence, and revolt allow us to probe deeper still into shifts in attitudes after the Black Death. From 1348 to 1353, social movements with concrete aims of redressing economic grievances, challenging political authority, or questioning social hierarchies disappear almost completely across Europe. In central Italy, the Black Death suddenly killed off workers' newly founded zeal to topple governments or challenge burgeoning capitalist exploitation, as had been witnessed in revolts of wool-workers in Siena and Florence from 1342 to 1347.[18] Immediately afterwards, I have found only a few minor riots. In Barberino Val d'Elsa, south of Florence, for example, tempers flared at the end of summer 1348, leading to a barroom brawl and a minor riot involving a handful of men. The cause of the conflict, however, pre-dated the plague, stemming from attempts to redress corrupt election results of the previous year, when a much larger revolt had engulfed this walled town. Two years later, city chroniclers reported a conspiracy to topple the government of the Bentivoglio in Bologna. But it amounted to little, was quickly repressed, and has left no trace in the rich judicial archives of Bologna. In France and Flanders, revolts, even minor skirmishes, from the Black Death to the Jacquerie of 1358 are as difficult to uncover. In the immediate aftermath of the plague, a tax revolt in Rouen was an exception. Although merchants began it, others, perhaps workers, paid the price, leaving 36 swinging from the gallows. And in the year of the Black Death, the new count of Flanders, Louis de Male, attacked the prerogatives of the weavers, especially in Ghent, which in turn provoked an unsuccessful counter-attack. It was not until 1359, however, that the weavers – along with other craftsmen of Ghent, Ypres, and elsewhere in western Flanders – united and organized a successful rebellion against the count's earlier encroachment on their municipal liberties.

To be sure, the Black Death did give rise to violence: flagellant movements and the burning of Jews swept across German-speaking areas, Spain, France, and the Low Countries from September 1348 to 1351, while in Sicily, Catalans were the chosen scapegoats of 1348.[19] But this violence differed markedly from the pre-plague organized protests of artisans and peasants with prior planning, numerous assemblies, and elected leaders. Rather than advancing the struggle for concrete goals or redressing specific political, economic, or social grievances, the violence of 1348 to 1352 looked to forces outside their societies – the scapegoat and the heavens – to resolve their fears, anger, and insecurity.

By 1353 the number of social protests and revolts began to mount again, occurring in Rome, Poitou, Gaeta, and Viterbo. In 1354 and 1355 their number increased more impressively, especially in Italy – Pavia, Modena, Bologna, Rimini, Rome, Siena (at least three times), Casole, Monteritondo, Massa Marittima,

Montepulciano, Grosseto, Lucca, Pisa, Venice, Udine, Piedmont, L'Aquila (two revolts), Castrogiovanni (today, Enna in Sicily), Syracuse, and Catania. The most famous of the revolts of the 1350s came, however, from the north, the Jacquerie of late May 1358, that spread through the Beauvaisis, Picardy, the Île de France, Champagne, and as far east as Bar on the borders of France. Along with Étienne Marcel's Parisian insurgents, the Jacques inspired revolts in cities such as Caen and Rouen. A year later, fullers, weavers, and cobblers waged war against the count of Flanders, humiliated him, and took over city councils in Ypres, Bruges, and Ghent. By August 1361 the weavers had restored their power in all cities of maritime Flanders.

The realities of the Hundred Years War were certainly behind these northern revolts, and the difficulties of financing increased warfare, with a tax base greatly diminished because of the plagues' onslaughts. But other causes seem to have been paramount, especially for the Jacquerie; none of its accounts mention taxes. Instead, the chroniclers point to the betrayal by the local nobility and their reneging on their customary protection of their peasants. For the north of France, the massacres of the Jacques and the defeat of Étienne Marcel may have blunted temporarily the desire for revolt, but peasants responded to the raids of brigands and "extraordinarily onerous taxes" with their feet, abandoning their work and heading for Paris. Moreover, in several villages, which had been the battlefields of the Jacquerie, peasant resilience and self-defence continued; they organized their own resistance to the onslaughts of the English, defeating the invading cavalry two times at Longueil-Sainte-Marie in the Beauvaisis.

Further north, taxes provoked open and successful revolts at Tournai in 1359, 1364, twice in 1365, and again in 1366, and at Valenciennes in 1364; by their examples, such revolts spread to "all the towns of Hainault" in 1365. But the south of France was the more important theater of class struggle in the 1360s. The combination of political instability, roaming brigands, war, and new taxes weighed heavily on the mountainous areas of the Massif Central. Soldiers, peasants, and townsmen formed bands called *Tuchins* (at least by their adversaries) to redress personal grievances and pursue economic advantage, but also to challenge the crown and its rising taxation in this milieu of hardship, war, and half-hearted truces between the French and English. This was especially true still further south in the regions of Toulouse, Carcassonne, and Beaucaire, where groups also called Tuchins revolted and took over villages and even the city of Nîmes.

Still other revolts raged through southern France in the 1360s. In 1364, 300 men of Carcassonne, "armed with various weapons and with the consent and guidance of their town councilors," made war on the royal castle of their region, setting fire to its gates and entering it. Seven insurgents were arrested. A few days later, the town council organized 2,000 men of Carcassonne to march to the prison holding the rebels, where they killed the royal officers and liberated the seven. In the same year *plebes* from the market towns of Gimont and Simorre in the region of Toulouse staged their own Jacquerie, which succeeded in deposing aristocratic rule in the region. According to a royal letter of remission, "like mad men" they assembled and battled against the ruling lord of the region; they stormed his castle; burnt it to the ground; took his lady, three children, the servants, and moveable goods to Simorre, where they burnt the servants, hanged the others from trees, and "committed many other very great, inhumane and detestable acts of evil." For the next 30 years the crown tried to bring these insurgents to trial and to have them pay a 25,000 franc fine. Finally, with the letter of remission above, the crown admitted failure and gave up its pursuit of the insurgents.

As important as the battlefields of the Hundred Years War were to instability and revolt, they were hardly the only areas of Europe to see popular rebellion rise during the latter half of the fourteenth century. In 1355 a combination of social forces from the richest magnate families in Siena to the *popolo minuto* successfully ended Italy's longest-standing city-state regime, that of the Nine. Afterwards, the governments of Siena fell as readily as those of Italy after the Second World War. In five months alone, 1368–9, no fewer than four governments were toppled and replaced with new regimes. In all of these permutations, artisans and workers played a significant role and secured governmental offices and privileges for themselves. Revolts in Siena culminated in 1371 with the uprising of the wool-workers organized around their neighborhood association, the Club of the Caterpillar. After this failure, rioting and serious threats to political stability from the lower classes in Siena died down or disappeared altogether, but, unlike in Florence and most other Italian city-states, these social classes maintained a presence in Siena's government well into the fifteenth century.

Perhaps the most lasting of the conclusions drawn in Michel Mollat and Philippe Wolff's *Ongles bleus* has been their emphasis on the sharp pan-European cluster of revolts a generation after the Black Death, in the years 1378 to 1382. For France and Flanders, tax revolts in the south, the *Harelle* in Rouen, the *Maillotins* in Paris, and the "troubles" of the Low Countries support their case. But I would argue that popular insubordination and rebellion built up from the mid-1350s to the 1370s. In fact, in Italy, after a steady rise in the number of revolts, they fell temporarily during the so-called cluster of 1378 to 1382. The Florentine revolt of the Ciompi in 1378 was an outlier.

Because of the Revolt of the Ciompi, historians have paid greater attention to popular revolt in Florence than elsewhere in Italy. Insurrections, however, were much more numerous in other regions of central Italy in the 1360s and 1370s. These included tax revolts, such as those at Bologna and Ravenna in 1357; insurrections of artisans and workers in the wool industry at Lucca, Perugia, and Siena; and various attempts by underlings (*sottoposti*) and the *popolo minuto* to change the political systems of their city-states – in Siena in 1368 (at least four times), Lucca in 1369, Cortona and Perugia in 1371 and Bologna in 1377. But by far the most numerous of these revolts stemmed from popular outrage over the violence, arrogance, and injustice of aristocratic behavior and rule, whether it came from the Church, a military presence, or the old local families.

The most important sweep of revolts occurred in the early and mid-1370s. In sheer numbers, these revolts dwarf those of Florence, as well as the supposed cluster of European-wide revolts listed by Mollat and Wolff. In one year alone, 1375, 60 cities in the Marches of Ancona, Tuscany, Umbria, Emilia Romagna, and the Papal States revolted and "freed themselves from the yoke of church rule"; that is, a third more than Mollat and Wolff found for all of Europe in the 1378 to 1382 period.[20]

The *Cronaca malatestiana* of Rimini counted even more: by March 28, 1376, 1,577 walled towns and villages (*buone castella*) from Milan to Naples had thrown off the rule of the rectors, and this was not counting small or tower villages (*delle piccolo e di certe torricelle*). According to Gene Brucker, this war against the papacy was "one of the most radical revolutions in Florentine history . . . a revolution of internal politics, a critical phase of the struggle between an old order and the new." Ernesto Screpanti has gone further, seeing it as a class struggle in central Italy "against the old aristocratic classes and the papacy, a war against nascent capitalism and the dying medieval order."[21] As the conservative anonymous diarist of the Machiavelli family observed for Bologna in 1376, "the aristocrats (*grandi*) were hounded out of office and in their place merchants and artisans remained as lords."

By contrast, I know of only a handful of riots in Italy that broke out during the supposed cluster – the Florentine Ciompi; a revolt of the *popolo* in Genoa, which may not in fact have involved artisans or workers; the undefined crowd in Rome that pressured the cardinals to elect an Italian pope in April 1378; a small tax revolt against the imposition of a land tax (*aestimum*) in Parma in 1380; and an insurrection of "the people" to overthrow the ruling family in Treviso around 1380 (the chronicler is not clear about the date). In this last-named revolt, only one official was singled out and killed, a Pirinzolo, who allegedly during their last war had captured Trevigian women and forced them "to pull up their slips to their groins so that he could ruminate on their private parts (*ad propria remandere*)."

So how do we account for the rise of insurrections across much of Europe from the late 1350s to the 1370s and its contrast to the violence of the Black Death's immediate aftermath? Most explanations have centerd on England and demography. With a sudden shrinkage in the tax base, governments were forced to raise taxes sharply to pay for more costly wars. At the same time, the dramatic demographic collapse meant that laborers were in a better bargaining position *vis-à-vis* their bosses, landlords, and the state. While this argument helps to explain much for post-plague revolt in England (although hardly everything, as Hilton and others have shown), it settles less for Italy, where post-plague tax revolts did not rise sharply in number until the 1390s and then were located principally in the countryside. Moreover, the most famous of the revolts south of the Alps – the Tumulto dei Ciompi – turned on just the opposite demographics: Florence's wool industry declined more sharply than its population. Thus a key demand of the Ciompi was the imposition of production quotas on their bosses to boost production and thereby secure employment for an industry with a surplus, not a scarcity, of workers. Nor was Florence the only place where a labor surplus was a pre-condition for popular insurrection during the post-plague fourteenth century. According to Philippe Wolff, one of the factors behind the tax revolts and anti-Semitic riots in Barcelona in 1391 was a recent influx of immigrants into the region that had driven down artisan wages.[22]

Further, the vast majority of revolts in post-plague Italy turned on politics; they were neither tax revolts as in the north nor disputes at the point of production as with the exceptional Ciompi. Instead, across large areas of Italy, commoners battled to end aristocratic abuse and to demand a share of governmental offices and political control. Similar revolts were also rife in the north with no connection to any demographic shift in the balance between social classes. For instance, in 1384 the sons of the noble family of the Hers humiliated and killed a townsman [*quemdam oppidanum*] of Saint-Trond by turning loose their hunting dogs on him. Those of the town responded collectively, marched to these sons' castle, and burned it to the ground. More importantly, the final and definitive assault that would establish a government of craftsmen in Liège and bar patricians from its council in 1386 erupted not from grievances tied to post-plague demographic realities but rather from a growing indignation over patrician injustices and inequality – the patricians' sale of justice. As the firebrand Gilles de Laveux prompted the crowd: "You all are as sure as I am that their sentences depend not on justice but on who can put up the most money." Taxes were not mentioned nor demands made about wages and working conditions. Gilles, however, did make concrete demands that in fact were shortly instituted: a committee of tradesmen throughout the *bonnes villes* of the Liègeois was set up to review patrician justice over the previous 20 years and to adjudicate cases of upper-class corruption.

But like the tax revolts and demands to change work practices, these popular revolts all turned on a new optimism, that commoners could change their worlds in concrete and practical ways. This common thread linking the rush to revolt north and south of the Alps came not with the Black Death itself but with the sharp, even if temporary, disappearance of plague followed by the decline in plague mortality and morbidity from the mid-1350s to 1400. Doctors and city councils saw these improvements brought on by the body's immune system and natural selection as of their own making. The same duality and timing in the plague's influence is seen in the post-plague turn in popular violence from mass flagellation and the burning of the Jews to social rebellion that addressed concrete social, economic, and political injustices head-on. They too saw that by their actions they could profoundly alter the here and now – conditions of work and political liberty.

From Johan Huizinga's *The Waning of the Middle Ages*, a growing school of historical thought has viewed the Renaissance dimly: beneath a thin veneer of intellectuals, mainly from Tuscany, lay a world transfixed by "fear, anxiety, and insecurity." This milieu persisted without significant variation from the catastrophes of the fourteenth century until the eighteenth century, when the French Enlightenment, as Delumeau and others have argued, supposedly rescued Europe from its Black Death nightmare. The views and actions of doctors, chroniclers, testators, and popular insurgents examined above cut against "this motionless history" of late medieval and early modern mentalities. The Black Death had more than one psychological and cultural outcome: the first horrific reactions of the plague's immediate aftermath were not its enduring ones. The Black Death was not like syphilis, smallpox, or a number of other infectious diseases that linger on, leaving their physical marks, returning yearly, killing slowly, and gradually debilitating its societies physically and mentally.[23] Instead, once the Black Death struck it rarely remained in a territory for more than several months, especially during the late fourteenth century, and until the mid-fifteenth century or longer its periodic returns showed a rapid adaptation between the pathogen and human host: mortalities sank and the disease became one principally of children. In this way the Black Death – the particular character of this fast killer – provided the subsoil of a new Renaissance mentality.

NOTES

1. Samuel K. Cohn, Jun., *The Black Death Transformed: Disease and Culture in Renaissance Europe* (London: Arnold, 2002). This book provides the basis for much of this chapter and readers may consult it for specific references. For recent and higher estimations of plague deaths, see Ole J. Benedictow, *The Black Death, 1346–1353: The Complete History* (Woodbridge, Boydell, 2005).
2. Matteo Villani, *Cronica con la continuazione di Filippo Villani*, ed. Giuseppe Porta, 2 vols (Parma: Fondazione Pietro Bembo, 1995), II, p. 273.
3. See Samuel K. Cohn, Jun., "The place of the dead in Flanders and Tuscany: towards a comparative history of the Black Death," in *The Place of the Dead: Death and Remembrance in Late Medieval and Early Modern Europe*, ed. Bruce Gordon and Peter Marshall (Cambridge: Cambridge University Press, 2000), pp. 17–43.
4. Giovanni Boccaccio, *Decameron*, vol. 4 of *Tutte le opere di Giovanni Boccaccio*, ed. Vittore Branca (Milan, 1976), pp. 10–11.
5. Ann Carmichael, *Plague and the Poor in Renaissance Florence* (Cambridge: Cambridge University Press, 1986), pp. 26 and 79.
6. Boccaccio, *Tutte le opere*, p. 10.
7. Brigadier-General W. F. Gatacre, *Report on the Bubonic Plague, 1896–97*, 2 vols (Bombay: Times of India, 1897). The same can be said for the clinical reports of the much smaller plague of Glasgow in 1900; see A. K. Chalmers, *Corporation of Glasgow, Report on certain cases of plague occurring in Glasgow in 1900 by the Medical Officer of Health* (Glasgow: Corporation of Glasgow, 1901). In rare instances, such as a plague in Chile in 1903, pustules were observed in some cases. Unlike their appearance in the late Middle Ages, however, in the twentieth century they have signaled benign cases of plague and not its most deadly form.
8. "Ein anonymer Tractatalus *optimus de pestilentia*," *Archiv für Geschichte der Medizin* XVI (1925), p. 104.
9. Alessandro Simili, "Saladino Ferro da Ascoli," in *Atti e Memorie dell'Accademia di Storia dell'Arte Sanitaria* 29 (1963), p. 40; "Eine consilium . . . Jacobus de Manderano (Monterone) 1448," *Archiv für Geschichte der Medizin* XVI (1925), p. 172; "Fragestellungen zur Pestätiolgie," *Archiv für Geschichte der Medizin* XVI (1925), p. 57.
10. Ira Klein, "Urban Development and Death: Bombay City, 1870–1914," *Modern Asian Studies* 20 (1986), p. 744.
11. Robert Pollitzer, *Plague* (Geneva: World Health Organization, 1945), p. 30.
12. Michael Smith and Nguyen Duy Thanh, "Plague," in *Manson's Tropical Diseases*, 20th edn, ed. Gordon Cook (London: Saunders, 1996), p. 920.
13. Cited in Hans Zinsser, *Rats, Lice, and History* (New York, 1935), p. 89.
14. *Cronaca di Pisa di Ranieri Sardo*, ed. Ottavio Banti Fonti per la Storia d'Italia, no. 99 (Rome: Istituto Storico Italiano, 1963), p. 209.
15. As with the Paris Medical Faculty, d'Agramont tried to uphold the profession's exclusive prerogative on advising on curative measures but suggested that all preventive measures could safely be followed without medical help. See Arrizabalaga, "Facing the Black Death," in *Practical Medicine from Salerno to the Black Death*, ed. Luis Garcia-Ballaster *et al.* (Cambridge: Cambridge University Press, 1994), pp. 270–2, and "L'Epistola de Maestre Jacme d'Agramont," *Archiv für Geschichte der Medizin*, XVII (1925), pp. 120–1.
16. For this discussion, see Cohn, *The Black Death Transformed*, pp. 225–30.
17. See Samuel K. Cohn, Jun., *The Cult of Remembrance and the Black Death: Six Renaissance Cities in Central Italy* (Baltimore: Johns Hopkins University Press, 1992), and "The place of the dead in Flanders and Tuscany."

18 The following is drawn from *Lust for Liberty: The Politics of Social Revolt in Late Medieval Europe* (Cambridge, Mass.: Harvard University Press, 2006).
19 The literature on the post-plague massacres of the Jews is extensive; see my "The Black Death and the Burning of the Jews," *Past and Present* (forthcoming, 2007). No one to my knowledge, however, has commented on the anti-Catalan and anti-foreign massacres that flared throughout Sicily in the plague's immediate aftermath in 1348; see A. Giuffrida (ed.), Michele da Piazza, *Chronica* (Palermo: I.L.A.-Palma, 1980), pp. 91–2. Nor was Italy completely free of anti-Semitic violence in the plague's immediate aftermath. There were persecutions in Mantua and Parma; further, Cecil Roth, *The History of the Jews of Italy* (Philadelphia: Jewish Publication Society of America, 1946), p. 142, has suggested that this violence possibly spread to other cities.
20 *Chronicon Placentinum ab Anno CCXXII usque ad annum MCCCCII auctore Johanne de Mussis cive Placentino*, vol. 16 of *Rerum Italicarum Scriptores*, ed. Ludovico Muratori *et al.* (Milan, 1730), col. 521. By contrast, Michel Mollat and Philippe Wolff, *The Popular Revolutions of the Late Middle Ages*, trans. A. L. Lytton-Sells (London: Allen & Unwin, 1973), pp. 139–41, list only 42 across Europe and some of these, such as the wars led by Philippe van Artevelde, I would not classify as popular revolts.
21 Gene Brucker, *Florentine Politics and Society 1343–1378* (Princeton: Princeton University Press, 1962), pp. 294–5, and E. Screpanti, *L'Angelo della rivoluzione: i Ciompi fiorentini all'assalto del cielo, Giugno-agosto 1378* (forthcoming), p. 64.
22 Philippe Wolff, "The 1391 Pogrom in Spain: Social Crisis or Not?" *Past & Present*, no. 50 (1971), p. 16.
23 On the effects of these diseases on populations, see William McNeill, *Plagues and Peoples* (New York: Anchor Books, 1976) and Alfred Crosby, *Ecological Imperialism: The Biological Expansion of Europe, 900–1900* (Cambridge: Cambridge University Press, 1986).

SUGGESTIONS FOR FURTHER READING

Primary sources

Boccaccio, Giovanni. *Decameron*, ed. Vittore Branca. Milan: Mandadori, 1976.
Cohn, Samuel. *Popular Protest in Late Medieval Europe*. Manchester: Manchester University Press, 2004.
Horrox, Rosemary. *The Black Death*. Manchester: Manchester University Press, 1994.
Villani, Matteo. *Cronica con la continuazione di Filippo Villani*, ed. Giuseppe Porta, 2 vols. Parma: Fondazione Pietro Bembo, 1995.

Secondary sources

Brucker, Gene. *Florentine Politics and Society 1343–1378*. Princeton: Princeton University Press, 1962.
Carmichael, Ann. *Plague and the Poor in Renaissance Florence*. Cambridge: Cambridge University Press, 1986.
Cohn, Samuel K., Jun. *The Cult of Remembrance and the Black Death: Six Renaissance Cities in Central Italy*. Baltimore: Johns Hopkins University Press, 1997.
—— *The Black Death Transformed: Disease and Culture in Renaissance Europe*. London: Arnold, 2002.
—— *Lust for Liberty: The Politics of Social Revolt in Late Medieval Europe*. Cambridge, Mass.: Harvard University Press, 2006.

—— "The Black Death and the Burning of the Jews," *Past and Present* (forthcoming, 2007).
Crosby, Alfred. *Ecological Imperialism: The Biological Expansion of Europe, 900–1900*. Cambridge: Cambridge University Press, 1986.
Delumeau, Jean. *La peur en occident (XIVe–XVIIIe siècles): Une cité assiégée*. Paris: Fayard, 1978.
—— *Le péché et la peur: la culpabilisation en Occident (XIIIe–XVIIIe siècles)*. Paris: Fayard, 1983.
—— *Rassurer et protéger: la sentiment de sécurité dans l'Occident d'autrefois*. Paris: Fayard, 1989.
Haverkamp, Alfred. "Die Judenverfolgungen zur Zeit des Schwarzen Todes im Gesellschaftsgefüge deutscher Städte," in Haverkamp (ed.), *Zur Geschichte der Juden im Deutschland des späten Mittelalters und der frühen Neuzeit*. Stuttgart: Anton Hiersemann, 1981, pp. 27–93.
Huizinga, Johan. *The Waning of the Middle Ages: A Study of the Forms of Life, Thought and Art in France and the Netherlands in the Dawn of the Renaissance*, trans. J. Hoppman. New York, 1945 [Dutch edn, 1924].
Luce, Siméon. *Histoire de la Jacquerie d'après des documents inédits*, 2nd edn. Paris: H. Champion, 1894.
McNeill, William. *Plagues and Peoples*. New York: Anchor, 1976.
Mollat, Michel and Philippe Wolff. *The Popular Revolutions of the Late Middle Ages*, trans. A. L. Lytton-Sells. London: Allen & Unwin, 1973.
Plague Manual: Epidemiology, Distribution, Surveillance and Control. Geneva: World Health Organization, 1999.
Pollitzer, Robert. *Plague*. Geneva: World Health Organization, 1945.
Rodolico, Niccolò. *La Democrazia fiorentina nel suo tramonto (1378–1382)*. Bologna: N. Zanchelli, 1905.
Roth, Cecil. *The History of the Jews of Italy*. Philadelphia: Jewish Publication Society, 1946.

PART II

A WORLD IN MOTION

CHAPTER FOUR

THE MANUFACTURE AND MOVEMENT OF GOODS

Joanne M. Ferraro

The manufacture and movement of goods did much to shape the culture of the Renaissance. Wealthy families expressed their success in business and their status in their civic worlds publicly through elaborate building programs, portrait painting, and other forms of artistic representation. They also filled their private, interior spaces with furnishings and precious objects that reflected their self-confidence, their pride, and their ambitions. The manufacture and movement of goods advanced this remarkable efflorescence of high culture in important ways. They generated surplus wealth, establishing the conditions for social and economic mobility. Most important, they helped constitute the culture of material life itself.

Historians studying the economy approach the material Renaissance differently from those studying culture. Their interest lies mainly in tracking the expansion and contraction of production and exchange, while cultural historians pay close attention to patterns of consumption and to assigned meanings of material display. The evolving discussions of these two specializations converge best in studies at the higher end of the social hierarchy, where oligarchs, nobles, and ecclesiastical and princely dynasts possessed the material wealth to show off the luxury products Italy produced or imported. But scholars of consumption have a harder time linking the cultural and material Renaissance to ordinary people whose limited purchasing power largely excluded them from the markets for goods. This chapter endeavors to illuminate the ways in which the manufacture and movement of goods intersected with high and low culture, bringing together current debates about production and consumption.

EARLY GLOBALIZATION

Italy's trading links, first with the medieval Levant and Byzantium and later with the sixteenth- and seventeenth-century Atlantic, encouraged cultural exchange and fostered new modes of living. Venice serves as a model of this early globalization. From the eleventh century on this important trading city on the Adriatic was the home base of a merchant community that traveled across European, Levantine, and Asian landscapes, bringing back both material goods and stories of other ways of life. By the twelfth century Venice had established colonies on the islands of the Aegean. In the Fourth Crusade in the early thirteenth century its troops sacked Constantinople, availing themselves and their commanders of rich, Byzantine spoils. The Venetians achieved Mediterranean dominance by 1381, and in the following century their trading networks stretched to the Black Sea, as well as to the towns of Acre, Alexandria, Cairo, Damascus, and Aleppo, and continued onwards to East Asia. Venetians not only amassed great wealth, they also brought Byzantine and Levantine material goods and culture to Italy and the rest of Europe. Cuisine, modes of dress, art, and architecture were infused with new energies.

The impact of trade on the Venetian diet offers a compelling example of the ways in which the lives of rich and poor were transformed. Armenians and Jews who settled in the city brought eggplant and asparagus to Venetian tables, while merchants brought bananas from Egypt, chickpeas from Turkey, and spinach from Persia. Many new Venetian recipes came from Baghdad. Some of the new food products brought with the Crusades, like wheat, rice, and olive oil, had been known in Europe since Antiquity but were lost in the Middle Ages. Others were new, like Venetian *saor*, fried sardines and onions soaked in vinegar and mixed with raisins from Zante, and "Saracen" sauces made of ground almonds, raisins, ginger, cinnamon, cloves, cardamom seeds, and nutmeg. The Aegean supplied sugar, raisins, and malvasia wine. Cattle from eastern Europe arrived via Dalmatia, supplying offal or tripe for the poor. Dalmatian cheese also became an important staple. Products from the Black Sea filled Venetian grain warehouses. Turkey, chili pepper, and chocolate came as luxury products from the Americas. Maize, which arrived in 1540, became an important basic staple.

Imported objects found their way into the homes, the wardrobes, and the pharmacopoeia of the wealthy: porcelain and pearls from East Asia; gems, mineral dyes, perfumes, ceramics, silks, cottons, brocades, and carpets from Egypt, the Levant, and Asia Minor. Levantine medicinal remedies also entered the market, with cloves to soothe toothache, mace as an astringent and a diarrheic, and a variety of recipes to ward off sexual impotence. By the sixteenth century the maritime republic had become a principal emporium for the exchange of international products and raw materials. It controlled 60 percent of the European spice market; it exported grain, leather, and wines to England as well as the raisins used in plum pudding; it sent cotton and raw silk to German markets, and other raw materials to the textile industries in the Valpadana, Milan, Cremona, and Bologna.

Venice was not alone in fostering early globalization. Genoese trade also created the conditions for cross-cultural encounters, first with the Levant and then, during the sixteenth century, with Iberia, the Americas (sugar, hides, medicines, cochineal), the Atlantic coast, Antwerp and London (textiles), and Sicily (grain). The Genoese economy waxed strong through the sixteenth and seventeenth centuries, when finance and international banking reached their heyday and Genoese merchants dominated international fairs.

DEFINING LIMITS

Identifying global leaders like Venice and Genoa, drawing their trade maps, and reciting the long list of luxury products they imported and exported is an easier task than measuring the consumption patterns of the goods exchanged. Cultural historians, borrowing from anthropology and semiotics, have been more successful in illuminating what products and objects meant to buyers than in assessing consumer purchasing power. Indeed some families in the Italian cities and countryside accumulated vast wealth, which they spent in part on ostentatious display that helped form their public identities, but scholarly discussion of their demand for art and architecture, books, collectables, and luxury goods captures the experience of only a small percentage of the population.

Before turning to production and consumption, then, it is important to draw attention to the limited market for expensive products. The first was widespread poverty. The vast majority of people in late medieval and early modern Europe lived at the subsistence level, subject to periodic famines, the disruptions of war and disease, and the burden of consumption taxes, rents, debased coinage, and obligations to their landlords or employers. Their standard of living was precarious at best, hardly qualifying them as consumers. For example, while the small Adriatic port of Pescara was linked through trade with the Atlantic and the great wealth of Spain, in 1564 three-quarters of its inhabitants lived in makeshift shelters. In Genoa the homeless poor sold themselves as galley slaves, while in Venice the indigent often lived in small water craft or under bridges. While not everyone was so destitute, most people had little purchasing power for handicrafts and perhaps none for luxuries. Moreover, they had little or no coin or currency, relying on their own raw materials at home and exchanging goods and services within local economies rather than the global networks of manufacture and trade that have been so well documented. Even those peasants who accumulated some reserves were rarely consumers; instead they set their sights on purchasing a plot of land, embellishing their villages, staging community and religious fests, or simply upholding the mandates of the Church to avoid placing too much emphasis on material goods.

Besides widespread poverty, industrial technology and transportation limited the manufacture and movement of goods. Manufacturing power rested on medieval machines, fulling and paper mills, mechanical bellows, tilt hammers, the loom and anvil, and other handcraft technology. For the vast majority of the Renaissance population, printing and clockmaking were of limited impact. Of greater importance were Walloon worsted fabrics and the technological advancements of warfare, including the firearms industry in sixteenth-century Brescia, artillery, new fortifications, and the development of the bronze cannon. In short, there was no "Renaissance" in economic development for the majority of people. The economy expanded and contracted at its own pace, quite apart from the material consumption and artistic production that have endowed the historical period with its name.

Agriculture in Italy, and Europe as a whole, remained the foundation of the economy, and foodstuffs were the principal items of production and consumption. The main diet was bread and gruel, with some vegetables and salted meat. The income of ordinary people went largely for cereal consumption and simple foodstuffs, low-grade textiles, perhaps a bed, a few linens, and cooking utensils. There were only a few basic staples, which varied according to climate and environment. Southern Europeans, adopting exports from the Levant, relied on wheat, olive oil, and wine in contrast to inhabitants of the northwest, who consumed more protein, and rye (for ale) and barley, or central Europeans, who lived on porridge, beer, and sausage. Eastern Europe initiated commercialized agriculture for export in the sixteenth century and maintained a high cereal diet. Maize from the New World re-energized the markets for foodstuffs in the sixteenth century, sparing large populations in places like the Veneto from famine. While salt was in abundant supply from Istria, Sicily, and Cyprus, spices reached a more limited market via Venice. Of all the spices pepper attracted the greatest demand, reaching its heyday in the sixteenth and seventeenth centuries. It was the one commodity besides grain that resembled an article of mass consumption, but no food was more important than grain.

After food, shelter and clothing were the greatest necessities for ordinary people. The historian Fernand Braudel has amply covered this terrain in *The Structures of Everyday Life*. He tells us it was not until the eighteenth century that a day laborer or small farmer in Burgundy enjoyed several household items: the pot-hanger, the pot in the hearth, the frying pans, the dripping pans, the board for kneading bread, the chest, the bedstead with four pillars, the feather pillow and the eiderdown, the bolster, maybe a cover for the bed, the coat, the gaiters and a few tools, like a shovel or pickaxe. Prior to the eighteenth century, however, the household inventories of these common laborers consisted of only a few old clothes, a stool, a table, a bench, the planks of a bed, and sacks filled with straw.

My own preliminary work with Venetian inventories and notarial documents suggests that conditions for the majority of the population in northern Italy were much the same. Used clothing, bed linen, and a modest chest for storage were among the most common items for ordinary people. One Jewish widow who wrote her will in 1672 seemed to be doing little better than the Burgundian farmer. Stella, the widow of Caim Coen, left a woolen blanket and cloak to her brother's daughter. Her nephew received two cotton garments, one old and one new, while another two nephews receive four old garments, an iron to heat the bed, three pots, a candle holder, and some Hebrew books. In the rural Veneto at the end of the sixteenth century a family of five agricultural workers on the Capello estate lived in two rooms with two beds.[1] Patricia Fortini Brown also finds that the inventories of the Venetian poor during the sixteenth century contained little more than a pine chest, a few chairs, and beds, often old and broken. The walnut chests and other luxurious containers, majolica, pewter, and silver found in the inventories of the wealthy were absent among the least fortunate strata in Italian society.

Housing for the majority in Italy between 1300 and 1600 was a far cry from the elaborate palaces and country villas of the ruling classes. Made from lumber and earthen materials, few dwellings remain today for observation. They were little more than precarious shelters for peasants and their livestock, who frequently lived together in a room or two with sparse furnishings and cooking utensils. Floors were simply dirt, strewn with straw, flowers, and herbs. Peasants wore homespun linen or coarse wool but not necessarily any shoes. Perhaps what was most important to common folk was used clothing, which could be remade to fit new needs. Few could afford to make purchases of anything other than absolute necessities.

PRODUCTION

Italy's productive output during the fourteenth century to the early seventeenth has dominated discussion and debate for over fifty years. Economic historians have given us a highly complex picture of *manufactures*, or hand-made products, through specialized research in each of the peninsula's principal cities and regions. It is difficult to reproduce a synthetic whole for Italian economic development, and rather more accurate, instead, to refer to multiple economies involved in manufacture and exchange. Some, as discussed earlier, established global networks, others were regional, while still others circulated within circumscribed urban and rural spheres. These economies were located along the now celebrated trans-oceanic trade routes, the roads connecting large cities, the mountain passes linking Italy to northern Europe, and the established physical places for markets, fairs, and shops. But they were also present within the complex, itinerant networks of thousands of rural peddlers who carried their wares to cities, towns, villages, and farms as well as to the domestic households that dotted the rural Italian landscape. The history of the men and women who earned their living by peddling is difficult to retrace and has been mostly lost, but their history touched the majority. Ironically, it is the history of the minority that grew rich in banking, manufacture, and trade and subsequently invested great portions of their wealth in collectables, art, and magnificent building programs that has filled the volumes of economic and cultural history. Yet at least three-quarters of the population was situated in the countryside, lived a marginal existence, and drew income from agricultural labor and household production. It is not only class difference that helped determine their marginal place in history, but gender as well, for the work that took place in the feminized space of the home has achieved less recognition than that within the masculine sphere of the urban guild.

The chronology of Italy's economic development is generally discussed in phases that do not necessarily correspond with periodizations of cultural history. The first phase, *c.* 1100–1300, witnessed an expansion in all sectors of the economy. The beginning of the second phase, in contrast, brought food shortages and, ultimately, the devastating pestilence of the Black Death in the middle of the fourteenth century, when manufacture and trade came temporarily to a halt. It is the period between 1350 and 1620 that has generated the most scholarly debate, the very economy that corresponds with the cultural and artistic apogee termed the "Renaissance." Historians have disagreed on whether the post-plague economy recovered, stagnated, or spiraled downwards.[2] Was the cultural hiatus known as the Renaissance founded against the backdrop of depression or economic resilience?

The earliest response to this question, advanced during the 1950s and 1960s by Robert Lopez, Harry Miskimin, and Carlo Cipolla, was the depression thesis.[3] These scholars characterized the post-1350 plague years in Italy as an era of diminishing profits, stagnating industries, and shrinking trade. Merchants gradually withdrew from commerce, purchased land in the countryside, and adapted a *rentier* mentality. These historians characterized the real estate investments of urban elites as retrograde, a retreat from high-risk enterprise, and a "refeudalization" or hearkening back to the period preceding the growth of urban manufacture and global trade. Lopez emphasized that the zenith in art and elite investment in culture coincided with a period of economic depression that weighed most heavily on the majority of the population.

A flurry of research between the 1960s and 1980s, however, challenged the depression thesis and revealed a more positive restructuring of economic activities. Perhaps the most important outcome of this scholarship was a shift away from a focus on urban–rural dichotomies to an emphasis on regional structures like the Veneto, Lombardy, and Piedmont. This scholarship demonstrated that urban and rural economic activities were intertwined in important ways. Cities relied on country dwellers to replenish their labor force as well as to supply them with a variety of products made in rural homes. Other revisions followed. Among them, the move to invest in real estate was actually a window of opportunity, for by the sixteenth century the swollen population demanded greater cereal production. Lombardy, the Vercellese, Piedmont, the Veneto plains, Ferrara, Mantua, and Emilia made significant strides in land reclamation and agricultural production. Irrigation networks were improved, dairy herds were expanded, and rice and maize were planted, along with mulberry trees for the silk industry. By the eighteenth century both Lombardy and Piedmont became models of progressive farming.

Historians who challenged the depression thesis also demonstrated that the economy was not in a slump after 1350. However, it did experience a temporary hiatus. The Black Death drastically reduced the population, hence the diminution of manufacture and trade, but the economy gradually recovered and diversified, experiencing an "Indian summer" until 1620. Sixteenth-century Venice provides the most successful example. It was perhaps the most industrialized city in Europe. Wool and silk producers, printers, shipbuilders, stonemasons, fullers, mill workers, glassmakers, leatherworkers, smiths, lead crystal workers, and employees of sugar refineries and wax- and soap-works all found employment in this celebrated city on the lagoon. In neighboring Lombardy the cities of Milan, Cremona, Pavia, Como, and Lodi produced a variety of textiles, ceramics, soap, paper, and leather goods, while Brescia was a center for arms manufacture. In the mountains north of Brescia and in the Apennine range north of Genoa mining and metallurgy yielded a number of manufactured metal goods, including buttons, farm implements, and cutlery. Warfare heightened the demand for cuirasses, swords, pikes, arquebuses, cannons, and iron bullets, while cast iron was used to make utensils, cauldrons, saucepans, grates, andirons, fire-backs, and ploughshares. These industries thrived throughout the sixteenth and seventeenth centuries, creating work for a peasant labor force at the ovens, forges, and waterwheels, as well as a demand for diggers, miners, and carters. The silk industry thrived in several major cities in both the north and south, while the Kingdom of Naples produced leather, wool, silk, laces, braids, frills, and other luxury products. Perhaps the only industry that declined during this period was cotton manufacture, which supplied clothing to ordinary people. Its contraction was not because of a depression, however, but because consumers preferred to purchase low-cost German cloth rather than to weave it at home.

Finally, the period between 1620 and 1690 proved a turning point in the history of manufacture. The urban economies of northern and central Italy underwent a restructuring in response to the rise of English, French, and Dutch competition.

While they still functioned as hubs of trade, not all continued to be homes of manufacture. Venice, Florence, Bologna, and the cities of southern Italy specialized in luxury silks. However, the centers of production for most industries shifted after 1620 from the major cities to the towns and villages of their regional states.

Domenico Sella made the most compelling case for the resilience of rural industries in his study of early modern Lombardy.[4] The towns north of Milan and around Turin produced low-quality woolens, cotton, and linen. Needlework thrived everywhere. Papermaking flourished in small towns along watercourses. Milan specialized in silk thread, cut crystal, ribbon, and trimmings. Lodi made decorative ceramics. Cremona became famous for stringed instruments. Unlike the urban centers, which suffered from restrictive guilds, small villages in the foothills, endowed with water-power energy and ample wood, became promising centers of production. Following Sella's lead, historians of the Venetian territorial state have also drawn important attention to rural industry. In the Veneto a number of towns prospered from fulling wool cloth, dyeing, silk, curing and tanning leather, glass, and cutting diamonds. Throughout northern Italy, small towns from Carnia to Brianza achieved regional recognition for their output of linen, canap, wool, silk, and silk thread. Foundries in the mountain areas of Lombardy and Tuscany produced metal sheets, bars, rods, and nails. Copper mines in Val Iperina north of Venice experienced growth, as did paperworks and sawmills.

Sella's findings underline the integration of Italy's rural and urban economies, an important structural characteristic of both the medieval and early modern periods in the peninsula's history. Lucy Riall states the reason for this most eloquently:

> [the] juxtaposition between urban and rural life is a false one. Renaissance society was not in fact urban but largely rural: the rural population greatly outnumbered that of cities, many of which incorporated fields and orchards within their territory . . . Furthermore, the economy of the countryside (*contado*) was closely integrated into urban life in Renaissance Italy.[5]

From at least the thirteenth century Lucca, Florence, Milan, Pisa, Cremona, Piacenza, Bologna and other cities and towns relied upon labor from neighboring rural areas for the production of their textiles. Thus, any discussion of the manufacture of goods must take into account the contributions of the countryside, where labor was situated in the household or nearby in the fields and farmyards. It was the proto-industries centered on domestic production that supplied the basic products for daily life, among them, grain, produce, thread, fabric, buttons, rope, soap, paper, and iron utensils.

Sella's findings are particularly important to the history of women and children, whose participation in the processes of production, at least in economic narratives of the fourteenth to seventeenth centuries, has not been adequately recognized.[6] With a few exceptions the literature on Italian economic development largely focuses on men. By contrast, the histories of women and children – because they generally worked in their own homes and outside of guild structures – are less visible to researchers. Beyond this limitation, while the literature on women and gender has grown immensely in the areas of social and cultural history, economic studies still lag behind. Thus the economic literature could stand both a thorough analysis of women's contribution to production and consumption as well as a gendered reading of overall developments, a proposal well beyond the scope of this chapter. Still, it would be fruitful to point out the areas where such analysis could be developed.

If in smaller numbers than men, and rarely in guilds, women were at work in Italy's major cities. They were spinners, weavers, embroiderers, mercers, barbers, bakers, petty retailers, sellers of produce (eggs, chickens, and cheese), innkeepers, hawkers, and peddlers. Venice's guilds did find room for women: as fustian weavers, comb-makers, cappers, tailors, doublet-makers, secondhand dealers, ironmongers, and haberdashers. They were also prominent in the Florentine and Bolognese textile industries. In Florence in 1604 women comprised 62 percent of the wool weavers; that number rose to 83 percent in 1627.[7] In Bologna in the eighteenth century women played a significant role in the silk industry, running production centers and participating in guilds. In Venice women made cloth sails at the Arsenal, the city's great shipyard. Others were involved in the preliminary processes of silkmaking, such as reeling, winding, throwing, and boiling silk filament.

Most women, however, worked at home for little or no compensation in real wages; as a result they elude the archival record. The household was important both as a unit of consumption and of production, providing work not just to men but also to women and children. Women prepared food, spun, sewed, planted, plowed, harvested, and tended animals in addition to manufacturing clothing, linen, thread, and many other textiles and performing specific tasks in the production of flax and hemp (useful for sheets, table linen, underwear, sacks, overalls, peasant trousers, sailcloth, and rope) and plants for dye. They also made soap; washed, bleached and dyed fabric; and gathered feathers to make pillows. With the gradual diffusion of the mulberry tree from medieval Sicily and Andalusia to sixteenth-century northern Italy, rural women unwound cocoons of silk, combed them, spun them, and sold thread to urban merchants.

The economic literature contains other sporadic references to the work of women and children, but they are not part of any systematic study. Carlo Cipolla tells us women worked as wetnurses and produced commodities at home that in modern times are produced industrially and traded on the market, such as bread, pasta, woolens, and socks. Sella tells us metallurgy in the Apennine range north of Genoa was sustained by a peasant labor force that included women and children as they were "poor and cheap to hire." Women also carried stones and bricks in building yards. In mining areas they carried wood and salt, sorted and washed ore, and prepared charcoal briquettes for use in smelting. In the Bresciano women made silk thread, silk buttons, and stockings and linen. Finally, women were intrinsically involved in costume and dress, activities that touch on raw materials, production, culture, and social hierarchy. We are only just beginning to learn about them from historians of fashion and used clothing.

How might we develop a gendered reading of Italy's economy? Above all, such a gendering of Renaissance economic history would require a re-examination of the tacit categories that have shaped prior research. This would include a questioning of such dichotomies as global versus local, urban versus rural, incorporated versus unincorporated labor, shop versus home production, paid versus unpaid work, agricultural versus non-agricultural labor, and production versus reproduction. Indeed, when we dismantle these dichotomies it becomes evident that the role of women in the late medieval and early modern economy was far more extensive than has been previously recognized.

CONSUMPTION

Cultural historians have greatly contributed to our understanding of elite investment in art, architecture, domestic interiors, fashion, and collectables. But was such consumption anything more than a manifestation of fundamental elitism? Richard Goldthwaite advanced the thesis in his *Wealth and the Demand for Art* that the birth of "consumer society" took place in early Renaissance Italy rather than in northern Europe in the seventeenth and eighteenth centuries. He argues there was a "continuing accumulation of wealth" through the seventeenth century, and a "trickle-down effect" where the consumption craze spread from the elite to people of lesser status.[8] Venice, Genoa, and Florence, Goldthwaite points out, still enjoyed strong economies in the sixteenth century. The first witnessed growth in luxury textiles, glass, metallurgy, and chemicals as well as an agrarian expansion with new crops such as rice and maize; the second attached its growing fortunes to the expanding Spanish Empire; the third grew rich in wool and silk manufacture as well as banking. Goldthwaite also builds on Sella's conclusions for Spanish Lombardy, seeing an accumulation of wealth in the smaller towns that achieved regional significance in arts and crafts. Southern Italy as well witnessed the conditions for accumulated wealth through growth in the production of both raw and finished silk. While Italy saw its global markets contract, its internal markets were still vital, and, according to Goldthwaite, this helps explain why internal demand was "vigorous," stimulating growth in manufacture. Goldthwaite's evidence rests on the growing liturgical demands of the Catholic Church, which sponsored new building programs, decorations, and other art forms as well as the art collecting and connoisseurship of secular elites. Their consumption, he argues, energized both the Renaissance economy and Renaissance culture, presaging the modern age. In a similar fashion, in her *Worldly Goods*, Lisa Jardine focuses on the entrepreneurial spirit of the Renaissance and the desire to own and collect worldly objects from tapestries and books to jewels, exotic goods, and opulent buildings.

The consumer models Goldthwaite and Jardine advance make for fascinating reading and contribute significantly to our understanding of elite values, yet other scholarly findings concerning the overall standard of living weigh against extending their examples beyond their own data. Jardine's book about collectors who fuel the economy and help produce a new commercially driven cultural world applies to only a tiny class of consumers, and Goldthwaite's evidence centers on Florence, a city whose archival repositories are exceptionally rich with the account books of both the wealthy oligarchs and the ecclesiastical institutions that were investing in art.

Evidence for Italy's other consumers is more scattered and raises questions. First, elite spending patterns varied. Florentine patricians made their houses larger and more luxurious, amassing great art collections. However, rich Venetians did not demand as much art as the Florentines did, while the poorer Sienese elites did. Second, there is not enough scholarly evidence to substantiate that wealth trickled down to the middle and lower segments of society in areas beyond Florence. Real wages declined throughout the Renaissance, while indirect taxes on foods and wares rose, thus limiting purchasing power. Moreover, ordinary people across the Italian peninsula experienced the limitations of their social place as well as the burdens of taxes and poverty. Spinners and washers of wool, for example, were guildless inhabitants of the countryside who probably did not reap the profits of the industry. During the Genoese silk boom of the fifteenth and sixteenth centuries spinners had to rent their tools from big silk merchants. The rent amounted to half of what they produced. Moreover, they were paid either in inferior currency or in goods, often with great delays. Elsewhere, wool weavers in Brescia suffered because the big merchants were concerned with keeping high profit margins and earning quick returns by importing finished products. Whether in textiles or in the iron industry, artisans did not control the raw materials, and thus their purchasing power was severely hindered. Third, inflation coupled with stagnant wages and repeated famine hardly make luxury or surplus goods the driving force in the economic machine of the sixteenth century. Taxes, grain prices, the cost of armies, rural catastrophes, and the disruption of war were among the major burdens of the people. Finally, the wealth that fueled the Renaissance in material culture came not just from international trade or the manufacture of luxury goods. It also derived from the power of political office and social privilege, which permitted the ruling elites to buy up tax gabelles, engineer tax exemptions, manipulate money exchange and debased coinage, dip into municipal treasuries, and engage in widespread lending – all activities that siphoned resources from ordinary people. My own findings on the behavior of the ruling families of Brescia are a prime example.

There are many challenges in gauging levels of consumerism and the market for manufactured goods. They include analyzing wages and prices in balance with tax and fiscal structures, as well as taking into account the disparities resulting from gender, class, occupation, and sources of income. It is difficult to speak of consumerism in the private sector before the eighteenth century because Italian – and European – society was fundamentally poor.

Historians who study the activities of markets cannot register the desire for goods unless it was sustained by purchasing power, and this was indeed the rare luxury of a few. Cipolla's analysis of the level and distribution of income in relation to the level and structure of prices indicates that a small percentage of the European population controlled the majority of *assessed* wealth (wealth that historians can measure with some approximation, in contrast to the less visible transfers that occur with gift exchange, charitable donations, or piracy). Peasants spent 60–80 percent of their income on food, while the rich expended 15–35 percent and the prosperous spent 35–50 percent. Ordinary people owned only a few garments in their entire lives, most of which were produced at home. What expendable income remained beyond subsistence was earmarked for rents and taxes, but it was more usual to be in debt than not. The world of luxury cloth, jewelry, banquets, public spectacle, abbeys, fortifications, and lavish building programs belonged to a few elite dynasts and families, the major cities, and those at the apex of the ecclesiastical hierarchy.

Yet there is undoubtedly value in the study of investments in culture. While one line of historians had argued that the *rentier* spirit put a damper on manufacture and trade, Goldthwaite found that the new building programs opened avenues of production that linked the Renaissance economy to the new cultural forms that make the Italian cities unique to Europe. Moreover, the building programs of Renaissance elites, the objects they acquired, and the artwork they commissioned represent not simply cultural investment but rather culture itself. They illuminate, for example, the very humanist encounter with Antiquity that has defined the Renaissance as an age. Moreover, the goods they created and consumed are an important means of understanding identity, values, and attitudes. For Italian elites, whether *rentiers* or merchants, status was expressed through appearance. From Chieri to Asti, from Vicenza to Venice, from Verona to Como, from Naples to Salerno, luxury goods were made for the wealthy with one express purpose: they defined their elite status publicly by setting them apart from other social orders.

Venetian patrician women, often the target of sumptuary prohibitions, provide a good example. They adorned their dresses with gold and silver embroidery and silk linings. They wore high-heeled shoes that demanded longer, more expensive garb and big sleeves requiring more fabric. Their fans were often of gold and silver, such that sumptuary legislation in 1526 admonished them to use simply bone or ivory. Jewels, pearls, alabaster chains and belts, and furs were essential. Dark colors expressed their dignity. Precious stones and gems manifested their wealth. Tapestries, paintings, ivories, bronzes, furniture, and other decorative arts adorned their palaces. Venetian women did not define this standard on their own; they did so in conjunction with the patrician men of their class, who were in consensus about how to project their status both publicly and privately.

Lauro Martines captures this kind of elite consciousness in his *Power and the Imagination*:

> [Princes, oligarchs, and rich men] sought to affirm themselves by means of more imposing *palazzi*, more organized and splendid facades, wider and higher internal spaces, a display of finer manual work of all sorts (from marquetry to hammered metal and leather), a higher finish to things, more rounded edges and polished surfaces, and larger accumulations of objects. There was an escalating taste for grander arches and doorways, carved chimney pieces, coffered ceilings, polychrome ceramic floors, wall hangings, marble plaques, armorial bearings on polychrome enameled terra-cotta, new kinds of sideboards (*credenze*), racks for caps and headpieces, and colorful earthenware (*majolica*).[9]

What did all this mean? Braudel views the luxury consumption that defined interior space in fifteenth-century Italy – colonnades, immense carved and canopied beds, and monumental staircases – as a form of social magnificence that validated political power. Patricia Fortini Brown sees sixteenth-century Venetians accumulating objects and works of art in order to define and defend their family identities and social rank. The façades of their palaces expressed their family identity. Material culture was a means to fulfilling private aspirations. Yet there was an underlying tension, the need to express communal solidarity, even if social, economic, and political equality was a fiction. In my own work I have identified a slightly different trend: first a growing concentration of wealth throughout Italy between the fifteenth and seventeenth centuries. This concentration not only divided the rich from the poor but also led to a restructuring of the distribution of wealth within the elite. Within each Italian city the richest oligarchs marginalized the less fortunate families whose patriarchs and sons could not compete for high office because of shrinking fortunes.

To Goldthwaite, Jardine, and Fortini Brown we may add the findings of Paula Findlen, who, like Jardine, agrees that the collection and celebration of objects – such as ancient manuscripts, paintings, sculptures, and books – was a critical feature of the Renaissance. Worldly possessions helped define the status of Italian nobles and patricians. Findlen does not concur with Goldthwaite that such consumption represents the origins of modernity; rather, she sees it as representing a "wide range of interactions." She maintains, however, that "new concepts of possession and new concepts of culture created and defined the Renaissance." In particular, artefacts were a separate form of patrimony from household goods; they were an important investment to bequeath to one's heirs. Thus Findlen finds that cultural objects were not simply an intellectual or aesthetic passion but rather a valuable asset and potential investment.[10]

The study of material culture in its anthropological context has enhanced our understanding of the creation of elite identity, of gender and class constructs, and of high Renaissance culture. Consumption patterns reflected the growing consolidation of wealth and power of Italy's elites, not just through manufacture or trade but by possession of the reins of power to harness tax resources, public finance, and more. The material culture of Italy's elite families was richly endowed with social meaning. They aimed to set themselves apart, defining both themselves and also other particular groups through dress codes and elaborate spending and through associations with the grandeur of the classical past. In contrast, the private lives and sentiments of ordinary folk still elude the historian's grasp. What seems certain is that the culture of the Renaissance made very little difference in their lives.

NOTES

1 Archivio di Stato di Venezia (hereafter ASV), *Notarile*. Nicolò Velano. *Busta* 1004, No. 165, 6 February 1672; ASV, *Avogaria di Comun. Miscellanea Penale. Busta* 97, *fascicolo* 5, 1593.

2 For a thorough historiographical review and analysis, on which this chapter depends, see Judith Brown, "Prosperity or Hard Times in Renaissance Italy," *Renaissance Quarterly* 42 (1989): 761–80. See also Salvatore Ciriacono, "Economie urbane e industria rurale nell'Italia del Cinque e Seicento. Riconversione o stagnazione?" *Rivista Storica Italiana* 113 (2001): 5–36.

3 R. S. Lopez, "Hard Times and Investment in Culture," in *The Renaissance. A Symposium* (New York: Metropolitan Museum of Art, 1953); R. S. Lopez and H. Miskimin, "The Economic Depression of the Renaissance," *Economic History Review* 14 (1962): 408–9; H. A. Miskimin, *The Economy of Early Renaissance Europe, 1300–1430* (Englewood Cliffs, N.J.: Prentice-Hall, 1969); C. M. Cipolla, "Economic Depression of the Renaissance?"

Economic History Review 15 (1963): 519–24; C. M. Cipolla, "The Economic Decline of Italy," in C. M. Cipolla, *The Economic Decline of Empires* (London: Methuen, 1970), 196–214.

4 D. Sella, *Crisis and Continuity. The Economy of Spanish Lombardy in the Seventeenth Century* (Cambridge, Mass.: Harvard University Press, 1979).

5 Lucy Riall, "Italy," in Peter Stearns (ed.) *The Encyclopedia of European Social History from 1350 to 2000* (New York: Charles Scribner's Sons, 2001), vol. 1, 322–3.

6 An especially helpful survey of early modern women's economic roles is M. Wiesner, *Women and Gender in Early Modern Europe* (Cambridge: Cambridge University Press, 1993), 82–114. For Italy, see J. Brown, "A Woman's Place was in the Home: Women's Work in Renaissance Tuscany," in M. W. Ferguson, M. Quilligan, and N. J. Vickers (eds) *Rewriting the Renaissance: The Discourses of Sexual Difference in Early Modern Europe* (Chicago: University of Chicago Press, 1986), 206–24; J. M. Ferraro, "Representing Women in Early Modern Italian Economic History," in J. Hartman and A. Seeff (eds) *Attending to Early Modern Women: Structures and Subjectivities* (Madison, N.J.: Associated University Press, forthcoming).

7 J. C. Brown and J. Goodman, "Women and Industry in Florence," *Journal of Economic History* 40 (1980): 73–80.

8 R. A. Goldthwaite, *Wealth and the Demand for Art in Italy, 1300–1600* (Baltimore: Johns Hopkins University Press, 1993), 16.

9 L. Martines, *Power and the Imagination: City States in Renaissance Italy* (New York: Vintage Books, 1979), 257.

10 P. Findlen, "Possessing the Past: The Material World of the Italian Renaissance," *Renaissance Quarterly* 103 (1998): 89, 86, 87 n. 20, 93, 95.

SUGGESTIONS FOR FURTHER READING

Allerston, Patricia. "Wedding Finery in Sixteenth-Century Venice," in Trevor Dean and K. J. P. Lowe (eds) *Marriage in Italy, 1300–1650*. Cambridge: Cambridge University Press, 1998.

—— "Reconstructing the Second-hand Clothes Trade in Sixteenth- and Seventeenth-Century Venice." *Costume* 33 (1999): 46–56.

Braudel, Fernand. *The Structures of Everyday Life. Civilization and Capitalism, 15th–18th Century*. New York: Harper & Row, 1979.

Brown, Judith. "A Woman's Place Was in the Home: Women's Work in Renaissance Tuscany," in Margaret W. Ferguson, Maureen Quilligan, and Nancy J. Vickers (eds) *Rewriting the Renaissance: The Discourses of Sexual Difference in Early Modern Europe*. Chicago: University of Chicago Press, 1986.

—— "Prosperity or Hard Times in Renaissance Italy." *Renaissance Quarterly* 42 (1989): 761–80.

Brown, Judith and Jordan Goodman. "Women and Industry in Florence." *Journal of Economic History* 40 (1980): 73–80.

Brown, Patricia Fortini. *Art and Life in Renaissance Venice*. New York: Prentice-Hall, 1997.

—— *Private Lives in Renaissance Venice*. New Haven and London: Yale University Press, 2004.

Cipolla, Carlo M. "Economic Depression of the Renaissance?" *Economic History Review* 15 (1963): 519–24.

—— "The Economic Decline of Italy," in Carlo M. Cipolla *The Economic Decline of Empires*. London: Methuen, 1970, 196–214.

―― *Before the Industrial Revolution. European Society and Economy, 1000–1700*. New York: Norton & Company, 1980.
Ciriacono, Salvatore. "Protoindustria, lavoro a domicilio e sviluppo economico nelle campagne venete in epoca moderna." *Quaderni Storici* 52 (1983): 57–80.
―― "Economie Urbane e industria rurale nell Italia del Cinque e Seicento. Riconversione o stagnazione?" *Rivista Storica Italiana* 113 (2001): 5–36.
De Vries, Jan. "The Industrial Revolution and the Industrious Revolution." *Journal of Economic History* 54 (1994): 249–70.
Ferraro, Joanne M. *Family and Public Life in Brescia, 1580–1650. The Foundations of Power in the Venetian State*. Cambridge: Cambridge University Press, 1993.
―― "Representing Women in Early Modern Italian Economic History," in J. Hartman and A. Seeff (eds) *Attending to Early Modern Women: Structures and Subjectivities*. Delaware: University of Delaware Press, forthcoming.
Findlen, Paula. "Possessing the Past: The Material World of the Italian Renaissance." *Renaissance Quarterly* 103 (1998): 83–114.
Frick, Carole C. *Dressing Renaissance Florence. Families, Fortunes, and Fine Clothing*. Baltimore: Johns Hopkins University Press, 2002.
Goldthwaite, Richard A. *Wealth and the Demand for Art in Italy, 1300–1600*. Baltimore: Johns Hopkins University Press, 1993.
Jardine, Lisa. *Worldly Goods. A New History of the Renaissance*. New York: Norton, 1996.
Lopez, Robert S. "Hard Times and Investment in Culture," in *The Renaissance. A Symposium*. New York: Metropolitan Museum of Art, 1953.
Lopez, Robert S. and Harry Miskimin. "The Economic Depression of the Renaissance." *Economic History Review* 14 (1962): 408–9.
Martines, Lauro. *Power and the Imagination: City States in Renaissance Italy*. New York: Vintage Books, 1979.
―― "The Renaissance and the Birth of Consumer Society." *Renaissance Quarterly* 51 (1998): 193–203.
McKendrick, Neil, John Brewer, and J. H. Plumb. *The Birth of a Consumer Society: The Commercialization of Eighteenth-century England*. Bloomington: University of Indiana Press, 1982.
Miskimin, Harry A. *The Economy of Early Renaissance Europe, 1300–1430*. Englewood Cliffs, N.J.: Prentice-Hall, 1969.
Pomeranz, Ken. *The Great Divergence*. Princeton: Princeton University Press, 2000.
Sella, Domenico. *Crisis and Continuity. The Economy of Spanish Lombardy in the Seventeenth Century*. Cambridge, Mass.: Harvard University Press, 1979.
―― "Il economia," in Gaetano Cozzi and Paolo Prodi (eds) *Storia di Venezia*, vol. 6. Rome: Istituto della enciclopedia italiana Treccani, 1994, 651–712.
―― *Italy in the Seventeenth Century*. London and New York: Longman, 1997.
Stearns, Peter. *Consumerism in World History. The Global Transformation of Desire*. London: Routledge, 2001.
Ventura, Angelo. *Nobiltà e popolo nella società veneta del '400 e '500*. Bari: Laterza, 1964.
Wall, Richard. *Family Forms in Historic Europe*. Cambridge: Cambridge University Press, 1983.
―― "The Household," in Peter Stearns (ed.) *The Encyclopedia of European Social History*, Vol. 4. New York: Charles Scribner Sons, 2001, 109–24.
Wiesner, Merry. *Women and Gender in Early Modern Europe*. Cambridge: Cambridge University Press, 1993.

CHAPTER FIVE

CITIES, TOWNS, AND NEW FORMS OF CULTURE

Alexander Cowan

INTRODUCTION

The sixteenth-century Italian diplomat and humanist Giovanni Botero was in no doubt of the importance and functions of cities in his time:

> A city is said to be an assembly of people, a congregation drawn together to the end they may thereby the better live at their ease in wealth and plenty. And the greatness of a city is said to be, not the largeness of the site or the circuit of the walls, but the multitude and number of the inhabitants and their power. Now men are drawn together upon sundry causes and occasions thereunto them moving: some by authority, some by force, some by pleasure, and some by profit that proceedeth of it.[1]

Like Botero, historians of the Renaissance have often focused on the vitality of cities in this period. Yet Renaissance Europe was an essentially rural world. The great majority of the population continued to live and work close to the land, in villages and hamlets scattered across the continent. In spite of the substantial quantities of capital represented by the value of international trade, banking, and industrial production, land continued to underpin the economic, social, and political structures of late Renaissance Europe. The significance of the urban growth that took place in the late medieval and early modern periods lies above all in its cultural importance, not only in individual urban centers but also in the relationship between them. "Culture" is used here in its widest sense, embracing not only the "high culture" of painting, sculpture, architecture, literature, and highly developed intellectual ideas, but also day-to-day behavior, the consumption of food and drink, the use of artefacts, and the belief systems that underpinned them. The movement of goods, people, and ideas was stimulated by the presence of towns and cities as nodal points in local and international trading networks.

The scale and geographical distribution of urban growth in western Europe was far from uniform. The first upsurge in urbanization had taken place in the eleventh and twelfth centuries and had been most visible in central and northern Italy, southern Germany, and the southern Netherlands. Italy was undoubtedly the region where cities were most prominent. In 1500, the peninsula was home to five of the six urban centers with populations of over 60,000: Venice, Milan, Florence, Rome, and Naples. In western Europe, only Paris was in this league, though the largest European city by far was Istanbul, with a population of nearly half a million at this time. Yet even towns with much smaller populations, at times places with only a few hundred people, functioned as urban centers – a fact that makes it difficult to assess the extent to which Europe was urbanized during the Renaissance. According to a recent urban history of Europe, just over 11 percent of the population lived in urban centers with populations of 5,000 or more around 1500. But the sixteenth century witnessed the development of large urban centers, with which this chapter is primarily concerned. These cities succeeded in attracting and retaining immigrants from considerable distances. The period from 1470 to about 1630 – the era historians have come to call "the long sixteenth century" – was characterized by a general urban demographic expansion, which benefited above all international trading centers, some of which grew at an unsustainable rate. The population of Seville, which experienced a spectacular boost to its economy as the major point of departure and arrival for the Spanish colonies in the Americas, rose by 150 percent in the first half of the sixteenth century. In the second half of the sixteenth century it had already ceased to grow as fast. By the seventeenth century, it was scarcely growing at all. Antwerp grew at a similar rate to Seville, but subsequently lost almost half its population because of major economic and political instability in the region. In the seventeenth century, the European economy experienced a significant slowdown. A small number of commercial centers, notably London and Amsterdam, continued to grow strongly, but many others did not, particularly those in the Baltic, the Mediterranean, the southern Netherlands, and the Iberian peninsula. Most seventeenth-century urban growth took place in regional administrative centers such as Dijon and Palermo, and in the capital cities of newly emergent centralized states: Vienna, Florence, Turin, Mannheim, Heidelberg, Copenhagen, Berlin, Dresden, Leipzig, Munich, and Madrid. More general economic changes in the Mediterranean, exacerbated by the effects of a major plague outbreak in the 1570s, brought economic growth to an end in centers such as Florence and Venice, but, paradoxically, not their capacity to function as centers of consumption. Rome should be considered as a case apart. Given its location and the fiscal base of its economy, it was quite unlike any other European city. The absence of the papacy from the city for much of the Middle Ages had impoverished Rome, leaving several of its seven hills depopulated. The return of the popes during the fifteenth century began an intense period of building to accommodate the princes of the Church. New ecclesiastical buildings of all kinds were constructed, comprising major churches, Jesuit colleges, and confraternity buildings. The numbers of inhabitants were greatly inflated at certain times of the year by the arrival of pilgrims from all over Europe.

In the late Renaissance only a small number of new towns were established. None of these rivaled their predecessors in their capacity for sustained growth. Their specialized nature predicated a limited lifespan. They tended to fall into the categories of citadel towns or monuments to personal aggrandizement. Citadel towns were constructed in sensitive military zones, such as Palmanova along the borders of the Holy Roman Empire in the northeastern Veneto, and Neufbrisach and Philippeville in the Rhineland. Built on geometric plans that represented the most complete concrete expression of classical designs for the ideal city, their small scale and internal and external organization facilitated rapid deployment of garrisons to defend what was in effect a fortress rather than a functioning town. The services provided by the non-military population were dedicated to the citadel town's primary function. It was never intended that they should become centers of trade. The fortified perimeters were a constraint on any potential growth, and the unstable military conditions that had originally justified their construction were a major deterrent to long-term commercial activity.

Monuments to personal aggrandizement had more potential for economic development, and this was in the minds of their founders. Like many personal projects though, they foundered when their patrons either lost interest or died. Once again, their location was not conducive to organic economic growth. Pienza was constructed between 1463 and 1469 on the orders of Pope Pius II on the site of Corsignano in Tuscany, his native village, both as a celebration of his elevation to the papacy and as a stimulus to economic development in the area. But with Siena, a major commercial and political center, so close by, Pienza had little potential for development. The existing inhabitants complained that they were forced to move and prevented from continuing to work in the fields. A century and a half later, Cardinal Richelieu attempted a similar project in the Poitou, locating his new town next to a family castle. He had intended to make it the administrative capital of his duchy and to establish a college there to educate young noblemen in French, the arts of war, and courtly behavior. The walls of Richelieu and the buildings of the Grande Rue still remain as a monument to this abortive urban ambition.

URBAN GROWTH AND THE ENVIRONMENT

The growth in the population of individual towns and cities brought about a number of changes in the urban environment. There was no direct correlation between the numbers of new urban residents and the rate at which the urbanized surface area of a specific center expanded, any more than it can be argued that additional land beyond the existing limits of the urban fabric was specifically earmarked for further development to accommodate newcomers. There were physical, institutional, and mental constraints on expansion *extra muros*. As the term suggests, most urban centers that could afford to do so maintained a fortified *enceinte* of some kind. These walls exercised a number of functions. They were defensive. Both the Hundred Years War (1337–1543) and the Italian Wars (1494–1559) had exposed the extent to which larger urban centers were vulnerable to siege. As a result, urban fortifications in many parts of northern and central Italy and western France were renewed. While such threats receded in these specific areas during the sixteenth and early seventeenth centuries, political instability elsewhere in Europe encouraged the renewal of urban fortifications on the Italian model as part of a rolling but often uncoordinated program dictated in part by perceived external threats and in part by the availability of finance for this purpose. Cities were proud of their walls. It was no coincidence that contemporary woodcuts and engravings of European cities of the kind published by Merian, and Braun and Hogenberg, emphasized their fortifications. Cities were represented as entities that were distinctly separated from the surrounding countryside. Even Venice, which famously had no defensive walls, was universally portrayed in the middle of its lagoon, which served as a physical barrier to any invading force as effectively as any wall. Visitors and citizens alike praised the beauty or size of urban fortifications in their writings. The German humanist Konrad Celtis described his native Nuremberg at the end of the fifteenth century as wearing about herself "a strong girdle of a three-fold wall and trench . . . The ground between the parallel walls is soft and grassy; a little brook runs through it, and deer graze upon it."[2]

Walls were also physical barriers to establish the extent of the jurisdiction of the urban authorities. In this context, what counted most was not so much the barrier itself but the points at which it could be crossed – the gates. Towns required both protection from outside threats and access to enable individuals and goods to pass in and out. There was also a need to control movement; to raise customs revenues; to check on the identity and provenance of strangers, particularly in times of disease or warfare; and to establish the area covered by urban taxation and guild regulations. Once again gates were built as imposing structures to enhance the imposing impression given by the walls. Accounts of royal entries frequently begin with a description of the liminal point at one of the city gates where the visitor was greeted by representatives of the urban elite. When Charles IX of France visited Montpellier in 1564, a viewing position was built for him outside one of the gates, where, "seated among the principal members of his court, he received the homage of all the estates of the city according to their orders and ranks, accompanied by the customary speeches."[3]

In general, urban growth was accommodated within the existing walls. In some cases, additional building was facilitated by the presence of open spaces enclosed by overly ambitious medieval fortifications. The Florentine wall, for instance, which had been built over a 50-year period at the end of the thirteenth and the beginning of the fourteenth centuries, enclosed a space six times as large as that protected by its predecessor. Many of these open spaces were used to keep livestock, giving some quarters of late medieval towns a semi-rural appearance. Other spaces remained open because they were marshy, such as the Parisian district of the Marais (literally 'marshland'), which had been enclosed by the walls of the late fourteenth century. The confiscation of Church property, and the closure of convents and the buildings of other religious institutions in those parts of Europe that became Protestant during the sixteenth century, also released space for rebuilding and further urban development.

Paradoxically, the greatest stimulus to the transformation of open spaces within the walls into built-up areas owed little directly to demographic growth. In some ways, the opposite might be said to have been the case. The construction of new urban quarters made it possible for parts of the existing housing stock to be modified to accommodate the immigrants who were largely responsible for increases in the urban population. The spatial organization inherited by the towns of the fifteenth century was a combination of lateral and vertical zoning. In general terms, the wealthy tended to live close to the center or along major thoroughfares leading out of the town, such as the London streets leading down to London Bridge, at the time the only crossing of the river Thames. Street names such as the Merceria in Venice and Lombard Street in London reflected occupational clusters (retailers, bankers) located close to one another for convenience. Some artisan activity took place on the edges of urban areas, not only because they were linked to raw materials brought in from outside but also because the urban authorities wished to avoid pollution from smoke or smells, both of which were believed to be responsible for the spread of disease. The link was explicitly recognized by the Venetian health board in their 1501 statement that in order to keep the city healthy, all sources of "fetor and stenches," such as rotten meat, had to be removed.[4]

This lateral zoning was complemented by more complex patterns of accommodation in which families and individuals from different parts of the social spectrum, with important disparities in the types of housing that they could afford to buy or rent, lived in close proximity to each other. The calle de Moncada in the Ribera district of Barcelona, while famous for its fine merchant housing, also accommodated artisans and families working at the port.[5] "Vertical zoning" only describes part of this phenomenon, where the wealthy lived on the second and third stories of buildings, while those lower down the social scale lived on the ground floors, when they were not taken up by shops or storage, and above all in the upper stories. Buildings were also socially and physically divided between the front and the back. Subsidiary entrances to large buildings gave access to a labyrinth of apartments and single rooms at the back. The spaces between streets were also often linked by lesser structures housing the poor.

Demographic pressures inevitably led to increases in urban population densities. To increase their rental income, landlords added extra stories to buildings to accommodate the influx or subdivided existing apartments. Between 1525 and 1553, the total housing stock in the Parisian parish of St-Germain l'Auxerrois rose by 10 percent.[6] Additional struts were built out into the city's streets to support the enlargement of existing buildings, adding to the traffic congestion already created by narrow streets and temporary structures for artisans and shopkeepers. A sixteenth-century Antwerp merchant recorded that traffic jams caused so much congestion that there was gridlock for at least half an hour in some streets, requiring substantial detours to avoid them. Conditions such as these were among the incentives to the wealthy to move to newly built urban quarters in which they could live in comfort away from the noise, smell, and proximity of the lower orders. As Leon Battista Alberti put it in his *On the Art of Building*: "the city will be more secure and less disrupted if those in power are separated from the feckless mob of poultry salesmen, butchers, cooks and the like."[7]

Some urban growth did take place beyond the limits of the walls. This was dependent on several factors. The presence of pre-existing suburbs provided a node around which further expansion took place. Often such an expansion was an amplification of long-standing migration patterns, differing only in scale from earlier times. The oldest London suburb, Southwark, which lay at the southern end of London Bridge, attracted so many settlers that its population in the seventeenth century rivaled that of many substantial provincial English towns. There was little to distinguish it from an urban center. Many migrants were attracted to settle in the suburbs because of the availability of relatively low-cost accommodations and unregulated employment. This was their first point of contact with the town, where they could expect to find a more open society even though it was intensely competitive. Housing was frequently cheaper than within the walls, reflecting lower land values and poor-quality construction. There were also more employment opportunities in industries such as brewing and dyeing. The expansion of demand for cheap textiles in particular offered work and a meager salary to many of these immigrants. Merchants took advantage of the availability of cheap labor beyond the regulatory control of the guilds, especially in the service industries: taverns, lodging houses, coopers, victuallers, and carpenters; ambulant traders, bathhouse keepers, and prostitutes. The distinction between town and suburb was less clear-cut than it might have been because the low level of military threats in many regions discouraged the urban authorities from maintaining their fortifications. Many unofficial openings were created as townspeople and suburban dwellers alike made use of the stones for building materials and took advantage of the absence of controls to move in and out of the town at will. Some houses were built straddling the walls. The long-term future of this suburban development was entirely dependent on a sustained lack of interest in the walls by the urban authorities. Any decision to remodel fortifications implied that buildings outside would be destroyed. Space was needed for the new stone-faced earthworks, bastions, and ditches. Often secondary earthworks were constructed at some distance from the main fortifications to keep soldiers at a distance. It became essential to keep the areas in front of them entirely clear to allow for a clear line of fire.

London is a case apart from other urban centers in terms of its expansion from the fifteenth century, not only in terms of scale – its population was to reach half a million by the end of the seventeenth century – but also because of the way in which housing grew up along the northern bank of the Thames both to the east and the west. The eastern expansion took place because of the growth of London as an international trading center. Most of the suburbs in the East End were poor and contained a substantial number of overseas immigrants, particularly from the Low Countries. In character and appearance, these suburbs were similar to those elsewhere, with piecemeal development of low-level housing in poor condition, industrial activity, and a marked degree of poverty. Over half the households in the first half of the seventeenth century fell below the threshold for the hearth tax. To the west of the city the picture was quite different. The presence of an alternative urban pole around the court and Westminster Abbey encouraged those who had interests in both the city and at court to build houses along the bank of the Thames so that they could travel easily in both directions, first by water and later by land. Over time, new quarters developed to the north of these axes.

It is abundantly clear that the internal remodeling of urban centers owed far more to improvements in material wealth among a small minority and changes in social and political organization than it did to general demographic changes. On a general level, there was a movement away from timber structures with straw or thatched roofs to buildings in brick or stone with tile or slate roofs. This was not enough to avoid ravages by fire, such as the disaster that destroyed 470 houses in Valladolid in 1561, but the greater use of stronger building materials permitted larger structures to be erected, which were increasingly designed to be part of a more ordered visual environment. Some were public buildings or churches. Others were constructed to accommodate the wealthy, and although much of the remodeling was piecemeal, either inserted into the existing urban fabric or constructed next to it, this often took place either as part of an overall conception of an ordered city or at least reflected architectural practices that subscribed to the same philosophy. The theoretical models for the Renaissance city were easy to find. The Piazza dell'Annunciata in Florence was directly based on the forum in classical Rome. The writings of Vitruvius strongly influenced the idea of a harmonious city, which was first introduced to an Italian humanist audience in the fifteenth century by Alberti, Sebastiano Serli, Leonardo da Vinci, and Filarete, among others. This concept brought together principles of mathematical symmetry, aesthetics, and the anatomical belief that each part of a healthy body functioned in harmony and balance with all the others. As a living organism of humans, animals, buildings, and spaces, the ideal city had to be organized, at least in key areas, to ensure that each of its functions complemented the others. The expression of the principles of balance, order, and symmetry in individual buildings, street frontages, squares, and vistas was intended to contribute to an optimum urban form, but it also sent out messages of social order and harmony that were used by the ruling authorities to underpin their power.

The new buildings were intended to be seen as well as used. Their size and harmonious appearance required observation from some distance, across a broad street, or a fine square, or at the apex of converging streets. Reality and artifice overlapped in designs for buildings, paintings, and stage sets. The latter were particularly important, for while they used the rules of perspective to convey the impression of large numbers of buildings receding into the distance within a very compact space, they also emphasized the principle that the spaces between and in front of buildings were also intended for the dramatic presentation of the elite, both to each other and to observers. This development can be traced in the reshaping of squares. Tommaso Garzoni's *Piazza Universale*, first published in 1585, posited a space within which one could meet men of every occupation and of none. Even as he was writing, the authorities in many towns were doing their best to empty major squares of the bustle of everyday activity, most of it commercial, in order to create a more controlled environment. The Piazza San Marco in Venice, which linked the lagoon to the center of government and acted as the forecourt to the Doge's private chapel (St Mark's Church), had doubled for centuries as a market and as the processional stage for civic ritual. In the course of the later sixteenth and early seventeenth centuries, the square was cleared of its market stalls and other temporary constructions. It was enlarged and paved, and commerce was relegated to two high-rent arcaded blocks flanking it, the so-called old and new *Procuratorie*. Similar developments took place in Bologna, Florence, Urbino, and Perugia. Where Italy led, northern European cities were to follow in the seventeenth century. Henry IV of France introduced two new squares into Paris, the Place Royale (now the Place des Vosges) and the Place Dauphiné. In London, the Italian model of the square encouraged the Earl of Bedford to employ the architect Inigo Jones to develop the piazza at Covent Garden in the 1630s.

Significantly, though both Covent Garden and the Place Royale were not planned as residential squares but as business centers, they rapidly became sought-after residences for a courtly elite, whose need to reflect their high social status arose from their association with princely authority in a capital city, rather than the international commerce that had been traditionally at the heart of urban wealth. In both Paris and London, merchants preferred to remain within the existing urban fabric, close to their places of business, while the great houses of the Marais and along the Strand in London were built for the aristocratic families whose names they or associated streets still bear today (The Hôtel de Rohan and the Hôtel de Soubise in Paris, Bedford Square and Southampton Row in London). Elsewhere, too, princely capitals attracted elite administrators whose residences in new urban quarters were intended to some degree to reflect the prestige of their employers as much as their own. Philip II's viceroy in Naples, Don Pedro de Toledo, constructed the city's Spanish quarter in the 1530s along a street linking the port to a carefully positioned garrison of Spanish troops located outside the city. New quarters were built on three sides of Turin at the end of the sixteenth century by Emmanuel Filibert of Savoy in spaces enclosed by his capital's new fortifications. The impulse to build new residential quarters in international trading centers was not entirely absent. Antwerp and Amsterdam are the best-known examples. In the former, Gilbert van Schoenbeke created two districts around a public weigh house and a new market in the 1540s, while the growing importance of Amsterdam in the early seventeenth century was reflected by the regents' decision to build three semi-circular canals to facilitate commerce and provide space for the houses of the wealthy. In Bordeaux, the Dutch merchants who dominated the city's wine trade in the seventeenth century eschewed the cramped conditions for housing and storage within the urban center and developed their own community in the suburb of the Chartrons.

URBAN CULTURES

Throughout the Renaissance, urban societies were far more complex than their rural counterparts. Factors of scale played their part. Large and growing concentrations of population permitted a degree of social differentiation far greater than those to be found in village communities. Both had their individual social hierarchies, but urban societies were characterized by three attributes that distinguished them from rural society: a very high level of occupational diversity; the presence of overlapping networks of social relationships, many of which were associated with specific areas of the city; and a distinct level of mobility. These formed the context for the presence of a multiplicity of urban cultures. While each form of culture permitted individuals to develop a sense of identity that was partly defined by the ways in which it differed from other urban cultures, the lives of many urban inhabitants were shaped by a recognition that they belonged to several overlapping cultures at the same time.

The numbers of individual craft guilds in each urban center were only a partial measure of occupational diversity. There were large numbers of unskilled workers and servants of both sexes whose activities lay outside the purview of guilds: peddlers, market stallholders, minor shopkeepers, not to mention numbers of minor officials employed by the urban or princely authorities in tasks ranging from keeping order, collecting taxes, or supervising workshops in orphanages, to keeping and storing records. In some centers, such as Augsburg, guilds were abolished. In others, such as Turin, they were introduced only late into the seventeenth century. In both cities, as elsewhere, artisans engaged in the same occupation demonstrated many forms of unofficial solidarity even outside their places of work. They wore easily identifiable clothing. In some cases they carried specialized tools. The rope-maker who was the victim of a well-known practical joke in sixteenth-century Rome believed that he had really been arrested by the police when the special knife he always carried for his work was confiscated as an offensive weapon. They frequently engaged in common social activities such as drinking and gambling after work. Court records concerning violence arising from the combination of the two confirm that these were frequently disputes between work associates. Such disputes were part of a broader honor system that linked men who shared the same working traditions and pride in the quality of their work. This sense of honor became more intense, among journeymen in particular, from the sixteenth century as socio-economic change altered their status from a stage in a career from apprentice to master craftsman to one of permanent dependence on employers.

Guild membership provided additional layers of cultural identity. Statutes, many of them dating back to the central Middle Ages, regulated the conditions in which members worked, the nature and duration of their training as apprentices, the hours worked and wages paid, and the quality of what was produced. Above all, they promised to protect members from unofficial external competition. A strong sense of pride in work was engendered by regulatory practices, which not only identified examples of poor workmanship but also destroyed them in public. The London Clockmakers' Company ordered a gold watch to be defaced on the grounds that if they did not do so, "great fraud would be put upon ye person who happened to buy it, and on abuse and disparagement redound to the Art and all good and honest artists."[8] The culture of guild membership also embraced the spiritual, the private, and the public. Medieval guilds enabled their members to carry out confraternal activity in specially dedicated chapels. Their dedication to patron saints particularly associated with individual occupations, such as St Barnabas, who was believed to have a special responsibility for shoemakers, gradually took on less meaning in the course of the sixteenth century when religious change among both Catholics and Protestants offered laymen alternative forms of religious expression. In Catholic areas, the establishment of new confraternities offered laymen greater energy and religious focus than the traditional occupational groupings. In spite of these changes, the guilds' moral and practical concern for collective welfare remained. The ordinances of the tailors' guild in Newcastle upon Tyne required a full complement of guild torches to be carried at all members' funerals, and a half complement for those of their wives. This public demonstration of solidarity and collective identity also found its expression through guild participation in religious and secular processions to mark key points in the Christian calendar and the mayoral year, as well as the visits of prominent outsiders. The significance of these processions to the artisans who took part was often reflected by conflicts between different guilds over precedence.

Membership of corporate bodies was not limited to artisans. Associative culture was particularly important to wealthier members of society. In some ways, these brotherhoods, colleges, and associations were minor versions of the legal entity represented by the town itself. Like the guilds, these groups were organized on occupational lines. In the case of long-distance merchants, associational groups originated as guilds, but rapidly distanced themselves socially, particularly in cases where their status was recognized by an external authority. The London Merchant Adventurers and the Hostmen of Newcastle upon Tyne, who monopolized first the control of coal exports along the river and then the reins of power on the town council, both received charters from the English monarchy. There was a contrast between the Mediterranean and northern Europe in this context, however. Formal merchants' groups were absent in the south, possibly because of the social prominence and great wealth of the international merchants and bankers of Venice, Florence, Milan, or Genoa, who comprised the ruling elites of their cities and considered themselves as gentlemen and consequently socially distinct from the "vile and mechanical arts." This attitude was intensified in the course of the sixteenth and seventeenth centuries, when members of the ruling elites in the Italian cities largely gave up trade as a source of income and considered the activity to be ignoble and thus unacceptable for a gentleman. Only Venice was an honorable exception to this trend. In northern Europe, long-distance merchants retained a strong associative culture. In Lübeck, for instance, the city's international merchants revived the Kaufleutekompanie (merchant brotherhood) along medieval associative lines in 1581 almost fifty years after it had been dissolved during the upheavals of the Reformation. They met regularly for feasts at which the brotherhood's ceremonial silverware was used. The inclusion of the words and music for Lutheran hymns in their account books suggests that occupational solidarity was also expressed in religious terms.

The Italian obsession with making a distinction between "civil" and "mechanical" occupations encouraged a number of professional groups to develop their own associations in such a way as to distinguish themselves from men who worked using their hands. Groups of notaries, physicians, and surgeons, often known as colleges, developed during the fifteenth and sixteenth centuries. Like the guilds, they were regulatory in nature and intended to enhance the status of their members while limiting the entry of newcomers and preventing non-members from competing with them. The surgeons had more difficulty than the physicians in establishing this higher status. Some commentators regarded the surgeons as *mecchanici et illiterates*. They may well have felt that their concern was justified by cases in which barber-surgeons benefited from the growth in demand for their services during outbreaks of epidemic disease to promote themselves to specialist surgeons. Such was the case of Alessandro Castello, a member of the Venetian College of Surgeons from 1593, who took the opportunity to dress as a gentleman while working with plague victims in the 1580s, even though he had grown up in his father's barber's shop.

NEIGHBORHOODS AND PARISHES

Occupation was only one defining factor in shaping urban culture. Neighborhood and parish were equally important identifiers. Furthermore, a man's social status was closely related to the geographical area within which he had social relationships. The higher his status, the larger the area in which he traveled. His residence and habitual place of activity were likely to be some distance apart, particularly where new quarters had been constructed some distance from key buildings in which a member of the elite might be expected to be active: the town hall, centers of trade and business, places of entertainment. In urban centers with overlapping elites, the range of movement between different poles of activity was even greater. Merchants living on the right bank of the Seine in Paris were accustomed to travel to the King's palace in the Louvre and to the homes of their aristocratic friends, relatives, and business associates in the Marais. In London, the distances were even greater, linking the city with Whitehall and the West End. For high-status Venetians, the scattered distribution of islands in the lagoon and the ease of travel by water created even more extensive networks. Patricians and wealthy merchants and lawyers visited their female relatives in convents all over the city, as well as in the outlying islands of Murano and Burano.

For those living lower down in society, there was much closer proximity between homes and places of work and access to local services – markets, bakehouses, washhouses, and places of worship. In itself, this proximity was not enough to create the network of relationships that comprised urban neighborhoods. They were organic areas, within which clusters of services and activities had developed of their own accord around key activities such as small-scale local marketplaces. Moreover, certain activities that took place within these "official" neighborhoods – parishes, quarters, wards, *gonfalone* – did draw adult males together, particularly in the fifteenth and early sixteenth centuries. The burgher militia was an active part of a town's defenses. Possession of the requisite arms was often one of the criteria for being accepted as a burgher, along with the capacity to pay taxes. Over time, however, urban militias trained together less frequently and their duties were subsumed into those of professional garrisons. Evidence of informal neighborhoods is far more plentiful. It has been suggested that such neighborhoods could be defined by what could be seen or heard from homes of places of work, a distance of some 50 yards. Within this area, there was considerable solidarity among people who depended on each other for mutual support. There was also a heightened sense of the "other." Religious conflicts between Catholics and Calvinists in sixteenth-century Dijon, for example, took place between groups from contiguous streets who were distinguished as much by their occupations and homes as by their religious allegiances. The form of bull-running that took place in Venice was far more than a ceremonial journey from their stable on the edge of the city to the square where they would be attacked by dogs as a public entertainment. The introduction of a large animal into the narrow streets on the way was a noisy intrusion of daily business and was carried out aggressively by the youths of one area as a form of insult to the other areas through which they passed, a classic form of inter-neighborhood conflict that only served to underline local solidarities.

A great deal of emphasis has been placed in this discussion on male solidarities as expressions of urban cultures. Renaissance urban society was indeed highly gendered, even if the sexes mixed in many workplaces and in the streets. At this level, it might be possible to consider a specifically female urban culture, but there is little that can be said about this in detail, other than that in general terms the female networks that shaped their members' identities lacked any formal basis, with the exception of those institutions for women established by the Catholic Church – convents, orphanages, homes for former prostitutes, and other exclusively female charitable institutions. Even where the operation of such institutions lay in the hands of women, such as the senior nuns who ran convents, they did not take overall responsibility for their institutions' spiritual health, financial stability, or general organizing principles. The cloistering of a Munich convent in 1632 by Franciscan *reformati* was recorded by one of the nuns with the words "on that evening they locked us in."[9]

Informal women's networks were determined by social status. Like their menfolk, higher-status women traveled much further distances within their city in order to carry out a variety of activities. They interacted with male institutions, particularly with lawcourts, where they pursued a variety of interests in lawsuits that were frequently associated with their domestic circumstances. They lobbied to restrain husbands on the grounds that they had exceeded their authority over their wives by using excessive violence or abusive behavior. They took action to protect their dowries on the grounds that their husbands had not fulfilled their responsibilities to keep the household financially safe, and it was therefore necessary to prevent them from misusing property they did not own. They requested legal separations or compensation for rape or a breach of promise of marriage. In the uncertainties of the Reformation and Counter-Reformation, they sought reassurance that the marriages they believed they had contracted were legally valid. As widows, or in the absence of their husbands on business, many higher-status women traveled some distance to transact a wide variety of business through notaries and shopkeepers.

Much of their social activity, like that of women lower down the social scale, was directed towards visiting neighbors, friends, and, above all, relatives. Marriage represented less of a break with the bride's natal family than might have been expected, and many of the affective links that remained were the province of mothers, aunts, and elder sisters. Evidence for this can be found in the bequests made in women's wills. Organized religion was an alternative cultural focus. Church buildings represented safe and attractive places to visit. In Catholic areas in particular, churches and other ecclesiastical institutions received a great deal of support and patronage from powerful women.

Lower down the social scale, informal women's networks developed around gendered spaces such as local markets, and communal bakehouses and wash-houses, as well as attendance at births. It has been argued that the street was also a gendered place, but one in which women were tolerated at best. While men could stand around in the street, women were expected to move through it. Only certain privileged spaces on the threshold between the street and buildings, such as doorways, balconies, and windows, were places where it was acceptable for women to stop and speak together. The role of gossip in socio-cultural terms has been greatly underrated, largely because it is normally such an ephemeral phenomenon and therefore passes unrecorded. Permission to exchange gossip was a sign of social inclusion within a well-defined group. It was often a means of transmitting important information through oral networks. Exchanging gossip, as well as a way of passing the time and a free form of entertainment, was a useful way of reinforcing pre-existing links between friends, family, and neighbors. Contrary to a widespread belief among men, it was not the prerogative of women. Nor was the subject matter of male and female gossip necessarily differentiated. Subjects such as impending marriages and births were of considerable interest to men as well as women; only the emphases differed. More importance was often given to work, business, or politics among male gossip. Frequently, too, this gossip was low level and therefore less likely to be reflected in the written record in a way that cases of defamation have come down to us. In the case of a couple's marital status or the presence of a marriageable girl in a household, however, speculative gossip did occasionally reach the written record in the form of witness statements in marital cases before civil or ecclesiastical courts.

THE IMPACT OF MIGRATION

The third major characteristic of the Renaissance town, alongside the multiplicity of occupations and of cultures, was the impact of migration. This was far from a one-way process, and while the contribution of in-migration was undoubtedly central to the demographic and economic growth of urban centers from a cultural point of view, the movement of people in and out of towns was equally important. Towns were great cultural diffusers as well as consumers. Their position as nodes within a network of commercial centers placed them in association with flows of goods, practices, and ideas that moved across Europe in the wake of major economic and political changes. As secular and administrative centers, they not only attracted large numbers of settlers but also many temporary visitors from smaller urban centers or from the surrounding countryside. The latter often carried back with them new ideas, tastes, and items of material culture.

The role of towns and cities as centers of cultural diffusion was enhanced by the impact of in-migration. Individuals and families moved to Europe's larger urban centers for several reasons. No matter whether they were rich or poor at the outset, they all moved for economic reasons. Some did so for reasons of subsistence. They believed that there was a greater possibility of surviving in the town of their choice than by remaining in their place of origin. Their reasons for choosing this solution were often determined by some awareness of the town and its potential because they had visited it before, or because they had maintained contact with relatives or neighbors who had successfully moved there in earlier years. The multiplicity of unskilled employment, the availability of housing at low rents, and the potential of other occasional sources of income through theft, prostitution, and begging were also attractions. Towns offered anonymity to those escaping social obligations, and some degree of protection to others who crossed the lines of socially acceptable behavior. Single pregnant mothers often made their way to suburbs, where they could find accommodation with innkeepers until they had given birth. The growth in domestic service drew on the growing pool of young female migrants.

Occupational diversity and the training available through formal or informal forms of apprenticeship offered single young males a way to take the first steps on a career of betterment in manufacture, business, or administration. Like many of the subsistence migrants, their move was determined in part by pre-existing relationships between their parents and potential employers. There was a long tradition, for example, of young men from Westphalia moving to Lübeck to train as merchants. Wolter von Holstein was sponsored by the merchant Johann Kampferbeke in the early sixteenth century. The latter provided him with a home and training, before supplying a substantial capital sum to establish him in trade. On a much smaller scale, but with considerable implications in the spread of material culture, individual specialist artisans in the luxury trades were recruited by princely rulers to travel long distances in order to embellish their palaces. The Court in Turin recruited tapestry-makers from Flanders. The interchange of painters, sculptors, musicians, and architects between the capitals of minor Italian rulers, Rome, Florence, and Venice, is particularly well known in this context. Migrants who moved in order to escape religious persecution also sought destinations that were economically favorable to them. Many were merchants whose migration patterns were consistent with those of the later Middle Ages, seeking to settle where business opportunities were good in locations where they already had business contacts, partners, or even family members.

The social and cultural implications of this in-migration were considerable. The urban authorities tended to view the large-scale arrival of outsiders with considerable suspicion, fearing that they would bring disease, unorthodox ideas and behavior, and would place extra pressures on resources. In times of crisis, the presence of migrants was perceived as an element of instability. Long-standing loyalties were under threat from those lacking roots and whose often evident "foreignness" through language, behavior, or dress marked them out. To a certain extent, these fears that the stability of urban society was being undermined were justified, but this was based on an inaccurate perception of an unchanging society. In reality, migration was a constant phenomenon that fluctuated according to circumstances inside and outside the town. Urban societies had strong integrative mechanisms, which undoubtedly facilitated a process of cultural exchange between newcomers and long-term urban residents. These integrative mechanisms operated at different levels of society. They were the least strong among the very poor. However, the marginal circumstances in which immigrants from different origins were thrown together created a new kind of society in itself, which provided a framework for newcomers to find work, accommodation, and friendship networks. Apprenticeship and other forms of training socialized newcomers, drawing them into occupational subcultures. There was a close association between marriage and the acquisition of burgher status by newcomers. One-seventh of all licenses to marry in London involved brides who were born elsewhere. There was a substantial concentration of immigrant husbands listed in the marriage registers of seventeenth-century Amsterdam. For both men and women, marriage permitted them to enter the established circles of urban society, with access to their partners' kinship networks. Sponsorship by a burgher father-in-law was widespread in the cases of outsiders who applied for burgher status. Integration through marriage was not the only option. Close associations were also forged through godparent ties, guardianships for the children of their neighbors and work associates, or making small loans to reinforce friendship networks.

Certain groups integrated more easily than others. Those who had not traveled far often retained strong links with their places of origin, which were reinforced through marriage. Others retained a strong sense of separateness. In sixteenth-century Aix-en-Provence, it was the immigrant shoemakers and tailors who fitted in most easily, while the plasterers and leather workers did not. There was also a strong sense of separateness among many communities of immigrant merchants. Paradoxically, these physical and social concentrations may have facilitated more cultural exchange than conditions of closer integration. In many parts of Europe, the medieval urban authorities had either encouraged groups of foreign merchants to live together, store their goods, and do business in compact complexes of buildings, or required them to do so. These arrangements benefited the foreign merchant communities in many ways, but left them under the strict control of the local authorities. The Fondaco dei Tedeschi, a palazzo for German merchants in Venice, is the classic example, but concentrations of foreign merchants were to be found all over the continent. While these conditions created an obstacle to greater social integration, the temporary and short-term nature of visits by many foreign merchants also made them reticent about greater personal engagement. Most of the Genoese merchants who worked in Antwerp in the sixteenth century remained in the city for a maximum of five years. They were present as representatives of their families who had been sent out to gain valuable commercial experience. On the other hand, even in this short time, as well-educated young men from patrician families, their cultural activity in Antwerp had much wider implications. Using Italian models, they established and participated in "academies." In effect, these were reading circles in which individuals came together to discuss ancient and modern texts, scientific ideas, politics, and philosophy.

As locations for cultural change and the diffusion of new ideas, large urban centers were without parallel in Renaissance Europe. Their size and economic and social complexity created two major conditions facilitating cultural change – the complexity of overlapping urban cultures and the constant movement in and out of people, goods, skills, and ideas. The two met at more than one point, through permanent or semi-permanent immigration, at ports and marketplaces, in churches, princely palaces, and the houses of the wealthy. To be sure, princely courts were also centers of Renaissance activity, but it was within the context of city life that the Renaissance had its deepest influence, as urban landscapes were reconfigured along classical lines and merchants and artisans joined humanists and patricians in conversations of no little consequence for the future development of Europe. Thus, the Renaissance city was both a source of new ideas and one of the first places in which those ideas reshaped the experience of men and women in the early modern period. Economic growth was the underlying precondition, but within this broader framework, towns and cities became forces of their own in the making of the Renaissance world.

NOTES

1 *A Treatise Concerning The Causes of the Magnificency and Greatness of Cities Divided into Three books by Sig. Giovanni Botero in the Italian Tongue, Now Done into English by Robert Peterson* (At London: Printed by T. P. [i.e. T. Purfoot] for Richard Ockould and Henry Tomes . . . , 1606), p. 1.

2   G. Strauss, *Nuremberg in the Sixteenth Century: City Politics and Life Between the Middle Ages and Modern Times* (Bloomington: Indiana University Press, 1976), p. 13.
3   Jean Philippi, quoted in Arlette Jouanna, "Des 'gros et gras' aux 'gens d'honneur,'" in G. Chassinand-Nogaret (ed.) *Histoire des élites en France du XVIe au XXe siècle* (Paris: Tallendier, 1991), p. 17, my translation.
4   J. Wheeler, "Stench in Sixteenth-century Venice," in A. Cowan and J. Steward (eds) *The City and the Senses: European Urban Culture from 1500* (Aldershot: Ashgate, forthcoming).
5   James Amelang, "People of the Ribera: Popular Politics and Neighborhood Identity in Early Modern Barcelona," in Barbara Diefendorf and Carla Hesse (eds) *Culture and Identity in Early Modern Europe (1500–1800)* (Ann Arbor: University of Michigan Press, 1992), pp. 119–37.
6   R. Descimon, "Paris on the Eve of St. Bartholemew," in P. Benedict (ed.) *Cities and Social Change in Early Modern France* (London: Routledge, 1989), p. 81.
7   L.B. Alberti, *On the Art of Building in Ten Books*, trans. J. Rykwert, N. Leach, and R. Tavernor (Cambridge, Mass.: MIT Press, 1988), Book IV.
8   M. Berlin, "'Broken All in Pieces': Artisans and the Negotiation of Workmanship in Early Modern London," in G. Crossick (ed.) *The Artisan and the European Town 1500–1800* (Aldershot: Ashgate, 1995), p. 82.
9   U. Strasser, "Cloistering Women's Past: Conflicting Accounts of Enclosure in a Seventeenth-century Munich Nunnery," in U. Rublack (ed.) *Gender in Early Modern German History* (Cambridge: Cambridge University Press, 2002), p. 227.

SUGGESTIONS FOR FURTHER READING

Benedict, Philip, ed. *Cities and Social Change in Early Modern France*. London: Unwin Hyman, 1989.
Braunfels, Wolfgang. *Urban Design in Western Europe. Regime and Architecture, 900–1900*. Chicago: Chicago University Press, 1988.
Brown, Judith and Robert C. Davis, eds. *Gender and Society in Renaissance Italy*. London: Longman, 1995.
Calabi, Donatella and Stephen Turk Christensen, eds. *Cities and Cultural Exchange, 1400–1700*. Cambridge: Cambridge University Press, 2006.
Clark, Peter and Bernard Lepetit, eds. *Capital Cities and their Hinterlands in Early Modern Europe*. Aldershot: Scholar Press, 1996.
Cowan, Alexander. *Urban Europe 1500–1700*. London: Arnold, 1998.
—— ed. *Mediterranean Urban Culture 1400–1700*. Exeter: Exeter University Press, 2000.
Cowan, Alexander and J. Steward, eds. *The City and the Senses. European Urban Culture from 1500*. Aldershot: Ashgate, 2006.
Crossick, Geoffrey, ed. *The Artisan and the European Town: 1500–1800*. Aldershot: Scholar Press, 1995.
Diefendorf, Barbara and Carla Hesse, eds. *Culture and Identity in Early Modern Europe (1500–1800). Essays in Honor of Natalie Zemon Davis*. Ann Arbor: University of Michigan Press, 1992.
Kittell, Ellen and Thomas Madden, eds. *Medieval and Renaissance Venice*. Chicago: University of Illinois Press, 1999.
Martin, John Jeffries and Dennis Romano, eds. *Venice Reconsidered. The History and Civilization of an Italian City-state, 1297–1797*. Baltimore: Johns Hopkins University Press, 2000.
Muir, Edward and Guido Ruggiero, eds. *Sex and Gender in Historical Perspective*, Baltimore: Johns Hopkins University Press, 1990.

O'Brien, Patrick *et al.*, eds. *Urban Achievement in Early Modern Europe. Golden Ages in Antwerp, Amsterdam and London.* Cambridge: Cambridge University Press, 2001.

Pinol, Jean-Luc, ed. *Histoire de l'Europe urbaine*, 2 vols. Paris: Seuil, 2003.

Pollak, Martin, *Turin 1564–1680. Urban Design, Military Culture and the Creation of the Absolutist Capital.* Chicago: University of Chicago Press, 1991.

Rublack, Ulinka, ed. *Gender in Early Modern German History.* Cambridge: Cambridge University Press, 2000.

Schutte, Anne Jacobson *et al.*, eds. *Time, Space and Women's Lives in Early Modern Europe.* Kirksville, Mo.: Truman State University Press, 2001.

Trachtenberg, Marvin. *Dominion of the Eye: Urbanism, Art and Power in Early Modern Florence.* Cambridge: Cambridge University Press, 1997.

Tracy, James, ed. *City Walls. The Urban Enceinte in Global Perspective.* Cambridge: Cambridge University Press, 2000.

Zimmerman, Susan and Ronald F. E. Weinstein, eds. *Urban Life in the Renaissance.* Newark: University of Delaware Press, 1989.

CHAPTER SIX

EUROPEAN EXPANSION AND THE NEW ORDER OF KNOWLEDGE

Francisco Bethencourt

The Renaissance cannot be reduced merely to the philological, literary, artistic, and scientific innovations that took place over the geographical axis Italy–France–Germany–Flanders–the Low Countries–England from the fourteenth to the sixteenth centuries. This traditional approach not only excludes much of the continent (Iberia, Scandinavia, central and eastern Europe, and the Ottoman Empire) but also the decisive role of overseas expansion towards other continents. Many authors, namely Jean Delumeau, Anthony Grafton, and Peter Burke, have pointed out the importance of the expansion for the European Renaissance. But the dominant approach has not changed: most historians (not to mention the cultivated public) continue to view the impact of the expansion as marginal, though at times it is seen as significant in the development of such disciplines as astronomy, geography, and cartography.

This chapter, by contrast, argues that the European expansion played a central role, affecting crucial areas of the new order of knowledge. First, I will briefly evaluate the real dimensions of the phenomenon, with its diversified economic, political, and social impact in other continents. Then, I will reconstitute the different conditions for cultural exchange outside Europe. Finally, I will focus on the impact of the overseas experience and its influence on the intellectual development of Europe. We will consider five areas where the effects of that experience were most visible: geography, natural history, linguistics, literature, and political thought.

EXPANSION

The exploration of the west coast of Africa by the Portuguese started immediately after the conquest of Ceuta in 1415. Aiming to bypass the caravan trade of gold from Timbuktu and the slave trade from sub-Saharan Africa to the Maghreb, the Portuguese discovered and populated the archipelagos of Madeira, the Azores, Cape Verde, and São Tomé; created trade posts and forts in Mauritania, the Gulf of Guinea, and Angola; and established political relations with the Akan states and the Kingdom of Congo – in this case the royal family was Christianized. In the process they improved the caravel, developed nautical instruments (like the astrolabe), and mapped the sky of the southern hemisphere; they mastered the system of winds and currents of the Atlantic Ocean, and eventually sailed around the Cape of Good Hope into the Indian Ocean. These achievements opened the way for the voyages of Christopher Columbus (1492) and Vasco da Gama (1497).

The next phase of the European expansion developed much faster and involved not merely the establishment of trading posts and forts on islands, or along the coasts of newly discovered territories, but actual colonization and territorial dominion. The establishment of the Spaniards in the main Caribbean Islands was followed by the conquest of Mexico by Cortés (1519–21) and of Peru by Pizarro (1531–33). Successive voyages of exploration and settlement created a Spanish network that spread from the former territorial domains of the Nahua and Tahuantinsuyo states to Central, South, and North America. Cortés launched the exploration of the Pacific Ocean immediately after the conquest of Mexico, but it took almost 40 years to master the system of winds and currents necessary to allow the round trip. It was only after the voyage of Urdaneta (1564–65) and the foundation of Manila (1571) that a regular connection was established between Mexico and the Philippines. Throughout the sixteenth century 250,000 people emigrated from Spain to America, while the native population suffered a huge decline provoked by war, the transfer of populations, and European diseases: Mexico declined from 15 million people before the conquest to 1.3 million people in 1600, Peru from 9 million people to 0.8 million during approximately the same period. A mixed population developed rapidly because Spanish women represented less than 15 percent of the total emigration throughout the sixteenth century. The slave trade from Africa to Spanish America involved 75,000 people during the same period. Several thousand Asian people, who arrived from the 1570s on, complete the picture of the demographic and ethnic impact of the Spanish conquest (Sánchez-Albornoz 1994).

The cultural impact of conquest was immense. The introduction of Christianity, and European culture more generally (as it was expressed, for example, in the visual arts and in literature), drove the indigenous peoples of the New World to learn new ways of thinking and new practices, with the result that their own traditional systems of beliefs, along with indigenous arts and craft traditions, were either transformed or destroyed. The codification of the native languages by the missionaries, and the teaching of Castilian and even Latin in the new schools, diffused writing skills, reinforcing what Serge Gruzinski (1988) has called the "colonisation of the imagery." The capitals of the vice-royalties, Mexico and Lima, reached 70,000 and 20,000 people respectively by 1600. These cities became homes to numerous institutions, including the universities, created in 1551. Colleges of the religious orders were established in the main cities, addressed to Spaniards, Creoles, and Indians from the local elites, not to mention the schools for young Creoles, Indians, and mestizos set up through the initiative of religious orders and civil authorities. The existence of printers and publishers facilitated the diffusion of European cultural models, even as censors sought to control the expression of local intellectual creativity.

The Portuguese expansion in Asia also proceeded at a rapid pace. The Portuguese reached China in 1513 and Japan in 1543, although, in comparison with the Spanish in America, the Portuguese conquests in Asia were much more limited due to the complexity of Asian powers, the presence of Turkish armies, and the widespread use of artillery. The conquest of Hormuz (1507–15), Goa (1510), and Malacca (1511) defined the backbone of a maritime empire that could control part of the inter-regional trade from the Persian Gulf to Southeast Asia. By the end of the sixteenth century the Portuguese dominated some of the main ports on the eastern coast of Africa, the Gulf, and the west coast of India, and the passage from the Indian to the Pacific Ocean, not to mention Macao near Canton (China) and coastal Ceylon. There were strong Portuguese communities outside the Estado da Índia in the Bay of Bengal, in Southeast Asia, and in Japan. But the Portuguese expansion also reached other continents: the occupation of the Brazilian coast, begun slowly in the first decades of the sixteenth century, gained momentum with the establishment of a general government in 1549. Throughout the second half of the sixteenth century Brazil attracted most of the Portuguese emigrants, aware of the high mortality in the carreira da Índia and of the new opportunities opened by the development of sugar-cane plantations. The Portuguese also migrated to Spanish America, mainly after the unification of Iberian crowns in 1580. More than 200,000 people emigrated from Portugal during the sixteenth century, but the geography of settlement changed through time. North Africa could count 15,000 Portuguese before defeat and retreat from 1541 to 1550; in 1600, the Atlantic Islands contained 95,000 Portuguese, Brazil 30,000, the west coast of Africa less than 1,000, and the Estado da Índia 10,000. The mixed population in Portuguese Asia was comparatively higher than in Spanish America, due to much lower percentages of women in the carreira da Índia. In 1600 the number of Portuguese in Goa was not much more than 2,500 in a total population of 75,000. African slaves transported to Brazil reached 50,000 throughout the sixteenth century. Slaves had already been crucial for the growth of the sugar plantation system in Madeira (later replicated in São Tomé) during the last decades of the fifteenth century.

In Asia, the influence of the Portuguese was much greater than the number of settlers alone suggests. In Japan, by the end of the sixteenth century, missionaries claimed to have converted some 300,000 people, a fabulous record that had no parallel in other regions, even those under Portuguese political dominion. Ceylon, Goa, and the Fishery Coast (southwest of India) were the clearest cases of evangelizing success. The presence of missionaries at the courts of the Ethiopian, Mogul, Persian, and Chinese rulers meant a regular cultural exchange at the top level. Brazil had a social environment much more similar to the eastern cost of North America than to Spanish America, because natives were nomadic or semi-nomadic populations, without a structured urban political society. The integration of native populations was generally the result of violent expeditions, which provoked huge migrations. Under those conditions, cultural exchange was mostly limited to tools, language, and gastronomy. Many Portuguese spoke Tupi and they integrated the products of the land in their culinary habits. They transferred manioc to Africa in the same way the Spaniards transferred tomatoes and maize to Europe. In the Portuguese territories overseas there were schools and colleges, mostly created by religious orders, but no universities (a distinct contrast with Spanish America). In Goa, Macao, and Nagasaki there were also printers, but in Brazil they were forbidden by the king.

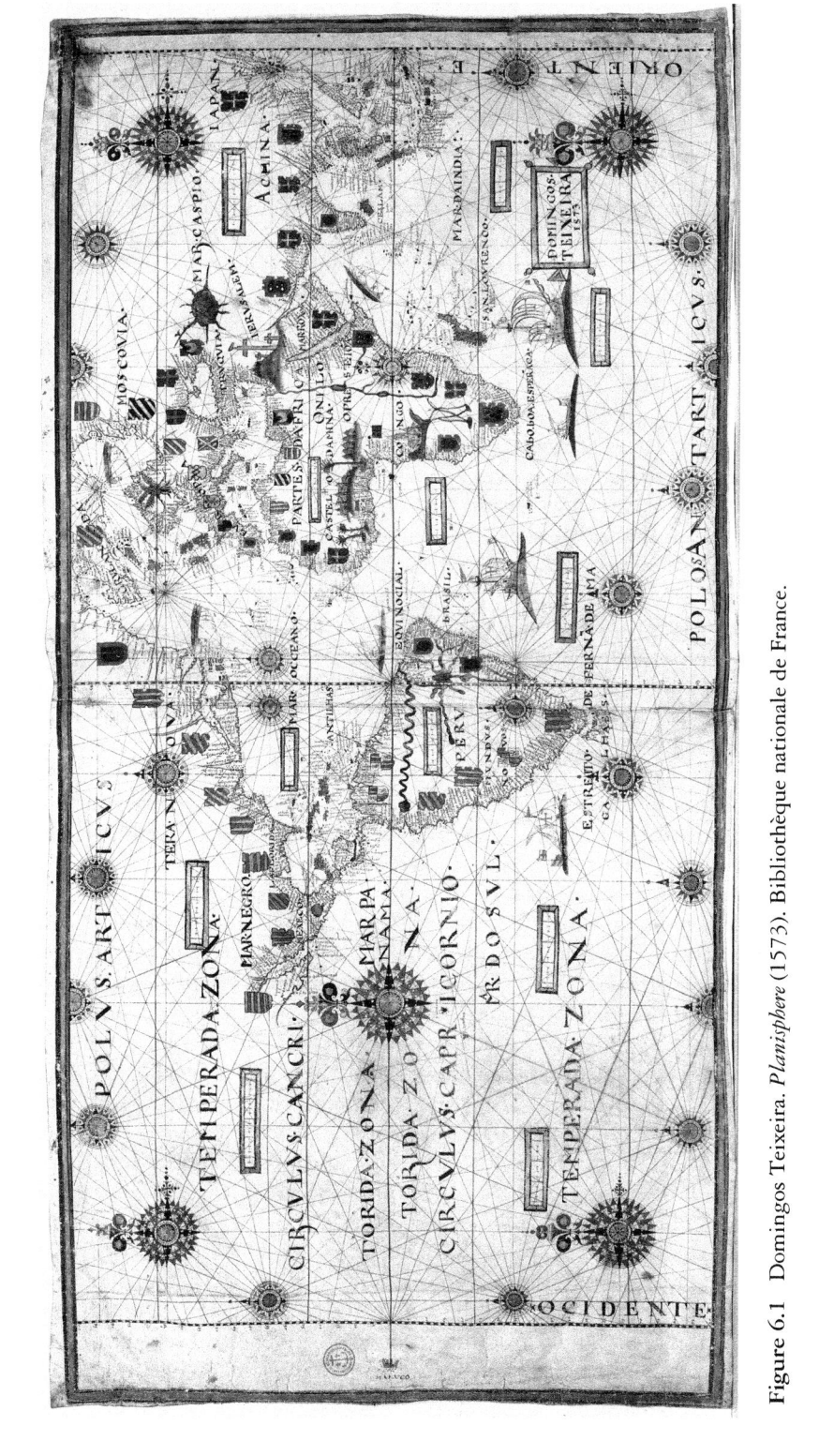

Figure 6.1 Domingos Teixeira. *Planisphere* (1573). Bibliothèque nationale de France.

EXCHANGE

A revolution in military architecture began in Europe after the Italian wars exposed the fragility of traditional vertical fortifications. Lower, inclined walls, prepared to receive successive canon discharges and protected by bastions with possibilities of cross-fire, defining a polygonal configuration with flat surfaces and sharp angles, were the main features of the new fortifications. In 1541 in Mazagan (now El-Jadida, Morocco) and in 1546 in Diu (India), this new style was deployed for the first time outside Europe. In Mazagan, the huge dimensions of the fort (the main walls were 384, 296, 342, and 240 meters long) allowed the architects/engineers (Benedetto da Ravenna, Miguel de Arruda, and João de Castilho) to improve the "bent walls" between the bastions. The new trend had not yet been reflected in a major printed text, despite the rapid circulation of drawings and news about the latest developments, such as the Fortezza da Basso in Florence, built in 1532 by Antonio da Sangallo. Benedetto da Ravenna, an engineer and specialist in artillery who worked extensively on military architecture for Charles V, was not only aware of the new trend in Italy but also had personal experience of the advances in military architecture in the eastern Mediterranean, where in 1522 in Rhodes he fought the Turks. But Mazagan also represented the fusion between the fort and the city, built inside the walls, designed as an ideal geometric city, and structured around a trapezoidal central square. In 1546, in Diu, immediately after a devastating siege that left almost all the fortifications in ruins, the humanist governor Dom João de Castro ordered the building of a new fort directed by Francisco Pires, chief engineer of the Estado da Índia. The same lessons of Renaissance military architecture can be seen in the huge polygonal bastioned fort, adapted to the topography of the rocky coast. These are the two most significant examples of Portuguese military architecture overseas, but similar examples can be found in hundreds of forts built on the islands and coasts of Africa, Asia, and America (Moreira). In a certain way, the Portuguese Empire can be defined as an empire of fortifications.

The geometric city, which was systematically built in America by the Spaniards after the reconstruction of Tenochtitlán (Mexico), is one of the most important cultural Renaissance features in the European expansion. Richard Kagan has rightly defined Spanish America as an empire of towns. By 1580, 240 municipalities had been founded, which meant the creation of a town with jurisdiction over a territory comprising hamlets and villages inhabited by natives. Towns were laid out according to a grid or checkerboard plan, with symmetric straight streets structured by a central square, where the most important buildings were located – the town hall, the prison, the main church, and the *picota* or pillory (a column for the public punishment and display of criminals, symbol of the royal justice). The impact of this configuration of the *urbs* (the architectural city) in the new *civitas* (the community of the residents) is obvious: the main symbols of *policía* (police, security, regulation of the common good) were central to all neighborhoods, defining the Spanish order. The square also concentrated the main market and the main religious and civic ceremonies, reinforcing the role of the urban setting for political and cultural values. We have to keep in mind that the Spanish conquest was followed by huge transfers of native inhabitants to the new towns, because the authorities were persuaded that resettlement was the best strategy to ensure long-lasting conversion and permanent political control. This policy explains the Spaniards' frantic activity in America, building and rebuilding towns – Alain Musset has called these "nomadic cities" – as the Spaniards searched for better strategic and environmental settings. The result is that while in Europe the Renaissance model(s) of the city had few opportunities to be built from scratch (Sabbioneta is one of the few examples), in America we have hundreds of examples, due to the conditions of conquest and the need felt by the European imperial power to impose political control through urban planning.

Regular two-story houses with multiple courtyards at the back, such as those represented in depictions of Mexico City, could create a pattern of order and harmony, which must be related to the symbolic power of the main civil and religious buildings. Size and style are the significant aspects of these buildings. The hospital of San Nicolas (built 1502–52), the *alcázar* (the palace of Diego Columbus, built 1515–23), and the cathedral of Santo Domingo (built 1521–40) had a major impact in an area where the native population was decimated and did not have buildings of the same size and material. The projection of European styles in these main buildings reinforced the assertion of authority, technical skill, and knowledge. In these first important colonial buildings we can see the richness of the Plateresque style, blending Gothic, Renaissance, and *Mudéjar* elements. While the structure, the arches, and the vaults of the cathedral are mainly Gothic, the vocabulary of the façade and the principal portal are Renaissance and include the decorative elements that justified the designation Plateresque (a metaphor referring to ornate silverwork). The hospital of San Nicolas reveals the same transition from Gothic to Renaissance, combining a Gothic structure with a Renaissance portal and courtyard. The *alcázar* of Santo Domingo, a rectangular, two-story, long H-shaped building, integrates the medieval military style of the Iberian *reconquista* and the elegant Italian Renaissance double loggia, placed at the center of both façades. This *alcázar*, already inspired by the villa Farnesina in Rome, became a model for Cortés's palace in Cuernavaca (built 1523–28), the manor house of the huge domain he had reserved for himself on the best lands in the region. In this case the medieval military style was emphasized, both in size and decorative elements, reducing the expression of the double loggia at the centre of the building.

The civil and religious buildings in New Spain and Peru also reveal a scale larger than was usual in Iberia, because the Spaniards had to come to terms with the huge ceremonial buildings of the Nahuas and Incas. In Mexico City, the hospital of Concepción de Maria (begun in 1524, attributed to Prada Vazquez and Diego Dias of Lisbon, who probably contributed to the palace of Cortés in Cuernavaca) features a clear Renaissance style, which shows a rapid transition from the first hospital in Santo Domingo. The viceregal palace of Mexico, built by Cortés on the site of Moctezuma's palace and purchased in 1562 by the crown, was subsequently transformed by Claudio de Arciniega and other architects. Its 300-meter-long façade underlines the imposing horizontal size of the two-story building (a third floor was added in 1926), engaging in a curious dialogue with the massive vertical cathedral built on an adjacent side of the square (110 [x] 55 meters), the towers of which, completed quite late, measure 67 meters high. Influenced by the *alcázar* of Toledo, begun in 1537 by Alonso de Covarrúbias, the palace features military-style rusticated walls, corner towers, plain windows, and spacious rectangular courtyards, following models of the Italian Renaissance. The austerity of the façade contrasts with the densely decorated doorway at the center, crowned by the royal coat of arms. Lima's viceregal palace, completed in 1603 (now destroyed), was even more imposing than the Mexican one, with balconies decorating half of the first floor. The central doorway had a similar Renaissance stone portal framed by pilasters and columns, supporting a pediment with the royal coat of arms. The façade and the doorway were also an open quotation of Renaissance classicism chosen by Juan de Herrera (and Philip II) for the Escorial (built 1563–82).

In New Spain, the rapid integration of Renaissance elements in architecture – mainly in the façades, portals, and cloisters of religious and civil buildings, but also in the single nave of the Augustinian churches – has to be related to the success of the Renaissance style in painting. The convent of Actopan, one of the most impressive edifices of the Augustinian order anywhere, is probably the best example. In this convent, founded in 1546, we can find 300,000 square meters of refined Renaissance frescoes painted from the 1540s to the 1570s, with the representation of the Old and New Testament, the Augustinian Saints, and the main scholars, bishops, archbishops, and cardinals of the order. We have to keep in mind that this was an establishment of superior education for Augustinian friars, although other convents of the order, like the one founded at Atotonilco, could also boast impressive sets of frescoes. But the interesting fact is that the painters were Indians, as in the case with other Augustinian, Franciscan, and Dominican convents in Mexico. It required skilful artisans to master the painting techniques of the Renaissance – not only the teachings of perspective and composition but also the totally new manner, for the native artists, of representing nature and the human body, not to mention European decorative motives.

In the Estado da Índia, Renaissance urban planning had an impact on the main cities of Goa, Colombo, Daman, and Bassein, through the introduction of geometric streets structured by main squares, two-story dwellings, and flat and continuous façades to create uniform blocks of houses. Even if the gridiron was not as strict as in Spanish America, the Portuguese city layout disrupted the traditional Hindu and Muslim urban features. Urban architectural constraints were not extended to rural areas, where palaces and leisure houses could boast balconies, terraces, and verandas more adapted to the conditions of the warm and humid climate. High pyramidal roofs indicate the adaptation to local Islamic influence, contributing also to the ventilation of the houses. The most significant civil and religious buildings reveal larger-scale plans than in Portugal, a tendency shared by the Spanish architecture in America. Manueline style, a specific blend of gothic structures, *Mudejár*, and Renaissance decorative elements, defined the first period of construction in the Estado da Índia, although we can follow the transition to Renaissance influence in the sequence of churches built in Goa between 1517 (São Francisco) and 1557 (Nossa Senhora do Monte). The construction of the hospital of Goa, the palace of the viceroys, and the shipyard (with an urban arrangement of the seafront that included warehouses and dockyards) represents the achievement of the Renaissance city. Helder Carita (1999) has already interpreted the tower houses of the captains as symbolic expressions of the Portuguese identification with the Kshatriya warrior

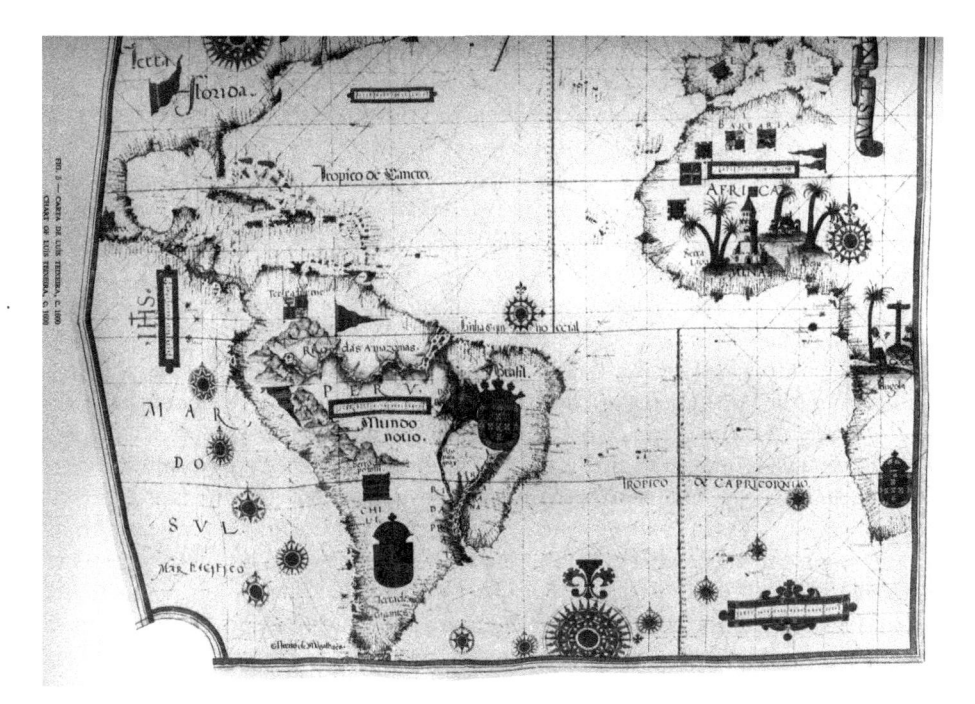

Figure 6.2 Luis Teixeira. *The Atlantic Chart*, c. 1600. Biblioteca Nazionale, Firenze.

caste, but they were not so distant in design from the first military palaces in Spanish America.

The Spanish conquest imposed a new framework of artistic styles, not leaving much space for native creativity. However, local patterns of representing nature may be identified in the façades of Augustinian churches in Cuitzeo and Yuriria in Mexico. More interesting is the fresco representing the Annunciation at the Franciscan church of Cuauhtinchan. The image follows the medieval canon, but it is placed between an eagle and a jaguar both of which watch the scene. We cannot dismiss the relationship of these animals with the two major and complementary divinities of the Nahua pantheon, Huitzilopochtli and Tezcatlipoca, representing light and darkness. If we have here a quite straightforward juxtaposition of two different worlds, in the extraordinary frescoes of the Augustinian church of Ixmiquilpan we have a much more complex cultural exchange. The fight of the Centaurs has already been interpreted by Gruzinski (1994) as a quotation from the *Metamorphoses* of Ovid, with Indian warriors dressed in pre-Hispanic fashion, masked as jaguars and eagles, using traditional weapons. The traditional representation of the human body, the absence of perspective, and the grotesque decoration indicate the persistence of the old manner, while the movement of the warriors, the expressions on their faces, and the European decorative elements show the acquisition of Renaissance patterns.

Nonetheless, in Spanish America hybridism was marginal in both architecture and painting – excluded from canvases and altarpieces, it appeared sometimes in frescoes inside churches, as we have seen. Native artistic traditions were mainly expressed through the magnificent illuminated codices produced after the conquest or the regional maps of the *relaciones topográficas* (depicted around 1580), where we find symbolic and codified ways of representing the human body, the genealogy of the old rulers, the landscape, and the towns (Mundy 1996). In Portuguese India hybridism was comparatively more visible, not only in architecture, with the inscription of native forms in façades of churches, verandas, and roofs of houses, but also in painting, mainly through facial expressions, positions of the body, and ornamental elements. But it was in the field of decorative arts that cultural exchange became more expressive, contributing to the enrichment of Renaissance forms not only in India but also in western Africa, Ceylon, Japan, and China.

From 1480 to 1530 local artisans created delicate ivory spoons in Sierra Leone and Benin for the Portuguese (and European) market. If the stylish forms of the spoon are already hybrid, the extraordinary ornamental elements (fishes, birds, antelopes) are African. The oliphants (hunting horns sculpted on ivory) were considered even more precious objects and were displayed in Kunstkammern or cabinets of curiosity throughout Europe. They were ornamented with an exuberant representation of flora and fauna, men (dressed as Europeans with fire guns), and geometric elements (reflecting the patterns of African works of raffia). Some of these oliphants included inscriptions in Latin and depicted typically European hunting scenes, with deer, wild boars, or bears chased by dogs, meaning that the African artists were inspired by European images, several of them already identified. The third type of these Afro-Portuguese ivories is the host-box, where scenes of the life of Christ or the Virgin Mary were depicted according to the Western canon. The fourth type is the salt cellar, perhaps the most African of these forms because it is closer to the traditional local forms of juxtaposed half-boxes. Again we have geometric forms, but the creative element is the representation of the Portuguese, with their long noses, hats, European dress, and fire guns (Bassani and Fagg 1988).

In Asia the typical production of decorative arts for the European market can be observed through Chinese porcelain, which followed the traditional forms complemented by inscriptions, monograms, emblems, and coats of arms. The region of Gujarat, in India, with a powerful tradition of textiles and jewelry, also presented a vast range of objects addressed to the European market, adapting their traditional forms to the new requests from the Portuguese merchants. Many of the items collected for Kunstkammern, such as the magnificent chessboards covered by turtle shell and mother-of-pearl with extraordinary representations of nature and human scenes at the back, or the vessels, basins, plates, bottles, and jars completely covered by mother-of-pearl, did not present significant changes in form. The portable oratories, reliquary boxes, trunks, arks, coffers, chests of drawers, desks, boxes, and table lids made out of exotic woods, mother-of-pearl, ivory, turtle, rock crystal, and lacquer, ornamented by an ingenious jewelry work of silver and gold, already included European religious or lay scenes. The designs of salt cellars produced in different regions of Asia engaged in a dialogue with the European forms. Sri Lanka was a competitive producer for the European market, due to its refined jewelry and traditional ivory work, its ability to create sophisticated coffers, and its sensibility for delicate small objects, like spoons, forks, and fans. Some of the most sought-after exotic objects, like bezoars, shells, gourds, coconuts, or rhinoceros horns, were mounted either in India or in Europe with complicated jewelry work. The jewelers of Goa played an important role in this process, not only as mediators, purchasing all over Asia the most significant objects, but also as creators of new forms, having specialized in the work of filigree (Trnek and Silva 2001).

Most of these objects defined a lifestyle: they belonged to what Eiko Ikegami called the arts of civility. The impressive amount and variety of tableware indicates that the Portuguese in Asia ordered extensively for the European market, but they also invested in receiving and entertaining their compatriots and native counterparts (artisans, merchants, bankers, ambassadors, political agents). The wide use of tableware by the Portuguese in Asia indicates the central role of gastronomy in the arts of civility, which were related to other forms of art, like dance and music, and which contributed to create an aesthetic environment, simultaneously private and public, that opened an exchange between the Portuguese and the local forms of cultural expression. It is interesting to note how selected silver tableware traveled to India to embellish the receptions of governors, captains, bishops, judges, inquisitors, and principals of religious orders, but also how Chinese porcelain services were exported in impressive quantities to Europe, becoming fashionable among the elites throughout the sixteenth century – we know that the Portuguese introduced porcelain in Italy as a gift to popes and cardinals, specifically during the Council of Trent. In Europe the introduction of porcelain followed the diffusion of table manners and the increasingly widespread use of forks.

FEEDBACK

From 1505 to 1508, Duarte Pacheco Pereira wrote the *Esmeraldo de situ orbis*, which is simultaneously a chronicle of Portuguese discoveries, an account of his travels, and a repository of cosmographical, geographical, and nautical observations. Pacheco Pereira (*c.* 1460–1533) – a man of action, navigator, and explorer of the Atlantic for the Portuguese kings and captain in Africa and in India, where he fought and won crucial battles – was celebrated by Camões in the *Lusiads* as the Lusitanian Achilles. But he was also a man of culture, with some knowledge of classic literature, read in translation. Experience was a key notion in his book, considered as the only criterion of truth, removing illusions and doubts. Pereira explicitly criticized the superstitions and fables of ancient cosmographers (Pliny, Ptolemy, Pomponius Mela, John Sacrobosco), who had assumed that the land south of the equinoctial circle was uninhabitable and who had suggested similarities of climate, land, and people under the same latitude. Pereira indicated the different complexion and phenotype features of Guinean and Brazilian peoples living under the same parallel. He boasted that the ancients only knew the world from Spain to the Arabian Gulf, while the Portuguese explored most parts of the world.

The notion of experience, as the criterion of truth, was invented and integrated into Renaissance epistemologies quite late (Carvalho 1983). Pacheco Pereira must be placed next to Leonardo da Vinci; they were preceded, in the fifteenth century, by Alphonse, king of Aragon; Duarte, king of Portugal; and the Portuguese chronicler Zurara. But fifteenth-century references to "experience as mother of all things" were scarce and too general, lacking the precision with which Pacheco Pereira (and da Vinci) developed this concept. Pacheco portrayed the connection between experience and knowledge as a kind of rape: "the best part of knowledge of so many regions and provinces came to belong to us, who took their virginity." It is a curious quotation for post-colonial studies, relating European observation (another word introduced quite late) with gender, possession, use, and knowledge. Pereira's radical text, however, remained in manuscript until the nineteenth century, a fact that likely restricted the possibilities of the direct diffusion of his ideas.

In 1535, one generation later, Gonzalo Fernández de Oviedo published the first part of his *História General y Natural de las Indias*. The author did not hesitate to criticize the fables of ancient writers (Ptolemy, Pliny, and Avicenna were quoted), and claimed that he was writing according to his personal observation and experience, as an eyewitness of most of what he was writing about. Oviedo's personal life as courtier, navigator, explorer, and royal high officer in Spanish America is obvious in his writings (the abridged and the extended version of the history of Indies, a chivalry novel, compilations of battles, genealogies). But Oviedo was extremely careful to place himself under the protection of the Catholic Church, never contradicting sacred history and geography. This was in contrast to the autonomous field of profane geography, created by humanists like André Thevet, who criticized not only the fables of the ancient geographers integrated by the scholastic order of knowledge but also the fables of the Old Testament, like Jonah's whale, Samson's lion, and Ezekiel's pygmies (Lestringant 1991). The primacy of experience over authorities was constantly heralded by Thevet in his books – *Cosmographie du Levant* (1554), *Les singularitez de la France Antarctique* (1557), *Cosmographie universelle* (1575), *Vrais portraits et vies des hommes illustres* (1584) – to the point that he boasted of imaginary voyages besides the real ones he made to Jerusalem and Constantinople (1549–52) and to Brazil (1555–56). He understood the notion of experience as experiment and proof (like Montaigne), asserting the importance of practical knowledge to redefine the theory of the world. Even though he decided to exhibit an erudition that he did not possess and insisted on a cosmographic model that had exhausted its possibilities in the 1550s, Thevet played an important role not only as geographer but also as ethnographer, since he produced accurate descriptions of Indian rituals and mythologies. He also "invented" the Indian monarchy, promoting and consecrating temporary war chiefs as "illustrious men," placed in his gallery of the main emperors, kings, and captains of all times, a theoretical political device necessary for colonial projects.

The value of experience (and experiment in sciences) was a fundamental notion that shaped a new order of knowledge, based on quantitative calculation and qualitative comparison. It must also be related to other innovations in Europe that defined this epistemic revolution. The replacement of roman by arabic numbers, already in progress throughout the fourteenth and fifteenth centuries, meant the liberation of new capacities for mental calculation. It was crucial for the development of accounting and theoretical mathematics, but we have to acknowledge as well the impact of the reintroduction of Euclidean geometry in the thirteenth century, opening new possibilities for the abstract representation of space. Astronomy benefited from these developments, as well as cartography.

Navigation in open sea required the use of nautical instruments, like the compass and the astrolabe, not to mention the mapping of the sky in the southern hemisphere to calculate distances and to map the coastlines, harbors, islands, canals, and reefs. We also have to consider the impact of maritime cartography on terrestrial cartography based on triangular observation of distances, applied in Portugal and Spain from the 1530s to the 1560s.

But Renaissance mental revolution cannot be defined only by these quantitative new trends; it was also defined by qualitative comparison. The accumulation of information about other people and other continents – their economies, trading customs, habits, religions, political systems, flora and fauna – introduced a completely different scale of reasoning, allowing systematic comparison to develop in different areas of knowledge.

The impact of European expansion in geography is evident, for example, in the contrast between the *Historia rerum ubique gestarum*, written by Aeneas Silvio Piccolomini (1405–64) when he was already Pope Pius II and printed in Venice in 1477, and the *Delle relationi universali*, written by Giovanni Botero and printed (the complete version) in Vicenza in 1595. Piccolomini based his description of the peoples of the world on Ptolemy, Strabo, Pliny, Curtius, and Pomponius Mela, with updated references – namely, from Marco Polo or Odorico da Pordenone, concerning India and Cathay (China). The ancient geographers (but also Pierre d'Ailly) inspired Piccolomini's introduction on cosmography, the three parts of the world (Asia, Africa, and Europe), and their boundaries. Piccolomini's published text actually dealt only with Asia and Europe, since he never wrote the promised section on Africa. In it, moreover, the author preserved the older visions of the world divided into inhabited and uninhabited regions, of continents surrounded by water, and of the oceans, in turn, surrounded by land without possibilities of navigation to the northern or southern poles. Even if the author was conscious of the limits of these references – he raised the issue of the Baltic Sea, never described before – he was totally dependent on ancient knowledge, revealed by the names of people and places he reproduced without questioning their evolution over time and the constant migration of populations. He described a world lost a long time before, into which he tried to introduce new political and religious information. Anachronism was limited by the fact that Piccolomini focused a good part of his description of Asia on the regions controlled by the Turks, a topographic obsession that would have a long life in Renaissance Europe. The description of Europe was less strange, since he had traveled extensively, knew many regions personally, and incorporated new knowledge, although the British Islands and Hispania were placed in a quite marginal position. What is striking is that the book was obviously not an enterprise of leisure or a work written in pursuit of pure knowledge, but rather a religious and political initiative that justified the investment of time by a pope who died while organizing a crusade against the Turks.

The *Universal Relations*, written by Botero more than a century later, reveals a dramatic change. The names of peoples and countries can be recognized without much effort by a reader of the twenty-first century with good geographical knowledge; the descriptions of territories and boundaries were quite accurate, especially for Europe, but also for most of Asia and a good portion of America – it was the interior of Africa that remained almost totally unknown. General knowledge of the world was portrayed through updated maps of the four continents, designed with precise degrees of latitude and longitude, even if there was a persistent inaccuracy concerning the western coasts of South and North America, not to mention the misleading representation of "Terra Australis" covering the bottom of the southern hemisphere. The division into four parts corresponded to the physical and human geography of the world (first part), the political geography (second part), and the religious geography (third and fourth parts). The density of description of the peoples of Europe, Asia, America, and coastal Africa is striking and makes clear how much knowledge had been accumulated over the previous hundred years on the various political systems, forms of administration, trade, economic behavior, habits, and beliefs of peoples throughout the world. Striking, too, was Botero's attention to quantitative criteria in his descriptions: he reported on the sizes of the kingdoms, the numbers of their inhabitants, cities, castles, the wealth of their rulers, and their military capacity, offering systematic demographic, economic, and political comparisons between China and Europe. The procedure is exactly the opposite of the *Historia rerum*: Botero offered updated information, including references to the past, whenever he considered it convenient for his demonstration. The program of the book was curiously close to that outlined by Piccolomini: the knowledge of the peoples of the world was considered instrumental in creating the intellectual conditions for political expansion and religious dominion. Only Botero had the possibility of developing this program. It is true that throughout the sixteenth century a huge number of travel accounts, chronicles, and correspondence (from missionaries, explorers, commercial agents, governors, and captains) had been printed or circulated in manuscript form. Several miscellanies had been organized, namely by Montalboddo (1507), Grynaeus (1532), and Ramusio (1550–59), but Botero could read the main texts directly in Portuguese or Spanish, many of them published in the second half of the sixteenth century. He also benefited from the work of his predecessors, namely Francesco Sansovino (*Del governo dei regni e delle republiche cosí antiche come moderne* [1561]), but Botero's book was better organized and included all the known world, a phenomenon that was also evident in the cartographic revolution of the Renaissance (see Chapter 7 in this volume by John A. Marino).

The impact of the European expansion on the development of the study of natural history – botany, zoology, and mineralogy – was also significant. The discovery of the New World and the travels to Asia created a new consciousness of how limited classical and earlier European understandings of the world's flora and fauna were, stimulating new research. From the thirteenth century onwards several travellers in Asia, including Marco Polo, John of Montecorvino, Jordanus of Séverac, Niccolo de' Conti, and Lodovico de Varthema, had described plants and fruits like jack, talipot, palmyra, durian, cinnamon, and coconut. In 1515, the first systematic accounts – geographic, political, economic, and ethnographic – of the territories around the Indian Ocean by the Portuguese Tomé Pires and Duarte Barbosa included lists of spices and descriptions of medicinal plants (Pires was a pharmacist). But it was only in 1563 in Goa that a real treatise on the botany of Asia was published, by Garcia d'Orta (*c.* 1501–68), a new Christian and head physician of the Estado da Índia, who lived in that city from 1534 to 1568. The *Colóquios dos Simples e Drogas e Coisas Medicinais da Índia* consisted of 59 dialogues between the author and a colleague, Doctor Ruano, who had just arrived from Europe, his head filled with a classical knowledge that had made no room for the new discoveries. The book described for the first time some diseases like cholera, but its major focus was on Asian flora and the medicinal uses of some plants. It engaged also in the description of animals and their behavior and the main features of minerals, like diamonds. It included numerous ethnographic references, especially to the caste system. Cristóvão da Costa (c. 1525–94), known under the Spanish name Christobal Acosta, met Orta in India and lived in Cochin as head physician of the royal hospital until he returned to Europe in 1572. In 1578 in Burgos he published the *Tractado de las Drogas y Medicinas de las Indias Orientales*, a new text based on his own observations, a straightforward narrative that corrected and enlarged Orta's book. For the first time, the text included woodcuts representing some of the plants and fruits described in the text, based on Acosta's own drawings. These two authors described around a hundred plants, which had a major impact on a discipline that could boast only 600 plants inventoried by the classical heritage. Carolus Clusius published Latin versions of these two main texts, which guaranteed their diffusion in Europe: first editions in 1567 and 1582, reissued in a single volume in 1593, and also included (with Monardes' text) in Clusius' collected works, *Exoticorum libri decem*, in 1605.

The abundance of the completely unknown flora and fauna of the New World immediately attracted the attention of the Europeans. Although the book *De Orbe Novo*, published by Pedro Mártir de Anglería in 1511 (and successively extended until the complete edition in 1530), described some plants, fruits, and animals, the first extensive descriptions of flora and fauna were included in the *Sumario de la Natural Historia de Indias*, published by Gonzalo Fernández de Oviedo in 1526, and in the *Historia General y Natural de las Indias*, published by the same author in 1535 (the first volume). The *Sumario* is completely dedicated to the description of nature: food of the natives (corn, manioc); mammals, birds, snakes, lizards, insects, fishes, and seafood; plants, trees, and fruits (avocados, coconuts, guavas); medicinal uses of certain plants (like the guayacan to treat syphilis); minerals; and natural phenomena. The first volume of *Historia General* contains ten "books," from VI to XV, on nature. The descriptions were enlarged and new species were included (like coca, potato, cacao, cassava), including more than 200 items and illustrations for the first time. In 1565 Nicolas Monardes published a treatise on the flora of the New World, which was immediately translated into other languages. Here again Clusius had a major role republishing and illustrating the text. A great amount of information concerning medicinal uses of plants and remedies produced by the natives had been added, although many "wonders" were still included in the text.

A further major achievement was the fieldwork done from 1570 to 1577 in New Spain by Francisco Hernández, work that resulted in an enormous compilation and description of flora, fauna, and minerals. He had been sent to Mexico by Philip II, who had organized botanical gardens (coupled with zoological gardens) in Aranjuez and at the Escorial. The work was so massive that it was issued only in an abridged version in Castilian, published by Francisco Ximénez in Mexico in 1615, and in a Latin version published in Rome in 1651. But we have to acknowledge the importance of local tradition of botanical gardens in Mexico – much before Europe, where similar initiatives were only taken during the second half of the sixteenth century – and the crucial role of local informers, like those who wrote the manuscript of 1552 with the description and illustration of numerous species of plants and their medicinal uses. In Brazil, the major accounts of the coast, produced by Pero de Magalhães Gândavo (printed in 1576), Gabriel Soares de Sousa (manuscript from 1587), and Fernão Cardim (manuscripts from 1591–1601, taken by British corsairs and published in English by Purchas) presented extensive descriptions of nature. Just to give an idea of the scope of these works, Cardim alone described nearly 200 items, including mammals, snakes, birds, fish, seafood, vegetables, and trees for food, medicine, and timber.

The study of non-European languages started quite early, with the listing of hundreds of words in the travel accounts and descriptions of new lands that circulated in Europe throughout the fifteenth and sixteenth centuries in manuscript or printed form. In many texts of Castilian and Portuguese authors concerning other continents, a large number of local words were integrated to designate new food, fauna and flora, ethnicities, social groups, systems of belief, rituals, ceremonies, powers, arms, products, forms of trade, and transport. Not surprisingly, in the sixteenth century Catalans, Castilians, and Portuguese integrated a significant number of new nouns borrowed from other languages and lent their own words to Asian and American languages. In the Portuguese case, the integration of words from Arabic origin did not occur in the Middle Ages, as we might suppose, but rather during the sixteenth century when the Portuguese had intense relations in North Africa and used Arabic as the language of communication in the Middle East, Ethiopia, East Africa, India, and Southeast Asia. The renewed interest in Greek and Latin in Europe led to the systematic study of vernacular languages, defined through grammars and dictionaries (vernacular-Latin and Latin-vernacular). The Latin paradigm behind those enterprises – declension, conjugation, doctrine of the parts of the discourse – would influence the first identification of "exotic languages" by Europeans, all of them missionaries, who defined a new strategy of communication and preaching that required knowledge of local languages.

The model of universal communication based on the Latin paradigm motivated the production of grammars and vocabularies of different languages (we only indicate here some significant publications): Nahuatl was included in a bilingual book on Christian doctrine printed in 1539 in Mexico and was the subject of a grammar published by Alonso de Molina in 1555; Quechua, in Peru, was the subject of a grammar published by Domingo de Santo Thomas in 1560 in Valladolid (including extensive vocabulary), while a trilingual (Quechua, Aymara, and Castilian) manual of Christian doctrine was published in 1584 in Lima; Tamil, in South India, was one of the first languages to be printed in vernacular characters by Europeans in 1577 (the author, Henrique Henriques, left an enormous number of manuscripts in Tamil, including dictionaries, grammars, manuals of confession, manuals of Christian doctrine, catechisms, hagiographies, and a life of Christ, while Tamil converts to Christianity like Vicente da Nazaré, Jorge Carvalho, and Tomé da Cruz printed a short manual of Christian doctrine in Tamil and Portuguese); Tupi-Guarani, the language of native Americans along most of the Brazilian coast, was the subject of a grammar written by José de Anchieta and published in 1595, contributing to transform a regional language into "general language," a typical strategy of the Europeans in America. Japanese was also the subject of a grammar written by João Rodrigues and published in 1604, ten years after the first abridged grammars and dictionaries of Japanese, and one year after the massive dictionary of Japanese, which had resulted from 50 years of work and collaboration of Europeans and Japanese, some of them Jesuit brothers, reproduced by their printer in Nagasaki.

Yet the impact of the European expansion on the Renaissance is most evident in literature. Travel accounts, reports of major navigations, and descriptions of other continents were crucial to the creation of the intellectual conditions that led to the emergence of the utopian literary genre. Raphael Hythloday, a character created by Thomas More in 1516 to report the habits, values, and forms of government of the people living on the island Utopia, was supposedly a Portuguese navigator, learned in Greek and Latin, dedicated to the study of philosophy, with a passion for traveling. He had sailed with Amerigo Vespucci and decided not to return to Europe after his last voyage. Curious to know foreign people and strange countries, he traveled with five friends for several years in the Atlantic and Indian Ocean, arriving finally at Calicut, where he took a ship back to Lisbon. It was during his travels that Hythloday discovered the island of Utopia, the location of which was never indicated (More regretted not having asked the obvious question . . .). It was precisely the recent profusion of texts concerning the New World, Africa, and Asia, collected in 1507 by Francesco da Montalboddo in *Paesi nuovamente ritrovati* (a bestseller with successive editions in Vicenza, Venice, and Milan; immediately translated into Latin, German, Flemish, and French), which opened the possibility of imagining a utopia – an "extraordinary place" or a "no-place" – where an ideal society could be set up and used to criticize British or European societies and forms of government.

The power of this new genre was recognized by other authors, who also used the information collected in *Paesi nuovamente ritrovati*. François Rabelais, in his *Pantagruel*, published in 1532, made his hero follow the typical maritime voyage of the Portuguese to India through Porto Santo, Madeira, the Canary Islands, Senegal, Cape Verde, Gambia, the Cape of Good Hope, and Melindi, before he arrived at the port of Utopia (in honour of Thomas More). In the complete edition of the work published in 1552 Rabelais returned to the same subject and described a new voyage undertaken by Pantagruel. This imaginary itinerary reproduced the French and English search for a northwest passage to India, explored for example by Jacques Cartier in 1534 and 1535/36. In 1602 Tommaso Campanella wrote *La città del sole*, taking advantage of a century of publications on other continents. For this new utopia he used the available knowledge of the Amerindian, Iranian, Indian, Chinese, and Japanese habits and religious beliefs to imagine a somewhat frightening theocratic society based on communal property, hierarchy based on age and merit, controlled sexual reproduction, and eugenics. In his *Questiones* (fourth question), published in 1637, Campanella quoted Thomas More and asserted the importance of utopian imagination to reflect on natural law and man in a state of nature.

The literary impact of the European expansion is not measurable just by the new utopian genre. Other literary genres, like chivalric novels, were also opened to new information on "exotic" peoples and countries. In 1516, the same year More published his *Utopia*, Ludovico Ariosto issued in Ferrara the first edition of *Orlando Furioso*. A fantastic poem inspired by the chivalric genre, its innovation lay in the supposed unity of man in his diversity, the relationship between vital experience and contemplative activity, and the references to the Oriental world that went beyond the tradition of crusades. The marvelous world built by Ariosto included precise geographic information on India, Ceylon, and Malacca, as well as explicit reference to the circumnavigation of Africa.

Travel writing created its own sphere of geographic, scientific, and ethnographic themes that inspired philosophers and politicians throughout the sixteenth century, and managed to provide a continuous line of new material for intellectual reflection through the nineteenth century (Rubiés 2002). Michel de Montaigne established the conditions for an anthropological vision of the world when he built a relativist perception of different cultures. Writing on a specific people of the New World he stated: "I do not find anything barbarian or savage in that nation . . . but each of us name barbarian what does not belong to our habits; we do not have any other criteria of truth and reason than the example and idea of the opinions and habits of our country. There is the perfect religion, the perfect police, the perfect use of all things." He contested also the designation "savage," arguing that people living in the order of nature ignored trade, letters, numbers, judges, political domination, richness or poverty, contracts, successions, dresses, agriculture, metal, wine, or cereals, but at the same time they ignored artificial life, lies, betrayal, dissimulation, meanness, envy, depreciation, or forgiveness. Montaigne considered the ritual dimension of cannibalism as an act of revenge, stating that "we judge their errors, but we are blind to our own." He attacked explicitly the European forms of justice, namely the Inquisition: "more barbarian than to eat a man dead is to eat a man alive, to torment a body full of feeling, to roast it or leave it to be bitten and torn apart by dogs and pigs (as we have read and seen recently, not among our old enemies, but among neighbors and fellow citizens, and what is worse, under pretext of piety and religion)." Montaigne evaluated the pride, dignity, and military resistance of the Aztec and the Inca "empires," underlining the magnificence of their cities, gardens, arts, and industries. He pointed out the sacrifice and integrity of local Asian princes facing Portuguese conquest and admired Chinese superiority concerning sciences, arts, and police. He also praised the stoic example of the dying Moroccan king who won the battle against King Sebastian of Portugal, commanding his troops all day until the final victory and his last breath.

Montaigne was not alone in his cultural relativism and criticism of the European expansion. Bartolomé de las Casas (1484–1566) represented a much more radical approach, because he was at the center of the Spanish expansion and vigorously condemned the process of conquest, supporting the Indians' rights to their own cultural system, political system, control of territories, and ownership of land. He openly asserted that Cortés and Pizarro should have been persecuted as criminals. From 1515 on he consistently presented his opinions to the king and the royal court, forcing open debates, in a constant balance between his political engagement – which included theoretical and historical writings – and his practice on the field, namely as a Dominican preacher and bishop of Chiapas (nominated in 1544). Although Las

Casas' opinions were systematically debunked, he managed to influence Francisco de Vitoria and the Salamanca school – Domingo de Soto, Luís de Molina, and Francisco Suárez – who reflected on the natives' rights and the notion of just war, two crucial issues for the development of Ius Gentium, a new domain of juridical theory between natural law and human law, concerning the whole world as a commonwealth.

The debate on international law was a further consequence of European expansion. Spaniards and Portuguese claimed that the oceans should be reserved for their exclusive navigation, according to the papal division of the world between the two kingdoms in 1493, redefined by the Treaty of Tordesillas one year later. The constant protest of the French kings against this shared monopoly influenced a first wave of juridical opinions on the freedom of navigation, which can be seen in the Latin and French translations of Girolamo Benzoni's *La Historia del Mondo Nuovo* (first published in 1565). The issue was again tackled at the beginning of the seventeenth century, when the shareholders of the Dutch Vereenigde Oost-Indische Compagnie wanted to know if the capture of and resulting booty from Portuguese ships in Asia could be legally accepted. Contrary to the Portuguese vision, the young Hugo Grotius argued in favor of the notion of *mare liberum* and the legitimacy of defensive and offensive action to reinforce the principle of free navigation.

The consequences of the European expansion in establishing a comparative field for political theory were extremely important. Damião de Góis, a Portuguese humanist who was a friend of Erasmus and who participated in the intellectual circles of Pietro Bembo and Johannes Magnus, wrote the first accurate account by a European on Ethiopia in 1532 (*Legatio magni Indorum Imperatoris Presbyteri Ioannis*) and a text developed in 1540 (*Fides, religio, Moresque Æthiopum sub imperio Preciosi Ioannis*), printed with a protest against the oppression of the Lapps. Although Góis always supported Portuguese conquests and intercontinental trade, even engaging in debate on the subject with Paolo Giovio, he decided to reproduce all the correspondence between the Ethiopian rulers and the Portuguese kings (and the popes), since the first direct contacts. The second embassy sent by the Negus in 1526 was an ambiguous one, with a native ambassador, the Coptic bishop Saga za-Ab, and a second ambassador, the Catholic priest Francisco Álvares, who had been in Ethiopia with the Portuguese diplomats (Aubin 1996). The Coptic bishop was immediately marginalized as a heretic by the Portuguese, who finally sent Francisco Álvares to Rome in 1533 as the legitimate ambassador to the pope. In the *Fides* Damião de Góis decided to include a long text by Saga za-Ab, where the bishop specified all the differences between the Catholic Church and the Coptic Church concerning doctrine and rituals (perhaps the reason for having the book in the Portuguese Index the following year). In the same year of 1540, Francisco Álvares finally published his book on Ethiopia in Portuguese. Although providing precious and accurate information on the political system, cultural habits, and daily life of the Ethiopians, Álvares did not include a detailed account of the Coptic religion, trying to blur the differences and contributing to the diplomatic fiction of Ethiopian obedience to the Roman Church. Góis consciously proposed a vision that emphasized religious differences and gave voice to the Coptic bishop who had been excluded by the Portuguese political and religious elite. The crucial point, however, is that Góis wrote and published a pamphlet in the same book on behalf of the Lapps, supposedly oppressed by the noblemen and prelates in Scandinavia, who did not want to convert them because they (the noblemen) wished to maintain an unfair tax system. We know that this was not an inconsequential issue for Damião de Góis: he exchanged an insistent correspondence with Erasmus asking him to intervene on this political matter. It is a seminal case in European thought, in which external colonialism was implicitly related to internal colonialism.

The text by Francisco Álvares on Ethiopia was a major success in Europe and helped Jean Bodin to study sovereignty in a comparative way. In his *Six Books on the Republic*, Bodin corrected Paolo Giovio on the supposed division of Ethiopia into five kingdoms (in reality provinces), evaluated the relations between the Negus and the governors of provinces, and reflected on the absence of fortresses, which showed the possibility for a king to exercise his power over vast regions and peoples without depending on castles or fortified cities, always sources of revolt and sedition. But one has to acknowledge that these examples were quite scarce: Bodin built up his book almost totally inspired by the examples of the past – Greek and Roman times. It was Giovanni Botero who developed the comparative analyses of political systems, introducing old and new examples from different parts of the world – even if Botero, from a theoretical point of view, was not at all as innovative as Bodin, who reflected deeply on the relationship between law and sovereignty, creating the basis for the notion of the legal state. In the book *Della Ragion di Stato*, published in Venice in 1589, Botero reflected on contemporary empires when he addressed the main questions: How to establish, maintain, and enlarge a firm dominion on populations? Is the longevity of states favored by united or by fragmented territories? He pointed out the risks of a huge, integrated state, which could stimulate an aggressive coalition of its neighbors and would have great difficulty controlling the spread of seditions, the corruption of its parts, or collapse in front of a successful invasion: Botero gave the example of the fall in 30 months of the Visigoth monarchy in Spain before the Arabs and the erosion in a few years of the Byzantine Empire before the Turks. In contrast he praised the possibilities of a fragmented empire (he gave the example of the Portuguese), which could isolate the corrupted, seditious, or invaded parts, mobilizing forces from one part to the other according to the real political and military needs. But what Botero managed to establish with his volume was a completely new comparative framework of political thought, which defined the pattern for the next centuries, a breakthrough that has not been sufficiently acknowledged.

In all these fields – military architecture, urban planning, arts of civility, literature, linguistics, geography, natural history, and political thought – the impact of the European expansion on the Renaissance was extremely important. If we had to indicate a work representative of the major shifts in the order of knowledge, we would privilege the *Itinerario*, written by Jan Huygen van Linschoten and printed in Amsterdam in 1596 (followed by successive editions in English, Latin, German, and French). It included precise information on the Indian Ocean's geography, ethnography, botany, mineralogy, economy, politics, and linguistics, establishing an extraordinary relation between text, maps, and images (of nature and people). It is a new image of the world, written by a Catholic (former secretary of the archbishop of Goa) who became a Calvinist when he returned to the Netherlands, deciding to reveal the secrets of the maritime routes to Asia and within Asia held by the Portuguese. But it is impossible to see in only one book all the major changes introduced by the European expansion. It was the growing autonomy of the different fields of knowledge, from botany to political theory, that revealed the dependence of the Renaissance on the European experience in other continents.

SUGGESTIONS FOR FURTHER READING

Primary sources

Acosta, Christobal de. *Tractado de las drogas y medicinas de las Indias Orientales*. Burgos, 1578.
Álvares, Francisco. *Verdadeira informação das terras do Preste João*, 1st edn 1540. Lisbon: Agência Geral do Ultramar, 1974.
Anglería, Pedro Mártir de, *Decadas del Nuevo Mundo*, ed. Ramón Alba. Madrid: Polifemo, 1989.
Ariosto, Ludovico. *Orlando Furioso* (ed. Marcello Turchi), 1st edn 1516. Milan: Garzanti, 1974.
Benzoni, Girolamo. *La Historia del Mondo Nuovo*. Venice: F. Rampazetto, 1565.
Bodin, Jean, *The Six Bookes of a Commonweale*, translated by Richard Knolles. London: G. Bishop, 1606.
Botero, Giovanni. *Relationi universali*, 4 parts, 2nd edn. Vicenza: Heredi di Perin, 1595.
Botero, Giovanni. *Della Ragion di Stato*, ed. Chiara Continisio. Rome: Donzelli, 1997.
Campanella, Tommaso. *La Città del Sole*, ed. Alberto Savinio. Milan: Adelphi, 1995.
Clusius, Carolus. *Exoticorum libri decem*. Leyden: Ex Officina Plantiniana Raphelengii, 1605.
D'Orta, Garcia. *Colóquio dos simples e drogas e coisas medicinais da India* (ed. Conde de Ficalho), 1st edn 1563, 2 vols. Lisbon: Imprensa Nacional, 1891–95.
Fernández de Oviedo, Gonzalo. *Sumario de la natural historia de las Indias* (ed. Manuel Ballesteros), 1st edn 1526. Madrid: Historia 16, 1986.
Fernández de Oviedo, Gonzalo. *Historia general y natural de las Indias* (ed. Juan Perez de Tudela Bueso), 1st edn 1535, 5 tomes. Madrid: Atlas, 1992.
Góis, Damião de. *Fides, Religio, Moresque Ætiopum sub imperio Preciosi Ioannis (. . .) Deploratio Lappianæ gentis*. Louvain: Ruigeri Rescij, 1540.
Grotius, Hugo. *The Free Sea*, ed. David Armitage. Indianapolis: Liberty Fund, 2004.
Grynaeus, Simon, *Novus orbis regionum ac insularum veteribus incognitarum*. Basileæ, 1532.
Hernández, Francisco. *Obras completas*, 2 tomes, ed. German Solominos d'Ardois. Mexico: Universidad Nacional de Mexico, 1960.
Las Casas, Bartolomé. *Obra indigenista*, ed. José Alcina Franch. Madrid: Alianza, 1985.
Linschoten, Jan Huygen van, *Voyage to the East Indies*, ed. A. C. Burnell and P. A. Tiele, 2 vols. London: Hakluyt Society, 1885.
Menardes, Nicolas. *Dos libros. El uno trata de todas las cosas que se traen de nuestras Indias Occidentales*. Seville, 1565.
Montaigne, Michel de. *Œuvres complètes*, eds Albert Thibaudet and Maurice Rat. Paris: Gallimard, 1962.
Montalboddo, Francesco da. *Paesi nuovamente ritrovati*. Vicenza, 1507.
More, Thomas. *The Yale Edition of the Complete Works of St Thomas More*. Vol. IV, *Utopia*, eds Edward Surtz and J. H. Hexter. New Haven: Yale University Press, 1965.

Pereira, Duarte Pacheco. *Esmeraldo de situ orbis*, ed. Joaquim Barradas de Carvalho. Lisbon: Fundação Calouste Gulbenkian, 1991.

Piccolomini, Enea Silvio. *Cosmographia*. Paris: Apud Collegium Plesseiacum, 1509.

Rabelais, François. *Oeuvre completes*, eds Jacques Boulenger and Lucien Scheler. Paris: Gallimard, 1955.

Ramusio, Giovanni Battista, *Navigazioni e Viaggi*, 1st ed. 1550–1559, ed. Marica Milanesi, 6 vols. Turin: Einaudi, 1978–1988.

Sansovino, Francesco, *Del governo dei regni e delle republiche cosi antiche come moderne*. Venice, 1561.

Thevet, André, *Les vrais portraits et vies des hommes illustres*, 2 vols. Paris, 1584.

Thevet, André. *Cosmographie de Levant*, 2nd edn. Lyon: Jean de Tournes and Guillaume Gazeau, 1556.

Thevet, André. *Les singularités de la France Antarctique* (ed. Frank Lestringant), 1st edn 1557. Paris: Chandeigne, 1997.

Thevet, André. *La cosmographie universelle*, 2 vols. Paris: Pierre L'Huillier and Guillaume Chaudière, 1575.

Vinci, Leonardo da, *The Notebooks*, ed. Irma A. Richter. Oxford: Oxford University Press, 1952.

Secondary sources

Aubin, Jean. "Le Latin et l'Astrolabe," in *Recherches sur le Portugal de la Renaissance, son expansion en Asie et ses relations internationales*, vol. I. Paris: Centre Culturel Calouste Gulbenkian, 1996.

Bailey, Gauvin Alexander. *Art of Colonial Latin America*. London: Phaidon, 2005.

Bassani, Ezio and William Fagg (eds). *Africa and the Renaissance: Art and Ivory*. New York: Centre for African Art, 1988.

Broc, Numa. *La géographie de la Renaissance*. Paris: C.T.H.S., 1986.

Buescu, Maria Leonor Carvalhão. *O estudo das línguas exóticas no século XVI*. Lisbon: ICLP, 1983.

Burke, Peter, *The European Renaissances: Centres and Peripheries*, Oxford: Blackwell, 1998.

Burke, Peter. *Languages and Communities in Early Modern Europe*. Cambridge: Cambridge University Press, 2004.

Carita, Helder. "Arquitectura civil indo-portuguesa e a paisagem urbana de Goa," in Artur Teodoro de Matos (ed.) *Os espaços de um império*, vol. 2. Porto: CNCDP, 1999, 77–89.

Carvalho, Joaquim Barradas de. *À la recherche de la spécificité de la Renaissance Portugaise*, 2 vols. Paris: Fundação Calouste Gulbenkian, 1983.

Castedo, Leopoldo. *Historia del Arte Iberoamericano*. Vol. 1: *Precolombina. El arte colonial*. Madrid: Alianza, 1988.

Cooper, Michael. *Rodrigues: The Interpreter. An Early Jesuit in Japan and China*. New York: Weatherhill, 1974.

Delumeau, Jean, *La civilisation de la Renaissance*, Paris: Arthaud, 1967.

Desmond, Ray. *The European Discovery of the Indian Flora*. Oxford: Oxford University Press, 1992.

Godinho, Vitorino Magalhães. "Portuguese Emigration from the Fifteenth to the Twentieth Century: Constants and Changes," in P. C. Emmer and M. Mörner (eds) *European Expansion and Migration: Essays on the Intercontinental Migration from Africa, Asia, and Europe*. New York and Oxford: Oxford University Press, 1992, 13–48.

Grafton, Anthony. *New Worlds, Ancient Texts. The Power of Tradition and the Shock of Discovery*. Cambridge, Mass.: Belknap Press, 1992.

Gray, Edward G. *New World Babel: Languages and Nations in Early America*. Princeton: Princeton University Press, 1999.
Gray, Edward G. and Norman Fiering (eds). *The Language Encounter in the Americas, 1492–1800*. New York: Berghahn Books, 2000.
Gruzinski, Serge. *La colonisation de l'imaginaire*. Paris: Gallimard, 1988.
Gruzinski, Serge. *L'aigle et la sybille. Fresques indiennes des couvents du Mexique*. Paris: Imprimerie National, 1994.
Gruzinski, Serge. *Les quatre parties du monde. Histoire d'une mondialisation*. Paris: La Martinière, 2004.
Guedes, Maria Natália Correia (ed.). *Encounters of Cultures. Eight Centuries of Portuguese Mission Work*. Vatican: Portuguese Episcopal Conference, 1996.
Ikegami, Eiko. *Bonds of Civility. Aesthetic Networks and the Political Origins of Japanese Culture*. Cambridge: Cambridge University Press, 2005.
Kagan, Richard. *Urban Images of the Hispanic World, 1493–1793*. New Haven: Yale University Press, 2000.
Kubler, George and Martín Soria. *Art and Architecture in Spain and Portugal and their American Dominions, 1500 to 1800*. Harmondsworth: Penguin, 1959.
Lestringant, Frank. *L'atelier du cosmographe ou l'image du monde à la Renaissance*. Paris: Albin Michel, 1991.
Moreira, Rafael. *A Arquitectura Militar na Expansão Portuguesa*. Porto: CNCDP, 1994.
Moreira, Rafael. "From Manueline to Renaissance in Portuguese India," *Mare Liberum* 9 (1995): 401–7.
Moreira, Rafael. "A fortaleza de Diu e a arquitectura militar no Índico," in Artur Teodoro de Matos (ed.) *Os espaços de um império*, vol. 2. Porto: CNCDP, 1999, 139–47.
Mundy, Barbara E. *The Mapping of New Spain. Indigenous Cartography and the Maps of the Relaciones Geográficas*. Chicago: University of Chicago Press, 1996.
Musset, Alain. *Villes nomades du nouveau monde*. Paris: EHESS, 2002.
Reveal, James L. *Gentle Conquest. The Botanic Discovery of North America*. Washington: Starwood, 1992.
Rubiés, Joan Pau. "Travel Writing and Ethnography," in Peter Hulme and Tom Youngs (eds) *The Cambridge Companion to Travel Writing*. Cambridge: Cambridge University Press, 2002, 242–60.
Sánchez-Albornoz, Nicolás. *La población de América Latinas desde los tiempos colombianos al año 2025*, 3rd edn. Madrid: Alianza, 1994.
Scott, John F. *Latin American Art: Ancient to Modern*. Gainsville: University of Florida Press, 1999.
Silva, Nuno Vassalo e (ed.). *The Heritage of Rauluchantim*. Lisbon: Museu de São Roque, 1996.
Teixeira, Manuel C. and Margarida Valla. *O urbanismo português, séculos XIII–XVIII*. Lisbon: Horizonte, 1999.
Trnek, Helmut and Nuno Vassalo e Silva (eds). *Exotica. Os descobrimentos portugueses e as câmaras de maravilhas do Renascimento* (Catalogue of the exhibition). Lisbon: Fundação Calouste Gulbenkian, 2001.

CHAPTER SEVEN

THE INVENTION OF EUROPE

John A. Marino

The "idea of Europe" developed dramatically during the Renaissance. Global expansion and imperialism transformed what once had been a rather vague geographical and historical conception founded upon mythological and literary traditions into the self-conscious representation of a relatively well-defined civilization. The sharp division between ancients and moderns, between East and West, and between local and international politics became the lens through which inhabitants of the old continent viewed their new contact and conquest of America, Africa, and Asia, which in turn reinforced, accelerated, and contested their emerging notions of Europe and their identity as Europeans in the Renaissance.

SETTING TEMPORAL AND SPATIAL LIMITS

The Middle Ages had given birth to an earlier idea of European civilization. Diverse peoples forged a common culture on the western peninsula of the Eurasian landmass in the aftermath of the late Roman Empire through the exchange of peoples, goods, and ideas, and from political rivalries. Upon the contraction and expansion of its economic and demographic base, a new society different from that of the ancient world emerged, yet one culturally dependent on the heritage of classical, biblical, and Germanic traditions. That society adopted a classificatory conception of itself founded upon a functional division of labor or duties into three hierarchical castes or orders – priests, warriors, and workers – that was shared by the great arc of Indo-European language-speaking peoples between the Arctic and the Mediterranean from the Atlantic to the Urals and beyond to India. The piecemeal development of Europe as a place and an idea proceeded – as it has continued to do today from the end of the Second World War into the twenty-first century – in stops and starts through cooperation and competition, integration and conflict.

A decisive turning point in the conception of Europe occurred, however, in the fifteenth century in the reconstruction of society after the crisis of the fourteenth century, the demographic and cultural shock of the plague, and the schism and fracturing of the Church. Four new developments from the mid-fifteenth century had dramatic repercussions for the theory and practices of Europe during the long sixteenth century from 1450 to 1650: (1) printing and its effect on the dissemination and standardization of knowledge; (2) the Turkish conquest of Byzantium and the expansion of Ottoman power toward Western Christendom; (3) the Iberian–Genoese maritime, commercial, and colonial expansion outside of the Mediterranean basin to West Africa, the Americas, and Asia; and (4) the rise of the New Monarchies and the increased national competition by their ruling elites for power and resources. While all periods contributed to the idea of Europe through gradual and incremental developments, the "new world order" of the Renaissance made the idea of Europe a commonplace in European thought and practice by the mid-seventeenth century.

The humanist Aeneas Silvius Piccolomini, who became Pope Pius II (1458–64), famously equated the medieval term *Respublica christiana* with "Europe." Indeed, he is often seen as the thinker most responsible for putting the word "Europe" into common usage. Moreover, where Dante had avoided the adjectival form by calling Europeans "inhabitants of Europe," and Boccaccio had proposed the abortive neologism "Europico," Pius is credited with being among the first to use the adjective "europeus" ("European"). From his vast humanist learning, the Sienese pope called for a united, Christian Europe to launch a crusade against the Ottoman Turks, recounted his broad international diplomatic experience, and described in chorographic texts on *Europa* (1458) and *Asia* (1461) the similarities and differences between the two continents, observing in his *Germania* (1457/58) that "the inhabitants of Asia are always considered inferior to the inhabitants of Europe." Similarly in his *Mémoires* on the reigns of Louis XI and Charles VIII from 1468 to 1498, Philippe de Commynes did not distinguish between "Christendom" and "Europe," with the newer word winning out. In Thomas More's *Utopia* (1516) – "In Europe, and especially in those parts where the faith and religion of Christ prevails" – Europe is larger than Christendom, which was under siege in the Balkans by the Turks. Erasmus, on the other hand, still preferred the unity of Christendom and did not much use the word "Europe" until after the decade-long advance of the Turks in the 1520s, with the capture of Belgrade (1521), Rhodes (1522), Hungary and the greater part of Dalmatia following their victory at Mohács (1526), and the siege of Vienna (1529). Thus, in letters from 1529 and 1530, Erasmus referred to "the most powerful princes from all of Europe" and even uses the adjectival form "European." In his *De Europae dissidiis et bello turcico dialogus* (1526), the Spanish humanist Juan Luis Vives compares the Turkish invasion of Europe to the wars between the ancient Persians and Greeks, even predicting on such classical precedent an inevitable Turkish defeat. In championing the call to arms against Ottoman expansion, Renaissance humanism identified Europe with Christendom at the very moment when the term "Europe" first found wide acceptance.

By the mid-seventeenth century, the papal *possesso* of Innocent X in 1644 made it clear how commonplace the idea and representation of Europe had become. The inaugural procession of the new pope from the Vatican through the streets of Rome to take "possession" of the Lateran Basilica was styled a "Gran Teatro del Mondo," and among the numerous ephemeral exhibits along the road of march was a stage set/fireworks display of "Roma triumphans" in front of the Palazzo Borghese. The two coats of arms of the ecclesiastical and secular powers loom above the temporary stage designating papal Rome, at the center of the Christian world, ruler over the four continents, each portrayed with her traditional gendered iconography. In first place, stage right, as we see below, stood Europa, crowned and holding a scepter and orb, in front of a bear. Such public festivals continued to glorify the theme of Europe at the head of the four continents both in Catholic principalities (such as the 1658 Neapolitan commemoration of the royal birth of the Spanish infante, Philip Prosper, with the four continents center-stage as four decorative horse-drawn carts, and the wedding of Cosimo III de' Medici to Margherita Luisa of Orléans in Florence in 1661 with cavalry and infantry representing the four continents), as much as in Protestant lands (such as the Amsterdam town hall marble frieze of 1656–58 depicting people of the four continents bringing goods and tribute to a female Amsterdam enthroned on a ship, and a festival arch in London during the 1661 English Restoration coronation of Charles II displaying figures of the four continents).

France provides the exception that proves the rule, since earlier representations of Europe among the four continents (with a fifth group of the northern peoples) in

Figure 7.1 The Four Continents at Palazzo Borghese from Innocent X's *possesso* in Laurentius Gunnari Banck, *Roma triumphans: seu actus inaugurationum & coronationum Pontificum Romanorum, & in spetie: Innocentii X. Pont. Max. brevis descriptio cum omnibus triumphis & cerimoniis eidem actui additis* (2nd edn, Franekerae: Typis & sumptibus, Johannis Arcerii, 1656). The Newberry Library, Chicago.

a ballet during the 1626 carnival under Louis XIII were no longer present when Louis XIV styled himself King of the Romans in the 1662 festival of the great *carrousel*, at the head of four other nations – Persians, Turks, Indians of India, and Americans. Where Dutch pamphlets after Louis XIV's attacks on the United Provinces in 1672 referred to "Europe," the French described Louis as the most Christian king and defender of the *respublica christiana*; where William of Orange's motto as *"handhaver der Europese vrijheid"* ("preserver of the liberty of Europe") was taken up by English propaganda after the Glorious Revolution in 1688 as the fight for "the freedom of Europe and the Protestant religion," the French preferred the term "Chrétienté." The political and diplomatic struggle between France and Spain in the mid-seventeenth century and between Catholic France and its Protestant neighbors led Louis to prefer his traditional title as head of Christendom.

As a place, however, Europe was a reality born of physical boundaries and frontiers. The physical geography of mountains and plains, rivers and seas, and climate and rainfall divided the continent into six natural units: first, three peripheral arcs (a "Nordic arc" from Iceland through the tips of Norway, Denmark, Sweden, the Baltic States, Finland, and Russia to the White Sea; an "Atlantic arc" from Portugal and northwestern Spain through Brittany and the British Isles; and a "Mediterranean arc" from Gibraltar along the Spanish and French coast through northern Italy, the Adriatic, the northern Balkans, and the Aegean coast of Anatolia to Cyprus); and second, three interior regions (the northern European plain stretching from the French and English basin to the Polish plains; an alpine divide between north and south; and the great continental steppe from the Oder to the Urals). Climate and soils determined medieval crops, livestock, and farming techniques from horses and the heavy moldboard plow in the northern plains to viticulture, olive trees, and the lighter scratch plow south of the Garonne and the Alps. In turn, material life gave rise to divergent social and economic structures in the continent's various regions.

Medieval boundaries were, nevertheless, not hard and fast, but rather permeable and shifting. Forests and heathlands, swamps and marshlands were reclaimed and dynastic territories consolidated. At the same time, the European river network constantly opened up the interior and often connected regions in loose political confederation, such as along the Rhine and Danube (the old lines of ancient Roman expansion), the Ebro valley in Iberia, and the Po valley in northern Italy. Germanic peoples expanded east beyond the Elbe and the Oder to Slavic and Baltic lands; Christians from Castile and Leon launched their *Reconquista* of Iberia; the Normans conquered Sicily and southern Italy; Angles and Saxons established colonies along the frontiers of Wales, Scotland, and Ireland; Russian contacts with Byzantium, Islam, and the Judeo-Khazar state spread from the Baltic to the Black Sea; and Byzantine Greeks inherited the Eastern Roman Empire that stretched from Trebizond through ancient Ionia (coastal Anatolia) and the Levant to Egypt before its erosion by Muslim expansion and crusaders' aggression. The Venetians traded with Byzantium and later the Ottomans, and Genoese slaved along the Black Sea by selling military manpower from Central Asia and the Caucasus to the Mamluks in Egypt, while Italian merchants brought back to western Europe Asian products such as pepper and spices as well as Arabic (really Indic) ideas such as the positional decimal numeral system for the developing practice of double-entry bookkeeping. At the same time, the three principal Iberian states of Portugal, Castile, and Aragon each formed fluid partnerships with the Genoese in rivalry with one another to exploit and colonize first North Africa within the Mediterranean basin and then West Africa outside it.

Mental and cultural frontiers were as decisive as geographical, political, and economic ones. The continent was linguistically diverse, though of the some 50 to 70 languages (not counting hundreds of regional dialects) most Europeans spoke vernaculars in the Indo-European family (Romance, Germanic, Slavic, Celtic, Hellenic, Baltic, and Albanian). Finno-Hungarian languages (Finnish, Estonian, and Hungarian), Euskera (the Basque language), and Turkish were the notable exceptions. But they all made use of only three alphabets: Greek, Latin, and Cyrillic. Before the fracturing of Latin Christianity during the sixteenth-century Reformation movements, the heirs of the Roman Empire were divided into three major cultural and religious polities, Orthodox Christian and Islamic in the East and Latin Christianity in the West, with enclaves of Judaism among all three. In the Latin West, the traditions of the Greco-Roman Mediterranean, the Judeo-Christian world, and native peoples and tribes (Germans, Celts, Scyths, Goths, Scandinavians, and Slavs) met and meshed as a new basis for unity spread through the Latin Church, Roman law, and the Latin language.

Where the material life of agricultural production set the norms and rhythms for the vast majority of peasant society over time, medieval avenues of trade and communication forged a unity through the exchange of ideas and practices in three socio-cultural milieux – the Church, the nobility, and towns. The ecclesiastical organization of the Church and the spread of religious movements from monasticism to the mendicant orders; the long-distance travel of pilgrims to Rome or Santiago de Compostela; the spread of universities, scholasticism, and the international circulation of teachers and students; the diffusion of styles of art and architecture; and the survival of the imperial ideal of a universal government in Germany and beyond served to consolidate the cultural unity of Europe in the late Middle Ages. Equally important was the spread of the techniques and ideology of warfare, court culture and its refined tastes for luxury goods, music, the arts, tournaments, and festivals; local and international fairs; merchant associations such as the Hanse in northern Europe; commercial companies such as the Bardi, Peruzzi, Medici, or Fugger with branches across the continent; communal organization and the spread of urban literacy – all means of fusion coexisted with the political divisions and almost permanent state of war to make Europe a land of unity in a sea of diversity. The Renaissance rediscovery of antiquity in both its Greco-Roman and New Testament–Church Fathers traditions fostered the illusive ideal of European peace and unity – first with the papacy and the Eastern Orthodox Church at the Council of Ferrara–Florence (1438–45), later in the sixteenth century between Protestants and Catholics, and throughout the period as a military alliance, rarely achieved among national rivalries, against the Ottoman Turks who had planted Islam in the Balkans and threatened both Vienna and Italy. Contact with peoples, goods, and ideas from Asia, Africa, and America increased European assertions of primacy, lordship, and mission, all of which were tied up in dynastic rivalries as the Habsburg juggernaut attempted to impose its hegemony over the continent, only to have it collapse in the devastation of the Thirty Years War.

REPRESENTING THE IDEA AND PERSONIFICATION OF EUROPE

During this two-century period of transformation, 1450–1650, the representation of Europe can be traced in three main forms: the visual arts (through cartography, iconography, and public rituals or festivals), printed books (literary and political tracts), and diplomacy. From this explosion of references and practices on the idea of Europe, two major representational images of the continent emerged: (1) Europa Virgo Crowned, a motif that first appeared in 1537 as a symbol of the Spanish world and that was reanimated with pro- and anti-Spanish adaptations after 1587; and (2) Europe as one of the Four Continents, which now included, in addition to Europe, Africa, and Asia in the earlier three-continent model of the world, the figure of America, a motif that became especially popular in the third quarter of the sixteenth century. The geographical-cultural meaning of modern Europe also developed in the sixteenth century through the active invention of humanists, who filtered their contemporary experience in European courts, Turkish conflict, exploration of the New World, and state rivalries through their learning from ancient texts, such as Ptolemy's *Geographia*.

Cartographic representation of the continent in world maps is the first place to see Europe. The earliest medieval world maps, such as Ambrosio Macrobius's fifth-century zone map, as reproduced in a 1492 Venetian book, and Isidore of Seville's seventh-century T-O map from a 1472 Augsburg book, represent Europe and the world most often in schematic, symbolic form. For the zonal map tradition, Macrobius's five climatic zones, derived from Pythagorean cosmography, influenced early Renaissance preconceptions about the impossibility of crossing the Torrid Zone because of its heat and the impossibility of life in the uninhabitable frigid polar zones. For the T-O map tradition, the mystical meaning of the peopling of the three continents by Noah's sons and the figural meaning of the crucifixion with the T as a cross within the O of the inhabited world pointed to the Christian's spiritual world more than to the structural realities of the physical earth. The medieval world maps (*mappae mundi*) conflated time and space in a moralized, didactic representation of a biblical, narrative history according to the dominant Christian world-view.

Medieval *mappae mundi* conventions began to change with knowledge of the wider world through the discovery of ancient texts and direct contact through commerce, war, and the exchange of ideas with Byzantine and Islamic societies in the Mediterranean. Sometime before 1300, and produced often in the fourteenth and fifteenth centuries, portolan maps (medieval navigation charts) influenced the visual construction of the Christian West on the world map and literally put the name "Europe" on a separate, continental map. Then, at the beginning of the fifteenth century, humanist scholars brought Ptolemy's *Geographia* from Constantinople to Florence and translated it into Latin. Ptolemy's *Geographia* had been rediscovered during the late thirteenth-century Greek revival in Byzantium and circulated in manuscript editions throughout the fourteenth and fifteenth centuries in a number of versions – some without maps, some with its original 27 maps, and after 1427 some with as many as 65 maps and plans. It was first printed with maps at Bologna in 1477, and early printed world maps followed Ptolemy's cartographic principles. To introduce the Second Age of Man, the world after the Flood, for example, the *Nuremberg Chronicle* of Hartmann Schedel reproduces the Ptolemaic world map surrounded by the sons of Noah, who look over the corners of the map to their respective parts of the world – Japhet to Europe, Shem to Asia, and Ham to Africa. Schedel's *Liber Chronicarum* was published in June 1493 soon after Columbus's letter on his first voyage had been published in April 1493, but the wide and rapid dissemination of the news of Columbus's discoveries by the end of that year in 11 editions in six cities and in three languages would change everything. From the early sixteenth century, the Portuguese established the *Armazém da Guiné*, a hydrographic office, to provide nautical charts for their ships. The anonymous world chart of 1502 called the Cantino Map, which was probably produced there and smuggled to Modena by an agent of the duke of Ferrara, contains accurate details of the Portuguese-explored African coast, India from Vasco da Gama's voyage of 1497–99, and even the fragmentary shore of Brazil discovered by Cabral in 1500. As details of Africa, Asia, and the New World became available, map-makers incorporated the new findings,

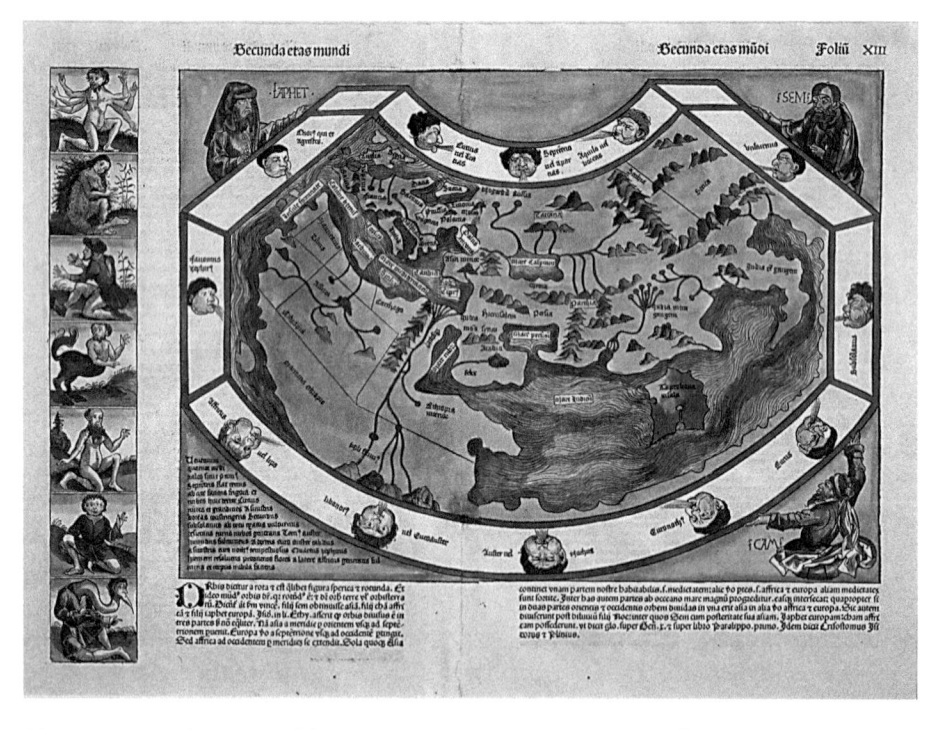

Figure 7.2 Ptolemaic world map in Hartmann Schedel, *Liber Chronicarum* (Nuremberg: Anthonius Koberger, 1493). Private collection, courtesy of Mandeville Special Collections Library, University of California.

and Martin Waldseemüller's *Universalis cosmographia* (Strasbourg, 1507) was not only the first map to name the New World "America," but also was the first printed map to include the coastline of Africa on the basis of Portuguese exploration, cover 360° of latitude, put Japan as an island off China, and make space for the as yet undiscovered Pacific Ocean (Figure 7.3). Working at St Dié in Lorraine, Waldseemüller did not center the known world near his homeland along the Rhine nor in Nuremburg as did Schedel's *Chronicle*, but along an axis reaching up from the Strait of Hormuz into Persia and a misshapen Caspian Sea. Early printed world maps did not necessarily situate the center of the world in Jerusalem, Mesopotamia, or Europe. Matteo Ricci's late sixteenth-century Chinese world map, derived from Ortelius and Mercator, for example, had its center in the South Pacific well east of the Philippines.

Waldseemüller was also the first to print a map of Europe as a whole, with the original 1511 first state map lost but the extant second state map published in Strasbourg in 1520 (Figure 7.4). Waldseemüller's 1520 *Carta itineraria Europae* reproduces the coats of arms of the European states along the map's borders and is dedicated to the newly elected emperor, Charles V, whose two primary titles from the Holy Roman Empire and Spain are represented by fully armed soldiers bearing their respective flags standing guard in the upper left and right corners. Europe itself is oriented to the south with Germany at the bottom looking up to Greece, Italy, and Spain at the top. Waldseemüller's map was probably influenced by two earlier maps of Central Europe, the Eichstätt map of Nicolas Cusa (c. 1491) and the *Rom-Weg Karte* (c. 1492–1501), a map of German and Dutch pilgrim itineraries to Rome by Erhard Etzlaub. Thus, in addition to the coastal particulars from portolan maps, the Waldseemüller map is able to incorporate significant details of the continental interior of mountains, forests, rivers, towns, and names of regions.

The printed map of Europe as a separate continent falls into three periods: (1) 1511–54, from Waldseemüller's first map of Europe to Gerard Mercator's influential scientific synthesis; (2) 1554–70, from Mercator to the printed atlas of Abraham Ortelius; and (3) after 1570, with Ortelius's *Theatrum Orbis Terrarum* setting the standard for what followed. Sebastian Münster, working in Basel, was the most important cartographer diffusing images of Europe in this first period. His first map of Europe was published in Frankfurt in 1536 in *Mappa Europae*, a concise cosmography and manual for map-making. Published in Basel, a first state map of a south-oriented Europe (*Europa Prima Nova Tabula*) appeared in his Latin edition of Ptolemy, *Geographica Universalis*, in 1540; the second state map (*Moderna Europae Descriptio*) appeared in 1544 in his *Cosmographei oder beschreibung aller Länder*, one of the most popular books of the sixteenth century with 40 editions in six languages up to its last edition in 1628, although the second state map of Europe was replaced in 1588 by a more modern map based on Ortelius. Maps of Europe became a pan-European phenomenon during the first period in the first half of the century with other extant examples from Venice (Benedetto Bordone, 1528; Giovanni Domenico Zorzi, 1545), Nuremberg (Heinrich Zell, 1536), Zurich (Johannes Stumpf, 1548), and Lyons (Guillaume Gueroult, 1553). Mercator's first state 1554 map of Europe (and his second state 1572 map), published in Duisburg from 15 copper plates, marks the beginning of the second period in maps of Europe because it is the first

Figure 7.3 Martin Waldseemüller. *Universalis cosmographia secundum Ptholomaei traditionem et Amerii Vespucii aliorum[m]que lustrationes* (St Dié: s.n., 1507). The Library of Congress, Washington, DC.

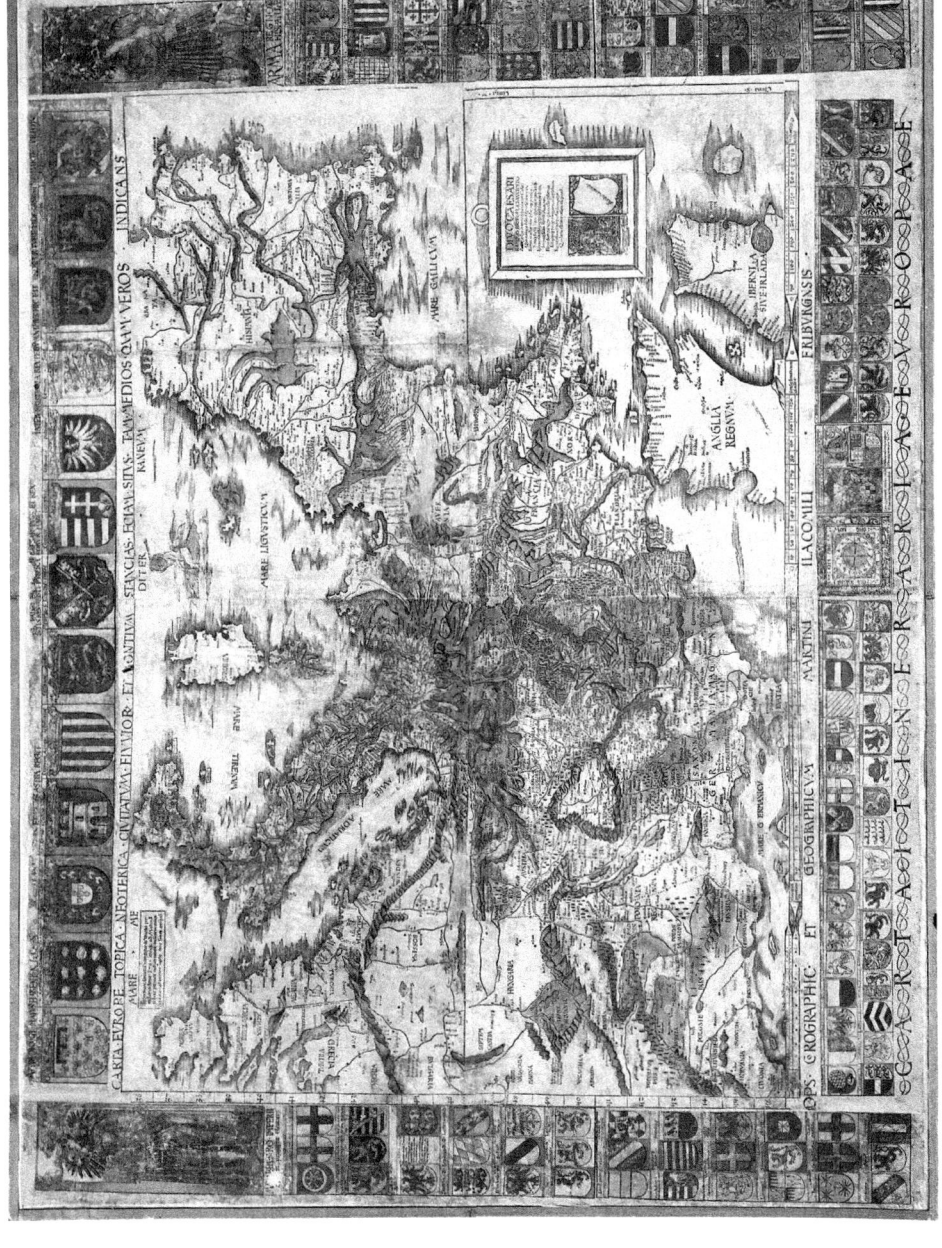

Figure 7.4 Martin Waldseemüller. *Carta Itineraria Europae*, 1520. Tiroler Landesmuseum Ferdinandeum, Innsbruck, Austria.

map to revise Ptolemy by correcting the exaggerated east–west distance of the Mediterranean. This large wall map of Europe (measuring approximately 165 × 134 cm) was dedicated to Charles V's minister Antoine Perrenot, lord of Granvelle and bishop of Arras, and remained the definitive map of Europe through the seventeenth century. While attempting to flatten the globe and minimize distortions at the edges of the map, Mercator had not yet reached the level of accuracy in the projection method of his revolutionary 1569 world map. The 1569 world map's title explains that it is a "New and More Complete Representation of the Terrestrial Globe Properly Adapted for Use in Navigation," similar to linear perspective's representation of three-dimensional space on a two-dimensional surface. By progressively increasing the separation between adjoining meridians and parallels by ten degrees, Mercator's cylindrical projection straightened out rhumb lines on a flat map, but created greater distortions as one moved away from the equator. (In seamen's language, rhumb lines are lines that intersect all meridians at the same angle and define a constant bearing, which is the angle between a course and a meridian.) Ortelius's *Europae* in his 1570 *Theatrum* begins the third period in printed maps of Europe (Figure 7.5). This map's importance comes from its accuracy (based upon Mercator's 1554 map and a host of other earlier exemplars) and its size (plate size of 342 × 466 mm), so that it became the model for all later maps of Europe. After its first printing in Antwerp in 1570, it appeared in some 42 editions of the *Theatrum* until 1612: the first state map from 1570 to 1581 in 3,300 copies; a second state map replaced it from 1584 to 1612 in 4,950 copies. Mercator's *Atlas* of 1585, rather than Ortelius's *Theater*, however, was to give its name to book collections of maps.

Sixteenth-century cartographers, with an imaginative eye on Europe in the world map, even turned the map of the continent into a female figure. The iconographic image of Europa Virgo Crowned first appeared in 1537 as an untitled map of Europe in the shape of a woman designed by Johann Putsch of Innsbruck and published in Paris by Christian Wechel (Figure 7.6). With Spain as her head, the coats of arms of Aragon and Navarre tattooed on her cheeks, Bohemia her heart, Italy her right arm holding Sicily in the form of an orb, and the whole figure studded with the coats of arms of the various states, this was clearly the Europe dominated by Charles V's Habsburg Empire in the year after his triumphal march through Italy following his victory in Tunis. Guillaume Postel, Michael Eitzinger (who mapped the Netherlands as a Lion, *Leo Belgicus*, in 1579), and Ortelius all commented on Putsch's European Virgin Queen, but it only began to be imitated in two maps of 1587: one at Catholic Cologne by the Netherlander Mathias Quad that included cartouches on the left describing Europe with the coats of arms of the seven electors and on the right a German translation of the myths of Europa with the imperial arms, and the other at Protestant Wittenberg as a woodcut, "Europa Prima Pars Terrae Forma Virginis," in Heinrich Bünting's *Itinerarium Sacrae Scripturae* in a much-simplified version with the coats of arms removed and the names of the various kingdoms predominant, redone as a copper engraving in 1638 and 1650 editions. In commemoration of the intended marriage of the Austrian Habsburg emperor Rudolf II and the Spanish infanta Isabella, the hardened Bünting visage with the more detailed Quad raiment even appeared in the center of a silver bowl made in Nuremburg in 1589. The simpler image of Bünting was reworked in a more aggressive regal pose, and this

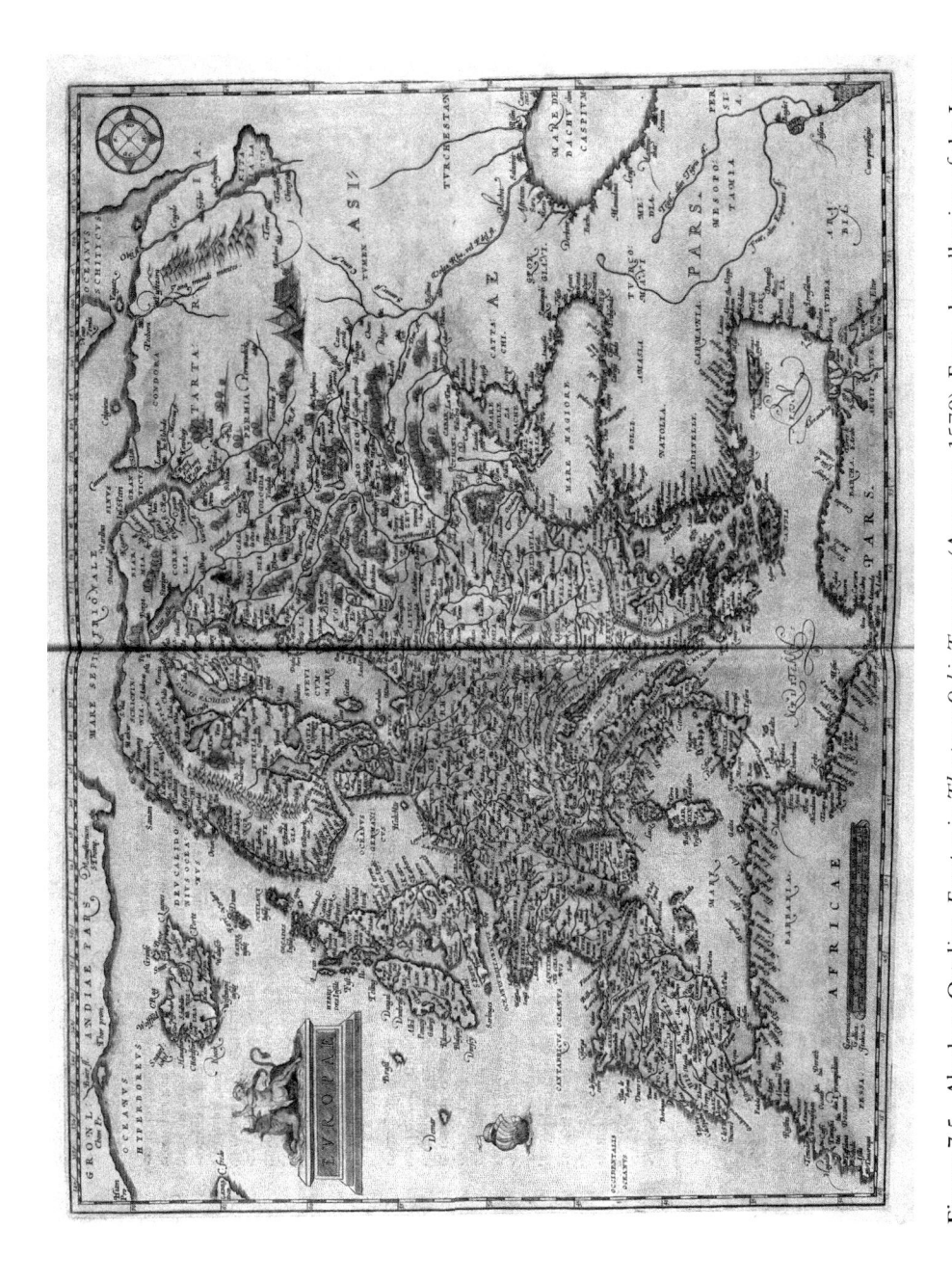

Figure 7.5 Abraham Ortelius. *Europae* in *Theatrum Orbis Terrarum* (Antwerp, 1570). From the collection of the James Ford Bell Library, University of Minnesota, Minneapolis.

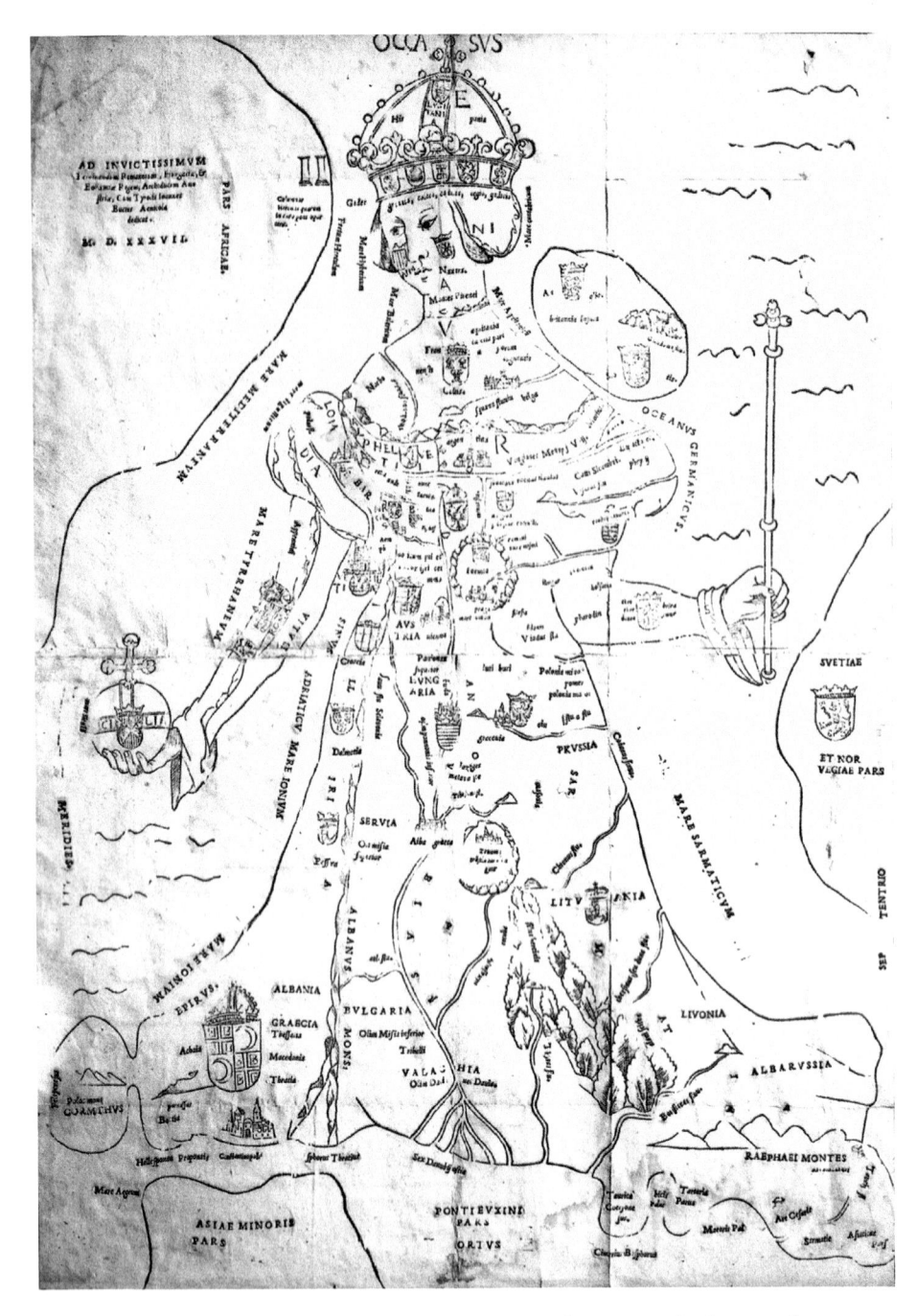

Figure 7.6 Johann Putsch. *Europa Virgo Crowned*, 1537. Tiroler Landesmuseum Ferdinandeum, Innsbruck, Austria.

– *The invention of Europe* –

Europa Virgo replaced an earlier map that first appeared in the 1550 edition of Sebastian Münster's *Cosmographei* in the 1588 and subsequent 1592, 1598, 1614, and 1628 editions. In 1598 two anonymous anti-Spanish pamphlets, *Het Spaens Europa* (one published at Amsterdam, the other without place), have Spanish Europe brandishing a sword instead of holding her scepter. In the second version, the dispersal of the Spanish Armada around the British Isles discomfits an image of Philip II while a lone Sea Beggar holds off a menacing, clerical fleet led by a three-headed Antichrist pope (Figure 7.7). Europe on a map continued to be used positively or negatively, with the Virgo still symbolizing Spanish power in Manila in 1761, and reappearing in 1804 in a Dutch print from Haarlem depicting the Napoleonic repartition of Europe.

Printed maps heavily influenced the creation of images and allegorical figures of Queen Europe reigning over the Four Parts of the World. After 1570, the Four Continents assumed allegorical shape on the title page of the new atlases such as Ortelius (Antwerp, 1570), Georg Braun and Franz Hogenberg's vol. 5 (Cologne, 1598), Quad (1600), and Willem Janszoon Blaeu's Latin edition (Amsterdam, 1645). In the Ortelius frontispiece, a naked America with spear, bow, and arrows lies at the feet of the other continents and in cannibalistic primitivism proudly displays a

Figure 7.7 *Het Spaens Europa*, anonymous Flemish print, 1598. Stewart Museum, Montreal, Canada.

severed human head in her left hand. Next to her is a bust of Magellanica, the yet undiscovered landmass to the south where the fires of Tierra del Fuego were sighted. Asia and Africa stand on pedestals to the sides, in front of columns supporting the high porch where Europe sits crowned and enthroned. Europe presides under a pergola garlanded with grape-vines; her right hand holds a scepter and her left clutches a rudder (in the shape of the cross) to steer the large globe. In the Braun and Hogenberg frontispiece, Europe crowned stands prominently in the left front with scepter in hand and Asia attentively gazing from behind; America and Africa attend on the other side of the title cartouche. Below, burghers, one of them a turbaned Turk, are in discussion. World maps also often presented the theme of European dominance over the continents in marginalia. In Peter Plancius's 1594 world map, Europe commands from the upper left corner and is surrounded by a cornucopia and the symbols of civilization from the arts, sciences, and warfare. So too, the wall maps of Pieter van den Keere (1611) and Henricus Hondius (1630) both glorify Europe as receiving tribute from the other continents. In 1653, the four corners of Nicolaes Visscher's world map reproduce the Flemish engraver Adriaen Collaert II's personifications after Martin de Vos's *The Four Parts of the World* (*c.* 1595). The regal queen Europe holds her scepter and the grape-vine symbol of civilization, while cattle graze peacefully, horses buck, two wild bears sniff each other out, and two armies collide in the background. Where Europe sits upon a large globe, her sister continents ride upon their respective native animals – Asia on a camel, Africa on a crocodile, and America on an armadillo.

Working in the same Antwerp workshop as Collaert, Philip Galle had engraved a crowned Europe in his 1579 emblem collection, *Prosopographia*. And not surprisingly, Elizabeth I was portrayed as Europa in a 1598 Dutch engraving now in the Ashmolean Museum. Cesare Ripa's *Iconologia*, first published with illustrations in 1603, included a figure of Europa holding in one hand "the temple, to indicate that in her at present is the perfect and true Religion, and superior to all others," while her other hand points to crowns, papal tiara, and scepter to show that "in Europe reside the greatest and most powerful Princes in the World, such as the Emperor and the pope, whose authority extends over everyone where the Most Holy and Catholic Christian Faith is established." Europe is seated upon the crossing of two overflowing cornucopias and backed by spears and horse. Later editions add mathematical and musical instruments, books, a palette, and the owl of wisdom – all to illustrate her superiority in arms, letters, and all the liberal arts. Crowned Europa is ubiquitous, even appearing brandishing a tree-sized branch of a grape-vine and raising her scepter in the *c.* 1610 plasterwork cornice above a fireplace in the Queen's Room, Burton Agnes House, Yorkshire, and on tapestries *c.* 1630–40 from either Tours or Blois in the Hôtel de ville of Beaugency. The image of the Four Parts of the World only grew over time, with the 16 recorded paintings of the theme before 1650 almost tripling to 43 paintings in the second half of the seventeenth century and the eighteenth. The crowned queen is a pan-European representation of the sixteenth-century European conquest of the world and symbolizes Europeans' belief in their salvific mission of spreading Christianity and civilization.

These images of the continent Europa as a crowned queen competed with another earlier image of Europa from Greek mythology. The title of Ortelius's 1570 map

Europae is printed on the pedestal of a statue of the bull carrying off Europa on the waves, while in Nicolaes Visscher's 1652 map, *Nova Europae*, a combined image of queen and abducted virgin above the title placard has Europa sitting enthroned on the bull and surrounded by her attributes of orb, sword, shield, and flags. In 1577, John Dee published *General and Rare Memorials pertaining to the Perfect Arte of Navigation*, a treatise against pirates and foreign fishermen in English waters, whose frontispiece represents Europe with her name on the ship of state carrying Queen Elizabeth sitting at its helm and with the mythological semi-goddess Europa on the bull in the water alongside. An unusual map of the Virgo Europa – with Spain still her crowned head, but Italy now holding a scepter in her right hand – rides the continent in the shape of a woman on a bull in a 1588 pamphlet published by Michael Eitzinger at Cologne, the same year that he saw a new edition of his *De Leone Belgico* through the press (Figure 7.8).

The Greek myth of the Rape of Europa carried off by Zeus in the form of a bull, as told by Ovid (*Metamorphoses* 2: 833–875), was a popular subject in Renaissance art. While Dürer's drawing (*c.* 1495) and paintings by Titian (*c.* 1559–62) and Veronese (*c.* 1570) may be the most well-known examples, there were some 40 paintings of this theme in the fifteenth and sixteenth centuries, and even a bronze sculpture *c.* 1520 by the Paduan Il Riccio (Andrea Briosco) now in the Budapest Museum of Fine Arts. The British Museum has a maiolica dish *c.* 1550 with the scene painted on it, and a 1580s painted stucco relief is in Bucovice (Butschowitz) Castle near Brno in Moravia. The drama and pathos of the abduction may tempt us to read the myth anachronistically with marriage by abduction unwanted and violent, but, at a time of familial control and arranged marriage, the image confirmed an alternative mode of attaining one's desire by either or both partners, as the hopeful expressions of many a triumphantly rendered Europa suggest. Above all, we should remember that the myth does not end with the flight to Crete; rather, the abduction leads to new story threads. The search for Europa by Phoenix and her other brothers, the marriage of her brother Cadmus to Harmony, the founding of Thebes by Cadmus, Europa as queen and mother of Crete, Europa's three sons by Zeus – Minos, king of Crete and later a judge in the underworld; Rhadamonthus, one of the judges in the underworld along with his brother Minos; and Sarpedon, king of Lycia in Asia Minor – as well as the sacred bull himself, are all ancient, generative myths that lie at the foundation of civilization, power, and authority in this world and the next. The story does not disappear or dissipate over time, but seventeenth- and eighteenth-century art counts 84 works in Italy, 39 in the Netherlands, 47 in France, and 15 in Germany.

The influence of the visual arts went beyond the printed map and the painted or sculpted object to ritual practice in public displays that reached a wide audience in city streets and squares. Festivals around Europe had been incorporating the theme of Habsburg rule over the continents and Europe Crowned Queen of the Four Parts of the World from the mid-sixteenth century. Antwerp, which had become the great port for the Portuguese Asian trade and center of a significant publishing, engraving, and map-making enterprise, had numerous such live performances of Europa and her sister continents. In 1549, Antwerp greeted the royal entry of Charles V and his son Prince Philip on their visit to the emperor's ancestral home with

Figure 7.8 Michael Eitzinger. *De Europae virginis, tauro insidentis, topographica atque historica descriptione* (Cologne: Godefridum Kempensem, 1588). Austrian National Library, Vienna: E27.766-C.

homage from actors representing the three Old World continents, but not America. In 1564 during Antwerp's annual July "Ommegang" festival, the Four Continents were represented in a tableau vivant. And in 1594, the entry of Archduke Ernst saw the Four Parts of the World on the skirt of the female figure of Spain represented with Austria and the Low Countries in an allegorical painting of the Habsburg states. In Portugal itself in 1619, the guild of Lisbon merchants sponsored a four-fronted arch with each front representing a continent for the royal entry of Philip III; again in 1623 for the canonization celebration of St Ignatius Loyola, Lisbon had four ambassadors from the Four Parts of the World pay homage. In another canonization celebration for St Ignatius, albeit in much humbler circumstances in the provincial town of Pont à Mousson in Lorraine, local Jesuits also included a Four Continents display. In Florence, the obsequies for the death of Philip II in 1598 included paintings of the Four Continents in the church of San Lorenzo and mourning figures of them in Santa Croce; as similarly in Naples for the same obsequies in its Duomo, Domenico Fontana designed a commemorative mausoleum centerpiece whose four corners each had niches to shelter statues of the four continents. Later in Naples in 1639 to celebrate the birth of the Spanish infanta, Maria Theresa (Philip IV's eldest daughter and the future wife of Louis XIV), an elaborate viceregal celebration centered around a new play performed for the occasion, the *Rapimento d'Europa*. The ideas that printing had spread were made real in festival drama, paintings, and statues. Thus, long after the event, Franz Francken's 1636 painting, *Allegory on the Abdication of Charles V in Brussels*, was able to recreate the 1556 abdication ceremony of the emperor at Brussels with Crowned Europe leading the continents in their homage.

Cartographers and their inventions were well known to the great writers of the sixteenth century and references to Europa as the demi-goddess carried off to Crete or as queen of the continents can be found in a wide linguistic range. Francesco Colonna's Latin *Hypnerotomachia Poliphili* extolled the Ovidian tradition of the Rape of Europa. In combining the myth and the parts of the world together, Rabelais has Pantagruel, commenting on the Virgilian lottery (Bk. 3, Chap. 12), deliver a paean to Jupiter, who "bulled, and lastauriated in one day the third part of the world, beasts and people, floods and mountains; that was Europa." Later Frère John finds Panurge's beard to look like a map of the world with Asia, Africa, and Europe (Bk. 3, Chap. 28), and likewise Pantagruel swearing an oath on his honor invokes the three continents, "nothing greater could I stake even were I sole and peaceful ruler in Europe, Africa, and Asia" (Bk. 3, Chap. 46). In the *Lusiads*, Camoens praises Europe as "the home of strong and warlike peoples" and "more advanced and more renowned in its governance than the others." In his poetry Ronsard emphasizes that despite her small size Europe still rules the world. Shakespeare refers to the Rape of Europa three times, and to Europe the continent ten times with two general meanings – by way of extent in space, such as "JACK FALSTAFF with my familiars, JOHN with my brothers and sisters, and SIR JOHN with all Europe" (*Henry IV, Part II*, II, 2) and "Whose bloody deeds shall make all Europe quake" (*Henry VI, Part I*, I, 1), or as a superlative, "It is the best horse of Europe" (*Henry V*, III, 7) and "Thou hast slain the flower of Europe for his chivalry" (*Henry VI, Part III*, II, 1). Commenting on the illusions of the theater in *Don Quixote* (Pt. I, Chap. 48), Cervantes refers to contemporary disregard for the dramatic unity of place, with plays having their first act open in Europe, the second in Asia, the third in Africa, and if there were a fourth, in America. Nevertheless, poets such as John Donne in "The Second Anniversary" found the ability to traverse the boundless globe in a couplet irresistible, "The Westerne treasure, Easterne spicerie, / Europe, and Afrique, and the unknown rest." In his essay "On Cannibals," where one finds his lone use of the word "Europe" as a geographical expression with Africa and Asia, Montaigne castigated the topographers for their lying exaggerations: "would they make detailed accounts of the places which they had actually been to. But because they have the advantage of visiting Palestine, they were want to enjoy the right of telling us tales about all the rest of the world." In such examples from the sixteenth-century canon in Latin and the French, Portuguese, English, and Spanish vernaculars, Europe is everywhere in the imaginative literature of the Renaissance.

Renaissance writing on politics and society looked to Aristotle's *Politics* as their starting point. Aristotle had contrasted the peoples of Europe and Asia from the Greek experience resisting the Persian invasions. For Aristotle (*Politics* 1327b), Europeans were spirited but lacked intelligence and skill, while Asians were the opposite – they lacked spirit but were intelligent and inventive. The result was that Europeans kept their freedom, but lacked political organization and could not rule others; Asians, on the contrary, were always in subjugation and slavery to their rulers. And of course, his Greeks, in between Europe and Asia, constituted, in all their attributes, the perfect mean. Medieval scholastics reasserted the dichotomy between European freedom and Asian despotism, a topos that Machiavelli's insights reaffirmed with his characteristic twist. In *The Prince* (Chap. 4), Machiavelli compares government in Turkey and France. His knowledge of Ottoman administration allows him to use their own word "sanjaks" (*sangiachi*) to identify Turkish political districts and to conclude that the difference between the king of France and the sultan *vis-à-vis* their subjects makes the state of the Turk difficult to conquer but, once conquered, easy to hold; whereas France would be easy to conquer but difficult to hold. In the *Art of War* (Bk. 2), Machiavelli extends Aristotle's argument on Europeans and Asians to the three continents by explaining why there have been many famous warriors in Europe, few in Africa, and still fewer in Asia. For Machiavelli "these two parts of the world have had one or two princes and few republics, but Europe alone has had several kingdoms and infinite republics." Because excellent men of *virtù* derive from their ruler, "it follows that where there are many rulers many valiant men arise; where few, few." Rivalry between states breeds warlike men of military *virtù*.

Thinking more about peace than war, Andrés Laguna, a Castillian born in Segovia with a medical degree from Bologna, published his *Europa εαυτην τιμωρουμένη hoc est misere se discrucians suamque calamitatem deplorans* ("Discourse on Europe") in Cologne in 1543 under the influence of Erasmus's *Querela Pacis* (*Complaint of Peace*), which in 1517 had not used the word "Europe." The title page of Laguna's treatise announces "This lugubrious declamation was delivered at a funeral ceremony at the Faculty of Arts of the University of Cologne . . . on Sunday 22 January 1543." Cologne was a "holy city" that boasted of the relics of the three Magi (who had become associated with the three continents – Balthazar, Africa; Melchior, Asia; and Caspar, Europe) and the inscription and cult of St Ursula and her 11,000 martyred companions (whose legend recounted their three-year, pan-European voyage and pilgrimage from England to Cologne, Basel, and eventually Rome). In Erasmian manner, Laguna's speaker not only eulogizes the deceased by describing her recent unhappy and pallid visage, but even calls upon her to appear and speak. Europa is presented in terms of the traditional organic metaphor of a body, whose head is the pope and the various Christian states its members. But the disease of war has ravaged her body and only the good doctor's remedy of peace between the Christian states can restore her to life. Some 25 years after Erasmus's *Complaint of Peace*, where Peace speaks of Christian division and the need to fight the real enemy, Turkey, sectarian differences have split Germany, religious war has wracked the continent, and in the most recent outbreak of war between Francis I and Charles V the French have allied themselves with the Turks. Laguna, who had earlier written a "Voyage to Turkey," knew well that the incompatibility between Erasmian peace and the inevitability of the emperor's military campaigns was much greater and more dangerous for Europe than at the time of Erasmus's lament over the unity of Christianity.

The Dutch Revolt from Spanish Habsburg rule that constituted an Eighty Years War (1568–1648) of secession had a ceasefire in 1609 that established a Twelve-Year Truce until 1621, when hostilities arose again in the European-wide fighting between 1618 and 1648 called the Thirty Years War. War and peace in the context of the renewed religious warfare of the late sixteenth through mid-seventeenth centuries again stimulated writers with pan-European perspectives. Johannes Althusius, a German Calvinist with a law degree from Basel, published *Politica methodice digest* (Herborn in Nassovia, 1603) that saw eight editions and was the first great theoretical work on federalism based upon the idea that all human politics and society were a symbiotics/symbiosis or "the art of living together." In reference to the peacemaking ambassador Cineas in Plutarch's life of Pyrrhus of Epirus, Emeric Crucé, a Parisian humanist in the Erasmian tradition, published *Le Nouveau Cynée ou Discours d'Estat* (Paris, 1623), which was the first call for a lasting peace in Europe through general alliances between nations in a kind of united nations that would meet in Venice under the leadership of the pope. The Duke of Sully, Maximilien de Béthune, a Huguenot treasurer of Henry IV, published *Le grand dessein de Henri IV* (Amsterdam [but really from retirement at his chateau], 1638), which proposed pragmatic peace recognizing the three dominant religions of Catholicism, Calvinism, and Lutheranism as established fact and identifying the permanent major states that would send representatives to a European senate. Jan Amos Comenius (Komenský) was a Protestant exile philosopher, theologian, and educator from Moravia, whose universal peace proposals from 1633 to 1638 would establish a confederation of states founded on the science of the education of Europe and were collected in his *Opera Didactica Omnia* (Amsterdam, 1657). Both sides, but especially the minority Protestants, were active in peace and confederation proposals during the seventeenth-century religious wars.

From the time of the Peace of Lodi in 1454, diplomacy among the Italian states had meant a balance of power and the establishment of resident ambassadors to keep the peace and protect themselves from the great powers of France and Turkey. The French invasions of Italy in 1494 precipitated a centuries-long struggle between France and Spain for dominance in Europe. As the Spanish star rose with union of the crowns of Aragon and Castile in 1469 and their new-found wealth in the New World, the marriage of the eldest daughter of Ferdinand and Isabella to the Habsburg Holy Roman Emperor Maximilian's son gave them a grandson, Charles, born in Ghent in 1500, who was to inherit the largest empire in Europe since the fall of Rome. With his American holdings, moreover, he was able to create a new world order around the dynastic union. In the diplomatic precedence practiced at courts, which recognized a semi-official hierarchy of the four European crowns – Holy Roman Emperor, King of the Romans, King of France, King of Spain – the union of emperor and Spanish king in the person of Charles V subordinated France to Spain. Theory was reinforced in fact with the Spanish victory in Italy (at Pavia in 1525, the Sack of Rome in 1527, and his crowning as emperor at Bologna in 1530) and in France (at St Quentin in 1557 and the subsequent Treaty of Cateau-Cambrésis in 1559). But the failure of Charles to pass his dynastic holdings undivided to his son Philip in 1556 meant that the Spanish king was no longer the German emperor and, consequently, theoretically inferior in diplomatic status to the defeated French Valois dynasty, a fact that the Spanish were able to contest because of the reality of their power. With Spanish power on the wane in the mid-seventeenth century after the Thirty Years War, Philip IV had to renounce these pretensions to priority to Louis XIV in 1662. The rise and fall of the Spanish Habsburgs in Europe fits roughly within the arc of the long sixteenth century, and their rivalry with France was the driving force behind the diplomatic theorizing about the idea of Europe.

The representation of Europe as more than a mere geographical expression had gained momentum in these 200 years as ideas and images of Europe – in sets of twos, groups of threes, and then quartered in fours – reinforced one another. Binary logic had divided the world by directions (north/south, east/west); by zones (habitable/inhabitable, temperate/antipodes); by peoples (civilized/barbaric, democratic/despotic, free/slave); by caste and class (patrician/plebian, haves/have-nots). Trinities of space and time had created typologies of place (the three sister continents, the three brothers who were sons of Noah, the three Magi) and habits of history around the three rings of religion (Judaism, Christianity, Islam), the three ages (ancient, medieval, modern), and the three philosophers (Aristotle, Averroes [Ibn Rushd], Aquinas). The sign of the four welcomed America to make the continents four sisters and the world four-cornered to join the four rivers of paradise, the four elements, the four winds, the four seasons, the four humors, and the four moral virtues. Numerology, iconography, and emblemology were all Renaissance games par excellence that revealed deeper, often hidden meanings.

Those meanings all pointed to power, authority, and control. The images carry a double valence of virtue and gender; the virgin queen is pure and good, strong and beneficent, triumphant and secure in war and peace. She is defined as much by her own attributes as those of her sisters; she is the opposite of nakedness, primitivism, and exoticism. Before Europe's other became the new sister of America, the exotic East of "orientalism" from Islam and Asia, as well as the danger and untamed wilds of Africa, played upon the personification of Europe. She is the goddess of power, beauty, and wisdom: a composite Juno, Aphrodite, and Athena. Her reign brings order to the world and draws abundance from the earth. And in the new world order of the Habsburg imperial project of the sixteenth century, it is Habsburg Europe that imposes her will on subjects near and far, defends and restores the Old Faith, and spreads the arts of civilization. The history of her reign is the story of those who embrace and resist her advances in the push and pull between center and periphery, imperial and local rule.

FINDING THE PRESENT IN THE PAST

Like the Renaissance idea of Italia, Europa was a geographical designation, not a political reality. Its boundaries were indeterminate and its people diverse. As for Italia, geography invented a history for Europa. Ortelius's *Parergon*, the ancient and historical map appendix to the *Theatrum*, which first began to appear with three supplementary maps in 1579, prominently announced on the foot of its first separate title page in 1595 that "Geography is the eye of history" (*Historiae Oculus Geographia*), a motto that Ortelius had included in his introduction to the original 1570 *Theatrum*. The 39 historical maps in the separately published 1624 edition constituted a sacred and classical atlas of the topography of ancient lands, biblical geography, classical history, and three particular views of "paradises" on earth. Geography incorporated history in a narrative exposition of such historically provocative comparisons as that posed by "A Geographical Map of the Old World" (*Aevi Veteris, Typus Geographicus*), first published in 1590. It presents "the entire geography known to the ancients until the salutary year 1492" centered in the much larger, contemporary world map. Small round maps of the four continents rim its corners and "spectator(s)" can see a juxtaposition of past and present knowledge, with the highlighted Old World centered, yet dwarfed, in the expanse of ocean.

Among Ortelius's ancient maps, Europe itself is discovered first in 1579 among the three original *Parergon* maps in an "Image of the Roman Empire" (*Romani Imperii Imago*) with "a short account of the origins, development, and culmination of the Roman Empire" and a genealogical tree of the seven Roman kings – "all shown on this map for the benefit of those studying history." It had previously appeared in a separate publication in 1571. But Ortelius created such maps less for the study of history than for the making of history. A map added in 1595, "Europe, or Old Celtica" (*Europam, sive Celticam*), is "a new map of ancient Europe" and based on classical sources – Hecataeus of Miletus, Pliny, Pomponius Mela, Ptolemy, Strabo, and Dionysius of Alexandria. It uses the same base map as that for the Roman Empire and shows the continental unity of the land of the Celtae from Iberia to Russia. The northern coast of Russia along the Barents and Kara seas is inaccurate, especially around the Urals and the mouth of the River Ob, which, nevertheless, has a legend showing Ortelius's attempts at accuracy: "In ancient times it was thought that through this river mouth the Caspian sea empties itself." If the far reaches of Tartaria had not yet been mapped, Ortelius's attention to the best available information is impressive, with the Ob, Volga, and Don forming the eastern border of Europe with Asia. From the middle of the fifteenth century, the geographical and ethnographical division between Europe and Asia and the distant European East of Scythia, Sarmatia, Ruthenia, the state of Moscow, and Kievan Rus had been of central concern to educated Eastern European elites, such as the Poles Jan Długosz (1415–80), Jan of Głogów (1455–1507), and Maciej of Miechów (1457–1523). And even if Ortelius shows the imaginary Isles of the Blessed ("Fortunatae insulae") in the top left above the British Isles rather than off Africa in the Canaries as Europe's traditional western border, the dreams of bliss that they promised might still be hoped for. Legends from the ancient geographers may have been slow to die, but the visualization of new constructs such as Celtic Europe fueled the imagination of a common continental history.

From a place, continental maps created a people. After Gerardus and Cornelis de Jode's 1593 *Nova Totius Europae Tabula* portrayed 20 "costumed men and wives," including even a scantily clad African, soldiers from Turkey and Persia, and women from Turkey and Macedonia in a cartouche, many seventeenth-century mapmakers continued to decorate the borders of their maps of Europe with natives dressed in traditional regional costumes. Such a Europe was not a binary world of civilized and barbarian, us versus them, but a much more nuanced and complex world that included male and female couples from every corner of the continent, such as Hondius-Jansson's 1623 *Nova Europae descriptio* with its English, French, Belgian, Castilian, Venetian, German, Hungarian, Bohemian, Polish, and Greek husbands and wives. National consciousness and rivalries were at play, creating a European identity from its constituent parts.

Over the course of the long sixteenth century, Europeans traveled around the world and into the past literally and literarily to find themselves; the last three plates in Ortelius's 1624 *Parergon* reproduce earthly paradises to provide rest and recreation from their page-turning journeys in print: "After this long and tedious peregrination over the whole world, I should think of some place to rest, where exhausted students, faint and wearied by their long and tiring journeys might recreate themselves." Two of the three plates present paradises lost: Tempe of Thessaly at the foot of Mount Olympus where "people dwell . . . meet in companies . . . and having done divine service and ceremonies in due form and manner, they banquet and make merry," and Daphne, a pleasant suburb of Antioch in Syria, which Apollo, "preferring it above all other places in the world, honoured and graced more than ever any other." The third of these earthly paradises, the *Parergon's* last plate, first appeared in the *Theatrum* in 1601 and reproduced an earlier 1591 engraving of El Escorial, the palace of Ortelius's patron Philip II, set above a 36-line poem by Michael van der Hagen of Antwerp. The text lauds Philip himself, "the greatest Ruler of the Occident," and the Spanish king's colossal construction of the college–church–monastery–palace as exceeding the seven wonders of the ancient world. The trajectory of Spanish Habsburg power in the sixteenth century had forged such "glory," "honor," "riches," and "splendor" that defied mortal thoughts and words, one of the "paradises" on earth. "Who can match the King, and Spain?" From Antwerp within his realm, all praise continued to flow, with calls that his "great Power continue to grow." While from across the rivers in Holland or from outside his kingdoms in France, England, and Electoral Saxony, a different Europe grew.

When 12 new states entered the European Union on May 1, 2004, to change the balance of power and broaden the ideological and practical project of debate and politics maturing since the Second World War, a new chapter in the invention of Europe was put in play. Much as in the Renaissance, objective truths and subjective myths, universalist ambitions and local realities once again look to the past to reinvent the present. The dispute between the Greeks and Italians on where to establish the European Union's capital – Athens or Rome – is not so much a battle for clout and patronage as it is over the meaning and origins of Europe as a democratic or imperial federation. Similarly, the papacy's attempts to make the European constitution acknowledge the role of Christianity, expansion of the union to former Soviet states in the east such as Ukraine and Georgia, or division over the admission of Turkey reflect the ever-evolving questions: What is Europe, both spatially and temporally? What does it mean to be European, both politically and culturally? Is there continuity with Europe's history in its present unification or is there a disjunction between Europe's past and its present course?

The invention of today's Europe is a continual process of rediscovering common values as much as markets, of finding Europe before as much as after nationalism, and of returning to the radical, self-conscious identity-formation begun in the Renaissance. Today's Europe is an idea and an ideal born of hope in the ashes of war that Europeans could resolve to stop consuming themselves. Yet, it is a Europe still threatened by the bitter fruits of militant colonial conquest and by the fearful betrayals from crusading religious fervor begun in the Renaissance quest to rule the four corners of the world. If Europe is to exorcise its inner demons that still reject the other because (with Montaigne's irony) "they do not wear pants" or (in today's French secularism) they do wear scarves, Europe will have to discover how history is the heart and soul of geography, and that multi-culturalism is not political correctness but historical fact. Pariah peoples such as Jews, Armenians, and gypsies have been essential participants in European development; Turks in the Balkans and around the Black Sea integral actors in modern European history and culture; and Asians, Africans, and Americans critical, if often coerced, contributors to the material and ideological making of Europe. From the time of the old continent's rebirth in the Renaissance, history has invented Europe's future.

SUGGESTIONS FOR FURTHER READING

Abulafia, David and Nora Berend (eds). *Medieval Frontiers: Concepts and Practices*. Aldershot: Ashgate, 2002.

Boer, Pim den. "Europe to 1914: The Making of an Idea," in Kevin Wilson and Jan van der Dussen (eds) *The History of the Idea of Europe*. Milton Keynes: Open University and London: Routledge, rev. edn 1995: 13–82.

Boorsch, Suzanne. "America in Festival Presentations," in Fredi Chiappelli (ed.) *First Images of America*, 2 vols. Berkeley: University of California Press, 1976, 1: 503–15.

Borri, Roberto. *L'Europa nell'antica cartografia*. Ivrea: Priuli & Verlucca, editori, 2001.

Broecke, M. P. R. van den. http://orteliusmaps.com/ort_background.html 2002.

Broecke, Marcel van den, Peter van der Krogt, and Peter Meurer (eds). *Abraham Ortelius and the First Atlas. Essays Commemorating the Quadricentennial of his Death, 1598–1998*. Goy-Houten (Utrecht): HES Publishers, 1998.

Buisseret, D. *The Mapmakers' Quest: Depicting New Worlds in Renaissance Europe*. Oxford and New York: Oxford University Press, 2003.

Chabod, Federico. *Storia dell'idea d'Europa*. Bari: Laterza, 1962.

Curcio, Carlo. *Europa: Storia di un'idea*. Turin: ERI, 1978.
Dürst, Fred. "The Map of Europe," in Marcel Watelet (ed.) *The Mercator Atlas of Europe*. Pleasant Hill, Oreg.: Walking Tree Press, 1997: 31–41.
Fagiolo dell'Arco, M. "Le forme dell'effimero," in F. Zeri (ed.) *Storia dell'arte italiana, pt. 3: Situazioni momenti indagini*. Vol. 4: *Forme e modelli*. Turin: Giulio Einaudi, 1982: 203–35.
Geremek, Bronisław. *The Common Roots of Europe*, trans. Jan Aleksandrowicz, J. K. Fedorowicz, R. Hunt, A. Kolakowska, and S. Mitchell. Cambridge: Polity Press, 1996.
Goffart, Walter. *Historical Atlases: The First Three Hundred Years, 1570–1870*. Chicago and London: University of Chicago Press, 2003.
Hale, John R. *The Civilization of Europe in the Renaissance*. New York: Atheneum, 1994.
Hamon, D. and I. S. Keller. *Fondements et étapes de la construction européenne*. Paris: Presses Universitaires de France, 1997.
Harley, J. B. and David Woodward. *The History of Cartography*. Vol. 1: *Cartography in Prehistoric, Ancient, and Medieval Europe and the Mediterranean*. Chicago: University of Chicago Press, 1987: 266–75 and 281–501.
Hay, D. *Europe: The Emergence of an Idea*. Edinburgh: Edinburgh University Press, 1957.
Heffernan, Michael J. *The Meaning of Europe: Geography and Geopolitics*. London and New York: Arnold, 1998.
Heijden, H. A. M. van der. *De oudste gedrukte kaarten van Europa*. Alphen aan den Rijn: Canaletto, 1992.
Le Goff, Jacques. *Europe est-elle née au moyen âge*, trans. Janet Lloyd. *The Birth of Europe*. Malden, Mass.: and Oxford: Blackwell Publishing, 2005.
Levin, Michael J. "A New World Order: The Spanish Campaign for Precedence in Early Modern Europe." *Journal of Early Modern History* 6, 3 (2002): 233–64.
Lopez, Roberto S. *Naissance de l'Europe*. (Trans. *The Birth of Europe*.) New York: M. Evans, 1967.
Marino, John A. "Celebrating a Royal Birth in 1639: The Rape of Europa in the Neapolitan Viceroy's Court." *Rinascimento* (2004): 53–67.
Mikkeli, Heikki. *Europe as an Idea and an Identity*. New York: St Martin's Press, 1998.
Pagden, Anthony (ed.). *The Idea of Europe: From Antiquity to the European Union*. Washington, DC: Woodrow Wilson Center Press and Cambridge/New York: Cambridge University Press, 2002.
Power, Daniel and Naomi Standen (eds) *Frontiers in Question: Eurasian Borderlands, 700–1700*. Basingstoke and New York: Macmillan Press/St Martin's Press, 1999.
Prosperi, Adriano. "Europa 'in forma Virginis': aspetti della propaganda asburgica del '500." *Annali dell'Istituto storico italo-germanico in Trento* 19: 243–75; reprinted in *America e Apocalisse e altri saggi*, Pisa and Rome: Istituti editoriali e poligrafici internazionali, 1999: 127–52.
Rak, Michele. "A dismisura d'uomo: Feste e spettacolo del barocco napoletano," in Marcello Fagiolo (ed.) *Gian Lorenzo Bernini e le arti visive*. Rome: Istituto della Enciclopedia Italiana fondata da G. Treccani, 1987: 259–312.
Redondo, Agustin. "El *Discurso sobre Europa* del doctor Laguna (Colonia, 1543), entre amargura y esperanza," in J. Martínez Millán (ed.) *Carlos V y la quiebra del humanismo politico en Europa (1530–1558)*, 3 vols. Madrid: Sociedad Estatal para la Conmemoración de los Centenarios de Felipe II y Carlos V, 3: 261–75.
Romano, Sergio. *Europa: Storia di un'idea dall'Impero all'Unione*. Milan: Longanesi, 2004.
Swerdlow, N. M. "The Recovery of the Exact Sciences of Antiquity: Mathematics, Astronomy, Geography," in Anthony Grafton (ed.) *Rome Reborn: The Vatican Library and Renaissance Culture*. Washington, DC: Library of Congress, 1993: 125–67; esp. 158–64.

Waldseemüller, Martin. *Carta itineraria Europae*, facs. edn of Strassburg, 1520. Bonn: Kirschbaum Verlag, 1972.

Wintle, Michael. "Europe's Image: Visual Representations of Europe from the Earliest Times to the Twentieth Century," in M. Wintle (ed.) *Culture and Identity in Europe: Perceptions of Divergence and Unity in Past and Present*. Aldershot: Avebury, 1996: 52–97.

—— "Renaissance Maps and the Construction of the Idea of Europe." *Journal of Historical Geography* 25, 2 (1999): 137–65.

Woodward, David. *"The Four Parts of the World": Giovanni Francesco Camocio's Wall Maps*. Minneapolis: James Ford Bell Lectures, no. 34, Associates of the James Ford Bell Library, 1997.

—— "Reality, Symbolism, Time, and Space in Medieval World Maps." *Annals of the Association of American Geographers* 75, 4 (1985): 510–21.

CHAPTER EIGHT

JOSÉ DE ACOSTA

Renaissance historiography and
New World humanity

Anthony Grafton

José de Acosta, S.J. (1540–1600) became famous in a richly human way, for writing about a shiver and a laugh. Early in Book Two of his *Natural and Moral History of the Indies*, which appeared in 1590, he described how his experiences on the way to the New World had taught him to see even the greatest ancient writers as fallible human beings:

> I shall tell you what happened to me when I went to the Indies. As I had read the exaggerations of the philosophers and poets, I was convinced that when I reached the equator I would not be able to bear the dreadful heat; but the reality was so different that at the very time I was crossing it I felt such cold that at times I went out into the sun to keep warm, and it was the time of year when the sun is directly overhead, which is in the sign of Aries, in March. I will confess here that I laughed and jeered at Aristotle's meteorological theories and his philosophy, seeing that in the very place where, according to his rules, everything must be burning and on fire, I and all my companions were cold.[1]

Acosta's declaration of independence from Aristotle made his work a favorite of such quintessentially modern readers as Francis Bacon, who learned from him to see that the Greeks had been far less cosmopolitan than modern Europeans.

The intellectual innovators who made this massive, pious book by a dedicated Jesuit a solid seller, not only in Spain and Italy but also in the most advanced cities of northern Europe, from London and Enkhuisen to Frankfurt and Oppenheim, were not misrepresenting Acosta when they saw him as a proponent of modernity. He made clear, at more than one point in his work, that he did not regard the Greek and Roman texts as a full and perfect body of knowledge. New World nature, for example, included many wonders that even the most learned ancients had not known. Modern writers like Francisco Hernandez (1515–87), who wrote from direct experience, offered rich information about these splendidly varied and useful flora: "it is a wonderful thing," Acosta commented,

> to see so many differences in shape and taste and properties never before known and heard of in the world before the discovery of the Indies, and of which Pliny

and Dioscorides and Theophrastus and other scholars achieved no knowledge despite their diligence and curiosity. In our day there has been no lack of inquiring men who have written treatises on these plants of the Indies and on grasses and roots and their properties and the medicines extracted from them, who may be consulted by anyone who wishes a more complete knowledge of these matters.[2]

While many of Acosta's learned contemporaries pulled and stretched Plato's account of Atlantis, in order to prove that this greatest of ancient philosophers had known about the New World, Acosta dismissed such efforts:

These writers are so convinced by Plato that they treat his writings as if they were the books of Moses or Esdras, and where Plato's words do not conform to truth they insist that it all has to be understood in a mystical and allegorical sense and can be nothing else. To tell the truth, I have no such reverence for Plato no matter how divine they call him . . . What I find obvious is that everything he says about that island, beginning with the dialogue of Timaeus and continuing to the dialogue of Critias, cannot be told as truth except to children and old women.[3]

Acosta, moreover, made clear from the start of his work that much of what he offered readers came from his own first-hand observation:

Those who sail to these parts nowadays are wont to write splendid things about this heaven, namely, that it is very brilliant and has many and very large stars. Indeed, remote things are often described with exaggeration, but I think the contrary, and consider it obvious that there are more stars on the northern side and that they are greater. Nor do I see any stars here that are brighter than the Little Bear and the Great Bear.[4]

And he did not hesitate to argue that the practical men who navigated the world could impart vital information about nature and its properties. In describing the behavior and properties of the compass, for example, he repeated what he had learned from a "very skilled pilot, a Portuguese," who had described how the needle "northeasts, that is, inclines towards the east," as his ship moved towards the equator. Learned men could not offer crisp, factual information of this kind, nor could their philosophical training help to explain them:

For my part I would gladly ask university graduates, who presume to know so much, what this can be, and would have them tell me the cause of this effect: why a bit of iron, after being rubbed on a lodestone, acquires the virtue of always pointing north, and this with such a skill that it knows the different climes and places in the world where it will be fixed and where it must lean to one side or the other, for there is no philosopher or cosmographer who knows it so well.[5]

The compass itself – to say nothing of the pilots who read it – knew more, Acosta argues, than the erudite schoolmen with their passion for devising elaborate, book-based causal explanations.

Yet Acosta's ways of dealing with older authorities were more complex than his often-quoted claims to possess new knowledge suggest. In the same passage in which he mocked those who still followed Aristotle and believed that the Torrid Zone was uninhabitable, Acosta pieced together a neat little mosaic of evidence from multiple texts – Roman, imperial-age Greek, and Islamic – to show that other ancient and medieval writers had not shared Aristotle's erroneous belief:

> Pliny places Taprobana, or Sumatra as it is now called, under the equator, as indeed it is, and says of it that it is not only rich and prosperous but heavily populated with men and beasts. From this we may understand that, although the ancients considered the heat of the Torrid Zone to be intolerable, they did realize that it was not as uninhabitable as they represented it. The excellent astronomer and cosmographer Ptolemy and the famous philosopher and physician Avicenna came much closer to the truth, for both believed that there were very moderate dwelling places under the equator.[6]

More generally, Acosta also made clear that he could explain why even the greatest ancient authorities had sometimes gone wrong. Every thinker wrote at a particular time and place, within a particular context, and this setting imposed limitations on what they could know and say.

In some cases the limitations were simple and factual. Aristotle "must be pardoned for" his error about the Torrid Zone,

> for in his time only the first part of Ethiopia, which is known as the exterior part, had been discovered; it is near Arabia and Africa. The other, interior Ethiopia was not known in his time, nor had he any knowledge of that immense territory located where the lands of Prester John now are, and still less had they knowledge of the rest of the land that is below the equator and continues until it passes the tropic of Capricorn and ends in the Cape of Good Hope, so well known and famous thanks to the Portuguese navigations.[7]

In other cases, however, context meant something more complex: the whole matrix of assumptions, interests, and beliefs within which every author lived and worked. Augustine, Acosta observed, could not contemplate for a second the idea that a continent on the side of the world opposite to his might be inhabited. The explanation for his blindness lay not simply in the limits of man's power to know the truth, but in the strength of the biblical tradition. Augustine envisioned the history of humanity, exactly as the Old Testament presented it, as the descent of a race from a single couple. He could not imagine the existence of a populated continent not connected by land to Europe, Asia, and Africa:

> Surely his motive was taken from the innermost parts of sacred theology, through which Holy Writ teaches us that all mankind descends from the first

man, who was Adam. Therefore, to say that men were able to pass over to the New World by crossing that infinite expanse of the Ocean Sea seemed an incredible thing and completely nonsensical.[8]

Like the Victorian scientist T. H. Huxley, who described the collision of a fine theory with a fact it could not accommodate as the greatest of tragedies, Acosta appreciated just how solid and weighty a fact had to be before it could destroy a theory as compelling as the one on which Augustine reared his Christian philosophy of history: "And, indeed, if palpable events and the experience of what we have seen in our own time had not opened our eyes, this reasoning would have been considered irrefutable to the present day."[9]

Acosta, in other words, did not simply reject the ancients *en bloc*. He wove a complex tapestry, a rich and colorful representation of the New World and its peoples. In it many ancient authorities appeared again and again. Some came in for criticism, but more of them supplied vital elements of structure, style, and explanation. Pliny the Elder, for all his ignorance of New World flora and fauna, provided the most useful of the lasts on which Acosta formed his book. Like his Roman predecessor, the modern Jesuit set the story of human action against a richly recreated geographical, geological, zoological, and botanical background – one that embedded human life in a natural context but also called attention to the many ways in which humans had transformed the natural world. Acosta's title called attention to this debt, since Pliny had labeled his great book a *Natural History* – even as it declared that Acosta was also doing something Pliny had not attempted.

What enabled Acosta to tack so adroitly, not only between ancient texts and modern experience but also among the ancient texts themselves, was his mastery of a particular set of historical and philological techniques. When he insisted that Aristotle could not have known about certain parts of the landmass of the earth, and that Augustine's narrow-mindedness could be understood only by working one's way into his vision of the cosmic and human past, he applied tools that generations of Renaissance humanists before him had forged and honed. The long effort to purge understandings of the past of anachronism that began with Petrarch and his contemporaries had yielded, for some thinkers at least, a new and cogent understanding that the past was a foreign country – one whose inhabitants had dressed and thought, as well as spoken and written, in ways radically different from contemporary Christians in Europe. This understanding underpinned Lorenzo Valla's brilliant demonstration that the *Donation of Constantine*, the eighth-century charter for papal monarchy in the Western Empire, could not have been written in the fourth-century age of Constantine the Great, and Erasmus's systematic efforts to show that Jesus and his followers had sought to create not a new theology but a new form of community and a new kind of moral life.[10]

No one adopted the techniques of humanistic education and scholarship more enthusiastically than Ignatius Loyola and the other founders of the Jesuit order. They made the order's colleges brilliantly successful centers for training in the disciplines of humanism, and required ambitious young Jesuits to master, and then to teach, philology and history in the early stages of their careers. And they emphasized the teaching of practical subjects, like cosmography, as an integral part of the curriculum.

Acosta himself, a famous master of classical oratory, served in and founded Jesuit colleges across the enormous province of Peru. It is hardly surprising, then, that humanist skills underpinned his accomplishments as a historian, or that he found it possible to navigate so adroitly between ancient texts and more modern sources of information.

Recent scholarship on Acosta has concentrated, for understandable reasons, less on the resources that he found in the humanistic tradition than – rather as he might have written about Augustine – on the ways in which that tradition limited his powers of observation and fixed his point of view towards the New World and its peoples. Acosta – so Edmundo O'Gorman and Walter Mignolo have argued in powerful works – did not try to understand the inhabitants of the New World with the full contextual subtlety that his method demanded in principle, and that he showed in practice when writing about the ancient Greeks and Romans. Though he drew his information on the New World, ultimately, from the records kept by native inhabitants, he did not take them as historians in their own right or as his equals, and build his account from theirs. Rather, as Acosta explained in his description of his use of informants, he had

> resorted to experienced men who were very knowledgeable in these matters, and from their conversation and abundant written works I was able to extract material that I judged sufficient to write of the customs and deeds of those people and of the natural phenomena of those lands and their characteristics.[11]

He meant not that he had consulted Indians or the records that they had inscribed in codices, but rather that he had consulted European authorities or their works: the histories compiled by Polo Onegardo, antiquary and student of Peruvian tradition, and Juan de Tovar, a fellow Jesuit and an expert on the Mexican past.[12] As to the codices, with their hieroglyphic records of Inca and Aztec traditions, Acosta dismissed them as inferior records, not comparable in precision or reliability to European written records: "But because their figures and characters were not as adequate as those of our writing and letters, this meant that they could not make the words conform exactly but could only express the essential part of ideas."[13] Here – as in his rejection of Indian religion as mere "idolatry" and his failure to grasp the qualities of New World architecture and other technologies – Acosta revealed not personal failings, or personal failings only, but the larger blindness of the humanistic tradition. No wonder, then, that in recent years scholars have chiefly sought to read Acosta's texts, like other writings of Jesuits on peoples outside Europe, "against the grain" – to recover, so far as the scrutiny of authorial strategy allows, the nature of the actual contacts with Andean (or Chinese, or Indian) religion that these texts encoded in terms familiar to their European audience at the Roman heart of the Jesuit order and elsewhere.

Yet these studies, for all their merits, do not do much to insert Acosta's book and others like it into one of the contexts that shaped their form and content: the development of European historiography in the fifteenth and sixteenth centuries. Acosta made clear, from the start of his work onwards, that he regarded it as a substantial, serious work, one meant to reveal two sorts of things that earlier accounts had not: the "causes and reasons" of "natural phenomena that fall outside the philosophy formerly received and argued" and "the deeds and history of the Indians themselves." Previous writers, he noted, had lacked the "philosophy" needed to carry out the former task and the direct acquaintance with language and peoples needed to carry out the latter. By contrast, his *History*, at once profound and precise, would contribute both to the rightful praise of God's glory and to the expansion of Christianity among the Indians. In the 1570s and 1580s, the period Acosta spent in the New World, scholars across Europe – especially the Basle scholar Theodor Zwinger and his Viennese collaborator Hugo Blotius – were defining the literature of travel, a literature, ideally, founded not on books but on skillful first-hand observation, as a primary source of knowledge about society, politics, institutions, and customs. Acosta's work forms part of the same vast, doomed effort to deprovincialize Europe – an effort necessarily carried out from a European standpoint and with European tools.

Acosta attacked this project from a particular standpoint, and adopted particular methods. He set out, as we have seen, to write a history. And history, in the late 1550s and 1560s, the years of Acosta's intellectual formation, was undergoing an onslaught from brilliant revisionists across Europe, but especially in Italy and France. Writers like Francesco Patrizi, François Baudouin, and Jean Bodin argued that history needed to be recast in multiple ways if it was really to offer Europeans the profound moral and political knowledge that historians had claimed for their art since ancient times. All of them agreed, moreover, on some of the reforms that the discipline needed. History must be critical. The historian must find and use only reliable sources. This had always posed a problem, as Tacitus had pointed out, since fear, partiality, and governmental censorship obscured the truth of events even in the periods when they took place. The problem had become even more acute in the mid-sixteenth century, however, since the brilliant bad boy of European historiography, Annius of Viterbo, had published an array of attractive, but fake, narratives of Egyptian, Assyrian, and early Italian history, which he ascribed to ancient Near Eastern priests and other reliable writers and embedded in a commentary that argued for their superior reliability. Across Europe, historians and theologians worked hard to show that Annius's texts were frauds – even if one of those who did so most effectively, Ioannes Goropius Becanus, did so in the interest of his own thesis that Dutch, closely related to Scythian, had been the language spoken in the Garden of Eden. Any historian who hoped to satisfy the new criteria must know exactly what he was putting in the foundation before he began to rear the structure.

History, moreover, could not limit itself to the doings of Europeans. After all, as Baudouin pointed out:

> We cannot understand our own history unless we also know that of the barbarians. If we are French, or British, or German, or Spanish, or Italian, we cannot speak of our countrymen if we do not know the history of the Franks, the Angles, the Saxons, the Goths, the Lombards. And since our countrymen have often encountered Saracens and Turks, we dare not be ignorant of Saracen and Turkish history. We must not immediately classify as barbarous or condemn as unknown everything that is alien from our customs or from the eloquence of the Romans and the Greeks.[14]

A full knowledge of history should begin, so every theorist agreed, with the Creation of the world. Ideally, it would cover the history of all the great empires of the world: Egyptian and Assyrian; Macedonian and Roman; Turkish as well as Spanish. And it would constantly draw comparisons among the different states and periods it described. The point of studying multiple monarchies, Bodin urged, was not simply to amass facts but to work out which constitutions had proved most effective and durable for which peoples.

History, in the third place, must not confine itself to narrative. History, of course, did not refer only to the study of the human past, but to any form of empirical inquiry – natural as well as social. And even human history – so many revisionists insisted – could be understood only in a larger natural setting recreated using the tools of science. Whether the student of history set out to draw up a universal time-line for students or a monographic account of a single war, he had to use the two "eyes of history" – geography and chronology – to locate his account on larger scales in space and time. More ambitiously still, historical thinkers like Bodin insisted that human history must be located within a natural context. Drawing on traditions of medical thought that went back to the Hippocratic corpus and had been extensively developed in medieval and renaissance astrology as well as medicine, Bodin argued that climate – the climate in which each people had its origins – determined that nation's character in fundamental ways. Even those who did not agree with Bodin's theories – like the influential medical man and scholar Girolamo Cardano – agreed that climate and disease often shaped human history. Cardano and other medical men, moreover, developed their own vivid new ways of describing and explaining the course of disease in individual cases and collective outbreaks.

The Jesuits, always eager to be at the cutting edge of intellectual life, were fully aware of these developments. Just after Acosta published his *History*, another Jesuit, Acosta's near contemporary Antonio Possevino, brought out a compendium that he entitled, modestly, *A Handbook for the History of All Nations*. Possevino drew – to the point of plagiarism – on Bodin. Though he could not follow the French scholar on certain delicate points, he completely agreed that the study of history had to be both critical and cosmopolitan, and that the two ways of reading could actually reinforce one another. Like many Jesuits, Possevino had the good fortune to explore both nature and society in places far outside the central lands of western Europe. His travels revealed a world of unsuspected wonder. The first Greek historian, Herodotus, had made his earlier readers suspicious by his vivid accounts of Egyptian civilization and Scythian barbarism. Direct experience showed Possevino that the critics were wrong:

> As to the fabulous things that Herodotus is accused of inventing: first, I say that those who have never set foot in foreign lands find many things incredible. Once they have traveled in Asia, Africa, and India, they will change their opinion. It would be truthful to say that this has happened to me more than once in my European travels. For as a youth in France, reading about Gothic matters in Olaus Magnus, I thought he was relating mere dreams. When I went on a number of missions to Gotland and Sweden, many years later, I found that much that I had thought invented was true. The same thing

happened to me when I had to do with Muscovites, Tartars, and Turks. Therefore what we read in Herodotus must be weighed in a fair scale.[15]

The new history was at home in Jesuit colleges. In fact, though Possevino borrowed liberally from Bodin, he also added something of his own to the mix. Bodin drew most of his information about the natural world and about non-European societies from books, including a fair number of older compendia. Possevino, by contrast, learned about both nature and culture in the field. His travels in northern Europe and Muscovy, the latter of which he described in a vivid book of his own, had given him a salutary shock. Seeing tribesmen travel on skis, use dogs to pull sleds, and read runes, he came to think that Herodotus's descriptions of nomads were entirely plausible. Acosta's work, then, exemplified a particular Jesuit style of scholarship.

Acosta made clear, again and again, that he saw his book not only as a modern Pliny for the New World but also as a work of critical history in the new style. He began, as we have seen, by asserting that he based his text on reliable informants.[16] When he excused Aristotle and Augustine for their ignorance, he followed Bodin, who had made a similar, if more controversial, argument about Tacitus. If modern readers hoped to assess ancient sources properly, Bodin explained, they must abandon the prejudices natural to the time and place in which they lived. The great Hellenist Guillaume Budé had denounced Tacitus for writing against the Christians.[17] Bodin reversed this verdict, on historical grounds: "Tacitus acted impiously, because he was not a Christian, but he was not impious when he wrote against us, since he was bound by the pagan superstition."[18] In fact, Tacitus would have committed an impiety if he had failed to defend his own religion – especially when he was conditioned to do so by the sight of Christians and Jews, accused of abominable crimes and dragged off for punishment.[19]

More important still, Acosta followed the theorists of history in the very way in which he laid out his ambitious, comprehensive book. Traditional history – even the history of Thucydides or Polybius – was narrative rather than analytical in its basic approach to the past. The reader learned more rapidly from history than from philosophy, so the usual account went, precisely because the historian offered not precepts, which were wordy and endless, but examples of moral and prudential principles applied in action. When Thucydides felt the need to demonstrate that Greek states in periods earlier than his own were smaller and weaker than the Athens he knew, or Polybius wanted to analyze the precise role of the funeral ceremony in perpetuating the Roman state, they inserted analytical digressions that formally interrupted their histories.

The mid-sixteenth-century theorists, by contrast, saw that the forms of writing about the past instructively had multiplied in their own time. Political theorists like Machiavelli and antiquaries like Flavio Biondo had developed new ways of writing about state institutions, religious rituals, and beliefs, and the discipline of history needed to take account of – indeed, to incorporate – these new approaches. Francesco Patrizi, for example, noted that Gasparo Contarini and other political specialists "write in a certain novel way about the magistrates of the Romans and the Greeks, and others about the form of the Roman Republic, and those of the Athenians, the Lacedaemonians, the Carthaginians, and the Venetians ... This is a most useful kind of writing." Contemporary antiquaries, for their part, had taught him to see history as thick description rather than taut narrative: "Some historians have not so much described events as customs, ways of life, and laws . . . And there is another sort, those who, especially in our day, write in another way about the clothing of the Romans and the Greeks, the forms of armament they used, their ways of making camp, and their ships, their buildings, and other things of this sort, which are necessary for life."[20] The new history Patrizi called for would be cast, at least in part, in synchronic rather than diachronic form, and would concentrate as much on analysis as on narrative. Acosta's *History*, with its long passages on New World institutions, beliefs, and practices, and its substantial narratives of Inca and Aztec history, exemplified the wedding of divergent practices that the theorists had demanded. As he explained:

> because the aim of their history is not only to inform of what is happening in the Indies, but to dedicate that information to the benefit that knowledge of such things can bring, which is to help these people to their salvation . . . I will therefore first describe in the book that follows things pertaining to their religion, or superstition and rites, and idolatries and sacrifices, and then I will deal with their polity, form of government and laws, and customs and deeds.[21]

When Acosta applied the new techniques of history to the New World, then, he pushed an existing set of methods to what may well have been their limit. Naturally, he did not succeed either in understanding the Indians he knew and describing them in their own terms: that was not part of his remit, or of anyone else's in the period. Naturally, too, his historicism proved to have limits: there was much about the New World and its inhabitants that he could not, in his own view, do anything but judge (and condemn). Yet the new historians' method permitted him to say and show things about humanity, in the Old World and in the New, that previous narratives could hardly have incorporated. It also seems to have led him to make arguments that modified, in revealing ways, the programmatic statements made in his other works about the New World.

We can begin, as Acosta did, with the question of sources. His humanistic training ensured that he would take a strong interest in local languages, but not that he would master them in order to do so – any more than most of the humanists who saw Hebrew as the oldest language, the source of all the rest and the harborer of many mysteries, actually mastered Hebrew grammar and syntax. But he did try to find out, for example, if the Indians had words of their own for the objects, tools, and animals that the Spaniards had brought with them. As he explained, linguistic evidence of this kind had a special value for the history of New World culture:

> I have found this a good rule for discovering what things the Indians had before the Spaniards came and those they did not, for they gave their names to the things they already had and with which they were familiar; things that they received newly were given new names, which are usually Spanish ones, though pronounced after their fashion, like the words for horse, wine, wheat and so on.[22]

In making this point, Acosta may have drawn on Bodin, who also saw that much of history "lay buried in language" – especially in the names of peoples and places. But he also drew on a longer humanist tradition. A century and a half before his time, Valla had pointed out that the modern Latinist had to use modern words, like "horologium" for clock and "pyxis nautica" for compass, because the ancients had lacked these devices – and, accordingly, had lacked words for them.[23] Language offered a font of evidence at a point where the accounts written by Indians and Europeans alike left Acosta without the information he needed. And the fact that it could serve this purpose reveals much about how Acosta understood language itself. Each people had a stock of words, which corresponded to the things it knew; as more things became known, more words were framed to refer to them. Language, then, was a human creation – European and Indian language alike.

But Acosta also had in mind larger and more precise questions about historical method. As he admitted at the start of his *History*, he had to explain how it was at all possible for the Indians to preserve any records of their past:

> The history itself will explain how the ancient sayings and doings of the Indians have come to be known, since they had no writing like us, for it is no small part of their abilities to have been able to preserve records of ancient times even though they did not use letters of any kind.[24]

Here too he followed the critical theorists of history. In 1561, for example, Baudouin had pointed out that the Romans had preserved their early history not in writing, since the Gauls had destroyed all written records when they sacked the city, but through the banquet songs they memorized and performed, and he compared these to the songs of the ancient Germans and the modern inhabitants of the New World.[25] Possevino made clear that assessment of a historian's reliability was a primary and essential task for the critical reader – though he concentrated more on signs of piety and ecclesiastical approval than on source criticism.[26]

Acosta devoted a long section of Book Six of his *History* to the writing systems of the New World:

> Those who have tried to investigate these matters in the proper way have found many things worthy of consideration. One of the members of our Society of Jesus, a very sensible and clever man, brought together in the province of Mexico the old men of Texcoco and Tula and Mexico and conferred with them at length, and they showed him their collections of books and their histories and calendars, a sight very much worth seeing. For they had their pictures and hieroglyphs with which they represented things in the following way: things that had shapes were painted in their own image, and for things that did not have actual shapes they had characters signifying this, and hence were able to express whatever they wanted. And for a reminder of the time when each thing happened they had those painted wheels, each containing a century, which as I said before was of fifty-two years; and they painted these things beside those wheels, corresponding to the year in which memorable events occurred, using the pictures and characters I have described. For instance, by placing a picture

of a man with a red hat and jacket in the sign of the cane, which was the century at the time, they marked the year when the Spaniards came into their land; and they did the same with other events. But because their figures and characters were not as adequate as those of our writing and letters, this meant that they could not make the words conform exactly but could only express the essential part of ideas. But they also have the custom of repeating in chorus orations and speeches made by the ancient orators and rhetoricians, and many songs that their poets composed, which would have been impossible to learn through those hieroglyphs and characters . . . And I say this because some persons who read such long and elegant speeches in Mexican history will easily believe that they were invented by the Spaniards and not really composed by the Indians; but once they understand the truth they will not fail to give proper credit to the Indians' histories.[27]

This rich passage offers one of the fullest discussions of research techniques to appear in any early modern work of history, and surely the most detailed discussion ever offered of the interviewing of witnesses. It evokes fascinating scenes of collaboration between the Jesuit expert and the native wise men, who explain their codices and the ways in which they use them. Yet it also seems strained, even ambiguous. On the one hand, Acosta argues that the Indians had technical ways of preserving memories – and even of making precise records of long speeches. On the other hand, however, he also concedes that these records were "not as adequate" as European, alphabetic ones – only to insist once more on their basic integrity, where speeches were concerned.

The research and thinking that went into this section of the *History* – as Acosta himself suggested – began with an exchange of letters with Juan de Tovar that took place in 1586. In 1572, Philip II had requested a formal inquiry into the history and society of New Spain, and since 1576 Tovar had taken part in this enterprise. He provided Acosta with a substantial narrative of the history of New Spain.[28] Worried about its credibility, Acosta addressed a series of pointed questions to his fellow Jesuit. "What certainty or authority," he wanted to know, "does this narrative or history have?" How could the native inhabitants of New Spain, who did not have a system of alphabetic writing, preserve the memory of events over a long period? And how could they preserve the precise wording of the speeches of their "ancient rhetoricians"?

Tovar answered encouragingly and in detail. True, the Mexicas had used images rather than alphabetic script to record their tradition, and images were less precise than words. But their symbols had enabled them to record "all the events and memorable occurrences that they had in their histories" – that is, in their calendar wheels, and Tovar enclosed a copy of one of them. At the same time, their highly trained memories preserved their ancestors' eloquent speeches without any deviation, metaphor by metaphor and word by word. These offered a supplement to the written record – or rather, oral and written records, taken together, formed a single, reliable narrative, the core of a proper history.[29] Tovar characterized the Mexicas' hieroglyphs for Acosta as "not sufficiently like our writing, so that everyone would report what was written, without any variation, in the same words. They only agreed on the general ideas."[30] That in turn explained, in his account, why the Mexica wise men who traditionally had the task of explaining the codices had to commit ancient speeches and other traditional materials to memory. Only by doing so could they explicate and comment on the pictographic codices that alluded to them. Tovar, in short, tried not to demonstrate the inferiority of Mexica images but to show that they had formed only part of a coherent Mexica way of preserving the past. When Acosta described Indian hieroglyphs as inferior to alphabetic writing, then, he did not reproduce what Tovar told him, but modified his source's words, subtly but powerfully, as he broke up what had been Tovar's coherent account of Mexica tradition.

Acosta made clear, moreover, exactly why he treated the remains of Indian tradition so high-handedly. In a long chapter that preceded his discussion of Mexica tradition, he discussed the question of pictographic writing more generally. The Chinese, he noted, used a pictographic writing system, and the evidence about this – as gathered by "the fathers of our society, who are even now in China learning their language and system of writing" – was clear: "since things themselves are innumerable, the letters or pictures used by the Chinese to denote them are almost infinite in number. For the person who needs to read and write in China, as the mandarins do, must know at least 85,000 pictures or letters, and those who must be perfect in that kind of reading have to know some 120,000."[31] The Jesuit fathers, Acosta noted, had been "studying this subject day and night for almost ten years with almost superhuman effort, for the love of Christ and the desire to save souls overcome all obstacles."[32] They had come to appreciate the incredible difficulty of the written language, which boys could not learn without physical compulsion. In fact, they had realized that the demands of learning to write in pictographs had prevented the Chinese from developing the "divine" or "natural" sciences, or even creating schools and universities.[33]

Acosta himself, moreover, could attest that pictographic writing could not accommodate new things with new names. For when he met some Chinese visitors in Mexico, and asked them to write "José de Acosta has come from Peru" in their language, they could not do so in a precise and unequivocal way.[34] Acosta, in other words, conflated the practices of the Indian priests to those of the Chinese – which he mocked, on the basis of fragmentary reports, even as other members of his order were gaining a far deeper and more respectful command of Chinese culture. From his point of view they were all structurally similar, and they all exemplified the difficulty and, in the end, the inadequacy of pictographic writing.

In this case, at least, Acosta's comparative approach both imposed costs and yielded profit. Inspired by a Counter-Reformation polemic against Renaissance myths about the powers of hieroglyphs and pictographs and the erudition and profound wisdom of the ancient eastern priests who had used them, he made clear that he could not accept Mexica annals as anything like the equivalent of western records – any more, presumably, than he could have accepted Chinese annals. No wonder, then, that this critical historian noted that: "It is not very important to know what the Indians themselves are wont to tell of their beginnings and origin, for what they relate resembles dreams rather than history."[35] Acosta knew, and admitted, that recreating the earliest periods of Indian history by conjecture – and especially retracing the route by which the Americas had been peopled – posed tremendous difficulties: "For I ask myself with what motive, with what means, with what strength, could the men of the Indies have crossed such an immense sea? Who could have been the inventor and inspirer of so great a crossing? Truly I have debated this point with myself and others many times and have never found an answer that satisfies me." Yet he preferred the route of conjecture, however frail, to that of working with the remains of imperfect, and imperfectly transmitted, Indian legends: "I will state what I believe, and since there is no testimony for me to follow I shall have to proceed by the thread of reason, though it be very thin, until it disappears from before my eyes."[36] His own view – one that may have rested on early maps of the New World, and that certainly served Spain's imperial interests – was that the ancestors of the New World's human and animal inhabitants had come on foot across land bridges. So much, one could reasonably think, for Acosta's critical approach to history: all he took away from his encounter with Tovar's first-hand knowledge of native traditions was a self-righteous feeling of superiority to them.

In another respect, however, the comparative approach gave Acosta the possibility of acknowledging that Indian traditions and their ways of preserving them were complex. In his formal treatise *On Winning Salvation for the Indians*, which he drafted in 1576, he argued that barbarians fell into three categories: those, like the Chinese, with their plentiful books and splendid academies, "who are not very distant from right reason and the customs of the human race"; those, like the Aztecs and Incas, who had true states but "do not know the use of letters or of written laws, or of philosophical or civil studies"; and "forest-dwelling men, like beasts, who hardly have any human feelings." Each required its own form of treatment.[37] By the time he wrote the *History*, by contrast, Acosta knew that *quipus*, the knotted cords used by the Incas, were not the only form of records kept in the New World, and saw resemblances, as well as similarities, between the barbarous Indians of Mexico and the almost civilized barbarians of China. Acosta's comparative historical method could, in short, have yielded some striking changes in his evaluation of "barbarian" cultures.

In practice, moreover – as witnessed by the body of his *History* – Acosta proceeded in an eclectic, flexible way when he chose which witness to believe. In keeping with standard precepts, he preferred first-hand accounts to second-hand ones, and appreciated the expertise that practical men could bring to the task of observation. He thus noted emphatically that he had been able to draw his account of the Straits of Magellan from the direct account of a professional navigator who had been there, its credibility assured by his direct observation:

> Only one has crossed from the Southern Sea, which is the flagship that I mentioned, from whose chief pilot, named Fernando Alonso, I had a very long account of everything that I have written. And I have seen the true description of the coast of the strait, which they made as they were sailing through it, a copy of which they took to the king in Spain and to his viceroy in Peru.[38]

Yet he also recognized that first-hand accounts could disagree – especially when it came to the description of something so vast and baffling as a new continent:

And there are divergent opinions by some who say that it is all flooded land, full of lakes and swamps, and others who insist that there are great and flourishing realms there and situate Paititi and El Dorado and Los Cesares in that region and say that it contains wonderful things. I heard a member of our society, a person worthy of belief, say that he had seen great cities and roads as broad and well traveled as those between Salamanca and Valladolid.[39]

At times, moreover, Acosta found Indian witnesses highly credible even when other Europeans did not, and gave the evidence that backed up his assessment:

The Indians say that [coca] gives them strength, and it is a great treat for them. Many grave men think this is a superstition and pure imagination. To tell the truth, I do not think it pure imagination; rather, I believe that it produces strength and spirit in the Indians, for effects can be seen that cannot be attributed to imagination, such as doubling the workload with a handful of coca without ingesting anything else and other similar feats.[40]

His actual method of inquiry, in short, was much more complex than his discussion of Indian tradition, and rested less on unexamined assumptions about Indian writing than on careful, case-by-case weighing of what he read and heard.

Like his responses to witnesses and sources, Acosta's evaluative comments on Indian society and culture ranged widely, and revealingly. He warmly praised such Indian accomplishments as the light woven bridges that enabled them to cross great lakes, the self-sufficient households whose male heads were trained in all the crafts, and their excellent system of education. Indian technology and architecture bore witness, as he showed in an antiquarian excursus, to the courage and industry, as well as the ingenuity, of their creators:

The buildings and constructions that the Incas made, in fortresses, temples, roads, country villas, and the like, were many and required enormous labor, as the ruins and fragments that remain today make plain. These can be seen in Cuzco and Tihuanaco and Tambo and other places, where there are stones so immense in size that we cannot imagine how they were cut and brought and placed where they are. In order to construct the buildings and fortresses that the Inca ordered built in Cuzco and different parts of his kingdom, a large number of Indians came from every province, for the toil was enormous and is frightening to contemplate. They did not use mortar, nor did they have iron or steel to cut and carve the stones, nor machines and instruments to drag them, and yet with all this the stones are so cleanly put together that in many places you can scarcely see the joining of one to another; and many of these stones are so large, as I have said, that it would be called an impossible thing were it not actually witnessed. In Tihuanaco I measured one that was thirty-eight feet long and eighteen wide and about six feet thick, and in the wall of the fortress in Cuzco, which is of masonry, there are many much larger stones. And what is most astonishing is the fact that, although the stones in the wall to which I refer are not cut uniformly but are very unequal among themselves in size and workmanship, they fit together with incredible smoothness and without the use of mortar. All of this was done by the work of many people and with terrible travail in the course of the work, for to fit one stone with another, the way they are adjusted, they had to test it many times because the other stones were not of the same size and thickness.[41]

In this case, Acosta applied to New World buildings the skills that Old World antiquaries forged and honed as they set out to survey Roman ruins. Like Brunelleschi or Alberti, who scanned the Pantheon, the Colosseum, and the Forum in order to work out exactly how the Romans had raised columns and built coffered roofs, Acosta read the Inca buildings in order to work out the dreadful experiences that the craftsmen who built them must have undergone and to identify the distinctive skills they had brought to these projects. Yet here, as elsewhere, Acosta's eloquent evocation of Indian prowess had a comparative barb in its tale:

But although the buildings were large, they were usually badly arranged and utilized and seemed no better than mosques or other barbarian buildings. They did not know how to build arches in their constructions, nor did they grasp the use of mortar to do so.[42]

In other contexts, Acosta proved capable of more wholehearted eulogy. In describing the zoo of Moctezuma, for example, he made clear, in a magnificently laudatory digression, that the Mexica ruler had placed, at the center of his palace complex, an encyclopedic collection of the works of both nature and art:

Even if he had owned nothing more than his private zoo, it was a magnificent thing and its like has never been seen. For with all those fish and birds and reptiles and beasts there was something resembling a new Noah's Ark in his house; and for the ocean fish he had saltwater pools and for the river fish sweet water pools, and food for the game birds and predatory birds, and for the wild beasts the same in great abundance, and a large number of Indians were occupied in maintaining and breeding these animals. When he saw that it was no longer possible to maintain some kind of fish or bird or wild animal, he had its likeness richly worked in precious stones or in gold or silver or sculpted in marble or stone. And for different kinds of living he had different houses and palaces: some were for pleasure, others for mourning and sorrow, and others for governing. And there were different rooms in his palace according to the rank of his lords, who served him with remarkable order and distinction.[43]

And when he described the fantastic and fantastically profitable silver mines of Potosi, he hailed the agility and courage of the Indian miners:

They climb [60 foot ladders] by catching hold with both hands, and in this way ascend the great distances I have described, often more than 150 estados, a horrible thing about which it is frightening even to think.[44]

In these cases, Acosta still used comparisons, but he carried them out implicitly, without much rhetorical emphasis, and they served a different function. When he described the Aztec palace zoo, for example, he mapped it – and the palace life of which it was a part – onto the European palaces and *Kunst und Wunderkammern* that he had known before he traveled west. Moctezuma's effort to capture all living beings – and his use of art to fill gaps in the collection of actual specimens – matched that of such encyclopedic collectors as the Habsburgs, in whose terms the Aztec's no doubt radically different enterprise was described. Similarly, when Acosta dramatized the heroic qualities of Indian miners at Potosi, he borrowed – quite explicitly – from Pliny, whose *Natural History* had also included a shocked response to the lengths to which humans would go to exploit the wealth deposited in the earth. In passages like these, Acosta made clear that he saw in the Indians qualities exactly comparable to those that he esteemed in his fellow Europeans. Comparison, in other words, was a double-edged tool – even if, from the anachronistic standpoint of modern ethnography, both of its edges were somewhat blunt. When he wanted, Acosta could use comparison either to emphasize the distance that separated Indians from Europeans, ancient and modern, or to close it. Nothing in Indian culture was more alien to Europeans – or, to those who encountered its full, living form, more horrifying – than the practices of Indian religion. Acosta described these, as Jesuit custom required, in considerable detail, vividly restaging rituals. He made clear that many of these ceremonies filled him – as they should fill any self-respecting Christian – with horror, or that he saw them as directly inspired by the devil. At times, his accounts emulated the graphic Roger Corman stage directions of those earliest of Renaissance ethnographies, the first treatises on witchcraft:

> The method used by the heathen sorcerers and priests to consult the gods was in the manner that the devil had taught them: usually it was at night, and they entered turned away from the idol, walking backward. And, bending low and bowing their heads, they assumed an ugly posture and thus consulted with him. Usually the reply was a sort of horrible whistle, or a scream, which struck them without horror, and everything that they were told and commanded was intended for their deception and perdition.[45]

True, not all areas of Indian religion made the hair of a European visitor rise in terror. Acosta was fascinated, and puzzled, by what he saw as the Indians' tendency to invest places and objects with religious meaning. He did his best to tease out the logic of these associations, and he did not describe them with the Lovecraftian horror that suffused his accounts of divination:

> But among the Indians, especially those of Peru, the sinfulness and perdition involved in all this was exaggerated to the point of folly; for they worship rivers, fountains, ravines, rocks, large stones, hills and the mountain peaks and consider them worthy of great devotion. And, last, they worship anything in nature that seems to them notable and different from others, as if recognizing some special deity in it. In Cajamarca de la Nasca they showed me a large hill of sand, which was the particular place of worship, or huaca, of the ancients. When

I asked what divinity was there, they told me that they worshiped the wonderful circumstance that a very tall hill of sand existed among others that were all rocks. And indeed it was astonishing to think how such a great hill of sand was placed in the middle of massive hills made of stone.[46]

Some ceremonies, moreover – for example, the ascetic rituals of self-inflicted denial and pain by which young boys and girls emulated, and even outdid, the members of western religious orders – strikingly reminded Acosta of Christian counterparts.

At this point Acosta's analysis takes a stunning – and revealing – twist. Apparently Christian features of pagan worship, as the Dominican Diego Durán had argued, were actually diabolic imitations, vicious parodies, of the rituals of true religion.[47] To attend or read about such rites was to approach direct traffic with the devil: the more harmless the practice, the deadlier its implicit deception of those who took part. Yet Acosta also insisted, with passionate directness, that the Indians were no closer to the devil than the ancient inhabitants of Europe had been. Once again, comparison proved Acosta's best weapon – and once again, comparison took his attention away from the particular. Close study of the most informative accounts of pagan religion – the compilations of the Fathers of the Church and even the full treatments of ancient myth and religion by Greek and Roman compilers – showed that the ancients had also followed Satanic dictates. Like the Indians, they had engaged in human and animal sacrifice:

> If any reader is astonished by some of the Indians' rites and customs, and scorns them as ignorant and wicked or detests them as subhuman and diabolical, let him look to the Greeks and Romans, who ruled the world, and he will find the same or very similar customs, and sometimes worse ones, as can easily be understood not only from our Christian authors Eusebius of Caesarea, Clement of Alexandria, Theodoret of Cyrene, and others, but also from their own writers such as Pliny, Dionysius of Halicarnassus, and Plutarch. But since the prince of darkness is the teacher of all the heathen, it is no new thing to find cruelty and filth and folly and madness among them, learned from that teaching and that school.[48]

Just as every baby must be snatched from the devil by baptism, so every non-Christian people had to be snatched from the devil by conversion. The Greek worshipers of the Unknown God whose altar Paul saw in Athens were no better – if no worse – than the Indians who resembled them, in some ways, so strikingly. The diabolic temples in which New World inhabitants invoked devils, pierced their tongues, and flailed their bodies resembled the groves in which the inhabitants of Arcadia had worshiped Great Pan, no better and no worse: both were the playing field of the devil, and of human nature unransomed by the Savior.

The critical and comparative method that Acosta brought with him to the New World, in other words, did not lead him even to try to think his way into the logic of New World beliefs and practices – into the otherness that this same method enabled him to find in Greek and Roman antiquity. Indeed, it often induced him to do the reverse: to identify the particularities he observed in the New World with the deeds, beliefs, and institutions of other pagans, known from classical texts or Jesuit annual letters from Asia.

In another respect, however, Acosta's new history had a radical impact – and one that he himself intended. Like the theorists – above all Bodin – Acosta believed that human history must be understood in its natural setting. Unlike the theorists, he had to lay in that setting himself, since he had only partial and confusedly overlapping maps and accounts of topography, botany, and biology to draw on. Faced with this formidable task, he collected information from texts, collated it with his own experiences and those of others, and made a remarkably good job of presenting the wonders of New World nature, lucidly and briefly, in his book. Acosta's treatments of some natural phenomena – like the trade winds – surpassed all of their predecessors in precision and vividness:

> In Capira, when I was crossing the isthmus from Nombre de Dios to Panama, I saw one of these monkeys jump from one tree to another that was on the other side of the river, which astonished me. They seize a branch with their tails and leap wherever they wish . . . The pranks, antics and capers performed by these animals would be a long time in the telling; the skills they can acquire when they are trained seem worthy of human intelligence rather than of brute animals. I saw one in Cartagena, in the governor's house, about whom they told me things that were scarcely credible, such as sending him to the tavern for wine and putting the money in one hand and the jug in the other, and that there was no way he would relinquish the money until they gave him the jug with wine in it. If on the way boys shouted at him or threw stones, he would set the jug aside and take up stones and throw them at the boys until he saw that the coast was clear, and then he would carry his jug again.[49]

Acosta followed Pliny in using carefully chosen literary devices, such as long catalogues of stones, plants and animals; easy, matter-of-fact transitions; and occasional admissions of ignorance to suggest that his chapters on natural history were actually exhaustive in content and seamless in coverage. He thus created the effective impression that he had reconstructed the complete natural setting for New World history – a goal no single book could possibly meet.

When Acosta set the Indians into their natural world, he did not, as one might now expect, treat them as what Germans traditionally called a "Naturvolk" – a people more primitive than Europeans. Like Pliny, he did not treat the conquest of nature by technology as a clear sign of superiority. Nature, for Acosta, was far more complex and beautiful than anything made by men. As to human creations, "even though they are built with great skill after one has grown accustomed to seeing them they appear worthless and almost arouse distaste."[50] He also clearly believed that the change in Indian population in the time since the arrival of the Europeans had not represented a simple response to environmental factors. Population had declined, catastrophically, in the fertile lowlands of South America, while growing rapidly in the infertile but mineral-rich mountains. The transformation of Indian society as a whole represented a clear case of free will, exercised in ways that went counter to the pressures exerted by the natural world – a movement every bit as free, however far-fetched this now seems, as the movement of Europeans into the New World.

On the individual level, rather than the social, Acosta made one fundamental point clear. As he described a mountain ascent in the Andes and its consequences, he emulated Cardano and other sixteenth-century medical men, who narrated their own case histories in living color and gruesome detail:

> When I climbed the Staircases, as they are called, the highest part of that range, almost in an instant I felt such mortal anguish that I thought I would have to throw myself off my mount onto the ground . . . This was soon followed by convulsive retching and vomiting that made me think I would give up the ghost, for after vomiting up my food and a watery residue there came bile and more bile, some yellow and some green, and I even vomited blood from the violence felt by stomach.

Far from showing stoical detachment, some of Acosta's Christian companions "asked for Confession along the way, thinking that they were dying." In the end, though, Acosta and his fellows realized that though altitude sickness was painful, "commonly it does not result in any great harm."[51] Here and elsewhere Acosta made clear that Christians were every bit as subject to nature, to the vagaries of climate and disease and to the weakness of the flesh, as Indians. Indeed, both Indians and Europeans who inhabited the mountains, as Acosta observed, lost their vulnerability to this disorder. One profound lesson of Acosta's work, then, was the same one that Bartolomé de las Casas had drawn from different evidence: all mankind was one.

Acosta himself made clear that, in the end, the real purpose of his history was to teach this vital point. Many Europeans, he remarked, saw the Indians as mere brutes:

> Many and very notable abuses have been committed upon them as a consequence of this false belief . . . I see no better way of refuting this pernicious opinion than to describe their order and behavior when they lived under their own law. In it, although they had many barbaric traits and baseless beliefs, there were many others worthy of admiration; these clearly give us to understand that they have a natural capacity to receive good instruction and that they even surpass in large measure many of our own republics.[52]

In the course of telling his immense, dramatic story, Acosta occasionally expressed disdain for Indian practices and beliefs, and he normally insisted on setting even the institutions and customs he praised before a European conceptual background. Yet in doing so he had a high ideal in mind: not cultural alterity but human solidarity.

Solidarity, of course, did not imply equality – especially in the realm of religion. On the contrary, it demanded intervention. Knowing that the Indians were human and capable of thought and feeling, Acosta also knew that he had an absolute duty to convert as many of them as possible to Christianity – and to destroy, in the end, many of the customs and institutions that he had inquired into so carefully and described so vividly. Here too he thought and worked within the intellectual traditions that had shaped his enterprise as a historian. The point of the new history that Bodin and others had called for was practical, not theoretical: they wanted to identify the constitutional arrangements that could restore peace and order to a Europe torn by religious war. The point of the new history that Acosta wrote was to lay down foundations for what would genuinely be a new world: a Christian New World, one in which the energy, skill, and practical intelligence of the Indians were turned to new purposes. Like many historians of his time – a number of whom studied the past in order to predict when the world might come to an end – Acosta, as he recreated the past, looked forward to a radically different future.

NOTES

1. José de Acosta, *Historia natural y moral de las Indias* (Seville: Juan de Leon, 1590), II.9, 102–3; *Natural and Moral History of the Indies*, trans. Frances Lopez-Morillas, ed. Jane Mangan, with an Introduction and Commentary by Walter Mignolo (Durham, N.C. and London: Duke University Press, 2002), 88–9.
2. Acosta, *Historia*, IV.26, 259; 216.
3. Acosta, *Historia*, I.23, 67–8.
4. Acosta, *Historia*, I.5, 25.
5. Acosta, *Historia*, I.15, 57.
6. Acosta, *Historia*, II.9, 103; 89.
7. Acosta, *Historia*, I.9, 38; 35.
8. Acosta, *Historia*, I.8, 34; 32.
9. Acosta, *Historia*, I.8, 34; 32.
10. For Valla, see most recently Alfred Hiatt, *The Making of Medieval Forgeries: False Documents in Fifteenth-century England* (London: British Library; Toronto and Buffalo: University of Toronto Press, 2004); for Erasmus, see e.g. Cecilia Asso, *La teologia e la grammatica: la controversia tra Erasmo ed Edward Lee* (Florence: Olschki, 1993).
11. Acosta, *Historia*, Proemio al lector, 10; 9.
12. Acosta, *Historia*, VI.1, 396; 330.
13. Acosta, *Historia*, VI.7, 408; 340–1.
14. François Baudouin, *De institutione historiae universae et eius cum iurisprudentia coniunctione prolegomenon libri duo* (Paris: A. Wechel 1561), 36–7.
15. Antonio Possevino, *Apparatus ad omnium gentium historiam* (Venice: apud Io. Bapt. Ciottum, 1597), 39 r.–v.
16. Acosta, *Historia*, Proemio al lector, 10; 9.
17. Jean Bodin, *Methodus ad facilem historiarum cognitionem* (Paris: Martin le Jeune, 1566), 75.
18. Bodin, *Methodus*, 75.
19. Bodin, *Methodus*, 75.
20. Francesco Patrizi, *Della historia diece dialoghi* (Venice: Arrivabene, 1560), 11 r.
21. Acosta, *Historia*, Prologo a los Libros sigiuentes, 300; 250.
22. Acosta, *Historia*, IV.34, 278; 232.
23. Lorenzo Valla, *Gesta Ferdinandi regis Aragonum*, ed. Ottavio Besomi (Padua: Antenore, 1973).
24. Acosta, *Historia*, Proemio al lector, 11; 11–12.
25. Baudouin, *De institutione historiae universae*, 73–74.
26. Possevino, *Apparatus*, 4 v.–6r.
27. Acosta, *Historia*, VI.7, 407–9; 340–1.

28 See José J. Fuente del Pilar, "Prologo," in Juan de Tovar, *Historia y creencias de los indios de Mexico* (Madrid: Miraguano, 2001), 37–47.
29 The letters of Acosta and Tovar, which are included in Tovar's manuscript, appear in J. García Icazbalceta, *Don Fray Juan de Zumárraga, primer obispo y arzobispo de México*, ed. R. Aguayo Spencer and A. Castro Leal (Madrid: Porrúa, 1947), 89–93.
30 García Icazbalceta, *Zumárraga*, vol. 4, 92.
31 Acosta, *Historia*, IV.5, 403; 336.
32 Acosta, *Historia*, IV.5, 403; 336.
33 Acosta, *Historia*, IV.5, 402–5; IV.6, 405–6; 335–9.
34 Acosta, *Historia*, IV.5, 404–5; 337.
35 Acosta, *Historia*, I.25, 82; 72.
36 Acosta, *Historia*, I.16, 57; 51.
37 José de Acosta, *De procuranda Indorum salute*, ed. L. Perena *et al.*, 2 vols. (Madrid: Consejo superior de investigaciones cientificas, 1984), vol. 1: 60–8.
38 Acosta, *Historia*, III.13, 155; 130.
39 Acosta, *Historia*, III.25, 182; III.23, 152.
40 Acosta, *Historia*, IV.22, 252–3; 211.
41 Acosta, *Historia*, VI.14, 419–20; 350–1.
42 Acosta, *Historia*, VI.14, 420; 351.
43 Acosta, *Historia*, VI.24, 440–1; 369.
44 Acosta, *Historia*, IV.8, 217; 181.
45 Acosta, *Historia*, V.12, 331; 277.
46 Acosta, *Historia*, V.5, 313; 261–2.
47 Diego Durán, *Book of the Gods and Rites and the Ancient Calendar*, trans. and ed. Fernando Horcasitas and Doris Heyden (Norman: University of Oklahoma Press, 1971).
48 Acosta, *Historia*, Prologo a los libros siguientes, 301–2; 251. For detailed discussion of early modern efforts to account for idolatry, see the articles by Carina Johnson, Peter Miller, Sabine MacCormack, Martin Mulsow, Joan Pau Rubies, and Jonathan Sheehan, in *Journal of the History of Ideas* 67, 4 (2006).
49 Acosta, *Historia*, IV.39, 241.
50 Acosta, *Historia*, I.3, 23; 22.
51 Acosta, *Historia*, III.9, 142–3; 119–20. For Acosta and altitude sickness, see Thayne Ford, "Stranger in a Strange Land: Juan de Acosta's Scientific Realizations in Sixteenth-century Peru." *Sixteenth Century Journal* 29 (1988): 19–33 at 30–2.
52 Acosta, *Historia*, VI.1, 395–6; 329.

SUGGESTIONS FOR FURTHER READING

Asso, Cecilia. *La teologia e la grammatica: la controversia tra Erasmo*, ed. Edward Lee. Florence: Olschki, 1993.

Bleichmar, Daniela. "Books, Bodies, and Fields: Sixteenth-century Transatlantic Encounters with New World Materia Medica," in Londa Schiebinger and Claudia Swan (eds) *Colonial Botany: Science, Commerce and Politics in the Early Modern World*. Philadelphia: University of Pennsylvania Press, 2004.

Brizzi, Gian Paolo (ed.). *La "Ratio studiorum": modelli culturali e pratiche educative dei Gesuiti in Italia tra cinque e seicento*. Rome: Bulzoni, 1981.

Carey, Sorcha. *Pliny's Catalogue of Culture: Art and Empire in the Natural History*. Oxford: Oxford University Press, 2003.

Codina Mir, Gabriel. *Aux sources de la pédagogie des Jésuites: le "modus parisiensis."* Rome: Institutum Historicum S.I., 1968.
Couzinet, Marie-Dominique. *Histoire et méthode à la renaissance: une lecture de la Methodus ad facilem historiarum cognitionem de Jean Bodin.* Paris: Vrin, 1996.
Dainville, François de. *La naissance de l'humanisme moderne*, vol. I. Paris: Beauchesne et ses fils, 1940.
Elliott, J.H. *The Old World and the New, 1492–1650.* Cambridge: Cambridge University Press, 1970.
Elman, Benjamin. *On Their Own Terms: Science in China, 1550–1900.* Cambridge, Mass.: Harvard University Press, 2005.
Erasmus, H.J. *The Origins of Rome in Historiography from Petrarch to Perizonius.* Assen: Van Gorcum, 1962.
Ford, Thayne. "Stranger in a Strange Land: Juan de Acosta's Scientific Realizations in Sixteenth-Century Peru." *Sixteenth Century Journal* 29 (1988): 19–33.
Gemegah, Helga. *Die Theorie des spanischen Jesuiten José de Acosta (ca. 1540–1600) über den Ursprung der indianischen Völker aus Asien.* Frankfurt: Peter Lang, 1999.
Ginzburg, Carlo. *No Island is an Island.* New York: Columbia University Press, 2000.
Gliozzi, Giuliano. *Adamo e il nuovo mondo: la nascita dell'antropologia come ideologia coloniale: dalle genealogie bibliche alle teorie razziali (1500–1700).* Florence: La nuova Italia, 1977.
Grafton, Anthony. *Defenders of the Text: The Traditions of Scholarship in an Age of Science, 1450–1800.* Cambridge, Mass. and London: Harvard University Press, 1991.
Grafton, Anthony. "The West and the Rest," in Anthony Grafton, *Bring Out Your Dead: The Past as Revelation.* Cambridge, Mass. and London: Harvard University Press, 2002.
Grafton, Anthony, April Shelford, and Nancy Siraisi. *New Worlds, Ancient Texts: The Power of Tradition and the Shock of Discovery.* Cambridge, Mass. and London: Harvard University Press, 1992.
Gruzinski, Serge. *The Mestizo Mind: The Intellectual Dynamics of Colonization and Globalization*, trans. Deke Dusinberre. New York and London: Routledge, 2002.
Hiatt, Alfred. *The Making of Medieval Forgeries: False Documents in Fifteenth-century England.* London: British Library; Toronto and Buffalo: University of Toronto Press, 2004.
Hodgen, Margaret. *Early Anthropology in the Sixteenth and Seventeenth Centuries.* Philadelphia: University of Pennsylvania Press, 1964.
Lupher, David. *Romans in a New World: Classical Models in Sixteenth-century Spanish America.* Ann Arbor: University of Michigan Press, 2003.
MacCormack, Sabine. *Religion in the Andes: Vision and Imagination in Early Colonial Peru.* Princeton: Princeton University Press, 1991.
Mignolo, Walter. "On the Colonization of Languages and Memories: Renaissance Theories of Writing and the Discontinuity of the Classical Tradition." *Comparative Studies in Society and History* 34 (1992): 301–35.
Mignolo, Walter. *The Darker Side of the Renaissance: Literacy, Territoriality, and Colonization.* Ann Arbor: University of Michigan Press, 1995; repr. 2003.
Molino, Paola. "Alle origini della Methodus Apodemica di Theodor Zwinger: la collaborazione di Hugo Blotius, fra empirismo ed universalismo." *Codices Manuscripti* (forthcoming).
Moreau-Reibel, Jean. *Jean Bodin et le droit public comparé dans ses rapports avec la philosophie de l'histoire.* Paris: Vrin, 1933.
Nadel, George. "Philosophy of History before Historicism." *History & Theory* 3 (1964): 291–315.
O'Gorman, Edmundo. *Cuatro historiadores de Indias. Siglo xvi.* México, Secretaría de Educación Pública, 1972.

Parry, J. H. "Juan de Tovar and the History of the Indians." *Proceedings of the American Philosophical Society* 121 (1977): 316–19.

Pomata, Gianna and Nancy Siraisi (eds) *Historia: Empiricism and Erudition in Early Modern Europe*. Cambridge, Mass.: MIT, 2004.

Ricard, Robert. *The Spiritual Conquest of Mexico: An Essay on the Apostolate and the Evangelizing Methods of the Mendicant Orders in New Spain, 1523–1572*. Berkeley: University of California Press, 1974; repr. 1982, 1996.

Siraisi, Nancy. *The Clock and the Mirror: Girolamo Cardano and Renaissance Medicine*. Princeton: Princeton University Press, 1997.

Stagl, Justin. *A History of Curiosity: The Theory of Travel, 1550–1800*. Chur: Harwood Academic, 1995.

Zupanov, Ines. *Disputed Mission: Jesuit Experiments and Brahmanical Knowledge in Seventeenth-century India*. New Delhi: Oxford University Press, 1999.

PART III

THE MOVEMENT OF IDEAS

CHAPTER NINE

THE CIRCULATION OF KNOWLEDGE

Peter Burke

This chapter is concerned with "knowledge" in the sense both of ideas and of information. It will include the knowledge of techniques and styles that was so important in the movement we call the "Renaissance," the increasing knowledge of other cultures in the "age of discovery," and the great debate about religion now described as "the Reformation." A short study needs a sharp focus. I have chosen circulation in the geographical sense, from place to place, rather than the movement of information and ideas between social groups. This chapter in the historical geography of knowledge will concentrate on circulation over long distances and over the long term, distinguishing where necessary between different circuits (art and humanism, religion and politics, north and south, east and west) as well as different media of communication (oral and visual, manuscript and print). This was the age of the so-called "print revolution," but, as scholars have increasingly emphasized in the last generation, oral transmission remained important at this time, and so did other traditional media such as communication through images and the circulation of manuscripts.[1]

The term "circulation" may suggest a simple diffusion or flow of knowledge from one part of Europe to another. This implication is misleading. "Dissemination" might therefore make a better metaphor, implying that seeds germinated into something else, and so allowing both for misunderstandings and for deliberate adaptations of ideas – in other words, for creative reception.

In what follows I shall examine the circulation of texts, images, and people in order to reach some provisional conclusions about routes, about "nodes," the cities that were located at the intersection of routes, and finally about forms of sociability that facilitated intellectual exchanges.

THE CIRCULATION OF BOOKS AND MANUSCRIPTS

In a discussion of circulation in a book on the Renaissance, pride of place should perhaps go to the manuscripts of the Greek and Latin classics that were recovered in this period (recovered by western Europeans, since the Greek texts were well known in Byzantium). In the fifteenth century, humanists such as the Florentine Poggio Bracciolini began to search for manuscripts of the classics in libraries in monasteries and elsewhere. Among Poggio's finds were texts by Cicero, Quintilian, Lucretius, and Petronius – texts the monks apparently did not know they possessed. Another humanist, Giovanni Aurispa, returned from Constantinople in 1423 with 238 Greek manuscripts. In the sixteenth century the great hunt continued and the French humanist Guillaume Budé, for instance, searched for classical manuscripts for the library of King Francis I.[2]

The circulation of information in private letters must not be forgotten. The so-called "Republic of Letters" (in the sense of an international community of scholars) was held together mainly by letter-writing. Erasmus, for instance, corresponded with his fellow humanists in many countries, once confessing to writing so many letters that "two wagons would hardly be equal to carrying the load." Among his most frequent correspondents, leaving aside his fellow countrymen, were Germans (Beatus Rhenanus and the lawyer Ulrich Zasius), Englishmen (Thomas More and John Colet), Frenchmen (Guillaume Budé), Italians (Andrea Ammonio), Spaniards (Juan Luis Vives), Portuguese (Damião de Gois), Czechs (Jan Slechta) and Hungarians (Miklós Oláh).

The letters written by and to the late sixteenth-century Netherlands scholar Justus Lipsius – of which over 4,300 survive – illustrate the strength of the humanist commonwealth of letters even more vividly than the correspondence of Erasmus. The correspondence of Lipsius, who taught both in Calvinist Leiden and Counter-Reformation Leuven, ranged across the Catholic and Protestant worlds from Lisbon to L'viv. On the Catholic side, we find Lipsius in touch with the Jesuit scholars Martin Delrio and Antonio Possevino, the French magistrate Jacques-Auguste de Thou, the Polish nobleman Jan Zamojski and the Spanish poet Francisco de Quevedo. Among the Protestants, his correspondents included the Danish nobleman Henrik Rantzow, the German professor Nathan Chytraeus, the French scholar Isaac Casaubon, and the Hungarian writer János Rimay. The diversity of mother tongues posed no problem, since the letters were generally written in Latin.

Letters were sometimes printed in the period, including some by Erasmus – edited by himself – as well as many to and from Lipsius. The invention and spread of printing obviously made a great impact on the circulation of information. Three consequences of printing may be distinguished. In the first place, the new technology vastly multiplied the number of copies of texts and so brought down their price. In the second place, by multiplying copies, printing contributed to the preservation of information. In the third place, printing standardized copies of texts, allowing a class of schoolboys, for instance, to use virtually identical versions of, say, a speech by Cicero.[3]

By 1500, presses had been established in more than 250 places in Europe – 80 of them in Italy, 52 in Germany and 43 in France. Between them these presses produced about 27,000 editions by the year 1500, which means that – assuming an average print run of 500 copies per edition – about 13 million books were circulating by that date in a Europe of 100 million people. Among the most important centers of the production and distribution of books were Venice, Antwerp, and Paris, while in Spain and the German-speaking world printing was dispersed among a number of cities such as Barcelona and Seville, Cologne and Leipzig. The spread of books across frontiers was assisted by international partnerships such as that of Anton Koberger in Nuremberg with colleagues in Basle, Strasbourg, and Lyon.

Religious works predominated, but a substantial minority of the books printed in the fifteenth and sixteenth centuries had something to do with the movement we know as the Renaissance. The Latin classics – Cicero, Virgil, Livy, Horace, and so on – were printed relatively early. On the other hand, it was only in the early sixteenth century that editions of ancient Greek texts in the original language began to be published, especially at the press of Aldus Manutius in Venice. Many of the editions of classical texts published during the Renaissance were translations. Greek texts were translated into Latin: the humanist pope Nicholas V, for instance, commissioned Latin versions of Herodotus, Thucydides, and Xenophon, while the Medici encouraged the philosopher Marsilio Ficino to translate the works of Plato.

Greek and Latin texts were also translated into a number of vernaculars. More than a thousand translations of Greek and Latin classics into five vernaculars (Italian, French, Spanish, German, and English) were published between 1450 and 1600. The French humanist Louis Le Roy, for instance, translated Aristotle's *Politics* and Plato's *Republic*. Plutarch's *Lives* were translated into French by Jacques Amyot and into English by Sir Thomas North (who did not work from the Greek but from Amyot's French, a not uncommon practice at this time). Ptolemy's *Geography* and the works on mechanics by Hero of Alexandria (so important for the designers of Renaissance festivals) were translated into Italian in the sixteenth century, while medical works by Galen appeared in Italian, French, and English.

Although most educated men knew Latin, there remained a public for the translation of ancient Roman texts into the vernacular. Alongside the many versions of Virgil's *Aeneid* – which was often read as history rather than as fiction – can be found compendia of practical information such as Vitruvius on architecture or Columella on farming (both these authors were translated into Italian, German, and French).

Many of the texts we associate with the Italian Renaissance were turned into other vernaculars in the period itself. Among the works most frequently translated were Machiavelli's *Discourses*, *The Prince*, *The Art of War*, and *History of Florence*, Castiglione's *Courtier*, and Guicciardini's *History of Italy*. Machiavelli and Guicciardini were each translated into six languages at this time (Latin, French, Spanish, German, Dutch, and English) and Castiglione into five (without counting the Polish version, *The Polish Courtier*, which was more of an imitation than a translation in the strict sense of the term).

Among the most frequently translated religious writers were Kempis, Erasmus, Luther, and Calvin. The late medieval text known as *The Imitation of Christ* and attributed to the Netherlander Thomas à Kempis was another of the best-sellers in the age of the Renaissance, remarkable not only for the number of languages into which it was translated (including Catalan, Slovene, Hungarian, Welsh, and modern Greek) but also for the number of times it was translated into the same language.

Another best-selling text was Erasmus's *Enchiridion* or *Manual of a Christian Soldier*, a work of piety that was translated into Czech, German, English, Dutch, Spanish, French, Italian, and Portuguese. Two exemplary monographs describe the reception of Erasmus in Spain and Italy. Both distinguish between a first phase of open and even official enthusiasm, described by the French scholar Marcel Bataillon as the "invasion" of Erasmus's ideas, supported by the diffusion of his books (published by well-known printers such as Cromberger in Seville or Marcolini in Venice), and a second phase of circulation underground after his works had been placed on the Index of Prohibited Books.[4]

The Index was an attempt to fight print by means of print, broadcasting information about the texts that Catholics were not supposed to read. The extent to which it was effective or counter-productive remains controversial. What is clear is that the flow of smuggled books was impossible to stop and also that censorship was virtually unworkable in the Protestant world, not for lack of will (especially in Geneva) but because the Protestants lacked a central authority. So far as censorship was concerned, the lack of a pope was a serious disadvantage.

Translations made a major contribution to the spread of the ideas associated with Reformation and Counter-Reformation alike. Luther reached the learned public with the works he wrote in Latin, a wide German public with his vigorous pamphlets in the vernacular, and an international public via his translators. The catechisms produced by Luther and the Jesuit Roberto Bellarmine, both aimed at a wide audience of listeners as well as readers, were among the works translated into most languages in this period. Luther, for example, was read in Latvian, Estonian, and Sami, and Bellarmine in 40 languages, 17 of them non-European. Between 1456 and 1632 the Bible was translated – wholly or in part – into 34 modern European languages. A few texts crossed the cultural frontier between the Catholic and Protestant worlds, like the *Combattimento spirituale*, a work of devotion by the Italian priest Lorenzo Scupoli that became popular in translation in Protestant England in the seventeenth century.

Among the community of scholars, the circulation of information was greatly helped by the practice of translation into Latin. At least five hundred such translations were printed by the year 1620. The majority of these texts are religious, works of piety by the Puritan William Perkins or the Franciscan Luis de Granada, for instance, but a substantial minority of translations provided geographical, political, historical, or scientific information, ranging from Botero on cities and empires to Palladio on antiquities or Galileo on mathematics. Latin translation was above all a means by which the ideas of Italian and Spanish writers were made available to a public that spoke German, Dutch, or English.

The fact that a few of the texts mentioned above were published in translation in east-central Europe deserves emphasis. Erasmus's *Enchiridion* was available in Czech and Polish. Works by the political writers Fadrique Furio Ceriol and Giovanni Botero were translated into Polish, while Calvin's *Institutes*, like the Jesuit Edmund Campion's *Ten Reasons*, could be read in Czech and Hungarian.

Some travel books were translated into half a dozen languages or more in this period, thus spreading both information and ideas about other continents (including many prejudices). The travels of Marco Polo appeared in print in nine translations, the travels of "Sir John Mandeville" (probably fictional) in eight, and those of the Italian Ludovico Varthema (who went as far east as Sumatra) and the Spaniard Juan González de Mendoza (who wrote about China) in six translations (the letters of

Columbus and Cortés were also translated into several languages at this time). Accounts by different travelers were assembled into anthologies that were virtual encyclopedias of geographical information, such as the three fat volumes of *Navigations and Voyages* (1550–9), published in Italian by Giovanni Battista Ramusio, or in England Richard Hakluyt's *Principal Navigations* (1589, the enlarged three-volume version 1598–1600), or the still larger collection of voyages compiled by the printer Theodore de Bry of Frankfurt.

Many modern texts also circulated in manuscript even after the invention of printing. Poems, for instance, might be passed from hand to hand among friends rather than published, either because the author was reluctant to be viewed as writing for money or because the verses would lose most of their significance if they were taken out of the context for which they had been written. Graffiti on walls or on the pedestal of the famous statue in Rome known as "Pasquino" provided irreverent public comments on recent events, and some of these pasquinades were copied and even printed in order to reach wider audiences. Different forms of relatively secret knowledge also circulated in manuscript form, including accounts of experiments by alchemists and the reports of spies and ambassadors to their paymasters.

Many of these manuscripts were copied, often without the knowledge or permission of the original writers. In sixteenth-century Rome, for instance, it was possible to buy copies of confidential reports by Venetian ambassadors to the Senate. Newsletters circulated in manuscript not only to avoid censorship but also because this "interactive" medium allowed the selection of news to be adapted to the interests and needs of particular subscribers.[5]

Manuscripts from other cultures were also in circulation, written in Hebrew, Arabic, and Turkish, for instance, or in the pictograms used by the Aztecs before the Spanish conquest. In the late sixteenth century, for example, the English geographer Richard Hakluyt bought from his French colleague André Thevet a manuscript known as the *Codex Mendoza*, still a major source for the history of pre-Colombian Mexico.

THE CIRCULATION OF IMAGES

The enthusiasm of Renaissance artists and humanists for classical sculpture is well known, for statues and fragments of statues such as the equestrian Marcus Aurelius on the Capitol in Rome, the Laocoön group (discovered in Rome in 1506), the Venus de' Medici and the Belvedere Torso. Many copies of these statues were made and some of them were exported from Italy. Francis I sent the painter Primaticcio to Rome to buy or copy antiquities for him, and he also received copies of statues as gifts.[6] Sculpture was difficult and expensive to transport, but plaster casts circulated more freely. Together with ancient Greek and Roman coins, many of which were dug up all over the former Roman Empire, the casts allowed artists in other countries to discover ancient art.

Italian sculptures were prized in the Hungary of King Matthias in the late fifteenth century, and in the Poland of King Sigismund I in the early sixteenth. Sculptors from the Netherlands, whether they migrated or stayed at home, produced tombs for rulers and nobles in cities such as London, Roskilde, and Stockholm, and as far east as Königsberg.

Paintings posed less of a transport problem than statues, and the increasing circulation of works by artists of the Italian Renaissance made artists and patrons in France, Spain, the Netherlands, central Europe, and elsewhere familiar with the new style. Leo X sent Francis I several paintings by Raphael, while Titian worked for Philip II without leaving Venice.

There was also movement in the other direction, from Flanders to Italy. Around the middle of the fifteenth century Leonello d'Este, Marquis of Ferrara, acquired several paintings by the Fleming Rogier van der Weyden, while the Florentine banker Tommaso Portinari brought to his native city an altarpiece by Hugo van der Goes, commissioned when Portinari was in Bruges. The great collector Cardinal Domenico Grimani owned works by Flemish and German artists. The collections were a source of information as well as pleasure. For instance, the Croat painter Giulio Clovio discovered the work of Dürer through Grimani's collection.

Collections were frequently dispersed or swallowed up by other collections, thus contributing to the circulation of paintings and statues. Italian collectors such as the Estes of Ferrara and the Gonzagas of Mantua were followed by collectors in other countries, among them Mary of Hungary, Philip II, Rudolph II, Charles I, Cardinal Granvelle, and the Earl of Arundel. The images that were easiest and cheapest to transport were of course drawings and prints.[7] Drawings were used in artists' workshops as a repertoire of images to employ when needed as well as a means of training apprentices, but they circulated by inheritance or sale and sometimes crossed frontiers. The Dutch artist Karel Van Mander brought drawings by his compatriot Bartholomeus Spranger from Vienna to Haarlem, for instance, and showed them to Goltzius. Architectural drawings by the Italian Sebastiano Serlio circulated in manuscript before they appeared in print between 1537 and 1551.

Printed images (woodcuts or engravings or etchings on metal) began to be made a generation before Gutenberg printed texts, and they were sold cheaply to a wide audience by itinerant pedlars as well as in shops and at fairs. Prints were often designed to communicate both ideas and information, as in the case of maps. For example, prints made by Lucas Cranach and others were a powerful weapon employed by Martin Luther and his followers against the pope.[8]

Prints that were sold separately included engravings of classical sculptures, of the buildings of Rome, and of the paintings of masters such as Leonardo and Raphael. Prints were equally important as illustrations to books: to herbals, for instance, or treatises on anatomy, or astronomy or calligraphy. Pattern-books like the ones published by Serlio or the Dutch artist Hans Vredemann de Vries presented possible clients with a choice of façades, fireplaces, grotesques, fountains, gardens, and so on. Handbooks for artists such as Cesare Ripa's *Iconologia* (1593) advised them how to represent personifications of history, the virtues, and so on.

Prints made a major contribution to the spread of knowledge and ideas about the different parts of the world. The illustrations to Ptolemy's *Geography* were regularly updated, even if the basic text remained the same. Globes and atlases encouraged a more global consciousness as well as presenting precise information in an accessible way. The *Theatrum orbis terrarum* ("Theatre of the Globe"), a collection of 53 maps first published by the Flemish cartographer Abraham Ortelius in Antwerp in 1570, sold well and was regularly revised and enlarged. By 1598, when Ortelius died, at least 28 editions of the book had been published in five languages.[9]

On a different scale, city plans and views became increasingly available in print, among them the huge one of Venice by Jacopo de'Barbari and that of Amsterdam by Cornelis Anthonisz. A collection of views could be found in the *Civitates orbis terrarum* ("Cities of the Globe") published by Georg Braun and Frans Hogenburg between 1572 and 1617. Many readers' impressions of the world beyond Europe were derived from the illustrations to Theodor de Bry's collection of voyages mentioned above, such as the engravings after John White's drawings of the Indians of Virginia, apparently made on the spot in the 1580s. Collections often included not only works of western art but also exotic objects, natural or the work of human hands, from Asia, Africa, and the New World, thus giving viewers some sense not only of the wonders of nature but also of the achievements and the variety of the world's cultures.[10]

Engravings also allowed the circulation of information and ideas in the opposite direction, from Europe to the Ottoman and Persian empires, to the Americas, and to India, China, and Japan, from the later sixteenth century onwards. Take the case of China. Jesuit missionaries such as the Italian Matteo Ricci brought the atlas of Ortelius and the *Civitates* of Braun and Hogenburg in their baggage in order to spread European secular culture as well as Christianity, or to spread Christianity more effectively by associating it with European secular culture.

Ricci, who was a kind of "Renaissance man" whose interests ranged from rhetoric and the art of memory to mathematics and astronomy, also drew and displayed his own world map. An unknown Chinese copied it and made prints of it, thus making a number of Chinese aware that their culture's image of the world was not the only one. A famous work of piety by the Spanish Jesuit Jeronimo Nadal, *Images from the Gospels*, with illustrations by Anton Wierix of Antwerp, was used in order to convert the Chinese to Christianity. However, some Chinese at least seem to have paid more attention to the landscape background than to the religious foreground, producing a revolution in landscape painting by making painters aware of alternatives to their own tradition.[11]

THE CIRCULATION OF PEOPLE

Ideas and information spread not only via texts and images but also through the circulation of people, as individuals or in groups, as in the case of the great diasporas of the Renaissance in which Greeks left Byzantium for Italy, Muslims and Jews were expelled from Spain, and Italian, French, and Flemish Protestants found refuge in England and elsewhere. Despite the language barriers, many refugees were able to communicate their ideas orally. The importance of oral communication in Renaissance Europe as a whole should not be underestimated, despite the lack of sources for its study, except in cases when institutions supported it: universities, for instance, or the "academies" or discussion groups that proliferated during the Renaissance in Italy and elsewhere. Thanks to the publication of so many sermons of this period, ranging from those of Bernardino of Siena to those of John Donne, posterity has some sense of the importance of preaching. By contrast, the many transactions on the bourses of the period, however important they once were, have left few traces even in archives, like so many political and religious discussions on the marketplace or in the tavern, recorded only when the suspicion of heresy or subversion led the authorities to ask witnesses what had been said.

In this section I shall privilege circulation across frontiers. The following statements about the circulation of people are based on prosopography; in other words, the collective biography of some 500 particularly mobile artists, scholars, and writers of the Renaissance. The study of these lives should make it possible to say something relatively precise and concrete about the routes along which certain kinds of knowledge traveled in the period, and especially about the cities that were the most important nodes in the network or networks of communication.

Architecture may not travel, but architects do, and Italian architects and masons worked not only in western Europe but also in Bohemia, Poland, and as far east as Muscovy. The sedentary painters of the period, such as Giovanni Bellini in Venice or Lucas Cranach in Wittenberg, were matched by nomads such as El Greco, whose route from Crete to Toledo took him through Venice and Rome, or the Flemish artist Bartholomeus Spranger, who came from Antwerp and lived in Italy before settling in central Europe, first in Vienna and later in Prague. Italians were often invited to court by foreign rulers, as Tsar Ivan III of Muscovy invited Aristotele Fioravanti, or Francis I invited Leonardo, Andrea del Sarto, Rosso, Primaticcio, and Cellini.[12] As in the case of China mentioned earlier, the awareness of an alternative style – in this case following the migration of artists rather than their prints – had far-reaching effects. In the case of Valencia, the arrival of the Italian artist Paolo da San Leocadio in 1472 is said to have "changed Valencian painting almost overnight."[13]

Artists from a number of European countries traveled in the reverse direction. Some went to Italy to study, as in the cases of the Netherlanders Pieter Brueghel, Marten van Heemskerck, and Jan Scorel, or the Welshman Inigo Jones. The Spaniard Alonso Berruguete saw the cartoon for Michelangelo's *Battle of Cascina* when he was in Florence in 1503. Some of these foreigners entered the studios of well-known Italian artists: the Fleming Jan Van Calcar and the Spaniard Juan Fernández de Navarrete both worked with Titian.

Already in this period, before the rise of Amsterdam in the seventeenth century, the Netherlands, north and south, played an important role in the process of cultural exchange. Artists from the Netherlands traveled to England (Hans Eworth, William Scrots), to the Baltic (Willem Boy, Cornelis II Floris, Johan Gregor van der Schardt), and to central Europe (Roland Savery, Spranger, Adrian de Vries, Hans Vredeman de Vries).

Many scholars also traveled widely, thanks to the mobility permitted by the university system as well as to the difficulty of finding employment and the need for good humanists to study in Italy. As we shall see, many were attracted by the universities of Padua and Bologna, as well as by the cities of Rome, Venice, and Florence. A number of scholars led itinerant lives. Jakob Monau, for instance, moved from his native Breslau (Wrocław) to Leipzig, Heidelberg, Wittenberg, Padua, and Geneva, while the Hungarian Johannes Sambucus (also known as János Zsámboky) worked in Vienna, Wittenberg, Paris, Padua, Bologna, and Prague. A few humanists went still further afield. Johannes Dantiscus was active in Danzig (now Gdańsk), Cracow, Venice, Jerusalem, Vienna, London, Lyon, and Madrid. Damião de Gois circulated between Lisbon, Antwerp, Padua, London, Cracow, and Moscow, while Nicholas Clenardus went from Leuven to Paris, Salamanca, Evora, Granada, and Fez.

In the early stages of the Renaissance, minor Italian humanists enjoyed a prestige that would probably have been denied to them had they stayed at home, like Bonfini at the court of King Matthias. Later Italians tended to move for religious reasons. Giordano Bruno's travels took him from the south of Italy to Paris, London, Frankfurt, and Venice, volubly expounding his unorthodox ideas all the way. Italian Protestants fled to Switzerland, Poland, or England, where they were sometimes active as translators.

Printers too were mobile, especially German printers, a European diaspora that might be compared in numbers and intellectual importance to the diasporas of Greeks and Protestants previously mentioned.[14] For instance, the Cromberger family settled in Seville and was active there from 1500 to 1552, as well as opening branches in Lisbon and Evora and establishing a monopoly of the book trade with Mexico. They published Italian classics, among them Petrarch, Boccaccio, and Castiglione, as well as Spanish writers.

Other famous examples of expatriate German printers include Johann and Wendelin von Speyer, who introduced the press to Venice in 1467; Johan Siberch of Cologne, the first printer in Cambridge; and Johann Trechsel and Sebastian Gryphius (or Greif), both of whom established themselves in Lyon. Gryphius published accessible editions of the classics, as well as of Renaissance scholars such as Valla, and employed writers such as Rabelais and the poets Clément Marot and Maurice Scève.

Foreign travel was expensive, so that patrons had a contribution to make to the process of intellectual exchange by making it possible for poets and artists to go abroad. Thus the poet Samuel Daniel visited Italy with his patron Sir Edward Dymoke, while Inigo Jones went with Lord Arundel. Appropriately enough, diplomats played an important role as mediators. When Sir Edward Stafford was appointed ambassador to France in 1583 he took Daniel with him, and also Richard Hakluyt as his chaplain and secretary. Pierre Belon and Guillaume Postel both traveled to Istanbul in the suite of a French ambassador, thus launching their careers as orientalists. It is time to examine the routes taken both by people and by ideas.

Italian Jesuits worked in Poland-Lithuania, Muscovy, India, China, and Japan, founding colleges and writing accounts of the countries in which they established missions – Antonio Possevino on Muscovy, Matteo Ricci on China, and so on. Jesuits have often been mentioned in this chapter: the reason is that the network of colleges that they established in Europe – including eastern Europe, from Braunsberg (Braniewo) and Elbing (Elbląg) to Kiev and Vitebsk – and also beyond Europe, from Goa to São Paulo, encouraged the movement of teachers, while the rule that each Jesuit establishment should write annual letters to the headquarters in Rome meant that a good deal of information was transmitted, much of which was soon translated and printed to reach a wide audience interested in the success of Catholic missions.

The movement of travelers beyond Europe made a major contribution to the spread of ideas and information.[15] They include not only the people now remembered primarily as travelers, such as the Flemish diplomat Ogier Ghiselin de Busbecq or the Italian Ludovico de Varthema, but a number of scholars such as Pierre Belon (who visited Egypt), Nicolaus Clenardus (who learned Arabic in Morocco), and João de Barros (who was in Guinea from 1522 to 1525). They also include some writers, marked by their imperial experiences, including Mateo Alemán, author of a famous Spanish novel, who lived in Mexico; Cervantes (who spent five years as a captive, mainly in North Africa); the Spanish poet Alonso de Ercilla (who lived in what is now Chile and wrote a poem about it); and the Portuguese poet Luis de Camões (some of whose adventures in Morocco, Goa, the Moluccas, China, and Mozambique between 1553 and 1569 are reflected in his epic *The Lusiads*).

ROUTES AND NODES

It is often said that heresy follows trade routes. The point can be generalized still further, emphasizing the importance of pre-existing routes, whether economic, political or military, for the transmission of all kinds of information and ideas. The Silk Road from China to the West facilitated the movement of news and religious doctrines along with the caravans of traders. The annual Frankfurt Fair was a center of trade in knowledge or at least in books. Books and paintings as well as cloth and silk traveled along the routes between Bruges and Florence, Lyon, and Italy. I say "routes" rather than "roads" because many people traveled by boat or ship. The transport of bulky goods was much cheaper by water than by land, and ships transmitted news as well. Lyon owed much of its cultural as well as its economic importance to its position at the confluence of the Rhône and the Saône as well as of land routes between Paris and Italy.

Routes were shaped by political as well as economic factors. It was the existence of a Venetian empire that led El Greco to pass through Venice on what turned out to be his way from Crete to Toledo. Ideas as well as troops passed along the so-called "Spanish Road," which connected the Netherlands with Lombardy at a time when both were ruled by Spain. The rise of permanent ambassadors in this period led to the circulation of a good deal of political knowledge via the diplomatic bags.

At this point it may be useful to try to identify the major nodes of communication in Renaissance Europe. A node may be defined as the point of intersection of different routes, or in the case of prosopography, the point of intersection of individual trajectories. Looking at the travels of our 500 artists, writers, and scholars, it turned out that there were 18 cities altogether in which ten or more of them resided as foreigners. Eight of these cities attracted 20 or more foreigners each, of which five attracted more than 40 apiece (see Figure 9.1).

It is hardly surprising to find that Rome attracted the most, 83 altogether. All roads led to Rome, since it was at once the headquarters of the Church, a museum city full of classical antiquities, a center of printing (including polyglot printing, linked to Catholic missions), and a center of cultural patronage. In the second

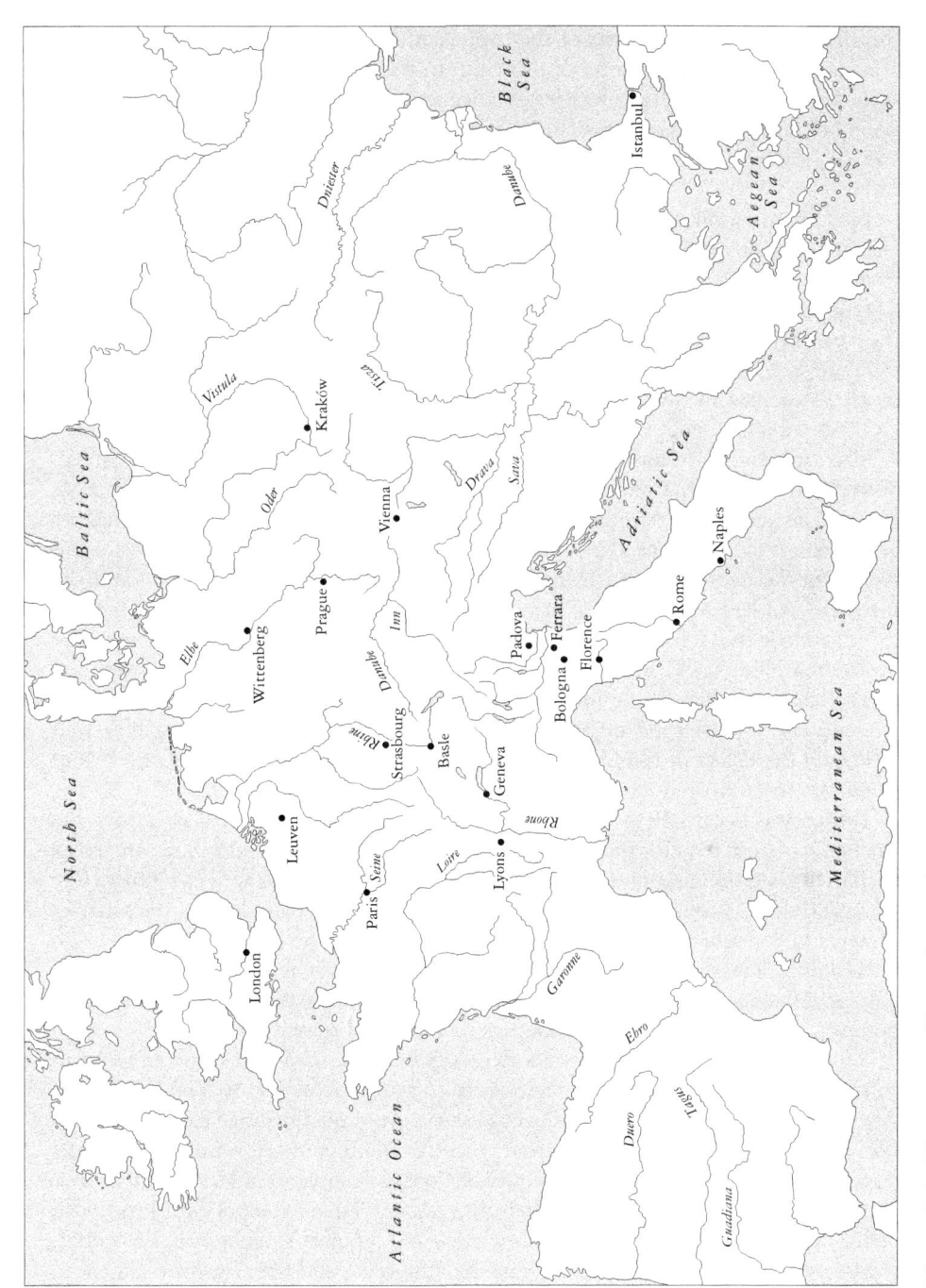

Figure 9.1 The centers of humanist activity.

place came Padua, a university city in which 61 of the sample studied, including a number of Englishmen.[16] In the third place Paris, with 46 foreigners, thanks to its combination of the attractions of the capital of a major European state with those of a university city and a center of printing. In the fourth place, with 40 foreigners each, were two very different cities: Venice and Bologna, the first combining the functions of a port, the capital of an empire, and a printing center, while the second was essentially a university town but one that attracted many students from outside Italy.

Next in importance came Basle, on the Rhine, another university town, a frontier city and a print center (a not unusual combination). Basle attracted 36 foreigners from our sample, whether Netherlanders (Erasmus), Frenchmen (the humanist Claude Chansonette and the poet François Malherbe), Germans (Paracelsus) or Italians (the Protestant refugees Celio Secundo Curione and Pietro Perna). It was followed by Florence (with 21 foreigners); Wittenberg (with 16); Ferrara and Prague (with 15 each); Cracow and Vienna (13 each); Istanbul, London, and Naples (12 each); and finally Geneva, Leuven, Lyon, and Strasbourg (with ten each).

The attractions of Florence to both artists and humanists scarcely need listing. Wittenberg was both a university town and, for Lutherans, a holy city, attracting Hungarians such as the religious writer Péter Bornemisza and the humanist Johannes Sambucus, Poles such as the political thinkers Andrzej Frycz Modrzewski and Krzysztof Warszewicki, and Danes such as the astronomer Tycho Brahe and the historian Anders Vedel. These students obviously helped Luther's message to spread outside the German-speaking world. Geneva played a similar role as the center of international Calvinism, attracting Frenchmen such as François Hotman, Netherlanders such as Philip Marnix, and Germans such as Paul Melissus (Calvinist students also went to the University of Heidelberg until the city was re-catholicized following the defeat of the Elector Palatine Frederick V at the battle of the White Mountain in 1620).

Ferrara was essentially a university town and so was Leuven, while Cracow was the home of both a major university and the Polish court, attracting foreign artists such as Santo Gucci and musicians such as Valentin Bakfark, as well as scholars like Conrad Celtis or Johannes Aventinus. In the case of Prague, despite the Charles University, foreigners were attracted almost entirely to the court during the reign of Rudolf II, a major patron of natural and occult philosophy (Tycho Brahe, Johann Kepler, Michael Maier, Michael Sendivogius) as well as the arts (Bartholomeus Spranger, Adrian de Vries, Giuseppe Arcimboldo, and so on).[17]

London, Naples, and Istanbul were all courts and capitals. What attracted Holbein to London, for instance, was the proximity of the court of Henry VIII. Ciriaco of Ancona and Gentile Bellini were active at the court of the Ottoman sultan, while in the years before 1453 the humanists Francesco Filelfo and Giovanni Aurispa had gone to what was still the Byzantine city of Constantinople in order to study Greek and to search for Greek manuscripts. In the case of Naples, the political links with Spain explain the presence of Spanish writers and scholars such as Juan de Valdés, the poets Garcilaso de la Vega and Francisco Quevedo, and the Argensola brothers, who wrote plays, poems, and works of history. As for the cities not in the list, a major surprise is that Antwerp, with nine foreigners, just missed inclusion.

It has to be remembered that the group of 500 is composed only of artists, scholars, and writers. Other kinds of people, most obviously merchants, traveled to major cities and brought knowledge and skills with them. Cities were magnets for local talent as well as for foreigners, as names like Leonardo da Vinci or Desiderio da Settignano, referring to villages near Florence, may remind us.

Some cities outside Europe, notably Goa, Macau, and Nagasaki, attracted relatively few famous foreigners, although Camões visited Goa in 1553 and Ricci was there 30 years later. All the same, these cities played a crucial role in the transmission of ideas both eastwards and westwards, partly through the books published there by Jesuits and others, partly through the export of oriental goods to the West (notably porcelain from China and Japan), and partly through the information that returning merchants, missionaries, and soldiers gave to writers such as João de Barros, the historian of the Portuguese in Asia.

CIRCLES AND SOCIABILITY

Of course, the nodes, like the prosopographical method itself, give us no more than a skeleton that needs to be fleshed out, so far as surviving documents permit. Renaissance cities were not only magnets for talent but also spaces for encounter and intellectual exchange – in marketplaces, palaces, colleges, taverns, and elsewhere. They allowed the formation of social and intellectual circles, networks of patronage and of discussion. What might be called the "micro-circulation" of ideas through personal networks is linked to their "macro-circulation" through the nodes.

Take the example of the English humanist physician Thomas Linacre. Linacre went to a monastic school, Christ Church Canterbury. The prior of Christ Church had recently studied in Padua, which may well have encouraged Thomas's aspirations. Like some other scholars mentioned earlier, he had the opportunity to visit Italy in the suite of an embassy (in this case to the pope). He took the opportunity to study not only at the University of Padua but also in Florence with the humanist Angelo Poliziano. In Rome he met another leading humanist, Ermolao Barbaro, and in Venice he came to know the scholar-printer Aldus Manutius. On returning to England he established himself in London, moved in court circles, and taught Thomas More Greek, together with his older colleague William Grocyn, who had also visited Italy and met Aldus.

Like Linacre, Grocyn, and John Colet (whose visit to Rome made him aware of humanist scholarship), Erasmus was a member of Thomas More's circle in London. He also formed part of the network of the printer Johann Froben in Basle. Froben employed the scholar Beatus Rhenanus (the biographer of Erasmus) in his press and Paracelsus as his physician. Thanks to their common friend Froben, Erasmus and Paracelsus met, although we do not know what they talked about.

Again, there is a fascinating circle of "artists, jewelers, heretics" that has recently been reconstructed by the historian Massimo Firpo. It centers on the Venetian painter Lorenzo Lotto, whose religious ideas appear to have been somewhat unorthodox. Among Lotto's acquaintances were the architect Serlio and the jeweler-poet Alessandro Caravia, both of whom were also suspected of holding unorthodox beliefs.

Another unorthodox circle surrounded the Spanish humanist Juan de Valdés when he was living in Naples and included the noblewomen Vittoria Colonna, Caterina Cibò, and Giulia Gonzaga.[18]

A new literary genre of the sixteenth century allows historians to reconstruct some of these personal networks. It is the "album amicorum," a kind of visitor's book in which friends would write comments or proverbs as well as signing their names. A cluster of albums from the Netherlands in the later sixteenth century has survived in which a number of names recur, among them a few artists (Lucas de Heere, Hubert Goltzius, Georg Hoefnagel, and Otto van Veen, the teacher of Rubens); a few merchants (including the printer Christophe Plantin, a Frenchman who settled in Antwerp); and a number of humanists, including the geographer Abraham Ortelius, the poet Janus Dousa, Philips van Marnix (an adviser to William the Silent), the philologist Bonaventure de Smet (who called himself "Vulcanius"), Justus Lipsius (a central figure in the neo-stoic movement), and Hugo Grotius, best known today for his theory of international law but also a good example of the Renaissance "universal man."[19] Women sometimes participated in these networks. Of 186 albums from the Netherlands that were begun before 1600, 13 belonged to women, among them Philips' daughter Marie de Marnix.

Women were still more prominent in the conversation groups, not yet called salons, such as that of Princess Margaret of Navarre at her court (including Marot, Rabelais, and Serlio, among others) or that of the poetess Louise Labé in Lyon (including Maurice Scève).[20] The picture painted by Castiglione in his *Courtier* of women directing the conversation – even if they allowed men to do most of the talking – was at least on occasion a realistic one.

The intellectual consequences of the formation of circles such as these are not easy to tease out. We might describe this as the "Yates problem," since the scholar Frances Yates devoted a good deal of effort to reconstructing circles of Renaissance artists and humanists in Paris, Heidelberg, and around the itinerant scholar Giordano Bruno, who lived at various times in Geneva, Lyon, Paris, London, Wittenberg, Prague, and Frankfurt.[21] Yates's work has sometimes been criticized for moving too smoothly from the fact that certain people met one another regularly to the conclusion that they shared certain beliefs. Experience suggests that an intellectual circle may flourish precisely because of differences in opinions of the kind evoked so vividly by Castiglione. What participation in a social circle allows historians to say about particular individuals is no more than that they must have been aware of certain ideas and that they found dialogue on these topics to be possible. However, this conclusion, cautious as it is, is also a significant one.

As one might have expected, the evidence for the circulation of information in this period is fragmentary and also biased, privileging formal institutions over informal groupings, the medium of print over oral and even handwritten communication, and the knowledge of social and political elites over that of ordinary people, especially women. All the same, an examination of the course of change over more than two centuries suggests that knowledge of many different kinds – religious and secular, theoretical and practical, knowledge of nature and knowledge of society – was coming from further afield, that it was accumulating, that it was traveling more rapidly, and that it was reaching more people than ever before. The increase and the spread of knowledge about the world beyond Europe were particularly dramatic, taking the form of maps, dictionaries, and grammars of Asian, African, and American languages as well as travelogues and histories. Whether this increase in knowledge led to a decline in prejudice and a better understanding of that world it is obviously impossible to say, but that problem is not peculiar to the age of the Renaissance.

NOTES

1 Robert W. Scribner, "Oral Culture and the Diffusion of Reformation Ideas," *History of European Ideas* 5 (1984): 237–56; Harold Love, *Scribal Publication in Seventeenth-century England* (Oxford: Oxford University Press, 1993); Fernando J. Alvarez Bouza, *Corre manuscrito: una historia cultural del Siglo de Oro* (Madrid: Marcial Pons, 2001).
2 R. R. Bolgar, *The Classical Heritage and its Beneficiaries* (Cambridge: Cambridge University Press, 1954); L. D. Reynolds and N. G. Wilson, *Scribes and Scholars. A Guide to the Transmission of Greek and Latin Literature*, 2nd edn (Oxford: Clarendon Press, 1974).
3 Elizabeth Eisenstein, *The Printing Press as an Agent of Change* (Cambridge: Cambridge University Press, 1979).
4 Marcel Bataillon, *Erasme et l"Espagne* (Geneva: Droz, 1937); Silvana Seidel Menchi, *Erasmo in Italia, 1520–1580* (Torino: Bollati Boringhieri, 1987).
5 Brendan Dooley and Sabrina Baron (eds) *The Politics of Information in Early Modern Europe* (London: Routledge, 2001); M. Infelise, *Prima dei Giornali: Alle origini della pubblica informazione* (Rome and Bari: Laterza, 2002).
6 Francis Haskell and Nicholas Penny, *Taste and the Antique* (New Haven and London: Yale University Press, 1981); Leonard Barkan, *Unearthing the Past. Archaeology and Aesthetics in the Making of Renaissance Culture* (New Haven and London: Yale University Press, 1999).
7 Francis Ames-Lewis, *Drawing in Early Renaissance Italy*, 2nd edn (New Haven and London: Yale University Press, 2000).
8 David Landau and Peter W. Parshall, *The Renaissance Print 1470–1550* (New Haven and London: Yale University Press, 1994), 237–40; R. W. Scribner, *For the Sake of Simple Folk: Popular Propaganda for the German Reformation*, 2nd edn (Oxford: Oxford University Press, 1994).
9 Numa Broc, *La géographie de la Renaissance*, 2nd edn (Paris: Éditions du CTHS, 1986).
10 Anthony Alan Shelton, "Cabinets of Transgression: Renaissance Collections and the Incorporation of the New World," in John Elsner and Roger Cardinal (eds) *The Cultures of Collecting* (London: Reaktion, 1994), 175–203.
11 Henri Zerner, *Le stampe e la diffusione delle immagini e degli stili* (Bologna: CLUEB, 1983); J. F. Cahill, *The Compelling Image: Nature and Style in Seventeenth-century Chinese Painting* (Cambridge, Mass.: Harvard University Press, 1982), 75; Jonathan Spence, *The Memory Palace of Matteo Ricci* (London: Faber, 1985).
12 On Francis as a patron, see R. J. Knecht, *Renaissance Warrior and Patron*, 2nd edn (Cambridge: Cambridge University Press, 1994).
13 Jonathan Brown, *The Golden Age of Painting in Spain* (New Haven and London: Yale University Press, 1991), 20.
14 Ferdinand Geldner, *Die deutsche Inkunabeldrucker*, 2 vols (Stuttgart: Hiersemann, 1968–70).
15 Joan Pau Rubiés, *Travel and Ethnology in the Renaissance: South India through European Eyes, 1250–1625* (Cambridge: Cambridge University Press, 2000).

16 Jonathan Woolfson, *Padua and the Tudors: English Students in Italy, 1485–1603* (Cambridge: Clarke, 1998).
17 T. D. Kaufmann, *The School of Prague: Painting at the Court of Rudolf II* (Chicago and London: Chicago University Press, 1988).
18 Massimo Firpo, *Artisti, gioiellieri, eretici: Il mondo di Lorenzo Lotto tra Riforma e Controriforma* (Rome and Bari: Laterza, 2001).
19 Chris L. Heesakkers and Kees Thomassen, *Voorlopige lijst van alba amicorum uit de Nederlanden voor 1800* (The Hague: Koninklijke Bibliotheek, 1986); on Smet, see A. Roersch, "L'album amicorum de Bonaventure Vulcanius," *Revue du 16e siècle* 14 (1927): 61–76.
20 Lucien Febvre, *Amour sacré, amour profane: autour de l'"Heptaméron"* (Paris: Gallimard, 1944); L. Clark Keating, *Studies on the Literary Salon in France, 1550–1615* (Cambridge, Mass.: Harvard University Press, 1941).
21 Frances Yates, *Giordano Bruno and the Hermetic Tradition* (London: Routledge, 1964); also her *The Rosicrucian Enlightenment* (London and Boston: Routledge, 1972).

SUGGESTIONS FOR FURTHER READING

Ames-Lewis, Francis. *Drawing in Early Renaissance Italy*, 2nd edn. New Haven and London: Yale University Press, 2000.

Barkan, Leonard. *Unearthing the Past: Archaeology and Aesthetics in the Making of Renaissance Culture*. New Haven and London: Yale University Press, 1999.

Bataillon, Marcel. *Erasme et l' Espagne*. Geneva: Droz, 1937.

Bolgar, R. R. *The Classical Heritage and its Beneficiaries*. Cambridge: Cambridge University Press, 1954.

Bouza, Fernando J. Alvarez. *Corre manuscrito: una historia cultural del Siglo de Oro*. Madrid: Marcial Pons, 2001.

Broc, Numa. *La géographie de la Renaissance*, 2nd edn. Paris: Éditions du CTHS, 1986.

Burke, Peter. *A Social History of Knowledge from Gutenberg to Diderot*. Cambridge: Polity Press, 2000.

Dooley, Brendan. *Morandi's Last Prophecy and the End of Renaissance Politics*. Princeton: Princeton University Press, 2002.

Dooley, Brendan and Sabrina A. Baron, eds. *The Politics of Information in Early Modern Europe*. London: Routledge, 2001.

Eisenstein, Elizabeth L. *The Printing Press as an Agent of Change*. Cambridge: Cambridge University Press, 1979.

Evans, R. J. W. *Rudolf II and his World: A Study in Intellectual History, 1576–1612*, 3rd edn. London: Thames & Hudson, 1997.

Firpo, Massimo. *Artisti, gioiellieri, eretici: Il mondo di Lorenzo Lotto tra Riforma e Controriforma*. Rome and Bari: Laterza, 2001.

Haskell, Francis and Nicholas Penny. *Taste and the Antique*. New Haven and London: Yale University Press, 1981.

Infelise, Mario. *Prima dei Giornali: Alle origini della pubblica informazione*. Rome and Bari: Laterza, 2002.

Kaufmann, T. D. *The School of Prague: Painting at the Court of Rudolf II*. Chicago and London: Chicago University Press, 1988.

Kenny, Neil. *The Uses of Curiosity in Early Modern France and Germany*. Oxford: Oxford University Press, 2004.

Lach, Donald. F. and Edwin J. Van Kley. *Asia in the Making of Europe*, 3 vols. Chicago: Chicago University Press, 1965–93.

Landau, David and Peter W. Parshall. *The Renaissance Print 1470–1550*. New Haven and London: Yale University Press, 1994.

Love, Harold. *Scribal Publication in Seventeenth-century England*. Oxford: Oxford University Press, 1993.

Pettegree, Andrew. *Reformation and the Culture of Persuasion*. Cambridge: Cambridge University Press, 2005.

Reynolds, L. D and N. G. Wilson. *Scribes and Scholars: A Guide to the Transmission of Greek and Latin Literature*, 2nd edn. Oxford: Clarendon Press, 1974.

Rubiés, Joan Pau. *Travel and Ethnology in the Renaissance: South India through European Eyes, 1250–1625*. Cambridge: Cambridge University Press, 2000.

Scribner, Robert W. *For the Sake of Simple Folk: Popular Propaganda for the German Reformation*, 2nd edn. Oxford: Oxford University Press, 1994.

Seidel Menchi, Silvana. *Erasmo in Italia, 1520–1580*. Torino: Bollati Boringhieri, 1987.

Spence, Jonathan. *The Memory Palace of Matteo Ricci*. London: Faber & Faber, 1985.

Woolfson, Jonathan. *Padua and the Tudors: English Students in Italy, 1485–1603*. Cambridge: Clarke, 1998.

Zerner, Henri, ed. *Le stampe e la diffusione delle immagini e degli stili*. Bologna: CLUEB, 1983.

CHAPTER TEN

VIGRIL AND HOMER IN POLAND

Michael Tworek

In 1566 Łukasz Górnicki, a humanist and royal secretary to the Polish king Sigismund Augustus, published his *Dworzanin polski* (*The Polish Courtier*), an adaptation of Castiglione's famous book, a bestseller that had already been translated into French, Spanish, English, German, and Latin. Like his contemporary Jan Kochanowski – another major Polish humanist who would achieve fame in this very same period – Górnicki played a major role in the introduction of Italian humanist ideas and practices to Poland. Yet, as we shall see, Górnicki and Kochanowski, despite the fact that they had studied in Padua and moved in overlapping circles of scholars and courtiers in both Italy and Poland, developed humanist practices and their understanding of language and its expression in fundamentally different ways. The transmission of humanist learning to Poland, in short, was shaped both by individual differences in temperament and experience as well as by certain fundamental tensions within European culture more broadly.

By the sixteenth century many noble families of Poland and Lithuania were eager to incorporate "all things ancient" into every aspect of their lives. Instead of erecting fortified castles, they hired Italian architects and built palaces and villas in accordance with the latest architectural fashions. The royal capital of Cracow had been transformed from a medieval town into a flourishing Renaissance city. Interest in humanism was widespread. Both noble and bourgeois alike sent their sons to study at the finest Italian universities.

Górnicki, born in 1527 into a modest burgher family in Oświęcim (infamously known today for its concentration camp, Auschwitz), originally found his way into the worlds of Greece and Rome through the guidance of his uncle, Stanisław Gąsiorek, a royal courtier and poet at the court of King Sigismund I. Gąsiorek, who was also known as Kleryka, achieved fame for his series of panegyrics for the Polish king and his son, the future Sigismund Augustus. His rise in the Polish court made it clear that a humanist education was enormously valuable, and it was only natural that he urged his nephew to pursue a similar course.

Jan Kochanowski, born in 1530 into a noble family in the region of Radom, just to the south of Warsaw and near what would become his country estate of Czarnolas, also studied in Italy. Under the influence of his mother, Anna – whom Górnicki described in *The Polish Courtier* as a "lady full of elegance and wit" – Kochanowski developed an early interest in humanism, as did his siblings Mikołaj and Andrzej, both of whom also went on to study in Italy and become noted humanists themselves. Andrzej translated Virgil's *Aeneid* into Polish, Mikołaj Plutarch's *Lives*.

Yet it was Cracow, a major center of humanist studies in east-central Europe, that served as the first stop for both Kochanowski and Górnicki. Kochanowski began his studies at the university there in 1544 at the age of 14. At the end of the fifteenth century, two eminent humanists, Conrad Celtis and Filippo Buonaccorsi (better known as Callimachus), helped cement the place of humanistic studies in the university's curriculum, and their lectures attracted large numbers of students. Callimachus, who was a close friend of Marsilio Ficino and later an important figure in the Polish royal court, provided Cracow with a direct connection to the ideas and texts of Florentine Platonism, the influence of which lingered within several humanist circles of the city all the way into Górnicki's and Kochanowski's time.[1] Dynastic connections also played a role in the making of Renaissance Cracow. Bona Sforza, the Italian wife of Sigismund I, became a generous patron of the arts immediately upon her arrival in Poland in 1518, bringing with her Italian architects and painters; her influence on Cracow was extensive. It was hardly accidental that the works of several of Cracow's graduates would prove revolutionary and contribute greatly to the larger philosophical discussions and scientific discoveries of the sixteenth and seventeenth centuries. Copernicus, for example, had studied there in the early sixteenth century, and his famous book *De revolutionibus orbium caelestium*, which was written in the humanistic milieu of the ecclesiastical court of Warmia, was published in Basle in 1543, the year before Kochanowski's own arrival at the university.

While Górnicki did not study at the University of Cracow, he was undoubtedly influenced by its teachings. He had arrived in Cracow in 1538, six years earlier than Kochanowski, and had enrolled at the parochial school of St John's to begin his preparatory studies in the humanities. Undoubtedly the bustling humanist activities of the university carried over to St John's, and Górnicki would have had ample opportunity to interact with scholars there. Through his uncle's help, moreover, Górnicki entered into the service of the bishop of Cracow, Samuel Maciejowski, a famous patron of the arts. It was at Maciejowski's Italian-styled palace in Prądnik, a village near Cracow, that Górnicki would receive the inspiration for the characters and setting of his *The Polish Courtier*:

> Near Cracow is a brook called Prądnik. It was here that Samuel Maciejowski, the bishop of Cracow and a royal chancellor, ordered that his beautiful home be built in the Italian style for many good reasons. Most especially of all, so that the private seclusion of the surroundings of Cracow would provide him with a place where he could host distinguished people and the ambassadors of great kings.[2]

Awed by the magnificent depth of the palace's great rooms and the stately presence of ornately decorated columns in view of the scenic stream, Górnicki, like other visitors, appreciated the splendor as well as the respect that such a place would have commanded for Maciejowski. In addition to appreciating the bishop's learned tastes, the young Górnicki would come to honor Maciejowski as a teacher and "father."

This bishop, a second Socrates, always surrounded himself with respected, learned, and dedicated people, on whom he spared no expense. In gathering them around him with great eagerness, his manor became the only school for knightly people (*rycerskich ludzi*), with whom he lived and treated as sons rather than as servants. It brought great joy to the bishop that so many young and talented men were willing to spend their best years in his company.[3]

While in the bishop's household, Górnicki encountered many of the most learned and influential men of all of Poland. As he cleaned the dining tables and filled the cups of the bishop's guests, Górnicki listened to men of great culture and learning such as Jan Dersniak, Andrzej Kostka, and the urbane Wojciech Kryski. All of these men belonged to *akademiej padewskiej między Polaki* (the Paduan Academy of Poles) – an informal group of humanists who had received their educations in Padua and were the leading proponents of a classical education and Italian manners at courts throughout Europe. The young Górnicki even had the opportunity to hear the reactionary yet humorous banter of Stanisław Lupa Podlodowski, who praised the values of Old Poland – fighting, merriment, and distrust of foreigners – while criticizing the Italianate tastes of men such as Kryski. The discussions of these courtiers on the importance of classical literature, the use of Polish language, wit, and philosophy, as well as on contemporary political problems, formed the perfect backdrop for shaping Górnicki's adaptation of Castiglione's work. Moreover, the fascinating narratives of ancient heroes and the witty discussions of these brilliant men, as well as the power they exercised, certainly filled the youthful Górnicki with inspiration. In time, he impressed Bishop Maciejowski, who encouraged him to continue his studies in Padua.

There were other reasons for moving on from Cracow. Though a flourishing center of humanist learning in the region, which continued to attract members from the Polish gentry well into the early seventeenth century, the university simply could not compete with Italian universities such as Bologna and Padua, whose liberating intellectual atmosphere continued to attract new minds and cultivate bold ideas. The on-again/off-again resurgence of scholasticism at the university in Cracow, with professors who taught in the older fashion taking over some of the key professorships and positions in the administration of the institution, certainly did not attract the more discerning among the elite. Equally, an Italian education was an intellectual and social badge of honor for ambitious young men that no institution in the Polish-Lithuanian Commonwealth could offer.

At about the same time Kochanowski realized that he also would have to travel to Italy to further his education. Kochanowski, however, did not immediately set out for Italy. Instead, in 1549, he headed first to Königsberg in northern Ducal Prussia, the location of a recently established academy dedicated to humanistic studies, as well as to the spread of Lutheran ideas into Poland and Lithuania.[4] During his brief stay, he befriended the academy's director, Georgius Sabinus, a German humanist and reformer, who was also the son-in-law of one of the most eminent humanist leaders of the Reformation, Philip Melanchthon. More important, however, he found a munificent benefactor in the person of Albrecht Hohenzollern, the duke of Prussia and the academy's founder, who strongly supported his humanist aspirations and subsequently supplied him with generous funds. The young Pole's humanist interests and religious sympathies must have also appealed to Albrecht's ambition of creating a group of highly educated and reform-minded Polish nobles loyal to him in Poland and Lithuania.[5] When Albrecht died later in 1568, Kochanowski dedicated his *Proporzec, albo Hołd pruski (The Banner, or the Prussian Homage)* to him, praising the former duke's virtues but, above all, his generosity. Armed with the duke's blessing and funds, Kochanowski departed from Königsberg for Italy in late 1550.

Górnicki and Kochanowski's stays in Padua appear never to have overlapped. Górnicki studied there from 1546 to 1549; Kochanowski reached Padua in April, 1551, and was there until 1557 before traveling in France and Germany, ironically, just before Górnicki returned to Padua for a brief stay. Though never classmates, Kochanowski and Górnicki both benefited from the remarkable clustering of scholars and humanists in this northern Italian city whose university was renowned throughout Europe for its accomplishments and advances in medicine, law, and philosophy. Many of the foremost scholars in these fields, such as the philosopher Pietro Pomponazzi and the anatomist Andreas Vesalius, had taught at Padua earlier in the sixteenth century. Consequently, the university's impeccable credentials provided many of its former students with honors and lucrative political positions in their native lands "simply because they [had] been to Padua."[6] A well-trained humanist was a valuable commodity in the princely and ecclesiastical courts of Poland and Lithuania, and, as their later successes as courtiers proved, Kochanowski and Górnicki were no exceptions. Studying with humanists of the highest caliber, such as Francesco Robortello, Bernardino Tomitano, and, above all, Carlo Sigonio, both men acquired a thorough knowledge of Greek and Latin authors, especially Homer and Plato, as well as Cicero, Horace, and Seneca. It was in their studies of the works of Cicero and Seneca that both Kochanowski and Górnicki first established their reputations as scholars, publishing noted translations and working on editions of the writings of these Romans. Through their shared interest in these two Roman writers, both became friends with Andrzej Patrycz Nidecki, a noted scholar of Cicero, who edited a collection of fragments of the Roman statesman's lost works. Since neither Górnicki nor Kochanowski was studying for a degree, they were free to explore any of the vast number of subjects offered in Padua, and could have joined in any of the numerous philosophical discussions in the city. In a sense, Kochanowski's and Górnicki's education in Padua brought them into contact with many aspects of what could be considered a cosmopolitan European culture.

When Kochanowski returned from Italy and his travels in France and Germany, he served as secretary and companion to many powerful and influential figures in Poland and Lithuania. Through his contacts with the Firlejs and Radziwiłłs, among the wealthiest families in Europe, he had gained entry into the courts of princes and bishops who had intimate ties with the crown. He befriended Piotr Myszkowski, Maciejowski's successor as bishop of Cracòw, who also held the postion of royal vice-chancellor and who would become one of Kochanowski's most supportive patrons. It was through Myszkowski's patronage that Kochanowski obtained the prestigious post of royal secretary to the humanist king, Sigismund Augustus. Serving as a secretary in the royal chancellery, Kochanowski found himself immersed in a dynamic mélange of the newest and most significant ideas and movements of the time. Traveling with the royal entourage on important diplomatic visits, he had many opportunities to visit the cities of Vilnius, which would become a leading center of learning in the coming decades, and Warsaw, a city that would soon supplant Cracow as the royal capital. Kochanowski's close proximity to the king and the royal court allowed him to witness the workings, difficulties, and evolutions of the Polish state, which foreign visitors from across Europe had dubbed the "nobleman's paradise." Regional and national *sejms* (parliaments) provided convenient theaters where Kochanowski could see his peers act out the drama of Polish political life, from highly polished, classical-styled orations to bumbling drunken tirades. By the same token, Kochanowski was familiar with the intellectual discussions that permeated the court on the future of the kingdom: balancing royal prerogatives with the nobility's rights, cementing the growing personal union between the Polish Crown and the Grand Duchy of Lithuania, and granting equal political rights to all classes of the population. The political works of Wawrzyniec Goślicki and Andrzej Frycz Modrzewski, both contemporaries of Kochanowski, became well known not only in educated circles in Poland but also throughout the courts of Europe. An educated observer of his surroundings, Kochanowski witnessed at first hand some of Poland's most important political transformations, including the Union of Lublin in 1569, which united Poland and Lithuania into the largest political entity in sixteenth-century Europe. Extending from the Baltic to the Black Sea, the new Polish-Lithuanian Commonwealth experienced its *Złoty Wiek* (Golden Age), a period of widespread prosperity and cultural creativity to which both Kochanowski and Górnicki contributed, each in his own unique way, free of the political disappointments and social tragedies that future Polish writers would inevitably face.[7]

During the 1560s and 1570s, Kochanowski's renown as a poet in the Polish-speaking world reached heights that echoed Virgil's in ancient Rome. Kochanowski's close friends and fellow humanists frequently praised his works, such as *Zgoda* (Concord), the *Pieśni* (Hymns), the *Fraszki* (Trifles), and the *Satyr albo Dziki Mąż* (Satyr or the Wild Man), as "witty," "tasteful," and "learned." Through his outstanding knowledge of Greek and Latin poetry and mastery of his native tongue, he was said to have transformed the Polish language from brick into marble. What had "appeared small at first," Górnicki noted about Kochanowski's literary achievements, "did not seem so small or distant now."[8]

Yet Kochanowski gradually tired of court life. Although Kochanowski was still a favorite at Myszkowski's court at Prądnik, the king had nevertheless passed him up for higher posts and never recognized him as the official royal poet. For a time Kochanowski remained a courtier of Sigismund Augustus, perhaps in the hope of some unexpected change of luck. The death of Sigismund, the lengthy interregnum that followed, and the election and the brief, disastrous reign of a French king, Henry Valois, who ruled the Polish-Lithuanian Commonwealth from 1573 to 1574, dimmed Kochanowski's court ambitions indefinitely. Disappointed with court life, the aging courtier resigned his last prebend in 1575. He then married Dorota of Przytyka, the daughter of Stanisław Lupa Podlodowski, who had been a familiar figure at the court of bishop Maciejowski when Górnicki had served there as a young man. Kochanowski and his wife settled at his estate at Czarnolas, near his boyhood home. For a time, both his poetic and domestic endeavors blossomed, and publication after publication of his works followed. Though Kochanowski was no longer officially tied to the royal court, he did correspond and maintain contacts with important dignitaries who came to his estate to pay to homage to the poet who had become Poland's "lord of language." One of these honored and frequent guests was Jan Zamoyski, a Paduan-educated nobleman who became one of the most powerful and richest men of the Commonwealth as chancellor and grand *hetman* (military commander) to the newly elected king, Stefan Batory. An outstanding student of ancient Roman history and government, as well as an astute politician, Zamoyski understood the value of having a famous and talented poet in his service. Becoming Kochanowski's strongest supporter and patron in the poet's later years, Zamoyski commissioned him to write a play based on the Trojan War, entitled *The Dismissal of the Greek Envoys*. Yet, despite Zamoyski's enticing and sometimes playful requests that he return to court permanently, Kochanowski stayed at his country manor. Soon, the birth of two daughters fulfilled Kochanowski's dream of becoming a father.

Though slightly older than Kochanowski, Górnicki had enjoyed similar success as a writer and as a courtier. Just as Kochanowski was moving into retirement, Górnicki had reached the pinnacle of his career. After his return from Italy, he entered the royal chancellery in 1552. In 1559, he became part of King Sigismund Augustus's retinue as a royal secretary. Górnicki frequently traveled with the king to Gdańsk, Königsberg, and Vienna, all cities with important ties to the Polish kingdom. Górnicki's time at court also allowed him to form and strengthen friendships with leading humanists such as Stanisław Orzechowski and Marcin Kromer, the authors of historical and political tracts on republicanism, not to mention Kochanowski himself. Górnicki impressed the king with his diligence and skill, and Sigismund appointed him royal librarian and charged him with collecting and organizing the royal library, filling it with the newest and finest books from across Europe. Taking advantage of the explosion in publishing and the book trade in this period, Górnicki enriched the collection with a variety of books, ranging from the philosophical writings of Petrarch, Ficino, and Erasmus to the dialogues of Mikołaj Rej, the best-known Polish writer before Kochanowski and Górnicki. Fortunately, Górnicki's efforts did not go unrewarded. As a token of his appreciation, the king ennobled Górnicki and, in a few years, would make him *starosta* (governor) of a province. Not surprisingly, his success as a courtier would also follow him into his literary endeavors.

His success no doubt shaped his adaptation of *The Courtier* into Polish. Significantly, Górnicki's *Courtier* was not, as has been noted, so much a translation as a learned and culturally sensitive paraphrase of a classic text whose author, in Górnicki's opinion, had written with utmost wisdom and eloquence. With the mores and needs of his readers in mind, Górnicki skillfully transposed the discussions of the Court of Urbino to a Polish milieu.[9] While centering the discussions of his characters on the ideal courtier as Castiglione had (albeit an ideal Polish courtier), Górnicki removed the more abstract debates on the nature of painting, sculpture, and music that were central to the Italian original, because Poles "did not know about them" nor were they "useful to an educated Pole."[10] Yet the most dramatic change was Górnicki's erasure of female characters. The women, such as Lady Emilia Pia, who had played important roles in Castiglione's work, were replaced in Górnicki's adaptation by noblemen who guided the conversation. Women, as Górnicki made explicit in his adaptation, were simply not intelligent enough for the learned discussions of men. Whether this was, in fact, Górnicki's personal opinion is not clear – he had, after all, praised Kochanowski's mother – but the exclusion of women undoubtedly reflected the realities of Polish court life where women were, in general, held in less regard than in Italy. In his *Courtier*, Górnicki's ideal Polish lady was a "humble" and submissive one. Nonetheless, Górnicki's adaptation did preserve what is perhaps the central ideal of Castiglione's work: the notion of *sprezzatura* or the ability to make art seem effortless. As Górnicki put it:

> From that I understand grace, as well as gratitude, are essential in human affairs: everyone knows how difficult it is to perform well when the occasion demands it. Truly, a person is befuddled when he sees another performing a feat with the utmost of ease. On the other hand, when this same person struggles with a task, straining himself horribly, it is unpleasant and pitiful to listen and watch. As a result, the deed, though wholly worthwhile, begins to lose its value quickly.[11]

Górnicki also preserved Castiglione's sense of the importance of a humanist education. As he put it in his adaption:

> Returning to my courtier, I would have him well educated not only in the literature (*in litteris*) of the Latin and Greek languages, which the humanists (*humaniores*) recommend, but also in other fields that are written about today, as well as understanding other languages such as German, Italian, French, and Spanish. Equally, he should know all poets, orators, and historians with great thoroughness. In all of these areas, he must study and remember them well, so that he can be knowledgeable and familiar with the history and manners of every place.[12]

For several years Kochanowski must have been happy on his estate. But, then, in 1579, he suffered a personal loss. His daughter Orzula, named in honor of St Ursula, whose legend was so popular in Europe at this time, died unexpectedly in her infancy. Deeply saddened by this loss, Kochanowski abandoned himself to grief.[13] In sixteenth-century Poland, as in much of Renaissance Europe, excessive grief in a man would have "concerned his friends" as well as his family, "who feared to be dishonored by his immoderate expression of sorrow."[14] Despite the social disapproval, Kochanowski ultimately turned to poetry to express publicly the emotional torments of his tragedy. Completed and published in 1580, this testament would be his last gift to Orszula. Kochanowski's touching expression of paternal love for his child, entitled the *Treny* (*Laments*), was a cycle of 19 poems, written not in Latin but in the emerging vernacular – Polish (Figure 10.1).

It would have been one thing for Kochanowski, when Orzula died, simply to describe the pain of grief, while ultimately failing to convey to readers its effect on him. Kochanowski, however, wanted to speak of grief's cruelty in a manner so

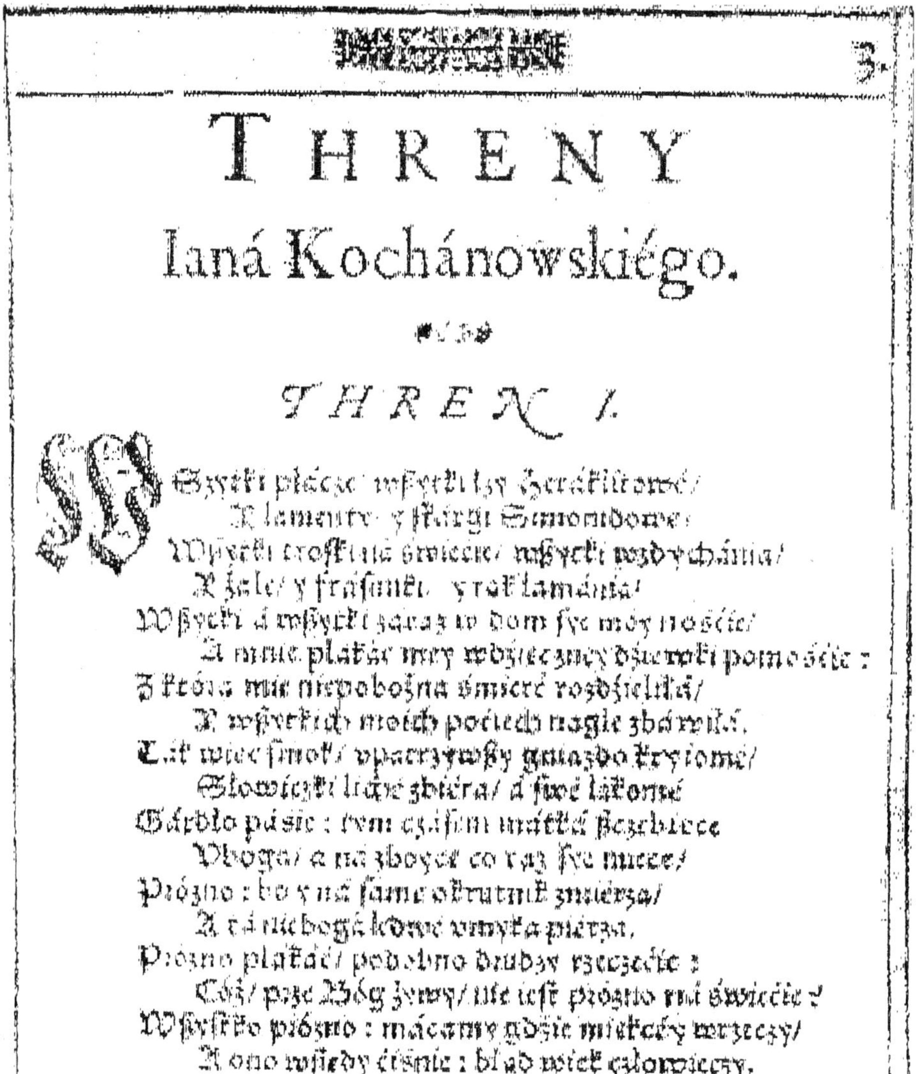
3.

THRENY

Ianá Kochánowskiégo.

THREN I.

Wszytki płácze / wszytki łzy Heráklitowe /
I lamenty / y skárgi Simonidowe /
Wszytki troski ná świecie / wszytki wzdychánia /
I żale / y fráſunki / y rąk łamánia /
Wszytki á wszytki záraz w dom ſie mój noście /
A mnie płákáć mey wdzięczney dźiewki pomoście :
Z którą mię niepobożna śmierć rozdźieliłá /
I wszytkich moich pociech nagle zbáwiłá.
Tak więc ſmok / vpátrzywszy gniázdo kryiome /
Słowiczki liczne zbierá / á ſwe łákome
Gárdło páśie : tym czáſem mátká szczebiece
Vboga / á ná zboycę co raz ſie miece /
Prózno : bo y ná ſámę okrutnik zmierza /
A tá niebogá ledwe vmyka pierza.
Prózno płákáć / podobno drudzy rzeczećie :
Cóż / prze Bóg żywy / nie ieſt prózno ná świećie ?
Wszytko prózno : mácamy gdźie mięcey w rzeczy /
A ono wszedy ciśnie : błąd wiek człowieczy.
Niewiem co lżey / czy w ſmutku iáwnie żáłowáć /
Czyli ſię z przyrodzeniem gwáłtem mocowáć.

A ii Thren

Figure 10.1 Jan Kochanowski. First page of the *Treny* (1580). The British Library.

moving and elegant that his readers could not help but mourn with him. As he labored over the *Treny*, he attempted to find words that would convey every subtlety, every shade, and every nuance of his grief:

> All Heraclitean tears and woes,
>   All plaints and dirges of Simonides,
> All the world's sorrows, griefs and cares,
>   All lamentations and wringing of hands,
> All but all enter my house at once
>   To help me mourn my precious girl
> Whom impious Death has gripped,
>   Suddenly ending all my joy.[15]

Death had robbed Kochanowski of his "precious girl," taking with her all of his comfort and happiness. Profound grief was Death's cruel reward to fathers who had loved their children too much. He questioned the necessity of this "gift," begging Death to remember that Orzsula had not deserved to bear its high cost:

> Oh merciless, cold and remorseless
> Sovereign of departing shades!
>   Orszula died innocent of life's ways:
> The poor child briefly saw the light,
>   Now she journeys into endless night.
> Better if she'd never been!
>   What had she but birth and death?
> Destroying the joy her parents shared
>   She left them anguish and despair.[16]

How could a child, he asked, who only "briefly saw the light" of the world, have suffered Death's penalty? In his poem, Kochanowski conveyed how Death's silence in response to his question angered him, while rage multiplied the weight of his grief. If only Orszula had never existed, then he would not have to hold onto "anguish and despair" instead of her loving embrace. His grief was so strong that he was unable to contain his anger at his daughter. Grief was all that Orszula had bequeathed to her father, and not even those closest to him could convince him otherwise:

> "You mourn in vain" – they say. But
>   Then what, by God, is not vain on earth?
> All is futile! We grope for relief
>   But pain pinches us on every side.
> Error rules our lives![17]

But was his uncontrollable grief pointless, as these lines suggest? Ultimately the *Treny* argued against this perspective. Were not all earthly things "vain" and "futile," he pressed on, if humans could not grieve for ones they had most cherished? Such advice itself was "futile," for it forgot that the "pain" pinching him now in his time of sorrow also was one that could pinch all of humanity. As Kochanowski developed his poem he came to view grief as an "error" that controlled humanity regardless of what one did to prevent or hide it. To him, his own reaction provided convincing evidence enough. It seemed that perhaps his studies and travels to Italy, his talent and fame as a poet, his praise of antiquity, and his service as a courtier, even his very existence, had become worthless in light of this irreparable malady:

In my misfortunes and sorrow,
Which pierce me to the marrow,
I must forsake my lute and scroll,
Perhaps my soul.[18]

In seeking to understand his "misfortunes and sorrow" for Orszula's death, Kochanowski found no solace in his two most prized possessions, the "lute" of his poetic talents and the "scroll" of his humanist learning. Their inability to console became all too apparent. The conundrum that Kochanowski faced was undoubtedly difficult, but he soon realized that his grief was the result of an even greater error, one of which he and all of humanity were culpable:

Oh human error, foolish pride!
How quick to reason
When things go well,
   The head not ill.

Wealthy – we laud the poor,
Content – we sport with sorrow,
While the mean spinner weaves –
   Death's a joke.

But faced with loss or dearth,
We tangle words and deeds
And notice Death
   When she's too near.[19]

Confronted with the stark reality of Orszula's death, Kochanowski had tangled both "words and deeds," realizing the full extent of human fickleness. His previous "words" of consolation and elegies to others now rang hollow. Had not Kochanowski's literary idols, Cicero, Horace, and Seneca, praised those who stoically maintained their virtue and calm in the face of distress? As a "good" humanist, he drew from the philosophical justifications and the literary models of his ancient masters' works and wove Stoic, Epicurean, and Platonic thought into his earlier poetry. Whether expressed in a clever epigram (*Fraszki*), a hymn or song (*Pieśni*), or a longer, more epic consolatory piece (*O Śmierci Jana Tarnowskiego*), Kochanowski's earlier sentiments on grief remained remarkably consistent. Yet, in attempting to find consolation for himself, these same humanist traditions offered him no comfort.

Perhaps it was their wisdom that had been misguided instead. Kochanowski's own experience had shown this dramatically. In fact, Kochanowski knew that he was not the only one to have tangled "words" and "deeds":

> Why weep, fluent Arpinas, when fleeing
> From home – if not just towering Rome
> But the whole world lies
>   Beneath your learned eyes?
>
> Why do you mourn your daughter so?
> Since you only fear disgrace,
> Your other perturbations –
>   But a celebration![20]

The same principles that Cicero had advocated to others in their times of adversity and loss had failed him too, Kochanowski recognized. When Cicero's beloved daughter Tullia died, Kochanowski's idol had also wept bitterly. Did not Cicero fear the horrible "disgrace" that came upon those who could not control their emotions? Perhaps Kochanowski and Cicero had not reacted so differently to the death of their daughters:

> You've proved to all, but not
> Yourself – you too, angelic scribe,
> Cannot match deeds to words when your soul,
>   Like mine, is fouled.[21]

Yet, instead of learning from Cicero's failure, Kochanowski succumbed to foolish pride and fell prey to hypocrisy. Grief now carried Kochanowski down the same path as those he had in earlier times consoled. Within the confines of sorrow, his duty to his family, his dignity as a nobleman, and his status as a courtier no longer seemed to matter. As if trapped in a wakeful coma, he was unable to temper his behavior or emotion in the *Treny*. In an explosion of desperation, Kochanowski asked himself, and his readers, a question that would shape the rest of the *Treny*:

> Is it better openly to grieve
> Or struggle fiercely against nature's course?[22]

Górnicki's ideas in his *The Polish Courtier* offered a striking counterpoint to Kochanowski's public display of grief. For Górnicki's work emphasized the necessity of decorum, and the ability of the courtier to control his emotions. Regardless of the misfortune, Górnicki explained, a courtier like Kochanowski must not descend into despair, nor react or speak with uncharacteristic "straining." The "feat" was controlling struggles of grief. By recording his grief in an exposed and unrepentant manner, Kochanowski had already risked too much, proclaiming his grief and anger to all. For not only was such behavior unbecoming and harmful for him, it was also unpleasant to the eyes and ears of those around him. What was needed on the part of this bereaved father was *przystałość* (grace), the aim of any courtier. Like a noble stoic, Kochanowski must bear his burden, accept his loss, and continue with his life as though nothing had happened. Striving for grace had not always been difficult for Kochanowski. When Górnicki had visited his country house during his retirement, Kochanowski thanked him for the honor of entertaining the "Polish Castiglione," who had enlightened their peers to the therapeutic effects of grace:

> With the arrival of my Górnicki, the joyful lyre struck
>   Gave forth sweet sounds without even a pluck.
> The Graces delighted, the learned Muses sung upon high,
>   Spring returned as Winter grumbled its goodbye.[23]

The fundamental difference in the temperament between these two Polish humanists – Kochanowski so open with his feelings and Górnicki so guarded – echoed a larger tension within European culture in the late sixteenth century. For it was in this period that many humanists and religious reformers began to place greater and greater emphasis on the value of openness and sincerity in one's language, an ideal that Kochanowski certainly embraced. In this regard, Kochanowski was the more modern of the two humanists. Górnicki's ideals as expressed in *The Polish Courtier* were in keeping with an earlier Renaissance emphasis on the prudential self – and it was certainly this emphasis that helped him navigate the treacherous waters of the court. Kochanowski, by contrast, was more open with his emotions. The tension between these two ideals was widespread in the late Renaissance and likely played some role in Poland, as elsewhere in Europe, in shaping new notions of the individual as an agent caught between the pressures of dissimulation and the ideal of transparency – a difficult but increasingly necessary negotiation in the courts of Europe.[24]

After fierce and intense internal torment, Kochanowski did find solace for his grief in *Treny*. Rejecting all consolations and appeals from his friends, Kochanowski at last looked to a "neglected" corner of his life for repose in the midst of his distress:

> So I'll shed tears
> Having lost all hope
> To be saved by reason.
> Only God halts pain.[25]

Abandoning the hope of finding relief in hiding his grief, Kochanowski realized that only his faith could ease the pain of his heartache. Through searching deep within himself for his grief's cure, he finally recognized that humanity's "virtue and happiness . . . [came] entirely from God."[26] The God of Kochanowski's *Treny* appeared quite different from the God of his first Polish hymn. Not surprisingly, personal tragedy was at the heart of this change. In an outward and contrite manner, Kochanowski recognized his failing as the source of his grief:

> I have greatly erred,
> But Your benevolence

Outweighs my sins
Grant me mercy now![27]

Kochanowski's grief brought to the surface the inherent conflict between reason and religious faith, as well as the larger tension between sincerity and prudence, which the "ambivalence" of humanism had obscured.[28] The life, death, and salvation of humanity remained solely in God's will, rendering demands and whims of society irrelevant in the face of a stern master. Suffering had reminded Kochanowski of this, prompting him to seek out divine grace in search of solace. Complete surrender to divine will was Kochanowski's collateral for the hope of relief, and in return he received some familiar advice in the form of a dream from an important figure of his past, his deceased mother:

Do not despair! So judge your losses and dashed hopes
As not to forget your reason and serenity are more precious![29]

Appearing in a dream with young Orszula in her hand, Kochanowski's mother urges him not to lose his mind over grief anymore. She reminds her son that worse misfortunes have befallen others. "Fortune" had no human master. Echoing the words of Cicero, Kochanowski's mother tells her son to "bear man's fate like a man." Strangely, his mother's pleas for "reason and serenity" also echoed Górnicki's, while anticipating those of another mother to her son in a tragedy of an English playwright at the dawn of the seventeenth century. Clearly, the most important speaker in the *Treny* was the one that was most conspicuously absent in *The Polish Courtier*: a woman. So, why did Kochanowski turn to his mother rather than to his friend?

Aside from familial considerations, the difference lay in their understanding of Kochanowski's personal struggle. "Heal yourself, Master!" she commanded. With her powerful words, Kochanowski validated his personal struggle with loss and grief throughout the *Treny*. He was the "master" of himself, his emotions, and his unadulterated expression of them. While urging her son's return to more rational behavior, Kochanowski's mother offered this counsel for the sake of his serenity, not for those around him. He was her son first, not a poet, a scholar, or a courtier. Seeking personal serenity would thus be the most sincere way of being prudent and the most prudent form of sincerity. However, as he searched for the serenity that his mother urged, Kochanowski soon discovered that the peace and repose he sought would prove more elusive than he could have imagined.

Towards the middle of 1583, news reached Kochanowski that a band of marauders, possibly Tartar soldiers, had killed Jakub Podlodowski, his brother-in-law and close friend, in a raid within the borders of the Commonwealth. Kochanowski immediately set out for Lublin, where he would find King Stefan Batory, leaving his wife, then pregnant, and Czarnolas for the last time. His goal was to convince the king to exact justice for this murder; he believed that his close relations with Batory and his entourage would guarantee that justice would be served to those who had murdered Podlodowski. Unfortunately, neither the king nor Kochanowski's allies at court were to help him. At this moment their hands were tied by larger, more pressing political matters such as playing off the threat of both Muscovy and the Habsburgs to the

Commonwealth while also placating the Ottomans. The pleas of an old courtier seemed to fall on deaf ears at that moment. Akin to his sorrow over Orszula's death, it seemed that "fortune," yet again, did not favor Kochanowski when the personal stakes were at their highest. He would not live long enough to regain "fortune's" favor. While still furiously waiting for another opportunity for redress, Kochanowski died suddenly in Lublin on August 22, 1584. In the midst of such bitter and unpleasant circumstances, Kochanowski's unexpected death brought no shortage of mourning to his numerous friends and admirers, not the least among them Górnicki.

The death of his close friend Kochanowski took place at a decisive crux in Górnicki's life. As a governor of an important province, the lord of a sizeable estate, a distinguished member of the royal entourage, and, perhaps more importantly, a respected and learned writer, Górnicki had reached the heights of professional success that he had laid out in *The Polish Courtier* in the years leading up to Kochanowski's death, embodying his own picture of a courtier to perfection. In addition to fulfilling his numerous obligations, Górnicki had also married and started a family. In a display of seemingly perfect symmetry, the happiness of his personal life soon matched the achievement of his career as a humanist and courtier with the birth of his children. Yet, Kochanowski's death appeared as an omen for a string of tragedies that soon fell upon Górnicki. In 1587 Górnicki's master and latest benefactor, King Batory, died, possibly poisoned, amidst squabbles with the unruly Polish *szlachta* (nobility) over strengthening his authority. Not long after the king's death, Andrzej Patrycz Nidecki, one of Górnicki's closest friends from his school days in Cracow and Padua, also died suddenly. Then, shortly afterwards, he lost his wife, Barbara. After a lifetime all but free from tragic ordeals, Górnicki now found himself awash in the same ocean of grief that had overwhelmed Kochanowski. In confronting death in an elegy to his wife, Górnicki now seemed to be echoing his old friend's dirges and laments on pain and grief:

> O blood thirsty death, why did you not murder me
> And take my life away instead of the one I held dear?
> [. . .]
> Be it so, cruel one, you still stole from me;
> For in stealing my love, you took a greater toll from me.
> Finish me now, you savage, as your act of contrition,
> And, holding me as your spouse, cut me down mercilessly![30]

Still, no matter how painful and bitter the loss of his loved ones was to him, Górnicki's poem was tame, even emotionally restrained, in comparison to Kochanowski's wrenching expressiveness in the *Treny*. Though his private grief might have been every bit as intense as Kochanowski's, Górnicki managed to remain remarkably stoic, at least publicly. Within a short time he returned to his courtly and literary pursuits as if tragedy had never touched his life, though it was perhaps no accident that he devoted his scholarship to Seneca, translating two of the stoic's works into Polish: his *Troas* and *On Philanthropy*. Using his political experience and following in the footsteps of his predecessors, Orzechowski and Kromer, he also turned to documenting the history of the Polish state as well as suggesting improvements for it in his last years. Though published many years after his death in 1603, his political works, not surprisingly, still echoed the ideals that he, Kochanowski, and many other humanists in Poland and throughout Europe had learned from the masters of antiquity as well as from each other, that harmony and balance were the keys to happiness.

Górnicki's *The Polish Courtier* and Kochanowski's *Treny* contributed to an important conversation about grace and grief, sincerity and prudence, fortune and death. Theirs was a dialogue, in the end, that echoed broader tensions in European culture as men and women struggled with questions of civility and power in the early modern world. Not surprisingly, the Renaissance would find various resolutions to these tensions, not only in Italy and western Europe but in Poland as well.

NOTES

1 Harold B. Segel, *Renaissance Culture in Poland: The Rise of Humanism, 1470–1543* (Ithaca: Cornell University Press, 1989), 22–3.
2 Górnicki, Łukasz, *Dworzanin polski* (Wrocław: Zakład im. Ossolinskich, 1954), 14–15.
3 Górnicki, *Dworzanin polski*, 15.
4 George Hunston Williams, *The Radical Reformation* (Philadelphia: Westminister Press, 1962), 404–7.
5 Janusz Pelc, *Kochanowski: Szczyt renesansu w literaturze polskiej* (Warszawa: Wydawnictwo Naukowe PWN, 2001), 34–5.
6 Paul Grendler, "The University of Padua 1405–1600: A Success Story," in *Books and Schools in the Italian Renaissance* (Aldershot: Variorium, 1995), 13–14.
7 Czesław Miłosz, "Foreword," in *The Polish Renaissance in its European Context* (Bloomington: Indiana University Press, 1988), xii.
8 Górnicki, *Dworzanin polski*, 14.
9 Peter Burke, *The Fortunes of the Courtier: The European Reception of Castiglione's Cortegiano* (University Park: Pennsylvania State University Press, 1996), 90.
10 Gornicki, *Dworzanin polski*, 7.
11 Górnicki, *Dworzanin polski*, 39.
12 Górnicki, *Dworzanin polski*, 54.
13 Jan Kochanowski, "Dedication," *Treny: The Lamentations of Kochanowski*, trans. Adam Czerniawski (Oxford: European Humanities Research Centre of the University of Oxford, 2001), 2–3.
14 Margaret King, *The Death of the Child Valerio Marcello* (Chicago: University of Chicago Press, 1994), 148.
15 Kochanowski, *Treny*, 4–5.
16 Kochanowski, *Treny*, 6–7.
17 Kochanowski, *Treny*, 4–5.
18 Kochanowski, *Treny*, 34–5.
19 Kochanowski, *Treny*, 34–5.
20 Kochanowski, *Treny*, 34–5.
21 Kochanowski, *Treny*, 36.
22 Kochanowski, *Treny*, 5.
23 Jan Kochanowski, "Ad Lucam Gornicium," in *Złacińska śpiewa Słowian Muza*, ed. Grzegorz Żurek (Warszawa: Panstwowy Instytut Wydawniczy, 1982), 236–7.

24 John Martin, "Inventing Sincerity, Refashioning Prudence: The Discovery of the Individual in Renaissance Europe." *The American Historical Review* 102 (Dec. 1997): 1309–42; also Martin, *Myths of Renaissance Individualism* (New York: Palgrave, 2004).
25 Kochanowski, *Treny*, 40–1.
26 William J. Bouwsma, "The Two Faces of Humanism: Stoicism and Augustinianism in Renaissance Thought," in *A Usable Past: Essays in European Cultural History* (Berkeley and Los Angeles: University of California Press, 1990), 51.
27 Kochanowski, *Treny*, 42–3.
28 Bouwsma, "The Two Faces of Humanism," 58.
29 Kochanowski, *Treny*, 49.
30 Łukasz Górnicki, "Lament on the Death of My Wife," *Pisma* (Warszawa: PIW Warszawa, 1961), 325–6.

SUGGESTIONS FOR FURTHER READING

Primary sources

Górnicki, Łukasz. *Dworzanin polski (The Polish Courtier)*, ed. Roman Pollak. Wrocław: Zakład im. Ossolinskich, 1954.

Górnicki, Łukasz. *Pisma (Writings)*, ed. Roman Pollak. Warszawa: Panstwowy Instytut Wydawniczy, 1961.

Kochanowski, Jan. *Dzieła wszystkie (Collected Works)*. Wrocław: Zakład Narodowy im. Ossolinskich, Wydawn. Polskiej Akademii Nauk, 1982.

Kochanowski, Jan. *Treny: The Laments of Kochanowski*, trans. Adam Czerniawski. Oxford: European Humanities Research Centre of the University of Oxford, 2001.

Secondary sources

Axer, Jerzy, ed. *Łacina jako język elit (Latin as the Language of the Elite)*. Warszawa: OBTA/Wydawnictwo DiG, 2004.

Barycz, Henryk. *Historja Uniwersytetu Jagiełłonskiego w epoce humanizmu (The History of Jagiellonian University in the Age of Humanism)*. Kraków: Nakładem Uniwersytetu Jagiełłonskiego, 1935.

Białostocki, Jan. *The Art of the Renaissance in Eastern Europe: Hungary, Bohemia, Poland*. Ithaca: Cornell University Press, 1976.

Bouwsma, William J. "The Two Faces of Humanism: Stoicism and Augustinianism in Renaissance Thought," in *A Usable Past: Essays in European Cultural History*. Berkeley and Los Angeles: University of California Press, 1990.

Davies, Norman. *God's Playground: A History of Poland*, vols. 1 and 2. New York: Columbia University Press, 1982.

Fitzman, Samuel, ed. *The Polish Renaissance in its European Context*. Bloomington: Indiana University Press, 1988.

Grendler, Paul. "The University of Padua 1405–1600: A Success Story," in *Books and Schools in the Italian Renaissance*. Aldershot: Variorium, 1995.

King, Margaret L. *The Death of the Child Valerio Marcello*. Chicago: University of Chicago Press, 1994.

Kot, Stanisław. *Polska złotego wieku a Europa: Studia i szkice (The Golden Age of Poland and Europe: Studies and Outlines)*, ed. Henryk Barycz. Warszawa: Państwowy Instytut Wydawniczy, 1987.

Lempicki, Stanisław. *Renesans i Humanizm w Polsce: materialy do studiow (The Renaissance and

Humanism in Poland: Materials for Studies). Kraków: Spoldzielnia Wydawniczo-Oswiatowa, 1952.

Lichański, Jakub Zdzisław. *Łukasz Górnicki: sarmacki Castiglione. (Łukasz Górnicki: The Sarmatian Castiglione).* Warszawa: Wydawnictwo DiG, 1998.

Mączak, Antoni, Henryk Samsonowicz, and Peter Burke, eds. *East-Central Europe in Transition: From the Fourteenth to the Seventeenth Century.* Cambridge: Cambridge University Press, 1985.

McClure, George W. *Sorrow and Consolation in Italian Humanism.* Princeton: Princeton University Press, 1991.

Mersereau, John Jun. "Jan Kochanowski's *Laments*: A Definition of the Emotion of Grief," in Zbigniew Folejewski *et al.*, eds, *Studies in Russian and Polish Literature: In Honor of Wacław Lednicki.* 'S Gravenhage: Mouton & Co., 1962.

Mikoś, Michael J. *Polish Renaissance Literature: An Anthology.* Columbus: Slavica Publishers, 1995.

Pelc, Janusz. *Kochanowski: Szczyt renesansu w literaturze polskiej. (Kochanowski: The Epitome of the Renaissance in Polish Literature).* Warszawa: Wydawnictwo Naukowe PWN, 2001.

Pirie, Donald, ed. *Jan Kochanowski in Glasgow.* Glasgow: Campania, 1985.

Porter, Roy and Mikulás Teich, eds. *The Renaissance in National Context.* Cambridge: Cambridge University Press, 1992.

Segel, Harold B. *Renaissance Culture in Poland: The Rise of Humanism, 1470–1543.* Ithaca: Cornell University Press, 1989.

Weintraub, Wiktor. "Kochanowski's Renaissance Manifesto." *The Slavonic and East European Review* 30, 75 (1951): 412–24.

Welch, David. *Jan Kochanowski.* New York: Twayne Publishers, Inc., 1974.

Ziomek, Jerzy. *Renesans (The Renaissance).* Warszawa: Wydawnictwo Naukowe PWN, 1995.

CHAPTER ELEVEN

MONTAIGNE IN ITALY

François Rigolot

On June 22, 1580, Michel de Montaigne, age 47, left his castle in Aquitaine for Paris. In his luggage he carried two freshly printed copies of his *Essays*: one was destined for the French king, Henry III, and the other would be given, five months later, to Pope Gregory XIII. Montaigne had set out on a long journey, which would take him to Italy through eastern France, Switzerland, Germany, and Austria. After publishing his first two books of *Essays* in Bordeaux, he certainly felt he deserved a vacation; but he also had other reasons to leave his home, family, and province. Later, in his third book, he will confess that he hardly enjoys "domestic servitude" and is rather lukewarm with regard to the "duties of marital love" ("devoirs de l'amitié maritale": III.9.975b, 745).[1] By moving to unknown territory his hope was to find an excitement of the mind that would relieve him not only from daily routines but also from the deep-seated melancholy that had overwhelmed him since the death of his friend Étienne de La Boétie, a lawyer, political philosopher, and poet, in 1563. In the essay "On the Education of Children," he recommended that young people travel abroad to open their minds and form their own judgments:

A cette cause, le commerce des hommes y est merveilleusement propre, et la visite des pays estrangers, . . . pour en rapporter principalement les humeurs de ces nations et leurs façons, et pour frotter et limer nostre cervelle contre celle d'autruy. (I.26.153a)

For this reason, mixing with men is wonderfully useful, and visiting foreign countries . . . to bring back knowledge of the characters and ways of those nations, and to rub and polish our brains by contact with those of others. (112a)

Above all, an extensive "field trip" would allow Montaigne to check and expand on his bookish knowledge of Latin and Italian languages and cultures. Like many of his contemporaries, he was eager to see with his own eyes what was left of Rome, a city that had occupied a large space in his classical education.

In the late sixteenth century traveling to Italy had become somewhat fashionable, especially after the Treaty of Cateau-Cambrésis (1559) between Henry II of France and Philip II of Spain, and the *pax hispanica* that had ensued. Highways were more secure and accommodations less uncomfortable. Rome, the defunct capital of an illustrious empire, was a mighty sightseeing attraction for all cultivated northern Europeans. At the same time, as a Frenchman raised in the Catholic faith but exposed to Lutheran and Calvinist propaganda, Montaigne also wanted to form a personal opinion about the real nature of papal Rome. Was the Holy See, as the reformer Martin Luther claimed earlier in the sixteenth century, the "Beast of the Apocalypse" gloating over the "Babylonian Captivity of the Church," or had it recovered much of its moral strength and political respect under the auspices of the Catholic or Counter-Reformation?

If a visit to Rome was the major motivation for his journey, Montaigne was also most eager to see Venice. He remembered how enthusiastically his friend Étienne de La Boétie had written about the Serenissima ("Most Serene Republic"), celebrating its political freedom and civic virtues in his *Discourse on Voluntary Servitude*, a treatise against tyranny that Montaigne meant to publish and place at the very center of his first book of *Essays*:

> Qui verroit les Venitiens, une poignée de gens vivans si librement que le plus meschant d'entr'eulx ne voudroit pas estre le Roy de tous, ainsi nés et nourris qu'ils ne reconnoissent point d'autre ambition sinon à qui mieulx advisera et plus soigneusement prendra garde à entretenir la liberté . . .

> Anyone who saw the Venetians, a tiny nation living in such liberty that the worst rogue among them would not wish to be their king, born and bred with a single avowed ambition to excel their fellows in meticulous and vigilant care to uphold liberty . . .[2]

In his chapter on friendship, published before he set out on his 17-month trip, Montaigne mentioned that if La Boétie had had the choice, he would rather have been born in Venice, a republic, than in his home town of Sarlat in the Périgord. Upon returning from his trip, Montaigne showed his approval by adding three significant words to the 1582 edition of the *Essays*: "et avoit raison" [and he was right] (I.28.194a, 144), thus confirming the legitimacy of La Boétie's praise of Venetian democracy.

Montaigne may have been entrusted with a secret diplomatic mission by the king of France prior to his arrival in Italy. In the *Journal de voyage en Italie*, his account of his trip to Italy, he tells us that he met with several important political figures and high-ranking officials in Florence, Rome, Venice, and elsewhere, but there is little archival evidence to claim that his meetings were planned with anything but a social purpose in mind. Indeed he had a very personal reason to travel, closely related to his health problems: he was desperately looking for mineral waters that could provide relief to the agonizing attacks of his kidney stones. In France, he had explored nearly all the spa resorts of Gascony and the Pyrenees to no avail. In eastern France and Germany he made brief stops at famous "stations thermales" on his way. But in Tuscany, he sojourned for almost three months at the thermal baths of La Villa, near Lucca, where he seems to have found at least some relief from his ills.

Montaigne, who was accompanied by a small group of relatives and servants, crossed the Alps through the Brenner Pass, traveled down the Adige river valley from Trent to Verona, and visited Vicenza, Padua, and Venice. He continued to Florence, via Ferrara and Bologna, and reached Rome after brief visits to Siena and Viterbo. After spending several months in the Eternal City, he crossed the Apennines to visit Loreto, a famous pilgrimage site dedicated to the Virgin Mary, and devotedly placed a silver votive tablet for his family in the shrine. From there he went back to Florence, via Ancona and Urbino, and reached the Baths of La Villa near Lucca for two extended stays (May 7–June 21 and August 14–September 12, 1581) interrupted by an excursion to Florence, Pisa, and Lucca. At La Villa he received a letter informing him that he had been elected Lord Mayor of Bordeaux. Although he did not hurry back home (he wanted to return to Rome one last time), he left Italy for France and arrived at his château on November 30, 1581. A long vacation of seventeen months and eight days had finally come to an end.

AN ANTI-GUIDEBOOK GUIDEBOOK TO ITALY

Most sixteenth-century guidebooks to Italy were written in Latin and published in Germany. The Baedekers of the day were authored by geographers, mathematicians, and well-known scholars like Joseph Furttenbach, Paul Hentzer, Sebastian Münster, Hilarius Pirckmair, Franz Scott, Hieronymus Turler, or Theodor Zwinger. A few, such as Leandro Alberti's *Descrittione di tutta Italia* (1550) and Jean-Antoine Rigaud's *Bref Recueil des choses rares, notables, antiques, citez, forteresses principales d'Italie* (1601), by contrast, were written in vernacular languages. Usually they followed a rigorous method of exposition giving exhaustive information to the traveler, the so-called *methodus apodemica*. In Hentzer's *Itinerarium Italiae* (1592), for instance, the text opens with an invocation to God and then offers a general description of the whole peninsula; topographical representations of the cities; commentaries on the major customs; descriptions of the seas, rivers, mountains, and forests; a list of the principal public and private monuments; and, finally, a description of political institutions. A similar movement can be found in Sebastian Münster's *Cosmographia universalis* (1556), which opens with a description of the country and its regions and then provides an account of the variety and diversity of its natural features, a list of strange or unknown animals, a list of its most notable cities, and an account of its customs, laws, and religions. Montaigne owned a French translation of Münster, but we do not know if he purchased it before his trip or upon his return. One thing is certain: when Montaigne arrived in Germany, he wished he had brought one of these guidebooks, especially Münster's, with him, so that he could be "alerted of the rare and remarkable things that could be visited in each place" (*JV* 32; *TJ* 28).[3]

In Zwinger's *Methodus apodemica*, published about three years before Montaigne began his trip to Italy, one reads the following initial statement:

> I shall describe not the things I have observed myself but those I *should have* observed when I traveled through these places, in other words, whatever is worthy of memory.[4]

Unlike the authors of guidebooks, Montaigne wanted to stay away from general considerations. Instead, he cared for what he called "singularities": not what he *should have seen* but what he *actually saw* on his own, at the risk of missing some important monuments, "worthy of memory," like the Piazza del Duomo in Milan, which he simply forgets to mention. Montaigne's *disinvoltura* is well known, and it would be surprising to find in his *Journal* a catalogue of all the canonical tourist sights of Italy. Precisely, the traveler did not care to mention the detailed descriptions anyone could find in the guidebooks of the time. For instance, when he visited the Villa d'Este at Tivoli he wrote:

> J'y consideray toutes choses fort particulierement; j'essayerois de le peindre icy, mais il y a des livres et peintures publicques de ce suject. (*JV* 128)

> Here I examined everything most particularly. I would try to describe it here, but there are published books and pictures on the subject. (*TJ* 98–9)

Montaigne's companions had only one goal in mind: they were eager to reach Rome as soon as possible. Unlike them, the essayist chose to take his time and enjoy the unexpected sites along the road. No pre-set itinerary could ever force him to repress his desire for digressive promenades. At one point, in Rovereto, his *Wanderlust* becomes irresistible and he considers making dramatic changes in his travel plans. Montaigne's secretary, who may have been in fact the author of a substantial portion of the *Journal*, writes:

> Je croy à la verité que, s'il eust esté seul avec les siens, il fust allé plutost à Cracovie ou vers la Grece par terre que de prendre le tour vers l'Italie; mais le plaisir qu'il prenoit à visiter les pays inconnus, lequel il trouvoit si doux que d'en oublier la foiblesse de son aage et de sa santé, il ne le pouvoit imprimer à nul de la troupe, chacun ne demandant que la retraite. (*JV* 61)

> I truly believe that if he [Montaigne] had been alone with his own attendants he would rather have gone to Cracow or toward Greece by land than make the turn toward Italy; but the pleasure he took in visiting unknown countries, which he found so sweet as to make him forget the weakness of his age and of his health, he could not impress on any of his party, and everyone asked only to return home. (*TJ* 51)

Montaigne's meandering route throughout Italy is no surprise when one considers the essayist's temperament and the *aesthetics of negligence* he admittedly found so appealing in Ovid's *Metamorphoses*. Whether writing or traveling, Montaigne was powerfully attracted by a digressive mode. In his chapter "On Vanity," written after his return from Italy, he noted:

> Ay je laissé quelque chose à voir derriere moy? J'y retourne; c'est tousjours mon chemin. Je ne trace aucune ligne certaine, ny droicte ny courbe. (III.9.985b)

Have I left something unseen behind me? I go back; it is still on my road. I trace no fixed line, either straight or crooked. (753)

A similar mood is constantly found in the *Journal*. When his companions complained to him that he often led his party, by various country roads, back very close to where they had started, he would reply that "he could not miss or go off his path since he had no plan but to travel in unknown places; and that, provided he did not fall back upon the same route or see the same place twice, he was not failing to carry out his plan" (*JV* 61; TJ 51).

MONTAIGNE'S "DIARIO DI VIAGGIO"

About one-third of the *Journal de voyage* is written in Italian by Montaigne himself. Once he had settled at the "Bagno de la Villa," he switched from French to the local vernacular:

> Assaggiamo di parlar un poco questa altra lingua massime essendo in queste contrade dove mi pare sentire il più perfetto favellare della Toscana, particolarmente tra li paesani che non l'hanno mescolato et alterato con li vicini. (*JV* 167)

> Let us try to speak this other language a little, especially since I am in this region where I seem to hear the most perfect Tuscan speech, particularly among those natives who have not corrupted and altered it with that of their neighbors. (*TJ* 126)

Thus, from the outset, Montaigne insists on the tentative nature of his linguistic experience. Significantly, his first word in "this other language" ("*questa altra lingua*") is the Italian equivalent of a French verb he used repeatedly in his own *Essays*: "*assaggiare*" for "essayer," meaning to try, but also attempt, test, and taste. He will "essay" or "assay" himself on a few pages ("*un poco*") by using the local way of speaking ("*parlare*," "*favellare*"). Here again chance is favored over mastery, and spontaneity over control and perfection. He had already expressed a similar attitude in his *Essays*: "Le parler que j'ayme, c'est un parler simple et naïf, tel sur le papier qu'à la bouche" ("The speech I love is a simple, natural speech, the same on paper as in the mouth": I.26.171a, 127).

In fact, Montaigne will continue to write "in Tuscan" until he leaves Italy. After crossing the Mont-Cenis Pass into France, he switches back to his maternal tongue, again stressing his lack of mastery in handling a foreign language:

> Ici on parle François: ainsi je quitte ce langage estrangier, duquel je me sers bien facilement, mais bien mal assurement, n'ayant loisir, pour estre tousjours en compaignie de François, de faire nul apprentissage qui vaille. (*JV* 227)

Here we speak French; so I quit this foreign language, which I use easily but with very little sureness, not having had the time to learn it at all well, since I was always in the company of Frenchmen. (*TJ* 172)[5]

Several studies have been devoted, with various approaches and degrees of success, to the essayist's linguistic proficiency.[6] What is important here is the traveler's sheer pleasure in adopting Italian for his daily conversation as well as the continuation of his diary. Mastering a foreign tongue is a fine thing, but that is not always possible. To be sure, what really matters to Montaigne is the ability to connect directly with the customs and people he encounters. Only pedants, he writes, value linguistic correctness: "c'est aux paroles à servir et à suyvre" ("it is for words to serve and follow": I.26.171a, 127).

Years after his return to France, Montaigne will write again about his knowledge of Italian. He will confess that it always remained foreign to him; that, although he could manage for casual business, he was never able to express subtle ideas or profound thoughts in Dante's tongue. In the last book of his *Essays*, he reflected back on his Italian experience by saying:

> En Italie je disois ce qu'il me plaisoit en devis communs; mais aux propos roides je n'eusse oser me fier à un Idiome que je ne pouvois plier ny contourner outre son alleure commune. J'y veux pouvoir quelque chose du mien. ("Sur des vers de Virgile": III.5.873b)

> When I was in Italy I said whatever I pleased in ordinary talk, but for serious discourse I would not have dared trust myself to an idiom that I could neither bend nor turn out of its ordinary course. I want to be able to do something of my own with it. ("On some verses of Virgil": 665)

Montaigne's false modesty is clear. Obviously, his written Italian was much better than what he says about it. In 1588, upon rereading his own "Apology for Raymond Sebond," he will re-examine the linguistic question, again emphasizing his preference for communicative power over linguistic purity:

> Je conseillois, en Italie, à quelqu'un qui estoit en peine de parler Italien, que, pourveu qu'il ne cerchast qu'à se faire entendre, sans y vouloir autrement exceller, qu'il employast seulement les premiers mots qui luy viendroyent à la bouche, Latins, François, Espaignols ou Gascons, et qu'en y adjoustant la terminaison Italienne, il ne faudroit jamais à rencontrer quelque idiome du pays, ou Thoscan, ou Romain, ou Venitien, ou Piemontois, ou Napolitain, et de se joindre à quelqu'une de tant de formes. (II.12.546b)

> In Italy I advised a man who was at pains to speak Italian, that provided he sought only to make himself understood, without wishing to excel otherwise, he should simply use the first words that came to his mouth, Latin, French, Spanish, or Gascon; and that by adding the Italian ending, he would never fail to hit some dialect of the country, either Tuscan, or Roman, or Venetian,

or Piedmontese, or Neapolitan, and to meet some one out of so many forms. (408)

Thus, as he traveled through Italy, Montaigne showed he could be an *assayist* as well as an *essayist*, examining and determining the contextual usefulness of speech according to its social desirability and functionality.

MONTAIGNE AND VERONICA FRANCO

On November 7, 1580 Montaigne, who was visiting Venice, received a small volume of printed letters from "la Signora Veronica Franco" (*JV* 68; *TJ* 56). The famous courtesan and writer had just published her *Lettere familiari a diversi*, dedicated both to Cardinal Luigi d'Este and the French king Henry III. Interestingly, Montaigne had also presented his *Essays* as a substitute for a collection of familiar letters he would have composed in Seneca's style if his great friend, Étienne de La Boétie, had still been alive:

> J'eusse prins plus volontiers ceste forme [épistolaire] à publier mes verves si j'eusse eu à qui parler. (I.40.253c)

> I would have preferred to adopt this [epistolary] form to publish my sallies, if I had had someone to talk to. (185–6)

Montaigne is fond of epistolary style because it is unpretentious, devoid of rhetorical ornaments, and represents the writer's self in unmitigated ways. This is precisely what he will find in Franco's *Lettere*: an artless art, as close as possible to natural conversation, which springs spontaneously from an alert and animated mind. The *cortegiana* Veronica Franco deals with a variety of topics, ranging from moral to political and philosophical issues. She praises Venetian society for its permissiveness but fights against the exploitation of women; she satirizes well-endowed patricians who obsessively indulge in self-pity; she rebukes a mother who wrongly believes her daughter will find happiness as a courtesan.

In other words, just as Montaigne's *Essays* nostalgically praise and mimic the epistolary style, Franco's letters can be read "as separate *essays*, which by addressing a wide selection of topics, provide traces of a courtesan's interactions with her milieu."[7] Letter 22, for instance, starts with a frank and lucid picture of prostitution in Venice but moves quickly to a critique of rhetorical practices, depicting seductive ornaments as deceitful artifices akin to the make-up worn by prostitutes.[8] In a similar vein, anything that smacks of inflated, overblown, pompous style is alien to Montaigne's aristocratic taste. Natural elegance, an essential aesthetic quality akin to ethical honesty, is what he prizes most in Castiglione's depiction of the ideal courtier. The learned should learn one essential thing: how to refrain from showing off with their erudition. Montaigne is merciless about those who misuse the art of true eloquence. His repeated attacks against demagogic oratory are well known. It is a deceitful and lying art ("un' art piperesse et mensongere": I.51.305a, 221a), he declares, approvingly quoting Socrates who "wisely defined rhetoric as the art of deceiving and flattering" ("l'art de tromper et de flatter": 305c, 222c). Like Montaigne, moreover, Socrates too had compared oratory with cosmetics.[9] Among all Italian writers, Montaigne singles out Aretino for "his turgid style, bubbling over with conceits, ingenious indeed but farfetched and fantastic" ("une façon de parler bouffie et bouillonnée de pointes, ingenieuses à la verité, mais recherchées de loin et fantasques": I.51.307a, 223a). Both Michel and Veronica loathe self-adornment, the key artifice for seduction of which the *cortegiana* is precisely the symbol. Interestingly enough, in his *La Retorica delle puttane* Ferrante Pallavicino will soon advise men how to foil the prostitutes' "*artificiose parole*" and other powerful charms ("*astuzia*" and "*ingordigia*").[10] The French essayist and the Italian *cortegiana* shared a remarkable aversion for the excessively learned mannerism typified by the Italian Neo-Platonists of their age. In a late essay, Montaigne writes:

> Les sciences traictent les choses trop finement, d'une mode trop artificielle et differente à la commune et naturelle. Mon page faict l'amour et l'entend. Lisez lui Leon Hebreu et Ficin: on parle de luy, de ses pensées et de ses actions, et si il n'y entend rien . . . Laissons là Bembo et Equicola. (III.5.874b)

> Learning treats of things too subtly, in a mode too artificial and different from the common and natural one. My page makes love and understands it. Read him Leone Ebreo and Ficino: they talk about him, his thoughts and his actions, and yet he does not understand a thing in it . . . Let us leave Bembo and Equicola alone. (666)

On his own copy of the 1588 edition Montaigne coins a neologism to downgrade the pretensions of artificial creations: "If I were of the trade (that is, if I were a philosopher), I would naturalize art as much as they *artify* nature" ("je naturaliserois l'art comme ils *artialisent* la nature": 666c, 874c). Thus it is appropriate to interpret Veronica's gesture in this very light: she sent her collection of letters to the French essayist who was also committed to "de-artifying" both the courtier's and the courtesan's artful artificiality.

We may notice that Montaigne talks about his relationship with Veronica Franco purely in literary terms. The respectful, almost ceremonious tone he chooses to address her is revealing ("la Signora Veronica Franco, gentifemme Venitienne": *JV* 68). The *cortigiana onesta* has turned into a veritable *donna del palazzo* or court lady, a "*femme d'esprit*" endowed with moral qualities as in Castiglione's *Book of the Courtier*. When Montaigne receives the volume of *Lettere*, he gives "two crowns" to the messenger for his commission. Some commentators have remarked that, according to police registry, this was the price paid to prostitutes for their services. Others have concluded that this was an offensive gesture, or at least a glaring blunder on Montaigne's part.[11] Quite on the contrary, Montaigne may have willfully used his knowledge of current fares to enhance the fact that he did not want to pay the courtesan but the "*femme de lettres.*" He was fully aware of the kind of trade Venetian women were famous for. Indeed he was surprised, even amazed by the number of high-class prostitutes who behaved as if they were genuine "princesses." His secretary writes:

[Monsieur de Montaigne] vit les plus nobles de celles qui en font traficque [de leur beauté]; mais cela luy sembla autant admirable que nulle autre chose d'en voir un tel nombre, comme de cent cinquante ou environ, faisant une despense en meubles et vestemens de princesses; n'ayant autre fonds à se maintenir que de cette traficque; et plusieurs de la noblesse de là mesme, avoir des courtisanes à leurs despens, au veu et sceu d'un chacun. (*JV* 69)

[Monsieur de Montaigne] saw the noblest of those who make a traffic of it [their beauty]; but it seemed to him as wonderful as anything else to see such a number of them as a hundred and fifty or thereabouts spending like princesses on furniture and clothes, having no other funds to live on except from this traffic; and many of the nobles of the place even keeping courtesans at their expense in the sight and knowledge of all. (*TJ* 56)

Montaigne does not hesitate to evoke the fascinating world of Venetian prostitution, but he deals with it separately, and makes sure his readers will not be mistaken about the true nature of his relationship with Veronica Franco. To this effect, the secretary notes that his master was struck that evening with a kidney stone ailment, and "passed two big stones, before supper, one after the other" (*TJ* 56). The essayist was in pain, obviously not in a mood for a sexual tryst. The only "traficque" between the two writers was not to be sexual, but exclusively textual. Veronica was no longer, as the pun went, the "*ver unica [puttana]*" (the truly unique whore) who had bestowed her favors on the French king Henry III after his election as king of Poland in 1573. To Montaigne, she had become a kindred literary spirit, or what Alfred Glauser aptly called "une Vénus de papier."[12]

Veronica Franco was from Venice, and that was also important to Montaigne, who greatly admired the Serenissima. To him as to his great friend, Étienne de La Boétie, Venice was the symbol of freedom and the exemplary model of the republican ideal. Even though Montaigne found Venice "different from what he had imagined" and "a little less wonderful" than his friend had thought it was (*JV* 69; *TJ* 56), he still felt that its "*franchezza*," with both the meaning of "freedom" and "authenticity," could be embodied by a woman whose very name, Franco or Franca, symbolized his aspirations. He may well have remembered that one of Veronica's verse epistles began as follows:

Questa quella Veronica vi scrive,
che per voi, non qual già *libera e franca*,
or d'infelice amor soggetta vive.

This letter is written to you by that Veronica
who now lives *neither free nor frank*
but as a slave of unrequited love.[13]

– *François Rigolot* –

MONTAIGNE'S VIEWS ON ITALIAN ART

Among all the Renaissance travelers to Italy Montaigne has often been singled out for his so-called "lack of interest" in Italian art. In his canonical edition of the *Essays* Pierre Villey wrote: "He [Montaigne] is largely insensitive to the artistic beauties which Italy offered him in profusion."[14] In the nineteenth century, Chateaubriand and Stendhal, two great lovers of Italy, had already expressed their amazement at the sixteenth-century traveler's almost complete silence on the major masterpieces he had encountered on his way.[15] Even when Montaigne notices works of art, he is often content simply with recording their presence, without passing an aesthetic judgment on them.[16] This may come from the aristocrat's reluctance to delve into art criticism, an activity restricted to "specialists" and "technicians" whom he usually treats with disdain. Or it may have, in part at least, been a result of his decision to write a significant portion of the *Journal* in Italian, since the foreign idiom did not provide an ideal medium for expressing a refined aesthetic sensibility.[17]

There are other reasons, however, why his *Journal* is devoid of notes and comments on the works of art the traveler visited in Italy. Montaigne's temperament is alien to any kind of discourse that might smack of pedantry, a subject about which he wrote a whole essay (I.25). Like most of his aristocratic contemporaries, he loves Baldesar Castiglione's *cortegiano*, whose natural elegance, *sprezzatura*, and *aurea mediocritas* appeal to him as essential qualities of the "*honnête homme*" (II.48.292c; II.17.640c). Any unnecessary demonstration of knowledge disheartens him. Why should he consign in his private notes names of painters, sculptors, and architects? He does admire a number of them: Bramante, Brunelleschi, Gianbologna, and Giotto, but rarely mentions their names. The exception is Michelangelo, whose statues of the Medici in San Lorenzo's New Sacristy strike him as "very beautiful and excellent" (*JV* 81; *TJ* 65). In Rome, he goes to the Vatican "to see the statues enclosed in the niches of the Belvedere and the beautiful gallery that the Pope is erecting for paintings from all parts of Italy" (*JV* 99; *TJ* 79). Yet his aesthetic contemplation is interrupted by an incident experienced by many tourists in Rome, even today: "he lost his purse and what was in it" (ibid.). This was not the result of a snatch-and-grab robbery, as the secretary explains:

> He thought what had happened was that in giving alms two or three times, the weather being very rainy and unpleasant, instead of putting his purse back into his pocket, he had slipped it through the slashings of his breeches. (*JV* 99; *TJ* 79)

Montaigne is so fascinated by a city he has so carefully studied with maps and books that he feels he no longer needs the guide he has hired (*JV* 100; *TJ* 79). One recalls his long, reflective meditation on the ruins of Rome, as reported by his secretary, though Montaigne's voice is clearly evoked:

> Il disoit qu'on ne voyoit rien de Rome que le ciel sous lequel elle avoit esté assise et le plan de son giste; que cette science qu'il en avoit estoit une science abstraite et contemplative, de laquelle il n'y avoit rien qui tombast sous les

sens; que ceux qui disoient qu'on y voyoit au moins les ruines de Rome en disoient trop; car les ruines d'une si espouvantable machine rapportoient plus d'honneur et de reverence à sa memoire: ce n'estoit rien que son sepulchre. (*JV* 100)

He said that one saw nothing of Rome but the sky under which it had stood and the plan of its site; that this knowledge that he had of it was an abstract and contemplative knowledge of which there was nothing perceptible to the senses; that those who said that one at least saw the ruins of Rome said too much, for the ruins of so awesome a machine would bring more honor and reverence to its memory: this was nothing but its sepulcher. (*TJ* 79)

There is no trace of anti-Italian feelings in Montaigne's discourse on Italy. He may at times voice reserve or mild criticism about the mores he encounters, yet, unlike many of his contemporaries, he only has positive comments to make about a culture he tries to understand as best as he can.[18]

Montaigne's reluctance to lavish praise on artistic masterpieces may also be attributed to a "puritan" form of thinking that fundamentally questions the utility of artistic representations. The triumph of representational skills is traditionally associated with the power of art to arouse passions. This was common theoretical currency in the Renaissance. A great painter could so enthrall the minds of people that they could even fall in love with a painting that did not represent real human beings. In his *Treatise on Painting*, Leonardo da Vinci tells the following episode:

I made a religious painting which was bought by one who so loved it that he wanted to remove the sacred representations so as to be able to kiss it without suspicion. Finally his conscience prevailed over his sighs and lust, but he had to remove the picture from his house.[19]

Pliny's well-known account of the evolutions of painting had a long-standing impact on the criteria used along the centuries to assess the quality of visual art. In his *Natural History* Pliny tells us that painting began with tracing an outline round a man's shadow, using a single color ("monochrome"), then discovered light and shade, and the contrast of colors, climaxing with the masterpieces of Apelles, so lifelike that "they challenged Nature herself."[20] The very progress of the *techne* showed an evolution from badly representational flat pictures to polychrome lifelike images, which had the power to seduce and deceive. In the moral context of a Stoic or Christian culture, the power of art to deceive the viewers and rouse their passions was deemed dangerous indeed. Seneca, a writer Montaigne revered and quoted copiously, had already raised the ethical issue in the context of Homer's representations.[21] The artist's chief aim was to instruct, and one way to safeguard his reputation was to interpret his works *allegorically*. By introducing allegorical interpretations of their works, painters could therefore side-step the moral objections of their critics, finding an identity in which moral worth and aesthetic freedom were simultaneously established by an ability to produce a marvelous, even uncanny, lifelike illusion.[22]

– *François Rigolot* –

The moral, political, and metaphysical implications of Plato's condemnation of art weighed heavily on Renaissance moral philosophers. The implication that the painter's subject is a lie, because twice or thrice removed from reality (that is, from the realm of Ideal Forms), remained central to any Renaissance theory of representation. We know that a painting is an illusion, but if we, like Leonardo, are attracted by it and cannot refrain from gazing at it, if it haunts our thoughts and our dreams, then the sign has become more pregnant and meaningful than its referent.[23] As the Latin oxymoron goes, the picture has become a *falsa veritas*, a false or "fictional" truth, and this can threaten individual psychology as well as social order, as the Anglican clergyman Robert Burton made clear in his *Anatomy of Melancholy* (1624). Enthusiasm for illusionist representations became disturbing as the Reformation developed in northern Europe. The same *energeia* that was so praised by patrons prompted the destruction of art, as a radical remedy for idolatry.

Montaigne, of course, held no extremist views on the subject. Yet he constantly opposed the idea of "nature" as the original, undisturbed creative character of things, to "art" as the human use of skill, allegedly used to improve on nature. He certainly did not care much for the dominant mannerist style, which he found in Italy. To him, any exaggerated or affected forms in literature or the fine arts smacked of unnaturalness, an inability to accord with the normal representation of events or things. At the same time, Montaigne is often considered by art and literary critics as the most important representative of European mannerism. To Arnold Hauser, for instance, he occupies "a key position in the whole movement."[24] In his classic monograph on Montaigne's *Essays*, Richard A. Sayce devoted a chapter to the "discussion of the confused question of mannerism and baroque" in the context of the essayist's writing strategies.[25] Beyond the "essential classicism" of Montaigne's taste, Sayce found several characteristics in his style that, "if they are not mannerist, at least correspond very closely to what is generally said about mannerism . . .: oblique and labyrinthine forms, paradox, [and] word-play."[26] More recently, Giancarlo Maiorino has reopened the question of Montaigne's place within "baroque" culture. Focusing on "the emergent concept of form as process," Maiorino includes Montaigne among the "founding fathers" of the Baroque, mostly because of his interest in representing the "boundless furtherance of life."[27]

Montaigne himself borrows a variety of shifting metaphors from the arts as he describes his own artistic endeavor. At the beginning of the central chapter, "De l'Amitié" ("Of Friendship": I.28), he compares his *Essays* with visual "grotesques," which he defines as "fantastic paintings whose only charm lies in their variety and strangeness" (183a, 135a). Raphael's Stanze, which he visited at the Vatican, were commonly identified as a major example of mannerist "grotesques"; that is, peripheral decorations imitated from the Roman frescoes discovered in the ruins of Nero's Villa Aurea (the so-called "grottoes").[28] Similarly, Montaigne wanted his writings to appear as artless divagations, stemming from a self-conscious resistance to the canon of artistic rules. They were based, he claimed, upon his own autonomous, individualistic imagination, or, in Bellori's words, upon a "fantastica idea non appogiata all'imitazione."[29]

In Italy, if our traveler showed a somewhat reserved interest in the fine arts, he never missed an opportunity to voice his enthusiasm for the mechanical arts he discovered on his way, especially technical innovations like fountains and waterworks. Already in Augsburg, Constance, and Neufchâteau he had marveled at ingenious examples of hydraulic machinery, but in Italy his admiration becomes boundless, especially at Tivoli's Villa d'Este, where art seemed to have perfectly reproduced Nature itself. He loves the gushing of water launched by jets in the fashion of whirlpool baths and meticulously describes the operation of the famous automated water organ:

> La musique des orgues, qui est une vraye musique et d'orgues naturelles, sonnant tousjours toutesfois une mesme chose, se fait par le moyen de l'eau qui tombe avec grande violence dans une cave ronde, voustée, et agite l'air qui y est, et le contraint de gaigner pour sortir les tuyaux des orgues et luy fournir de vent. (*JV* 128)

> The music of the organ, which is real and a natural organ, though always playing the same thing, is effected by means of the water, which falls with great violence into a round arched cave and agitates the air that is in there and forces it, in order to get out, to go through the pipes of the organ and supply it with wind. (*TJ* 99)

The beauty of the Villa Lante at Bagnaia was even more intriguing, because the architect, Tommaso Chinucci, had added new inventions to the already well-known ones: "e così aggiugendo sempre nuove invenzioni alle vecchie" (*JV* 210). There, in this perfect *locus amoenus*, art, beauty, and pleasure reached an exemplary status ("ha posto in questo suo ultimo lavoro assai più d'arte, di bellezza, e leggiadria": ibid.). In Montaigne's description superlatives abound to connote the extreme diversity of art and ingeniosity of artists: "infiniti disegni," "assaissimi modi diversi," "bellissimi," "lavorati molto artificiosamente" (ibid.). Similarly, at the Villa Farnese in Caprarola Montaigne registers "many noteworthy and beautiful things" ("parecchi cose ragguardevoli e belle": *JV* 211). He is especially fascinated by a grotto in which water is sprayed so artfully that it gives the appearance to the eye and the ear of the most natural rainfall:

> Fra le altre [cose c'è] una grotta la quale spruzzendo l'acqua in un laghetto con arte fa parere, et alla vista et al suono, la scesa della pioggia naturalissima. (*JV* 211)

> Among other [things there is] a grotto, which, spraying water artfully into a little lake, gives the appearance to the eye and the ear of the most natural rainfall. (*TJ* 163)

Art, therefore, conspires with nature to produce a perfect illusion. *Ars est celare artem*: true art must remain subservient to Nature. From an aesthetic and metaphysical point of view there are obvious differences between the value of the fine arts and the relevance of technology. In Plato's *Republic*, artful pictures, being "thrice removed from Nature," are denied ontological validity (X, 597e). From this perspective even

Michelangelo is but the imitator of a duplicitous imitation. Plato's painter wishes he could be mistaken for a carpenter (X, 598c). As we have seen earlier, the same type of suspicion about art can be found in Montaigne's *Essays*, but technical inventions, inasmuch as they may bring something useful to humanity, can be saved from philosophical skepticism.

In a passage of the essay "Of Coaches," Montaigne discusses the political responsibilities of rulers and reminds the king that he has nothing he can claim as his own: "he owes his very self to others" (III.6.903b, 689). Later, on his copy of the 1588 edition, Montaigne added a quotation from Cicero, which offers a penetrating commentary on the concept of utility: "Nulla ars in se versatur" ("No art is directed to itself": 903c, 689). Interestingly enough, he decided to modify the sense of the original quotation by giving it a more positive rendition: "Toute art jette sa fin hors d'elle" ("all art has its end outside of itself" (903c, 689)). Examples chosen to illustrate this maxim are revealing:

> La juridiction ne se donne point en faveur du juridiciant, c'est en faveur du juridicié. On faict un superieur, non jamais pour son profit, ains pour le profit de l'inferieur, et un medecin pour le malade, non pour soy. (903c)

> The authority to judge is not given for the sake of the judge, but for the sake of the person judged. A superior is never appointed for his own benefit, but for the benefit of the inferior, and a doctor for the sick, not for himself. (689c)

To the narcissistic tendencies of self-serving aesthetics Montaigne opposes the vigorous outward-looking thrust of a new, pragmatic sensibility.[30] On ethical grounds, he conflates the Ciceronian advice and the Evangelical formula favored by Erasmian humanists: "Agape ou zetei ta eautes" (Charity does not seek its own advantage). Rabelais, for example, had chosen this motto for his young hero Gargantua. This is perhaps one of the key lessons Montaigne learnt in Italy: art must avoid self-complacency; it is not meant to look vainly inward; its ultimate redeeming value is to improve upon nature for the shared benefit of human society. That is why the myth of Pygmalion is so dear to his heart and so central to what one could venture to call Montaigne's antimannerist mannerism.[31]

Thus, most of Montaigne's comments and observations about the discoveries he makes as he travels through Italy are quite revealing about contemporary reactions to a number of intellectual positions embraced by Renaissance humanists. The French essayist breaks with the approach of traditional guidebooks. His trip is very much his own, reflecting his idiosyncratic interests rather than his effort to follow a set itinerary. There is a quality of wandering here. And his attitude about language, which comes out especially clearly in his encounter with Veronica Franco, is also concerned with his own approach, his naturalness, his view that words should serve us and not we them. He constantly prefers chance over mastery, as he emphasizes his preference for communication over linguistic purity. His attacks against demagogic oratory, his mocking of pretentious self-adornment, his aversion for excessively learned mannerism point to a recurring concern: the essayist's commitment to debunk artificiality. Like his more famous *Essays*, Montaigne's *Journal de voyage* shows a common man's temperament alien to any kind of discourse that might smack of pedantry. At the same time, there is no trace of anti-Italian feeling in his critique of mannerism. Finally his attitude towards art has a similar drift, with Montaigne deeply concerned with the matter of illusion and the fear that the sign will become more important than the thing it is meant to represent. All this tells us much about Montaigne's view of the Renaissance and the Reformation as a new, forward-looking, pragmatic sensibility is developing in the northern Europe of Bacon and Descartes.

NOTES

1 Pagination for the text and translation refers here and below to *Les Essais*, ed. Pierre Villey (Paris: Presses Universitaires de France, 1978) and *The Complete Essays of Montaigne*, trans. Donald M. Frame (Stanford: Stanford University Press, 1965) with a fair degree of modification.

2 Étienne de La Boétie, *De la Servitude volontaire ou Contr'Un*, ed. Malcolm Smith (Geneva: Droz, 1987), pp. 47–8; *Slaves by Choice*, trans. Malcolm Smith (Egham Hill, England: Runnymede Books, 1988), p. 50.

3 All page references to the French text are to the edition of the *Journal de voyage* (*JV*), ed. François Rigolot (Paris: Presses Universitaires de France, 1992); all references to the English text are to the edition of *Montaigne's Travel Journal* (*TJ*), ed. Donald M. Frame (San Francisco: North Point Press, 1983) with a fair degree of modification. For the textual history of this work, including the thorny question of Montaigne's authorship, see the Introduction to *JV*, especially pp. v–vi, xxxiv–xxxvi.

4 *Methodus apodemica* . . . (Basle, 1577), quoted by Luigi Monga, "Itinéraires de Français en Italie à l'époque de Montaigne," in *Montaigne e l'Italia* (Geneva: Slatkine, 1991), p. 448, note 13; my translation.

5 Frame translates "on parle" to "they speak," but it can also mean "we speak," a preferable reading given the fact that Montaigne switches himself to French as he writes this sentence.

6 Concetta Cavallini, *L'Italianisme de Michel de Montaigne* (Fasano: Schena Editore, 2003).

7 Margaret F. Rosenthal, *The Honest Courtesan. Veronica Franco, Citizen and Writer in Sixteenth-century Venice* (Chicago: University of Chicago Press, 1992), p. 126.

8 "Franco literalizes the ancient misogynist trope that had equated rhetorical excess and epistolary flattery with a dressed-up whore." Ibid., p. 127.

9 Plato, *Gorgias* (465b) in *Works*, ed. W. R. M. Lamb (Cambridge, Mass.: Harvard University Press, 1961), V, p. 319.

10 *LA RETORICA DELLE PVTTANE Composta conforme li preccati di Cipriano. Dedicata alla università delle Cortegiane più celebri*, ed. Laura Coci (Parma: Fondazione Pietro Bembo/Ugo Guanda Editore, 1992), p. 8.

11 Madeleine Lazard, *Michel de Montaigne* (Paris: Fayard, 1992), p. 271, and Jean Lacouture, *Montaigne à cheval* (Paris: Éditions du Seuil, 1996), pp. 208–9.

12 Alfred Glauser, *Montaigne paradoxal* (Paris: Nizet, 1972), p . 21. In his essay "Sur des vers de Virgile," Montaigne writes: "Venus n'est pas si belle toute nue, et vive, et haletante, comme elle est icy chez Virgile [in *Eneid*, VIII, ll.387–404]" (III.5.849b). In his essay "De l'experience," he adds: "A faute de memoire naturelle *j'en forge de papier*, et comme quelque nouveau symptome survient à mon mal, je l'escris" (III.13.1092c).

13 Veronica Franco, *Poems and Selected Letters*, ed. and trans. Ann Rosalind Jones and Margaret F. Rosenthal (Chicago: University of Chicago Press, 1998), Capitolo 20, ll.1–3, pp.196–7.
14 *Les Essais*, introduction, p. xxvii.
15 Chateaubriand, *Mémoires d'outre-tombe*, ed. M. Levaillant (Paris: Gallimard, 1964), XXX, 7, vol. 2, pp. 243–4; Stendhal, *Promenades dans Rome* in *Voyages en Italie*, ed. V. Del Litto (Paris: Gallimard, 1973), p. 1052.
16 See Lino Pertile, "Montaigne in Italia: arte, tecnica e scienza dal *Journal* agli *Essais*," in *Saggi e Ricerche di Letteratura Francese* 12 (1973): 50, note 4.
17 Richard A. Sayce, "The Visual Arts in Montaigne's *Journal de voyage*," in *O un amy! Essays on Montaigne in Honor of Donald Frame*, ed. Raymond C. La Charité (Lexington, Ky.: French Forum Publishers, 1977), pp. 220–1.
18 The most famous collection of anti-Italian poems is Joachim Du Bellay's *Les Regrets*, written in Rome and published in 1558, eds J. Joliffe and M. A. Screech (Geneva: Droz, 1966). See Henry Heller, *Anti-Italianism in Sixteenth-century France* (Toronto: University of Toronto Press, 2003).
19 Quoted by Ernst Gombrich, *Art and Illusion. A Study in the Psychology of Pictorial Representation* (Princeton: Princeton University Press, 1961), p. 94.
20 Pliny, *Natural History*, ed. and trans. H. Rackham. Loeb Classical Library (Cambridge, Mass., 1952), vol. IX, book XXXV, sections v, xi, xxxvi, pp. 271, 283, 331.
21 See John Francis D'Alton, *Roman Literary Theory and Criticism* (New York: Longmans, Green & Co., 1931), pp. 485ff.
22 Lucy Gent, *Picture and Poetry 1560–1620. Relations Between Literature and the Visual Arts in the English Renaissance* (Leamington Spa: James Hall, 1994), p. 45.
23 Leonard Barkan, *The Gods Made Flesh: Metamorphosis and the Pursuit of Paganism* (New Haven: Yale University Press, 1986), pp. 9–11.
24 Arnold Hauser, *Mannerism. The Crisis of the Renaissance and the Origin of Modern Art* (Cambridge, Mass.: Harvard University Press, 1965), p. 327. Also, "Montaigne and Giordano Bruno are unquestionably the two most important and representative philosophers of mannerism" (ibid., 51).
25 Richard A. Sayce, *The Essays of Montaigne. A Critical Exploration* (London: Weidenfeld & Nicolson, 1972), ch. 13, pp. 313–26.
26 Ibid., p. 324.
27 Giancarlo Maiorino, *The Cornucopian Mind and the Baroque Unity of the Arts* (Philadelphia: Pennsylvania University Press, 1990), p. 45 and *passim*. As a complement to the bibliography on the subject, see A. Touré, "Montaigne: écrire baroque," in *Montaigne, penseur et philosophe (1588–1988)* [Actes du Congrès de littérature française tenu en ouverture à l'année de la francophonie, organisé par l'Université de Dakar, 20–22 mars 1989], ed. Claude Blum (Paris: Champion, 1990), pp. 113–28.
28 See Nicole Dacos, *La Découverte de la Domus Aurea et la formation des grotesques à la Renaissance* (London: Warburg Institute, 1969).
29 Quoted by Walter Friedländer, "Die Entstehung des antiklassischen Stiles in der italienischen Malerei um 1520," *Repertorium für Kunstwissenschaft* 46 (1925): 51.
30 This dichotomy is analyzed in terms of the opposition between *maniérisme* and *baroquisme* by Gisèle Mathieu-Castellani in a significant contribution to this discussion. See her Introduction to *La Poésie amoureuse de l'âge baroque* (Paris: Livre de Poche, 1990), pp. 5–38.
31 For the development of this notion see "Montaigne's Anti-mannerist Mannerism," in *Le Visage changeant de Montaigne. The Changing Face of Montaigne*, eds Keith Cameron and Laura Willett (Paris: Champion, 2003), pp. 207–30.

SUGGESTIONS FOR FURTHER READING

Primary sources

Montaigne, Michel de. *The Complete Works of Montaigne*, trans. Donald M Frame. Stanford: Stanford University Press, 1965.

―――― *Les Essais de Montaigne. Édition conforme au texte de l'exemplaire de Bordeaux, préparée par Pierre Villey*. Paris: Presses Universitaires de France, 1978.

―――― *Travel Journal*, trans. Donald M. Frame. San Francisco: North Point Press, 1983.

―――― *The Essays*, trans. M. A. Screech. London and New York: Penguin, 1991.

―――― *Journal de voyage de Montaigne*, ed. François Rigolot. Paris: Presses Universitaires de France, 1992.

Secondary sources

Balmas, Enea, ed. *Montaigne e l'Italia*. Geneva: Slatkine, 1991.

Brush, Craig. "The Essayist is Learned: Montaigne's *Journal de voyage* and the *Essais*." *Romanic Review* 62 (1971): 16–27.

Cameron, Keith and Laura Willett, eds. "Montaigne's Anti-mannerist Mannerism," in *Le Visage changeant de Montaigne. The Changing Face of Montaigne*, Paris: Champion, 2003, pp. 207–30.

Cavallini, Concetta. *L'Italianisme de Michel de Montaigne*. Fasano: Schena Editore, 2003.

Friedrich, Hugo. *Montaigne*. Paris: Gallimard, 1968.

Garavini, Fausta. *Itinerari a Montaigne*. Florence: Sansoni, 1983.

―――― "Montaigne, écrivain italien?" *Etudes montaignistes en hommage à Pierre Michel*, eds Claude Blum and François Moureau. Geneva: Slatkine, 1984, 117–29.

Pertile, Lino. "Montaigne in Italia: arte, tecnica e scienza dal Journal agli Essais." *Saggi e Ricerche di Letteratura Francese* 12 (1973): 47–92.

Rigolot, François. *Les Métamorphoses de Montaigne*. Paris: Presses Universitaires de France, 1986.

―――― "Montaigne's Anti-mannerist Mannerism," in *Le Visage changeant de Montaigne. The Changing Face of Montaigne*, eds Keith Cameron and Laura Willett. Paris: Champion, 2003, 207–30.

Rosellini, Aldo. "Quelques remarques sur l'italien du *Journal de voyage* de Montaigne." *Zeitschrift für Romanische Philologie* 83 (1967): 381–408.

Sayce, Richard A. *The Essays of Montaigne. A Critical Exploration*. London: Weidenfeld & Nicolson, 1972.

―――― "The Visual Arts in Montaigne's Journal de voyage," in *O un amy! Essays on Montaigne in Honor of Donald Frame*, ed. Raymond C. La Charité. Lexington, Ky.: French Forum Publishers, 1977, 219–41.

Starobinski, Jean. *Montaigne in Motion*, trans. Arthur Goldhammer. Chicago: Chicago University Press, 1985.

CHAPTER TWELVE

"SHARED STUDIES FOSTER FRIENDSHIP"

Humanism and history in Spain

Katherine Elliot van Liere

In 1575, near the zenith of Spain's imperial fortunes, the Spanish royal chronicler Ambrosio de Morales (1513–91) published a curious work entitled *The Antiquities of the Cities of Spain*. He described it as a supplement to his *General Chronicle of Castile* (1574–87), but unlike the *Chronicle*, the *Antiquities* was not a narrative history. Organized topographically rather than chronologically, it elucidated the origins of over 60 Castilian cities and settlements, drawing on classical sources such as Pliny's *Natural History*; the geographers Ptolemy, Strabo, and Pomponius Mela; and the *Itinerary* of Antoninus Pius (a Roman emperor who had traveled through Spain in the second century). Most notably, the *Antiquities* contained transcriptions of more than 170 Latin inscriptions from Roman altars, gravestones, arches, mile markers, and other monuments across Castile. Some of these were derived from earlier written sources, like the *Travels* of fifteenth-century epigrapher Cyriaco d'Ancona, but most came either from Morales' own field observations or from students and colleagues who did similar fieldwork on his behalf. The monuments of Morales' native province of Córdoba were particularly well represented. Finally, the *Antiquities* contained a 200-page methodological "Discourse" on how to evaluate these various types of ancient texts and artefacts. This survey of Castile's Roman antiquities belonged to a genre that had blossomed in Renaissance Italy over a century earlier, with such works as the *Roma instaurata* of Flavio Biondo (d. 1463). It had roots in Petrarch's fourteenth-century investigations of Rome's ancient ruins and inscriptions, and indeed in the explorations that the Roman antiquarian Varro had recorded in the first century BC. It was, however, the first work of this nature to be published in Spain (Figure 12.1).

Some modern observers have gone so far as to call Morales the founder of Spanish archaeology. This label exaggerates both Morales' originality and his

Figure 12.1 (opposite) Portrait of Ambrosio de Morales. Frontispiece from Ambrosio de Morales, *Viage de Ambrosio de Morales por orden del Rey D. Felipe II a los reynos de Leon, y Galicia, y principado de Asturias para reconocer las reliquias de santos, sepulcros reales, y libros manuscritos de las catedrales y monasterios*, ed. H. Florez (Madrid: Antonio Marín, 1765; facsimile: Madrid, 1985). The British Library.

AMBROSIO DE MORALES
Presbítero Historiographo Regio
Fr. HENRICUS FLOREZ AVG. B. M. F. C.

expertise. Morales was well read in the field of antiquities. He knew and recommended to his readers the researches of contemporary Italian antiquarians Aldo Manuzio (d. 1515), Onofrio Panvinio (d. 1568), and Carlo Sigonio (d. 1584). But he himself was not as skilled an interpreter of ancient relics as any of these scholars, nor was he fully consistent in applying the critical standards of humanist antiquarianism in his own historical research. Alongside the study of coins and inscriptions and the reading of Greek and Roman cosmographers, Morales' methodological discourse advised his readers to consult the legends of the saints and the oral testimony of local peasants. It gave ambiguous advice on how to rank the different kinds of evidence drawn from artefacts and how to reconcile discrepancies between written and unwritten sources, and no advice at all on how to distinguish genuine ancient artefacts from forgeries. In his own historical writing Morales gave ample attention to the Roman era, using classical sources, but he also perpetuated a number of legendary traditions, such as the coming of James the Apostle to Spain, that had no physical and a dubious textual basis. Nonetheless, Morales was introducing in Spain a tradition of historical research that represented a significant advance on medieval historiography. When married to philological criticism, the study of "antiquities" offered a powerful tool for critical historical research.

In the neighboring kingdom of Aragon, Morales' contemporary Antonio Agustín (1517–86) produced another seminal work on Spanish antiquities, the *Dialogues on Medals, Inscriptions, and other Antiquities* (Tarragona, 1587). This posthumous publication followed more than 20 scholarly works in Latin, including emendations to classical texts and studies in legal history, Roman history, Church history, and canon law. In the early sixteenth century the study of coinage, or numismatics, had taken its place alongside epigraphy, legal history, and textual criticism as one of the essential tools of the humanist enterprise of reconstructing ancient culture. Agustín was an avid collector and an astute numismatist, and his *Dialogues* sought to popularize among his countrymen the critical tools he had acquired in years of studying historical artefacts and inscriptions, and to show how they could be applied to interpreting both the Roman and the Spanish past (Figure 12.2).[1]

Few works published on Spanish history before this time made extensive use of antiquarian research. Medieval scholars had been deeply curious in their own way about their land's remote past, and the term "antiquities" had been used for centuries to denote the era of the peninsula's first known inhabitants. But in the eclectic historiographical tradition of the Middle Ages, which can be traced back to Isidore of Seville (*c.* 636), "antiquities" bore quite a different meaning, denoting a largely mythical era when Iberia was reputedly settled and populated by biblical and classical heroes. In this tradition Noah's grandson Tubal had founded Cetubal, the peninsula's first city, and subsequent rulers had included the Greek hero Hercules, whose descendants Hispanus and Liberia had given their respective names to the peninsula. The winged monster Geryon and the Titan Atlas sometimes appeared in this imaginative cast of settlers as well.

In the later fifteenth century, a handful of Spanish humanist scholars began to approach the early history of Spain with a more critical spirit and to dispel some of these medieval foundation legends. The Catalan bishop Joan Margarit i Pau (d. 1484) and the grammarian and chronicler Antonio de Nebrija (d. 1522) made extensive

Figure 12.2 Portrait of Antonio Agustín. Frontispiece from Agustín's *Dialogos de medallas, inscriciones y otras antiguedades* (Madrid, 1744). The British Library.

use of ancient geographers like Strabo, Ptolemy, Diodorus Siculus, and Pliny in trying to identify Spain's ancient settlements. Both observed Roman sites first hand and questioned the traditional identifications of some Hispano-Roman sites, such as that of the famous Numantia with Zamora. Nebrija, the foremost Spanish humanist of his day, also lectured and wrote on such antiquarian questions as Roman roads, coinage, and weights and measures. Yet despite their awakening humanist interests, these fifteenth-century historians made no radical revisions to the medieval "antiquities" tradition. While their use of ancient geographers was novel, their almost exclusive reliance on texts still made them susceptible to both legendary history and outright forgery. The most dramatic example of the latter in Nebrija's day was the 1498 *Commentaries* of Annius of Viterbo (Giovanni Nanni). This learned but unscrupulous scholar presented his work as a specimen of the new antiquarian learning, claiming to have discovered ancient Chaldean texts that vindicated and expanded on the familiar medieval legends about Spain's origins. They showed Hercules to be the son of the Egyptian god Osiris, thus backdating Iberian antiquity to an even more illustrious age. Spanish scholars continued to accept Annius' fabrication at face value well after the German scholar Beatus Rhenanus (d. 1547) proved it spurious.

By bringing antiquarianism to bear on the study of Spain's past, Morales and Agustín heralded a more critical approach to historical research. They were not alone. Jerónimo de Zurita's *Annals of the Crown of Aragon* (1562–85), the other major work of national history written in this period, made unprecedented use of archival sources. Zurita (1512–80), the royal chronicler for the kingdom of Aragon, began his narrative with the eighth-century Muslim invasion, arguing that earlier times were simply shrouded in too much uncertainty. But he made substantial use of classical sources for geographical questions. All three writers thus broke away from the fictions of Annius, whether by ignoring them (Morales and Zurita) or by condemning them outright (Agustín). It is not surprising that when a new generation of critical historians arose in the Enlightenment, they hailed Morales, Agustín, and Zurita as the forerunners of critical Enlightened historiography. We should not accept these laudatory judgments too readily; Spanish historical scholarship did not become decisively modern and critical in the sixteenth century. For all their fascination with antiquities, Morales and Zurita both continued to accept as authentic many texts that were later shown to be unreliable or forged. Many of their successors in the seventeenth century were even less critical. Indeed, the late sixteenth and seventeenth centuries witnessed spectacular bursts of new "ancient" forgeries even cruder than those of Annius, due largely to the renewed interest in sacred history sparked by the Counter-Reformation. The legends perpetuated by Annius, and newer ones just as far-fetched, continued to find adherents in Spain until the early twentieth century. But no matter how crooked the course of later developments, the humanist researches of these sixteenth-century scholars represented a signal contribution to Spanish scholarship.

Who were these Spanish antiquarians, and what inspired their common interest in antiquities? This chapter does not pretend to offer a comprehensive survey of sixteenth-century Spanish historical or antiquarian studies. It seeks rather to reconstruct the social context in which these studies were pursued. While in 1500 Antonio de Nebrija had still been an anomaly as an Italian-trained humanist in Spain, by 1550 it is possible to speak of a community of Spanish humanist historians. This community was quite different from its Italian counterparts. Not only was it much smaller, but it had no geographical center. In Italy, Rome's inexhaustible collection of antiquities served as a perpetual magnet for scholars, while a host of Roman patrons, from the popes to wealthy Roman churchmen like Gentile Delfini and Angelo Colocci, provided patronage and comfortable villas where these scholars could gather to observe and discuss collections of antiquities first hand. No city played an equivalent role in Castile or Aragon. Antiquarians were scattered among a handful of cities, and patrons were scarcer. Nor did the universities play a formative role in Spanish antiquarian studies. The scholars in question came mainly from aristocratic circles, and they were professionally diverse. While some were salaried chroniclers, others worked as bishops, royal bureaucrats, or teachers of rhetoric, biblical studies, or mathematics. For many, antiquarian and historical studies were a part-time pursuit. The majority never became as well known as Morales, Agustín, or Zurita because they published little or none of their historical research.

Despite their geographic dispersion, these scattered Spanish devotees of Roman antiquity formed a remarkably tight-knit scholarly community. Today we might call it a "virtual community," for what held it together was written correspondence. Zurita knew both Morales and Agustín, and all three were part of an even wider epistolary network that stretched across Castile, Aragon, and Italy. This network certainly did not approach the scale of the Enlightenment's "republic of letters," nor did it include every humanist historian in Spain, but a considerable number of the period's leading humanist scholars were connected to it. For most of them this scholarly network was more valuable than an academic affiliation. In an electronic age, when we marvel at how easily we can communicate with our own peers across the globe, it is easy to forget that international correspondence was just as essential for Renaissance scholars. It let them exchange not only ideas and reflections on each other's work, but also the necessary materials for that work. With their letters they regularly shared transcriptions and lent books, manuscripts, and coins, and they sustained crucial contacts with patrons. Their modes of correspondence were certainly slower, more expensive, and more erratic than our own. Without a regular postal service, they had to rely on personal couriers and the networks of the Church and crown. Letters sometimes took months to arrive or disappeared in transit. Yet despite these inconveniences, correspondence played a crucial role in the production of historical knowledge. The surviving letters of these humanist scholars can tell us a great deal – not just about how they supported one another's work but also about the difficulties they faced in a land where humanism had arrived late and never put down deep institutional roots.

THE INFLUENCE OF ROME

The closest place to a geographical center for Spanish historical and antiquarian studies in the sixteenth century was Rome. The eternal city's cultural attraction for Spanish scholars began in the fifteenth century, but waxed in Spain's imperial age, along with Spanish political influence in Italy. Although not all of Spain's antiquarians traveled to Italy, Rome was a crucial influence on them all, directly or indirectly. One of the first Spanish humanists in the sixteenth century to be formed by a lengthy stay in Italy was Juan Ginés de Sepúlveda (1491–1573). He followed in Margarit and Nebrija's footsteps by studying at the Spanish College of Bologna (Colegio de San Clemente), an institution that helped to form some of Spain's best scholars during the Renaissance. This residential college within the University of Bologna had served a population of elite Spanish students since its foundation in the fourteenth century. Serving mainly law students, the Spanish College was never a center of humanist studies *per se*, but it did give many ambitious scholars entrée to the rich and varied academic milieu of Bologna. Sepúlveda, who devoted most of his career to translating and interpreting Aristotle, got his start there under the great Aristotelian philosopher Pietro Pomponazzi. He also wrote his first historical work there (and the only one to be published in his lifetime): a commissioned history of the Spanish College and a life of its founder.[2]

It was Rome, however, that inspired Sepúlveda's interest in new kinds of historical research. He pursued his philosophical studies and translations there from 1525 to 1536 under Pope Clement VII's patronage. Sometime during this decade he took religious orders, a natural move for a scholar in papal service. Living in Rome inspired in Sepúlveda a lively interest in Roman antiquities. He frequented the circle around the antiquarian Angelo Colocci, whose villa housed one of Rome's greatest collections of antique statuary and sarcophagi. Sepúlveda survived the gruesome Sack of Rome in 1527, and might have spent the rest of his days in the eternal city, but a 1529 meeting with Charles V, Holy Roman Emperor and king of Spain, brought an irresistible opportunity to continue his studies in his native land. Returning to Spain in 1536 to serve as Charles's royal chronicler, Sepúlveda would apply his admiration for Roman culture to a vigorous defense of Spanish imperial expansion, both in his chronicles of recent Spanish history and in his famous debate with Dominican Bartolomé de las Casas.

While serving as Charles V's chronicler, Sepúlveda exchanged letters with Spaniards in Rome, including Antonio Agustín, and with humanist scholars in Spain. He may also have conveyed some of his passion for classical antiquities to the future Philip II of Spain, whom he served for a while as a tutor. In 1543 Sepúlveda was assigned to accompany the royal party escorting Maria of Portugal to Salamanca for her wedding to Prince Philip. When this journey took him along the Roman Mérida–Salamanca road, which preserved some intact Roman mile markers, Sepúlveda eagerly seized the opportunity to investigate the remains of the Roman road, measure the distances between the markers, and transcribe as many of the remaining inscriptions as he could. He reported his detailed conclusions in a letter to Philip, complimenting the heir on his own appreciation for antiquities and reminding him how Sepúlveda had showed the prince an iron measure of a Roman foot that had been carefully measured against ancient stone originals in Angelo Colocci's Roman collection.[3]

Sepúlveda's letter itself did not turn the future Philip II into a lover of antiquities. For one thing, despite the efforts of Sepúlveda and Philip's other Latin tutors, the young prince never mastered the language. This published Latin letter was intended mainly to publicize Sepúlveda's activities to a European scholarly audience, and it is possible that Philip never even saw it. Still, there seems some reason to believe the letter's confident assurance that the prince was already genuinely interested in "news of ancient things." When Philip became king in 1558 he did show more interest in ancient history than his father. Charles had initiated the *Coronica General* only after repeated appeals from the Cortes of Castile. Most of his chroniclers, including Sepúlveda, wrote recent or contemporary history. Under his son Philip, the balance shifted more toward the investigation of ancient times. This was evidenced not only in narrative works like those of Zurita and Morales, but also in projects like the *Relaciones topográficas*, a monumental royal report on the topography, sociology, and history of Castile's towns and villages undertaken in the 1570s. The royal questionnaire on which this report was based asked explicitly about the town's earliest history and what vestiges of antiquity it preserved. It may not be too far-fetched to imagine that the tutor Sepúlveda's personal influence was one early source of Philip's interest in such matters.

Just as Sepúlveda was leaving Rome to return to Spain, Antonio Agustín was beginning a similar trajectory, commencing studies in Bologna that would propel him to Rome, into a prestigious ecclesiastical and scholarly career, and eventually back to Spain. The son of one of Aragon's leading noble families, Agustín had studied in Alcalá from the age of nine, and then in Salamanca from 1528 to 1535. At eighteen he began a sojourn of nearly three decades in Italy. In Bologna he studied with the great legal humanist Andrea Alciato. After a brief stay in Padua, where he learned Greek, he returned to Bologna to take up a fellowship at the Spanish College. In these years he began to conduct a rich correspondence in Latin with a diverse circle of Spanish and Italian intellectuals. Soon after earning his doctorate in canon and civil law from Bologna in 1541 he entered a lifelong career in the Church, which afforded him lifetime financial security and the luxury of devoting his spare time to scholarship. His initial interests in legal humanism led naturally to other historical and antiquarian pursuits, for legal humanists investigated Roman political, social, and even monetary history as part of the historical context for Roman law. Over the next four decades Agustín wrote more than 30 works (many, like the *Dialogues*, still unpublished at his death), beginning with a critical commentary on the *Digest of Roman Law* and branching out into many other areas of civil and canon law, Roman history, Church history, and antiquities. In Rome he benefited immeasurably from contact with a lively intellectual circle that included such eminent scholars and collectors as Gentile Delfini, Fulvio Orsini, and Carlo Sigonio. Four of his published works were collaborations with his good friend Orsini.

All the while Agustín maintained his Spanish identity, kept in touch with Spanish scholars back in the mother country, and sometimes offered them material assistance. In 1549, while Agustín was serving as a judge in the Rota (papal court of appeals), Sepúlveda approached him as a likely ally in his quest to find an Italian audience for his controversial treatise on natural servitude. Las Casas and the Dominicans, who opposed his ideas, were making it difficult to publish the work in Spain. Although he had probably never met Agustín, Sepúlveda wrote to him in Rome asking if he would circulate the work there, and Agustín not only complied but praised the treatise and had it printed at his own expense. By the mid-1550s, Agustín had begun an extensive correspondence with the historian Jerónimo de Zurita, an old friend from Zaragoza. In 1561, Agustín came into contact with another circle of Spanish scholars when he attended the third session of the Council of Trent as the newly appointed bishop of Lérida. One of his most pleasing contacts there was with fellow bishop and jurist Diego de Covarrubias (1512–77), who shared his interests in numismatics, Roman history, and early Spanish history. Covarrubias had published his own treatise on ancient coinage in 1556. After both returned to Spain from Trent in 1564, they corresponded about the interpretation of coins.[4]

Perhaps Agustín's most valuable scholarly contact among the Spanish expatriate community was his fellow noble antiquarian Don Diego Hurtado de Mendoza (1504–75). When Don Diego arrived in Venice in 1539 as the new Spanish ambassador, Agustín traveled there from Padua expressly to greet him. Born into a noble family that had long cultivated a tradition of classical studies, Don Diego had acquired his first taste for ancient learning and literature at home in Granada, where he had grown up in the Alhambra. He had studied in Salamanca, Rome, and Padua, and was almost unique among the Spanish nobility in knowing not only Latin but also Greek and Arabic. After serving as Spain's ambassador to England and Venice, he became imperial delegate to the first session of the Council of Trent (1545–6) and ambassador to the papacy (1547–54). A highly unusual combination of noble diplomat, soldier, bibliophile, and man of letters, he amassed one of the largest private libraries of any Spaniard in the sixteenth century, and next to Agustín was probably the greatest Spanish coin collector. As a scholar, he was admittedly a dilettante, and his writings (unpublished during his lifetime) were more literary than antiquarian. His greatest service to sixteenth-century scholarship was generous patronage. In Trent and in Rome he acted as a Maecenas to expatriate Spanish *eruditos*. He also lent books and coins to scholars in both Spain and Italy, some of whom employed a small army of copyists to copy his works for their own use. Though he never joined him in Italy, Ambrosio de Morales also enjoyed Hurtado de Mendoza's patronage, and in gratitude he dedicated his *Antiquities* to him. In his dedication, Morales praised Don Diego's "singular understanding of Roman antiquities" and credited him with teaching Morales all he knew about antiquities and numismatics and furnishing him generously with Hispano-Roman coins and inscriptions.[5] Such dedications tend to exaggerate, but Hurtado de Mendoza was clearly a strong support to Morales' studies.

THE SPANISH UNIVERSITY MILIEU

Not all Spanish antiquarians had firsthand experience of Italy. Ambrosio de Morales never left Spain, but his noble Cordoban family had its own Italian connections. His maternal uncle, the humanist polymath Fernán Pérez de Oliva (1494?–1533), who had studied in Rome and Paris, was a formative influence on the young Morales. He personally directed Ambrosio's university studies in Salamanca between 1526 and 1531. But it was Morales' years in Alcalá, where he first went around 1540, that afforded him the most valuable contact with fellow humanists and historically minded scholars. Alcalá was the one academic community in Castile that came close to serving as a geographic locus for these kinds of studies. Neither history nor antiquities was a formal academic subject, but individuals from different faculties discovered these common interests and pursued them outside the regular curriculum.

Morales' 1575 *Discourse on Antiquities* attests to a diverse network of students and teachers who shared his passions for coin collecting, monument hunting, and epigraphy, and offered substantial support to his researches. Even before becoming a university lecturer of rhetoric in 1549, Morales had a large roster of private students. One of these, the Dominican friar Alonso Chacón, went to Rome in the 1580s and published extensively on Roman antiquities. The other students whose collaboration Morales warmly acknowledged in his *Antiquities* were mostly young noblemen who shared his passion for digging and transcribing but never published anything. Like Morales and Mendoza, these young men acquired an interest in antiquities and collecting from aristocratic family circles. Morales' favorite was Diego de Guevara, son of the famous courtier Felipe Guevara. Both father and son were avid collectors and interpreters of antiquities, coins, and art, and Felipe wrote treatises on numismatics and painting. Juan Fernández Franco, a Cordoban like Morales, may have been the most helpful of all Morales' students. He not only introduced his teacher to many sites of antiquities in Andalusia but wrote several volumes of his own on antiquities and epigraphy, and a treatise on numismatics, all of which remained unpublished for centuries.

Because Morales was fortunate enough to have so many like-minded scholars close by in Alcalá, he wrote fewer letters than some of this fellow scholars. But one of his closest scholarly friendships, with Alvar Gómez de Castro (1515–80), was sustained largely by letters, at least after Gómez left Alcalá around 1550 to lecture in Toledo at the newly founded Colegio de Santa Catalina. Although best known for his biography of Cardinal Cisneros and his translations of Greek and Latin poetry, Gómez de Castro was also an assiduous epigrapher and collector of coins and antiquities. He and Morales corresponded throughout the 1550s and 1560s, with Morales picking his friend's brain especially eagerly in the 1560s as he began to do research for the *General Chronicle*. They discussed coins and inscriptions that each had seen first hand, as well as the shortcomings of earlier written histories. Like so many of Morales' circle, Gómez de Castro wrote copiously about antiquities and circulated his writings generously among his friends, but never published them. He was the first to describe the monumental remains being excavated at Talavera la Vieja in the early 1570s (the details of which Morales published in his *Antigüedades*). He took at least one large stone for his private collection of coins and monuments in Toledo, a collection he eventually bequeathed to a grateful Antonio Agustín.

Morales' contacts with historical scholars outside Alcalá were equally crucial, and these extended well beyond his indebtedness to Don Diego de Hurtado de Mendoza. In later years he communicated on historical and antiquarian subjects with fellow chronicler Jerónimo de Zurita and with Diego de Covarrubias, the scholarly bishop befriended by Agustín in Trent. The three must also have crossed paths repeatedly in the 1560s and 1570s when all were frequently at court. Covarrubias read an early draft of Morales' *Discourse on Antiquities*, and shared with him Greek versions of Plutarch and Polybius from his private collection, helping him to appreciate how unreliable the existing Latin translations were. Morales warmly acknowledged both Covarrubias and Zurita's advice in the *Antigüedades*, and Zurita's generosity with his collection of Aragonese coins and antiquities. When the first volume of Zurita's *Annals of the Crown of Aragon* was criticized by royal censors in 1562, Morales defended Zurita's scholarship in a vigorous "Apologia," which also cited Covarrubias's judgment that the censure was unfair.[6]

Salamanca, where Diego de Covarrubias had spent 25 years, was Castile's other great university, but it was much less lively than Alcalá as a center of historical scholarship. Covarrubias was one of a few exceptional graduates who dedicated themselves to humanistic studies. A jurist like Agustín, he had studied in Salamanca between 1523 and 1533, then taught canon law there from 1533 to 1548. Although Covarrubias shared many of Agustín's interests in numismatics, legal history, and Roman and early Spanish political history, these interests did not reflect the university curriculum at Salamanca. Covarrubias's own early education in Salamanca, like that of Morales, was largely a family-run affair; his uncle ran a private boardinghouse in Salamanca for young scholars, and it was the private tutors he provided who first steered Covarrubias's interests toward humanistic studies. (The same family operation later produced the great lexicographer Sebastián de Covarrubias, author of the classic Castilian dictionary.) As a professor of law at Salamanca, Covarrubias adhered to the traditional (pre-humanistic) Bartolist method, which was pragmatic rather than historical in approach. Most of his published works consisted of traditional commentaries on canon and civil law. It was only in the years after he left the university to serve as a royal judge, and then as a bishop and eventually as president of the Council of Castile, that he had the freedom to exercise his historical and antiquarian interests. Some of these found expression in a 1556 treatise on coinage, and in the fourth book of his *Various Resolutions* (1570), which dealt with Roman social and legal history. But many of Covarrubias's antiquarian pursuits remained unpublished. His professional duties left him little time for research. Still, he continued to exchange letters on these subjects into the 1570s, not just with Morales and Agustín but also with Italian humanist Pier Vettori and others.

Covarrubias may not have found many kindred spirits in his years at Salamanca, but he did find one in the distinguished lecturer of Greek and rhetoric, Hernán Núñez de Guzmán (1473?–1553). In 1545, three years before leaving Salamanca to pursue a legal career, Covarrubias visited the royal court in Valladolid bearing a letter of recommendation from Núñez de Guzmán. The letter, addressed to Núñez's friend Jerónimo de Zurita, praised both Covarrubias's character and his humanist credentials. Núñez is more often known as "el Pinciano" (the Latin name for his presumed birthplace, Valladolid) or "the Greek Commander," denoting his rank as commander in the military Order of Santiago. At least 70 when he wrote to Zurita on Covarrubias's behalf, Pinciano was one of the few scholars left in Salamanca who had known Antonio de Nebrija personally. From his perspective, colleagues as learned as Covarrubias were far too rare in the university. Although not an antiquarian *per se*, Pinciano was a keen textual critic and a devotee of classical history. He shared the antiquarians' passion for Spain's Roman history, and corresponded enthusiastically with Sepúlveda and Zurita about how to interpret the classical sources. Like Covarrubias, he pursued these studies more in spite of than because of the academic milieu, and his letters suggest that a scholar with these interests did not find much support from his colleagues in Salamanca.[7]

Like many of his contemporaries, Pinciano acquired his humanist interests not at a Spanish university, but through family influence and study abroad. He came from a noble Granadan family with close ties to the monarchy and to the Mendoza, whose sons he probably tutored. He had studied in Bologna, possibly at the Spanish College, and returned to Spain a first-rate humanist textual critic and proficient in Arabic, Greek, and Latin. He taught both at Salamanca and at Alcalá, where he collaborated on Cisneros's Polyglot Bible and knew both Nebrija and Cisneros. When he moved to Salamanca permanently in 1522, he was disappointed at the contrast with Alcalá. Although Salamanca had had a chair of Greek for some time, Pinciano complained in a letter to his old Alcalá colleague Juan de Vergara that languages were underappreciated; law, Aristotelian philosophy, and medicine dominated the intellectual scene. In 1535 he lost a bitter suit with the university over the appointment to a chair of grammar, and while he continued to do some teaching, he devoted himself more and more to private study.

Despite his frustrations with the university, Pinciano was wealthy enough to pursue his scholarly interests without a tenured chair. These interests were quite diverse, but most revealed an interest in the cultural history of his native land. His most popular publication was an anthology of Spanish proverbs (1555), which became so well known that Cervantes cited it 50 years later in *Don Quixote* as the standard by which to measure Sancho Panza's prodigious knowledge. Pinciano's more scholarly works were humanist commentaries and editions of classical texts, but these also favored Spanish authors: a commentary on the works of Hispano-Roman philosopher Seneca (1536); an edition with commentary of the *Geography* of Hispano-Roman cosmographer Pomponius Mela (1543); and a commentary on the *Natural History* of Pliny (1544), who, though not Spanish, had much to say about the natural history and topography of Hispania. These humanist commentaries did not find a particularly appreciative audience in Salamanca. The university senate (*claustro*) actually attempted to ban the commentary on Pomponius Mela after its publication, on the (somewhat obscure) grounds that it contained remarks prejudicial to the university. This move apparently failed, but it deepened Pinciano's resentment toward his colleagues.

He did, however, find interested readers and critics outside. His correspondence with Sepúlveda and Zurita shows how an isolated scholar could use letters as a lifeline to a distant community of sympathetic peers. It also shows that these scholarly exchanges traded not just superficial compliments, but rigorous criticism. And they did not always end amicably, especially when the scholars concerned were as proud and self-confident as these two men. The Sepúlveda–Pinciano correspondence is a problematic source, for all that survives is Sepúlveda's half, self-selected and edited for his published letter collection. The exchange started out in 1541 with mutual admiration, humor, and signs of affection. The conventions of the Latin "familiar letter" that both writers employed dictated much of this, so Sepúlveda's letters may well exaggerate the degree of their friendship. Sepúlveda read and praised Pinciano's edition of Pomponius Mela. This evidently prompted Pinciano to send him the commentaries on Pliny in manuscript form, for Sepúlveda wrote again with extensive suggestions on how to revise these. Pinciano put some of these into effect, and politely acknowledged Sepúlveda's assistance in the final version. But he also criticized some of the suggestions quite harshly, questioning Sepúlveda's philological skills and his understanding of Aristotle. Sepúlveda, who prided himself as an expert on Aristotle, took this very badly, and his last letter in 1544 suggests that the row may have ended the epistolary friendship.

SCHOLARSHIP AT COURT

Pinciano enjoyed a more productive, sustained, and amicable epistolary friendship with Jerónimo de Zurita, whose assistance he acknowledged warmly in his published Pliny commentaries. Zurita had studied at the University of Alcalá, probably a few years after Pinciano had left there, but never pursued an academic career. Born into a noble Aragonese family like Antonio Agustín, he joined the court of Charles V before he was 20 and remained a courtier all his life. Like Pinciano (and unlike Sepúlveda, Agustín, Covarrubias, and Morales), he was a layman with no ties to the Church. However he and Pinciano first met, they were regular correspondents by 1537 when Zurita was serving as secretary of the Council of the Inquisition. Over the next decade Pinciano wrote more than 50 letters to Zurita, and Zurita must have returned many more than the one that survives. Zurita was not yet a chronicler himself, but he took a keen interest in the textual problems of Pinciano's emendations to Pomponius Mela and Pliny, which formed the dominant theme of the correspondence. (Zurita appears to have been working on his own emendations to Pliny in this period, according to exchanges with his friend Juan de Vergara, although unlike Pinciano he never published them.) Zurita lent Pinciano a priceless manuscript of Pliny, which Pinciano apologetically returned more than two years late. Zurita was not Pinciano's only contact at court in these years. The letters refer warmly to other scholars at court such as Honorato Juan, one of Prince Philip's tutors, and the bibliophile royal secretary Gonzalo Pérez. They refer much less warmly to the chronicler Florián de Ocampo, Morales' predecessor, who also read and criticized some of Pinciano's work. The outspoken Pinciano found Ocampo uncritical, dishonest, and thoroughly unlikable, despite Zurita's apparent affection for him.

Unlike the Sepúlveda–Pinciano exchange, Pinciano's letters to Zurita were clearly not intended for publication. They were gossipy, full of personal and financial business, and written in the vernacular, although Pinciano apologized to Zurita for not addressing him "continually" in Latin as he deserved, and both peppered their Castilian epistles generously with classicizing Latin fragments. Theirs was not an exchange between social equals; Pinciano, though noble and 40 years Zurita's senior, deferred to the courtier by addressing him as "muy magnífico señor." But there was clearly affection as well as scholarly respect between them. More than the capricious and self-regarding Sepúlveda, Zurita offered Pinciano long-distance intellectual fellowship that boosted his confidence and enriched his work. Pinciano acknowledged this by quoting to Zurita the Latin adage "Paritas studiorum conciliat amicitiam" ("shared studies foster friendship").

Zurita played two distinct roles in this community. He was a scholar whose published history eventually embodied some of the most substantial historical research of his generation. But perhaps even more valuable to his peers (especially before his *Annals* were published in 1562), he served as a crucial mediator of news and material resources for a large group of scholar-correspondents. As a courtier with personal access to the king and to networks of royal patronage, Zurita helped to keep these far-flung humanists in touch with events and people at court, to provide them with news of their families, to help them deal with legal and financial problems at home, and, if they were in the crown's pay, to make sure that their salaries were properly disbursed. His material position was enviable compared with many of his fellow scholars. Zurita often had works copied and sent to Pinciano. Once Pinciano slyly told Zurita to borrow a book from a fellow courtier on false pretenses and have it copied without the owner's knowledge. This constant sense of the scarcity of books, and the reliance on copyists, reminds us that even in this later Renaissance era the "culture of print" had not wholly displaced the manuscript culture of medieval learning – least of all in Spain, where, even in the largest university town, booksellers and libraries were relatively thin on the ground.

Zurita gained something from the exchange too, for the scholarly perks of life at court in this period were still limited. Before 1570 there was no royal library; Philip II began to put one together in the 1570s (the Royal Library of El Escorial), largely by amassing the private collections of Zurita's correspondents. Thus Zurita eagerly sought books from his friends abroad, as well as sending books out. Pinciano was one of his lifelines to the scholarly world outside the court. Pinciano sent him Latin books from Salamanca on a range of subjects, including early Greek history, natural history, and the geographical works of Ptolemy. Sometimes he fulfilled specific requests, and sometimes he combed through recent acquisitions in local bookshops to find works he thought Zurita might fancy. The supply was seldom abundant. Pinciano would apologize that nothing new had appeared in Salamanca for weeks, or that one book he had specially ordered from Bologna had been snapped up by another customer before he could get his hands on it. Often he paid copyists to duplicate rare books for his friend.

Pinciano was not the only correspondent with whom the bibliophile Zurita traded books. Zurita supplied other Spanish scholars with books and manuscripts, and made use of his many Spanish contacts in Italy to feed his own appetite for humanist and historical literature. The royal chaplain Agustín de Cazalla, later burned as a Protestant in the Inquisition's great *auto-de-fe* in Valladolid in 1559, supplied Zurita with shipments of books, including a Greek text of the works of Jewish historian Josephus. An even more important source was Juan Páez de Castro (1520?–70), a polymath from Guadalajara who operated as a virtual inter-library loan agent in Italy in the 1540s and 1550s.[8] Páez was a mutual friend of Zurita, Cazalla, and Pinciano, although it is not clear where the friendships began. All had taught or studied at Alcalá, though not simultaneously. In the 1540s Páez appears to have been a scholarly drifter, appearing now in Salamanca, then in Valladolid, but in 1545 Zurita arranged for Páez to go to Trent in the service of his friend Diego Hurtado de Mendoza. In 1547 Páez moved on to Rome in Cardinal Francisco de Mendoza's service. It was probably there that he also befriended Antonio Agustín. Zurita wrote regularly to Páez in Italy, sending the most recent works of their scholar friends in Spain, including Pinciano's annotations on Pliny, and inquiring about expatriates like Cazalla and Hurtado de Mendoza. Páez responded with political and ecclesiastical news, requests for financial arbitration for himself and other Spaniards, and more books. Páez and Zurita were able to meet in Rome at least briefly, as the latter passed through in 1550 on his journey south to the archives of Naples and Sicily. During his years in Italy, and in his travels through the Low Countries in the 1550s, Páez eventually amassed a substantial library of books and manuscripts. Pinciano also sent books to Páez from Salamanca. In 1564 Agustín brought part of Páez's collection to Spain, where most of it ultimately ended up in the Escorial library.

Páez never published a book of his own, nor can he be called an antiquarian; his wide-ranging interests centered on books, not on artefacts. He did share with Sepúlveda, Morales, and Zurita the distinction of being named a royal chronicler, but he never rose to the occasion. He was given this title in 1555, upon rumors of the death of Florián de Ocampo, the first author of the *General Chronicle of Castile*. But Páez could not decide what to do with the commission. At first he wondered whether he should write modern history or carry on the early history that Florián had begun. Then he changed his mind about returning to Spain to take up the position, first arranging to have his books sent to Madrid, but later telling Zurita (from Brussels in 1556) that he would request a license to keep residing abroad. Two months after that he cheekily told Zurita that he really did not think the job would involve much work at all, for he expected Zurita himself to provide him with all the necessary materials and information. Páez finally returned to Spain around 1560, and spent his last ten years in retirement collecting historical materials and advising Philip II on how to organize his royal library. Although he never completed a narrative history, he left massive notes toward that end, and his energetic defense of the Escorial library project ultimately benefited many other scholars. He joined Ambrosio de Morales in writing a lively defense of Zurita's historical writing when it came under criticism from a royal censor in 1562. Finally, in the year he died (1570), he drafted the royal questionnaire for the *Relaciones topográficas*, which encouraged every town in Spain to inquire into its historical roots and antiquities.

AMICITIA UNDER STRAIN

Jerónimo de Zurita could have applied the epigram "Paritas studiorum facilitat amicitiam" to his epistolary friendships with Pinciano, Juan Páez, and quite a few others. During the three decades that he researched and wrote the *Annals of the Crown of Aragon*, he carried on a wide correspondence with other scholars. The most intense of these exchanges was with his old friend Antonio Agustín.[9] Agustín followed the progress of Zurita's *Annals* with keen interest, first from Rome and then from Catalonia and Aragon. He found it decidedly superior to any existing Spanish histories, including the recent work of Morales. The Agustín–Zurita letters offer one of the best windows into Zurita's critical and historiographical interests. When their correspondence began is uncertain, but both men were from Zaragoza and may well have met there in their youth. They could have deepened their acquaintance at Alcalá in the late 1520s, and in Rome where they coincided in the 1550s. The two addressed each other as social equals, and when Agustín made ready to return to Aragon after his 20-year stay in Italy, he wrote to Zurita that he was more eager to see him than any of his other old friends.

Despite his decision to begin his history of Aragon with the eighth-century Arab conquest, Zurita was obsessed with the question of Roman origins, and he had no more learned adviser on this subject than Agustín. A recurring topic in his letters to Agustín was the use of Roman coins to ascertain which Spanish settlements originated as Roman *coloniae*. The two compared evidence from their large private coin collections for the spellings of different place-names, and collated these with textual evidence from Strabo, Ptolemy, Pliny, Varro, and other ancient writers. Agustín and Zurita also shared an interest in the Visigothic era, particularly the history of its Church councils. But unlike many medieval chroniclers of Spain, who saw the Visigoths, Spain's first Christian rulers, as the founders of Hispania, neither seems to have seen the Visigothic period as a crucible of "Spanish" identity *per se*. They were also eager to know more about the *pre*-Roman era, and lamented that their ignorance of Punic and Celtiberian writing (and that of "other nations which we do not know") kept them from deciphering this chapter of their national past. The fact that Agustín refers to these unknown, pre-Roman, pre-Christian inhabitants as "the ancient Spaniards" suggests a remarkably broad conception of what constituted the historical "Spain."

Agustín's letters to Zurita also hint at the conditions for a humanist scholar living in a northern provincial Spanish city. After his years in Italy, Augustín could not help finding his episcopal residences in Lérida and Tarragona remote. His initial enthusiasm about returning to his native land quickly gave way, in his letters, to laments about isolation from the vast scholarly resources of Renaissance Rome. He complained that it was hard to acquire books. Thankfully Zurita, by the 1570s, was able to provide regular loans of rare books from Madrid and Zaragoza, through the same couriers who exchanged their letters. Many of these came from the libraries of Páez de Castro and Hurtado de Mendoza, to which Agustín had enjoyed regular access in Rome. (These collections passed into the crown's possession after their owners' respective deaths in 1570 and 1575.) When Zurita lent him a volume, Agustín often paid to have it copied, just as Pinciano had done in Salamanca. For Agustín these loans were a lifeline. Although he had a considerable private library of his own, he regularly noted the gaps in his collection and the paucity of books around him. When he learned in 1576 of his promotion to the see of Tarragona, Agustín told Zurita how he looked forward to making use of the cathedral archives and library, possessed of "lots of ancient texts," and to investigating the "great quantity of antiquities and inscriptions" that the city had to offer. Yet Agustín was not satisfied by the intellectual stimulation in Tarragona. As Christmas 1578 approached, he pleaded with Zurita not to forget to send him the next shipment of promised books "so that I will have a more pleasant way to pass my time in the coming holidays than in conversation with the people of this land." This was a rather unjust insult to his countrymen, for Agustín was not the only antiquarian scholar in Aragon. His own observation that new inscriptions were "being discovered daily" acknowledged the presence of others with similar interests. One noble contemporary, the Duke of Villahermosa (1526–81), shared Agustín's passion for numismatics and sent him a copy of his own unpublished treatise on the subject, which Agustín may have drawn on in his *Dialogues*, although he did not acknowledge it.[10] But in general Agustín dismissed these amateur noble coin collectors as dilettantes.

For all his reluctance to accept advice from other scholars, Agustín was eager to offer it to Zurita. For more than two decades (until Zurita died in 1580), he lavished copious advice on Zurita concerning sources, chronology, the identification of place-names, orthography, language, rhetorical style, and the practical business of seeing his *Annals* into print. "I want to see the *Annals* finished and printed during your life-time," he wrote at one point, sounding more impatient than the author himself, and when Zurita's publishers seemed slow in issuing the second volume, Agustín tried to persuade him to have the work published in Tarragona. At first Zurita seemed to invite such advice from his friend. He even lamented that Agustín was not there in person to give him even more direct assistance. But Agustín's criticism could be harsh. One particularly intense disagreement arose over rhetorical style. Although Zurita chose to write the work first in Castilian (a Latin version was also planned, but never published), Agustín felt strongly that he should follow humanist rhetorical conventions, even in the vernacular. He urged Zurita to imitate Cicero and Caesar, not the "base" style of Tacitus, and to refrain from excerpting long passages verbatim from his original sources. These originals were worth preserving in libraries, Agustín counseled, but the narrative itself should be free of such clutter: "I would prefer to see good history told in a different style, for these are not books of science (*ciencias*), or doctrine, in which it is really important to see exactly what each author says in his [original] source."

Meanwhile Agustín offered ever more detailed criticism of Zurita's interpretation of particular sources, demanding to know which sources he was using to derive specific factual claims. After a while Zurita began to take Agustín's exhaustive critique as a personal assault. Although Zurita may have invited the criticism initially, it now seemed that Agustín was persisting in it not as an act of friendship but as an unwanted intrusion at the crown's behest. In the final year, their correspondence degenerated into a sad exchange of insults, Zurita's rage barely contained by formal expressions of politeness. He accused Agustín of taking perverse pleasure in criticizing not only Zurita's work but that of his friends Ambrosio de Morales and Alvar Gómez de Castro. He bewailed the "bloodiness and rigor" of Agustín's attacks on himself and Alvar Gómez. Once his indignation was aroused, Zurita added a bitter litany of complaints about Agustín's scholarly and personal failings over the last years. He drew an invidious comparison between Agustín's apparently private pursuit of learning for its own sake and his own dogged determination to publish his histories as a "service to the kingdom," imperfect though they might be. He disliked the way Agustín had chosen to structure his *Dialogue on Coins* (Agustín was now readying the manuscript for publication), setting it in an imagined Spanish context instead of a more authentic Italian one, with genuine Italian interlocutors, where it would better reflect the true genesis of Agustín's knowledge of coins and medals, and be of greater "utility to the universal church." Worse still, he accused Agustín of being reckless with the scholarly resources of others, hoarding borrowed coins and books for far too long without regard to their owners' feelings. The monks of the Aula Dei Monastery, he pointedly recalled, were still awaiting the return of three long-overdue books that Agustín had borrowed years earlier and had failed to put to any good use.

The bitterness of this broken friendship, which apparently followed Zurita to the grave, reminds us that Pinciano's dictum did not always hold true. Shared studies could strengthen friendships, perhaps even create them. But the double-edged sword of scholarly criticism could also sever the bonds of *amicitia*. In a later age, when the European "Republic of Letters" took on a vigorous life of its own, comprising hundreds of members and sustained by scholarly journals and academies, one quarrel between two scholars did not jeopardize the whole republic. The humanist scholarly community of sixteenth-century Spain, however, was still a smaller and more fragile affair, a finite web of individual relationships that had to be carefully reconstructed with each new generation.

NOTES

1 Antonio Agustín, *Diálogos de medallas, inscripciones y otras antigüedades* (Tarragona: Felipe Mey, 1587). (A facsimile edition was published in Madrid: Jano, 1987.)
2 Juan Ginés de Sepúlveda, *De vita et rebus gestis Aegidii Albornotii* (Bologna, 1521).
3 Juan Ginés de Sepúlveda, *Epistolarum libri septem*, ed. Juan J. Valverde Abril, Bibliotheca scriptorum Graecorum et Romanorum Teubneriana, 1252 (Munich and Leipzig: K. G. Saur, 2003), Ep. 3, 6 (XXVIII).
4 Agustín was the most prolific correspondent among the scholars discussed here. Published selections of his letters include Antonio Agustín, *Epistolario de Antonio Agustín*, ed. Cándido Flores Selles (Salamanca: Universidad de Salamanca, 1980); F. Miquel Rosell, ed., "Epistolario Antonio Agustín, ms. 53 de la Biblioteca Universitaria de Barcelona," *Analecta Sacra Tarraconensia* 13 (1937): 113–202.
5 Ambrosio Morales, *Las Antigüedades de las ciudades de España que van nombradas en la coronica con las averiguaciones de sus sitios y nombres antiguos* (Valencia : Librería Paris-Valencia, 2001), pp. lxiii–lxx.
6 Ambrosio Morales, "Apologia y respuesta al memorial de Alonso de Santa Cruz," reprinted (with separate pagination) at the end of Jerónimo de Zurita, *Anales de la Corona de Aragón*, vol. 6 (Zaragoza, 1610), pp. 5r–31v. This volume also contains the defense of Zurita's history by Páez de Castro mentioned on p. 256.
7 For Pinciano's correspondence, see Hernán Núñez de Guzmán, *Biblioteca y epistolario de Hernán Núñez de Guzmán (El Pinciano): una aproximación al humanismo español del siglo XVI*, eds Juan Signes Codoñer, Carmen Codoñer Merino, and Arantxa Domingo Malvadi, Nueva Roma, 14 (Madrid: Consejo Superior de Investigaciones Científicas, 2001). Pinciano's letter of recommendation for Covarrubias (April 15, 1545) is carta 53 (pp. 345–6). Sepúlveda's letters are cartas 67–72 (pp. 359–78). The correspondence with Zurita is cartas 7–65 (pp. 277–357). Pinciano's letter to Vergara (March 20, 1522), cited on p. 253, is carta 2 (pp. 263–8).
8 See Gregorio de Andrés, "31 Cartas inéditas de Juan Páez de Castro, cronista de Carlos V," *Boletín de la Real Academia de la Historia* 168 (1971): 515–71.
9 Diego Dormer, *Progresos de la Historia en el Reyno de Aragón, y elogios de Geronimo Zurita, su primer coronista* (Zaragoza: Herederos de Diego Dormer, 1680), reprints many of these letters. The Agustín–Zurita correspondence occupies pp. 379–431.
10 Martín de Gurrea y Aragón, *Discursos de medallas y antigüedades* (Valladolid: Editorial Maxtor, 2003). This is a facsimile of the first printed edition of 1902.

SUGGESTIONS FOR FURTHER READING

Primary sources

Agustín, Antonio. *Diálogos de medallas, inscripciones y otras antigüedades*. Tarragona: Felipe Mey, 1587. (A facsimile of this first edition was published in Madrid: Jano, 1987.)
—— *Epistolario de Antonio Agustín*, ed. Cándido Flores Selles. Salamanca: Universidad de Salamanca, 1980.
Dormer, Diego. *Progresos de la Historia en el Reyno de Aragón, y elogios de Geronimo Zurita, su primer coronista*. Zaragoza: Herederos de Diego Dormer, 1680.
Ginés de Sepúlveda, Juan. *Epistolarum libri septem*, ed. Juan J. Valverde Abril. Bibliotheca scriptorum Graecorum et Romanorum Teubneriana, 1252. Munich and Leipzig: K. G. Saur, 2003.
Miquel Rosell, F., ed. "Epistolario Antonio Agustín, ms. 53 de la Biblioteca Universitaria de Barcelona." *Analecta Sacra Tarraconensia* 13 (1937): 113–202.
Morales, Ambrosio. *Las Antigüedades de las ciudades de España que van nombradas en la coronica con las averigüaciones de sus sitios y nombres antiguos*. Valencia: Librería Paris-Valencia, 2001. (Facsimile edn; first published in Madrid: Benito Cano, 1792).
Núñez de Guzmán, Hernán. *Biblioteca y epistolario de Hernán Núñez de Guzmán (El Pinciano): una aproximación al humanismo español del siglo XVI*, eds Juan Signes Codoñer, Carmen Codoñer Merino, and Arantxa Domingo Malvadi. Nueva Roma, 14. Madrid: C.S.I.C, 2001.
Ocampo, Florian de and Ambrosio Morales. *La coronica general de España*, 5 vols. Alcalá de Henares: Juan Iniquez de Lequerica, 1574–86.
Zurita, Jerónimo. *Anales de la Corona de Aragón*, 6 vols. Zaragoza: Lorenzo de Robles, 1610.

Secondary sources

Bataillon, Marcel. *Erasmo y España*, 2nd edn, trans. Antonio Alatorre. Mexico City: Fondo de Cultura Económica, 1966.
Carlos Villamarín, Helena. *Las antigüedades de España*. Spoleto: Centro Italiano di Studi sull' Alto Medioevo, 1996.
Caro Baroja, Julio. *Las falsificaciones de la historia (en relación con la de España)*. Barcelona: Seix Barral, 1992.
Cochrane, Eric. *Historians and Historiography in the Italian Renaissance*. Chicago: University of Chicago Press, 1981.
Coroleu, Alejandro. "Humanismo en España," in Jill Kraye (ed.) *Introducción al humanismo del renacimiento*. Madrid: Cambridge University Press.
Ferrary, Jean-Louis. *Onofrio Panvinio et les antiquités romaines*. Rome: École française de Rome, 1996.
Kagan, Richard. "Clio and the Crown: Writing History in Habsburg Spain," in *Spain, Europe, and the Atlantic World: Essays in Honour of John H. Elliott*. Cambridge: Cambridge University Press, 1995, 73–99.
—— "Philip II, History, and the *cronistas del rey*," in Fernando Chueca Goitia *et al.* (eds) *Philippus II Rex* (English-language supplement). Madrid: Lunwerg Editores, 1998, 19–29.
Mayans y Siscar, Gregorio. *Vida de Don Antonio Agustín*. Madrid, 1734.
Mora, Gloria. *Historias de mármol: la arqueología clásica española en el siglo XVIII*. Anejos de Archivo Español de Arqueología 17. Madrid: C.S.I.C., 1998.
Redel y Aguilar, Enrique. *Ambrosio de Morales, estudio biográfico*. Córdoba: Imprenta del Diario, 1909.

Rowland, Ingrid. *The Culture of the High Renaissance: Ancients and Moderns in Sixteenth-century Rome*. Cambridge: Cambridge University Press, 1998.

Sánchez Madrid, Sebastián. *Arqueología y humanismo: Ambrosio de Morales*. Córdoba: Universidad de Córdoba, 2002.

Spivakovsky, Erika. *Son of the Alhambra: Don Diego Hurtado de Mendoza, 1504–1575*. Austin: University of Texas Press, 1970.

Tate, Robert Brian. "Mythology in Spanish Historiography of the Middles Ages and Renaissance." *Hispanic Review* 22, 1 (1954): 1–18.

Vaquero Serrano, María del Carmen. *El Maestro Alvar Gómez. Biografía y prosa inédita*. Toledo: Caja Castilla la Mancha, 1993.

CHAPTER THIRTEEN

NICCOLÒ MACHIAVELLI AND THOMAS MORE

Parallel lives

David Harris Sacks

Renaissance thinkers frequently distinguished two forms of writing about the past:

> one, which setteth down men's doings and adventures at length, is called ... history; the other, which declareth their natures, sayings, and manners, is properly named their lives. The one respect[s] more the things and the other the persons: the one is more common, and the other more private: the one concerneth more the things that are without the man, and the other the things that proceed from within: the one the events, the other the consultations.[1]

This chapter is about lives – i.e. about "the marks and indications of the souls of men" as Plutarch put it in considering the lives of famous Greeks and Romans – and it follows Plutarch's model in drawing parallels between them. Great events, Plutarch says, "do not always furnish us with the clearest discoveries of virtue or vice in men, sometimes a matter of less moment, an expression or a jest, informs us better of their characters and inclinations."[2]

From the perspective of their life histories, the parallels between Niccolò Machiavelli and Thomas More are quite striking. Although there is no evidence that they knew, or that they should have known, anything of each other, they were near contemporaries who had similar educations and experienced similar public careers. Machiavelli was born in 1469 and More in 1478. Each lived into his late fifties, Machiavelli dying in 1527 and More in 1535. Their lives, then, traversed one of the most momentous periods in European history, years that not only witnessed the voyages of Bartolomeu Dias to the Cape of Good Hope; of Vasco da Gama to the Indian Ocean; of Christopher Columbus, John Cabot, and Amerigo Vespucci across the Atlantic, and of Ferdinand Magellan around the world, but that also saw religious passions spread across Europe by the protests and theological challenges of Martin Luther and his followers against traditional Roman Catholic beliefs and practices. These same decades were dominated by new developments in the building of the state and the reshaping of society in both England and Italy, and by the need for new intellectual and practical skills to understand these changes, promote them, and bring them under control.

Although Machiavelli was born in the great republican city-state of Florence and More in the national capital of an island kingdom at the periphery of the European continent, their backgrounds had much in common. Their families each were of middling rank with ties both to the city and the country, but at their core both were urban men, shaped in their outlooks and their aspirations by their experiences of life in well-peopled commercial centers with strong traditions of local self-government. Their fathers each had training in the law, although Bernardo Machiavelli lived mainly from farm and rental properties, unlike John More, who was a successful practicing lawyer and eventually a judge. Both Machiavelli and More also enjoyed humanistic educations as youths and had some experience of the university, but unlike More, who for two years studied at Canterbury College, Oxford, Machiavelli appears never to have been formally enrolled at the University of Florence. Nor did he learn any Greek, a language with which More was very adept. Both men also had a taste for literature and a talent for writing it, but both eventually turned their attention to practical subjects and to public service grounded in legal training. While Machiavelli cannot be shown to have had a formal legal education, More, in contrast, entered Lincoln's Inn in 1496 and was admitted to the bar five or six years later.

In 1498, when Machiavelli was 29 years old, he was appointed second chancellor to the Florentine Republic, a state whose political order was at that very moment being newly reconstituted following Savonarola's fall; Marcello Virgilio Adriani, Machiavelli's mentor, former teacher, and his likely patron, had become first chancellor only a few months before, and Machiavelli's own appointment came within days of Savonarola's execution and burning. Shortly after, Machiavelli was also elected secretary to the Republic's Council of Ten for War. The two posts, although subject to supervision of his superiors in the city, gave Machiavelli important governmental and diplomatic duties and made him a key adviser to the Republic in its public affairs. In 1502, when the Republic created the office of perpetual Gonfalonier for the city, and appointed Piero Soderini, a citizen of established family, to head the government and militia, Machiavelli was maintained in these posts. His service, under increasingly challenging political and diplomatic conditions, continued until 1512, when Soderini was ousted from office at the return of the Medici from their 18 years of exile from Florence.

More's rise to office was slower, although it seems likely that he sat in the Parliament of 1504, when he was only 26 years old. In 1510, he was appointed to his first important public office, that of undersheriff in London. In this capacity he sat as judge in the Sheriff's Court, whose jurisdiction covered commercial cases in what was not just the most populous city in England with 50,000 to 60,000 inhabitants, but the greatest trading and financial center in the British isles and one of the leading port cities in northwestern Europe. This post made More, similar to Machiavelli, an important adviser to the government of his native city on legal and commercial matters. Within a few years, his activities in holding it brought him to the attention of Cardinal Wolsey, the lord chancellor, and of King Henry VIII himself. With Wolsey's patronage, More was sworn as one of the king's councilors in 1517. For some years thereafter he accumulated new offices and their incomes at a steady pace; they were granted largely as rewards for his main service as the king's intimate secretary and personal adviser. He was knighted in 1521 and made speaker of the House of Commons in 1523. In 1529 he was appointed Wolsey's successor as lord chancellor, the highest office of state. This post made him not only the senior legal official in the kingdom but also one of the first men of the realm. As chancellor he not only presided over administrative and judicial functions of the Chancery, but also over the Star Chamber and House of Lords, and necessarily was one of the most important figures at the Council table. He held the post until he resigned in 1532.

There is also some similarity to the endings of the two men's careers. When Machiavelli left office in 1512, he did not just fall from favor with the Medici. Nor was he simply dismissed from his post as chancellor of the second Chancery and from his duties as secretary to the Council of Ten. He was also fined 1,000 gold florins, barred from leaving the Florentine territory for a year and from entering the Palazzo during this period, after which he was forced during another month to account to his tormenters in painful detail for his expenditures of the funds that had been assigned to him under Soderini to pay Florence's soldiers. Not long after, Machiavelli's name appeared in a list of men believed to be possible allies in a conspiracy to overthrow and replace the new regime. He was arrested, imprisoned for a month, and interrogated under torture by application of the *strappado*. Although he remained hopeful of returning to office in his native city and openly sought governmental service under the Medici, he never achieved this goal. In 1520, however, he was commissioned by Cardinal Guilio de' Medici to write the history of Florence, a work he completed in 1525 and presented to his patron, who by then had become Pope Clement VII. Along with writing the *Florentine Histories*, the last dozen years of Machiavelli's life were devoted to producing *The Prince*, the *Discourses on Livy*, the *Art of War*, a version of the *Golden Ass* in rhyme, several comedies in prose, including the *Mandragola*, and a number of more minor works.

More also spent the last years of his life out of office. However, having risen higher than his Florentine contemporary, almost to the very pinnacle of temporal power in his homeland, his end was much more dramatic, coming as it did on the scaffold, after being found guilty of high treason for refusing to swear the Oath of Succession acknowledging the legitimacy of Henry VIII's divorce from Catherine of Aragon and marriage to Anne Boleyn and renouncing the authority of the pope. More had entered the office of chancellor already holding the view that his king's marriage to his first wife was legitimate, a position that Henry VIII tolerated at first. More then served for two and a half years, making major reforms in the operations of the Chancery itself, while using his official powers and great influence to arrest and interrogate early "Lutherans," figures he regarded as heretics, and then turn them over to the ecclesiastical authorities for trial. At the same time, he initiated a highly vituperative literary campaign against the early English reformers, figures such as the Lutheran William Tyndale, the Bible translator, and Simon Fish, the anti-clerical critic of Purgatory and of the ecclesiastical institutions and practices it spawned. In addition, More used his very considerable political skills quietly but effectively to oppose the king's wish for divorce and to resist the growing attacks on the Church's independence that the move for divorce had engendered.

But by the middle of 1532, with the king's demands for a successful conclusion to his divorce case ever more pressing and his attacks on the liberties of the clergy ever more severe, More's position became untenable and he chose retirement, hoping perhaps to keep his peace as well as his conscience as the king's "great matter" proceeded. On leaving office, he professed himself pleased "that neither gracious prince could disallow his doings, nor was he odious to the nobility, nor unpleasant to the people, but yet to thieves, murderers and heretics grievous." In the epitaph he wrote for himself soon after resigning, he attributed his departure in part to his advancing age – he was 54 years old at the time – and to "a certain sickly disposition of his breast . . . creeping upon him." "Weary of worldly business," he said, he gave up "his promotions" and "obtained at last by the incomparable benefit his most gentle prince . . . that thing which from a child . . . he wished and desired, that he might have some years of his life free, in which he little and little withdrawing himself from the business of life, might continually remember the immortality of the life to come."[3]

More, like Machiavelli, also used his last days to express in writing his views on the issues that most concerned him. In keeping with the sentiments he expressed in his epitaph, religious themes were the main focus. Although it cannot be said that the Florentine had paid no attention to the Church in his books and commentaries, he focused on it mainly as a human institution, and on its leaders and officials as worldly politicians. The subject matter of More's late works concentrated primarily on the Church's divine mission and the doctrines for which it stood. During this period, however, he sought to steer clear of the greatest controversy of the day, the building crisis in church-state relations generated by the king's divorce. But with his resignation from office he renewed the battle he had started against Tyndale and wrote other polemical works against the English reformers, continuing by other means his war on heresy and his support for the independence of the Church. While dodging the worst of the dangers to his life created by his persistence, he also produced his *Apology*, which defended the actions he had taken in his career to support the Church and expressed his most deeply felt religious convictions.

However, by spring 1534, with the King married to Anne Boleyn and their daughter Elizabeth already half a year old, it became impossible to avoid swearing the Oath of Succession, and More was imprisoned in the Tower to spend the last 15 months of his life there until his execution on July 6, 1535. While awaiting his end he wrote additional works of religious contemplation, as well as a series of moving letters about his faith addressed to his daughter Margaret. His Tower writings were first published only in 1557 in his nephew William Rastell's edition of More's *English Works*. They include: "A Dialogue of Comfort against Tribulation"; "A treatise to receive the blessed Body of our Lord, sacramentally and virtually both"; "Certain devout and virtuous Instructions, Meditations, and Prayers"; "Treatise upon the Passion," which was unfinished; and a translation into English, by his granddaughter Mary Basset, of a work in Latin also on the passion originally entitled *De tristitia, tedio, pavore et oratione Christi ante captionem eius*, and given the title *Expositio Passionis* in the Louvain edition, first published in 1565.

Despite the differences we see in the manner in which the two men lived their last years, we can also detect a similarity in how they were observed and depicted in portraits when they were still alive. Hans Holbein the Younger's portrait of Sir Thomas More was painted in 1527 (Figure 13.1). Holbein, born in Augsburg in 1497 and trained there in the workshop of his father, Hans Holbein the Elder, was

Figure 13.1 Hans Holbein the Younger (1497/1498–1543), *Sir Thomas More*, 1527 © The Frick Collection, New York.

closely connected with More's long-time friend Desiderius Erasmus, having painted him on several occasions in the 1520s. He produced his picture of More, whose assistance he received in seeking royal service, during his first sojourn in England. In this portrait of More we see the sitter, chancellor of the Duchy of Lancaster by this time, as a man of affairs holding a letter in his right hand and wearing a golden chain from which hangs the Tudor rose. While his hat is very similar, as we shall see, to the one worn by Machiavelli, More is dressed as a courtier in fur and velvet. Nevertheless, the painting is far from conventional in its portrayal of More as a high royal official. The deep inward concentration in his expression and the clear look in his dark eyes reveals a man of introspective intensity, while the tiny wisps of hair just peeking below the edge of More's hat suggest that the strong sense of the sitter's self-control goes together with a hint of personal independence and capacity to break the bounds of rigid conformity.

Figure 13.2 Ridolfo del Ghirlandaio. *Portrait of Machiavelli*. Altomani & Sons, Milan.

Within a year or two of Holbein's portrait of More, we have an equally impressive probing image of Machiavelli painted by Ridolfo del Ghirlandaio (Figure 13.2). Born Ridolfo Bigordi in Florence in 1483, apprenticed with Fra Bartholomeo in the workshop of the San Marco there, Ghirlandaio was employed by the Medici family from the mid-1520s, and painted this probing image of Machiavelli as he was in his last years. The portrait, probably painted around 1525, depicts the former secretary of the fallen Republic as a man in his fifties wearing an austere black cloak and soft four-cornered hat. While the hat is similar to More's, Machiavelli is dressed as a scholar and writer, not in the luxurious robes of a state official. In his right hand we see him holding a pair of gloves, a gesture of friendship meant to symbolize his openness to the amicable exchange of good will with others. But his dark eyes, looking downward, and his intense expression convey a sense of a self-disciplined and self-possessed person in deep reflection, qualities similar to those Holbein saw in More.

Although the parallels between these two lives are noteworthy, it is their differences that have been most remarked upon. By historical reputation Thomas More is neither a state servant, nor an energetic wielder of political power, nor a determined defender of the Church's worldly privileges, as some modern historians have come to consider him, but first and foremost a devout Catholic who wore a hair shirt, and a man of conscience, more concerned for the welfare of his soul than for the safety of his person. On this understanding, his humanism shared more with the passionate Augustinianism of Martin Luther, whom he vigorously opposed, than with the sweet reasonableness of Desiderius Erasmus, who was his lifelong friend. Almost immediately after his execution in 1535 he became the subject of hagiographical accounts, initially by members of his family circle, depicting him as defending his conscience and the true faith of the Holy Catholic Church. Until recently, these early views dominated the judgment of him, although latterly he has been treated as an eloquent defender of personal and political liberty against the tyrannical rule of the omni-competent state as much as, or more than, an advocate for his faith. In 1886 he was beatified by Pope Leo XII, and in 1935, in honor of the 400th anniversary of his execution, he was canonized by Pope Pius XI.

Machiavelli's posthumous popular reputation is almost the opposite. In numerous literary works his name appears in the character of the Machiavel, a godless, cunning schemer and devious dissembler greedy for domination over others, the embodiment of unscrupulousness and self-serving duplicity for whom the ends of personal advantage justify any means. Transformed into the adjective "Machiavellian," his very image represents political expediency at its worst. A tale told about a dream he is purported to have had captures the essence of this characterization. He is said to have imagined seeing a small throng of impoverished people dressed only in rags. When he asked their identities, he was told they were the blessed souls of heaven. On their departure, they were replaced by a large assemblage of noble figures in royal and courtly attire discussing political affairs. He recognized Plato, Plutarch, Tacitus, and other learned men of antiquity. Inquiring about them, he was told they were the worldly-wise, persons inimical to God and damned to Hell. He was then asked which group he wished to join. According to the tale, he replied "that he would be far happier in Hell, where he could discuss politics with the great men of the ancient world, than in Heaven" with the saintly beggars.[4]

A similar view of the man as a purely worldly figure is revealed in the treatment of Machiavelli's remains after his death. Although he never returned to a position of political power, his reputation was sufficiently restored by the time of his death to warrant his burial in the Basilica di Santa Croce in Florence, which also holds Dante, Michelangelo, and Galileo, among others. Two-and-a-half centuries later, in 1787, he was honored with the erection of a magnificent tomb, by the sculptor Innocenzo Spinnazi. It shows a neoclassical sarcophagus on which sits the allegorical figure of Politics holding a portrait plaque with the image of Machiavelli. The inscription reads: *"TANTO NOMINI NVLLVM PAR ELOGIVM."* ("For so great a name no eulogy is adequate.") Here we see Machiavelli celebrated as an Enlightenment hero, a figure of worldly fame, a model for modernity, for whom conversing about politics and the state represents the epitome of human achievement.

More fell further than his Florentine contemporary, and did so more precipitously. Since he died a traitor's death, beheaded by the king's executioner at the Tower of London, he received no burial in a great church in his native city, nor was a public tomb ever erected for him. And since he ended his life defending the Church of Rome against what became the official established Church of England, he was honored at first only among those most intimately associated with him through family. His headless body was buried in obscurity in the Church of St Peter ad Vincula in the Tower, while his head was boiled and placed in view on Tower Bridge for a month as a warning to all who might seek to follow his example. Later, his daughter Margaret Roper bought it from the man assigned to throw it into the Thames. According to tradition, it was buried with her in 1544, cradled in her arms. In contrast to Machiavelli's imposing sarcophagus, there is presently only a very modest monument to More in St Peter ad Vincula, erected after he was declared a saint in 1935. A small portrait bust of him sits atop a simple plaque where he is identified as "Knight, scholar, writer, statesman Lord Chancellor of England 1529–32. Beheaded on Tower Hill, buried in this Chapel 1535. Canonised by Pope Pius XI 1935." As for More's severed head, it is uncertain whether its final resting place is in Chelsea Old Church, where More had worshiped when alive and where the epitaph he wrote for himself in 1532 can be found, or, as seems more likely, in the Roper family vault in St Dunstan's, Canterbury, where fragments of a skull that might have been his were found in 1978.

On November 5, 2000, during the Roman Catholic Church's Jubilee year, Pope John Paul II declared More to be the patron saint of politicians. Notably, in English history November 5 is Guy Fawkes' Day, celebrated raucously with bonfires and effigy burnings on the anniversary of the discovery of the Roman Catholic Plot of 1605 to blow up England's Houses of Parliament and murder the Protestant king of England and Scotland. The contrast between Fawkes's execution for treason in contemplating mass murder for his cause with More's eloquence in defense of his personal conscience and his dignified martyrdom for peacefully standing up for his beliefs against the tyranny of the secularizing state and the heresies of its rulers, perhaps accounts for the timing of John Paul's announcement. Insofar as More enjoys worldly fame as a political figure, therefore, it is for qualities seemingly antithetical to Machiavelli's: ends over means, patience over cunning, principle over expediency, conscience over advantage, and, most of all, God and His will over the world and its temptations.

Nevertheless, even here there are some parallels. Although Machiavelli was by no means a deeply devout Christian, or much concerned with movements for Church reform in his day, he was not irreligious. He was certain, for example, that the introduction of religion among mankind "caused good orders" in society, from which, he believed, follows "good fortune" and "the happy successes of enterprises." "As the observance of the divine cult is the cause of the greatness of republics," he says in his *Discourses*, "so disdain for it is the cause of their ruin. For where the fear of God fails, it must be that either the kingdom comes to ruin or that it is sustained by the fear of a prince, which supplies the defects of religion."[5] Rather than rejecting religion himself, he was deeply skeptical of the effects that religious enthusiasm, such as aroused in Florence by Savonarola, might have on the passions of human beings and believed that the Christianity of his day had "lost all devotion and all religion," through the wickedness and failed policies of its priests and officials.[6] Despite his skepticism, he became a member of the Company of Piety in Florence in 1495, which like other religious confraternities was devoted to prayer for the salvation of its members' souls. It should be no surprise, therefore, that in the hour of his death on June 21, 1527 he confessed his sins to a priest, seemingly a Franciscan friar name Matteo, who remained with him until he drew his last breath; he was duly buried the next day in Santa Croce, the church of the Franciscan order in Florence.

Where Machiavelli believed in the importance of religion not just to public order, but also to the spiritual welfare of his own soul, More was as aware as Machiavelli of the dark forces of human motivation that drove politics and underpinned history. In his *History of King Richard the Third*, he tells the tale of Richard, Duke of Gloucester's betrayal and murder of the children of his brother, King Edward IV, heirs in succession to their father's crown. Composed in 1513, the same year as Machiavelli completed *The Prince*, More's narrative describes the cunning and ruthless machinations of the "malicious, wrathful, envious, and . . . ever forward" duke, and stresses that "the desire of [for] a kingdom knows no kindred."[7] In a deathbed speech to councilors that More provided for Edward IV, More lays out a view of the workings of the will to domination in human affairs. He represents Edward as saying:

> Such a pestilent serpent is ambition and desire of vainglory and sovereignty, which among states where he once enters creeps forth so far, 'til with division and variance he turns all to mischief. First longing to be next the best, afterwards equal with the best, and at last chief and above the best. Of which immoderate appetite of worship, and thereby of debate and dissention, what loss, what sorrow, what trouble.[8]

Here we see More communing with many of the same classical historians and ancient political thinkers on whom Machiavelli relied when living in political exile at his farm at San Casciano after he had been ousted from office, imprisoned, and tortured. Both men, it seems, donned "clothes that are fit for a royal court," and "thus properly clad," entered "the ancient courts of the men of old," and there "convers[ed] with them, and ask[ed] them why they acted as they did."[9]

As state servants, Machiavelli and More conducted their lives in an era that witnessed the stirrings of what the great Swiss historian Jacob Burckhardt saw as "the modern political spirit of Europe," during which the state became, more than ever before, "a work of art," the object and "outcome of reflection and calculation."[10] These developments led to the absorption and consolidation of territories and centralization of power under more and more tightly integrated political and administrative regimes. In Florence, they were driven as much by the exigencies of internal conflict such as the Pazzi Conspiracy (1478) against the hegemony of the Medici and by the reform efforts of Savonarola, also targeted against Medician rule, as by the Italian wars that eventually drew virtually every European state, including the papacy, into their vortices. In England, this period encompassed the last years of the Wars of the Roses and the establishment of the Tudor regime, under which the monarchy systematically asserted and enforced its superiority over all independent sources of military, political, and judicial power in the kingdom. At the same time, the English undertook to secure their country's place in the emerging system of European states, a goal conditioned by the commercial requirements of England's cloth industry and major ports as well as by the need to protect itself from foreign enemies and to advance its interests in international affairs more broadly.

To be the servant of a prince or republic in a world dominated by these intrinsically divisive issues was as much a test of principle as of skill, and it was difficult, if not impossible, to negotiate one's way between the Scylla and Charybdis of factional rivalry and ideological difference. But to those, like Machiavelli and More, whose humanist educations and philosophical sensibilities attuned them to the lessons that might be gained, the experience gave deep insight into the driving forces in human social relations. As a Florentine official, Machiavelli was closely connected with his native city's external affairs in the era of the Italian wars. His duties set him special responsibility for the Florentine militia as well as its foreign relations and provided him with an intimate familiarity not just with the actions of public men engaged in advancing their interests but also with their motivating passions. In his main political works, especially *The Prince*, he drew significantly on the insights into human behavior he had gained in this service. In praising the political skills of Cesare Borgia, for example, Machiavelli relied not just on his close observation of Borgia's actions as a ruler and military commander but also on personal knowledge of the man acquired during his diplomatic mission to Borgia's court in 1502 and 1503. There he learned that Borgia's *virtù*, his capacity to act effectively according to the circumstances, depended as much on his cunning and ruthlessness as on his sound judgment and willingness to provide good government. Although Machiavelli recognized that Borgia was no friend to Florence, he presented him as a model of princely rule, someone to be emulated by those who would succeed in gaining or maintaining effective rule.

Unlike Machiavelli, who wrote *The Prince* after he had ended his days as a Florentine official, More gained his experience as a state servant following the publication of *Utopia*. Indeed, at the time he completed writing this book in 1516, he was weighing the offer from Henry VIII to join his court. More's acceptance would bring him into the royal council in 1517 and then to the series of increasingly important offices that culminated in his elevation to the lord chancellorship in 1529. More would resign from the king's government in 1532 when Henry VIII's attacks on the autonomy of the Church left him unable, by his lights, to make government policy "as little bad as possible," to quote the remark of his namesake in *Utopia*.[11]

Despite the focus on the practical realities of state service expressed in *Utopia*, the learning about statecraft that More brought to the discussion was largely book learning, dependent especially on his reading of Cicero and Quintilian and of the Roman historians. His knowledge of agrarian conditions in the England of his day, so concretely described elsewhere in Book I of *Utopia*, must also have come largely at the second hand, since his private life to this point was lived mainly in the populous urban setting of London. Until More became a royal servant, his most important practical experience derived from professional activities in this great city, especially his employment as London's undersheriff. This post made him the chief law officer of the Sheriff's Court, a site where disputes about debts, contracts, and property rights among artisans and merchants filled the dockets. From that vantage point, More saw among his fellow London citizens the same self-interested and selfish desires for ever-greater power and material advantage that Machiavelli witnessed among the leading figures in Italy in his day.

More's *Utopia*, with its attention to the rapaciousness of landlords in forcing their tenants from the land, enclosing their estates for sheep pasture, monopolistically controlling the sale of wool, and then ravenously indulging themselves in luxury with the windfall profits generated by the wool trade, bore witness to the dominating presence in England's agrarian economy of many of the same moral failings prevalent in the urban world in which he lived and worked. Although the ways of getting and spending might be different in country and town, More implies that the toll imposed on human well-being by the corrupting power of greed and of pride was the same. He treated this subject with special insight and subtlety, if also with more than a hint of anti-Jewish sentiment, in his *Treatise upon the Passion*, written as already noted while he was awaiting an almost certain execution. In that unfinished work he speaks, somewhat surprisingly, of Judas as a "jolly merchant," who alone among the disciples was willing to deliver Christ to the priests and judges of the Jews. With his knowledge of the self-interested material motivations and the manipulative market practices of merchants, More reconstructed what he believed must have been Judas's internal monologue as he considered the price he could charge for this commodity: "This ware" is "all in your own hands. You have a monopoly thereof." While it is so fervently sought for by so many rich persons "you may . . . make the price of your own pleasure" and become rich yourself "with this one bargain."[12] Judas, the great betrayer, the ultimate traitor, is here also represented as the symbol of unrestrained greed, the monopolist, the sole seller who charges his eager customers what he wishes for his wares, and who in consequence knows no limits to his desires or his power.

As More retells this famous story, however, he also sees that advantage arises where there is a sole buyer, a condition known to modern economists as "monopsony," the opposite of "monopoly," which in Greek means "sole seller." The priests and judges, More says, "were on their side covetous too." As much as they wanted Jesus, "they thought the merchant was needy, & that to such a needy merchant, a little money would be welcome, & money they offered him, but not much." The bargain and sale was grounded in greed on either side, with each maneuvering to gain personal advantage over the other. The sum offered to Judas was, of course, 30 pieces of silver, which More says was the equivalent of only about ten shillings of English money. "To show himself a substantial merchant and not an huckster, he gently let them have it . . . at their own price," a ware so "precious . . . that all the money and plate in the whole world were too little to give for it."[13] Cheating pride, a striving for undeserved honor, defeated Judas's purpose, just as his unbounded greed and his profound disloyalty – his "treason" as More called it[14] – had promoted it.

Implicit in this picture of Judas, who More calls "the fool," is a contrast between the spirit of brotherhood that should have informed his relations with Christ, making him one with the rest of the disciples, and the specter of his grasping selfishness and his prideful hunger for personal honor that haunts his dealings with the avaricious and bloody-minded priests and judges of the Jews, and divides him from God. In this view, the questing for monopoly was the antithesis of the pursuit of virtue and good fellowship. It introduced one not just into Judas's world but also the Devil's, where the calculation of costs and benefits was subject to self-delusion, striving for self-advantage led to self-defeat, and there was no final victory, save for death.

More made a somewhat similar point earlier in his career in the pages of *Utopia*, in addressing the reasons behind England's inability to aid the hungry when famine struck in his day. In a remarkably prescient analysis, very much in keeping with our own present-day understandings of how food shortages produce their dire affects, Raphael Hythodaeus, the fictive traveler whom we meet in the work, argues that it is only the want of "cursed money" in the hands of the poor, not the lack of the needed supplies, that prevents those suffering starvation in a year of failed harvests from finding the food they need to live. "If at the end of the famine the barns of the rich were searched," he argues, "positively enough grain would be found in them to have kept all those who died of starvation or disease even from realizing that a shortage ever existed." Generalizing from this case, he concludes that the selfishness of the greedy, "burdened with great masses of wealth," and above all their pride keep them from recognizing where their "true interests" lie and what the "authority of Christ our Savior" requires.[15]

In his *Treatise upon the Passion*, More equated original sin with pride as the source of Lucifer's fall, and then of Eve's and Adam's. He asked his readers to

> ponder well . . . what horrible peril there is in ye pestilent sin of pride, what abominable sin it is in the sight of God, when any creature falleth into the delight and liking of itself: as the thing whereupon continued, inevitably faileth not to follow first the neglecting, & after the contemning, and finally with disobedience and rebellion, the very full forsaking of God.[16]

In articulating a similar view in *Utopia*, speaking in the voice of Hythlodaeus, he maintained that:

> pride measures her advantages not by what she has but what other people lack. Pride would not deign to be made a goddess if there were no wretches for her to sneer at and domineer over. Her good fortune is dazzling only by contrast with the misery of others, her riches are valuable only as they torment and tantalize the poverty of others. Pride is a serpent from hell that twines itself around the hearts of men, acting like a suckfish to hold him back from choosing a better way of life.[17]

According to Hythlodaeus, however, the Utopians, held in check by the regime imposed on them by their conqueror and lawgiver Utopus, had been lucky enough to escape from the threats to their well-being that spring from this lust for domination.

Where More was fiercely passionate in his commitment to orthodox Christianity, Machiavelli, of course, was skeptical and quite tepid, although no atheist. Judging from the copy of Lucretius' *On the Nature of Things* (*De Rerum Natura*) that he transcribed, as well as his association with several important Florentine students of Epicureanism (including his father's own best friend), he shared with many advanced humanist thinkers a deep interest in Epicurean theories. We find echoes in Machiavelllli's writings, especially *The Prince* and *The Discourses*, of Lucretius' commentaries on the evolutionary character of human social development, on the role of worldly pleasure in driving history and natural processes, on the importance of fear in giving religion its social and political utility, and, perhaps most important of all, on the place of chance or Fortune in shaping events. As he says in *The Prince*, "I am disposed to hold that fortune is the arbiter of half our actions, but that it lets us control roughly the other half."[18] In contrast, More in *Utopia* gently satirized the Epicureanism of the Utopians as marking the limitations to virtue and understanding that resulted from their lack of true knowledge of Christ. Hence where More might be said to have taken St Augustine's eternal city of God, on whose characteristics he had lectured publicly in London early in his career, as his model of a best commonwealth, Machiavelli looked more to pagan Rome for his. Nevertheless, in reaching his conclusions Machiavelli shared an understanding with More of the present condition of human nature and the problems it posed for the maintenance of public order in the state.

Although the originality of Machiavelli appears to reside in the overt ruthlessness of the political advice he offered, many of his most profound insights and most notorious claims result from his deep skepticism regarding the human capacity for virtue as understood in the traditions of Christianity. An individual's virtue in the Christian sense demanded true goodness of soul – "wholly possessed by zeal for Christian piety," as More's friend Erasmus put it in his *Praise of Folly*. "They squander their possessions," Erasmus's Goddess Folly says there; they "ignore insults, submit to being cheated, make no distinctions between friends and enemies, shun pleasure, sustain themselves on fasting, vigils, tears, toil, and humiliations, scorn life, desire only death."[19] From Machiavelli's perspective, therefore, they lacked *virtù*, which he regarded as the primary requirement for effectiveness in a political ruler. Against the qualities of self-effacement – the capacity to live "neglected, inglorious, and disliked" as Folly put it[20] – *virtù*, which derives from the ancient Roman concept of *virtus*, emphasized the possession of ability, skill, prowess, strength, courage, energy, spiritedness, or determination. The root of the term lies in "*vir*," the Latin word for "man." In Machiavelli's view, only this kind of neo-Roman manly excellence could assure the stability of the state and provide security and this-worldly well-being to its inhabitants. A ruler, he argued, needed to recognize the moral limitations of his subjects:

> He cannot rely on what he sees happen in peaceful times, when citizens have need of his government, because then everyone comes running, everyone is ready with promises, and everyone wants to die for him, when the prospect of death is far off. But in troubled times, when government needs the services of the citizens, few are then to be found. And it is especially dangerous to test their loyalty, because it can be done only once. A shrewd ruler, therefore, must try to assure that his citizens, whatever the situation may be, will always be dependent on the government and on him; and then they will always be loyal to him.[21]

Those who would attempt to govern a state by traditional doctrines of moral virtue would only bring it to ruin, whatever reward they might receive in the afterlife for their individual charity or personal goodness.

Take, for example, the advice Machiavelli offers the prince on whether it is better to be feared or loved. Cicero famously had raised this question in his treatise *On Duties*. There he argued that "there is nothing at all more suited to protecting and retaining influence than to be loved, and nothing less suited than to be feared." Humans hate those they fear, he said, and whom one hates one wishes to see dead. In consequence, "no amount of influence can withstand the hatred of a large number of men." Equating love with the exercise of goodwill, the Roman concluded that "fear is a poor guardian over any length of time; but goodwill keeps faithful guard for ever."[22] Machiavelli took the contrary view that while it is "desirable to be both loved and feared . . . it is difficult to achieve both, and, if one of them has to be lacking it is much safer to be feared than loved." Human beings, he explained, "are less hesitant about offending or harming a ruler who makes himself loved than one who inspires fear," but also insisted that a ruler could "make himself feared in such a way that, even if he does not become loved, he does not become hated." To achieve this, he recommended refraining "from laying hands on the property of citizens and subjects, and on their womenfolk," and recommended that "if it is necessary to execute anyone, this should be done only if there is a proper justification and obvious reason."[23] Every ruler, he believed, "should want to be thought merciful, not cruel," but if it proves necessary,

> he should not worry about incurring a reputation for cruelty; for by punishing a very few he will really be more merciful than those who over-indulgently permit disorders to develop with resultant killings and plunderings. For the latter usually harm a whole community, whereas executions ordered by a ruler harm only specific individuals.[24]

"Whether men bear affection," he concluded, "depends on themselves, but whether they are afraid will depend on what the ruler does. A wise ruler would rely on what is under his own control; not on what is under the control of others."[25]

Machiavelli's reasoning on this point derived directly from his dark view of the human condition. Cicero had maintained that "for one man to take something from another and to increase his own advantage at the cost of another's disadvantage is more contrary to nature than death, than poverty, than pain and than anything else that may happen to his body of external possessions," since "it destroys the common life and fellowship of men."[26] Behaving with goodwill toward fellow human beings, he maintained, was what made humans, human; it was ordained by the immortal gods and natural to mankind. In contrast, Machiavelli insisted that:

> this may be said of men generally: they are ungrateful, fickle, feigners and dissemblers, avoiders of danger, eager for gain. While you benefit them they are all devoted to you: they would shed their blood for you; they offer their possessions, their lives, and their sons . . . when the need to do so is far off. But when you are hard pressed, they turn away . . . For love is sustained by a bond

of gratitude which, because men are excessively self-interested, is broken whenever they see a chance to benefit themselves.[27]

Hence "men sooner forget the killing of a father than the loss of their patrimony." But fear induced by the "dread of punishment" changes the calculus of self-interest, and "is always effective."[28]

Similarly, Machiavelli argued that while "everyone knows how praiseworthy it is for a ruler to keep his promises, and live upright and without trickery . . . experience shows that . . . rulers who have done great things are those who have set little score by keeping their word, being skilful rather in cunningly deceiving men. They have gotten the better of those who have relied on being trustworthy." Rulers, he argued, could follow two possible strategies in governance: they could use law or they could use force. "The first is appropriate for men, the second for animals; but because the former is often ineffective, one must have recourse to the latter," and act like a "fox to recognize traps and a lion to frighten away wolves." In this light, Machiavelli insisted that "a prudent ruler cannot keep his word, nor should he, when such fidelity would damage him, and when the reasons that made him promise are no longer relevant." However, such "foxiness should be well concealed: one must be a great feigner and dissembler." And since "men are so naïve, and so much dominated by immediate needs . . . a skilful deceiver always finds plenty of people who let themselves be deceived." As with love and fear, Machiavelli's rationale is grounded in his view of human nature and its failings. "This advice," he concludes, "would not be sound if all men were upright; but because they are treacherous and would not keep their promises to you, you should not consider yourself bound to keep your promises to them."[29]

Despite his dark view of the human condition, Machiavelli was no "Machiavel" – no worldly incarnation of Satanic evil – and the form of rule he sought to inculcate was no tyranny in the classical sense. Rule was not to be pursued to satisfy the boundless desires of those in power nor power wielded solely for the advantage of those in command, whether the regime was a principality under the sway of a single individual or a republic governed by a small group. It was necessary instead for rulers to be men of *virtù*, possessing the skill to maintain their state and advance its interests. He "understood that a ruler . . . cannot always act in ways that are considered good, because, in order to maintain his power, he is often forced to act treacherously, ruthlessly or inhumanely, and disregard the precepts of religion." He had to "be prepared to vary his conduct as the winds of fortune and changing circumstances constrain him." Although a skillful ruler should seem to be "merciful, trustworthy, humane, upright and devout," he believed that "always cultivating" these moral virtues "is harmful." When "it becomes necessary to refrain," Machiavelli argued, the ruler "must be prepared to act in the opposite way," but he was not to "deviate from right conduct if possible," and was precluded from committing acts of cruelty for cruelty's sake or transforming citizens into abject slaves. "It cannot be called virtue (*virtù*)," Machiavelli insisted, "to kill one's fellow citizens, to betray one's friends, to be treacherous, merciless and irreligious," no matter how well the exercise of such practices enabled the ruler to hold sway over his state. "Power may be gained that way, but not glory."[30]

Nevertheless, Machiavelli was sure that there could be no virtue without *virtù*. What will cause a ruler to be "despised," he says, is to be "considered inconstant, frivolous, effeminate, pusillanimous, and irresolute: a ruler must avoid contempt as if it were a reef. He should contrive," therefore, "that his actions should display grandeur, courage, seriousness and strength, and his decisions about . . . private disputes irrevocable. He should maintain this reputation, so that no one should think of lying to him or scheming to trick him."[31] In the absence of effective control over the aggressiveness of individuals scrambling to advance their private interests, the state, on which those very same subjects depended for their own welfare, would fall victim to communal conflict and become vulnerable to conquest by enemies. In consequence, it would also become impossible to guide the people in pursuit of prudent policies and marshal their collective energies to ward off misfortune.

For Machiavelli *virtù* grants those who possess it the power to challenge fortune. "Fortune," he averred, "is a woman," who yields more readily to the aggressive and impetuous than the cautious. Nevertheless, he also insisted that prudent anticipation of her inconstancy could limit the damage she might cause. She is like "one of those dangerous rivers," he argued, "that, when they become enraged, flood the plains, destroy trees and buildings, move earth from one place and deposit it in another. Everyone flees before it, everyone gives way to its thrust, without being able to halt it in any way." Nevertheless, "this does not mean," he insisted, "that, when the river is not in flood, men are unable to take precautions, by means of dykes and dams, so that when it rises, it will either not overflow its banks or, if it does, its force will not be so uncontrolled or damaging."[32]

Machiavelli was thinking, almost certainly, of the River Arno, along whose banks Florence stood and which was subject to serious flooding. He may also have been recalling the project of flood control in which as Florence's second chancellor he had participated in the years 1503 to 1505 along with Leonardo da Vinci. Although this scheme failed, it strongly suggests a model of prudential rule of the kind that Machiavelli favors. Reducing the risk of flood on a river through the building of dykes and dams was intrinsically a communal act. It not only required advanced planning, effective application of engineering skills, and the marshaling of large resources, but also a common understanding of the need and collective action under strong leadership. The analogy is grounded on an understanding of the state as a political community with its own independent corporate life, and of the autonomy of politics conducted within it. In drawing attention to it, Machiavelli was asking his readers to accept that the security and well-being of the subjects or citizens of the state demanded that its rulers follow prudent practices and uphold this-worldly values often incommensurable with – and sometimes even quite remote from – the personal virtues and moral duties required of good Christians in their everyday lives.

In *Utopia*, More took a very similar view of government and its aims. Speaking in the voice of Hythloday, he saw the maintenance of harmony in the state as the ideal toward which the best form of a commonwealth should strive. The social and political institutions adopted by the Utopians, Hythloday said, had

> made their community most happy, and as far as I can tell, capable of lasting forever. Now that they have torn up the seeds of ambition and faction at home,

along with most other vices, they are in no danger from internal strife, which alone has been the ruin of many other nations that seemed secure. As long as they preserve harmony at home, and keep their institutions healthy, the Utopians can never be overcome or even shaken by their envious neighbors, who have often attempted their ruin.[33]

As described by Hythloday, many of these institutions – arguably those that More says he "would like rather than expect to see" – were aimed to reduce to a minimum the incentives to sin without however eliminating them. But, as Hythloday also acknowledged, the sin of "pride is too deeply fixed in human nature to be easily plucked out." Hence, short of living in this "new island of Utopia," sinfulness would remain a controlling feature of social life, or so More implies. And since "it is impossible to make everything good unless all men are good" – something More allows he does not "expect to see for quite a few years yet" – rigid adherence to principles could accomplish but little and might in the end do more harm than good.[34]

How then should a virtuous man act when called upon to play an active role in governing the commonwealth? At the time More was writing *Utopia*, this was no mere hypothetical question. Between beginning the work in 1515, while residing in Antwerp during an adjournment in the diplomatic negotiations in which he was assisting under commission from the king, and completing it after he had returned to London in 1516, Henry VIII had formally offered More a post among his councilors. More almost certainly added the discussion about whether a virtuous man should accept service in princely councils, a discussion that occupies much of the dialogue in Book I of *Utopia* in part as his way to think through what would be gained and what would be lost in his own efforts to live a virtuous and godly life should he accept the king's patronage.

In the debate, More represents the opposing sides in the *personae* of two alter egos, the fictional Raphael Hythloday, whose surname means "expert in nonsense," and a character called Thomas More, whose own surname might be a figure for the concept of "folly" itself, as Desiderius Erasmus famously made clear in dedicating his *Praise of Folly* (*Moriae Encomium* in Latin) to his good English friend. In this "dialogue of counsel," as it has been termed, Hythloday insists that any princely counselor seeking to promote true virtue at the council table would be laughed at as a fool by his fellows.[35] Their aim would be the advancement of state power and self-interest, not of peace or of the general good. In response More, the character, argues against the employment of what he calls "school philosophy which supposes that every topic is suitable for every occasion." "There is another philosophy," he says, "better suited for the political arena, that takes its cue, adapts itself to the drama in hand, and acts its part neatly and appropriately." He argues that whatever play is being performed, Hythloday should act his role in it the best he can. More designates this doctrine "civil" philosophy, a viewpoint derived from the ancient theorists of rhetoric and their Renaissance followers, where the exercise of eloquence and the maintenance of what usually is called "decorum" were understood to be critical to the proper performance of the duties a citizen owed to the commonwealth. "That's how things go in the commonwealth and in the councils of princes," More insists. "If you cannot pluck up bad ideas by the root, or cure long-standing evils even to your heart's content, you must not therefore abandon the commonwealth," but instead "strive to influence policy indirectly, urge your case vigorously but tactfully, and thus what you cannot turn to good, you may at least make as little bad as possible."[36]

In the end, as we have seen, More accepted the king's offer, in effect adopting the position advocated by his own namesake in this dialogue of counsel. Whether or not he believed that "the new island of Utopia" represented "the best state of a commonwealth" (he almost certainly did not), he believed there was such a best state and that a virtuous man had a duty to use his reason and his talents to promote its values as well as he could, even if those values could only be partially instantiated in present circumstances. Like Machiavelli, he also recognized important distinctions between the public, political qualities of those who ruled and the private, personal ones. In characterizing the virtues of Edward IV, More found him "of heart courageous, politic in council, in adversity nothing abashed, in prosperity rather joyful than proud, in peace just and merciful, in war sharp and fierce, in the field bold and hardy, and nonetheless no farther than wisdom would, adventurous." As a youth, however, Edward, More tells us, was "greatly given to fleshly wantonness" and in his old age to an "over liberal diet." Nevertheless, "this fault" did "not greatly grieve the people" since his pursuit of private pleasure was "without violence" and he left the realm in his latter days in a "quiet and prosperous estate: no fear of outward enemies, no war in hand nor . . . looked for, the people toward the Prince not in constrained fear, but in a willing and loving obedience among themselves, the commons in good peace."[37]

As More revealed in *Utopia*, a collective and peaceful life lived in a well-governed state represented for him the most we can hope for while we remain bound in this fallen world. The tools required were law and rhetoric, in the practice of both he was exceptionally adept. Each in its own way was an instrument for making men's actions less bad than they might otherwise have been – law by imposing order and raising the costs of wrongdoing, and rhetoric by persuading the sinful that their interests coincided with the commonweal and by harnessing their desires as the means to advance it. Law arguably bested rhetoric, since it could compel what it was impossible to institute by persuasion. Once a law was enacted it established the terms of debate. But until it was enacted, persuasion offered the means to set its terms, as More, the royal councilor, politician, and sometime member of Parliament well understood. When he achieved high office and the religious and political conflicts of the Reformation loomed, he battled, often as ruthlessly as anyone guided by Machiavelli's advice, to purge the realm of crime and error and impose his vision of discipline and organization on the political scene. He was in this sense as much a product of the new temporal order of the sovereign state as any of Henry VIII's servants and as modern and secular a figure as Machiavelli himself.

Nevertheless, there were significant differences between More's concept of the state and Machiavelli's. For the latter, the state was well on its way to becoming a wholly secular territorial entity with well-defined boundaries within which its government possessed an autonomous capacity to maintain its power over its subjects, to advance its own worldly interests, and to enjoy a monopoly of rule. Although Machiavelli often used the word "state" to mean no more than the condition the prince or government of a particular place might seem to uphold or improve, he also treated the principalities and republics of which he wrote as free in practice, if not always in law, from the superior authority of any outsider, whether temporal or spiritual. It was a time-bound community, embedded in the history of human events to which its actions contributed even as they were conditioned by them.

Whatever power More conceded to worldly rule, however much he saw its necessity, he did not acknowledge its autonomy. For him, the English kingdom to which he owed his obedience and loyalty was not only subject to God's law, and under His divine will, but also remained a subsidiary component of the commonwealth of Christendom, whose spiritual life was under the authority of the Holy Church. Where Henry VIII claimed sovereign authority to make laws and dispense justice in ecclesiastical as well as secular matters without a right of appeal beyond English borders – that is, to rule, as Parliamentary statute had put it, over "an empire . . . governed by one supreme head and king . . . unto whom a body politic, compact of all sorts and degrees of people, divided in terms and by names of spirituality and temporalty, be bounden and owe to bear next to God a natural and humble obedience"[38] – More held that such a view was:

> directly repugnant to the laws of God and His Holy Church, the supreme government of which, or any part whereof, may no temporal prince presume by any law to take upon him, as rightly belonging to the See of Rome, a spiritual pre-eminence by the mouth of Our Savior himself, personally present upon the earth, only to Saint Peter and his successors, Bishops of the same See, by special prerogative granted.[39]

England – indeed every state – was "but one member and small part of the Church," and as such "might not make a particular law disagreeable with the general law of Christ's universal Catholic Church . . . than the City of London, being but one poor member in respect of the whole realm, might make a law against an act of Parliament to bind the whole realm."[40]

The community to which More believed "all Christian men" owed their ultimate allegiance was timeless, because the truth itself was universal and beyond history. Against "all the bishops, universities, and best learned men" of the kingdom who had endorsed the king's claims to supreme authority over the English Church, he called not only on what he regarded as the vast majority of "well-learned bishops and virtuous men" now living, but also upon "those which already be dead, of whom many be now holy saints in heaven."[41] Had More's contemporaries attributed to him a dream equivalent to the one Machiavelli was supposed to have experienced, he would almost certainly have been depicted seeking out the "saintly beggars" said to have been eschewed by his Italian antitype. Rather than associating More with the philosophers and historians of antiquity, the tale would have designated among his preferred companions such figures as St Augustine, whose efforts in *The City of God* and other works to reconcile ancient wisdom as embodied in Platonism with Christian truth had so stirred the Englishman's understanding in his early years. In this same imagined company, no doubt, would have been More's namesakes: St Thomas of Canterbury, martyr for the independence of the Universal Church, and, above all, St Thomas the Apostle, "doubting Thomas," who bears witness with the evidence of his own eyes to the truth of the resurrected Christ.

Machiavelli and More each were doubtful about the intrinsic goodness of the human condition. Both believed in the ability of worldly rule to limit, but not eliminate, the harm that could be caused to human welfare by unrestrained pride and greed. But where Machiavelli was a skeptic with a profound belief in the powers of human ingenuity – of politics itself – to make life less bad than it might otherwise be, More eventually recognized, as he acknowledged on the scaffold in 1535, that while he was "the King's good servant," he was "God's first."[42]

NOTES

1 "Amiot to the Readers," in Plutarch, *The Lives of the Noble Grecians and Romanes, Compared*, trans. from Greek into French by James Amyot and from French into English by Thomas North (London, 1579; STC 20065), sig. *iiii[c]ʳ. Note that I have modernized spelling and punctuation in all quotations from early modern English sources. In the cited passages, "common" means "more public"; "without," "external to."

2 Plutarch, "Alexander," trans. John Evelyn, in *Plutarch: The Lives of the Noble Grecians and Romans*, trans. John Dryden and rev. Arthur Hugh Clough (New York: Modern Library, 1932), p. 801.

3 Thomas More, *The vvorkes of Sir Thomas More Knyght, sometyme Lorde Chancellour of England, written by him in the Englyshe tonge*, ed. William Rastall (London 1557; STC 18076), p. 1421.

4 Maurizio Viroli, *Niccolò's Smile: A Biography of Machiavelli*, trans. Antony Shugaar (New York: Farrar, Strauss & Giroux, 2000), p. 3. The story of Machiavelli's dream, which is almost certainly fictional, is based on the famous "dream of Scipio" communing with the ancient heroes reported in the sixth book of Cicero's *De Republica*. But the earliest accounts of Machiavelli's dream can be traced in sixteenth-century sources back almost to the time of Machiavelli's own death; see Roberto Ridolfi, *The Life of Niccolò Machiavelli*, trans. Cecil Grayson (London: Routledge & Kegan Paul, 1963), pp. 249–50, p. 330 n. 24.

5 Niccolò Machiavelli, *Discourses on Livy*, trans. Harvey C. Mansfield and Nathan Tarcov (Chicago and London: University of Chicago Press, 1996), I.11.4, p. 35.

6 Machiavelli, *Discourses*, I.12.2, p. 38.

7 Thomas More, *The History of King Richard III*, ed. Richard Sylvester, *The Complete Works of St. Thomas More*, 15 vols, eds Richard Sylvester et al. (New Haven: Yale University Press, 1963–84), II, p. 41. This comment is placed in the mouth of the deceased Edward IV's queen, Elizabeth Woodville, mother of the two princes.

8 More, *History of King Richard III*, pp. 12–13.

9 Niccolò Machiavelli to Francesco Vettori, Florentine envoy to the Holy See, December 10, 1513, in Machiavelli, *The Prince*, eds Quentin Skinner and Russell Price (Cambridge: Cambridge University Press, 1988), p. 93.

10 Jacob Burckhardt, *The Civilization of the Renaissance in Italy: An Essay*, trans. S. G. C. Middlemore, 3rd rev. edn (London: Phaidon Press Ltd, 1950), p. 2.

11 Thomas More, *Utopia*, trans. and ed. George M. Logan and Robert M. Adams (Cambridge: Cambridge University Press, 1989), p. 36.

12 Thomas More, *Treatise on the Passion* (1534), in Sylvester et al. eds, *Complete Works*, vol. 13 (ed. Garry Haupt), p. 78.

13 More, *Treatise on the Passion*, p. 79.

14 More, *Treatise on the Passion*, p. 49 and *passim*.
15 More, *Utopia*, p. 109.
16 More, *Treatise on the Passion*, p. 7.
17 More, *Utopia.*, pp. 109–10.
18 Machiavelli, *The Prince*, p. 85.
19 Desiderius Erasmus, *Praise of Folly and Letter to Maarten van Dorp, 1515*, trans. Betty Radice, ed. A. H. T. Levi (London: Penguin Books, 1993), p. 128.
20 Erasmus, *Praise of Folly*, p. 113.
21 Machiavelli, *The Prince*, p. 37.
22 Cicero, *On Duties*, trans. and ed. M. T. Griffen and E. M. Adkins (Cambridge: Cambridge University Press, 1991), bk. I, chap. 23, pp. 70–1.
23 Machiavelli, *The Prince*, p. 59.
24 Machiavelli, *The Prince*, p. 58.
25 Machiavelli, *The Prince*, p. 61.
26 Cicero, *On Duties*, bk. III, chap. 21, p. 108.
27 Machiavelli, *The Prince*, p. 59.
28 Machiavelli, *The Prince*, p. 59.
29 Machiavelli, *The Prince*, pp. 61–2.
30 Machiavelli, *The Prince*, pp. 31, 62.
31 Machiavelli, *The Prince*, p. 64.
32 Machiavelli, *The Prince*, pp. 85, 87.
33 More, *Utopia*, p. 110.
34 More, *Utopia*, pp. 36, 110, 111.
35 J. H. Hexter, *More's* Utopia: *The Biography of an Idea*, 2nd edn (New York: Harper & Row, 1965), part 3, pp. 99ff.
36 More, *Utopia*, pp. 35–6.
37 More, *History of King Richard III*, p. 4.
38 "An Act that the appeals in such cases as have been used to be pursued in the see of Rome shall not be from henceforth had or used but within the realm": *Statutes of the Realm*, 24 Henry VIII c. 12 (1533), in G. R. Elton, ed., *The Tudor Constitution: Documents and Commentary* (Cambridge: Cambridge University Press, 1960), p. 344.
39 William Roper, *The Life of Sir Thomas More*, in *Two Early Tudor Lives*, eds Richard S. Sylvester and David P. Harding (New Haven and London: Yale University Press, 1962), p. 248.
40 Roper, *The Life of Sir Thomas More*, p. 248.
41 Roper, *The Life of Sir Thomas More*, p. 249.
42 "The Paris Newsletter" (1535), in Nicholas Harpsfield, *The life and death of Sr Thomas Moore, knight, sometimes Lord high Chancellor of England*, eds Elsie Vaughan Hitchcock and R. W. Chambers. Early English Text Society, orig. ser., no. 186 (London: Oxford University Press, 1932), appendix II, p. 266.

SUGGESTIONS FOR FURTHER READING

Primary sources

Cicero, Marcus Tullius. *On Duties*, ed. and trans. M. T. Griffen and E. M. Adkins. Cambridge: Cambridge University Press, 1991.
Erasmus, Desiderius. *Praise of Folly and Letter to Maarten van Dorp, 1515*, trans. Betty Radice, ed. A. H. T. Levi. London: Penguin Books, 1993.

Harpsfield, Nicholas. *The Life and Death of St. Thomas Moore, Knight, Sometimes Lord High Chancellor of England*, eds Elsie Vaughan Hitchcock and R. W. Chambers. Early English Text Society, orig. ser., no. 186. London: Oxford University Press, 1932.

Machiavelli, Niccolò. *The Chief Works and Others*, 3 vols, ed. and trans. Allan Gilbert. Durham, N.C.: Duke University Press, 1965.

—— *The Prince*, eds. Quentin Skinner and Russell Price. Cambridge: Cambridge University Press, 1988.

—— *Discourses on Livy*, trans. Harvey C. Mansfield and Nathan Tarcov. Chicago and London: University of Chicago Press, 1996.

More, Thomas. *The vvorkes of Sir Thomas More Knyght, sometyme Lorde Chancellour of England, written by him in the Englyshe tonge*, ed. William Rastall. London 1557; STC 18076.

—— *The Correspondence of Sir Thomas More*, ed. Elizabeth Frances Rogers. Princeton: Princeton University Press, 1947.

—— *The Complete Works of Saint Thomas More*, 15 vols, eds Richard S. Sylvester *et al*. New Haven and London: Yale University Press, 1963–97.

—— *Utopia: Latin Text and English Translation*, eds George M. Logan, Robert M. Adams, and Clarence H. Miller. Cambridge: Cambridge University Press, 1995.

—— *Utopia*, trans. Ralph Robynson, ed. David Harris Sacks. Boston and New York: Bedford/St Martin's, 1999.

Roper, William. *The Life of Sir Thomas More, in Two Early Tudor Lives*, eds Richard S. Sylvester and David P. Harding. New Haven and London: Yale University Press, 1962.

Secondary sources

Ackroyd, Peter. *The Life of Thomas More*. London: Chatto & Windus, 1998.

Berlin, Isaiah. "The Originality of Machiavelli," in Myron P. Gilmore, ed., *Studies on Machiavelli*. Florence: Sansoni, 1972, 149–206.

Bock, Gisela, Quentin Skinner and Maurizio Viroli, eds. *Machiavelli and Republicanism*. Cambridge: Cambridge University Press, 1990.

Bradshaw, Brendan. "More on Utopia," *Historical Journal* 36 (1985): 1–27.

Burckhardt, Jacob. *The Civilization of the Renaissance in Italy: An Essay*, 3rd rev. edn, trans. S. G. C. Middlemore. London: Phaidon Press Ltd, 1950.

De Grazia, Sebastian. *Machiavelli in Hell*. Princeton: Princeton University Press, 1989.

Elton, G. R. "Thomas More, Councillor"; "Thomas More and the Opposition to Henry VIII"; "The Real Thomas More?," in G. R. Elton, *Studies in Tudor and Stuart Politics*, 4 vols. Cambridge: Cambridge University Press, 1974–92, vol. 1, 129–35, 155–72; vol. 3, 344–55.

Fox, Alistair. *Thomas More: History and Providence*. New Haven and London: Yale University Press, 1982.

Gilbert, Felix. *Machiavelli and Guicciardini: Politics and History in Sixteenth-century Florence*. Princeton: Princeton University Press, 1965.

Greenblatt, Stephen, "At the Table of the Great: More's Self-fashioning and Self-cancellation," in Stephen Greenblatt, *Renaissance Self-fashioning: From More to Shakespeare*. Chicago: University of Chicago Press, 1980, 11–73.

Guy, John A. *The Public Career of Sir Thomas More*. New Haven and London: Yale University Press, 1980.

Hexter, J. H. *More's Utopia: The Biography of an Idea*, 2nd edn. New York: Harper & Row, 1965.

—— *Visions of Politics on the Eve of the Reformation: More, Machiavelli and Seyssel*. New York: Basic Books, 1973.

Marc'hadaour, Germain and Richard S. Sylvester, eds. *Essential Articles for the Study of Thomas More*. Hamden, Conn.: Archon Books, 1977.

Marius, Richard. *Thomas More: A Biography*. New York: Knopf, 1984.

Pocock, J. G. A. *The Machiavellian Moment: Florentine Political Thought and the Atlantic Republican Tradition*. Princeton: Princeton University Press, 1975.

Ridolfi, Roberto. *The Life of Niccolò Machiavelli*, trans. Cecil Grayson. London: Routledge & Kegan Paul, 1963.

Skinner, Quentin. *Foundations of Modern Political Thought*, 2 vols. Cambridge: Cambridge University Press, 1978.

—— *Machiavelli* (Past Masters). Oxford: Oxford University Press, 1981.

—— "Sir Thomas More's *Utopia* and the Language of Renaissance Humanism," in Anthony Pagden, ed., *The Languages of Political Theory in Early Modern Europe*. Cambridge: Cambridge University Press, 1987, 123–57.

Viroli, Maurizio. *Niccolò's Smile: A Biography of Machiavelli*, trans. Antony Shugaar. New York: Farrar, Strauss & Giroux, 2000.

Wootton, David. "Friendship Portrayed: A New Account of Utopia." *History Workshop*, no. 45 (1998): 29–47.

PART IV

THE CIRCULATION OF POWER

CHAPTER FOURTEEN

COURTS, ART, AND POWER

Malcolm Vale

It is something of a paradox that an age often regarded as one of economic contraction, social upheaval, intellectual disorientation, and – at least in Northern Europe – terminal cultural decline, should provide us with so many examples of innovation. Between 1250 and 1500, western Europe witnessed the birth and coming of age of diplomatic, military, financial, navigational, technological, devotional, artistic, and educational practices that were to mold and shape the early modern world. We cannot, I would contend, understand the Renaissance world without some awareness and appreciation of what preceded it. Knowledge of the later Middle Ages – an allegedly epidemic-wracked, war-torn, and strife-ridden epoch – is vital to our understanding of Renaissance culture because it offers us striking visual evidence of a novel kind. For the first time since the end of the Roman Empire, images that look as if they represent the features of living individuals appear in western art. As ever, sculpture had led the way towards verisimilitude during the thirteenth century – in the West Choir of Naumburg cathedral (c. 1240–50) and in the works of the brothers Pisano (1258–1319). But it is only in the early fourteenth century that recognizable, identifiable portraits begin to emerge, first of all in devotional art, namely in wall paintings, altarpieces, and Books of Hours. Much of this artistic patronage stemmed from the very highest echelons of society, although it was not entirely confined to them. Much of it was associated with the courts of rulers. The princely households of the later Middle Ages formed, at the very least, the seedbed from which the courts of the Renaissance were to grow. Courts, great and small, were populated by high-status patrons, clerical and secular, drawn from the ranks of both hereditary and more recent nobility, and from the growing legal and financial bureaucracies of the age. As power centers, filling the space around the person of the prince, the courts of Europe acted as forums of many kinds, above all as a means whereby images of rulers and their immediate entourages were presented. In the iconography of power, the court played a fundamental role. It is the purpose of this chapter to trace some of these developments into the Renaissance and to consider the legacy of later medieval civilization and its princely courts to the world of humanism, individualism, princely power, and the "new" monarchies of the sixteenth century.

This was, of course, a time-span in the history of art that saw striking developments in more general modes of representation, leading to what has been called "a much closer congruence between art and reality." In both Italy and northern

Europe, an art of what appears to be greater realism emerged, associated with Giotto and Simone Martini in the fourteenth century, and with Jan van Eyck, Rogier van der Weyden, Masaccio, Antonello da Messina, the Bellinis, and many other Italian and Netherlandish artists in the fifteenth century. The evidence presented here will largely be drawn from northern Europe, above all from the Low Countries, which, during the last quarter of the fourteenth century and second quarter of the fifteenth, had become the dominions of the dukes of Burgundy: Philip the Bold (1363–1404), John the Fearless (1404–19), Philip the Good (1419–67), and Charles the Bold (1467–77). Today, the very word "Burgundy" probably conjures up thoughts of a French province famous for its wine growing, its Cluniac and Cistercian monasteries, and its French-speaking, French-cultured ducal dynasty – one of the wealthiest and most powerful of the princely houses of the later Middle Ages. But the "Burgundy" of the later Middle Ages clearly consisted of much more than the French duchy (Figure 14.1). The Burgundian dominions, between 1363 and 1482, formed a large territorial configuration comprising lands stretching from North Holland and Guelders in the north to the Swiss and Savoyard borders in the south. This was a new power in European politics, an embryonic third kingdom, or "middle" state, lying between France and the German Empire, whose rulers never wore a crown and whose lifespan was relatively brief. This was no nation-state, but one of those composite polities to which historians of early modern Europe have drawn our attention. Its structure – as a federation of territories under one prince, each governed according to its own laws and customs, with a resplendent court and court culture – did not perish when the last Valois duke of Burgundy, Charles the Bold, perished on the battlefield at Nancy in 1477.

The political and institutional structures of the Burgundian dominions did not lend themselves easily to "centralization" or to government and administration from any one fixed center. The piecemeal and haphazard means whereby these territories were acquired – by marriage, conquest, absorption, exchange, or purchase – worked against centripetal tendencies. Power centered upon the person of the ruler and those immediately around him. There was a paradox at the heart of the Burgundian "state": while bureaucratic, legal, and financial departments of state (chancery, accounting offices, law courts) evolved, with fixed locations and formal structures, the power center of the whole edifice constantly moved around, represented by the ruler and his or her court. This was not confined to the Burgundian case – much the same could be said of other Renaissance polities, including the England of Henry VIII, the Spain of Ferdinand and Isabella, even the France of Charles VIII, Louis XII, or Francis I. Power could be exercised on the move, in the most informal of ways and in the most informal of circumstances – when the ruler was getting up, being shaved, in the hunting field, on the road, or on his way to and from Mass. Louis XI of France (1461–83) often attended to business while in the saddle, granting offices to suitors and suppliants while indulging his passion for the hunt, and some of the surviving papers of his secretary, Jean Bourré, reflect this essentially informal manner of operating. There was a constant tension between the emergent bureaucratic government of the modern state and the fundamentally personal and fluid nature of princely rule. That rule was conducted through the institution that was closest in every sense to the person of the prince: the household.

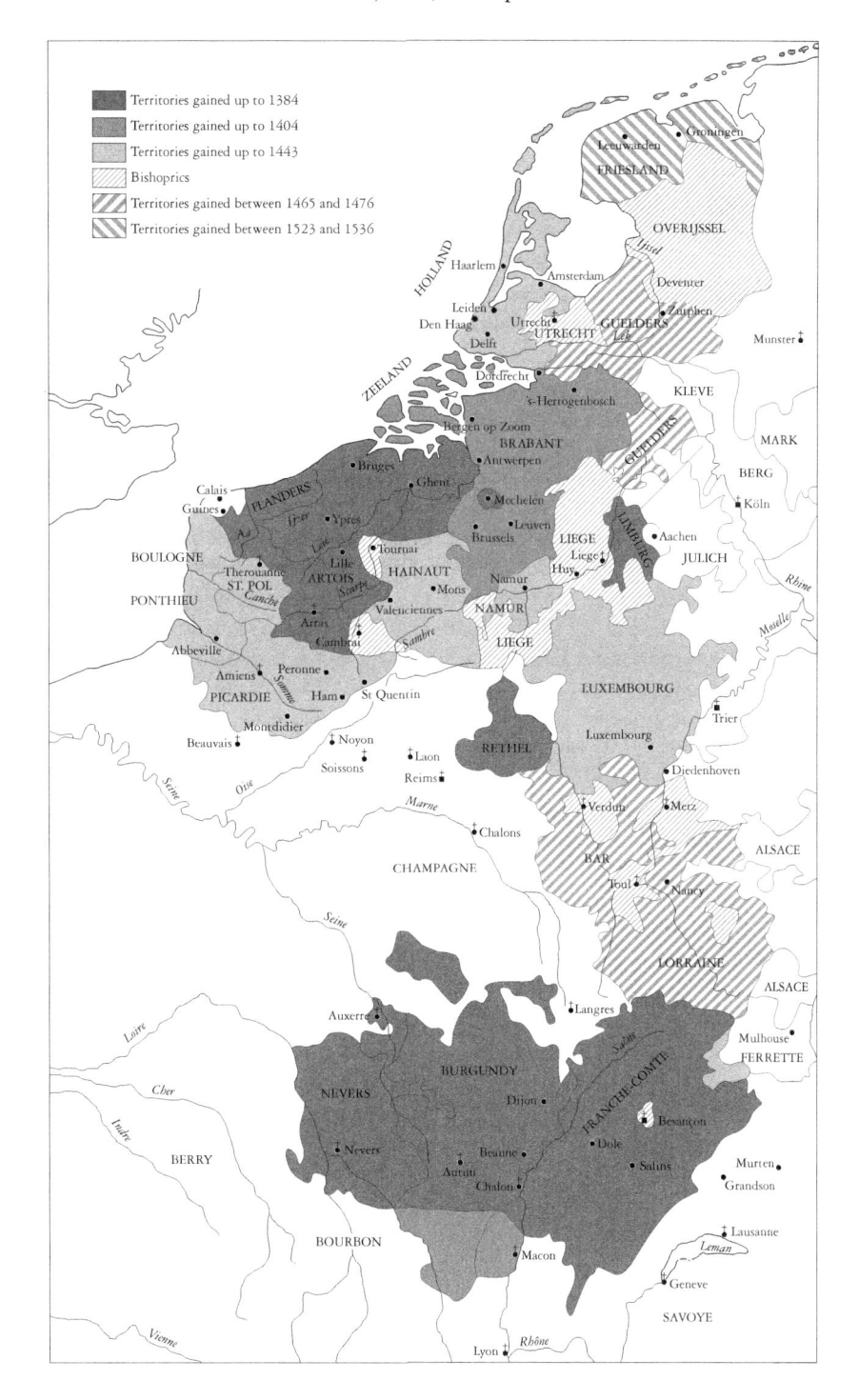

Figure 14.1 Burgundy in the late Middle Ages.

In the Burgundian lands, as in many other political formations of the later medieval and early modern periods, the household formed the spine or backbone of the ruler's court. The court would otherwise have been an amorphous, amoeba-like body, with no institutional framework. It could be argued that it was from the upper household – the formal, ceremonial, Domus Magnificencie ("household of magnificence") – that the Renaissance court emerged. Below it lay the Domus Providencie ("household of provision"), which provided for all the daily, material, and physical needs of the ruler and his entourage. The two spheres were by no means totally distinct and there was some overlap of both functions and personnel. But the holding of household office – whether ceremonial, domestic, or honorific – was a hallmark of court position and status across Renaissance Europe, from Brussels to Urbino and from Westminster to Prague. Castiglione, at the court of the Montefeltro, was well acquainted with the practice. The Burgundian household was, however, to some extent exceptional for the degree to which domestic functions, sometimes of a distinctly ritualized and ceremonial nature, were exercised by members of the nobilities of the Burgundian lands, serving at court by turns. This was one means of containment and control of potentially bellicose and dissident nobles, a practice that appeared to be relatively successful in the Burgundian period. There was, for instance, no major noble revolt, with the exception of a resistance to ducal policy in Holland and Zeeland in 1456, during the lifespans of the two last Valois dukes of Burgundy (1419–77). The kingdom of France, on the other hand, in which household service to the ruler did not play so prominent a part in the lives of the nobility, witnessed the full-scale rising known as the War of the Public Weal in 1465, and subsequent conflicts in Brittany and the southwest. There was nothing that came close to a nobility of service in royal France. Only under the new Habsburg rulers of the Low Countries after 1477 did the former Burgundian territories experience significant noble disaffection, especially in Flanders, and the nobility were to play a major role in the Dutch revolt after the executions of the counts of Egmont and Hoorne in 1568. It was perhaps unsurprising that the Habsburgs were concerned to stress continuities with their Burgundian predecessors and, ultimately by means of an ordinance of 1548, to attempt to emulate their court and household organization.

Yet the court was not solely formed by the household. Its composition extended beyond it to include, for example, nobles who did not hold office there, guests, visiting representatives from other powers, and young men such as Francesco d'Este of Ferrara or Rodolfo Gonzaga of Mantua, sent to be "nurtured" at the court of Burgundy. All European courts, well into the modern period, also possessed an "occasional" character that took them beyond the personnel of the prince's immediate entourage. Full, solemn, or plenary courts were convened at the major liturgical feasts of the Church's calendar, in both Catholic and, later, Protestant countries. Christmas, Easter, Pentecost, and often All Saints, Epiphany, or feast days associated with saints of especial significance to a given dynasty (St George, St Stephen, St Michael, St Wenceslas) witnessed the gathering of "full" courts to which subjects and vassals came from all parts of a ruler's dominions. Such was the size of these assemblies that, following Burgundian and earlier precedent, they tended increasingly to gravitate towards the cities and towns of a kingdom or principality. Not only the full courts, but the everyday courts of Philip the Good and Charles the Bold of Burgundy could be very large, sometimes numbering a thousand people, and the business of lodging and feeding them, as well as stabling their horses, posed logistical problems to the household administrations of many rulers. The cities of the Low Countries often saw the peripatetic court of Burgundy in their midst, and facilities and resources had to be put in place for its arrival and residence. This was the period that saw the rise of the princely residence, to the extent that, in the German-speaking world, the Residenzstadt became a characteristic urban phenomenon of the age. Not only did Italian princely dynasties – Visconti, Sforza, Medici, Montefeltro, Gonzaga, Este, or Malatesta – develop the Renaissance palace, but northern rulers also had their networks of residences, which might incorporate or restyle former castles and hunting lodges. The dukes of Burgundy and their Habsburg successors also launched campaigns of palace building and, from the second quarter of the fifteenth century onwards, new or substantially rebuilt residences were constructed at Lille, Ghent, Bruges, Mechelen, and Brussels, where the Coudenberg Palace became their preferred winter domicile and, as far as there ever was one, the effective centre of government of the Burgundian and Habsburg Netherlands. Court therefore constantly met city, and the juxtaposition, coexistence, and, in some cases, integration of interpenetrating court and civic cultures became dominant and defining features of the Renaissance cultural landscape.

As we have seen, with the demise of the Valois dynasty between 1477 and 1482, it was to Burgundian precedent and Burgundian culture that the Habsburgs were often to refer and allude during the following century. In Chapter 24 of his unfinished autobiographical epic *Der Weisskunig* (The White King), the Habsburg emperor Maximilian I (1493–1519) says (or is made to say): "When a man dies, only his deeds live after him. He who provides no remembrance (*gedachtnus*) for himself during his lifetime has no remembrance after his death and . . . is forgotten with his passing bell, and therefore the money that I spend on my remembrance is not lost." Maximilian was referring, among other things, to the art of portraiture and its propaganda value. As evidence, outliving the lifetime of its creator, art – for Maximilian – was as much for commemoration's sake as for its own. He was much concerned about the means whereby rulers were commemorated: without tolerably accurate likenesses of a prince, taken during his lifetime, how was he to be remembered and depicted after his death? The Renaissance cult of fame was not the only spur to image-making among princes: continuity with the medieval past was also maintained. Dynastic as well as pious concerns continued to prompt the depiction of ancestors. By the later Middle Ages an increasing desire that those likenesses should be consistently lifelike, recognizable, and quite widely disseminated was apparent. It could also be claimed that the technical innovations of the early Netherlandish painters – above all Jan van Eyck (d. 1441) and Rogier van der Weyden (d. 1464) – enabled an unprecedented (though still contrived and illusionistic) degree of realism to be injected into the art of portraiture.

Now the Emperor Maximilian I (d. 1519) (Figure 14.2) was not the ruler only of the Austrian Habsburg lands. In 1477, when archduke of Austria, he had married into the house of Burgundy. His marriage to Mary, sole heiress of Charles the Bold, last Valois duke of Burgundy, made Maximilian and his house heirs not only to the Netherlandish dominions but also to the cultural traditions of the Burgundian court.

Figure 14.2 Albrecht Dürer (1471–1528). *Kaiser Maximilian I.* © Kunsthistorisches Museum, Vienna, Austria/The Bridgeman Art Library. The emperor is portrayed at the end of his life, in 1519, holding a pomegranate, symbol of eternal life, and accompanied by a depiction of the imperial coat of arms, encircled by the collar of the Burgundian Order of the Golden Fleece, at the top left-hand side of the picture.

Although shorn of their original French heartland in the duchy of Burgundy itself, the Burgundian dynasty survived, absorbed by the Habsburgs, as rulers of the Netherlands (including the French-speaking areas in Flanders, Hainault, and Artois). Now if there was an art form for which the Netherlandish painters of the Burgundian dominions were most noted by contemporaries, including Italians, then it was the portrait "head" or "likeness." Maximilian was to make good use of this inheritance, in painted – or, as his money ran out – in cheaper printed, or engraved form. There was nothing particularly new or "Renaissance"-like about this desire of princes for commemoration, nor for the perpetuation of images that could contain didactic and propagandist messages. But a number of questions present themselves if we attempt to see relationships between art and power, art and politics, or art and ideology at this time. The identity of those who produced the images is often important: the dukes of Burgundy, unlike many of their predecessors, did not rely upon monks and other clergy for their image projection. Panel painters, manuscript illuminators, sculptors, and so on were, very largely, laymen by this time – some, indeed, were retained by the dukes as members of their household. There were, of course, artists such as the Fra Angelicos, Fra Filippo Lippis, and Brothers Hugo van der Goes at this time, but they were in a small minority. The great age of the monastic scriptorium as an exclusive source of illuminated books had, for instance, waned forever. Did this therefore mean that a different repertoire of images was devised, or simply that old images were used in a new way? What were the sources upon which these rulers drew for their representation? What purposes did those images serve? Did the Burgundian dukes introduce any new features into the iconography of princes, or did they merely build upon and develop an existing legacy? Did the fact that the Valois dukes constituted a new power in western Europe have any influence upon their iconology and on the manner in which they were represented in art? Finally, what, if anything, do these representations of the powerful tell us about the nature and exercise of princely power in northern Europe during the later Middle Ages and early Renaissance?

A desire among many ruling houses to emphasize continuity with their predecessors meant that they tended to adopt (and adapt) traditional modes of representation that themselves had a very long ancestry. Take the image of the Emperor Otto III enthroned (Figure 14.3), flanked by his lay and ecclesiastical household officers, in the Reichenau Gospel book made between 998 and 1001, now at Munich. On the left-hand page, personifications of Roma and of the provinces of his empire perform homage to Otto. The analogs to this theme were not only classical but also biblical, and the image clearly owed something to representations of God the Father and the enthroned Christ in Majesty. A later medieval version of this age-old theme appears in a tinted drawing of the Emperor Charles IV and the seven ecclesiastical and lay electors in Gelre Herald's Armorial or Wapenboek of *c.* 1390–1400. A similar frontal pose is adopted, and the Luxembourg emperor (who was also king of Bohemia) sits enthroned bearing the imperial sword and orb. A closely contemporary example is the Westminster portrait of Richard II of England, where an identical pose is shown. These images closely resemble the impressions of rulers on their seals of majesty where, in contrast to the equestrian figures often pictured on the reverse, a strictly frontal pose was always *de rigueur*. These icon-like images were, as we shall see, to enjoy a very long history. It has been suggested that they were "calculated to overawe or unnerve." There is little sign of conditional tenure of power here. Holbein's Whitehall Henry VIII, for example, which stems from this tradition, was said to have had a terrifying effect upon the spectator.

Another variant of this authoritarian theme is found in the later Middle Ages: the prince presiding over a chapter or assembly of his own order of chivalry. Burgundian images of the chapters of the new Order of the Golden Fleece (founded in 1430) achieved their most grandiose expression under Charles the Bold (1467–77), but this imagery continued to be projected, and elaborated, by his Habsburg successors. This kind of iconography of the ruler owes something to representations of

Figure 14.3 Holy Roman Emperor Otto III enthroned (980–1002), accompanied on his left by two clerics, probably Heribert, Chancellor of Italy, and Leo, the future bishop of Vercelli, c. 998 (vellum) © Bayerische Staatsbibliothek, Munich, Germany/The Bridgeman Art Library.

Figure 14.4 Rogier van der Weyden (attributed) from Jacques de Guise, *Chroniques de Hainaut. Philip the Good of Burgundy and his Court*, 1448. Art Resource NY.

the Virgin enthroned as queen of heaven. But it also provides us with glimpses of a world of court ceremonial that can otherwise only be reconstructed from written sources. The artefacts and objects associated with the Golden Fleece are thus invaluable historical documents. An adaptation, or modification, of this uncompromisingly icon-like style of imagery is detectable in the Burgundian development of the presentation frontispiece in manuscript painting. In this, the prince, surrounded by his higher household officers and courtiers (who, in the Burgundian case, were largely synonymous), is shown receiving a copy of a manuscript book from its writer, translator, or editor. It forms a kind of dedication page, intended to honor a patron. It also had a long ancestry. In its later medieval form it is found at the court of Charles V of France (1364–80), but there were earlier medieval precedents. Sometimes a frontal pose is chosen, but in the majority of cases a three-quarters view is preferred. The book production of a single manuscript workshop (which was also a kind of publishing house) at Mons in Hainault during the 1440s and 1450s provides us with the best examples, in the secular manuscripts produced by Jean Wauquelin and Jacquemart Pilavaine. The duke – Philip the Good of Burgundy – sits or stands flanked by his court, echoing earlier representations, but in a far more realistic style. A striking example of a disposition of the court that echoes earlier precedents is found in the presentation page of the *Chroniques de Hainaut* (Figure 14.4), offered to the duke by Wauquelin in 1448. To Philip's left stand the secular nobles, all household officers, and on his right the clerical, legal, and financial members of the court. There may here be some affinity with the portraits of the donor found on devotional altarpieces or in Books of Hours – the author, scribe, or translator (rendered in profile) kneels in obeisance to the ruler, as the donor of an altarpiece or the owner of a Book of Hours would kneel or genuflect in adoration or veneration of Christ, the Virgin, or the saints. Bending the knee in the presence of the ruler had become an essential part of court etiquette and protocol by this time.

Although the original text and de luxe edition of such books went to the ducal library, copies were made for more general dissemination, usually containing the original dedication and the presentation miniature. Whoever was the owner of the copy, he or she was thus reminded of the piety, generosity, and wisdom of the original patron or dedicatee of the manuscript. This was the custom at most European courts. So these were not purely private images, intended for a one-man (or one-woman) audience. Some continuity with imperial iconography is apparent – in these Burgundian images, the grouping of lay and ecclesiastical courtiers follows Ottonian precedent – but the courtly scene has been translated into the more "realistic" idiom of the mid-fifteenth century. Eyckian art enabled rulers – and everyone else – to be represented more faithfully. This could be both an advantage and a disadvantage if, as was the case with Duke Filippo Maria Visconti of Milan (1412–47) or King Charles VII of France (1422–61), the ruler was physically unprepossessing. But a desire for verisimilitude was apparently paramount, especially in northern Europe. We might relate this to the notion of remembrance that Maximilian emphasized. True and faithful likenesses (or at least fair approximations to them), owing to the technical innovations of the Netherlandish masters, could now be achieved. The ruler is set in the interiorized, almost domestic setting of his household. One could, again, perhaps draw parallels with the representation of religious and devotional themes, such as depictions of the life of Christ in a domestic context. A genre of princely iconography, which laid less overt stress upon the iconic, yet essentially human, image of the ruler, seems to be evolving here. Sacrality and humanity was, as in Christian iconography, held in a state of creative tension in the imagery of secular rulers.

Another source of images, upon which the dukes of Burgundy and their subjects drew, was the series of figures or portraits illustrating the descent of a ruling house. We have both visual and documentary evidence for this kind of pictorial genealogy from the mid- to late thirteenth century, and there may well be earlier examples. In the earliest cases, heraldic emblems, rather than figures or portraits, were used to identify individuals without ever attempting to represent their true features. Burgundian portraiture (like other aspects of Burgundian culture) built upon these pre-existing traditions. A lost series of wall paintings, depicting the counts and countesses of Flanders from their remotest ancestors to the last pre-Burgundian count, Louis de Male (d. 1384), in the chapel of the counts at the collegiate church of Our Lady at Courtrai, provides a good example. These were commissioned by the count between 1372 and 1374 from his painter, Jan van Hasselt. Each figure was accompanied by an inscription in Flemish, not French, stressing the Netherlandish, as well as French, identity of the ruling house, recording their regnal years and places of burial, with a shield of arms denoting their family origins and in some cases

Figure 14.5 Genealogical portrait panels of the counts and countesses of Flanders, 1480, from the abbey of Ter Duinen at Koksijde © Irpa-Kik, Brussels.

marriage alliances. The series began in the mists of time with Lideric the *forestier* and became rather more accurate chronologically by the twelfth century.

The emphasis here was clearly upon dynastic continuities, especially significant during periods – as were the later Middle Ages – of frequent change of ruling houses. Even the kingdom of France, blessed with a continuous line of Capetian kings from 987 onwards, underwent a succession crisis in 1328. Dynastic change was particularly marked in the Low Countries in the thirteenth and fourteenth centuries, where the indigenous house of Avesnes in Hainault and Holland gave way to a branch of the Wittelsbachs of Bavaria, and they in turn to the Valois dukes of Burgundy after 1428. In Flanders and Artois the houses of Dampierre and Nevers succeeded each other, to be subsumed by the Burgundian dukes after 1384. In Brabant, a cadet branch of the house of Burgundy was already in place at the beginning of the fifteenth century, to be superseded in turn by Philip the Good of Burgundy himself after 1430. Burgundian concern to identify and link themselves with their predecessors in their new Netherlandish dominions was exemplified by the addition of their own images to these portrait series. At Courtrai the ducal painter Melchior Broederlam was commissioned in 1407 to insert figures of Philip the Bold of Burgundy (d. 1404) and his wife, Margaret of Flanders, in the series. These, like the existing image of Louis de Male, appear to have been "true likenesses" according to later witnesses who saw the paintings before their destruction. The sequence then appears to have been arrested until 1467, when a request was sent to Brussels for cartoons on which to base portraits of John the Fearless and Philip the Good, who had not yet been depicted. Some impression of what these pictorial genealogies looked like may be gained from the surviving panels from the Cistercian abbey of Ter Duinen (Bruges, Groot Seminarie), which were "renewed" at the request of Mary, duchess of Burgundy, in 1480 (Figure 14.5).

Representations such as these formed part of a much more general later medieval and early Renaissance tendency. But their purpose in the Burgundian dominions perhaps went further than mere commemoration of ancestors, founders, or benefactors. Burgundian rule in the Low Countries had been established by various means, some more legitimate than others: from marriage alliance and lawful inheritance in Flanders and Artois, to coercion in Holland and Hainault, to negotiated agreement with the Estates in Brabant. The ruler's legitimacy was therefore promoted by these visual means and the idea of an unbroken succession, whereby a new dynasty emphasized its connections with its predecessors, seems evident here. Perhaps the most famous example of this practice was to be found in Bohemia, near Prague, at the castle of Karlstein, where the Luxemburg emperor Charles IV had commissioned a series of 60 figures representing his ancestors, stemming (he believed) from the Trojans, passing through many entirely spurious and fictitious characters. The Luxemburgs had superseded the indigenous Bohemian dynasty of Přemysl in the early fourteenth century. An account survives, by the Brabançon chronicler Edmond de Dinter, of the guided tour he was given to this early family portrait gallery by Wenceslas, king of Bohemia himself. This must have taken place in October 1412, during a diplomatic mission to Bohemia. Although it is quite probable that its "first aim was almost certainly to divert and interest," Wenceslas (in one of his increasingly rare sober moments) was also concerned to make a point: to show an envoy from Brabant that the house of Luxemburg had a good claim to that duchy through an ancestry that included a number of dukes and duchesses of Brabant. Similar sentiments may have lain behind the dynastic series that we know to have existed in Flanders, Hainault, and Holland during both the pre-Burgundian and Burgundian periods.

The function of these images must depend upon who actually commissioned them, who saw them, and upon the setting or context in which they were originally conceived. There is clearly a world of difference between images of the prince on the pages of relatively private objects such as Books of Hours and other manuscripts, and those displayed in audience chambers, courts of justice, or the halls of échevins, guildsmen, or town councillors. Clearly these public sequences of portraits were constantly added to, and attempts were made to achieve lifelike images of present or recent rulers. These were public images, which were intended to be seen, whether by courtiers, guests, or diplomatic envoys; or by members of town councils and courts of justice; or by residents of religious houses and their guests, as in the series depicting the counts and countesses of Flanders at the abbey of Ter Duinen. At both Ghent and Ypres, the town councillors had commissioned such series in their meeting halls, and in 1419 the Ghent échevins simply copied the paintings in the chapel of the counts of Flanders at Courtrai for their own hall. The prince might be absent, but his presence was enshrined, as it were, in his likeness and those of his ancestors, presiding over the deliberations of these burgher assemblies.

Another type of artistic evidence is by far the most difficult to interpret and explain. It is sometimes represented as a prime example of "Renaissance" individualism. This is the "independent" portrait or portrait miniature, with no known association or evident purpose, increasing in numbers and popularity during the fifteenth century. Some were undoubtedly conceived for private and personal use – the secular equivalent of the small devotional picture. It has been suggested that "these paintings had little function, once painted and delivered; and they came to rest in odd places." Some were quite small and easily portable; others rather larger and more substantial objects. In some cases, function and meaning might be deduced from the attributes, emblems, or insignia borne by the sitter. But many are simply portrait heads, or heads and shoulders: they represent the painted equivalent of the portrait bust, well known from Italian marble, alabaster, and bronze sculpture from the early fifteenth century onwards, but also found in the north. Portraits in bronze of Philip the Good of Burgundy and his successors survive (Figures 14.6, 14.7). The more portable of these painted images on panel and canvas may have served as gifts: there is evidence for the exchange of likenesses from *c*. 1350 onwards. For example, an exchange of portraits between Charles V of France and the Emperor Charles IV seems to have provided material for one of the wall paintings in the Karlstein. One use of such images was of course during marriage negotiations, when artists were employed to record the features and at least some of the attributes of prospective brides. It is also known that portrait sketches and drawings circulated, as reminders or remembrances of both the living and the dead, and as sources for subsequent depictions of these rulers (for example, in the celebrated sixteenth-century *Recueil d'Arras*). All presupposed the absence of the sitter or subject.

Some were clearly intended to be hung up; others took the form of panels closing one upon another, as free-standing objects, like a diptych or triptych. Surviving

Figure 14.6 Philip the Good of Burgundy from the tomb of Emperor Maximilian I, Hofkirche, Innsbruck, begun 1502. His Burgundian predecessors join the ranks of mourners around Maximilian's memorial, together with his other ancestors, actual and mythical, including King Arthur. Eriche Lessing/Art Resource NY.

works may be misleading: some may be parts of dismembered or cut-down paintings that once consisted of more than one panel. The fact that some of these images, for example that of Francesco d'Este, bastard of Ferrara, by Rogier van der Weyden, painted *c.* 1450 (Figure 14.8), have heraldic insignia, or marbling, or inscriptions painted on their reverse sides are revealing. They may not have been intended to be

Figure 14.7 Charles the Bold, Duke of Burgundy (1433–77), father of Mary of Burgundy, first wife of Emperor Maximilian I. Design by Sesselschreiber, sculpture Leonhard Magt, cast Stephan Godl (1521). From the tomb of Emperor Maximilian I, Hofkirche, Innsbruck. Erich Lessing/Art Resource NY.

hung, but picked up and turned over. Household and other accounts offer valuable evidence for the function and housing of such panels. Dr Lorne Campbell has noted that in 1404, Anthony of Burgundy, duke of Brabant, was supplied with hooks, chains, and a reel "pour pendre les tableaux de la portraicture dudit seigneur" (to hang the panels of the portraiture of the said lord). If hung from a ceiling or beam

Figure 14.8 Rogier van der Weyden. *Portrait of Francesco d'Este of Ferrara*, c. 1460. Metropolitan Museum of Art, New York. An illegitimate son of Leonello, Marquis of Ferrara, he was at the court of Burgundy in the Low Countries until 1475.

on long chains, both sides of a portrait could be viewed. But what about those apparently isolated and "functionless" panels that have come down to us? Some were copied and given to other rulers and subjects. But where were they put? Some found their way into the later medieval and early Renaissance equivalent of the seventeenth-century cabinet of curiosities. Charles V of France, for instance, possessed four "heads" of himself and three contemporary princes in the "petit estude" (small study) in the Hôtel St-Pol at Paris by 1380. There is little sense of any very close relationship between art and power in many of these likenesses or remembrances, which were not apparently intended for public display. They pose, perhaps, all the problems of the presentation photograph: what on earth do you do with it? Whether or not they possessed other powers – talismanic, devotional, votive, or otherwise – is a matter for speculation. But it was not always unhelpful for a ruler to have images of those with whom he dealt on the European political and diplomatic stage, into whose families he and his immediate kinspeople married, and whom he customarily saw only rarely. Perhaps the simple reminder or souvenir might prove to be a perfectly adequate explanation without delving too deeply – in the manner of Erwin Panofsky, for example – into the iconographical jungle. Panofsky tended to see symbolism and "hidden meaning" everywhere in fifteenth-century paintings. He took the iconographical approaches and methods, developed largely in relation to Italian Renaissance art by a previous generation of art and cultural historians such as Aby Warburg (1866–1929), into the field of early Netherlandish painting. But less elaborate and arcane explanations may sometimes suffice. The function of the portrait, as a means of commemoration and recall of an individual's features, prompts many questions about the motivations that lay behind them. Jan van Eyck may himself have given us an answer by painting the words "Leal Souvenir" ("faithful remembrance") on the stone parapet of his *Portrait of a Man* in the London National Gallery.

In conclusion, what do all these images, which evidently performed different functions in different contexts, tell us about princely power – and especially that of the dukes of Burgundy – in the later Middle Ages? It has been a common tendency among historians to argue that princely power was under threat – from both nobles and townsmen – during this period. Hereditary rule inevitably posed problems of succession if direct heirs failed or proved inadequate; elective monarchy (as in the German Empire) could be inherently unstable; and the dynastic shifts to which we have already referred meant that new houses (albeit directly or indirectly related to old ones) had to stake their claims and legitimate their authority. The opposition of both nobles and towns to princes may have been exaggerated by historians, especially in the Burgundian dominions, but it remained a potential, if not actual, thorn in every prince's side. There were of course more tangible, more subtle, and perhaps more effective ways of staking claims and legitimating authority than the propagation of images. But if the practice of creating pictorial genealogies, and of distributing portraits of past and present rulers, is set into a political context, then we might begin to see a closer relationship between art, politics, and power.

Some of these depictions were prompted by the desire of individuals or groups among a prince's subjects to demonstrate their loyalty to the ruling dynasty. This may also be one explanation of the portrait series of their rulers commissioned by échevins and patrician town councillors in the Burgundian Netherlands. Sometimes princely images were imposed by higher authority, as in Philip the Good's and Charles the Bold's dealings with the more rebellious elements in the city of Ghent. Subjects apparently wished to know what their rulers looked like: if it could be argued that princes made fewer public appearances (for all kinds of reasons) in the fifteenth century, then the demand for more widely disseminated and consistent images may have become all the greater. Edward IV of England, for example, caused a considerable stir in Bruges in March 1471 when he pioneered the twentieth-century "walkabout" by going on foot from the city to the port of Damme, greeting the inhabitants on his way, to embark for England. As far as we know he did not provide any Flemish painter with what might be called a "likeness-opportunity" on that occasion. But it is known, for instance, that Charles the Bold discontinued his father's practice of holding public audiences. Opportunities to see the prince, apart from the rather infrequent formal entries into towns (the *joyeuse avènement* or *Blijde Inkomst*) may therefore have been diminishing. Surrounded by his court, screened and protected by his ever-growing bodyguard of archers, the duke of Burgundy had become a more remote figure by the end of the fifteenth century. Philip the Good had a sort of observation post created for himself in one of the gables of his palace at Brussels from which he could see the inhabitants of the lower town, but they could not see him. With the possible exception of Filippo Maria Visconti of Milan and his Sforza successors, however, few fifteenth-century rulers occupied Kremlin-like palaces, totally isolated from the surrounding population. But the tendency towards withdrawal had begun, and access to the prince had already become a key political issue, not only in the Burgundian dominions.

Art can present an image of power that is designed to impress and, in some cases, to mislead. Many celebrated images, designed to impress and overawe, seem to stand in a direct line of descent from the frontal ruler-portrait of the later Middle Ages. Henry VIII and Elizabeth I of England, as well as Louis XIV of France, employed these icon-like images to propagate a vision of royal authority that expressed its "absolute" qualities. But this often represented a departure from reality. Images could purposefully mislead, attributing far greater power to their subject than was ever actually exercised in the living theater of monarchy. A French monarch might be shown presiding over a *lit de justice* in the plenary assembly of France's supreme court of appeal, the Paris Parliament — but that court possessed a right of remonstrance, or objection, to the crown's edicts that it did not hesitate to exercise. Behind the grandiose, imperial images lay an *ancien régime* in which venality, corruption, and the constant, institutionalized sale, purchase, and inheritance of office and favor set very real limits on the scope of a king's or prince's authority and its exercise. Sometimes an inverse ratio between power and its representation in art prevailed. The grander the image, it can sometimes be argued, the lesser the power. Van Dyck's dramatic portraits of Charles I of England provide an excellent example. Propaganda took over when political reality ceased to correspond to the manner in which rulers were represented. When that propaganda finally failed to convince and persuade, styles of rule that had been forged in the later Middle Ages and Renaissance could meet their nemesis, as they did in England between 1649 and 1688 and in France between 1789 and 1793. The traditional images and insignia of power — the imperial eagle; the scepter of Charles V (1364–80) of France, topped with an image of

Charlemagne; or the *main de justice* of St Louis (1226–70) – no longer gave substance to timeless and unquestioned power. The practice of appropriating imperial imagery was thus not confined to the ruling dynasties of later medieval and Renaissance Europe. But, with their backward-looking references and allusions, represented and depicted in novel and forward-looking ways, Renaissance images of power brought together the old and the new. In the process, an iconography of rulers and their courts that was to endure for centuries was fashioned.

SUGGESTIONS FOR FURTHER READING

Adamson, John (ed.). *The Princely Courts of Europe: Ritual, Politics and Culture under the Ancien Régime, 1500–1750*. London, 1999.
Armstrong, C. A. J. "The Golden Age of Burgundy: Dukes that Outdid Kings," in A. G. Dickens (ed.), *The Courts of Europe*. London, 1977, 54–75.
Asch, Ronald G. and Adolph M. Birke (eds), *Princes, Patronage and the Nobility: The Court at the Beginning of the Modern Age, ca. 1450–1650*. London and Oxford, 1991.
Blockmans, Willem Pieter and Walter Prevenier. *The Promised Lands: The Low Countries under Burgundian Rule, 1369–1530*. Philadelphia, 1999.
Campbell, Lorne. *Renaissance Portraits*. New Haven and London, 1990.
Cole, Alison. *Art of the Italian Renaissance Courts: Virtue and Magnificence*. London, 1995.
Costa Gomes, Rita. *The Making of a Court Society. Kings and Nobles in Late Medieval Portugal*. Cambridge, 2003.
Dickens, A. G. (ed.). *The Courts of Europe: Politics, Patronage and Royalty, 1400–1800*. London, 1977.
Duindam, Jeroen. *Myths of Power: Norbert Elias and the Early Modern European Court*. Amsterdam, 1995.
—— *Vienna and Versailles. The Courts of Europe's Dynastic Rivals, 1550–1780*. Cambridge, 2003.
Elias, Norbert. *The Court Society*. Oxford, 1983.
Gunn, Steven and Antheun Janse (eds), *The Court as a Stage. England and the Low Countries in the Later Middle Ages*. Woodbridge, 2006.
Harbison, Craig. *The Art of the Northern Renaissance*. London, 1995.
Huizinga, Johan. *The Autumn of the Middle Ages*. Chicago, 1996.
Jaeger, C. Stephen. *The Origins of Courtliness: Civilizing Trends and the Formation of Courtly Ideals, 939–1210*. Philadelphia, 1985.
Kaiser Maximilian I. *Weisskunig*, eds H. T. Musper, R. Buchner, H. O. Burger, and E. Petermann, 2 vols. Stuttgart, 1956.
Kaufmann, Thomas da Costa. *Court, Cloister and City: The Art and Culture of Central Europe, 1450–1800*. London, 1995.
Martindale, Andrew. *Heroes, Ancestors, Relatives and the Birth of the Portrait*. The Hague, 1988.
Mueller, Jan-Dirk. *Gedechtnus: Literatur und Hofgesellschaft um Maximilian I*. Munich, 1982.
Nijsten, Gerard. *In the Shadow of Burgundy: The Court of Guelders in the Late Middle Ages*. Cambridge, 2004.
Panofsky, Erwin. *Early Netherlandish Painting. Its Origins and Character*, 2 vols. New York and London, 1971.
Paravicini, Werner (ed.), *Alltag bei Hofe*. Sigmaringen, 1995.
—— *Zeremoniell und Raum*. Sigmaringen, 1997.
Prevenier, W. and W. Blockmans. *The Burgundian Netherlands*. Cambridge, 1986.

Vale, Malcolm. *War and Chivalry: Warfare and Aristocratic Culture in England, France and Burgundy at the End of the Middle Ages*. London, 1981.

—— *The Princely Court. Medieval Courts and Culture in North-West Europe, 1270–1380*. Oxford, 2001 (2nd edn 2003).

Van Oostrom, Fritz Pieter. *Court and Culture: Dutch Literature, 1350–1450*. Berkeley, Los Angeles and Oxford, 1992.

Warnke, Martin. *The Court Artist: On the Ancestry of the Modern Artist*. Cambridge and Paris, 1993.

CHAPTER FIFTEEN

THE IMPERIAL RENAISSANCE

Thomas James Dandelet

CAESAR IN THE RENAISSANCE

Early in the second half of the fourteenth century, just as the Renaissance was dawning in Italy, the great Italian humanist Petrarch wrote *The Lives of Illustrious Men*. A collection of biographies of 30 famous ancient Romans, the book began with the life of Romulus, founder of Rome, and ended with the life of Julius Caesar, the de facto founder of the Roman Empire.

Written by one of the intellectual luminaries of the Renaissance, Petrarch's work served as an early literary guide to the two primary political streams that flowed out of ancient Rome: the republican tradition and the imperial tradition. Certainly for Petrarch and many of his admirers, such as the Florentine humanists Coluccio Salutati and Leonardo Bruni, it was the republican tradition that they celebrated and sought to revive and emulate in their own city-states. The great majority of Petrarch's famous men came from the republican period, for example; only Julius Caesar could be tied to the imperial tradition.

This emphasis on the revival of the ancient Roman republican political tradition in Renaissance thought and institutions has also dominated much contemporary scholarship on the Renaissance. American Renaissance scholars in the post-war period in particular have devoted the lion's share of their time and writing to exploring the histories of the two most famous Italian Renaissance republics, Florence and Venice. When they did turn to regions of Italy with no Renaissance republican political tradition like Rome and Naples, for example, the political dimension of the Renaissance was treated largely as the unrealized imperial fantasies of a few popes and kings in the late fifteenth and early sixteenth centuries. In this scholarly tradition the imperial Renaissance in these cities was largely over by 1527 and the sack of Rome, although papal imperial ambitions continued for a while longer, especially in the realms of artistic or architectural production. In short, the Renaissance in Rome, Naples, and other regions of Europe has generally taken a back seat to the republican Renaissance of Florence and Venice precisely because those renaissances were not republican.

And yet, as Petrarch's *Illustrious Men* reminds us, the Renaissance, from its very beginning, also contained the seeds of the imperial tradition that was always the other political option for Europeans committed to a revival of Roman antiquity. In fact, the imperial theme, with its great political lure and temptation of reviving large-scale imperial ambition, actually came to dominate the political imaginations of European Renaissance princes just as it had dominated ancient Rome throughout the centuries after Caesar. Indeed, this Renaissance of empire largely supplanted the republican tradition and the Renaissance republics by the middle of the sixteenth century. It was the revival of empires, not republics, both imagined and real that came to dominate the literary, artistic, and political agendas of Europe's most powerful states, political theorists, and monarchs. To the extent that this imperial Renaissance shaped the political ambitions and agendas of western European monarchs and empires throughout the sixteenth, seventeenth, and even eighteenth centuries, it is not too much to say that this Renaissance continued far beyond the normal chronological boundaries of republican Renaissance history, which frequently ends in the early sixteenth century. Subsequently, taking the Renaissance of empire seriously also substantially revises and expands our traditional understanding of the impact and longevity of the Renaissance itself.

Petrarch's elaborate treatment of the life of Julius Caesar already hinted both at the Renaissance fascination with the imperial theme and at the way that the republican period became almost a prelude to the central imperial moment. In his *Illustrious Men*, for example, Petrarch dedicated the first volume, or 870 pages in a modern Italian edition, to the lives of 29 men. But his second volume of 695 pages was dedicated to just one man, Julius Caesar. Petrarch's life of Caesar announced very clearly that the founder of the Empire was being resurrected as perhaps ancient Rome's most compelling and greatest political figure. In Petrarch's own words, "Certainly I find the name of Caesar to be glorious."[1]

And Petrarch was not alone in this sentiment. Rather, the revival of interest in Caesar grew throughout the fifteenth and sixteenth centuries due to both his prominence as an ancient author and his political and military role as one of ancient Rome's most successful strategists and generals. This interest was embodied in the numerous editions of Caesar's *Commentaries* that began to appear in the fifteenth century and that were repeatedly published throughout the sixteenth and seventeenth centuries. To cite just a few examples, Caesar's *Commentaries* were first published in Venice in 1471, in Rome in 1472, in Milan in 1478, in Treviso in 1480, and in Florence in 1508. In the decades that followed, no fewer than 18 editions would be printed in Venice alone, and by the later sixteenth century northern editions of the *Commentaries* were published in Frankfurt and Antwerp.

The vernacular editions, moreover, increasingly took on the tone of instruction manuals that were relevant to the military strategists and generals of the sixteenth century. The volume edited and illustrated by Andrea Palladio and his sons in 1575, for example, was dedicated to Giacomo Boncampagno, the general of the papal state and son of Pope Gregory XIII. In the introduction Caesar is called "the greatest captain that ever commanded," and the author "clearly proposes the imitation of his great deeds."[2]

Not all Renaissance writers shared such enthusiasm for Caesar, of course. Humanist republicans like the Florentine historian and statesman Francesco Guicciardini viewed Julius Caesar as the tyrant who was largely responsible for bringing the republican tradition to an end in ancient Rome. It is this rejection of the imperial tradition that is most often noted by scholars of humanist political thought. Yet, many Renaissance humanists clearly saw reviving the imperial memory and example of Caesar and the Roman Empire as important and legitimate options when seeking political models and inspiration.

GHOSTS OF ANCIENT ROME: EMPIRES OLD AND NEW

This revived literary interest in Caesar, while consistent with the deep fascination that Renaissance scholars had with other authors, memories, and models of the ancient Roman Empire, was distinct in the way that it held an unflattering mirror up to the primary late medieval and early Renaissance pretenders to Caesar's title and imperial capital, the Holy Roman Emperors of the German lands and the popes of Rome.

From the time that the king of the Franks, Charlemagne, was crowned with the title of Holy Roman Emperor by Pope Leo III on Christmas day 800, his successors had claimed to be the legitimate heirs to the ancient Roman emperors. But as rulers of often fragmented territories primarily in central Europe, with only modest economic, military, and political power, the Holy Roman Emperors of the late medieval and early Renaissance periods were mere shadows of the ancient emperors. And their empire was a shadow of that of ancient Rome.

For these emperors, the memories of the ancient Caesars and ancient Rome were like ghosts that haunted them and reminded them and the rest of Europe of what they and their empire were not. While the ancient Caesars had ruled over an empire that dominated the entire Mediterranean world and all of western Europe, the late medieval emperors held onto an often tenuous rule over parts of Germany, France, and Italy. While the ancient empire had conquered numerous other ancient empires, such as Greece, Egypt, and Carthage, and imposed Roman law, currency, institutions, language, religion, art, architecture, and armies on their subject lands, it was difficult for the medieval emperors to hold even the German lands together.

Similarly, Renaissance popes, from the time of the papacy's return to Rome under Martin V in 1417, were confronted constantly with their own shortcomings when they looked upon the city of Rome itself, a city of ancient ruins. They knew all too well that in comparison to the Rome of the ancient Caesars, once the largest city in the ancient world boasting a population of one million, they ruled over a shadow city that only gradually came to have a population of 50,000 by 1500 and a shadow state whose largest cities like Bologna claimed almost complete autonomy from Rome.

Still, just as early Renaissance authors like Petrarch sought to revive and imitate the ancient Latin eloquence of Cicero and Virgil, so too did the new popes and emperors of fifteenth- and sixteenth-century Europe begin to aspire to the real political, military, economic, and cultural might of the ancient empire. Indeed, they sought to exorcise the old ghosts of imperial Rome by becoming rulers of empires and imperial cities that both imitated and surpassed their ancient predecessors.

– *Thomas James Dandelet* –

RENAISSANCE ROME AS NEW IMPERIAL CITY

Not surprisingly, the dream of imperial revival first took root in Renaissance Rome where humanists, artists, and a number of popes began to cultivate the memory and knowledge of ancient Roman grandeur. Renaissance popes of the fifteenth century, particularly Eugenius IV, Pius II, Nicholas V, Sixtus IV, Paul II, and Alexander VI, nurtured humanists who revived ancient Roman learning and classical Latin. Some of these humanists, like Flavio Biondo in his treatise *Roma triumphans*, promoted the idea that Rome was destined from its earliest pagan beginnings to be the sacred center of the world. By reconstructing the geography and rituals of imperial Rome, Biondo and others intentionally sought to hasten the day when Rome would once again be pre-eminent. For most of these fifteenth-century humanists and popes, there was a self-conscious desire to be agents and witnesses of the greatness of ancient Rome reborn.

The new learning of the Roman humanists was given institutional focus in the new Roman Academy established by Pomponio Leto, Bartolomeo dei Sacchi, and others in the mid-fifteenth century and formally sanctioned by Sixtus IV in 1478. Its members, often making their living as secretaries in the papal *Curia*, wrote eloquent Latin poetry and letters, issued new editions of classical texts, and produced ancient Greek and Latin plays that were performed on the new impromptu stages of Rome.

Largely a literary movement and ideal in the early decades after Martin V's return to Rome, by the late fifteenth century and the early sixteenth, there were concrete, or rather marble, signs of a program of urban renewal in Rome that had distinctive imperial dimensions. Paul II had built the classically inspired palace of San Marco in the late 1460s, and the new papal chancellery building, erected in the mid-1480s just a short distance down the road from St Peter's Basilica, was a spectacular new building of imperial dimensions and beauty.

On a smaller scale, but of purer classical form, the Tempietto next to the church of San Pietro in Montorio, designed by the architect Bramante, *c*. 1500, was a classical domed chapel that marked one of the spots where St Peter was thought to have been martyred. For Renaissance Rome, the Tempietto's singular beauty and elegance of form also marked the revival of ancient Roman architectural splendor. Indeed, it foreshadowed the greatest of all Roman Renaissance building projects, namely the building of new St Peter's Basilica, begun in 1506 with Bramante as its chief architect.

The Tempietto also points to another rising imperial presence in Rome; namely, the Spanish monarchy. It was King Ferdinand of Aragon who paid for the Tempietto, as well as for the restoration of the church of San Pietro in Montorio next door. King of Naples and Sicily by 1504, Ferdinand was the new imperial power in Italy at the beginning of the sixteenth century. He was praised by Machiavelli as one of the new monarchs of Europe, and his rule would lay the foundations for the eventual Spanish imperial domination of Rome and most of Italy. His patronage of the Tempietto, moreover, prefigured later Spanish patronage of Bramante's largest Roman project – namely, the new St Peters.

Ferdinand's rule coincided with the pontificate of the Spanish pope, Alexander VI. His family, the Borgia, had its own raw imperial ambitions, perhaps most dramatically embodied in their own Caesar, Cesare Borgia, the pope's son and military general. Cesare's successful mission of subjugating independent-minded princes and towns in the Papal States was carried out with the military skill and brutality that won him Machiavelli's praise. The victories were celebrated with triumphs modeled after those of ancient Rome, and the celebrations of 1500 included images that recollected the victories of Julius Caesar.

This claiming of the mantle and memory of Caesar, with its accompanying dream of reviving ancient Roman power and grandeur, reached new heights with the pope whose choice of papal names came with clear imperial associations in mind. Julius II (1504–13) expanded the territories of the Papal States through military conquests that surpassed even those of Cesare Borgia. His pontificate embodied the full-blown secular ambitions of the Renaissance papacy, and he was the first pope overtly to compare himself and Rome with the ancient emperors and city.

Unabashedly drawing on the rituals and iconography of ancient Rome, Julius II presented himself to the world as a new Julius Caesar, especially after his famous conquest of Bologna in 1506. Returning to Rome as the conqueror in 1507, Julius made a carefully choreographed triumphal entry into the city following the ancient triumphal procession routes. Ephemeral triumphal arches were erected in his honor, and many other decorative trimmings of an ancient triumph were added to emphasize the parallels with ancient Roman victories. If there was any doubt left about the meaning of the event or the character of Julius II, the pope had a commemorative medal struck that was inscribed on one side with the name Julius Caesar Pont[ifex].[3]

Just as Julius II sought to fashion himself a new Caesar, he also wanted to continue and hasten the refashioning of Rome as an imperial capital. To this end he instituted an artistic program in the Vatican palace that evoked ancient imperial grandeur. Raphael of Urbino decorated the pope's apartment with frescoes such as the "School of Athens," and his workshop decorated other major reception rooms in the palace with historical paintings that celebrated the first Christian emperor, Constantine. At the same time, Michelangelo was at work on the Sistine Chapel decoration and a monumental sculptural ensemble that was meant for the tomb of Julius II in the center of the new St Peter's.

Michelangelo also acted as the primary architect who shaped the most important Christian temple in the new Rome, St Peter's Basilica. Appointed as the chief architect of St Peter's in 1546, and serving in that role until his death in 1564, Michelangelo expanded upon Bramante's original design begun under Julius II in 1506. The result was the largest church in Christendom, topped by a monumental dome that surpassed even that of the ancient Pantheon in size and grandeur.

Other building projects of an imperial scale were begun by earlier popes and architects, but transformed by Michelangelo into truly imperial spaces, including the Capitoline Hill. The ancient political center of republican and imperial Rome, the Capitoline by 1550 was in multiple senses a place to commemorate and celebrate the greatness of ancient and contemporary Rome alike. Various popes had given important pieces of ancient Roman sculpture to the Palazzo dei Conservatori that flanked one side of the piazza. Paul III (1534–49), moreover, had the ancient bronze equestrian statue of Marcus Aurelius moved to the Capitoline, where it was placed in the center of the piazza, directly in front of the Palazzo del Senatore. It put a definitive imperial stamp on the Capitoline, as did the renovated façades that Michelangelo designed for both the Palazzo dei Conservatori and the Palazzo Nuovo that was built directly across from it. Using the colossal order that dominated monumental imperial architecture, Michelangelo made of the Capitoline Hill one of the most dramatic imperial spaces of the Renaissance.

Although the Capitoline restoration and the new St Peter's embodied in their magnificence, size, and classical style the imperial ambitions of the Renaissance papacy, they also revealed the papacy's limitations as a pretender to imperial status and its ultimate dependence on its main rival for that role – namely, the Holy Roman Emperor, Charles V (1500–57). More specifically, it was Charles V and his Spanish successors who played the roles of primary financial patrons of St Peter's and other major building projects when the popes after Julius II discovered that they simply did not have the money to finish many of the projects of such imperial dimensions.

Indeed, it was Charles V and later kings of Spain and rulers of the Spanish Empire who became the chief military protectors and foreign financial benefactors of Rome in the sixteenth and seventeenth centuries. Many building projects and the general economic and population boom in Rome from roughly 1535 to 1650 were products of this patronage. Contributions from Spanish imperial lands, for example, provided two-thirds of the funds for new St Peter's. In this sense, Rome was very much a synthesis of papal and Spanish imperial ambitions, a fusion of ancient Roman imperial form with contemporary Spanish imperial financial and military protection. This phase of the Roman Renaissance, moreover – the Spanish imperial phase – lasted well into the seventeenth century, well beyond the conventional chronology used to describe Renaissance Rome.

IMPERIAL CROSSROADS

While Renaissance popes clearly reached for ancient imperial greatness primarily in their roles as sovereign princes of the Papal States and Rome, their actual political and economic power fell far short of imperial Roman dimensions. This had been true of every secular and ecclesiastical prince in western Europe since the fourth century. But this was to change dramatically with the appearance of the central political figure of the high Renaissance, the Holy Roman Emperor Charles V.

The grandson and heir of King Ferdinand of Spain and the Holy Roman Emperor Maximilian, Charles inherited from them the largest collection of kingdoms and territories that any European monarch had ruled over since the time of Charlemagne. More specifically, the premature death of his father Philip the Fair in 1506, and the madness of his mother, Juana, daughter of Ferdinand and Isabella of Spain, left Charles, at the tender age of 17, ruler over the following territories: Castile and its New World possessions, Aragon, Navarre, Naples, Sicily, Sardinia, part of Burgundy, the Netherlands, and the Habsburg lands in Germany. To these he would add the duchy of Milan, the former Aztec Empire in Mexico, and the former Inca Empire in Peru in the course of his lifetime (Figure 15.1).

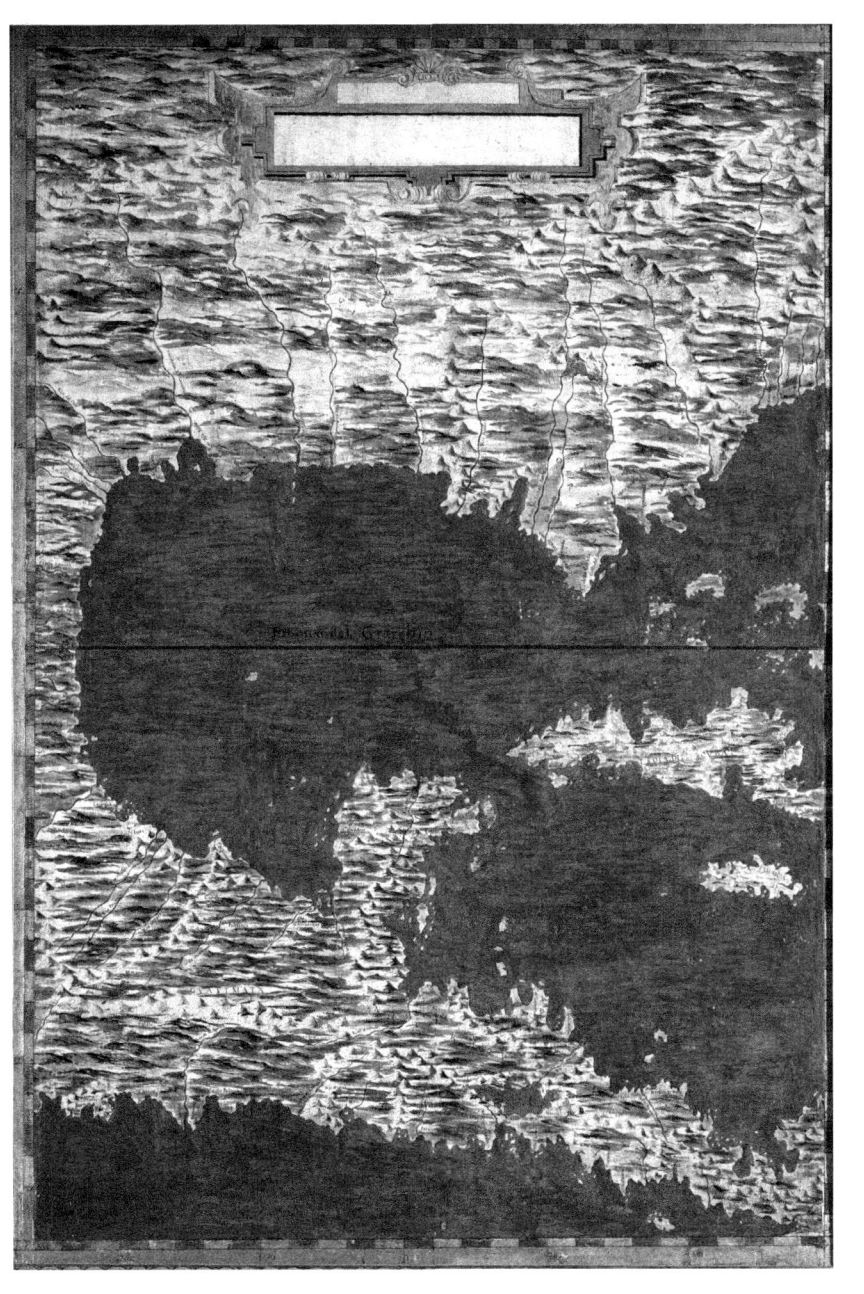

Figure 15.1 Egnazio Danti (1536–86). Map of Mexico and Central America, from the Sala dell Carte Geografiche (Hall of Geographical Maps) c. 1570 (oil on panel). © Palazzo Vecchio (Palazzo della Signoria) Florence, Italy/The Bridgeman Art Library.

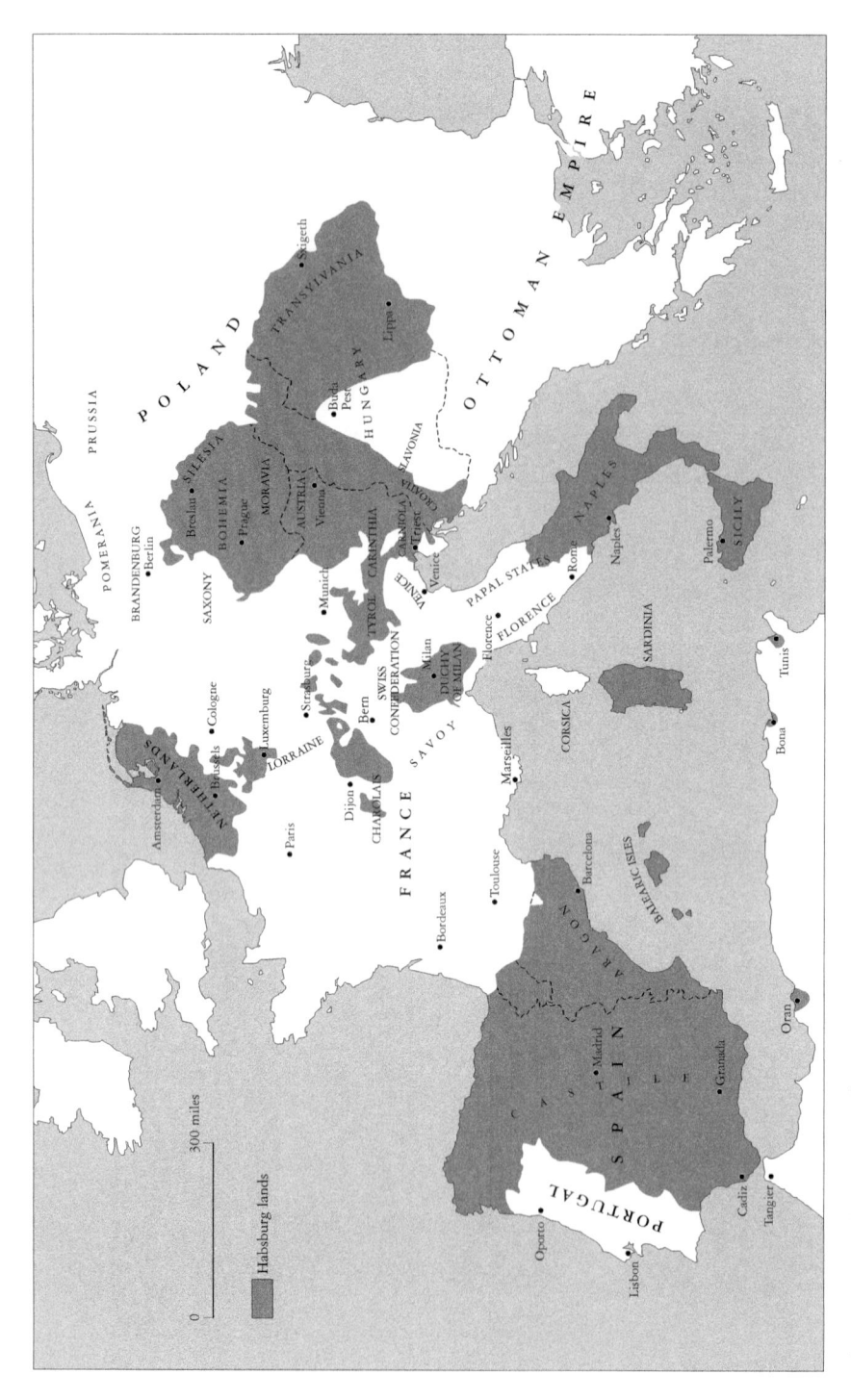

Figure 15.2 The Empire of Charles V, showing only European possessions and not including the Empire's American possessions.

The enormity of this collection of territories made it the object of much political reflection, not to mention fear, in the first half of the sixteenth century. Comparisons with ancient Rome and the ancient Caesars were inevitable: the Florentine diplomat and historian Francesco Guicciardini, for example, noted in his *Political Discourses* that Charles V was "not only in name and title Caesar, but (also in) theory, authority, and power similar to the ancient Caesars." Moreover, Guicciardini went on to note that "the laws state that he is ruler (*signore*) of all the world; he has the example of the ancient Caesars."[4]

As a global emperor and "ruler of all the world," Charles V represented a central crossroads in the history of European empire. Like the two-faced God of Roman antiquity, Janus, his empire had one face looking back toward the Middle Ages and antiquity, and another looking forward into the future of modern European global empires. More concretely, the possessions of Charles V represented a new hybrid empire that was actually the fusion of three empires: two old empires that were rooted in medieval Europe and one new empire taking shape in the New World.

The first of the old empires, the Holy Roman Empire, was ironically the weakest link in this Renaissance political hybrid. While it gave Charles the title of emperor and a collection of central European lands known as "the Empire," the political reality was that Charles had the least amount of real power in the German lands, and they functioned least like an empire. The fact that his title came through an election presided over by seven electors, six from German lands and one from Bohemia, underlined his dependence on them. Moreover, many of the German princes, like Frederick of Saxony, revolted against his authority by supporting Martin Luther and his Reformation after 1517, thereby revealing the limits of imperial power in central Europe. Charles expended a vast amount of money and men trying to impose his rule on the German territories, but with little success. Indeed, the German lands represented the most bitter and costly political failure for Charles V. They also revealed the illusory nature of the Holy Roman Empire.

Fortunately for Charles V, the other medieval empire in his inheritance, the Mediterranean empire of the kingdom of Aragon, proved more reliable and resilient. This was a quintessential medieval Mediterranean empire, although it never claimed any imperial title or status. Still, it shared the features of other medieval merchant empires like Venice and Genoa, which were described by sixteenth-century political writers such as Giovanni Botero as "middle-sized" empires that owed their success to the fact that they were neither too large nor two small.

In the case of Aragon, its Mediterranean possessions – which included the islands of Sicily (1409), Sardinia, the Aeolian islands, and after 1504, the Kingdom of Naples – brought it considerable agricultural wealth; strategically important port cities like Palermo, Messina, and Naples; and the military and maritime talents of Italian soldiers and sailors. The Italian states also provided a much closer link to ancient Rome and the ancient monuments and memories of the empire. For their part, the kings of Aragon fashioned themselves as the protectors of southern Italy in the face of the constant threat posed to Italian coastal towns and cities by Barbary pirates and the Ottoman Empire.

This was a role that Charles V embraced enthusiastically and with some success. In 1535, for example, he led a naval force against one of the most feared and hated foes of the Italians, the corsair admiral Chaireddin Barbarossa. Barbarossa rose to Mediterranean prominence at roughly the same time that Charles V came into his inheritance. From his fortress city in North Africa, Tunis, his fleet was perpetually attacking merchant and military ships and sacking the coastal cities of Italy and the eastern coast of Iberia. In 1535, this spurred Charles V to sail against Tunis, where his forces scored a decisive victory that drove the nemesis out of the city and left the fortress in imperial hands.

Although the victory in Tunis was short-lived, the long-term importance of the Barbary and, more particularly, Ottoman naval threat in the Mediterranean was that it provided one of the major spurs to the development of the naval capabilities and strength of the Spanish Empire. More generally, the rise of the Ottoman Empire in the East has to be seen as one of the central forces that encouraged the growth of Renaissance empires. It provided a level of imperial competition in the Mediterranean that shaped not only the Spanish Empire but also the old Venetian maritime empire and the Holy Roman Empire on its eastern front.

Victories against this expanding and perpetual nemesis were highly prized, and the taking of Tunis in 1535 thus provided the emperor with rich symbolic booty since it begged comparisons with the African victories of the ancient Caesar. This became evident in the triumphal processions that Charles V, shortly after returning from Africa, made through Italy, where he was greeted by crowds from Messina to Genoa. The leading men of those cities were well-versed in the humanistic treatises and new editions of ancient Roman history that described ancient triumphs, and they subsequently decorated their streets with triumphal arches reminiscent of the victory parades of antiquity that celebrated their new Caesar (Figure 15.3).

The emperor and his courtiers, too, were quick to make use of the symbols, rhetoric, and images of the ancient empire and emperors to bolster the image and agenda of this new Caesar. In fact, they went further to claim that with his New World possessions, Charles had even surpassed the Caesars of old. Accordingly, the insignia of Charles carried the image of the gates of Hercules representing Gibraltar, and the motto *Plus Ultra* referring to the fact that his empire stretched beyond the traditional boundaries of the ancient Roman Empire.

While the Italian and Mediterranean kingdoms of Aragon provided Charles V with what he himself described in a political will and instruction to his son as the key to all of his strength, it was the Castilian part of his inheritance that constituted the wealthiest and fastest-growing part of his empire between 1520 and 1550. With empires being defined in their basic form as sovereign states that have conquered and submitted to their own rule a number of other previously sovereign states, the empire of Charles V truly became the first indisputably modern global empire when his Castilian subjects, Cortés and Pizarro, conquered the Aztec and Inca empires in 1520 and 1535 respectively.

These were certainly the most distinctive and dramatic acquisitions of the hybrid empire. The American possessions, including the Caribbean islands taken earlier by Columbus in the name of the Spanish monarchs Isabella and Ferdinand, represented the first expansion beyond Europe into realms where the Spaniards imposed, through extensive colonization, their distinct law, language, religion, economic system, government, military authority, agricultural organization, and social organization.

Figure 15.3 Andrea Mantegna. *Triumph of Caesar, IX*. Julius Caesar on his triumphal chariot. Hampton Court Palace, London. Alinari/Art Resource NY.

At the same time, through military occupation and coercion, the Castilian subjects of Charles V extracted increasing amounts of natural resources and raw products from the Americas. Gold, silver, cocoa, tobacco, and sugar all flowed back to Spain in increasing quantities throughout the sixteenth and seventeenth centuries.

It was this New World empire, moreover, that spurred the greatest amount of reflection and comparison with ancient Rome. Chroniclers of the conquest such as Bernal Díaz made frequent reference to ancient Rome, and the conquistador of Mexico, Hernán Cortés, who saw himself as even greater than Caesar, clearly viewed himself and his men in an ancient imperial mirror. This is not to say that these "Romans in a New World" did not make distinctions between themselves and ancient Rome. On the contrary, they frequently used the Romans as a point of contrast to underline their own superiority; but Rome remained their main point of historical reference.[5]

This was also true of Spanish humanists who never traveled to the New World, but whose influence as authors of new humanist histories of Spain was widespread.

More specifically, the royal historians Florian de Ocampo and Ambrosio Morales, who served as courtiers to Charles V and Philip II respectively, wrote a new four-volume *History of Spain* that provided an extensive analysis of the Roman period of Spanish history.

As disciples of the Italian-trained humanist Antonio Nebrija, both Ocampo and Morales were central examples of the close connection between the Italian and Spanish Renaissance. Still, their history was very much a Spanish imperial history since they went to great lengths to claim even the ancient Roman past for Spain and to emphasize the importance of ancient Spaniards, such as the Roman emperors Hadrian and Trajan, in the successes of the ancient empire. In short, the history of Ocampo and Morales created a Spanish myth of ancient Rome that presented the Spaniards as the natural heirs and legitimate successors to the ancient Roman Empire.

LIVY, TACITUS, AND SUETONIUS IN THE RENAISSANCE

At the same time, these historians and other Spanish humanists were very dependent on ancient Roman histories of the empire for their own work. Interest in the history of ancient Rome throughout Renaissance Europe was naturally accompanied by a revival of interest in the ancient historians of the empire. More specifically, Renaissance humanists in the later fifteenth century began to publish new editions of Livy (1469), Tacitus (1470), and Suetonius (1470). Like the works of Caesar mentioned earlier, the histories were popular throughout Europe and new editions appeared repeatedly throughout the late fifteenth, sixteenth, and early seventeenth centuries.

Various parts and new editions of Livy's history, *The Decades*, went to press in Venice at least 12 times between 1502 and 1581, for example, while three earlier editions had appeared in Rome between 1469 and 1477. Other editions would be printed in Florence, Paris, Cologne, Strasbourg, and Basle, all in the sixteenth century. Similarly expansive and international publishing histories were also true of the *History* of Tacitus and the *Lives of the Twelve Caesars* by Suetonius.

All of these historians were products of the Roman Empire, and their histories, even when they focused primarily on the republican period, as Livy's did, nonetheless reflected an imperial view of the Roman past. Empire in these texts was generally treated as the natural evolution of the expansion of the Republic. And the authors all shared a pedagogical or moral purpose that ultimately aimed to point out both the qualities and failings of the central groups and individuals that occupied the ancient Roman stage.

For humanists inhabiting the new empires of the Renaissance, the ancient histories were particularly compelling as mirrors and guides. The first translation of Livy into Spanish appeared in 1552 in the imperial city of Strasbourg. It was the work of a German subject of Charles V, Arnaldo Birckman, a humanist book dealer from Cologne. Birckman dedicated the book to Philip II, noting in the introduction that the prince could find in Livy many important lessons for obtaining the great prudence necessary to govern his state and properly lead his military forces.

This pedagogical theme was expanded upon much further in the first Spanish translation of the *History* of Tacitus, published in 1614 in Madrid. Dedicated to the duke of Lerma, the principal adviser of Philip III, this text also provided lengthy annotations in the margins of the text that explicitly pointed out the political lessons of various episodes from Rome's imperial past. Moreover, the lengthy ten-page dedication of the translator, Baltasar Alamos de Barrientos, underlined the usefulness and, indeed, essential nature of ancient Roman history for both the practice and theory of the contemporary imperial state.

THE SPANISH AND PORTUGUESE EMPIRES

The vast territories that comprised the Spanish Empire after the death of Charles V provided an obvious explanation for the intense interest in Roman imperial history and imagery in Renaissance Spain. When Charles V died in 1557, the old emperor left to his son Philip II the largest empire that any Europe monarch had ever ruled over: the Iberian kingdoms of Castile, Aragon and Navarre; the Italian kingdoms of Naples and Sicily; the duchy of Milan; and the island of Sardinia; in the New World the kingdoms of Peru and Mexico, along with the Caribbean islands originally occupied by Columbus; and in northern Europe the Netherlands and part of Burgundy. To these Philip II would add the Philippine Islands and all of the Portuguese Empire after 1580. With the addition of the Asian territories, Philip II became the ruler of the largest global empire the world had ever known. However, Charles V did not leave his son the German lands and the title of Holy Roman Emperor, both of which were obtained by Charles V's brother, Ferdinand.

This decision on the part of Charles V left Europe in the middle of the sixteenth century with three primary empires: the old Holy Roman Empire, the new Spanish Empire, and the other new Iberian power that had also emerged in the late fifteenth century and the early sixteenth – namely, the Portuguese Empire.

For Philip II, the most powerful monarch of the later half of the sixteenth century, the loss of the title of emperor was clearly unwelcome. Indeed, his own imperial self-conception led him to lobby the papacy for the new title of emperor of the Indies. Although the papacy turned down this request, perhaps fearing a further expansion of Philip II's ambitions, it could not resist the much more important and dramatic expansion of the Spanish monarch's power; namely, his acquisition of the Portuguese Empire in 1580. The event that precipitated this development was the death of King Sebastian, the last male heir to that throne, who was killed during an ill-fated battle in North Africa in 1578.

The Portuguese Empire was the other major European power that was growing into a global empire in the late fifteenth century and the early sixteenth. A number of Atlantic islands – the Azores and Madeira especially – had been conquered and colonized in the early fifteenth century. Using African slaves bought at Portuguese trading forts on the West African coast, Madeira produced large amounts of sugar, and provided a colonial laboratory for later American plantation practices.

American territories were added to the Portuguese Empire in 1500 when the explorer Pedro Alvares Cabral claimed Brazil for the Portuguese crown. Lacking the large bullion deposits that the Spanish were quick to discover in Mexico and Peru, Brazil was nonetheless rich in natural resources, and by the later sixteenth century the Portuguese were extracting large amounts of wood and sugar from the New World.

Yet another source of imperial wealth for the Portuguese came from new Indian Ocean possessions taken in the decades after 1488, the year the Portuguese explorer Bartolomeu Días had rounded the Cape of Good Hope. Later voyages by Vasco de Gama in 1498, Cabral in 1501, and Antonio de Abreu in 1511 led to the eventual establishment of trading fortresses/factories in Cochin, Goa, Calicut, Ormuz, Madagascar, Ceylon, Macau, and the Moluccas. Outposts in these territories allowed the Portuguese to dominate the lucrative spice trade with Europe. Combined with the sugar plantations established in Brazil in the sixteenth century, the spice trade brought Portugal enormous new wealth and made Lisbon a truly imperial capital.

Thus, when Philip II of Spain claimed the Portuguese throne for himself in 1580, based upon the fact that his mother was a Portuguese princess, he merged yet another vast empire with his own. The lands and economies that he brought together constituted the first truly global modern empire, which represented the pinnacle of Renaissance empire building.

IMPERIAL INSTITUTIONS

While humanist political theory provided important intellectual backing for the imperial Spanish monarchy, the concrete tools of imperial control included armies and navies of a size that dwarfed most medieval precedents and that began to equal or surpass those of ancient Rome. The Spanish Empire in the century between roughly 1550 and 1650 built up a naval presence of some 100 ships in the western Mediterranean and another 100 in the Atlantic and Pacific. In special campaigns such as the famous battles of Lepanto (1571) or the English Armada (1588), the Spanish navies counted over 200 ships manned by over 25,000 sailors and soldiers. On land, Spanish armies could number over 100,000 men, and the logistical capabilities and weapons technology, especially of cannon and guns, grew increasingly sophisticated over the course of the sixteenth century.

The expanded military forces clearly required financing on a scale that was unprecedented in the medieval period. And it was largely money from the gold and silver mines of Mexico and Peru that provided the funds for the Spanish imperial military. In the century after the discovery of the mines at Potosí in Peru (1545) and Zacatecas in Mexico (1548), the Spanish monarchy received growing revenues from the New World mines that largely underwrote the imperial military expansion.

The far-flung territories of the Spanish Empire were held together by a number of institutions that had roots in medieval Europe, but that were transformed by the Spanish Empire to serve early modern imperial needs. First among these was the monarchy itself. The kings of Spain in the sixteenth and seventeenth centuries increasingly fashioned themselves through ceremony, art, and architecture as imperial figures who ruled over a global empire. A visitor to the new Retiro Palace of Philip IV of Spain, for example, could visit the Hall of Realms that displayed painted maps of all of the monarch's global possessions. Like the Retiro Palace, earlier precedents – including the Renaissance palace of Charles V in Granada and the monumental palace of the El Escorial of Philip II outside of Madrid – embodied and projected an imperial image of the monarch that contrasted quite strongly with those of the itinerant monarchs of the Middle Ages.

The Spanish monarchy forged the model for the imperial monarchy in the sixteenth and seventeenth centuries. While ruling over a collection of territories with differing legal traditions, privileges, and institutions, the Spanish kings imposed their will on all of their territories through the overarching institutions of monarchy, Church, and military. Because the monarchy served as the central power broker that controlled most of the lucrative military, ecclesiastical, and judicial appointments in all of its territories, it became the dominant unifying institution in these territories.

This authority was extended to distant territories by the following royal institutions: royal governors (viceroys), royal courts (*audiencias*), and various ecclesiastical organizations including bishops appointed by the king, religious orders such as the Jesuits, Franciscans, and Dominicans that answered to the monarchs; and the Inquisition, whose head was appointed by and answered to the monarchy. Viceroys and inquisitions existed in the kingdoms of Mexico, Peru, Sicily, and Aragon, while royal governors ruled in the king's stead in the Netherlands and Milan.

This did not mean that Spanish imperial lands were uniform in their institutions, laws, or religious culture. Just as the Roman Empire was characterized by a variety of local traditions, so too was the Spanish Empire. But at the same time, the Spanish Empire in the sixteenth century, like ancient Rome at its height, was extremely confident in the superiority of its own civilizing mission. A few important internal critics like Bartolomé de las Casas notwithstanding, the Spanish monarchy clearly sought to impose its language, law, religion, and culture on its subject peoples to the greatest extent possible, and they were quick to use their superior arms to enforce their will.

This imperial hubris, especially in the Americas, led to the exploitation of human labor and the extraction of natural resources on a scale that was unprecedented in medieval Europe. Moreover, the introduction of African slave labor, first in Brazil and then in the Caribbean primarily to work the sugar plantations, revived slavery as a critical part of imperial agricultural economy on a level that had not been seen in the West since the Roman Empire. Slavery, colonization, the exploitation of native labor, and the plundering of the natural resources of the Americas: these were clearly the dark side of the Renaissance of empire.

It was in the Americas, in particular, that Spanish imperialism proved itself opportunistic, improvisational, and syncretic. While using the traditional institutions of Church and state that were so effective in bolstering and advancing monarchical rule in Iberia, the Spanish monarchs and their agents were also quick to incorporate and co-opt native elites through the distribution of favors and rewards when possible. In the realm of religion, too, the friars were quick to point out the similarities between native religious belief and practice and that of various Native American peoples, and to incorporate American myth, ritual, and imagery into the new religion of empire: Roman Catholicism.

Even in Italy, the historical center of imperial memories and models that inspired the Spanish Empire, the kings of Spain sought successfully to draw the Italian ruling class to itself. Using its considerable power of patronage, the monarchy brought the great majority of Italy's leading families into the Spanish imperial orbit. Families like the Doria and Spinola in Genoa; the Medici dukes in Florence; the Colonna, Orsini, Borghese, and Farnese in Rome; the Caracciolo in Naples; the Gonzaga and Este of Ferrara; and the Montefeltro of Urbino, all developed strong ties to the Spanish court. Some, like the Doria and Colonna, sent their sons to study in Salamanca and Alcalá, while others, like the Gonzaga, sought to have the Spanish monarchs stand as godfathers to their children. Many adopted Spanish customs in dress, spoke Castilian, and were thought of as being Hispanicized.

Through the many titles, commissions, and favors that the Spanish monarchs bestowed on these families, the Spanish Empire also came to dominate many of the Italian states that were not formally part of the empire. The duchies of Savoy, Urbino, Ferrara, and Florence, together with the Papal States, and the Republic of Genoa, were overwhelmingly attached to the Spanish Empire as client states. They represented the informal empire of the Spanish, and it was this very intentional practice of beneficent informal imperialism that furthered Spanish imperial designs throughout their far-flung territories.

CONSTANTINE AND THE RENAISSANCE OF CHRISTIAN EMPIRE

The key to the imperial confidence or hubris of the Spanish monarchy lies not in their claiming the mantle of any of the ancient Roman emperors mentioned thus far. For no Caesar of the first, second, or third century could provide the Spanish monarchs with the moral imperative or historical model that they sought as leaders of the *Republica Christiana*. That role fell to Constantine, the first Christian Roman emperor (272–337).

Just as the memories and texts related to the pagan Caesars were being revived in Renaissance Europe, so too were memories and monuments of Constantine. New Latin editions of the *Life of Constantine* and the *History of the Church* by Eusebius, Constantine's first Christian biographer and the fourth-century bishop of Caesarea, were published in 1547 and 1553. For the Renaissance of empire, no Roman emperor was more important as a model of imperial behavior than the first great patron and protector of Christian Rome, who had given the Roman Church enormous amounts of property, built numerous important basilicas, and even given the papacy the imperial Lateran palace. Most famous among his many gifts was the Basilica of St Peter's that still stood at the beginning of the sixteenth century.

Ironically, it was the decision of Julius II to tear down Constantine's basilica to build a new church that revealed the papacy's need for a new Constantine. With the Protestant Reformation removing English and much German patronage from Rome, and the French monarchy refusing to send aid, it fell to the new Caesar, Charles V, and to his successors, the Spanish monarchs, to fill the role of the new Constantine as patrons and protectors not just of Rome but of the Roman Catholic world more broadly.

This was a historical parallel that was overtly proposed in the *Ecclesiastical History* of Cesare Baronio. Writing in 1593, Baronio dedicated volume III of his 12-volume history to Philip II. It is a 684-page volume devoted exclusively to the history of Constantine, and in the four-page dedication, the author makes clear parallels between the role of Constantine as great protector and propagator of the Church and the similar contemporary role of Philip II. Baronius presented the work with the suggestion that Constantine provided a good example for Christian monarchs of his own day. In fact, Baronius was making a point that Pope Gregory XIV had stated more clearly two years earlier when he noted in a letter to Philip II of Spain that as "almost a new Constantine" the Spanish king had a particular duty to maintain and defend the authority of the pope and the city of Rome.

A political entity of such vast and unprecedented proportions as the Spanish Empire inevitably invited such historical imperial comparisons. At the same time, it inspired a growing body of political analysis and a guiding political rational, much of it in the guise of political theology. Of the numerous political theorists who arose in the Spanish Empire and contributed to this growing body of imperial political theory, none was more important than the Jesuit Francisco Suarez. The greatest of Spanish political writers in the late sixteenth and early seventeenth centuries, his influence and importance as an intellectual architect of Spanish imperial authority in the reign of Philip II was well known.

In works like his *Defense of the Faith*, more specifically, Suarez wrote against the perceived theological errors of Henry VIII and the Anglican Church. The four-volume text draws on an extensive knowledge of patristic sources to support the papacy's claim to have authority over all secular powers in matters of Church doctrine, law, and episcopal appointments. He is especially fond of the example of Constantine to support his argument against what he sees as the error of the Protestants concerning the subjection of the secular to the spiritual and of monarchs to the pope. He notes: "It is known in the history of Constantine that he said that he attended the council to be judged by the bishops, not to judge them." Writing more specifically about the pope he notes that many kings and emperors "often professed and recognized the chair of Peter in the Roman Pontiff and his universal jurisdiction over all the Church, as shown by Constantine."[6]

The importance of men like Suarez for Spanish empire building was clearly understood by monarchs like Philip II, who recalled the Jesuit from Rome to become the head of the theology department at the leading university in Portugal, Coimbra, shortly after the Spanish annexation of that kingdom.

The Constantinian Renaissance, promoted primarily by the close relationship between the Spanish Empire and the papacy, had strong resonance in other parts of Europe as well. By the late sixteenth century, other pretenders to the title of new Constantine had emerged, and the following decades witnessed a succession of battles for imperial domination among European monarchs. In their turn, the British, Dutch, and French would all try their hand at being the new Romans and the new Caesars and Constantines in the New World and Old World alike. Thus the Renaissance of empire went on, perpetuating imperial institutions, ideologies, economies, and material culture for centuries to come.

NOTES

1. Francesco Petrarca, *Le Vite degli Uomini Illustri*, vols. 1 and 2, trans. Donato degli Albanzani da Pratovecchio, ed. Luigi Razzolini (Bologna: Romagnoli, 1874).
2. Andrea Palladio, *I Commentari di C. Giulio Cesare* (Venice: Pietro de Franceschi, 1575).
3. Charles Stinger, *The Renaissance in Rome* (Bloomington: Indiana University Press, 1998), p. 236.
4. Francesco Guicciardini, *Discorsi Politici, in Opere Inedite di Francesco Guicciardini*, eds Piero and Luigi Guicciardini (Florence: Barbara, Bianchi e comp., 1857), pp. 384–8.
5. David Lupher, *Romans in a New World* (Ann Arbor: University of Michigan Press, 2003).
6. Francisco Suarez, *Defensa de la Fe Catolica y Apostolica Contra los Errores del Anglicanismo* (Madrid: Instituto de Estudios Politicos, 1970), pp. 322–3.

SUGGESTIONS FOR FURTHER READING

Primary sources

Guicciardini, Francesco. *Discorsi Politici, in Opere Inedite di Francesco Guicciardini*, eds Piero and Luigi Guicciardini. Florence: Barbara, Bianchi e comp., 1857.

Petrarca, Francesco. *Le Vite degli Uomini Illustri*, vols. 1 and 2, trans. Donato degli Albanzani da Pratovecchio, ed. Luigi Razzolini. Bologna: Romagnoli, 1874.

Suarez, Francisco. *Defensa de la Fe Catolica y Apostolica Contra los Errores del Anglicanismo*. Madrid: Instituto de Estudios Politicos, 1970.

Secondary sources

Abernethy, David B. *The Dynamics of Global Dominance: European Overseas Empires, 1415–1980*. New Haven and London: Yale University Press, 2000.

Blockmans, Wim and Nicolette Mout, eds. *The World of Emperor Charles V*. Amsterdam: Royal Netherlands Academy of Arts and Sciences, 2004.

Boxer, Charles. *Portuguese Conquest and Commerce in Southern Asia, 1500–1750*. London: Variorum Reprints, 1985.

Dandelet, Thomas. *Spanish Rome*. New Haven and London: Yale University Press, 2001.

Dandelet, Thomas and John Marino, eds. *Spain in Italy, 1500–1700*. Leiden: Brill, 2006.

Elliott, John. *Spain and Its World*. New Haven and London: Yale University Press, 1989.

Kagan, Richard. *Spain, Europe, and the Atlantic World*. Cambridge: Cambridge University Press, 1995.

Kamen, Henry. *Empire, How Spain Became a World Power, 1492–1763*. New York: HarperCollins, 2003.

Lotti, L. and R. Villari, eds. *Filippo II e il Mediterraneo*. Rome: Laterza, 2003.

Lupher, David. *Romans in a New World*. Ann Arbor: University of Michigan Press, 2003.

Pagden, Anthony. *Spanish Imperialism and the Political Imagination*. New Haven and London: Yale University Press, 1990.

—— *"Lords of All the World": Ideologies of Empire in Britain, France, and Spain, 1400–1800*. New Haven and London: Yale University Press, 1995.

—— "Fellow Citizens and Imperial Subjects: Conquest and Sovereignty in Europe's Overseas Empires." *History and Theory* 4, 44 (2005): 28–46.

Pomper, Philip. "The History and Theory of Empire." *History and Theory* 4, 44 (2005): 1–27.

Russel, Peter. *Prince Henry the Navigator*. New Haven and London: Yale University Press, 2000.

Stinger, Charles. *The Renaissance in Rome*. Bloomington: Indiana University Press, 1998.

Temple, Nicholas. "Julius II as Second Caesar," in Maria Wyke, ed., *Julius Caesar in Western Culture*. Oxford: Blackwell Press, 2006, 110–30.

Tracy, James. *Emperor Charles V, Impresario of War*. New York: Cambridge University Press, 2002.

CHAPTER SIXTEEN

RENAISSANCE TRIUMPHALISM IN ART

Randolph Starn

To say that art represents power can mean that art is powerful, that it shows where power lies, or that it serves the powers that be. The relationship between the visual arts and power in all these senses is an old theme in Renaissance studies. Giorgio Vasari, the courtier artist turned art historian, first codified the idea of the Renaissance as a period and a process in his *Lives* of Italian painters, sculptors, and architects (1550, expanded edition 1568). Vasari's story of a "rebirth" of ancient art from 1300 to his own time has a political edge as propaganda for his native land and his patrons, the Medici dukes of Tuscany. Jacob Burckhardt's *Civilization of the Renaissance in Italy* (1860), the charter text of Renaissance studies, opens with chapters on "the state as a work of art." For Burckhardt, the art of statecraft and the political uses of art were driving forces of Italian Renaissance culture.

Recent interpretations of the Renaissance, in a renaissance of their own, have given the old theme a new lease of life. Art historians these days are as likely to be as concerned with functions as with forms. Attention has shifted from style and iconography to the contexts in which art was commissioned, made, and apprehended. As a result, the visual culture of the Renaissance has come to look like a world of image-makers and media managers – in this respect at least like our own world. The implications of the comparison across time are mixed. While it picks up on long-standing convictions about the "modernity" of the Renaissance, it also signals a fall from grace. Art does not transcend mundane interests "for art's sake"; Renaissance artists were not the brave new world's seekers after truth and beauty, let alone cultural freedom fighters. Every age gets the history it deserves, and this skeptical, not to say cynical, view takes out on the past our disenchantment with the flood of images that assails us at every turn. On the positive side, we can see art from this perspective as an active force in the world, not as a mere adornment or luxury, or as an obliging mirror. Renaissance patrons of the arts and the artists they engaged knew this; it was one reason for the greatest boom in western art since classical antiquity.

However we choose to define it, the art/power nexus runs deep in Renaissance culture. Much recent scholarship has concentrated on patronage; that is, on the commissioning and the making of art. Since Renaissance art was mostly made to order, this is a productive line of inquiry. Even so, solid evidence for the patron's "program" is usually hard to come by, and patronage studies tend to veer between being highly speculative and overly deterministic. One way or another, how do we decide where "art" or "power" begins or ends? There is a large scholarly literature on ritual and ceremony as a rich but transient vehicle of both. Building projects and urban planning have been studied for what they can tell us about power, as have, at another extreme of scale, medals, illuminated manuscripts, and portrait miniatures. We obviously need to frame and focus.

I've chosen to single out a particularly pervasive and revealing complex of images and ideas. As known from the textual record and surviving art of classical antiquity, the rituals of triumphal celebration were an archive and a tool kit for Renaissance displays of power. The celebration of the hero, the victory parade, and the amassed trophies of conquest were its basic components, but there were any number of variations. The first post-classical triumphal procession we know of was staged in Italy for the Holy Roman Emperor Frederick II in 1247; a century later Petrarch (1304–74), the scholar-writer who practically invented what came to be called humanism, composed a widely read poem on the triumphs of the virtues, complete with triumphal chariots. In fifteenth-century Italy, classicizing triumphs were represented in print, paint, and sculpture, and by the sixteenth century processions of many sorts – not only those celebrating military and political victories but also those mounted for visiting dignitaries, saints' days, civic festivals, even weddings – were being called "triumphs" all over Europe.

This Renaissance "triumphalism" was more than an antiquarian exercise or a catch-all for flattering superlatives. It had overarching features, functions, and structuring principles. On the model of language we can think of it as the product of a distinctive grammar and vocabulary. In anthropological terms it is a master myth of the sort that seeks to make an unruly world seem coherent; in politics we might call it an ideology of legitimation and control. As much as a repertory of forms, Renaissance triumphalism was a formula for the themes and variations that provide one key, to be sure not the only key, to the representation of power in Renaissance art.[1] Or so I want to suggest in this chapter.

TOTAL TRIUMPH:
THE PAPER PARADES OF EMPEROR MAXIMILIAN I

Let us begin with an early sixteenth-century triumph of triumphalism. Between 1515 and 1523 no fewer than three sets of woodcuts, more than 300 sheets in all, were produced for the Emperor Maximilian I (r. 1493–1519): an *Arch of Honor* dedicated to the real or imagined victories of the emperor and his Habsburg dynasty, a *Triumphal Procession*, and a *Great Triumphal Chariot*.[2] The Italians had studied, described, portrayed, and occasionally re-enacted the ancient Roman triumph since at least the fourteenth century. Maximilian's projects grafted onto Italian precedents the trappings of chivalric festivity in northern Europe – mounted knights in showy armor, mummery, and speechifying, emblazoned shields and pennants. These spectacular hybrids trumpeted the revival of a Holy Roman Empire under the Habsburgs – on paper, where failed military adventures, uprisings, and empty treasuries had no place. The simulated architecture, sculpture, and painting, together with poetry and prose inscriptions, were imperial in their own right: a union of medieval traditions and humanist culture.

The woodcut sets are too large and too elaborate to take in all at once – another imperial touch. However, we can find most of the triumphal repertory in a detail showing the crowning of Emperor Maximilian in the *Great Triumphal Chariot* series. Albrecht Dürer, profoundly influenced by his travels in northern Italy and already in his own time the most famous German artist, designed the eight-sheet series that extends over nine feet. The detail on the facing page shows Maximilian, scepter in hand, orb and sword at his feet, seated on a cushioned throne mounted on a combination triumphal chariot and festival float.

The emperor is about to be crowned by a winged female figure, a Victory Goddess, as her crowned attendants above and below reach out with wreaths of their own; the crown he already wears is a medieval affair, as is the pearl-lined, jewel-studded cape. The canopy over the central scene is part exotic flower and part fabric, supported improbably on an organic-and-metallic stem. This glorified umbrella presents a flaming sun-face with a Latin motto on either side proclaiming that on earth the emperor is like the sun in the heavens; from the canopy's front edge, just beneath a wreathed shield bearing an imperial double eagle and insignia of the knightly Order of the Golden Fleece, hangs a cymbal-shaped holder for a chain attached to a scrolled plaque that reads in Latin "The heart of the king is in the hand of God." Other Latin inscriptions name 12 virtues, from Justice and Temperance at the top to Gravity and Perseverance on the scrolls on the ground; Magnificence and Honor, inscribed on the wheels, are ready to roll. The protruding feathers of the winged Victory crowning the emperor list victories over the French, Hungarians, Swiss, Bohemians, Germans, and Venetians. (In fact, Maximilian was more often than not defeated on the battlefield and owed his greatest successes to marriage alliances.) Emblematic animals snarl and cry out in tribute while doing duty as allegorical stand-ins: three eagles, icons of the empire and Olympian Jupiter, king of the gods; the lion's head as a rearguard and symbol of fortitude; two griffins embossed on the wheel and a dragon creeping along its edge; a bird perched at the curled end of the flowering canopy. A simulated tapestry decorated with pomegranates, symbols of fertility and abundance, hangs along the chariot's side.

If this long description of just one woodcut sheet misses something, as it no doubt does, that is part of the intended effect. More is more in the triumphalist mode. The virtuoso dexterity and the layering on of meaning were clearly meant to inspire awe and wonder, but the woodcuts were also power-brokers and pawns in a political transaction. The free imperial city of Nuremberg had commissioned the *Great Triumphal Chariot* in the first place as a gift to the emperor; Dürer's workshop reproduced the design later in a mural in the city hall. As a bid for and a sign of a relationship of mutual obligation, the imagery put on paper the rituals of medieval entries and ancient triumphs whereby cities leery of force and hoping for peace and a share of the spoils "welcomed" a commander or an overlord. The Nuremberg triumphs sought to bring about the happy outcome that they fictively represented; they were instruments of power as much as laws, taxes, and armies were. No one understood this better than Emperor Maximilian, who had himself staged as chivalric hero and classical triumphator in inverse proportion to his chronic money and

Figure 16.1 Albrecht Dürer. *Great Triumphal Chariot* (1518–22), detail, woodcut (Peter Vischer the Elder).

military troubles. Accolades in art and literature were relatively cheap. So much the better that in its representations at least the triumph never ceases, never fails to overcome resistance and to celebrate perpetual victory.

FROM THE TRIUMPH TO TRIUMPHALISM

The triumphal projects of Emperor Maximilian fall between Italian multimedia experiments and their spread across Europe later in the sixteenth century. Over the long term we have records or representations of dozens of triumphal-style processions with a more or less full complement of appurtenances. Maximilian's grandson Charles V was constantly on the move during his long reign as king of Spain (1516–56) and emperor (1519–56), and more than 50 triumphal entries were held for him. On his return from a minor expedition against the Muslim states of Tunisia (1535–6) one Italian city after another received him as *triumphator*, New Charlemagne, Crusader King, and Herald of Peace and a New Golden Age. Together with the festivities for his formal coronation as emperor (1529–30), this triumphal progress up the Italian peninsula raised the stakes in a competition to turn out the most perfect triumph according to increasingly codified formulas. The chief competitors with the Habsburgs in this ritual potlatch were the popes, the Medici grand dukes of Florence, and the kings of France.

By mid-sixteenth century, then, the triumph was a complete media package that could be produced on demand. However, it was also a tool kit stocked with motifs that could be adapted to fit virtually any representation of victorious achievement, real or imagined. The heterogeneous ensemble of assumptions, formal patterns, and objectives constituted a triumphalist code going beyond and beneath any particular instance. Three case studies suggest how it can be decoded in a very wide range of materials and forms.

BODIES POLITIC: REINVENTING THE HERO

The triumphant victor-hero does double duty as a protagonist and a star attraction in Renaissance art. Different actors could play the role, not only soldiers and rulers but also gods, demigods, saints, and sinners. Since antiquity, then in the Middle Ages, and again in the Renaissance, what we can understand as a kind of biopolitics literally embodied authority in the leader, the head and members of the state, the corporations of communes, guilds, neighborhoods, and extended families of the collective social body. The powers of kings, princes, and nobles were inherently corporeal as family heads, heirs of real or feigned dynastic ties, soldiers, and incarnations of majesty; so were those of priests as the intermediaries of the divinity and humanity of Christ on earth. In the medieval political theology of the king's "two bodies," the crown and the state were temporarily resident in the mortal body of the ruler that they outlived and transcended. Renaissance images of corporeal authority, particularly the male figure as the primary host, talisman, and exemplar of strategic political and social interests, were all the more insistent because authority was so often called into question, makeshift, and provisional. The genres in western art most intent on representing the politically charged body – the state portrait, the equestrian monument, and narrative history painting – all emerge in their characteristic post-classical forms in the years around 1500.

Raphael's three-quarter-length portrait of Pope Julius II (1503–13), much copied in its own time and much imitated in later papal portraits, is arguably the most influential of official portraits of the Renaissance (Figure 16.2). It is famously an exhibit of Renaissance "individualism" or "naturalism," seemingly an expressive study of an individual caught in a moment of reflection, but it is also a power play centered on the papal office and the person of the pope. Like Raphael in paint, contemporary writers paid close attention to the pope's physical appearance and volcanic character, likely to erupt at any moment. In an anonymous satire (actually written by Erasmus of Rotterdam), St Peter shut the gates of Paradise to the raging warrior pope, who once led a siege in person. Yet the contemporary accounts, like the portrait, envelop the person of the pope in the temporal and spiritual personae of the papacy. He is "like a Caesar, the Julius of his name," and sits in Raphael's portrait on a throne modeled after ancient thrones; he is *divino* and makes "all tremble," as the portrait might well have done. He is not just St Peter's successor but "the greatest champion of Peter's patrimony that ever was"; for "Peter's greater glory" he had initiated the rebuilding of his temple and summoned the greatest artists to Rome.[3] The Julius of the portrait, with traces of the papal coat of arms on the green cloth behind him, wears St Peter's ring (among others) and the formal garb of the papal priest-and-monarch. The pope evidently offered this likeness to the Virgin Mary in an appeal for divine intervention to liberate Italy and the Church from foreign invasion; it was probably placed on the altar of one of this pope's favorite Marian churches in Rome, Santa Maria del Popolo. If Julius was not triumphant when the portrait was painted, sometime between the summer of 1511 and the middle of 1512, he soon meant to be.

We know of at least three copies of Raphael's *Julius*, one of them attributed to the great Venetian master Titian. (The National Gallery version in London was not accepted as Raphael's original until restoration work and x-ray analysis confirmed its authenticity in the late 1960s.) The copies pay tribute to a triumph in art, but they may have been produced to satisfy a Renaissance demand for portraits of famous people or to hang like the official likenesses in our public buildings. Variations on Raphael's Julius-type persist in papal portraiture until the invention of photography, and arguably beyond that. The papal prototype was taken over for secular rulers, from the Habsburg kings of Spain to the kings of France and the English monarchs Henry VIII and Elizabeth I. We can take this crossover to the secular sphere as a profanation, irony, or yet another demonstration that the laity have learned as much about power as religion from the Church.

The equestrian statue is the quintessential heroic monument. In traditions running from antiquity through the Middle Ages the armored rider was the symbolic icon of real systems of social domination and political control, the figurative embodiment of brute force dignified by the heroic pose. The horse-drawn chariot and the prancing charger were basic equipment for ancient triumphs and ceremonial entries – the subversive travesty of Jesus's Palm Sunday entry into Jerusalem on an

Figure 16.2 Raphael. *Pope Julius II* (1511–12). The Trustees, The National Gallery, London.

ass was quite deliberate. St George battled the dragon on horseback, mounted crusaders charged the infidels, the Knights of the Round Table fought for king, quest, and romance. We have had trouble representing heroes ever since the triumph of the internal combustion engine.

A few equestrian monuments survived from antiquity, most famously the statue of Marcus Aurelius in Rome now on the Capitoline hill – it was spared because it was mistakenly identified as the first Christian emperor, Constantine. By the end of the fifteenth century equestrian monuments *all'antica* in sculpture or, on the cheap, in paint had become again a privileged emblem of military prowess in the murals painted by Paolo Uccello and Andrea del Castagno in the cathedral of Florence and in the bronze statues by Donatello and Andrea Verocchio on the piazzas of Padua and Venice. More exactly, they conferred a stature on the mercenary captains to whom they were dedicated that those soldiers-for-hire could hardly claim in the flesh. In the 1490s Leonardo da Vinci designed a colossal bronze horse for a monument to the founder of the upstart Sforza dynasty of Milan, and in the middle of the sixteenth century Catherine de' Medici sought out the aged Michelangelo to cast a bronze equestrian monument to her husband, Henry II of France, who had been killed in the not-so-mock battle of a joust. The work was actually done by Michelangelo's disciple, Daniele da Volterra. This piece, and the equestrian figures painted by Titian and Velazquez in the service of the Habsburg court of Spain, internationalized the form. The best testimony to its effectiveness is that equestrian monuments were favorite targets of future rebels and revolutionaries.

History painting was the hero's wide-angle lense. The battle scene was its greatest challenge. The twists and turns of painted bodies had to convey every exertion and emotion, quite literally, a tour de force. The happenstance of battle had somehow to look coherent; there could be no doubt about the winner – the patron paid for that – but victory should not look too easy. Vasari prayed for a triumph over the difficulties of a battle scene he was painting in the Vatican, so as "to win such a victory with my brushes as those Christian warriors did with their weapons."[4]

The battle scenes in Piero della Francesca's pictorial epic of the True Cross in the church of San Francesco in Arezzo (*c*. 1454–65) are pivotal examples of the battle piece en route to an ever more neo-classical form (see Figure 16.3).[5] On one hand, his warriors recall the knights in medieval manuscript illuminations of biblical battles, the Trojan War, and the Crusades. The rainbow colors, rearing carousel horses, blazoned banners, clashing swords and spears, warriors colliding with armor, shields, and bodies underfoot – these are medieval stereotypes that were still alive and well, especially in northern art. On the other hand, Piero clearly drew on the choreography of battle known from ancient sarcophagi and surviving monumental reliefs such as those on the Trajanic and Antonine victory columns and the Arch of Constantine in Rome. By the early sixteenth century the antique manner, self-consciously imperial, had won out in the great painted halls of state in the wake of the foreign invasions of Italy and the Italian wars.

Of course power is as much about defeat and exclusion as winning and heroes, about things we are not supposed to see or are meant to see only as witnesses or objects of superior force. The "people" do not much appear in Renaissance art. When they do, it is usually where they are unavoidable, as in scenes of daily life or stories that require them – shepherds in Bethlehem, for example, or ruffians on the road to Calvary. The swaggering soldiers and the broken-down veterans of German woodcuts contemporaneous with Emperor Maximilian's triumphs are the anti-heroes that triumphalism elides from the picture.[6] Renaissance women in art are mostly

Figure 16.3 Piero della Francesca. *Battle of Heraclius* (c. 1454–65). S. Francesco, Arezzo.

high-born marriage material, allegorical figures, fashion plates, or sex objects. A famous exception proves the rule: Queen Elizabeth, who said that the heart of a king beat in her breast, enacts these feminine roles in her many portraits.[7] We must not forget the abject antiheroic obverse of Renaissance triumphalism. In a grimly unsparing drawing by the Swiss artist Urs Graf (Figure 16.4) a splendidly cocksure soldier on the left drains a flask with his back to a panorama of savage destruction. Faceless charging armies bristle with lances and pikes. The distant glimpse of a peaceful scene on the upper right is belied by the clutter of slashed bodies, the hangman's handiwork in the trees, and the torched buildings in the middle distance.

Trophy art

"To the victor belong the spoils" – the ancient maxim fits an empowering strategy in Renaissance art. In ancient triumphal processions the spoils – plundered treasure,

Figure 16.4 Urs Graf. *Battlescene* (1521). Öffentliche Kunstsammlung, Basel.

weapons, prisoners, the vanquished's insignia of rule and religion – were carried through the streets, placed on altars as offerings to the gods, or distributed to the victors. In the late sixteenth century an Italian writer complained about a Renaissance mania for trophies in paint, plaster, stone, and metal; besides commemorating military and political victories, designs of heaped-up tools and symbols touted "triumphs" of art, the crafts, and the profession.[8] The critic might have gone further. Even when the triumphal apparatus was not so explicit, Renaissance art made a point of flaunting the proofs and rewards of victory of one kind or another. The very idea of a "Renaissance" depended on capturing the legacy of antiquity, and the arts played a key part in making the idea visible.

Small artefacts and the "minor arts" are routinely left out of histories of Renaissance art and consigned to specialists. However, medals, illuminated manuscripts, and jewelry, to cite just three, were far from marginal either in the artistry lavished on them or their function as tokens of power. There is a case to be made for the medal as the Renaissance art form par excellence.[9] The prototypes were ancient coins and seals, which were avidly sought out by Renaissance collectors, but the Renaissance medal was a creative adaptation spreading in the fifteenth century from the smaller courts of northern Italy. Its value was not like a coin's, dependent on its metallic content; bronze was preferred to silver and gold because it was easy to work and relatively inexpensive. It was not issued by or for an office or an institution; the Renaissance medal was commemorative, individually commissioned in a bid for fame and glory or to advertise honors received, alliances concluded, or family celebrations such as weddings or the birth of an heir. By the sixteenth century most medals were stamped from dies rather than cast, and in this form a kind of medal mania spread from Italy to the north. They were courtly calling cards, seals of friendship, tokens of ambition, and a portable medium for the spread of a Renaissance style. There are collections of Renaissance medals with hundreds, even thousands of exemplars in many European museums.

At the other extreme of scale, Michelangelo's *David* (1501–4) is, next to Leonardo's *Mona Lisa*, the best-known work in all of Renaissance art – and for our purposes, one of the best examples of trophy art (see figure on facing page).[10] The *David* is one of our reinvented heroes, the more strikingly so for its sheer size – 16 feet tall – and the brazen nudity that are all out of proportion to the biblical shepherd boy. Even supposing that Michelangelo had a live model in some overgrown apprentice, the figure evokes the colossal sculptures of antiquity, most famously the Colossus of Rhodes, one of the seven wonders of the ancient world. This is only the beginning of a heady proliferation, a virtual trophy case, of references. David was a Florentine favorite, a poster boy of Florentine republicanism and a familiar subject in fifteenth-century Florentine art. Comparisons between earlier Florentine sculptures of David and Michelangelo's reveal that Michelangelo incorporated their features and magnified them in what amounted to a virtuoso triumph over his predecessors. Appropriating another tradition in order to go beyond it, Michelangelo's *David* is no sprouting shepherd about to topple Goliath with a slingshot; rather, he is a Hercules, the personification of the virtue of fortitude as represented in carved stone relief on a door frame of the cathedral of Florence. Furthermore, Michelangelo carved his masterpiece out of the huge marble block that had been intended for one of a series of stone prophets on the cathedral and was subsequently abandoned after a botched attempt two generations earlier. Thus Michelangelo's sculpture took on (in all senses of the words) a wide array of forms and meanings: Florentine pride in the slayer of the Philistine, the personification of tyranny; the fortitude of Hercules; the suggestion of prophecy and salvation in the story of David, whose lineage were ancestors of Christ. The republican government that had expelled the Medici family, the unofficial rulers of the city, commissioned the work. After a public debate, it was located in front of the town hall together with other icons of the sorry fate of tyrants. There it still stands, more exactly a replica still stands there (the original is in the museum of the Accademia in Florence), because it became in turn a trophy of the defeat of the Florentine republic in the 1530s at the hands of the Medici dukes and their Spanish allies.

We have already cited battle scenes as a heroic narrative type, but many other Renaissance pictorial narratives can be seen as trophy art. As an art of captured motifs and meanings, they reclaimed and elaborated on myths, legends, and history for some patron's greater glory. Here again the lines were deliberately blurred. Fantasy and history, sacred and profane, ancient and modern, ideal and ideology fitted easily together. Genealogical epics pictured the deeds of biblical patriarchs, Greeks, Trojans, Romans, and medieval worthies as a pedigree for their would-be descendants. Material was lifted and updated in the latest styles from the Bible, saints' lives, collections of miracles, chronicles, and the ever-expanding trove of classical history and literature. Renaissance pictorial narrative cycles were time machines for reintroducing the past into the present.

Figure 16.5 Michelangelo. *David* (1501–4). AICT/Allen T. Kohl.

The Vatican palace was their showplace. Tourists hurtling toward the Sistine Chapel frescoes rush past the spectacular concentration of more or less contemporary narrative cycles (1508–24) painted in the papal apartments by Raphael and his workshop. The *stanze*, as they are known from the Italian for "rooms," were added to the palace in the late fifteenth century and the early sixteenth to house living quarters, administrative functions, reception halls, and a chapel, but the fresco cycles in most of them illustrated the trials and divinely ordained triumphs of the papacy. Since the popes claimed authority from scripture and tradition, all the more so after 1517 in the face of the Protestant Reformation slogan "Scripture Alone," an art saturated with references to tradition was not a merely aesthetic choice, or for that matter an altogether traditional one. It was to demonstrate the vitality of tradition that the popes had drawn the best, most modern, which is to say most "Renaissance," artists and scholars to Rome since the mid-fifteenth century.

The *stanze* are probably the most intensively studied ensemble in Renaissance art, in part because the pictorial machinery met expectations so well. The result is an open invitation to learned iconographical readings of their textual and visual sources. Together with connoisseurship, iconography was a dominant concern in the rise of the modern discipline of art history and is still a privileged method among art historians. Unwittingly or not, the iconographical approach is the beneficiary and at the same time the servant of an art of multi-layered signs and symbols that catered to ideological interests, nowhere more than in Rome. The iconography of the *stanze* works by amassing a plentitude of iconographical booty to reproduce simple formulas in complex forms and limited meanings in an endless proliferation of means. All iconographical roads do lead to Rome in the *stanze*: to the destiny of the city as the seat of empire, the resting place of St Peter, the seat of salvation through the sacrifice and resurrection of Christ as ministered by the priesthood of the Church Militant and extolled by the heavenly chorus of the Church Triumphant.

In practice, the iconographical details work like hypertext, Renaissance style. To follow the links to similarities, analogies, and affinities is to rehearse the Renaissance papacy's message. So, to take just one example, the personifications and impersonations that figure so prominently throughout the *stanze*. We see contemporary "witnesses" in the historical scenes painted there, and where historical popes take part in the action they are played by the reigning pontiffs. The image links past and present, the type with its archetypes to convey the simulation of a living tradition. Truth does not reside in mere history. In the frescoed room dedicated to the Emperor Constantine and completed by Raphael's workshop after his death in 1520, art illustrates a legitimating historical event that never happened. The so-called Donation of Constantine, the document by which the Emperor Constantine supposedly gave Pope Sylvester the regalia and the territories of the Roman Empire in the West, was proved to be an early medieval forgery in the middle of the fifteenth century. Undaunted by the mundane reality, Raphael's workshop staged the requisite reality in paint. As a dividend, the reigning pope Clement VII, in the guise of Pope Sylvester, receives the emperor's donation in the form of an actual trophy, a statuette of an allegorical "Eternal Rome" (see figure on facing page).

With few exceptions narrative picture cycles did not come north until the later sixteenth century, and even then not in the Italian manner of paint on fresh plaster from which we get the term *fresco* painting. Disconnects of this sort are as much a theme of Renaissance studies as are connections across a widely shared Renaissance culture. Some factors are fairly obvious – different social and political structures; the lasting hold of a brilliant medieval culture in the north; the erratic circumstances of conflict and recovery there in the fifteenth century. Other reasons are technical: in the case of fresco painting, conditions of climate, building materials, and working procedures. So far as Renaissance culture is concerned, northern Europe was a debtor region with respect to Italy and remained so even after northerners took their booty back home from the Italian wars. Perhaps the closest parallels to narrative picture cycles in the north were tapestries. These were trophy pieces in their own way.

Figure 16.6 Raphael's workshop. *Donation of Constantine* (1523–4). Direzione Dei Musei, Citta del Vaticano.

Flanders and the Netherlands were the main centers for the production of these trophies of courtly magnificence. Woven up to wall size from fine wool or silk, sometimes with threads of silver and gold, they were a far more expensive wall-covering than paint. Fresco painters had their apprentices and hired hands, but tapestries required teams of designers, dyers, weavers, and embroiderers working for years at a time. A room of the best Arras hangings cost several times more than

Michelangelo's frescoes on the Sistine Chapel ceiling. Henry VIII maintained at least five storage rooms containing more than a hundred tapestry panels, and traveled with a full supply to decorate drafty castles and palaces and the royal tent. His celebrated meeting in 1519 with the French king Francis I – the Field of Cloth of Gold – took its name from the display of tapestries and rich fabrics in which the two monarchs vied to outdo each other. Besides the glitter, the privileged company might have feasted their eyes on scenes of battle and the hunt, history and legend. By this time some of the most sought-after designs were those of Italian artists. It was another triumph of the Italian Renaissance style.[11]

TRIUMPHAL CITYSCAPES

Processions were integral to the rites of triumph as proof and demonstration of victory. By drawing participants and witnesses into the public arena, they secured de facto approval or, in any event, awed the opposition; in their marching order, they represented social hierarchies as well as communal solidarities. The processional routes of Renaissance triumphs were laid out like stage sets in plaster, cloth, and paper. In the most ambitious productions the city itself became a festival apparatus and staging ground. But since the ephemeral triumph lasts only so long as the performance, the most enduring processions and the only foolproof ones were the oxymoronically permanent stagecraft we find in art and literature and, most impressively, in real and imagined cityscapes. There was no controversy that architecture, which included what we call city planning, was first among the arts. To dictate and carry out a plan, to impose a commanding will on the city is still a classic dream of power. The utopias of Renaissance imagining were well-ordered cities; a new style in urban palaces, streets, and squares was one of its lasting triumphs.

The size and population of Renaissance cities look minuscule compared with today's metropolises and megalopolises. Only four cities in western Europe had as many as 100,000 people in 1500; Florence, the dynamo of Renaissance culture and a pioneer of systematic urban design, had around 65,000. The urban percentage of the population hovered around 15 percent in the most heavily urbanized areas of northern and central Italy and the Low Countries; it ranged from just 2 percent to a little more than 3 percent in most of northern Europe. Cities were still the exception, islands in a rural sea, but partly for that reason all the more conspicuous and dynamic as economic and administrative centers and magnets for talent and ambition. The ancient Roman practice of laying out grid-like street patterns and centralized public buildings to order and control the strategic cities of the empire had given way in the Middle Ages to what urban historians call the Organic Cityscape – meaning growth by accretion, irregular patterns depending on the lie of the land or the happenstance of property rights. The planned city is a Renaissance invention, or reinvention.

Northern and central Italy were leaders in this, understandably so as one of the most urbanized areas in Europe, rich in independent or semi-independent city-states. We find ordinances for civic improvement in the thirteenth century and still see the results in the historic quarters of towns like Florence or Siena. Civic boosters broadcast city pride in descriptions of their towns as models of good government. In the 1330s the Sienese painter Ambrogio Lorenzetti painted panoramas of a prosperous city together with the admonitory civic virtues and, in counterpoint, the menacing vices in the Palazzo Pubblico in Siena. The republican government of Florence, it has been argued recently, had already begun a campaign centered on the urban center's piazzas to "rationalize" and thereby to dominate and control public space. The redoubts of rebel magnates and the quarters of otherwise respectable citizens were seized and demolished in what was billed as a victory against the forces of partisanship and disorder.[12]

A few new cities were planned and some were actually built. Those that remained on the drawing board evaded the inconveniences of reality. In his treatise on architecture (1460–4) the Florentine artist and architect Antonio Filarete designed the ideal city of "Sforzinda," so named to flatter a patron and a new dynasty, the Sforza dukes of Milan. Filarete's city has the overall shape of an octagonal star with a round piazza at its center, the hub of the streets radiating out from it. The urban complex is "beautiful and good and perfectly in accord with the natural order," writes Filarete; an idealized nature, of course, but also, with the emphasis on "order," a politicized one that dictated the distribution of civic functions and social groups. Its piazzas and markets anchor and provision its neighborhoods; the neighborhoods circle a carefully proportioned "civic center" with the main public buildings and a cathedral housing cosmic and religious symbols. Twenty years later, while serving the Sforza dukes, Leonardo da Vinci sketched plans for a city with the technical ingenuity and visionary form that we would expect of him. He devised a drainage system, a network of roads and pathways, and a three-tiered disposition of urban space. What he seems to have intended was a geometrically ordered city where the parts corresponded to and demarcated social hierarchy: producers, professional classes, and ruling officials. It would be worthy, boasts Leonardo, of "the triumphs of the Caesars."[13]

One of the more direct connections between triumphalism and the historic cityscape – the palace – is so familiar that we hardly think of it as a Renaissance invention. The name comes from the site of a residence of the Roman emperors on the Palatine Hill in Rome that housed the imperial *aulae* or "halls of state" for receptions, audiences, and assemblies. On ceremonial occasions it was a landmark on the *via triumphalis* leading through the Forum – the arches of Titus, Septimius Severus, and (much later, in the fourth century CE) Constantine, still visible today, were part of the processional route. The ancient forms were only dimly remembered in the Middle Ages at least in the West, but here again, the papacy, by far the most highly developed European "state" before the sixteenth century, led the way in the long process of recovery and transformation. The new fifteenth-century wing of the Vatican commissioned by Pope Nicholas V (1447–55) set the pattern for later palaces: a central courtyard, state rooms on a second floor, sumptuous decorations celebrating the authority of its residents. On the exterior, the palace in its most complete form anchored a complex of avenues with a monumental façade of neoclassical colonnades and pediments facing an open square. It was the primary seat, stage, and destination of power attained (or wished for), not a defensive fortress like the old castles of power besieged. For the very same reason it was fair game for enemies of the established order, as the French royals at Versailles and the Tuileries found out in 1789. After the fall of communism in 1989 the new Czech president, the former dissident Vaclav Havel, occupied the old Habsburg residence on the hill above Prague, which had been taken over by the Communist regime, and instituted a changing of the republican guard in front of the triumphal arch built by a descendant of Emperor Maximilian I in 1619.

TRIUMPHALISM'S REASONS

There is obviously no single explanation for a pervasive triumphalist code in Renaissance art. While taking on the old theme of art and power in Renaissance studies in this chapter, I have mostly drawn on the scholarly work of the past 30 years or so, and that means a scholarship that is largely, even relentlessly, monographic. The emphasis on specific cases and contexts rather than overarching connections reflects a boom of professionalization and specialization that a volume like the present one confidently reproduces. The results have deepened our understanding and swept away old crusts of cliché, but they have also created a Humpty Dumpty problem – how, or whether, to put the pieces together again. The notion of triumphalism is a way of doing that in keeping with another characteristic trait of Renaissance studies today: the interdisciplinary interest that this volume also reflects. Given that the relationship of power and art is complex and multifaceted, how are we to account for the triumphalism and its variations in art?

The most acute Renaissance analysts of power knew that appearances could substitute for, even become a surrogate reality. Niccolò Machiavelli, always the provocateur, insisted that power was not so much a material force as a mask worn to suit the occasion. Triumphalism was a perfect cover for chronic weaknesses. It will not do to project modern institutions and technologies onto the Renaissance. Most recent scholarship is very clear on the limited means and methods for the exercise of power in the Renaissance. Arbitrariness and violence were a bottom line, but then as now they were seldom signs of strength beyond their exercise and some shift in fortune, a favorite arbiter in Renaissance ideas about the ways of the world. So far as politics is concerned, it is worth remembering that by the "state as a work of art" Burckhardt meant a politics and an art of compensation. As he saw it, political authority in Italy, particularly the authority of its braggadocio princes, was in doubt, challenged from above and below, rattled by intrigue and violence. The standard objection to Burckhardt that Renaissance political actors did not have the freedom of action to play politics as "the outcome of calculation and reflection" – hedged in by the constraints his self-proclaimed realist critics like to cite – actually supports the argument that cagey artfulness was not just a style but a survival skill and a political necessity. The contrast with the north in this respect was not so sharp considering that the fifteenth century was a period of "new monarchs" rising out of dynastic intrigues, revolts, and war. In triumphal display we should be ready to see through the mask to limited means, fear of defeat, and wishful thinking.

So much the better that triumphalism offered a winner's view of the world going far beyond an inventory of discrete motifs and sources. This suggests something important about power and art in the Renaissance. More exactly, it reinstates the proposition that, despite the complications and exceptions that scholars like to make much of, Renaissance culture can still be thought of as greater than the sum of its parts; not only that, it points to an assertive, specifically "Renaissance" construction of reality. To put it another way, triumphalism, as we have sketched it out in this chapter, was triumphal several times over. It was a victorious appropriation of antiquity, rigged to the authority of a perceived Golden Age and plotting past and present in terms of a (successful) struggle for dominance and the satisfactions (supposedly) derived from it. This winner-take-all view was both expandable and divisible. It was convertible across genres and transportable from Italy to the north. Perhaps it is worth noting for comparison in the global context in which European history is being recast in our own time that the fifteenth and sixteenth centuries were also a period of triumphalist image-making elsewhere in the world – the Ottoman and Mogul empires, for example, and indeed the empires of the New World.

But why triumphalism *in art*? It was not at all exclusively visual of course. Petrarch's long poem on the *trionfi* of the virtues and *Roma Triumphans* (1457–9), the last book of the Roman humanist historian Flavio Biondo's history of Roman antiquities, were only the most influential of many literary and historical texts taking triumph as a theme. It is significant for our purposes, however, that both works were soon illustrated and became source texts for artists. We might expect as much of a period and a culture so closely associated with triumphant achievements in the visual arts.

This is not the place to rehearse in detail the arguments for innovation in the arts and the primacy of vision in the Renaissance. The emphases differ, but there is not much serious disagreement about the phenomenon itself. Some accounts stress technical developments in theory and practice that culminate in what most scholars agree was the invention of a system of perspectival construction in the 1420s by Florentine architect Filippo Brunelleschi. Other versions hinge on daily social practices, particularly in Italy, that called for measurement, discrimination, and acuity in the piazza, the marketplace, and the counting house. Economic historians have weighed in ambivalently on the economics of conspicuous consumption that created a market for art, either because of prosperity or conversely because of limited openings for more productive investments. New ideas and attitudes (many of them old, recycled from the ancients) justified the display of magnificence and a cardinal rule of Renaissance culture: "I am seen, therefore I am." Ironically, the Church was probably the most important school of this profane rule of thumb. It was far and away the most important patron of the arts, and over the centuries it had developed the most coherent rationalization of the power of the image against iconoclastic revulsion against image worship as a form of idolatry. Following the sixth-century pope St Gregory the Great, religious images were the Bible of the illiterate and, in any case, capable of making religious teachings vivid, memorable, and moving. Seeing was believing.

It would not be hard to rewrite these interpretations in a triumphalist key. In one way or another they are about mastery of the visible world through the power of the eye. This heady goal had its abstract, even metaphysical underpinnings in the notion that the visible world showed forth the ideal principles implanted in creation and revealed in history. It was for the ability to make those principles visible and to appropriate them in its own activity that humankind was most like God. On an instrumental level one-point perspective in art, for example, deploys a geometrical grid on the perceived world, arranges it as an extension of the viewer's attention, and engineers the apprehension of three dimensions in a picture's two dimensions. So might the artist-beholder command the microcosm and some reflection of the macrocosm too. Never mind that our eyes see only a small fraction of the total spectrum of light, that they play tricks on us, or that the perspective scheme pretended that we see from the fixed perspective of one eye. These "mistakes" are a measure of the earnestness of the enterprise.

They are also, paradoxically, indicative of a clear victory over the ancients to whom the Renaissance system of perspective was unknown. We have come to understand that "the rise of the artist" in prestige, independence, and cultural standing was much more uneven than Renaissance enthusiasts once believed. Even Michelangelo could be threatened by his patrons and forced to scramble for his pay. How much more interesting, then, and how much in keeping with triumphalist panache, that the Renaissance art world's own narrative was a triumphant one. Artists had first delivered the arts from a Gothic night, then emulated the ancients, and finally surpassed them. By the early sixteenth century a third-rate humanist could salute a triumph of the arts in the north. In 1519 Hellius Hessus, the stylish Latin disguising his uncouth German name Heller the Hessian, wrote of a project in Nuremberg that "not even the Muse would be capable of such labor or of doing justice to this immortal work, which neither Praxiteles nor Myron nor Polyclitus nor Chares nor Scopas could duplicate. Although fame commends these . . . greater glory shall fall to our own times."[14] The work he was referring to was an elegant *Gothic* burial shrine for St Sebald, the eleventh-century Nuremberg patron saint renowned for turning icicles into firewood. A Renaissance triumph indeed.

NOTES

1 For an extended discussion of triumph rituals and the concept of triumphalism in a more limited context of late sixteenth-century Italian "halls of state," see Randolph Starn and Loren Partridge, *Arts of Power: Three Halls of State In Italy, 1300–1600* (Berkeley, Los Angeles, and Oxford: University of California Press, 1992), pp. 157–68.

2 See the overview and analysis by Larry Silver, "Paper Pageants: The Triumphs of Emperor Maximilian I," in Barbara Wisch and Susan Scott Munshower (eds) *Art and Pageantry in the Renaissance and Baroque. Pt. I: Triumphal Celebrations and the Rituals of Statecraft* (University Park: Pennsylvania State University, 1990), pp. 292–331.

3 For contemporary descriptions and a full analysis of the portrait: Loren Partridge and Randolph Starn, *A Renaissance Likeness: Art and Culture in Raphael's* Julius II (Berkeley, Los Angeles, and London, 1980).

4 Quoted by John Hale, *The Civilization of Europe in the Renaissance* (London: HarperCollins, 1993), p. 139.

5 Marilyn Aronberg Lavin, *Piero della Francesca: San Francesco, Arezzo* (New York: George Braziller), 1994.

6 J. R. Hale, *Artists and Warfare in the Renaissance* (New Haven and London: Yale University Press, 1990).

7 Roy Strong, Gloriana: *Portraits of Queen Elizabeth* (London: Pimlico, 2003); Cristelle L. Baskins, *Cassone Painting, Humanism and Gender in Early Modern Italy* (Cambridge: Cambridge University Press, 1998), is an indispensable guide to "gender politics" in Renaissance art.
8 Giovanpaolo Lomazzo quoted in Starn and Partridge, *Arts of Power*, pp. 164–5.
9 G. F. Hill, *Medals of the Renaissance* (Oxford: Clarendon Press, 1920), is the classic work.
10 Charles Seymour, Jun., *Michelangelo's David: A Search for Identity* (Pittsburgh, Pa.: Pittsburgh University Press, 1967), is a useful casebook of documents and interpretations; the 500th anniversary of the sculpture and its controversial cleaning completed in 2004 have drawn fresh attention to the sculpture.
11 Thomas Campbell, *Tapestry in the Renaissance: Art and Magnificence* (New Haven and London: Yale University Press, 2002).
12 Marvin Trachtenberg, *Dominion of the Eye: Urbanism, Art, and Power in Early Modern Florence* (Cambridge: Cambridge University Press, 1997); for Siena, see Randolph Starn, *Ambrogio Lorenzetti: The Palazzo Pubblico* (New York: George Braziller, 1994).
13 Filarete and Leonardo, as quoted by Wolfgang Braunfels, *Urban Design in Western Europe: Regime and Architecture, 900–1900* (Chicago: University of Chicago Press, 1988), pp. 75, 79.
14 Quoted by Hale, *Civilization of Europe in the Renaissance*, p. 407.

SUGGESTIONS FOR FURTHER READING

Baskins, Cristelle L. *Cassone Painting, Humanism and Gender in Early Modern Italy*. Cambridge: Cambridge University Press, 1998.
Braunfels, Wolfgang. *Urban Design in Western Europe: Regime and Architecture, 900–1900*. Chicago: University of Chicago Press, 1988.
Brown, Patricia F. *Venice and Antiquity: The Venetian Sense of the Past*. New Haven: Yale University Press, 1997.
Campbell, Stephen J., ed. *Artists at Court: Image-making and Identity, 1300–1550*. Chicago: University of Chicago Press, 2004.
Dale, Kent V. *Cosimo de' Medici and the Florentine Renaissance: The Patron's Oeuvre*. New Haven and London: Yale University Press, 2000.
Eriksen, Roy and Magne Malmanger, eds. *Basilike Eikon: Renaissance Representations of the Prince*. Rome: Edizioni Kappa, 2001.
Goldthwaite, Richard A. *Wealth and the Demand for Art in Italy, 1300–1600*. Baltimore: Johns Hopkins University Press, 1993.
Hale, John R. *Artists and Warfare in the Renaissance*. New Haven and London: Yale University Press, 1990.
—— *The Civilization of Europe in the Renaissance*. London: HarperCollins, 1993.
Hill, G. F. *Medals of the Renaissance*. Oxford: Clarendon Press, 1920.
Partridge, Loren and Randolph Starn. *A Renaissance Likeness: Art and Culture in Raphael's Julius II*. Berkeley, Los Angeles, and London: University of California Press, 1980.
Randolph, Adrian. *Engaging Symbols: Gender, Politics and Public Art in Fifteenth-century Florence*. New Haven: Yale University Press, 2002.
Seymour, Charles, Jun. *Michelangelo's David: A Search for Identity*. Pittsburgh, Pa.: Pittsburgh University Press, 1967.
Starn, Randolph. *Ambrogio Lorenzetti: The Palazzo Pubblico*. New York: George Braziller, 1994.
Starn, Randolph and Loren Partridge. *Arts of Power: Three Halls of State in Italy, 1300–1500*. Berkeley, Los Angeles, and Oxford: University of California Press, 1992.

Trachtenberg, Marvin. *Dominion of the Eye: Urbanism, Art, and Power in Early Modern Florence*. Cambridge: Cambridge University Press, 1997.
Welch, Evelyn S. *Art and Society in Italy, 1350–1500*. Oxford: Oxford University Press, 1997.
Wisch, Barbara and Susan Scott Munshower, eds. *Art and Pageantry in the Renaissance and Baroque*. Pt. I: *Triumphal Celebrations and the Rituals of Statecraft*. University Park: Pennsylvania State University Press, 1990.
Zapalac, Kristin S. *Political Iconography and Religious Change in Regensberg, 1500–1600*. Ithaca: Cornell University Press, 1990.

CHAPTER SEVENTEEN

THE OTTOMAN EMPIRE

Daniel Goffman

The "Renaissance" has long been imagined as a western European phenomenon, even a doggedly Eurocentric one. It was born in Italy on the eve of the European "age of discovery," and carried from there to the rest of Europe. It has been intimately coupled to, and in important ways fused with, the colonialism, imperialism, and sense of superiority associated with early modern and modern western Europe. The concept, though, is slippery. It has been used to refer to an artistic movement, to an intellectual movement, and to a cultural transformation. It also has been said to mark the beginning of modernity and the critical moment in European history when the past became historicized. Recently, some scholars have tried to broaden the meaning of the Renaissance by arguing that other Renaissances occurred in other parts of the world, and especially in the Islamic Middle East. Others have attempted to modify the significance of the Renaissance (as well as the definition of early modern) by redirecting our focus from artist to patron, from art to commerce and produce, and from regional to global. This latter reinterpretation pays particular notice to the role of the Ottoman Empire in the creation of a Renaissance in Italy and the rest of Europe. Scholars have noted a Renaissance consciousness of the Ottoman East and the movement of diverse commodities from the Ottoman world into the European one. They have paid less attention, however, to the fact that thousands of Italians, Frenchmen, and Englishmen lived in Ottoman lands and had to negotiate with Ottoman authorities and communities. How did their accommodations with and adjustments to that world influence their own art, literature, and world-views? What might they have learned from that encounter about dealing with others and constructing empires? In other words, how deeply and in what ways did the Ottomans (and others) participate in the creation of Renaissance and early modern Europe?

In the past decade or so, scholars have broadened their definition of "Renaissance" in an attempt to break away from the word's Eurocentric derivation. There are several catalysts for this endeavor. The field certainly has responded to more general critiques of historians' views of Europe's relationship with the rest of the world. For example, while postcolonial scholarship originally focused its withering attack upon historiography on the "age of imperialism," in recent years it has turned its attention to the "age of discovery." In this context, scholars have observed that early European encounters with Americans and Asians are better characterized as negotiations rather than conquests. In most cases, European success was far from certain; in some cases, Europeans suffered setbacks that suggested to contemporaries that western Europe was as likely to be conquered as to conquer others.

This postcolonial venture into the early modern, then, also has problematized postcolonial studies. A fundamental premise of the field has concerned power relationships; that is, the ability of Europe to impose its military, economic, political, and intellectual will upon the rest of the world. Scholars, though, have questioned the appropriateness of this framework to the early modern era. After all, Europeans ventured into the west, east, and south Asian worlds only when the Ottoman, Chinese, or Mogul rulers allowed them to do so. Furthermore, they remained very much on the defensive in the Mediterranean seas until well into the seventeenth century. Consequently, scholars have coined new phrases, such as "Ottomanism" and "imperial envy," to convey the sense of fear, awe, inferiority, and jealousy that first Italians, and then other Europeans, often felt toward the worlds they encountered and with which they attempted to negotiate.

Using this framework, literary scholars have begun to recognize how non-European civilizations influenced the writers of the day. Those who study Elizabethan drama, for example, have found profound traces of the Ottomans in the plays of Christopher Marlowe and William Shakespeare and have uncovered the genre of "Turk plays." Those who study early English expansion have discovered an early modern obsession with the Islamic Mediterranean in the many narratives of Englishmen captured by and living in that world. It is not surprising, then, that Renaissance scholars also have begun to extend their gaze beyond the European subcontinent in their search for new ways to conceptualize the caldron that we call the Italian Renaissance.

Of all the polities that Italians and other Europeans living through the Renaissance contacted, they found the Ottoman Empire both the most threatening and the most fascinating. The empire was threatening both because it was emphatically not Christian, and because of its aggressive expansion into southeast Europe and the eastern Mediterranean during the very years of the Italian Renaissance, the same areas into which Italian city-states such as Genoa and Venice had expanded in earlier centuries. It was fascinating because of its ability (or so it seemed) to construct a large, successful, and relatively centralized state during the very years that Italian and other Christian European states were struggling (and failing) to construct such entities.

Until recently, scholars by and large failed to note this contemporary fascination with the Ottoman world. Instead, they concentrated almost exclusively upon the Ottoman Empire as an outside threat to a Europe just emerging from a dark age and about to embark upon an unprecedented domination of non-European worlds and civilizations.[1] This concern reflected not only an early modern European fear of the Ottomans – that "terror of Europe" – but also the sense of European superiority that accompanied the nineteenth-century "age of imperialism." In other words, we have remained largely oblivious to a long, elaborate, and in some ways fruitful relationship between the Ottoman and Italian (and other European) worlds, and have regarded this expanding neighbor to the east, if at all, as an external menace, a Terrible Turk.

One consequence of this perception has been that, outside of the sphere of international relations, scholars have considered the Ottoman Empire hardly at all in their examinations of fifteenth- and sixteenth-century Italy. A key condition for the Italian Renaissance, in the scholarship of Jacob Burckhardt, Garrett Mattingly, and others, has been the existence of a political vacuum – broken only with the French invasion of the peninsula in 1494 – within which the Italian states and elites could act as patrons, struggle among themselves, and autonomously develop new artistic, intellectual, and diplomatic apparatuses. This sense of distance between the Italian and eastern worlds long persisted in our scholarship despite the Byzantine loss of Constantinople in 1453, the slow yet inexorable Genoese and Venetian loss of their empires in the Black Sea and eastern Mediterranean in the latter half of the fifteenth century, and the shocking Ottoman landing at the Italian port town of Otranto in 1480.

In reality, if there was a vacuum at all in Italy during the Renaissance, its dealings with eastern states and economies chronically punctured it. By focusing on the Christian world exclusively, and consequently imagining that the Ottoman conquest of Constantinople severed Italy from the east even as French and Spanish distractions and the Alps severed Italy from the north, we have washed out a rich and essential relationship between these worlds that we too narrowly divide as Christian and Islamic. An Italian physical retreat from the eastern Mediterranean certainly occurred. The change of rule in Istanbul represented only the most spectacular of a series of withdrawals. Equally dismaying for the Genoese was the loss of easy access to the Black Sea; equally disastrous for the Venetians was the loss of islands and ports in the Aegean and eastern Mediterranean seas. Nevertheless, the tangible need of the Italian states for their empires was more commercial than political, and the Genoese and the Venetians – as well as other Italian states – found ingenious ways to sustain and even expand their commercial and other links with the Ottomans and other Islamic polities.

In short, even though historians and literary critics have succeeded in constructing a portrayal of the early modern European and Mediterranean worlds that integrates the idea of the Ottoman Empire, they have not given us much sense of what that empire looked like, or precisely how Venetians, French, and English men and women, and other Christian Europeans familiarized themselves with it and applied knowledge gained in that encounter to their own lives and societies. Two examples, one considering Renaissance diplomacy and the second examining how individual Englishmen navigated the Ottoman world, may suggest ways to make more sense of this encounter and to understand more concretely how Ottoman civilization might have contributed to the transformations that ushered in early modern Europe.

The argument that a new diplomacy arose in fifteenth-century Italy is one of the many fruitful explorations that derived from the Burckhardtian concept of a Renaissance genius arising out of a political vacuum. This line of reasoning presents a self-contained Italian world, in which the increasingly secular squabbles between the rulers of Rome, Venice, Florence, Mantua, Genoa, and other city-states demanded a more sophisticated and permanent system of diplomacy than the often *ad hoc* structure that existed in the medieval Catholic world. The French invasion of 1494, the argument continues, initiated the movement of this new diplomacy, characterized by the legal fiction of extraterritoriality, the placement of permanent emissaries in foreign capitals, and regular reports about the politics, society, and ambitions of rival rulers to states north and west of the Alps. By the end of the early modern period, a version of the system of diplomacy that still exists today was in place throughout western Europe.

This is a tidy and persuasive hypothesis that has held historiographical sway for half a century. Furthermore, the general outline of its story is accurate; a new diplomacy did emerge in Italy during this period, and the new structures did travel northwestward into Europe. Nevertheless, the argument's most fundamental premise – that the independent, politically fragmented, and self-sufficient nature of the Italian peninsula in the fifteenth century was the creative spark that motivated this new diplomacy – is only partially true. Italy remained an integral part of the eastern Mediterranean world in the fourteenth, fifteenth, and sixteenth centuries, and a chief stimulant toward innovation in methods of diplomacy was an urgent need of Italian states to adapt themselves first to a Seljuk and Turcoman, and then to an Ottoman world in the making. Furthermore, these adaptations depended upon the ambiguities, flexibilities, and porosity of eastern Mediterranean frontiers.

The vocabulary through which Ottoman documents describe foreigners suggests this ambiguity and flexibility. For example, although each of these terms later came to connote different types of foreigners or subjects, a fifteenth- or sixteenth-century Ottoman statesman might have referred to an outlander as *ecnebi*, *firenk*, *yabanci*, *misafir*, *muste'min*, *gavur*, or even *zimmi* – terms that refer, with varied and shifting connotations, to foreigners, visitors, or non-Muslims. Such an official might have described this outlander's community as a *taife* or a *millet*. Today, we might understand that, in the Ottoman world, a *muste'min* referred to a temporary visitor to the empire, a *gavur* to an enemy infidel, and a *zimmi* to a non-Muslim inhabitant of the empire. We might think of a *taife* as a group, and a *millet* as a religious community of non-Muslim Ottoman subjects (Armenian Christians, Greek Orthodox Christians, and Jews). During the formative years of the empire, however, these clear distinctions seem not to have existed. The term *zimmi* is a case in point. In a rapidly expanding realm in which identity was in persistent flux, there was confusion over the question of who constituted a subject, who did not, and at what point a person who had not been a subject became a subject.[2]

The attempt to integrate the Christian community of Chios into Ottoman society after the conquest of that island in 1566 serves as an example. Even before the conquest, the Ottoman government had demanded a *harac* (a head tax) upon the islanders, a surcharge that by that year had fallen some 30,000 gold coins into arrears. A year and a half after the conquest of the island, the government ordered an official to go there and personally examine each household in order to impose the *harac* upon them.[3] These and other sources testify not only to the Ottomans' attempts to integrate a newly conquered non-Muslim population into their society but also to that people's resistance to such incorporation. Over time, the loyalties of Chians to previous Genoese rulers (who also had not shared their religion, being Catholic rather than Greek Orthodox) dissipated, and they came to accept their integration into the Ottoman world.

The agreements through which the Ottoman state attempted to normalize its relationship with newly conquered peoples and foreign entities reflect the ambiguity with which this government dealt with its diverse populations. Today, we refer to such agreements – when they pertain to foreign states – as "capitulations." Nineteenth-century Ottomans referred to them as *imtiyazat-i ecnebiye*. These terms are virtually synonymous. Nevertheless, neither accurately reflects the meaning of these documents for the early modern period. In its formative years, the usual term was *ahidname-i humayun*, or imperial pledge. Furthermore, the Ottomans did not limit the use of this term to guarantees that the state made in reference to foreign governments. Instead, the term covered many sorts of pledges made with many types of communities. The state often (but not exclusively) employed another term, *taife*, to refer to the group to whom such pledges were made. For example, Mehmed II, after conquering Constantinople in 1453, granted to the patriarch of the Greek Orthodox *taife* an *ahidname* that pledged a particular relationship (considerable religious and juridical autonomy) between the sultan and that subject population of the empire; two decades later, this same sultan had an *ahidname* written up that granted considerable economic and political autonomy to the Genoese *taife* of the island of Chios. As late as the 1620s, the Ottoman government granted an *ahidname* to Catholic monks (that protected them principally from Greek Orthodox Christian rivals) who traveled across the southeastern European parts of the empire to minister to and gather revenue from the Catholic Ottoman *taife*.[4] Using exactly the same terminology, Mehmed II granted *ahidnames* (predominantly commercial in nature) to the Florentine, Genoese, and Venetian *taifes* in the 1450s, and his successors wrote up such an *ahidname* with the French *taife* in the 1530s (probably not ratified until decades later), with the English *taife* in the 1580s, and with other states (that is, *taifes*) thereafter.

In short, in its formative centuries, the Ottoman government consistently used the same terminology and the same form in pledges to subject communities, foreign communities, and independent states. This refusal to differentiate between types of communities probably derived in large part from the rapidity with which the polity expanded. The Ottomans swiftly integrated into their society the remnant of the Byzantine Empire, a variety of other Christian states in southeastern Europe, rival Turkic states, large portions of the Genoese and Venetian empires, and much of the Arab world. Why acknowledge the independence of states when they soon would be absorbed into Ottoman society? Furthermore, the Ottomans found, in Islam, legal justification for granting considerable autonomy to conquered peoples. Thus, the *harbi* – that is, the foreign, non-Muslim enemy – received an *aman*, or safe conduct, upon taking up residency in the empire, and was transformed into a *muste'min*, or foreign inhabitant. After a period of time, this foreign inhabitant often became a *zimmi* – that is, an Ottoman subject. In other words, Ottoman experience with non-Ottoman groups combined with an Islamic world-view to envision the foreigner not as an "other," a member of a community that was, perhaps innately, different from the Ottomans, but as a wayfarer on her or his way toward incorporation into Ottoman society.

Italians and other Europeans, of course, sought to resist such absorption, and we see a "middle-grounds" struggle between competing notions of pledges and contracts in their challenge to Ottoman attitudes. They did so by attempting to adjust the terms of their *ahidnames*. Over time, such manipulations helped transform the very meaning of the word, as these certificates more and more resembled treaties rather than Ottoman assurances of fair treatment. For example, envoys began negotiating the right for certain foreigners to reside in the empire indefinitely without sliding from the class of *muste'min* into that of *zimmi*. Thus, a Venetian merchant could reside in Aleppo, for example, for decades, even a lifetime, and remain a member of the Venetian "nation" in that city.

Even though European states began routinely insisting on this codicil in their *ahidnames*, on the ground and in relations with local officials, such legal protection did not always suffice, because the terms of the agreements embodied a developing disparity between Islamic law and Ottoman customs on the one hand, and the historically concrete on the other. As, first, Italian settlements, and subsequently those of French, English, and Dutch, progressed, differing interpretations of the rights and obligations of alien sojourners led to frequent clashes between officials and foreigners in Istanbul and elsewhere. The roots of the tension lay in the fact that these alien traders and diplomats, of whom many spent decades in Ottoman port towns and cities, established their own enclaves (often referred to as "nations" or "factories") and more and more expected to retain capitulatory advantage over their Ottoman and non-Ottoman rivals. Many Ottoman officials, operating within an Islamic world-view and striving not to lose their competitive edge in the marketplace, saw things differently and continued to seek to collect allegedly exorbitant duties and other surcharges, and to convert such habitués into Ottoman subjects.

Almost 60 years after the Ottoman conquest of Chios in 1566, for example, a Jewish tax collector on that island insisted on treating the community of Venetian merchants residing there, as well as those who visited from Crete and other islands, as Ottoman subjects, seeking from them that same *harac* and other taxes that the government collected from non-Muslim subjects. Whereas earlier the policy of the Ottoman government had been to encourage the integration of Chian subjects into the polity, now it ordered local officials to desist from imposing these surcharges upon the Venetians. In the words of the decree (and in seeming contradiction to Islamic law): if Venetian subjects "dwell on Chios for a long or short time, I do not give consent for the *harac* and other taxes to be imposed on them."[5]

Such Ottoman representatives attempted to bend the terms of pledges in a variety of ways. Capitulatory guarantees more and more granted a type of "most-favored-nation" status to their recipients. Such terms tended to increase tensions between Ottomans and non-Ottomans. For example, they meant that duties on goods for the English, the French, and other foreigners tended to be lower than those imposed on Ottoman subjects. Ottoman merchants fought such inequities, often through local officials. In 1624, for example, the consul of Venice in the port town of Izmir complained that the collector of customs there persisted in artificially raising the value of cotton yarn in order to collect a higher export duty.[6] Such measures were largely futile, however, and the competitiveness of local merchants was gradually eroded.

The rearguard actions of Ottoman subjects continued in a number of spheres. For example, even though the capitulatory agreements more and more covered not only aliens themselves but also their dependants (such as janissary guards, doormen, and translators), in the early seventeenth century Ottoman administrators who were responsible for administering the community of foreigners at Galata, just across the Golden Horn from Istanbul, persistently ventured to collect the head tax from them as if they were unprotected Ottoman subjects (Figure 17.1). Also in Galata, janissary watchmen, candlemakers, and customs collectors tried to collect taxes on meat and suet bought and butchered for the Venetian community as if it were a non-Muslim subject community. Finally, these same officials repeatedly attempted to categorize as non-Muslim subjects (that is, *zimmis*) Venetian and French merchants who leased shops in the bazaars of Istanbul.[7] Such behavior certainly threatened the self-rule of these communities of foreigners. Nevertheless, the Ottoman officials were behaving in neither venal nor deviant ways. They intended neither to extort, nor to exclude, nor to convert. Rather, without subverting either religious or civil autonomy, their methods were designed to integrate these long-term sojourners into Ottoman society in accordance with Islamic law.

Discrepancies between *ahidnames* and Islamic and local laws created even more confusion in the Ottoman provinces than in the capital city. In the first decade of the seventeenth century, for example, a certain cavalryman named Ali seized a Venetian merchant, Yakmo, on a Bosnian byroad, dragged him off to his home, slit his throat, tossed his "rotting carcass" into a sack, and buried it in his garden.[8] No one doubted that Ali had committed murder, and the local magistrate had him brought to justice. The difficulty was that a municipal judge in the small Bosnian village near which Ali had abducted the merchant ordered Yakmo's goods sold and his money and documents confiscated, in accordance with his reading of Islamic laws governing inheritance but contrary to the Venetian *ahidname*. In two other cases, Ottoman tax collectors on the island of Chios and in the port town of Izmir attempted to collect head taxes from Venetian merchants.[9]

Nor was it only Muslim Ottomans who felt confused by (or perhaps took advantage of) the legal discrepancies between the various legal traditions current in the early modern Ottoman world. Christians and Jews were prominent in the collection of taxes in Ottoman domains, and such agents doggedly sought the head tax and other dues from foreigners, as we have seen with the Jewish tax collector on Chios. Such conflicts also intruded into the lawcourts, as when in 1613 Christian Ottoman subjects living in Izmir refused to accept foreign legal testimony against them, arguing that such "witnesses must be from the *zimmis* of this place." The state disagreed, ruling that "all misbelievers are alike" in such matters.[10]

The opportunity to worship constituted an essential part of foreign settlement in the Ottoman world. Even though Islamic law precluded the construction of new churches and synagogues, the myriad non-Muslim places of worship erected in Istanbul, Izmir, Salonika, and elsewhere suggests frequent evasion of this law. Furthermore, Christian and Jewish communities could maintain and repair existing structures, as is apparent in the many Byzantine churches that survived the conquest of Constantinople in 1453.[11] In the capital city and elsewhere in the empire, Italians and members of other foreign communities repaired churches and other places of worship. In 1622, for example, the Venetian community repaired an ancient structure, over the protests of "some people" who argued that it was a new church.

Donna di conto Greca della Citta di Pera

Figure 17.1 Nicolay. *Le navigationi et viaggi nella Turchia*. The Bodleian Library, Oxford.

The government responded that the church "is an old one. It has not been recently built." Two years later, Venetians in the town of Gallipoli petitioned to repair the grounds, gardens, and walls attached to their church. The government again consented, as long as the church had not been built "since the conquest." In a similar fashion, it protected a Venetian monk and the monastery in which he lived in Jerusalem when some "rebellious people" tried to seize the property with the excuse that the monk had converted to Islam.[12] In well-established cities such as Jerusalem as well as in rebuilt cities such as Izmir (the ancient Smyrna), Christian and Jewish communities, both indigenous and foreign, had little trouble finding abandoned or ruined pre-Ottoman churches and synagogues to rebuild. In short, the Ottoman government routinely defended the right of non-Muslim inhabitants as well as foreign communities to worship, and made it possible to build the structures necessary for them to do so.

In a state system based upon monotheistic belief but lacking religious uniformity, such a policy became an essential element in communications between states and societies. Western Europe, divided after 1517 between Protestantism and Catholicism and committed to the idea that a society must embrace its monarch's religion (*cuius regio eius religio*), eventually had to adopt the practice, long followed in the Ottoman world, of allowing foreign diplomatic communities the freedom of worship. Without such a right, no ambassador, consul, or other representative could accept long-term residency. Indeed, such a policy constitutes an essential element in extraterritoriality. The English government, for example, could never expect a Spanish ambassador to worship in an Anglican church any more than could the Ottoman government expect an English ambassador to worship in a mosque. In each case, the state learned to accept the idea of immunity from the religious (and legal) obligations of the host country and recognize the concept of diplomatic extraterritoriality.

These examples reflect the relative openness of the Ottoman world as well as the inescapable misunderstandings of a frontier zone between civilizations. Some foreigners simply melted into this almost aggressively malleable land. Many, however, insisted upon the legal and cultural security that their political and social autonomy afforded and strove to preserve and even augment collective self-rule. In doing so, they merely emulated the practices of countless other Ottoman communities and associations. Unlike Ottoman subjects, though, the innovations that their activities produced were transferable to their home countries. In short, these sojourners developed methods and procedures that became templates for many of the institutions that we associate with the new diplomacy of the Italian Renaissance.

In order to protect foreigners from Ottoman law (upon which Ottoman officials based their demands), for example, European governments began negotiating the right to govern their subjects living in Ottoman cities according to their own laws rather than Ottoman laws. This innovation was then exported, first to Italy during the Renaissance and subsequently to the rest of Europe. In the religiously homogeneous societies of western Europe, such extraterritoriality became an essential mechanism in communications between governments, and especially across the Catholic/Protestant divide.

Europeans also began posting permanent representatives in Istanbul; their job was not only to represent expatriate communities with the central government but also to find out as much as possible about Ottoman policy and the workings of Ottoman society. Such an ambassadorial system, with its resident envoys and cultural and political attachés, also became an essential element in early modern and modern diplomacy. Furthermore, the Italians and other Europeans realized that it was not enough to have official representatives in the Ottoman capital city. They also had expatriate communities in other Ottoman cities and began appointing official representatives in each. There was considerable variation in the relationship between such consuls and compatriot ambassadors and home governments. Nevertheless, in each case a fundamental mission was to protect and communicate. This network became the basis for the consular system that is also a feature of modern diplomacy. All of these innovations represented attempts to protect their subjects from a culture and society that western Europeans considered strange and arbitrary, and from the local authorities who represented it.

Recent studies of the Italian Renaissance have examined the influence of the East, especially on consumer culture and the widening possibilities for goods and ideas. They have found evidence for this influence in paintings, woodcuts, and essays produced by Renaissance artists and writers. There has been little acknowledgement, however, that two parties were involved in such transmissions. This was not just a period of expanding global commerce; it also saw a consequent growing presence of western Europeans in the Ottoman and other worlds. As we have seen, Renaissance Italian states learned a great deal about negotiating with others through their experiences in the middle grounds between the retreating Genoese and Venetian empires and the expanding Ottoman one. Comprehending what these Europeans learned on the frontier, and how they went about acquiring this knowledge, demands an intimate understanding of the world in which they lived.

If Italians had dominated such encounters during the fifteenth and much of the sixteenth centuries, by 1550 the states of the Atlantic seaboard had begun to dislodge their Mediterranean rivals. It is no coincidence that this displacement coincided with the transalpine migration of the Renaissance. Just as France, the Netherlands, and England explored and adopted many of the artistic and intellectual innovations of the Italian Renaissance, so did they uncover a parallel world of exotic goods and begin to probe the lands from which they came. They did so first in Ottoman realms.

By the 1580s, for example, the English government (working through and with the newly formed English Levant Company) had assigned a resident envoy to Istanbul, through whom it negotiated its own *ahidname* with the Ottoman government. Soon Englishmen had established communities, and English authorities had appointed consuls in Aleppo, Izmir, and the Morea as well as in the Ottoman capital. By the 1620s, an English commercial and political network, which emulated Italian ones even as it enhanced them, stretched across the Islamic Empire. The English, even more than the Genoese and Venetians a century earlier, were unable to impose their will upon the Ottomans because the structure of English trade left so much to the English Levant Company, and the Company in turn left so much to its representatives and factors resident in the Ottoman Empire. These men had to compete with a swarm of rival traders, both compatriot and non-English; they did so by developing a keen sense of the world in which they worked. The most effective English merchants learned Ottoman languages, Ottoman personalities, and Ottoman culture. Rather than colonize or impose their own administrative and commercial behavior on the Ottomans, these Englishmen learned how to adapt themselves to this unfamiliar world.

The most dramatic and significant example of English adaptation to (and attempt to exploit) the Ottoman world occurred between 1645 and 1647. It involved both the sitting English ambassador, Sir Sackvile Crow, and the envoy sent to replace him, Sir Thomas Bendysh. The first of these men was a loyal supporter of Charles I. The loyalties of the second were more ambiguous. The principal catalyst for the crisis occurred in 1645, when Charles, low on funds, supplies, and manpower, and bottled up in Oxford, ordered his ambassador in Istanbul, Crow, to seize the monies and goods of the English nations residing in the Ottoman cities of Istanbul, Izmir, and Aleppo. The instructions link London traders to parliamentarians, asserting that "diverse Merchants inhabitants of our City of London, . . . now or lately trading at Constantinople or elsewhere in Turkey, are actually in arms against us or aiding assisting or abetting to the present Rebellion." It consequently accuses them of "high treason," declares their "Goods, Merchandizes, & Estates . . . forfeited & confiscated unto us," and orders Crow to ask the Ottoman sultan "to give you authority to seize & take into your custody, the merchandizes, goods, specialties, & estates of all such merchants in Rebellion against us & trading in his Dominions." Charles, finally, asks Crow to request from the sultan the authority "to apprehend and imprison the persons of such Merchants in Rebellion against us."[13] With this action, the English Civil War spilled over into the Levant.

For personal reasons as well as a sense of loyalty to his king, Crow purposefully set about confiscating the wealth of English merchants and imprisoning the most refractory of them. As the king himself realized, without a police force or an army of his own Crow could act only with the support of Ottoman authorities, from whom he secured imperial rescripts.[14] Among other actions, the ambassador convinced the Ottoman central government to send a *çavuş* (imperial representative) to Izmir with an order to the *kadi* (municipal judge) of the town to seize the goods of all English merchants there. In this undertaking, Crow had behind him the king of England, the government of the Ottoman sultan, and a bevy of Englishmen loyal to Charles. Those who rallied against his plan, however, included all of the principal men in Izmir – including the French and Venetian consuls, the heads of the Armenian and Jewish communities, the collector of customs, and various English ship captains – as well as the English consul in Izmir and many English merchants there and in other Ottoman cities who either opposed Crow or were sympathetic to those forces arrayed against Charles in England.

Crow's agent in Izmir reported to the ambassador the immediate consequences of the intra-communal quarrel:

This morning [June 16, 1646], the Caddies son, with his Neipe and principall Officers came . . . but before wee began [to seize the goods] 'twas spoken in the caddies own hous, & all over the Town, our design to seiz what we could finde; about 7 a clock his son came & entred the Consul hous, & opened all the Warehouses. . . . Before we had entred at this house, the whole Town was in an uprore, being fomented by Jews, and som of the young frie left behinde, and proclaimed in the Streets, that the Town would bee undone, the Trade lost and go to wrack, if this was suffered; so that before the Consulls door were so many of the scum of the Town, the Streets were packed thick of them. On the other side, a more unruly enemy threatned worse things. The Master of the Golden Lyon [renamed the Hopewell] . . . lands 40 men at Barnardistons house, and vowed hee would have his money or goods, or swore he would beat down the Town.[15]

This passage suggests a complicated world, in which lines of authority were blurred and local authorities could undermine the will of central authorities, whether Ottoman or foreign. The Ottoman municipal judge (*kadi*) seems to have tried to act on his government's orders. Local foreigner and Ottoman communities and men from vessels riding in the harbor, however, combined to overwhelm his efforts. Neither Sir Sackvile Crow nor the king of England, nor even the Ottoman sultan could dominate encounters in this realm. Those foreigners who succeeded in this environment learned to adapt themselves to it.

Crow's actions in the summer of 1646 threw the English community in the Levant into confusion and fright. His assault also had consequences in England. Most dramatically, the Parliament and the English Levant Company (with the probably compelled blessing of the king) dispatched Sir Thomas Bendysh to replace Crow. Bendysh arrived in Istanbul, after a layover in Izmir, in late September 1647. His appearance triggered a protracted quarrel between these two pretenders to the ambassadorship. In an audience with the Ottoman sultan, Ibrahim, on October 3, Bendysh ostensibly declared that Crow was a rebel against his king who carried forged credentials.[16] During the next couple of weeks, Bendysh continued his campaign to convince Ottoman officials of Crow's illegitimacy. Eventually, he succeeded. On October 23, a group of Ottoman soldiers arrested Crow at his garden in the Istanbul suburb of Galata, marched him through the streets of the city, and shipped him off in a small Ottoman vessel to Izmir. Here, he was spirited aboard an English ship and, several months later, the ex-ambassador was in London, where he spent the next 13 years in the Tower.

This account of how Sackvile Crow sought to seize the assets of his compatriots in Ottoman domains, and how English nations residing in Ottoman cities defeated him, exposes more than just an intriguing element in the English Civil War. It also reveals a great deal about the middle grounds within which this community operated, for those who triumphed did so not because of their connections in England but because of their understanding of the particular Ottoman city in which they worked, as well as their ability to maneuver through the many layers of Ottoman law, power, and authority. English diplomats, traders, and clerics could not colonize this world (although some certainly dreamed of doing so); instead, they had to adapt themselves to it and learn how to work within it.

Curiously, their own political and social worlds may have eased these journeys into Ottoman civilization, because this supple and surprisingly haphazard Ottoman political organization mirrors, in important ways, the organization of the Renaissance Italian peninsula (as well as the early modern European state) as we currently understand it. Scholars of the Italian Renaissance have shifted their interpretation of that world's political history from an emphasis upon relationships between a strong center and the periphery in states such as the Duchy of Milan, the Republic of Venice, and the Kingdom of Naples to a more subtle and complicated representation. In the words of one scholar, these polities constituted "territorial systems in which local communities were connected not only to the centre but also to one another through a variety of economic and political networks that continued, in many cases, to guarantee them a degree of autonomy in relation to the growing power of the prince."[17] This vision of the Italian territorial state as decentralized, dominated by local interests, and diverse is removed from the formerly depicted strong central authority or even despotic prince of the Italian Renaissance. Our current understanding of the Ottoman world is equally remote from the more familiar representations of a firmly centralized and increasingly despotic Ottoman realm.

For many Renaissance Italian political philosophers and Italian statesmen, the Ottoman Empire constituted a vital illustration of, as well as a model for, the princely state. Niccolò Machiavelli's celebrated statement is representative of early sixteenth-century views: "The entire monarchy of the Turk is governed by one lord, the others are his servants; and, dividing his kingdom into sanjaks, he sends there different administrators, and shifts and changes them as he chooses." For Machiavelli, then, the Ottoman state, while a monarchy, resembled a paper tiger – strong and fierce as an icon but essentially unstable and liable to collapse once its leader is detached. Giovanni Botero, often referred to as the "anti-Machiavelli," certainly disputes his predecessor's admiration for the Ottoman state. Writing in the 1580s, some 70 years after Machiavelli, he declares that "the government of the Ottomans is completely despotic." The inhabitants, he continues, "account themselves [the sultan's] slaves, not his subjects; . . . and there is no personage so great that he stands secure in his life or in his estate unless it so pleases the Grand Signor."[18] Even though Machiavelli and Botero express differing views of the Ottoman state (with the first describing a legitimate, if brittle, monarchy and the second an illegitimate despotism), in their agreement that the polity depended upon a strong, feared, and controlling ruler they seem to contradict the Venetian and English experiences of an Ottoman world diverse and dominated by local interests.

Botero, Machiavelli, and other humanists had a strong understanding of the Ottomans; they based their descriptions of that world on attitude and expectation – framed largely in terms of humanistic knowledge of the ancient world – rather than anecdote and legend. Whereas these writers had gained their understanding of the ancient world from recovered classics, they almost certainly obtained their knowledge about the Ottomans from compatriots who had visited and lived in the empire. The conclusions of political commentators such as Machiavelli and Botero, for example, mirror the reports (*relazioni*) of Venetian *baili* (ambassadors), many of whom had spent years in Istanbul representing the Venetian state. These reports consistently praise the "Grand Turk" for his magnificence, power, fabulous wealth, and the legal edifice upon which his authority rests, even though they remain wedded to the anomalous idea that the sultan's power was rooted in Christian genius and energy. As the *bailo*, Marcantonio Barbaro typically remarked in 1573, "the wealth, the power, the government, in short, . . . the entire state of the Ottoman Empire is founded on and entrusted to people who were all born into the Christian faith and who, by various means, were enslaved and borne off into the Mohammedan sect."[19]

This understanding of the Ottoman state as centralized, potent, and even despotic seems distant from the experiences of Venetian and English visitors. For them, it never was sufficient to possess a capitulation granting reduced customs or autonomy. Even an imperial decree focusing upon a particular issue was often ineffective. Instead, the diplomat or merchant had to navigate through an array of interests, authorities, and personalities. Whether it was a Venetian consul protesting the integration of his compatriots into the Ottoman world or an English merchant contesting imprisonment and the seizure of goods, successful resistance depended upon the individual's familiarity with a varied and multifaceted civilization.

The image of an inordinately forceful central Ottoman state, effectively organizing society around itself, clashes with current views of the structure of that empire no less than it contradicts the experiences of contemporary visitors. The Ottoman sultan seems to have been in continual negotiation with members of his household as well as with other powerful patricians, and factionalism better than despotism represents this early modern state. Ottoman society reflected this complicated political core. Even in Istanbul, visitors such as Sackvile Crow and Thomas Bendysh worked and clashed with municipal judges, customs officials, and various religious and communal leaders as well as the Sublime Porte. Outside of the capital city, the lines of authority were even more convoluted, and they varied according to location and situation. The visitor to the Ottoman Empire, then, found a political system that in essential ways resembled contemporaneous states in Italy and elsewhere in Europe. This was a world to which visiting Englishmen and Venetians had to accommodate themselves, one from which they could learn a great deal, and one that must have seemed considerably less foreign than we have previously supposed.

The Ottoman Empire was an integral part of the early modern Mediterranean and European worlds, and first Italians, and then other Europeans, had to engage with that civilization at many levels in addition to the military and the intellectual. As a consequence, the Ottomans constituted a significant factor in the Italian, English, and other Renaissances. Renaissance diplomacy, for example, emerged principally out of the experiences of the Italian trading states with, first, the Byzantines – and then even more so with the Turkish emirates and the Ottomans in the fourteenth, fifteenth, and sixteenth centuries. The urgent need for the Florentines, Genoese, and Venetians to find ways to retain a commercial presence in that expanding empire – more than an Italian political vacuum or the French invasion of 1494 or the political ambitions of the Papal States or some other Christian European political structure – stimulated the formation of extraterritoriality, resident embassies, and routine reports on foreign and often hostile states. In short, the ideas of the "Renaissance" and "Europe" did not emerge only in contrast or opposition to other people, places, and ideas, or by the conquest of distant territories and dominion over different people. Equally important was accommodation with states and societies that the Italians, the French, the Dutch, and the English could not dominate or control. During those very years when Europe was in formation, foreigners – and especially the Ottomans – impressed fear, admiration, and envy upon the inhabitants of western European states. Italian understanding of this reality appears in the rather desperate construction of a new diplomacy along its borderlands with the Ottoman world; English comprehension of this reality appears in the inability of that state's agents to control their compatriots, as well as in the deep and thick ambivalence of the many "Turk" plays produced in sixteenth- and seventeenth-century England, including Marlowe's *The Jew of Malta* and Shakespeare's *Othello*. Finally, even the state structures of the Ottoman Islamic and Christian European worlds may have had far more in common than contemporary and more recent observers would lead us to believe.

Why have we been so slow to acknowledge how much these worlds shared? The fault may lie in part with the humanists themselves, who learned how to historicize the past and consequently profoundly to separate themselves from it. With this growing conviction of the past as a foreign land came a growing belief that traveling in foreign lands was like traveling in the past. Thus, just as Renaissance Europe began separating itself from the past and considering itself superior to it, so did Renaissance Europe begin to detach itself from other parts of the world and consider itself superior to them. In this situation, it became easy for even the accomplishments of others to seem imitative or inauthentic. Such seems to be the case with the Ottomans. Humanists and other western Europeans certainly admired many of their accomplishments, such as their ability to integrate diverse religions and peoples into their body politic. Nevertheless, Europeans effectively learned how to draw on the idea of historicity to wash out such achievements, and the Renaissance, in its inspiration as well as its accomplishment, became conceived as a uniquely European phenomenon.

Ottoman civilization was an equal partner in Mediterranean and European history, rather than an antagonistic backdrop as it generally has been considered up to now. This is not to deny difference. In fact, Ottoman relevance to western Europe probably lies in its role in creating a middle-ground tension and profound sense of difference. This tension, precipitated through contact with an intimidating civilization, forced institutional and individual creativity, as we have seen in both the Italian and English cases. Struggles to make sense of and assimilate this great power (literary critics refer to it as "imperial envy") on the part of Italian city-states, the English, and others led to new attitudes toward relationships between states and society and the development of a new diplomacy, as well as other innovations. Such legacies, unfortunately, have been largely forgotten. Instead, we remember only the negatives of this relationship: that Europeans feared the "Turk," that the "Turk" thrust himself into the heart of Europe, that Europe reduced the "Turk" to nothing more than a barbarian, and that if the European learned anything at all from the "Turk" it was how to conquer and colonize.

NOTES

1 This attitude is shared by nineteenth-century masterpieces such as Jacob Burckhardt's *The Civilization of the Renaissance in Italy* (Modern Library, 2002) (first published in 1860), more recent classics such as Garrett Mattingly's *Renaissance Diplomacy* (New York: Dover Publications, 1988) (first published in 1955), and current scholarship such as Daniela

Frigo (ed.), *Politics and Diplomacy in Early Modern Italy: The Structure of Diplomatic Practice, 1450–1800*, trans. Adrian Belton (Cambridge: Cambridge University Press, 2000).
2. The term "subject" may not accurately describe an inhabitant of the empire, but I do not know a better word.
3. See Başbakanlık Osmanlı Arşivi, Mühimme Defteri 5, p. 492, n. 1329; and 7, p. 174, n. 464.
4. See Başbakanlık Osmanlı Arşivi, Ecnebi Defteri 14/2, p. 62, no. 2.
5. See Başbakanlık Osmanlı Arşivi, Maliyeden Müdevver 6004, p. 51, doc. 1.
6. See Başbakanlık Osmanlı Arşivi, Maliyeden Müdevver 6004, p. 34, doc. 1.
7. See Başbakanlık Osmanlı Arşivi, Ecnebi Defteri 13/1, p. 28, no. 6; Ecnebi Defteri 13/1, p. 29, no. 4; Ecnebi Defteri 13/1, p. 35, no. 5; and Ecnebi Defteri 26, p. 144, no. 3 and p. 54, no. 3.
8. Başbakanlık Osmanlı Arşivi, Ecnebi Defteri 13/1, p. 52, no. 3.
9. Başbakanlık Osmanlı Arşivi, Ecnebi Defteri 13/1, p. 70, no. 7 and 16/4, p. 65. This was a chronic problem, on which see also 13/1, p. 120, no. 1; 13/1, p. 150, no. 1; and 16/4, p. 56, no. 1.
10. Başbakanlık Osmanlı Arşivi, Ecnebi Defteri 13/1, p. 101.
11. Debate over the destructiveness of the Ottoman conquest is ongoing (on which, see Nancy Besara, *Creating East and West: Renaissance Humanists and the Ottoman Turks* [Pittsburgh: University of Pennsylvania Press, 2004], pp. 60–2). However many Greeks died and however many Byzantine structures were razed, the survival of these churches rules out a policy of demolition.
12. Başbakanlık Osmanlı Arşivi, Maliyeden Müdevver 6004, p. 33, doc. 2, p. 102, doc. 3, and p. 20, doc. 1.
13. British Library, Egerton MS 2533, fos. 438 and 439.
14. Rescripts on this topic are preserved as Başbakanlık Osmanlı Arşivi, Mühimme Defteri 90, p. 43, n. 130 and 90, p. 44, n. 139.
15. *Subtilty and Cruelty: or a true Relation of Sr Sackvile Crow, His Designe of seizing and possessing himselfe of all the Estates of the English in Turkey. With the Progresse he made, and the Meanes he used in the execution thereof, with such other papers as are since discovered related thereto*, 2nd edn (London, 1657), pp. 60–1.
16. *Calendar of State Papers, Venice*, vol. 28, p. 21, no. 43.
17. Elena Fasano Guarini, "Geographies of Power: The Territorial State in Early Modern Italy," in John Jeffries Martin (ed.), *The Renaissance: Italy and Abroad* (London: Routledge, 2002), pp. 90–1.
18. Giovanni Botero, *Relationi universali*, pt. 2, bk. 4 (Venice, 1591), as quoted in Lucette Valensi, *The Birth of the Despot: Venice and the Sublime Porte*, trans. Arthur Denner (Ithaca: Cornell University Press, 1993), pp. 95–6.
19. As quoted in Valensi, *Birth of the Despot*, p. 24.

SUGGESTIONS FOR FURTHER READING

Besara, Nancy. *Creating East and West: Renaissance Humanists and the Ottoman Turks*. Pittsburg: University of Pennsylvania Press, 2004.

Brotton, Jerry. *The Renaissance Bazaar: From the Silk Road to Michelangelo*. Oxford: Oxford University Press, 2002.

Burckhardt, Jacob. *The Civilization of the Renaissance in Italy*. New York: Modern Library, 2002 (first published 1860).

Colley, Linda. *Captives: Britain, Empire and the World, 1600–1850*. New York: Anchor Books, 2004.

Darling, Linda T. "The Renaissance and the Middle East," in Guido Ruggiero, ed., *A Companion to the Worlds of the Renaissance*. London: Blackwell Publishers, 2002, 55–87.

Eldem, Edhem, Daniel Goffman, and Bruce Masters. *The Ottoman City Between East and West: Aleppo, Izmir, and Istanbul*. Cambridge: Cambridge University Press, 1999.

Encyclopaedia of Islam. New edn, prepared by a number of leading orientalists; edited by an editorial committee consisting of H. A. R. Gibbs *et al*. Leiden: Brill, 1960– .

Frigo, Daniela, ed. *Politics and Diplomacy in Early Modern Italy: The Structure of Diplomatic Practice, 1450–1800*, trans. Adrian Belton. Cambridge: Cambridge University Press, 2000.

Goffman, Daniel. *Britons in the Ottoman Empire, 1642–1600*. Washington: Washington University Press, 1998.

Guarini, Elena Fasano. "Geographies of Power: The Territorial State in Early Modern Italy," in John Jeffries Martin, ed., *The Renaissance: Italy and Abroad*. London: Routledge, 2002, 90–1.

Jardine, Lisa. *Worldly Goods: A New History of the Renaissance*. New York: Nan A. Talese, c. 1966.

MacLean, Gerald. "'Performing East': English Captives in the Ottoman Maghreb," *Actes du Ier Congrès International sur Le Grande Bretagne et le Maghreb: Etat de Recherche et contacts culturels*. Zaghouane, Tunisia: Fondation Temimi, 2001.

Mattingly, Garrett. *Renaissance Diplomacy*. New York: Dover Publications, 1988.

Peirce, Leslie. *The Imperial Harem*. Oxford: Oxford University Press, 1993.

Stevens, Paul. "England in Moghul India: Historicizing Cultural Difference and its Discontents," in Balachandra Rajan and Elizabeth Sauer, eds, *Imperialisms: Historical and Literary Investigations, 1500–1900*. New York: Palgrave, 2004.

Valensi, Lucette. *The Birth of the Despot: Venice and the Sublime Porte*, trans. Arthur Denner. Ithaca: Cornell University Press, 1993.

Vitkus, Daniel. *Turning Turk: English Theater and the Multicultural Mediterranean, 1570–1630*. London: Palgrave Macmillan, 2003.

CHAPTER EIGHTEEN

RELIGIOUS AUTHORITY AND ECCLESIASTICAL GOVERNANCE

Constantin Fasolt

There is a standard story about religious authority and ecclesiastical governance in early modern Europe. It runs somewhat like this:

In medieval Europe religious authority lay in the hands of clerics. Clerics were regarded as superior to the laity, and they were governed by the papacy in Rome. When there were disagreements about the faith, the papacy had the last word. Dissenters were condemned as heretics and handed over to lay governments for punishment. Orthodoxy was ruthlessly enforced and there was no religious liberty.

That changed during the Renaissance and Reformation. Lay people began to grow dissatisfied with the enforcement of orthodoxy and claimed a growing share of religious authority for themselves. When Martin Luther proposed a new kind of theology, their dissatisfaction erupted into outright rebellion. After about a century of violent religious wars, the papacy had to admit defeat.

The outcome was settled more or less around the time of the Peace of Westphalia (1648). Priests and bishops continued to exist. But they were divided into different confessions and the papacy lost the ability to impose its will by force. Education, persuasion, and enlightenment took the place of the Inquisition and the stake, and religious liberty was enshrined as a natural right. That was a great step forward in the history of humanity's progress from ignorance and oppression.

The problem with this story is that it does not explain what happened to religious authority during the Renaissance and Reformation. It assumes that medieval people somehow knew what we call religious liberty, and that the difference between them and us is simply this: they did not have it, and we do. It tells us why they did not have religious liberty (because the clergy wanted to exercise control over their faith) and how we managed to gain it for ourselves (because the monopoly of the papacy over religion was broken up and the Church was separated from the state). But it does not explain how religious authority changed when it was handed over to the laity. It rather conceals a transformation in the criteria by which we judge what counts as faith and what as knowledge. It thereby reassures us that we can trust our understanding of concepts like "religion," "authority," "Church," and "state" by projecting them back onto the past.

There are other ways in which the standard story can be criticized: it is incomplete and it embodies an idea of progress no longer as convincing as it was a hundred or two hundred years ago. Historians are busily unearthing a cornucopia of details to fill in the blank spots. They have been doing so almost since the professional study of history came into its own in the nineteenth century, with works like Ranke's *History of the Reformation in Germany* and Burckhardt's *Civilization of the Renaissance in Italy*, two classics of modern historiography not coincidentally devoted to the Renaissance and Reformation. They are still debating whether or not some kind of progress has in fact occurred; if so, to what extent; if not, what it is lacking. They are shaking off the national and confessional hostilities that used to burden them. Social history, cultural history, anthropology, and the study of what has been called "confessionalization" have established much common ground.[1] Today, our understanding of religious authority and ecclesiastical governance in early modern Europe is therefore detailed, rich, and subtle beyond what Ranke or Burckhardt could have imagined.

But telling the story in more detail and exercising greater care in calling its outcome good or bad is not enough. The problem facing historians today lies neither in the details nor in their evaluation. It lies in the lack of an alternative that can be sketched as briefly as the standard story but does not presuppose what ought to be explained. Before we can explain how religious authority changed in the Renaissance and Reformation, we therefore need to take a closer look at how it operated during the Middle Ages.

RELIGIOUS AUTHORITY IN MEDIEVAL EUROPE

Religious authority in medieval Europe was shaped by three main factors. First, knowledge was based on writing; second, most writing was in Latin; and third, the ability to read and write was limited to clerics. It is misleading to view medieval Europe as a place where knowledge rested on memory and oral tradition. Memory and oral tradition mattered more than today, but not as much as in societies where there is no written literature at all (like those of hunters and gatherers). Not only was there writing in medieval Europe, but writing was scripture – and scripture was not mere letters on the page, but *Scripture*, the Bible, the sacred Word of God. It is equally misleading to believe that clerics were ordained priests or consecrated bishops. Clerics came in all sorts of shapes and sizes. Many of them were simply students, not unlike Chaucer's clerk, and some of them were indistinguishable from the laity. They were literati in the elementary sense of knowing how to read and write in Latin. But they were never more than a small sector of society. Their literacy was a privilege that distinguished them sharply from the great majority of the population. Medieval society was hierarchical in many ways. But the most obvious way was the subordination of the illiterate laity to the literate clergy.

Medieval society was therefore marked by a characteristic tension. On the one hand, writing was viewed as a source of truth. On the other hand, writing was accessible only to a small group of people. Ordinarily this is considered a great deficit.

That is not altogether wrong. There is an obvious sense in which the hierarchical organization of medieval society kept ordinary people in thrall to priests and knights. This is the same sense in which ordinary people were being kept in thrall to priests and knights in all of those large-scale agro-literate societies, as they have been called, that were the predominant form of social organization across the globe from about the fourth millennium BCE until the nineteenth century, when the Industrial Revolution, capitalism, and massive urbanization changed the most basic rules of the games that humankind has played since its emergence from prehistory.[2] But simply to equate hierarchy with oppression is to misunderstand the role that writing plays in authenticating truth, both in modern, literate societies and in societies most of whose members were illiterate. Perhaps more important, it is to ignore the conceptual foundations of oppression in egalitarian societies.

An analogy may help to clarify this point. It is taken from the activity of measuring — not coincidentally an activity crucial to modern science. Assume you use a ruler to measure the length of your foot. How do you know your measurement is true? The answer is, of course, "from observation" — namely, the observation made in placing the ruler next to the foot and noting the marks on the ruler that correspond to the length of the foot. Up to a point that answer is enough. But a further question can be asked: "How do you know your ruler is reliable?" Usually that question need not be asked. But it is always possible, and sometimes it must be answered, especially when it concerns disputes about the measurement of something that matters to society at large. The standard way of answering that question is to compare your ruler to the standard meter bar kept at the International Bureau of Weights and Measures in Sèvres, near Paris.[3]

Now it might seem that this answer, too, depends on observation — the observation made when you put your ruler next to the standard meter bar. But in this case observation is not enough, for if it were you might go on to ask a further question: "How do you know the standard meter bar itself is reliable?" That question, however, is nonsensical.[4] The standard meter bar is reliable by definition. The reason has nothing to do with lengths or observations. The reason is that an agreement has been reached to use this object as a means of last resort with which to settle disputes about the accuracy of measurements of lengths. That agreement makes it the standard meter bar. The actual length is not the point. The agreement is. So long as the agreement holds, no matter how long the bar may be, its length is that of one meter.

The measurement of lengths — or, more precisely, the authentication of the truth of measurements of length by means of the standard meter bar — furnishes an instructive instance of a kind of truth that rests neither on reason nor on observation, but on a consensus without which neither reason nor observation could begin to do their work. In medieval Europe a similar consensus governed the use of writing. Writing was something other than a mere means of communication or a depository of knowledge. It functioned like a ruler by which one's views were measured. The clergy held the ruler and used it to measure the views of the laity. Sometimes there were disputes about the reliability of the ruler. In order to resolve such disputes, there had to be agreement on a standard with which the reliability of the ruler could be judged. That standard was the Catholic faith as declared by general councils and the papacy.

In the age before printing was invented, writings were copied by hand. They differed from case to case. Even the Bible existed in different versions. But there was only One Holy Catholic Church and only one pope in Rome. The pope derived his authority directly from an unbroken chain of apostolic succession that went straight back to St Peter. He looked like any other bishop. But his authority was unique in the same sense in which the authority of the standard meter bar is unique. It rested on a consensus to use his word as a means of last resort with which to judge the reliability of all other words. His word was true by definition, just as the standard meter bar by definition is one meter long. The question whether or not his word was actually true was nonsense, quite like the nonsense of asking whether the standard meter bar is actually one meter long. He was that spiritual man of whom St Paul had written: "he that is spiritual judgeth all things, yet he himself is judged of no man" (1 Corinthians 2:15). Canon law concluded: "the first see shall not be judged by anyone."[5] And one of the most distinguished experts on canon law declared: "so long as he does not go against the faith the pope can do and say whatever he pleases. He can even deprive someone of his rights, for there is no one who may ask him: 'Why are you doing this?' . . . His will stands in the place of reason, and whatever pleases him has the force of law."[6]

Viewed in this way, the hierarchical organization of the medieval world makes better sense than can be grasped so long as the use of writing is thought to consist entirely of communication, and knowledge to stem entirely from reason and observation. The certification of the truth by means of writing and the authentication of the truth by the papacy met the same basic need as the measurement of lengths by means of rulers and the authentication of the standard meter bar by the International Bureau of Weights and Measures: it assured the integrity of a system of reference and meaning. The papacy's authority did not rest on the truth of its pronouncements, but on a consensus that its pronouncements settled disputes about the standards with which the truth was ascertained. Just as the surreptitious substitution of some other meter bar for the true standard meter bar must be prevented in order to maintain the integrity of the system of measuring lengths, the substitution of false popes needed to be prevented in order to maintain the integrity of the system of ascertaining the truth. Without the papacy's ability to guarantee the unity of the faith, writing could not be trusted to fulfill its function as a ruler with which all truths were measured. Communication would have broken down in irresolvable disputes and society would have fallen apart.

The idea of religious liberty could therefore not have made much sense to medieval people. Demanding a right for every person to hold whatever religious beliefs seem right to them would have threatened their ability to distinguish true from false. They had to consider the demand for religious liberty meaningless or dangerous in the same sense in which we would find it meaningless or dangerous if someone were to protest against the tyranny of the standard meter bar and claim that every person has an inalienable right to determine how long the meter ought to be. We recognize that our measuring devices need to conform to standards in order to fulfill their purpose. We sanction the punishment of people who intentionally use false measuring devices. And we do not regard the choice of the standard meter bar as a natural right. In the same way the people of medieval Europe believed that statements about the truth had to conform to writing, and that the truth of writing was guaranteed by its conformity to the official declarations of the Church. The authority of the Church was universal in the same sense in which the authority of the standard meter bar is universal: it rested on a consensus of society as a whole without which society could not have existed. That does not mean that each and every person was forced to hold the same religious views. Quite the contrary – the variety of different ideas about religion that flourished throughout the Middle Ages and the freedom with which those ideas could be explored were almost certainly greater than in the modern age. Conformity is not the same as identity. A wooden stick about a meter long and a precision tool calibrated to measure a thousandth of a millimeter can both serve the purposes of measuring, so long as they conform to the same standard meter. A shepherd in the Pyrenees, a local parish priest, and a Dominican professor of theology could all proclaim ideas about the truth. By no means were their views identical nor did they need to be. But the freedom with which they were allowed to state their different views depended on their consent to the principle that all claims on the truth were ultimately subject to the judgment of the papacy. Heresy did not consist of holding erroneous views or disagreeing with the pope, any more than using badly calibrated rulers threatens the system of measurement. Heresy consisted of the heretic's refusal to bow to the authority of the Church.[7]

HOW RELIGIOUS AUTHORITY CHANGED

The question is, of course, why did that change? What turned religious hierarchy and conformity to the papacy from an apparently useful means of guaranteeing truth into a form of religious oppression? The answer turns on the spread of literacy. Schools and universities were founded in growing numbers throughout the later Middle Ages. The use of paper made from rags reduced the cost of books below what it had been so long as writing surfaces were being made from skins of animals. And the invention of printing with moveable type in the fifteenth century furnished the people of Europe with an efficient and unprecedented means of multiplying copies of the same text. More schools, cheap paper, and printed books meant that the laity learned how to read and write. Soon it learned to read and write for its own purposes, not only in Latin but also in the various European vernaculars. Illiterate merchants became obsolete and an increasing share of secular business was carried out in writing. As a result the difference between the clergy and the laity lost its hierarchical significance. What had been a crucial marker in the organization of a hierarchical society became a distinction without a difference and a source of unjustifiable inequity.

In their general outline these changes are well known. But in order to appreciate their significance it is not enough to know that writing spread. The point is that the spread of writing led to a change in the criterion of truth. While writing was the prerogative of a small sector of society, the criterion of truth consisted of conformity to the Church as represented by councils and the pope. The chief problem for the maintenance of religious authority was not how to make sure that everyone shared the same beliefs – impractical to the point of impossibility in a society as highly differentiated and lacking in modern means of communication as medieval Europe was – but rather how to make sure that everyone acknowledged the authority of the papacy to act as a judge for all. Different degrees of conformity to the papally sanctioned truth were thought to be not only tolerable but a legitimate expression of the hierarchical dispensation of the truth. Medieval orthodoxy required submission to the pope as the ultimate arbiter of truth, but not much else besides. What the believer actually thought was somewhat beside the point, just as it is somewhat beside the point how accurate your ruler really is, so long as you do not dispute the standard meter bar.

That changed when writing became a common possession of society and printing put the same texts into the hands of every reader.[8] The difference between the clergy and the laity was watered down and the criterion of truth shifted from conformity to the Church toward the sense expressed in writing. Now orthodoxy meant having the same understanding of the faith as every other member of the Church, not merely following the lead of the papacy. Truth could no longer be conceived in terms of conformity, and mere submission to authority – no matter how sincere – lost its ability to certify orthodoxy. The papacy was forced to vacate the office of religious standards, and identity of sense ascended to its throne.

Three periods in the history of religious authority in early modern Europe can therefore be distinguished. The differences between these periods do not turn on the spread of literacy as such, but on the effects the spread of literacy had on the consensus of society. In the first period the shift away from conformity to the lettered by the illiterate toward mastery of writing's sense by all got underway and gathered speed. But it did not yet pose an explicit threat to the clergy's exclusive right to judge religious truth in the established way. This period is commonly known as the Renaissance. During the second period, the traditional reliance on conformity to the Church came under direct assault from people claiming that religion required all believers to grasp the sense of Scripture for themselves. This period is commonly known as the Reformation. The third period was marked by a proliferation of conflicting views on what the sense of Scripture was, along with a prolonged attempt to solve those conflicts by force. This period is commonly known as the Age of Religious War. It ended when agreement was reached on a new method of exercising religious authority. Roughly speaking, that happened at the Peace of Westphalia in 1648. Let me describe these periods in more detail.

THE RENAISSANCE

The Renaissance is often seen as a movement of cultural innovation that was centered in Italy and took its inspiration from classical antiquity. The very term "Renaissance" ("rebirth") stresses the degree to which contemporaries understood themselves to be witnessing the return of something that had existed once before. That view has much to recommend it. In painting, architecture, thought, and letters the models of classical antiquity gained a new prominence. At the same time, the models elaborated in the high Middle Ages – Gothic architecture and scholastic theology, for example – came in for critical attention.

The most important point, however, is the degree to which the turn to classical antiquity advanced a shift in the criterion of truth. The Renaissance began in Italy because in the Italian city-states the use of writing had for a long time spread much further beyond the limits of the clergy than elsewhere in Europe, and the border dividing the clergy from the laity had long been more porous than further north. The more thoroughly the clergy in Italy came to be integrated into lay society and the more successfully the laity managed the literate methods of the clergy, the less they were able to rely on conformity to clerically sanctioned interpretations of Scripture as a foundation for religious authority.

Classical antiquity offered a ready-made alternative. The distinction between clergy and laity that loomed so large in medieval Europe did not exist in ancient city-states as such. Of course there had been priests and temples. But ancient politics was carried out on the principle that all citizens were equal members of the polity. Regardless of whether they ruled themselves in free republics or were subject to an emperor, citizens were not divided into clergy and laity. In liberty as well as under tyranny citizens enjoyed equality. Classical antiquity had also produced a significant body of literature of which so much survived that it could fruitfully be mined for guidance in the quest for a consensus on the truth when truth could no longer be equated with conformity to the clergy. It helped that the clergy based much of its own authority on ancient writings. Classical antiquity thus seemed to offer a solution to the problem posed by the erosion of the line dividing the clergy from the laity.

The fourteenth-century humanist Petrarch was one of the first and greatest minds to advance that line of thought. When Petrarch drew a new theory of virtue from reading the works of Cicero, something quite different from mere reverence for ancient models was at stake. The point was that the virtue on which Cicero had written was one and the same for every human being. That does not mean that Cicero had not distinguished between different kinds of virtue. There were four virtues – wisdom, courage, temperance, and justice – on the list of cardinal virtues alone. It rather meant that wisdom, courage, temperance, and justice did not vary according to one's standing in society, especially not according to one's membership in the clergy or the laity. From Cicero's perspective it made no sense to say that wisdom was peculiar to the clergy, and courage to the knights, much less that justice ought to be meted out in different ways (by Roman law, canon law, or local custom) and in different courts (temporal or spiritual) depending on whether one belonged to the clergy or the laity. Petrarch agreed. Each and every member of the polity ought to be wise, courageous, moderate, and just. If some were not as virtuous as others, that could no longer be interpreted as a legitimate manifestation of the hierarchical gradations of a society composed of different ranks and orders where the virtues of clerics and monks ranged at the top and those of peasants at the bottom. It rather amounted to a failure to live up to standards that were the same for all. Thus Petrarch replaced a hierarchy of virtues that corresponded to the ranks and orders of a hierarchical society with an identical morality for all.

Something similar may be said about the humanist movement that swept Europe in the fourteenth and fifteenth centuries. Humanists valued language above all else. They taught the laity how to express themselves clearly, elegantly, and persuasively – in speaking as well as in writing, in Latin as well as in the vernacular – and they did so by drawing on the models of classical antiquity. Following the definition of Paul Oskar Kristeller, humanism may therefore be defined as an educational movement giving pride of place to the study of classical grammar, rhetoric, poetry, history, and moral philosophy.[9] Much ink has been spilled over Kristeller's definition of humanism. According to Hans Baron, humanism had a definite content, quite apart from the classical forms in which that content was expressed: it taught republican virtue.[10]

From the perspective taken here, the difference between Kristeller and Baron looks like a false dilemma. Humanism's turn to classical forms of expression amounted in and of itself to a substantial change. Each of the five disciplines whose study it encouraged put the laity in a position of equality with the clergy by eroding the hierarchical distinction between the lettered and the illiterate, regardless of whether the outcome was a republic of virtue or a princely tyranny. Grammar allowed the citizen to read and write correctly; rhetoric allowed him to convince his fellows of whatever truth he had grasped; in poetry he spoke about the self in search of meaning; in history he wrote about the relationship between himself and the community; and in moral philosophy he studied how to settle on a proper course of action without conforming to any superior authority or taking his guidance from the clergy. Humanism advanced a shift in religious authority (to that extent Baron was right), not by endorsing any particular ideas of right or wrong (to that extent Kristeller was right), but by changing the criteria by which all such ideas were judged.

A few lines from Petrarch's letters will show how closely the use of language, the practice of virtue, and the assumption of religious authority lay side by side during the Renaissance:

> I urge and admonish that we correct not only our life and conduct, which is the primary concern of virtue, but our language usage as well. This we will do by the cultivation of eloquence. . . . How much help eloquence can be to the progress of human life can be learned both in the works of many writers and from the example of daily experiences. How many people have we known in our time who were not affected at all by past examples of proper speech, but then, as if awakened, suddenly turned from a most wicked way of life to the greatest modesty through the spoken word of others! [. . .] Make for yourself a refuge within your mind where you may hide, rejoice, rest without interruption, and live together with Christ, who through the sacred priesthood made you in your youth His confidant and table companion. You will ask, "and with what skills do I do that?" It is virtue alone that is powerful enough to accomplish it all; through her you will be able to rejoice and to live happily wherever you are.[11]

By turning to classical antiquity, Italians thus took a large step forward toward a new understanding of religious authority. But in their view the turn to classical antiquity and the movement to educate the laity did not conflict with the authority of the Church. They rather helped to improve the Church and to extend its reach by spreading the use of letters from the clergy to the laity. A good many of their numbers were clerics themselves, studied canon law, and worked for the papacy, including not only Petrarch but also Leon Battista Alberti, often taken as the embodiment of Renaissance man himself. One of the greatest of them all, Aeneas Silvius Piccolomini, even ascended to the papacy as Pope Pius II.

From the perspective of the history of religious authority, the Renaissance therefore needs to be viewed as part and parcel of the great movements to reform the Church that reverberated throughout late medieval history. Historians who assume that Church history must be distinguished from the history of the state find it difficult to agree with that point. But that is an anachronistic imposition of modern ideas on late medieval times. The Italian Renaissance and late medieval Church reform did not merely happen at the same time. They went hand in hand and they belong in the same chapter. Both were replete with criticisms of corruption in Church government, both sought to improve the Church by improving letters, and neither meant to overthrow established forms of ecclesiastical governance. When the conciliar movement tried to subject the papacy to the control of general councils it did not do so in order to abandon the distinction between the clergy and the laity, but, quite the contrary, in order to renew the laity's allegiance to the clergy. It is no mere coincidence that the clerics assembled at the Council of Constance burned Jan Huss as a heretic at the stake. It rather shows how closely the conciliar movement was tied to the cause of maintaining the authority of the Church. The Renaissance peaked at the same time as the great councils met in Constance (1414–18), Basel (1431–49), and Florence-Ferrara (1438–45) in order to reform the Church. The same councils played a crucial role in advancing the cause of humanism by spreading books and manuscripts of ancient learning to the participants. From Petrarch to Erasmus, Renaissance, Church reform, and humanism were closely intertwined.

THE REFORMATION

That changed during the Reformation. The Reformation shifted the center of gravity in the historical development of early modern Europe from Italy to Germany and turned what had been a reasonably happy alliance between Renaissance and Church reform into a frontal assault on the established structure of the Church. In Germany the laity was less familiar with writing than elsewhere in Europe and not as closely integrated with the clergy as in Italy. This was in part because the local vernacular differed from Latin more sharply than was the case in Romance-speaking Italy, France, and Spain, or even in England where the Norman Conquest had turned French at least temporarily into the language of government. It was also because the German clergy, thanks to its disproportionately noble origins and dioceses that were the size of middling states, was far more highly raised above the laity. In Italy the laity's comparatively thorough command of writing and its close integration with the clergy had allowed the shift from hierarchical conformity to individual mastery of sense to proceed in small increments, without major disruptions. In Germany, the same shift was compressed into a smaller span of time and faced with greater obstacles. That gave it the force of an explosion.

The explosion took symbolic shape in the person and theology of Martin Luther. His story – from the indulgence controversy in 1517 and the great tracts of 1520

(*Address to the Christian Nobility of the German Nation*, *On the Babylonian Captivity of the Church*, and *On Christian Liberty*) to his confrontation with Emperor Charles V in Worms, translation of the Bible while in hiding on the Wartburg, marriage to the former nun Katharina von Bora, and opposition to the rebelling peasants – is so familiar that it need hardly be repeated here. But two points particularly telling for the nature of religious authority deserve to be spelled out.

One is the clarity with which Luther treated the sense of Scripture as the sole foundation of religious authority. He rejected religious authority of any other kind with uncompromising candor. He detested the confusion of religious authority with conformity to the Church. He had nothing but contempt for the imitation of Christ as it had flourished in the later Middle Ages. And he heaped scorn on a distinction that had been close to the heart of medieval religiosity; namely, between commands and counsels of perfection.[12]

Conformity to the Church and resemblance to Christ could be imagined in different degrees. A common medieval teaching had therefore been that not all Christians needed to follow Christ's commands to the letter. When Christ said to the rich man, "if thou wilt be perfect, go and sell that thou hast, and give to the poor" (Matthew 19:21), that was not really a command. It was merely a counsel of perfection. Monks followed it by giving up their private property when they entered the monastery. Mendicant friars like St Francis vowed even stricter poverty than monks. Monks and friars therefore resembled Christ more closely than did the laity, who kept their property for themselves. They approached perfection. But precisely because they approached perfection, their way of life was not obligatory for all Christians.

From Luther's point of view that was a travesty of Christian teaching. Christians were not obliged to make themselves resemble Christ at all. Christ was God, and no human could be like God. Imitation was useless at best and blasphemous at worst. If Christ had wanted Christians to imitate his conduct, Luther thought, all Christians ought to have practiced the art of preaching, assembled a cast of 12 Apostles, and died on the cross, for that was what Christ had done – and none of them should have been cobblers, tailors, husbands, ploughmen, princes, hangmen, or beadles, for Christ was an unmarried carpenter.[13] True Christians did not imitate Christ. They understood his promises and they followed his commands without exception or condition. That did not mean that Christians were perfect. It meant the opposite: that no one achieved perfection in this life.

The freedom with which this view of the Gospel allowed Luther to put himself on the same footing as the papacy and challenge the authority of the Church remains breathtaking. "I have no quarrel with any man concerning his morality, but only concerning the Word of truth," he wrote to Pope Leo X, not as a monk at the bottom of the hierarchy ought to have written to its ruler but as one reader to another, simply concerned to grasp the sense of Scripture. "In all things else I will yield to any man whatsoever: to give up or deny the Word I have neither the power nor the will."[14] The obligation of a Christian was not to follow the papacy but to grasp the sense of the Gospel Christ had preached and to believe his promises. Salvation depended on the Word. Here the shift from conformity to the Church toward identity of sense was made complete, and authentication of the truth by the papacy was replaced with authentication of the truth by Scripture. Scripture, in Calvin's deservedly famous phrase, was "self-authenticated."[15]

The second point worth stressing is the clarity with which Luther recognized that the sense of Scripture could not be used as a criterion of truth unless hierarchy was replaced with dichotomy. In hierarchy there can be many different ranks and orders that are related to each other by the degree to which they resemble the example set at the top. That degree can infinitely vary. The obligation to master a certain sense, however, admits only two possibilities: either you have mastered it or you have not. There is no in-between, no middle ground, and there is certainly no possibility for anything like a hierarchy of truths ascending to heaven step by step, much less a hierarchy of social orders resembling the hierarchy of truth.

Dichotomies therefore proliferate in Luther's thought. Take the distinction that he drew in *Christian Liberty* between the inner and the outer man.[16] The inner man enjoys freedom from the law because he lives by faith. The outer man must serve his neighbor and obey the government. Thus every Christian is at one and the same time a sovereign lord and abject slave. But it is neither possible nor safe to confuse the dichotomy between inner and outer (lord and slave) with the higher and lower elements of hierarchy. The question is, of course, how the life of the inner man is to be reconciled with that of the outer man. But the answer to that question is a mystery that will not be revealed until the final resurrection. In this life, all Christians are both inner and outer, saint and sinner, *simul iustus et peccator*.

Or take the parallel dichotomy between the kingdom of God and the kingdom of the world.[17] No Christian may resist evil. That is one of Christ's commands; all Christians must follow it without exception. But they must follow it only where their own interest is at stake, and their own interest lies solely in the kingdom of God. Meanwhile they live with their neighbors in the kingdom of the world. Where their neighbors are concerned, they may resist evil. Indeed, they are commanded to resist it for the love of neighbor – of course not on their own initiative (which no one could safely take without risking to confuse the love of neighbor with the love of self), but only at the command of their God-given rulers. "For you attend to yourself and what is yours in one way, and to your neighbor and what is his in another. As to you and yours, you keep to the Gospel and suffer injustice as a true Christian. But where the next man and what is his are concerned, you act in accordance with the [command to] love and you tolerate no injustice against him."[18] That is the reason why God ordained the sword and gave it to rulers over the kingdom of the world. So long as those rulers and their soldiers kill for the sake of peace, and not for their own advantage, their killing does not conflict with the command not to resist evil at all. On the contrary, their killing is a work of love.

Dichotomies between self and other, inner and outer, the Christian and the Christian's neighbor, the kingdom of God and the kingdom of the world thus allowed Luther to replace hierarchy (built on conformity to a shared standard) with equality (built on identity of sense). In terms of hierarchy Christians had been asked to explain how closely their conduct resembled the conduct of Christ. The answer resulted in hierarchical distinctions between different forms of conduct with different degrees of merit, depending on how closely they approached perfection. In Luther's terms Christians were asked in whose name their conduct – any kind of conduct – was carried out: their own name or the name of Christ? There were no degrees of merit; there were only two possibilities. No Christian was to resist evil in his own name; all Christians were to resist it for the love of God and neighbor. As Calvin put it:

> There is a twofold government in man: one aspect is spiritual, whereby the conscience is instructed in piety and in reverencing God; the second is political, whereby man is educated for the duties of humanity and citizenship that must be maintained among men. These are usually called the "spiritual" and the "temporal" jurisdiction (not improper terms) by which is meant that the former sort of government pertains to the life of the soul, while the latter has to do with the concerns of the present life. . . . There are in man, so to speak, two worlds, over which different kings and different laws have authority. Through this distinction it comes about that we are not to misapply to the political order the gospel teaching on spiritual freedom, as if Christians were less subject, as concerns outward government, to human laws, because their consciences have been set free in God's sight; as if they were released from all bodily servitude because they are free according to the spirit.[19]

Soldiers, priests, cobblers, married and unmarried folk could all be equally good Christians, no matter what they did in the present life. The question was not what they did, but the sake for which they were doing it. Depending on that sake, they were full members of the society of right-minded people, or banished from it entirely.

THE AGE OF RELIGIOUS WARS

In a few startling phrases, Luther once advocated religious liberty as clearly as could be desired: "No ruler ought to prevent anyone from teaching or believing what he pleases, whether it is the Gospel or lies. It is enough if he prevents the teaching of sedition and rebellion."[20] But Luther could say so only because he did not reckon with the possibility that reasonable people might come to different conclusions about the sense of Scripture. Nothing would have been more repugnant to him than to abandon Scripture as the ground on which all Christians were to take their stand in public no less than private. He was convinced that Scripture had a single sense, and that its sense was clear to all believers. He never wavered from that conviction, even though it caused an irreparable breach with Zwingli and divided him bitterly from the peasants who thought he would support them in their rebellion against their rulers. He stood his ground on Scripture with the same uncompromising certainty that he was in the right as members of the medieval Church had stood their ground on the rock of St Peter. And so did his opponents.

The third period in the history of religious authority in early modern Europe was therefore marked by persistent religious wars. Different interpretations of Scripture's sense were propounded in increasing numbers and no single interpretation won general agreement. Lutherans, Zwinglians, Calvinists, Hutterites, Mennonites, Socinians, and others spread the Gospel in mutually exclusive ways while Catholics were sharpening their own interpretation of the sense of Scripture at the Council of

Trent and devising new means, such as the Jesuits, the Roman Inquisition, the so-called second scholasticism, and missions abroad, in order to keep Catholicism pure, spread its reach, and recover regions lost to Protestants in the great struggle known as the Counter-Reformation. None could agree with any of the others, yet all, including Catholics, insisted with increasing fervor on orthodoxy.

From the Schmalkaldic War in the late 1540s – or even the Peasants War of 1524–5 – via the French wars of religion in the second half of the sixteenth century, and Philip II's great Armada of 1588 down to the English Civil War (1642–8) and the Thirty Years War (1618–48), the inhabitants of Europe found themselves locked in bloody struggles to make one kind of sense prevail over the others. They only stopped when it was clear to all that none were able to prevail. Exhaustion convinced them to admit that Scripture could no longer serve as a criterion of truth. And peace did not return until they had agreed on sovereignty as the new criterion.

Accordingly the nature and exercise of religious authority were reconfigured in ways that proved enormously successful until the havoc wrought by sovereign states in the twentieth century led to growing doubts about their legitimacy. A line was drawn that had never been drawn like this before: the line between the private and the public realm. In itself that line was not a new invention. It figures prominently in antiquity and Roman law. It figures even more prominently in the distinction the medieval Church had drawn between the sacramental power priests exercised by virtue of their ordination (*potestas ordinis*) over the conscience of Christians in the privacy of the confessional (*forum internum*) and the power of jurisdiction (*potestas iurisdictionis*) the papacy exercised by virtue of its plenitude of power (*plenitudo potestatis*) over the whole Church in the public domain (*forum externum*). What was new was the use of that distinction to confine religious authority completely to the private sphere. Henceforth religious authority was going to be grounded in the self, subject solely to individual choice, and wholly removed from the enforcement of laws in the public realm.

That does not mean that religion disappeared from the public sphere, that governments no longer took an interest in questions of faith, or that religious liberty was instantly granted to all. By social habit, if nothing else, but usually as a matter of public policy as well, adherence to one or another religious faith continued to have momentous consequences, both advantageous and disabling, for different sectors of the citizenry. All states had more or less explicit affiliations with one or another kind of church; the Peace of Westphalia gave territorial rulers a formal right to choose the faith to be observed within the borders of their lands (the so-called *ius reformandi*); dissenters suffered serious disabilities; atheism was universally condemned; and Jews were never admitted to full and equal membership in the community.

And yet the middle of the seventeenth century marked a watershed in the history of religious authority.[21] For the first time, religious faith was ruled out as a criterion with which to distinguish members of the community from outsiders. It no longer made a difference to the organization of society whether religious faith was authenticated by the papacy or by mastery of the sense of Scripture. A new consensus relegated both kinds of authentication to the private sphere and severed them from laws and law enforcement. Hierarchy gave way to two kinds of sovereignty: the sovereignty of states and rulers in public and the sovereignty of individuals in private.

And social order came to be founded on dichotomies like self and other, domestic and foreign, peace and war, private and public, religious and secular, moral and legal. These are the means by which Europe emerged from a great civil war over the nature and exercise of religious authority and laid the conceptual foundations on which the modern world was built.

CONCLUSION: A SINGLE STORY CAN BE TOLD

A single story can therefore perhaps be told about the history of religious authority in early modern Europe without casting that story as progress from ignorance and oppression to reason and liberty. That story could plausibly begin with the Fourth Lateran Council in 1215 and end with the Peace of Westphalia in 1648.

The Fourth Lateran Council met in 1215 under the presidency of Pope Innocent III. It is properly remembered as the greatest council of the high medieval Church, and the canons that it laid down may be regarded as the single most important body of legislative work completed in high medieval Europe.[22] The canons began with a formal declaration of the doctrine of the Trinity, and they included the dogma of transubstantiation. They condemned alternative positions as heretical and laid down inquisitorial procedures by which the spread of heresies was to be brought under control. Bishops were obliged to investigate their flock, even where no formal charges of heresy had been brought. Secular governments were sworn on pain of losing their authority to assist the Church in seeking out and punishing heretics. All adult Christians were ordered on pain of excommunication to confess their sins and take communion at least once per year. A crusade against the infidels was planned. And temporal rulers who had crossed the papacy, such as the counts of Toulouse, the barons of England, and the enemies of Emperor Frederick II of Hohenstaufen, were subjected to ecclesiastical discipline. At the Fourth Lateran Council the Catholic faith as declared by the papacy served Europe as a universal standard by which all forms of conduct could be judged, to which all Christians could be expected to conform, and to which recalcitrants could be made to conform by force.

About four centuries later, from 1643 to 1648, the Congress of Westphalia assembled close to 150 diplomatic representatives from Germany, Sweden, France, Spain, and many other states to meet in separate gatherings in Münster and Osnabrück. Three different interpretations of the sense of Scripture – Catholic, Lutheran, and Calvinist – were given equal standing. The freedom of every person's conscience (*conscientia libera*) was explicitly endorsed. People whose faith differed from that of their territorial ruler were assured that they would be "tolerated" (*patienter tolerentur*) and given a formal right to emigrate without damage to life, property, or reputation. Conflicting religious parties were prohibited from using force to make their views prevail and the Church was denied the right to exercise any jurisdiction over the clauses of the Peace.[23] The papacy protested and annulled what it regarded as a peace with heretics. But its annulment went unheeded and for a century or more it was condemned to political insignificance.[24] Henceforth individual persons were aiming to become sovereign rulers over their own bodies and minds, as John Stuart Mill was going to put it later on,[25] and questions of public order, including questions of religion whenever religion threatened the peace, were going to be decided by sovereign rulers enforcing the law at home and defending the territory of their state by military force.

The history that unfolded between the Fourth Lateran Council and the Congress of Westphalia consisted of the Renaissance, the Reformation, and the Age of Religious War. The meaning of those phases for the nature of religious authority can be summed up like this. The Renaissance developed new criteria of religious authority by moving from conformity to the Catholic faith, as authenticated by the papacy, to grasping the sense of Scripture, but it did not assault the established order of the Church. During the Reformation, the sense of Scripture escaped from the control of the Church and was deployed in opposition to its established structures. Scripture still served to underwrite public authority, but the distinction between clergy and laity lost its hierarchical significance. The Age of Religious War offered conclusive proof that the shift from conformity to sense made peace impossible to keep unless the exercise of public authority was founded on something other than religion, regardless of whether religion was authenticated by the papacy in Rome or by the self-authentication of Scripture. Religious authority was therefore limited to the private sphere, and the maintenance of public order was turned over to sovereign rulers. Thus religious liberty became an inalienable individual right on the condition that private individuals would keep their religion to themselves, surrender the use of force to sovereign states, and use no other grounds on which to make demands upon the public sphere than reason and observation.

NOTES

1 John W. O'Malley, *Trent and All That: Renaming Catholicism in the Early Modern Era* (Cambridge, Mass.: Harvard University Press, 2000) is good on the historiography.
2 Ernest Gellner, *Plough, Sword and Book: The Structure of Human History* (Chicago: University of Chicago Press, 1988).
3 I simplify greatly, but the principle is the same, regardless of whether the standard used to authenticate the reliability of instruments of measurement consists of a metal bar, the wavelength of a specified color of light, or any other thing. For details, see http://www.bipm.org/en/si/history-si/evolution_metre.html (accessed July 8, 2005).
4 For a deservedly famous demonstration of the reasons why it is nonsensical, see Ludwig Wittgenstein, *Philosophical Investigations*, section 50, trans. G. E. M. Anscombe (Oxford: Blackwell, 1953), pp. 24–5.
5 "Prima sedes non iudicabitur a quoquam." Gratian, *Decretum*, D.21 c. 7, in *Corpus Iuris Canonici*, ed. E. Friedberg (Leipzig: Tauchnitz, 1879), vol. 1, col. 71.
6 William Durant the Elder, *Speculum iudiciale*, 1.1, De legato 6.52, quoted from Constantin Fasolt, *Council and Hierarchy: The Political Thought of William Durant the Younger* (Cambridge: Cambridge University Press, 1991), p. 67. Note the explicit exception for a heretical pope.
7 "A heretic, by canonical definition, was one whose views were 'chosen by human perception, contrary to holy scripture, publicly avowed and obstinately defended.'" R. I.

Moore, *The Formation of a Persecuting Society* (Oxford: Blackwell, 1987), p. 68, with reference to Gratian, *Decretum*, C.24 q.3 cc.27–31, in *Corpus Iuris Canonici*, vol. 1, cols. 997–8.

8. Anthony Grafton, Adrian Johns, and Elizabeth L. Eisenstein, "*AHR* Forum: How Revolutionary Was the Print Revolution?" *American Historical Review* 107 (2002): 84–128.
9. Paul Oskar Kristeller, *Renaissance Thought, 1: The Classic, Scholastic, and Humanist Strains* (New York: Harper & Row, 1961), pp. 3–23.
10. Hans Baron, *The Crisis of the Italian Renaissance: Civic Humanism and Republican Liberty in an Age of Classicism and Tyranny*, 2nd edn (Princeton: Princeton University Press, 1966).
11. Petrarch, *Letters on Familiar Matters*, quoted from *University of Chicago Readings in Western Civilization*, vol. 5: *The Renaissance*, eds Eric Cochrane and Julius Kirshner (Chicago: University of Chicago Press, 1986), pp. 32, 33, 45.
12. Martin Luther, "On Secular Authority," in *Luther and Calvin on Secular Authority*, trans. Harro Höpfl (Cambridge: Cambridge University Press, 1991), pp. 4, 8.
13. Luther, "On Secular Authority," pp. 18–19.
14. Luther, "Letter to Pope Leo X," in *University of Chicago Readings in Western Civilization*, vol. 5: *The Renaissance*, p. 327.
15. "Let this point therefore stand: that those whom the Holy Spirit has inwardly taught truly rest upon Scripture, and that Scripture indeed is self-authenticated." John Calvin, *Institutes of the Christian Religion*, bk. 1, chap. 7, sec. 5, ed. John T. McNeill, trans. Ford Lewis Battles, 2 vols (Philadelphia: Westminster Press, 1960), vol. 1, p. 80.
16. Martin Luther, *Christian Liberty*, trans. W. A. Lambert (Philadelphia: Fortress Press, 1957), pp. 7–8, 21–2, and *passim*.
17. Luther, "On Secular Authority," pp. 8–14 and *passim*.
18. Luther, "On Secular Authority," p. 15 (brackets in the original).
19. Calvin, *Institutes of the Christian Religion*, bk. 3, chap. 19, sec. 15, vol. 1, p. 847.
20. Luther, "To the Princes and Lords," in *University of Chicago Readings in Western Civilization*, vol. 5: *The Renaissance*, p. 340.
21. For a good explanation of this periodization, see Theodore K. Rabb, *The Struggle for Stability in Early Modern Europe* (New York: Oxford University Press, 1975).
22. Raymonde Foreville, *Latran I, II, III et Latran IV* (Paris: Editions de l'Orante, 1965).
23. *Instrumentum pacis Osnabrugense*, art. V, paras. 1–2, 34–7, 48; art. VII, para. 1, in Karl Zeumer, ed., *Quellensammlung zur Geschichte der Deutschen Reichverfassung in Mittelalter und Neuzeit*, 2nd edn (Tübingen: Mohr, 1913), pp. 403, 410, 412, 415–16.
24. Konrad Repgen, "Der päpstliche Protest gegen den Westfälischen Frieden und die Friedenspolitik Urbans VIII." *Historisches Jahrbuch* 75 (1956): 94–122.
25. "Over himself, over his own body and mind, the individual is sovereign." John Stuart Mill, *On Liberty*, ed. Gertrude Himmelfarb (Harmondsworth: Penguin, 1974), p. 69.

SUGGESTIONS FOR FURTHER READING

Baron, Hans. *The Crisis of the Italian Renaissance: Civic Humanism and Republican Liberty in an Age of Classicism and Tyranny*, 2nd edn. Princeton: Princeton University Press, 1966.

Bellomo, Manlio. *The Common Legal Past of Europe, 1000–1800*, trans. Lydia G. Cochrane. Washington, DC: Catholic University of America Press, 1995.

Berman, Harold J. *Law and Revolution: The Formation of the Western Legal Tradition*. Cambridge, Mass.: Harvard University Press, 1983.

Bossy, John. *Christianity in the West, 1400–1700*. Oxford: Oxford University Press, 1985.

Burckhardt, Jacob. *Die Cultur der Renaissance in Italien*. Basle: Schweighauser, 1860.

Dickmann, Fritz. *Der Westfälische Frieden*, 4th edn, ed. Konrad Repgen. Münster: Aschendorff, 1977.

Elias, Norbert. *The Civilizing Process*, trans. Edmund Jephcott. Oxford: Blackwell, 1994.

Evennett, H. Outram. *The Spirit of the Counter Reformation*, ed. John Bossy. Birkbeck Lectures. Cambridge: Cambridge University Press, 1968.

Febvre, Lucien. "The Origins of the French Reformation: A Badly-put Question?" in Peter Burke, ed., *A New Kind of History and Other Essays*. New York: 1973, pp. 44–107.

Febvre, Lucien and Henri-Jean Martin. *The Coming of the Book: The Impact of Printing, 1450–1800*, trans. David Gerard. London: NLB, 1976.

Figgis, John Neville. *Studies of Political Thought from Gerson to Grotius, 1414–1625*, 2nd edn. Cambridge: Cambridge University Press, 1916.

Gellner, Ernest. *Plough, Sword and Book: The Structure of Human History*. Chicago: University of Chicago Press, 1988.

Grafton, Anthony, Adrian Johns, and Elizabeth L. Eisenstein. "*AHR* Forum: How Revolutionary Was the Print Revolution?" *American Historical Review* 107 (2002): 84–128.

Johns, Adrian. *The Nature of the Book: Print and Knowledge in the Making*. Chicago: University of Chicago Press, 1998.

Koselleck, Reinhart. *Critique and Crisis: Enlightenment and the Pathogenesis of Modern Society*. Cambridge, Mass.: MIT Press, 1988.

Kristeller, Paul Oskar. *Renaissance Thought, 1: The Classic, Scholastic, and Humanist Strains*. New York: Harper & Row, 1961.

Moore, Robert Ian. *The Formation of a Persecuting Society: Power and Deviance in Western Europe, 950–1250*. Oxford: Blackwell, 1987.

Oakley, Francis. *Omnipotence, Covenant and Order: An Excursion in the History of Ideas from Abelard to Leibniz*. Ithaca, N.Y.: Cornell University Press, 1984.

—— *The Western Church in the Later Middle Ages*. Ithaca, N.Y.: Cornell University Press, 1979.

Oberman, Heiko A. *Luther: Man between God and the Devil*, trans. Eileen Walliser-Schwarzbart. New Haven: Yale University Press, 1989.

O'Malley, John W. *Trent and All That: Renaming Catholicism in the Early Modern Era*. Cambridge, Mass.: Harvard University Press, 2000.

Peters, Edward. *Inquisition*. Berkeley: University of California Press, 1988.

Rabb, Theodore K. *The Struggle for Stability in Early Modern Europe*. New York: Oxford University Press, 1975.

Ranke, Leopold von. *Deutsche Geschichte im Zeitalter der Reformation*, 6 vols. Berlin: Duncker und Humblot, 1839–47.

Rosenstock-Huessy, Eugen. *Out of Revolution: Autobiography of Western Man*. London: Jarrolds, 1938.

Skinner, Quentin. *The Foundations of Modern Political Thought*, 2 vols. Cambridge: Cambridge University Press, 1978.

Tierney, Brian. *The Idea of Natural Rights: Studies on Natural Rights, Natural Law, and Church Law, 1150–1625*. Atlanta, Ga.: Scholars Press, 1997.

Trevor-Roper, Hugh R. "Religion, the Reformation and Social Change," in *The European Witch-craze of the Sixteenth and Seventeenth Centuries and Other Essays*, by Hugh R. Trevor-Roper. New York: Harper & Row, 1969, pp. 1–45.

Trinkaus, Charles Edward. *"In Our Image and Likeness": Humanity and Divinity in Italian Humanist Thought*, 2 vols. Chicago: University of Chicago Press, 1970.

Weber, Max. *The Protestant Ethic and the Spirit of Capitalism*, trans. Talcott Parsons. New York: Scribner, 1958.

CHAPTER NINETEEN

MOTHERS AND CHILDREN

Caroline Castiglione

In her late sixteenth-century dialogue, *The Worth of Women*, the Venetian writer Moderata Fonte captured a central dilemma of Renaissance motherhood in an evocative hypothetical question. In the midst of grave difficulty, a mother has the power to save only her husband, or her son, or her father. She must choose between them. As the fictional interlocutor framed the dilemma: "[W]hose life should I most value – he who gave me life, he who joined himself to me in marriage, or he to whom I gave birth?" While the women had inconclusively debated the relative worth of difficult husbands and disloyal sons, unanimity greeted the following solution to the gruesome riddle:

> If you are a loving mother, you must rescue your dear son from the cruel enemy ranks, for, if you choose to give life to your husband or your aged father, you are endangering your own life. A mother's love is instinctive, natural love, while a woman's love for her father contains an element of duty, that for her husband, an element of principle. And, by as much as love outweighs duty and principle, so the bond of maternity outweighs those of marriage or filial obligation.

The enthusiasm for this solution among Fonte's fictional conversationalists is unique in the text. Like many Renaissance dialogues, *The Worth of Women* does not often steer the reader to a clear conclusion, especially regarding women's relationships. But here the unanimous remedy for the divided loyalties of womanhood privileged an instinctive bond over relationships of obligation. The contrast between the natural goodness of a mother's love and the shortcomings of the social order would become a commonplace in the early modern world, an enduring ideological configuration of womanhood embedded in European modernity.[1]

Fonte's celebratory assertion of maternal love evolved amidst the bureaucratic expansion of Italian states in the aftermath of invasion and war. It also emerged alongside the increasing engagement of women in the reforming agenda of the Roman Catholic Church. Its detractors were many, its allies unwitting, its proponents certainly unaware of how long their heirs would wrestle with its impact on women's lives. Those who praised it saw it as a resolution of the contradictions of female identity: daughter, wife, mother, Christian, legal advocate, financial counselor, mediating figure at the nexus of two families. That any relationship could resolve this constellation of social roles was impossible, of course, but the increasing numbers of sources that celebrate maternal feeling suggest a heightened engagement with its potential to clarify women's lives – to offer women who became mothers a well-defined identity that could serve as a sort of moral fulcrum in a world that imposed so many conflicting expectations upon them.

CRUEL MOTHERS AND THE FAILURES OF INSTINCTIVE LOVE

Three decades ago the historian Christiane Klapisch-Zuber argued that Florentine women of the Renaissance faced significant impediments to forming the kind of maternal bonds that motivated Fonte's imaginary mother. Although historians have disputed her conclusions, Klapisch-Zuber's path-breaking research set the parameters of debate about womanhood and motherhood in pre-modern Italy. She characterized fifteenth-century Florentine women as mere "visitors" to Florentine houses, which were made by and for men through the laws of patrilinear inheritance. Some elite women's experience of mothering was severely limited because of the custom of using wet nurses, since breastfeeding was believed to weaken the health of the mother and sexual intercourse was thought to contaminate the mother's milk. This practice raised Florentine women's fertility, but it also may have limited the development of the mother–child bond. Even the choice of the wet nurse typically rested with the father of the child.[2]

Other legal impediments precluded a strong relationship between Florentine mothers and children. Married in their teens to men often a decade or more older, elite women in fifteenth-century Florence were often widowed at a young age. In such a scenario, the widow would be pressured by her natal family to reclaim her dowry and leave behind her children with her husband's family (to whom they legally belonged, unless he had left her custody in his will). Her natal family would then arrange a new marriage for her. In returning to her natal kin she acted the dutiful daughter while, in the eyes of her deceased husband's family, she was typically portrayed as the "cruel mother." As one prominent merchant bitterly noted of his sister-in-law: "[she] left the house with her dowry of 900 *fiorini* and left her children on the straw, with nothing." The patrilinear family and the dowry system itself created this problematic moral dilemma for widowed mothers, forcing them to choose between alternatives that were unsatisfactory either to their natal or their marital kin, but often, undoubtedly, to themselves. Florentine men did not face the same contradictions after the death of their spouses. For a father without a wife, there was no contradiction between remaining loyal to his lineage, loving his children, and marrying a new woman.[3]

A young widow who chose to remain with her children and reject remarriage was seen as a manly hero since her ethos of self-sacrifice was associated with the constancy of a father's love. She was, in the words of the historian Giulia Calvi, "a fine asexual and virile model" for humanity. Her true obstacles to remaining with her children may have been her husband's refusal to designate her guardian, or pressure from her natal family due to the dowry system, but fifteenth-century writers such as Leon Battista Alberti argued that love itself varied according to gender: "I most certainly do not believe that there is any love more secure, more constant, more complete, or greater than the love of a father for his children." Alberti (and later Montaigne) voiced reservations about a mother's love, noting its defective origins in her physical body. Such love was considered weaker than the love that arose in the mind of the father. Like a cat, a Renaissance mother might love her young intensely and instinctively, but not for long. Some male writers thus extrapolated the dilemma created for young widows by the dowry system into a weakness inherent in all maternal love.[4]

Yet, as other scholars have argued, this emphasis on patrilineality and the dowry system overlooks other structures, social and legal, through which women were able to achieve at least a modicum of autonomy. Thomas Kuehn, for example, has demonstrated that Florentine women could inherit property beyond their dowry under certain circumstances, and demonstrated considerable independence in tending to the distribution of their own assets in their wills. Women, in other words, were not merely visitors in patriarchal households, and this certainly had a bearing on their experience of motherhood. Even the impact of the most potentially disruptive event for Florentine mothers, the loss of their children at the death of their spouse, is difficult to assess, but wills and testaments suggest that affective ties between a mother and her children could continue long after her physical separation from them. In the late sixteenth century, for instance, Maddalena Nerli Tornabuoni still recognized the children from her first marriage in her will, many years after her husband had denied her the custody of those same offspring. While she no longer resided with them, she may have found ways to tend to their care informally and from a distance.[5]

Similarly, the dowry system itself could provide women in the Renaissance with considerable autonomy. As Stanley Chojnacki has shown, women's control of their dowries gave them bargaining power, especially when it came time to decide the destiny of children who frequently needed the money from the mother's dowry to establish themselves as adults. Mothers used this financial autonomy to argue for more latitude for their children's choices – including whether they wished to marry or to choose the religious life. The ever-increasing size of dowries eventually generated its own perils – falling rates of marriage for aristocrats, increasing numbers of women in convents between the late sixteenth and first half of the seventeenth centuries. But in the earlier period women's control of the dowry gave them some autonomy in their mothering, and they used that independence to broaden their children's choices.[6]

These practices suggest that elite families were more bilinear than patrilinear, and that they drew on the allies and the resources of both maternal and paternal lineages in order to situate the next generation of children. Mothers were the nexus point between two dynasties, playing important networking and diplomatic roles. In Rome, the activities of women – and especially the activities of mothers – were critical in advancing dynastic aims, an activity so complex that the historian Renata Ago has suggested that it was a "team sport," in which the efforts of both women and men were necessary for success. Mothers were expected to engage in informal diplomacy, even during pregnancy, unless nausea or other complications curtailed their public appearances. Roman aristocratic women (like their Florentine counterparts) also maintained an active engagement in childrearing, and were frequently in charge of arranging the marriage of daughters.[7]

Renaissance women – it appears – often remained actively involved in the lives of their children during and beyond childhood. If women were lucky, after all, motherhood was a life sentence, where the bonds between mother and child endured until her death. Alessandra Strozzi's letters to her sons provide insights into this lifelong relationship. She endured the twin burden of widowhood and the exile of her marital kin, including her two older sons. In Florence, she advanced her sons' interests, pursued political connections to rescind their exile, and advised them on their business affairs. To her deep regret, she eventually had to send her teenage son, Matteo, away from her home to join his exiled brothers in the family business. She was deeply attached to this youngest child, whom she had raised alone after the death of her husband. Her love for him prompted her to stall his departure in a variety of ways. His eventual death in his early twenties while exiled with his brothers was a great blow to her, which she openly shared in her letters to her surviving sons. *Vis-à-vis* her daughters and her potential daughters-in-law, Strozzi talks about women quite a bit like her Florentine contemporary, Leon Battista Alberti in his *Libri della famiglia*. But regarding her boys, and her youngest boy in particular, Strozzi was an emotionally committed mother, although such sentiments were seen to stand in the way of the larger dynastic and financial ambitions of the family. In the end, not even Alessandra, as manly a widow as one was likely to find in the Renaissance, was able to privilege her feelings for her youngest son over the larger ambitions of the Strozzi.[8]

THE MOTHER ADVOCATE AND HER UNLIKELY ALLIES, 1550–1650

By the mid-sixteenth century, Italians had endured decades of invasion, occupation, and war. Despite the catastrophic ambitions of the peninsula's combatants and Spain's growing influence in Italian politics, many of the independent northern and central Italian states re-emerged from half a century of conflict with their sovereignty more or less intact. Moreover, during the late sixteenth century, Italian states significantly extended their authority to towns and villages under the jurisdiction of their capitals. In the same period the Church, too, largely in response to the challenge of Protestantism, expanded its institutional reach into Italian society. Both of these initiatives had significance for women, many of whom facilitated ecclesiastical and secular institutions' interventions in family life.

In Tuscany, for instance, a significantly reorganized bureaucracy, the Magistrato dei Pupilli (The Magistracy for the Protection of Children), intervened to secure the well-being of children who had lost their father (or both parents). In her exploration of this particular magistracy, the historian Giulia Calvi has shown that these magistrates typically intervened only under certain circumstances. A husband who explicitly stated in his last will that his wife was in charge of their children created a scenario that was unlikely to involve the Magistrato dei Pupilli. She and his kin would typically work out arrangements on their own. If a husband failed to specify who would be their guardian, or if a mother was not designated guardian but insisted upon it nonetheless, the children's destiny might be decided by the Magistrato. The typical custody battle decided by the Magistrato was between the children's mother and the deceased father's brother. Mothers who brought petitions claimed that the well-being of women and children constituted the measure by which the stability of families (and thereby society) should be judged. Evidently they were often persuasive. In about 70 percent of the cases in which the father died intestate or the custody was disputed, the Magistrato found in favor of the mother, granting her custody of the children. The success of some women could constitute potential leverage for other mothers in conflict with marital kin.[9]

What legal precedents facilitated the settlement of so many disputes in the mothers' favor? Magistrates relied on what could be called a legal loophole in statutory law: ideally no orphan should be the ward of a person who is potentially his or her heir. When a Tuscan father died, his children were poised to inherit his patrimony, unless those children also died. In the case of the children's death, the property would typically pass to their father's brother or to other male kin. In this inheritance scheme, a widow could not inherit from her husband, unless her husband designated her as his heir in his will. Women and magistrates employed this legal particularity to insist that by her very marginality to her husband's inheritance, a widowed mother was the most appropriate parent: she could not profit from the death of her offspring in the same way her brother-in-law potentially could.[10]

A mother's love for her offspring was therefore "above suspicion." A good mother practiced *carità* and *affetto* toward her children. Her love was given for its own sake. Extraneous to her financial interest, her love was "pure" and "free" (*gratuito*). In the rare case when a woman was named her husband's heir, she was not given guardianship of the children. Her financial interests in such cases were believed to compromise her maternal love. Another potential compromise was her remarriage, but about half of the women who pursued custody after their remarriage were granted it by the Magistrato. As Margherita Corselli, a wealthy widow in the 1630s, explained, she "loved her son more than herself," and thus her remarriage could not threaten her relationship to her child, which took precedent over all other relationships, and could only be compromised by the birth of another child by her second husband.[11]

In addition to their disinterestedness, women came to be seen as superior parents to men. This was easier to assert than to prove, but attempts were made. The case was easiest for a mother to make with children under the age of three, or with her daughters, whose education, it was widely believed, could best be provided for by her mother. But some women also argued that this was the case with all children regardless of their sex or their age. In the case of six-year-old Domenico, whose health was frail, the argument made on behalf of maternal custody was that his male relatives, although motivated by paternal love, "are incapable of learning to do the things that children require." A second husband testified that common sense (*ragion comune*) dictated that a son belonged to his mother – in this case, to his second wife, regardless of her new marriage to him.[12]

The success of Tuscan widows suggests a significant shift in attitudes about mothering between the late sixteenth century and the early seventeenth. In the fifteenth century, the cruel mother had been the stereotype of female failure; in the sixteenth and seventeenth centuries, by contrast, the "cruel uncle" was evoked as the villain from whom the children (and sometimes their mother) had to be protected. His failings went beyond the general child-rearing incompetence of his gender (whether claimed, feigned, or real). A particularly acrimonious dispute in the Tuscan countryside elaborated the dangers the uncle posed. In the late 1630s, Agnese Griffoli of Montepulciano argued that her brother-in-law's shady financial maneuvers were eroding her children's inheritance, and he refused to give a financial accounting of his dealings. Agnese also charged that he withheld sufficient food and clothing from them. Even a paternal relative begged the magistrates to place the children exclusively under their mother's control, or "we won't have them with us for very much longer." Agnese hoped to protect her offspring's inheritance and to move with her children to another house, separate from that of her brother-in-law. The level of domestic tension was clearly considerable, as phrases and accusations from the trial testimony suggest: "Agnese can salt the food any way she wants"; or "[her] cat eats the pork guts that Agnese cleans for sausage making." According to her brother-in-law she tended to hoard sausages and hams. Nonetheless, years of petition-writing secured for Agnese some financial measures to protect the children's inheritance, and she won the right to leave her brother-in-law's house with her children. Arguments for the latter refer to the request to "live on their own" (or as another widow put it, "avere casa da per sé") – a chance to manage the upbringing of the children in a house of her own, which would "be better [done] by her, the mother, than by anyone else."[13]

Similarly successful negotiations between magistrates and women also emerge from the records of ecclesiastical courts to which many women in this period appealed in efforts to fashion more tolerable marriages. The clarification at the Council of Trent about what constituted legitimate marriage helped some women find exits from marital hells, and other women assert the validity of their claim that they were indeed married, whatever their nay-saying male partners might say. Decisions from the Patriarchal Court of Venice suggest that in addition to the minimal canonical requirements for marriage (free consent and consummation) magistrates also insisted upon a minimal financial support for wives, alongside limitations on the amount of physical violence to which the woman might be subjected. A separation might be granted in cases where women were excessively threatened financially or physically by their husbands. These latter claims are similar to those made by widows to the Magistrato, and suggest a minimal standard for what was necessary for women and children to survive in the home. Thus, both state and Church courts assumed the role of imposing these standards from outside the family, suggesting the mutually beneficial cooperation between women and magistrates that emerged in (and beyond) the sixteenth century.[14]

The parallels between the arguments Renaissance women brought before both the secular and the ecclesiastical courts and Fonte's *fictional femme* forte are clear. Such claims undermined the notion that successful parenting required a man, or a celibate manly widow. If we consider the cornerstone of the modern affective family its psychological and physical extrication from issues of inheritance, its hyper-consideration of the well-being of the child as an assessment of its success, and a tendency toward matrilinearity, then magistrates and petitioning women were at least experimenting in the late sixteenth and seventeenth centuries with what became the family's core elements in the modern era. It was elaborated however, not to launch modern motherhood or the modern family, but rather as a corrective to legal and familial structures that had made it so difficult for a woman in this period to make a morally coherent life for herself, especially given her conflicting roles as mother, daughter, and remarried woman. Even in Tuscany where women's options in the late Renaissance appear to have been extremely limited, an important magistracy saw the dilemma resolved in motherhood, and mothers as capable and even preferable to their male in-laws in that task.[15]

Renaissance juridical institutions, therefore, fostered among women a rich legal culture, not only as they prepared to go to court on their own behalf but also as they talked with their mothers, their sisters, their daughters, and their friends about what their possibilities were. As Thomas Kuehn has demonstrated, legal literacy was integral to the culture of late medieval and Renaissance Italian elites, including elite women. In the later Renaissance and early modern period, therefore, women were drawing on forms of practical and collective knowledge about the nature of courts with which they had been long familiar. Inevitably, therefore, as both state and Church courts became more central in the administration of the early modern state, women themselves became stronger advocates for themselves and their families; they learned how to navigate new legal and bureaucratic systems, and they gained specific knowledge of the means of advancing their own cases in the expanding juridical arenas of Italy. I have called the constellation of such practices among peasants in the early modern Italian state "adversarial literacy," and this concept applies to the strategies of Renaissance women as well, as we see varied cases of women petitioning before the Magistrato dei Pupilli in Tuscany and of their counterparts in Venice appealing to the ecclesiastical courts.[16]

Yet the cultural values upon which Renaissance women forged a new maternal identity did not rest exclusively on their legal knowledge. They drew upon religious imagery and ideals as well. The idea that a mother's love for her child was greater than (or the same as) her love for herself likely finds its origins in the medieval devotion to Mary as co-participant in the Passion of Jesus, or as St Catherine summarized it: "the Son was physically pierced, and so was his mother, since his flesh was hers." Advocating mothers celebrated maternal tenderness to the point of conflating the well-being (or suffering) of the child with the well-being (or suffering) of the mother, a domestic devotion surely inspired by the earlier Marian one. Another source of inspiration for Mary's maternal tenderness was the *Madonna lactans*, an image in which Mary prepares to feed the baby Jesus. Although such depictions of Mary increasingly fell out of fashion in the late sixteenth century, the theme persisted in works such as Sofisniba Anguissola's tender and realistic image of 1588. Anguissola shows Mary supporting her breast between her index and middle fingers in order to nurse the baby Jesus, who is distracted by his viewing the audience. Artemisia Gentileschi captured a similar tenderness and nursing technique in her early seventeenth-century painting, *Madonna Feeding the Christ Child*. Mary supports

Figure 19.1 Artemesia Gentileschi (1593–1652). *Madonna Feeding the Christ Child*, 1610–11, Spada Gallery, Rome.

the older infant Jesus with her left arm, using her right hand to pull down her garment and manipulate her exposed breast into the same naturalistic V-hold, a position still used by mothers today (Figure 19.1).[17]

Maternal advocacy thus drew upon older religious devotions to Mary as the physical mother of Jesus. As Donna Spivey Ellington has shown, late medieval devotion to Mary also emphasized her emotions, activities, and speech during and after her life on earth. This earlier Mary contrasted with the "silent, self-controlled, and obedient" Mary of the Catholic Reformation. Thus, older aspects of Marian devotion continued to serve as inspiration even as newer images of Mary emerged. In the late sixteenth century, for example, Lucrezia della Rovere Colonna commissioned paintings for her natal family chapel that emphasized the importance of the matrilinear descent of Jesus through Mary and praised the tenderness of maternal love as exemplified by the Virgin. Lucrezia likewise employed subtle choices in the chapel in order to critique her marital family, the Colonna, who had behaved despicably toward her and her daughters. By including the Massacre of the Innocents, a biblical scene not associated with the Marian cycle, Lucrezia's patronage emphasized the most painful possible loss associated with motherhood, seeking consolation in the solidarity of maternal suffering, since one of her daughters had been kidnapped and raped by a member of her husband's family. Lucrezia reinforced the visual criticisms with specific written ones that she included in her will.[18]

Whether through their patronage of the visual arts or through their recourse to written protest, mother advocates drew on old and new cultural paradigms to protect their children (and themselves). Mothers effectively emphasized long-standing contradictions in their society, including the potential conflict between patrilinear interests and the well-being of young heirs. Like Fonte's heroine, such women were in crises that necessitated the drawing of strict boundaries between the ideals of mothering and the threats posed to it by men with more power than love for children.

MOTHERING ON THE EPISTOLARY HORIZON

The correspondence of Anna Colonna Barberini (1601–58), devoted daughter, enthusiastic matron-patron, wife and mother, opens up for us a view of motherhood that drew on both legal and religious traditions and practices at the end of the Renaissance. Indeed, certain of Anna's views appear to reflect Fonte's arguments about women. And, even if we cannot assume that Anna knew of those specific arguments, her assiduous attention to many of the same matters, and her use of the terms *affetto* and *amore* echo the comments of her elite female peers elsewhere in Italy. How did Anna configure the meaning of mothering, especially in relationship to the other social roles in her life?

Anna's enthusiasm for Catholic Reformation piety, her spiritualized motherhood, and her consistent attention to bilinear aristocratic family interests were commitments that she reinvented throughout her life. As a bride, Anna was older than usual. She was 26 when she married, and two years older than her groom, Taddeo (1603–47), the nephew of the reigning pope, Maffeo Barberini, elected Pope Urban

VIII in 1623. Anna's words and her actions attest to the aristocratic woman's delicate balancing of her activities on the part of natal and marital kin, the goals of her religious piety, and the considerable physical and psychological demands of raising the Barberini heirs amidst the reality of high childhood mortality. She attended to this latter task with the utmost seriousness and anxiety. The Roman aristocratic family was certainly bilinear in its practices, but her activities were multivalent, consuming her days – or, as she summarized life during her children's early years: "I don't have time to eat."[19]

Unfortunately for Anna, the demands of being a dutiful Colonna were very high, and the Colonna exigencies followed her throughout the years of intense activity on behalf of the Barberini. While the Barberini ruled the Papal States, her branch of the Colonna family were in financial free-fall. Her letters describe her goals for the Colonna, of securing, that is, valuable assistance for them from various members of the Barberini family. Her motivating metaphors intertwined familial and religious iconographies of devotion. Anna's loyalty to her *casa paterna* is expressed clearly in her metaphorical shorthand for it: "bones and blood." The potential alienation of Colonna fiefs, a financial loss as well as a public humiliation, struck her as particularly painful because it represented the loss of what was acquired by the "bones and blood" of the ancestors. In the midst of her brothers' many difficulties, she confessed how much she would like to distance herself from the anxiety-provoking weight of their affairs, but she could not since (as she put it) "she had a great obligation to the bones of my Father . . ."[20] Like Fonte's fictional character, Anna's sense of daughterhood was expressed as duty, inescapable duty.

Her mothering consumed more of her day than the Colonna, and it was fraught with different dilemmas. Although a woman of Anna's social status was unlikely to have breastfed her young children (especially given the closeness of their ages), her letters from the early 1630s suggest that finding and retaining wet nurses for her children, and attending to them through a variety of physical ailments, was a time-consuming and nerve-wracking task. She had legitimate reason to worry. Her first child, Camilla, died in 1630 before she reached the age of two. By 1633, Anna struggled actively for the survival of the remaining children: Carlo (about three years old); Maffeo (about two years old); Lucrezia (about a year old or less). During their illnesses she moved from her own apartments in the Barberini palace to sleep on a makeshift bed in the children's room. Since children were breastfed for as long as two to three years, Anna faced the difficulty of securing enough acceptable wet nurses for all three children. Breast milk was believed to have an impact on the physical and moral development of the child, thus choosing the wet nurse was a particularly crucial choice. Anna related these mothering dilemmas to Taddeo, describing the children's ordinary ailments, such as Maffeo's teething difficulties and his fever as well as the physical demise of Carlo's wet nurse, whose ill-health she described with emotion and as a divine punishment for Anna's sins. In the midst of the crisis over Carlo's wet nurse, Maffeo's fever continued and the physician suggested that Anna secure a new nurse for him as well, or "she could lose the child." Anna was clearly carrying the responsibility of the choice of wet nurse, although she consulted with the Barberini physician, and she expected the long accounts of her wet-nursing dilemmas to be of interest to her husband. Anna interviewed and observed scores of women, eventually calling upon the niece of the wet nurse of Taddeo himself, a woman eliminated from consideration because she arrived at the Barberini *casa* with a seven-month-old baby girl who "looked like a cat."[21]

While Anna sometimes referred to her attention to the children and the Barberini *casa* as an obligation, she more frequently framed her actions in terms of her *amore* and *affetto* for Taddeo and the children. She expressed satisfaction at her activities on their behalf, and genuine delight that by the early 1640s her children's health was mostly good. She also acknowledged, however, that this love of hers could also be seen as a fault, but a fault she hoped others would share: "I know that I am too fond of these children . . . but I wish there were also others who were thinking about them." Such feelings prompted her to disagree (or justified her disagreements) with some of the Barberini expenditures. "Motherly affection" inspired her to advance her opinion, and despite the shortcomings of the origins of her insights (they were rooted in her excess) she showed herself in no way willing to abandon them. Her love allowed her to frame her critique of the Barberini in terms of a higher good (the physical and financial survival of the children), revealed to her by the affection that she bore them.[22]

By contrast her critique of the Barberini as insufficiently concerned about the children was typically linked in her letters to Barberini expenditures. Were Taddeo and his brothers, the Cardinals Francesco and Antonio, sufficiently concerned with the financial future of the Barberini offspring? She reported with dismay how much she disagreed with the decisions of the family Congregazioni. The decisions were only made to "spend more, no one ever talks about paying." She knew the problem of increasing financial disarray of the Barberini first hand – she reported that she was pressed by creditors of the family for payment as early as 1633, partly a problem caused by the shortcomings of the Barberini accountant, but a sign to her that the family spent more than it could reasonably expect to pay. Although there was a social logic to the Barberini's costly magnificence, Anna regarded them as financial miscalculations that would be borne by the next generation: "These children," she wrote in 1642, "will not be as well off as people think they will be."[23]

Anna's letters reveal the extent to which a highly motivated and active mother juggled conflicting obligations, but privileged the interests of the children over other interests. As was the case for Fonte's fictional heroine, there was a tone of duty in Anna's account of her obligations to the Colonna family, and to the larger Barberini dynasty as well. However, her love for her children is more closely intertwined with her love for Taddeo than was the case for the Tuscan widows petitioning for custody, probably because she was not yet widowed. Demarcating the "nuclear" from larger dynastic interests of the *casa* was difficult – since Anna had no word for family in the sense we mean it today. In medieval and early modern Europe, as in antiquity, the family (*familia, famiglia*) included not only the basic kinship group but the servants as well. Thus, Anna had recourse to the term *figli*, whose needs were understood and defended by an excessively affectionate mother. For Anna, as for the women in Tuscany fighting for custody of their children, the *figli* have a potential set of conflicting interests within the larger *casa*. She hoped this alternative nameless unit could be ruled by an "absolute padrone" – Taddeo. He completed the unit she had in mind, which was not whole without him. She admitted that in his absence she sat down and wept with the children, although this emotional revelation was embedded in a letter stuffed with concerns about the financial future of the children – economics and heightened emotions were frequently entangled in her mothering. She felt more acutely the need for Taddeo when the two boys (Carlo and Maffeo) were trying to sort out their futures – Maffeo was supposed to be the cleric, although as he reported to his mother, the idea repelled him if he wasn't going to be able to perfect his horseback riding, his true passion. During Taddeo's absence, Maffeo was named the abbot of Subiaco, and should have been tonsured immediately, but Anna refused – she would not make such a decision without her husband.[24]

Anna's letters allow us to see the day-to-day struggle of maternity in the midst of the conflicting demands of a married, rather than a widowed, woman. Her recourse to affection appeared frequently as the justification for her very decisive opinion about what the Barberini should be doing and how they should be doing it. We have no evidence for doubting the love she expressed for her offspring, but the word "love" does seem at times to serve as a compensatory rhetorical cover for the fact that in many ways Anna did not measure up to some of the qualities of Mary (and thereby women) that were most praised after the late sixteenth century, especially humility and obedience. Instead she remained embedded in the close identification with her offspring associated with the cult of Mary–Jesus in the late Middle Ages, where mother and child were conflated. Anna had recourse to the language of maternal love and affection, yet she did not view its possibilities as gender-specific. She expected that Taddeo and his brothers could be motivated by it as well. Maternal love was the standard by which the behavior of family members should be judged. Anna's alternative recourse to a political model of fathering did not actually capture the kind of family she clearly hoped to help bring into being. If Taddeo were the absolute padrone (as one must assume he was not, as she implied by her request) it is likely that maternal love would be the taskmaster. He was to rule so the children could come first. This goal underscores her entire critique of the larger dynastic ambitions of the Barberini.

While emerging models of female sanctity placed greater emphasis on obedience, the paradigm of motherly affection was employed by women to expand their autonomy in the family, especially *vis-à-vis* their marital kin. In Tuscany, such ideals among advocating widows were employed in gender-specific ways, as emotional bonds and caretaking skills that women practiced better than men, especially where young children were concerned. Anna Colonna imagined the gender-neutral possibilities for the love she bore the Barberini offspring. From the day-to-day details of toddler survival, the good accounting necessary for their financial survival, and the attention to the life choice most suitable for each child, Anna expected Taddeo's close involvement alongside her own. Litigation and the literature of the *querelles des femmes* suggest some of the other ways that women reconfigured mothering. The model of the Virgin Mary and the many paintings showing her as lovingly devoted to her son played a role in this refashioning as well. What is clear is that the idea of motherhood had undergone major changes from the early fifteenth century to the early seventeenth, at least among elite women. These women learned how to carve out an increasingly important role for themselves in the shaping not only of their own but also of their children's lives. In this context, they celebrated their natural, instinctual love for their sons and daughters. That they did so contributed significantly to the emergence of the family as an affective sphere in which mothers played the critical role.

NOTES

1 Moderata Fonte, *The Worth of Women*, ed. and trans. Virginia Cox (Chicago: University of Chicago Press, 1997), pp. 67–8.
2 Christiane Klapisch-Zuber, *Women, Family, and Ritual in Renaissance Italy* (Chicago: University of Chicago, reprint edn, 1987), pp. 111, 117, 143–4, 153, 156. On the recourse to wet nurses in Europe, see Olwen Hufton, *The Prospect Before Her: A History of Women in Western Europe. Vol. I: 1500–1800* (New York: Alfred A. Knopf, 1996), pp. 197–8.
3 Klapisch-Zuber took the expression "cruel mother" from Giovanni Morelli, *Women, Family, and Ritual*, p. 127; "[she] left the house . . . ," from Lapo di Giovanni Niccolini dei Sirigatti, ibid., p. 126; see also pp. 120–1, 129.
4 "a fine asexual model," Giulia Calvi, summarizing the position of Ambrose, *Il Contratto morale: madri e figli nella Toscana moderna* (Rome: Laterza, 1994), p. 22; for Calvi on Montaigne and Alberti, see pp. 30–1; for the original passage from Alberti, see *I Libri della Famiglia*, eds Ruggiero Romano and Alberto Tenenti (Torino: Giulio Einaudi, 1969), p. 33: "Ma per certo non credo amore alcuno sia piú fermo, di piú constanza, piú intero, né maggiore che quello amore del padre verso de' figliuoli."
5 Thomas Kuehn, *Law, Family, and Women: Toward a Legal Anthropology of Renaissance Italy* (Chicago: University of Chicago Press, 1991), pp. 197–257; Elaine G. Rosenthal, "The Position of Women in Renaissance Florence: Neither Autonomy nor Subjection," in *Florence and Italy: Renaissance Studies in Honour of Nicolai Rubinstein*, eds Peter Denley and Caroline Elam (London: Committee for Medieval Studies, Westfield College, University of London, 1988), pp. 369–81; Giulia Calvi, "Maddalena Nerli and Cosimo Tornabuoni: A Couple's Narrative of Family History in Early Modern Florence," *Renaissance Quarterly* 45, 2 (1992): 312–39. For the early modern period the evidence suggests that women continued to use wills to designate objects as personal possessions rather than family property, and to bequeath property based on affective ties. See Sandra Cavallo, "Proprietà o possesso? Composizione e controllo dei beni delle donne a Torino (1650–1710)," in *Le Ricchezze delle donne: Diritti patrimoniali e poteri familiari in Italia (XIII–XIX secc.)*, eds Giulia Calvi and Isabelle Chabot (Turin: Rosenberg & Sellier, 1998), pp. 187–207. For an innovative reading of women's wills, see Giovanna Benadusi, "Investing the Riches of the Poor: Servant Women and Their Last Wills," *American Historical Review* 109. 3 (2004): 805–26.
6 Stanley Chojnacki, *Women and Men in Renaissance Venice: Twelve Essays on Patrician Society* (Baltimore: Johns Hopkins University Press, 2000), esp. pp. 14, 96, 129, 140, 149. Throughout the early modern period, the restitution of the dowry could potentially create conflict between mothers and children. See Calvi, "Maddalena Nerli and Cosimo Tornabuoni," and Giulia Calvi and Isabelle Chabot, *Le Ricchezze delle donne*.
7 Renata Ago, *Carriere e Clientele nella Roma barocca* (Rome: Laterza, 1990) and her "Giochi di squadra: uomini e donne nelle famiglie nobili del XVII secolo," in *Signori, patrizi, cavalieri in Italia centro-meridionale nell'età moderna*, ed. Maria Antonietta Visceglia (Rome: Laterza, 1992), pp. 256–64; Marina d'Amelia, "Becoming a Mother in the Seventeenth Century: The Experience of a Roman Noblewoman," in *Time, Space, and Women's Lives in Early Modern Europe*, eds Anne Jacobson Schutte, Thomas Kuehn, and Silvana Seidel

Menchi (Kirksville, Mo.: Truman State University Press, 2001), pp. 223–44; on pregnancy and the diplomatic work of women, see Benedetta Borello, *Trame sovrapposte: la socialità aristocratica e le reti di relazioni femminili a Roma* (Naples: Edizioni scientifiche italiane, 2003), pp. 31–2.

8 *The Selected Letters of Alessandra Strozzi*, trans. and ed. Heather Gregory (Berkeley: University of California Press, 1997), for her attachment to her youngest son, pp. 46–7, 54–5, 62–5; on his death, p. 83: "I hope God doesn't let me live long enough to go through this again"; on her views of women, see especially pp. 158–9.

9 For the discussion of how issues of custody were related to the recasting of maternal love, this essay is indebted to Giulia Calvi, *Contratto morale*. Calvi analyzed about 1,500 cases in which the father died intestate or the custody was disputed. For recourse to the Magistrato, pp. 18–19; 68–9; for summary of cases, pp. 23–4, 77–9, 130–4; for the history of Magistrato, pp. 70–5. On the possible implications of judicial cases beyond the families involved, see Joanne M. Ferraro, *Marriage Wars in Late Renaissance Venice* (New York: Oxford University Press, 2001), pp. 6–9.

10 On guardianship and inheritance conflict in statutory law, see Calvi, *Contratto morale*, pp. 27–8. The Magistrato dei Pupilli could also remove children altogether from their families and place them in an institutional setting. For such institutions in Florence, see Sharon T. Strocchia, "Taken into Custody: Girls and Convent Guardianship in Renaissance Florence," *Renaissance Studies* 17, 2 (2003): 177–99; Nicholas Terpstra, "Mothers, Sisters, and Daughters: Girls and Conservatory Guardianship in Late Renaissance Florence," *Renaissance Studies* 17, 2 (2003): 201–29.

11 On the description of a mother's love "above suspicion," etc., see Calvi, *Contratto morale*, pp. 28–30; on women's marginality to inheritance, pp. 31–2; on the compromise of her love by potential inheritance, p. 126; on success of remarried widows in pursuing guardianship, pp. 130–4; on Margherita Corselli, pp. 148–9.

12 On Domenico and the supposed incompetence of fathers, see Calvi, *Contratto morale*, p. 115; on *ragion comune* argument, pp. 140–1. Calvi has also elaborated the potential incest risk magistrates saw for older daughters at the remarriage of their mothers. Because the second husband was seen as a threat to stepdaughters, magistrates were more likely at that juncture to remove older girls from the home than their brothers. See her detailed discussion of the issues of custody after a mother's remarriage in "Reconstructing the Family: Widowhood and Remarriage in Tuscany in the Early Modern Period," in *Marriage in Italy, 1300–1650*, eds Trevor Dean and Kate J. P. Lowe (Cambridge: Cambridge University Press, 1998), esp. pp. 286–7, 292–3.

13 On the contrast between cruel mothers and cruel uncles, see Calvi, *Contratto morale*, pp. 158–9; on Agnese's case and the desire of mothers to have a house of their own, pp. 92–105; "we won't have them," p. 94; on the accusations regarding food, p. 93; "live on their own," p. 96; "avere casa da per sé," p. 92; "better done," p. 94.

14 On the significance of the state in monopolizing violence in Tuscan households, see Calvi, *Contratto morale*, pp. 160–1; Ferraro, *Marriage Wars*, pp. 9, 29–30. Daniela Hacke qualifies the interpretation of the alliance between women and magistrates and notes that the expansion of courts such as the Patriarchal Court in Venice had a mixed impact on women, allowing them to seek solutions to bad marriages, but also subjecting them to "reforming and disciplining." See her *Women, Sex, and Marriage in Early Modern Venice* (Aldershot: Ashgate, 2004), p. 233. Another nuanced view of the rapport between ecclesiastical courts and women is Emlyn Eisenach, *Husbands, Wives, and Concubines: Marriage, Family, and Social Order in Sixteenth-century Verona* (Kirksville, Mo.: Truman State University Press, 2004). Eisenach underscores the extent to which clerics hoped to remake society through remaking the family, often with the cooperation of women.

15 Calvi frames this as the emergence of the "moral mother" based not upon the assertion of a right, but on the basis of "affective relations" between mother and children. See Calvi, *Contratto morale*, pp. 158–61. Samuel Cohn has argued that "Florence was simply the worst place to be a woman." See his *Women in the Streets* (Baltimore: Johns Hopkins University Press, 1996), p. 1.

16 Caroline Castiglione, *Patrons and Adversaries: Nobles and Villagers in Italian Politics, 1640–1760* (New York: Oxford University Press, 2005).

17 On the conflation of Mary and Jesus, Donna Spivey Ellington, *From Sacred Body to Angelic Soul* (Washington, DC: Catholic University of America, 2001), p. 44, 71–72, 77–81, 91, 95. Naomi Yavneh, "To Bare or Not Too Bare: Sofonisba Anguissola's Nursing Madonna and the Womanly Art of Breastfeeding," in *Maternal Measures: Figuring Caregiving in the Early Modern Period*, eds Naomi J. Miller and Naomi Yavneh (Aldershot: Ashgate, 2000), pp. 65–81. While Artemisia's depiction was probably influenced by her father's *Madonna and Child* from 1609 (Bucharest, Muzeul de Arte), his exaggerated attempt at depicting the same preparatory nursing gestures leaves Mary's breast looking like a grafted-on orange, manipulated into a position as high as her neck, to which the child does not seem to have a realistic chance of latching on. Interestingly, the arch of the baby's back suggests that it was going to be a struggle. See figures 1–6 in R. Ward Bissell, *Artemisia Gentileschi and the Authority of Art* (University Park: Pennsylvania State University Press 1999).

18 On the contrast between the Mary of the Middle Ages and the Mary of the Catholic Reformation, see Ellington, *From Sacred Body*, esp., pp. 143–8; "silent," p. 148. On how women may have heard sermons, and the patronage of the della Rovere chapel see Carolyn Valone, "The Art of Hearing: Sermons and Images in the Chapel of Lucrezia della Rovere," *Sixteenth Century Journal* 31, 3 (2000): 753–77; on matron-patrons, see "Women on the Quirinal Hill: Patronage in Rome, 1560–1630," *The Art Bulletin* 76, 1 (1994): 129–46.

19 "I don't have time . . . ," Biblioteca Apostolica Vaticana, Barb. Lat. 10043, 96r. A limited but interesting scholarship on Anna has emerged: Giuseppe Lodispoto Sacchi, "Anna Colonna Barberini ed il suo monumento nel monastero di Regina Coeli," *Strenna dei romanisti* 43 (1982): 460–78. The most accessible and thorough accounts of Anna's religious vocation and her patronage of the Roman convent, Regina Coeli, are by Marilyn Dunn. See her articles, "Piety and Patronage in Seicento Rome: Two Noblewomen and their Convents," *The Art Bulletin* 74, 4 (December 1994): 644–64; "Spiritual Philanthropists: Women as Convent Patrons in Seicento Rome," in *Women and Art in Early Modern Europe: Patrons, Collectors, and Connoisseurs*, ed. Cynthia Lawrence (State College, Pa., 1997), pp. 154–88. Anna's relationship to her distant cousin, Cesare, and her dispute with the Barberini for her dowry after the death of her husband is outlined in Simona Feci, *Pesci fuor d'acqua: Donne a Roma in età moderna: diritti e patrimoni* (Rome: Viella, 2004), pp. 197–226.

20 Barb. Lat. 10043, 52r.; "she had a great . . . ," 96r.

21 My rendering of the children's age follows Patricia Waddy, including the tentative years for Camilla's short life (1628–30?). Waddy lists the surviving children's birth for these years: Carlo (1630–1706), Maffeo (1631–85), Lucrezia (1632–98), Nicolò (1635–?). P. Waddy, *Seventeenth-century Roman Palaces: Use and the Art of the Plan* (Cambridge, Mass.: MIT Press, 1990), Table 50; on her moving to the children's quarters see Barb. Lat. 10043, 9v.; on their illnesses, 1r., 3r.; on the wet nurses, 6r., 8v., 11r., 16r., 19v., 22r., 26r., 28v., 33r., 36r.; on the possible death of Maffeo, 12r.; on the search for the wet nurses and their shortcomings, 9r. and 11r.

22 Barb. Lat., 10043, see 63v. on their health; on her delight with their good health, 64r.;

on remaining health problems with Maffeo, 81r.; "I know that I am too fond," 82r.; on her disagreements about expenditures, 22r.–23r.
23 Barb. Lat. 10043, "spend more, no one ever talks," 23r.; on the creditors and other problems, 13v., 20r.; "These children," 82r.
24 Barb. Lat. 10043, on absolute padrone and missing Taddeo, 83r.–83v.; on Maffeo, 115r.–115v., 125v.

SUGGESTIONS FOR FURTHER READING

Ago, Renata. "Maria Spada Veralli, la buona moglie," in Renata Ago and Giulia Calvi (eds) *Barocco al Femminile*. Rome: Laterza, 1992, 51–70.

—— "The Family in Rome: Structure and Relationships," in Peter van Kessel and Elisja Schulte *et al.* (eds) *Rome, Amsterdam: Two Growing Cities in Seventeenth-century Europe*. Amsterdam: Amsterdam University Press, 1997, 85–91.

Ambrosini, Federica. "Toward a Social History of Women in Venice: From Renaissance to the Enlightenment," in John Martin and Dennis Romano (eds) *Venice Reconsidered*. Baltimore: Johns Hopkins University Press, 2000, 420–53.

Borello, Benedetta. *Il Trame sovrapposte: la socialità aristocratica e le reti di relazioni femminili a Roma*. Naples: Edizioni scientifiche italiane, 2003.

Brown, Judith C. and Robert C. Davis, *Gender and Society in Renaissance Italy*. London and New York: Longman, 1998.

Calvi, Giulia. "Sans espoir d'hériter: Les mères, les enfants, et l'État en Toscane, XVIe–XVIIe siècles." *CLIO: Histoire, Femmes, et Sociétés* 21 (2005): 43–68.

Cavallo, Sandra. "Proprietà o possesso? Composizione e controllo dei beni delle donne a Torino (1650–1710)," in Giulia Calvi and Isabelle Chabot (eds) *Le Ricchezze delle donne: Diritti patrimoniali e poteri familiari in Italia (XIII–XIX secc.)*. Turin: Rosenberg & Sellier, 1998, 187–207.

Chabot, Isabelle. "Seconde nozze e identità materna nella Firenze del tardo Medioevo," in Silvana Seidel Menchi, Anne Jacobson Schutte, and Thomas Kuehn (ed.) *Tempi e spazi di vita femminile tra medioevo ed età moderna*. Bologna: Il Mulino, 1999, 493–523.

Chojnacki, Stanley. *Women and Men in Renaissance Venice: Twelve Essays on Patrician Society*. Baltimore: Johns Hopkins University Press, 2000.

Crabb, Ann. "How to Influence Your Children: Persuasion and Form in Alessandra Macigni Strozzi's Letters to Her Sons," in Jane Couchman and Ann Crabb (eds) *Women's Letters Across Europe, 1400–1700: Form and Persuasion*. Aldershot: Ashgate, 2005, 21–41.

D'Amelia, Marina. "La presenza delle madri nell'Italia medievale e moderna," in D'Amelia (ed.) *Storia della Maternità*. Rome: Laterza, 1997, 3–52.

—— "Becoming a Mother in the Seventeenth Century: The Experience of a Roman Noblewoman," in Anne J. Schutte, Thomas Kuehn, and Silvana Seidel Menchi (eds) *Time, Space, and Women's Lives in Early Modern Europe*, Kirksville, Mo.: Truman State University Press, 2001, 223–44.

Ellington, Donna Spivey. *From Sacred Body to Angelic Soul: Understanding Mary in Late Medieval and Early Modern Europe*. Washington, DC: Catholic University Press, 2001.

Grieco, Sara F. Matthews. "Persuasive Pictures: Didactic Prints and the Construction of the Social Identity of Women in Sixteenth-century Italy," in Letizia Panizza (ed.) *Women in Italian Renaissance Culture and Society*. London: Modern Humanities Research Association, 2000, 285–314.

Hufton, Olwen. "Motherhood," in Olwen Hufton, *The Prospect Before Her: A History of Women in Western Europe*. Vol. I: *1500–1800*. New York: Knopf, 1996, 177–220.

Hughes, Diane Owen. "Representing the Family: Portraits and Purposes in Early Modern Italy," in R. I. Rotberg and T. K. Rabb (eds) *Art and History: Images and their Meaning*. Cambridge: Cambridge University Press, 1986, 7–38.

Kuehn, Thomas. "Daughters, Mothers, Wives, and Widows: Women as Legal Persons," in Anne J. Schutte, Thomas Kuehn, and Silvana Seidel Menchi (eds) *Time, Space, and Women's Lives in Early Modern Europe*. Kirksville, Mo.: Truman State University Press, 2001, 97–115.

Lombardi, Daniela, "Famiglie di antico regime," in Giulia Calvi (ed.) *Innesti: Donne e genere nella storia sociale*. Rome: Viella, 2004, 200–21.

Miles, Margaret. "The Virgin's One Bare Breast: Nudity, Gender, and Religious Meaning in Tuscan Early Renaissance Culture," in Susan Suleman (ed.) *The Female Body in Western Culture: Contemporary Perspectives*. Cambridge, Mass.: Harvard University Press, 1986, 193–208.

Miller, Naomi J. and Naomi Yavneh. *Maternal Measures: Figuring Caregiving in the Early Modern Period*. Aldershot: Ashgate, 2000.

Pomata, Gianna. "Family and Gender," in John A. Marino (ed.) *Early Modern Italy*. Oxford: Oxford University Press, 2002, 69–86.

Rossi-Doria, Anna. *A che punto è la storia delle donne in Italia?* Rome: Viella, 2003.

Valone, Carolyn. "Mothers and Sons: Two Paintings for San Bonaventura in Early Modern Rome." *Renaissance Quarterly* 53, 1 (2000): 108–32.

Wiesner, Merry E. "Pregnancy, Childbirth, and Motherhood," in *Women and Gender in Early Modern Europe*, 2nd edn, 78–89. Cambridge: Cambridge University Press, 2000.

Zarri, Gabriella (ed.) *Per Lettera: La scrittura epistolare femminile tra archivio e tipografia: secoli XV–XVII*. Rome: Viella, 1999.

CHAPTER TWENTY

THE RENAISSANCE GOES UP IN SMOKE

Robert C. Davis

Just as in the mid-twentieth century, H. Rap Brown could famously observe that "violence is as American as apple pie," one could also certainly make the claim that, in the mid-sixteenth century, violence was as Italian as pizza pie. Individual aggression, group contention, and general mayhem were this era's constant and necessary subtext, the backdrop against which both the most brilliant artistic and intellectual innovations as well as the most sordid political maneuvering were worked out. Some social historians of Italy have highlighted the centrality of violence to the age of the Renaissance: Jacob Burckhardt, for one, devoted considerable space in his *Civilization of the Renaissance in Italy* to the connection that he found between violence and the secular, pragmatic individualism that he saw as an essential element of Renaissance character.[1] Though he continually deplored their apparent addiction to brutality and vendetta, Burckhardt still had to admit that those Renaissance individuals he so admired – Federico da Montefeltro, Sigismondo Malatesta, Lorenze de' Medici, Francesco Sforza – were very much products of a culture that rewarded personal aggression. Few of the era's bright lights came to power and almost none of them stayed long enough to make his or her mark in Renaissance learning and culture without an easy and frequent recourse to homicide, war, torture, or the threat of all three.

Yet, if Italians had been prone to violence in the centuries before Machiavelli codified their behavior in *The Prince*, things got a lot worse later on in the 1500s: wars raged across the peninsula, public order collapsed, and large swathes of territory saw the return of a private, retributive justice on a scale not seen since the precommunal era. Though endemic throughout Italy, violent disorder may have reached its peak (or nadir) between 1550 and 1600 in the Papal States, where society at times appeared on the edge of a complete breakdown. Frequent poor harvests, constant baronial unrest, fragile borders, and an often erratic judicial system conditioned by the relatively short tenure of many popes in this period, all conspired to reduce this state lying at Italy's heart to near anarchy. Attempts by Rome to extend its control into the hinterlands through administrative and military means ran into sporadic, but often violent, reactions from feudal lords.[2] For pursuing their resistance to Rome's encroachments, these rural potentates had plenty of ex-soldiers available, especially after the Peace of Cateau-Cambrésis ended 60 years of Habsburg–Valois conflict in

1559. Known as *masnadieri*, these rogues on the loose had no other training than that of arms and no allegiance to any particular state or person; the cultural values they had developed from three generations of warfare made violence for them a form of eloquent expression and even casual thuggery seem like a noble calling.

How much these thousands of *masnadieri*, wandering around Italy after 1559, might have contributed to the decline or collapse of the humanist values that had distinguished Renaissance civic life in the 1400s is still an open question. Certainly their threatening presence made it much more difficult for Italians to realize Leonardo Bruni's vision of a society where "all enjoy the same liberty, governed only by law and free from the fear of individuals."[3] When it came to spreading disorder and violence they certainly had lots of help from home-grown assassins, highway robbers, and simple vengeance seekers, all of whom had long been endemic to the Italian social scene. As far back as the early fifteenth century, even modest-sized towns like Vicenza and Verona might have a thousand or more of their local men in exile at any one time, the majority of them for murder. Such native outlaws did not proliferate completely on their own, however, but were instead created in their profusion by the very states that then had to deal with them, in what has been labeled "widespread judicial dysfunction."[4] In pre-modern Italy, where prisons were fundamentally holding cells for those awaiting trial or sentencing, banishment had been the favored form of punishment since communal times for both criminal and civil misconduct. It was exile, rather than incarceration, that served society as its traditional, intermediate penalty between fines and mutilation or execution. In communal times, banishment was often the lot of the losing side during regime change; often as not, these political outlaws, known as *fuorusciti*, could, like Florence's Bianchi faction, find comfortable, if bitter, lodgings with some rival commune until their side's fortunes improved. Once the largest Italian communes began to coalesce into states, however, there were fewer hospitable refuges for such exiles. When, with the Peace of Lodi of 1454, the major Italian states pledged to withdraw at least their open support from these miscreants, such outlaws increasingly took to hiding out in "the bush: *le macchie*," in insecure borderlands, or in the service of those feudal lords who liked the idea of running their own private army. Since exile also meant the confiscation of one's possessions, this new breed of banned men, appropriately known as *banniti* or *banditi*, were often in desperate straits. Many had little choice, if they were to survive, but to act like bandits in fact, making their living by "kidnapping, robbing, and murdering," as one contemporary diarist put it – as well as running protection rackets, rustling livestock, and renting themselves out as thugs for hire.[5]

Not all *banniti* were sent into exile: some went on their own, even if unwillingly. Those who had committed revenge killings usually fled before they could be arrested by the courts, which then promptly made their hasty flight into official exile. It also seems, however, that even men who had committed relatively minor crimes were increasingly choosing bandit status, in response to pressures that had nothing to do with their misdeeds. Over the course of the sixteenth century, as the bigger Italian states worked hard at building up a naval presence, the big fleets of war galleys they constructed created an insatiable demand for oarsmen. Paid volunteers and slave labor only went so far in filling the benches with *galeotti*, so the judges and lawmakers of Venice, Florence, Rome, and Naples obligingly began sentencing even petty thieves and troublemakers to long stints at the oar. For many a small-time crook, the self-imposed life of a *bannito*, though he might be starving, violent, and on the run, may still have seemed almost attractive when compared to three or four years of living death as a *galeotto*.[6] The result was an upsurge of those who took to the *macchie*, such that by 1581 the diarist Romolo Allegrini, in the papal city of Perugia, could observe that "they say that there are more than 4,000 people of Perugia [who are] either banned and condemned men." Allegrini was no doubt speaking of the entire district rather than just Perugia proper, with its population at the time of fewer than 20,000; even so, he was implying that somewhere between 10 and 15 percent of the men from his locale were in exile or on the run.[7]

All these various outlaws – *masnadieri, banniti, fuorusciti* – perpetrated a tremendous amount of violence, either for their own sake or on behalf of someone else. Just how much violence is unclear and awaits a more formal, quantitative study of their crimes, though suggestive figures do exist for a few times and places. Peter Blastenbrei has, for example, found that between the 1560s and 1580s Rome, with its population of around 90,000, had roughly three verifiable (that is, recorded) instances of serious violence per day. Blastenbrei also notes that Rome's annual murder rate in those years typically ranged around 70 per 100,000, or around three times that of present-day Washington DC, the current American leader in this dubious category.[8] Yet this was downright tranquil compared to nearby Perugia, the university town and provincial capital of Umbria, where Romolo Allegrini recorded 35 homicides in the city and its suburbs in 1584 alone – "and in the [surrounding] *contado* yet many more, some by bandits and some by [their] enemies" – a homicide rate that works out to more than double even Rome's.[9]

Not that such figures fully encompass the violence of the period, not by any means. Besides private violence, of the homicidal sort noted by Allegrini, a good deal more mayhem was carried out at the public level on behalf of states or by pseudo-state entities – not just by standing armies, police, and militias, in other words, but also by irregular posses, bands of feudal retainers, and even by such outside interlopers as Muslim or Protestant corsairs. A great deal of the turmoil can be blamed on the process of national consolidation, as the centralizing authorities in Venice, Florence, Rome, Naples, or Palermo attempted to extend their fiscal and judicial reach in the face of often violent resistance by feudal magnates, displaced peasants, and sometimes the rulers of neighboring states. Yet when the authorities themselves freely meshed their offices with their own clan loyalties, sense of personal honor, and instincts for vendetta, using state force to legitimize their own private ends, it often became unclear (as it still is) just what violence was being employed for state building and what for the self-aggrandizement of those in positions of power.[10]

Still, in the manner of governments throughout history, those who ran the Italian statelets tended to overlook their own direct or oblique complicity in the rising tide of violence and instead put the blame on external factors. They complained about an idle nobility and scheming neighbors, but one culprit they especially singled out was more technological than social. As far as the papal legate in Perugia was concerned, it was simple: "The outrages and villainies that the bandits and delinquents commit are caused by the ease [with which] they can get ahold of arquebuses."[11] Specifically, he was talking about that form of firearm known to Italians as the *archibugio a ruota*, or wheel-lock arquebus, a weapon that for several decades at the end of the Renaissance seemed poised to undermine if not indeed overthrow the existing social and political order. Invented around 1510 in southern Germany, most likely in Nuremburg, the wheel-lock has been treated by many historians, both military and social, as little more than a evolutionary stepping stone between the original, hand-held matchlock, invented in the late 1400s, and the relatively enduring flintlock, which first made its appearance in France around 1620. It is true that the wheel-lock, whose firing mechanism was based on a spring-wound steel wheel that, when released by the trigger, spun and generated sparks against a flint, was far from the efficient, mass-producible weapon that its successor would become. When first conceived, the wheel-lock was at the outer limits of current manufacturing technology: to keep all its parts functioning, the weapon had to be constructed with precision and aligned with great care; even then, it was always prone to jamming or misfiring. Not for nothing had some of the first wheel-lock producers been trained as clockmakers, for no one else had either the technical ability or the precision skills to produce a working weapon that was even occasionally reliable.[12] Their efforts, especially with fowling pieces, created objects that are now highly prized works of art – delicate, well-balanced, crafted of rare woods finely inlaid with gold, silver, and ivory – but as weapons wheel-locks had minimal impact on the evolving military tactics of the 1500s: they were too hard to maintain, too limited in range and projectile, and (obviously) too expensive to issue to common soldiers.[13] For all of the sixteenth century and indeed much of the seventeenth, despite the advent of the mounted pistoleer (again in Germany, in the 1540s), it was the much heavier, if clumsier, matchlock musket or *schioppo*, as Italians called it, that provided hand-held firepower for European armies.

The wheel-lock arquebus may not have done much to change tactics on the battlefield, but sixteenth-century observers still saw it as a weapon of mass destruction when it got into civilian hands. This it clearly did, for despite its high price and relatively limited range, the wheel-lock was very much in demand among private individuals, and for several good reasons. Dispensing with the lit fuse of the matchlock allowed the wheel-lock to be used in the rain, wind, or other bad weather, and, most importantly, it could be carried loaded and primed for immediate shooting. When crafted for civilian use, these *archibugi* tended to be much more manageable than the cumbersome *schioppi*, even if they had less stopping power. A version called the *archibugietto* was a light, graceful weapon with a weight only about a third that of a musket; craftsmen were also soon turning out *archibugi corti*, or *terzette* (sometimes *terzaroli*), essentially forerunners of the pistol. Usually defined as a gun with a barrel under two (later three) palms in length, these had the huge advantage over other firearms in that they could be, and usually were, carried concealed.[14]

The authorities were right to be worried, not just about the greater versatility of the *archibugio a ruota*, but also about its rapid spread through Italian society, both legally and illegally. In 1535, barely a decade after the wheel-lock's invention, the newly minted duke of Florence, Alessandro de' Medici, apparently had quite a collection of them "sent from Germany." Benvenuto Cellini, goldsmith and raconteur, boasted that Alessandro, out of sheer admiration, once gave him free run of that collection, to pick out for himself "the best and most beautiful arquebus I had ever seen or owned." Cellini was evidently in a position to recognize quality, since this was not his first wheel-lock: in 1532 he had set out on a trip to Naples, via Lago Albano, "with an *archibuso a rota* across the pommel, primed and set, to defend me."[15] Cellini no doubt knew what he was doing: the road to Naples via Monte Casino was notoriously plagued by bandits since well before his day. At this point in time, arming himself with what was still essentially a collector's curiosity gave him a definite edge over highway robbers (*grassatori di strada*), who themselves were still unlikely to carry any firearms at all. Cellini's advantage was doubled because he was traveling mounted: his *archibuso a rota* gave him a mobility on horseback, for either attack or defense, that he would never have had with the heavy and cumbersome matchlock musket.

It was this quality of the wheel-lock, that a man could ride with one "wound in readiness to fire," that made it initially attractive and later essential for anyone traveling on Italian highways, especially as the safety of the roadways deteriorated over the course of the sixteenth century. Unfortunately, what worked for travelers worked just as well if not better for the bandits themselves. The *archibugi a ruota* were too easily stolen, from houses, shops, or hapless travelers, who could expect to lose their wheel-lock even before they lost their lives. Before long, bandits were reportedly more likely to have *archibugi* than horses, though it was not unknown for an especially unlucky wayfarer to come across a mounted gang: "six men on horseback, all armed with *archibusi a rota*." By no later than the 1570s the wheel-lock had so associated itself with bandits to have become their identifying symbol. Witnesses often made statements along the lines of, "I knew he was a bandit, for he was carrying an *archibugio proibito*," thereby pairing the forbidden, or banned, weapon (depending on the laws in force at a given place and time, this could mean either any kind of wheel-lock or simply a short one) with its banished carrier.[16]

It would seem that few self-respecting *banniti* contented themselves with the firepower of a single arquebus. Some sported double-barreled versions, but more commonly bandits and goons for hire went about their business bristling with two or three *archibugi corti* stuffed into their sash or belt, balanced by an *archibugio longo* slung over one shoulder: the well-furnished bandit was then *benissimo armato d'archibugi*, as one observer put it.[17] Clearly, in their line of work – robbery and assassination, mostly – outlaws had no time to reload, and in any case they needed backup for the inevitable jams or misfires for which the wheel-lock was renowned. When the weapons did fire off according to plan, a bandit could go against his enemy or prey with a fusillade of bullets – many loaded their *archibugi* with pellets and barbs appropriately called *lagrime* ("tears") – firing one gun after another as rapidly as circumstances allowed. If their target was still standing (or breathing) when the smoke cleared, they would then try to finish him off by hacking him to pieces with their machetes, or *pistolesi*.

Certainly the wheel-lock's advent into Italian society made recourse to violence much swifter and the results of that violence more deadly in 1600 than in 1500. With both bandits and many supposedly law-abiding citizens toting firearms, harsh words readily escalated into shootings rather than mere blows or (somewhat) less fatal stabbings. One had to get to know an entire new language of gesture and threat to understand when mere arguments were spiraling towards a shootout and to recognize which moves were ritual and which might be, as it were, loaded. An *archibugio longo* slung on the shoulder or held butt on the ground was ubiquitous but (fairly) pacific. When someone crotched it under his arm, and thereby "brought down his gun: *fa abbassar l'archibugio*," he brought the barrel (and the weapon) into play, and the discourse suddenly shifted to the likes of, "Don't come forward or I'll kill you."[18] It was only when a shootout was imminent, however, that men would demonstratively "lower the dog, *calar il cane*" – that is, click the flint holder that was popularly called "the dog" into place against the wheel of their arquebus.[19] When a group squared off like this, cocked and ready to fire in a second, fairly radiating menace, it would take much cooler heads than were usually available to avoid a shootout.

Out in the countryside, where police were few and one had to look out for oneself, it was a common practice to go about armed (*andare armato*) – not just on the highways, for self-defense, but also in the villages, to ensure respect. Although the *archibugio longo a ruota* was sometimes legal and sometimes forbidden, many ordinary peasants and villagers apparently carried one. They did so fairly openly, literally and figuratively using their weapons as a prop of ordinary comportment, holding them in their hands, under their arms, slung over their shoulders, or as staffs when standing around talking. The short *archibugio prohibito*, on the other hand, was solely found in the hands of those at opposite ends of the social scale – rural nobility and outlaws. As we have seen, elites and the better-off bandits found the illegal *terzarolo* ideal for use on horseback. It was the outlaws, though, who really turned the *archibugio corte* and their other weapons into something of a fashion statement, turning themselves into walking arsenals of sundry arquebuses, machetes, and daggers, while setting off the menacing effect by presenting themselves, with "braids and little tassels of hair on the right side or the left," "adorned with bunches of feathers," "wearing one of their mustaches longer than the other," and going around with their hats on backwards or sideways.[20]

Not everyone in the countryside wanted or could afford to tote a wheel-lock, but just knowing that *banniti* and rogue nobles were likely to be armed must have made a persuasive case for getting a weapon, much as it does among gun advocates in America today. At times, the authorities seemed to acquiesce to this logic. In June of 1580, for example, as bandit unrest was starting to threaten harvests in the Papal States, the pope's legate in Perugia conceded the point and ruled that, at least out in their fields, even peasants without the appropriate license could go about armed with "*archibugi da ruota* that are of proper size, so that they can better guard themselves from said bandits and also be ready to help the authorities, when there is need." The authorities' sporadic desire to arm peasants may have led to a rural militia, of sorts, but the weapons they permitted had a tendency to end up in the hands "of people of bad quality and those who do not know how to use them."[21] An anonymous jeremiad written in Perugia in the 1580s claimed that, as a result:

> The abuse of the *Archibugi a ruota* has got so bad these days, both among great men, who carry them for defense, and among their inferiors, who use them in the country, that . . . at present no one undertakes *vendette* or attempts to unburden himself of even the lightest offense with any other weapon than this,

such that we see that the sword and other arms that were used in a knightly fashion for these purposes have almost fallen into oblivion. Everywhere you go, you hear the reports of arquebus shots, either fired from a thicket, or from a window in a house, or . . . in the middle of the public streets . . . The police [*la Corte*], finding every one well furnished with this weapon, cannot carry out their duties . . . and no place or person is safe these days in the country, since there is not a cattle drover or shepherd who does not have his arquebus slung over his shoulder.[22]

The authorities tended to agree with this unsettling picture, the more so since the police did periodically have to beat a retreat in the face of superior outlaw firepower.[23] Many a legate or governor, sent from Rome to run the papal provinces, lamented about "how many unpleasantries, murders, and other evils are daily caused by [people] carrying *archibugi a ruota*, both of the legal and illegal size," noting that "[these] have so increased in number in the Papal States that almost no other sort of weapon is used, with evident damage and harm to the people."[24] This flourishing of wheel-locks in civilian hands continued in the face of a steadfast state repression, which dated back essentially to the time the weapon itself was invented: already in 1517, the Holy Roman Emperor Maximilian I forbade his subjects from either making or owning "self-striking hand-guns that ignite themselves" – words that evidently referred to the wheel-lock mechanism.[25] Venice's Council of Ten moved as early as 1533 to suppress the use of the arquebus by making even non-lethal gun attacks a capital crime; wheel-locks were singled out somewhat later in the papal territories, but by the 1550s Rome also had bans in place against anyone who would even carry them, much less use them.[26] Over the next three decades these laws were steadily refined and extended by a succession of popes and governors of Rome, a long-term process that, while not especially successful, does at least reveal something of the intentions and concerns of the lawmakers.

From its inception, the authorities recognized the particular danger posed by the short-barreled wheel-lock. Like the sawn-off shotgun of the twentieth century, the *archibugio corte* was denounced as having no socially redeeming features: useless for hunting, easily concealed, and amenable for being carried two or three at a time, its only purpose was "for committing various crimes."[27] The papal legates and governors consequently came down hard on these weapons, ordering "the immediate punishment of the gallows" and confiscation of all property for anyone caught carrying an *archibugio* with a barrel less than two (later three) palms long, loaded or unloaded, inside or outside of town.[28] Eventually, just keeping a *terzetta* in one's house or shop was made a capital crime, as was knowing someone who did and failing to denounce him.[29] Periodically, to show how serious they were, the papal authorities would take someone found with an *archibugio corte* and hang him on the spot.[30]

Yet, as one papal governor complained, "Despite the prohibitions and other edicts issued concerning this [violation], we see from experience that many still dare to carry these prohibited weapons."[31] One reason they dared was that, in theory at least, an *archibugio prohibito* was not actually prohibited if one had a permit to carry one. Licenses and dispensations were issued for those who supposedly had a special need – for self-defense while traveling through bandit-infested country, for example.

Considering the gravity with which the state treated the *terzetta* question, such permits should have been issued only by a select few legates and governors, but, as it happened, a host of authority figures dispensed the permits, and much too readily – for profit, one assumes, but probably also as a means of asserting their own status by demonstrating precisely that they could. If legatine edicts are to be believed, the papal highways were choked with men armed both with *archibugi corti* and permits to carry them signed by every imaginable sort of petty nabob, including (in the single case of Perugia):

> the Lord Masters of Rome, the assistants [*famiglia*] of the Lord Priors, the Council Ministers, the Lord Feudators, the Lord Religious Knights, the two Triumphal Councillors of the Chamber, the soldiers of the Fortress, the [state] Monopoly holders and Customs Officers (that is, them personally and their hired substitutes), and the Officials of villages.[32]

One of the first things every new governor in Rome or the provinces had to do, upon taking office, was to "revoke and annul all existing licenses to carry *archibugi a ruota* . . . in whatever way and for whatever purpose issued," particularly aiming at "those licenses obtained from any persons who do not have authority to issue them."[33] But just who had the authority to license others to carry *archibugi prohibiti*? It was a vexed question, the more so since anyone who had the right was also implicitly authorized to arm himself and his personal attendants, or *famiglia*, without asking anyone's permission. The threat, then, was not only the *dilatione dei archibugi*, the spread of arquebuses (though this was troublesome enough), but also the building up of private armies, nodes of power whose loyalty to the ever-changing occupant of the Throne of St Peter could never be completely assured. Yet cutting back on those allowed to issue these permits ultimately meant that ever more of the remaining, still licit *archibugi corti* were concentrated in ever fewer and (for this very reason) potentially ever more threatening hands.

It may well have been such fears that led the papacy in the 1570s to take the rather drastic step of turning the entire Papal States into a sort of wheel-lock-free zone, with a total ban on all sorts of arquebuses, both long and short. Henceforth the weapon would be outlawed, not only in the hands of the usual suspects – bandits, barons, and goons – but also the state's own police, officials, and soldiers, who could not "use nor carry similar sorts or arms, that is, *Archibugi a Ruota* of any sort, but who can only carry, in the Countryside, the *Archibugi a Micchio* [the Matchlock] according to their permits." To ensure, as one edict put it, "that this sort of weapon falls into disuse," the whole Roman wheel-lock industry was abolished at a stroke, with orders given to "artisans and master craftsmen of every sort not to make or adapt Wheels or other sorts of similar arquebuses, nor make the [firing] chambers, nor even keep made ones in their shop or house." All citizens who owned an *archibugio a ruota*, whether long or short, were to pull off the wheel and turn it in to the local *castellano*; then they could, if they had the right permit, hire someone to convert the remaining gun frame into a matchlock. Though foreign visitors to Rome (and there were many, even outside of Holy Years) were allowed to keep their wheel-locks, they were expected to break down the mechanism at the border and carry the wheel separate from the chamber and barrel. Once "arriving in a city or village, they must give [the wheels] to the gate guardian, who would carry them to the other [i.e., opposite] gates, where they will have them again when they leave."[34]

The major flaw in such laws was, of course, that they only had any real traction with those who were already likely to obey them. Although law-abiding citizens could be scared into surrendering their wheel-locks this way, the threat of summary execution would not have much effect on hard-core bandits who were already capitally condemned anyway. Efforts were consequently made to render harmless the weapons of these *scelerati*, by depriving them of the powder and shot they needed to function. Smaller production sites around papal territories were to be shut down, and the manufacture and storage of gunpowder and bullets were to be concentrated in Rome, where the state's monopoly could be more jealously guarded. Those who dared to "make, or have made powder for *archibugi*, [or] who sell it or have it sold, [or] buy it or have it bought . . . without a permit" would be heavily fined; if they were caught making or selling powder or shot "in suspect places, where bandits are known to frequent," they would be sent to the galleys; the police could even arrest someone just for "carrying more powder and shot than he could reasonably employ for his own use." Knowing that wheel-locks were high-maintenance weapons, papal authorities also went after those who were capable of keeping them operating and tuned-up, requiring anyone working on *archibugi a ruota* to have a license expressly for that craft. Such permits were supposedly hard to come by, especially out in the countryside, where it was feared, evidently with some reason, that many a small-town artisan could be bullied by the village lord into doing the necessary gun work for the local bandit gang, even if "he didn't want to fix them."[35]

These papal sanctions against the wheel-lock were not really extraordinary: other European states passed similar laws at about the same time. Somewhat more radical, however, was the papacy's determination in 1578 to ban the weapon from its own army, the more so since just two years earlier "soldiers enrolled in the militia rolls approved by the sergeant major" had been specifically allowed to carry it.[36] The rationale given was that the *archibugio a ruota* was too expensive and, anyway, "for the infantry no other arquebus pays off except that with the fuse, as a weapon both more secure and of less responsibility for the soldier," though Rome also knew that soldiers, besides committing a good deal of mayhem on their own, were also a ready source of wheel-locks for the civilian population.[37] Still, giving up this leading-edge, if somewhat capricious, tool of warfare must have seemed a real sacrifice to some, especially considering that neighboring states like Florence and the ever-hostile Naples made no similar move (though the more distant Venice did ban the wheel-lock for a spell).[38] The decision may have been based, at least in part, on the revulsion, often stated, that the *archibugio a ruota*, even more than the matchlock, was "ruining" not just the honorable conduct of war, but the very notion of honor itself; that the comportment appropriate to estimable men, who redress wrongs face to face, on or off the battlefield, was impossible in a world where "there is not a cattle drover nor shepherd who does not have his arquebus slung over his shoulder"; and that, in a state which was essentially a theocracy, governance should not just establish order and a healthy economy but should also be driven by a strong moral and spiritual vision.

Still, it was a rather quixotic move, at a time when so many states were jostling for pre-eminence (or at least survival) in a Europe almost continually at war, and where the imperative to exploit any technological edge, however minor, was immense. True, the *archibugio a ruota* may not have had much competitive advantage over the matchlock among infantry on the battlefield, but it could and did flourish in certain niche areas. The *terzette* was a big help to mounted troops – the pistolers – in attacking other cavalry, whereas the matchlock was quite difficult to use effectively on horseback: those who carried one, later known as dragoons, essentially had to dismount before they could fire.[39] Just as important as this ease of use, however, especially in the civilian sphere, was the wheel-lock's prestige quality. Far more noble a firearm than the clumsy matchlock, the wheel-lock attracted elites who wanted to carry them for hunting, dueling, and swaggering. The determination of elites to own them, with a permit if possible but without if necessary, turned more than a few of the gentry into outlaws, and not only because headstrong lords persisted in going around armed. In a legal system fueled by denunciations, anonymous or otherwise, accusing an enemy of carrying or secretly owning an *archibugio prohibito* was a popular means of slander: if true, the punishments were – sometimes literally – crippling; even if false, it was never easy to disprove.[40]

Before too long, Rome began to abandon the ideal of the wheel-lock-free state. Already by the early 1590s, the distinction between *archibugi* and *archibugetti piccoli* was reintroduced, and once again only possessing the latter represented a capital offense, while having an *archibugio longo* meant just a fine or a turn or two on the *strappado*. By the end of the decade one increasingly comes across the term *archibugio di giusta misura*, the "proper-sized arquebus," which at least in the countryside and with a permit was acceptable. A generation or so later, just on the verge of the invention of the flintlock, Rome appears resigned even to allowing *archibugi longhi a ruota* in town. Papal authorities in the seventeenth century were less concerned about forbidding the wheel-lock altogether than defining the occasions in which an arquebus, whether wheel-lock or matchlock, could properly be fired. Hunting, by select individuals in specific times and places, was permissible and indeed central to a growing firearms culture; carrying a loaded weapon at night, or shooting it off to gain attention, to celebrate, or *per burla* – as a joke – were all clearly not acceptable.[41]

Over the course of the 1600s there was a significant tailing off of papal edicts against the *archibugio*, whether *da ruota* or anything else, but it would be too optimistic to conclude from this that firearm violence had actually declined in the Papal States. Rather, it would seem that the authorities in Rome were increasingly willing to fight only the battles they could hope to win, which certainly excluded any general bans against new weapons technology. That the *"terzarolo da rota o da focile* [a rifled pistol]" had thoroughly and irresistibly penetrated Roman culture – and the weird places it could consequently turn up – is evident from some mid-seventeenth-century edicts that were aimed at, among others, "ecclesiastics, regular and cloistered [clergy] of whatever institution," who, despite their "state, rank, order, condition, or pre-eminence, however sublime and most worthy of respect" nevertheless apparently liked to arm themselves while saying mass or while taking part in the religious "processions, functions, and devotions" that linked the various pilgrimage basilicas of Rome.[42] If the States of the Church had to worry about its own clergy packing firearms during religious services, one can imagine how prevalent the habit must have become among nobles and artisans. As to the more common folk, even if they were effectively denied access to gunpowder weapons, they were still more than willing to settle their differences with knives, stilettos, and daggers, which by the eighteenth century if not earlier had developed a widespread cult following among the Roman *bulli*, or youthful gangsters.

In the countryside, meanwhile, the wheel-lock and its successor flintlock became permanent features of the landscape, so common in the hands of peasants and outlaws as to no longer merit special mention. Thus, both the weapons and the bandits they had so come to symbolize more or less evaporated from the edicts issued by Roman authorities, though this is not to say that the papal backwaters became safer or more law-abiding places. By degrees, the papacy ceded responsibility for keeping the peace to the great landowners who had so successfully resisted efforts to tame them in the sixteenth century. Some of these families ruled virtual mini-kingdoms and essentially answered to no one; under their care, the bandit bands that had marauded through the *macchie* during the sixteenth century evolved into private armies in the seventeenth. Throughout the 1600s, the wise voyager, even on the main roads, always carried an *archibugio a ruota* and still traveled in large groups whenever he could. Banditry became so diffused in, and so identified with, Roman territories that by the later eighteenth century it would turn into something of a tourist attraction for foreign connoisseurs of the wild and romantic; the exploits of these desperados inspired scores of popular ballads, many of which were published and hawked from village to village. Revenge killings remained common, among peasants as with their feudal lords, as old traditions of personal honor, clan loyalty, and bonds of fealty largely usurped the rule of Roman law and communal authority that had predominated in much of this region during the Renaissance centuries.

Some scholars have held that this was the era of Italy's "refeudalization", when large parts of the peninsula – especially, though not exclusively, in the center and south – apparently reversed a long-standing course towards urbanization and centralization, gave up on the mercantile economy and its purported values of secular individualism, and returned to an ethos permeated with notions of hierarchy, private justice, and subservience. The term, both loaded and clunky, may say less about baroque Italians' actual embrace of neo-feudal norms than about the unhappiness of many historians with Italy's apparent turning away from "Renaissance values" after the mid-1500s. Still, there has been no shortage of potential culprits glimpsed behind the Italians' retrograde retrenchment: some have blamed the massive Spanish presence in Italy after 1559; others have pointed to the loss of international trade routes, the increasing cost of warfare, and a newfound post-Tridentate piety.[43] And the *archibugio a ruota*? Although this firearm may not have changed battlefield tactics much, it did, by widely arming the civilian population, significantly corrode Italian codes of conduct and respect for social order that had been in place for centuries. Through empowering those at both ends of the social scale at the expense of the merchants and artisans who for so long had made up the significant and stabilizing middle ground of Italian society, the wheel-lock may well have had its own role to play in hastening the demise of the Renaissance paradigm and demolishing the balance between classes that, however imperfect, had informed Italian culture for the centuries of its rebirth. As such, this new technology helped make Italy not only a more violent, but also a poorer and more conservative place, long after the sixteenth century's shocks of war and religious upheaval had faded from collective memory.

NOTES

1 For example, pp. 17–22, 62–4, and 262–79 in Jackob Burckhardt, *Civilization of the Renaissance in Italy*, trans. S. G. C. Middlemore, 3rd edn (London: Phaidon, 1950).
2 On this jurisdictional patchwork, see Caroline Castiglione, *Patrons and Adversaries: Nobles and Villagers in Italian Politics, 1640–1760* (Oxford: Oxford University Press, 2005), pp. 28–34.
3 Leonardo Bruni, "Oration on Palla Strozzi," in Mary Ann Witt *et al.* (eds), *The Humanities, Cultural Roots and Continuities* (Lexington, Mass.: D. C. Heath, 1980), vol. 1, pp. 224–6.
4 James Grubb, "Catalysts for Organized Violence in the Early Venetian Territorial State," in Gherardo Ortalli (ed.), *Bande armate, Banditi, banditismo e repressione di giustizia negli stati europei di antico regime* (Rome: Jouvence, 1986), pp. 389–90.
5 Giovanni Battista Crispolti, "Memorie di Perugia dall'anno 1578 al 1586," in Ariodante Fabretti (ed.), *Cronache della città di Perugia* (Torino, 1891), vol. 4, p. 97.
6 During the 1570s and 1580s roughly a quarter to a third of rowers were slaves, half to two-thirds were *forzati*, or convicts, and the remaining quarter or so were paid volunteers, known as *buonavoglia*. Often, however, convicts could outnumber slaves by as many as six to one. See Salvatore Bono, *Schiavi musulmani nell'Italia moderna. Galeotti, vù cumprà, domestici* (Naples: Edizioni Scientifiche Italiane, 1999), pp. 166–75.
7 Romolo Allegrini, "Memorie di Perugia dall'anno 1580 al 1591," in Ariodante Fabretti (ed.), *Cronache della città di Perugia* (Torino, 1894), vol. 5, p. 9.
8 Peter Blastenbrei, "I Romani tra violenza e giustizia nel tardo Cinquecento," *Roma moderna e contemporanea: Tribunali, giustizia e società nella Roma del Cinque e Seicento* 1 (1997): 67–79.
9 Allegrini, "Memorie di Perugia," pp. 42–51.
10 Michele Di Silvo, "Per via di giustizia. Sul processo penale a Roma tra XVI e XIX secolo," pp. 13–35 in *Rivista storica del Lazio*, vol. 9 (2001): *Giustizia e criminalità nello Stato Pontificio*; Giancarlo Baronti, *La Morte in piazza. Opacità della giustizia, ambiguità del boia e trasparenza del patibolo in età moderna* (Lecce: Argo Editrice, 2000), pp. 47–82.
11 Archivio di Stato di Roma, Collezione bandi (henceforth ASR, CB), vol. 410, 5 November 1585.
12 Thomas F. Arnold, "The Wheel-lock Pistol," *Quarterly Journal of Military History* 8 (1995): 74.
13 Geoffrey Parker, *The Military Revolution: Military Innovation and the Rise of the West, 1500–1800*, 2nd edn (Cambridge: Cambridge University Press, 1996), pp. 17–21.
14 Thus, *archibugio corte di doi palmi* mostly turns up in the edicts that outlawed such weapons: see ASR, CB, bu. 410, 28 June 1573, titled "Prohibition against keeping or carrying *Archibusetti a Rota* of barrel [length] shorter than two palms"; also, ibid., bu. 8, *Bandi generali* of 28 April 1591. In the 1600s, the terms *terzarolo* and *terzetta* were joined and eventually superseded by *pistole*: see ASR, Tribunale del Governatore di Roma, Processi Criminali (henceforth TGPC), bu. 11 (1601), filza 4, fol. 256r.

15 Benvenuto Cellini, *Vita di Benvenuto Cellini, orefice e scultore, scritta di sua propria mano*, ed. Ulrico Martinelli (Milano: Villardi, 1930), pp. 126, 146.
16 On robbing someone for his wheel-lock, see ASR, TGPC, bu. 175 (1581), filza 20, fol. 840r.; also ibid., bu. 111 (1566), filza 17, fol. 722 r.; bu. 169 (1580), filza 8, fol. 1r.; bu. 204 (1586), filza 3, fol. 227r.; bu. 250 (1592), filza 16, fols. 742r.–v.; bu. 252 (1592), filza 6, fol. 238r.; bu. 257 (1592), filza 33, fol. 910r.
17 For example, ASR, TGPC, bu. 244 (1591), filza 2, fol. 22r.–v.; also ibid., bu. 177 (1582), filza 4, fol. 546r.
18 Thus: ASR, TGPC, bu. 116 (1613), filza 8, fol. 221r.; also ibid., bu. 199 (1584), filza 35, fol. 839r.
19 For example, ASR, TGPC, bu. 199 (1584), filza 35, fol. 842v.; ibid., bu. 204 (1586), filza 3, fol. 227v.; ibid., bu. 204, filza 16, fol. 766r.; ibid., bu. 244 (1591), filza 2, fol. 34r.; ibid., bu. 270 (1593), filza 5, fol. 157r.
20 Archivio di Stato di Perugia, Editti e Bandi (henceforth ASP, EB), bu. 8, 7 October 1584; ASR, TGPC, bu. 215 (1587), filza 16, fol. 1039v.; ibid., bu. 299 (1596), filza 20, fol. 622r.; Allegrini, "Memorie di Perugia," p. 50.
21 ASP, EB, bu. 8, 11 June and 31 August 1582.
22 Perugia, Biblioteca Augusta, ms. 289: "Ripartimento delle battaglie nel stato ecclesiatico," fols. 50r.–v.
23 Thus, ASR, TGPC, bu. 205 (1586), filza 10.
24 ASP, EB, bu. 13, 7 November 1578.
25 Quoted in Arnold, "The Wheel-lock Pistol," p. 74.
26 Julius R. Ruff, *Violence in Early Modern Europe, 1500–1800* (Cambridge: Cambridge University Press, 1991), pp. 50–1; ASP, EB, bu. 5, 6 September 1556; ASR, CB, bu. 410, 31 October 1558.
27 ASR, CB, bu. 410, 28 June 1573.
28 ASP, EB, bu. 8, 2 December 1578; also, Archivi di Stato di Spoleto, *Editti e bandi*, 1561–80, 28 November 1578.
29 ASR, CB, bu. 8, 28 April 1591. This was eventually sweetened somewhat by promising a quarter share of the culprit's possessions to whoever denounced him: ibid., 26 January 1625.
30 See Allegrini, "Memorie di Perugia," pp. 31, 65.
31 ASR, CB, bu. 410, 28 June 1573.
32 ASP, EB, bu. 7, 15 November 1572.
33 ASP, EB, bu. 8, 26 October 1579; ibid., bu. 9, 26 January 1597.
34 ASP, EB, bu. 13, 7 November 1578; also ibid., 2 December 1578; ASR, CB, 28 June and 5 December 1573.
35 ASR, CB, bu. 410, 5 November 1585, 18 February 1587 and 1 March 1587; ASR, TGPC, bu. 169 (1580), filza 28, fol. 704r.; for an edict in Perugia against the traffic in stolen lead: ASP, EB, bu. 8, 18 December 1579.
36 ASR, CB, bu. 410, 28 June and 5 December 1573; ASP, EB, bu. 7, 30 June 1576; ibid., bu. 13, 7 November and 2 December 1578.
37 Perugia, Biblioteca Augusta, ms. 289, fol. 51v.
38 Ruff, *Violence in Early Modern Europe*, p. 51.
39 Arnold, "The Wheel-lock Pistol," p. 74.
40 For example, ASR, TGPC, bu. 205 (1586), filza 8, fol. 27v.; ibid., bu. 244 (1591), filza 2, fol. 26r.
41 ASR, CB, bu. 8, 28 April 1591, 15 September 1599, 15 July 1624; bu. 410, 6 August 1635; ASP, EB, bu. 9, 16 October 1590; bu. 12, 11 March 1609.
42 ASR, CB, bu. 8, 26 January 1625; bu. 410, 15 February 1654.

43 See Domenico Sella, *Crisis and Continuity. The Economy of Spanish Lombardy in the Seventeenth Century* (Cambridge, Mass.: Harvard University Press, 1979), especially Sella's concluding "Afterword on Refeudalization," pp. 148–72.

SUGGESTIONS FOR FURTHER READING

Baronti, Giancarlo. *Coltelli d'Italia. Rituali di violenza e tradizioni productive nel mondo popolare.* Padoa: Franco Muzzio editore, 1986.

—— *La Morte in piazza. Opacità della giustizia, ambiguità del boia e trasparenza del patibolo in età moderna.* Lecce: Argo Editrice, 2000.

Black, C. F. "Perugia and Papal Absolutism in the Sixteenth Century." *English Historical Review* 96 (1981): 509–39.

Blastenbrei, Peter. "I Romani tra violenza e giustizia nel tardo Cinquecento." *Roma moderna e contemporanea: Tribunali, giustizia e società nella Roma del Cinque e Seicento* 1 (1997): 67–79.

Blok, Anton. "The Peasant and the Brigand: Social Banditry Reconsidered," in Robert P. Weiss, ed., *Social History of Crime, Policing and Punishment.* Aldershot: Ashgate, 1999, 15–27.

Calzolari, Monica *et al.*, eds. *Rivista storica del Lazio: Giustizia e criminalità nello Stato Pontificio* 9 (2001).

Caravale, Mario and Alberto Caracciolo. *Lo Stato pontificio da Martino V a Pio IX.* Turin: UTET, 1978.

Castiglione, Caroline. *Patrons and Adversaries: Nobles and Villagers in Italian Politics, 1640–1760.* Oxford: Oxford University Press, 2005.

Cirinei, Alfredo. "Bandi e giustizia criminale a Roma nel Cinque e Seicento." *Roma moderna e contemporanea: Tribunali, giustizia e società nella Roma del Cinque e Seicento* 1 (1997): 81–95.

Guilmartin, John jun. *Gunpowder and Galleys. Changing Technology and Mediterranean Warfare at Sea in the Sixteenth Century.* Cambridge: Cambridge University Press, 1974.

Hale, John. "Violence in the Late Middle Ages: A Background," in Lauro Martines, ed., *Violence and Civil Disorder in Italian Cities, 1200–1500.* Los Angeles: University of California Press, 1972, 19–37.

—— *War and Society in Renaissance Europe 1450–1620.* Montreal: McGill-Queen's University Press, 1998.

Hanlon, Gregory. *Early Modern Italy, 1550–1800.* New York: St Martin's Press, 2000.

Hughes, Steven. "Fear and Loathing in Bologna and Rome: The Papal Police in Perspective." *Journal of Social History* 21 (1987): 97–116.

Muir, Edward. *Mad Blood Stirring: Vendetta and Factions in Friuli during the Renaissance.* Baltimore: Johns Hopkins University Press, 1993.

Ortalli, Gherardo, ed. *Bande armate, Banditi, banditismo e repressione di giustizia negli stati europei di antico regime.* Rome: Jouvence, 1986.

Parker, Geoffrey. *The Military Revolution: Military Innovation and the Rise of the West, 1500–1800,* 2nd edn. Cambridge: Cambridge University Press, 1996.

Polverini Fosi, Irene. *La società violenta: Il banditismo dello Stato pontificio nella senconda metà del Cinquecento.* Rome: Edizioni dell'Ateneo, 1985.

Ruff, Julius R. *Violence in Early Modern Europe, 1500–1800.* Cambridge: Cambridge University Press, 1991.

Sella, Domenico. *Crisis and Continuity. The Economy of Spanish Lombardy in the Seventeenth Century.* Cambridge, Mass.: Harvard University Press, 1979.

Tallett, Frank. *War and Society in Early-modern Europe, 1495–1715.* London: Routledge, 1992.

PART V

MAKING IDENTITIES

CHAPTER TWENTY-ONE

HUMAN EXCEPTIONALISM

Kenneth Gouwens

In his landmark study *On the Fabric of the Human Body* (1543), Andreas Vesalius launched a withering critique of Galen, the ancient physician whose anatomical writings had held sway for nearly fourteen centuries. Through dissecting human cadavers and comparing his findings with the texts, Vesalius had identified over 200 errors, which he attributed overwhelmingly to Galen's reliance upon apes:

> It is now clear to me from the reborn art of dissection, from diligent reading of Galen's books and their restoration in several places . . . that he never dissected a human body; but deceived by his monkeys (*simiis*) . . . he frequently and improperly opposed the ancient physicians trained in human dissection.[1]

Although he notes in passing that Galen had erred even in his descriptions of apes, Vesalius focused his attack upon the contrast between human and simian anatomies.[2] Following Aristotle, Galen had stated that "there is an exact similarity between the parts of a human and those of a monkey."[3] Working from that assumption, although he did signal the outwardly visible distinctions in fingers and in the bend of the knee, Galen had overlooked major discrepancies in internal organs.

In the preface to *De fabrica*, Vesalius casts himself less as an innovator than as an heir and vindicator of ancient wisdom. He emphasizes the conventionality of his methods: at Padua and Bologna, "I demonstrated and taught in such a way that there was nothing in my procedure that varied from the tradition of the ancients."[4] He narrates anatomy's decline in the intervening centuries: over time, physicians lost respect for the use of the hand in medicine, and so they delegated manual work to subordinates. Meanwhile, the surviving fragments of ancient anatomical writings came to be viewed as an authority independent of direct observation and yet, somehow, more reliable than it was. But now anatomy is recovering much of its ancient splendor, and his own efforts to harmonize direct observation with textual knowledge participate in that recovery.[5] Both in the lavishly illustrated *Fabrica* and in the *Epitome* (1543), a brief rendition of his findings pitched at non-specialists, Vesalius made clear that he was extending an ancient tradition rather than displacing one.[6] Thus he strikes a pose characteristic of Renaissance intellectuals: that of the savvy reader of texts whose encounter with antiquity is integral to his or her creative reconceptualization of present-day orthodoxies.

This chapter explores the larger intellectual framework within which Vesalius was writing, with particular attention to Renaissance conceptions of human dignity. When specifying what made humans distinct from and superior to other earthly creatures, sixteenth-century authors could cite numerous classical and Christian precedents.[7] Certainly there was nothing new or controversial about Vesalius's assertion that human beings are "the most perfect of all creatures," the human body being the "lodging-place and instrument of the immortal soul."[8] If anything, he attenuated and limited the traditional providential rhetoric about the design of the human body, concerning which Galen had waxed eloquent.[9] But in attributing crucial importance to the differences between humans and apes, Vesalius made his point in a way that resonated particularly with a major topos in the literary and artistic discourse of his own age.

If the human/ape distinction was a commonplace of Renaissance thought, it had special prominence in theoretical writings on the imitation of ancient models.[10] In his *Ciceronianus* of 1528, Erasmus famously ridiculed as "apes" those humanists whose imitations of Cicero were superficial. But what, exactly, did it mean in the Renaissance to call a rival an "ape"? By addressing this question, which has received surprisingly little scholarly scrutiny, we may better appreciate just what was at stake in Renaissance controversies over imitation. Moreover, humanists' deployment of simian metaphors will help to set in sharper relief what they wrote about humankind's distinctness from and superiority to all the rest of earthly creation.

Renaissance Europeans had a range of images of apes upon which to draw. Only around 1700 did they come to know, or at least conceptualize, the hominoid "great apes" (e.g., gorillas, chimpanzees, orang-utans).[11] But other simians – Egyptian baboons, tailed monkeys, Barbary apes – had been known since antiquity, and stories had circulated about their perceived habits.[12] For example, in his *Natural History*, Pliny the Elder cited Mucianus's curious report that "the species which have tails become quite melancholy when the moon is on the wane," but "leap for joy at the time of the new moon and adore it."[13] Authorities including Pliny often noted the propensity of apes for imitating humans, but for doing so without much skill. While this flawed imitation could be viewed as an entertaining diversion, often it was taken more seriously, as an offensive pretense to human status. Ennius's observation, famously cited by Cicero, neatly summarizes the unease that the comparison of humans and simians could evoke: *simia quam similis turpissima bestia nobis* ("how similar is the ape, a most-foul beast, to us!").[14]

Medieval lore elaborated upon both the ridiculous and the unsettling aspects of this similarity. Bestiaries claimed that the word *simia* arose from the animal's strong likeness (*similitudo*) to humans – an etymology widely accepted despite Isidore of Seville's explicit rejection of it.[15] The twelfth-century natural historian Alexander Neckam defined the ape as a "joke of nature" (*naturae ludentis opus*) that silently critiqued human vices. At times Christian theologians referred to sinners as apes, and to Satan as God's ape.[16]

The stories and interpretations thus ranged widely, in some cases portraying simians as diabolical, in other cases dismissing them as silly and disgusting. In all accounts save the most fanciful, however, apes lacked the ability to speak: the faculty that, for Cicero, distinguished humans from the beasts and first gave rise to civilization. This view, dominant and rarely controversial until the twentieth century, resonated with particular intensity in the learned culture of Renaissance humanism. By the sixteenth century, the humanists' sophisticated theories of language, their valorization of human dignity, and their systematic scrutiny of both physical and textual evidence led them to define the human/simian boundary with unprecedented clarity and precision.

Humanists held a wide range of beliefs and values, but on one point few of them dissented: eloquent speech had the power to make people better. One's ability to speak was intricately interrelated with one's internal disposition: a well-ordered mind and beautiful, cultivated speech necessarily went together. It followed that by studying and imitating ancient models of eloquence, humans could become more civilized – and, in so doing, distance themselves all the more from savages (who lacked the ability to speak well) and from the beasts (who could not speak at all).

In a letter to his friend Tommaso da Messina concerning the pursuit of eloquence, Petrarch blazoned the transformative power of reading the ancients aloud:

> I cannot tell you of what worth are to me in solitude certain familiar and famous words not only grasped in the mind but actually spoken orally. . . . When through the power of an unusual sweet temptation I am moved to read them again, they gradually take effect and transfigure my insides with hidden powers.[17]

He recalled the stories of Orpheus and Amphion, who through "outstanding eloquence" could "inculcate gentleness and patience in all things," and he referred in passing to Cicero's *De inventione*. There, Tommaso would doubtless have known, Cicero attributed the origins of human civilization to one great and wise man who, "on account of his reasoned argument (*rationem*) and oratorical talent (*orationem*), transformed his listeners from being like beasts to being kind and gentle."[18]

If the trope of the civilizing power of eloquence dated back at least to Isocrates, Cicero's formulation of it was most influential in the Renaissance. In the *De oratore*, recovered in full in 1417 and canonical thereafter, Cicero's interlocutor Crassus explicitly defined the ability to speak among themselves as that which separates humans from the beasts:

> For the one point in which we have our very greatest advantage over the brute creation is that we hold converse one with another, and can reproduce our thought in word. Who therefore would not rightly admire this faculty, and deem it his duty to exert himself to the utmost in this field, that by so doing he may surpass men themselves in that particular respect wherein chiefly men are superior to animals?[19]

Extravagant claims about the power of persuasive speech served the interests of humanists well, particularly after the revival of classical oratory in the fifteenth century. Expert in eloquence, they could hawk to potential employers wares said to have the power to improve moral character, a promise underwritten by Cicero and other ancient authorities. Unsurprisingly, what humanists actually delivered, whether in the classroom or on behalf of a city-state or a wealthy patron, fell short of the ideal, but the remarkable time and energy that they spent reading and imitating less marketable classical models (Martial's epigrams, for example, or Catullan poetic invectives), less in their official duties than in private study and social gatherings, attest to humanists' thoroughgoing commitment to revive ancient culture and thereby elevate the culture of their own age.

Just as humanists viewed their encounter with antiquity as active, the texts and artifacts speaking to them and working change within them, so too they conceived the imitation of classical models as a creative enterprise. Reflexive copying missed the point, for only by making classical *sententiae* one's own could one reap their full benefit. Thus it was no empty figure of speech when Erasmus ridiculed certain Latin stylists as "apes of Cicero": by imitating their model without adequately internalizing his style, these *Ciceroniani* were missing out on the civilizing, humanizing encounter with antiquity that was central to Renaissance humanism.[20]

Erasmus was not the first Renaissance humanist to make this distinction between the human and the simian. Already in the fourteenth century, in a letter to Boccaccio, Petrarch had explicitly invoked apes when describing how best to imitate literary models. Describing the skills of his amanuensis, Petrarch expressed his hope that the youth would develop his own personal style, but was concerned that at the moment he "delights in imitation, and at times is so enraptured by another poet's sweetness and so entangled, contrary to good poetic practice, in the rules of such a work that he becomes incapable of freeing himself without revealing the originals."[21] The imitator should write something similar rather than identical to the model. Insofar as possible, one should guard against the tendency to copy one's models exactly. The composition should not resemble the model the way a painting does, "where the greater the similarity the greater the praise for the artist," but instead should resemble it the way a son does his father.[22] Mastery of this skill is key for creative expression:

> Thus we may appropriate another's ideas as well as his coloring but we must abstain from his actual words; for, with the former, resemblance remains hidden, and with the latter it is glaring, the former creates poets, the second apes.[23]

Boccaccio, by contrast, cast simians in a more favorable light in his compendious *Genealogy of the Pagan Gods*.[24] Particularly noteworthy is his brief chapter refuting the charge "that poets are merely apes of the philosophers."[25] "The apes' natural and invariable habit," he writes, "is to imitate as far as they can everything they see, even to the actions of men." The poet, however, is far removed from the simple sort of imitator who "never sets foot outside his model's track." If these critics had instead called poets "apes of nature" (*simiae naturae*), that would have been less bothersome, "since the poet tries with all his powers to set forth in noble verse the effects, either of Nature herself, or of her eternal and unalterable operation." He concedes that in so doing, poets are apes. He closes the chapter on a striking note: "it would be better for such critics if they would use their best efforts to make us all become apes of Christ, rather than jeer at the labors of poets, which they do not understand." Here, as elsewhere in the *Genealogia*, Boccaccio deploys simian metaphors with surprisingly positive overtones.[26]

A few decades later, around 1400, likening a writer to an ape could still be imagined to be a compliment. In his *Life* of Coluccio Salutati, the chronicler Filippo Villani praised him for his imitation of Cicero's "familiar" letters, which Salutati had helped to recover from oblivion in 1389: "in the texture of his prose he has been so successful that he has rightly been said to be an ape of Cicero."[27]

Around 1489, however, Angelo Poliziano used precisely that turn of phrase in an unambiguously negative way. Having received from Paolo Cortesi a collection of contemporary letters modeled on those of Cicero, Poliziano responded with a letter of his own, which offered a scathing critique of Cortesi's stylistic preferences. Thus he writes: "If I understand you, you approve only those who copy the features of Cicero. To me the form of a bull or a lion seems more respectable than that of an ape, even if an ape looks more like a man." He clarifies his point:

> Those who compose only on the basis of imitation strike me as parrots or magpies bringing out things they don't understand. Such writers lack strength and life; they lack energy, feeling, character; they stretch out, go to sleep, and snore. There is nothing true in them, nothing solid, nothing efficacious. Someone says: "You don't represent Cicero." What of it? I am not Cicero; I think I represent myself.[28]

To play the ape, then, suggests for Poliziano a flawed sort of imitation that neither is internalized nor allows the expression of inner disposition. The ape may look more human than do other animals, but the surface appearance deceives. Imitating a single model militates against forming one's own distinct style.

In response, Cortesi offers a measured defense of imitating Cicero alone. Since the study of elegance has been neglected for so long, "no one can at present speak with elegance and variety unless he places before him a model to imitate," and the best model is Cicero.[29] He explains the sort of imitation he has in mind:

> By likeness . . . I mean not as an ape is like a man but as a son is like a father; for in the first instance the ridiculous imitator reproduces the deformities and faults of body only, on account of his misconception of likeness; while in the other he reproduces the face, gait, posture, carriage, form, voice, and figure and yet he keeps something individual, something natural, something different so that the two, when compared, seem to be unlike.[30]

Whereas apes merely mimic the idiosyncrasies of a given human's bodily movement, one's imitation of even a single model, if properly practiced, allows for differentiation: "all art is the imitation of nature but nature brings it about that both likeness and unlikeness are born of the same seed."[31] Those who attempt to imitate Cicero have at least chosen a worthy model. Thus, Poliziano ought not to hinder him from imitating Cicero, but instead should "criticize my ignorance because I cannot imitate him well – although I prefer to be a sycophant and an ape of Cicero rather than the son of another."[32]

This partial rehabilitation of the simian metaphor is anomalous even for Cortesi: in his dialogue *Concerning Learned Men* (c. 1490), he dismissed the Venetian humanist Andrea Contrario's botched efforts at imitation by calling him not an *alumnus Ciceronis* but instead a *simia Ciceronis*.[33] More typical was the German poet and satirist Sebastian Brandt, who devoted a chapter of his *Ship of Fools* (1494) to the "lazy ape" (*Schluraffe*). Beyond being ridiculous, Brandt's *Schluraffen* embodied the vice of idleness, and he envisioned a boatload of them sailing off toward *Schluraffenland*.[34] But these slothful simians would look fairly innocuous when compared to Erasmus's "apes of Cicero."

Already in 1517, in a letter to Guillaume Budé, Erasmus had used the expression *Ciceronis simios* in a general sense, to indicate all those whose elaborate prose draws attention to itself rather than to its subject matter – a group including imitators not only of Cicero but of Apuleius. Excessive ornamentation detracts from clarity, which "should be the chief aim of everyone who wishes his style to be admired."[35] The flaw is more than just cosmetic, for literary style reveals inner disposition: "Language above all is the mirror of the mind, and the mind should be without spot."[36]

In the *Ciceronianus* (1528), Erasmus uses the simian metaphor with greater specificity and more emphatic condemnation. The way "those miserable Ciceronian apes" (*isti Ciceronis simii*) imitate is that they "scrape up a few phrases, idioms, figures, and rhythmical patterns from here and there and then exhibit just a top surface or veneer of Cicero."[37] Like Poliziano, whose exchange with Cortesi he recapitulates, Erasmus portrays these "apes" as ridiculous in their piecemeal imitation.[38] But he goes farther: not only do these *simii* make fools of themselves and annoy their betters, they also cause collateral damage to Cicero's good name, as well as to the reputations of his more faithful imitators. He notes how fathers scold sons of whom they are ashamed, and then suggests that "[t]his is the way Cicero would probably feel towards those miserable apes, and this is the way we ought to feel, we who are eager to be known as his true and worthy sons."[39]

Beyond defaming Cicero and his worthy heirs, *isti simii* also "create obstacles for the young in their studies and in their moral development."[40] Only after the "undecorous uproar of certain apes has been rejected" can one proceed to imitate Cicero in his totality.[41] That which is nearer to the appearance (*imaginem*) of Cicero, however, may not be the best, a point Erasmus's interlocutor Bulephorus illustrates thus:

> No animal is more like man in all its physical features than the ape; if it had the power of speech in addition, it could be taken for a man. Nothing is less like a man than a peacock or a swan; but you would, I imagine, prefer to be a swan or a peacock rather than an ape.[42]

To this the interlocutor Hypologus replies that he would rather be a camel or a buffalo than the "handsomest of apes."[43] There follows a brief bestiary, contrasting creatures that have pleasant voices with those that make sounds that superficially resemble a human voice. Thus, the nightingale, lark, and horse are to be preferred, respectively, to the cuckoo, the crow, and the donkey. In this context, the ape stands out in sharper relief: superficially hominoid, it does badly what humans do well, rather than striving after and displaying an excellence proper to itself.

In his ever-larger editions of *Adages*, Erasmus came to include at least 11 that concern apes, none of them flattering. To take but one example, in glossing *tragica simia*, he writes that the expression:

> was proverbial as an offensive description of a man who held high office and was rich and powerful, though in other ways undeserving. Ape, like manikin, is the word for what is scarcely a man and more like a pale copy of one; and it is called "tragic" because of the noise and bustle of high position and the wearing of a kind of mask.[44]

The locution has been used by Demosthenes, and also by Jerome, who "shows in his letters that this was a jibe often leveled at Christians, though only by the irreligious and by gentiles, as though they made a show of piety in face and bearing, while being themselves rascals."[45]

As for Erasmus, so too for Luther an ape's gestures are deficient imitations of models, and people's efforts to "ape" their betters look ridiculous. Lecturing in 1534 on Psalm 101:1, for example, he praised his patron, Frederick the Elector of Saxony, for his idiosyncratic wisdom, but cautioned: "in acting this way he did make and leave behind him a very large number of apes."[46] Wanting similarly to be reputed wise, they imitated his contrary manner, but only to comic effect. Thus Luther writes:

> What is more ridiculous than for a monkey to try to do a man's work? What can be more stupid than that a stupid person should want to do the work of a clever man? . . . The Greeks say: "Even if a monkey wore royal apparel, it would still remain a monkey."[47]

Here Luther evidently refers to Lucian's fable of apes who danced in purple robes, an image he may well have drawn from Erasmus, who had cited it in *Praise of Folly* and glossed it in the *Adages*.[48] For Erasmus, as for Lucian, this apish masquerade is comic as an obvious imposture. But for Luther, the deception is more insidious:

> If God raises up an outstanding man, among either the spiritual or the temporal authorities, the devil brings his apes and simpletons to market to imitate everything. And yet it all amounts to monkey-business (*Affenspiel*) and tomfoolery.[49]

Whereas for Erasmus, apes of Cicero inadvertently damaged Cicero's legacy and hindered the literary and moral edification of the youth, for Luther, aping had wider-ranging significance for the political order. Thus in lecturing on the story of Jacob and Rachel in Genesis 29, he cautioned against taking Jacob's example as permission for lawlessness, any more than one should attempt to imitate Achilles's slaying of Hector ("if you try this, Hector will slay you").[50] One must not transgress common custom and law unless and until God orders one to become a Jacob or a hero:

Otherwise such people become apes who invite destruction for themselves and for others. Thus when a well-known incendiary who was pusillanimous by nature became an ape and wanted to imitate the illustrious deeds of other heroes, he revealed his folly and brought destruction on himself. For stupid men of this kind accomplish nothing else than the destruction of states and the confusion and disturbance of the world.[51]

The religious consequences of aping are even more dire. One should imitate the saints by attending first to their faith, and only thereafter to their works. In the pope's church, however, "we see nothing else than an outward imitation of the works which the saints did."[52] Mimicking the external appearance without the Word and without faith, people "become apes of the saints."[53] Their error results from misunderstanding "flesh" in a material rather than a spiritual sense. "This disease," Luther says, "has lurked in human nature in all eras. By means of it we are made apes, with the result that we follow the deed and the examples of the fathers and forsake their spirit."[54] The malady was already evident when those who saw Abraham offering sacrifices imitated his actions without honoring the First Commandment. When people "become apes of their fathers," imitating only their outward works, their doing so is "the origin of all forms of idolatry."[55]

In sum, Luther resembles Erasmus in pointing to the hollowness of the "apish" gestures he describes, but differs markedly in his assessment of them not merely as bad and inadvertently destructive, but instead (to invoke a Nietzschean distinction) as outright evil. The exemplar of flawed imitation, for Luther, is the Evil One himself: "wherever Christ builds a temple and gathers a church, Satan habitually imitates Him like an ape (*tamquam simia*) and inventing idolatrous forms of worship and idolatrous traditions similar to the true doctrine and the true forms of worship."[56] Dreams are particularly dangerous sources of deception: they may arise from God, but also "from the devil, who is God's ape."[57] One should be wary of dreams even if they are in some respects accurate, for Satan "lies even in telling the truth."[58] But then, Satan "can deceive those who are awake as well as those who are asleep."[59] In short, the devilry is in the details.

While Renaissance thought encompassed a range of views about the misery and dignity of humankind, the writers who have been our focus – from Petrarch and Boccaccio, to Poliziano and Cortesi, to Erasmus and Luther – all believed that human beings, made in God's image and likeness, occupied a special place in creation above that of animals. While their anthropologies differed significantly, they all saw humans as embodying potentials that apes did not share. For all of them, too, the faculty of speech played a particularly crucial role, whether for its potential to improve the listener or as the key means by which God communicated His Word to humankind. By the later sixteenth century, however – particularly in the writings of Montaigne – all of these postulates were called into doubt.

Among rhetoricians, aping still signified flawed imitation, but its invocation became less controversial. In 1577 Gabriel Harvey published two Latin orations, *Ciceronianus* and *Rhetor*, that he had delivered as the praelector of rhetoric at Cambridge. In the former, he seasons enthusiastic endorsement of studying Cicero with advocacy of eclectic imitation and offers a *mea culpa* for his own youthful failings as an imitator:

> I valued words more than content, language more than thought, the one art of speaking more than the thousand subjects of knowledge; I preferred the mere style of Marcus Tully to all the postulates of the philosophers and mathematicians; I believed that the bone and sinew of imitation lay in my ability to choose as many brilliant and elegant words as possible, to reduce them into order, and to connect them together in a rhythmical period. In my judgment – or perhaps I should say opinion rather than judgment – that was what it meant to be a Ciceronian.[60]

Roman humanists, Harvey writes, "have contrived a sort of misguided imitation founded on an erroneous opinion," so that they should be called "apes (*simias*) or shadows or even bastard offspring of Cicero."[61] Harvey himself favors Peter Ramus, along with Erasmus, Johann Sturm, and Joannes Thomas Freigius, over "any number of Italians."[62] In the *Rhetor*, Harvey dismisses the Ciceronians as ridiculous and outmoded: "those little crows and apes of Cicero were long ago driven from the stage by the hissing and laughter of the learned, as they so well deserved, and at last have almost vanished."[63] By the 1570s, then, "apish" imitation of Cicero was no longer the flashpoint it had been in Erasmus's time.[64]

Meanwhile, Montaigne was launching his most radical philosophical critique of human exceptionalism. In the *Apology for Raymond Sebond* (begun 1575), amidst challenges to the reliability of perception, he writes: "Presumption is our natural and original malady. The most vulnerable and frail of all creatures is man, and at the same time the most arrogant."[65] Puffed up with vanity, imagining himself equal with God, man "attributes to himself divine characteristics, picks himself out and separates himself from the horde of other creatures . . ."[66] Yet these claims are groundless:

> How does he know, by the force of his intelligence, the secret internal stirrings of animals? By what comparison between them and us does he infer the stupidity that he attributes to them?
>
> When I play with my cat, who knows if I am not a pastime to her more than she is to me? [We entertain each other with reciprocal monkey tricks (*singeries*). If I have my time to begin or to refuse, so has she hers.][67]

Montaigne even questions the uniqueness to humans of the faculty of speech:

> This defect that hinders communication between [the beasts] and us, why is it not just as much ours as theirs? It is a matter of guesswork whose fault it is that we do not understand one another; for we do not understand them any more than they do us. By this same reasoning they may consider us beasts, as we consider them.[68]

Later in the *Apology*, when he cites Ennius's famous dictum about apes, he puts it to an idiosyncratic use, in support of a challenge to humans' physical uniqueness:

Those [beasts] that most resemble us are the ugliest and most abject of the whole band: for in external appearance and shape of the face, it is the apes (*guenons*): "How similar the simian, ugliest of beasts!" . . . for the insides and vital parts, it is the hog.[69]

It would be a mistake to take such passages as Montaigne's definitive word on the subject.[70] He invokes apes not to raise them up, but to bring humans down. For example, when discussing ambition in "Of presumption," he cites a contemporary's aphorism "that the French are like monkeys [*guenons*] who climb to the top of a tree, from branch to branch, and never stop moving until they have reached the highest branch, and show their rear ends when they get there."[71] And in the essay "Of cruelty," written precisely when he was completing the *Apology* (1578–80), Montaigne stated explicitly: "As for that cousinship between us and the animals, I do not put much stock in it. . . ."[72] His final position may better be gleaned, however, from the ultimate essay in his collection, "Of experience." There, he proposes an approach to knowledge that is grounded in self-scrutiny, and that offers a measured restatement of human dignity: "It is an absolute perfection and virtually divine to know how to enjoy our being rightfully. . . . The most beautiful lives, to my mind, are those that conform to the common human pattern, with order, but without miracle, without eccentricity."[73]

Like the assertions of human exceptionalism that Montaigne interrogated, so too his own skeptical questioning of them drew extensively upon classical models. The Renaissance recovery of ancient texts facilitated renewed attention, after all, not only to the dominant voices that had championed human dignity but also to dissonant ones that had challenged human presumption. In constructing his "new Pyrrhonism," Montaigne appropriated ideas and strategies from the minority report of Sextus Empiricus, whose skeptical writings had appeared in Latin translations in 1562 and 1569.[74] Thus, if antiquity had bequeathed to Renaissance intellectuals the building blocks for their own master narratives, it also equipped them with some powerful tools and techniques for dismantling those narratives.

A positive conception of "aping" did persist in theoretical writings on art such as Giovanni Paolo Lomazzo's ponderous *Treatise on the Fine Arts* (1585). Lomazzo asserts that painting is an art since it takes "works of nature for its models and is the imitator or, as it were, the ape of nature, constantly striving to imitate its quantity, modeling, and color."[75] In a move reminiscent of Boccaccio's in the *Genealogia*, he goes on to associate this sophisticated "aping" of nature with the *imitatio Christi*.[76] Lomazzo's views were soon eclipsed, however, by aesthetic doctrines propounded in the Carracci Academy in Bologna (founded 1582), which left little room for the *ars simia naturae* metaphor.[77]

In the seventeenth century, the *ars simia naturae* topos lingered on in the writings of the alchemist and Rosicrucian Robert Fludd, for whom the old systems of correspondences remained fundamentally meaningful.[78] In the first volume (1617) of his unfinished *History of the Macrocosm*, an etching depicts a nude woman holding on a chain an ape, which sits on the terrestrial globe while using a compass to measure a smaller globe (Figure 21.1). Fludd glosses the image thus:

– *Human exceptionalism* –

Nature, not Divine, but the closest handmaid of God, has under her a servant or attendant who by imitating her mistress, impressing upon herself in agreement the likenesses of things produced by Nature, marvelously follows and imitates Nature's vestiges and delineations.[79]

By Fludd's time, however, not all found such systems of correspondences so compelling. In general, the attitude of the learned toward the natural world was being transformed. Scientists were coming to view nature instrumentally, yet (in accordance with Genesis) as the domain over which humans held dominion by divine fiat.[80] *Ars simia naturae* was falling from favor, as the trope of "jokes of nature" soon would, and for much the same reason – the decline of analogical and poetic readings of nature, which were being replaced by "an increasingly vertical taxonomy that explained natural operations in functional rather than symbolic terms."[81]

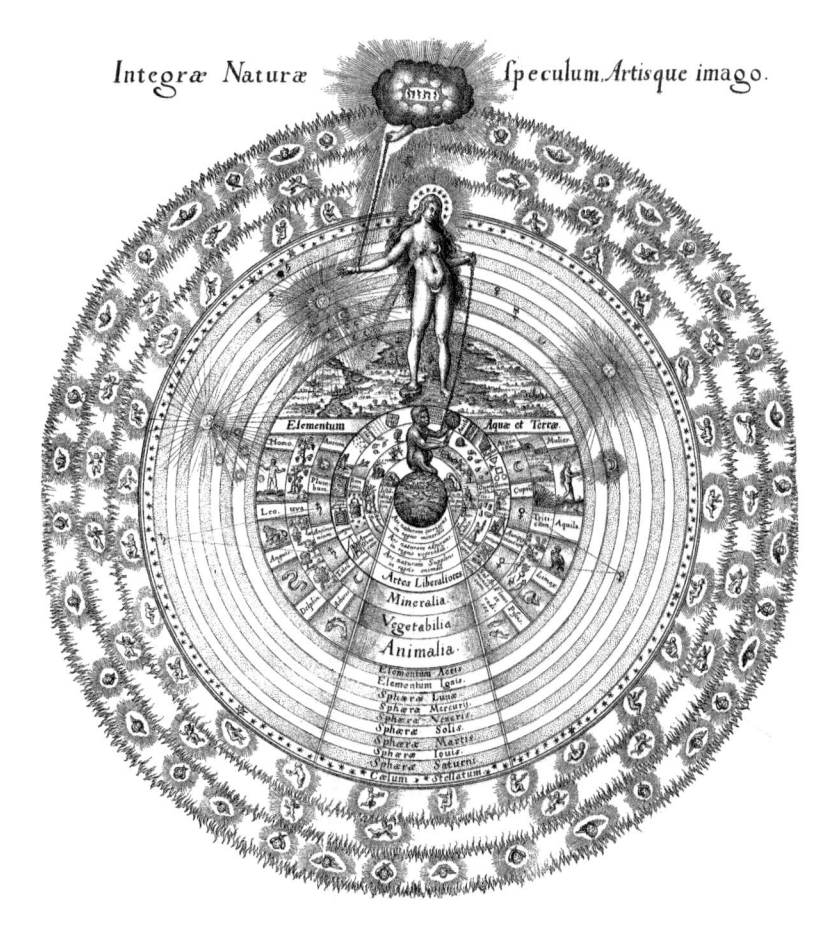

Figure 21.1 "Integrae naturae speculum" from Robert Fludd, *Utriusque cosmi historia*, 1617. The British Library.

If mainstream natural scientists and philosophers no longer read simian imitation as an instance of nature's serious playfulness, artists could still exploit it for parody, as had been the case for centuries. Apes had appeared often in Renaissance paintings, as for example in Carpaccio's *Return of the Ambassadors* (*c.* 1499; Figure 21.2), although their significance is not always easy to read. Is Carpaccio's monkey purely decorative? Might its presence serve to create an ironic distance from the main narrative? Or, does its indifference to that narrative serve as a foil to heighten the viewer's illusion of participation in the action?[82] More obviously parodic, if no easier to parse, is an early 1540s woodcut by Niccolò Boldrini, based on a design attributed to Titian, which rendered the figures in the famous *Laocoön* statue group as monkeys (Figure 21.3). Scholars have interpreted this image variously, e.g., as criticism of the talents or aesthetic ideals of either Baccio Bandinelli, or Michelangelo Buonarroti, or Giorgio Vasari.[83] Janson read this image as an attack on critics of Vesalius, meaning: "This is what the heroic bodies of classical antiquity would have to look like in order to conform to the anatomical specifications of Galen!"[84] The serious import (if any) of this woodcut remains moot, but its ludic dimension is inarguable.

Figure 21.2 Vittore Carpaccio. *Scenes from the Life of Saint Ursula: The Return of the Ambassadors* (detail), 1490–4. Accademia, Venice, Italy/Scala Archives.

Figure 21.3 Niccolò Boldrini, parody of *The Laocoön*, woodcut, *c.* 1540–5. Board of Trustees, National Gallery of Art, Washington, DC.

By the seventeenth century, the parodic use of simians would extend to their depiction as portrait painters – perhaps a satire of the burgeoning business of portraiture, but not an invocation of "serious play."[85] But simians fared even worse in the works of art theorists. Giovanni Pietro Bellori's influential *Lives of Modern Painters, Sculptors, and Architects* (1672) thoroughly dismissed the *ars simia naturae* trope. Tellingly, the book includes an engraving by Albert Clouet that depicts an idealized female figure, explicitly identified as *imitatio sapiens*, trampling an ape underfoot (Figure 21.4).[86] Thus, if apes remained ambiguous signifiers more generally, for seventeenth-century aesthetic theorists their imitative abilities were belittled, and they were left without even a shred of dignity.

It was in the realm of philosophy, however, that human exceptionalism was most forcefully and influentially reasserted in the seventeenth century. Although René Descartes did not entirely dismiss the possibility of animals having emotions, he denied that they had a rational soul or self-consciousness.[87] Thus he wrote: "I cannot share the opinion of Montaigne and others who attribute understanding or thought to animals."[88] He was equally emphatic in denying that any of the beasts had the ability to speak:

> We ought not to confound speech with natural movements which betray passions and may be imitated by machines as well as be manifested by animals; nor must we think, as did some of the ancients, that brutes talk, although we do not understand their language.[89]

Figure 21.4 Albert Clouet. Engraving: "Imitatio Sapiens," taken from Giovanni Pietro Bellori, *Le vite de' Pittori* . . . (Rome, 1672). The British Library.

Yet in the Enlightenment, the Renaissance and early modern distinction between humans and apes – which was itself a central part of the intellectual context in which Vesalius developed his critique of Galen – would also come under attack. The first major blow came from Linnaeus who, in the mid-eighteenth century, subsumed apes and humans alike under the new rubric *mammalia*.[90] Even more revolutionary was Darwin's evolutionary theory, which raised the specter of common human and simian ancestry.

One may lament, with present-day philosopher Stephen Toulmin, the extent to which a Cartesian concern with "abstract rigor and exactitude" in the pursuit of knowledge triumphed at the expense of Montaigne's skeptical, situational approach.[91] We may need, as Toulmin suggests, to "reappropriate the wisdom of the 16th-century humanists" for our own age.[92] In the intervening centuries, the triumph of Cartesian rationalism has served to justify philosophers' assertion of a strict separation of humans from simians.

In the late twentieth and early twenty-first centuries, however, philosophers, anthropologists, and cognitive psychologists have gone farther than ever before toward effacing the distinction between humans and apes – not only in the realms of emotions and of language but even in the realm of dignity.

As in earlier centuries, so too today simian behavior holds the mirror up to human folly. Thus advertisements for products ranging from suitcases to business software portray "savage baggage handlers" and inept co-workers, respectively, as apes.[93] Psychology experiments, meanwhile, have documented apes engaged in a variety of behaviors that uncannily resemble "human" ethical lapses, such as compulsive gambling, exchanging sex for money, and deceiving "friends" for personal advantage (a trait that has been termed "Machiavellian Intelligence").[94] Thus, the parallels drawn between humans and simians can still evoke a memorable mixture of amusement and unease.

More significantly, sophisticated challenges to human exceptionalism are now appearing in learned discourse with unprecedented frequency. In 1993, Peter Singer and Paola Cavalieri launched "The Great Ape Project," an interdisciplinary enterprise combining animal rights advocacy with philosophical and psychological arguments for the "personhood" of apes.[95] More recently, the Chimpanzee Cultures website features the news that "a paper published online in *Nature* offers the first evidence for the transmission of traditions in non-human primates."[96] And the age-old trope of simians' physical likeness to humans has gained new support with the discovery that the human and chimpanzee genomes have alphabets that are upwards of 97 percent identical. What, then, remains that is distinctly human, and that is likely to be thought so in future centuries?

In time, a new scholarly consensus may or may not dictate that we expand our identity from a human to a hominoid scale. Simians may or may not come to be recognized as having cognitive abilities on par with those of human beings. What is clear, however, is that the faith that Renaissance humanists placed in the transformative and civilizing power of language, and their assumption that human beings were unique among all creatures in their dignity and their aspiring creativity, now ranks among the most endangered species of thought.

NOTES

1 Vesalius, trans. C. D. O'Malley, in his *Andreas Vesalius of Brussels 1514–1564* (Berkeley and Los Angeles: University of California Press, 1964), 321. *Pace* Vesalius, Galen had in fact occasionally taken part in human dissections. See Andrea Carlino, *Books of the Body: Anatomical Ritual and Renaissance Learning*, trans. John Tedeschi and Anne C. Tedeschi (Chicago: University of Chicago Press, 1999), 143–9.
2 Andreas Vesalius, *De humani corporis fabrica libri septem* (Basel, 1543; repr., Brussels: Culture et civilisation, 1964), fol. 3v.; trans. in O'Malley, *Andreas Vesalius*, 320–1.
3 Carlino, *Books of the Body*, 144.
4 Vesalius, *Fabrica*, 3r.
5 Nancy G. Siraisi, "Vesalius and the Reading of Galen's Teleology," *Renaissance Quarterly* 50 (1997): 1–37, esp. 3, where she suggests that even in sharply criticizing a prior authority, Vesalius may have been imitating the practice of Aristotle and Galen.
6 He dedicated both texts to powerful patrons – Charles V and his son, Philip, respectively – under whose aegis the works might be afforded some protection. The dedicatory letter of the *Epitome* offers an abbreviated and somewhat gentler critique of Galen "who, although easily chief of the masters, nevertheless did not dissect the human body; and the fact is now evident that he described (not to say imposed upon us) the fabric of the ape's body, although the latter differs from the former in many respects." *The Epitome of Andreas Vesalius*, ed. and trans. L. R. Lind (New York: Macmillan, 1949), xxxv.

7 Jill Kraye, "Moral Philosophy," in *The Cambridge History of Renaissance Philosophy*, ed. Charles B. Schmitt and Quentin Skinner (Cambridge: Cambridge University Press, 1988), 306–16.
8 *Fabrica*, fol. 4v.
9 Siraisi, "Vesalius," 30.
10 For an authoritative assessment of literary imitation, with copious bibliography, see Thomas M. Greene, *The Light in Troy: Imitation and Discovery in Renaissance Poetry* (New Haven: Yale University Press, 1982).
11 H. W. Janson, *Apes and Ape Lore in the Middle Ages and Renaissance* (London: Warburg Institute, 1952), 331–2, and 335–6, for whom Edward Tyson's detailed physical description of a young specimen in 1699 marks "the formal entry of the anthropoid ape into the consciousness of Western civilisation."
12 Janson, *Apes*, 15. In the present chapter, as in the translations herein cited, "ape" and "monkey" are used synonymously.
13 Pliny, *Natural History*, ed. and trans. John Bostock and H. T. Riley; online at www.perseus.tufts.edu.
14 Cicero, *De natura deorum*, 1.35.97.
15 Isidore of Seville, *Etymologiae*, II.2.30.
16 Janson, *Apes*, 16–19.
17 Lett. I.9, in Petrarch, *Rerum familiarium libri I–VIII*, trans. Aldo S. Bernardo (Albany: State University of New York Press, 1975), 49–50.
18 Cicero, *De inventione* I.ii.2. There was no room in this scheme for the silver-tongued devil, although there could be what Cicero called (I.ii.3) a "depraved imitator of virtue" (*prava virtutis imitatrix*); my translation.
19 I.32–3 in Cicero, *De oratore*, ed. and trans. E. W. Sutton and H. Rackham, 2 vols (Cambridge, Mass.: Harvard University Press, 1967), 1:25.
20 Of course, "humanism" and the "human" are not isomorphic, but humanists' appropriation of Cicero entailed reproducing commonplaces about civilization and humanity. For a positive appraisal of Ciceronianism, see John Monfasani, "The Ciceronian Controversy," in *The Cambridge History of Literary Criticism*, vol. 3, *The Renaissance*, ed. Glyn P. Norton (Cambridge: Cambridge University Press, 1999), 395–401.
21 Petrarch, *Letters on Familiar Matters*: Rerum familiarium libri *XVII–XXIV*, ed. and trans. Aldo S. Bernardo (Baltimore: Johns Hopkins University Press, 1985), 300–2 (bk. 23, lett. 19), at 300. Latin in Petrarch, *Le Familiari*, 4 vols. Vol. 1: "Introduzione e libri I–IV," ed. Vittorio Rossi (Florence: Sansoni, 1968), 4: 203–7, at 205.
22 Petrarch, *Letters*, 205. Cf. Seneca, *Epistulae morales*, 84.8.
23 Petrarch, *Letters*, 302; Latin in *Le Familiari*, 4: 206.
24 Giovanni Boccaccio, *Genealogiae* (New York: Garland, 1976; reprint of 1494 Venice edition).
25 Book XIV, chap. 17 ("Philosophorum simias minime poetas esse"); *Genealogiae*, 108v. Translated in Charles G. Osgood, *Boccaccio on Poetry: Being the Preface and the Fourteenth and Fifteenth Books of Boccaccio's* Genealogia Deorum Gentilium *in an English Version with Introductory Essay and Commentary* (Princeton: Princeton University Press, 1930), 78–80 (notes, 176–7). The quotations that follow in this paragraph are drawn from Osgood's translation.
26 Janson, *Apes*, 290–3, analyzes as well Boccaccio's creative retelling of two myths (one about Vulcan, the other about Epimetheus) in ways that similarly treat apes and aping positively. He calls Boccaccio "the originator of the Renaissance concept of *ars simia naturae*, as against the mediaeval *simia veri* with its invidious distinction between reality and representational art, the 'forgery of reality'" (*Apes*, 293).

27 For the Latin, see Izora Scott, *Controversies over the Imitation of Cicero in the Renaissance* (Davis, Calif.: Hermagoras Press, 1991), 8, n. 39. Janson, *Apes*, 293, notes that Filippo Villani also praised a certain "Stefano," a follower of Giotto, as "the ape of nature" since he "so excelled at imitating nature that even physicians would study the wonderfully precise details of arteries, veins, and sinews in his representation of the human body."
28 Greene, *Light in Troy*, 150.
29 Scott, *Controversies*, 20.
30 Scott, *Controversies*, 20.
31 Scott, *Controversies*, 21.
32 Scott, *Controversies*, 20; trans. slightly modified.
33 Paolo Cortesi, *De hominibus doctis dialogus*, ed. and trans. Maria Teresa Graziosi (Rome: Bonacci, 1972), 62–4; cited by John F. D'Amico, *Renaissance Humanism in Papal Rome* (Baltimore: Johns Hopkins University Press, 1983), 129 and 287 n. 53.
34 Janson, *Apes*, 203. Elsewhere in the *Narrenschiff*, apes also illustrate folly and vanity.
35 *The Collected Works of Erasmus*, eds James K. McConica *et al.* (Toronto: University of Toronto Press, 1974–): *Correspondence*, trans. R. A. B. Mynors *et al.* (series henceforth abbreviated *CWE*).
36 Lett. 531, in *CWE*, *Correspondence*, 4: 233.
37 Erasmus, *Ciceronianus*, trans. Betty I. Knott, in *CWE* 28: 369.
38 *CWE* 28: 443–5, esp. 445: "The letter Cortesi produced with all his care was prolix rather than Ciceronian, and Poliziano, treating it as irrelevant, made no reply. But Poliziano, who was called unciceronian, offers a much better representation of Cicero, and in a shorter letter at that, because his opinions are shrewd, while his language is appropriate, stylish, and expressive." Similarly, Erasmus's interlocutors prefer Jerome to Lactantius, even though the latter is much more an ape of Cicero. Erasmus, *Opera Omnia* (Amsterdam: North-Holland Publishing Company, 1981), vol. 1–2, 705 (series henceforth abbreviated *ASD*). D'Amico, *Renaissance Humanism*, 129–30, offers a more positive assessment of Cortesi's theory of imitation that emphasizes its Aristotelian basis.
39 *CWE* 28: 374, slightly altered.
40 *CWE* 28: 386; *ASD* 1–2, 639.
41 *CWE* 28: 376. Cf. Horace, *Ep.* I.19.19–20.
42 *CWE* 28: 398; *ASD* 1–2, 649.
43 *ASD* 1–2, 649.
44 *CWE* 34: 87 (adage II.viii.95).
45 *CWE* 34: 87.
46 Martin Luther, *Works*, ed. Jaroslav Pelikan *et al.*, 55 vols (St Louis, 1955–86), 13: 158 (henceforth abbreviated *LW*); *D. Martin Luthers Werke: Kritische Gesamtausgabe* (Weimar: H. Böhlau, 1883–), 51: 210 (henceforth abbreviated *WA*). I render *affen* as "apes" rather than *LW*'s "apish imitators."
47 *LW* 13: 159.
48 Erasmus, *Moriae encomium*, bk. 17: "simia semper est simia, etiam si purpura vestiatur." Cf. Diogenianus, VII, 94.
49 *LW* 13: 159, alt.; *WA* 51: 211.
50 *LW* 5: 309; *WA* 43: 641.
51 *LW* 5: 309; *WA* 43: 641–2.
52 *LW* 8: 132; *WA* 44: 676.
53 *LW* 8: 132–3; *WA* 44: 676.
54 *WA* 43: 307.
55 *LW* 4: 328.

56 *LW* 4: 236; *WA* 43: 305. Cf. *LW* 21: 212, n. 2, and 4: 237.
57 *LW* 6: 331; *WA* 44: 247.
58 *LW* 6: 331.
59 *LW* 7: 121.
60 Gabriel Harvey, *Ciceronianus*, ed. Harold S. Wilson and trans. Clarence A. Forbes (Lincoln: University of Nebraska, 1945), 69.
61 Harvey, *Ciceronianus*, 82.
62 Harvey, *Ciceronianus* ("sexcentum Italis").
63 Gabriel Harvey, *Rhetor*, ed. and trans. Mark Reynolds, 2001. Accessed online: <http://comp.uark.edu/~mreynold/rhetor.html>.
64 Ciceronianism (at least when broadly and positively defined) did remain, however, a vital scholarly practice: see Monfasani, "Ciceronian Controversy."
65 Michel de Montaigne, *The Complete Essays of Montaigne*, trans. Donald M. Frame (Stanford: Stanford University Press, 1965), 330.
66 Montaigne, *Essays*, 331.
67 Montaigne, *Essays*, 331 and n. The bracketed material, which Frame places in a footnote, was added in the 1595 edition of the *Essais*.
68 Montaigne, *Essays*, 331.
69 Montaigne, *Essays*, 356.
70 R. W. Serjeantson, "The Passions and Animal Language," *Journal of the History of Ideas* 62 (2001): 425–44, at 443, reads Montaigne's discussion of animal communication as "fundamentally moral in purpose."
71 Montaigne, *Essays*, 490.
72 Montaigne, *Essays*, 317.
73 Montaigne, *Essays*, 857.
74 On Montaigne and Renaissance skepticism, see Richard H. Popkin, "Theories of Knowledge," in *Cambridge History of Renaissance Philosophy*, 668–84, at 678–84; Kraye, "Moral Philosophy," 314–16; cf. Brian Cummings, "Animal Language in Renaissance Thought," in *Renaissance Beasts: Of Animals, Humans, and Other Wonderful Creatures*, ed. Erica Fudge (Urbana: University of Illinois Press, 2004), 164–85, at 179–82, whose interpretation is not persuasive.
75 Janson, *Apes*, 302.
76 Boccaccio, *Genealogia*, XIV.17.
77 Janson, *Apes*, 304.
78 Janson, *Apes*, 325–8.
79 Janson, *Apes*, 305.
80 Genesis 1:28.
81 Paula Findlen, "Jokes of Nature and Jokes of Knowledge: The Playfulness of Scientific Discourse in Early Modern Europe," *Renaissance Quarterly* 43 (1990): 292–331, at 325.
82 Patricia Fortini Brown, *Venetian Narrative Painting in the Age of Carpaccio* (New Haven: Yale University Press, 1988), 184–5: "Participation is heightened by small oases of non-participation: a monkey sits on the steps to the right and observes a guinea hen."
83 See the measured survey of interpretations in Una Roman D'Elia, *The Poetics of Titian's Religious Paintings* (Cambridge: Cambridge University Press, 2005), 50.
84 Janson, *Apes*, 361.
85 Janson, *Apes*, 308–12.
86 Giovanni Pietro Bellori, *Le vite de' pittori, scultori et architetti moderni* (Rome, 1672), 253; see Janson, *Apes*, 303–4.
87 Peter Harrison, "Descartes on Animals," *Philosophical Quarterly* 42 (1992), 219–27.

88 Cummings, "Animal Language," 185, n. 60 (letter to the Marquess of Newcastle, 23 November 1646).
89 *Philosophical Works*, cited by Cummings, "Animal Language," 180.
90 Londa Schiebinger, *Nature's Body: Gender in the Making of Modern Science* (Boston, Mass.: Beacon Press, 1993), chap. 2.
91 Stephen Toulmin, *Cosmopolis: The Hidden Agenda of Modernity* (Chicago: University of Chicago Press, 1990), x–xi and *passim*, e.g. (201): "The seduction of High Modernity lay in its abstract neatness and theoretical simplicity: both of these features blinded the successors of Descartes to the unavoidable complexities of concrete human experience."
92 Toulmin, *Cosmopolis*, xi.
93 The quotation is from a TV commercial aired *c.* 1970 in which a gorilla unsuccessfully tries to destroy an American Tourister suitcase.
94 On the last of these, see Richard W. Byrne and Andrew Whiten, "Machiavellian Intelligence," in *Machiavellian Intelligence II: Extensions and Evaluations*, eds Whiten and Byrne (Cambridge: Cambridge University Press, 1997), 1–23.
95 *The Great Ape Project: Equality beyond Humanity*, eds Paola Cavalieri and Peter Singer (New York: St Martin's Press, 1993).
96 http://biologybk.st-and.ac.uk/cultures3/ (accessed 16 June 2006).

SUGGESTIONS FOR FURTHER READING

Primary sources

Erasmus, Desiderius. *The Ciceronian: A Dialogue on the Ideal Latin Style/Dialogus Ciceronianus*, trans. Betty I. Knott. Collected Works of Erasmus, 28. Toronto and Buffalo: University of Toronto Press, 1986.
Vesalius, Andreas. *The Epitome of Andreas Vesalius*, ed. and trans. L. R. Lind. New York: Macmillan, 1949.
See also the extensive translated primary materials in the secondary works below by Fudge, Greene, Janson, O'Malley, Osgood, Scott, and Trinkaus.

Secondary sources

The Cambridge History of Renaissance Philosophy, eds Charles B. Schmitt and Quentin Skinner. Cambridge: Cambridge University Press, 1988.
Cavalieri, Paola and Peter Singer, eds. *The Great Ape Project: Equality beyond Humanity*. New York: St Martin's Press, 1993.
Corbey, Raymond. *The Metaphysics of Apes: Negotiating the Animal–Human Boundary*. Cambridge: Cambridge University Press, 2005.
Findlen, Paula. "Jokes of Nature and Jokes of Knowledge: The Playfulness of Scientific Discourse in Early Modern Europe." *Renaissance Quarterly* 43 (1990): 292–331.
Fudge, Erica. *Perceiving Animals: Humans and Beasts in Early Modern English Culture*. New York: St Martin's Press, 1999/Urbana: University of Illinois Press, 2002 (pbk).
Fudge, Erica, ed. *Renaissance Beasts: Of Animals, Humans, and Other Wonderful Creatures*. Urbana: University of Illinois Press, 2004.
Gouwens, Kenneth. "Perceiving the Past: Renaissance Humanism after the 'Cognitive Turn.'" *American Historical Review* 103 (1998): 55–82.
Greene, Thomas M. *The Light in Troy: Imitation and Discovery in Renaissance Poetry*. New Haven: Yale University Press, 1982.

Janson, H. W. *Apes and Ape Lore in the Middle Ages and Renaissance.* London: Warburg Institute, 1952.

Nussbaum, Martha C. *Upheavals of Thought: The Intelligence of Emotions.* Cambridge: Cambridge University Press, 2001.

O'Malley, C. D. *Andreas Vesalius of Brussels 1514–1564.* Berkeley and Los Angeles: University of California Press, 1964.

Osgood, Charles G. *Boccaccio on Poetry: Being the Preface and the Fourteenth and Fifteenth Books of Boccaccio's* Genealogia Deorum Gentilium *in an English Version with Introductory Essay and Commentary.* Princeton: Princeton University Press, 1930.

Schiebinger, Londa. *Nature's Body: Gender in the Making of Modern Science.* Boston, Mass.: Beacon Press, 1993.

Scott, Izora. *Controversies over the Imitation of Cicero in the Renaissance.* Davis, Calif.: Hermagoras Press, 1991 (orig. pub. 1910).

Serjeantson, R. W. "The Passions and Animal Language." *Journal of the History of Ideas* 62 (2001): 425–44.

Siraisi, Nancy G. "Vesalius and the Reading of Galen's Teleology." *Renaissance Quarterly* 50 (1997): 1–37.

Spitz, Lewis W. "Man on this Isthmus," in Lewis W. Spitz, *Luther and German Humanism.* Aldershot: Variorum, 1995, essay XI.

Toulmin, Stephen. *Cosmopolis: The Hidden Agenda of Modernity.* Chicago: University of Chicago Press, 1990.

Trinkaus, Charles. *"In Our Image and Likeness": Humanity and Divinity in Italian Humanist Thought*, 2 vols. Chicago: University of Chicago Press, 1970.

CHAPTER TWENTY-TWO

WORTHY OF FAITH?
Authors and readers in early modernity

Albert Russell Ascoli

This chapter will consider how the traditional (classical Roman and European medieval) definition of the "author" as "one worthy of faith" (the faith of the reader, obviously) is put increasingly to the test during the early modern period, as the notion of literary writing gradually moves from epistemological (vatic) and/or ethical-rhetorical models toward what Terry Eagleton has called "the ideology of the aesthetic" – that is, toward suspension of readerly belief in the moral fidelity and intellectual credibility of the literary writer. In a classic formulation, the literary author as a distinctive "personal" and individual presence, indeed as willful demi-deity "making worlds," first emerges in what we sometimes still call the Renaissance: first in the Italy of Dante and Petrarch, and then, gradually, spreads throughout the nascent vernacular traditions of western Europe. What follows will rehearse some clichés of the topic, one hopes in an appealing way, and lay out to shift the terms of the discussion in others. In particular, I will focus on the intuitively obvious, yet not always thoroughly explored, point that any notion of authorship is intricately tied to ideas, and realities, of readership. More especially, I will explore, on the one hand, the question of authorial control over the meaning of a text as this takes shape in the experience of its readers and, on the other, how such readers may either trustingly embrace the offered sense of the text or willfully recast it.

The topic of late medieval and early modern authorship can be confronted in any number of productive ways. It can be written in terms of the shift from Latin to vernacular literature (or of the parallel developments in both); of the increasing prestige (the "rebirth" as it were) of classical literary and philosophical models; of the gradual process of secularization and the formation of a lay cultural elite; of the development of new models of education that also involve a certain expansion in the number of literate subjects; of the cataclysmic shift from manuscript to print culture; of the struggle between an incipient bourgeoisie and an evolving aristocracy. Any history of authorship will vary according to the time and/or place one focuses on, to the forms of social organization under which the writing occurs (republic or principate, city-state or nation-state, etc.), and to the religious affinities of the writer and/or reader (especially after Luther) – not to mention the question of the ethnicity, gender, and/or class of the writers and readers involved.[1]

The tale I will tell here will only address some of these issues, and most of them tangentially. Rather, I will take a simpler, but I still believe telling, path. My writers are the most typical types of authors in this period – white, male, upper class – as, basically, are their readers. Beginning with a standard late medieval definition of what an author is and how he ideally relates to his readers, I will then examine a series of symptomatic texts reaching from the fourteenth to seventeenth centuries where the authorial struggle to command the "faith" of the reader is played out in a wide variety of ways. For reasons of conviction I begin well before the established starting bells of early modernity (the press; voyages of discovery; Protestantism; the proto-modern nation-state). For reasons of training, I will weight my discourse heavily, though not exclusively, to Italian cases. And as for readers, I will take the easy way out: my writers are also understood to be readers, and their texts to represent, however one-sidedly, a variety of relationships into which these two inextricably intertwined figures, at once lovers and enemies, masters and servants, may enter.

In book four of the *Convivio* (*Banquet*, *c*. 1303–6), Dante Alighieri offers two definitions of what an "autore," an author, is, only one of which will concern us here (4.6).[2] The primary definition he provides is a slightly modified version of the principal medieval etymology of the word: "au[c]tor" comes from a Greek word, *autentin*, meaning "worthy of faith and obedience." This definition was, by all historical accounts, the best known in the Middle Ages, which had it originally from Cicero, who used it in reference to the (rhetorical) authority of a legal witness, that person's ability to command *fides* (trust or faith) in court. In context, Dante's use of the word refers to two types of (non-literary) "authorities": Aristotle as the personification of philosophical belief – worthiness and the Holy Roman Emperor, specifically the late Frederick II (d. 1250), whose judicial commands must be obeyed. The combination of "faith" with "obedience" in authority, however, ultimately comes from the Christianization of the Roman legal concept, whereby God becomes *the* archetypal figure of the Author, creator of the "book of the world," omniscient and omnipotent, worthy to be both absolutely believed and perfectly obeyed. And there is good reason to think that at base Dante is imagining his own poetic making as deriving from, and modeled on, that of his own Maker.

Dante's use of the loaded term "autore" is complex, since it at once disavows its relevance to himself and tacitly appropriates it, raising himself up to the level of the great classical *auctores*. The stated aim of the discourse on authority in book four is to show that he is showing due respect, faith, and obedience for *other*, non-literary *authors* (i.e., Aristotle and Frederick) as he treats the topic of "nobility" as a quality inherent in the individual rather than handed down genealogically. This humble posture is mirrored in the form of the text too, since in it Dante places himself in the role of a reader, and specifically of a commentator upon classical philosophical and literary authorities, secondarily, and, primarily, upon one of his own *canzoni*, which begins "the sweet rhymes of love."

Here, however, there is an obvious complication: throughout the prose of the *Convivio* Dante adopts the posture of the traditional medieval "lector," the modern, humble commentator on the (long-dead) classical, and biblical, *auctores*, whose texts are not read for the "personal" content they might contain, the individual intentions they might realize, but for the truths they bear. But in declaring his respect for the writings of Aristotle his transparent purpose is to win "faith and obedience" for his own views on nobility ("treating of nobility," he says, "I have to show myself to be noble" [4.8]). And in writing a commentary on "the "sweet rhymes of love," he is placing his own works in the position previously reserved for Aristotle, Virgil, and other *autores*.

Dante, in the *Convivio* and elsewhere, stages himself as both reader and as writer. As reader of the works of the ancient *auctores*, his clear purpose is to learn how to become one of them: a point dramatized most obviously in the *Comedy* when the character named "Dante" meets "Virgil" and salutes him as "master and author," saying that he has learned to be a poet from his readings ("from you I have taken the beautiful style that has brought me honor" [*Inferno* 1.85–7]). Indeed, by the end of his long journey in the Roman poet's company, it is clear both that he has gone beyond Virgil as a writer and that in fact he has turned the tables, becoming the author of the character "Virgil."

In entering into direct personalized relationship with Virgil and, elsewhere, in simultaneously occupying the roles of poet and reader of his own poems, Dante levels the distance between *auctor* and *lector*, and apparently implies the potential for his own readers to do the same in reading him. In this passage from early in *Convivio*, the point is stated baldly:

> I intend as well to show the true meaning of those [the *canzoni* to be commented upon] which may not be seen by some unless I recount it, because it is hidden under the figure of allegory: and this [exposition] will not only give good pleasure when heard, but also subtle teaching, both in how to speak [i.e., to write poetry in this way] and how to understand the writings of others. (1.2.17; my translation)

This passage already reveals some of the problematic consequences of Dante's restructuring of the relationship between writer and reader. On the one hand, by collapsing the difference between them, he suggests the potential for any (modern) reader to become an author, to raise himself up to the level of the ancients (and at the same time to lower them down to his). On the other, in explicitly dictating the meanings of his poems, revealing his hidden intentions, he clearly attempts to wrest control over the text from the possible (mis)interpretations of his own readers – a natural consequence of his understanding of what he himself has willingly done in reading Aristotle, Virgil, and even the Bible itself.

While Dante's theory and his practice bring into view a "new," dynamic image of the writer/reader relationship, what is at stake is not a fixed idea about what that relationship will consist of, but rather a fluid set of possibilities, beginning with the potential interchangeability of the two roles, as well as the special case of the "self-reader." This relationship may vary according to multiple parameters: intimacy vs. suspicion, understanding vs. misunderstanding, identification vs. reification, supplication vs. interpellation, and so on. In looking at what comes after, then, we will see not a single version of the relationship, but the contingent instantiation of one or more of the possibilities inherent in the complex.

Dante's proximate and eminent successor, Petrarch, who disingenuously declares himself to have read little or nothing of Dante, seems instead to have learned a great deal about the entanglement of readership and writership from him. In an infamous epistolary response to a gift of the *Comedy*, accompanied by accusations of envy from his peer/pupil Boccaccio, Petrarch indicts Dante, without naming him, for wasting his writings on an ignorant vernacular audience unable to understand in the least what it is reading (*Familiar Letters*, 21.15). Nonetheless, Petrarch certainly learned the trick of dramatizing himself in conversation with ancient writers of the past (for example, in the *Secretum* and *Familiar Letters*, book 24) from Dante and his "Virgil," similarly using it at once to appropriate their authority for himself and to transform it by historicizing and personalizing it. In a famous example, Petrarch writes a letter to "Cicero," turning the Roman orator into the Italian laureate's reader, at once praising him for his abilities as a writer and scolding him for his political and moral failings.

In fact, Petrarch, far more than Dante, not only dramatizes the dependence of the writer on his readers (most notoriously in the unfinished *Letter to Posterity*), but also emphasizes the failings of the latter and asserts his superiority to and control over them. In the first of his *Familiar Letters*, Petrarch asserts that his authorial personality disappears as he changes his style to match the needs of each individual reader:

> [In my letters], I . . . had to correspond with many [friends and acquaintances] who differed considerably in character and station. As a result, the letters were so different that in rereading them I seemed to be in constant contradiction. . . . Indeed, the primary concern of a writer is to consider the identity of the person to whom he is writing. . . . [W]riting entails a double labor: first to consider to whom you write, and then what his state of mind will be at the time he undertakes to read what you propose to write. These difficulties compelled me to be very inconsistent.

And yet, this careful matching of style to audience also silently attributes extraordinary power and versatility to the protean author, who is able to understand precisely the needs of each individual reader and to adapt his style not only to that person's personality in general but also to his state of mind at the specific moment of reading. The posture of self-effacement thus poorly conceals an absolute will to control the way in which one will be read in every individual instance.

An even more complex and conflicted staging of the writing self in relation to its readers appears in the opening sonnet of his *Canzoniere*:

> You who hear in scattered rhymes the sound of
> those sighs with which I nourished my heart during my first
> youthful error, when I was in part another man from what I
> am now:
> for the varied style in which I weep and speak
> between vain hopes and vain sorrow, where there is anyone
> who understands love through experience, I hope to find
> pity, not only pardon.

> But now I see well how for a long time I was the
> talk of the crowd, for which often I am ashamed of myself
> within;
> > and of my raving, shame is the fruit, and
> repentance, and the clear knowledge that whatever pleases
> the world is a brief dream.

Very much like *Convivio*, this poem constitutes a retrospective rereading and reinterpretation of the writer's life and his works, but it does so without erecting any formal barriers between the past self who wrote and the present reader who looks back on and interprets that writing. The present "I" is only "in part" different from the past one. And the "interpretation" of past poetic writings is itself a poem, one which is set *before* the lyric collection it introduces and glosses, reversing the proper historical order. That "I" is, in other words, in open oscillation between the roles of reader, writer, and subject of Petrarch's poetic texts.

This poem also serves as an example of the dialogue that Petrarch consistently attempts to create with his "other" readers (the readers who are not himself), modern as well as ancient. From the outset, the poem is directed to a plural audience (in Italian the initial "you" is a plural form, "voi"). Rather than using the dominating imperative typical of Dante's apostrophes to his readers in the *Comedy*, Petrarch opens with hopeful subjunctives: "where there is anyone who understands love through experience, I hope to find pity." In the brief compass of the poem's 14 lines a range of dialogic possibilities are opened up, and in most the poet is more in the reader's power than otherwise. The reader can be an equal, who shares an experience and offers empathetic pity, or a superior, who can grant "pardon." The majority of readers, however, respond to Petrarch's writing by scripting him to their own taste: "for a long time I was a tale told by all people." In this image, the readers turn the tables on Petrarch, becoming a sort of collective author of a *favola* – tale or fable – that defines and debases him. Finally, and reversing direction yet again, the last line, which seems to culminate in Petrarch's humiliation, projecting his complete submission to readerly authority, suddenly turns the tables on his readers, reducing them to part of the englobing *mondo* whose readerly pleasures are no more than a "brief dream," and reinstituting the authorial "I" in a position of judgmental superiority over them.

In comparing Dante's and Petrarch's modes of staging the reader/writer dialectic, we might say that where Dante lifts one medieval reader (himself) up to the level of the classical author and assumes the possibility of perfectly realizing his writerly intentions not only in the works he produces, but also in the responses they receive, Petrarch tends to bring the classical reader down to his own level and to stress the internal conflicts and flaws that collapse the distance between them, both morally and textually. Despite these radical differences, there is no question that the drive to control the terms of the reader/writer relationship is just as strong in Petrarch as it was in Dante. To offer a variant on a very old contrast between them: if the latter's readers were rapidly converted into Dante critics, unable, except obliquely and deviously, to use the Dante–Virgil relationship as a model for their own relationship to Dante, the former, to echo W. H. Auden's phrase, "became his admirers." By this

I mean (as Auden certainly did not), that, on the one hand, Petrarch ventriloquized a full gamut of readerly responses to his writing, and pre-emptively assumed the role of "his own harshest critic," and, on the other, that vast numbers of his later readers "became him" in the sense that generation after generation wrote lyric poetry on the model of Petrarchan authorship.

If Dante's work patently demands the "faith" of his readers in its revelatory truths, commanding moral obedience to its strictures while precluding the close imitation of its author's prophetic art, Petrarch's clearly does not demand either faith or obedience, but sets up a model of self-reproducing, narrowly circumscribed, poetic authorship whose traces are still visible today. Petrarch defines poetry as an ornamental, "exquisite" speech, rejecting the vatic – theological claims of near contemporaries – such as Mussato, Boccaccio, Salutati, and, of course, Dante – and setting it in opposition both to the revelatory but crude language of biblical scribes (*Familiar Letters*, 10.4) and the suasive powers of political rhetoric (13.6). Where Dante joins artisanal mastery of the poetic art with the power/knowledge of the *autore* from *autentin*, Petrarch prefers a version of the former in specific opposition to the latter, cordoning off the poet's profession as at once limited and unique. Whatever the intrinsic convictions that moved him to adopt this stance, there is no doubt, in fact, that it also serves as a means of isolating and protecting him from the claims, attacks, and appropriations of readers.

The author–reader relationship as it appears in both Dante and Petrarch is one of a doubling between the two figures and at the same time of a struggle for control between the two of them. In describing the power dynamic shaping this relationship, I have only alluded in passing to the specific configuration – that of "servant" intellectual and master patron – which, at least since Jacob Burckhardt's account of the "alliance" between tyrants and artists and Hans Baron's counter-discourse about the "resistance" of Florentine humanists to Milanese tyranny, has been at the center of scholarly discourse on Renaissance authorship. It would take more space than is here available to describe the way in which both writers are intimately concerned both with attempting to shape the moral and political behavior of the readerly powers-that-be and with avoiding the apparently inevitable subjection to them. It is certainly the case that the figure of the prince-patron as privileged reader of Renaissance texts increasingly comes to the fore in the fifteenth century and beyond, to a certain extent displacing, or at least competing with, the central question of the relationship between ancient authorities and their modern readers/imitators.

Machiavelli provides an excellent starting point for considering the complex situation of the author in the sixteenth century. In various ways he offers the perfect sequel to Dante's and Petrarch's attempts to convert themselves from readers of the ancient authors to their authoritative peers. Most famously, in the letter to Francesco Vettori describing the composition of *The Prince*, Machiavelli writes:

> When evening comes . . . I enter the ancient courts of ancient men, where, received by them in a loving manner, I batten on that food which alone is mine and for which I was born, where I am not ashamed to talk with them and to ask of them the reasons for their actions, and they, in their humanity, answer me. (December 10, 1513; my translation)

Yet with Machiavelli this form of the author–reader dialectic is in the service of, and subordinate to, increasingly desperate attempts to persuade another sort of reader, men of power, that his "gift of counsel" deserves their "faith and obedience," that his words possess the force of truth (and the truth about force!). In the dedicatory letter to *The Prince*, Machiavelli justifies his apparent presumption in offering unsolicited advice to the Medici family as follows:

> Nor would I wish that it be considered presumptuousness if a man of low and base estate dares to discourse about and to give rules concerning the government of princes; because, as those who paint landscapes place themselves low on the plain to consider the nature of mountains and high places, while to consider that of low places they place themselves high upon the peaks, similarly, to know well the nature of the populace it is necessary to be a prince, while to know well that of the princes it is necessary to be one of the people. (My translation)

Having ostentatiously failed to command the attention of his ideal princely reader, Machiavelli would then address his next major work, the *Discourses*, to those who are *not* princes, but deserve to be (presumably because they take him seriously), and would expose the mechanism by which the writing of history can be seen as a tissue of obsequious lies designed to placate powerful readers:

> [N]or should anyone deceive themselves because of Julius Caesar's glory, hearing him so greatly celebrated by writers, because those who praise him are corrupted by his good fortune and frightened by the duration of the Roman empire which, ruled under that name, did not allow writers to speak freely about him. But whoever wishes to know what free writers would have said about him, should see what is said about [the unsuccessful conspirator] Cataline. (1.10; my translation)

An ideal sequence may appear to be completed when, frustrated at the failure to win the trust of those who shape the world, Machiavelli turns to literature, or rather to comic drama, as a poor second best, as appears in the prologue to his comedy the *Mandragola* (c. 1517):

> And if this matter is not worthy of a man who wishes to appear weighty and wise, because of its insubstantiality, excuse him thus: that he strives with these vain thoughts to make his sad time sweeter, because he has nowhere else to turn his face, since he is cut off from . . . other undertakings. (my translation)

Then follows a degraded vision of the author/audience relationship as one of mutual bad-mouthing, where parity is parodied, and the rejected author seemingly embraces an uneasy alliance with the "vulgar herd." Machiavelli's constant appeal, however rhetorical, to "the effectual truth of things" (*The Prince*, chapter 15) as the basis for belief in him as author paradoxically culminates with a retreat into a world of literary-theatrical fiction whose pretense to credibility is, as he puts it, "enough to break your jaw with laughing."

Machiavelli's contemporary and, in his express view, chief peer and rival, Ludovico Ariosto, is in many ways the paradigmatic example of the early modern "author-God," ostentatiously exercising control over the denizens of his chivalric world through his first-person narrative emanation, as well as over his readers, for example by repeatedly creating and frustrating the desire for narrative closure through his elaboration of the medieval romance technique of *entrelacement*. Ariosto's authorial role is, however, and by now predictably, articulated in relation to a gamut of readers – his Estense patrons (Cardinal Ippolito and then Duke Alfonso I), his unnamed beloved, and the "ladies and knights" who are his courtly peers. Moreover, there is his own feigned role as faithful reader-rehearser of the chronicles of Bishop Turpin and his empirical but dissimulated vocation as reader-continuer of Boiardo's *Innamoramento di Orlando*.

Curiously, notwithstanding his stance of poetic omnipotence, Ariosto repeatedly represents the author–reader relationship as one of misunderstanding and antagonism, of which he himself is chief victim. The culmination of this process, which can be documented throughout his *Orlando furioso*, comes with the final encomiastic tribute to Cardinal Ippolito d'Este, whose life is woven into the prophetic tapestries decorating the pavilion of Trojan Cassandra, under which the dynastic wedding of Ruggiero and Bradamante is celebrated. Mythical Cassandra, whose prophetic truths are always disbelieved, always taken as signs of madness, is, I argue, the poet's feminized figuration of himself and the poetic art generally – his/its impotence in the face of courtly masters unwilling to face the harsh truths about themselves and their world which the *Furioso*, however obliquely, would show them. More famously, in the lunar episode Ariosto makes St John the Evangelist and author of the Apocalypse (to whom Dante repeatedly assimilates himself as "theologian-poet") depict the poet–patron relationship – from Homer through Virgil and Lucan to his own days – as utterly mercenary, a tissue of lies predicated on poets who puff up reputations for pay or tear them down for revenge. The process by which Dante, modern reader, claims for himself the "faith and obedience" owed not only to Virgil and the classical *auctores* but, far more ambitiously, to the human authors of the Bible, comes full circle as Ariosto not only exposes the whole of literature as a tissue of lies, but even implies that the Gospel of John itself is a mendacious exercise in compensated obsequiousness.

Perhaps Ariosto's most extraordinary exercise in asserting and subverting the poetic author's claims on the belief of his readers comes in a little-known passage from the so-called *Five Cantos* (an incomplete addition to or a continuation of the *Furioso*). The passage in question concerns the success of Gano (that is, Ganelon), Carlomagno's privy counselor, in winning his sovereign's unwarranted trust, to the end of dividing the Christian heroes from each other by making each believe that his faith in the others has been grossly betrayed. The whole canto is shot through with the language of faith and belief, always in an ironic vein, and the climax comes as Gano prepares his greatest deception of Carlo:

> I once read in a very old book, the name of whose author I cannot remember, that Alcina [the malevolent fairy] gave to Ganelon an herb ... that constrains everyone to belief in the words of whosoever eats it. God showed that herb to

Moses on Mount Sinai, so that he could then use it to make the hard people humble and pious. Then the demon showed it to evil Mohammed, for the perdition of the African and Eastern peoples: he kept it in his mouth as he preached and it drew those who heard him to his false laws. (3.21–2)

The passage presents itself as an allegory of courtly rhetoric, capable of persuading the ingenuous sovereign-reader of whatever it asserts, regardless of truth value or ethical content. Moreover, as in the *Furioso*, the power of language to command unwarranted belief spreads out to include the revealed truths of Christianity – no distinction can be discerned between the persuasive powers of Moses and those of Mohammed, as of their respective sacred books – both command assent of their hearers/readers based on the magical power of their words.

The passage cuts in two directions simultaneously: it promulgates a perverse fantasy of the author to command the faith and obedience of the most powerful of princes, while it also reveals that such trust is founded on sheer linguistic performance, suspended above a moral-epistemological void. The Ariostan narrator makes it clear that he and the poem he speaks for and from form a privileged instance of the problem depicted. Invoking the "old book" of "an author whose name [he] cannot remember," he parodically invokes the medieval cult of authority, figuring himself as credulous reader, while implying that the belief of his own reader is thoroughly misplaced. Thus, even as Ariosto previews a collapse of the assumptions (political, moral, metaphysical) in which his culture is grounded, and with them all possibility of a trusting relationship between author and reader, he allows the reader to confine this crisis to the marginal space of a "literary" text: his own. Ariosto's understanding of authorship is beginning to be "literary" in a modern sense, in that it refuses its own claims as a mode of knowledge and of moral action, openly inviting its readers' disbelief – at once recalling and undermining Dante's "witness-author."

Closely related to this Ariostan travesty of the author as one "worthy of faith" are two major French texts of the sixteenth century – the prologue "of the Author" to François Rabelais's *Pantagruel* (1532) – and Michel de Montaigne's address "To the Reader" at the opening of his *Essays* (first edition, 1580). Rabelais's prologue presents *Pantagruel* as a sequel to and a rewriting of the anonymous *Chronicles of Gargantua* in such a way as to evoke, however ironically, the appropriative reinterpretation of the Hebrew Bible in the Christian New Testament. Following a tradition later taken up by Cervantes, Rabelais's book is said to be the creation of a pseudonymous author stand-in, Alcofribas Nasier, thereby distancing the "truth" of the text from its historical author and suggesting an elaborate rhetorical strategy of simultaneous self-presentation and self-effacement.

Immediately relevant here is how this boastful first-person author-figure puts both the Gargantua tradition and his own sequel to it into a lineage of books (including the near-contemporary *Orlando furioso*) that have performed miraculous cures on credulous readers:

Most illustrious . . . noblemen . . . who gladly devote yourselves to all gentle and honest pursuits, you have recently seen, read, and come to know *The Great and Inestimable Chronicles of the Enormous Giant Gargantua*, and as true believers

> have nobly believed them . . . I would have every man put aside his proper business . . . in order to devote himself entirely to this book . . . I have known high and mighty noblemen . . . [whose] refuge and comfort, and their method of avoiding a chill was to re-read the inestimable deeds of the said Gargantua . . . But what shall I say of the poor victims of pox and gout? . . . Their one consolation was to have some pages of this book read to them. . . . It is peerless, incomparable, and beyond comparison. . . . The world has thoroughly acknowledged the great returns and benefits proceeding from this Gargantuine Chronicle. For more copies of it have been sold by the printers in two months than there will be of the Bible in nine years.

This passage parallels Ariosto's ironic assimilation of poetic to biblical writing. In this case, however, the question of authorial credibility and readerly credulity is dramatized through direct address. Having referred to the miraculous benefits of the Gargantua chronicles for those readers who have believed in them, and having indeed compared their popularity favorably to that of the Bible, the narrator invites the reader's blind faith in this new and even better text:

> I, your humble slave, offer you now another book of the same stamp, though one a little more reasonable and credible than the last. But do not suppose – unless you wish to be willfully deceived – that I speak of it [*Pantagruel*] as the Jews do of the Law. I was not born under that planet, nor have I ever come to lie, or to affirm a thing to be true which was not. I speak of it as a lusty Onocrotary – no I mean Crotonotary of martyred lovers and Crocquenotary of love. *Quod vidimus testamur* [We testify to what we have seen].

Through the reference to the Law of the Old Testament, the oblique reference to the traditional iconography of Christ as pelican (onocrotary), and the echoing of St John's claim to bear eyewitness testimony to the contents of the Book of Revelations, Rabelais turns *Pantagruel* into a simulacrum of the New Testament, and his alter-ego into a truth-telling biblical witness-author, worthy indeed of "faith and obedience."[3]

The first effect is to create an ironic contrast between the obvious lies of Alcofribas and the biblical witness of St John, discrediting the bravado of the literary author and redrawing an ever-sharper line between literature's fictions and the revealed truths of the Bible. In closing, however, the prologue takes a disturbing turn:

> Therefore, to make an end of my prologue, I offer myself, body and soul, tripe and bowels, to a hundred thousand basket-loads of fine devils in case I lie in so much as a single word in the whole of this History. And, similarly, may St. Anthony's fire burn you, the epilepsy throw you, the thunder-stroke and leg-ulcers rack you, dysentery seize you, and may the erysipelas . . . through your arse-hole enter up, and like Sodom and Gomorrah may you dissolve into sulfur, fire, and the bottomless pit, in case you do not firmly believe everything that I tell you in this present Chronicle.

Again, the transparent bad faith of Alcofribas exposes his truth claims upon his reader as vacuous. On the other hand, something else happens: having in the first part of the prologue attempted to draw the reader into believing by the promise of miraculous benefits, the narrator now reverses field: *unless the reader believes* every word of the text he will suffer all of the ills, and then some, previously said to be cured by this book. Promise turns into threat. In so doing, it reveals a principal mechanism by which the Bible sets out to command readerly faith by alternately holding out the prospects of salvation and of damnation. Textual authority is represented as the product of the violent constraint of readerly belief – and thus the possibility of readerly resistance is tacitly entertained, even invited.

In contrast with, but also dialectically tied to, Rabelais's assault on canons of authorial credibility is the preface to Montaigne's *Essays*:

> This book was written in good faith (*bonne foy*), reader. It warns you from the outset that I have set myself no goal but a domestic and private one. I have no thought of serving either you or my own glory . . . If I had written to seek the world's favor, I should have bedecked myself better and should present myself in a studied posture. I want to be seen here in my simple natural, ordinary fashion, with straining or artifice, for it is myself that I portray. My defects will here be read to the life, and also my natural form, as far as respect for the public has allowed. Had I been placed among those nations which are said to live still in the sweet freedom on Nature's first laws, I assure you I should very gladly have portrayed myself here entire and wholly naked. Thus, reader, I myself am the subject of my book; you would be unreasonable to spend your leisure on so frivolous and vain a subject.

Montaigne's first-person claims to offer an image of himself "to the life," or almost, ostensibly contrasts with the indirections and distortions of the pseudonymous Alcofribas, as does the intimate second-person singular address to the reader ("tu"), constructing "him" as friend or even family member. Yet, one can understand this authorial self-portrait as an alternative tactic for confronting a very similar set of circumstances. Most notably, Montaigne evokes the traditional category of the author–reader relationship based in trust, in faith, only irrevocably to transform it. The "good faith" of the book is not a guarantee that its author either knows or tells the truth, nor does it claim for him the stoic constancy of faithful promise steadfastly maintained over time. Rather, it claims for its author *good intentions*, whether realized or not, and its commitment to the truth – compromised from the outset by cultural strictures on what is representable – is to record precisely his inconstant, fallible, private, ordinary humanity. Much as Petrarch insulates himself from readerly judgment by a strategic retreat into the privileged yet restricted domain of poetry, Montaigne cordons himself off in the world of private selfhood, anticipating and thwarting readerly doubts and attacks by an apotropaic confession of frivolity and vanity, not unrelated to Machiavelli's disclaimer in the prologue to *Mandragola*, and by representing himself not as imitable model but as singular instance. Where Dante's "self-reading" figures the author as "worthy of faith and obedience" in matters of objective truth and political consequence, Montaigne's only claim is to self-knowledge, or, rather, to representations of the self's incomplete and frequently erroneous efforts to know itself. Tellingly Montaigne's subsequent defense against possible accusations of lying is the negative one of asserting that his memory is too weak to maintain a falsehood successfully ("Of Liars" [1.9]).[4] The reader has no grounds for complaint that his faith is being abused, because each utterance, true or not, is a "faithful" representation of the inconstant author and the unstable universe in which he dwells.

If Rabelais, like Ariosto, takes the crisis of readerly faith in authorial witness to a point of extreme crisis, where no text, not even the Bible, is above suspicion, and where the author overtly expresses his will to domination over the reader, Montaigne posits a thoroughly subjective text, neutral to objective truth, and embraces the reader as "another self." As against both of these, Torquato Tasso, writing in the growing shadow of the Counter-Reformation Church (itself in large measure a violent response to a "crisis of faith"), sets out to "save the appearances" in his crusader epic, *Jerusalem Delivered* (1581).

In many ways, Tasso can be seen as returning us to Dante's totalizing conception of the author and of the author–reader complex, at once reconciling literary representation with theological truth and constructing the epic author as the God of his own verbal universe. Indeed, Tasso's formulation in his *Discourses on the Art of Poetry* of the poet as "maker" in the image and likeness of the Judeo-Christian God is perhaps the most famous of its kind:

> In this marvelous domain of God that we call the world we see the sky ... adorned with so great a variety of stars; and, descending from realm to realm, we see ... on earth streams and fountains and lakes and meadows and fields and forests and mountains, and here fruits and flowers, there wastelands and emptiness. Nonetheless, the earth, which encloses so many and diverse things in its bosom, is one; and its form and essence are one; and one, the knot by which it joins and binds its parts in discordant concord. ... Just so, I think, the excellent poet – who is called divine for no other reason except that by working like the supreme Artificer he comes to share in his divinity – can shape a poem in which, as in a little world ... we find heavenly and hellish assemblies and see sedition, discord, wanderings, adventures, enchantments, cruelty, boldness, courtesy, kindness and love ... And still, the poem which contains such a variety of matter is one; its form and its plot are one.

The force of the passage is all the greater in this context because it stands as a critique of the ungainly multiplicity of Tasso's precursor and *bête noire*, Ariosto. For the same reason, however, its emblematic power is compromised, both because of its polemical aims and because the divine analogy it advances is, in the end, sheerly formal, making no essential claims for a correspondence between God's truth and Tasso's own fabrications. Indeed, in the same treatise, Tasso makes no truth claims at all for poetry, but instead follows Aristotle's *Poetics* in advancing the criterion of mimetic verisimilitude; that is, the convincing *appearance of truth* that elicits the reader's temporary and strictly provisional belief. Ironically, his argument in favor of a Christian subject for a contemporary epic, such as his own *Jerusalem Delivered*, is not that it participates in Christian truth but rather that it enables the appealing representation of miraculous events, because readers are more likely to invest these with verisimilitude than the improbable marvels that appear in pagan literature.

In the light of this paradoxical vision of totalizing authorial mastery and of an art entirely aimed, not at representing "the true," but at eliciting readerly assent, we should now consider Tasso's remarkable version of the author–reader dialectic. If Ariosto, Rabelais, and Montaigne stage the writer–reader relationship within the confines of their texts (or on their immediate paratextual margins), in *Jerusalem Delivered* Tasso has scaled back the narrating "I" nearly to vanishing point, in keeping with Aristotelian canons of mimetic illusion. This does not mean, however, that the idea of the author as reader of his own work is absent from Tasso. What *has* happened is that Tasso's "readerly" moments have, once again, as if returning to the Dantean precursor, been formally separated from the writerly ones. Against even Dante's hybrid creations, the *Vita Nuova* and *Convivio*, where readerly and writerly voices alternate within an overarching formal structure, Tasso's self-readings are presented in the form of entirely separate texts: the so-called "poetic letters" of 1575–6 that discuss the process of writing and revising the poem with a series of interlocutors; the theoretical and regulatory *Discourses on the Art of Poetry* (1567; later revised as the *Discourses on the Heroic Poem*, 1594); the *Allegory of the Poem* (published 1581); and the *Apology in Defense of Jerusalem Delivered* (1585), which responds to various critical attacks against his work, including numerous invidious comparisons with none other than Ariosto.

The very large number of these works in which Tasso discusses either *Jerusalem Delivered* specifically or the rules of literary composition more generally suggests a new and dramatic evolution of the figure of the author as critical reader able to "explain himself." Tasso's critical writings document every phase of the composition of the poem: before, during, and after. The first *Discourses* substantiate his credentials as an author in command not only of his own compositions, but in fact of the art of poetry in general, within whose rules he will elaborate his own intentions. The "poetic letters" document the process of composition, the careful selections and revisions made along the way from the beginning to the end of writing. The *Allegory* and the *Apology* constitute versions of the more familiar authorial gesture of giving retrospective definition to the meaning of the text.

This sense of obsessive authorial drive to determine the meanings of his text is only reinforced by a consideration of the elaborate and highly documented revisionary process through which Tasso's epic took shape (in which even what we now call *Jerusalem Delivered* was only one, and not the final, step). The poem began as a handful of stanzas known as the *Gierusalemme*, which date from Tasso's sixteenth year (1560). It was then elaborated into an epic poem known as the *Goffredo* between 1573 and 1575, being revised in the period 1575–6 and finally published from an unauthorized manuscript in 1581 while Tasso was confined as a madman to the Ospedale of Sant'Anna in Ferrara by Duke Alfonso II d'Este. Although Tasso subsequently accepted and defended the *Liberata* as *if* it constituted his definitive redaction, that did not stop him from carrying out a further, drastic revision culminating with the publication of *Jerusalem Conquered* in 1593.

The more obsessively Tasso attempts to shape and control his text and to demonstrate his control over his art, his book, and its meanings, the clearer it becomes that his purpose in doing so is antithetical to Dante's. Where Dante affirms his own role as author by a critical reading of his text, thereby to establish authority over his readers, Tasso goes to ever-greater lengths to show that what he writes is precisely what his readers require that he write. In other words, Tasso responds to Ariosto's perception that his readers systematically misunderstand his text and convert it to their own meanings by attempting to demonstrate that *what he means is exactly what his readers want him to mean.*

The problem, however, is that the readerly demands put on him are of two, radically antithetical, kinds. On the one hand are the demands of the consuming public of readers who refuse to confront books that do not give them pleasure through a series of suspect devices that Tasso associates with Ariosto and with the popular genre of romance (marvels, digressions, erotic entanglements, and so on). On the other are the demands of "cultural authorities" that require strict adherence to a range of ever-stricter codes: particularly those governing poetic composition (especially Aristotle's *Poetics* and the proliferating sixteenth-century glosses on it), and those which, in the wake of the Council of Trent, command rigorous ethical and doctrinal orthodoxy. These two idealized readers are, obviously, in constant conflict with one another, as the protracted efforts of the *Discourses on the Art of Poetry* to mediate between them clearly reveal (for example, in the tortuous efforts to square the poetic use of fiction, the marvelous, and multiple plots with the imperative for truth, verisimilitude, and formal unity show). Indeed, even the authoritative codes come into conflict with one another, so that adherence to classical, pagan poetic doctrines can, at times, put one at odds with Tridentine Catholic orthodoxy.

This conflict is further reflected in the oft-discussed lines in the exordium to the *Gerusalemme*, where the authorial "I" puts in his one prominent appearance in the poem, attempting to negotiate between the demands of the heavenly Muse for scrupulous adherence to an orthodox faith and the need to cater to the debased tastes of the "world":

> O Muse, who do not bind your brow with impermanent laurels in Helicon, but rather up in Heaven among the blessed choirs you have a golden crown of immortal stars: inspire my breast with celestial ardors; make clear my song; and pardon me if I weave ornaments into truth, if I adorn in part my pages with other delights than yours. You know that the World runs there where seductive Parnassus most pours out its delights, and the truth, seasoned in sensuous verses, has persuaded the most skittish by enticing them. (I.4.–5; my translation)

Such ambivalence accounts well for the protracted revisionary process, in which Tasso attempted to accommodate now one, now another imaginary or actual reader's objections.

Perhaps the most exemplary of Tasso's attempts to make his poem ventriloquize the voice of an authoritative readership is his decision (documented in the "poetic letters") to send copies of the *Goffredo* to a number of leading intellectuals for their comments, in order to ascertain that the poem conformed to generally established rules for poetic composition. During this same period, Tasso voluntarily submitted not his poem but himself for examination by the Holy Inquisition, not once, but twice (1575 and 1577), with the express purpose of ascertaining that his beliefs conformed to post-Tridentine doctrinal imperatives.

Given his accomplishment in both literary composition and literary theory, Tasso appears as among the most explicitly masterful of the authors surveyed in this chapter, perhaps on a par with Dante himself. Yet his self-awareness as author expresses itself consistently as an anxiety, even a terror, that his writerly autonomy will put him at odds with empirical readers, and especially with those two most critical groups of readers: the inquisitors (who twice exonerated him) and the literary critics (who did not!). Where Dante's self-reading goes to prove that he is worthy of the "faith and obedience" traditionally due to the *auctores*, Tasso's efforts as critical reader of his own work are consistently aimed at proving that, as writer, he has due respect for the authority of his readers, particularly his "official readers." The irony of the matter, of course, is that notwithstanding very real pressures from the Church, his Estense patron, and the literary establishment, those official readers are at least as much an internalized creation of Tasso's own imagination as they are a reality.

To sum up: in the course of this chapter we have followed a path, at once linear and circular, from Dante's emergence as writer and reader from the Middle Ages, where *auctor* and *lector* alike were – normatively – vehicles by which a relatively homogeneous culture ventriloquized its values, to the self-critical, individualized world of the Renaissance, and thence to Tasso's attempted return to a world where authorial intentions and readerly understandings coincide with the "official story" put out by the potent machinery of a nascent state apparatus.

By way of a coda, let us turn briefly to Cervantes' *Don Quixote*, a book notoriously predicated on an excess of readerly faith, to the point where such excess becomes the very substance of the narrative. Cervantes' work has often been used to mark an epoch in the history of authorship, and particularly of author–reader relations, as the founder of what would become the literary genre par excellence: the novel (whose name, at least in English, tellingly evokes "the new"). This entire chapter could, in retrospect, be taken as the prehistory not only of Quixote's pathos-drenched habits of reading but also of the elaborate narrative apparatus that Cervantes erects to buffer and complicate his own and his readers' relations to the book: the "found" manuscript, written in Arabic by the imaginary Cide Hamete Benengeli; the demystificatory dedicatory letter and parodic celebratory verses attributed to the great fictional personages of the chivalric tradition; the remarkable Part II, predicated not only on Cervantes' rivalry with the usurper-author, Avellaneda, but also on Quixote's and Sancho's knowledge that they themselves have become characters in a book, and on their encounter with vicious aristocratic "readers" (the duke and duchess) bent on exploiting these characters for their own vacuous amusement. The novelty and modernity of *Quixote* have their sources, then: one may point particularly to Montaigne's brilliant stratagem of making the author's "good faith" not the guarantor of the texts but its subject. From the perspective developed here, Cervantes does the same for the reader's "faith and obedience." That is not to deny either the beauty or the importance of *Don Quixote* – far from it. Cervantes' book undoubtedly offers among the most incisive readings and elaborations of the early modern author–reader dialectic; never more so, of course, than in making its ostensible author a man of another faith entirely.

NOTES

1. I use the masculine pronoun for writers, since the occupation was normatively gendered male in the period.
2. I deal extensively with the importance of the second etymology, the poetic author from *avieo*, in Ascoli, *Dante and the Making of a Modern Author* (forthcoming).
3. In the first edition the reference to St John was explicit – the revision seems to have been a response to the understandable outrage of ecclesiastical and academic authorities.
4. Timothy Hampton, on p. 190 of his *Writing from History: The Rhetoric of Exemplarity in Renaissance Literature* (Ithaca, N.Y.: Cornell University Press, 1990), astutely points out a later passage in which Montaigne blames on bad memory departures from the truth which in others would have been caused by "bad faith" ("Of Experience": 3.13).

SUGGESTIONS FOR FURTHER READING

Primary sources

Ariosto, Ludovico. *Cinque Canti / Five Cantos*, trans. David Quint and Alexander Sheers, intro. David Quint. Berkeley: University of California Press, 1996.

Montaigne, Michel de. *The Complete Essays of Montaigne*, trans. Donald Frame. Stanford: Stanford University Press, 1965.

Petrarca, Francesco. *Rerum Familiarum Libri*, vol. 1, trans. Aldo S. Bernardo. Albany: State University of New York Press, 1975.

—— *Petrarch's Lyric Poems: The 'Rime Sparse' and Other Lyrics*, trans. Robert M. Durling. Cambridge, Mass.: Harvard University Press, 1976.

Rabelais, François. *Gargantua and Pantagruel*, trans. J. M. Cohen. Baltimore: Penguin Books, 1955.

Tasso, Torquato. *Discourses on the Poetic Art*, in *The Genesis of Tasso's Narrative Theory: English Translations of the Early Poetics and a Comparative Study of Their Significance*, ed. and trans. Lawrence Rhu. Detroit: Wayne State University Press, 1993.

Secondary sources

Abrams, M. H. *The Mirror and the Lamp*. New York: Oxford University Press, 1953.

Chartier, Roger. *The Order of Books*, trans. Lydia G. Cochrane. Stanford: Stanford University Press, 1994; first published in French, 1992.

Durling, Robert M. *The Figure of the Poet in Renaissance Epic*. Cambridge, Mass.: Harvard University Press, 1965.

Eisenstein, Elizabeth. *The Printing Press as an Agent of Change: Communications and Cultural Transformations in Early Modern Europe*. Cambridge: Cambridge University Press, 1979.

Ferguson, Margaret W. *Dido's Daughters: Literacy, Gender, and Empire in Early Modern England and France*. Chicago: University of Chicago Press, 2003.

Foucault, Michel. "What is an Author?" in Donald F. Bouchard, ed., *Language, Counter-*

memory, Practice: Selected Essays and Interviews, trans. Donald F. Bouchard and Sherry Simon. Ithaca: Cornell University Press, 1977, 113–38.

Greenblatt, Stephen. *Renaissance Self-fashioning: From More to Shakespeare*. Chicago: University of Chicago Press, 1980.

Greene, Thomas M. *The Light in Troy: Imitation and Discovery in Renaissance Poetry*. New Haven: Yale University Press, 1982.

Grosz, Elizabeth. "Sexual Signatures: Feminism after the Death of the Author," in *Space, Time, and Perversion: Essays on the Politics of Bodies*. London: Routledge, 1995, 9–24.

Hampton, Timothy. *Writing from History: The Rhetoric of Exemplarity in Renaissance Literature*. Ithaca: Cornell University Press, 1990.

Helgerson, Richard. *Self-crowned Laureates: Spenser, Johnson, Milton and the Literary System*. Berkeley: University of California Press, 1983.

Hoffmann, George. *Montaigne's Career*. Oxford: Oxford University Press, 1998.

Holmes, Olivia. *Assembling the Lyric Self: Authorship from Troubadour Song to Italian Poetry Book*. Minneapolis: University of Minnesota Press, 2000.

Jauss, Hans Robert. *Toward an Aesthetic of Reception*, trans. Timothy Bahti, intro. Paul de Man. Minneapolis: University of Minnesota Press, 1982.

Lerer, Seth. *Chaucer and his Readers: Imagining the Author in Late-medieval England*. Princeton: Princeton University Press, 1993.

Lowenstein, Joseph. *The Author's Due: Printing and the Prehistory of the Copyright*. Chicago: University of Chicago Press, 2002.

Minnis, A. J. *Medieval Theory of Authorship: Scholastic Literary Attitudes in the Later Middle Ages*, 2nd edn. Philadelphia: University of Pennsylvania Press, 1988.

Noakes, Susan. *Timely Reading: Between Exegesis and Interpretation*. Ithaca: Cornell University Press, 1988.

Orgel, Steven. *The Authentic Shakespeare*. New York and London: Routledge, 2002.

Petrucci, Armando. *Writers and Readers in Medieval Italy: Studies in the History of Written Culture*, trans. Charles Radding. New Haven: Yale University Press, 1995.

Quint, David. *Origin and Originality in Renaissance Literature: Versions of the Source*. New Haven: Yale University Press, 1983.

Reiss, Timothy J. *The Meaning of Literature*. Ithaca, N.Y.: Cornell University Press, 1992.

Richardson, Brian. *Printing, Writers and Readers in Renaissance Italy*. Cambridge: Cambridge University Press, 1999.

Spitzer, Leo. "Note on the Poetic and Empirical 'I' in Medieval Authors." *Traditio* 4: 414–22. (Also in *Romanische Literaturstudien, 1936–56*. Tübingen: Niemeyer, 1959, 100–12.)

Stillinger, Thomas Clifford. *The Song of Troilus: Lyric Authority in the Medieval Book*. Philadelphia: University of Pennsylvania Press, 1992.

Stock, Brian. *Augustine the Reader: Meditation, Self-knowledge, and the Ethics of Interpretation*. Cambridge, Mass.: Harvard University Press, 1996.

Wall, Wendy. *The Imprint of Gender: Authorship and Publication in the English Renaissance*. Ithaca: Cornell University Press, 1993.

Weimann, Robert. *Authority and Representation in Early Modern Discourse*, ed. David Hillman. Baltimore: Johns Hopkins University Press, 1996.

Zatti, Sergio. *The Quest for Epic: From Ariosto to Tasso*. Ed. Dennis Looney. Trans. Sally Hill, with Dennis Looney. Toronto: University of Toronto Press, 2006.

CHAPTER TWENTY-THREE

THE RENAISSANCE PORTRAIT
From resemblance to representation

Bronwen Wilson

At the end of the sixteenth century, the Bolognese artist Agostino Carracci engraved a portrait of Giovanni Gabrielli, known as "il Sivello." In the proof, the head of the celebrated actor is completed, though the torso is only tentatively sketched. A shadow conceals half Gabrielli's face in darkness as he looks out across the parapet toward the viewer; he holds a mask that faces away from his body, an attribute of his profession, and also a reference to his reputation as an actor who could play all the characters of a cast single-handedly. Were he hidden from view, a contemporary reported, the audience would believe there to be "a group of six persons of differing speech, voice, age and condition."[1] In the completed engraving, Agostino reversed the direction of the mask, its smooth surface and gaping eye-socket evoking a skull (Figure 23.1). Transformed into a *vanitas*, and gesturing, through the bust-length format and inscription below, to ancient funerary monuments, the engraving is a reflection on conventions at the heart of Renaissance portraiture. Turned to face the sitter, the mask seems to question his identity, and thus motivate his inquisitive turn toward the viewer. The engraving not only conveys il Sivello's skill as a simulator but also suggests that portraits, like people, could be deceptive.

Gabrielle Paleotti, the archbishop of Bolgona, certainly thought so. In his treatise on images of 1582, he criticized the vanity of portraiture, from idealized physiognomies to extravagant accessories.[2] Two years later, Gian Paolo Lomazzo complained in his treatise that "merchants and bankers who have never seen a drawn sword and who should properly appear with quill pens behind their ears, their gowns about them and their day-books in front of them, have themselves painted in armour holding generals' batons."[3] And Girolamo Cardano, the famous prognosticator, asserted in his autobiography, written shortly before his death in 1576, that "several painters who have come from afar to make my portrait have found no feature by which they could so characterize me, that I might be distinguished."[4]

This recognition of the deceptive qualities of portraiture runs counter to the traditional claim made for the Renaissance portrait, that mimesis enabled the image to express the sitter's soul or character. For Giorgio Vasari, whose revised *Lives of the Artists* was published in 1568, the genre was emblematic of the generative capacity of the artist who emulates both nature and God.[5] As David Summers explains:

Figure 23.1 Agostino Carracci. *Solus instar omnium*/Joannes Gabriel Comicus Nuncupatus SIVEL (Giovanni Gabrielli, called il Sivello).

Renaissance images were presumed to make us see more than we are shown and, more specifically, to make us see something higher than we are shown. We see a higher, spiritual inwardness in external forms.... The apparent sitter in a Renaissance portrait was thus an external appearance showing an inward truth, and so, it might be said, were Renaissance works of art in general.[6]

Yet many scholars have challenged this view by underlining how Vasari's idealism, and the authority given to his views by art historians, has concealed the ideological work — systems of patronage, gender and sexuality, the politics of aesthetics — that is sedimented in portraits.[7]

But how did contemporaries understand the distinction between external appearances and inwardness? This chapter argues that portraiture, as it evolved, contributed to a sense of the portrait not as an expression of self-sufficiency but rather as an expression of the desire for legibility. As I posit, representational strategies that organized how sitters were perceived, and the increasing desire of viewers to interpret appearances, overlapped with a broader shift during the fifteenth and sixteenth centuries from the idea of the portrait as a likeness to the notion of the portrait as representation. The relation between portraiture and the changing status of the subject was altered by diverse and specific geographical and political concerns. However, accounting for the complex shifting mechanisms of social change — state formation, religious debates, bodily discipline, an increasingly courtly context, contact with foreigners, representational technologies — is beyond the scope of this chapter. Instead, I consider the evolving status of the portrait by surveying some of the structural and material characteristics of the genre: its concerns with death, documentation, authenticity, the form of the face and its changeability, the frame, the mirror, physiognomy, and transparency.

NEGOTIATING INTERIORITY

The Renaissance portrait was harnessed to the myth of the modern individual by Jacob Burckhardt.[8] For Burckhardt, the individual was liberated from the yoke of faith and communal medieval life, and portraits were the visual expression of the "will-to-power" of those dynamic figures who fueled the changes he ascribed to the period.[9] His essay on the portrait was published posthumously, in 1898, and four years later, in "The Art of Portraiture and the Florentine Bourgeoisie," Aby Warburg acknowledged his debt to Burckhardt's cultural-historical approach.[10] However, it was Burckhardt's thesis about a pivotal change in subjectivity that became a topos. More than a century after the publication of *The Civilization of the Renaissance*, John Wyndham Pope-Hennessy ascribed the "beginning of the modern portrait" to "the Renaissance vision of man's self-sufficient nature."[11] The Renaissance portrait, he maintains, "reflects the reawakening interest in human motives and the human character, the resurgent recognition of those factors which make human beings individual." Particularization in images came to be seen as a symptom of a self that was internal to the body.

In recent decades scholars have challenged this view of the subject, arguing instead that selves are constituted by representations that are external to them, and incorporated through speech acts, movements, and gestures. Working from a theoretical understanding of the subject in which there is no self prior to the symbolic order of language and representations, scholars – perhaps most notably Stephen Greenblatt – have stressed the constitutive role of control mechanisms, the ambiguous, permeable, and performative nature of identity in the period.[12]

Harry Berger has recently shifted the focus to self-representation. In contrast to Greenblatt's concept of self-fashioning, which views the self as a cultural artefact, self-representation is something you do with yourself. Thus Berger stresses the performative nature of portraits, the "fiction of the pose" that attests to the sitter's struggle to embody the ideal types that managed identities.[13] Berger is critical of scholars who identify a candidate for the sitter of a portrait and then deploy this biography as evidence of the artist's ability "to depict the interior character of the subject," as Stephen Pepper has recently said of Annibale Carracci.[14] It is a "referential fallacy," Berger insists, to believe that there is something legible about the interior.[15] Even *sprezzatura*, that art of prudent dissemblance, is only a "performance of exemplary inwardness that's assumed to be inauthentic by the performers no less than by their audiences."[16] For Berger, inwardness is mere artifice.

If the body is understood as a system of discourse, however, is there a tendency to overlook or misinterpret how Renaissance men and women understood themselves? This is the question asked by Katharine Maus, who argues that the Renaissance self was increasingly conceptualized in relation to inwardness. According to the sources on which she draws, "persons and things inwardly *are*," whereas "persons and things outwardly only *seem*."[17] John Martin has also been concerned with the long history of interiority. What changed in the sixteenth century, he argues, was the increasing importance of sincerity and a sense of the self that was bound to a new "understanding of the relation of one's thoughts and feelings to one's words and actions."[18] Both sincerity and prudence were ways of being that emphasized the threshold between one's heart and one's façade. Even if interiority is a fiction, both Maus and Martin suggest we should remain attentive to how that fiction was constructed. The premise of this chapter, then, is that portraits were themselves instrumental in this process.

LIKENESS AND DEATH

Agostino Carracci's engraving, as noted earlier, is a commentary on the meanings embedded in the reactivation of ancient conventions in the fifteenth century. Jan Van Eyck's *Leal Sovvenir* (Faithful Remembrance) of 1432 is an early example in which a naturalistic bust-length portrait of a man is separated from the observer by a parapet that is painted to resemble marble incised with ancient epigraphy (Figure 23.2). The enigmatic French inscription suggests the portrait may have been painted posthumously, a possibility furthered by the trompe-l'oeil porphyry painted on the back of the panel. Taken together, the inscriptions and visual references to the durability of stone and their memorial functions contrast with the transience of life.[19] This was a commonplace by the end of the sixteenth century, and Agostino's engraving of

Figure 23.2 Jan Van Eyck. *Leal Sovvenir* (portrait of a man), 1432. The National Gallery, London.

il Sivello plays with notions of permanence and presence (Figure 23.1). The Latin text *"Solus instar omnium"* is inscribed on the parapet with the actor's name, as if calligraphy penned on paper brings forward the ephemeral and reproducible nature of print. The meaning of the text, "singlehandedly capable of representing all," in combination with the mask held by the actor, similarly underscore the mutable and fleeting nature of appearances.

In this context, the contrast between the striking realism of il Sivello's face and the mask prompts associations with that other emblem of the Renaissance portrait, the death mask, an object that also invokes ancient origins. Cast portraits of ancestors appeared in "infinite numbers" and "every house in Florence," as Giorgio Vasari famously reported, "so well made and natural that they seem alive."[20] An intriguing example is the likeness of Lorenzo de' Medici, the de facto ruler of Florence until his death in 1492 (Figure 23.3). The death mask is centered on a black wood panel, and a text is painted in gold Roman letters below:

Mortre crvdele che n qvessto chorpo venne
Che dopo morte el mondo ando sozopra
Mentre che 'l vise tvto i pace 'l tenne

[Cruel death that comes to this body
That after death, the world went in confusion
While he lived, all was kept in peace]

Taken from a poem by Angelo Poliziano, humanist and member of the Medici circle, the text encourages the beholder to consider Lorenzo's countenance in relation to his deeds.[21] The form, taken from a mold, replicates the topography of his face with its broad nose, pointed chin, and textured surface incised with wrinkles and facial hair. Through contact with the face of the sitter, the likeness is an indexical icon, unmediated by the artist. Excessively realistic, the image is haunted by the trace of the deceased, an effect intensified by recalling the traditional juxtaposition of sculpted likeness and inscribed parapet.

In contrast to the material remains of the body impressed in the death mask, the lifelike wax figures (*boti*) commissioned by Lorenzo attested to his living presence.[22] These surrogate objects – *ex votos* made by *fallimagini* (image makers) – were testaments to his survival following the attack on April 26, 1478, in which his brother, Giuliano de' Medici, was assassinated by Pazzi conspirators in the Florentine cathedral. Produced in multiples, the effigies were dispersed to different sacred sites. The three *boti* were still visible, according to Vasari, whose account of them appears in his life of Andrea Verrochio.[23] In a church on via di S. Gallo, Lorenzo was dressed in the bloodied clothes and bandages he wore when he appeared in the windows of his house following the attack. Another *ex voto* was sent to Santa Maria degli Angeli in Assisi. A third, displayed above the door of the Santissima Annunziata, was dressed in the official Florentine gown. Lorenzo's *ex voto* was only one of the effigies that crowded around the miracle-working icon of the Annunziata. So great was the profusion of wax bodies that hung from the rafters of the church that they were said to disrupt worshipers. Significantly, all three figures were sent to churches with miracle-working images where the presence of the *boti* substituted

Figure 23.3 Death mask of Lorenzo de' Medici. Attributed to the Benintendi, Polo Museale, Fiorentino.

for Lorenzo, and even rendered the exchange with the sacred more effective through the enduring presence of the *ex voto*. The wax *ex votos* were not replicas of an authentic individual, but surrogates dressed in the diverse categories of his composite and ambiguous identity.

Resemblance through contact with the face and body, seen in the death mask and wax *ex votos*, was combined in another kind of likeness: the transitional effigy. In the English context, funeral effigies of the king were distinctive in function from the permanent tomb monuments for which they seem to have served as models.[24] Funeral effigies, sometimes cast from the face of the deceased, served as substitutes for the monarch during the period between death and burial. In contrast to the permanent media used for tombs, the ephemeral status of the facsimiles required less durable materials, such as wood and plaster, but realistic effects were created by paint, wigs, and costumes that facilitated recognition. As extant effigies of Henry VII (reigned 1485–1509) demonstrate, casting could be used to produce striking verisimilitude. The death mask of the Tudor king, at Westminster Abbey, was modeled into a polychrome bust.[25] Imprinted with the surface of the king's face, the specter of his mortal body was transformed into a living image by an unknown artisan familiar with the Italian practice of constructing wax *ex votos*.

The death mask was probably the source for Pietro Torrigiano, who was commissioned to sculpt a terracotta bust of Henry and his tomb effigy three years after his death. In contrast to the prototype, Torrigiano modeled the terracotta, idealizing the physiognomy, dressing him in hunting clothes, and adjusting the turn of the head and gaze of his eyes to construct an impression of the king, a fiction that solicits the observer's interpretation.

The variety of images generated by the death of Henry VII condense into a few years the evolving status and expectations for the portrait. An icon, traditionally a portrait of a saint, contains the presence of the sacred through its likeness to an original image. Likeness can be manifested in the image through contact (the face of Christ in Veronica's veil), through copying (images of the Virgin that trace their genealogy to Luke's portrait of her), or through their miraculous appearance. The icon resembles the original sitter, or earlier image, without mediation. By the sixteenth century, however, the function of likeness was increasingly subordinated to representation, and this change is evident in contemporary writing about portraiture. In the 1390s, Cennino Cennini recommended casting a living person's face as a means to simulate nature in his *Craftsman's Handbook*.[26] By 1504, however, the humanist Pomponius Gauricus criticized this practice as a reproductive mode in his treatise on sculpture. Physiognomy, he explained, was "a way of observing by which we deduce the qualities of souls from the features of bodies."[27] Thus a portrait should represent the sitter *ex se*, "out of itself"; it should convey the sitter's *animacio*, or animation.[28] Like Gauricus, Vasari was opposed to casting because it was unmediated by the artist. If the cast likeness was ubiquitous, as Vasari tells the reader, it serves as a foil for his account of the arts as a history of the artists' styles.[29] The presence of the sitter, as Hans Belting explains, was replaced by "an idea that is made visible in the work: the idea of art, as the artist had it in mind."[30] In this process, the role of the beholder was altered; it was activated in response to how the work acted. The resemblance of the ritual object – ancestor portrait, wax *ex voto*, transitional effigy – to the body of the sitter, was succeeded by the artist's representation of the sitter. Iconic likeness gave way to artistic representation.

Replication and the production of multiples enabled images to function as portraits of the deceased, to stand near the divine, or to move in a procession. In the era of representation, however, replication could nullify authenticity. This is exemplified in the intriguing case of the competition for an effigy of the French king Henry IV, following his murder in 1610. Michel Bourdin won the competition and his wax portrait was used for the lying-in-state of the king. The portrait became damaged, however, as a result of efforts to make molds of it for the production of copies. Bourdin therefore sued François de Bechefer, whose unauthorized images of the king made the rounds of provincial fairs, even turning up in Amsterdam in the Oude Doolhof (Old Labyrinth), where they were displayed in 1630s.[31] Distanced from contact with the king's body and removed from the ritual context, Bechefer's portraits were mere reproductions.

If the formless nature of wax, terracotta, and plaster enabled resemblance in the fifteenth century, in the following century the malleability of media became associated with idealization and dissimulation. The mutability of wax could be used to signify both ideal beauty and also the conflict between exterior appearances and interiority. For example, in *Romeo and Juliet*, Juliet's suitor, Paris, is compared to the perfection of a wax portrait, which is invoked as a sign of his idealized beauty. The medium was also used to signal the changeability of appearances. As Friar Laurence says to Romeo: "Thy noble shape is but a form of wax/Digressing from the valour of a man."[32] The portrait, like the medium, no longer conveys the truth of appearances; instead, it signifies their mutability.

DOCUMENTATION AND THE BODY

Van Eyck's complex play of inscriptions and resemblance in *Leal Souvenir* has elicited speculation about the sitter's identity (Figure 23.2). Since 1949, when Erwin Panofsky proposed that the man was the composer Binchois, a dozen scholars have generated as many potential candidates for the sitter and almost as many *métiers*, but both his name and profession remain unknown.[33] A Greek inscription has been translated as "Tymotheus," perhaps the name of the sitter, but other possibilities include "tum otheos," then god, or I honor God, or even a transliteration of Latin into Otheos, the Trojan deity from Christine de Pizan's *L'Epître d'Othéa*.[34] The texts are in different languages and each is distinguished from the other through its style and form: the Greek letters are painted graffiti, *Leal Souvenir* pretends to be carved in stone, and the artist's signature – "Done in the year of Our Lord 1432 on the 10th day of October by Jan Van Eyck" – is signed in Latin as if with a stylus. The signature and precise depiction of the sitter's features call attention to the artist's position as a witness and his work of transcription. Whatever the meaning of the texts, and regardless of whether the portrait is made from life or not, the pictorial catalog of forms and modes of writing, emphasized by the scroll held by the sitter, with its illegible text, contributes to the documentary nature of the image.

State formation during the fifteenth and sixteenth centuries required monitoring the movements of individuals and thus new forms of documentation. Badges and documents carried the signs, seals, insignias, and marks of authorities as efforts were made to identify pilgrims, students, journeymen, beggars, merchants, soldiers, and diplomats. Diverse forms of passports emerged in Italy and northern Europe as a means to identify that a person was in fact who she or he claimed to be. Legal cases throughout Europe confirm that it was costume, and also scars and unusual marks, such as moles, that were used to identify individuals. This "archaeology of identification," as Valentin Groebner describes it, was a process of categorizing distinctive and unchanging marks that "separated the 'inner' from the 'outer.'"[35]

Individuals, moreover, did not identify with their faces alone, as the case of Matthias Schwarz (1496–1574) demonstrates.[36] A bookkeeper in Augsburg for the Fuggers, wealthy traders who imported textiles, Schwarz recorded changes in his life by commissioning portraits. But his "Gestalt," as he calls his external form, was expressed through the diversity of clothing he wears throughout his Trachtenbuch, or costume book. Consisting of 137 portraits by different artists painted between 1521 and 1560, the book traces his life from his early infancy, dressed in diapers, through his apprenticeship, to the attire he wore as a traveling merchant. Proud of his ability to disguise himself – he calls himself a "juggler" – he describes the coat that could be reversed from green to red, which enabled him to travel unrecognized through rebellious terrain during the Peasants' War.[37] Portraits were commonplace at the age of 30 – the age at which Christians envisioned their bodies and souls would be rejoined at the Last Judgment. In the Trachtenbuch, Schwarz takes this literally: he is seen nude from both the front and the back (Figure 23.4).

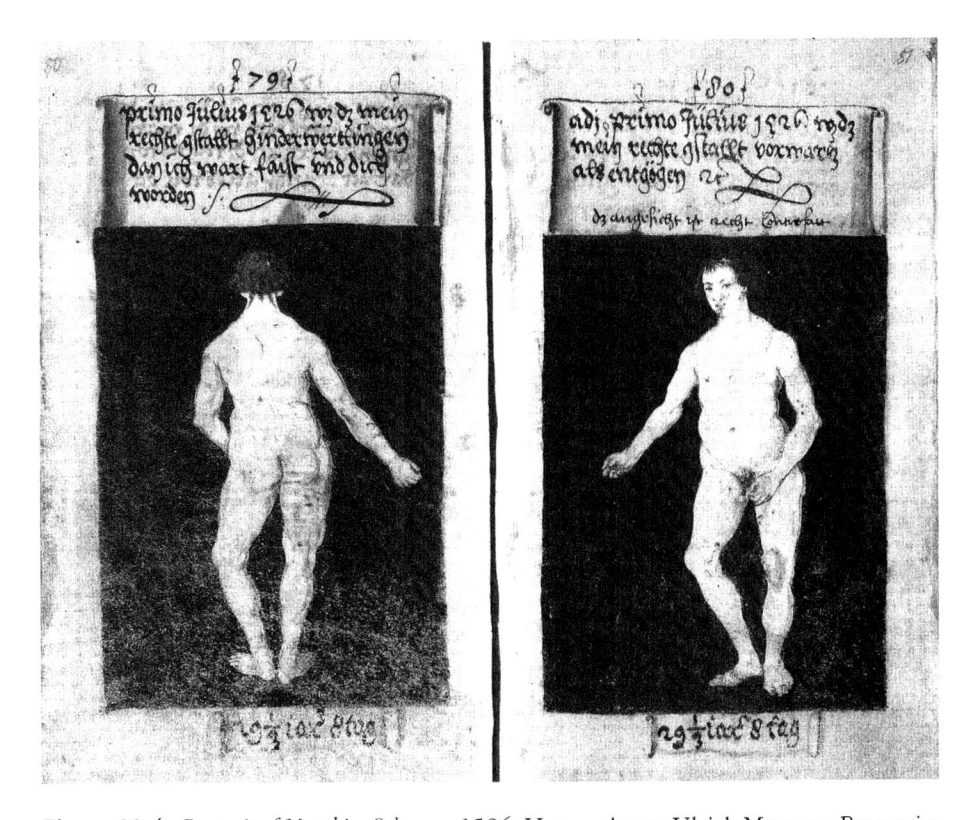

Figure 23.4 *Portrait of Matthias Schwarz*, 1526, Herzog Anton Ulrich Museum, Brunswig.

He also commissioned numerous panel portraits. Christoph Amberger documents the date he painted Schwarz (4.15 p.m. on March 22, 1542) and also the sitter's age and birthdate (45 years 30 days and 21¾ hours; 6.30 p.m. on February 19, 1497).[38] These details are arranged in columns on a loose sheet of paper as if pulled from a ledger, and affixed to the casement behind him. Instead of as self-preoccupation, Groebner interprets Schwarz's project as self-documentation, "simply a part of a larger system of personal records."[39] By exploring the practices of trade, of accounting, and of recording, his collection of portraits is evidence of how early sixteenth-century selves did not have fixed identities, but multiple ones. And yet, Schwarz's use of clothing to negotiate his identity was not a fiction but a bodily practice. As Gabriele Mentges argues, his costume book is an "attempt to demonstrate, by means of attire, the claim to autonomous agency within the framework of the current social norms of dress."[40] Schwarz reports that his book is intended to furnish a historical record of costume. Thus the process of reflecting on himself in different guises must have called attention to the function of his body as a threshold between who he appeared to be and the memories of those embodied experiences that constitute identity.

MODERATING EXPOSURE

With the wax *ex votos*, repetition contributed to the efficacy of the surrogate object by multiplying its continued proximity to the sacred. For the sacred icon, by contrast, it is concealing the face that activates the aura. This revelatory function is described by Leonardo da Vinci: as the image of the divine being is unveiled, the faithful worship the deity "who is represented in the picture . . . exactly as if this goddess were there as a living presence."[41] Covering portraits was widespread and their disclosure activated by the use of covers, bags, and curtains. For example, Diego Hurtado de Mendoza, the Spanish ambassador to Venice, concealed Titian's portrait of his mistress behind a silk veil. For Pietro Aretino, who described the object in a letter of 1542, the covered portrait resembled a reliquary ("aguisa di reliquia") and the woman a "goddess".[42] Elisabetta Condulmer, a Venetian courtesan, kept her portrait in the *portego* of her house where it was protected by a *timpano*, a frame with a curtain. Drawing the fabric to one side, Condulmer could reveal her image.[43] In contrast to the living presence in the icon, Condulmer's sixteenth-century patrons would have been able to compare the sitter in person to her representation.

Portraits could be hung from chains and attached by a hinge on one side to a wall, with both sides of the painting contributing to the beholder's interpretation. For example, a portrait of a man in the Courtauld Institute of Art Gallery, by a follower of the Master of Flémalle (*c.* 1440–50), has a branch of holly with the motto "Je he ce que mord" (I have that which bites) depicted on the reverse.[44] These were likely the device and the motto of the sitter, which, seen first, determine how the observer interprets the portrait. Double-sided portraits were forerunners of painted covers, probably developed in northern Europe in the fifteenth century, that could be opened with hinges or slid along grooves inside the frame.

Lorenzo Lotto experimented with panels on which he painted allegories. For example, his bust-length likeness of Bernardo de' Rossi, bishop of Treviso (1505), was once covered with an allegorical landscape.[45] A healthy new tree, growing from the left side of an otherwise dead trunk, divides the scene into two parts. On the right, a storm causes a shipwreck at sea and casts a threatening shadow over the forest where a Satyr lies drunk, wasted by wine and lust. The bishop's coat of arms, resting on the trunk, has been turned away from these dangers and a cherub plays with instruments of knowledge in front of it. Obstacles on the left – a cliff, a bleak plateau, a barricade of rocks with brambles – convey the hard spiritual work of the patron whose success is indicated by the path and sunlit hill beyond.

Drawing the allegorical panel to the side would have revealed the stark portrait of the bishop. The cover thereby encourages the viewer to interpret de' Rossi's pursed facial features, taut pose, and clenched fist as signs of his steadfast and determined character. The combination of likeness and allegory recalls the two sides of a medal, in which the portrait on the obverse is considered in relation to an *impresa*, that device in which an image and motto are converted into a symbol of the sitter's character. Medals, two-sided portraits, and covers prompt the observer to consider one image in relation to the other.

Similar conventions were used by Albrecht Dürer for his portrait of Hieronymus Holzschuher in 1526, but here the use of a cover marks a significant reconceptualization (Figure 23.5). A panel once covering the portrait displays the coat of arms of the patron interwined with those of his wife. Removing the panel reveals a closely cropped bust-length portrait of Holzschuher with his name and age recorded in the upper left. If Dürer was rehearsing a traditional format, the extraordinary naturalism of the portrait suggests this is a rhetorical gesture. For the undulating topography of Holzschuher's physiognomy, the contrast between the fine wrinkles, wispy curls of hair, and tufts of fur on the jacket, and the reflection of the room in the lights of the sitter's eyes, demonstrate Dürer's act of painting. In contrast to the icon, or the external likeness of the bishop, here it is the work of the artist that is unveiled.[46]

This is the effect of painting, as Leonardo observes, since the reaction of "worshipping and praying to a deity, who is represented in the picture ... does not happen with any other science or other works of man."[47] The use of covers is proof of the superior value bestowed upon painting, which "alone retains its nobility, bringing honours singularly to its author and remaining precious and unique."[48] In this light, Holzschuher's appearance is coextensive with the revelation of Dürer's art.

SELF-REFLECTIONS

Portraits made images widely available in which the face and shoulders of the sitter were the focus, precisely those parts of the viewer's own body that cannot be seen without the use of a mirror.[49] The countenances of de' Rossi and Holzschuher, revealed by their respective covers and returning the viewer's gaze, bring forward the mirror-like impact of the image. Activating the presence of the sitter, the covers also point toward the representational weight of the face. This effect is magnified in self-portraiture, in the process of engaging with one's reflection in a mirror.

Renaissance artists often included representations of themselves in narrative works. For example, Domenico Ghirlandaio cast himself as the young shepherd

Figure 23.5 Albrecht Dürer. *Portrait of Hieronymus Holzschuher* (1526). Gemaeldegalerie, Staatliche Museen zu Berlin, Berlin, Germany/Scala Archives.

in *The Adoration of the Shepherds*, the altarpiece he painted for the Sassetti Chapel at Santa Trinità in Florence (1483–6). Kneeling on his left leg, and supported by the right, he points toward the infant in the center, but looks in the opposite direction, beyond the frame, toward the fresco portrait of Francesco Sassetti, who kneels on the right. By projecting himself into the sacred narrative, but also interacting with his patron, Ghirlandaio's painted surrogate mediates between his work and the person who commissioned it. The connection across the frame expresses the ambiguous nature of Renaissance identity, the artist's professional, social, and pious obligations.

Figure 23.6 Albrecht Dürer. *Self-portrait*, c. 1491. Universitätsbibliothek, Erlangen.

In 1508 Dürer depicted himself and his friend Konrad Celtis in *The Martyrdom of Ten Thousand*. Standing out in their black clothes from the surrounding slaughter, the two men are at the center of the narrative painting. Dürer holds a stick to which a large sheet is affixed with an inscription: "This was done in the year 1508 by Albrecht Dürer, German." Soliciting the viewer's attention, Dürer oberves the viewer from inside the narrative, a display of authorship that Victor Stoichita describes as "the self-portrait as visitor."[50]

The origins of Dürer's act of identification with his image – recognizing himself as a subject, and not as a figure in the work – have been connected to a sheet, drawn about 1491 and now in Erlangen. As Joseph Leo Koerner has shown, this can be understood as the moment in which the self was materialized through the bodily act of drawing (Figure 23.6). The artist's right hand is pressed toward his head, as if steadying it, while he stares at the convex mirror once positioned before him, where the observer is now placed. Dürer delineates his facial features and gesture as if his reflection were an object before him, or a study for a figure in another work. Indeed, the pose rehearses, and also anticipates, other images, including the famous angel in *Melencolia I* (1514; see Figure 2.2) who supports its head with its left hand. This engraving has been used as an iconographic key to interpret both the Erlangen sheet and the print as self-portraits of the artist's melancholic nature, and the gesture as an attribute of the "abstracted inwardness" of the Renaissance genius. Yet this is an anachronistic view of both the self and late medieval theories of the humors in which the relation between the inside and the outside of the body is not clearly drawn. A historical reading of self-portrayal, as Koerner explains, "would record less Dürer's unique and innermost being than melancholy's self-manifestation through the medium of the artist's body."[51] Instead of self-portraiture, the drawing is better understood as prosopopoeia, when an object speaks for an agent. The Erlangen sheet is evidence, significantly, of the transition from "objects to subjects, things to signifiers."[52] The self-portrait, then, is not an idea invented by a self-conscious subject; instead, it is the image that reveals the self.

Through the repeated process of drawing himself as a model, Dürer came to see himself as a subject of representation instead of an object. This evolving practice enabled the visitor portrait in the *Martyrdom* and Dürer's inscription, in 1498, on his self-portrait in the Prado: "I painted this in my image, when I was 25 years old." In contrast to Ghirlandaio, who negotiates his position within the work, or the transitional Erlangen drawing, Dürer's use of the first person in the Prado portrait creates the "fiction of autonomy," a fiction that is intensified when the sitter is also the artist.[53]

A similar conceit appears on the frame of the portrait of a man who wears a red headdress in the National Gallery in London. The inscription states: "Jan van Eyck made me on 21 October 1433," and the addition of the artist's motto, "Als Ich Can," with its pun, "As I (Eyck) can," also on the frame, suggests he may be the sitter.[54] The visual evidence supports the claim of the text since the uneven focus in the eyes conveys the artist's concentrated focus on his reflection in a convex mirror seen later in Dürer's Erlangen sheet. The first inscription situates Van Eyck outside the work, as neither the sitter nor the observer, whereas the second inscription, "As I can," proposes that the artist is in the work, the likeness seen inside the frame. And yet, in contrast to Dürer's use of the first person in the Prado painting, Van Eyck's inscriptions are ambivalent; together they suggest, once again, the ambiguous nature of identity, that the artist could be the maker of the work, the likeness in it, and a witness to it.

In Parmigianino's self-portrait, painted in 1524, it is the mirror itself that is the subject of the work. According to Vasari, the artist was "fascinated by his own reflection in a barber's convex mirror [and] he decided to produce it exactly"; that is, the profile of the mirror itself, and not only himself.[55] The reflection transforms the artist's left hand into his right, its scale and importance exaggerated by replicating the shape of the convex mirror. In a culture preoccupied with status, self-portraiture was a means of negotiating one's social standing, and Parmigianino stresses his hand as an instrument of the mind.[56] Advertising his talents, the young painter plays with the expectations of the genre. The edge of a circular frame appears on the far right, a gesture to the mirror he uses to produce his reflection or a reference to the painting within the painting. The corner of a rectangular window in the upper left suggests the conventional format for portraiture, which is furthered by the function of the table as a parapet upon which his hand rests.

The emergence of the self-portrait underscores how the change from resemblance to representation was generated through the work of painting. It was the material practice of drawing one's face in the mirror that contributed to the fictions of autonomy ("I painted this in my image," "Als ich Can") and interiority (melancholia). With the self-portrait, authorship was conjoined to the body of the artist reflected in the mirror, the game that Parmigianino exploited through the distortions to his hand.

CONSTITUTING CHARACTER

In a large medal made by Costanzo di Moysis, the Ottoman sultan Mehmed II appears in a bust-length portrait on the obverse, and on horseback on the reverse. The medal translates the signs of Mehmed's eastern identity – the kaftan and fluted *örfi*, surrounded by a turban – into political currency for a western audience, using models that were Mediterranean wide, as Lisa Jardine and Jerry Brotton explain, "to provide an archetype of the oriental power-figure."[57] The profile format highlights his arched brows, bird-like nose, and pointed chin that one Turkish poet described as "a parrot's beak resting on cherries."[58]

The independent portrait was not a form of imagery usually exploited by Muslim rulers; as Esin Atil explains, a likeness "was considered a 'reflection' of the person, devoid of his soul," and thus Islamic artists conveyed information about historical and fictive persons through iconographic conventions and compositional devices such as seating arrangements.[59] Until the nineteenth century "all representations of rulers were executed from memory and based on accepted models of an ideal type" authenticated by research into the individual's "physical characteristics." Nevertheless, Mehmed II capitalized on the political efficacy of the genre, commissioning painted portraits and medals that came to define his physiognomy.[60] Ancient prototypes, including coins of Alexander the Great, were familiar in the East, and thus Mehmed's interest in portraiture is not outside of his Islamic inheritance.[61]

With its two sides, the medal combines Mehmed's distinctive physiognomy with the actions of a condottiere, a potent symbol of martial prowess. Indeed, a century later, Giovanbattista della Porta would describe the sultan's distinctive profile – his "hooked and notable nose, that almost reached his upper lip" – as a sign of a great leader and his "great soul."[62] Della Porta was looking at medals and also printed portrait-books for his famous treatise on physiognomy, first published in Latin in 1586.

Portrait-books were a new serialized format, published throughout Europe in the last four decades of the century, in which a pictorial likeness was typically paired with a biographical text. These were organized into professional, social, and religious categories – kings, captains, popes, illustrious ancients, emperors, sultans, artists – as printmakers responded to a market for images of famous men and women. The faces were not drawn from life, but copied from other prints, painted portraits, coins, and monuments. Mehmed II is one of 122 woodcuts copied from Paolo Giovio's famous collection of portraits and published in Theobold Mueller's *Musaei Joviani Imagines* in 1577. Faces of men appear on both the front and back of the sheets, enabling viewers to compare the physiognomies of sitters, such as Mehmed II and Giuliano de' Medici, who appear across from one another.

Pietro Bertelli drew on the medal of Mehmed II for his portrait of the sultan in his *Vite degl'imperatori de'Turchi con le loro effiggie*, published in 1599 (Figure 23.7). The sultans are defined as a group by their turbans, which highlight the singularity of their faces. Each portrait is accompanied by a brief history of the sitter's deeds. Substantive details of military pursuits are interwoven with a scintillating synopsis of the sultan's character and customs: the strangling of male siblings by the ascending sultan, sexual appetite, and of course the seraglio. Bertelli rarely makes explicit correlations between the likeness of the sultan and his biography. However, Mehmed II is an intriguing exception. The text embellishes what had become a familiar description of his profile: he had "a face of an ugly yellow color, with fierce eyes, arched eyelashes, and a nose so hooked that it seemed on the point of touching his lips. . . . He was notably cruel in war as in peace, since for the smallest reason he would murder those young men in the seraglio that he had loved lasciviously."[63] The bird-like eyes and nose, and skin color imputed to yellow bile and choleric personalities, are drawn from ancient theories of the humors and physiognomy. These general characteristics, however, are understood as signs of Mehmed's individual character, and the format urges the reader to look for the signs of the biography in his distinctive facial features. In so doing, the portrait of the sultan becomes evidence of his singular personality, his famous profile now confirming the claims in the text.

The portrait-book is emblematic of the belief that interior character and physiognomy were co-extensive, as Francesco Sansovino explains in his *L'historia di casa Orsina*, published in 1565 and a forerunner of the genre. The prolific Venetian writer advocates the use of portraits of celebrated people to accompany their biographies, since "one profits from the presence of esteemed people no less than from the memory of their honored deeds."[64] For Sansovino, the portrait is a mnemonic device, a way to recall the sitter's history. The portrait is charged with reviving the presence of an absent individual, and with propelling the memory of that person into the present. Significantly, he directs his readers to the visual evidence of the sitters' faces:

> although having frequently seen for themselves that actions [of individuals] do not correspond to their faces, and that sometimes under beautiful faces one discovers dreadful and horrible thoughts, the reader will come to marvel . . . [and] to contemplate the miracles that nature knows to produce in the countenances of man. And finding the forces of our souls implicated together with [Nature] in the making of the face, in the way that smell, taste, and color are bound together in the making of a fruit, the judgment of human hearts is most undoubtedly found in the face.[65]

Even if physiognomy cannot always be trusted as an indicator of character, the engravings, he asserts, demonstrate the virtuous and noble character of the men.

Sansovino sometimes begins by referring to the accompanying engraving, as in the case of Camillo Orsino da Lamentana: "This face, so dry and of an emaciated

MAVMET 2.° Imp. VIIII morì l'anno 1 4 8 1 di età d'
anni 5 3 hauendo regnato anni 3 2.

Figure 23.7 Pietro Bertelli. *Portrait of Mahometto II*, from Pietro Bertelli, *Vite degl'imperatori de'turchi con le loro effiggie* (1599). The British Library.

color, demonstrative of the quality of a nervous man, and by nature agile and strong, is the true portrait of Signor Camillo Orsino."[66] The man depicted in the portrait is indeed a gaunt figure, whose weedy beard exaggerates his lean face. He is dressed in armour and looking toward the viewer with sharp eyes; the text prompts us to interpret his gaze as incisive and his visage as a sign of vigor and assiduity. Significantly,

Sansovino describes the physiognomy he sees in the engravings, and interprets it on the basis of the biographies of the sitters. Lamentana's character is not revealed through his physiognomy, but is constituted from external evidence.

Portrait-books, produced in multiples and circulated widely, with their distinctive sequence of images paired with the biography of the sitter, prompt viewers to forge connections between the actions and character of individuals and their facial features. If initially the face is a way to remember the text, in turn viewers learned to distinguish between faces. The portraits introduce the histories, distinguishing the life of one person from the actions of the next in the reader's mind.

This is the function of the portraits that introduce the biographies of the artists in Vasari's *Lives*. Each woodcut becomes a signifier of the moral character and style of the artist that is described in the accompanying text. The portraits create a matrix of legibility, as Georges Didi-Huberman observes, for Vasari's history of art is a history of individual style.[67] The person's face becomes fused with his or her history in the reader's mind, the face a distinctive landscape. Contemporaries may have believed that outward appearances were expressions of inward character, as the sources repeatedly state, but an analysis of the evolving representational strategies and uses for portraits demonstrates that the genre was itself a contributing factor; interiority was being constructed from the outside in.

THE RETURN OF RESEMBLANCE

Indeed, "the face is a weak guarantee," as Michel de Montaigne remarked, "yet it deserves some consideration."[68] In his essay "Of Physiognomy," the French essayist explored how people perceive faces, how they "infer certain inward dispositions from the cast and formation of the face and those lineaments." He confessed to being drawn to beautiful faces, even though he knew that an ugly one might conceal a beautiful interior. People can alter their faces, he added, concealing their true nature, beliefs, and desires. Montaigne's views reflected widespread suspicions about appearances. In Shakespeare's *Macbeth*, for example, Duncan laments "there is no art/ To tell the mind's construction in the face."[69] Paolo Pinzio, whose *Fisionomia* was published in 1550, contrasted the "clear and open" character of animals with that of humans who can conceal their vices and obfuscate their true natures.[70] And in his treatise on physiognomy, Della Porta described the human face as a threshold between the observer and the "uncertain and inconstant consciousness."[71] A surge in publications across Europe, on topics ranging from physiognomy and gesture to comportment and dissimulation, attests to efforts to negotiate the increasingly fraught boundaries of the body.

The growing interest in physiognomy in the late Renaissance was a response to dissimulation as writers and reformers negotiated the boundaries of the body from two opposing points of view. On one side, authors pointed to the need to dissimulate. The high stakes of one's religious identity during the long Reformation required both the performance and expression of faith but also the ability to conceal those beliefs.[72] The social demands of the court similarly necessitated prudence, what Torquato Accetto would describe in the seventeenth century as the ethics of disguise.[73] Wearing a mask had become more than self-protection; it had become a way of life. On the other side were those who advanced sincerity as an ethical imperative. Montaigne, for instance, while acknowledging that some situations call for dissemblance, valued transparency, being open with one's face toward others, and being true to one's temperament.[74]

The Woman in Red, painted by Giovanni Battista Moroni about 1555–60, points to the difficulties of negotiating social expectations (Figure 23.8). The woman poses in accordance with the long history of comportment, engaging the viewer with her eyes, but with the modesty required of women that deflects attention from her gaze. The slashed sleeves and white lace collar and cuffs call attention to the pearls and jewels she wears around her neck and wrists, and the fan in her left hand that she fingers idly. She perches on a chair, buttressed by the metallic bodice that anchors her to the lavish marble pavement, as if to silence the noisy rustle of the slippery crisp rose silk. Moroni's attentiveness to the materiality of the costume suggests, to use Montaigne's words, that "we perceive no charms that are not sharpened, puffed out, and inflated by artifice."[75]

Concerns about artifice were at the heart of debates about painting and manifested in the call for naturalism in painting following the Council of Trent. These were articulated in Paleotti's treatise on painting in which he explains that images impress themselves on the intellect, the will, and memory.[76] Images are mediators between the body and psyche, and thus portraits had the potential to manage viewers' identities. For Paleotti, it was the affective character of images that rendered idealization and other forms of display immoral. For Lomazzo, portraits similarly impress themselves on the viewer, but he emphasizes the political efficacy of idealization, and thus recommends the genre be limited to the powerful. He describes the mirror-effect of portraits in his treatise: "as the human face answers a smile with a smile, so does it wait upon tear; if you would have me weep, you must first of all feel grief yourself."[77] For Francesco Bocchi, also writing in 1584, "there is no doubt that the passions of the mind cannot be concealed in the human body and that they are evident in external appearances, now of prudence, now of liberality, and then, as often happens of their opposites."[78] And this expression, or attitude of the person's face in the representation, is stamped in the mind of the observer. As these writers indicate, portraiture had come to be seen as a threat because of the effects it was believed to have on the beholder.

Naturalism was one response, as suggested by two portraits of blind women, attributed to Annibale Carracci and dated to about 1590.[79] Figure 23.9 illustrates one of the two images in which the sitters are painted with unconventional directness and close to the picture plane, their faces tightly cropped. At first glance, the women, with their closed eyes, recall death masks. Yet there is neither the pallor of a death mask, nor the illusion of the dead depicted as alive. The palpable texture of their flesh and upright poses indicate the sitters were aware that their portraits would be seen. And yet, the women's faces don't signify in conventional ways. Neither theatrical nor absorptive in Michael Fried's terms, their very corporeal presence disrupts our speculation, as if to probe the very fiction of portraiture.[80]

Images of the blind were more often represented with their eyes open, including examples painted by Annibale. However, these are two of six extant portraits of men

Figure 23.8 Giovanni Battista Moroni. *Portrait of a Lady (La Dama in Rosso)*, c. 1555–60. The National Gallery, London.

Figure 23.9 Annibale Carracci. *Portrait of a Blind Woman*, c. 1490. Private Collection, Bologna.

and women in which their closed eyes signify their blindness. Anna Ottani Cavina proposed that the group of images was likely associated with the Compagnia dei Ciechi (Company of the Blind), one of the many associations for the poor established during Gabrielle Paleotti's religious reforms in Bologna.[81] The Company consisted of up to 80 blind men and women, and only members of the company were permitted to collect and distribute alms. The group of extant portraits and their format – small, and painted in oil on paper – suggest the process of social classification connected with reforms that sought to distinguish between the so-called legitimate and the illegitimate poor.[82]

Although details of the commission are unknown, the portraits were in the collection of Paleotti's heirs, suggesting this is a special case in which the archbishop's ideas about portraits are particularly relevant. Paleotti viewed the genre with suspicion, believing it was unchristian to commission a portrait of oneself, a practice he compared to the self-love of Narcissus.[83] Critical of portraits being commissioned by the wrong sorts of people, such as heretics, prostitutes, and illicit lovers, Paleotti insisted instead that only models of virtue and piety should be represented. The human face should be depicted with all its singular defects, moreover, since true representations demonstrate dignity, self-restraint, and thus worth. His demand for radical realism, through which a portrait's external likeness or shape had a moral truth, transformed the artist into the author of a silent sermon.

The irregular surface of the skin, uneven lips, and wrinkled neck of the women, created by Annibale's descriptive facture, engages the viewer's haptic sense. Although not a death mask, the face is therefore like one; the portraits are iconic, but also indexical as if formed by the painter's hand through touch, as if the artist were himself blind.[84] Naturalistic, and freed from conventional accoutrements of status, the portraits engage the viewer directly, as if unmediated by art. In contrast to Moroni's portrait, *The Woman in Red*, here there is no mask, no dissemblance.

The images therefore prompt questions about interiority during the decades in which inwardness was being forged in response to prudence. Central here is the eye to the right of one of the portraits, which contributes to the impression that the women are aware of being seen (Figure 23.9). The representation of the eye may be a sign, as Cavina suggests, of "inner vision," the heightened piety of the blind, or perhaps an indication of the artist's interest in realism.[85] The eye also recalls *ex votos*, and perhaps functioned as a sign for the company, whose members prayed as they solicited alms. With their eyes closed, the women perform the gesture of prayer, and thus convey the transparency between interior virtue and external appearances sought by Paleotti and other reformers. Annibale's extraordinary realism forces the observer to look, to acknowledge the other, even if the eye compels us to look askance.

The Renaissance portrait, as this chapter has proposed, drew attention to the representational weight of the human face and body. In so doing, the genre contributed to a growing split between external appearances and claims about interiority. In contrast to studies that focus on the social or political function of portraits, their content or symbolic meaning, such as the accoutrements of status, my goal has been to highlight some of the representational strategies of the genre during a period in which concerns with likeness became subordinated to representation. Thus I have introduced how artists, using diverse media, worked to document, frame, expose, and interpret the body, and I have suggested how those conventions intersected with the iconography of death, the mirror, biography, character, dissimulation, and sincerity. I have been arguing, then, that portraits contributed to the changing status of the subject through the repeated engagement with the boundaries of the body. Theories of interiority have an ancient lineage, and those writers, such as Aristotle, Horace, and Martial, are echoed in the writing of Gauricus, Vasari, Sansovino, Paleotti, Lomazzo, and Bocchi.[86] In the Renaissance, however, it was the repeated practice of engaging with the image, and the projection of evidence from outside, that constituted interiority.

NOTES

1. Giovanni Anastasio Mosini [pseudonym of Giovanni Antonio Massini] in *Arte di Bologna di Annibale Carracci {1646}*, ed. Alessandro Marabottini (Rome: Edizioni dell'elefante, 1979), xxxviii–ix.
2. Gabriele Paleotti, *Discorso intorno alle imagini sacre et profane {1582}* in Paola Barocchi, ed., *Trattati d'arte del cinque cento fra manierismo e controriforma* (Bari: Laterza, 1960–62), vol. 2, 332–53.
3. Giovanni Paolo Lomazzo, *Trattato dell'arte de la pittura {1584}* (Hildesheim: G. Olms, 1968). Lorne Campbell's translation, *Renaissance Portraits: European Portrait-painting in the 14th, 15th, and 16th Centuries* (New Haven: Yale University Press, 1990), 209–10.
4. Girolamo Cardano, *The Book of My Life* (De vita propria liber), trans. Jean Stoner (New York: Dover, 1962), 20.
5. Giorgio Vasari, *Vite de' più eccellenti architetti, pittori et scultori italiani*, in *Art Theorists of the Italian Renaissance* [electronic resource] (Cambridge, UK: Chadwyck-Healey, 1998).
6. See David Summers, *The Judgment of Sense: Renaissance Naturalism and the Rise of Aesthetics* (Cambridge: Cambridge University Press, 1987), 110–11.
7. Harry Berger, "Fictions of the Pose: Facing the Gaze of Early Modern Portraiture," *Representations* 46 (spring 1994): 87–120.
8. Jacob Burckhardt, *The Civilization of the Renaissance in Italy: An Essay* (London: Phaidon Press, 1960); *Beiträge zur Kunstgeschichte von Italien: das Altarbild – das Porträt in der Malerei – die Sammler* (Basel: G. F. Lendorff, 1898).
9. Philippe-Alain Michaude, *Aby Warburg and the Image in Motion*, trans. Sophie Hawkes (New York: Zone Books, 2004), 31–2.
10. Aby Warburg, "The Art of Portraiture and the Florentine Bourgeoisie (1902)," *The Renewal of Pagan Antiquity: Contributions to the Cultural History of the European Renaissance*, trans. David Britt (Los Angeles: Getty Research Institute for the History of Art and the Humanities, 1999), 186.
11. Sir John Wyndham Pope-Hennessy, *The Portrait in the Renaissance* (New York: Bollingen Foundation/Pantheon Books, [1966]), 3.
12. See Stephen Greenblatt, *Renaissance Self-fashioning from More to Shakespeare* (Chicago: University of Chicago Press, 1980), esp. 1–10.
13. Harry Berger, *Fictions of the Pose: Rembrandt against the Italian Renaissance* (Stanford: Stanford University Press, 2000), 20.
14. Stephen Pepper, "Annibale Carracci's Venetian Portraits," *arte/documento* 13: 199–203.
15. Berger, *Fictions of the Pose*, 27, 4.

16 Harry Berger, *The Absence of Grace: Sprezzatura and Suspicion in Two Renaissance Courtesy Books* (Stanford: Stanford Univesity Press, 2000), 4.
17 Katharine Eisaman Maus, *Inwardness and Theater in the English Renaissance* (Chicago: University of Chicago Press, 1995), 5. For Berger's critique, see *Absence of Grace*, 1–5.
18 John Jeffries Martin, *Myths of Renaissance Individualism* (New York: Palgrave Macmillan, 2004), 113. See also his "Inventing Sincerity, Refashioning Prudence: The Discovery of the Individual in Renaissance Europe," *American Historical Review* 102, 5 (December 1997): 1308–42.
19 E. James Mundy, "Porphyry and the 'Posthumous' Fifteenth-century Portrait," *Pantheon* 46 (1988): 37–43. Similar, if less subtle, claims were made through the depiction of decaying corpses on the reverse of portraits of couples in Germany. See Campbell, *Renaissance Portraits*, 54. See also Jodi Cranston, *Poetics of Portraiture* (Cambridge: Cambridge University Press, 2000), 37–44.
20 Vasari, *Vite*, Vol. 1, Part 2, 485.
21 On Medici portraits and for Poliziano's text, see Karla Langedijk, *The Portraits of the Medici, 15th–18th Centuries* (Florence: Studio per edizione scelte, 1981–7), vol. 2, 1154.
22 On the figures and for historiography, see Hugo Van der Velden, "Medici Votive Images and the Scope and Limits of Likeness," in Nicholas Mann and Luke Syson, eds, *The Image of the Individual: Portraits in the Renaissance* (London: British Museum Press, 1998), 126–37.
23 Vasari, *Vite*, Vol. 1, Part 2, 485.
24 David Piper, *The English Face* (London: Thames & Hudson, 1957), 28–9.
25 On the effigy and terracotta bust, see Carol Galvin and Phillip Lindley, "Pietro Torrigiano's Portrait Bust of King Henry VII," *The Burlington Magazine* 10, no. 1029 (1988) 892–902.
26 Cennino Cennini, *The Craftman's Handbook*, trans. D. V. Thompson (New York: Dover, 1954), 123–7.
27 Pomponius Gauricus, *De sculptura* (1504), ed. and trans. André Chastel and Robert Klein (Geneva: Droz, 1969), 128–9; Campbell's translation, *Renaissance Portraits*, 27.
28 Joseph Leo Koerner, *The Moment of Self-portraiture in German Renaissance Art* (Chicago: University of Chicago Press, 1993), 9; Gauricus, *De sculptura*, 204–5; Frank Zöllner, "Leonardo da Vinci's Portraits: Ginevra de' Benci, Cecilia Gallerani, La Belle Ferronière and Mona Lisa," in *Rafael i Jego Spadkobiercy. Portret Klasyczny w Sztuce Nowozytnej Europy* (Torùn, 2003) (Sztuka i kultura, 4), 157–83.
29 See Georges Didi-Huberman, "Ressemblance Mythifiée et Ressemblance Oubliée chez Vasari: la Legende du Portrait 'Sur le Vif,'" *Mélanges de l'Ecole Française de Rome, Italie et Méditerranée* 106, 2 (1994): 383–432.
30 Hans Belting, *Likeness and Presence: A History of the Image Before the Era of Art*, trans. Edmund Jephcott (Chicago: University of Chicago Press, 1994), 459.
31 Edward V. Gatacre and Laura Dru, "Portraiture in 'Le Cabinet de Cire de Curtius' and its Successor Madame Tussaud's Exhibition," *Ceroplastica* (Congr. Florence, 1975 [1977]), 617; Jean Adhémar, "Les Musées de Cire en France, Curtius, le 'Banquet Royal', les Têtes Coupées," *Gazette des Beaux Arts* 92 (1978) 212, note 4; P. Vitry notes that Bourdin was one of three successful competitors in "Deux Familles de Sculpteurs de la Première Moitié du XVIIe Siècle: les Boudin et les Bourdin," *Gazette des Beaux Arts*.
32 Shakespeare, *Romeo and Juliet*, ed. Blakemore Evans (Cambridge: Cambridge University Press, 2003) 3.3. 126–7, 155–6.
33 These range from merchant to sculptor, navigator to herald, poet to notary. See Jacques Paviot, "The Sitter for Jan van Eyck's 'Leal Sovvenir,'" in *Journal of the Warburg and Courtauld Institutes* 58 (1995): 210–15. For critiques of this kind of art historical detective

work, see Berger, *Fictions of the Pose*, and Didi-Huberman, "The Portrait, the Individual, and the Singular; Remarks on the Legacy of Aby Warburg," in Mann and Syson, eds, *Image of the Individual*, 165–88.

34 Paviot, "Sitter," 215.
35 Valentin Groebner, "Describing the Person, Reading the Signs in Late Medieval and Renaissance Europe: Identity Papers, Vested Figures, and the Limits of Identification, 1400–1600," in Jane Caplan and John Torpey, eds, *Documenting Individual Identity: The Development of State Practices in the Modern World* (Princeton: Princeton University Press, 2001), 20–1.
36 Valentin Groebner, "Inside Out. Clothes, Dissimulation and the Arts of Accounting in the Autobiography of Matthaeus Schwarz (1498–1574)," *Representations* 66 (1999): 52–72; Gabriele Mentges, "Fashion, Time and the Consumption of a Renaissance Man in Germany: The Costume Book of Matthäus Schwarz of Augsburg, 1496–1564," *Gender & History* 14, 3 (November 2002): 382–402.
37 Groebner, "Describing the Person," 24.
38 Campbell, *Renaissance Portraits*, 25.
39 Groebner, "Insides Out," 114, 117.
40 Mentges, "Fashion, Time," 391.
41 Leonardo da Vinci, "Of the Imitable Sciences," in Martin Kemp, ed., *Leonardo on Painting: An Anthology of Writings* (New Haven: Yale University Press, 1989), 20.
42 Pietro Aretino, *Lettere sull'arte*, ed. Ettore Camesasca (Milan: Edizioni del Milione [1957–60]), vol. 1, 225–6, cited by Mary Rogers, "Sonnets on Female Portraits from Renaissance North Italy," *Word and Image* 2 (1986): 293. My thanks to Allyson Burgess Williams for this reference.
43 Patricia Fortini Brown, *Private Lives in Renaissance Venice: Art, Architecture, and the Family* (New Haven: Yale University Press, 2004), 175.
44 Campbell, *Renaissance Portraits*, 66.
45 The panel, *Allegory of Virtue and Vice*, and portrait were painted two years after an assassination attempt on the bishop. The former is in the National Gallery in Washington, DC, and the latter in Naples at the Capodimonte.
46 So striking is Dürer's realism, protected by the cover, that the portrait was taken for a forgery when it was discovered in the nineteenth century. Henning Bock *et al.*, *The Complete Catalogue of the Gemaldegalerie, Berlin* (New York: Abrams, 1986), 74.
47 Leonardo da Vinci, "Of the Imitable Sciences," 20.
48 Ibid., 19.
49 Susan Stewart, *On Longing: Narratives of the Miniature, the Gigantic, the Souvenir, the Collection* (Baltimore: Johns Hopkins University Press, 1984), 125.
50 Victor Stoichita, *The Self-aware Image: An Insight into Erly Modern Meta-painting*, trans. Anne-Marie Clasheen (New York: Cambridge University Press, 1997), 205.
51 Koerner, *Moment of Self-portraiture*, 25.
52 Ibid., 32.
53 Ibid., 9.
54 Campbell, *Renaissance Portraits*, 12, 216; Anthony Bond, Joanna Woodall *et al.*, *Self-portrait: Renaissance to Contemporary* (London: National Portrait Gallery, 2005), 84–5.
55 Vasari, *Vite*, Vol. 2, Part 3a, 232; Stoichita's translation, *Self-Aware Image*, 217.
56 Joanna Woods-Marsden, *Renaissance Self-portraiture: The Visual Construction of Identity and the Social Status of the Artist* (New Haven: Yale University Press, 1998), 35. See also 133–7.
57 Lisa Jardine and Jerry Brotton, *Global Interests: Renaissance Art between East and West* (Ithaca: Cornell University Press, 2000), 42.
58 Franz Babinger, *Mehmed the Conqueror and his Time* (Princeton: Princeton University Press,

1978), 424. On Mehmed's portraits see Esin Atil, "Ottoman Miniature Painting under Sultan Mehmed II," *Ars Orientalis* 9 (1973): 103–20.
59 Esin Atil, "The Image of Süleymân," in Halil Inalcik and Cemal Kafadar, eds, *Süleymân the Second and His Time* (Istanbul: Isis Press, 1993), 334.
60 Günsel Renda, "Portraiture in Islamic Painting," in *Islamic Art, Common Principles, Forms and Themes, Proceedings of the International Symposium held in Istanbul in April 1983*, 227.
61 Filiz Cağman and Zeren Tanindi, "Approval and Disapproval of Images in Islam," in *The Topkapi Saray Museum; The Albums and Illustrated Manuscripts*, trans. J. M. Rogers (London: Thames & Hudson, 1986), 23–4.
62 Giovanbattista della Porta, *Della Fisonomia dell'Uomo* (Parma: Ugo Guanda, 1988), book 2, ch. VII, 164.
63 Pietro Bertelli, *Vite degl'imperatori de'Turchi con le loro effiggie* (Vicenza: Pietro Bertelli, 1599), 31.
64 Francesco Sansovino, "Degli huomini illustri di Casa Orsina," *L'Historia di Casa Orsina* (Venice: Bernardino and Filippo Stagnini, 1565), Libro Quarto, 63r.
65 Ibid.
66 Ibid., 81.
67 Didi-Huberman, "Ressemblance Mythifiée."
68 Michel de Montaigne, "Of Physiognomy," in Donald Frame, ed., *The Complete Essays of Montaigne* (Stanford: Stanford University Press, 1965), 811.
69 Shakespeare, *The Tragedy of Macbeth*, ed. Nicholas Brooke (Oxford: Oxford University Press, 1998), 1.4.11–14, 109.
70 Paolo Pinzio, *Fisionomia* (Lyon, 1550), 50–1.
71 Giovanbattista della Porta, *Della Fisionomia dell'Huomo del Signor Giovanbattista Della Porta Napolitano, Libri Sei* (Venice: Christoforo Tomasini, 1644), 70v.
72 Maus, *Inwardness*, 15.
73 Torquato Accetto, *Della dissimulazione onesta*, ed. Salvatore Silvano Nigro (Turing: Einaudi, 1997).
74 Montaigne, "Of Physiognomy," 814.
75 Ibid., 793.
76 See Pamela Jones, "Art Theory as Ideology: Gabriele Paleotti's Hierarchical Notion of Painting's Universality and Reception," in Claire Farago, ed., *Reframing the Renaissance: Visual Culture in Europe and Latin America, 1450–1650* (New Haven: Yale University Press, 1995), 127–39.
77 Lomazzo, *Scritti sulle arti*, ed. Roberto Paulo Ciardi (Florence: Marchi & Bertolli, 1973–4), vol. 2, 95.
78 Francesco Bocchi, *Ragionamento sopra l'eccellenza del San Giorgio di Donatello* (1584), in Barocchi, 1960–2, vol. 3 (1962), 134–5; cited by Summers, *Judgment of Sense*, 144.
79 On the paintings see Anna Ottani Cavina, "Annibale Carracci's *Paintings of the Blind*," *Emilian Painting of the Sixteenth and Seventeenth Centuries: A Symposium. National Gallery of Art, Washington* (Bologna: Nuova Alfa Editoriale, 1987), 90–9; "Annibale Carracci's Paintings of the Blind: An Addition," *Burlington Magazine* 131 (1989): 28.
80 Michael Fried, *Absorption and Theatricality: Painting and Beholder in the Age of Diderot* (Chicago: University of Chicago Press, 1980).
81 On the Compagnia, see Andrea Farnè, *Le Opere Pie a Bologna: ruolo e storia della compagnia de'poveri vergognosi. Storia, patrimonio, possibilità attuali e prospettive future dell'Opera Pia Poveri Vergognosi* (Bologna: Le Coq Editori, 1989), 121–5.
82 On reforms, see Nicholas Terpstra, "Confraternities and Public Charity: Modes of Civic Welfare in Early Modern Italy," in John Patrick Donnelly and Michael W. Maher, eds,

Confraternities and Catholic Reform in Italy, France, and Spain (Kirksville, Mo.: Thomas Jefferson University Press, 1999), 97–121.
83 On Paleotti, see Hannah Baader's commentary, 303–06, "Gabriele Paleotti: Ähnlichkeit als Katgorie der Moral (1582)," in Rudolf Preimesberger, Hannah Baader, and Nicola Suthor, *Porträt* [Geschichte der kalassischen Bildgattungen in Quellentexten und Kommentaren Bc. 2] (Berlin: Reimer, 1999), 297–306.
84 See Jacques Derrida, *Memoirs of the Blind: The Self-portrait and Other Ruins*, trans. Pascale-Anne Brault and Michael Naas (Chicago: Chicago University Press, 1993).
85 Cavina, "Annibale Carracci's Paintings," 96.
86 See John Shearman, "Portraits and Poets," in *Only Connect . . . Art and the Spectator in the Italian Renaissance* (Princeton: Princeton University Press, 1992), 108–48; Summers, *Judgment of Sense*.

SUGGESTIONS FOR FURTHER READING

Primary sources

Da Vinci, Leonardo. "Of the Imitable Sciences," in Martin Kemp, ed., *Leonardo on Painting: An Anthology of Writings*. New Haven: Yale University Press, 1989.

Lomazzo, Gian Paolo. *Scritti sulle arti*, ed. Roberto Paulo Ciardi. Florence: Marchi & Bertolli, 1973–4.

Montaigne, Michel de. "Of Physiognomy," in *The Complete Essays of Montaigne*, ed. and trans. Donald Frame. Stanford: Stanford University Press, 1965.

Paleotti, Gabriele. *Discorso intorno alle imagini sacre et profane*. Bologna: Arnaldo Forni, 1990 (first published 1582).

Vasari, Giorgio. *Vite de' più eccellenti architetti, pittori et scultori italiani*, in *Art Theorists of the Italian Renaissance* [electronic resource]. Cambridge, UK: Chadwyck-Healey, c. 1998.

Secondary sources

Belting, Hans. *Likeness and Presence: A History of the Image before the Era of Art*, trans. Edmund Jephcott. Chicago: University of Chicago Press, 1994.

Berger, Harry. "Fictions of the Pose: Facing the Gaze of Early Modern Portraiture." *Representations* 46 (spring 1994): 87–120.

——— *Fictions of the Pose: Rembrandt Against the Italian Renaissance*. Stanford: Stanford University Press, 2000.

Boehm, Gottfried. *Bildnis und Individuum: über den Ursprung der Porträtmalerei in der italienischen Renaissance*. Munich: Prestel-Verlag, 1985.

Bond, Anthony and Joanna Woodall et al. *Self-portrait: Renaissance to Contemporary*. London: National Portrait Gallery, 2005.

Burckhardt, Jacob. *Beiträge zur Kunstgeschichte von Italien: das Altarbild – das Porträt in der Malerei – die Sammler*. Basel: G. F. Lendorff, 1898.

Campbell, Lorne. *Renaissance Portraits: European Portrait-painting in the 14th, 15th, and 16th Centuries*. New Haven: Yale University Press, 1990.

Cranston, Jodi. *The Poetics of Portraiture in the Italian Renaissance*. Cambridge: Cambridge University Press, 2000.

Didi-Huberman, Georges. "Ressemblance Mythifiée et Ressemblance Oubliée chez Vasari: la Legende du Portrait 'Sur le Vif.'" *Mélanges de l'Ecole Francaise de Rome, Italie et Méditerranée* 106, 2 (1994): 383–432.

Greenblatt, Stephen. *Renaissance Self-fashioning from More to Shakespeare*. Chicago: University of Chicago Press, 1980.

Groebner, Valentin. "Inside Out. Clothes, Dissimulation and the Arts of Accounting in the Autobiography of Matthaeus Schwarz (1498–1574)." *Representations* 66 (1999): 52–72.

—— "Describing the Person, Reading the Signs in Late Medieval and Renaissance Europe: Identity Papers, Vested Figures, and the Limits of Identification, 1400–1600," in Jane Caplan and John Torpey, eds, *Documenting Individual Identity: The Development of State Practices in the Modern World*. Princeton: Princeton University Press, 2001.

Koerner, Joseph Leo. *The Moment of Self-portraiture in German Renaissance Art*. Chicago: University of Chicago Press, 1993.

Mann, Nicholas and Luke Syson, eds. *The Image of the Individual; Portraits in the Renaissance*. London: British Museum Press, 1998.

Martin, John Jeffries. "Inventing Sincerity, Refashioning Prudence: The Discovery of the Individual in Renaissance Europe." *American Historical Review* 102, 5 (December 1997): 1308–42.

—— *Myths of Renaissance Individualism*. New York: Palgrave Macmillan, 2004.

Maus, Katharine Eisaman. *Inwardness and Theater in the English Renaissance*. Chicago: University of Chicago Press, 1995.

Preimesberger, Rudolf, Hannah Baader, and Nicola Suthor. *Porträt* [Geschichte der kalassischen Bildgattungen in Quellentexten und Kommentaren Bc. 2] Berlin: Reimer, 1999.

Rosand, David. "The Portrait, the Courtier, and Death," in *Castiglione: The Ideal and the Real in Renaissance Culture*. New Haven: Yale University Press, 1983, 91–129.

Simons, Patricia. "Portraiture, Portrayal, and Idealizaton: Ambiguous Individualism in Representations of Renaissance Women." In Alison Brown, ed. *Language and Images of Renaissance Italy*. Oxford: Clarendon Press, 1995.

Stoichita, Victor. *The Self-aware Image: An Insight into Early Modern Meta-painting*. Trans. Anne-Marie Clasheen. New York: Cambridge University Press, 1997.

Summers, David. *The Judgment of Sense: Renaissance Naturalism and the Rise of Aesthetics*. Cambridge: Cambridge University Press, 1987.

Warburg, Aby. "The Art of Portraiture and the Florentine Bourgeoisie (1902)," in *The Renewal of Pagan Antiquity: Contributions to the Cultural History of the European Renaissance*, trans. David Britt. Los Angeles: Getty Research Institute for the History of Art and the Humanities, 1999.

Woodall, Joanna, ed. *Portraiture: Facing the Subject*. Manchester: Manchester University Press, 1997.

Woods-Marsden, Joanna. *Renaissance of Self-portraiture: The Visual Construction of Identity and the Social Status of the Artist*. New Haven: Yale University Press, 1998.

CHAPTER TWENTY-FOUR

OBJECTS AND IDENTITY

Antonio de' Medici and the Casino at
San Marco in Florence

Jacqueline Marie Musacchio

The material culture of Italian Renaissance life encompassed objects as diverse as monumental fresco cycles, sculpted portrait busts, and domestic devotional tabernacles, as well as decorative and functional maiolica, painted furniture, both daily and festive clothing, and innumerable objects in between; all had a prominent place in the construction of individual, familial, and corporate identity. These objects increased in variety and number during the Renaissance, in ways we are only now beginning to understand; indeed, after many years of scholarly neglect the demands and patterns of consumption in this pre-industrial age have become subjects of close study. Although a surprising number of objects survive, few do so in their original settings and a great many of them are lost, understood today only through vague or indecipherable references in inventories, diaries, or letters, comments in literature or legislation, or representations in contemporary paintings, prints, or sculptures.

This neglect can also be attributed to modern biases; many of these objects fall into the category of "minor" or "decorative" arts, while others are not considered under the umbrella of the arts at all. But no such distinction existed in the Italian Renaissance. Artists worked on special commissions to produce altarpieces for churches, but they also made window shades, enameled girdles, and painted drug jars to sell from their workshop shelves to whomever walked in and wanted to buy them. When examined with care, every one of these objects reveals information about contemporary taste and patronage, often in regard to broad categories of people otherwise lost to history, such as middle-class women or members of religious orders whose individuality was suppressed by societal norms. Yet the possibility of reading history from things is neglected in much of the scholarship on this period.[1] Fortunately a number of recent publications demonstrate the benefits of enlarging what might be deemed the confines of traditional art history to include a close look at exactly these things, thereby illuminating the lives of a wide range of previously unknown or ignored individuals. The work of Mary Hollingsworth on Cardinal Ippolito d'Este and Caroline P. Murphy on Felice della Rovere, to cite only two cases, places art history within a wider cultural context, employing methodologies more typical of economic and social history or biography to shed new light on their subjects. Particularly interesting, in these cases, are the relationships between the individuals and their settings; indeed, the world of goods can reveal much about the lives of individuals, especially when these goods were intended by their otherwise disenfranchised owners as a means to assert identity.[2]

If the Renaissance truly was, as Jacob Burckhardt famously alleged, a remarkably accepting time for bastards,[3] we should know far more about figures like Antonio de' Medici, the illegitimate son of Florentine Grand Duke Francesco I de' Medici and the woman who became his second wife, Grand Duchess Bianca Cappello. Yet Antonio has been only a minor figure in Medici studies. He does, however, become more three-dimensional when seen within the context and contents of his home, the Casino at San Marco in Florence. The Casino contained a performance space, the setting for the numerous entertainments with which Antonio was associated, as well as a wide range of objects, from alchemical supplies and porcelain plates to rhinoceros horns and a vast array of portraits, both Medicean and more broadly European. The activities that took place at the Casino, and the objects that filled it, reflected Antonio's life as an impresario, experimenter, and aesthete, a man who was denied the ducal throne and had his parentage disparaged but who nonetheless impressed and influenced those around him. The Casino was critical to this; it gave him a way to manipulate his public identity and affirm his princely identity to the outside world.

Such manipulations were especially necessary for a figure such as Antonio, since both he and his mother had a problematic relationship to the Medici family. Bianca Cappello was a Venetian noblewoman who eloped to Florence with the penniless clerk Pietro Buonaventuri in 1563. Shortly after they arrived, Bianca met the ducal heir Francesco de' Medici and began what became a 14-year-long affair; Pietro's acceptance of his wife's new role was rewarded with lucrative employment and extravagant favors. However, in 1565, Francesco married Giovanna of Austria, daughter of the deceased Habsburg Emperor Ferdinand I and sister of current Emperor Maximilian II. The match elevated Medici status in the larger European arena, but did not make a happy marriage: while Giovanna gave birth to eight children, Bianca and Francesco continued their affair. Pietro was murdered in 1572, with the tacit approval of Francesco, whose power only grew greater after he succeeded his father as Grand Duke in 1574. Now as a widow and the Grand Duke's lover, Bianca enjoyed even greater freedom, and she gave birth to Francesco's first son, Antonio, in 1576. Two years later, a mere two months after Giovanna's unexpected death, Francesco and Bianca married. They celebrated the union publicly in 1579 with several days of festivities, during which Bianca received the titles of True and Particular Daughter of the Venetian Republic and Grand Duchess of Florence. Yet Antonio's path to the ducal throne was hardly secured, since his legitimate half-brother, Filippo, born to Francesco and Giovanna in 1577, was considered the rightful Medici heir by many.

Certainly before, and even after, she became Grand Duchess, Bianca was conscious of her status at court and keen to enhance it. Her affair with Francesco was common knowledge, and for much of it both were married to others. By usurping the place of Francesco's first wife, a deeply devout woman whose Habsburg ancestry was critical to the city in both political and economic terms, Bianca angered the Florentines. They questioned her morality and expenditures, condemned her as syphilitic, and blamed her for almost anything that went wrong in the city.[4] A verse sung in

Florence's streets capitalized on the rhyme between *veneziana*, or Venetian woman, and *puttana*, or whore.[5] Francesco only further exacerbated the situation; he was seen, quite rightly, as aloof and disinterested in Florence and the Florentines, preferring instead to spend time in his experimental laboratories. In fact, Francesco's reign was marked by economic decline and strained political relationships, at least partly brought on by his apparent dislike of governing. This all worked against the grand ducal couple, so much so that an ambassador to the court reported back to the Duke of Urbino that Bianca and Francesco found little favor with their Florentine citizens.[6]

Bianca's extensive and expensive patronage activities combated some of these allegations. Because she eloped without parental consent, she had no assets of her own; Francesco essentially funded her both before and after she became his wife. She used this money wisely. In addition to real estate and clothing purchases, Bianca employed architects, painters, sculptors, weavers, and musicians to ornament her residences and arrange elaborate court festivities. These residences became the centers for meetings, musical and theatrical performances, and celebrations to entertain both Florentines and court guests. The events were calculated to impress and influence, reflecting positively both on the Medici and Bianca herself. In gratitude for her munificent patronage – or, at times, in the hopes of it – major figures such as Marco Fabrizio Caroso, Moderata Fonte, Vincenzo Galilei, Francesco Sansovino, and Torquato Tasso dedicated poems, songs, and books to Bianca. Her close ties to the arts certainly set her apart from Francesco's first wife, Giovanna, who spent little time or money on such activities. But Bianca's interests were not all self-serving; she received a Golden Rose for her piety and charity from Pope Sisto V, she corresponded with holy women Maria Maddalena de' Pazzi and Caterina Ricci, and she supported the Jewish population during the formation of Florence's ghetto. Indeed, Bianca's upbringing as the privileged daughter of a Venetian noble household must have provided some impetus for her behavior. Similarly, the privations of her first impecunious months in Florence probably had a role, as did the model of Francesco's generous patronage. But the strongest motivation must have been her finely honed instincts for self-preservation and self-aggrandizement, which prompted her to use what funds she had to her greatest possible advantage.

Bianca knew that the best way to secure this advantage was to ensure that her son, Antonio, became the next grand duke of Florence. She tried to elevate the boy in Francesco's affections as much as possible, especially once it became apparent that she could not bring another, legitimate, pregnancy to term. Letters purported to be from five-year-old Antonio to his father betray an improbable grasp of language and grammar, no doubt intended to impress Francesco with the boy's precocious intellect.[7] And letters from Francesco back to his young son seem to indicate a true degree of affection, with admonitions to be obedient accompanied by special gifts; Antonio was cautioned not to sweat when he played ball and sent some dried fish as a treat.[8] In 1580 Francesco purchased the Marquisate of Capestrano for Antonio and four years later, at Francesco's persistent urging, the king of Spain recognized Antonio as Francesco's son and made Capestrano a principality and Antonio a prince. Bianca apparently had a role in the king's decision; she sent him a precious silver and ebony Calvary altarpiece as part of her campaign.[9] Bianca's motivations are easy to understand, since her success was inexorably tied to that of her son. But Francesco's desire to see Antonio named a prince must have been due, in part, to the death of his legitimate son, Filippo, in 1582, which left Antonio as his only male offspring. Nevertheless, Francesco's affection for the boy certainly seemed genuine to others; that same year a Venetian ambassador, analyzing the familial relationships among the Medici, noted that Francesco loved Antonio the most among his four surviving children.[10] To promote his young prince, Francesco legitimized him and named him as heir; Antonio traveled with an honor guard and received drawing lessons from Jacopo Ligozzi. This made it clear to ambassadors and Florentines alike that Francesco was grooming the boy to inherit the ducal throne.

All of this changed in October 1587, when Antonio was eleven years old: Francesco and Bianca died unexpectedly, less than a day apart, and Francesco's younger brother, Cardinal Ferdinando, became Grand Duke. The overall health of the ducal couple had been compromised for some years, Francesco's by his various experiments and severe dietary regime and Bianca's by fertility treatments and a probable case of edema. But the cause of their deaths remains mysterious; some believe they contracted a virulent infection in the Tuscan countryside and died after a short illness, while more recent investigations imply that Ferdinando poisoned the couple for his own political gain.[11] In either case, Antonio's opportunity to become Grand Duke died with them. Ferdinando took great care to consolidate his own power while further diminishing Antonio's. In March 1588 he renewed Antonio's title of Prince of Capestrano and granted him Francesco and Bianca's bequests; in return, Antonio recognized Ferdinando as Grand Duke and, when he came of age in 1594, he renounced this inheritance, retaining only the right to use it for the rest of his life and a yearly stipend, and entered the celibate order of the Knights of Jerusalem.[12] Meanwhile, Ferdinando relinquished his cardinal's hat in 1589 to marry Cristina of Lorraine, with whom he had nine children, including his eventual heir, Cosimo II. Although Antonio had four illegitimate children, Ferdinando's careful plotting ensured that his own son inherited the throne, rather than Antonio or Antonio's children, and Antonio's inheritance returned to the Medici. This was the best possible scenario for Ferdinando, allowing him to retain the duchy and its assets for his own immediate bloodline while appearing magnanimous to his orphaned nephew.

But privately Ferdinando also signed a declaration stating that he did not recognize Antonio as Francesco's son and he almost certainly concealed Francesco's testament, which named the boy heir; indeed, Antonio may have never known of his father's precise testamentary wishes.[13] While Ferdinando was loyal to Francesco during his brother's lifetime, that loyalty did not extend beyond the grave. Fortunately for Ferdinando, family ambition and personal ambition were allied here. It was in the best interests of the Medici that an older male of unimpeachable origin become Grand Duke, rather than a recently legitimized eleven-year-old boy. For Ferdinando, considered a candidate for the papal tiara at the conclave of 1585, the grand ducal crown was an excellent consolation prize. And his treatment of Bianca's memory hinged on these ambitions. Shortly after Ferdinando became Grand Duke, he described his deceased sister-in-law as *pessima*, or wicked; his secretary was even more explicit and referred to her as a concubine.[14] Ferdinando arranged for the removal of Bianca's heraldry from prominent locations, replacing it with either the Medici *palle* or Giovanna's Habsburg device.[15] His efforts to erase her from the Medici family expanded beyond her heraldry; in fact, several texts published in the early seventeenth century omitted Bianca from the family altogether.[16] Indeed, two months after her death Urbino's ambassador to Florence observed that Ferdinando had extinguished even the memory of Bianca.[17] And of course, without Bianca Antonio did not exist, and his potential to challenge the ducal throne disappeared.

But Ferdinando knew he could not completely eliminate Bianca from the historical record. So he needed some assurance that later Florentines would not find fault with the succession of his bloodline. To achieve this, he cast aspersions on Antonio's birth, fabricating a cache of supporting documents based around a stated deathbed confession from one of Bianca's associates.[18] The documents alleged that Antonio was neither Bianca's nor Francesco's son, but instead a baby Bianca obtained after faking a pregnancy in her desperation to produce an heir. Yet there were no persistent rumors to this effect while Francesco and Bianca were alive or immediately thereafter. Even the adamant anti-Mediceans Bastiano Arditi, who wrote a condemnatory diary, and Giovanvettorio Soderini, who circulated a letter with verses describing Bianca as a whore, witch, and enchanter, did not accuse her of such a crime.[19] Furthermore, accounts of Bianca's life written during Ferdinando's reign, by the Italian novelist Celio Malespini and the English traveler Fynes Moryson, capitalized on the titillating – and often fictional – aspects of her biography but never questioned Antonio's birth.[20] Nevertheless, as these allegations spread, they formed the basis for a number of romantic novels, operas, plays, and paintings. This revised history peaked following the publication of Riguccio Galluzzi's authorized history of the Medici duchy in 1781, a comprehensive text that was the first to utilize Ferdinando's fabricated documents to their fullest advantage.[21]

The later dissemination of this information would have pleased Ferdinando. He was eager to establish his family on a surer footing than Francesco had left it, and he did everything in his power to achieve this goal, even if it meant stepping over his nephew and spreading rumors about the boy's birth. The documents are silent about Antonio's feelings. But the tragedies of Antonio's childhood, losing both his parents at age eleven and falling victim to his uncle's machinations, must have had a grave impact on him throughout his life. It is certainly not surprising that contemporaries described the boy as melancholic and silent.[22] Yet as Antonio grew older he was unswervingly dutiful to both his uncle and to the Medici family. Antonio undertook trips abroad and reported pertinent information back at his uncle's behest. His proximity was recognized and his influence on the Grand Duke was courted by others. In fact, Antonio was an important part of Ferdinando's household, and then that of Ferdinando's son, Cosimo II, and, at the end of his life, that of Cosimo's son Ferdinando II, the last two largely dominated by the widowed Grand Duchesses Cristina of Lorraine and Maria Maddalena of Austria. Antonio even named his own daughter Maria Maddalena, certainly in homage to the Grand Duchess herself.

However dutiful a Medici Antonio may have been, the simple fact that he never received the ducal throne as his father intended casts him as a marginal member of the family, a legitimized bastard left to a peripheral existence amid swirling rumors about his mother's character. Elite bastards like Antonio reacted to their status in different ways. For those who were lauded by their parents and provided with every privilege, as Cesare, Juan, and Lucrezia Borgia were by their father, Pope Alexander VI, illegitimacy was only a peripheral issue. Others were more sensitive to the circumstances of their birth, and their behavior reflected that sensitivity. The illegitimate Leon Battista Alberti, denied much of the inheritance his father left him by his Alberti relations, used the dialogue in his *Della famiglia* as a way to come to terms with his own position and the treatment of illegitimate children in general.[23] Felice della Rovere used her hard-won assets to purchase property that announced her connection to her father, Pope Giulio II, and to establish herself as an influential member of Roman society; she particularly treasured a diamond-studded crucifix Giulio gave her, and spent many years trying to retrieve it after she was forced to relinquish it as ransom during the Sack of Rome.[24] Even illegitimate girls of noble families who entered convents brought family possessions to fill their cloistered cells.[25] That these very disparate bastards all sought tangible ways to assert their identities is a poignant reminder of the burden of illegitimacy during this period, and the effort it sometimes took to overcome it. Antonio, technically a cleric himself and therefore similar in many ways to the cloistered girls cited above, was no exception. For some illegitimate children – or adults – the physical connection to their natal family through objects may have been the most obvious way to exert some control, no matter how minor, over their birthright.

Antonio's public efforts to emphasize his part in and contribution to the Medici family began in earnest in 1600, at the marriage of his half-sister Maria to Henri IV of France.[26] This marriage was of enormous benefit to Florence, and its arrangement was the political coup of Ferdinando's reign. Antonio was responsible for one part of the accompanying celebrations, a pastoral comedy performed on October 6, 1600 in the Palazzo Pitti chamber associated with Antonio's name.[27] Ferdinando would not have asked Antonio to stage such an important event without prior experience, although there is no evidence of his earlier efforts in this field. On this occasion, the performance was Ottavio Rinuccini's *Euridice*, with music by Iacopo Peri; it has been described as the earliest surviving opera, demonstrating Antonio's appreciation and patronage of new developments in music.[28] Following these Florentine celebrations, Antonio traveled as part of Maria's entourage to her new home in France, not returning until early January of the following year.

Ironically, at this same time Antonio's status as a Medici was increasingly minimized by the Grand Duke's own growing family, and he had to be aware of the efforts to disparage – or even erase – his very identity. This must have caused considerable angst on his part. But he had very few ways to establish his own Medicean identity. In fact, his only real option was to take advantage of the possibilities inherent in his home, the Casino at San Marco. Built by Bernardo Buontalenti in 1567, the Casino was the original location of Francesco's various laboratories.[29] Francesco certainly considered these laboratories, and the space they first occupied, as one of his most valuable assets, and he planned for Antonio to inherit the Casino and its contents from an early date.[30] Ferdinando acquiesced to this part of Francesco's bequest, certainly at least in part because the Casino was a good location for his increasingly marginalized nephew. Although elaborate and well furnished, it could not compete with the other grand ducal residences at the Palazzo Pitti, the Palazzo Vecchio, and the Palazzo Medici in terms of history or status, and it was removed from the center of the city, far down the via Larga across from the San Marco complex. But this did not seem to bother Antonio; after renovating and rearranging the building to suit his needs, Antonio moved into the Casino in 1597.

He began holding musical events and banquets there by 1602, entertaining both the ducal household and visiting dignitaries; the Casino's somewhat distant location did not prohibit Antonio from contributing to some of the more important Medici activities of the period. The visitors Antonio hosted included cardinals Montalto and del Monte (1602), his own brother-in-law, the Duke of Mantua (1603), Archduke Maximilian (1604), Alfonso and Luigi d'Este and their mother, Antonio's aunt Virginia (1605), and Cardinal Gonzaga (1610). They were entertained with productions of Jacopo Pagnini's *I morti e i vivi* (1602 and 1603), Michelangelo Buonarroti the Younger's *Nascita d'Ercole* (1605) and *La Tancia* (1611), Francesco d'Ambra's *La Cofanaria* (1613), and Giovanni Villifranchi da Volterra's *La Greca Schiava* (1618), among others.[31] Because most of the musicians in the city were in the service of the Grand Duke, Antonio's use of them for his entertainments must have met with official approval, further indication that his Casino activities were considered an important part of Medici life. And even with his limited income, Antonio managed to act as a patron in a variety of ways. He supported the training of the *castrato* Giovanni Gualberto Magli, and he employed Domenico Visconti as his personal musician; Magli had a chamber in the Casino, and Visconti, who dedicated a book of madrigals to Antonio, received a residence nearby.[32] Visconti's expression of thanks (and its accompanying hope for future patronage) was not uncommon; a number of composers, including Antonio Brunelli and Raffaello Rontani, dedicated work to either Antonio or his mistress.[33] Antonio also sponsored the Accademia degli Elevati, a group of progressive musicians and literati prominent in Florence at that time.[34] This range of activities demonstrates Antonio's esteem in the musical community and the way he used his patronage to improve his standing in the grand ducal household.

Of course, this behavior was very much like that of his mother. Like Bianca, Antonio was an outsider among the Medici, so it makes sense that his memories of the way Bianca defined herself, both through her activities and her objects, influenced his behavior. This is particularly clear in the Casino, where Antonio used its well-furnished chambers to express his identity to the outside world. As a boy Antonio would have been well acquainted with Bianca's various chambers. And Bianca in turn knew Eleonora of Toledo's former apartment in the Palazzo Vecchio; Eleonora's chambers had had a decidedly public function, and Bianca certainly wanted hers to achieve the same status.[35] Like Eleonora before her, Bianca created spaces that reflected both her individual and her marital identities. In addition to commissioning work by Francesco Morandini, Jacques Bylivelt, Bernardo Lomazzi, and Alessandro Allori to fill her chambers, Bianca received many objects as gifts from prominent figures in Italian and European politics and religion. These included a diamond collar from the Venetian Senate, a mother-of-pearl goblet from Pope Gregorio XIII, an elaborate mirror from King Philip II of Spain, a crystal and gold sculpture of Christ and the Virgin from Cardinal Luigi d'Este, and a gold goblet by Benvenuto Cellini and two Mexican feather mosaics from Cardinal Ferdinando.[36] A courtier sent her Botticelli's two small Judith panels, and dealers supplied her with antiquities, medals, and gems to complement these items.[37] This fantastic assemblage served her well; invitations to see Bianca's splendid chambers were extended to visiting dignitaries, on whom they made a great impression. One ambassador described her rooms as "full of the most delicious things."[38] Such a reaction could only elevate Bianca's reputation, something she both craved and, given her rather negative public perception, required.

Antonio must have been aware of his mother's motivations. A meticulous inventory of the Casino, prepared 13 days after his death in 1621, reveals a great deal about how Antonio constructed his identity. The chamber where he died contained an extraordinary amount of money and documents. Since the bedchamber of an Italian Renaissance home was traditionally the location for the most prized possessions, this is not surprising. But it may have been that, sensing mortality, Antonio tried to order his affairs. He had documents regarding his agreement with Ferdinando following the death of Francesco and Bianca, as well as information about the legitimization and inheritance of his own four children, and investitures and dispensations from various rulers, indicating Antonio's substantial national and international reputation. This chamber also contained a privilege to excavate mines near Prato, numerous books and manuscripts, alchemical supplies, a wild boar's tooth, and a box of pine nut medicinals from Peru.

The diversity of these objects is telling. Like his father before him, Antonio was extremely interested in experimentation, and this interest was reflected throughout his home. He continued Francesco's work in the Casino's laboratory; his reputation in the field, and his willingness to patronize others engaged in similar activities, was widely recognized.[39] Galileo Galilei's discovery of scaling laws was announced in a letter to Antonio in 1609, and Galileo's description of Jupiter in another letter anticipated the more public description in his *Starry Messenger* of 1610.[40] Antonio even had glass telescopic lenses, evidence that he not only read about Galileo's discoveries but also actively pursued their possibilities on his own. In 1612 Antonio Neri dedicated his treatise on glass production, *L'arte vetraria* (*The Art of Glass*), to Antonio, and several copies of it were in the Casino. Antonio's engagement with these various endeavors did much to bolster his reputation in certain circles. He was in fact an avid experimenter. A receipt for the purchase of aquavit, as well as the supplies to produce it, indicates Antonio's interest in tempering metals.[41] He wrote an unpublished metallurgy treatise, partly based on the work of the early sixteenth-century Swiss physician and scientist Paracelsus, and at least three manuscript versions of this treatise were kept in the Casino.[42] In addition, there were instruments, books, manuscripts, recipes, chunks of minerals, gold coins, and envelopes and ampoules filled with what was described, intriguingly, as alchemical dust.

During this period, alchemy was closely tied to porcelain production. Antonio's father, Francesco, was the first westerner to produce porcelain successfully, although his was soft-paste, rather than true, hard-paste porcelain. These experiments took place at the Casino, with the assistance of Bernardo Buontalenti and Flaminio Fontana, beginning around 1575; some 59 pieces survive, all painted in imitation of coveted eastern wares.[43] Antonio inherited more than 4,000 various ceramic wares from his father, encompassing real imported porcelain, Francesco's own productions, and Italian maiolica painted to resemble both.[44] Although Antonio did buy ten pieces of Iznik ceramics, most of his purchases were probably of less expensive earthenware or maiolica, their cost an important consideration for a Medici bastard on a limited stipend.[45]

Because of these financial constraints, Antonio never lived on the scale of his legitimate Medici relations. But he did the best he could with what he had. Indeed, the fabulous items scattered throughout the Casino make it clear that, despite his economic situation, Antonio lived like the prince he rightfully was. A dozen items in the Casino were described as explicitly ancient, ranging from a bronze flask to a marble Hercules. This seems like a small number, considering both the contemporary appreciation of antiquities and the obvious example of his uncle Ferdinando, who had an extensive collection from his time as a cardinal in Rome. But it may well have been Antonio's financial inability to compete with Ferdinando that limited his acquisition of antiquities beyond what he inherited. He certainly seemed more interested in other things, accumulating an eclectic assemblage of fantastic but comparatively inexpensive items, many of which must have come to him as part of his inheritance from his parents, now rearranged in the Casino to best meet his own needs. Antonio had a carved ox horn; a model of a sled, a German child's pistol, an ostrich egg bowl, a gilt copper elephant with a clock that chimed the hours, a dried head, said to be from a dragon, and a silver lizard. Like his mother with her feather mosaics, Antonio was interested in the new world; in addition to his Peruvian medicinals, he had a greenstone mask from Teotihuacán.[46] Antonio had a license for a chapel in the Casino, and he furnished it with hangings, vases, candleholders, a Pietà tapestry, and an altar frontal with the Medici arms. He had a spinet, an organ, and a lyre, as well as various musical texts, testimony to the performances that took place in the Casino, almost certainly in the Hall of Comedies, which was decorated with a perspective scene.[47] And there were several objects from Antonio's travels on Ferdinando's behest with the Imperial troops in the 1590s, including a Hungarian coat of mail and an intarsiated gun from Archduke Mattias of Austria.

Of particular interest are the paintings, sculptures, and decorative arts in the Casino, the great majority of which were kept in the gallery, a showplace that all his guests would have visited. Most of these date to an earlier period and were likely from his parents' estate, such as the *Adoration of the Magi* paintings by Leonardo and Botticelli, Pontormo's *Expulsion of Adam and Eve*, and Rosso Fiorentino's *Moses and the Daughters of Jethro*. These were major paintings by major artists; the Casino also contained work by Michelangelo, Raphael, Albrecht Dürer, and Lavinia Fontana, among others. Sculpture at the Casino included a version of the famous Marsyas statuette known as the *Scared Nude* (*Ignudo della paura*) for its stance resembling a frightened figure; another version of this statuette had been in the collection of Antonio's most illustrious ancestor, Lorenzo *il Magnifico*. There were a number of sculptures by Giambologna and his workshop, including, when Antonio first arrived at the Casino, a fountain with *Samson Slaying a Philistine*. This fountain was disassembled on the order of Ferdinando in 1601 – certainly a reminder that he really owned all that Antonio had – and sent to Spain as a gift to the Duke of Lerma.[48] But Antonio retained many smaller and obviously less valuable bronzes by Giambologna, including those of a bull, a horse, and Hercules battling Antaeus. He also had a statuette of Morgante, one of the dwarves popular in the ducal households. Antonio would have known these dwarves; indeed, a dwarf's bedchamber was near his suite in the Pitti, and Antonio was portrayed with an unidentified dwarf in a now-lost painting.[49]

The statuette of Morgante is one example of the most notable, and the most revealing, aspect of Antonio's estate: the great number of portraits. There were at least 139 portraits in the Casino, distributed among 30 different chambers, but the highest concentration was in Antonio's gallery. These portraits included most current and past Medici, the Duke and Duchess of Mantua, the queens of England, France, Spain, and Cyprus, the kings of France and Spain, emperors Frederick III and Charles V, popes Paul III and Pius V, and various members of the House of Austria. They did not form a strictly unified group, conceived from the start to work together thematically and compositionally. Instead, the earlier ones must have come from his parents' estate, while others, depicting Antonio's contemporaries, must have been acquisitions he made himself. His choices are revealing. As the resident and, ostensibly, the owner of the Casino and its contents, Antonio could have removed any of the portraits he did not want, hanging others he deemed more appropriate in their place. However, although he had two long affairs and fathered four children, only a single portrait of one of his lovers, and none at all of his children, was found in the Casino. Instead, the faces of the Medici and their Italian and European allies stared down at him on a daily basis. Clearly Antonio saw the Casino as a way to promote his princely identity. These portraits surrounded Antonio with an extended family, and, ironically, in their static nature they were more benevolent than his real family. Their very presence allowed Antonio to claim not only his blood relation with the Medici but also his links to other European houses. Although he had no legal recourse to what should have been his inheritance, and his throne, Antonio could celebrate and advertise his status via the portraits in his Casino, a subtle but effective message.

The inspiration for this very deliberate display was almost certainly the *Serie aulica*, or courtly series, the collection of portraits of Medici family members and relations originally commissioned by his father, Francesco, and then continued by later Grand Dukes to line the Uffizi corridors and convey Medicean power and prestige to all who passed.[50] Neither Bianca nor Antonio formed part of the Uffizi series, although Allori had been hired to paint their double portrait for inclusion in it right before the ducal couple died; in fact, as we will see, Antonio had that painting in the Casino. But in the Uffizi, a posthumous double portrait of Giovanna of Austria and her son, Filippo, hung – and still hangs – in the position accorded to Francesco's wife. With this very blatant omission, Antonio could not avoid the fact that he and his mother were not part of the official face of the grand ducal family. This was not because he was illegitimate; bastards were nothing new to the Medici family tree, and, for example, his equally illegitimate predecessors Duke Alessandro and Pope Clemente VII were both represented in the *Serie aulica*. But Bianca and Antonio were an alternative to Ferdinando's bloodline, and as such they were not appropriate for inclusion in this display of familial authority. The Casino provided Antonio with a place to right the historical record and create his own *Serie aulica*, a far from methodical grouping, but one that was appropriate to his own needs.

The critical figure in Antonio's modified *Serie aulica* was, of course, his father. The Casino contained at least ten portraits representing Francesco. With these, Antonio was able to assert his lineage in no uncertain terms. But the most popular subject among Antonio's portraits, represented eleven times, was Maria de' Medici, Antonio's half-sister and arguably the most important Medici on an international scale. Antonio's connection to Maria was critical; not only did he participate in her wedding but they were closest in age among Medici of their generation, having grown up in adjoining chambers in the Palazzo Pitti.[51] Their relationship must have been one reason Antonio found favor with successive Grand Dukes; even when Maria's power in France was waning, it did not make sense to mistreat her favored half-brother. The Casino also contained portraits of Maria's husband Henri IV, and son Louis XIII, as well as the earlier French royals Henri III and Caterina de' Medici. The French presence in the Casino must have been due to the ties Antonio felt to his half-sister, both personally and politically. And certainly Maria and Francesco were Antonio's most important ties to his birth family, providing him with a secure Medici identity by their very presence, so their predominance seems logical.

The only other person represented with such frequency was Antonio's mother, Bianca, the subject of ten more portraits. The many portraits of Bianca at the Casino disprove the often-repeated assertion that Ferdinando destroyed all representations of Bianca in his efforts to expunge his sister-in-law from the family history. Such a *damnatio memoriae* would have been impossible on a purely practical level, since many of Bianca's portraits were in individual or foreign hands. But both Antonio's inventory and an inventory of the paintings in the Uffizi Tribuna in 1589 indicate that even those in Medici hands were not destroyed.[52] Given the number in the Casino, it seems more than likely that the majority of Bianca's portraits were relegated there immediately after her death. This makes the one remaining example in the Tribuna especially interesting, since that location was reserved for the most precious items in the family collection; it would seem more likely that this particular painting would be among the first to go. No matter how they got there, however, Antonio must have been pleased to find the portraits in the Casino when he arrived; their continued presence in it represents the more sentimental side of his personality. A display of her portraits did nothing for his reputation; considering the way in which she was erased from Medici history, this display may even have hurt him. But her portraits allowed Antonio to correct the injustices of the past, celebrating his mother as only he could do. In fact, in addition to these portraits of Bianca, Antonio had three of her mother, two of her father, and one each of her brother, her daughter, and her daughter's son. Furthermore, the Casino contained a painting of the Ca' Cappello in Venice and another of Cappello heraldry, as well as a carved red coral ring with the Medici and Cappello arms.[53] Antonio also had a number of specifically Venetian items, almost certainly from his mother's estate, including a desk, an ebony and intarsia mirror, a group of walnut chairs, a chest painted with Ovidian stories, a boat, and paintings of a Doge, Venetian women, and the Piazza San Marco. Bianca eloped from Venice at age 15 and never returned, but these items suggest that she missed her native city and her family, and the type of goods she grew up with there, and that she acquired Venetian objects to fill her chambers. Bianca was certainly conscious of her Venetian connections and kept up a steady correspondence with cousins in Venice, who regularly acted on her behalf.[54] Antonio in turn adopted her love of all things Venetian, and the presence of her portraits and possessions in the Casino must have been of some comfort to him.

Antonio was in a unique situation at the Grand Ducal court, and he was certainly the only member of it who would have lived surrounded by so many portraits of Maria and Bianca. Some of these portraits were particularly revealing. For example, he had paintings that emphasized the importance of these women as bearers of lineage through the inclusion of their respective sons. These portraits corresponded to a well-known Medicean trope, explicitly and visibly making a statement about succession, similar to Bronzino's earlier portraits of Francesco's mother, Eleonora of Toledo, with both Francesco and his younger brother Giovanni.[55] Antonio's painting of himself with his mother was sent to the Casino in 1590; it was the portrait by Allori, originally intended for the *Serie aulica*.[56] This painting does not seem to be in the Medici collections today, a telling fact in itself since otherwise relatively few objects ever left. It may be the three-quarter-length composition now in Dallas (Figure 24.1). The composition was essential for the vilified Bianca, who, as Grand Duchess, posed with her son as a way to affirm his place in the Medici lineage, cementing both his future and her own. Images were indeed key to public perception; through the use of carefully determined compositions and details, an artist could invest an illegitimate sitter with just as much prestige as a legitimate one.[57]

Both Bianca and Maria (together with her son Louis) were also represented in a set of extravagant wall hangings dominated by life-size representations of six Medici women by Jacopo Ligozzi – Antonio's former drawing instructor – and displayed in the aptly named Hall of the Ladies in the Casino.[58] The other four women were grand duchesses Eleonora of Toledo, Giovanna of Austria, Cristina of Lorraine, and Maria Maddalena of Austria. According to the inventory, the costumes were embroidered in gold – Maria's had real pearls – and the heads and hands of each woman were painted with oils and inserted into the hanging. Each portrait was based on recognized types, most likely paintings in Antonio's own collection, although no representation of Bianca with the Grand Ducal crown alongside her, as she was shown in the hanging, seems to survive.[59] Aligning Bianca with these women – four fellow grand duchesses and the queen of France – gave her a credibility she otherwise seems to have lost by the early seventeenth century. Antonio must have felt secure with his own position in the Medici household to make such a bold statement regarding his mother. But the inventory indicates that a blue curtain could be pulled to cover the hangings, and, perhaps, Bianca's was hidden in this way from certain visitors. Antonio could not risk angering his Medici relatives, especially after he put so much care into his Casino.

Besides these portraits of his parents and his half-sister, Antonio's collection included other prominent Medici: there were four portraits of Grand Duke Cosimo I and three each of Grand Duke Ferdinando and his wife, Cristina of Lorraine. There were even four portraits of Antonio's father's first wife, Giovanna of Austria. There were three of the current Duke of Mantua, Vincenzo, and one of his wife, Antonio's other half-sister, Eleonora. And there were portraits of the next generation of Medici, Ferdinando's sons Cosimo II and Francesco II. In addition, there were four portraits of Antonio himself. In several surviving examples, he stands full length, with a partly

Figure 24.1 Workshop of Alessandro Allori. *Portrait of Bianco Cappello and Antonio de' Medici*, c. 1587. Dallas Museum of Art.

curtained backdrop, near a table with an important attribute; this pose was typical of Grand Ducal portraits, and this was certainly deliberate. However, in one case, instead of the famous jeweled Grand Ducal crown, Antonio's portrait includes his smaller, less elaborate crown on the table beside him.[60] This crown provided him with the status of prince of Capestrano, but by his adulthood this was a limited and largely ceremonial claim, and indeed one he had relinquished years earlier when he joined the knighthood. But he never relinquished his Medici identity, as the many portraits and heraldic objects in the Casino indicate.

The Casino's contents clearly reflected Antonio's self-professed Medicean identity. But he was full of contradictions. Antonio was a Medici, yet he was denied the ducal throne. His paternity was disparaged, and he was ousted from the line of succession, yet he had the favor of three Grand Dukes. He was a courtier who staged extravagant theatricals, yet he was a Knight of Jerusalem. And he was a learned collector whose home was used to impress visiting dignitaries, yet he did not actually own the things around him, only maintained them during his lifetime. As the figure at the center of this paradox Antonio had few opportunities to maneuver, and indeed could only retain the privileges he did have by keeping his silence about the disasters that had befallen him. Those around the Medici were certainly aware of his unique situation, and they remained aware of it long after his death. Around 1670, the scholar Alessandro Segni compiled devices for all members of the Medici family. Antonio's device was a hovering globe with the text "motu nulli molesta suo," or, "of no trouble to anyone in its movement," a motto that reflects his situation very well.[61] Antonio went about his life quietly, promoting the Medici and himself as best he could from the sidelines of the Medici household. In this way, his Casino constituted a sort of experiment, as carefully controlled as the alchemical investigations both he and his father before him conducted. Antonio was, essentially, walking a fine line between asserting and disguising his identity. He surrounded himself with an extended family of portraits, establishing his connections to the Medici and to western Europe's princely houses by creating his own *Serie aulica*. Yet any overt claims to a Medicean pedigree had to be tempered with some acknowledgement that both he and his mother were not considered full partners in that lineage and the advantages it entailed.

Had his father lived a few years longer, or died with his political allies more firmly established, Antonio might have become the third Grand Duke of Tuscany. But it truly seems that Antonio's interests were not political. If he bore ill will to Ferdinando for essentially removing him from the line to the ducal throne, he did not exhibit it in an obvious fashion. Indeed, Ferdinando and his heirs seemed content to have Antonio around. Antonio in turn may have been content simply to continue his social and scientific activities, in the well-appointed Casino, with no impediments. Although the example of his mother, who used her patronage and her chambers to construct her public persona, was very much on Antonio's mind, he also followed the example of his more private father, by choosing a withdrawn existence and asserting himself in a quieter fashion.

Antonio died on May 2, 1621. Unlike his mother, whose body was relegated to an as-yet unidentified location, Antonio was buried in San Lorenzo's Old Sacristy, near his father. His body was placed in a niche to the right of the altar, a location described during the exhumation of Medici corpses in the nineteenth century as one reserved for *spuri*, or illegitimate offspring. Obvious care had been taken to honor him; Antonio was buried within three caskets, two wooden and the inner lead, and he rested under aromatic plants wearing his knight's cloak and a gold medallion with his portrait, name, and title on one side and precise age at death, 44 years, eight months, and one day, on the other. A lead plaque described him as Francesco's

– *Objects and identity* –

son, with no reference to his illegitimate status and certainly no reference to any of the later rumors about his birth.[62] It seems most likely that Grand Duchess Maria Maddalena, the namesake of Antonio's daughter and the woman who tended to the inventory of Antonio's estate, arranged for this careful interment, something it seems doubtful he would have warranted had he not been considered Francesco's true son.

As a Knight of Jerusalem Antonio could not marry and therefore had no legitimate heirs. But he managed to legitimize his four children and arranged for them to retain certain of his objects during their own lifetimes. Indeed, one of the most interesting of these is the portrait of Bianca and Antonio, originally intended for the *Serie aulica*, and then sent to the Casino, which was in the estate of Antonio's son Giulio in 1670.[63] After Antonio's death his daughter joined a convent and his three sons continued to live amongst the Medici, probably much as Antonio himself had, first in the palace on the via Larga and then, when it was sold to the Riccardi in 1659, in the Palazzo Vecchio.[64] The fact that Antonio was able to arrange this speaks well as to the esteem in which he was held by his more powerful relations. And his insistence that his children be allowed to use some of his estate further indicates the importance he placed on these material possessions and their meanings.

Sadly, despite his prominent role in the Medici household, his intellectual achievements, and his sumptuous Casino, Antonio's positive reputation did not last very long. In fact, it suffered in the same way that his mother's did; as accusations regarding her allegedly faked pregnancy grew in popularity over the centuries, both their reputations fell. Antonio's most careful experiment – his own identity – disappeared as a result. After Antonio's death, a number of the best paintings in the Casino were transferred to the Uffizi.[65] But both the building and most of its contents passed to Cardinal Carlo de' Medici, a younger son of Ferdinando; at Carlo's death, the rest were assimilated into the Medici holdings at large. Cardinal Carlo commissioned a fresco cycle for several of the Casino's main rooms, illustrating the lives of the first four Grand Dukes. The painted life of Antonio's father, Francesco, ends in 1578, before he constructed the Uffizi (1581) or received the Order of the Golden Fleece (1585), and nine years before his actual death.[66] Although Antonio was born in 1576, and the Casino had most recently been his own residence, he, along with his mother Bianca, is completely absent from this celebratory familial cycle. Antonio's carefully crafted identity failed him almost immediately after his death.

In many ways, the problems created by the dispersal of Antonio's Casino and the obliteration of his identity parallels the challenges implicit in any study of the material culture of the Renaissance. Many monumental objects – churches, palaces, villas, altarpieces, and fresco cycles – still survive and often can be reconstructed with their original messages intact. But the less monumental objects, those that made up the material culture of an individual's life, cannot be recreated as easily and, in their destroyed, dispersed, or otherwise devoid state, their original meanings are lost. Because Antonio's Casino and its contents reverted back to the Grand Ducal holdings at his death (and eventually to the state following the death of the last Medici, Anna Maria Luisa, in 1743), these various objects, now completely out of context, carry a very different meaning today. But Antonio's inventory enables a recreation and understanding of not only the Casino at San Marco but also of Antonio de' Medici himself. And it makes one pause to consider the many other individuals whose objects and identities have been lost over time.

NOTES

1 Steven Lubar and W. David Kingery, eds, *History from Things. Essays on Material Culture* (Washington and London: Smithsonian Institution Press, 1993).
2 Mary Douglas and Baron Isherwood, *The World of Goods* (London: Routledge, 2002).
3 Jacob Burckhardt, *The Civilization of the Renaissance in Italy* (London: Phaidon, 1995), 13–14.
4 For her alleged misdeeds, see Maria Luisa Mariotti Masi, *Bianca Cappello. Una Veneziana alla corte dei Medici* (Milan: Mursia, 1986), 97; Bastiano Arditi, *Diario di Firenze e di altre parti della cristianità (1574–1579)*, ed. Roberto Cantagalli (Florence: Istituto Nazionale di studi sul Rinascimento, 1970), 34, 177–9; Agostino Lapini, *Diario fiorentino di Agostino Lapini dal 252 al 1596*, ed. Gius. Odoardo Corazzini (Florence: Sansoni, 1900), 197 note 1; and G. Pardi, "Disegno della storia demografica di Firenze," *Archivio storico italiano* 74 (1916): 197.
5 Nicolas Tenhove, *Memoirs of the House of Medici, from its Origin to the Death of Francesco, the Second Grand Duke of Tuscany, and of the Great Men Who Flourished in Tuscany within that Period*, trans. Sir Richard Clayton (Bath: G. G. and J. Robinson, 1797), 2: 510.
6 Luciano Berti, *Il principe dello studiolo. Francesco I dei Medici e la fine del Rinascimento fiorentino* (Pistoia: Maschietto & Musolino, 2002), 44.
7 P. F. Covoni, *Don Antonio de' Medici al Casino di San Marco* (Florence: Tipografia Cooperativa, 1892), 3–8.
8 Archivio di Stato Florence, *Mediceo del Principato* 5130, 1 recto, 4 recto, and 6 recto.
9 Rosemarie Mulcahy, *Phillip II of Spain: Patron of the Arts* (Dublin: Four Courts Press, 2004), 74–5.
10 Arnaldo Segarizzi, ed., *Relazioni degli ambasciatori Veneti al Senato* (Bari: Gius. Laterza & figli, 1916), 3: 2:19.
11 Gaetano Pieraccini, *La stirpe de' Medici di Cafaggiolo* (Florence: Vallechi, 1924), 2: 125–61; Guglielmo Enrico Saltini, "Della morte di Francesco I de' Medici e di Bianca Cappello. Relazione storica," *Archivio storico italiana* 18 (1863): 19–81; and Francesco Mari, Aldo Polettini, Donatello Lippi, and Elisabetta Bertol, "The Mysterious Death of Francesco I de' Medici and Bianca Cappello: An Arsenic Murder?," *British Medical Journal* 333 (2006): 1299–1301.
12 Covoni, *Don Antonio*, 12–19 and 37–44; Guglielmo Enrico Saltini, *Bianca Cappello and Francesco I de' Medici* (Florence: Rassegna Nazionale, 1898), 414–18.
13 Covoni, *Don Antonio*, 15–16; Giuseppe Vittorio Parigino, *Il tesoro del principe. Funzione pubblica e private del patrimonio della famiglia Medici nel cinquecento* (Florence: Olschki, 1999), 141–4.
14 Jacopo Riguccio Galluzzi, *Istoria del Granducato di Toscana sotto il governo della casa Medici* (Florence: Gaetano Cambiagi, 1781), 2: 426; G. E. Saltini, ed., "Istoria del gran duca Ferdinando I scritta da Piero Usimbardi," *Archivio storico italiano* 18 (1880): 378.
15 Paola Barocchi and Giovanna Gaeta Bertelà, eds, *Da Cosimo I a Cosimo II 1540–1621* (Florence: SPES, 2002), 123.
16 See, for example, Robert Darlington, *A Survey of the Great Dukes State of Tuscany. In the Yeare of our Lord 1596* (London: Edward Blount, 1605).

17 Masi, *Bianca Cappello*, 297.
18 Roberto Cantagalli, "Bianca Cappello e una leggenda da sfatare: la questione del figlio supposto," *Nuova rivista storica* 49 (1965): 636–52; Parigino, *Il tesoro*, 140–5.
19 Arditi, *Diario*, 23 and Saltini, "Della morte," 61–79.
20 Celio Malespini, *Duecento Novelle* (Venice: Al segno dell'Italia, 1609), 80v.–85v., 275v.–280v.; and Fynes Moryson, *Shakespeare's Europe*, ed. Charles Hughes (London: Sherratt & Hughes, 1903), 94–5.
21 Galluzzi, *Istoria*, 2: 270–4.
22 Segarizzi, *Relazioni*, 3: 2: 84.
23 Thomas Kuehn, "Reading Between the Patrilines: Leon Battista Alberti's *Della Famiglia* in Light of his Illegitimacy," *I Tatti Studies* 1 (1985): 161–87.
24 Caroline P. Murphy, *The Pope's Daughter* (London: Faber & Faber, 2004).
25 Silvia Evangelisti, "Monastic Poverty and Material Culture in Early Modern Italian Convents," *The Historical Journal* 47 (2004): 1–20.
26 Covoni, *Don Antonio*, 110–24; Sara Mamone, *Firenze e Parigi: Due capitoli dello spettacolo per una regina* (Milan: Silvana, 1987).
27 Laura Baldini Giusti, "Nelle stanze della principessa Maria all'ultimo piano . . . ," in Caterina Caneva and Francesco Solinas, eds, *Maria de' Medici (1573–1642). Una principessa fiorentina sul trono di Francia* (Livorno: Sillabe, 2005), 36–40; Robert Lamar Weaver and Norma Wright Weaver, *A Chronology of Music in the Florentine Theater 1590–1750* (Detroit: Information Coordinators, 1978), 19–20.
28 *Le musiche di Iacopo Peri nobil fiorentina sopra l'Euridice del Sig. Ottavio Rinuccini rappresentate nello sposalizio della cristianissima Maria Medici regina di Francia e di Navarra* (Florence: Marescotti, 1600). For this performance see also Tim Carter, "Jacopo Peri's 'Euridice' (1600): A Contextual Study," *Music Review* 43 (1982): 83–103; and Mario Sperenzi, *Teatro e spettacolo nella Firenze dei Medici. Modelli dei luoghi teatrali* (Florence: Leo S. Olschki, 2001), 199.
29 P. F. Covoni, *Il Casino di San Marco costruito dal Buontalenti ai tempi medicei* (Florence: Tipografia Cooperativa, 1892).
30 Barocchi and Gaeta Bertelà, *Da Cosimo*, 269.
31 Angelo Solerti, *Musica, ballo, e drammatica alla corte Medicea dal 1600 al 1637* (Florence: Bemporad & figlio, 1905), 28–36, 58–62; Weaver and Weaver, *Chronology*, 20, 91–7, 101; Warren Kirkendale, *The Court Musicians in Florence during the Principate of the Medici* (Florence: Olschki, 1993), 148.
32 All references to Antonio's estate inventory are from Archivio di Stato Florence, *Guardaroba Medicea* 399. See also Tim Carter, "Music-printing in Late Sixteenth- and Early Seventeenth-century Florence: Giorgio Marescotti, Cristofano Marescotti and Zanobi Pignoni," *Early Music History* 9 (1990): 66.
33 Carter, "Music-printing," 66.
34 Edmond Strainchamps, "New Light on the Accademia degli Elevati in Florence," *Musical Quarterly* 62 (October 1976): 526–8.
35 Bruce Edelstein, "The Camera Verde. A Public Center for the Duchess of Florence in the Palazzo Vecchio," *Mélanges de l'Ecole française de Rome. Italie et Méditerranée* 115 (2003): 51–87.
36 Saltini, *Bianca Cappello*, 340–1; Detlef Heikamp and Ferdinand Anders, *Mexico and the Medici* (Florence: Edam, 1972), 16, 30 note 45.
37 Raffaello Borghini, *Il Riposo* (Florence: Giorgio Marescotti, 1584), 353; Paola Barocchi and Giovanna Gaeta Bertelà, *Collezionismo Mediceo: Cosimo I, Francesco I, e il Cardinale Ferdinando: Documenti 1540–1587* (Modena: F. C. Panini, 1993), 208–9, 225–6.
38 Barocchi and Gaeta Bertelà, *Collezionismo*, 256. For Bianca's chambers, see Saltini, *Bianca*

Cappello, 339; Berti, *Il principe*, 48–9; Barocchi and Gaeta Bertelà, *Da Cosimo*, 269 note 1.
39 Detlef Heikamp, "La galleria degli Uffizi descritta e disegnata," in Paola Barocchi and Giovanna Ragionieri, eds, *Gli Uffizi. Quattro secoli di un galleria. Atti del Convegno Internazionale di Studi* (Florence: Olschki, 1983), 2: 505.
40 Galileo Galilei, *Opere*, ed. Antonio Favaro (Florence: Babera, 1890–1909), 10: 228–34, 277–8.
41 Suzanne B. Butters, *The Triumph of Vulcan: Sculptors' Tools, Porphyry, and the Prince in Ducal Florence* (Florence: Olschki, 1996), 1: 262.
42 Ibid., 1: 230; Alfredo Perifano, *L'Alchimie à la cour de Côsme Ier de Médicis: Savoirs, culture et politique* (Paris: Honoré Champion Éditeur, 1997), 49 note 2.
43 Galeazzo Cora and Angiolo Fanfani, *La porcellana Medicea* (Milan: Fabbri, 1985).
44 Marco Spallanzani, "Un dono di 506 porcellane medicee," *Faenza* 90 (2004): 55 note 2, and *Ceramiche alla corte dei Medici nel cinquecento* (Modena: Franco Cosimo Panini, 1994), 191–2.
45 Spallanzani, "Un dono," 56; see also Fausto Berti, *Capolavori della maiolica rinascimentale. Montelupo "fabbrica" di Firenze 1400–1630* (Montelupo Fiorentino: Aedo, 2002), 291–6.
46 Eduardo Matos Moctezuma and Felipe Solis Olguin, *Aztecs* (London: Royal Academy of Arts, 2002), 404.
47 Kirkendale, *Court Musicians*, 303, 318.
48 Charles Avery, *Giambologna. The Complete Sculpture* (Oxford: Phaidon, 1987), 25, 215.
49 Hélène Chauvineau, "Nella camera del granduca (1590–1660)," in Sergio Bertelli and Renato Pasta, eds, *Vivere a Pitti. Una reggia dai Medici di Savoia* (Florence: Olschki, 2003), 799; Karla Langedijk, *The Portraits of the Medici, 15th–18th Centuries* (Florence: Studio per edizioni scelte, 1981–7), 1: 306.
50 Langedijk, *Portraits*, 3: 1557.
51 Baldini Giusti, "Nelle stanze," 37; Fiorella Facchinetti, "Le vicende costruttive in Palazzo Pitti," in Marco Chiarini, ed., *Palazzo Pitti. L'arte e la storia* (Florence: Nardini, 2000), 35.
52 Giovanna Gaeta Bertelà, *La Tribuna di Ferdinando I de' Medici. Inventari 1589–1631* (Modena: Franco Cosimo Panini, 1997), 15.
53 For this ring see Maria Sframeli, ed., *I gioielli dei Medici dal vero e in ritratto* (Livorno: Sillabe, 2003), 95.
54 Maria Gubini Leuzzi, "Straniere a corte. Dagli epistolari di Giovanna d'Austria e Bianca Cappello," in Gabriella Zarri, ed., *Per lettera. Le scrittura epistolare femminile tra archivio e tipografia secoli XV–XVII* (Rome: Viella, 1999), 413–14.
55 The importance of these portraits is discussed most recently in Janet Cox-Rearick, "*La Ill.ma Sig.ra Duchessa felice memoria*: The Posthumous Eleonora di Toledo," in Konrad Eisenbichler, ed., *The Cultural World of Eleonora di Toledo, Duchess of Florence and Siena* (Aldershot: Ashgate, 2004), 225–66.
56 Simone Lecchini Giovannoni, *Alessandro Allori* (Torino: Allemandi, 1991), 75; Langedijk, *Portraits*, 1: 317, 319 and 3: 1524–5.
57 This is evident in Bronzino's portrait of Bia de' Medici, illegitimate daughter of Duke Cosimo I de' Medici, whose paternity was declared via Cosimo's medallion around her neck; see Sframeli, *I gioielli*, 68–70.
58 These hangings were destroyed, but watercolor copies were made in the eighteenth century; see Karla Langedijk, "Jacopo Ligozzi al Casino di San Marco e al Poggio Imperiale: Il paramento delle granduchesse," in Mina Gregori, ed., *Rubens e Firenze* (Florence: La Nuova Italia Editrice, 1983), 103–11.

59 For a portrait of Bianca, attributed to Ligozzi and compositionally similar to the hanging, see Günther Heinz, "Studien zur Porträtmalerei an den Höfen der Österreichischen Erblande," *Jahrbuch der kunsthistorischen Sammlungen in Wien* 59 (1963): 143, 223–4.
60 Langedijk, *Portraits*, 1: 301–6.
61 Langedijk, *Portraits*, 3: 1564.
62 G. Sommi Picenardi, "Esumazione e ricognizione delle ceneri dei principi medicei fatta nell'anno 1857. Processo verbale e note," *Archivio storico italiano* 1 (1888): 350–1.
63 Langedijk, *Portraits*, 3: 1525.
64 Covoni, *Don Antonio*, 167–72, 187–9.
65 Gaeta Bertelà, *La Tribuna*, 73–4.
66 Anna Rosa Masetti, "Il Casino Mediceo e la pittura fiorentina del Seicento, 2," *Critica d'Arte* 9: 53–4 (1962): 90–1; Julian Matthias Kliemann, *The Heroic Fresco. Ancestral Fresco Cycles in Italian Patrician Residences from the 1400s to the 1600s* (Cinisello Balsamo: Silvana, 1993), 180.

SUGGESTIONS FOR FURTHER READING

Avery, Charles. *Giambologna. The Complete Sculpture*. Oxford: Phaidon, 1987.
Bertelli, Sergio and Renato Pasta, eds. *Vivere a Pitti. Una reggia dai Medici di Savoia*. Florence: Olschki, 2003.
Burckhardt, Jacob. *The Civilization of the Renaissance in Italy*. London: Phaidon, 1995.
Butters, Suzanne B. *The Triumph of Vulcan: Sculptors' Tools, Porphyry, and the Prince in Ducal Florence*. Florence: Olschki, 1996.
Eisenblicher, Konrad, ed. *The Cultural World of Eleonora di Toledo, Duchess of Florence and Siena*. Aldershot: Ashgate, 2004.
Evangelisti, Silvia. "Monastic Poverty and Material Culture in Early Modern Italian Convents." *The Historical Journal* 47 (2004): 1–20.
Goldthwaite, Richard A. *Wealth and the Demand for Art in Italy 1300–1600*. Baltimore: Johns Hopkins University Press, 1993.
Heikamp, Detlef and Ferdinand Anders. *Mexico and the Medici*. Florence: Edam, 1972.
Jardine, Lisa. *Worldly Goods: A New History of the Renaissance*. London: Macmillan, 1996.
Kliemann, Julian Matthias. *The Heroic Fresco. Ancestral Fresco Cycles in Italian Patrician Residences from the 1400s to the 1600s*. Cinisello Balsamo: Silvana, 1993.
Kuehn, Thomas. *Illegitimacy in Renaissance Florence*. Ann Arbor: University of Michigan Press, 2002.
Lubar, Stephen and W. David Kingery, eds. *History from Things. Essays on Material Culture*. Washington and London: Smithsonian Institution Press, 1993.
Luchinat, Cristina Acidini, ed. *The Medici, Michelangelo, and the Art of Late Renaissance Florence*. New Haven: Yale University Press, 2002.
Mulcahy, Rosemarie. *Phillip II of Spain: Patron of the Arts*. Dublin: Four Courts Press, 2004.
Murphy, Caroline P. *Lavinia Fontana: A Painter and Her Patrons in Sixteenth-century Bologna*. New Haven and London: Yale University Press, 2003.
—— *The Pope's Daughter*. London: Faber & Faber, 2004.
Nagler, A. M. *Theatre Festivals of the Medici 1539–1637*. New Haven: Yale University Press, 1964.
Thornton, Peter. *The Italian Renaissance Interior 1400–1600*. New York: H. N. Abrams, 1991.
Tomas, Natalie R. *The Medici Women: Gender and Power in Renaissance Florence*. Aldershot: Ashgate, 2003.

Welch, Evelyn. *Shopping in the Renaissance.* New Haven and London: Yale University Press, 2005.
Westfall, Richard S. "Science and Patronage: Galileo and the Telescope." *Isis* 76 (March 1985): 11–30.
Zambelli, Paola, ed. *Scienze, credenze, occulte.* Florence: Olschki, 1982.

CHAPTER TWENTY-FIVE

FOOD

Pietro Aretino and the art of conspicuous consumption

Douglas Biow

AN APPETITE FOR THINGS

Guardabasso, Malanotte, and Perdelgiorno, three household servants in Pietro Aretino's comedy *The Hypocrite* (1542), are – as servants are wont to be in Renaissance drama – hungry for attention, honor, and respect. But, above all, they are hungry for some food. And this is significant in the late Renaissance, for hunger itself had become a matter of immediate, daily concern. "The 'plague of God,' the 'rabid hunger,'" the literary and cultural historian Piero Camporesi observes, "cannot be dated with exactitude, but from as far back at least as the second half of the sixteenth century one gets the very bitter impression that, for two centuries and a half, hunger weighed upon the whole of Italy like a terrible nightmare."[1] In times of famine the rank and file suffered terribly. However, it is also important to note that economic and social historians have not always seen the Italian Renaissance as a period of such hard times. Richard Goldthwaite, for instance, has argued that both skilled and unskilled workers employed in the construction industry in Florence were paid well enough to feed themselves and their families, and some could earn enough to put a substantial margin of wealth between themselves and the poverty line. Goldthwaite's calculations suggest that workers after the Black Death (1348) were better off than before, and his conclusions, along with Brian Pullan's calculations about the standards of living of Venetian artisans, remind us that when we use literature as evidence, it is always difficult to tell what is real and what is imaginary.[2] There is hunger, which was experienced by people in the Renaissance, and, then again, there is hunger in literature, a commonplace as old as Homer's description of Odysseus' famished crew.

This chapter, which focuses on Aretino and his interest in different styles of consumption, deals with the intersection of the real and the imaginary. For if Aretino's characters were hungry, so, it is important to recognize, was Aretino – or at least the Aretino as he imaginatively and self-consciously represented himself in his letters. Indeed, in one letter he compared himself to a pregnant woman with all sorts of cravings that he has to satisfy, for instance by consuming the gift of "liver sausages" (6: 94). Like the characters in his irreverent play *The Hypocrite* Aretino had an immense, almost insatiable appetite for food, an appetite that found expression not only in his letters but also in his works of imaginative literature. When it comes to food, what distinguished Aretino from so many of his contemporaries was not only his gargantuan appetite – a "bestial appetite" (1: 140) that was not at all parasitical in nature, like the appetite of those satirically described in *The Hypocrite* – but also his willingness to fantasize so overtly about the art of consumption in his poetry and prose. If, as Ken Albala has observed in his study of eating habits in the European Renaissance, dietary literature with all its restrictions and prohibitions "must have generated a considerable amount of anxiety and guilt," Aretino seems to have been little affected or troubled by it all. He remained supremely free of all those "fears, prejudices, and preoccupations" that the dietary literature addressed.[3] Aretino ate heartily and with gusto, and he enjoyed talking about consumption as well. Moreover, in a culture in which different types of food could be shunned because they retained lingering associations with the lower classes, Aretino ate everything that came his way with an egalitarian love. He was open to all types of food associated with different strata of society, much as – to connect from the outset of this chapter two aspects of pleasure central to his life, both food *and* words – he was open to all types of linguistic registers, from the popular to the elite. Aretino was a great and conspicuous consumer, and he self-consciously portrayed himself as one. By doing so he inevitably offered himself up artfully as a figure worthy of consumption in print.

Furthermore, in focusing on Aretino and the topic of consumption, this chapter examines a major shift of the sixteenth century as Italy gradually became dominated by court culture. Aretino, who lived in Rome, Mantua, and, after 1527, Venice, witnessed this change and looked at it with unabashed hostility. For him the court was not only changing for the worse as it adopted increasingly elaborate rituals. The court, especially from the vantage point of his house near the Rialto in republican Venice, was debased through and through. It was a seedbed of ignominious skinflints and a place where people prostituted themselves for social advancement. For this reason, his interest in consumption figured squarely into his ongoing contentious relationship with the court and, in particular, with Baldassar Castiglione's *The Courtier*, which offered up such a singularly positive and often nostalgic view of court culture in the early sixteenth century. Furthermore, Aretino's interest in consumption, when measured against the alternately niggardly or overly ostentatious meals at the court, allowed him to advance his own aggressive, competitive need to place himself in the foreground in relation to others as an author of importance. The art of excess that he applauded was central to the art of the sixteenth-century *poligrafo*, the adventurer of the pen, who could exist outside the court and survive off the gifts of others, as well as the fruits of his prolific and supremely versatile writings.

That food figured so prominently in the writings of a major critic of the court should not strike us as entirely surprising. As Mikhail Bakhtin argued long ago in *Rabelais and His World*, the massive consumption of food in the European Renaissance, with its attention to both the sensuous and the copious, had much to do with carnival. A body eating anything and everything announced the body of carnival as a sign of popular culture. And that culture focused relentlessly on food as sex and sex as food: hence, Aretino's carnivalesque focus on the tavern, the abundance of food in popular feasts, the sensuousness of food, the unabashed pleasures of food as if it were sex, the oral pleasures of talking about food in the *copia* of language, the mixing of high and low foods in a manner that upset conventional food hierarchies (much as Aretino mixes up high and low linguistic registers in his writings), and the irreverent manner in which a religious vocabulary is employed to describe massive quantities of food, as if it were something truly sublime. By approaching consumption in this way, Aretino simultaneously acknowledged the value of popular culture and the importance of appetites. Such an emphasis constituted an explicit critique of elite culture and, in particular, of Castiglione's refined courtiers, who never took the bodily appetites into account. Nonetheless, Aretino embraced certain aspects of an elitist approach to the consumption of food. First, when he received food as a gift, he highlighted the status of the friend or acquaintance who had given it to him. Gifts, always signs of status, are the rewards one receives for being a valuable person in a recognizably stratified world. Second, Aretino often boasted of the high status of the company he kept when he dined. Third, he underscored the honor bestowed on him by having such a cornucopia of food at his disposal. Aretino did not need to be at the court to partake in festive rituals of conspicuous consumption, for he could provide those feasts for himself and others on his own, and he could do so selectively for his friends in bonds of mutual trust and loyal, private companionship. Finally, he publicized his habits of consumption in print, fashioning himself, therefore, as a man of importance and stature, even as he critiqued court society.

Thus, through his art of consumption, Aretino retained some vestige of courtly distinction. He acquired status and reputation through his own publicized consumption of so much food bequeathed to him as gifts of value. But he also violated the codes of courtly distinction in order to embrace the carnival and to critique aspects of the court he found devoid of value. Much as Aretino would continually and prominently display the gift of the valuable gold chain he received from Francis I in 1533, so he repeatedly and continually displayed the gifts of food he received as a sign of his distinction in a world where hunger was real, where popular culture fantasized about conspicuous consumption, and where conspicuous consumption indeed had an important function in courtly culture because it occurred in a restricted, controlled, and highly stratified context. Aretino, in brief, wanted everyone to know that he possessed what popular culture wanted and elite culture had in abundance – massive quantities of every type of food. Yet he also wanted everyone to know that such strategies of self-fashioning were not the privilege of a poor, working person, but rather of a member of the elite – a man favored by Andrea Gritti, the powerful Doge of Venice; Francis I, the king of France; and Charles V, the Holy Roman Emperor. In this respect, Aretino's representations of food enabled him to align himself with popular culture and find real value in it, yet to maintain a sense of distinction that aligned him with the elite, while simultaneously distancing himself from the very body politic of popular culture he embraced so openly in his writings.

– *Douglas Biow* –

THE APPETITE OF THE PARASITE: COURTLY CONSUMPTION AND THE HUNGER OF PROSTITUTES

Early in his career Aretino offered a striking impression of how important food was to him within the context of the imaginary. His first comedy, *The Courtesan* (1525; reworked and published in 1534), whose ambiguous title can be read as "The Courtiers' Play" or "Courtly Matters," was deliberately titled to echo and parody Castiglione's *The Courtier*, then circulating in manuscript form. As is well known, Castiglione set his dialogue in the court of Duke Guidobaldo Montefeltro of Urbino where a number of leading nobles, men and women, discussed the attributes of the perfect courtier. Yet, while the work was often read as encyclopedic, Castiglione's courtiers never – apart from a brief discussion of manners when eating – had anything to say about food. By contrast, in *The Courtesan*, Aretino's characters are obsessed with food. For example, when Rosso, the main parasite, is sent out to procure a gift of food for his master, the foolish Parabolano, he takes it upon himself to steal some lampreys from a Florentine fishmonger; then, later in the day, we see him leaving a tavern ostensibly licking his fingers, having in the meanwhile feasted on the purloined food with Cappa, a friend and fellow companion in intrigue. In the process Rosso bluntly asserts that food is not a substitute for sex. Quite the contrary, sex – in Rosso's mind – is a sorry substitute for the real sweetness of life, which is nothing other than the savory taste of food. Similarly, Rosso's companion Cappa holds forth that food is not a substitute for social status. Social status is instead a substitute for a basic longing that animates us all: the desire to be surrounded by immense quantities of succulent, odoriferous food. In the end, it seems, all you have to do is set up a tavern by a perfume shop, and everyone will drop the civet and run for the spits dripping with fat. For it is in the tavern where one finds acceptance. It is in the tavern where the hunger of ambition gets satisfied and one can rest in peace. It is in the tavern where one can fashion an identity that matters in the world and consequently acquire, as Rosso puts it, "a name." Indeed, as far as Rosso is concerned, there is absolutely no point in seeking to achieve glorious deeds worthy of a triumphal homecoming if you can satiate the craving for recognition by having your fill at the tavern.

Moreover, it is in the tavern, not the humanist's schoolroom, where children were disciplined and thus educated into acquiring habits and attributes that would serve them well in life and secure them a reputation. It is in the tavern where everyone is an equal and can feel like a lord, the master of his or her own destiny. The tavern is consequently the place of full-fledged "agency." And, as Rosso irreverently announces at the outset of the second act, it is in the tavern, the earthly "paradise," where one consumes the food that matters. That is because the tavern *is* paradise for Rosso, where lampreys – stolen lampreys nicely cooked – are deemed as angelic sustenance. The tavern is thus the place of earthly, rather than atemporal, "joy," the embodiment of all things that anyone could possible crave both now and forevermore. In this way Rosso's and Cappa's inflation of their own bellies comes with a corresponding deflation of virtually all societal norms, hierarchies, and cultural expectations. Everything of accepted value in Renaissance Italy – the spiritualized reflection of the self in the beloved, the fulfillment of coition, the making of a name for oneself through self-presentation, the longing to achieve triumphant deeds, the security of a position in a transparently hierarchical world, the search for distinction in the world through a fashionable education, and the joy of eternal life in heaven where the blessed feast on celestial ambrosia and are forever fulfilled – is systematically overturned and deemed wanting, a lackluster substitute for the cornucopia of food. In Rosso's and Cappa's carnivalesque view of things, food is the great reward, and hunger is the great equalizer. The belly – and thus the body – triumphs.

At the time that Aretino composed *The Courtesan* he was a courtier in the service of Pope Leo X, and much of the play – indeed, the essence of it – focuses on highlighting in an exaggerated way the flaws of the court, including the calculated cheapness of patrons when it comes to parceling out food. We hear this from no less than Flaminio, one of the few loyal, temperate courtiers in the play. Flaminio has become so thoroughly disillusioned with the way he has been treated that he ends up counseling an elderly man, Sempronio, to spare his son any extended contact with the court, which, he laments, is so full of ignominious cheapskates (II.v: 81). The debased court, we learn from Flaminio, has lost the art of affability that once accompanied communal meals and thereby brought lords and servants into a bond of trust and mutual respect. In the old days, we learn from the nostalgic Sempronio, there was always plenty to eat, whereas now, amid the squalor of the incorrigible skinflints, one "has to look after his own fire and water" (II.v). Now the wives of the lord, with a watchful greedy eye, "keep the keys of the wine cellars and ration the food – so much on feast days, so much on regular days" (II.v) "They even count the bowls of soup!" Flaminio plaintively exclaims. Worse, we later learn from the ever-hungry Rosso, the physical space in which the servants are constrained to eat is so dark, grungy, and filthy that it is difficult to eat even the paltry, uninviting food that is served. Small wonder, then, that the tavern becomes for Rosso a paradise and eating well constitutes the best form of revenge against his patron. Rosso can aggressively and sadistically act out the role of the parasite, but within the duration of the play he cannot act in a manner that will fundamentally alter his lifestyle or make his master truly suffer. In contrast to Castiglione, therefore, Aretino has come to set the record straight. Food matters. And when it comes to eating, the virtue of moderation in the court is the luxury of those who can ascertain with a high degree of predictability when their next meal is coming to them and that, in fact, they will be sitting at a well-stocked table when they do sit down to eat. It's not enough to get close to the master whom one aims to serve dutifully. Intimacy means little if you're not getting decently fed.

The Courtesan was not Aretino's only attack on Castiglione's *Courtier*. In his two sets of *Dialogues* (1534/36), Aretino's ribald parodies of the genre of how-to books, the experienced and worldly Nanna aims to fashion her daughter Pippa into a prostitute who will acquire fame – the perfect prostitute, as it were, for a society bent on producing the perfect courtier (as well as the perfect secretary, the perfect ambassador, and the perfect cardinal). In addition to the expectation that Pippa must never clean her teeth with a napkin, chew in a filthy way, or say dirty things in polite company, Pippa must never "be seen or heard peeing, easing [her] bowels, or dabbing [her] face with a handkerchief" (188). Like the fools in Shakespearian drama,

Aretino's Nanna and Pippa function as foils. They are figures who highlight both the virtues and vices of their culture. In this case Nanna and Pippa take advantage of the virtue of employing good manners in order to win a place in society at the very moment that they bring to the foreground the vice of greed, opportunism, and self-serving power that underpins the uses of good manners for the purpose of making money and advancing a "career." They thus reveal that others who fashion themselves for the gain of social advancement are also whores. "Indeed," Nanna observes in the dialogue, "Maestro Andrea used to say that whores and courtiers can be put on the same scales" (149). Like courtiers, whose habits of presentation give them a mark of distinction, thereby determining where they belong both in society and at the dinner table, prostitutes in Aretino's dialogue must always be careful about how they consume, much as – some two decades later – Giovanni della Casa will dictate in his *Galateo* how people of stable social standing must eat with proper decorum at the table. Unlike della Casa's gentleman, however, Aretino's prostitutes are not interested in their own sense of self, their own self-image, and their own sense of place. Shameless and immodest, they only care about the image they project. In Aretino's satire, it is the *posture* that matters, the *show* of representing good manners and appearing to care about cleanliness, even if one's predisposition would be to feast like a pig at a trough.

To this effect, Pippa must be told not to consume great quantities of wine even if she is thirsty, or for that matter not to consume conspicuously, because her predilection, we can assume, would be to eat heartily and without much consideration for the feelings of others at the table. We can safely make this assumption about Pippa's eating habits not only because she must be told what *not* to do – the expectation therefore being that she would otherwise do what she is not supposed to do and would consequently offend decorum – but also because everyone in Aretino's dialogues, including the interlocutors, thinks about consuming food. This is certainly true at the very beginning of the dialogues. It is hardly accidental that what partly initiates the discussion at the opening of the first dialogue is Antonia's admiration of Nanna's ability to buy all sorts of food since she has profited so well over the years from being an adept prostitute. "You can afford the most fantastic delicacies," she observes with some envy (5). Food is on Antonia's mind, just as it is on the minds – as well as in the bellies – of the people described in the dialogues. It is food, for instance, that people gorge on right away, as Nanna describes the first hours of her life after having entered the convent as a young girl – all, it turns out, in preparation for her eventually becoming a prostitute. No sooner has the door been shut behind her, cutting her off from her family, than the sisters of the entire convent, with countless monks and friars attending, settle down to "one of the most delicate feasts" possible, with "the sort of food" – Nanna assures us – "that the Pope in person has never tasted" (11), though the habits of consumption here leave much to be desired, and have more to do with street behavior than the presumably refined comportment of the Holy See. Being in the convent is no different than being in Rome's Piazza Navona with garrulous men and women squabbling and picking at the food. One piggish friar worked his jaws so much as he ate large quantities of food that his "cheeks bulged like a man blowing a trumpet"; then, to polish it off, "he brought a bottle to his lips and guzzled it down to the last drop" (12). "I could not describe all the wine guzzled and the pastries they wolfed down," Nanna remarks with incredulity as she describes the post-coital hunger of a group within the convent (30). Another friar, after delivering a sermon from the pulpit, "lapped up wine as a horse laps up water, and devoured pastries with the voracity that a donkey gobbles the tendrils of a vine" (48).

The pleasures of the life of the convent, we learn from the outset, are first and foremost the pleasures of the conspicuous consumption of food. And the pleasures of the consumption of food continue through Aretino's *Dialogues*, whether we are talking about Nanna indoctrinating others into the highly sexualized life of the convent, the delights and peccadilloes of adultery in marriage, or the lucrative work of prostitution. Humans are beasts, and the beast must be fed, whether in or outside the convent. As a recently married woman, whose lack of virginity has been cleverly disguised, Nanna and a friend, she recalls, feasted on a "light supper" that included no less than "a thousand tidbits – livers, sweetbreads, chickens' feet and necks, a salad flavored with parsley and pepper, nearly a whole capon, olives, red apples, goat's-milk cheese, quince jelly to settle our stomachs, and candies to sweeten our breath" (72). As it is for the lascivious married woman, so it is for the prostitute. Pippa may be warned by Nanna not to consume lavishly and copiously, but in the end eating this way is fun. Eat as much as you want, she is told, when you are with old men, for old men can't perform very well, if they can perform at all, and they take pleasure in seeing young women eat, so young women might as well take pleasure in consumption. "At dinners like this," Nanna advises, "you can gorge yourself without standing on ceremony" (194). Moreover, a prostitute needs to think about setting aside food on occasion for a later time. It's not just important to eat but to store up large quantities of comestibles. Appetites come and go, and though one can get one's fill at one meal, it's important to think about the days that follow. Hence, have the competing clients pay for the meals "royally" with the aim of setting aside a plethora of "leftovers" (265).

At the same time, the hunger described in the *Dialogues* is not only for food but also for sex envisioned as a form of food, as a type of consumption that propels people to behave in such a way that they can hardly have enough, with the exception perhaps of the prostitutes themselves who, because they are so often fed, only yearn for sex as one might a light snack. For virtually everyone else, however, sex is a feast. "But the joy he derived from shoving it into and pulling it out of every hole and aperture," Nanna informs us, "were mere gentilities compared to the slaughter that started when a herd of flunkies, undercooks, and hostlers rushed out of the vineyard house with the growl that famished hunting dogs make when they're let off the leash and, like monks hurling themselves on a plate of broth, pounce on the food." (300) "What a feast!" Antonia exclaims on hearing about one person after another aggressively stuffing a dildo and then a prick smack into the "ovens" her fellow prostitutes make available for them (26). Women who are unresponsive and lack the talent of taking on many positions offer a man who "tastes them" about as much savor as one "gets from broad bean soup cooked without oil or salt" (16). On occasion sex is so fulfilling that one can lose an appetite for food itself (24). In another instance, the coy appearance of chastity on the part of the prostitute may make an aroused client so frustrated that she appears to him as an "appetizer" that only whets his hunger for a "full meal." Different sorts of sexual activities, moreover, sometimes bring to mind different sorts of dining tastes. Anal intercourse, for instance, is so appetizing, Antonia insists, that it is deemed "a choice tidbit that people fight for more than lamprey. It's a dish for gourmets" (37).

Finally, Aretino's delight in talking about sex as food paralleled his interest in finding various ways of talking about food as sex. One could, after all, be linguistically blunt. And on one occasion Aretino explained why it is important to be blunt and avoid the niceties of indirection, the kinds of indirections that are required by decorum and constitute the *modus operandi* of a courtier. No doubt Aretino finds irreverent satisfaction in saying things as they are, in not beating around the bush; he surely takes pleasure in offending decorum here, much as he does elsewhere. But the pleasure of talking about sex, and in this instance the parts of the body that are repeatedly deployed in the dialogues as the privileged instruments of sex, is the pleasure in finding various and sundry euphemisms for it. And in keeping with the close connection established in the text between the hunger for food and the hunger for sex, many of those euphemisms have to do with food. A woman has cheeks like milk and honey, much as they are conventionally represented in elevated Petrarchan love lyrics, but – in keeping with the contrary genre of carnival songs, where food lasciviously doubles as body parts – a woman also has a vagina that is a "granary" (119), an ass that tastes of "mint and wild thyme" (89), and a "you-know-what" that is full of "honey" and tastes sweeter than the sugar sold by the sugar merchant himself who hungers for the prostitute's services. Similarly, a man boasts of having between his loins a veritable, if not edible, "sausage" (73), and he is capable of satisfying a woman with a piece of "larded bread" (59). If the variety of sexual positions and sexual lovers serves to arouse an appetite, so, too, linguistically the variety of ways that Aretino finds to talk about sex complements his notion about the importance of variety in increasing the appetite. We don't always want to eat homemade bread, Nanna observes, any more than we want to dine at home all the time, for "variety stimulates appetite" (6). Furthermore, the variety of ways of talking about sex as food feeds the underlying principle in the *Dialogues* that a well-told narrative is itself a form of feeding. Consequently, the response on the part of the listeners – or readers articulating the words out loud – is to yearn for that narrative full of calculated digressions and variations with a stimulated appetite, like a famished child groping for the breast. "I'm waiting for you to get to the heart of your story," Antonia informs Nanna, "and I feel like a baby waiting for his wet nurse to shove her tit in his mouth. Yes, all your dawdling seems more painful to me than the day before Easter is to someone peeling eggs after fasting through Lent" (18). The pleasure of sex mirrors the pleasure of verbalizing sex.

When it comes to matters of consumption, then, nothing in Aretino's *Dialogue* comes in moderation, and everything serves to offend decorum, in particular the decorum advanced in such books of professional self-development as *The Courtier*, which Aretino here deliberately parodies with characteristic satirical vengeance. Hence, if Castiglione's notion of conspicuous consumption revolves around objects of distinction and taste, from the elegant palace of Urbino to the duke's study, Aretino's notion of conspicuous consumption revolves around fulfilling one's appetite for both sex as food and food as pleasure to such an extent that people are inspired to behave in the most immodest and immoderate of ways. Appetite, Aretino reveals, is a strange thing. It can get the better of us and lead us to perform in a debased manner. When clients are properly cajoled and manipulated to a point of absolute frustration, for instance, their appetite can even lead them to the point where they'll eat a prostitute's excrement or consume the scabs of her syphilis (141). Appetite has no bounds in Aretino's dialogues, no zero degree of debasement.

At the same time, it is important to have an appetite and to recognize that one has an appetite, Aretino also seems to warn, for there is no denying the demands – indeed sometimes the most immoderate demands – of the body. In this light, if no one talks at any length about food in *The Courtier*, it is not just because talking about food – God forbid talking about the pleasures of sex! – would offend decorum by addressing so openly matters that have to do with satisfying the body rather than the mind. No one talks at any length about food in *The Courtier* simply because talking about it would also mean stating the obvious in a manner that would undermine the virtue of *sprezzatura* (the art of understatement, nonchalance, and studied coolness) that is so suavely put into practice in the text itself. We should, in short, just generally assume that these laudable, happy courtiers, whose sexual appetites are sublimated through talk about gender and gentle yet tense skirmishes with each other about women, are being well fed at the dinner table. Surely we should assume this is the case at the beginning of Book II of *The Courtier* when, before the courtiers have all gathered together in the late evening with the duchess to continue their games, "the Prefect decided they should eat, and took all the gentleman to supper with him" (95). However, this was not always the case in the sixteenth century, Aretino warns. The court, to be sure, is just what Castiglione describes – a place of show and prudential performance, and in this way it is certainly very real – but according to Aretino the life of the courtier is far more debased than anything Castiglione ever presented:

> Yes, we had a fine world in the old days, and my good godfather Motta gave me a neat comparison. "Nanna," he told me, "today's whores are like today's courtiers, who, if they wish to live in pomp and plenty, are forced to steal; otherwise they'd die of hunger. And for one courtier who has bread in his coffer, there are hordes that scrounge for crusts." (287–8)

In the *Dialogues*, as in *The Courtesan* and *Hypocrite*, Aretino once more invites us to witness the sorry state of the court. For, in truth, courtiers are a hungry lot, he would have us believe, and they are not just hungry for respect, honor, and distinction, as his comic figures Guardabasso, Malanotte, Perdelgiorno, Rosso, and Cappa make clear. Like prostitutes, and the parasites in classical and contemporary literature, they are hungry for food as well. To be sure, Aretino's comparison and representation may be more literary imagination and satirical characterization than anything else, but it was a colorful and ribald exaggeration that offered to the public at large a counterpart to Castiglione's image of the court as a place of perfected moderation with its decorous habits of consumption and finely controlled appetites.

FOOD FOR THOUGHT:
ARETINO'S ART OF CONSUMPTION

If there is a figure in the European Renaissance generally who embodies in the cultural imagination of the period what it means to have an enormous appetite for things it would have to be Christopher Marlowe's Faustus, the man who is willing to give up everything, even his own soul, so that he can sate his desire. He knows everything, but he must have more. His desire is for an absolute, a sort of anguished Lacanian "demand." But to single out an actual living person who embodied in the cultural imagination of the period what it meant to have an enormous appetite, one could do no better than choose Pietro Aretino, a man who was happy to have his home in Venice mistaken as a paradisiacal place of plenty where capons are eternally stuffed and sausages drip fat from spits and the booze flows freely. In one instance, for example, early on in his life in Venice, as he wrote off a letter of thanks to Messer Girolamo Agnello for the keg of wine sent him, he described how his house had been turned into a sort of tavern, and, through the offering of the delectable wine to others, he acquired fame. Wherever anyone goes, he reported, "they talk only of my perfect wine. It looks as if I have more renown on its account than I have on my own. I'd be a nobody if I hadn't produced this famous drink" (*The Letters of Pietro Aretino* 34 [hereafter *Letters*]).

Aretino loved food, and he loved receiving it in a culture where the exchange of gifts constituted a privileged form of making and reinforcing connections. "For in giving a gift," Aretino reminded his dear friend Jacopo Sansovino, the sculptor and architect with whom he often dined, "is found the love of him who sends them, the thoughtfulness of him who brings them, and the delight of him who receives them" (*Letters* 287). It is not only essential, therefore, that people like Girolamo Agnello provide Aretino with gifts of food and that, in receiving these gifts, Aretino cements relationships within extended networks of influence and patronage. It is also essential that Aretino in his letters publicizes how these gifts advance his standing, his own sense of distinction, and his sense of privilege and entitlement. Hence, his letters are full of expressions of gratitude for the gifts of food he receives. He receives *confetti* on a number of occasions, along with lots of peaches, some so wonderful that it seemed to him, "eating them, that he had eaten the very fruit" that would have made Adam forget about the taste of the apple (1: 233). He gets massive quantities of olives and olive oil, hares and veal, and thrushes so good that Titian, upon sniffing them, even cancels a dinner engagement to feast on them. There are strawberries "suffused with their natural crimson and scented with their native perfume" (*Letters* 76), as well as cucumbers, figs, muscatel grapes, pears, apricots, melons, plums, artichokes, squash, beans, suckling kids, jellies, almonds, citrons, and fish (herring, shrimp, and carp, among others). There are mushrooms (which he sometimes eats with the "delights of gluttony," *Letters* 76), chickens, a fair amount of spiced bread, turkeys, pear-shaped lemons, cheese, caviar, fennel, salami, snails, salads of all types, mixed in such a way that the "pungency and bite" of one kind matches another "until the whole is a mixture so tasty that it would satisfy satiety itself" (*Letters* 88). And there are gallons – one can deduce – of different types of wine. Some of the wine is so good that the guests in Aretino's house, he records, "seemed like a gaggle of gabblers who had collected around the wine barrels at Empty Talk Inn" (*Letters* 165).

Quantity also matters. "To see the abundance of the food" (1: 176) pleases the eye and the appetite, as is evident in so many paintings in the Italian Renaissance. Consequently, nothing is finer than being sent an enormous cheese — the sort of cheese that can elicit stupor, like the one Count Ludovico Rangone sends him:

> I assure you that I do not believe that from the udders of all the herds of cattle and the flocks of sheep that Apollo ever looked upon, would have come, in their whole lifetime, enough milk to make a cheese as enormous as the one that your and my Gian Tomaso Bruno made me a gift of in your name. When I saw it, the admiration it aroused in me, went into conference with the appetite which its excellence and handsome appearance evoked, and concluded that it would not be without never-ending astonishment that I would go about enjoying it, as long as it lasted and to the great honor of our courteous and generous lordship. (*Letters* 300)

Aretino's worth is therefore measured not only in the nature of the gift and its provenance (what is sent and who sends it are always critical and telling pieces of information that he needs to share with his reader); Aretino's worth is also measured according to the amount of the gift, its "*copia*," as he put it in one letter. The cheese is stupefying in its grandeur, and so it is right that Aretino, in keeping with his notion of gift-giving as an expression of love, should receive it. The cheese is larger than life, and so, conspicuously, is he. And, as we learn in another instance, he really adored cheese. On one occasion he took the rare measure of cautioning his household help, whom he usually treats, he claims, with decorous familiarity and generosity, not to dare touch his recent gift of cheese, about which he finds himself compelled to break out in Latin song by citing from Horace's *Ars poetica*.

Aretino ate not only a lot but also all sorts of foods. "It is true that my soul — if I had the means — would like to feast in royal grandeur, but my mouth, although it is still able to enjoy many dishes, takes its nourishment from simpler food. If it is a sin, then, to eat a whole salad, and with it a whole onion, I am done for, for I find in such things a delicate flavor, and that is more than those kitchen hawks who hovered around the table of Leo [X] ever did" (*Letters* 76–7). He refused to disdain "rude and rustic fare" (*Letters* 268). Even his dreams bring him to a fantasized tavern, where, citing his own *The Courtesan*, he exclaims: "To quote Cappa, 'He who has not ever been in a tavern does not really know what heaven is like.' And since my appetite had taken over my stomach, I decided to have a good meal" (*Letters* 111). To be sure, Aretino was perfectly capable of praising the simple life, in which "You eat to live and do not live to eat" (*Letters* 135), but in the same context he felt compelled to provide us with the names of all sorts of food available to anyone living the so-called simple life: salads, sausages, omelettes, roast pork, wine, eggs, fish, capons, and broilers. Nothing pleased him so much as food, and no food was too good for him or too debased. Onions have a place at his dinner table as do fine peaches and savory wines. In particular, wine — indeed a steady supply of it — gives him "the same pleasure that sends others in ecstasy when they reach the climax of making love"

(*Letters* 266). To this effect, Aretino has only words of mockery for the advice of doctors, who would limit the range of foods available for consumption according to the particular complexion of the individual (something that the other famous Aretine, Petrarch, had little tolerance for when he was informed not to drink water but wine instead). And Aretino has perfect evidence that the doctors must be quacks when it comes to limiting the intake of food. His own body, and his own tolerance for the food he consumes, tells him directly and unequivocally that he should just keep consuming what and as he does.

This was not a man, then, who disdained the pleasures of consumption of any sort of food, nor one who suffered the prohibitions and admonitions of doctors. As a result he was, he claimed, prepared to break out into song on tasting a thrush, and he asserted elsewhere that he was astounded that poets have not sung extended praises of salad (*Letters* 88). He was also ready to discourse on the different types of olives with the pedantry of a learned gourmand: "Spanish olives," he opines, "are ostentatiously large. Bolognese olives, not being juicy – as indeed Spanish olives are not juicy either – retain some of the bitterness that comes to them from the tree. Olives from Apulia could be called 'spit-breads' because they are so scrawny" (*Letters* 117). This was also a man who could attack the food sent to him with unrestrained pleasure. He had, to borrow the term from the letter above, a "bestial appetite," and he consumed with "ravenous pleasure" (1: 140–1). But it is important to stress that Aretino's habits of consumption are simultaneously high and low, elitist and popular. His body, often portrayed by Titian as distinctly robust (Figure 25.1), is large and bears the imprint of a man who has lavished attention on his table, but it is also a distinguished body, allied to the world of refinement as it is to the tavern. This is not the body of carnival but of the high and low *combined*. Aretino's habits of consumption are the locus of a synthesis as much as they are wide-ranging and all-inclusive. He was happy both with the food of the elite and the food of the tavern, and he could transform his house into a setting appropriate for the one and the other.

The pleasure Aretino took in what he ate also has much to do with where he was eating. It matters supremely that he is consuming his food at his own house and not at the court. What made the food of the simple life arguably satisfying, for instance, was that one consumed it in one's own domain, even if home might happen to be a rustic hut. Needless to say, in his letters, the court remains the privileged locus of anticipated indigestion. "The deuce with courts!" he exclaims in the letter in praise of the simple life: "They give you nothing but dry meat or stale cheese to eat. It is madness to live any other kind of life than this." His praise of the simple life may be a literary exaggeration, but his contempt for the court and praise of dining in his own house with food freely given to him was not. "Courts ah? Courts eh?" he writes to Monsignor Giovanni Agnello from Venice in 1537, "It is better for the belly to dine on bread and jests than to try to feast on the smell of fine viands on a silver platter. You cannot assuage the gnawing of your hunger with one chestnut or one walnut either before or after dinner. No, there is no suffering like that of a courtier who is weary and has nowhere to sit down, who is hungry and may not eat" (*Letters* 99). By contrast, bread simply tastes better when it is consumed at one's own home free of servitude and in which servants are treated decently, as if they were sons and

— *Food: the art of conspicuous consumption* —

Figure 25.1 Titian (Tiziano Vecellio) (*c.* 1488–1576). *Portrait of Pietro Aretino ('The Aretin')* (1545). © Palazzo Pitti, Florence, Italy/The Bridgeman Art Library.

daughters (*Letters* 43). In his house, people are urged to return as if to a "tavern where the bread is never locked up" and "the wine is never watered down" (*Letters* 252). Eating must also be done in company, for anyone who dines alone is just "gorging himself like a wolf" (*Letters* 266). It is always a delight to feed others, those who are friends and those in need (*Letters* 278). His house is always a *mensa del carnasciale*, a place of festive consumption (1: 176), as well as a place of refined dining among the elite. In this way Aretino's home becomes a sort of clearing house. The food sent to him doesn't just fill his body. The food sent to him also fills the bodies of others. Deliver a gift of food to Aretino and a larger, communal body is fed.

"Tell me what you eat and I will tell you what you are," Jean-Antoine Brillat-Savarin observed in the fourth aphorism of his *The Philosophy in the Kitchen* (1825). In Aretino's case we know a lot about what he ate, or what he would have us think he ate, and thus a lot about how he would like us to perceive him as a man who could combine both the high and the low and share it all with his friends. And what we get when we read about his habits of consumption is Aretino himself conspicuously put forward in all his anti-conformist, robust corporeality. His letters about consumption speak to his mode of conspicuous self-fashioning. His food *is* his personhood, his embodied essence. In this respect, in reading Aretino's letters we are invited to consume indirectly the popularized arch-consumer in literary form, participating, if only at a distance once removed, in the kind of consumption for which Aretino created a name for himself. Consuming his letters, as he put it in one instance, was like gathering cherries to eat (1: 523). We may or may not therefore be fully aware when we read Aretino's descriptions of his habits of consumption that our desire is someone else's, but we can still take pleasure in that mediated desire, mystified or demystified as it may be. The desire of the other – a desire that does not originate in us but is created through triangulated identification – is still fully pleasurable "even so."

Moreover, and more important, the consumption of Aretino's prose about wine and salads and olives and peaches and spiced bread and fennel is the consumption that we have been looking for all along as readers. Aretino's art of consumption in this regard encapsulates the narrative strategy of his letters as a collection, a *raccolta* to be taken symbolically as a harvesting, as he provides us with six separate volumes (the last printed posthumously) that privilege variety in subject matter and style, just as he privileges throughout his works a variety in foods and their preparations. Hence, even though the etymology of the word "satire" would not be disclosed until the first decade of the seventeenth century, it is nevertheless not too anachronistic to think of Aretino's letters – and by extension many of his works in general – within the context of that elusive genre, as a dish that is offered up with a variety of foods to be tasted. For with his letter writing, the gifts of food Aretino has received and shared are in their turn offered back to the public at large in representations as gifts about food to be received and shared in a language everyone can understand. And all this is done, Aretino is quick to point out, outside the confines of the court full of hungry, parasitic hangers-on and, as he also insisted, in a manner in which he could never be accused of grossly prostituting himself through the new, highly instrumentalized medium of print. One oral pleasure in this way feeds another. Consumption of food leads to literary production about food, and consequently – if the reader is willing to engage Aretino's art by buying it and buying into it – back to consumption once again. Aretino's art of consumption, then, is not strictly an art of food (for that one can read in the period everything from carnival songs to collections of *novelle*) any more than it is the art of edifying readers through literature as food. Instead, Aretino's art of consumption is ultimately the art of conspicuously consuming massive quantities of food so that we begin to think about how we become, through the process of reading all his varied letters in the vernacular, consumers ourselves. In this way, as in so many others, Aretino makes us conscious of our bodies, our habits of consumption, and our endless and unpredictable appetites for things in a culture so deeply invested in not just the art of eating but also the art of eating well.

NOTES

1. Piero Camporesi, *The Land of Hunger*, trans. Tania Croft-Murray (Cambridge: Polity Press, 1996), p. 120.
2. Brian Pullan, "Wage-earners and the Venetian Economy, 1550–1630," in Brian Pullan, ed., *Crisis and Change in the Venetian Economy in the Sixteenth and Seventeenth Centuries* (London: Methuen, 1968), pp. 147–74.
3. Ken Albala, *Eating Right in the Renaissance* (Berkeley: University of California Press, 2002), pp. 2–4.

SUGGESTIONS FOR FURTHER READING

Primary sources

Aretino, Pietro. *The Letters of Pietro Aretino*, trans. Thomas Caldecot Chubb. Hamden, Conn.: Archon Books, 1967.
—— *Tutte le commedie*, ed. G. B. De Sanctis. Milan: Mursia, 1968.
—— *Dialogues*, trans. Raymond Rosenthal. New York: Ballantine Books, 1971.
—— *Selected Letters of Aretino*, trans. George Bull. New York: Penguin, 1976.
—— *Poesie varie: Edizione nazionale delle opere di Pietro Aretino*, eds Giovanni Aquilecchia and Angelo Romano. Rome: Salerno, 1992.
—— *Le Lettere: Edizione nazionale delle opere di Pietro Aretino*, vols. 1–6, eds Giovanni Aquilecchia and Angelo Romano. Rome: Salerno, 1997–2002.
—— *La cortigiana*, trans. J. Douglas Campbell and Leonard G. Sbrocchi. Ottowa: Dovehouse Editions Inc., 2003.
—— *Lettere scritte a Pietro Aretino: Edizione nazionale delle opere di Pietro Aretino*, eds Giovanni Aquilecchia and Angelo Romano. Rome: Salerno, 2003.

Secondary sources

Albala, Ken. *Eating Right in the Renaissance*. Berkeley: University of California Press, 2002.
Andrews, Richard. *Scripts and Scenarios: The Performance of Comedy in Renaissance Italy*. Cambridge: Cambridge University Press, 1993.
Aquilecchia, Giovanni. "Pietro Aretino e altri poligrafi a Venezia," in Girolamo Arnaldi and Manlio Pastore Stocchi, eds, *Storia della cultura veneta*. Vicenza: Neri Pozza, 1980, vol. 3, pt. 2, 61–98.
Bakhtin, Mikhail. *Rabelais and His World*, trans. Hélène Iswolsky. Bloomington: Indiana University Press, 1984.
Bareggi, Claudia di Filippo. *Il mestiere di scrivere: Lavoro intellettuale e mercato librario a Venezia nel Cinquecento*. Rome: Bulzoni, 1988.
Brillat-Savarin, Jean-Antoine. *The Philosopher in the Kitchen*, trans. Anne Drayton. Harmondsworth: Penguin, 1988.
Burke, Peter. *Popular Culture in Early Modern Europe*. New York: Harper & Row, 1978.
Camporesi, Piero. *The Land of Hunger*, trans. Tania Croft-Murray. Cambridge: Polity Press, 1996.
Dionisotti, Carlo. *Geografia e storia della letteratura italiana*. Turin: Einaudi, 1971.
Elias, Norbert. *The Civilizing Process: The History of Manners*, trans. Edmund Jephcott, 2 vols. New York: Urizen Books, 1978.
Findlen, Paula, "Humanism, Politics and Pornography in Renaissance Italy," in Lynn Hunt,

ed., *The Invention of Pornography: Obscenity and the Origins of Modernity, 1500–1800*. New York: Zone Books, 1993, 49–108.

Frantz, David O. *Festum Voluptatis: A Study of Renaissance Erotica*. Columbus: Ohio State University Press, 1989.

Goldthwaite, Richard A. *The Building of Renaissance Florence*. Baltimore: Johns Hopkins University Press, 1980.

Gowers, Emily. *The Loaded Table: Representations of Food in Roman Literature*. Oxford: Clarendon Press, 1993.

Jeanneret, Michel. *A Feast of Words: Banquets and Table Talk in the Renaissance*, trans. Jeremy Whiteley and Emma Hughes. Chicago: University of Chicago Press, 1991.

Larivaille, Paul. *Pietro Aretino fra Rinascimento e manierismo*. Rome: Bulzoni, 1980.

McTighe, Sheila. "Foods and the Body in Italian Genre Paintings, ca. 1580: Campi, Passarotti, Carracci." *Art Bulletin* 86 (2004): 301–23.

Messisbugo, Cristoforo da. *Banchetti, composizioni di vivande e apparecchio generale*, ed. Gernando Bandini. Venice: Neri Pozza, 1960.

Quondam, Amedeo. "Le scene della menzogna: Corte e cortegiano nel 'Ragionamento' di Pietro Aretino." *Psicon* 8–9 (1976): 4–23.

Richlin, Amy. *The Garden of Priapus: Sexuality & Aggression in Roman Humor*, rev. edn. New York: Oxford University Press, 1992.

Ruggiero, Guido. *The Boundaries of Eros: Sex, Crime, and Sexuality in Renaissance Venice*. New York: Oxford University Press, 1985.

Talvacchia, Bette. *Taking Positions: On the Erotic in Renaissance Culture*. Princeton: Princeton University Press, 1999.

Waddington, Raymond B. "Introduction," in Pietro Aretino, *La cortigiana*, trans. J. Douglas Campbell and Leonard G. Sbrocchi. Ottawa: Dovehouse Editions Inc., 2003.

—— *Aretino's Satyr: Sexuality, Satire, and Self-projection in Sixteenth-century Literature and Art*. Toronto: University of Toronto Press, 2004.

CHAPTER TWENTY-SIX

SHAKESPEARE'S DREAM OF RETIREMENT

David Bevington

The idea that *The Tempest*, performed at Whitehall for King James on November 1, 1611 (and quite possibly earlier at the Globe Theater), is Shakespeare's "last" play in the sense of being a self-fashioned retirement party, is by now a commonplace. The idea has met with some skepticism as well. Shakespeare evidently did continue to write after completing *The Tempest*: he collaborated with John Fletcher on *The Two Noble Kinsmen* in about 1613, and seemingly on *Henry VIII*, also with Fletcher, in the same year.[1] Many persons do of course continue to do some work after they retire, and the work in this case was both part-time and presumably designed to ensure a smooth continuity between Shakespeare and his successor as chief dramatist for the King's Men, so that these undertakings do not in any way detract from the idea of *The Tempest* as Shakespeare's official retirement play.

One reason that this concept of a retirement play has run into critical resistance in recent years is that Prospero as a character has undergone a sea change, and generally for the worse. Traditionally regarded as a benign ruler and father, he has been seen of late as a patriarch of the most paternalistic stripe, a tyrant, an officious and even sadistic interferer into the lives of everyone around him, and a colonialist. Can such an oppressor be seen as a stand-in for Shakespeare on the verge of his retirement? To suppose as much would appear to signify the play's implicit endorsement of the capitalism, sexism, and colonialism that much recent criticism is at pains to deplore.[2] To the extent that one sympathizes with Caliban as the oppressed and Prospero as the embodiment of corrupted European patriarchal value systems, the hypothesis of a retirement celebration grows unworkable – unless one is prepared to consign both Prospero and Shakespeare himself to the unhappy category of dead white European males. Shakespeare is surely all of these things, in the literal sense, but since few critics are eager to abandon the idea of Shakespeare as a great and sensitive writer, the critical trend of late has been to separate him as author from his dramatic creation. The portrait of Prospero becomes Shakespeare's incisive critique of an oppressive social order as it encounters, and seeks to rule over, a newly discovered world across the seas.

Much is at stake, then, in the debate over Prospero as a colonialist – not simply whether the play endorses a kind of racism but also whether the vision of the play can be said to sum up the artistic accomplishments of England's greatest writer.

Perhaps it can, if we stop to consider that Prospero is not really a colonialist in the usual sense of that term after all. He did not come to the island with the intent to colonize it. He was put to sea against his own will and managed to reach the island only by good luck and the kindly intervention of Gonzalo, who supplied the miserable boat to which he and Miranda were consigned with food and water. Once on the island, he and Miranda apparently took Caliban in as virtually a member of their family; the enslavement, however harsh it seems to us, was motivated by a need to protect Miranda against a rape. When Prospero departs from the island at the end of the play, he leaves Caliban in possession of the island to which he has laid claim. In other words, Prospero sets up no commercial scheme by which he might exploit the island's inhabitant(s) or natural resources. The real colonialists in *The Tempest* are Trinculo, Stephano, Antonio, and Sebastian, all of whom immediately conceive of the idea of exploiting Caliban as a kind of marketable freak the moment they lay eyes on him (II.ii.28–31 and 68–71, v.i.267–9). Not surprisingly, these are the play's most unreconstructable rogues and villains.

This essay argues that the play does indeed attempt to sum up an artistic career, and in doing so will gladly concede many of the points that Prospero's critics urge against him. Prospero is assuredly, as Shakespeare presents him, dictatorial, controlling, and intrusive into the lives of others. He is even deceptive in his managerial tactics. But so are dramatists, if they are worth their salt. They invent characters and push them around, arranging whom they will meet and under what circumstances, fooling those characters with false shows, testing them relentlessly, humiliating them, and at last sentencing them to edifying punishments, or (more commonly in Shakespeare) to forgiveness and a second chance, even when that forgiveness seems scarcely deserved. If poets are, in Shelley's well-known formulation, the legislators of mankind, then dramatists are especially so in that they preside over the moral destinies of the characters they create in a way that no other mortals can hope to do. Dramatists are the gods of their own creation. And no dramatist is more so than Prospero on the island of *The Tempest*. The very qualities that Prospero stands accused of from a modern perspective are the very qualities that align him with the kind of intensely theatrical directing of people's lives that we find everywhere in this play.

This island of *The Tempest* is Utopian. It is also, pre-eminently, a world of imagination and of the theater, where the artist is free to do virtually anything, so long as it conforms to the ideals of his creativity and to the wishes of his audience. The island of *The Tempest* is not the real world, and it is not even a mimetic representation of such a "real" world. It is a place of imagination and creativity. Shakespeare's play relies on no literary source or sources to an extent that is unusual in in his works; apart from its apparent use of two accounts of shipwreck in the Bahamas,[3] *The Tempest* interweaves the adventures of its various characters in storylines that are original. The fact that those adventures in *The Tempest* continually remind us of Shakespeare's own earlier dramatic writings – a journey from the "fallen" social world disfigured by the bitter enmity of brothers to an imaginary landscape, a shipwreck, the close companionship of father and daughter, the rivalry between a young man and the father for the daughter's affection, the presiding of magical spirits over the affairs of mortals, the below-stairs antics of clownish characters, the resolution of the plot in marriage, and the return to a renewed world of social order – tends to support the hypothesis that Shakespeare is looking back over his own writing career and assessing what he thinks he has tried to accomplish. Shakespeare's adroit use of the classical "unities" of time, place, and action – 24 or 48 hours, one island, one multiple but interconnected plot – reads like the statement of an artist who wishes to show his critics like Ben Jonson that he is perfectly capable of writing a neoclassically constructed play, as he had done in his early *The Comedy of Errors*, albeit in his own ineffable way that glances "from heaven to earth, from earth to heaven" in order to "bod[y] forth/The forms of things unknown" (*A Midsummer Night's Dream*, v.i.13–15).[4] Then, too, the decision of John Heminges and Henry Condell, the editors of the 1623 Folio edition of Shakespeare's works, to give *The Tempest* pride of first place is suggestive of a special recognition that the play summarizes, perhaps better than any other, what Shakespeare's colleagues thought his playwriting was all about.

Containing as it does so many features that are compatible with a theory of its being a retirement play, *The Tempest* reads compellingly as the dramatist's fantasy about the concluding chapter of his life as artist and as father. Nowhere is this more true than in the central pairing of father and daughter. Shakespeare seems to be responding to a timeless fantasy: if one were to be deposited on a desert island with no hope of rescue, what books would one choose to have there in one's possession, and, above all, with whom would one wish to be marooned in this way? (Many *New Yorker* cartoons have capitalized on this theme.) As artist and magician, Prospero rejoices that he has been able, with the help of old Gonzalo, to take away his books from Italy into his exile; as a father, he rejoices even more that he is given the precious company of his only daughter. Stranded on the island of *The Tempest*, they live as a couple. They are all in all to each other. Prospero is Miranda's instructor, in language, mores, and the art of living. Miranda is her father's companion, his pupil, his hope for the future, and his helper in domesticity. Caliban is there, of course, and as a member of their small family at first, until his awakening sexual desire drives him to attempt a rape for which he is confined to a rock and is relegated to the ignominious status of "slave." Caliban thus forfeits, in the eyes of Prospero and Miranda, any claim he may have had to be a son and a brother. No mother is present. Prospero mentions his wife only once, in passing, and as part of a wry joke (spoken to Miranda) about fathers' perennial uncertainty as to whether a child presented to the father by his wife is undoubtedly his (I.ii.55–7). Shakespeare's island fantasy is thus notably selective in its representation of the nuclear family: no wife, and no son other than an intruding native. Caliban is at times an utterly engaging character, responsive to the beauty of the island and eloquent in defense of his claim to being the island's original inhabitant. Still, from the perspective of Prospero and Miranda, he is an impenitent creature "on whose nature/Nurture can never stick" (IV.i.188–9).

We are left, then, with the central pairing of father and daughter. The configuration is all the more compelling in this "last" play of Shakespeare's because it so movingly recapitulates narratives of fathers and daughters that have dominated the so-called romances leading up to *The Tempest*: *Pericles*, *Cymbeline*, and *The Winter's Tale*. It does so, moreover, in ways that seem consciously designed to heal the wounds of earlier interactions between fathers and daughters (as in *Othello* and *King Lear*), and to bring that continuing saga to a happy conclusion in which the father is benignly in charge from first to last.

A widower father having to cope with a daughter or daughters is, to be sure, a not unfamiliar situation even in Shakespeare's early plays. Baptista Minola, in *The Taming of the Shrew*, must find a way to marry off two daughters, unassisted by a wife; we assume that she is dead. The Duke of Milan in *The Two Gentlemen of Verona*, old Egeus in *A Midsummer Night's Dream*, and Shylock in *The Merchant of Venice* are blocking figures of the sort that Northrop Frye labels *alazon* characters; each stands in the way of his single daughter's romantic hopes only to be outmaneuvered at last in a replay of a familiar neoclassical plot.[5] Wives are scarcely ever mentioned (Shylock does recall his wife, Leah, at one poignant moment) and appear in all cases to be dead. Leonato, in *Much Ado About Nothing*, is a widower who is elated at the prospect of his daughter marrying the princely Don Pedro, then quite content with her engagement to young Count Claudio, and then, sadly, so mistrusting of Hero's reputation for virtue that he is ready (as are Claudio and Don Pedro) to believe the worst of slanders against young Hero; only when he is counseled by Friar Francis and has had time to recover his senses does he begin to regain faith in his daughter. Duke Senior in *As You Like It* is, to be sure, the kind of father that a daughter of marriageable age might best like to have if she could choose: wise, patient, understanding, ready and willing to see his sole daughter and hope of his posterity marry a young man whom he rightly considers to be eminently eligible. Yet Duke Senior is the exception to the rule, one whose benign understanding serves to highlight by contrast what is more often a distressing matter of generational conflict. The vulnerability of a father, and his fear of desertion or dishonor at his daughter's hands, is thus a continuing theme in Shakespeare.

Scholars used to wonder if casting limitations might explain the absence of wives in a time when acting companies had to rely for women's parts on a limited supply of sufficiently trained boys, but the role of Juliet's mother in *Romeo and Juliet*, among others, tends to undermine that materialist argument by showing that mothers could be supplied when needed. Presumably, then, Shakespeare chooses to pair widower fathers and daughters as a matter of artistic and personal choice, sometimes guided by his sources. All in all, we might say that Shakespeare presents us with a goodly number of widower fathers with single daughters in the comedies of the first half of his writing career, and that in these instances we can perhaps discern a growing awareness of the painful threat presented to such fathers by the daughters when those daughters come to marriageable age. For the most part, however, it is in the plays from the second half of Shakespeare's career as a dramatist that the father–daughter configuration assumes a salient role.

Among the great tragedies, *Hamlet* offers a prime example of how not to be the father of a daughter (or of a son, for that matter). Obviously Polonius loves and cares for Ophelia, and may well feel the burdens of responsibility as a parent in the absence of his wife. In his overly protective wariness of Hamlet as a potential son-in-law, Polonius is something of a transitional figure from Egeus, Shylock, and Leonato to the fathers of the late tragedies and the romances. The traditionally comic business of the "blocking" father – familiar to Shakespeare and his contemporaries from the works of the Roman playwright Plautus – may inform the wryly satiric stance that

Hamlet adopts toward the father of the young woman he has been courting. Polonius is something of an *alazon* figure, then, but with a devastatingly tragic dimension that culminates in the slaying of the father by the young man. That killing is not over Ophelia, to be sure, but the consequences for her are certainly dire.

Brabantio in *Othello* is more directly anticipatory of the father whose story Shakespeare will repeatedly, even obsessively, re-enact in his late plays. Brabantio's life with Desdemona has been like that of Shylock with Jessica, and anticipatory of that of Prospero and Miranda: they have shared the duties of their household, with the daughter acting as hostess and companion to her father. We learn from Othello's account of his wooing that during Othello's visits to Brabantio's house, Desdemona has been in and out of the room while the men talked, hearing part of Othello's travel accounts but not all. The "house affairs" (I.iii.149) have occupied so much of her attention that she has to ask Othello for a fuller account when they are able to be alone. In other ways, as well, we see that Desdemona occupies a central place in her father's heart – so much so that her elopement is, to him, a betrayal. To be sure, her marrying a black officer contributes materially to Brabantio's dismay, but we gather from his hostility toward Roderigo that he has not warmed to the idea of Desdemona's marrying under any circumstances. He allows belatedly that he would prefer Roderigo as a son-in-law, but only as an alternative to Othello. Some fathers find the marrying of their daughters a path strewn with emotional hazards, and Brabantio is such a father.

Once Desdemona is unreclaimedly married to Othello, Brabantio accepts his bitter fate, but only with a warning to his daughter's new husband. "Look to her, Moor, if thou hast eyes to see," he warns Othello. "She has deceived her father, and may thee" (I.iii.295–6). These are Brabantio's last words in the play. He has been utterly unable to heed her plea that he afford her the choice that Brabantio's own bride took as her due in the previous generation: the choice of leaving a father whom the daughter has loved and obeyed, and to whom the daughter still owes reverence and thanks, to give her loyalty to a new lord and husband (I.iii.183–91). Brabantio cannot hear this, cannot learn this hard lesson. We understand later that he has died of a broken heart. Whether he was afforded any brief grim satisfaction by learning, or at least intuiting, that Othello collapses into fatal mistrust of Desdemona, we do not know.

Even though King Lear is the father of not one but three daughters, the focus is once again on a single cherished daughter. The centrality of Cordelia to Lear's anxious craving for happiness is plainly crucial, and becomes increasingly so as the play goes on. *King Lear* is the nightmare for which *The Tempest*'s happy ending will eventually find a solution. Lear is, like so many other fathers in Shakespeare, a widower, and, as in *The Tempest*, his dead wife is mentioned only once, in Lear's bitterly ironic speculation that her tomb might sepulchre "an adulteress" since she has presented him with such unnatural daughters as Goneril and Regan (II.iv.129–31). Though more bitterly expressed, it is the same misogynistic joke as in Prospero's jesting allusion to his dead wife as having vowed that Miranda was indeed Prospero's child (*The Tempest*, I.ii.55–9). This male phobia of paternal uncertainty is at the heart of the father–daughter anxiety in Shakespeare's late plays.

The death of Cordelia, so hotly debated, deplored, and frequently excised in the stage history of the play, is also central to Shakespeare's fascination with the overdependency of the aging father on a favorite daughter. Lear has refused to heed the lesson that Brabantio could not learn: that he must let go in favor of a younger candidate for his daughter's chief loyalty and affection. Indeed, what Cordelia attempts to say to Lear in scene 1 of *King Lear* is precisely what Desdemona said to her father. Both daughters express their unceasing devotion and gratitude to their fathers, along with a quiet insistence that their wish to marry be respected. Both fathers make the mistake of interpreting what they hear as a betrayal. Both destroy their own happiness by clinging to what Freud characterizes as an incestuous tie – not in any overt physical sense, but as a longing so intense as to border on the compulsive. Both die of a broken heart. In Lear's case the nightmare is grotesquely magnified by Lear's being reunited with his loving daughter only to lose her once more and forever, but essentially the emotional crisis is the same. The presumed reason for Lear's final and devastating loss of Cordelia is that he has not learned how to let go his proprietary grasp on her. Having lost everything else – his throne, his worldly possessions, his sanity, his very sense of identity – Lear is prepared to bargain with the gods: he will be content as long as he can have Cordelia. His moment of reunion with her, as they are herded off to prison, is his one moment of genuine happiness in the play. "We two alone will sing like birds i'th' cage," he says to her:

> When thou dost ask me blessing, I'll kneel down
> And ask of thee forgiveness. So we'll live,
> And pray, and sing, and tell old tales, and laugh
> At gilded butterflies . . .
> And take upon 's the mystery of things,
> As if we were God's spies, and we'll wear out,
> In a walled prison, packs and sects of great ones,
> That ebb and flow by th' moon. (v.iii.9–19)

Nothing else matters to Lear; his happiness is wholly caught up in cherishing her company. What she says on the occasion of their capture is, however, considerably less euphoric. "We are not the first / Who with best meaning have incurred the worst," she says to him. "For thee, oppressèd king, I am cast down; / Myself could else outfrown false Fortune's frown" (lines 3–6). She expresses concern for her father's misfortunes, but says of herself only that she has learned something akin to the stoic truth that sustains Edgar as well. She has, after all, done what she vowed once she would vastly prefer not to do: give up her own marital life to devote herself solely to the care of her father. She has done so uncomplainingly, earnestly, even willingly, because her sisters have treated their father with such cruelty, but it was not what she had originally envisaged for herself. For reasons such as these, perhaps, Shakespeare decided that Cordelia must die – as she had not done in any of Shakespeare's sources, and as she would not do in Nahum Tate's Restoration stage adaptation. Her death is a bleak answer to Lear's unresolved possessiveness.

In Shakespeare's four late romances culminating in *The Tempest*, fathers and daughters are a constant focus, along with a mother-wife who is sometimes included in the family constellation, sometimes pointedly absent, and sometimes replaced by a wicked stepmother whose grotesque evil reads like still another distress signal concerning the maternal presence. Shakespeare appears to have chosen source plots that enabled him to explore further the issues and conflicts that he had dwelt upon in *Othello*, *King Lear*, and other plays. The incessant repetition of the family pattern may owe something to circumstances in Shakespeare's own life. He had married Anne Hathaway in November of 1582 when she was already three months pregnant; their first daughter, Susannah, was born in May of 1583. Two more children, the twins Hamnet and Judith, came along in February of 1585. William and Anne had no more children during their remaining 31-plus years of nominally married life. Medical reasons could perhaps explain such a long childlessness, but an absence of cohabitation may offer the likeliest explanation. Birth control methods were essentially non-existent, and families were often large. Some time in 1585 or afterwards, Shakespeare moved to London and took up the professional life of actor and dramatist. He never moved his family to London to be with him, even when he was wealthy enough to do so. He acquired New Place, one of the best houses in Stratford-upon-Avon, and bought the residence now known as Hall's Croft for his daughter Susannah and her physician husband, John Hall. Susannah seems to have been a favorite daughter, at least to the extent that Shakespeare was less generous to Judith, whose marriage to Thomas Quiney in 1616 was to a man with whom Shakespeare had quarreled. (Shakespeare did revise his last will and testament in March of that year to make some provision for the marriage.) Certainly his family was comfortably provided for, and presumably he got to Stratford from time to time during his working years, though the journey from London to Stratford was a long one, and his professional life in London afforded him little free time other than during unpredictable bouts of the plague. Anne's welfare was assured after his death. Yet Shakespeare mentions her in his will only as the recipient of their "second best bed." The tone of this provision seems churlish, in relation to other wills of actors and theater people during this same period, so that we have reason to wonder if the marriage was all that might have been hoped.[6] This is not to suggest that the late romances are coherently autobiographical. It is to wonder if Shakespeare chose the stories he dramatized as a way of pondering the prospect of retirement and eventual return to Stratford by means of his late plays, culminating in *The Tempest*.

The text of *Pericles* is corrupt and shows signs of multiple authorship. The Folio editors, Heminges and Condell, may have had good reason for excluding *Pericles* from the collection they published in 1623 of all of Shakespeare's known plays. Heminges and Condell were, as Shakespeare's lifelong colleagues, intimately acquainted with his work. Yet most students of the play find Shakespeare's hand to be prominent, especially in the final scenes, and it is here that we see most substantively the working out of a suggestively familiar family history. Pericles' first encounter on his many voyages is with the incestuous king of Antiochus and his beautiful but sin-ridden daughter. As the one overt instance of father–daughter incest in all Shakespeare, this relationship hovers menacingly over the play as a mute warning of the kind of unnatural error that the hero must avoid at all costs. The incestuous danger contrasts instructively with the more happy courtship that Pericles soon experiences at the court of Simonides, the king of Pentapolis. To be sure, this latter monarch seems also at first to be strongly attracted to his daughter and unwilling to give her up; he bridles at Pericles' overtures and appears to be unreasonably angry in much the way that Brabantio and Lear have behaved before him. Yet he soon reveals to us and to the alarmed young couple that he was only putting on a show of resistance. Every good story of courtship needs a complication to overcome, and so Simonides has play-acted the role of the sternly denying father, doing so in the best tradition of the Plautine *alazon* or blocking figure. His doing so strikingly anticipates the seemingly alarming behavior of Prospero toward young Ferdinand when they first meet in *The Tempest*. Shakespeare imagines in these two father figures an angry response to the daughter's suitor that may arise from a genuine anxiety about the loss of that daughter, but that is then rationalized as part of a genial process of acceptance over which the father seems to maintain control.

Even though Pericles' marriage to Thaisa is happy, its subsequent history is one that bears an uncomfortable resemblance to the circumstances of Shakespeare's own prolonged separation from his wife and family. When Pericles and his nine-months-pregnant wife undertake a sea voyage, Thaisa gives birth to their daughter, Marina, in the midst of a fearful storm and then dies in childbirth. Or so it appears. Urged by the mariners to commit Thaisa's body to the deep to satisfy their superstitious belief that Neptune will never be appeased until the body is thus disposed of, Pericles reluctantly agrees. He then consigns his infant daughter Marina to the care of Dionyza, wife of Cleon (the governor of Tarsus), who turns out to be one of the wicked stepmothers in these late plays — as nightmarish an image of motherhood as one could hope to find. Meantime the good mother, Thaisa, seemingly dead, washes ashore at Ephesus in her coffin and is resuscitated by a scholarly magician named Cerimon, who supports her wish to become a vestal priestess in the nearby Temple of Diana. Marina survives the threat posed by the wicked Dionyza, is seized by pirates, and is sold by them into a bordello on Mytilene, where she proceeds to convert potential customers by her radiant innocence. Eventually, Pericles' ship finds its way to Mytilene also, with Pericles himself in a deep and virtually catatonic depression. When the governor of Mitylene, Lysimachus, hits upon the plan of asking Marina to minister to the ailing Pericles, she does so in a virtual replay of Cordelia's bringing her father back to sanity. Following the tearful reunion of father and daughter, a dream vision instructs Pericles and Marina to visit the Temple of Diana at Ephesus, where they find Thaisa. This version of the father–daughter saga in the late plays thus provides a happy ending with husband, wife, and daughter all joyfully reunited. At the same time, the bleak depression that Pericles has suffered suggests the working out of an unconscious guilt for his having abandoned them both. Pericles is a man who, though admittedly constrained to do so, has literally thrown away his wife and left his daughter to the tender mercies of a wicked foster-mother. Whatever the mitigating circumstances, *Pericles* is certainly the fable of a father who freely confesses that his second chance at family happiness is an undeserved bliss.

The wicked foster-mother or stepmother is once again a central character in *Cymbeline*; so is the undeserving, perversely rejecting father. King Cymbeline refuses to countenance the marriage of his daughter, Imogen, to a gentleman of less than royal rank, Posthumus Leonatus. Because Imogen will not marry Cloten, the grotesquely witless son of the king's second wife, Imogen is in disgrace and Posthumus forced to go into exile. Her true mother is dead. Until his recent second marriage, Cymbeline has been, like Brabantio, Shylock, Prospero, and the rest, a widower with a single daughter. His two sons have strangely disappeared, having been taken away from the court by a disaffected courtier, Belarius, in order that they might be raised in the uncorrupted, pristine environment of the Welsh mountains. Imogen, lured to Wales by the prospect of finding her banished husband, happens across the cave where Belarius and her brothers dwell, and lives with them for a brief time disguised as a young man. She is quite unaware of their royal identity, as are they. Eventually all are reconciled to the king. Cymbeline is finally disabused of his infatuation with the wicked queen, who has in fact been attempting to poison or otherwise kill both king and daughter. Thus *Cymbeline* ends like *Pericles* in a happy family reunion, with two important variations: the wicked queen becomes the scapegoat figure embodying all the hatreds and misunderstandings that have afflicted the family for so long, and the king's sons are restored to him so that he will now enjoy the rich reward of a crown prince and heir.

The motif of the lost and recovered son, missing until now in the narratives of *Othello*, *King Lear*, and *Pericles*, but soon to be revisited in varying manifestations in *The Winter's Tale* (where the son is lost and not recovered) and *The Tempest* (where the lost son is transformed into a son-in-law), prompts us to ask what dreamwork may be involved here. Shakespeare had one son, the twin, Hamnet, born in early 1585. Hamnet died in 1596, at the age of 11. One can only begin to imagine what a crushing blow this loss must have been to the author of the *Sonnets*, with their insistent refrain of advice that the poet's friend "get a son" (Sonnet 7). This terrible event has posed a critical difficulty of sizeable proportions for Shakespeare biographers and interpreters, especially since the plays that evidently follow in 1596 and afterwards – *Much Ado About Nothing*, *The Merry Wives of Windsor*, *As You Like it*, *1* and *2 Henry IV* – say so little about the deaths of sons. The problem is compounded by the fact that some earlier plays, such as *1* and *3 Henry VI*, contain eloquent passages on the deaths of sons. The joining in death of Lord Talbot and his son John in *1 Henry VI* is just the kind of poetic tribute that one might look to for biographical interpretation, but it predates 1596 by a considerable margin. Attempts by Stephen Greenblatt and others to push forward the date of *King John* to 1596 or later are manifestly motivated by a wish that *King John* should come after Hamnet's death, so that Constance's lament ("Grief fills the room up of my absent child," etc., III.iv. 93–8) might resonate in that context, but even if the late dating were convincing we still have the contrary evidence of Shakespeare's manifest ability to write with poignant intensity on a son's death long before Hamnet died, and conversely his silence on the subject in the comedies and histories he wrote after 1596.[7]

The Shakespeare scholar Richard Wheeler has provided the best hypothesis yet, by examining two plays. In *2 Henry IV*, Lady Percy upbraids her father-in-law, the Earl of Northumberland, for his failure to show up at the Battle of Shrewsbury, where, at the end of *1 Henry IV*, the earl's son Hotspur has met his untimely end (*2 Henry IV*, II.iii.9–41). Wheeler cogently wonders if Shakespeare here reveals something of what it may have felt like if, as seems likely, he was unable to get to Stratford in time to see Hamnet before the boy died. This is speculation, of course, but it at least offers an explanation of a passage for which the chroniclers provide no source. More substantially, Wheeler points out that *Twelfth Night* deals with twins in a telling way. The twins, a male and a female, are separated by a storm and the young man is presumed drowned – as later is the case of Ferdinand in *The Tempest*. Viola, by taking upon her the male likeness of her twin brother, enacts his life as well as her own until, at the very end of the play, she brings her brother back to life through the stage magic of which she is a capable mistress. In a play of perhaps 1600 to 1601, then, some four or five years after the death of Hamnet, we find a dreamwork fantasy of bringing back to life a son who was accounted dead. We cannot of course be sure of a biographical connection, but it does at least provide a clue as to why Shakespeare chooses to dramatize the story of twins at this time. Twins are central earlier to *The Comedy of Errors*, but without the motif of a drowned son restored to life.

In a charming fictional biography of Judith Shakespeare, called *My Father Had a Daughter*,[8] Grace Tiffany imagines what it might have been like for Judith to encounter her father's play of *Twelfth Night* and to see it as a fable of the death of Judith's own twin brother, Hamnet. She is horrified at first by the seeming exploitation of such a deeply private matter, but eventually comes around to the view that her father was right after all to find a way of restoring Hamnet to a kind of life through art. The genre of fictional biography allows Tiffany to speculate freely in a way that opens up a potentially very personal reading of the play.

To read *The Winter's Tale* in these same terms is to uncover a situation that is even more poignantly close to Shakespeare's own family story as he approached retirement and a return to Stratford. Leontes, King of Sicilia, is a more guilty husband and father than we have yet encountered. Conceiving an insane jealousy of his wife, Hermione, seemingly because the nine months of her pregnancy now approaching full term correspond to the nine months that the king's best friend, King Polixenes of Bohemia, has been a guest at the Sicilian court, Leontes insists on putting his wife on trial for adultery even though he has no other evidence and even though his advisers all fervently counsel him to believe in her chaste goodness. The trial is too much for Hermione, and she dies after having given birth to a daughter. Or so it appears. Indeed, we are assured of the death of the queen with such certainty that we realize later we have been deliberately misled by the dramatist. The spirit of Hermione appears in a dream or vision to Antigonus, the hapless courtier charged with depositing the newly born Perdita in "some remote and desert place," bidding him that he carry out his unwelcome commission on the coast of Bohemia. "And so," says Antigonus, "with shrieks, / She melted into air" (II.iii.176, III.iii.35–6). Accordingly, we as audience feel a sense of repugnance toward Leontes' actions that far transcends our anxieties about Pericles or Cymbeline. Leontes is directly responsible for the death of his innocent wife. It is as though he has sentenced her to execution.

Indeed, Leontes accepts this harsh judgment. No one is harder on him than he is himself, aided by his counselor, Paulina, who reminds him daily over a period of some 16 years that he has killed his wife. The inescapable nature of this guilt is emphasized again and again: by the refusal of Leontes' advisers to countenance what he has done, by the unambiguous message of Apollo brought from the oracle at Delphi that "Hermione is chaste, Polixenes blameless, Camillo a true subject, Leontes a jealous tyrant, his innocent babe truly begotten" (III.ii.132–4), and by the death of the son Mamillius, whose swift demise from heartbreak over his mother's suffering is seen at once by Leontes as a sign that "Apollo's angry, and the heavens themselves / Do strike at my injustice" (III.ii.146–7).

Yet because this is a tragicomic romance, not a tragedy, forgiveness and reconciliation do eventually triumph, once penitence has had its long and painfully slow chance to remind Leontes incessantly that he has done the unforgivable. The daughter, Perdita, grows up as a shepherdess in Bohemia, and is so entrancingly beautiful that she wins the amorous affection of Florizel, the princely son of Leontes' now-estranged boyhood best friend, Polixenes. The play shifts into its comic mode as Polixenes attempts (like Egeus in *A Midsummer Night's Dream* and other *alazon* figures of the early comedies) to prevent a marriage he considers socially unworthy of the crown prince of Bohemia. The young people flee by means of a ship and make their way to Sicilia, where Perdita is reunited with her father in a touching replay of the reunions of Pericles with Marina and Cymbeline with Imogen. A last-minute contretemps threatens their happiness when Polixenes arrives in hot pursuit and insists on the arrest of the young couple, but this difficulty is soon straightened out by the revelation that Perdita is of royal lineage.

Why does Shakespeare describe this great moment of peripeteia through the conversation of three unnamed gentlemen (v.ii) rather than presenting it directly in the theater? In part, perhaps, he does so because he does not wish to upstage (in a literal sense) the still more dramatic moment of discovery, soon to come, when Hermione will be unveiled as a statue and will turn out to be alive after all. Another reason is that it enables Shakespeare to stress what is so indescribable about an event that he conjures up through language rather than through visible gesture. Speaking of the reunion of Leontes and Camillo, who has been with Polixenes in Bohemia all these sixteen years and is now home at long last, one gentleman describes how "There was speech in their dumbness, language in their gesture. They looked as they had heard of a world ransomed, or one destroyed. A notable passion of wonder appeared in them." The news that Leontes has reclaimed his lost daughter "is so like an old tale that the verity of it is in strong suspicion." The event exceeds the power of speech itself: anyone not privileged with having been present at these reunions has "lost a sight which was to be seen, cannot be spoken of." The story of poor Antigonus, who, they learn, was torn to pieces by a bear after having deposited the infant Perdita on the Bohemian shore, is "Like an old tale still, which will have matter to rehearse though credit be asleep and not an ear open" (v.ii.14–64). The wonderment calls our attention metatheatrically to what is so deliciously improbable about a play in which a shepherdess turns out to be a king's daughter, a statue comes to life, and the unforgivable is forgiven.

All this is prelude to the play's climactic final action in which the "statue" of Hermione comes to life. Once again, Shakespeare stresses the wonderment, the improbability. Paulina, presiding over the scene, insists that she is not "assisted / By wicked powers," as indeed she needs to do, since the act of seemingly bringing the dead back to life comes threateningly close to forbidden magic and blasphemy. She is, like Cerimon in *Pericles* and then Prospero in *The Tempest*, a learned magician whose theatrical "trickery" is essentially that of the dramatist in the theater. Her art requires something like willing suspension of belief. Her way of putting this is to insist, to her audience, "It is required / You do awake your faith" (v.iii.90–5). Indeed, we as audience do not know quite how to interpret what she has done. In a practical sense, she seems to have sequestered Hermione over a period of 16 years, letting no one (including us as audience) know that the queen is in fact alive, so that the sharp sorrow of penance will have its full course of time in which to work on Leontes' heart. As though she is an agent of the god Apollo of Delphi, her actions are shaped by the demands of the divine oracle: "the King shall live without an heir if that which is lost be not found" (III.ii.134–6). Yet in human terms this plot seems inconceivable, that Hermione would consent to so long a sequestration and that she and Paulina would insist on 16 years of penance. We are left with a vivid sense, especially in the theater, that a miracle has taken place. The dead queen has been brought back; a statue has come to life. The very staging of the scene, in which a practiced actress (a boy in Shakespeare's first production, presumably) must stand motionless for a long while and then begin to move, invites us emotionally to experience what miracle and wonderment can achieve in the theater.

If we ask why this great moment has captured Shakespeare's imagination, and what part this "miracle" plays in the continuing saga of sin and redemption in the late plays, we might well be tempted to wonder if this dreamwork fantasy has something to do with Shakespeare's own story of long separation from wife and family, his continuing interest in a precious relationship between the father and a favorite daughter, and the prospect of reunion with that family as the dramatist prepared to retire from his professional life. In no other late play is the father so guilty as is Leontes of having abandoned his wife. Nowhere else is the eventual forgiveness so undeserved and by that very token so indescribably dear. Nowhere else does Shakespeare express so touchingly what it might be like for a guilty husband such as Leontes to encounter his long-estranged wife and then discover in that moment that he does still love her. The statue which, in this Pygmalion story, is metamorphosed into Hermione appears to her beholders not as she was 16 years ago but as she is now. She has grown older with Leontes, albeit in separation. And she is desirably lovely. "Oh, she's warm!" exclaims Leontes as Hermione steps down from her pedestal and approaches her husband so that they can touch once more. "If this be magic, let it be an art/Lawful as eating," Leontes says (V.iii.109–11). As a fantasy, the story tells of a husband who is given a second chance by the radiant innocence and goodness of the wife he has attempted to destroy and whom he believes he has succeeded in killing. Leontes' story is that of Othello with a happy ending. It is a magical ending such as tragicomedy can provide.

Yet Mamillius is truly dead. No illusion can recover the lost son and heir. The dreamwork here may be suggestive of a pattern continued from earlier plays, in which lost sons are recovered: the presumably drowned twin of Viola in *Twelfth Night* and the sons of Cymbeline who have grown up in mountainous Wales. Eventually, dreamwork can (and should) come to terms with the necessity of letting go of a son who is simply gone. The loss points forward in this case to *The Tempest*, where the images of loss and recovery are masterfully combined: the supposedly drowned Ferdinand is restored to his guilt-ridden father, Alonso, who has been convinced that the presumed drowning was a divine punishment for Alonso's own culpabilities, whereas Prospero finds in the place of the son he never had a fine son-in-law.

As this theatrical sleight-of-hand suggests, *The Tempest* is in many ways a resolution of Shakespeare's many explorations of family conflict involving father, daughter, and son. Earlier, we have looked at ways in which *The Tempest* is a recapitulation of Shakespeare's artistry as dramatist: the medley of plot elements and character types that define his earlier dramaturgy, the metatheatrical reflections on the special mix of wonderment and social observation that is so quintessentially Shakespearean, the freeing of Ariel as a gesture of acknowledgment that a theatrical artist must eventually set aside the gift of creativity he has mysteriously been given for a time, and the like. *The Tempest* also recapitulates and then perfects the questions of family relationships with which Shakespeare has been so concerned.

Prospero does correctly what his predecessors have done so abysmally for the most part. Not without an emotional struggle, he sees that it is time for Miranda to marry a younger man. Prospero briefly play-acts the role of denying father, as did Simonides in *Pericles*, forcing Ferdinand into the slavish business of carrying wood; the menial task links Ferdinand imagistically with Caliban, who has also desired Miranda as his sexual partner. Caliban of course will not do; Ferdinand is eminently eligible, not least of all in that his marriage to Miranda will unite Milan and Naples and thus end (for a time at least) the civil conflict that led to Prospero's being banished from Milan some 12 years earlier. Prospero's play-acting the role of the *alazon* may represent in part a reluctance and sadness that even he feels as a possessive father about to lose his daughter to a younger man, but in the main his actions appear to be driven by the consideration that Ferdinand and Miranda should not be allowed to fall in love and consummate their desire too quickly.[9] Love prospers in the face of difficulty, in comedies at least, and Prospero is above all a theatrical artist, aware that the lovers' story needs the complication of a blocking father. "This swift business / I must uneasy make, lest too light winning / Make the prize light," he confides to us (I.ii.454–6). Prospero obligingly takes on the part of the gruff, angry parent, and yet even as he does so he repeatedly winks at us in asides to assure us that he is only playing a role.

The deceptions that Prospero practices on Alonso, Antonio, Sebastian, and the rest are similarly theatrical in their intent. These deceptions are admittedly not without a personal element of anger and desire for revenge; Prospero freely confesses such feelings to Ariel and is moved to practice forgiveness in part at least because Ariel tactfully suggests that compassion and tenderness are what humans should strive most to discover in themselves; Ariel too would become tender, he says, "were I human" (V.i.20). Yet forgiveness can be offered only to those who are truly sorry for what they have done. "The rarer action is / In virtue than in vengeance. They being penitent, / The sole drift of my purpose doth extend / Not a frown further" (V.i.27–30). Prospero's intent in deceiving Alonso about the seeming death of Ferdinand is, in part at least, to subject Alonso to the kind of bitter but eventually healing remorse that Leontes had to endure for 16 years in *The Winter's Tale*.

Whether Antonio and Sebastian are capable of true remorse is, to be sure, an uncertain matter at best, and yet Prospero has guided them too through a series of deceptive experiences aimed at probing the conscience. Through Ariel he has prevented these two bad men from assassinating Alonso and his party. Again with Ariel's able means, Prospero confronts the villains with a picture of their depravity in the shape of a frightening harpy and with a sermon assuring them that their every action is watched by a higher power. That power, as Ariel says, "delaying, not forgetting," insists on moral accountability in all those who come to the island (III.iii.73). On the Italian mainland, villainy will no doubt go on apace, but, in the world of the theater that the island represents, all are held responsible for crimes whether committed or intended. Stephano and Sebastian too, in company with the easily misled Caliban, are subjected to a kind of purgatorial chastening that in their case is suitably ludicrous; they are chased by hounds and submerged in a "filthy-mantled pool" until they are stinking of horse-piss and racked with convulsions (IV.i.178–263). In all of these practices, Prospero comes close to a kind of hubris in assuming a godlike role, and indeed he acknowledges this arrogance when he prepares to abjure his magical art and drown his book; the burden is a great one, and part of him longs to set it aside. Yet the responsibility is inescapably that of the theater artist, presiding over the lives of his characters like Destiny personified. The gods in *The Tempest* are creations of Prospero and Ariel; Prospero is the ultimate supernal authority on his island. He does briefly acknowledge a "providence divine" that has saved the lives of himself and Miranda and has brought Prospero's enemies to within reach of his magical authority (I.ii.160), but within that special theatrical world he is truly the sole ruler.

Alonso is restored to his supposedly drowned son; Prospero gains a son-in-law by overseeing the union of Ferdinand and Miranda. The son-in-law appears to be an entirely satisfactory answer. When he has been duly impressed by Prospero's skill (aided by Ariel) in staging a masque to celebrate the betrothal of the young couple, Ferdinand cannot contain his admiration. "This is a most majestic vision," he ventures. "Let me live here ever!/So rare a wondered father and a wise/Makes this place Paradise" (IV.i.118–24). Whether one reads the word as "wife" or "wise" (the possibility that the tall "s" is an "f" in the First Folio printing has led to some critical disagreement about this), the praise in either case is something any father would no doubt love to hear. Is this a kind of fantasy in which the dramatist imagines himself to have found a husband for his daughter who would willingly live out his days on a desert island in such fine company? In any event, the happy ending reads plausibly as an imagined scenario in which the lost son and heir (Hamnet) is amply compensated for by the finding of the perfect son-in-law.

Prospero's wife is not a part of the story. He mentions her only once,[10] and does so in the spirit of that familiar, anxious joke in which a man expresses his uncertainty as to whether the child presented to him by his wife is truly his own. "Sir, are not you my father?" asks Miranda, confused for the moment by her being told that her "father was the Duke of Milan and/A prince of power." Prospero takes the question in a wry sense that Miranda did not intend. "Thy mother was a piece of virtue, and /She said thou wast my daughter," he replies (I.ii.54–7). We understand, of course, that this is an old joke, and that Prospero has no uncertainty about Miranda being his true daughter. As the only mention of Prospero's wife, however, this is disappointing. The fantasy in *The Winter's Tale*, of recovering an abandoned wife who then turns out to be desirable in her advanced years, is simply not incorporated into a play that reads so plausibly as Shakespeare's farewell to his art. We seem to be back in the world of *Othello* and *King Lear* in which the father depends extraordinarily on the favorite daughter because the wife-mother is no longer there. One hesitates of course to suggest that this can tell us anything about Shakespeare's actual retirement to Stratford. At the level of an imagined experience, nonetheless, the absence of the wife-mother is striking.

NOTES

1 See John Margeson, ed., *King Henry VIII. The New Cambridge Shakespeare* (Cambridge: Cambridge University Press, 1990), pp. 4–14. Although the evidence for Shakespeare's collaboration on *Henry VIII* with Fletcher is essentially internal, it has met with increasing acceptance in recent years.
2 See, for example, Francis Barker and Peter Hulme, "Nymphs and Reapers Heavily Vanish: The Discursive Context of *The Tempest*," in John Drakakis, ed., *Alternative Shakespeares* (London and New York: Methuen, 1985), 191–205, and a reply by Meredith Skura, "Discourse and the Individual: The Case of Colonialism in *The Tempest*," *SQ* 40 (1989): 42–69.
3 See Virginia Mason Vaughan and Alden T. Vaughan, eds, *The Tempest*. Arden Shakespeare (Walton-on-Thames: Thomas Nelson, 1999), pp. 6, 41ff.
4 Citations are from David Bevington, ed., *The Complete Works of Shakespeare*, 5th edn (New York: Pearson/Longman, 2003).
5 Northrop Frye, *Anatomy of Criticism: Four Essays* (Princeton: Princeton University Press, 1957; rpt. Atheneum, New York, 1968), pp. 39, 40, 172, 176, 182, 217, 226–8.
6 E. A. J. Honigmann, "Shakespeare's Second Best Bed," *New York Review of Books*, November 7 (1991), p. 30.
7 Stephen Greenblatt, *Will in the World: How Shakespeare Became Shakespeare* (New York and London: W. W. Norton, 2004), pp. 289–90.
8 Grace Tiffany, *My Father Had a Daughter: Judith Shakespeare's Tale* (New York: Berkley Publishing/Penguin, 2003). On the death of Judith's twin brother, Hamnet, see Richard P. Wheeler, "Deaths in the Family: the Loss of a Son and the Rise of Shakespearean Comedy," *SQ* 51 (2000), 127–53.
9 See David Sundelson, "So Rare a Wonder'd Father: Prospero's Tempest," in Murray M. Schwartz and Coppélia Kahn, eds, *Representing Shakespeare* (Baltimore: Johns Hopkins University Press, 1980).
10 See Stephen Orgel, "Prospero's Wife," *Representations* 8 (1984): 1–13, reprinted in *The Authentic Shakespeare and Other Problems of the Early Modern Stage* (New York and London: Routledge, 2002), 173–210; and Schwartz and Kahn, *Representing Shakespeare*.

SUGGESTIONS FOR FURTHER READING

Primary sources

Shakespeare, William. *The Tempest*, ed. Frank Kermode. Arden Shakespeare. New York: Random House, 1964.
—— *The Winter's Tale*, ed. A. D. Nuttall. London: Edward Armold, 1996.

Secondary sources

Adelman, Janet. *Suffocating Mothers: Fantasies of Maternal Origin in Shakespeare's Plays, "Hamlet" to "The Tempest."* Chicago: University of Chicago Press, 1992.
Barber, C. L. "'Thou That Beget'st Him That Did thee Beget': Transformation in *Pericles* and *The Winter's Tale*." *Shakespeare Survey* 22 (1969): 59–67.
Eagleton, Terence. *Shakespeare and Society: Critical Studies in Shakespearean Drama*. London: Chatto & Windus; New York: Schocken Books, 1967.

Foakes, R. A. *Shakespeare: From the Dark Comedies to the Last Plays*. London and Charlottesville: University Press of Virginia, 1971.

Frye, Northrop. *Anatomy of Criticism: Four Essays*. Princeton: Princeton University Press, 1957.

—— *A Natural Perspective: The Development of Shakespearean Comedy and Romance*. New York: Columbia University Press, 1965.

Greenblatt, Stephen. *Will in the World: How Shakespeare Became Shakespeare*. New York and London: Norton, 2004.

Hartwig, Joan. *Shakespeare's Tragicomic Vision*. Baton Rouge: Louisiana State University Press, 1972.

Honan, Park. *Shakespeare: A Life*. Oxford: Oxford University Press, 1998.

Hunter, Robert Grams. *Shakespeare and the Comedy of Forgiveness*. New York: Columbia University Press, 1965.

Kahn, Coppélia. *Man's Estate: Masculine Identity in Shakespeare*. Berkeley: University of California Press, 1981.

Kernan, Alvin B. *The Playwright as Magician: Shakespeare's Image of the Poet in the English Public Theater*. New Haven: Yale University Press, 1979.

Kirsch, Arthur C. *Shakespeare and the Experience of Love*. Cambridge: Cambridge University Press, 1981.

Knight, G. Wilson. *The Crown of Life: Essays in Interpretation of Shakespeare's Final Plays*, 2nd edn. London: Methuen, 1948.

McMullan, Gordon and Jonathan Hope, eds. *The Politics of Tragicomedy: Shakespeare and After*. London and New York: Routledge, 1992.

Marshall, Cynthia. *Last Things and Last Plays: Shakespearean Eschatology*. Carbondale: Southern Illinois University Press, 1991.

Mowat, Barbara A. *The Dramaturgy of Shakespeare's Romances*. Athens: University of Georgia Press, 1976.

Palfrey, Simon. *Late Shakespeare: A New World of Words*. Oxford: Clarendon Press; New York: Oxford University Press, 1997.

Richards, Jennifer and James Knowles, eds. *Shakespeare's Late Plays: New Readings*. Edinburgh: Edinburgh University Press, 1999.

Traversi, Derek. *Shakespeare: The Last Phase*. New York: Harcourt, 1954; London: Hollis & Carter, 1979.

Vaughan, Virginia Mason and Alden T. Vaughan, eds. *Critical Essays on Shakespeare's "The Tempest."* New York: G. K. Hall; London: Prentice-Hall International, 1998.

Wheeler, Richard P. *Shakespeare's Development and the Problem Comedies: Turn and Counter-turn*. Berkeley: University of California Press, 1981.

—— "Deaths in the Family: The Loss of a Son and the Rise of Shakespearean Comedy." *Shakespeare Quarterly* 51 (2000): 127–53.

Woodbridge, Linda. *The Scythe of Saturn: Shakespeare and Magical Thinking*. Urbana: University of Illinois Press, 1994.

PART VI

BELIEFS AND REFORMS

CHAPTER TWENTY-SEVEN

SPEAKING BOOKS, MOVING IMAGES

Meredith J. Gill

A fifteenth-century bishop sits at his desk, pen poised, looking out the window (Figure 27.1). An other-worldly light – yet a light resembling the radiance of the evening sun – circulates within the interior where, among the artful clutter, one sees objects that fascinate and engage the senses: in the background, books, astrolabes, and works of sculpture; in the foreground, other instruments of measure – an hourglass and an armillary sphere – and musical manuscripts. Who, we might ask, is this scholarly person?

For the literate public of the fifteenth and sixteenth centuries, and for the Venetian confraternity members who looked upon the painting as they sang the offices in their oratory, Vittore Carpaccio captured well Augustine's Renaissance likeness. He captured a tension that we, too, apprehend, between the worldly and the other-worldly, conveyed in an intimation of the active versus the contemplative life. The artist described the joys of the senses, and, equally, their casting away. What is the point of things? Augustine seems to be asking, and it is a question which, in the literal terms of Carpaccio's painting, is Augustine's dilemma at this very moment. What is the character of salvation in relation to the passing of time, and in relation to the distractions of the here and now? And it is a dilemma centered on the saint's attention to the light streaming in.

Carpaccio based his portrayal on a widely available thirteenth-century letter attributed to Augustine and addressed to Cyril of Jerusalem in which he narrated how, at the very hour of Jerome's death in far-away Bethlehem, his cantankerous correspondent came to him in a light and a fragrance. Until Erasmus's conclusion, in 1516, that the letter was inauthentic and, perhaps worse, that the Latin was of such a quality as to make Cicero stumble, Renaissance readers believed the event to be true. Like paintings, apocryphal writings can bridge a fragile divide between belief and desire, between history and allegory, truth and fiction. Certainly, through the Reformation and beyond, Pseudo-Augustine's voice, alongside that of Augustine himself, was part of the colorful, nubby fabric of hagiographic culture. Pseudo-Augustine enterprisingly glossed Possidius's life of himself, which had been transmitted by Jacobus de Voragine in the later thirteenth century. Voragine, for his part, was believed to have known all of Augustine's writings by heart. Pseudo-Augustine also wrote eloquent letters and homilies on the solitary life and on the appropriate

Figure 27.1 Vittore Carpaccio (c. 1460–1526). *St Augustine in His Study* (1502–8) (oil on canvas). © Scuola di San Giorgio degli Schiavoni, Venice, Italy/The Bridgeman Art Library.

medieval costume and lifestyle of his fellow hermit friars, whose Order had only been founded in 1256. He wrote of mysterious and provocative meetings with holy persons, including the Christ child on the seashore, who admonished him on the futility of his curiosity. Pseudo-Augustine could be more Augustinian than Augustine himself, attuned to the inclinations of his age, a clever actor who seemed to play his character more assuredly than his real Late Antique forebear.

Augustine's name has long summoned his famous conversion among all his life experiences, and it is conventionally the conversion that is taken to be his saintly calling card. Yet how we define what happened to him in a garden in 386 is as much a reflection of ourselves as it is of him, and this is equally true for his Renaissance audiences, who saw in it a mirror of many of their own predilections. He describes the conversion in the *Confessions*, towards the end of Book 8, when, after a period of talking and weeping:

> Suddenly I heard a voice from a house nearby – perhaps a voice of some boy or girl, I do not know – singing over and over again "Pick it up and read, pick it up and read." My expression immediately altered and I began to think hard whether children ordinarily repeated a ditty like this . . . I stemmed the flood of tears and rose to my feet, believing that this could be nothing other than a divine command to open the Book and read the first passage I chanced upon; for I had heard the story of how Antony had been instructed by a gospel text . . . Stung into action, I returned to the place where Alypius was sitting, for on leaving it I had put down there the book of the apostle's letters. I snatched

it up, opened it and read in silence the passage on which my eyes first lighted: *Not in dissipation and drunkenness, nor in debauchery and lewdness, nor in arguing and jealousy; but put on the Lord Jesus Christ, and make no provision for the flesh or the gratification of your desires* [Rom. 13: 13–14]. I had no wish to read further, nor was there need. No sooner had I reached the end of the verse than the light of certainty flooded my heart and all dark shades of doubt fled away.[1]

Immediately, Augustine closed the book while marking his place, and told Alypius what had happened. Ever his responsive companion, Alypius read the next verse from Romans (14: 1), "*Make room for the person who is weak in faith,*" and took it to heart as his own oracle. Together they went in to Monica, most likely to tell her that they had decided to be reborn in baptism, which would happen the following spring. Augustine had resolved to change his life: "Many years earlier," Augustine notes, "you had shown her a vision of me standing on the rule of faith [3, 11, 19]; and now indeed I stood there, no longer seeking a wife or entertaining any worldly hope, for you had converted me to yourself."

Augustine had many conversions. In a sense, the first nine books of the *Confessions* comprise one conversion story. In the following four books (10–13), "he generalized from his experience so as to make it emblematic for all Christian conversions."[2] The work as a whole might be seen as conversion, an alchemy of self poured into the vessel of narrative. The word "conversion" is a metaphor derived from the realm of the arts and crafts, and meaning transformation; etymologically, it means a turning, and so it is one half of a process of which the other half constitutes alienation, aversion, or "disenchantment," to use Robert Markus's term. Augustine's other conversions came about while reading Cicero, through encounters with Manichaeism, skepticism, and Plotinus. He describes other persons' conversions from pagan polytheism, and this is worth noting because, in fact, what he describes happening to himself in the garden is really a kind of *re*conversion, since he had, after all, been raised by his mother as a Christian.

Conversion can only be represented indirectly, through signs; that is, as a personal and inward turning, it can only be conveyed through a veil of words. In works of art, the metaphorical languages multiply so that conversion may not – in many ways, it *cannot* – follow textual or literal sequence at all. Garry Wills has recently spoken of this episode of Augustine's as his "mythic" conversion in the sense that *of* his many "loquacious ditherings,"[3] this was one essentially of "vocation."[4] Augustine made celibacy – his setting aside of "debauchery and lewdness" – a precondition for the sacrament of baptism. This choice, which was linked to a philosophical tradition of asceticism, and was not a prerequisite for Christianity, was intimately connected to the allegorical stage of the garden. Evoking Eden and Gethsemane, Augustine's Milanese retreat was a theater for the contest of human will, for revelation, and for change. Augustine narrated his conversion ten years after the event when it had become an artful exegesis on the sin of Adam and Eve; for some commentators, the fig tree is the Tree of Knowledge that had given up its leaf to cover the pair's nakedness. Yet for Wills, the garden was not an *entirely* allegorical place, for the voice that the saint heard was real. Further, as Wills points out, drawing on William James's *The Varieties of Religious Experience* (1902), it is the *suddenness* of Augustine's experience that really needs explaining, since the phenomenon of conversion – if it is to be lasting – is gradual. The moment under the fig tree is, in any case, the distillation of the three themes of Augustine's story: sin and its misery; God's instigation of the stages of conversion; and the unfinished and precarious character of the conversion experience itself – for he was still, as he had expressed it earlier (4, 4, 9), "a question to himself."[5]

However we may debate the real or allegorical character of the event, Renaissance readers, writers, and artists seem to have understood what we understand today: that this was a conversion in which Augustine surrendered his will to God's by means of the book. His conversion followed that of the rhetorician Victorinus and of Antony, and it was succeeded by that of Alypius, an event, then, that was framed by the examples of others. But it was words – hearing and reading – that effected this conversion; and just as reading Paul had changed *his* life, so the *Confessions* were meant to prompt others to change theirs. While his conversion would prove to be imperfect, its climactic moment, brought about by text, was decisive and euphoric.

Augustine's epiphany in the garden was integrally bound to his representation in Renaissance times as the paradigmatic scholar, as the painter of Augustine's portrait in Malatesto Novello's copy of the *City of God* (Figure 27.2) suggests. Augustine's study leads out to a walled enclosure in which the small figure of Alypius stands between two trees, beneath a shimmering vision of the City of God. The precedent for Augustine's pictorial biography in Italy was, in fact, his monumental *arca* in San Pietro in Ciel d'Oro, Pavia, a reliquary writ large for his remains which, since 1327, had been the hard-won pride of Pavia's Order of Augustinian Hermits (Figure 27.3). Begun in the 1350s as a panegyrical counterpart to the life of Augustine written by Henry of Freimar, the tomb boasted an extraordinary addition – extraordinary compared to the only two fourteenth-century tombs of saints to precede it – an effigy of the saint within a funerary chamber in the middle story. Augustine is likened, then, to a contemporary churchman, whose tomb this resembles. As a seemingly recently living authority, he might compare to Petrarch's Augustinus of the *Secretum* who spoke with Petrarch in his own time and on his own terms.

From Pavia in 1365, Petrarch would note to Boccaccio how much glory Augustine's relics had brought to that city. He himself had a well-known and long-standing affection for the Hermits, with whom he had lodged several times. The event of his fabled ascent of Mont Ventoux in the spring of 1336, often interpreted as the clarion call of the Renaissance, was framed by an Augustinian sensibility in every sense: not only by Petrarch's devotion to the Order but also by a striking impulse towards intimacy with a figure who was so long gone. The Augustinian Fra Dionigi da Borgo San Sepolcro had given Petrarch his copy of the *Confessions*, and he would later bequeath the same book to his young Augustinian friend Luigi Marsili. The little volume of the *Confessions* was both a totem of the transformative nature of books and a tantalizing call in general to literary self-disclosure.

Augustine's tomb adapts these themes. At the front, underneath the gables, three relief panels initiate a sequence of scenes from the saint's life, scenes that present the Hermits' inflected image of their holy namesake, since they privilege instances of verbal persuasion and instruction, whether through preaching or reading. The conversion is central, succeeding Augustine and Alypius's witness of Ambrose preaching,

LIBER PRIMVS

BEATISSIMI AVRELII AVGVSTINI:
DE CIVITATE DEI LIB: PRIMVS INCIPIT

GLORIOSISSI
MAM CIVI
TATEM DEI
SIVE IN HOC
TEMPORV
CVRSV CV
INTER IM
PIOS PERE
GRINATVR

ex fide uiuens: siue in illa stabilitate sedis eternae qua
nunc expectat per patientiam quoad usq; iustitia conuerta
tur in iudicium deinceps adeptura per excellentiam uicton
a ultima; & pace perfecta hoc opere ad te instituto & mei
promissione debito defendere aduersus eos qui conditori ei?
deos suos praeferunt fili carissime Marcelline suscepi: ma
gnum opus & arduum: sed deus adiutor noster est. Nam
scio quibus uiribus opus sit ut persuadeatur superbis quā sit
sit uirtus humilitatis: qua fit ut omnia terrena cacumina
temporali mobilitate nutantia non humano usurpata fastu
sed diuina gratia donata celsitudo eius transcendat. Rex
enim & conditor ciuitatis huius: de qua loqui instituimus
in scriptura populi sui sententiam diuinae legis aperuit qua
dictum est. Superbis deus resistit: humilibus autem dat
gratiam. Hoc uero quod dei est superbae quoq; animae spiritu
afflatus: amatq; sibi in laudibus dici: parcere subiectis & de
bellare superbos. Vnde etiam de terrena ciuitate: quae du
dominari appetit & si populi seruiant ipsa ei dominandi
libido dominatur. Non est praetereundum silentio quicquid

Figure 27.2 Augustine. *De civitate Dei*, Cesena, Biblioteca Malatestiana, MS. D.IX.1, c. 15r. (375 × 255 mm, cc. I, 405, II') (1450).

Figure 27.3 Detail of *arca* of St Augustine (front), (1350s): Augustine and Alypius Attending Ambrose's Preaching; Augustine's Visit to Simplicianus and Augustine's Invitation to Read St Paul; Augustine's Baptism by Ambrose, Church of San Pietro in Ciel d'Oro, Pavia. Art Resource NY.

and before Ambrose baptizes him and he receives new clothes in the presence of his mother. Consistent with Henry of Freimar's emphasis on the Order's eremitic origins, Augustine is seen at the humble dwelling of the hermit Simplicianus, before he is invited by a hovering angel to read St Paul as he sits beneath his tree reading, head

Figure 27.4 Guariento di Arpo. *Scene from the Life of Augustine: Conversion of Augustine* (*c.* 1350s), Church of Eremitani, Padua. The Art Archive/Dagli Orti.

in hand. As a symbolic prologue to the whole, the subject of Augustine teaching rhetoric in Rome is a forthright statement of the Order's priorities, and it is the largest panel of all.

In the mid-fourteenth century, on the walls of the apse of the Eremitani in Padua, Guariento rendered four canonical moments in the Order's history, including the conversion and the *Ordination and Baptism*. As at Pavia, an angel carrying an open book represents the injunction "Tolle, lege," while Augustine looks up from his text; then coming indoors, he shares his discovery with Alypius, the two of them leaning together over the conspicuous (though tantalizingly blank) pages of the Bible (Figure 27.4). This is a sagacious Augustine, dressed already in doctor's ermine. The drama moves not from conversation with Simplicianus to conversion, as described in the *Confessions* and also in the *arca* relief, but from conversion to belief in action through the catalytic vehicle of the book that, in any case, is prominent in each.

In the early decades of the fifteenth century, the Umbrian artist Ottaviano Nelli completed the first major mural cycle of Augustine's life, decorating the sanctuary of the Augustinian conventual church at Gubbio with a vibrant visual homily. In

Figure 27.5 Ottaviano Nelli. *Augustine Receiving Instruction from Simplicianus and His Conversion* (c. 1420s). Church of Sant'Agostino, Gubbio. Foto Gavirati, Gubbio.

Nelli's version (Figure 27.5), Simplicianus appears again as a mentor, and as a hermit, an identity that historians of the Order gave to this future bishop for polemical reasons. Seated at the wall of Simplicianus's hovel, then reading by angelic invitation, Augustine proceeds to the approving greeting of Monica. In perhaps the most familiar rendition, from Sant'Agostino, San Gimignano, in the 1460s, Benozzo Gozzoli portrays the moment of the "Tolle, lege" in still more condensed fashion (Figure 27.6). Two young men – presumably the origins of the childlike voice – look on as a studious Augustine pores over his text, towards which Alypius is already pointing. Paired with the subject of the baptism on the privileged altar wall, Gozzoli's conversion shows an Augustine who is the ideal that the cycle as a whole advanced: a young Renaissance doctor who is the embodiment of faith and learning conjoined, the image of a reformed observant Augustinian whom the patron of the cycle, together with the citizens of San Gimignano, was enjoining on a renegade community of friars.

Each artist gives us an image of conversion by the book, an image of how reading could change one's life. For Augustine, God had brought about his conversion, as he had brought about Paul's, through signs – through sounds and sights. As further signs, for Augustine, the sacraments in which Christ is the active agent made still more clear the duty of struggling Christians to their individual receptivity to God. And so the baptism, which is directly juxtaposed with the conversion in these cycles, is the sign of signs, an affirmation of the totemic potency of the word. At San

Figure 27.6 Benozzo Gozzoli. *Conversion of St Augustine* ("Tolle, lege"), mid-1460s, Church of Sant'Agostino, San Gimignano. The Art Archive/San Agostino San Gimignano/Dagli Orti.

Gimignano, the baptism is divided from conversion on the apse wall by a window, so that a blast of light, with all its symbolic associations, punctuates our reading of both frescoes, modeling, perhaps, in whatever very distant fashion, "the light of certainty" that "flooded" Augustine's heart.

I am struck, however, in all of these instances, by two things: by the *un*dramatic nature of the conversion itself, on the one hand (or, at least, by its interiority, which contrasts markedly with the subjective power of the tear-drenched passages of the *Confessions*); and, on the other hand, by the bookishness that prevails – a bookishness that not so much sets this moment apart as it is a fulfillment of Augustine's scholarly career to that point. And in every case words abound. Both Nelli and Gozzoli accompany each fresco with an inscription telling us respectively "here" or "in what manner" – "*quem ad modum*" – Augustine embarked upon his enterprises.

In Gubbio, in the vault, and at San Gimignano, as the first panel, he is a schoolboy whose mother nudges him into the classroom. In San Gimignano, in fact, the inscriptions beneath the schoolroom and university scenes present us with an Augustine who is much more sanguine about his literary training than he really was. He hated Greek, he said, but came to love Latin literature after an uncertain start in his boyhood. His descriptions of the horrors of his school, for which he had no enthusiasm, and of his beating, are perhaps implied by Gozzoli in his first fresco. Yet the inclusion of a type of hornbook (without a handle) that was familiar to Renaissance classrooms in the setting of his African school suggests a pedagogical intent. As a teacher, Augustine was, in fact, something of a failure, and his attempts as a professor of rhetoric in Rome, which he mentions only briefly in the *Confessions*, were disappointed by his students' penny-pinching wiles. Yet while Augustine teaches rhetoric in Rome, the open page in the lap of the student at the left in Gozzoli's depiction proclaims a Ciceronian adage about the *scientia* of rhetoric. Beneath six panels out of 17, in fact, the fruits of rhetoric or its beneficial qualities are implied. The patron of the program, Fra Domenico Strambi, certainly had the background to devise such laudatory texts, and they were a satisfying token, no doubt, of the city's investment in Strambi's education, since the citizens of San Gimignano had sent him to university in Paris.

The relation among the inscriptions, the *Confessions*, and Gozzoli's representation of each event is, at times, contradictory, with each seeming to work at odds with the other. The artist places his protagonists in gracious halls, in front of loggias, and within Renaissance settings where they act with the confidence and autonomy of actors on a princely stage. The inscriptions, however, simply emphasize Augustine's intellectual prowess in rhetoric and philosophy conceived in modern terms – terms that the Order of Hermits would have liked; the *Confessions* themselves, though, seem far away. In this context, the conversion, while privileged in its placement, is not an epiphany so much as it is testimony to a life that was already well on its own way, already devoted to books, and approaching reconciliation with God.

That Augustine was a reader was very dear to his Renaissance audiences and to the patrons of these frescoes, the Hermits, in particular. It might well have been Petrarch, as much as it was really Augustine, who observed: "When I read, it was I who gained knowledge through myself. Or was it?"[6] Recently, Brian Stock and others have demonstrated just how astute Augustine was about reading, interpretation, and self-knowledge, and Stock, especially, has analyzed the reverberations of the saint's theory of reading – unsystematic though it may have been – in Petrarch and Thomas More.[7] In this sense, the Hermits got it right: the occasion of the conversion was as much about the vitality of the word as a means of self-examination as it was about the surrender of the will to God.

Conversion, after all, is invisible. To externalize the internal and to portray temporal sequence in the instant of visual encounter are challenges particular to the artist. Conversion's ineffable quality, as well as Augustine's relentless probing of the nature of salvation as an ongoing dynamic in his *own* conversion story, was understood by Renaissance artists, as by modern commentators, to be effectively embodied by other-than-literal signs. In fact, it was Pseudo-Augustine, in the thirteenth-century letter popular in the fifteenth century, who encapsulated, in a deeply Augustinian way, the conflicted celebration of the senses, and then their casting away, that Book 8 implied. In two mesmerizing portraits of Augustine in his study – Botticelli's of 1480 and Carpaccio's of 1502 – the saint is interrupted in his labors by a vision. According to Pseudo-Augustine's letter on which both paintings are based, a supernatural light and fragrance entered Augustine's study at night at the very moment that his correspondent had died. He had been pondering "how much glory and joy the souls of the blessed have who rejoice with Christ." Jerome admonished him:

> Augustine, Augustine, what are you seeking? Do you think that you can put the whole sea in a little vase? Enclose the world in a small fist? . . . Will your eye see what the eye of no man can see? Your ear hear what is received by no ear through sound? . . . What will be the end of an infinite thing? By what measure will you measure the immense?

In other words, Jerome seems to say, the realms of faith and salvation are not truly measurable in the here and now, by bodily means; rather – perhaps like a conversion experience – they are founded on higher principles in which the lower self must be abandoned. What is remarkable is that, apart from the presence of the light, Jerome himself is absent in both works. At Ognissanti, however, a portrait of Jerome by Domenico Ghirlandaio was placed on the opposite side of the doorway, so that both saints appear to receive light from its direction. Although the inscription attached to Botticelli's fresco is lost, Ghirlandaio's text begged the saint, "that radiant lamp, to enlighten us." The phenomenon of the light and its prophetic nature are underlined in the Venetian work more subtly, by the little dog's rapt alertness. The supernatural is shown here exclusively in terms of its sensory experience, not literally, with the insertion of heavenly persons, nor even, as portrayed by Botticelli, by clear, straight lines of incoming light that (tellingly) pierce the armillary sphere. But both Botticelli and Carpaccio depart from a tradition in which Augustine's book-strewn study is about to be shared with the tiny forms of other saints, as in Botticini's *St Augustine Visited by Sts Jerome and John the Baptist* (National Gallery of Art, London) and also Sano di Pietro's *St Augustine Visited by St Jerome* (Louvre).

While Ghirlandaio's patrons were probably the Umiliati, Botticelli's patron may have been Giorgio Antonio Vespucci (1434–1514), the uncle of Amerigo. He was a lover of books, a neighbor of Botticelli's, and an acquaintance of the philosopher Marsilio Ficino (1433–99). The Vespucci arms appear at the top of the fresco. Botticelli's musing, in Italian, on the open page of the geometry treatise ("dov'è fra Martino . . .") seems to play on words, and on a contrast between high and low language: between the vernacular, on the one hand, and Latinity, on the other. For Vasari, the subject's head showed a state of "profound cogitation and sharpest subtlety that is customarily found in persons of deep sense who are continually abstracted in the investigation of things that are very high and very difficult."[8]

Carpaccio's naturalistic supernaturalism was characteristic of Venetian artists of the late fifteenth and early sixteenth centuries who wished to give a convincing testimony to the miraculous and the visionary. "Mobile and intangible," as Millard Meiss once wrote, "light has always seemed the natural counterpart of the mind. In nature as in art, it stirs feelings and sustains moods."[9] At a philosophical level, this could be an extension of Augustine's own thinking relative to light and the divine, a perspective that Carpaccio and Botticelli share in their evocations of the events described in the letter.

Augustine's conversion is alluded to here in the masterly references to the ineffable nature of the divine through light, and in his own turning to that light; it is present in the interplay between the contemplative and the active, divine and mortal, otherworldly and worldly. Augustine's own theory of seeing, and of divine illumination in particular, had a very long trajectory into Renaissance times. From the Platonic teachings of Plotinus he had accepted the idea of the "intelligible" and the "sensible" worlds, and of the way in which the mind, or soul, governs both. He used the model of sight to work out the relationship between the body and the soul. In his commentary on Genesis, and in later writings such as *On the Trinity*, he tried to articulate this relation through the distinction between "corporeal" and "spiritual" sight. Spiritual sight (*visio spiritualis*) accompanies corporeal sight (*visio corporalis*) and informs it of its nature as sense experience. Spiritual sight can also happen without bodily seeing, as in imagining and dreams. Informed by corporeal seeing, they are capable, nonetheless, of revealing both the human and the divine, and they lead, potentially, to the third and highest kind of seeing, called by him "intellectual" (*visio intellectualis*), which defines the interpretive work of the mind. At this third and most discriminating level of sight, we perceive divine truths and we judge things as they should be judged (*On the Trinity*, 16, 6, 8).

At the heart of Augustine's theory of knowledge, alongside three-fold sight, is his concept of divine illumination. And it is here that Renaissance Neoplatonism intersects with the seductive combination of the sensory and the ineffable – the corporeal and the spiritual – that is, I think, at the heart of Botticelli's and, particularly, of Carpaccio's work. Carpaccio expresses something of Augustine's Neoplatonic musical theory, his notion of Creation as a "song of the great whole," for example, in the two musical scores, the sphere, and the hourglass in the foreground. These objects, in unison with those in the background, create a metaphor expressive of Augustine's ideas about the soul's ascent. The astrolabes connect with the hourglass in measuring human time, and to the armillary sphere, which tracks heavenly movements. The statue of the Risen Christ, which is centrally placed within the composition in its chapel, affirms the goal of human striving towards redemption.

Together, light and music share qualities of the divine, such as intangibility and immateriality, and they work as invisible ladders to God. Carpaccio's musical manuscripts in the foreground initiated, perhaps, a kind of re-enactment of this progress to God, since their odd and ostentatious placement close to the picture plane meant that they might have been read, or sung, by members of the *scuola* as they stood in the oratory. Augustine had once made a statement that became well known: "He who sings prays twice" (*Sermons on the Psalms*, 72, 1).

Yet it is the pure mechanism of light that sets the composition in motion, and it is light in this pictorial narration of Jerome's visitation that carries with it both scent and sound. The visible light of the material world was, for Augustine, the metaphor for the intellectual "light" of the higher, Platonic realm of intelligible forms. Both kinds of light make visible the objects seen by illuminating both them and the organ of perception – the eye or the mind. Contrasting the morals of the Manichees and the Christians, Augustine's very view of the philosopher incorporated this theory:

> The striving after God is therefore the desire of beatitude, the attainment of God is beatitude itself. We seek to attain God by loving him; we attain to him, not by becoming entirely what He is, but in nearness to Him, and in wonderful and sensible contact with Him, and in being inwardly illuminated and occupied by His truth and holiness. He is light itself; it is given to us to be illuminated by that light.[10]

Reason, for Augustine, is often portrayed Platonically, "as if it were a kind of vision." This is a position that is continuous with his doctrine of illumination, where "God's love first enables the mind to see and also directs it to recognize particular spiritual truths . . . What motivates the mind first to look in the various directions it does is love, such as a love of truth which in turn reflects God's love of persons."[11] This seems to be a perfect summation, too, of the promptings and full resonance of his conversion.

Augustine represented the very idea of Plato and of the Platonic for many of his Renaissance readers, who would have read him long before they read Plato. Since he seems to have had little or no direct acquaintance with Plato's writings, Augustine derived his Neoplatonism from Plotinus, and perhaps also from Porphyry and Iamblichus; indeed, this was one way that their influence entered the arena of Renaissance Neoplatonism. Humanists cited Augustine's statement in the *Confessions* that Plato's doctrine was close to Christian truths in their own philosophical self-defense. Petrarch called Plato "the prince of philosophy," acknowledging that:

> He is praised by the greater men, Aristotle by the bigger crowd . . . In divine matters Plato and the Platonists rose higher, though none of them could reach the goal he aimed at. But, as I have said, Plato came nearer to it. No Christian and particularly no faithful reader of Augustine's books will hesitate to confirm this, nor do the Greeks deny it, however ignorant of letters they are in our time; in the footsteps of their forebears they call Plato 'divine' and Aristotle 'demonious.'[12]

Later in the same work, Petrarch says that he believes "a pious reader will agree with him [Augustine] no less than with Aristotle or Plato," and that the saint "does not in the least doubt that he [Plato] would have become a Christian if he had come to life again in Augustine's time or had foreseen the future while he lived." As Petrarch adds approvingly, Augustine had counted himself among the Platonists.

The celebrated Marsilio Ficino was an exceptionally attentive reader of Augustine, as well as of Plato, whose "spirit," he wrote, though long dead in the West, had lived in Byzantium until his own times when it "flew to Italy." The advent of Greek scholars and their libraries in the Latin West after the fall of Constantinople must have contributed to the relatively sudden arrival of a Neoplatonic movement in Florence after the Peace of Lodi in 1454. The Byzantine scholar John Argyropoulos played a vital role, for he arrived in Florence in that year, but so, too, in his own distinctive way, had George of Trebizond in the 1420s, when he associated Catholicism with Aristotelian philosophy and the inferior Byzantine church with Platonism.

In his captivating painting, Carpaccio bestowed the likeness of another leading figure, the Greek humanist and cardinal Johannes Bessarion (d. 1472), on his Augustine, thereby making an extraordinarily subtle and philosophically nuanced commentary. In defending Plato against Byzantine Aristotelians, and in attempting to Christianize the Platonism of his own teacher, Georgius Gemistus, called Pletho, Bessarion had marshaled quotations from Augustine praising Plato and Platonists, drawing upon the Church Father's authority on matters of dogma. Bessarion's standing in the Church was reflected in his near election as pope in 1455, following his appointment as a papal legate by Nicholas V. These recognitions ensured that his philosophical outlook, in concert with his publications, had a wide public forum. His library in Venice was a hub of Greek learning and a unique repository of Neoplatonic scholarship. Alongside Ficino, Bessarion represented a major vehicle for the communication of Platonism among fifteenth-century Italian literati. He is very much responsible for the receptiveness of his contemporaries to the idea that, from the days of the primitive Church on, the language and character of theology were closer to Plato than to Aristotle. His reconciliation of Platonic teachings on the soul with Christian perspectives, and his analysis of homosexual love in Plato in terms of a classification of love as either divine or earthly, were milestones in the history of Renaissance philosophy. One month before Bessarion published his conclusions on Platonic love, Marsilio Ficino himself had issued his own commentary on the *Symposium*, his *Convivium de amore*.[13] Pletho had also deliberated on the strengths of Aristotle as opposed to Plato during the Council of Union in Florence in 1439. His readers at the time would have known of this ancient debate from its reverberation in early writers, including Augustine. Humanists such as Leonardo Bruni and Ficino, who stood by Augustine as their light, claimed that Plato was closer to Christian truth.

Marsilio Ficino was the most notable of Plato's translators and commentators, as he was, too, of Plotinus. In one letter he claimed that the Latin Platonists first drew him to Platonic philosophy; in another, in which he itemizes the Latin sources of Platonism, Augustine is given his due. Accompanying a copy of his masterpiece, the *Theologica Platonica*, which he sent to Archbishop Giovanni Niccolini, was another letter in which Ficino quoted Augustine on the Platonists. He continued:

Being first induced by the authority of the divine Augustine and then confirmed by the judgement of many Christian saints, I thought it would be worthwhile to philosophize in the Academy since I had to philosophize anyway.[14]

In the preface to the work, he quoted Augustine as saying that Plato is close to the Christian truth and, further: "For a long time I have believed in the authority of Augustine . . . and decided to produce an image of Plato most similar to the Christian truth."

The Church Father appears often in Ficino's *Theologica Platonica*. The works that Ficino cites or from which he quotes form the body of those texts that, for the most part, were also most often read in the Renaissance: the *Confessions*, the *City of God*, *Enchiridion*, *Against the Academicians*, *Questions*, *Soliloquies*, *The Immortality of the Soul*, *The Magnitude of the Soul*, *On Music*, *On True Religion*, *On Free Choice of the Will*, and *On the Trinity*. In concept and style, Ficino emulated Augustine and he shared, too, his ideas relative to the soul's relation to the body, the nature of sense perception, and the place of God in the mind as its ruler. Augustine's theory of divine illumination influenced him profoundly. His metaphors for the irrepressible movement of the soul derived from Augustine, and his accounting for the relations between will and love relative to intellect and knowledge also owes much to him. As Kristeller sums it up, if one were to refine Ficino's metaphysics down to its basic elements of God and the soul, Augustine's own first line from the *Soliloquies* comes to mind: "I seek God and the soul." Ficino, Kristeller says, even while noting the differences between them, "must be called, after Petrarch, one of the greatest Augustinians of the Renaissance."

In the second half of the fifteenth century, Ficino also popularized Augustine through his participation in vernacular humanism. Through the Tuscan vernacular, Ficino contributed to the dissemination of the tenets of humanism to a larger and less Latinate audience. Among this audience were Tuscan artists and their patrons. Like Bessarion, too, with whom he corresponded, Ficino was knowledgeable on Pletho, and translated not only Plato himself, a publication that appeared in 1484, but also all of Plotinus, in an edition that was printed in 1492. Ficino's translation of Plotinus was the first ever, and his Plato the first complete version of the philosopher's works. Both were reprinted well into the nineteenth century. These, together with his accompanying commentaries, would shape the conception of Plato for centuries to come. More immediately, Ficino not only made Plotinus and Plato accessible but, in collaboration with Cosimo de' Medici and his descendants, he defended them, aloud and in writing, rephrasing and interpolating them into his own astoundingly original creations. His opinions on the interpretation of Plato, in which he allowed for a variety of hermeneutical tactics, were founded on the Church Father's attitude to the Bible. Allegory, for him, was not necessarily a dominant strategy, and Augustine was a guide here too. Platonic theology had laid certain foundations for Christianity by way of an introduction to it, and Augustine, along with John the Evangelist and Dionysius the Areopagite, had witnesseed this rich amalgam. Since Ficino's outlook was, finally, Christian – he was ordained a priest in 1473 – the framework of his interventions furthered the study of patristics and of

Augustine in particular, especially since Ficino stated outright that he felt there to be a harmony between Christian religion and Platonic philosophy.

Ficino was passionate about music, both in terms of understanding its pleasurable harmonies and in terms of its cosmological associations. Unlike Plato, he also favored poetry, having even penned a youthful treatise on the poet's frenzy. Augustine's own interests in music attracted Renaissance theorists and artists, including, of course, Carpaccio and his patrons. His investigation *On Music*, as well as *On Order*, must surely have had an as yet unexplored impact on Renaissance architectural theory, as well. In these ways, Ficino's and Augustine's Neoplatonic enthusiasms mirrored one another. In his Platonic allegorizing of classical myths, as well, Ficino allowed for a subtle infiltration of Augustinian ideas into the world of the arts, and for an interpretive shaping of subject matter that might seem on the surface to have nothing to do with the content of Augustine's writings but that permitted a kind of Augustinian poetics.

More particularly, Ficino knew Leon Battista Alberti and the Pollaiuoli brothers, and his portrait was painted in manuscripts and in frescoes by Domenico Ghirlandaio and Cosimo Rosselli. As a patron of art, he had eclectic preferences. Inspired by Seneca, he commissioned an unknown artist to paint a weeping Heraclitus and a laughing Democritus flanking the globe on the walls of his study. This was possibly the origin of the motif in art. That Michelangelo's pensive portrait by Raphael in *The School of Athens* is linked to Heraclitus lends piquancy to this brooding but sympathetically rendered figure, especially in the context of Plato's own centrality in the same fresco – not something to be taken for granted – as equal and partner to Aristotle. There might be a deeper significance to this portrait of Michelangelo as well, in that both Plato and Aristotle portrayed Heraclitus as the dark outsider in their day. Raphael, then, salutes his colleague with a backhanded compliment that surely identifies the sculptor as a philosopher, but that also casts him meditatively apart.

Ficino's view, in fact, that Platonism preceded Plato himself, since it emerged in a distant ancient time that was coincident with Moses and the prophets, allowed for an inclusive idea of the sweep of human history, as well as for the notion that philosophy and religion represented equally worthy traditions. In this sense, the audacious iconographic framework of Michelangelo's Sistine ceiling, which furthers the teleological argument of the fifteenth-century narratives of the lives of Moses and Christ along the chapel walls, extending that argument backwards to pagan times, finds its clear reverberations in Ficino's integrated version of Neoplatonism. A sympathy between Ficino's ideas and those of Renaissance Augustinians is clear in the person of the mercurial Augustinian general and reformer, an observant at Lecceto, Giles of Viterbo (1469–1532), who often addressed the saint as "my Augustine." Giles's commentary on the Sentences *ad mentem Platonis* is perhaps its best articulation. This indebtedness, as well as Giles's popularity with Julius II as counselor and orator, incidentally makes plausible both a Neoplatonic and Augustinian reading of the Sistine ceiling.

Ficino's ideation of the visible world as hierarchically ordered, beginning with God and the angels, through the soul at the very center of the universe to the corporeal quality and material bodies below, also parallels Michelangelo's arrangement on the ceiling quite specifically, as well as complementing the artist's poetic conceits relative to the act of creation. As a discourse on the human soul's immortality, and on its hopes for redemption, the Sistine Chapel offered a visual analogue to the dogma of the immortality of the soul only made official at the Lateran Council of 1513, the year after the program was finished.

Ficino contributed his own strain of thought to the Platonic conception of the *idea*, the furtive concept in the mind of the artist that guided him in the ideation of his compositions. Sixteenth-century art theory could be connected in this way, via Ficino, to Cicero, Plotinus, and to Augustine himself, since these constituted Ficino's major influences. In elevating painting, sculpture, and architecture to the status of the liberal arts, Ficino saw his own Platonic philosophy as their equal in a novel flourishing of the humanities, the arts, and the sciences. In his emphasis on an interiorized ascent to God that sets aside earthly matters – a movement, then, from the corporeal to the incorporeal or intelligible – Ficino also paraphrases not just Plotinus but Augustine himself. Ficino's larger pursuit of a definition of love and of a theory of love, including its relationship to the will, has at its very roots a strong, common sympathy with Augustine, whose overarching quest for Wisdom, by which he meant God, may be encapsulated in terms of a journey to love. Whether in love poetry or painting, whether in secular or religious subjects, a definition of Ficino's presence in Renaissance culture must in some way include Augustine. In these ways, Ficino is a conduit, another voice, for Augustine's philosophy. It is very hard not to see, in Carpaccio's magisterial picture, a kind of Augustinian apotheosis in which an array of signs alluding to the arts and sciences, and including many books, is composed in relation to a conversion – a radical turning towards God – for which Neoplatonism itself had become a vehicle.

These have been, in their own ways, Renaissance stories of conversion by the book, stories of conversion to the ancients – or from one ancient to another – and in which certain conceptual paradigms, and a certain kind of interiority, propelled each man to examine and to reject aspects of his scholarly inheritance. Caught in an instant of recollection and revelation, Carpaccio's Augustine might well have aptly represented for men such as Bessarion, Ficino, and Giles their own humanistic enterprise in motion. Framed by a Christian context, yet seeking reconciliation with pre-Christian antiquity, reworking Platonic truths yet reveling in worldly beauties and the lessons of science, this Augustine's conversion asserted, finally, the value of words – words that arrive serendipitously and invisibly and yet, nevertheless, change one's life.

We have come a long way from conversion in the strict sense, having moved from a bookish moment to Platonic speculation, from Augustine as a slightly rebellious academic type to Augustine as philosopher and metaphysician of light. It was *this* Augustine, Augustine the metaphysician, and his larger theology of conversion or "sacramental conversion," who lived on in the religious imagination of the sixteenth and seventeenth centuries. The works of Caravaggio, most famously in his *Conversion of St Paul* (c. 1600), and of Georges de la Tour, in his *Repentant Magdalene* (c. 1640), radiate with profoundly Augustinian metaphors of sight and of light. In a reformatory climate of debate about the economies of will and grace, Augustine's advocacy of individual receptiveness to God and his description of the salvific nature of repentance assumed new urgency. Light as God's grace made visible, as the instrument of both conversion and insight, and its capacity to reflect both sensual pleasure and, equally, its casting away are the aspects of Augustinian conversion that would prevail in the early modern imagination. Light became the sign, then, of absolute conversion, a conversion that was both sacramental and lasting.

NOTES

1. *Confessions*, 8, 29, trans. Maria Boulding, O.S.B. (Hyde Park, N.Y.: New City Press, 1997), 206–8. Much of this chapter is based on my *Augustine in the Italian Renaissance: Art and Philosophy from Petrarch to Michelangelo* (New York: Cambridge University Press, 2005).
2. Frederick H. Russell, "Augustine: Conversion by the Book," *Varieties of Religious Conversion in the Middle Ages*, ed. James Muldoon (Gainesville: University Press of Florida, 1997), p. 13 (and further bibliography).
3. "Loquacious dithering": James J. O'Donnell, ed., *Confessions* (Oxford: Oxford University Press, 1992), vol. III, p. 70.
4. Garry Wills, "Augustine's Mythical Conversion." Presented at the conference "A Legacy of Provocation: Augustine Reconsidered," Princeton University (October 21–22, 2004).
5. Russell, "Augustine," p. 15. Cf. Book 10, 33, 50 where he has become, in God's eyes, "a problem" to himself.
6. Augustine, *The Usefulness of Belief*, 7, 17, quoted in Brian Stock, "Reading, Writing, and the Self: Petrarch and His Forerunners," *New Literary History* 26 (1995): 718.
7. See, in particular, Brian Stock, *After Augustine: The Meditative Reader and the Text* (Philadelphia: University of Pennsylvania Press, 2001).
8. Giorgio Vasari, *Vite de' Più Eccellenti Pittori, Scultori e Architettori*, ed. G. Milanesi (1878), vol. III, p. 311.
9. Millard Meiss, "Light as Form and Symbol in Some Fifteenth-century Paintings," *Art Bulletin* 27 (1945): 43–68; reprinted in *The Painter's Choice. Problems in the Interpretation of Renaissance Art* (New York: Harper & Row, 1976), pp. 3–18 (quotation 4).
10. *The Customs of the Catholic Church and the Customs of the Manichees*, 1, 11, 19; 1, 25, 46 (*Patrologia Latina* 32), in David Glidden, "Augustine's Hermeneutics and the Principle of Charity," *Ancient Philosophy* 17 (1997): 143.
11. Glidden, "Augustine's Hermeneutics," p. 143, n. 19.
12. Petrarch repeated Augustine's statement about Plato and truth in his *On His Own Ignorance and That of Many Others*, trans. Hans Nachod, in *The Renaissance Philosophy of Man*, ed. Ernst Cassirer *et al.* (Chicago: University of Chicago Press, 1948), pp. 101, 107–8.
13. James Hankins, *Plato in the Italian Renaissance* (Leiden and New York: Brill, 1991), 1, p. 261.
14. *Opera Omnia*, in Paul Oskar Kristeller, "Augustine and the Early Renaissance," *The Review of Religion* 8, 4 (May 1944): 354; see *Platonic Theology*, trans. Michael J. B. Allen with John Warden, ed. James Hankins with William Bowen, vols 1–3 (*The I Tatti Renaissance Library*, 2, 4 and 7) (Cambridge, Mass.: Harvard University Press, 2001–3).

SUGGESTIONS FOR FURTHER READING

Primary sources

Augustine. *St. Augustine: On Genesis*, trans. R. J. Teske. *The Fathers of the Church*, 84. Washington, D.C.: Catholic University Press, 1991.

—— *The Trinity*, Introduction, translation and notes by Edmund Hill, O.P., ed. John E. Rotelle, O.S.A. Brooklyn, N.Y.: New City Press, 1991.
—— *Confessions*, 3 vols, ed. James J. O'Donnell. Oxford: Oxford University Press, 1992.
—— *Confessions*, trans. Maria Boulding, O.S.B. Hyde Park, N.Y.: New City Press, 1997.

Secondary sources

Arbesmann, Rudolph, O.S.A. "Henry of Freimar's 'Treatise on the Origin and Development of the Order of Hermit Friars and its True and Real Title.'" *Augustiniana* 6 (1956): 37–145.

Bagemihl, Rolf. "Reading (into) Botticelli's Saint Augustine." *Source* 16, 2 (1997): 16–19.

Bowen, William R. "Ficino's Analysis of Musical Harmonia," in Konrad Eisenbichler and Olga Zorzi Pugliese, eds, *Ficino and Renaissance Neoplatonism*. Ottawa: Dovehouse Editions, 1986.

Bynum, Caroline Walker. "Why All the Fuss about the Body? A Medievalist's Perspective." *Critical Inquiry* 22 (autumn 1995): 1–33.

Cassirer, Ernst ed. *et al. The Renaissance Philosophy of Man*. Chicago: University of Chicago Press, 1948.

Celenza, Christopher S. "Late Antiquity and Florentine Platonism: The 'Post-Plotinian' Ficino," in Michael J. B. Allen and Valery Rees, with Martin Davies, eds, *Marsilio Ficino: His Theology, His Philosophy, His Legacy*. Leiden: E. J. Brill, 2002.

Courcelle, Pierre. *Les Confessions de Saint Augustine dans la Tradition Littéraire: Antécédents et Postérité*. Paris: Etudes Augustiniennes, 1963.

Ficino, Marsilio. *Platonic Theology*, 3 vols, trans. Michael J. B. Allen with John Warden, ed. James Hankins with William Bowen. *The I Tatti Renaissance Library*, 2, 4 and 7. Cambridge, Mass.: Harvard University Press, 2001–3.

Field, Arthur M. *The Origins of the Platonic Academy of Florence*. Princeton: Princeton University Press, 1988.

Gill, Meredith J. *Augustine in the Italian Renaissance: Art and Philosophy from Petrarch to Michelangelo*. New York: Cambridge University Press, 2005.

Glidden, David. "Augustine's Hermeneutics and the Principle of Charity." *Ancient Philosophy* 17 (1997): 135–57.

Hahn, Cynthia. "*Visio Dei*: Changes in Medieval Visuality," in Robert S. Nelson, ed., *Visuality Before and Beyond the Renaissance*. Cambridge: Cambridge University Press, 2000.

Hankins, James. *Plato in the Italian Renaissance*, 2 vols. Leiden and New York: Brill, 1991.

Jacobs, Fredrika H. "Carpaccio's Vision of St. Augustine and St. Augustine's Theories of Music." *Studies in Iconography* 6 (1980): 83–93.

Kristeller, Paul Oskar. "Augustine and the Early Renaissance." *The Review of Religion* 8, 4 (May 1944): 339–58.

—— *Renaissance Thought and Its Sources*. New York: Columbia University Press, 1979.

—— *Marsilio Ficino and His Work after Five Hundred Years*. Florence: L. S. Olschki, 1987.

Meiss, Millard. "Light as Form and Symbol in Some Fifteenth-century Paintings." *Art Bulletin* 27 (1945): 43–68; reprinted in Millard Meiss, *The Painter's Choice. Problems in the Interpretation of Renaissance Art*. New York: Harper & Row, 1976, 3–18.

Muldoon, James, ed. *Varieties of Religious Conversion in the Middle Ages*. Gainesville: University Press of Florida, 1997.

O'Malley, John W., S.J. *Giles of Viterbo on Church and Reform: A Study in Renaissance Thought*. Leiden: Brill, 1968.

Reeves, Marjorie. "Cardinal Egidio of Viterbo: A Prophetic Interpretation of History." In *Prophetic Rome in the High Renaissance Period*, ed. Marjorie Reeves. Oxford: Clarendon Press, 1992.

Reuterswärd, Patrik. "The Dog in the Humanist's Study." *Konsthistorisk tidskrift* 50, 2 (1981): 53–69.

Roberts, Helen I. "St Augustine in 'St Jerome's Study': Carpaccio's Painting and its Legendary Source." *Art Bulletin* 41, 4 (1959): 283–97.

Saak, Eric Leland. *High Way to Heaven: The Augustinian Platform Between Reform and Reformation, 1292–1524*. Leiden/Boston: Brill, 2002.

Stock, Brian. "Reading, Writing, and the Self: Petrarch and His Forerunners." *New Literary History* 26 (1995): 717–30.

—— *Augustine the Reader: Meditation, Self-knowledge, and the Ethics of Interpretation*. Cambridge, Mass.: Belknap Press of Harvard University Press, 1996.

—— *After Augustine: The Meditative Reader and the Text*. Philadelphia: University of Pennsylvania Press, 2001.

Trinkaus, Charles. *In Our Image and Likeness. Humanity and Divinity in Italian Humanist Thought*, 2 vols. Chicago: University of Chicago Press, 1970/Notre Dame, Ind.: University of Notre Dame Press, 1995.

CHAPTER TWENTY-EIGHT

RELIGIOUS MINORITIES

N. S. Davidson

In April 1559 the Treaty of Cateau-Cambrésis returned most of the Duchy of Savoy to Duke Emmanuele Filiberto. This territory in northwestern Italy, seized by the French during the Italian wars earlier in the century, included the Piedmontese valleys of the southwestern Alps that, since at least the fourteenth century, had been the home of the Waldenses, descendants of a dissident Christian group excommunicated in 1184. Under French occupation, the Waldenses had enjoyed freedom of religion, and even under ducal government, the local Catholic authorities initially limited their contacts with the heretics to doctrinal debates and preaching campaigns. But in 1560, the duke changed policy, expelling the Waldenses' ministers and executing three members of their church. The failure of these measures to convert the Waldenses in any numbers persuaded the duke to order a military invasion of their valleys in October. A general assembly of the Waldenses decided to resist militarily, and in February and March 1561 they inflicted two serious defeats on the ducal forces. In the wake of this setback, the duke opened negotiations with the Waldenses, and in June his representative and four Waldensian delegates signed the Peace of Cavour, by which the duke guaranteed the inhabitants of the valleys pardon, protection, and the free exercise of their religion within their own communities. In return, the Waldenses agreed to permit the continuing presence of the Catholic Church in the valleys and to refrain from preaching their faith outside their own churches.

In a few short years, therefore, the Alpine Waldenses had faced in quick succession the full range of possible reactions to their existence from the surrounding Catholic authorities: religious freedom, then a preaching campaign, followed by violent persecution and open warfare. Their remarkable success in forcing new concessions from a Catholic ruler in 1561 startled all who learned of it. For in the fifteenth and sixteenth centuries, religious minorities were only rarely allowed to live out their beliefs in peace and security. The history of minorities in Renaissance Europe was invariably shaped by the attitudes of their host communities.

Religious minorities were more common in medieval Catholic Europe than we might assume. Muslims had lived in Iberia since the Islamic conquest of the peninsula in the eighth century, and sizeable Muslim communities survived after 1400 in the kingdom of Valencia in eastern Spain and in the Nasrid kingdom of Granada in the south. Jews, too, had lived in Spain and Portugal for many centuries, exercising a wide range of occupations and enjoying regular commercial and social relations with their Christian neighbors. Jewish communities could also be found throughout the Holy Roman Empire and in many Italian cities. By the fifteenth century, identifiable Waldensian communities existed in Piedmont, Fribourg in Switzerland, the Dauphiné and Provence in the south of France, and Calabria and Apulia in the south of Italy. And in England, small communities of Lollards, inspired by the writings of the fourteenth-century Oxford theologian John Wycliffe, survived into the sixteenth century. In central and eastern Europe, meanwhile, the religious map was even more varied. The followers of the Bohemian reformer John Huss grew rapidly in numbers in the fifteenth century and survived well into the sixteenth century in Bohemia, Moravia, and Poland. The eastern territories of Poland were dominated by Orthodox Christians, who were also found in Hungary, Transylvania, Moldavia, the Balkans, and the Greek-speaking islands of the eastern Mediterranean. Jews and Muslims existed in many parts of the same area, as did members of the independent Armenian, Syrian, and even Coptic churches. The introduction of Protestantism in the sixteenth century added to this confessional mix in all parts of Europe, both east and west: this included followers of Martin Luther, Huldrych Zwingli, and John Calvin, as well as of more radical Anabaptist groups, such as the Mennonites and Hutterites, and the antitrinitarian Socinians. The proliferation of Christian confessions after the Reformation meant that almost every state came to contain at least one minority.

These minorities enjoyed a wide variety of relations with their host communities. In some territories, a single religious minority existed, surrounded by a large population of a different persuasion. Elsewhere, several competing religious groups lived in the same territory. The most cosmopolitan city in Europe was probably Venice, where Catholic, Orthodox, Armenian and Protestant Christians rubbed shoulders every day in the streets with Jews and Muslims. Within the Ottoman Empire, too, the Turks were willing to govern believers of all kinds. In some cases, religious differences became associated with specific linguistic or ethnic groups, and so reinforced pre-existing local divisions. In sixteenth-century Transylvania, for instance, German-speakers tended to adopt Lutheranism while Hungarian-speakers preferred Calvinism or antitrinitarianism. A century later, the Gaelic Highlands of Scotland still remained impervious to the Protestantism that was by then dominant in the rest of the country, since the Reformed Church was unable to provide ministers who spoke the local language.

In these cases, the religious differences affected well-established communities in the area. But many religious minorities were initially made up of migrants, especially in the sixteenth century, when Catholics fled from their homes to escape persecution by Protestants, and Protestants fled from their homes to escape persecution by Catholics (or by other Protestants). Migrants often exhibited cultural characteristics that differentiated them starkly from their neighbors, and this in itself could create a sense of separation from the host community. Jews in particular could be easily singled out by their language, their names, and their dietary habits as well as their religious practices, even many generations after they had settled in a new home. And such separation could provoke hostility if there were any suspicion that the incomers might owe a prior allegiance to some outside power. It was often claimed, for instance, by Christians in southern and eastern Europe that Jews could not be trusted, for it was believed that they shared with Muslims a desire to destroy Christian societies and would therefore happily ally themselves with the enemy should the Ottomans ever invade. One Venetian patrician expressed that fear clearly and insultingly in 1568 when he wrote that he did not want to see Christian territory fall into the hands of "Turkish dogs through the treacherous perfidy of Jewish dogs."[1] Similar doubts attached themselves in Spain to the 200,000 Muslims who chose to stay in Granada after the Christian conquest of 1492 and to Catholics in Protestant lands. Such suspicions were of course usually without foundation in fact – though in the Balkans, there is no doubt that leaders of both Catholic and Orthodox churches did become involved in plots to displace Ottoman sovereignty.

Religious minorities sometimes survived only in very small numbers. In Lutheran Strasbourg, for example, a city of between 20,000 and 25,000 in the sixteenth century, there were only a few hundred Catholics. But by the beginning of the seventeenth century almost one in five inhabitants of the Protestant city of Nîmes were Catholic, and as many as 40 percent of the population of the officially Calvinist United Provinces were still Catholic in the middle of the seventeenth century. And minority groups could grow, whether by conversions, natural increase, or immigration. The Jewish communities in Poland expanded from a figure of around 30,000 in 1500 to between 100,000 and 150,000 by 1575, mainly as a result of migration from western and central Europe. In some areas, what had once been a numerical minority could become numerically dominant. In the fifteenth century, a majority of the population of Bohemia and Moravia – formerly Catholic territories – adopted Hussite beliefs; in the sixteenth, Protestant confessions attracted the majority throughout central and eastern Europe, with the exception of Poland. As a result, Catholicism in these territories became marginalized, and more recent confessions struggled for supremacy against each other. Similarly, in parts of the Balkans where Christians had been in a majority in previous centuries, voluntary conversions to Islam had by the later sixteenth century changed the religious map, especially in the towns. The Kosovan town of Peć, for example, once the patriarchal seat of the Serbian Orthodox Church, already had a Muslim majority by the 1550s. But religious boundaries were rarely fixed, as the Catholic resurgence in much of eastern and central Europe demonstrated in the later years of the sixteenth century.

Since religious minorities were a familiar feature in Renaissance Europe, local authorities in each state had to decide how to deal with them. The usual starting point was the assumption – held by virtually all religious groups – that contact with alternative beliefs would serve to weaken faith in the established teaching and foment social disorder. In the mid-1550s, the Lutheran pastor Johann Wieland asked his congregation "What has light to do with darkness? What does Christ have in common with Belial? What business have believers with unbelievers?"[2] According to the Spanish Jesuit Juan de Mariana, writing in the 1590s, there could be neither friendship nor trust between those who disagreed about theology. Religion was "the bond of society," and confessional uniformity the essential precondition for social and political order. Reason and history taught the same lesson, he declared: "what communion or society can there be among men who do not recur to the same God of a certainty in a like ceremonial and worship, since each turns away from the others as impious, and is convinced that heaven is served by injuring them?" And he added, "nothing is farther from peace than that in one city, state or province there be several religions."[3] There could be no compromise with false belief; dissent should be eliminated, not accommodated.

Most minorities, therefore, found themselves lodged within a host society that wanted, and expected, uniformity, and that preference helps to explain the pressure put on dissenting groups by the secular and ecclesiastical authorities in all parts of Renaissance Europe. Many states passed laws against alternative religious beliefs. In Hungary, the Habsburg authorities issued legislation in 1525 ordering that all Lutherans should be burned; Catholic worship was outlawed in the Protestant Netherlands in 1581, but made compulsory in France in 1585. In many Catholic territories, the Church used the Inquisition to investigate and punish Christians who deviated from Catholic teaching. Against non-Christians, persecution took other forms. Jews in Catholic lands were obliged to wear distinctive clothing, and their economic, social, and educational opportunities were severely restricted. Similar pressure was applied in 1567 by Philip II of Spain against the *moriscos*, descendants of Muslims who had converted to Christianity after the final Christian conquest of the peninsula, but who were often suspected to be still loyal to their old faith. Their use of Arabic and wearing of traditional dress was prohibited, Moorish music and dances were banned, and women were ordered not to cover their faces.

Governments often established their own judicial procedures to prosecute dissent. In the German city of Cologne, for example, Anabaptists and Calvinists were routinely investigated, imprisoned, or even executed in the sixteenth century by the Catholic magistrates. More arbitrary measures were adopted in the last years of the sixteenth century in many parts of eastern and central Europe, where Catholic rulers sought to wear down the Protestant majority by destroying their meeting houses or transferring them to Catholic congregations. Religious minorities could even find themselves the targets of military aggression. The Papacy proclaimed a crusade against the Bohemian followers of John Huss in 1420 and against the Waldenses of southern France in 1487. On each occasion, the papal declaration was followed by an armed invasion of the heretics' home territories. In the following century, too, Catholics and Protestants fought a series of vicious civil wars in Germany, the Low Countries, and France.

In many cases, religious minorities were forcibly relocated from their homes. In 1492 and 1497, the Jews of Spain and Portugal were given the choice of converting to Christianity or leaving the country. This expulsion formed part of a wider campaign against Europe's Jewish communities in the fifteenth century, one that had begun in the cities in Austria and southern Germany in the earlier part of the century, taking in Cologne in 1424 and the Moravian royal cities in 1454. From the 1480s, Jewish communities were driven out of some Italian states, and there was a further round of expulsions in the 1490s from Malta, Geneva, Lithuania, Provence, Switzerland, Lower Austria, and many German states and imperial cities. This program continued in the sixteenth century. The Jews of southern Italy were expelled in 1510, and Protestants in Germany moved quickly to remove their Jewish communities from the 1530s. Italian cities such as Ferrara and Mantua, and papal territories in both Italy and France, served as a refuge for Jewish exiles from other states in the first half of the sixteenth century, as did Catholic ecclesiastical territories in the Empire in the second half of the century. But Pope Pius V ordered the expulsion of all Jews from his lands, with the exception of the port of Ancona, in 1569, and that order was renewed in 1593 by Pope Clement VIII, who excepted only Rome, Ancona, and Avignon from its provisions.

The Spanish Muslims, who had initially been allowed in the 1490s "to live in their own religion" by their new rulers, and to maintain their property, laws, and language,[4] came under increasing pressure from the Christian authorities to abandon their faith and customs, and a royal edict eventually ordered all unbaptized Muslims to leave Castile in 1502. In 1570, the descendants of Muslims in Granada who had been baptized were forcibly removed to new settlements in an attempt to break up their communities, and in 1609 the entire Spanish *morisco* population – almost 300,000 people in all – was ordered out of Spain altogether. The kingdom of Valencia, in the east of Spain, may have lost as many as 23 percent of its inhabitants as a result. But mass expulsions were not confined to non-Christian groups: Catholic authorities expelled Protestants, and Protestant authorities expelled Catholics and other Protestants. Anabaptists were expelled from Hungary in 1543 and 1556, for example, and in 1578 all Protestant ministers and schoolteachers were expelled from Vienna in an attempt to weaken and eventually to eliminate Protestant worship in the city. In 1588, all Protestants were expelled from Salzburg.

Not all religious communities submitted tamely to such hostility. On occasion in both the fifteenth and sixteenth centuries, the Waldenses in southern France successfully challenged their persecution on legal grounds. When such tactics were ineffective, they simply migrated: the Waldensian communities of southern Italy were created by groups driven from their Alpine homes by the actions of the Inquisition. Of the 150,000 or so unbaptized Jews who lived in Castile in 1492, perhaps two-thirds emigrated rather than accept Christianity, transferring to North Africa, Italy, central Europe, Poland, or Ottoman territories in search of a safe home. Other groups took up arms in their own defense. The Waldenses in particular had a record of violence against Catholicism: in the 1440s in the Alpine valleys, in the 1480s and 1530s–40s in southern France, and again in 1560 in Calabria. Attempts to force cultural uniformity on baptized Muslims in Spain similarly led to armed revolts in 1500 and from 1568 to 1570. These rebellions did not have the same success as that of the Waldenses in Savoy in the 1560s. But the Hussites in Bohemia were spectacularly successful in their response to the crusade of 1420: a series of crushing defeats was inflicted on the Catholic forces, and by June 1421 the Hussites had seized control of virtually the whole kingdom. Similarly, the Protestant Huguenots successfully established their own self-governing communities in the smaller cities and towns of southern and western France during the later stages of the Wars of Religion in and after the 1570s: they seized Catholic churches for their own use, appropriated royal taxes, and established their own reformed Estates-General.

But in societies where the authorities expected and demanded religious uniformity, many individual dissenters simply hid their beliefs from public view and lived in conformity with the majority around them. The charge of deception was often leveled at the descendants of Iberian Jews who had converted to Christianity. Many were no doubt sincere believers in the new religion chosen for them by their parents and grandparents. But some converts clearly did retain a commitment to their ancestral religion, and took the opportunity to revert to Judaism when they moved to societies where that religion could be practiced safely. One of the reasons the Waldenses were able to survive so long was that they continued to attend Catholic services, make their confessions, and receive communion. Their contact with their own pastors provided them with a supplementary devotional life, fostered and cherished away from public view. A similar form of religious subterfuge was adopted by many Christians in the confusing years of the early Reformation and there are examples in the records from later years too of Protestants in Catholic territories and of Catholics in Protestant territories conforming in public to the demands of the established Church – though by its nature, the scale of such dissimulation can never be measured accurately.

John Calvin labeled the Protestants who hid their faith in this way "Nicodemites" after the member of the Jewish council recorded in the Fourth Gospel who visited Jesus only by night for fear of revealing his true beliefs to the authorities.[5] For many, religious simulation must have seemed the safest tactic in societies where those in power were seeking to dictate the confessional commitment of the majority: as the dissident notary Girolamo Parto is reported to have said in Catholic Venice: "In this city you have to live as others do."[6] In Elizabethan England, too, many Catholics survived in the same way, conforming outwardly to Anglican requirements but dissembling their true beliefs; it seems as if the *moriscos* in Spain adopted a similar tactic in the sixteenth century, observing the external requirements of Christianity while continuing the prayers and fasts expected by Islam in private.

In all these cases, religious minorities were obliged to live out their faith as best they could in societies that demanded uniformity. But that demand for uniformity was never universal: at all times, the authorities of Church and state were prepared to accept the existence of some doctrinal diversity within their societies, if only temporarily. For dynastic and political reasons, for instance, members of royal families sometimes married outside their own faith, and chapels had then to be created for the incomers (usually wives) who did not share the approved confession of their partners. When the Catholic duke of Lithuania, Aleksander Jagiełło, married Helena, the daughter of the Orthodox Tsar Ivan III of Russia in 1495, it was agreed that she could retain her ancestral faith untroubled in her husband's land; even after Aleksander became king of Poland in 1501, Helena continued to worship as an Orthodox Christian. Governments also allowed resident ambassadors from other states to worship in their own way in their embassies. Elizabeth I allowed the French, Spanish, and Venetian ambassadors to attend Catholic services in London, some of which were also attended by English sympathizers. And under both Edward VI and Elizabeth, London hosted several communities and churches of exiles from the continent – exiles whose Protestantism did not always fit easily with that of the established Church of England. Italian universities took in Protestant students from northern Europe, even when the local authorities were conducting a vigorous campaign against native dissenters. Such visitors provided a significant source of revenue to the local economy, and as long as they avoided any open discussion or demonstration of the faith, they were usually assured of protection from religious prosecution. The University of Padua welcomed Orthodox Greeks as well as Protestants. Port cities too welcomed traders from other nations and religions. Muslim, Jewish, and Protestant merchants all visited Malta, for instance; they could stay as long as their business required and were protected from molestation by the Catholic authorities.

European societies also made use of slaves and servants drawn from other lands and religions. Many slaves were seized by ships in the Mediterranean: in the early years of the seventeenth century, more than 3,600 were captured by the Knights of Malta, for example – a figure representing over 12 percent of the island's total population. High numbers of slaves were recorded also at different times in Lisbon, Madeira, Majorca, and Palermo. Almost all the slaves in Malta were Muslims, and a special prayer room was established for them in 1599 in the prison where they were lodged at Valletta. But Christians throughout Europe employed servants or slaves of many different confessions, including other Christians. Bulgar and Russian slaves were recorded in fifteenth-century Venice, for instance, in addition to Saracens, Tatars, and Turks. Portuguese slavers even imported Hindus and Tamils from India for sale in Europe. Black Africans were used as slaves in southern Europe in increasing numbers, too: by the end of the fifteenth century, 83 percent of the slaves in Naples were black Africans. Some of these African slaves were Muslims, but others kept their traditional religions, and the trade continued well into the sixteenth century.

At times, governments were even willing to profit from the presence of religious minorities by charging them for the privilege of residence. Even though Jews had been expelled from Münster in the later fifteenth century, several Jewish families were permitted by the city's bishop to buy property in the city for their own use in 1536 in return for an annual fee. Charles V had similarly protected the *morsicos* of Granada from inquisitorial pressure ten years earlier after receiving from them the promise of a large subsidy of 90,000 ducats over six years. In Lower Austria, members of the noble Estates were given freedom of worship on their own lands by the Emperor Maximilian II in 1568 in return for funds to prosecute the war against the Turks; in Inner Austria, too, Protestant members of the Estates managed to secure religious concessions from the Archduke Charles ten years later in return for financial support.

It is clear, then, that Europeans accepted sometimes surprisingly large numbers of people of other faiths within their communities as a matter of routine. In 1434, the Council of Basle had encouraged the Church to work for the conversion of nonbelievers in Europe, recognizing perhaps that religious minorities could not just be legislated, or persecuted, out of existence, and preaching campaigns to convert members of Europe's Jewish communities were regularly organized by the Catholic Church – evidence that total and immediate religious uniformity in society was not always expected. A similar willingness to acknowledge the existence of a significant minority, if only temporarily, can be found in France in the 1560s, when it was unclear how the eventual balance of forces between Catholics and Protestants might settle, and the legal existence of more than one confession had therefore to be accepted. The Edict of Saint-Germain issued in 1562, for example – one of a series of attempts between 1560 and 1598 to ensure peace between the Catholics and the

Protestant Huguenots – was intended "to maintain our subjects in peace and concord while we wait for God by his grace to enable them to reunite, and to bring them together again in a single sheep-fold."[7]

That edict held the peace in France for only a short time, but such temporary and grudging expedients, allowing freedom of worship and a guarantee of security to both sides, were often adopted after periods of war between two confessions, when it was clear that the religious minority could not be eliminated and had instead to be incorporated into the constitutional structure of the state. In the case of the Edict of Nantes, issued in 1598, the effect was more longlasting: this permitted the Huguenots freedom of worship in those places where they were already dominant and allowed them to protect themselves there with fortifications and garrisons. But the settlement was not wholly welcomed by either Catholics or Protestants, nor was it seen as permanent. It was adopted not because there was general agreement that the minority had any established right to religious freedom, but because the military conflict had reached a stalemate. Both confessions still hoped for eventual victory and the total conversion of their opponents, and over time the concessions granted to the Huguenots were whittled away or withdrawn entirely.

Such legislation did at least mark a step away from the expectation that a society had at all times to hold to a single confession. In Basle, in order to defuse confessional conflict in the city and so maintain peace, the council issued decrees in 1526 and 1527 guaranteeing freedom of conscience to all. In 1563, the French Edict of Amboise similarly stated that "everyone can live and reside freely everywhere in their own houses without being investigated or molested, compelled or constrained because of their conscience."[8] Freedom of conscience was also explicitly recognized in article 13 of the Union of Utrecht, a document agreed by the rebellious provinces in the northern Netherlands in 1579, but designed to attract the adherence also of the Catholic southern provinces: "every individual shall be allowed to remain free in his religion and . . . no one shall be allowed to arrest or examine anyone on account of religion."[9]

But statements of this kind did not grant full religious liberty. The Union of Utrecht made no explicit reference to freedom of worship, and consequently only members of the established Dutch Reformed Church were allowed in later years to worship in public in the United Provinces. This pattern – freedom of conscience to all, but freedom of worship only to some – was in fact quite common in the sixteenth century. As a result many minorities were forced to restrict their devotions to the privacy of their own homes, out of sight – though certainly not outside the knowledge – of the majority community surrounding them. "House churches" of this kind could be found in several parts of Europe: Lutherans and Calvinists relied on them in Catholic Cologne, for example, while Catholics in later sixteenth-century England and Scotland gathered for worship in the homes of recusant gentry and nobles. Hamburg's Jews similarly worshiped in private houses from the 1580s. In politically fragmented areas, members of religious minorities were able to journey outside the borders of their own state to find a territory where they could pray in public. Calvinists in the Catholic bishopric of Speyer traveled to the Calvinist Palatinate, for example, while Catholics in the Palatinate traveled to Speyer. In addition to having their opportunities to worship restricted, religious minorities often found that their civil rights were limited as well. Lutherans were politically disenfranchised in Catholic Münster, for instance, while Catholics were excluded from guild membership and other civic rights in the eastern provinces of the Dutch republic. And throughout Europe, Jews found themselves obliged to wear distinguishing hats or marks on their clothes, barred from specified economic activities, and prohibited from full commercial, intellectual, and social contacts with their Christian neighbors.

Such attempts to make the faith and lives of minorities uncomfortable or difficult were inspired by the hope that they would in time be more inclined to convert to the approved religion. Even in states that permitted some freedom of conscience, the assumption that all members of a society ought to share a common set of beliefs still dominated the authorities' thinking. But at a day-to-day level, minorities sometimes found that members of their host communities took a more relaxed view and that they were able to benefit as a result from an informal confessional independence. Clerics disapproved when the laws were ignored, of course: in Strasbourg, for example, the long-serving president of the Lutheran Church Assembly complained in 1572 that "These days we have unfortunately fallen into the habit of leaving everyone free to take up not just the old [Catholic] religion, but also those that are expressly forbidden . . . all this publicly and without any prejudice to them."[10] But examples of such practical cooperation were surprisingly common. In 1536, the citizens of Lausanne agreed at a town meeting that everyone in the city should be free to attend either Catholic or Protestant services as their conscience should demand, and in the 1560s, as France descended into religious civil war, the residents of Nyons and Saint-Laurent-des-Arbres in the Dauphiné swore to "live in peace, friendship, and confederation" despite "the diversity of religion that is between them."[11] Neither of these agreements lasted for very long, but they indicate that religious plurality was a possibility in early modern European communities, both conceptually and in reality.

In other words, the laity did not always share the extreme fear of dissent expressed by their clerical leaders. Religious discord threatened economic prosperity and social order; communities could not flourish, and might even be destroyed, if neighbors were in constant conflict over religion. For many, therefore, practicality took precedence over ideological or doctrinal difference. And such relations sometimes went beyond mere passive coexistence. In Elizabethan England we know of Catholics who acted as godparents to the children of their Protestant neighbors and even served as executors of their wills, while in Strasbourg Protestants served as godparents for Catholic children. Marriages between Christians of different confessions were recorded in many communities, and Protestants frequently sent their sons to Jesuit colleges to complete their secondary education.

In many parts of Europe, in fact, religious minorities were protected against the authorities of Church and state by local councils or the nobility. There was thus no systematic opposition from officials in the northern Netherlands to the slow re-establishment of the Catholic hierarchy from 1583, and a number of Catholic monasteries continued to function in cities such as Utrecht until the early seventeenth century, despite the legal prohibition on Catholic worship. The support of individual Bohemian nobles for the radical Brethren, who broke away from the main body of Hussites in 1467, enabled them to survive when both Hussites and Catholics wanted their destruction. In neighboring Moravia, it was the Anabaptists who were protected by the nobility: by 1600, some 20,000 had settled in the territory, mostly on noble estates where other labor was in short supply, and where (it was argued) the crown had no jurisdiction. In much of central and eastern Europe, in fact, attempts by central governments to expel Protestants and enforce Catholicism were often resisted by nobles who had themselves adopted the new teaching. In Royal Hungary, where the majority of the population was Protestant by the later sixteenth century (Lutherans mainly in the western counties, Calvinists in the eastern), the nobility used their patronage rights to elect Protestant ministers to serve their own estates, while town councils often allowed several confessional groups to settle locally and to worship in their own churches. Although the Hungarian Diet was reluctant to legitimize these alternative confessions formally, they repeatedly refused to act against Lutherans and Calvinists, despite pressure to do so from their Habsburg monarchs.

A number of German Lutheran cities similarly welcomed non-Lutherans in the later sixteenth century for economic reasons. Nuremberg encouraged the migration of Calvinist merchants and artisans from the southern Netherlands, even offering them tax exemptions as an incentive; several other cities and territorial rulers in north Germany began to welcome renewed Jewish migration from the 1570s as part of a policy of developing trade. In 1577 Emperor Rudolf II issued a charter guaranteeing Jews security within Bohemia, and by 1600 the Jewish population in Prague exceeded 3,000. In Amsterdam, too, the city regents welcomed Portuguese merchants of Jewish descent in the 1590s, protecting them even when they reverted publicly to Judaism. And many Spanish landowners obstructed the expulsion of the *moriscos* by the royal government in 1609, or condoned their early return, reliant as they were on *morisco* labor to work their estates.

Of course, local autonomy could cut both ways. In Polish territory the privileges of self-government granted to noblemen, towns, and regions by the crown in the later Middle Ages to encourage settlement in the east enabled members of many different confessions, including Jews and Protestants, to reside and worship freely in some places. For instance, the town of Troki or Trakai (now in Lithuania) contained a Catholic church, a Uniate monastery, a Karaite Jewish synagogue, and a Muslim mosque by the mid-sixteenth century, to which was added an antitrinitarian group from the 1570s. But the same privileges also allowed their holders to discriminate against minorities: towns such as Warsaw and Toruń excluded Jewish residents entirely; others turned against Protestants in and after the 1590s, depriving them of their churches and preventing their ministers and teachers from exercising their full functions.

A common response to the conflicting demands of confessional uniformity and economic opportunity was to create separate residential zones for dissident religious groups within the community. In 1434, the Council of Basle had in fact explicitly prohibited the co-habitation of Christians and non-Christians, insisting that all "infidels . . . should be made to dwell in areas, in the cities and towns, which are apart from the dwellings of Christians and as far distant as possible from churches."[12] This requirement was only rarely observed in the fifteenth century. But in Spain, in 1478,

Ferdinand and Isabella required all Muslims and Jews in Castile to return to designated zones in their home towns. Jewish quarters in particular were sometimes literally separated from the rest of the community by a wall or some other physical boundary that obstructed easy movement in or out. It was the Jewish quarter of Venice, established in 1516 and called the "Geto" or "Ghetto," after the foundry that had formerly occupied the site, that was to give its name to such segregated areas elsewhere in Europe. The Venetian ghetto was surrounded by canals patrolled by boats, and entrance was through two gates only, which were locked at night. Ghettos were also established in papal territories in 1555 and in Florence and Siena in 1570–1.

Settlements of this kind were regulated by charters that set down the terms on which minorities were entitled to live within their host community. In Poland, such charters were issued to Muslims, Armenians, and other national groups as well as Jews. There were disadvantages in this arrangement of course, especially for the minorities, whose free movement was limited; Jews in particular were subjected to many additional humiliating social and economic restrictions. But there were advantages, too. The legal establishment of a recognized communal identity allowed minorities a greater degree of control over their own affairs and the opportunity to apply their own laws and customs within their own settlement without undue interference from the territorial government. They could also benefit from continued commercial and business links, at the same time reducing the frequency of social contacts with members of the majority faith that might increase the risk of conversion. Minorities could thus follow their own customs without fear of interruption, while the majority was spared the sight of lifestyles or forms of worship they did not share. In some cases, in fact, residential segregation of this kind was the result of a voluntary decision by minorities who chose to live in close contact with each other, even when it was not compulsory, and to create their own devotional, charitable, and social networks as alternatives to those of the surrounding majority. In Venice, for example, while practicing Jews were compelled to reside within the ghetto and Muslims in the Fondaco dei Turchi, Protestant Germans mostly gathered near the Rialto, and Orthodox Greeks near their church in Castello.

Occasionally, rulers deliberately created safe havens for minorities. The Jews expelled from Kraków in 1494 were resettled in the nearby town of Kazimierz, for instance. In 1548 and again in 1551, Duke Cosimo I of Tuscany issued an invitation to Greeks, Turks, Moors, Jews, Armenians, and Persians to migrate to Pisa and Livorno in order to develop the two ports, guaranteeing the incomers immunity from investigation by the Inquisition; the invitation was renewed in 1593 by his successor Ferdinand I, who extended it also to Protestants from England and the Low Countries. Two years later, Henri IV of France issued a privilege guaranteeing the practice of Judaism to the Jewish community of Metz, and in 1602, the Lutheran Count Ernst of Holstein-Schauenburg offered all religious groups freedom of religion if they settled in his little town of Altona. His purpose was to attract migrants who would help to develop the local economy, and by 1664, the population of Altona had grown to over 3,000, including Calvinists, Catholics, Jews, and Mennonites.

Some states adopted this policy of segregation, and applied it across their whole territory to resolve religious conflict. In 1531, the Second Peace of Kappel acknowledged the presence of the reformed faith within the Swiss Confederation after several years of debilitating warfare, and allowed each canton to choose its own religion. This settlement anticipated the Peace of Augsburg agreed in 1555, which similarly recognized the right of territorial units within the Holy Roman Empire to decide the religion of their own inhabitants. In France, several edicts issued after 1562 permitted Protestant worship in specified localities, a situation established on a longer term basis in 1598 by the Edict of Nantes; but Huguenots were at the same time required to respect the exercise of Catholicism, and both confessions were prohibited from discriminating against each other in education, health care, or welfare. In this way, the maps of Switzerland, the Empire, and France came to resemble a patchwork of separate, and largely self-governing, religious confessions. In the European provinces of the Ottoman Empire, too, non-Muslim communities regulated themselves: local religious leaders needed official endorsement from the Sultan, but that was normally a matter of routine (and a cash payment). Beyond that, Jews and Christians of all kinds exercised ecclesiastical, pastoral, and judicial authority over their own people, even though in other respects they enjoyed a lower status than Muslims in the eyes of the Ottoman authorities and were not entitled to hold any government or public offices.

These large-scale agreements in effect granted a measure of legal recognition to members of religious minorities. In some territories, though, two or more confessions were granted formal equality. The Compactata of Prague, drawn up in 1433, recognized both the Catholic and the Hussite churches, and members of both confessions were thereafter represented in the Bohemian Estates; Ferdinand I renewed the agreement when he was elected king of Bohemia in 1526. Under the terms of the Peace of 1555, the German imperial free cities were required to allow both Lutherans and Catholics to practice their faith in public, and in a few cities in Swabia in southern Germany a careful balance was thereafter established between the two confessions. Religious peace was essential if commercial links with these cities' traditional trading partners were to be maintained. In the city of Augsburg, therefore, Catholics and Protestants continued to live alongside each other, and members of both confessions sat on the city council in almost equal numbers. In some French towns, too, we find that Catholics and Protestants held office on local councils, assemblies, and judicial tribunals into the early seventeenth century.

These agreements did not solve all problems. Rights of access to burial grounds were often problematic: where two confessions were recognized in a single state, could both use the same cemetery? In Augsburg, a fascinating row blew up in 1583 when the council decided to adopt the reformed calendar approved by Pope Gregory XIII the previous year. Many Protestants refused to acknowledge the revised dates, and members of the two approved confessions therefore found themselves observing festivals such as Christmas, and even regular Sunday worship, on different days. A further feature of such bi-confessional agreements was that they necessarily excluded members of other confessions. There was no space for Protestants in the legal system of Bohemia after 1526, and Calvinists were excluded from the provisions of the Peace of Augsburg. The recognition of more than one confession did not therefore of itself involve an acceptance of the principle of freedom of conscience or worship. The proliferation of denominations after the Reformation did however sometimes force the authorities gradually to widen the range of acceptable beliefs. The Transylvanian Diet recognized Lutheranism as well as Catholicism in 1557, for example, and Calvinism in 1564, when ministers were ordered to tailor their preaching to the preference of the local congregation. Antitrinitarian beliefs were added to the mix at the Diet at Torda four years later. This Diet seemed on the surface to grant religious liberty: "no one should be compelled by force if their spirit is not at peace . . . no one . . . should abuse anyone on account of their religion . . . because faith is a gift from God."[13] Even here, though, it is worth noting that the local Orthodox population was not mentioned in the declaration, and in 1572 the Diet prohibited any further theological innovation.

Occasionally, though, we can see members of different religious groups trying to edge towards greater cooperation between themselves. In bi-confessional German cities such as Biberach or Ravensburg, for example, Protestants and Catholics made use of the same church buildings for worship, as they did also in rural Hungary. In some parts of Cyprus, too, Latin and Orthodox Christians shared a single church, designed with altars for the two communities in different parts of the building. In some parts of eastern Europe, non-Catholics sought to repair the divisions of the Reformation by holding their own doctrinal conferences. Throughout the 1550s and 1560s, representatives of the Lutheran and Calvinist populations of Poland and Lithuania held meetings with members of the local Bohemian Brethren to establish a common statement of belief, and in 1570 the three confessions signed a Consensus at the Polish town of Sandomierz in which they listed the matters on which they did agree, recognized each other's essential orthodoxy, encouraged attendance at each other's services, and looked forward to further doctrinal convergence in future. Non-Catholics in Bohemia similarly worked together, initially securing the abolition in 1567 of the fifteenth-century Compactata, which gave recognition only to Catholics and Hussites, and then eight years later issuing the document known as the *Confessio Bohemica* to serve as a common statement of belief for the Hussites, Bohemian Brethren, Lutherans, and Calvinists in the kingdom. This represented a genuine doctrinal compromise between its signatories, for it accepted both the Lutheran position on justification and the Calvinist position on the Eucharist. In the isolated region of southeast Transylvania, the antitrinitarian and Calvinist churches went one step further and formed a formal administrative union, so that members of both confessions could attend services together.

Such attempts at doctrinal unity were viewed with suspicion by some clerics, however, precisely because they involved surrendering the distinctive theological convictions of each confession. Among the laity, though, as we have seen, attitudes were often more relaxed, and examples of apparent confessional confusion were common. In Münster, for instance, Lutheran hymns were sung in Catholic churches, and communion was administered in both kinds on the Protestant model. According to the Jesuit Antonio Possevino, Catholics in Transylvania and Moldavia readily accepted married priests,[14] while in sixteenth- and seventeenth-century Kosovo we have reports of Catholic and Orthodox Christians attending the same services, praying at the same shrines, and even sometimes receiving the sacraments from each other's priests. Muslims in this area also adopted some Christian practices and were willing to serve as godparents to their Christian neighbors' children. According to one Catholic visitor, local people "seemed to glory in this diversity of religions."[15] Where more than one faith was (or had been) available, it is no wonder that some individuals preferred to construct their own package of beliefs rather than simply adopting one selected for them. Out in the parishes, therefore, in both west and east Europe, the notion of confessional purity was often compromised.

The existence of any minority forces the majority to make a choice between insisting on uniformity and accommodating diversity. This choice predated the Reformation, as Jewish, Muslim, and other Christian groups already posed a challenge to the monopoly of the Catholic Church in the Middle Ages. But the problem was clearly made more urgent by the growth of migration and international trade in the sixteenth century, and by the proliferation of Christian confessions in and after the 1520s. It would be pleasant to conclude that the fifteenth and sixteenth centuries saw a growing willingness to allow religious minorities to live and worship in peace. In some parts of Europe, that development may well be visible. But no consistent trend can be identified across the continent as a whole, and in the seventeenth century there were renewed attempts to enforce conformity on both willing and unwilling populations. The clerical authorities of virtually all Christian churches in this period wanted to exercise a monopoly of belief and behavior, believing that dissent was a temporary phenomenon that could be eradicated by targeted preaching or persecution. At the same time, secular governments needed to bring together the populations of their territories into a coherent and stable political union. Religious minorities stood in the way of both those ambitions, indicating as they did that an alternative faith was possible, and that personal and group loyalties could be given to more than one source of power. The first instinct of both ecclesiastical and temporal governments was therefore to eliminate minorities by either peaceful or violent means. But preaching campaigns took time, and forced conformity was rarely sincere or long-lasting. And when the resistance of the dissenters became more determined, the impracticality of a policy of religious uniformity became rapidly apparent.

In the event, it tended to be more pragmatic considerations that persuaded majorities to tolerate minorities in their midst: the fear of provoking social disorder or a costly civil war, the need to maintain good diplomatic and trading relations with neighboring states of different faiths, or the desire to maintain a semblance of unity in the face of military threats from outside. In these circumstances, minorities were more likely to survive if they avoided drawing attention to themselves and posed no obvious threat to the beliefs and way of life of the majority. But when the majority felt vulnerable – when a minority grew in numbers, for example, or seemed to undermine the supremacy of the dominant faith by its actions, either secretly or openly – the likelihood of prosecution, persecution, or violence could always recur. In some areas, minorities were able to shelter under the protection of municipal authorities or nobles, whose privileges enabled them to flout the clear religious preference of the state. But reliance on such protection placed the minority in a position of dependence and was never a sure guarantee of safety.

So minorities existed in what was always a precarious environment. They were confronted with another problem, too: whether to integrate with the surrounding majority or to isolate themselves from it. There were obvious advantages to be gained from integration, which provided access to greater economic opportunities and to the wider social, cultural, and political world of the majority. Regular interaction between members of different groups also tended to reduce confessional tensions and the sense of otherness that fed violence: conflict could be absorbed by sociability. But greater integration also increased the risk of assimilation and even of conversion, thus threatening the minority's very survival. As a result, the leaders of minorities often warned against closer relations with outsiders, believing that it was essential to separate themselves as an identifiable confessional community, with its own established institutional structure and clear membership rules. But the more minorities advertised their distinctiveness in this way, the more they were seen as a challenge by the majority, thus raising the risk of renewed persecution.

Both majorities and minorities therefore faced a dilemma: uniformity or diversity, integration or separation – and this helps to explain why relations between them were characterized so often by uncertainty and inconsistency. Laws against minorities were frequently ignored, but periods of coexistence could be followed suddenly by persecution and violence, and legal attempts to establish a framework for some sort of confessional peace were often short-lived. What was needed to create a more long-lasting pluralism was a willingness to separate questions of beliefs from questions of trust, and so reduce the significance of religious disagreements in daily life. This is what happened in cities with the richest collection of religious minorities, such as Venice or Amsterdam. Here governments allowed minorities a good deal of autonomy and relied on them to discipline and care for their own members. This policy did not try to disguise the differences between the religious communities, but it avoided the risks of fragmentation by recognizing the minorities within the legal structure of the city. Exclusion and inclusion were in this way combined: the dilemmas of both majority and minority were resolved, and peace was secured without sacrificing identity. But such practices were rare in Renaissance Europe.

NOTES

1 B. Arbel, *Trading Nations: Jews and Venetians in the Early Modern Eastern Mediterranean* (Leiden: Brill, 1995), p. 62.
2 Johann Wieland, *Fünff Christliches Predigten* (1593), quoted by C. Scott Dixon, "Urban Order and Religious Coexistence in the German Imperial City: Augsburg and Donauwoerth, 1548–1608," forthcoming in *Central European History* 40, 1 (2007). I am most grateful to Dr Dixon for sending me a copy of this article before publication.
3 Juan de Mariana, *De rege et regis institutione* (1599), in David George Mullan (ed.), *Religious Pluralism in the West: An Anthology* (Oxford: Blackwell, 1998), p. 118.
4 Capitulations of 1491, in L. P. Harvey, *Islamic Spain, 1250–1500* (Chicago: University of Chicago Press, 1990), pp. 315–22.
5 *Excuse de Jehan Calvin, à Messieurs les Nicodemites, sur la complaincte qu'ilz font de sa trop grand' rigueur* (1544).
6 Archivio di Stato, Venice, *Santo Uffizio* b. 37, "Parto Girolamo," denunciation of 27 March 1572, quoted by John Jeffries Martin, *Venice's Hidden Enemies: Italian Heretics in a Renaissance City* (Baltimore: Johns Hopkins University Press, 2003), p. 134.
7 A. Stegmann (ed.), *Édits des guerres de religion* (Paris: J. Vrin, 1979), p. 10.
8 Stegmann, *Édits des guerres de religion*, p. 34.

9 Benjamin J. Kaplan, *Calvinists and Libertines: Confession and Community in Utrecht 1578–1620* (Oxford: Clarendon Press, 1995), p. 270.
10 Lorna Jane Abray, *The People's Reformation: Magistrates, Clergy and Commons in Strasbourg 1500–1598* (Oxford: Blackwell, 1985), p. 183.
11 P. Benedict, "'Un roi, une loi, deux fois': Parameters for the History of Catholic-Reformed Co-existence in France, 1555–1685," in Ole Peter Grell and Bob Scribner (eds), *Tolerance and Intolerance in the European Reformation* (Cambridge: Cambridge University Press, 1996), p. 78.
12 Norman P. Tanner (ed.), *Decrees of the Ecumenical Councils* (London: Sheed & Ward, 1990), vol. I, pp. 483–4.
13 Graeme Murdock, *Calvinism on the Frontier 1600–1660: Calvinism and the Reformed Church in Hungary and Transylvania* (Oxford: Clarendon Press, 2000), p. 110.
14 Cesare Alzati, *Terra romena tra Oriente e Occidente: chiese ed etnie nel tardo '500* (Milano: Jaca Book, 1982), pp. 62–3.
15 Antonio Maria de Turre, *Orbis seraphicus: De missionibus fratrum minorum ad infideles* (Quaracchi, 1886), vol. II, p. 492.

SUGGESTIONS FOR FURTHER READING

Abray, Lorna Jane. *The People's Reformation: Magistrates, Clergy, and Commons in Strasbourg, 1500–1598*. Oxford: Blackwell, 1985.

Arbel, Benjamin. *Trading Nations: Jews and Venetians in the Early Modern Eastern Mediterranean*. Leiden: Brill, 1995.

Bell, Gary M. "John Man: The Last Elizabethan Resident Ambassador in Spain." *Sixteenth Century Journal* 7 (1976): 75–93.

Cameron, Euan. *Waldenses: Rejections of Holy Church in Medieval Europe*. Oxford: Blackwell, 2000.

Cameron, K., Mark Greengrass, and Penny Roberts, eds. *The Adventure of Religious Pluralism in Early Modern France*. Oxford: Peter Lang, 2000.

Ciappara, Frans. *Society and the Inquisition in Early Modern Malta*. San Ġwann, Malta: PEG, 2001.

Dixon, C. Scott. "Urban Order and Religious Coexistence in the German Imperial City: Augsburg and Donauwoerth, 1548–1608." Forthcoming in *Central European History* 40, 1 (2007).

Earle, T. F. and Lowe, K. J. P., eds. *Black Africans in Renaissance Europe*. Cambridge: Cambridge University Press, 2005.

Edwards, John. *The Jews in Christian Europe 1400–1700*. London: Routledge, 1988.

Evans, R. J. W. and T. V. Thomas, eds. *Crown, Church and Estates: Central European Politics in the Sixteenth and Seventeenth Centuries*. Basingstoke: Macmillan, 1991.

Grell, Ole Peter and Bob Scribner, eds. *Tolerance and Intolerance in the European Reformation*. Cambridge: Cambridge University Press, 2002.

Hanlon, Gregory. *Confession and Community in Seventeenth-century France: Catholic and Protestant Coexistence in Aquitaine*. Philadelphia: University of Pennsylvania Press, 1993.

Harvey, L. P. *Islamic Spain, 1250–1500*. Chicago: University of Chicago Press, 1990.

—— *Muslims in Spain, 1500 to 1614*. Chicago: University of Chicago Press, 2005.

Hsia, R. Po-Chia. *Society and Religion in Münster, 1535–1618*. New Haven: Yale University Press, 1984.

—— *Social Discipline in the Reformation: Central Europe 1550–1750*. London: Routledge, 1989.

Hsia, R. Po-Chia and Hartmut Lehmann, eds. *In and Out of the Ghetto: Jewish–Gentile Relations in Late Medieval and Early Modern Germany*. Cambridge: Cambridge University Press, 1995.

Hsia, R. Po-Chia and Henk van Nierop, eds. *Calvinism and Religious Toleration in the Dutch Golden Age*. Cambridge: Cambridge University Press, 2002.

Imber, Colin. *The Ottoman Empire, 1300–1650: The Structure of Power*. Basingstoke: Palgrave Macmillan, 2002.

Kaplan, Benjamin J. *Calvinists and Libertines: Confession and Community in Utrecht, 1578–1620*. Oxford: Clarendon Press, 1995.

——— "Fictions of Privacy: House Chapels and the Spatial Accommodation of Religious Dissent in Early Modern Europe." *American Historical Review* 107 (2002): 1030–64.

Kooi, Christine. *Liberty and Religion: Church and State in Leiden's Reformation, 1572–1620*. Leiden: Brill, 2000.

Maag, Karin. *The Reformation in Eastern and Central Europe*. Aldershot: Scolar, 1997.

Malcolm, Noel. *Kosovo: A Short History*. London: Macmillan, 1998.

Martin, John Jeffries. *Venice's Hidden Enemies: Italian Heretics in a Renaissance City*. Berkeley: University of California Press, 1993.

Mentzer, R. A. "Ecclesiastical Discipline and Communal Reorganization among the Protestants of Southern France." *European History Quarterly* 21 (1991): 163–83.

Mullan, David George, ed. *Religious Pluralism in the West: An Anthology*. Oxford: Blackwell, 1998.

Murdock, Graeme. *Calvinism on the Frontier, 1600–1660: International Calvinism and the Reformed Church in Hungary and Transylvania*. Oxford: Clarendon Press, 2000.

Wettinger, Godfrey. *Slavery in the Islands of Malta and Gozo: ca. 1000–1812*. San Gwann, Malta: PEG, 2002.

Whaley, Joachim. *Religious Toleration and Social Change in Hamburg, 1529–1819*. Cambridge: Cambridge University Press, 1985.

CHAPTER TWENTY-NINE

HUMANISM AND THE DREAM OF CHRISTIAN UNITY

Susan R. Boettcher

More than any other humanist of the early sixteenth century, Desiderius Erasmus redefined the intellectual landscape of western Europe. His effectiveness in doing so was largely a result of his self-conscious use of the printing press – especially in Venice and later in Basle – to promote himself and his ideas via intense relationships with printers like Aldus Manutius and Johann Froben. But his influence was primarily a consequence of the astonishing range of his widely respected scholarship. He assembled renowned collections of his letters as guides to the consummate Latin style. He wrote pedagogical texts in dialogue form, like the *Colloquies*, and others, like the *Adages*, that drew on the classical Latin heritage to educate even beginning students in correct Latin. Later in life he wrote works like the *Hyperaspistes*, in which he debated Martin Luther on the problem of the freedom of will. He also composed erudite, playful satires like *The Praise of Folly* that displayed his command of the canon of ancient culture even as they poked fun at the pretensions of the Church. Finally, a master not only of Latin and Greek but also of Hebrew, Erasmus proved to be an assiduous, perhaps brilliant, biblical scholar. In the prefaces to his critical editions of the New Testament, moreover, he expressed his desire that the Bible be translated so that everyone could read it for him/herself: "Christ wants his gospel to be spread as widely as possible. He died for all; he wants to be known by all. It would serve that end if his books were turned into all the languages of all the nations."[1] Erasmus's learning was elite, but his intended audience was no less than all of Christendom.

Erasmus died in 1536 with his scholarly reputation intact. Yet, with the development of the Reformation, the sentiment that many of his scholarly and moral commitments were no longer publicly tenable was rising. His biography, with its relationship to lay piety (the *devotio moderna*, with its emphasis on inner asceticism), its episode of life in a religious order, a sojourn at several universities, and the cultivation of a group of like-minded friends, was typical of a group of now mostly forgotten men – we think of Beatus Rhenanus or Wolfgang Capito – who developed not only critical tools for scriptural study but also an attitude of piety and reverence in the face of the unknown. In the end, such men felt, the humanist "republic of letters" would use its intellectual tools to solve divisive problems and draw the Church – itself a regular object of Erasmus's biting persiflage – more closely together.

— *Humanism and Christian unity* —

Figure 29.1 Hans Holbein the Younger. *Erasmus* (1523). The Art Archive/Musée du Louvre Paris/Dagli Orti.

But the Reformation engendered a new atmosphere of religious discourse, one that often took resort in punishing polemic and left no room for many of Erasmus's stylistic preferences: for a source-based classical knowledge analyzed independently of doctrinal presuppositions, elegant rhetorical verve for its own sake, or willingness to hold answers in abeyance to religious questions for which evidence could be found on both sides.

Thus the very push toward a unity of knowledge and belief present in Erasmus's writings, when carried out via the tools of humanistic learning, incorporated the seeds of bitter dissent. The cost of preserving text-critical methods in combination with the move toward Christian unity was an increasingly doctrinal orientation within later sixteenth-century Christianity, where discussants who disagreed with each other could no longer agree to table their disputes as the humanists had done, but perforce split themselves up into new religious groups called "confessions." The authors of the Reformation also sought to reach all of Christendom, but they spoke in increasingly shrill tones. The erosion of the cultural values of the humanists is clearly evident in the biographies of three reformers who had been substantially influenced by Erasmus, not least in terms of their tendencies toward irenicism. Martin Bucer, educated in the renowned humanist academy at Sélestat, pursued after his abandonment of the Dominican Order a theological program that stressed unity among evangelicals over doctrinal agreement; Philip Melanchthon, the first mate of the Wittenberg Reformation and one of Erasmus's correspondents, came to the university as a teacher of classical languages and was drawn to the evangelical movement through his contact with Luther, but was increasingly marginalized among his fellow theologians after Luther's death, largely as a consequence of his willingness to support the compromise-oriented Catholic doctrine of the Augsburg Interim in 1548; and Jan Laski, one of Erasmus's most influential popularizers in Poland, refused to condemn Anabaptists merely for the label attached to them, and insisted on questioning individuals as to the actual content of their beliefs. This intellectual openness nonetheless faded in the atmosphere of the post-Interim years. Bucer, Melanchthon, and Laski embody both the compatibility of humanist intellectual approaches with the Reformation and the increasing separation of humanistically inclined reformers from the Old Church. Even more, their divergent careers trace the growing impossibility of the unity proposed by the humanists, even among a group of individuals who shared a particular text-critical orientation and might have sought such a unity. Bucer's theology, which sought to resolve differences among Protestants, was pushed aside; 400 years passed before Protestants could view Melanchthon's support of colleagues who had pleaded for the existence of *adiaphora* in religion – matters whose treatment was indifferent to the rightness of belief – equably. Laski's development was more typical; he became an almost constant religious refugee after 1548, only partially due to Catholic persecution. Like his opponents, his ability to accept diverging interpretations of certain scriptures had been immeasurably reduced. Their and their fellow reformers' different readings and interpretations of the ancient texts meant that they could not remain in one church.

The lives of these reformers suggest a paradox: that precisely the push for unity embodied in humanism contributed to the most noticeable consequence of the Reformation: the division and thus manifest splitting of the western Church. The program of humanism was one aspect of a move toward unity that responded to the conditions of an age of extreme and often troubling fragmentation. Thus the tragedy of humanism as it was received by the Reformation was not one akin to the failure of Erasmus's ideas to influence the structure, belief, and piety of the Old Church but rather the fact that humanism carried with it the seeds of some aspects of its own demise. Erasmus and his positions were ultimately abandoned by Christians of all stripes, not because of their orthodoxy – if by this we mean their insistence on remaining within the bounds of the Old Church and its teachings – but rather because of their catholicity, a more tolerant mood that did not survive the doctrinal and political settlements of the mid-sixteenth century, not even within that church itself. The humanist practices of the Renaissance, as employed by the reformers, finalized rather than caused fragmentation – and they did so in the name of fostering Christian unity.

This concern with unity developed against the backdrop of a religious landscape marked by extreme diversity. Although the structuring ritual of the mass was shared, for example, its execution varied widely. Thus on a popular level, western Christianity was marked by a wide variety of local practices. Concerns about Purgatory, for example, gave rise to a rich culture of piety that involved pilgrimages long and short, the donation of art monumental and miniature, the performance of a vast assortment of prayers and penances, and the growth of the indulgence system that Luther so despised. While some widely accepted pious practices were shared – like the desirability of undertaking two of the most well-known pilgrimages, those to Santiago and Jerusalem – many or perhaps most pious practices were specifically bound to local places and were likely to appear unintelligible or even superstitious to outsiders, like local shrines and pilgrimage destinations that enjoyed a primarily regional or even local appeal. Central protagonists of these devotions were the Virgin Mary and the numerous ranks of the saints, who were thought to intercede for sinners with Jesus. Some, indeed many, holy people venerated locally were known only to local populations; only social elites had the money or the political clout to pursue official recognition of the apparitions and miracles they experienced at Rome. Marian devotions around the locations of individual apparitions allowed a universal protector to be individualized for the spiritual needs of local populations.

The diversity of beliefs and practices becomes even more apparent in the relation of most Christians to the sacraments. Many or even most laymen and laywomen may not have understood the subtleties of how salvation occurred and thus taken refuge in a heavily works-oriented piety. They may also have been confused about the efficacy of the sacraments, conflating them with sacramentals – blessings over special objects such as holy water or church bells – that could be used to insert the power of the divine into mundane settings. Manipulation of sacramentals was particularly common, for example, during childbirth, when midwives often attached amulets including text from the Gospel of John to the laboring woman's body, and in the case of a breech birth, baptized individual body parts as they were expelled from the womb to prevent the soteriological catastrophe of a stillbirth or death of an unbaptized child. Particular practices varied from community to community or even from midwife to midwife. Moreover, the prevalence of such practices was easily sustained in the presence of an often uneducated clergy whose members were not infrequently drawn, for lack of an alternative, from the unlearned portions of local communities themselves.

But late medieval Christianity was not only diverse on the popular level. Theologians too debated doctrinal issues about which there was often little consensus. For example, on the central matter of justification – the question of how humans will be saved – theologians subscribed to one of at least two differing teachings. Some taught that human effort must precede divine grace (*meritum de condigno*), while others thought that divine grace triggered a moral cooperation on the part of the human (*meritum de congruo*) – in either case culminating in salvation. Both theories were assumed to be in concert with the decision of the Church to condemn Pelagianism (the idea that human works alone were sufficient for salvation) at the Council of Ephesus in 431, and Semipelagianism (which, while denying human works sufficient, nonetheless left room for their minimal positive influence) at the Council of Orange in 529. The two orthodox theories varied in emphasis more than they really competed; they were associated with different strands in the teaching of theology in northern and southern Europe.

The subtle distinctions discussed here were not always entirely intelligible to lay contemporaries. Insofar as the indulgence system and the idea of remitting time in Purgatory urged people to affect their posthumous status by concrete actions and charitable donations, it is not unlikely that many Europeans, if they thought about doctrine, believed some version of Pelagianism – precisely the teaching that the Church condemned. Erasmus suggested that such confusion was entirely understandable given the stupidities of the period's academics: "The various devices of our schoolmen only render these subtlest of subtleties more subtle yet, so you'd have a better chance of getting out of a labyrinth than out of all the equivocations devised by the Realists, Nominalists, Thomists, Albertists, Occamists, Scotists, and I can't give all their names but you have the main ones."[2] An intensification of piety after the mid-fourteenth century, which appears at least partially to have been a response to the wide reception of the doctrine of Purgatory and the activities of itinerant preachers, made the split between university theology as an intellectual endeavor and as a matter of practice and belief to be communicated to the laity a more significant social problem than it had been a century earlier. One of the purposes of late medieval university teaching had been to instruct students in how to mediate theology to the laity through sermons and confessions. The very success of this activity in creating an interested audience backfired insofar as humanists like Erasmus could credibly charge their scholastic predecessors with a failure to speak in meaningful terms to an increasingly aware, involved laity. This apparent communication gap is an oft-cited trigger of the impulse toward Reformation.

Indeed, the disunity of university theology seemed particularly noticeable after the mid-fourteenth century, when theologians became party to a series of varying disputes later condemned as heresies in western Christianity, movements like Lollardy and Hussitism. While each started from impulses set in motion by social and intellectual elites, the allegiance of popular and national elements emerged quickly and was essential to their propagation – demonstrating both the interest of lay people in theological concerns and their ability to pursue their ends effectively. Lollardy, an elusive movement associated with the circle around John Wyclif at Oxford, incorporated ideas preserved primarily in transcripts of its followers' interrogation during heresy investigations; it appears to have involved an equal stress on rejection of key Church hierarchies, doctrines, and rituals and the insistence on the primacy of scripture. Followers are said to have shared a manuscript English translation of the Bible with each other. Although Lollardy was largely suppressed in England, its ideas took fertile root in Bohemia, where a similar dissatisfaction with Church finances and hierarchy was cultivated by a number of prominent preachers in the fourteenth century. Starting from the University of Prague and the teachings of Jan Hus, the movement successfully survived Hus's execution at the Council of Constance in 1415 to force a separate settlement with the Church that allowed the Hussites their own practices, most importantly the right to administer the cup to the laity in the Eucharist.

This settlement reminds us that as a final factor, the lack of unity of the western Church was determined as much by its organization and the contests its power arrangements engendered as by either doctrine and theology or popular practice of the faith. If the Church was not unified in practice, belief, or theology, the protests embodied in Lollardy and Hussitism demonstrate that its potential for unity also fell victim to its de-centered, sometimes amorphous, administrative structures. It is unclear from our perspective whether the frequent inability of the ecclesiastical center to control its periphery effectively had really been a disadvantage – one could argue that the ability of marginal movements to take over the center had long been a source of creativity and novelty. Lollardy and Hussitism were not so different from other movements that challenged the Christian hierarchy successfully without stepping over the line into heresy, like the thirteenth-century rise of the mendicant orders (such as the Franciscans and Dominicans) and the fifteenth-century observantine reforms of older orders (like the Augustinians). It might be argued that the lack of unity in praxis or doctrine made it easier for new ideas to take root, or even for the Church to respond effectively to challenges from within its ranks.

However we evaluate this situation, the point of the Reformation's appearance was one in which challenges from the periphery were perhaps even less welcome than they had been for some time, because the previous century had been a period of sustained administrative uproar and tedious efforts by the popes to return control to the center. Both Lollardy and Hussitism appeared in periods when the Church leadership was divided by the presence of separate papal administrations (the "western schism," which led to papal courts at Rome and Avignon). Conflicting administration of the Church after 1378 hampered effective evaluation and potential suppression of diverging viewpoints. Moreover, it spawned a third challenge to the central administration, the conciliar movement, an attempt to institute a level of control over Church government to be held in the hands of ecumenical councils as representative bodies rather than in the person of the pope. Whether we see conciliarism, an attempt to create a separate source of power to make Church policy, as a push toward unity – an attempt to mitigate the influence of the papacy as one of the most divisive forces in the Church – or a divisive move – an attempt to wrest control away from the center – it left the Church in uproar and suspicious of any attempts toward renewal from the geographical or intellectual margins. Conciliarism and responses to it were thus symptoms of a central ecclesiastical administration in turmoil.

If we consider all of these factors – piety and devotion, belief and doctrine, administration and government – we can see that the Reformation broke out in an environment of remarkable diversity crammed together under the capacious, inclusive tent of Old Church catholicity, a tent often more apparent than real. The success of the Reformation in influencing that Church permanently over half a millennium makes it easy to forget that the initial *calls for reform* were indeed calls for reform. The majority of the first generation of reformers sought not fragmentation for its own sake but rather a doctrinal coherency to be embodied in a single church. Bernd Hamm has termed this general desire for coherence, underway after the thirteenth century, a "normative centering" of European society in response to a general perception of chaos and desire for greater unity in large parts of spiritual and social life. We can see this impulse toward unity – among other places – in the lives and activities, in the publications and attitudes of the European humanists, especially in the northern European, sixteenth-century permutation of which Erasmus is the most outstanding representative.

One starting point for an examination of this unifying push lies in a defining impulse of humanism present already in the thirteenth century and growing mightily over time: its opposition to both the content and the teaching method of scholasticism, the dominant intellectual and educational method of the Middle Ages after the beginning of the thirteenth century, an educational style that emerged with the birth of the university in Europe. Its most well-known representative is Thomas Aquinas, but at the end of the fifteenth century other practitioners' names – Duns Scotus, William of Ockham, Albertus Magnus, Gabriel Biel, Bonaventure, Roger Bacon – were also on the tongue of every scholar. As an intellectual method it sprang from the renewed conviction – in dialogue with the reappearance of Aristotle's works in the West – that observed and revealed truth must coincide. The method that supported this conviction was the dialectic, in which scholars answered questions by confronting a proposition with its negation and reasoned via a series of patterned steps toward the answer to the question. In teaching, these steps of reasoning were articulated orally in a particularly formal, organized intellectual debate between two scholars (and their supporters) known as a disputation. Scholasticism often relied heavily on definitional jargon as an argumentative strategy, so that words in their individual meanings were often more important than words in their contexts.

Aspects of the humanist opposition to scholasticism reveal to us one of the ways that the concerns of the humanists, all their praise of the pagan antique notwithstanding, could become those of the reformers. Initially, humanists revered the ancients for their effective communication: this focus was rooted in schools set up for children of Italian civic elites to impart practical skills necessary for diplomatic or commercial careers (the so-called *ars dictaminis*, a particular sub-school of rhetoric focused on effective letter-writing); this method focused on imitation of antique, pagan authors as succinct, persuasive, effective stylists. When, centuries later, Erasmus chose to translate the *logos* – "the Word" – of the first lines of the Gospel of John as *sermo* rather than *verbum* (in divergence from the vocabulary of the Vulgate), he was making a choice stemming from a conviction of long duration among the humanists that communication was superior to content, the Word in motion (*sermo*) more true than the Word as substance (*verbum*).

But the reading of ancient authors led to a respect for rather more than effective communication among the humanists: not simply the "purer" language of the ancients but also their attitudes toward education and human behavior. Petrarch's aphorism from *On His Own Ignorance and That of Many Others* that it is better to will the good than to know the truth reflected an approach to virtue drawn from ancient writers (Cicero, Seneca, Horace) directly related to this only apparently primarily rhetorical concern: if the best language was language in use, the best life was actively virtuous – and better language could make men more virtuous. Thus the energy with which the humanists spoofed the allegedly inauthentic or at least inelegant Latin style of the scholastics and castigated them for their ignorance of Greek hid the centrality this critique of language held for the critique of morals more generally.

As a consequence of this viewpoint, scholastic education was not merely irrelevant – focused on abstract trivialities – but dangerous to society. If only language and usage became pure, the humanists felt, behavior could also become actively virtuous. To note that the Italian Renaissance detached such notions of virtue from the Christian morality found in scholasticism does not mitigate the centrality of its preference for active virtue over passive piety.

The educational strategies of scholasticism exacerbated this linguistic problem from the viewpoint of the humanists. Reading arguments made people argumentative. In contrast, the new models of reading that developed in the Renaissance, with particular emphasis on persuasion and virtue, were central to Erasmus's program. In *The Praise of Folly*, for example, he wrote:

> [All this theological disputing] is nothing but weaving and unweaving the web of Penelope. But I think Christians would be well advised if, instead of building up all those cumbersome armies with which they've been fighting indecisive wars for some time now, they sent against the Turks and Saracens some of our most vociferous Scotists, our most pig-headed Occamists, our most invincible Albertists. Then I think the world would behold a most hilarious battle and a victory such as was never seen before. Who is so cold-blooded that the clash of these mighty intellects would not excite him? Who so stupid as not to be stirred by these keen sarcasms? Who so piercing of visage as not to be overwhelmed by the smoke-screens of verbiage?[3]

Scholasticism, Erasmus and many of his contemporaries believed, divided Christianity and made it vulnerable to challenge with its understanding of language out of context and its disputative education style; with pure language and persuasive education to virtue, the northern Christian cousins of the Italian humanists would grasp the potential to reunite it.

Thus the humanist cultivation of ancient sources was not merely an aesthetic preference, it was equally an ethical one capable of being mobilized to moral ends, especially as the northern humanists increasingly turned their attention to the scattered Christian source base. Italian humanists had been notorious for their disdain for Vulgate Latin – Pietro Bembo, for instance, was said to fear that reading the Vulgate would corrupt anyone's good style; their northern cousins used knowledge gained from their reading of the ancients to reread and revise its texts in service of their intellectual and education programs. Thus fear of division, preference for ancient authors, and the desire to cultivate good style through a return to the sources were intimately related. The reformers picked up on the humanist impulse by investing the ancient languages with religious capital: if Petrus Mosellanus implied in 1518 that Christ had consecrated Greek, Latin, and Hebrew by his death on the cross, Philip Melanchthon in turn equated the turn to the sources with the capacity to savor Christ.[4] The entry into Italy of refugee scholars from the eastern Church after the Ottoman seizure of Constantinople in 1453 may have given a decisive push not only to the humanists' incipient interest in Greek but also to their desire for Christian unity. But the famous turn of the humanists *ad fontes* argued for a basis of knowledge that not only unified Christianity internally and the body of Christ with the pagan tradition; in its increasing interest in Hebrew language, it built a bridge to redefining the common heritage of Christians and Jews. The wider controversy – cultivated by scholastic theologians – over this possibility lay at the roots of the acerbic criticisms of Johannes Reuchlin, who defended the necessity of printing Hebrew books, not in order to assure that Jews had access to them but (at least ostensibly) to make sure that Christians would. The humanist focus on the critical text of the Bible fed directly into the activities of the reformers: the Complutensian Polyglot, a critical edition that utilized Hebrew manuscripts and Jewish converts to provide the most accurate translation possible of the biblical text, was sponsored by the humanist-minded bishop Ximenes de Cisneros. It spurred Erasmus to complete his own critical edition, published by Froben in four editions after 1516 – the second of which is regarded to have influenced Luther's (1522) Wartburg translation of the New Testament.

At the root of the humanists' charge that scholasticism was divisive was their scorn for scholastic methods of textual interpretation, particularly those focused on the Bible. Their programs and editions replaced medieval exegesis (often referred to as the "fourfold" method, which emphasized a series of metaphorical readings) with an emphasis on grammatical relationships and historical context as a key to understanding the scriptures. When Luther formulated his own program for proper biblical exegesis, following the maxim *was Christum treibet* (a phrase impossible to translate, which means something like "what propagates Christ"), he relied primarily on the literal and typological senses, but his Bible translations reveal an acute sensitivity to the historical sense for the purposes of communicating. In this, like many other reformers, he followed the humanists. When the Reformation emerged, humanists who followed the reception of their methods in the new religious movement used their contacts to support it. The initial excitement of many humanists sold wider audiences on the Reformation's merits. Humanism thus fought the Reformation's initial intellectual battles and won the day in the hearts and minds of broader groups among the elite.

As we have seen, the most important elements of the humanist reinterpretation of authority and attack on scholasticism were based on a moral idealism that sought to mobilize commonalities against the perceived divisiveness of the scholastic tradition and the incoherence of the Church. A second push for unity, however, occurred on the level of relationships with the uneducated. Of course, the quest for an accurate translation of the Scriptures was useless if it were not actually used; the French humanist Jacques Lefèvre d'Étaples despaired, after preparing a critical edition of the Latin psalms, that the monks praying them did not understand them. So humanist activity was pointless without a connected framework of ideas about education, which argued based on human commonalities to foster quotidian virtue. In *The Education of a Christian Woman*, the Spanish humanist Juan Luis Vives argued for the education of all women, regardless of social position, in a treatise intended as a reflection on the education of Princess Mary (later Mary I) of England. Humanists shared an emphasis on a program of education that stressed moral development equally with educational achievement. In 1523, Guillaume Budé (who authored *Commentaries on the Greek Language*, a text central to the classical revival in France) dedicated a similar treatise, *On the Study of Letters Rightly and Easily Established*, to

Francis I of France, arguing that the human mind would only develop blemished morals if it were kept in ignorance; study allowed students to learn discipline and improve their lives. In turn, the scholar of the humanities was fitted to live life rather than to spend his life disputing in universities, as the career of the Nuremberg humanist (and later opponent of the Reformation) Willibald Pirckheimer shows. More than simply an aficionado of Greek learning, Pirckheimer was a civic counselor and diplomat, as were hundreds or even thousands of less exemplary individuals who worked as urban or territorial clerks or teachers of youth. The necessity of education was further stressed by teaching texts like Erasmus's *Colloquia*. Humanist methods – here Erasmus was typical rather than path-breaking – were peculiarly central to the education of the sons of the urban patriciate who flooded European universities after the mid-fifteenth century – the audience whose openness to the ideas of the Reformation made the early movement largely an urban one.

A final push to unify the historical and contemporary Christian world came from the involvement of the humanists in printing programs. Fostering virtue through effective instruction would have been pointless if done in isolation; indeed, the productive burst of university education after the mid-fifteenth century can be connected to the production of printed textbooks for student use. Humanists quickly realized the value not only of printing schoolbooks to facilitate the spread of their ideas, but also of printed propaganda for their position. By publishing their correspondence, humanists created a "republic of letters" that not only allowed them to exchange their arguments and their information but also to create a lasting cultural charisma that outlived their short lifetimes. *Ad fontes* as a program in the face of so much opposition required aggressive advertising if it were to be successful. In the early stages of print, humanists immediately grasped its usefulness for propagating both their content and their propaganda. These letters, of course, served the practical purpose of connecting a far-reaching network of men with similar sympathies. Erasmus's own centrality in these epistolary networks is well known, but humanists throughout Europe, from Poland to Spain, and from Naples to northern Germany, exchanged ideas with one another, often with a deep sense of unity of purpose that they used to comfort each other when frustrated by intellects less convinced of the rightness of their program. Just as important as the knowledge they attempted to share with one another, however, was the image and style that they cultivated in their famous correspondences. Reading the letters of the leading lights was a way for more ordinary individuals far from the centers of ecclesiastical and political power to learn about and espouse this program for intellectual and spiritual reform.

The concerted attack of the humanists against scholasticism thus both reflected priorities that related to the development of commonalities and also led to other program points that enhanced this unifying mood by spreading their program to wider groups. This attack was critical because, to humanist observers like Erasmus, the world of late medieval Christianity appeared full of situations that were problematic and divisive at best, dangerous and destructive at worst. With ancient texts, pure languages, and appropriate interpretation, the nagging details of Christian theology would be put aside or would simply not be important. Admittedly, the program of the humanists to solve this problem from the top down did not generate the desired response. Indeed, the humanists' charge that scholasticism mired its practitioners in controversy was the source of even more dispute. Thomas More complained in 1518 that ignorant opponents of the inclusion of the Greek language in the educational canon at Oxford caused the university to be gripped by a spirit of contention. Humanists charged that divisive scholastics could only maintain their positions via edict; scholastics accused humanists of impiety and an unacceptable level of doctrinal heterodoxy – a pattern repeated in the generation before the Reformation at the universities of Salamanca, Alcalá, and Paris.

The first reformers (and the circles that engendered and later surrounded them) pursued precisely this humanist emphasis on unifying commonalities through accurate sources and Christian virtue in ways that the humanists themselves often found comprehensible and desirable. Humanists and would-be humanists in Nuremberg united themselves in a sodality that focused on the revival of interest in the ancient Church Father St Jerome. Its members believed that the cultivation of ancient rhetorical style would form men to lead virtuous worldly and Christian lives. Jerome served as a normative example precisely because of the connection in his life between linguistic prowess and imitation of Christ. Thomas More shared this preoccupation with the connection between ancient and sacred texts as a source of virtue. When Zwingli and other future Swiss reformers turned their attention, under the influence of Erasmus, to the study of the Holy Scriptures after 1515, they presaged a scholarly attitude that combined textual criticism with a narrow focus on the Bible in a form more commonly associated with Luther and his maxim of *sola scriptura*. But Erasmus had formulated this program already in his *Enchiridion militis christiani* of 1501, which argued that the virtue sought by the ancients was the same as the growing tendency of the man inspired by the Holy Spirit to be focused only on Christ. Here Erasmus united the impulses of the *devotio moderna* of his youth with the scholarly strategies that had characterized a long line of his intellectual predecessors stretching back to Petrarch.

But just as the entry of the humanists into universities caused strife wherever it succeeded, as the Reformation showed, the house of the humanists' push for unity was built upon sand. Even if humanist morals were generally uncontroversial, insistence on the creation of an authoritative text of the Bible for interpretation was a nightmare, the bounds of which the humanists only dimly realized. The source basis of the Bible was too much of a challenge for the limited source access of early modern humanists. "Authoritative" critical editions were based on limited sources, and were subject to tricks carried out by opponents of the movement. Erasmus initially omitted from his translation of the New Testament portions of the text of 1 John 5:7, a central proof-text for the Trinity, because he did not find them in the Greek manuscripts he used to prepare the edition. Shown a Greek manuscript in which they were included during his sojourn in England, he added them to a later edition, only to be informed that the manuscript he had been shown was a forgery. Even after onerous labor, the text of the New Testament was only as reliable as the manuscripts and the editors who prepared it. Reformers, in turn, assumed optimistically that the edifice of the Church could be restored to its strength if only the errors in the Vulgate were corrected; what they did not predict was the possibility that individuals with little or inadequate theological training would interpret the Bible themselves for the pursuit of all kinds of ends the Reformers found distasteful, from political revolt to polygamy and millenarianism.

Humanists knew about interpretive conflict but it did not trouble them inordinately, partially because they were still occupied in providing a source basis and partially because their debates were conducted primarily in letters and pamphlets, away from the structures of ecclesiastical power. But as the reformers discovered, even when different individuals and groups agreed upon a translation, the Scriptures simply could not serve as the basis for Christian unity in the way that humanists thought they might. The reformers' experiences in attempting to reform Catholic belief and practice proved what the humanists had known all along: language is power – but changing the language of the Old Church was tantamount to challenging its right to govern. Similar power struggles resulted inside the Protestant movement. The first major formal theological split in German Protestantism documented via a statement occurred at Marburg in 1528, when evangelical theologians assembled to establish the meaning of Jesus's statements about his institution of the sacrament during the Last Supper. What is the meaning of the declaration: "this is my body?" A probably apocryphal story has Luther carving the Latin words *hoc est corpus meum* into the table at the colloquy, in hopes it might fix the meaning in the face of those who felt that "is" means "signifies."

With this sort of debate Protestants found themselves in the same rhetorical position as the scholastic disputants they, like the humanists, disdained so vehemently. In the end, then, the resort to the sources created only an additional basis for the sort of divisive theological bickering humanists found so distasteful. Erasmus died convinced that the Reformation was bad for the progress of humanism, presumably because the reformers focused on doctrinal rather than philological and rhetorical concerns. Still it was his movement that laid the basis for developing requirements that theological students and future pastors be prepared for their careers with courses in Greek and Hebrew. When Wittenberg reformed its curriculum as a model for the newly emerging Protestant universities, it took over large pieces of the humanist curriculum wholesale. In the second half of the sixteenth century it was Protestants who most heavily continued the humanist program of providing critical editions of ancient Christian sources, in order to create a legitimate Protestant identity that took refuge in values about the importance and purity of the early Church that the northern humanists outlined earlier. Moreover, when the Jesuits – those quintessential Catholic reformers and the Protestants' most virulent opponents – came to take over the arts and humanities faculties humanists had invaded a generation or two earlier, they maintained many of the same priorities in their curricula.

But if the Reformation was really one result of humanism's emphasis on commonality, the subsequent "fragmentation" of the western Church remains to be explained. In light of the humanist program as a unifying response to the diversity and even incoherency of the medieval western Church, we should see this development less as an increase in the variety of different beliefs, practices, and administrative divisions that characterized western Christendom than as the result of an insistence on the necessity of an increasingly coherent and unified Christianity. That this goal could be accomplished only within separate camps that in turn insisted on the sole primacy of their own position was due not to inherently fragmenting qualities in the Reformation but rather stemmed from the often messy administrative structure of Church and state in the sixteenth century. In this framework, given the momentary resistance of the Old Church to renewal movements from the margins, any impulse toward increasing the coherence of the Church could only be carried out in a series of smaller churches, not in a single one. The need to create a supportive identity for these bodies led to a hardening of the boundaries between intellectual and theological positions that might earlier have coexisted but now required intensive enforcement of boundaries.

As counter-intuitive as this point may seem – that the fragmentation of the Reformation stemmed in part from the humanist impulse toward unity – it was undoubtedly the case, for at least two reasons. The first of these relates directly to the humanist program and the way that the Protestant reformers were influenced by it. Scott Hendrix, who recently argued that the Reformation is only apprehensible as a coherent movement if we take its defining characteristic to be the re-Christianization of Europe, has suggested that the biblically oriented humanism received by the early reformers took its definitions of the virtuous Christian life, which were rooted in the relationship to the early Church, and used them to argue that the diverse, perhaps superstitious practices typical of late medieval piety were pagan and even idolatrous. Protestant reformers thus transferred aspects of their critique of scholasticism to their emergent view of the world of piety and belief in which they found themselves. The resulting confessions were thus not so much differing belief systems as competing visions of the correct way to cleanse the one true Church of its iniquity. As Hendrix writes:

> the rise of the confessions can be seen as the structural outcome of the Reformation agenda, which anchored new ways of being Christian in the culture. The faith could only be re-rooted, it turned out, in diverse patterns of theology and piety, and in different sociopolitical contexts, which we call the confessional groups of early modern Europe.[5]

We may question whether Hendrix's view takes the rhetoric of the Reformation too much at face value. But insofar as re-Christianization was drawn from the humanist cultivation of virtue via resort to ancient sources, its pursuit in the Reformation was directly connected to humanism.

Hendrix's comments about the variety of contexts in which the Reformation took root point us to a second reason to see confessional fragmentation as the result of a struggle for unity, which has to do with the ecclesiastical administration. Indeed, the process of fostering fragmentation in order to create unity pre-dates the Reformation. In order to obtain the force necessary to suppress Hus, the papacy was forced to grant a series of concessions to particular national churches (especially those of Germany and France) that typically involved the devolution of rights for naming benefice holders or placing clergy – even as it allowed Bohemian Christians their own particularly distinct sacramental practices. Church "unity" was thus sustained only through the concession or even establishment of administrative or doctrinal diversity. These problems, which had to do with conflicts between local and papal administration, were not solved by the end of conciliarism but merely briefly papered over. The German *gravamina*, or lists of complaints about the Church made by local authorities in the years leading up to the Reformation and culminating in those presented at the Diet of Worms in 1521, like Henry VIII's reactivation of the English statutes of *praemunire* to dispossess the Catholic Church in England, point to financial and taxation issues that underline the continuing resistance of regions and forming nations to the financial and political priorities of the papacy. Papal concessions to the different national churches after the councils of Constance and Basle point to an upswing in the growth of secular state power after the Investiture Contest, so late fifteenth-century developments in ecclesiastical administration led into the development of national and territorial Protestant churches during and after the Reformation. The rulers of the Reformation did not invent their right to reform national and territorial churches – which they termed the *jus reformani* – out of whole cloth; here they carried on a tendency already growing in the late medieval period.

Humanistically inclined reformers were not held apart from such developments; indeed, they actually urged them onwards. Many of the most humanistically inclined reformers were close advisers of civic and princely authorities, not only on the level of education, but also with regard to correct doctrine and appropriate organization. Here again, we see men like Philip Melanchthon, Huldrych Zwingli, and Martin Bucer urging secular authorities to actions in support of the establishment of a single, true Christian Church within their territories. But a territorial or even national sovereign only had so much power. Consequently these wishes ended, contrary to their guiding impulses, in separation – particularly as their political sponsors, the emerging national monarchs and territorial lords, demanded an increased administrative coherence for the institutions that may have supported their own particular notions of a more local sovereignty but which they were also now called upon to finance. Alliances between larger territorial and national units (the Schmalkaldic League is a classic example) foundered as much on disconnects in political culture and diplomacy as they did on theological grounds. Administrative fragmentation of the Church – and the accompanying hardening of theological boundaries sponsored by states and churches as a means of establishing a religious identity to bolster membership in these emerging political bodies – was the price paid for a desired unity of belief and practice that could be shared only at the regional or national level. This is not to say that only monarchs and territorial sovereigns sponsored these divisions; indeed, theologians and lay people played their part as well. In many regions, particularly those that later became Calvinist, local populations welcomed the increasing "discipline" and consolidation that the Reformation brought. But they pursued these divisions, as contrary as it may seem, under the aegis of a search for Christian unity and in hopes of establishing a single, true Church. If the Reformation was a re-Christianization of Europe following the humanist emphasis on virtue, the development of smaller confessions that could be more effectively administered was a necessary consequence.

This process of the deliberate intertwining of Church and state in order to consolidate the ideological gains of the Reformation is usually termed "confessionalization," a term that describes the parallel developments of the different churches after the middle of the sixteenth century. The term refers to the process of facilitating the creation of administrative structures, existing ones, or newly mobilizing to spread the content of "confessions," official statements of belief of the various new bodies that sprang from the heritage of the Catholic Church. This process of codifying doctrine began with the formulation of the Augsburg Confession of 1530, a legal document intended to put the evangelical estates on a stable legal footing in the Holy Roman Empire. But it was followed by a number of other official statements of doctrine: among them the Heidelberg Confession of 1563, which established the teachings of the Reformed Church; the Canons and Decretals of the Council of Trent, 1545–63, which provided the first statement of doctrine that scholars term "Roman Catholic"; the English Church's Thirty-Nine Articles of 1571; and a more definitive Lutheran attempt, the 1580 Formula of Concord. The process of doctrinal confessionalization that pushed theology toward intellectual unity was thus fostered by the very state development that would make true unity in western Christendom impossible, at least at the administrative level.

Despite these divisions, we should be careful in deducing that the presence of more Church bodies and the parallel doctrinal codification automatically meant a greater fragmentation of the Church, whether in terms of belief, practice, or administration. It is hard to say anything at all about how the content of belief changed after the Reformation beyond the limited numbers of statements made by literate, expressive individuals. Popular belief in many regions may have changed little or not at all, at least in the short term. This problem is seen most clearly in discussions of the alleged "failure" of the Lutheran Reformation; visitation records suggest that local populations were unable to articulate even the most basic statements of what they believed, although there are too many problems with visitation records to take their general tone of disgust with local conditions at face value. Studies of Catholic villages in southwestern Germany show that the Reformation and Catholic Reformation had little effect on the practice of piety, except for a lull or temporary interruption in practices when the policies of the Council of Trent were being most actively applied. When the energy for reform and pressures to comply went away, however, pre-Reformation devotions re-emerged.

Considering the extent to which ideas about doctrine differed before the Reformation, the enumeration of a particular doctrine that would be valid and binding for all of the members of a particular group can be termed a consolidation as much as it can a fragmentation. The process of defining a system of belief, in that it involves inclusion as much as exclusion, must set boundaries and mark territory. The Catholic Church, for example, in the canon on justification included in the decision of the Council of Trent, enumerated a long list of beliefs whose holders were to be declared anathema. Some of these statements were clearly directed at "new" beliefs identified with various groups of evangelicals, but some of them, insofar as they had not been forbidden before the Reformation, might have been held within the bounds of orthodoxy. There was less room in the new confessions for diverging belief and practice than there had been before the Reformation, but at the same time the variety of beliefs that had led to conflict in the face of the late medieval intensification of piety was eliminated, in (illusory) hopes of restraining the potential for such conflicts.

In the end, then, we can see that although the humanist impulse toward unity appears to have ended in a fragmentation of the Church – insofar as this impulse was taken over by the Reformers and became the program of heads of states – overall the Reformation led to a consolidation both of territorial states and of the content of Christian doctrine, but in the form of the confessions rather than one church. By 1700, European Christianity was undeniably more coherent (at least in the sense of doctrine and practice) than it had been in 1500. Indeed, it is precisely this process of doctrinalizing and Christianizing Europe and Europeans via the processes of confessionalization that marginalized Erasmus's position by limiting the possibilities of a humanist scholarship separated from governing definitions of "right" religion as the sixteenth century wore on. There has been a tendency to view this development alternately as tragic – like the fate of Erasmus – or triumphant. Most likely, however, the average individual held neither view. It was unlikely, in the late medieval age of very limited government and relatively undeveloped modes of communication, that people felt themselves in any way personally connected with regimes or popes. While a widespread awareness of the Church as such must have prevailed, it may have been perceived in its administrative and doctrinal aspects as much as an absence as a presence. The progress of confessionalization, the "fragmentation" of the church body it reflected notwithstanding, brought the Church as an institution much more actively into the lives of everyday people. Insofar as this development also augmented piety and morals, it, too, can be seen as a fulfillment of the ideals of humanism.

NOTES

1. Desiderius Erasmus, "Foreword to the Third Edition," *The Praise of Folly and Other Writings*, trans. Robert Adams (New York: W.W. Norton, 1989), p. 134.
2. Erasmus, *The Praise of Folly*, p. 58.
3. Erasmus, *The Praise of Folly*, p. 60.
4. Cited in Erika Rummel, *The Humanist–Scholastic Debate in the Renaissance and Reformation* (Cambridge, Mass.: Harvard University Press, 1995), p. 115.
5. Scott Hendrix, "Re-rooting the Faith: The Reformation as Re-Christianization," *Church History* 69 (2003): 558–77, at p. 573.

SUGGESTIONS FOR FURTHER READING

Bataillon, Marcel. *Erasme et l'Espagne*. Paris: Droz, 1937.
Benedict, Philip. *Christ's Churches Purely Reformed*. New Haven: Yale University Press, 2002.
Brown, Christopher. *Singing the Gospel*. Cambridge, Mass.: Harvard University Press, 2005.
Christian, William A. *Local Religion in Sixteenth-century Spain*. Princeton: Princeton University Press, 1981.
Diefendorf, Barbara. *Beneath the Cross*. New York: Oxford University Press, 1991.
────── *From Penitence to Charity*. New York: Oxford University Press, 2005.
Dixon, C. Scott, ed. *The German Reformation*. Oxford: Blackwell, 1999.
Duffy, Eamon. *The Stripping of the Altars*. New Haven: Yale University Press, 1992.
Forster, Marc. *The Counter-Reformation in the Villages: Religion and Reform in the Bishopric of Speyer, 1560–1720*. Ithaca: Cornell University Press, 1992.
Fudge, Thomas. *The Magnificent Ride: The First Reformation in Hussite Bohemia*. Aldershot: Ashgate, 1998.

Gorski, Philip. *The Disciplinary Revolution*. Chicago: University of Chicago Press, 2003.
Grell, Ole Peter, ed. *The Scandinavian Reformation*. Cambridge: Cambridge University Press, 1995.
Hamm, Bernd. *The Reformation of Faith in the Context of Late Medieval Theology and Piety*. Leiden: Brill, 2004.
Hendrix, Scott. *Recultivating the Vineyard: The Christian Agendas of Reformation*. Louisville: Westminster John Knox Press, 2004.
Hsia, R. Po-chia. *The World of Catholic Renewal*. Cambridge: Cambridge University Press, 1998.
Karant-Nunn, Susan. *The Reformation of Ritual*. London: Routledge, 1997.
Kingdon, Robert McCune. *Adultery and Divorce in Calvin's Geneva*. Cambridge, Mass.: Harvard University Press, 1995.
Koerner, Joseph Lee. *The Reformation of the Image*. Chicago: University of Chicago Press, 2004.
Leonard, Amy. *Nails in the Wall*. Chicago: University of Chicago Press, 2005.
Luebke, David Martin, ed. *The Counter-Reformation*. Oxford: Blackwell, 1999.
MacCulloch, Diarmaid. *The Reformation*. New York: Viking, 2003.
Martin, John Jeffries. *Venice's Hidden Enemies*. Berkeley: University of California Press, 1993.
Moeller, Bernd. *Reichstadt und Reformation*, rev. edn. Berlin: Evangelische Verlagsanstalt, 1987.
Oberman, Heiko A. *Luther: Man between God and the Devil*. New Haven: Yale University Press, 1989.
Ozment, Steven. *The Age of Reformation*. New Haven: Yale University Press, 1980.
Pettegree, Andrew. *The Reformation and the Culture of Persuasion*. Cambridge: Cambridge University Press, 2005.
Rummel, Erika. *The Humanist–Scholastic Debate in the Renaissance and Reformation*. Cambridge, Mass.: Harvard University Press, 1995.
—— *The Confessionalization of Humanism in Reformation Germany*. Oxford: Oxford University Press, 2000.
Safley, Thomas, ed. *The Reformation of Charity*. Boston: Brill, 2003.
Schilling, Heinz. *Civic Calvinism in Northwestern Germany and the Netherlands*. Kirksville, Mo.: Sixteenth Century Journal Publishers, 1991.
Scribner, Robert W. *For the Sake of Simple Folk*, 2nd edn. Oxford: Clarendon Press, 1994.
Shagan, Ethan. *Popular Politics and the English Reformation*. Cambridge: Cambridge University Press, 2003.
Wandel, Lee Palmer. *The Eucharist in the Reformation*. Cambridge: Cambridge University Press, 2006.
Watt, Tessa. *Cheap Print and Popular Piety*. Cambridge: Cambridge University Press, 1991.
Williams, George Huntston. *The Radical Reformation*, 3rd edn. Kirksville, Mo.: Truman University Press, 1992.

CHAPTER THIRTY

CHRISTIAN REFORM AND ITS DISCONTENTS

Brad S. Gregory

In January 1510 John Colet preached a famous sermon to the Convocation of Clergy from the Canterbury Province in St Paul's Cathedral in London, where he served as dean.[1] His text was Romans 12:2: "Do not be conformed to this world, but be reformed in the newness of your minds, so that you may discern what is the good, well-pleasing, and perfect will of God." A man steeped in the Bible and one of the leading preachers in England, Colet ripped into his clerical colleagues for their pursuit of honors and benefices, their devotion to sensual pleasures, their entanglement in worldly preoccupations, and especially their selfish avarice: "every corruption, every ruin of the church, every scandal of the world, comes from the avarice of priests." After berating them for just the sort of conformity to the world that Paul had condemned, he took up the latter's admonition to reform and renewal, exhorting them to holy uprightness that they might be an example for the clergy and laity in their dioceses. The central problem was not the Church's teachings or ideals, but persistent inadequacy in living up to them: "The work is therefore not that new laws and constitutions be enacted, but that those enacted be observed."[2] Colet specified how important it was to adhere to laws regarding the ordination only of worthy candidates, the legitimate conferral of benefices, the prohibition of simony, the practice of clerical residency, the abstention of clergy from worldly pursuits, and other concerns that had troubled not only England but much of the Latin Church for centuries (as was implied by the way in which Colet seamlessly quoted the twelfth-century Cistercian reformer Bernard of Clairvaux). In Colet's view, the Church was beset by many problems, the clergy was overwhelmingly responsible for them, and such difficulties could be remedied if the clergy followed the prescriptions of canon law and the dictates of Christian morality.

Two years later, on 3 May 1512, Giles of Viterbo, the general of the Augustinian Order and one of the most renowned preachers in Italy, delivered the opening address of the council convened by Pope Julius II in the Lateran Basilica in Rome. It was the first such gathering since the implosion of the protracted Council of Basel in the late 1440s and the subsequent reassertion of ecclesiastical monarchy by the Renaissance popes. In the presence of the pope, the cardinals, and other prelates in attendance, Giles offered an encomium on the prospects for "a true, holy, and proper Council, to eradicate vices, to promote virtues, to capture the foxes who in this age swarm to ruin the holy vineyard, and at last to call fallen religion back to its old purity, its ancient light, its innate splendor, and its sources." Steeped in humanism as well as neo-Platonism, Giles, like Colet, saw similar problems plaguing the Church, as he made clear in a series of rhetorical questions: "When has ambition been more impudent? When has greed been more inflamed? When has licentiousness in sinning been more shameless? When has audacity in speaking, arguing, and writing against piety been either safer or more frequent?" Both in northern and in southern Europe the need for reform was urgent, for "unless by this council or some other means we impose moderation on our morals, unless we force our yearning for human things, the source of evils, to give way to a love for divine things, Christendom and religion are finished . . . and lost." In a hierarchical institution such as the Church, a particular burden fell on "the shepherds of the people, on whom indeed the entirety and fullness of Christianity and salvation depend," and who, in order to correct the Church's problems, "while shining with the light of the disciplines must teach others, and by practicing the devout behavior that they preach, must themselves in the first instance and above all lead the way by their actions." Like Colet, Giles thought that flaws were endemic in the Church, that the clergy bore a heavy responsibility for them, and that their solution required priests, prelates, and religious to live in a genuinely Christian manner. Neither man hinted that the Church ought to change its doctrines or prescribed practices, for as Giles famously put it, "human beings must be changed by the dictates of religion, not religion by human beings."[3]

By the time that John Colet and Giles of Viterbo delivered these sermons, such remarks had been commonplace for more than a century, stretching back into the period of the Schism (1378–1417) and indeed, the Avignonese papacy (1308/9–77). Their words can be read not only as part of a chorus confirming ongoing problems and the need for reform in the Church, the most pervasive institution in Renaissance Europe, but also as indications of ecclesiastical vitality. Had there not been problems, then widespread, repeated calls for their eradication would have made no sense; yet had there been uniform complacency and corruption, such problems would have met with sheer indifference rather than so many spirited calls for reform and multiple indications of renewal. In fact, the Church in the fifteenth and early sixteenth centuries was marked by serious problems as well as reform-minded dynamism, a paradoxical combination without which it is difficult if not impossible to account for what transpired in the Latin Christian world after 1520. The Renaissance popes tended to treat the papacy as a familial possession, relied more than ever on ecclesiastical judicial fees and the sale of Church offices for income, and often acted like secular Italian princes, yet they also stabilized the Holy See in its traditional city, began rebuilding Rome's churches and public spaces, and patronized Eucharistic and Marian devotion. Many of the religious orders experienced problems with recruitment and discipline, becoming the butt of satire, yet the Carthusians, the most ascetic contemplative order of all, had never been stronger. Across Europe, the Observantine movement eventually inspired hundreds of religious houses among the Benedictines, Franciscans, Dominicans, and Augustinians to take the original zeal of their respective founders as a model for renewal. Conscientious critics such as Colet and Giles of Viterbo attacked clerical avarice and mediocrity, evidence for which is legion, yet preachers such as Johann Geiler von Keisersberg in Strasbourg and Girolamo Savonarola in Florence, bishops such as John Fisher of Rochester in England, and scholars such as Agostino Giustiniani and Erasmus of Rotterdam demonstrated that learned, committed members of the clergy were alive and active in their respective ways. Members of the laity were criticized for their ignorance, indifference, and superstition, yet at the same time voluntary devotional practices such as pilgrimages, processions, meditation on Christ's passion, participation in confraternities, and the support of pious bequests were thriving, while in cities the advent of printing contributed to unprecedented levels of literacy among devout laymen and laywomen alike. And so it goes virtually everywhere one looks in the Church during the fifteenth and early sixteenth centuries. If one tilts the evidence and emphasis toward the problems, the Church appears as a gigantic, self-serving bureaucracy whose own leaders were selfishly exploiting it; if one tilts the evidence and emphasis toward the vitality, the Church looks as though it was in the midst of a major religious revival, with unparalleled lay participation and multiple strands of clerically led reform whose protagonists frankly acknowledged and were addressing many of its problems.

Colet and Giles of Viterbo belonged to a long-standing tradition of reform and renewal within the established Church, one that would continue in subsequent decades and culminate institutionally in another council, held intermittently over a period of nearly twenty years in the small town of Trent, beginning finally in late 1545. Yet the Tridentine representatives would convene in a Christian world radically different from that of 1512, when Giles preached to open the Fifth Lateran Council. Later that same year, one of Giles's fellow Augustinians, a German, received his doctoral degree in theology, an academic credential grafted to his wholehearted participation in the Observantine renewal. Within a decade, that Observant Augustinian and professor of sacred scripture, Martin Luther, would improbably find himself as the principal figure in a movement that, beyond decrying the Church's problems, would also repudiate many of its doctrines and ideals. The fundamental dividing line in Christian reform after 1520 would be between those who thought that Christendom's root problem was the failure of the established Church to live up to its teachings, and those who regarded many of its teachings as aberrant. It is deeply misleading to regard what would become known as the Protestant Reformation as merely or even primarily a reaction against abuses and corruption in the late medieval Church. While its spread is hardly imaginable without the Church's persistent problems, the doctrinal claims without which it would not have existed were only secondarily, derivatively, a reaction against the Church's concrete shortcomings. Reformers such as Colet, Giles, Erasmus, John Fisher, Johannes Eck, and many more besides, like their fifteenth-century predecessors such as Jean Gerson, Bernardino of Siena, Antonino Pierozzi, Nicholas of Cusa, and others, also deplored and inveighed against the same problems. The real point and principal claim of those sixteenth-century reformers who parted ways with them was that Roman Catholicism was a perverted form of Christianity even at its best, even if all Christians were enthusiastically following all of its teachings and knowingly participating in all of its practices. Widespread institutional abuses and immorality were at base symptomatic signs of a flawed foundation – namely, false and dangerous doctrines. In short, such reformers asserted, the Roman Church was not what it claimed to be: the established Church was not the church established by Christ, the church that proclaimed the truth and so held the keys to eternal salvation, but a patently all-too-human institution fatally compromised by centuries of self-serving clerical exploitation and the indulgence of extra-biblical superstition. In their own way the reformers who rejected Rome agreed with Giles's maxim that the dictates of religion should change human beings rather than human beings changing religion – and in their view, it was precisely because human beings had *already* so distorted the Gospel as recorded in scripture that Christianity was doing such a poor job transforming human hearts and human lives. Therefore a religion wrongly changed by human beings should be restored to the religion revealed by God, so that it could work as God had intended. And the means to such a restoration were to expose the invented beliefs, practices, and institutions that had twisted the one genuine source and standard for Christian faith and life – namely, the Bible. In a manner reminiscent of John Wyclif, who had repudiated the authority of the established Church, including the papacy, the Protestant reformers sharply distinguished scripture from tradition and turned the former against the latter wherever they perceived a divergence between the two.

This move marked a striking divergence from reforms by those who had accepted and continued to acknowledge the authority of the Roman Church. Almost always, traditional reforms had been additions to or modifications of existing institutions, devotions, or practices rather than wholesale replacements of them, which contributed to the exuberant variety – or, some might say, the ecclesial congestion – of the Church in the Renaissance era. Only a minority of the religious in each order became Observants, for example, and far from being received enthusiastically by all, the movement precipitated often bitter struggles within religious orders. New confraternities, such as the Oratory of Divine Love, which was founded in Genoa in 1497 and subsequently spread throughout the Italian peninsula, were added to those already established. Humanist chairs were founded at universities, beginning in Italy in the 1420s and spreading north of the Alps by late in the century, but without displacing a curriculum that – especially in northern Europe – retained at its apex the study of scholastic theology, itself divided between those who assumed realist versus nominalist epistemologies as their starting points. Renewals in piety such as the *devotio moderna*, from which came a bestseller of fifteenth-century spirituality, *The Imitation of Christ*, did not replace existing devotional traditions but became simply one more option among them. Variety and voluntarism marked Christian life. Lay Christians might belong to many confraternities or none; they might be fervently devoted to Christ's passion or not; they might go on pilgrimages or stay home, purchase or not purchase indulgences; they might say the rosary and endow Masses for deceased family members, or do neither. To a large extent, beyond the fulfillment of minimal religious duties such as annually confessing their sins and receiving the Eucharist, having their children baptized, and (it was hoped) attending Mass on Sundays and major feast days, their religious lives as laypeople were largely discretionary. The Protestant Reformation marked a major change, at least in principle, its various leaders seeking in their respective ways a drastic simplification of the Church's religious variety and leaving less up to the initiative of individual Christians.

The Church whose authority they rejected was an extraordinarily complex, multi-layered institution. Just as its long-standing abuses or manifest vitality can be exaggerated and thus yield a distorted picture, the same is true of its unity and variety. The Church was unified in its basic doctrines, liturgy, piety, and institutions, and yet extraordinarily variegated in the ways in which its institutions and practices were particularized in local circumstances. Although in a significant and substantial sense a whole (wherever one went, from Iceland to Spain to Poland, one found parishes and priests, bishops and dioceses, the Mass, the seven sacraments, the Creed, the *Pater noster* and *Ave Maria*, devotion to the saints and feast days in their honor, prayers for the dead, and an implicit acceptance of the traditions and authority of the Church, governed by the pope), this whole was far from being either uniform or homogeneous. The result of historical processes built up over centuries, the Church's elements did not always fit comfortably with one another, and the same institutions and practices might vary dramatically across countries and regions. Canon law tried to keep pace with ecclesiastical realities, but myriad particularities had to be haggled over – the relationships between parish churches and religious houses in towns, the rights to the appointment of vacant benefices in specific cases, the give-and-take between secular and ecclesiastical authorities at every level from single rural parishes and their village councils up through the concordats negotiated between popes and sovereign rulers. The unwieldy, particularistic, and cumulative character of the Church's institutions and practices helps to explain why systematic reform "in head and members," as it was articulated repeatedly in the late Middle Ages, was so elusive, and why reforms and renewals that did occur tended to be piecemeal. It is perhaps not inconceivable that a pope analogous to a Gregory VII or an Innocent III might have attempted a top-down, papally led reform of the entire Church. But considering the much weaker position of the papacy with respect to secular authorities after the schism of the 1370s and the formal political compromises extracted from secular rulers beginning in the 1430s, the much greater extent of the Church's bureaucracy, and the much wider range of devotional activities and ecclesiastical institutions in the fifteenth century compared to the late eleventh century or the early thirteenth, the implementation of such reform would almost surely have proved even more difficult than it had been for either of these medieval popes. In addition, the material and cultural self-interest of the Renaissance popes militated against heroically ascetic, self-denying reforms, commitment to which would have entailed a volte-face with respect to the opulent lifestyle that most popes had led as cardinals even before their respective elections to the Holy See.

If prospects for systematic reform *in capite et membris* were slender, the possibility of a gradual renewal of the Church via education and moral instruction was somewhat more encouraging. Or so thought humanist reformers. By the first two decades of the sixteenth century, Christian humanism was embodied in a network of geographically widespread communities of scholars with a significant institutional presence in universities, at rulers' courts, in monasteries, and in the ecclesiastical hierarchy itself. The humanists' disdain for medieval Latin in favor of Ciceronian eloquence was but a first means to an end. Epitomized by Erasmus of Rotterdam and what he called the *philosophia Christi*, humanist scholars concerned with religious reform sought in a variety of ways to apply the philological and literary tools of classical rhetoric, moral philosophy, and oratory to the problems afflicting the Church, with an eye toward religious renewal. Sacred philology enabled them to return to the early textual sources of Christianity, namely scripture – studied in the original Hebrew and Greek, not the Latin Vulgate translation – and the Latin as well as Greek Church Fathers, many of whose works were edited and published for the first time. Bypassing the methods and assumptions of scholastic philosophy and theology, humanist scholars criticized medieval devotion wherever it seemed divorced from their understanding of Christian virtues, as expressed famously by Erasmus in his *Praise of Folly* (1512), for example, and his *Colloquies* (1518). At the same time, in addition to inspiring a criticism of shortcomings, sacred philology was to provide a foundation for Christendom's renewal based on education and Christian moral formation, a perspective implicit in Erasmus's *Enchiridion* (1503).

In contrast to the apocalyptic sensibilities so common in Europe in the late fifteenth and early sixteenth centuries, the humanists' reform vision was patient, with the Christian scholar as its hero: pious philology would eventually, it was hoped, lead through editions, publications, translations, textbooks, teachers, education, and exhortation to a more virtuous clergy and less superstitious laity. The Church would be reformed and society renewed. Well beyond Erasmus's efforts as the leading humanist reformer north of the Alps, by the 1510s humanists were active throughout Europe on multiple fronts. A major revival of biblical and Greek Patristic erudition was in full swing among the dozens of Benedictine houses, especially in Italy, that belonged to the Congregation of Santa Giustina, including Montecassino itself after 1505. In the Holy Roman Empire, humanistic monks among the Benedictines and Cistercians labored in Austria, Bavaria, Thuringia, and Swabia.[4] In France, Jacques Lefèvre d'Étaples made substantial use of Greek in his commentary on St Paul's letters, which were published in 1512. By the same decade Hebrew was being taught alongside Greek in multiple universities, including Oxford and Cambridge in England, Louvain in the Low Countries, and Alcalá in Spain. Opened in 1509 and established by Francisco Jiménez de Cisneros, an Observant Franciscan and the most influential prelate in Spain, explicitly to serve theology and especially humanistic biblical studies, the University of Alcalá was home to the distinguished team of scholars who produced the Complutensian Polyglot Bible between 1514 and 1517.

It is impossible to know what would have happened to humanism as a reform initiative without the advent of the evangelical movement sparked by Luther. Notwithstanding their desire to make erudition serve education and moral formation, humanists posed challenges to the traditional organization of knowledge in conceptual, disciplinary, and institutional terms. Most consequentially, especially with regard to the northern universities with strong scholastic theological faculties such as Paris, Louvain, and Cologne, humanists applied their historically minded, critical philological methods to the Bible itself, raising serious questions about the relationship between philology and theology. In 1516 Erasmus published his eagerly awaited edition of the New Testament, boldly dispensing with the Vulgate in favor of his own, facing-page Latin translation of the Greek text on which it was based. A firestorm of controversy ensued. Yet despite the defensive denunciations of Erasmus and other "poets" by certain scholastic theologians, there is little reason to think that humanism presented insuperable intellectual obstacles to the established Church.

In the early thirteenth century, Aristotelian philosophy had been derided by some ecclesiastical leaders as incompatible with the faith. Yet it soon became the intellectual scaffolding of scholasticism, taking its place alongside and interacting with traditional, monastic forms of study and education that were more closely associated with the liturgy and prayerful meditation on scripture. So, too, the appropriation of humanist philological scholarship in combination with scholastic philosophy and theology later in the sixteenth century by members of the Society of Jesus and other religious orders, for example, as well as the ways in which humanism and scholasticism were combined by Fisher, Eck, and other Catholic theologians in the early sixteenth century, demonstrates that there was no fundamental incompatibility between the two. Actually to implement and carry through a wide-scale educational revolution that would transform piety and morals, in a tradition-minded society with low literacy rates, could only have transpired imperfectly and over the long term. But increasing numbers of schools and rising numbers of readers made for an unprecedented foundation, especially in the cities of northern Italy, southwestern Germany, and Flanders, during the fifteenth and early sixteenth centuries. Erasmus wanted ordinary folk to do their part, by learning to read so that scholars might supply them with vernacular translations of the Bible. This would enable even "the lowliest women" to read God's Word for themselves, as he wrote in 1516 at the outset of his edition of the New Testament. Because the essential teachings of scripture were clear, and were fundamentally ethical in character, "The journey is simple and it is ready for anyone.... The sun itself is not as common and accessible to all as is Christ's teaching."[5]

Viewed collectively and comparatively, what happened beginning in the late 1510s in Germanic lands suggests otherwise, despite an overwhelming emphasis on the Bible's importance for Christian faith and life. Within a decade hundreds of reformers, many of whom were influenced by humanism, rejected and denounced not merely the abuses but also the authority of the Roman Church, convinced that it had departed fatally from the Word of God, which they upheld as the only genuine source of Christian truth. But from the very outset of the movement that would come to be called the Protestant Reformation, they also rejected and denounced each other. Throughout the remainder of the sixteenth century and beyond these reformers were divided – exegetically and doctrinally, and therefore liturgically, ecclesiastically, socially, and politically – over the content of Christ's teaching and the Word of God as expressed in scripture. Consequently, after 1520 the nature of Christian reform differed dramatically from preceding decades, as those who repudiated the Roman Church asserted a wide range of conflicting calls for reform. Whether erudite former priests or zealous artisans, such reformers quickly occupied a competitive niche alongside those who still sought to address internally the problems of the Roman Church.

The clarity of different doctrines and coalescence of discrete bodies of believers ought not to be exaggerated in a decade as unsettled as the 1520s. But neither should either be minimized. Not all of the grievances and demands expressed in an avalanche of Germanic sermons, songs, and pamphlets were merely vague slogans about "the Gospel" and "the pure Word of God." Some, perhaps many, ordinary men and women were confused as they tried to sort through contradictory assertions purportedly based on God's Word – yet precisely because countervailing claims were so often sufficiently clear, they engendered confusion, indecision, and second-guessing among influential elites as well as common folk who had to decide what to do about them. Did God want Christians to obey secular authorities, rebel against them, or separate themselves from them? If the Roman Mass was a dangerously wayward, even idolatrous, perversion of Christian worship, what should take its place? Which sacraments had been established by Christ, and what was their nature and role in Christian life? In response to such questions and many more, the decade and indeed the entire Reformation era was marked by wildly discrepant views of what Christian truth was and thus about what Christians were to believe and do. Virtually all of the central, contested issues emerged in the 1520s, persisting in various forms into the seventeenth century and beyond. Different answers gave rise to divergent movements, churches, and traditions, which took shape in relationship to the exercise of political power and the forging of social ties among different groups of believers.

Luther was the first of the evangelical reformers and by far the most frequently published in the 1520s, a man who influenced even many reformers who rejected Rome and yet disagreed with him. In a journey underway years before he appeared as a public figure in late 1517 with the printing of his *Ninety-five Theses*, this Observant Augustinian friar and theology professor yearned for existential certainty of God's mercy and his own salvation. How could utterly sinful human beings be made acceptable to a just God, who sees all things, knows the human heart, and holds them to the Sermon-on-the-Mount standards established by Christ? Still tormented despite years of self-examination, ascetic practices, sacramental confession, and prayer, Luther found what he was seeking through an experience, inspired especially by certain passages in Paul's letters to the Romans and Galatians, of the way in which God saves human beings – not through their own strivings, however earnest or even heroic, but only and strictly through his grace and faith. Human beings are justified by faith alone, not because of their virtuous actions but despite their sinfulness, an experience that yields liberation, peace, and joy. Luther articulated this experience as a doctrine: a radical theology of grace would become his cornerstone for Christian reform as well as for his criticism and rejection of the authority of the Roman Church. If salvation were a matter of faith and grace alone, bestowed all at once as a free gift from God and mediated by his Word in scripture, then there could be no legitimate point to traditional, elaborate religious practices that implied a very different understanding of faith and grace. Luther drew a shocking conclusion, which his excommunication by Leo X in early 1521 could only have confirmed: the Roman Church had not protected and proclaimed the saving truth of the Gospel, but corrupted it. The pope was not the Vicar of Christ, but the Antichrist, whose perch on Peter's See could only mean that the Apocalypse was near. Those who saw matters correctly had a twofold duty: to proclaim the central Gospel truth of justification by faith alone as an eleventh-hour rescue mission for Christian souls before the second coming of the Lord, and to reject whatever traditional teachings, practices, and institutions compromised the Gospel rightly understood.

Because Erasmian humanists had criticized some of the same traditional practices in their efforts to improve Christian morals, many initially thought that Luther stood alongside Erasmus in the same cause. Mistaken impressions were soon corrected. Not only were the passionate preacher and the urbane scholar temperamentally worlds apart, but more significantly they held dichotomous views of human nature, as became obvious between 1524 and 1526 during the course of their published debate on the place of free will in Christian salvation. Erasmus cared less about how God's grace and human will interacted than about establishing at least a minimal role for free will in the process of salvation, without which countless exhortations in the Bible seemed meaningless. According to Luther, the correct theology of grace was the essence of Christianity, and Erasmus's moralism was a farce based on a deluded overestimation of the capacities of fallen human beings, who lacked any shred of free will in matters pertaining to salvation. Both argued based on abundant, learned reference to scripture. Luther appreciated and used humanist biblical scholarship, including Erasmus's edition of the New Testament, but for the Erasmian *philosophia Christi* he had only scorn.

More deeply influenced by humanism and Erasmus in particular was Huldrych Zwingli, who became the leader of evangelical reform in the Swiss city of Zurich in the early 1520s. From there his influence and that of like-minded colleagues spread to other Swiss and southwestern German towns. Zwingli and his followers applauded Luther's view of justification by faith alone, his conviction that scripture was the sole source of Christian doctrine, and his attack on and rejection of the Roman Church. Like Luther, they rejected traditional practices and institutions, including the papacy, monasticism, a sacerdotal priesthood, clerical celibacy, the Mass as a sacrifice, pilgrimages, prayers to saints, scholasticism, and five of the seven sacraments, retaining baptism and the Lord's Supper. Yet despite what they shared, their disagreements over the correct interpretation of the Lord's Supper were made public by 1525 and escalated in subsequent years until they reached a dramatic non-resolution at the Colloquy of Marburg in 1529. This impasse prevented doctrinal and therefore ecclesial unity between what were in fact already two different, nascent Protestant traditions. It also precluded a political alliance, deeply desirable in the face of a disgruntled Emperor Charles V, among the cities and territories drawn to these respective versions of the Reformation. Luther condemned the Roman doctrine of transubstantiation as an Aristotelian encroachment on the mystery of Christ's real presence in the Eucharist, but insisted on the latter as the straightforward reading of Christ's words of institution at the Last Supper. Zwingli and his colleagues argued that "This is my body" must be understood metaphorically, as were many other passages in scripture, and that it was manifestly impossible for Christ's resurrected body to be simultaneously in heaven and in thousands of churches. Scripture could not arbitrate this dispute, because both sides appealed to scripture and accused their opponents of misunderstanding it. The Eucharistic controversy revealed broader differences regarding the relationship between God and the world: whereas Luther attenuated traditional Catholic sacramentality – the conviction that divine presence is manifest and mediated through created, material reality – Zwingli rejected it altogether. Other disagreements distinguished the two reformers as well, including convictions about the place of images in Christian worship, the relationship between Law and Gospel in Christian theology, and the relationship of churches to political authorities; but incompatible convictions about sacramentality, manifest above all in their Eucharistic disagreement, were the crucial, irreconcilable differences that prevented Lutheran and Reformed Protestants from worshiping together or belonging to the same church. This remained so after John Calvin became the leading theologian of Reformed Protestantism and persisted throughout the Reformation era.

The embrace of scripture alone as the source of Christian truth, coupled with the repudiation of the Roman Church, led even in the first decade of the Reformation to many more claims and reform proposals than those offered by Luther, Zwingli, and their respective colleagues. Notwithstanding their disagreements and the consequent, early development of divergent Protestant traditions, Luther and Zwingli insisted on obedience to political authorities, cooperated with them in implementing reforms, and upheld the traditional practice of infant baptism as the mandatory rite of initiation into Christian life. Following Paul's letter to the Romans, both saw political authorities as divinely established and indispensable for the maintenance of public order, not to mention the controlled introduction of religious changes. But beginning in the early 1520s, many other central Europeans read the Bible and concluded otherwise.

Andreas Bodenstein von Karlstadt was Luther's senior colleague in Wittenberg and had known him for years before he became a public figure. He had conferred the doctoral degree on Luther in 1512, supported his early protest against indulgences, and accompanied him against Johannes Eck in the Leipzig disputation of 1519, when Luther articulated his principle of *sola scriptura*. Yet it was over the proper understanding of scripture that the two parted ways. By August 1520, months before Luther's formal excommunication by Leo X or imperial condemnation via the Edict of Worms, Karlstadt criticized the doubt that Luther had already cast on the apostolic authorship and canonicity of the New Testament letter of James, which Luther disliked for its apparent contravention of the doctrine of justification by faith alone. By the time that Luther returned from the Wartburg castle in 1522, Karlstadt disputed his views on the normative character of the Old Testament, Eucharistic practice, the confession of sins, and the permissibility of religious images.[6] What is sometimes characterized merely as a disagreement with Luther over the pace of reform – as though the two were in agreement about what Christian truth was, and differed only over the timing of its implementation – was in fact more fundamental. Their dispute over the use of religious images, for example, which in 1522 on the basis of copious biblical citations Karlstadt derided as sheer idolatry, was inseparable from issues as central as the connection between the Old and New Testaments, the place of the Mosaic commandments in Christian life, and the relationship between the Law and the Gospel. In contrast to Luther's pastoral approach to what he viewed as a secondary concern, Karlstadt refused to allow concessions for men and women unprepared to abandon their attachment to images, a practice he thought unequivocally condemned by scripture. Luther could (and did) use his influence to prevent Karlstadt from preaching and publishing in Wittenberg, but he could not (and did not) persuade him that his understanding of the Bible was mistaken.

Karlstadt's divergence from Luther was relatively mild compared to other claims about the imperatives of God's Word. While Luther and Erasmus were debating grace and free will, the German Peasants' War raged. A series of five major, interrelated upheavals that began in the Black Forest in mid-1524 peaked in the spring of 1525 and lasted in the Tyrol into mid-1526; these rebellions of villagers and town commoners comprised the greatest social unrest of the sixteenth century anywhere in western Europe. Historians continue to debate the motivation for the uprisings: were they chiefly socio-economic and political demands couched in strategic religious language, or a radicalization of "Christian freedom" extended to concrete social and political forms? A single, simple answer is unlikely, given a two-year series of episodes engaged by bands without a uniform program and involving multiple leaders, actors, and grievances spread over a vast geographical area. Wherever one places the emphasis, however, the scope and nature of the Peasants' War seen as a whole distinguish it from periodic peasant rebellions in central Europe in preceding decades. Some of the leaders in the Peasants' War understood themselves and their actions primarily in religious terms. As such, they saw the imperatives of true Christianity not merely as the setting right of wrong Roman doctrines and practices *per se* for the sake of eternal salvation, or the proper ordering of ecclesiastical life in a civic setting, but as the revolutionary overthrow of a hierarchical social and political order as patently unchristian as it was deeply ingrained.

Such was the radically anticlerical activism of Thomas Müntzer. His reforming career began with Luther's approval, but Müntzer quickly became one of his harshest critics, accusing Luther of a superficial understanding of God's Word that pandered to the powerful and perpetuated the suffering of the poor and powerless. God's elect were those who, beyond mere exegesis and scholarly apprehension of the "outer word," had endured his "inner word" and been transformed by it. Instructed directly by the Holy Spirit, genuine Christians could see that God would lead his righteous elect against the unrighteous in the imminent apocalypse. The explosive emergence of the peasants demanding redress of grievances seemed both its clear sign and its means. In July 1524 Müntzer delivered before Duke John of Saxony and his son, John Frederick, a sermon that threatened them with God's wrath, including their deaths, should they neglect to remake entirely existing political and ecclesiastical institutions. In May 1525, Müntzer led several thousand peasants into battle at Frankenhausen; they were slaughtered, and he was captured and executed.

Issues raised by Müntzer's distinction between the "outer" and "inner" Word of God, the latter including direct, divine inspiration and visions – both of which are abundant in the Bible – prompted serious questions for Luther, Zwingli, and other reformers about what it meant to understand God's will through his Word. All reformers who rejected the Roman Church, notwithstanding their emphasis on the literal sense of scripture, thought that understanding God's Word entailed more than simply a technical, philological determination of the meaning of the words in the Bible. In some manner, so that hearts would be touched and lives changed, the presence of the same Holy Spirit who had revealed the Word was necessary to its proper interpretation. But how, exactly? By what and whose criteria was the presence of the Spirit known? And why might not the Holy Spirit, which "blows where it wills," act in the Last Days as in biblical times, revealing fresh insights to God's chosen instruments? Even before Luther returned to Wittenberg from the Wartburg in 1522, the Zwickau prophets had visited his city claiming direct inspiration by God – and although Luther ultimately rejected their assertions, he did not dismiss them out of hand. Because Protestant reformers throughout the Reformation era were not secular philologists but rather Christians seeking salvation, none could dispense entirely with "spiritualist" claims. Instead, the question of just how the Holy Spirit guided and guaranteed the correct understanding of God's Word further complicated already complex issues of biblical interpretation. Matters were further vexed because those who advanced strong forms of spiritualism in the 1520s, such as Müntzer, the Zwickau prophets, and Caspar Schwenkfeld, disagreed among themselves. Among spiritualist reformers and groups from the 1520s through mid-seventeenth-century English Quakers and beyond, it was one thing to downplay scholarly biblical exegesis and concrete religious rituals in favor of the Spirit or "inner light." It was another thing entirely for such spiritualist Christians to agree about what was illuminated.

Other reformers involved in the Peasants' War shared Müntzer's concern for a Christian leveling of social and political relationships, but eschewed his exhortations to apocalyptic violence. Instead, without dwelling on means beyond God's agency, they envisioned a thoroughly egalitarian, post-revolutionary society, whether spread over the entire world or restricted to a particular region. The author of *On the New Transformation of the Christian Life*, most likely the Nuremberg printer Hans Hergot, touted a complete dismantling of all existing ecclesiastical institutions and political arrangements. A communitarian, Christian agrarian society would take their place, one that integrated Church and state at the local level of villages and coordinated these villages under elected territorial lords. Above these territorial lords would stand an elected chief lord, by means of which "a single flock will be established on earth." In contrast to Luther and Zwingli, Hergot stated that extreme unction and confirmation were two of three sacraments to be retained (he did not specify the third).[7] The peasant leader Michael Gaismair, a former secretary to the prince-bishop of Brixen, drafted a similar proposal for revolutionary reform of the Tyrol in early 1526, although he limited his sketch to that territory. All members of the new order would swear an oath "to pursue first of all the honor of God and then the common good," seeking to live by "laws which are wholly Christian, and which in all matters are founded only on the holy word of God." Accordingly, in this new order all traditional social and political privileges would be abolished, all walls that encircled cities and castles torn down, so that there would be "complete equality in the territory."[8] Political, social, and economic issues did not stand apart from religious concerns. Here were readings of scripture and reforming notions dramatically different than those of Zwingli as well as Luther.

In certain respects, Luther's frustrations with Karlstadt, Müntzer, and the Zwickau prophets were paralleled by Zwingli's disputes with fellow reformers in Zurich who became the first Anabaptists. Karlstadt and Müntzer had already criticized the practice of infant baptism. If salvation came by faith alone, what sense did the baptism of infants make? Pouring water on and pronouncing words over babies did not create Christians, but such a custom helped to explain why so many adult "Christians" led morally dissolute lives. They had never resolved to follow Christ. Extending the logic that spurned infant baptism as a meaningless ritual, the practice of adult baptism was begun by Conrad Grebel, Felix Mantz, and others in and around Zurich beginning in late January 1525 as the culmination of more than a year of conflicts with Zwingli about a host of issues. Only those who made the self-conscious decision to follow Christ in discipleship, having experienced the regenerative power of the Holy Spirit that accompanied God's gift of faith, should be baptized as the external sign of that interior baptism by the Spirit. Once again, the proper interpretation of scripture was central: no explicit sanction for infant baptism could be found in the Bible. Zwingli and others argued for it by analogy with the Old Testament practice of circumcision, but Anabaptists rejected such arguments with their own, contrary readings of scripture. Beyond matters of biblical exegesis and sacramental theology, the rejection of infant baptism had profound ecclesiological implications. If baptism was to be received only by committed adults who had been renewed by the Holy Spirit, then in all likelihood not everyone in a given locale or territory would belong to the Church. Zwingli's vision of city and Church as two sides of the same coin would disappear. Indeed, implicit in the rejection of infant baptism and the refusal of many early Anabaptists to swear civic oaths was a repudiation of the Constantinian model of the relationship between Church and state, which had prevailed since the fourth century. Such a repudiation was as objectionable to Lutheran and Reformed Protestant as to Roman Catholic authorities.

Anabaptists themselves proved to be a deeply fissiparous association of different groups even within the first decade of their existence. It was not as if, convinced that adult commitment followed by baptism was the prerequisite for genuine Christianity, Anabaptists agreed on the interpretation of scripture or the nature of Christian life. Contemporaneous with the Peasants' War, Grebel and Mantz advocated a principled Christian pacifism and separatism that would be echoed in the Schleitheim Articles (1527) authored by the former Benedictine monk Michael Sattler. But other early leaders among the Swiss Brethren, including Wilhelm Reublin and Johannes Brötli, defended and were militarily defended by the peasants in 1525, and Balthasar Hubmaier, the most theologically well educated of all the early Anabaptist leaders, upheld the right of political authorities to bear arms. A distinct stream of South German and Austrian Anabaptism took shape in the immediate aftermath of the Peasants' War, owed little to the Zurich context in which the Swiss Brethren arose, and was strongly marked by Müntzer's apocalyptic views. The clash in Nikolsburg, Moravia, in 1527 between Hubmaier and Hans Hut, an important South German Anabaptist leader who owed so much to Müntzer, epitomizes the tension between these two divergent Anabaptist streams. Another group, the followers of Jacob Hutter, grew out of heavily persecuted Austrian Anabaptism in the early 1530s. Based in Moravia, the Hutterites' most distinctive practice, the communitarian ownership of property, inspired partly by the example of early Christians from the Acts of the Apostles, led to denunciations by the Swiss Brethren, whom the Hutterites denounced in turn for their failure to follow the biblical example of the communal sharing of possessions. In 1530, the arrival in Emden of the apocalyptic preacher Melchior Hoffman marked the advent of a third distinct branch of Anabaptism in northern Germany and the Low Countries. Within five years, the notorious Anabaptist kingdom of Münster would establish communitarian property holding – and polygamy – as part of social and political ideas radically different than those of the Hutterites. Whatever their common commitments, the differences among Anabaptists – derived ultimately from competing interpretations of scripture and claims about the experience of the Holy Spirit in Christian life

– were sufficient to divide them doctrinally and socially into separate groups marked often by mutual hostility.

If scripture had been clear about issues of concern to sixteenth-century Christian reformers, then the repudiation of the Roman Church might reasonably have been expected to yield clarity about the content and imperatives of Christian doctrine. Instead, its complexities and ambiguities, combined with different assumptions, interpretations, and prioritizations among reformers, led to divisive disagreements from the very outset of the Reformation. To concentrate principally on the most influential reformers masks the fact that most assertions about Christian truth in the 1520s were as critical of Luther and Zwingli as they were of the Roman Church. The large majority of the anti-Roman claims articulated in the 1520s rejected not only Roman Catholicism but also the cooperation with political authorities espoused by Luther and Zwingli, in a spectrum that ranged from separatist pacifism to revolutionary violence. In the 1520s, backed by political authority, incipient Lutheran and Reformed Protestantism ended up with many more followers and much greater influence, to be sure, but *sola scriptura* saw many more radical than magisterial interpretations. In a sense, the full range of those who rejected the Roman Church in the 1520s might be seen as a dramatic reconfiguration of the traditional relationship between Catholic unity and variety: instead of different theological and devotional strands that coexisted within an inherited institutional and liturgical framework, different interpretations of scripture were articulated as incompatible doctrines, and correlatively gave rise to distinct and competing Christian groups. None of the interpretative disputes about scripture, the sacraments, or the Holy Spirit even remotely approached consensual resolution throughout the remainder of the era. Doctrinal disagreement marked the Reformation's inception and remained a fundamental religious, social, and political feature of early modern Christianity. Empirically, the denunciation of Rome proved to be not a panacea for the impasses of reform but an unanticipated Pandora's Box of contested biblical interpretations.

The central paradox of the Reformation is that its foundational assumption was simultaneously an insoluble problem. That scripture alone was proclaimed the authoritative basis for Christian faith and life meant the elimination of papal decrees, conciliar decisions, ecclesiastical institutions, long-standing practices, and other elements constitutive of the tradition in relationship to which the Bible had been implicitly understood for many centuries. At a stroke, this solved the problem of the papal logjam that had stymied efforts at ecclesiastical reform as a whole. Papal authority was viewed as the linchpin of the merely human traditions that had twisted rather than safeguarded God's Word for so long. But at the same time, insistence on scripture alone led not to a consensus about Christ's "common and accessible" teaching, as Erasmus had dreamed, now liberated from oppressive human inventions, but to a welter of incompatible claims about what the Bible said and implied for human life. Among those who rejected Rome, disagreements over scripture's meaning could not be resolved by appealing to mutually recognized authorities or institutional mechanisms, the elimination of which had been part of the point in distinguishing scripture sharply from tradition in the first place. But judgments had to be made in a context of incompatible doctrinal claims if any form of Protestantism was to exhibit any doctrinal or social coherence whatsoever. So *each* nascent church and discrepant group created its own institutions and recognized its own extra-biblical authorities, minimally to distinguish true from false teaching and sound from unacceptable Christian practice – precisely and ironically, two of the functions exercised by Roman ecclesiastical authorities through their church's institutions. From its inception, the open-ended heterogeneity of the Protestant Reformation derived from its foundational principle. Its protagonists proved conspicuously unable to agree about what God's Word said, and so about what Christians should be and do. What was heralded as the only genuine foundation for the reform of Christianity yielded not one but a profusion of competing claims about biblical truth and prioritizations within Christian life, paralleled by a profusion of divergent Protestant churches and groups alongside the Roman Catholic Church. This was so in the 1520s, it remained so throughout the Reformation era, and it has been so in western Christianity ever since.

NOTES

1 For the dating of this sermon to January 1510 rather than its traditional date of February 6, 1512, see John B. Gleason, *John Colet* (Berkeley and Los Angeles: University of California Press, 1989), pp. 181, 184, 370 n. 33.

2 John Colet, *Oratio habita a D. Ioanne Colet Decano Sancti Pauli ad Clerum in Conuocatione* ([London:] Richard Pynson, [1512]), pp. 3–7, 12–13; quotations on 7, 13.

3 Giles of Viterbo, in *Sacrorum conciliorum nova et amplissima collectio*, ed. Giovan Domenico Mansi *et al.*, vol. 32 (Paris: H. Welter, 1901), cols 669, 675, 671–2, 669.

4 For Italian Benedictines, see Barry Collett, *Italian Benedictine Scholars and the Reformation: The Congregation of Santa Giustina of Padua* (Oxford: Clarendon Press, 1985); for central Europe, see Franz Posset, *Humanist Monks: Monastic Humanism in Six Biographical Sketches* (Leiden: E. J. Brill, 2005).

5 Desiderius Erasmus, *Christian Humanism and the Reformation: Selected Writings of Erasmus*, ed. John C. Olin (New York: Fordham University Press, 1965), pp. 97, 96.

6 Ronald J. Sider, *Andreas Bodenstein von Karlstadt: The Development of His Thought, 1517–1525* (Leiden: E. J. Brill, 1974), pp. 97, 108–12, 143–6; Karlstadt, *Von abtuhung der Bylder, Vnd das keyn Betdler vnther den Christen seyn soll* [1522], repr. in *Flugschriften der frühen Reformationsbewegung (1518–1524)*, ed. Adolf Laube *et al.* (Verduz: Topos Verlag, 1983), vol. 1, pp. 105–27.

7 Hans Hergot, *On the New Transformation of the Christian Life* [1527], in *The Radical Reformation*, ed. and trans. Michael G. Baylor (Cambridge: Cambridge University Press, 1991), pp. 218 (quotation), 214.

8 Michael Gaismair, "Territorial Constitution for Tyrol," in Baylor, *Radical Reformation*, pp. 254, 255.

SUGGESTIONS FOR FURTHER READING

Augustin, Cornelis. *Erasmus: His Life, Works, and Influence*, trans. J. C. Grayson. Toronto, 1991.

Baylor, Michael G., ed. and trans. *The Radical Reformation*. Cambridge, 1991.

Bedouelle, Guy and Bernard Roussel, eds. *Le temps des Réformes et la Bible*. Paris, 1989.

Bentley, Jerry H. *Humanists and Holy Writ: New Testament Scholarship in the Renaissance.* Princeton, 1983.

Blickle, Peter. *The Revolution of 1525: The German Peasants' War from a New Perspective*, trans. Thomas A. Brady, Jun. and H. C. Erik. Midelfort. Baltimore, 1981.

Collett, Barry. *Italian Benedictine Scholars and the Reformation: The Congregation of Santa Giustina of Padua.* Oxford, 1985.

D'Amico, John F. *Renaissance Humanism in Papal Rome: Humanists and Churchmen on the Eve of the Reformation.* Baltimore, 1983.

Edwards, Mark U., Jun. *Printing, Propaganda, and Martin Luther.* Berkeley and Los Angeles, 1994.

Evans, G. R. *Problems of Authority in the Reformation Debates.* Cambridge, 1992.

Gleason, John B. *John Colet.* Berkeley and Los Angeles. 1989.

Hsia, R. Po-chia. *A Companion to the Reformation World.* Malden, Mass., 2004.

Matheson, Peter, ed. and trans. *The Collected Works of Thomas Müntzer.* Edinburgh, 1988.

Muller, Richard A. and John L. Thompson, eds. *Biblical Interpretation in the Era of the Reformation.* Grand Rapids, Mich., 1996.

Olin, John C. *The Catholic Reformation: Savonarola to Ignatius Loyola.* New York, 1969.

Pettegree, Andrew, ed. *The Reformation World.* London and New York, 2000.

Posset, Franz. *Renaissance Monks: Monastic Humanism in Six Biographical Sketches.* Leiden, 2005.

Rummel, Erika. *The Humanist–Scholastic Debate in the Renaissance and Reformation.* Cambridge, Mass., 1995.

Scott, Tom and Bob Scribner, eds and trans. *The German Peasants' War: A History in Documents.* Atlantic Highlands, N.J. and London, 1991.

Sider, Ronald J. *Andreas Bodenstein von Karlstadt: The Development of His Thought, 1517–1525.* Leiden, 1974.

Snyder, C. Arnold. *Anabaptist History and Theology: An Introduction.* Kitchener, Ontario, 1995.

CHAPTER THIRTY-ONE

A TALE OF TWO TRIBUNALS

David Gentilcore

In 1590 a Franciscan friar was charged before the Inquisition in Venice with "superstitious healing." His crime? As a cure for fevers he would dispense his own *brevi*: on each of 12 slips of paper he would write the name of one of the 12 apostles. The sick person was to open one of these folded papers each day, and then burn it if the fever persisted. If, however, the fever abated, the sick person should vow to fast on the vigil of the apostle whose name had appeared that day. The friar's good intentions were dismissed as irrelevant by the court; it saw the technique as an irreverent attempt to coerce the actions of the apostles through bribery and threats. His punishment? He was sentenced merely to recite psalms and fast on feast days and perform private penances. This minor incident tells us several things about the relationship between belief and authority in the Renaissance period. In general terms it was not an unabated war of oppression against "wrong" belief; the different forces involved were far from presenting a united front, and the actions they took were far from consistent. More specifically, it was not so much a campaign against certain categories of people as one directed against suspect beliefs and practices. As a result, punishment was not, at least not in the first instance, directed so much at the individual as at the offence, eradicating it through a process of reform and re-education.

In Italy, the rise of the merchant economy in the sixteenth century and the transition from a predominantly artisan economy that preceded it were the causes of profound social rifts and pressures. In fact, the century at the heart of this book, the sixteenth, ushered in a period of great shifts and changes throughout Europe: demographic (the plague pandemic), religious (heresy, and the Reformation and Counter-Reformation), political (warfare and the rise of nation-states), socio-economic (urbanization and impoverishment of the peasantry), and knowledge-based (humanism and the "scientific revolution"). Change brought unease, anxiety, and sometimes fear of witches, and of the poor. What was previously perceived as marginal was increasingly seen as organized, and therefore dangerous, leading to widespread attempts to identify, classify, control, reform, and repress. Society itself seemed corrupted, divine order overthrown. In response to the upheaval generated by the Protestant Reformation and the ongoing struggles of confessionalization that characterized the century, the period saw a widespread process of "social disciplining."

At the same time, however, the causes of fear could be dealt with and measures taken. The authorities felt confident in their abilities to counter threats.

Part and parcel of this disciplining process was the strengthening of pre-existing institutions to deal with the perceived threat, or else the establishment of new ones. Two of them will form the focus of this discussion: the Inquisition and the Protomedicato. While all readers will have heard of the Inquisition and have at least a vague (although possibly erroneous) notion about its aims and functions, few have any idea about the Protomedicato. While the Inquisition was a major tribunal, with unparalleled authority over a range of areas, with lengthy and complex legal procedures and the authority to order capital punishments, the Protomedicato was a minor tribunal, with very limited jurisdiction, abbreviated procedures, and lesser penalties like fines and temporary banishment. Nevertheless, as we shall see, both had a role to play in the reform of society and the maintenance of order, which were key elements in the exercise of authority during this period. Both had an impact on the ways in which people could think and what they could do in these troubled times, evident in a wide range of activities and areas of endeavor, from religion through to medicine and natural philosophy.

It is arguable that for most Christians prior to the Reformations religious practice was more important than belief. What one did, the actions one performed, were crucial to one's physical and spiritual health. Popular religion in particular was more concerned with the here and now than with the hereafter. It was primarily about protecting oneself and one's family from misfortune, disease, and hunger. For the official Church, however, it was also important to be a "good Christian" by participating in the rites of the Church and showing loyalty to them, especially the seven sacraments. The exact boundaries between prayer, medicine, and superstition were not clearly defined. With the Reformations, ecclesiastical authorities sought to separate these various elements – demarcating sacred and profane, natural and supernatural – but it was a near impossible task, and certainly one not achieved within the chronological limits of this book.

More straightforward was the demarcation of orthodoxy and unorthodoxy; that is, the elimination of heresy. In heresy, belief came to the fore, with the stress on personal piety. It is important to realize that a wide range of different movements and devotional trends coexisted throughout the Renaissance period. Up until the middle decades of the sixteenth century the division of the Church into Catholic and Protestant was by no means a foregone conclusion. In Italy, Protestant ideas and movements, though ultimately declared heretical, existed alongside less radical Catholic ones. It was only with the Council of Trent (1545–63) that the breach was sealed. In a process that took 18 years, what was now the Catholic Church defined its dogma and initiated disciplinary reforms.

The Council was a defeat for the traditions deriving from the thought of St Augustine and Christian humanism. It defied the whole Protestant concept of evidence and authority by rating ecclesiastical tradition on a par with the Bible. But it was also a beginning. It ushered in the Counter-Reformation, which meant putting the decrees into place throughout the ever-expanding Catholic world. This would be a long and difficult process, one that would encounter difficulties and resistance at many levels, from the poorest illiterate peasant, to local bishops, through to the Spanish kings. Despite the slower than expected pace of reform, basic features of the Church did change. The plague of non-resident bishops was ended. Indeed, Italian and Spanish bishops themselves provided adequate, and sometimes inspiring, leadership. Through the means at their disposal – episcopal tribunals, visitations, synods, seminaries, and parish missions – the bishops sought to implement the decrees of the Council in their own dioceses. A second key element in religious reform, in the modeling of belief and practice, consisted of the Inquisitions. They represent the most powerful instrument of authority against belief, before and after the Tridentine watershed. Two main forms existed: "Spanish" and "Roman" (also called "Papal"). The changing operations of the Inquisitions in Spain and Italy, combined with the role of Inquisitorial officials in the proceeding of other tribunals, offer an indication of how the campaign against heresy was waged.

In Spain the "Holy Office of the Inquisition" was founded in 1478 to punish converts from Judaism suspected of practicing their old religion in secret, a function that was soon extended to Muslim converts in the wake of the "Reconquest" of Muslim kingdoms in the south of Spain. Reconquest Spain was in no mood to tolerate the presence of other faiths (although to be accurate this was heterodoxy rather than heresy) and these home-grown "heresies," involving native inhabitants of the country, were dealt with harshly. Pre-existing local rivalries and tensions came to the fore in the campaign against Judaizers and Moriscos. By contrast, a group of perceived "outsiders" very rarely met with the Inquisition's ire: Gypsies. Although widely suspected of blasphemy, irreligion, and magical practices, Gypsies rarely came before the Inquisition, due to their very mobility and different language and culture. It was simpler to chase them out of town than to prosecute them.

While the Spanish Inquisition continued to prosecute suspected Judaizers (who made up most of the few people it put to death) and Moriscos (the latter especially by the provincial tribunals of Valencia and Granada), Martin Luther's split from the Church in 1520 gave the Inquisition a new focus: the elimination of Protestant ideas in the country. Spain had been affected by the currents of Italian and Dutch humanism, which widened horizons in religion and literature, influencing science, painting, and architecture. The spread of the Reformation led to a dramatic shift, a return to traditional doctrines, secular and religious. It instigated the reaction of the 1530s against these new currents of European thought. However, the absence of actual "Lutherans" posed something of a problem, so the Inquisition turned to harassing followers of Erasmus and his ideas, which they thought the inspiration behind Luther. It also went after a small group of mystics known as *alumbrados*, so-called because they claimed to be "illuminated" by the Holy Spirit. The charge was extended to other mystics, including, somewhat paradoxically in terms of their later contributions to the Counter-Reformation, investigations into the early activities of Ignatius Loyola and Teresa of Avila.

Together, what were identified as "major heresies" represent a large proportion of Inquisitorial activity – but less than half. More important for the Spanish Inquisition, at least in statistical terms, were the "minor heresies": heretical utterances, blasphemy, bigamy, and "superstitious offences." The focus here was on native Spaniards of Catholic heritage, the so-called "Old Christians," and it testifies to the important role of the tribunals of the Spanish Inquisition in enforcing the Counter-Reformation in terms of beliefs and behavior. This was a pastoral role of trying to make good Catholics out of ordinary Spaniards, trends which are reflected in overall trial numbers. The Spanish Inquisition was organized into provincial tribunals, from the heartland of New Castile to outlying dominions like Sicily or Lima, all of which sent regular reports and trial summaries to the Inquisition's head office in Madrid, a source that has proved a veritable gold mine for historians. According to these, trial numbers steadily increased during the reign of Philip II (1555–98), a time when religious uniformity was a cardinal point of state policy. Then a more relaxed period follows in the second decade of the seventeenth century. By this time the substantial minority of Moors had been driven out of the country, and the fanatical attitude toward foreign Protestants and toward deviations among the Old Christians had moderated. The religious militancy and dogmatism characterizing the first 50 years after the Council of Trent were replaced by a sense of bureaucratic routine. That said, the Spanish Inquisition's impact was never as profound as their laws and edicts might suggest. Even in Toledo, capital of the Spanish Church, where the Spanish Inquisition had set up an active tribunal as early as 1485, the beliefs and practices of its "Old Christian" (that is native Spanish Catholic) community continued to be diverse, with pockets of spiritual dissent, while those of its "New Christians" (the descendants of Jewish and Muslim converts) were only nominally Catholic throughout the sixteenth century.

As far as the Italian states are concerned, the key year was 1542, which saw the establishment of the "Sacred Congregation of the Holy Office of the Inquisition" in Rome. The Roman Inquisition was set up to deal with suspected "Lutherans," a blanket term for the followers of Protestant sects and, occasionally, their sympathizers. Its creation should be seen in the context of the gradual reorganization of the government of the Catholic Church by successive popes. A radical centralization was achieved by the setting up of "Congregations," commissions or ministries with the responsibility of preparing the pope's decisions in the various areas of their competence and jurisdiction. The members of the Congregations were cardinals, chosen for their expertise in the respective areas. By the short papacy of Sixtus V (1585–90) there were 15 Congregations: six responsible for temporal affairs, while others oversaw areas of activity like the enforcement of doctrinal orthodoxy (the Holy Office, founded 1542, as we have seen), book censorship (the Index of Prohibited Books, 1571), the bishops (1576), and the making of saints (Rites and Ceremonies, 1588).

The establishment of the Inquisition in Italy, followed by the opening of the Council of Trent three years later, forced some Italian Protestants to flee. Those who remained soon had to adapt to the changed circumstances, meeting in secret "conventicles." These were the main target of Inquisitorial operations in Venice and Friuli, for example, closer to Protestant areas of Europe. In Naples, by contrast, the relative absence of "Lutherans" meant that the accusation of heresy tended to refer to Muslims. Most of these were in fact Catholics who had been captured into slavery and then released or ransomed. They had to confess and officially re-convert to Catholicism. However, even the establishment of the Inquisition in the states of Italy did not instigate a campaign of repression. Take the 774 residents of Venice accused of various forms of Protestantism by the Venetian Holy Office in the years 1547 to

1583, studied by John Martin. This was a time when previous toleration and openness about Protestant ideas turned to repression, leading to the extinction of groups of followers. Almost half of the accusations (44 percent) were not considered worthy of further investigation by the Inquisition. One out of five (18 percent) led as far as the gathering of testimony but no further, while only two out of five (38 percent) resulted in a formal sentence. Despite the aim to eliminate Protestant heresy there was no witch hunt of Protestants in Venice. The Inquisition proceeded with caution, only interrogating the accused after a preliminary investigation had been carried out. But there was one thing the Inquisitions did not tolerate, and this was recidivism. Repeat offenders faced the full brunt of their authority. Close to a third of heretics found guilty for the first time were punished with some form of penance, while a number of those found guilty for a second time were sentenced to death. The same fate befell Domenico Scandella, the heretical Friulian miller studied by Carlo Ginzburg.

The impact of the Spanish and Roman Inquisitions was limited by numerous factors, from the closing of ranks by local communities to conflicting jurisdictions with other organs of Church and state. Venice, for example, admitted the presence and activity of the Papal Inquisition on its soil, but only under certain conditions and restrictions. We must also bear in mind the judicial propriety of the Inquisitions, Spanish and Roman alike, which has emerged out of the study of the trial registers and official correspondence. The judicial conduct of the Inquisitions was rarely as arbitrary as depicted in legend. Abuses could occur, as in any court, but serious ones were usually checked by the intervention of the central office in Spain ("*La Suprema*") or the papal Congregation. The rights of the accused were better guaranteed in the Inquisitorial process than in the ordinary judicial procedures of the secular courts of the major states of Europe. The Inquisitions did use torture, like other courts at this time, but only in certain circumstances and after following certain procedures. Studies have shown that the Spanish Inquisition used torture (in the form of the *strappado*) in around 10 percent of cases. Furthermore, decisions reached by the Inquisitions could be appealed; by comparison, most civil courts of the time provided for no appeal against the sentence for some types of crime. Finally, the death penalty was used only rarely, in contrast to the stereotype. If the Inquisitions were feared as tribunals, it was because of the economic and social consequences of even a light sentence: these might include the confiscation of property, banishment, or loss of certain rights, as well as the infamy heaped on the condemned person and his descendants. One wealthy Italian apothecary, Zuan Donà della Colombina from Vicenza, found himself reduced to making rosary beads in order to earn a living after being charged with heresy in the middle of the sixteenth century.

By the 1580s or so, the different Inquisitorial offices in the Italian states were no longer concerned with Protestant heretics, so few had they now become. What little dissent remained was an individual phenomenon, and some of this was so eccentric in nature that it is difficult to label it Protestant. By then heretical preoccupation had given way to trials for clerical and sexual misconduct, especially in Spain. The Inquisition set itself up as the guardian of Catholic morals, using the argument that morality came under the heading of faith. In addition to the prosecution of sexual offences, there were numerous trials falling under the rubric of "superstition" – illicit magic and witchcraft. During the seventeenth century "superstitious offences" represented about 40 percent of cases in the Italian tribunals – a higher proportion than in Spanish ones. Denunciations under this rubric included therapeutic magic; divination; harmful magic; sorcery; love potions; spells uttered against storms, wolves, or bullets; magic used in treasure hunting; and witchcraft and demonic magic. As far as the Italian Inquisitions were concerned, it was by far the largest single category of religious deviance they handled. Why all the fuss for mere superstition? A standard theological view was that practitioners of magic made an open pact with the devil, which gave them the power to cause harm, notably by casting spells. These caused fatal diseases in both people and animals. Moreover it was always illicit and sinful to have recourse to sorcerers to obtain good, such as the healing of the body, likewise the work of the devil. The only effective and licit means of dissolving the malefice were "ecclesiastical remedies": converting to God with a humble and contrite heart, prayer, and fasting. In addition to these remedies, Catholics were encouraged to give alms, use blessed water and the sign of the cross, and, in the most extreme case, have recourse to exorcism as proposed by the Church.

However, there was no unanimity within official circles. While the orthodox view considered the covenant with the devil as a reality, and aimed at annihilating Satan's minions, a newer, more relaxed view of sorcery gained prominence. This saw the devil as using such people because they did not know any better. It called for a re-education of cunning folk and their clients. Rather than regard the pact with Satan as "explicit," this view saw it as "tacit"; that is, done unknowingly or passively. In Italy and Spain superstitious offences were generally regarded as the result of ignorance, rather than apostasy to the devil. The Inquisitorial authorities soon adopted a skeptical attitude toward the crimes of witchcraft, sorcery, and magical spells, and felt called upon to quell the zeal of local officials. When an inquisitor was sent to Barcelona in 1549 to examine the activity of the local tribunal, he was appalled to find two suspected witches being held in jail. He sent a typical trial transcript back to the central office of the Inquisition with the comment: "I believe that most of the other cases are as laughable as this one indicates." He recommended that all those arrested be freed immediately and all confiscations be returned. Likewise by the early seventeenth century, Rome had issued special instructions to all its tribunals that required judges to view accusations with circumspection and duly weigh all evidence. There was no "witch-craze" in Spain or Italy. The notorious execution of a handful of Basque witches in northern Spain in 1611 is something of an exception; it certainly had no parallel in Italy. For the most part the denunciations arose out of the common context of community and family tensions. If people brought their complaints regarding witchcraft to the Inquisitions, it was not because they were terrorized by the tribunal but because it was a convenient tool for settling local scores. At the same time and somewhat paradoxically, the inquisitors' views of the real existence of witchcraft – in its devil-worshiping, night-flying, sabbath-attending variety – did have the effect in certain places of transforming local beliefs over the centuries into exactly the sort of thing the inquisitors were looking for, as both Carlo Ginzburg and Gustav Henningsen have suggested.

The interpretation of superstitious offences by the Inquisitions, as stemming from an erroneous set of beliefs that it was the Church's responsibility to eliminate, was closer to the popular interpretation of the power of magic and its uses in everyday life. Even smaller towns and villages would have had their cunning man or woman, variously called a *fattucchiara* or *magara* in Italy and a *hechicera* or *sabía* in Spain. Although individual practitioners could be quite specialized, in general terms these were people who treated disease, predicted the future, and even sought to influence events by making love potions or casting spells. They mixed beneficent and maleficent magic, for it was believed that those who could heal by means of incantations could also harm, an ambivalence that is an important element in popular religion. A typical cure might consist of three elements: (1) a healing invocation, which usually recounted an event in the life of Jesus, the Virgin, or the saints, related in some way to the sick person's affliction; (2) the reciting of prayers like the Our Father and Hail Mary, often in groups of three, by the practitioner, sometimes accompanied by the instruction to the sick person to light candles in church or have a mass said; and (3) the use of an oil made from various herbs, rubbed on the afflicted area, with which the practitioners might make the sign of the cross.

Three features are worth noting. The first, not immediately obvious in the above description, is the social element. A disease was ascribed to sorcery when it appeared strange and when sick people felt themselves to have been the victims of aggression. Ailments were usually of the chronic type, visible as a slow wasting away, stubborn headaches, heaviness of the eyes, general malaise, the halting of growth in children, or impotence in men. In such cases, sick people sought the advice of cunning folk to ascertain whether the cause was sorcery. The practitioners could function as brokers: mediators between the victims of spells and those who had cast them. They used forms of divination on behalf of their clients, in order to determine the presence of a spell and who had cast it. If the disease had been caused by a human actor, a particular wise woman (say), then the most efficacious cure depended on contacting and placating that same actor, whatever the Church might have had to say about it. Such women met with a mixture of fear, suspicion, and respect. I say 'she' here because the practitioners of these healing rituals were most often women. The second feature of this therapeutic magic is the importance of the ritual itself. This meant that, although a great variety of cures were available, there was no necessary correspondence between disease and remedy. One ritual formula might be used for more than one kind of disease and one disease might be treated by more than one formula. The third feature is the Christian content of the magic: appeals to the saints, having masses said, the lighting of altar candles and saying of standard prayers. Practitioners and clients alike regarded them, at least in part, as extensions of ecclesiastical rituals.

For all these reasons it is useful to speak of "popular religion" containing magical elements, but not to see it as a sealed-off world of its own. Indeed recent trends in historiography have emphasized the links, commonalities, and overlap between ecclesiastical and popular practices, while not ignoring the tensions and differences. Take the process of "signing" (Italian *segnare*), in the sense of making the sign of the cross. It was a common form of treating the sick, made by a priest on the ailing part of the body, part of a wide range of rites and benedictions known as sacramentals. These were eventually collated and standardized in the Church's *Roman Ritual*, the aim of which was to regularize the practice of the sacramentals by the clergy, especially in the field of exorcisms. But it also had the effect of encouraging their use. The perceived efficacy of the sacramentals in healing disease resulted in two things. First of all, priests were increasingly sought out by their parishioners to administer "signings" and blessings for the benefit of the sick. Priests came to be regarded as mediators between the sacred and the profane. Second, the perceived efficacy of the sacramentals also resulted in popular, lay interpretations of them. Local healers often imitated the sacramentals in their rituals. This flew in the face of Counter-Reformation Church teaching that only priests be permitted to use the sacramentals; the rest was sinful. The difficulty with the sign of the cross was that all Catholics were encouraged to do it, and frequently. So common was it as part of healing rituals that in parts of northern Italy "to sign" became synonymous with "to treat." When Domenica de Boaris was investigated by the episcopal court of Treviso in 1576 for "signing" sick children (accompanying this treatment with prayers, blessed palm branches, and a rue oil of hers), rather than punish her, the bishop issued her with a license to practice. In her case, the Church decided her use was in line with ecclesiastical teaching and indeed beneficial; other popular healers would not be so lucky.

This process of appropriation – the use of (in this case) Church devotions and rites by the laity for their own purposes and to meet their own needs – is typical of popular religion in this period. The study of appropriation as a process was first suggested by Roger Chartier as a means of getting to grips with a concept as slippery and potentially misleading as "popular culture." He proposed the study of the different cultural uses, by different levels of society, of a particular belief, action, ritual, or object. In the Renaissance context the rosary suggests itself as an obvious example: at once a belief, action, ritual, and material object. The practice of the rosary was spread by the Dominicans from the fifteenth century. At first, devotional literature stressed its symbolic nature, in terms of the meditation on the mysteries of the rosary. Families were encouraged to recite it together every evening. However, by the beginning of the seventeenth century the rosary was being presented as a well-defined ritual, and the indulgences, confraternities, processions, and masses associated with it were being emphasized. The healing miracles that occurred as a result were publicized in pamphlets and devotional works. At the same time, the repetitive and formulaic prayers making up the rosary were found to be effective in ways not approved by the Church. In southern Apulia, for example, it was said that if the prayers were said while holding the rosary behind one's back, in the dark, and one turned around, one would see scenes of hanged prisoners, tongues hanging out of their heads. This practice may have been a one-off association, made as the result of (mis-)interpreting a preacher's hellfire sermon. But another interpretation of the rosary was widespread, and largely tolerated: when it became a sacred object, like a saint's relic. The material object took on sacred powers of its own. People commonly touched their rosaries to the bodies of dead saints, to imbue the rosaries with their sacred power.

The careful involvement of the Church authorities in offences for magic and superstition was one of the reasons why the witch craze did not affect Spain or Italy in the same way it did northern Europe. Charges of performing illicit healing rituals, love magic, and harmful spells rarely led to charges of diabolical witchcraft. At the same time, traditionally held notions of the supernatural persisted because the basic structures of life and existential needs remained largely unchanged. The Counter-Reformation did manage to shape these beliefs and practices to a certain degree, but the process was necessarily a long one. The period covered by this book was essentially the first stage of this process, which entailed educating Catholics about the erroneous nature of such practices and the culpability of those involved in them. Popular forms of belief and practice, as they regarded healing, were also dealt with by the Protomedicato tribunals in Italy and Spain – for it is time to bring them into our discussion. However, while the Protomedicato tribunals sought to enforce their authority over the practice of all of the healing arts, they drew the line at healing practices judged to contain "superstitious" – that is magical or diabolical – elements, such as charms or invocations. This was left for the Church, in the form of the Inquisitions, to judge and prosecute. It was not just a question of recognizing the authority of a superior tribunal, like the Inquisition. Physicians considered their art to be a natural one, albeit one that was made possible by God-given knowledge and virtues; their expertise ceased when a disease was caused by magic (for they did acknowledge this possibility).

What can the Protomedicato tribunals tell us about the relationship between belief and authority? How do they compare with the Inquisitions? The role of "protophysician" and the tribunal he headed are symptomatic of the disciplining process in European society. As with the Inquisitions, we have a case of tribunals pre-dating the Reformations, in both Spain and Italy, whose powers and reach were nevertheless strengthened from the middle of the sixteenth century onwards. It would be too simplistic to single out the Protestant Reformation as the origin of this process; in many ways it may also have been a symptom of it. The expansion of the Protomedicato tribunals was also part and parcel of the medicalization of Italian and Spanish society during the fifteenth and sixteenth centuries, evident in the rise of university medical faculties, Colleges of Physicians, and hospitals. Still, by a strange coincidence, Bologna's Protomedicato tribunal was set up in the same year in which Luther nailed his theses to the church door in Wittenberg, 1517. Its functions were by no means new, but the founding of a specific tribunal sent out a signal that the response was no longer to be haphazard but methodical and rigorous. Such, at least, was the intent; the actual practice of such tribunals was always limited by the means at their disposal.

In their supervision and regulation of the medical field, one of the main functions of the Protomedicato tribunals was the prosecution of unlicensed healing. The Protomedicato tribunals represented both public authority, overseeing the other branches of medicine on behalf of the state, and a professional group, the physicians – two functions not always in harmony with each other. In prosecuting illicit or unlicensed medical practice, the activities of the Protomedicato tribunals were not primarily punitive; instead, like the Inquisitorial courts of the time, they sought admittance of guilt, repentance, and the offender's "return to the fold" by limiting their healing activities within licit bounds. The usual sanction against unlicensed healers was to oblige them to become licensed. Their approach toward offenders was, in practice, flexible and pragmatic, open to negotiation – quite in contrast to the sharp words and substantial financial penalties threatened in their official edits.

But then this was typical of the exercise of much authority in early modern Europe. The protophysicians (like the inquisitors) were aware that plaintiffs might be using them to settle disputes, rather than in the selfless pursuit of unlicensed healing (or witchcraft). In 1595, as one example among many, the "humble Laura Diola" petitioned the Bolognese Protomedicato for "the refund of three ducats from a Neapolitan man practicing medicine; he having taken to treat said Laura and having crippled her, she wished that her money be returned to her, especially since she heard of the bad practice of said Neapolitan." This was breach of contract, an exchange gone wrong; the fact that he was unlicensed was almost incidental in Laura's mind.

The impact of the Protomedicato tribunals on unlicensed healing was a work in progress, not something that was achievable once and for all. The sick continued to seek out a wide range of healers, according to their own needs and expectations; the practitioner's possession of a license (or not) was rarely their primary concern. Moreover, the impact of the different Protomedicato tribunals varied, given that there was no centralized authority to coordinate their activities – although despite this, the tribunals had remarkably similar objectives and functions.

When it came to the Protomedicato tribunals, Italian and Spanish physicians found themselves in a position of power. This was not always the case. They might find their thoughts and actions limited and shaped by the Inquisitions as well, more often than not in the form of "Indexes of Prohibited Books." These sound very ominous to us, the very essence of Catholic "thought control." The censorship of books by the Spanish and Roman Inquisitions is an often misunderstood area of their activities, and recent research into the process of censorship and the trade in books has revised our understanding. The Inquisitions had no monopoly in the matter of censorship, nor were they able to exercise a universal or even effective system of control over the circulation of books.

Throughout Europe episcopal authorities had their own system of licensing and censorship, as did the state authorities. For example, in the early 1500s, in one of the centers of the European book trade, the Venetian government practiced pre-publication censorship of books. When an author or publisher sought a license to publish, in a few cases the Council of Ten asked someone to read the work to make sure that it was free of religious, moral, or political error. This process was formalized by law in 1527. Later, once the Council of Trent was underway, Catholic state and religious authorities moved beyond isolated acts of confiscation and issued edicts and indexes of prohibited, Protestant books. By the late 1540s the Venetian Republic moved to draft such an index, as Milan, Lucca, and Siena had already done. Published in 1549, it was entitled (to give an idea of its thrust), a "Catalogue of various works, compositions and books, which as heretical, suspect, impious and scandalous are declared condemned and prohibited in this glorious city of Venice and in the entire most illustrious Venetian domain."

Although most of the Italian states had compiled their own indexes by this time, they were only put into effect in a half-hearted way. In part this was due to the lack of any guidance from Rome, symbolized by the absence of a papal index to act as a guide. This absence was a minor example of the general inadequacy of papal leadership at this time, which had only recently managed to call the Council of Trent. Pope Paul IV commissioned the Holy Office to prepare the first official Roman Index, which it did in 1559. It was longer than earlier indexes and included new categories of prohibitions, the first to manifest the "puritanism" characteristic of Counter-Reformation censorship. Newly prohibited were a number of authors and works that were not heretical, but were judged to be anticlerical, immoral, lascivious, or obscene. In addition, the Roman Index banned the printing and possession of bibles in any vernacular except with the Inquisition's permission. It also listed about 60 European publishers, primarily German and Swiss, whose total output was proscribed. However, its greatest significance lay in the fact that it was the first index to be promulgated unequivocally by the papacy in its capacity as spiritual leader of Catholic Christendom.

The pope demanded that it be implemented and enforced, and to a large extent it was, although no ruler wished to harm local print production and bookselling. Moreover, there was some dispute over what works were considered heretical and could be confiscated. An early grievance against the Inquisition was that a book could be classified as "prohibited" merely for containing the name of a heretic or an innocuous text by him. Things became slightly more straightforward in 1564, with the publication of a second Index in Rome after the close of the Council of Trent. Known as the "Tridentine Index," its contents mirrored the diversity of views expressed at Trent. The few changes over the earlier Index produced for Paul IV tended toward moderation. It became apparent that censors should more sensibly ban only sections of books and not books in their entirety. The expurgation of passages was a potentially mammoth task, but one undertaken with increased zeal following the institution of a full Congregation of cardinals to compile future Indexes, in 1571, and even more so with the publication of the third papal Index in 1596. It was not made any easier by the fact that the two Congregations, the Holy Office and the Index (the latter dependent on the former), did not always see eye to eye. In any case the authors of works were not their real concern; the focus remained on prohibiting the publication or dissemination of prohibited works.

Did it succeed? On one level, the functions of the local Inquisitions in this matter were limited by practical considerations. First of all the inquisitors were not experts on literature. By the time they got around to condemning something, it had already been circulating for five years or more. Since there were several licensing and censoring authorities, a printer or bookseller could sometimes defy the Inquisition, given that a particular book could be approved and licensed by one body – the bishop, say – while being condemned by another. Moreover, the actual search for books was not the result of active policing but depended on informed opinion and, even more importantly, chance denunciations, discoveries, and voluntary compliance by booksellers.

On another level, the combined forces of the Index and the Inquisition undeniably affected Italian intellectual developments – just how much remains an ongoing source of scholarly debate. They were by no means the only, nor perhaps the major, influence at work. Italy changed profoundly during the course of the sixteenth century, but only a part of this transformation can be attributed to the Counter-Reformation. The Counter-Reformation itself must be seen in the broader context of economic, intellectual, political, and religious change as both cause and effect. For example, with the advent of the Reformation, deviation in natural philosophy began to appear more dangerous. Heresy was seen to threaten social order, as we have seen, and departure from tradition in any aspect of learned culture could be seen by Church authorities as potentially disruptive of established authority. As part of the Catholic Church's moves to define dogma and control dissent, the Council of Trent took various decisions relating to ideas about the natural world and how to know it. It encouraged a knowledge of nature that stressed order and intelligibility over disorder and caprice, repudiating things like divination and magic, including astrology. It approved rules for the proper interpretation of Scripture, making the authority of the established interpretation of any biblical passage paramount. These decisions were to have considerable consequences when it came to dealing with apparent conflicts between biblical statements about the natural world and the assertions of natural science.

The study of natural philosophy nonetheless remained vibrant in Italy throughout the sixteenth century and beyond. Investigations into the body, in the form of anatomical demonstrations, were actively encouraged by the papacy. When the papal university of "La Sapienza" was rebuilt, it included both a church (St Ivo) and an anatomical theater, modeled after Padua's. Likewise, the subject of botany flourished at Italian universities. Rome was also the home of the flagship educational institution of the Society of Jesus, the Collegio Romano. During this same time the Jesuits, the leading Catholic teaching order of the period, introduced yet more mathematics and physics into their colleges. Many of the teachers were important names in the innovations of the scientific revolution, especially in the mathematical sciences. But Italian Jesuits were careful, too. They had a sensitive regard to such issues as matter theory and Copernicanism. Indeed, Italian natural philosophers tended to focus on the experimental, steering clear of broadly speculative or theoretical arguments in their investigations. For the most part they remained outside the mainstream of the new scientific thought, as it developed in the seventeenth century, wedded to a theoretical version of Aristotelianism. In this way they avoided clashes with Church authority.

How does Spain compare? In 1584 the secretary of the Inquisition in Logroño reported on "a Dr León, a medical doctor, who said he was a citizen of Valladolid, with two sons whom he was taking to study in Bordeaux. When he was asked why he was taking his sons to Bordeaux, where there was little security in matters of religion, and when there were so many good universities in Spain, he replied that if he did not find conditions suitable in Bordeaux he would take them to Paris." Nothing was done to impede the doctor. Several other Spanish scholars continued to study in France, but the Inquisition and the government turned a blind eye. This would be unremarkable were it not for the fact that in 1559 Philip II had forbidden all subjects of the crown of Castile from studying abroad (with the exception of the Italian universities of Bologna, Rome, and Naples and the Portuguese university of Coimbra). This legislation, combined with the censorship powers of the Inquisition, has been interpreted by historians as having turned Spain into a virtual police state. The legislation worked, in that it all but ended the matriculation of Spanish students into "heresy-ridden" French universities like Montpellier (as well as further afield). When Europe had been of one faith, scholars traveled freely across national boundaries; now there was an increasing tendency to remain within the safety of their own.

However, Spaniards were still able to travel outside of the country to study; that is, when their own finances permitted. The frontiers were never closed.

With regard to censorship, historians of the Spanish Inquisition have interpreted its impact on literature and the circulation of ideas in two contrasting ways: as either a success in purging heresy, with no negative influence elsewhere, or as a total suppression of creativity. Both views have in common the assumption that the censorship system functioned effectively, which is to overestimate the practical capabilities of the Renaissance state. As in Italy, neither the Index nor the censorship system produced an adequate machinery of control. To this we must add the consideration that most European states had comparable systems in place, yet none appears to have suffered significantly. Mechanisms of censorship on their own were of limited significance in altering intellectual development. During the sixteenth century, the Spanish Inquisition's impact on natural philosophy, for instance, was largely indirect. Spaniards who took learning seriously tended to go to Italy. Due to continued access to Italian and foreign scholarship, scientific enquiry did not collapse. Scientific books written by Catholics tended to circulate freely in Spain, and in any case the Index had a negligible impact on the overall accessibility of books. The picture changed somewhat during the seventeenth century, however, when many of the innovators in natural philosophy and medicine were English and Dutch scholars. Because they were Protestants, their books automatically fell within the scope of the Inquisitorial bans in Spain. Increasingly, the Inquisition was seen as an obstacle to learning by Spanish scholars, a barrier to the latest discoveries. Spanish science became conservative, its culture isolated, even if this isolation was due only in part to the Inquisition, given the country's nationalistic sense of mission and superiority during this period.

The effects of the Inquisitions' prohibitions were not on science or knowledge as such, but on certain of their features, approaches, and pursuits. And while the negative functions of the Inquisitions and Indexes in terms of repression and impediment have long been the subject of debate, historians of Italy and Spain are only now seeking to reconstruct their more "creative" function as agents of change in shaping early modern science and society. For instance, the Italian Church's prohibitions against astrology, referred to on p. 616, seem to have had the effect of driving a wedge between the figure of the scientist and the astrologer, before this epistemological shift happened elsewhere, bringing about a change in astronomy's form and status as a discipline. Although not exactly what the Church intended, it serves as an example of the impact it might have.

In conclusion, what can a comparison of the Inquisitorial and Protomedicato tribunals in Italy and Spain tell us about the relationship between authority and belief during the Renaissance? First of all, both suggest how the process of social disciplining usually associated with the Reformations actually predated them. That said, there is no doubt that they then gathered momentum, focus, and a sense of purpose from the middle of the sixteenth century as part of the reaction to the religious and social upheavals of the period. In fact, the exercise of authority in the control of belief in both the religious and medical fields is best seen as a process. On the one hand, both sets of tribunals worked with specific goals in mind, the re-establishment of divine order in their respective fields. On the other hand, neither was able to achieve them during the period covered by this book and, it could be argued, neither really aimed to. That is to say, they were both eminently practical in what they sought to achieve, cognizant of the limitations within which they worked. While the Inquisitions were successful in eliminating "Lutheranism," they had an uphill struggle when it came to popular religious beliefs and practices – but then these were perceived as less of a threat. So the tribunals ended up acting in a generalized role as overseer, responsible for maintaining "order."

Second, and following on from this, the tribunals were instruments of authority, not authoritarianism. The Inquisitions were not instruments of religious fanaticism tyrannically imposed on society. They were clearly more menacing than the Protomedicato tribunals: people were executed as a result of the Inquisitions' program of religious homogenization, even if it they had no monopoly on the burning of heretics (when we consider England, France, and Germany, where executions continued well into the seventeenth century). However, to speak in terms of effective thought control is to equate their actual impact with their own propaganda. Individual actors in the Inquisitorial and Protomedicato trial records alike rarely seem to be overwhelmed or terrorized by the tribunals; they generally negotiate, or try to, even from a position of relative weakness. The impact of authority on belief was not always that which was expected or sought. Tribunals varied from effective in some areas to ineffectual in others. Finally, the actions of the two sets of tribunals have to be seen in their complex geopolitical contexts. With neither the Iberian nor the Italian peninsula existing as a single, unitary state during the period, the historian must inevitably focus on the "local." The findings here suggest the continuing existence of a vast diversity of belief alongside (and despite) the Renaissance exercise of authority, and its search for conformity.

SUGGESTIONS FOR FURTHER READING

Baldini, Ugo. "The Roman Inquisition's Condemnation of Astrology: Antecedents, Reasons and Consequences," in Gigliola Fragnito, ed., *Church, Censorship and Culture in Early Modern Italy*. Cambridge: Cambridge University Press, 2001, 79–110.

Black, Christopher. *Church, Religion, and Society in Early Modern Italy*. Basingstoke and New York: Palgrave, 2004, 171–96.

Chartier, Roger. *The Cultural Uses of Print in Early Modern France*, trans.. L. Cochrane. Princeton: Princeton University Press, 1987.

Contreras, Jaime. "The Impact of Protestantism in Spain, 1520–1600," in *Inquisition and Society in Early Modern Europe*, ed. and trans. Stephen Haliczer. London: Croom Helm, 1987, 47–63.

Dear, Peter. "The Church and the New Philosophy," in S. Pumfrey, P. Rossi, and M. Slawinski, eds, *Science, Culture and Popular Belief in Renaissance Europe*. Manchester: Manchester University Press, 1991, 119–39.

Del Col, Andrea, ed. *Domenico Scandella Known as Menocchio: His Trials before the Inquisition (1583–1599)*. Medieval and Renaissance Texts and Studies. Binghamton: State University of New York, 1996.

Fragnito, Gigliola, ed. *Church, Censorship and Culture in Early Modern Italy*. Cambridge: Cambridge University Press, 2001.

Gentilcore, David. *From Bishop to Witch: The System of the Sacred in Early Modern Terra d'Otranto.* Manchester: Manchester University Press, 1992.

—— "'All That Pertains to Medicine:' Protomedici and Protomedicati in Early Modern Italy." *Medical History* 38 (1994): 121–42.

—— *Healers and Healing in Early Modern Italy.* Manchester: University of Manchester Press, 1998.

Ginzburg, Carlo. *The Cheese and the Worms: The Cosmos of a Sixteenth-century Miller.* Baltimore: Johns Hopkins University Press, 1980.

—— *Night Battles: Witchcraft and Agrarian Cults.* Baltimore: Johns Hopkins University Press, 1983.

Grendler, Paul. *The Roman Inquisition and the Venetian Press.* Princeton: Princeton University Press, 1977.

Henningsen, Gustav. *The Witches' Advocate: Basque Witchcraft and the Spanish Inquisition, 1609–1614.* Reno: University of Nevada Press, 1980.

—— "'The Ladies From Outside': An Archaic Pattern of the Witches' Sabbath," in B. Ankarloo and G. Henningsen, eds, *Early Modern European Witchcraft: Centres and Peripheries.* Oxford: Oxford University Press, 1993, 191–215.

Kamen, Henry. *The Spanish Inquisition.* London: Weidenfeld & Nicolson, 1965.

—— *Inquisition and Society in Spain in the Sixteenth and Seventeenth Centuries.* Bloomington: Indiana University Press, 1985.

—— *The Phoenix and the Flame: Catalonia and the Counter-Reformation.* New Haven and London: Yale University Press, 1993.

—— "Spain," in B. Scribner, R. Porter, and M. Teich, eds, *The Reformation in National Context.* Cambridge: Cambridge University Press, 1994, 202–14.

—— *The Spanish Inquisition: An Historical Revision.* New Haven and London: Yale University Press, 1997.

Lanning, John Tate and John Jay TePaske. *The Royal Protomedicato: The Regulation of the Medical Profession in the Spanish Empire.* Durham, N.C.: Duke University Press, 1985.

Martin, John Jeffries. "Per un'analisi quantitativa dell'Inquisizione veneziana," in A. Del Col and G. Paolin, eds, *L'Inquisizione romana in Italia nell'età moderna: archivi, problemi di metodo e nuove ricerche.* Rome: Ministero per i beni culturali e ambientali, 1991, 143–57.

—— *Venice's Hidden Enemies: Italian Heretics in a Renaissance City.* Berkeley: University of California Press, 1993.

Martin, Ruth. *Witchcraft and Inquisition in Venice, 1550–1650.* Oxford: Blackwell, 1989.

Monter, William. *Frontiers of Heresy: The Spanish Inquisition from the Basque Lands to Sicily.* Cambridge: Cambridge University Press, 1990.

Nalle, Sara. *God in La Mancha: Religious Reform and the People of Cuenca.* Baltimore: Johns Hopkins University Press, 1992.

O'Neill, Mary. "Sacerdote ovvero strione: Ecclesiastical and Superstitious Remedies in the Sixteenth Century," in S. L. Kaplan, ed., *Understanding Popular Culture: Europe from the Middle Ages to the Nineteenth Century.* Berlin and New York: Mouton, 1984, 53–83.

Pomata, Gianna. *Contracting a Cure: Patients, Healers and the Law in Early Modern Bologna.* Baltimore: Johns Hopkins University Press, 1998.

Rawlings, Helen. *Church, Religion, and Society in Early Modern Spain.* Basingstoke and New York: Palgrave, 2002.

—— *The Spanish Inquisition.* Oxford: Blackwell, 2005.

Reinhard, Wolfgang. "Reformation, Counter-Reformation, and the Early Modern State: A Reassessment." *Catholic Historical Review* 75 (1989): 383–404.

Ruggiero, Guido. "The Strange Death of Margarita Marcellini: Male, Signs, and the Everyday World of Pre-modern Medicine." *American Historical Review* 106 (2001): 1141–58.

Schilling, Heinz. "Confessional Europe," in vol. 2 of *Handbook of European History, 1400–1600*, eds T. Brady, H. Oberman, and J. Tracy. Leiden: Brill, 1994–5, 641–81.

Seidel Menchi, Silvana. "Italy," in B. Scribner, R. Porter, and M. Teich, eds, *The Reformation in National Context*. Cambridge: Cambridge University Press, 1994, 181–201.

—— "The Book and the Reformation in Italy," in J. F. Gilmont, ed., *The Reformation and the Book*. Aldershot: Ashgate, 1998, 319–67.

Tedeschi, John. *The Prosecution of Heresy: Collected Studies on the Inquisition in Early Modern Italy*. Binghamton: State University of New York Center for Medieval and Early Renaissance Studies, 1991.

Terrada, López, Alvar Vidal Martínez, and M. L. Martínez Vidal, eds. "El Tribunal del Real Protomedicato en la Monarquía Hispánica." *Dynamis* 16 (1996).

CHAPTER THIRTY-TWO

CHRISTIANITY IN SIXTEENTH-CENTURY BRAZIL

Alida C. Metcalf

In 1554 Pedro Correia and João de Sousa became the first Jesuit martyrs in Brazil. The men, both talented linguists, had traveled from the Jesuit residence in São Paulo deep into Guarani territory to the south and west. The details of their deaths – one shot with arrows, the other's head smashed with a war club – were soon known in São Paulo. There, the Jesuits had complex reactions to these deaths. On the one hand, they were greatly saddened by the loss of their best interpreter and by the treachery exhibited by the Guarani. On the other, they saw the deaths as "glorious" and worthy of emulation. "These blessed brothers suffered death in holy obedience, in the preaching of the Gospel, in peace, and for the love and charity of their neighbors," José de Anchieta wrote to Ignatius of Loyola, and "all of us wish mightily and ask God through constant prayer that we might die in this way."[1]

This image of a Christian missionary killed as he evangelized, which the sixteenth-century Jesuits of Brazil saw as glorious and worthy of emulation, is how we continue to imagine indigenous resistance to Christian evangelism in the Americas. One of the most powerful of such images was created in the 1986 film *The Mission*, where, in the opening scene, a Jesuit who seeks to open a mission among the Guarani above the Iguaçu Falls is rejected and returned: strapped to a wooden cross, he plunges to his death. Yet such instances of Christian evangelism meeting violent resistance should not completely shape how we view the expansion of Christianity into the Americas. A more common response was acceptance and adaptation. Christianity, as it was preached by the Jesuits, was not so much rejected as it was transformed. A hybrid spiritual experience that spoke to the needs of indigenous, mixed-race, and even Portuguese colonists in Brazil was the result. And imbedded in this new interpretation of Christianity were seeds of resistance to Portuguese colonialism, especially to the practice of slavery.

Another setting should occupy our thoughts as we contemplate Christianity and resistance to European colonialism in sixteenth-century Brazil. Thirty years after Correia and Sousa's deaths, in the *sertão* or wilderness of Brazil's capital Salvador da Bahia, a congregation had formed around a charismatic man known to his followers as "the Pope." This pope led his believers in trance-like rituals where they chanted in tongues, danced, fell to the ground in spasms, and were perfumed and cleansed with tobacco smoke. The men and women in this movement, known as *"Santidade"*

438   SOCIETAS AMERICANA.

Petrus Correa, et Ioannes Sosa, Lusitani Societatis IESU. sagittis confixi in Brasilia, apud Carigios; Mense Decembri. A 1554.
C. Screta del.   Melch. Küsell f.

PETRUS CORREA, & JOANNES SOSA.

Vales impetus habebas ad Mundum, tales habeas ad Authorem Mundi, scitè monet S. Ambrosius, conformiter ad illud Apostoli Rom 6. *Sicut exhibuistis membra vestra servire iniquitati ad iniquitatem, ita exhibete membra vestra servire Justitiæ ad Sanctificationem.* Cujus Apostolici moniti vim cernere est in Petro Correa luculenter expressam, quo sicut nihil fuit initio in vita sæculari immanius, & in miseros Brasilos truculentius, ita postliminio in vita Religiosa nihil illo benignius, & commodis eorundem procurandis impensius. Natus in Lusitania clarissimo sanguine, Regia stipendia secutus est in Brasiliam, animo Provincias illas Sceptro Lusitanico subjiciendi, seque & suos quâ posset arte & marte ex spolijs barbarorum ditandi. Nemo illo totâ Brasiliâ inter Lusitanos ditior, sed nemo etiam in indigenas sævior, quibus spoliandis, & post erepta omnia durissimæ servituti addicendis, mille artifex evaserat. Littora enim Brasiliæ navi oberrans, exposito proopportunitate capturæ in terram milite, inermes Brasilos veluti indagine cingebat, ferarum instar insectabatur, contráque omne jus & fas comprehensos. pro mancipijs ad durissimos Sacchari parandi, aliáque infimorum servitiorum opera Lusitanis divendebat, neq; melius quàm canes habebat. Hæc & alia id
genus

Figure 32.1 The martyrdom of Pedro Correia and João de Sousa, 1554. From Matthias Tanner, *Societatis Jesu. Americana.* Prague: Typis Universitatis Carolo-Ferdinandeae, 1675. Courtesy of the John Carter Brown Library at Brown University.

or "Holiness," believed that God was coming to free them from their servitude, that Mary and Jesus would soon walk on earth, and that evil slave-owners would soon themselves become slaves or converted into animals and birds of the forest. The congregation instituted confession, baptism, and schools for the children, and made rosaries for prayer.

Known as the *Santidade de Jaguaripe*, this movement is reflective of a hybrid religious tradition that began in Brazil as European Christianity fused with indigenous and African beliefs in the sixteenth century. It was a spiritual experience that characterized the lives of Indian and African slaves and the free poor, many of whom were of mixed race. Those who practiced it saw themselves as Christian, even if the Jesuits and the Holy Office of the Inquisition saw their beliefs as heretical or the work of the devil. Deeply interwoven into the spiritual expression of the Santidade de Jaguaripe were beliefs drawn from Christianity that rejected the dominance of the Portuguese colonists. The powerful message of the Christian apocalypse and millennium, coupled with indigenous myths of destruction and rebirth and with an indigenous tradition of wandering charismatic prophets, became a means through which the believers rejected the institution of slavery and the power of the Portuguese colonists.

The roots of the hybrid spiritual tradition that underlay the *Santidade de Jaguaripe* began with the "way of proceeding" of the first Jesuit missionaries as they presented Christianity to the Tupi- and Guarani-speaking peoples of Brazil. The Society of Jesus, or Jesuits, arrived in Brazil with the newly appointed royal governor, Tomé de Sousa, in 1549, when Brazil was hardly an unknown territory. Officially discovered in 1500, Portuguese, French, Spanish, and English ships, driven by the dyewood trade, had been calling along its long coastline to load the logs, known as Brazilwood, for 50 years. A few settlements had begun along the coast, such as at the Bay of All Saints, Pernambuco, Ilhéus, and São Vicente, and the Portuguese crown had even attempted private colonization schemes by granting huge tracts of land to individuals to colonize, few of which had met with much success. Anxious to protect his claim to Brazil, the Portuguese king decided to create a royal colony and to authorize the Society of Jesus to begin the evangelization of Brazil. The justification for the colonization of Brazil was, as articulated by the King of Portugal, "so that the people of that land would be converted to our holy Catholic faith."[2]

Of primary importance to the first Jesuits in Brazil was that the indigenous peoples of Brazil should willingly accept Christianity. This approach was consistent with Jesuit missions in Europe, where sermons and informal preaching were stressed, as well as in their early missions in the Middle East, India, Japan, and China. The essential message brought by the Jesuits was that unbelievers must be persuaded to convert to Christianity in order to enjoy eternal life. In the early letters from Brazil, Jesuits constantly describe how they talked, presented arguments, preached, taught through dialogues, and recited prayers to the Indians. Yet all of the first Jesuits lacked even the most fundamental requirements for this missionary work; none spoke the languages of Brazil, and none had studied the peoples whom they hoped to persuade. Missionizing, therefore, depended on local interpreters and informants. The ideal interpreter-informant was a man like Pedro Correia, who was experienced in the languages and cultures of Brazil. Living in Brazil since 1534, Correia had once made his living as a slave trader, but in 1549 he entered the Society of Jesus, quickly becoming their best interpreter.

Jesuits developed persuasive arguments to kindle a desire among Indians to convert to Christianity; these arguments were then translated into language and concepts preached to Tupi and Guarani peoples. Leonardo Nunes wrote that the Indians "greatly fear death and the day of judgment and hell," and that this led many to convert in order to be saved. Nunes urged his interpreter, Pedro Correia, "always to touch on this in the conversations, because the fear puts them in great confusion." Pedro Correia assured Indians, "if they believed in God that not only would our Lord give them great things in heaven . . . but that in this world on their lands he would give them many things that were hidden." A theme stressed by Vicente Rodrigues through his interpreters was that "the time of dreams had passed" and that it was time for Indians to "wake up and hear the word of God, our Lord."

Jesuits recognized that they had to move beyond language in order to present Christianity in appealing ways. One Jesuit believed that "because they love musical things, we, by playing and singing among them, will win them." João de Azpilcueta adapted the Lord's Prayer to "their way of singing" so that the Indian boys would learn it faster and enjoy it more. Manuel da Nóbrega, leader of the Jesuit mission in Brazil, disclosed not only that the Jesuits sang the "songs of Our Lord" in Indian tones and to the accompaniment of Indian instruments but that these rhythms came from "their celebrations when they kill enemies and when they walk around drunk." To Nóbrega this was perfectly justifiable, because if Indians gave up certain customs, such as cannibalistic ceremonies, they could retain traditions, such as music, if lifted up towards different, spiritual ends. Similarly, Jesuits began to imitate the style of preaching used by chiefs and shamans: using Indian intonations, they preached at dawn, walked through the village while preaching, and even beat their chests for emphasis. The year before he died, for example, Brother Pedro Correia headed west, paddling down the Tietê River for eight or nine days, and at every village he preached for two hours at dawn "because that was the time that the chiefs and shamans customarily preached."

Although the first letters written by Jesuits from Brazil extol the rapid progress of their mission, they met much initial resistance from village shamans. The resistance of shamans and wandering prophets to Christianity also shaped the hybrid religious tradition later visible in the *Santidade de Jaguaripe*. Village shamans typically countered Jesuit preaching with their own discourse. Using their authority as healers, shamans proclaimed that the Jesuits brought death. One Jesuit wrote that the shamans persuaded the Indians that "in baptism we put death into them" or that calling on Jesus or making the sign of the cross was the "sign" of death. When an Indian chief in Bahia died after having been baptized, the shamans spread the word that "holy baptism had killed him." Jesuits accused cunning shamans of extracting knives, scissors, and fishhooks from the bodies of ill Indians, claiming that the Jesuits had put them there. While many Jesuits saw the shamans as acting for the devil in, as they saw it, the devil's campaign against their Christian mission, it is clear from their letters that the Jesuits perceived themselves in a battle of words: Jesuit preaching vs. that of the shamans. "Satan, who rules in this land," wrote António Pires, "ordered and taught the sorcerers many lies and deceptions to impede the good of souls." João de Azpilcueta described how the shamans "tell the Indians that I teach them so that when they are our slaves, I will have less work."

A more potent form of resistance to the Christian message came from wandering prophets who periodically emerged among Tupi- and Guarani-speaking peoples. This was one of the few indigenous religious practices that the Jesuits accepted as evidence of a religious faith. After residing in Brazil only a few months, Nóbrega wrote that the Indians "worshiped nothing nor knew God" but that "from time to time a sorcerer [wandering prophet] appeared in the villages" and "preached that there was no need to work, that the crops would grow on their own, that arrows would hunt the game, that the old would become young, that warriors would kill many of their enemies and that the people would eat many captives." After hearing these words, which the wandering prophet distorted by speaking them through a gourd, he notes that the Indians "especially the women, began to shake, throw themselves on the ground, and froth at the mouth." Then, "the sorcerer would cure them and holiness (santidad) would enter them."

Jean de Léry, a French Calvinist who lived in Brazil for several months in 1557, wrote a detailed description of a ceremony led by wandering prophets who traveled from village to village proclaiming that "by their communication with spirits they can give to anyone they please the strength to vanquish enemies in war, and, what is more, can make grow the big roots and the fruits." Léry observed the use of *maracas* (rattles) and *petum* (tobacco) in the ceremony. These prophets shook the rattles continuously so that "the spirit might thereafter speak" and repeatedly took "a wooden cane four or five feet long, at the end of which was burning some of the dried herb *Petun* [sic]," and blowing the smoke in all directions they would say: "[s]o that you may overcome your enemies, receive all of you the spirit of strength." According to his interpreters, Léry writes, the songs lamented the passing of the ancestors and praised the day when the living would rejoin them. The songs referred to a previous flood "that had once swelled so high above their bounds that all the earth was covered, and all the people in the world were drowned, except for the ancestors, who took refuge in the highest trees."

The early Portuguese colonists coined the term *santidade* – "sanctity" or "holiness" – to describe such wandering prophets and their Messianic movements. Those who had lived in Brazil for a number of years recognized that *santidades* were dangerous for outsiders. Jesuit Brother Pedro Correia explained that after the arrival of a "saint" who promised health and victory in battle, and who decorated pumpkins to look like heads – complete with hair, noses, eyes, and mouths, and adorned with colorful feathers – the Indians, men and women, danced and sang around them all day and night. These dances were accompanied by copious amounts of drinking. Two of the best interpreters of São Vicente, recounts Pedro Correia in a letter, went to a village where a *santidade* was going on in 1551, and the "saints" ordered them killed – and they were.

Correia's mission, which led to his death in 1554, coincided with a turning point in the Jesuit mission in Brazil as the fathers and brothers realized that powerful preaching – whether modeled on the classical rhetorical tradition of the Renaissance, new forms of preaching that were developing in the Counter-Reformation, or the art of the great shaman preachers of Tupi Guarani society – was no longer enough.

Independent chiefs were successfully resisting the expansion of Portuguese farms and settlements. The inexplicable illnesses and plagues, which we now know were diseases unknown in the Americas and introduced by Europeans with catastrophic results, swept through Indian villages, convincing many that the shamans had been right: Jesuits were bringing sickness and death. Moreover, wandering prophets began to attack Jesuits. Anchieta described a prophet in the wilderness of São Vicente in 1557 who intended to destroy the Jesuit Church. "Wherever he goes," Anchieta writes, "all follow and they wander from here to there leaving their own houses." He acquires followers by blowing smoke from his mouth over them, Anchieta explains, and in this way he gives them his spirit and makes them his followers.

Thus when Nóbrega returned to Salvador following the death of Correia and Sousa, and found the new governor of Brazil, Mem de Sá (1557–72), prepared to force the Indians living around the capital city of Salvador into submission, he agreed to support the governor's violent campaign. Setbacks in their mission led Nóbrega and other Jesuits in Bahia to see the governor's use of force as a step forward in the conversion of Indians. In May of 1558, a disillusioned Nóbrega agreed that defeating the Indians was the first step to achieving conversion. He expressed anger that the Portuguese in Brazil were accommodating themselves to the ways of Indians – "the most vile and sad people of the world."

Governor Mem de Sá's military campaign brought war the likes of which had never before been seen in Brazil. He ordered the men of an entire Indian village killed, and the women and children brought back to Salvador as war captives, which meant certain slavery. "Never has another such war been waged in this land," wrote one Jesuit, and "not only these Indians, but the whole coast will be shocked and afraid." The Portuguese exploited the power of their horses, ships, and guns in battle and gained an edge over Indian villages around the shores of the Bay of All Saints and along the coast of Ilhéus to the south. Mem de Sá's campaign eliminated many independent and powerful Indian chiefs, who had negotiated directly with the governor. The campaign led to the consolidation of independent Indian villages into large mission villages (*aldeias*) under the control of the governor and the Jesuits. In these mission villages, Indians lived under the supervision of Jesuits, who not only taught them Christianity but transformed their ways of life. From this point on, the *aldeias* were the defining institution of the Jesuit mission in Brazil.

As the landscape of power changed along the coast of Brazil in the 1560s and 1570s, so too did the forms of indigenous resistance to Portuguese colonialism. Independent and autonomous chiefs began to disappear, as did the village shamans. In their place, new kinds of wandering prophets began to emerge who preached a new kind of spiritual experience, one that incorporated Christian beliefs and teachings into indigenous myths and rituals. One of these new *santidades* clearly articulated resistance to slavery. In 1559, Nóbrega described a *santidade* that erupted on a plantation in Bahia, initiated by an Indian who arrived from another village. An unnamed man called together all slaves on the plantation to listen to this wandering prophet, who predicted that he would destroy the plantation and the master of it, that he would convert all who wished into birds, that he would kill all the caterpillars that were then infesting their food plots, and that he would spare the Jesuits but destroy their churches.

The *santidade*'s rejection of slavery confronted a basic fact of the Portuguese colonization of Brazil. Very early on slavery became established in Brazil. So comfortable were Portuguese mariners of the early sixteenth century with the slave trade – after all, it was Portuguese merchants, captains, and sailors who had developed a highly profitable slave trade from Africa in the fifteenth century – that they immediately saw it as a possible commercial venture in Brazil. Indians were sailing across the Atlantic as slaves for at least two decades from 1502–20. Demand for slaves in Brazil intensified when the first *donatários*, holders of colonization grants, began to build their colonies in Brazil. Three thousand slaves labored in the captaincy of São Vicente in 1548, which then had 600 colonists and six sugar mills. One of the sugar mills in São Vicente, probably the largest and best appointed, had 130 slaves, the vast majority of whom were Indian; only seven or eight slaves were from Africa.

When the Society of Jesus arrived in Brazil in 1549, the Jesuits questioned the legality of the means used to enslave Indians. Theoretically, Indians might only be legally enslaved through a war declared to be "just" or through the purchase of war captives known as *resgate* (ransoming). Both just-war theory and the practice of ransoming were well known to Europeans and, therefore, familiar to the early colonists of Brazil. The just-war doctrine had its roots in the arguments of classical philosophers, early Christian theologians, and the scholastic theologians of the late Middle Ages, all of whom had debated the morality of waging war. Once the declaration of a just war had been made by a sovereign, it not only legitimized the violence but also the enslavement of the prisoners of war. Ransoming was a well-known practice in the wars between Christian and Muslim kingdoms in the Renaissance. In Brazil it took on an added meaning because it was associated with the cannibalistic ceremonies of coastal Tupi groups. Through *resgate*, captives held for a cannibalism ceremony were purchased from an Indian group. Since Tupi groups obtained such captives from their inter-tribal wars and raids, such captives were deemed prisoners of war and therefore accepted as already enslaved.

Jesuits complained that colonists widely abused the practice of *resgate* and that many coastal indigenous groups had been enslaved through *saltos* – attacks by unscrupulous slave raiders. The fact that the majority of Indian slaves in Brazil had been illegally enslaved, they believed, undermined the Jesuits' evangelical mission. Jesuits insisted that the indigenous peoples of Brazil were free, and that enslavement could only occur through a properly certified just war or through true *resgate*. But a stricter application of the principles of just-war theory and ransoming did little to reduce the incidence of Indian slavery in Brazil. Nor did the law promulgated by King Sebastião, in March of 1570, which decreed the liberty of the indigenous peoples of Brazil. Sebastião's law allowed the concept of enslavement following a war declared by the king or by the king's governor to be just, and colonists could take as captives Indians from groups who "customarily" attacked the Portuguese, or who waged war to obtain captives for cannibalism ceremonies. Colonists might seize such Indians, provided that within two months the captives were registered with crown officials, who would verify their status, and if unsatisfied with the documentation presented could free them. Even with these loopholes that clearly maintained the principle and practice of Indian slavery, colonists immediately petitioned the king, stating that it would be detrimental to comply with the law because they needed workers for their sugar mills and plantations. The king then compromised the law even further by asking his two governors in Brazil and the Jesuits to come to an agreement that would guarantee the colonists laborers for their estates as long as they avoided egregiously unjust methods of enslavement.[3]

Slavery posed complicated problems for the Jesuits as they built their schools and residences in the Portuguese settlements. Through their letters it is clear that they were likely the only Europeans in Brazil in the sixteenth century who questioned the legality of Indian slavery. This stance brought them into conflict with the Portuguese colonists who had become highly invested in Indian slavery. Jesuits began to refuse to absolve colonists who knowingly held slaves proven to have been captured illegally. In one letter, the Jesuit João Gonçalves reflected on a situation that had emerged in Bahia in 1555 when a slaver arrived with three boatloads of Indian slaves to sell in Salvador. A Jesuit priest spoke out against those who sought to buy the slaves and refused to hear the confessions of the crew who had transported them. Similarly, Nóbrega describes "closing the door" of confession to the Portuguese colonists because of the illegal slave trade. Yet, from his first months in Brazil, Nóbrega believed that slaves were necessary for the Jesuit's own mission. He proposed that the *colégio* (school and residence) of Bahia be supported by ten slaves: five slaves would farm, while five would fish. Nearly a decade later, in 1558, he wrote that the "best thing that could be given to the Colégio would be two dozen slaves from Guinea" who would raise foodcrops and fish to support the Jesuits and their students. The Jesuits became slave-owners even though many of the early Jesuits had serious reservations about slavery. The head of the Jesuit order in Rome, Diego Laínez, wrote to Nóbrega that the Brazilian province could own slaves to support their residences and schools "so long as the slaves were justly possessed," by which he meant legally enslaved. Given the Jesuits' criticism of the widespread illegal enslavement of Indians in Brazil, the majority of slaves owned by the Society in Brazil were Africans.

Santidades not only attacked slavery, but they began to compete with the Jesuits' mission. A *santidade* that spread in the *sertão* of Ilhéus in 1561 or 1562 was described by the Jesuit Leonardo do Vale as a "blindness" that occurred when an unknown wandering prophet, who called himself a saint, appeared. The *santidade* disrupted the order established by the Jesuits in their newly created *aldeias*, and Vale suggests that God punished the followers of the *santidade* in the *aldeias* with a devastating smallpox epidemic. This plague, the first documented outbreak of smallpox in Brazil, began in Ilhéus and moved up the coast, and was followed by famine in 1563/4.

The power of *santidades* spread beyond the *aldeias* and sugar plantations and into the homes of the Portuguese colonists. A Portuguese woman who had lived in Bahia all of her life confessed to a visiting inquisitor that she had believed in one of these *santidades* as a girl. Luísa Barbosa revealed that when she was 12 (which would have been in 1566), a *santidade* arose in Bahia in which the Christian as well as the non-Christian (she used the word pagan) Indians said that "in their *santidade* was a God . . . who told them not to work because the crops would grow of their own accord." They also believed that "those who did not believe in the *santidade* would turn into sticks and stones." Barbosa said that the followers believed that "the white people would be converted into game for them to eat" and that the "law" of the Portuguese was worthless. At the time she claimed that all of the Christian and non-Christian (pagan) Indians living in the household of her father as well as in other Portuguese households said and believed in such things, and that she herself believed too and joined in the rituals.[4]

The *Santidade de Jaguaripe* followed on the heels of these earlier *santidades*, at a time when Salvador, the capital of Brazil, seemed to have become a center of European Christianity. In 1584, just as the *santidade* began in the adjacent *sertão*, the Jesuit provincial reported his pleasure with the celebrations held in the city. One was in honor of the consecration of six heads of the famed 11,000 virgins, associated with the popular cult of St Ursula. The pope himself had sent the heads to Brazil as relics. A festival, with vespers and a sung mass, along with a procession and skits, drew in many who confessed and received communion. Later that year, when a drought threatened the city and its surrounding plantations and farms, the populace gathered for public prayers, a procession, and a sermon, after which, the provincial reported, "God manifested his signs of benevolence" and it began to rain. Yet, at this same time, in the *sertão*, a new *santidade* began.

Interweaving indigenous beliefs with Christianity and articulating resistance to slavery and the Jesuit mission, the *Santidade de Jaguaripe* became part of the spiritual life of slaves and the free poor who lived in and on the margins of the Portuguese capital. If we are to believe the head of the Society of Jesus in Brazil, the *Santidade de Jaguaripe* went further than any previous *santidade* by threatening to replace the Jesuit mission. The Jesuit provincial's annual letter of 1585 explained how he and his fellow Jesuits saw the *Santidade de Jaguaripe* as a deeply disturbing new kind of resistance that violently rejected Portuguese colonialism and grotesquely distorted Christianity. The Jesuit provincial called the *santidade* a new kind of superstition, a "pestilence," and an invention of the devil. The provincial wrote that the *santidade*'s rites so imitated Christian rituals that "the Devil could persuade" the less wise that "our ways in no way differ from their ways; and if there are nevertheless differences, our ways stray from the truth."[5]

The description of the *Santidade de Jaguaripe* in the provincial's letter emphasized the extensive imitation of Christianity and of the Jesuits' own missionary enterprise. The provincial cited the ordaining of "a supreme high priest of their rites, as we ordain the Pope," the consecration of bishops and priests, and the institution of the confession of sins. He thought it would truly amaze his Jesuit readers in Portugal, Rome, and elsewhere to know that the believers in the *santidade* had created schools free of charge, celebrated mass, prayed with rosaries, substituted gourds for the altar bell, and manufactured books from bark and boards.

The provincial also described rituals associated with tobacco. These were clearly drawn from the indigenous tradition, but the provincial found them disgraceful and bordering on insanity. He wrote that after drinking the "juice [i.e., smoke] of a certain herb [tobacco] . . . they fall suddenly, half alive, and tremble in all their limbs." Writhing on the ground, as if "mad," the believers "twist their mouths indecently," stick out "their tongues in an unsightly way," and "speak amongst themselves without moving their lips." The provincial recognized all of this as the work of the devil, but the believers, he noted, were convinced that when these agitations end "they are washed with water and made holy; and whoever has produced the more horrible signs is thought to have attained the more sanctity."

The provincial clearly understood the beliefs of the *santidade* to be a form of resistance: the believers say, he wrote, that "their ancestors are to be conveyed here in a ship," that their ancestors will liberate them from "the most wretched servitude into the sweetness of freedom that they desire," and that "at the ancestors' coming the Portuguese will then at last totally perish," but if any of the Portuguese are to survive "they will be converted into fish or pigs or similar beasts." Whoever believes all this, the provincial related, "is promised salvation; anyone who does not will be torn by wild beasts and birds." When the Indians heard of the *santidade* and fled from the Portuguese estates, the provincial exclaimed that "they burned the Portuguese houses, laid waste their fields, razed the sugar mills to the ground, and cruelly put to death many Portuguese."

Coincidentally, when the first inquisitor of the Lisbon Inquisition arrived in Brazil, landing in the capital city of Salvador in 1591, the memory of the *Santidade de Jaguaripe* of 1585 was still fresh in the minds of the residents. As a result of the inquisitor's call for denunciations and confessions of sins and heresies, residents of the city and the surrounding rural parishes denounced those who had participated in the *santidade* some years before. Although most of the denunciations came from the Portuguese-born colonists, who generally did not join the *santidade*, several men of mixed Indian and Portuguese race, known as *mamelucos*, and a few Portuguese came to the inquisitor to confess that they had believed its message and had celebrated its rituals. These were the free poor members of colonial society who saw themselves as Christian and yet were drawn to the *santidade* in the *sertão*. Most claimed to the inquisitor that they had pretended to believe and that they had followed the rituals on the outside only, while on the inside they remained firmly Christian.

A group of men sent to contact the *santidade* in the wilderness frontier and to persuade the believers to descend to the Portuguese colony reflect the complicated and ambiguous intersection between Christianity and indigenous beliefs and rituals then characteristic of Portuguese colonial life. The men – largely a group of small farmers and the free poor, many of whom were mixed-race *mamelucos*, but including some Portuguese men, one or two mulattos, and a group of Indian archers – all had conflicting feelings about their expedition. The story they recounted to the inquisitor suggests that they intended to deceive the believers in the *santidade* by persuading them to descend to the plantation of a sugar planter, where they would most likely be enslaved. Yet, reading between the lines, it is clear that many of the *mamelucos* and Indian archers had already heard about the pope and his believers in the *sertão*, were intrigued by the movement, and were inclined to join in. Cristovão de Bulhões, a mixed-race *mameluco*/mulatto who would have been 19 or 20 at the time, described to the inquisitor that he had heard it said among the Indians that "St Mary, Our Lady, Mother of God" would descend from heaven and would arrive among the Indians. It would, he thought, be a "true holiness." Another *mameluco* youth of approximately the same age learned from the slaves in the parish where he lived that "God was coming now to free them from their captivity and to make them lords of the white people" and that "those who did not believe . . . would be converted into birds and animals of the forest." This youth wanted to go and see the pope for himself so that "with his own eyes he might see" the place where "it was said that God was," because "it seemed to him that this was the true God."

The *mameluco* Domingos Fernandes Nobre, who led the expedition into the wilderness to meet the *santidade*, also confessed to the inquisitor. His confession reveals the intensity of the believers who were convinced that the world as they knew it was about to be destroyed and a new one created. It seems that the believers spent their days in trance-like states in processions and rituals. Nobre first met Antônio, the leader of the *santidade* who was known as the pope, leading "his followers in orderly ranks of three, the women and children following behind." They approached him with their hands raised "shaking, making movements with their feet, hands and necks, and speaking a new language." But Nobre confessed that he too "wailed and lamented" in the Indian custom and "jumped and celebrated" with Antônio in the "Indian way" and "played" the Indian instruments and "sang" their songs and "drank the smoke" – the "sacred smoke" of the followers of the *santidade*. He revealed that the believers called him São Luís, or "Son of God."

According to several who met him, Antônio, the leader known as the pope, had been raised by the Jesuits and was a baptized Christian. Bras Dias told the inquisitor that Antônio had been raised in a Jesuit mission village and that he had run away from the Jesuits and "invented" the movement's beliefs and rituals, while Domingos Fernandes Nobre reported to the inquisitor that Antônio was "raised in the house of the fathers of the Society of Jesus during the time when they had mission villages in Tinharé." Antônio, then, was not raised in a traditional Indian village, but in a Jesuit *aldeia*. The Jesuits first contemplated a mission in Tinharé, located between Bahia and Ilhéus, in 1561, at the request of one of the region's Indian chiefs whom they had baptized. When the Jesuits first visited, they estimated that the region – the island and the adjacent coast on the mainland – had 24 Indian villages. Soon the Jesuits created two *aldeias* in the immediate region: Nossa Senhora da Assunção and São Miguel. Each mission village had a Jesuit father and brother, and between the two mission villages there were 6,000 Indians. It was here that the *santidade* spread in the *sertão* of Ilhéus in 1561 or 1562, immediately prior to the outbreak of the first smallpox epidemic. From Jesuit letters, it is clear that both the *santidade* and the smallpox epidemic affected the two mission villages. After the epidemic and the famine that followed it, the Indians abandoned the *aldeias*.

If indeed Antônio was raised in one of these two mission villages in Tinharé he most certainly had direct exposure to Christian doctrine. As a boy he would have attended the mission school and might have even been a translator. He had certainly heard of the *santidade* in the *sertão* of Ilhéus. As a child he survived the smallpox epidemic, but most likely he lost many members of his family to it. It seems likely that he fled with the others when the Indians abandoned the two mission villages. Eventually he fled to the *sertão*, where his *santidade* began. There Paulos Dias reported that the followers called Antônio "God" and said that Antônio claimed to have descended from the heavens and to have created all of the animals of the earth; Cristovão de Bulhões said that Antônio referred to himself as "God and Lord of the world." Two other leaders mentioned in the inquisition sources are a woman, known as Maria or as Mother of God, and her husband, Aricute, also known as the "second pope."

Drawn from the indigenous tradition as well as from Christianity, the *Santidade de Jaguaripe* reflects the role of religious belief and ritual in resistance to Portuguese colonial society. The movement blended an array of religious messages heard by Indians, Africans, *mamelucos*, and even Portuguese colonists who lived in the heterogeneous world of Bahia. Myths that told of the origins of Tupi peoples and rituals of purification once led by wandering prophets existed alongside of Christian teachings on the apocalypse and re-enactments of the sacraments of baptism and the mass. Both the inquisitor and the Jesuit provincial accepted as evidence of Christian teachings some beliefs that were inspired by an indigenous creation myth. For example, when the inquisitor heard the believers proclaiming that a flood had destroyed the earth, he understood them to mean Noah's flood. Yet, among the coastal Tupi, a creation myth told of the destruction of the earth by a flood and the survival of the people's ancestors, who escaped in the eye of a palm tree. In a Tupinambá myth recorded in the sixteenth century, Tamanduaré, angry at his brother Aricute, strikes the earth, causing a huge fountain of water to erupt, which floods the land. Tamanduaré escapes into the mountains with his wife and they find refuge at the top of a palm tree. Aricute, similarly, survives by climbing a Jenipapeiro tree. From these two brothers are descended the Tupi peoples. In his account to the inquisitor, Paulos Dias, a *mameluco*, said that Antônio "was called in their language Tamanduaré." Others told him that a lesser leader, sometimes called the "second pope," was known by the Indian name, Aricute.

The Jesuit provincial dismissed the use of *petum* (tobacco) in the *santidade* rituals as indecent and madness, but it was a recovery of an important indigenous ritual once used by the traditional wandering prophets. "Drinking the smoke," by which the believers meant inhaling, had a sacred meaning in the *Santidade de Jaguaripe*, as Gonçalo Fernandes explained to the inquisitor. The believers "drank the smoke until they fell drunk" and through the smoke "the spirit of holiness entered them." Drinking the smoke was a means of achieving holiness, a way of inducting new believers, and a ritual of passing the spirit from one believer to another. This is similar to the use of tobacco by wandering prophets reported earlier in the sixteenth century, but not to the general, non-sacred use of tobacco by Indians and Portuguese by the 1580s. In one of his texts written after 1583, the Jesuit Fernão Cardim describes tobacco as the "holy herb" and cites its medicinal qualities. But Cardim's description of how the dried tobacco leaves were smoked through a palm straw or cane suggests that addiction had become common. "Sucking and drinking that smoke," he writes, induces pleasure and laziness, as whole parts of days and nights are spent lying in a hammock smoking. "It is very harmful to some," Cardim explains, and "makes them drunk and dizzy," while others "drool at the mouth." In contrast, the *Santidade de Jaguaripe* restored the sacred use of tobacco in rituals led by the traditional wandering prophets in their Messianic movements.

In the inquisition trials, the words *abusão*, literally abusion, and *erronia*, error, are used to describe the *santidade* to the inquisitor, suggesting that those who participated, or who observed the rituals, clearly understood that the religious movement directly copied Christian practices. The men on the expedition repeatedly told the inquisitor that the movement "imitated" and "counterfeited" the rites of the Christian church. Bras Dias reported that they placed crosses in piles of rocks, and around them they drew lines on the ground in all directions. Antônio baptized his wife and children, Bras Dias continued, by raising a bowl of water and pouring it over their heads, blessing them. He described baptisms in which men were given the name Jesus, and women, the name Maria. Domingos Fernandes Nobre noted that the followers of the *santidade* built churches that included altars adorned with candlesticks, a vestry, and a baptismal fount. Diogo Dias claimed that the believers had made a chair out of one piece of wood, which they used to confess the women; he added that the believers used prayer beads and read "in their way" from books made of leaves of wood. The Jesuits perceived the 1585 *santidade* as more dangerous than previous *santidades* because of these Christian influences. Whereas the belief that there was no need to plant, the use of smoke, the labeling of the Portuguese as evil, and the belief in the return of ancestors were common in previous *santidades*, the *Santidade de Jaguaripe* copied recognizable Christian sacraments, such as the mass and confession, in such a way that it challenged the Jesuits' own mission.

Christian teachings of the apocalypse, combined with Tupi and Guarani beliefs in a "land without evil," created the millenarian message of the movement. In Christianity, millenarian ideas appear in the prophecies associated with the Day of Judgment, as expressed in the Book of Revelation. In the Book of Revelation, the Messiah returns on a white horse leading heavenly armies to make war against a ten-horned beast, the false prophet, and thereafter creates a New Jerusalem where the faithful will live with God, the Messiah. Then Jesus inaugurates the "millennium," the 1,000-year reign of Christ on earth when the devil will be held in bondage. While it is unlikely that the believers in the *Santidade de Jaguaripe* had read this text, they were certainly familiar with the broad outline of the end of the world, as Christians understood it; the missionary priests of the Society of Jesus had preached these Christian beliefs to Indians, Africans, and *mamelucos* in Brazil since 1549.

Jesuits stressed heaven, hell, the Day of Judgment, and the second coming of the Messiah in their sermons. In a mission to Indians living beyond the new capital of Salvador in 1552, the children who served as interpreters told the Indians that those Christian Indians who had believed in the "true holiness (*santidad*)," which was the holiness brought by the Jesuits, were given "life forever in the heavens," while the evil Indians died and went to hell where they "burned with the devil." A basic part of Jesuit teaching in the catechism translated into Tupi was the concept of the Day of Judgment. In plain language the Jesuits taught that Christ will return from heaven on a cloud; no one, not even animals, will escape; all will die and then be reborn; and the good will be beautiful and the bad ugly. Christ will judge all and will take the good to heaven, where they will live forever, while the evil will go to the fires of hell and suffer eternally.

In the *Santidade de Jaguaripe* believers combined the indigenous tradition of a charismatic wandering prophet who preached that crops would grow of their own accord with the Jesuit teachings on the apocalypse. This places the *Santidade de Jaguaripe* squarely into the framework of millenarian movements. Scholars who study millenarian movements emphasize that believers seek to escape from a harsh present to a harmonious future where evil will not exist. Disasters, crises of subsistence, civil wars, colonialism, the rapid spread of capitalism, or relative deprivation have all encouraged the spread of millenarian movements. In them believers are prepared to sacrifice in order to be among those who will be saved in the next world, a world of peace, harmony, equality, and happiness. Believers may move away, try to create a new holy city, pool their possessions, fail to plant the crops needed for survival, or passively wait for the dawning of a new age. Because millenarians see the world as fundamentally evil, they expect a superhuman agent to defeat the evil loose in the world and desire intensely that those who caused that evil should pay for their sins. Although millenarian movements are religious in tone, they invariably become political, and conflict escalates when such movements challenge extant political authorities. Not infrequently this leads to deep and destructive conflicts with established authorities.

The millenarian urgency of Antônio's message can be seen in the confessions of those who believed. Luísa Rodrigues, the *mameluco* daughter of a Portuguese notary public, confessed that she believed out of ignorance that "Our Lady and Our Lord" would return to walk on earth. The only Indian believer interrogated by the inquisitor was a woman who told him that it was "true" that the followers said that "God Our Lord would descend from heaven, and that God would change this world and that when he came, all would die, and that after they died, they would rise." Gonçalo Fernandes confessed to the inquisitor that the followers believed that "their God was coming soon to free them from slavery" and "to make them lords of the white people." The "whites would become their slaves," he said, while those who did not believe "would be converted into birds and beasts of the forest." Álvaro Rodrigues, a veteran *mameluco* slave trader and sugar planter, saw the millenarianism of the *santidade* as its most dangerous feature. He described to the inquisitor how the believers no longer planted because they believed that their food and drink would grow for them and that their vegetables "would be bigger than those of others," and that they "would not run out." The leaders of the *santidade* told him that "they had no fear of swords nor of chains because the iron would change into wax and would not harm them."

The *Santidade de Jaguaripe* was destroyed sometime during 1586. In his annual letter of 1585, most likely written in early 1586, the Jesuit provincial states that the leader of the *santidade* had been captured by Indians from the *aldeias*, who then "dragged" him through the *aldeias* "for the mockery of everyone." He states approvingly that the governor of Brazil sentenced the one "who a little before had made himself God" to death and then allowed the Indians to hang him. The provincial thought it entirely appropriate that Antônio should "perish at the hands of those to whose souls he had brought destruction." Still Antônio's memory persisted and the provincial noted that the fathers and brothers of the Society of Jesus are still "totally occupied" with "suppressing" the sect. By August of 1586, the *Santidade de Jaguaripe* had been defeated, according to the governor. The governor ordered a church built by the *santidade* burned and all runaway slave believers returned to their owners. He sent the female leader known as Mother of God, her husband (the "second pope"), and a third leader to Lisbon. He dispatched an expedition to find the remaining congregations. The leader of this expedition, with little remorse, murdered the remaining leaders of the movement in front of their followers. But the fate of Antônio remains unknown. The governor claimed that he had escaped, as did others. The Jesuit annual letter seems to say, however, that Antônio was murdered by Indians in or near the *aldeia* of Santo Antônio.

The early modern missionaries who sought to evangelize the Tupi, Guarani, and later Gê-speaking peoples of Brazil were sometimes violently rejected, as the martyrdom of Pedro Correia and João de Sousa makes clear. But another pattern also emerged, wherein the teachings of Christian missionaries became part of the spiritual life of indigenous and mixed-race peoples living in Brazil. Adapted to their lives, and incorporating indigenous myths and traditions, including those introduced by African slaves, Christianity as practiced by Indian and African slaves or by the free poor did not replicate European Catholicism. Instead, as seen in the *Santidade de Jaguaripe*, Antônio became a new religious leader who combined the traditional roles of the wandering prophet with elements of Christianity. In his movement, believers became saints who received what the Jesuits promised – salvation in the afterlife – and something more: freedom from slavery in the present life. Brazil was a promised land and therefore must be purified from existing evils such as slavery. In this way Christian beliefs, combined with indigenous traditions, served not only to create a powerful new identity for those marginalized by colonial society but to articulate a rejection of slavery. In Brazil, as elsewhere in both Europe and the New World, Christianity functioned not only as a source of repression but also as a source of resistance to power.

NOTES

1 For fuller development of the ideas expressed in this essay, see my "Millenarian slaves" and *Go-betweens and the Colonization of Brazil*. All quotations from Jesuit correspondence from 1549–68 are my translations of letters in Serafim Leite, ed., *Monumenta Brasiliae*, 5 vols (Rome: Monumenta Historica Societatis Iesu), 1956.
2 Quotations from documents on the early colonization of Brazil are my translations from Carlos Malheiro Dias, Ernesto de Vasconcelos, and Roque Gameiro, eds, *História da colonização portuguesa no Brasil*, 3 vols (Porto: Litografia Nacional, 1924).
3 For the text of Sebastião's law see Georg Thomas, *Política indigenista dos Portugueses no Brasil: 1500–1640* (São Paulo: Edições Loyola, 1982), 221–2.
4 The Inquisition trials from sixteenth century Brazil are in Inquisição de Lisboa, Arquivo National da Torre do Tombo, Lisbon; portions of the books of confessions and denunciations have been published; see the Further Reading section.
5 This annual letter appears in *Annuae Litterae Societatis Iesu, Anni MDLXXXV ad patres et fratres eiusdem societatis* (Rome: in Collegio Eiusdem Societatis, 1587). I thank my colleague Colin Wells for helping me with the translation from Latin.

SUGGESTIONS FOR FURTHER READING

Primary sources

Cardim, Fernão. *Tratados da terra e gente do Brasil*, ed. Ana Maria de Azevedo. Lisbon: Comissão Nacional para as Comemorações dos Descobrimentos Portugueses, 1977.

Primeira visitação do Santo Ofício às partes do Brasil . . . Confissões da Bahia 1591–1593. Rio de Janeiro, F. Briguiet, 1935.

Primeira visitação do Santo Ofício às partes do Brasil . . . Denunciações da Bahia 1591–1593. São Paulo: Paulo Prado, 1925.

Primeira visitação do Santo Ofício às partes do Brasil . . . Confissões da Bahia 1591–1592, ed. Ronaldo Vainfas. São Paulo: Companhia das Letras, 1997.

Secondary sources

Alchon, Suzanne. *A Pest in the Land: New World Epidemics in a Global Perspective*. Albuquerque: University of New Mexico Press, 2003.

Alden, Dauril. "Changing Jesuit Perceptions of the Brasis during the Sixteenth Century." *Journal of World History* 3, 2 (1992): 205–18.

—— *The Making of an Enterprise: The Society of Jesus in Portugal, Its Empire, and Beyond 1540–1750*. Stanford: Stanford University Press, 1996.

Blackburn, Robin. *The Making of New World Slavery: From the Baroque to the Modern, 1492–1800*. London and New York: Verso, 1997.

Cohn, Norman. *The Pursuit of the Millennium: Revolutionary Millenarians and Mystical Anarchists of the Middle Ages*, 2nd edn. Oxford: Oxford University Press, 1970.

Daniels, Ted. *Millennialism: An International Bibliography*. New York: Garland Publishers Inc., 1992.

Dias, Carlos Malheiro, Ernesto de Vasconcelos, and Roque Gameiro, eds. *História da colonização portuguesa no Brasil*, 3 vols. Porto: Litografia Nacional, 1924.

Lanternari, Vittorio. *The Religions of the Oppressed: A Study of Modern Messianic Cults*, trans. Lisa Sergio. New York: Alfred A. Knopf, 1963.

Leite, Serafim. *Monumenta Brasiliae*, 5 vols. Rome: Monumenta Historica Societatis Iesu, 1956–68.

Léry, Jean de. *History of a Voyage to the Land of Brazil, Otherwise Called America*, trans. Janet Whatley. Berkeley: University of California Press, 1990.

Metcalf, Alida C. "AHR Forum: Millenarian Slaves? The Santidade de Jaguaripe and Slave Resistance in the Americas." *American Historical Review* 104 (1999): 1531–59.

—— "The *Entradas* of Bahia in the Sixteenth Century." *The Americas* 61 (2005): 373–400.

—— *Go-betweens and the Colonization of Brazil, 1500–1600*. Austin: University of Texas Press, 2005.

O'Malley, John. *The First Jesuits*. Cambridge, Mass.: Harvard University Press, 1993.

Schwartz, Stuart B. *Sugar Plantations in the Formation of Brazilian Society: Bahia, 1550–1835*. Cambridge: Cambridge University Press, 1985.

Souza, Laura de Mello e. *The Devil and the Land of the Holy Cross: Witchcraft, Slavery, and Popular Religion in Colonial Brazil*, trans. Diane Grosklaus Whitty. Austin: University of Texas Press, 2003.

Thomas, Georg. *Política indigenista dos Portugueses no Brasil: 1500–1640*. São Paulo: Edições Loyola, 1982.

Vainfas, Ronaldo. *A heresia dos Índios: Catolicismo e rebeldia no Brasil colonial*. São Paulo: Companhia das Letras, 1995.

CHAPTER THIRTY-THREE

TOWARD A SACRAMENTAL POETICS[1]

Regina Mara Schwartz

In his *De doctrina christiana*, Milton does not mince words about his loathing of the doctrine of transubstantiation: "The Papists hold that it is Christ's actual flesh which is eaten by all in the Mass. But if this were so, even the most wicked of the communicants, not to mention the mice and worms which often eat the Eucharist, would attain eternal life by virtue of the heavenly bread." Besides, such a corporeal understanding of the Mass brings down Christ's holy body from its supreme exaltation at the right hand of God. "It drags it back to the earth, though it has suffered every pain and hardship already, to a state of humiliation even more wretched and degrading than before: to be broken once more and crushed and ground, even by the fangs of brutes. Then, when it has been driven through all the stomach's filthy channels, it shoots it out – one shudders even to mention it – into the latrine." His account is colorful, if conventional. And yet, Milton gives the communion prominence of place in *Paradise Lost*, embracing the image of transubstantiation with gusto, for he frames the central meal in the epic – the meal of which Adam and Raphael partake in the Garden – as a communion:

> So down they sat
> And to their viands fell, nor seemingly
> The angel, nor in mist, the common gloss
> Of theologians, but with keen dispatch
> Of real hunger, and concoctive heat
> To transubstantiate; . . .
>   (*Paradise Lost* V.433–8)

What is Milton doing calling to mind theologians and Real Presence – which for him has become "real hunger" – and *transubstantiate* – such an overloaded term – for a simple luncheon on the grass? Raphael compares their meal to heaven's high feasts, where "Tables are set and piled with Angel's food,/Fruit of delicious vines, the growth of heaven," and the angels "eat, drink, and in *communion* sweet quaff immortality and joy," echoing Jesus's own words that allude to the heavenly communion: "Then he took the cup, gave thanks and offered it, saying, 'drink from it, all of you, this is my blood of the covenant which is poured out for many for the forgiveness of sins. I tell you, I will not drink of this fruit of the vine from now on until that day when I drink it anew with you in my Father's kingdom'" (Matt. 26: 27–9).

But the heavenly allusion anticipates, for Milton is describing the earthly, not the heavenly paradise, and in the *earthly* paradise what kind of communion is this? First, polemically, it takes place on a table and not an Altar:

> Raised of grassy turf
> Their table was, and mossy seats had round,
> And on her ample square from side to side
> All autumn piled, though spring and autumn here
> Danced hand in hand.
> *(Paradise Lost* V.391–5)

Second, the communion is not ministered by a priest in vestments, but by a naked woman:

> Meanwhile at Table Eve
> ministered naked and their flowing cups
> with pleasant liquors crowned
> *(Paradise Lost* V.443–5)

Eve crushes grapes – of all things – to drink. We are cautioned that the bountiful fruits of Paradise are really materially digested by the angel – "not in mist, the common gloss of theologians" (*PL* V.434–6). There are no words of institution, nor a sermon. But there is instead a conversation whose subject is, virtually, the nature of transubstantiation. For while they are eating, Raphael expounds Milton's own version of the doctrine, inflected by the rhetoric of neoplatonism, vitalism, monism, and alchemy:[2]

> One Almighty is, from whom
> All things proceed, and up to him return,
> If not depraved from good, created all
> Such to perfection, one first matter all,
> Indu'd with various forms various degrees
> Of substance, . . .
> But more refined, more spiritous and pure
> As nearer to him placed or nearer tending
>   So from the root
> Springs lighter the green stalk, from thence the leaves
> More aery, last the bright consummate flower
> Spirits odorous breathes: flowers and their fruit
> Man's nourishment, by gradual scale sublimed
> To vital spirits aspire . . .
> *(Paradise Lost* V.469–84)

And then the angel offers a demonstration of this wondrous digestion:

> Wonder not then, what God for you saw good
> If I refuse not, but convert, as you
> To proper substance; . . .
> *(Paradise Lost* V.491–3)

And finally, he explains to Adam what this whole process of sublimation, digestion, conversion is really about: it is not about the wafer turning into the body of Christ or the wine turning into the blood of Christ; it is about man becoming the body of God. But wait, isn't that the heart of the Eucharistic doctrine?

He adds that the whole universe is engaged in this digestive or sublimation process – but with this important difference: these changes are not effected by priests, they just happen naturally. Moreover, this process does not just characterize the meal in the garden; this eating and sublimating describes Milton's cosmology. His entire universe is a body engaged in ceaseless transformation and transubstantiation of a kind, a material, digesting, concocting, assimilating body that perpetually and naturally turns matter into spirit.

> Whatever was created
> Needs to be sustained and fed; of elements
> The grosser feeds the purer, Earth the Sea,
> Earth and Sea feed Air, . . .
> Nor doth the Moon no nourishment exhale
> From her moist continent to higher orbs.
> The sun that light imparts to all
> Receives from all his alimental recompense
> In humid exhalations
> And at Even Sups with Ocean.
> *(Paradise Lost* V.414–26)

Why does John Milton, who inveighed so vociferously against transubstantia-tion in his prose – with all of the conventional reformist rhetoric of the idolatry and cannibalism of eating and digesting god – depict, in his epic, the entire cosmos as in the very act of ceaselessly transubstantiating?[3]

The meanings that transubstantiation had accrued are stunning: the means of achieving communal justice and peace, for cleansing human fault, and for overcoming death. Entering the new, sacramental body, the communicant is no longer an exile from God, he can enjoy a share of his divinity; no longer an exile from community, he can help to constitute the body of the Church; and no longer in exile from creation, he is joined to it materially. The sacrifice satisfies justice, the participation assures love, the words of institution even overcome the failure of fallen language. In short, paradise is restored.

Many Reformers thought that this sacrament of mystery had been instrumentalized: it had come to signify the rule of the Church, not the body of God – in fact the phrase *corpus mysticum* that had once referred to the host was transferred by the

Lateran Council to the Church, and the *corpus Christi*, which had referred to the body of the Church, was now used to refer to the host. By the Tudor period, the sacrament had become so entangled with politics that *corpus mysticum* was even used in legal discourse to signify the body of the monarch and the nation. The original sense of the mystical body, of participation in a community governed by consent rather than rule, seemed threatened.

Nonetheless, the tradition always harbored not only *corpus* understood as a polity, but also *mysticum*, the mystery, and the longing for that mystery surfaces again and again, sustained in part by the rich resources of mystical theology, even as the doctrine winds its way through its instrumental history. This longing for a mystical participation in God is not lost during the Reformation any more than the hunger for justice, love, and a world alive and redolent with meaning is lost in modern secularism. Christopher Sutton's *Godly Meditations upon the Most Holy Sacrament of the Lord's Supper*, a popular devotional book in the seventeenth century, maintains that the bread and wine do not change at their consecration, but it still confesses the mystery: "we must acknowledge that the dignity of this sacrament is greater than words can express, yea, than the mind of man is able to conceive." At the advent of modernity, this longing begins to be transfigured, or, to use the term loosely, transubstantiated into the cultural substantial life of *ars poetica*.

When the medieval sacramental system of meaning was under attack and revision, and emphasis was placed on the logical contradictions of operations that had heretofore been deemed mysterious, the sacramental system was not altogether destroyed. The attraction of understanding the world and its beings as participating in the sacred, rather than manifesting dead matter, endured. Early modern writers, in their impulse to hold fast to the sacred even while modern sciences challenged its presuppositions, forged innovative responses to the looming threats of a godless world. One was to widen the sacramental beyond the ritual to the domain of art. If the locus of the medieval sacramental vision had been the ritual of the Eucharist, during the dawn of modernity it spread into wider cultural expressions. This is apparent in the religious poetry written by those who, doctrinally speaking, rejected the Catholic doctrine of transubstantiation. In their art, the sacramental understanding of justice as sacrifice is investigated under the purview of tragedy; the sacramental symbolic order reflected in the words of institution, "this is my body," is widened into the mystery of communication or conversation; the transformation of wine and bread into the blood and body of Christ becomes instead a vision of a material universe continually infused with the sacred; communion with the body of God becomes the erotic consummation with the lover. In this way, key impulses in sacred thought were transferred into the secular symbolic realm in this nondenominational "sacramental poetics," one that did not succumb to the identity labels of either a Catholic or a Protestant poetics. But the "sacramental poetics" that emerges is not only a thematic expansion of cravings – for redemption, for justice, for love, for communion – met by the earlier system. A poetry is sacramental, not because it is an object of worship (an idol, an artefact), and not because it is believed to be a sacred leftover of a divine presence (a relic), but "sacramental" because it does not contain what it expresses. Rather, such art expresses far more than it contains, pointing to a meaning greater than and beyond itself. While their world was shaken by challenges to the medieval system of sacramentality, the sixteenth- and seventeenth-century thinkers who lived at the dawn of modernity responded with creative solutions about the sacred, even while modern empiricism challenged its very existence.

While John Milton takes the Eucharist to the cosmos, John Donne takes it to the bedroom; between their imaginations, communion is stretched to the limits of the universe and contracted to the space of greatest intimacy.[4] As the Anglican Dean of St Paul's, and an ex-Catholic, Donne had to tow a doctrinal line rejecting the doctrine of transubstantiation, and yet he did deplore intolerance toward doctrinal differences. Moreover, he was obsessed with communion. Even Donne's seduction lyrics can allude to communion, inflecting a conventional "flea poem" with the imagery of the Eucharist, where "our two bloods mingled be":

Thou know'st that this cannot be said
A sin, or shame, or loss of maidenhead,
Yet this [flea] enjoys before it woo,
And pampered swells with one blood made of two,
And this, alas, is more than we would do.

To stop her from crushing the flea, the speaker invokes the Trinity – "Oh stay, three lives in one flee spare" – and the sacredness of marriage – "This flea is you and I, and this/Our marriage bed, and marriage temple is." She squashes it and he turns to the Passion – "Cruel and sudden, hast thou since/Purpled thy nail, in blood of innocence?" accusing her of the "sacrilege of three sins in killing three." The poem turns not only on the satiric incongruity of comparing the sacrifice of Christ with swatting a flea; something serious hovers as a remainder: physical love gets sanctified, even if comically, for the whole trope requires the leap that love-making is like communion.[5]

Donne's investment in the physical body cannot be overestimated: love-making recapitulates the union of God and man achieved in the incarnation and echoed in the Eucharist, and it is so redemptive that he even imagines making love beyond the grave. Then, too, when he preaches that in the afterlife Christ excludes marriage because there is no need of it in heaven – "there they need no mutuall help," he says – love-making is not expressly ruled out: "yet he excludes not our *knowing* [carnally], or our loving of one another upon former *knowledge* in this world, in the next; Christ does not say expressly we *shall* yet neither does he say that we *shall not* know one another there. Neither can we say, we shall not, because we *know* not how we should."[6] Donne's attachment to the body is also strong enough for him to suggest that the angels should envy us for having bodies, rather than we them: "Man cannot deliberately wish himself an angel," he writes, "because he should lose by that wish, and lack that glory which he shall have in his body." After all, "we shall be like the angels in the exalting of the faculties of our souls; But they shall never be like us in our glorified bodies."[7] Indeed, "the Kingdom of Heaven hath not all that it must have to a consummate perfection, til it have bodies too." God did not think heavenly glory "so perfect, but that it might receive an addition from creatures; and therefore made a world, a material world, a corporeal world, so they would have bodies in the

Heaven of Heavens, the Presence Chamber of God himself where the presence of our bodies is expected."[8] In many sermons he argues for the resurrection of the body with the soul. "A man is not saved, a sinner is not redeemd, I am not received into heaven, if my body be left out; The soule and the body concurred to the making of a sinner; and body and soule must concur to the making of a Saint."[9] And he vividly envisions the physicality of the resurrection:

> Where be all the splinters of that Bone, which a shot hath shivered and scattered in the Ayre? Where be all the Atoms of that flesh, which a Corrasive hath eat away, or a Consumption hath breath'd and exhal'd away from our arms and other Limbs? In what wrinkle, in what furrow, in what bowel on the earth, are all the graines of the ashes of a body burnt a thousand years since? In what corner, in what ventricle of the sea, lies all the jelly of a Body drowned in the generall flood? What coherence, what sympathy, what dependence maintaines any relation, any correspondence, between that arm that was lost in Europe, and that legge that was lost in Afrique or Asia, scores of years between?[10]

One implication of this grasp of the material immanent world is that for Donne, communion – between body and soul, man and God, and human lovers – may be rare. He dwells on how difficult it is to achieve, how transitory its moments are, how much the lover fails to apprehend his beloved due to his own self-absorption, and how much the would-be lover fails to love another and God due to his worldly preoccupations. Nevertheless, it is achievable in *this* world and in *this* time. What is remarkable is that Donne does not pursue this quasi-mystical project of combining by transcending the material world through asceticism. Rather, by fully embracing materiality, sexuality, and desire, he makes them the very medium of his transvaluation. This means that he differs from Milton for whom communion is an achievement before the world as we know it, a feature of prelapsarian paradise, and from George Herbert, for whom that communion will be achieved beyond this world – in an apocalyptic after-life.[11]

Unlike Milton's work, then, Donne's poetry does not lament the loss of a prelapsarian cosmos in which all ingests All and gives back its "alimental recompense," in which the sun sups at even with the ocean, as Milton so exquisitely expresses his longing for a natural Eucharist (*Paradise Lost* V.425–6). The poetry of Donne tends not to mourn a lost paradise where to behold the face of God was Adam's "highth of happiness" (*Paradise Lost* X.724) because it typically looks for the face of God in the face of the lover. This look yields the all in All:

> My face in thine eye, thine in mine appears,
> And true plain hearts do in the faces rest,
> Where can we find two better hemispheres
> Without sharp north, without declining west?
> Whatever dies, was not mixed equally;
> If our two loves be one, or, thou and I
> Love so alike, that none do slacken, none can die.
> ("The Good Morrow" 15–21)

In addition to its innuendo of sexual consummation, the poem suggests that full love, fully given, achieves a kind of resurrection; hence, redemption for the lovers.[12] Donne preached, "GOD is *Love*, and the Holy Ghost is amorous in his Metaphors; everie where his Scriptures abound with the notions of Love, of Spouse, and Husband, and Marriadge Songs, and Marriadge Supper, and Marriadge-Bedde."[13] And the learned divine knew his precedents in amorous theological metaphors: from the Song of Songs through Augustine and Gregory, Bernard of Clairvaux and William of Saint Thierry, St Francis and St Bonaventura, Eckhart and the Rhineland School, Jean Gerson and Denys the Carthusian, Nicholas of Cusa and Catherine of Genoa, Luis de León, John of the Cross, Teresa of Avila. This strain of Christianity was eloquently expressed by Dionysius the Areopagite:

> Why is it, however, that theologians sometimes refer to God as Yearning (*eros*) and Love (*agape*) and sometimes as the yearned-for and the Beloved? On the one hand he causes, produces, and generates what is being referred to, and on the other hand he is the thing itself . . . He is yearning on the move, simple, self-moved, self-acting, preexistent in the Good, flowing out from the Good onto all that is and returning once again to the Good.[14]

Pseudo-Dionysius resolutely refused to separate erotic desire from love: "Indeed some of our writers on sacred matters have thought the title 'yearning' to be more divine than 'love'. . . . So let us not fear this title of 'yearning' (*eros*) nor be upset by what anyone has to say about these two names, for in my opinion, the sacred writers regard 'yearning' and 'love' as having one and the same meaning."[15] Human desire is the same eros that came from God: divine love is the source of human craving, the author of our desire. For Dionysius, the very creation of the world is an explosion of erotic energy. God creates out of the overflowing of eros: "the very cause of the universe is the beautiful, good superabundance of his benign yearning (*eros*) for all, carried outside of himself in the loving care he has for everything. He is, as it were, beguiled by goodness, by love (*agape*) and by yearning (*eros*) and is enticed away from his transcendent dwelling place and comes to abide within all things.[16] As all is created from divine eros, so all yearns for its divine source. The logic is incarnational and Eucharistic: we seek God to combine with God. In this Platonic tradition love is characterized as full of both immanent and transcendent desire, consummated in physical and spiritual union, a union of mortals that grants access to union with the immortal. No competition between lowly carnal love and higher spiritual love; rather, it joins them to produce the fruit of human and religious love.[17]

Such an understanding of human love challenges us to rethink idolatry: when love of man or woman leads *to* God instead of away from God, it cannot be idolatrous. Hence, instead of finding passion dangerous, Donne's speakers confront another threat, inauthentic worship, false valuation. Sonnet XVIII ventures to describe what idolatry would be with more specificity: following through the trope of the Church as the bride of Christ, it suggests that embracing an institution instead of loving God may be idolatrous. The bride of Christ could be "richly painted" on "the other shore" – the Church of Spain, or "robbed and tore/Laments and mourns in Germany and here" – the Protestant Church, or she could be on Mt Moriah or even on the seven hills of Rome. But these are partial: the true bride of Christ knows no single place, but all places.

> Betray, kind husband, Thy spouse to our sights,
> And let mine amorous soul court Thy mild Dove,
> Who is most true and pleasing to Thee then
> When she is embraced and open to most men.

At her best, the bride of Christ is promiscuous, the sonnet says provocatively. The bride of Christ pleases God most when she gives to most; in this sense, "betrayal" is completely transvalued to become liberality. Embracing eros as divine takes the speaker to the logical conclusion that the more love the better. Dangers do not lurk from love, but from its lack, from not enough love, false love, and, above all, no love: for Donne, this is the devil.

Even if the titles of his poems were made by discerning editors instead of Donne, the subject of his lyric "The Community" alludes to a social group, holy communion, and common – all at once.

> Good we must love, and must hate ill,
> For ill is ill and good good still,
> But there are things indifferent,
> Which we may neither hate, nor love,
> But one, and then another prove,
> As we shall find our fancy bent.

The speaker begins by defining women as *adiaphora*, as "things indifferent" and therefore as available for use:

> But since she [Nature] did them so create,
> That we may neither love, nor hate,
> Only this rests: All, all may use.

Good women are betrayed to all eyes, and in that way, presumably, rendered bad. Bad ones "waste" and so do not remain bad, but disappear. So both are indifferent, he argues, neither good nor bad. But for all its playfulness, the poem becomes, in the final stanza, not only sexually but also theologically charged:

> But they are ours as fruits are ours,
> He that but tastes, he that devours,
> And he that leaves all, doth as well;
> Changed loves are but changed sorts of meat,
> And when he hath the kernel eat,
> Who doth not fling away the shell?

The offensive implication that having had the favors of a woman (her kernel) the man would fling her away conforms to the stance of the speaker as a libertine. But the language of "kernel" and "shell" also permeated discourse on the Eucharist, where the kernel signaled the substance and the shell the accidents. In that sense, the final couplet suggests, when you have the substance, why worry about the accidents? When you have taken in the true Christ, why worry about the status of the bread and the wine? The subject of the poem then, community, means not just the community of the women and men who have one another sexually; it also alludes to the body of believers, the Church community. In this sense, "changed loves" are not only new women, but the change wrought by loving Christ. In the end, the theological argument helps us make sense of the sexual one: asking who needs the shell when he has the kernel, the speaker has suggested that he does not need "all" these women because he has All in having his one true love.

Meat, instead of the elements of bread and wine, is precisely the way that Herbert refers to the body of Christ in his famous Eucharistic lyric, "Love."[18] Marked by its ease and deceptive simplicity at presenting a deep theological and emotional drama, "Love" is often thought of as Herbert's quintessential poem: it derives its rich texture from the echo of many biblical passages describing God's inviting man to a feast. Song of Songs 2: 4, "he brought me to the banqueting house, and his banner over me was love"; the 23rd Psalm, where God is a gracious Host; Matthew 26: 29; Luke 12: 37, where the master comes and serves his servants; Revelation 3: 20, the promised Messianic banquet: "Behold I stand at the door and knock; if any one hears my voice and opens the door, I will come in to him and eat with him, and he with me"; and Matthew 22: 1–10 and Luke 14: 7–24, the parables of the great supper. Herbert's unworthy guest alludes most directly to Matthew's version of the parable, "the king said to his servants, / The wedding is ready, but those invited were not worthy" (Matthew 22: 8)]. But Herbert has changed the plot. Luke 14: 16 says: "A man once gave a great banquet, and invited many; and at the time for the banquet he sent his servant to say to those who had been invited, 'Come; for all is now ready.' But they all alike began to make excuses . . . Then the householder in anger said to his servant, 'Go out quickly to the streets and lanes of the city, and bring in the poor and maimed and blind and lame.' And the servant said, 'Sir, what you commanded has been done, and still there is room.' And the master said to the servant, 'Go out to the highways and hedges, and compel people to come in, that my house may be filled. For I tell you, none of those men who were invited shall taste of my banquet.'" Herbert clearly changes that plot.

In Herbert's version, Love does not only invite a guest who refuses, making excuses, is pronounced unworthy and then replaced by someone else because the host gives up on them. *Love will not be refused.*

LOVE (III)

Love bade me welcome. Yet my soul drew back
        Guilty of dust and sin.
But quick-eyed Love, observing me grow slack
        From my first entrance in,
Drew nearer to me, sweetly questioning,
        If I lacked any thing.

A guest, I answered, worthy to be here:
                Love said, You shall be he.
I the unkind, ungrateful? Ah my dear,
                I cannot look on thee.
Love took my hand, and smiling did reply,
                Who made the eyes but I?

Truth Lord, but I have marred them: let my shame
                Go where it does deserve.
And know you not, says Love, who bore the Blame?
                My dear, then I will serve.
You must sit down, says Love, and taste my meat:
                So I did sit and eat.

The feast of love to which God has invited man alludes both to the earthly communion with the implied pun on "host" and to the heavenly marriage banquet it anticipates. In the course of this conversation, the guest claims that he is not worthy, tries to back away but love holds on to him, continuing to engage him in conversation. The guest agrees that Love created him, but insists that he has marred that created image. Alluding to the original sin, he wants to leave in shame; Love admits that the image of God in man *has* been marred, shame *has* ensued, but Love reminds him that she has borne the blame and has thereby imputed worthiness to him. This is not only a conversation *about* worthiness; rather, in the course of the conversation, the guest *becomes* worthy – worthy, first by acknowledging his lack of worth; worthy, next, by listening when he is told that his unworthiness has been accounted for; and worthy because he then understands that he belongs at the meal. All of these change him, begin to qualify him, for the communion. The conversation becomes a conversion. The drama of the poem focuses with exquisite intensity on the invitation and the question of its acceptance – not on the menu, not on the wine and bread – and its status. What is at the heart of Herbert's mystery of the Eucharist is that an utterance could ever be heard, that a call could ever be answered, an offer ever received, an invitation ever be accepted, a conversation ever take place. Clearly, for Herbert, an important aspect of this sacramental mystery is the mystery of language.

    The English Reformed poets did not inaugurate modernity by turning away from the medieval mystery of transubstantiation, but by making language its chief vehicle into other cultural formations with their "sacramental signification." In their understanding of language, what is said and its relation to the referent – the sign to the signified – is less important than the activity of saying. In this sacramental model, language is not understood as the servant of ontology, of "standing for a thing"; in the language of conversation, some *thing* is not passed from one to another, rather some *one* hears when we call. What is heard is left indeterminate, but whatever it is, it is the only utterance we make while we live: praise expressed as the mysterious hypostasis of joy and pain. In Milton's paradisal sinless Eucharist, the emphasis falls on longing and its frustration – on desire, and perhaps on hope, but not on an achieved redemption. For him, the doctrine of Real Presence leaves one with Real

Hunger. Donne is more hopeful that we can achieve communion here and now in common love. For Herbert, there is no option: we must accept the invitation; we must taste the meat.

If Milton, Donne, and Herbert infused the cosmos, lovers, and language with such sacramentality, perhaps transubstantiation of bread and wine seemed pale in comparison. Given that the Eucharist commemorates the redemption of man by Christ, it is remarkable to place the communion, that recalls Christ's death, in Paradise with the unfallen Adam – even more remarkable in the context of Reformation controversies. The Reformers had already changed the allusion to sacrifice: it was to be *remembered* at the communion, not *repeated*. The Altar became a Table. Calvary was to be called to mind, not re-enacted. But Milton's Eucharist does not even call it to mind! The body and blood of Christ are not a bleeding body, but a breathing body; indeed, a giant living pulsing universe, one whose breath joins the very breath of angels to become the spirit of God. In his remarkable imaginative feat, Milton has depicted a sinless man in the garden, with no need for the redemption signaled by the communion, engaging in communion. We are challenged to imagine a wondrous thing: a sinless Eucharist.

Is this nostalgia for the "old faith" of a more sacramental Christianity, even for Catholicism? Or is it a lament that the departure of transubstantiation at the Reformation signals the departure of the divine, of a world replete with meaning replaced by one emptied? Not really: God or the gods have left the world repeatedly. In ancient Greece, with the rise of democracy, Plato dismissed tradition to insist that the new order had to be justified in Reason. The gods left again with the decline of the ancient "pagan" world and the rise of the Judeo-Christian civilization. The standard reading of this shift is that the organic totality of the ancient universe, in which religion was an immediate element in people's lives, was lost, and religion came to refer to a transcendent power – no longer the pre-Christian gods, but the One transcendent God, the supreme Being. Again, the gods departed with the rise of modernity: here, a medieval universe full of sacramental meanings gave way to the notion of the infinite mechanistic universe. They left again with the rise of modern industrial civilization and the secular political order. Again, at the end of the nineteenth century, in the epoch of nihilism signaled by Nietzsche's "God is dead." And again, when postmodernity claimed the end of big narratives. It seems that God is abandoning the world, or dying, all the time. And because the gods are ever-departing, they are ever-returning only to depart again. Something else, however, is impelling this lament – the departure of a ritual that harbored the potential of reconciliation – and here, as I conclude, I would prefer to express it as a hope instead of as loss. A life-world, conversation, justice and love – the departure of these Eucharistic impulses would be very much worth lamenting, and these poets offer a reminder of their value as well as the hope that we will continue to desire these and strive for them – however sadly.

When we live in a world of conflicting identities – cultural, national, ethnic, religious, and gendered – each asserting their particularity against another, the result is invariably violent.[19] Conversely, the opposite demand for a universal is attended by another kind of violence: the risks of a political totalitarianism, a global imperialism, a violence that crushes particularity in its relentless drive toward universal control. Another option, a third option that we could try to imagine, is a particular that honors other particulars, one that opens out toward a potential universal without coercion. In the Eucharist, I seek such an example.[20] This is not to pretend that it has not served as the occasion for terrible strife – it has; nor that it has not been used to distinguish between those who are welcome and those who are not – it has done that, too. But in its intent to create a community that coheres – not from blood or territorial boundaries, not from history or from political allegiance, but through sharing divinity – it sought to overcome the pain of difference, to achieve reconciliation. The irony that this only led to further strife over the meaning and form of that very ritual is testimony to the stubbornness of human aggression. Nonetheless, even in the time of greatest conflict over the ritual, early modern thinkers sought to embrace the central impulses of the Eucharist: a life-world instead of a dead universe, conversation instead of conflict, justice instead of the triumph of evils, and love instead of utility. To translate these from a church ritual into more secular, cultural achievements could be, perhaps, to save them for a future time. Then too, perhaps the sacramental poetics conferred to us could be far more than a description of literary arts – a way of regarding the world, other peoples, and one another. I conclude with the hope that the potential of reconciliation harbored by communion could still inspire, in new cultural forms, a world of community.

NOTES

1. This chapter is drawn from my *When God Left the World: Sacramental Poetics at the Dawn of Secularism* (Stanford: Stanford University Press, 2006).
2. On Milton and vitalism, see John Rogers, *The Matter of Revolution: Science, Poetry and Politics in the Age of Milton* (Ithaca: Cornell University Press, 1996); for Milton and monism, see Dennis Danielson, *Milton's Good God: A Study in Literary Theodicy* (Cambridge: Cambridge University Press, 1982); on Milton and alchemy, see Michael Lieb, *The Dialectics of Creation: Patterns of Birth and Regeneration in Paradise Lost* (Amherst: University of Massachusetts Press, 1970).
3. John King in "Miltonic Transubstantiation," *Milton Studies* 36 (1988): 41–58, has contributed a different approach to this question, regarding Milton's allusion to transubstantiation as wholly ironic. He rightly notes how central the issue of communion was for Milton, paying heed, importantly, to Milton's revision in the 1674 edition of *Paradise Lost* where he substitutes the following passage for Book V, 637–9 in the first edition:

   > They eat, they drink, and in communion sweet
   > Quaff immortality and joy, secure
   > Of surfeit where full measure only bounds
   > Excess, before the all bounteous king, who showered
   > With copious hand, rejoicing in their joy. (V.637–41)

   See also John Ulreich Jr.'s discussion of Haemony as a Eucharistic symbol in "A Bright Golden Flow'r: Haemony as a Symbol of Transformation," *Studies in English Literature, 1500–1900* 17, 1 (winter 1977): 119–28.
4. Michael Schoenfeldt, "'That Spectacle of Too Much Weight': The Poetics of Sacrifice in Donne, Herbert, and Milton," *Journal of Medieval and Early Modern Studies* 31, 3 (2001):

561–84, points to Reformation writers' sense of inadequacy before the enormity of the subject of the passion.
5 See Theresa DiPasquale, *The Sacred and the Secular in John Donne* (Pittsburgh: Duquesne University Press, 1999); M. Thomas Hester, "'This Cannot Be Said': A Preface to the Reader of Donne's Lyrics," *Christianity and Literature* 39, 4 (1990): 365–85; Achsah Guibbory, *Ceremony and Community from Herbert to Milton* (Cambridge: Cambridge University Press, 1998). On the sacramental images, see Judah Stampfer, *John Donne and the Metaphysical Gesture* (New York: Funk & Wagnalls, 1970), pp. 173–4; Sally Sheppeard, "Eden and Agony in 'Twicknam Garden,'" *John Donne Journal* 7 (1988): 70; Terry G. Sherwood, *Fulfilling the Circle: A Study of John Donne's Thought* (Toronto: University of Toronto Press, 1984); Eleanor McNees, *Eucharistic Poetry: The Search for Presence in the Writing of John Donne, Gerard Manley Hopkins, Dylan Thomas, and Geoffrey Hill* (Lewisburg: Buckness University Press, 1992). On Donne's residual Catholicism, see Richard Strier, "John Donne Awry and Squint: 'The Holy Sonnets,' 1608–1610," *Modern Philology* 86 (1989): 357–85; and Dennis Flynn, *John Donne and the Ancient Catholic Nobility* (Bloomington: Indiana University Press, 1995).
6 Sermon no. 3, preached 19 November 1627: John Donne, *Sermons*, 10 vols, eds George R. Potter and Evelyn M. S. Simpson (Berkeley: University of California Press, 1953–62), VIII, pp. 98–9.
7 Sermon preached 8 May 1625: *John Donne, The Major Works*, ed. John Carey (Oxford: Oxford University Press, 1990), p. 360.
8 Sermon preached at Whitehall, 8 March 1622: Carey, *Major Works*, p. 306.
9 *Sermons*, VII, p. 103.
10 Sermon no. 3 preached 19 November 1627, *Sermons*, VIII, p. 98.
11 See Richard Strier, "Donne and the Politics of Devotion," in *Religion, Literature and Politics in Post-Reformation England, 1540–1688*, eds Donna Hamilton and Richard Strier (Cambridge: Cambridge University Press, 1996), p. 105; Anthony Lowe, "John Donne: The Holy Ghost is Amorous in his Metaphors," in John Roberts, ed., *New Perspectives on the Seventeenth-century Religious Lyric* (Columbia: University of Missouri Press), pp. 201–21. Albert C. Labriola's fine essay, "This Dialogue of One: Rational Argument and Affective Discourse in Donne's 'Aire and Angels,'" *John Donne Journal* 9, 1 (1990): 77–83, is one of the readings that deals most explicitly with the theological context of the poem.
12 Raymond-Jean Frontain and Francis M. Malpezzi, *John Donne's Religious Imagination* (Conway: University of Conway Press, 1995), p. 2: "Donne's Elegies and his Songs and Sonnets include some of the most erotically bumptious and strategically blasphemous love lyrics in the English language." William Shullenberger, in "Love as a Spectator Sport in John Donne's Poetry," in Claude J. Summers and Ted Larry Pebworth, eds, *Renaissance Discourses of Desire* (Columbia: University of Missouri Press, 1993), pp. 46–62, argues that a "liturgical and healing function" characterizes many lyrics. See William Kerrigan, "What Was Donne Doing?," *South Central Review* 4 (1987): 4–6. See also John Carey, *John Donne: Life, Mind and Art* (New York: Oxford University Press, 1981), pp. 37–46, and Thomas Docherty, *John Donne, Undone* (London: Methuen & Co., 1986), pp. 147–86, for the convergence of theological and erotic motifs in Donne.
13 Sermon preached before the king at Whitehall, 24 February 1625, Simpson and Potter, *Sermons*, VII, pp. 87–8.
14 Pseudo-Dionysius, *The Divine Names in Pseudo-Dionysius: The Complete Works* (New York: Paulist Press, 1987), pp. 82–3 (712C).
15 Pseudo-Dionysius, *The Divine Names*, p. 81 (709B).
16 Pseudo-Dionysius, *The Divine Names*, p. 82 (712B).

17 Heather Dubrow, *Echoes of Desire: English Petrarchism and its Counterdiscourses* (Ithaca: Cornell University Press, 1995), p. 207, notes that Donne "presents himself as both resident and alien in the realms of Petrarchism."
18 I refer to the third lyric on Love in *The Temple*.
19 I have explored some of the logic and rhetoric of such identity violence in *The Curse of Cain: The Violent Legacy of Monotheism* (Chicago: University of Chicago Press, 1997).
20 The philosopher Alain Badiou has sought such a "particular universal," and for him Paul is its quintessential example. See Badiou's *Saint Paul: The Foundation of Universalism*, trans. Ray Brassier (Stanford: Stanford University Press, 2003).

SUGGESTIONS FOR FURTHER READING

Primary sources

Donne, John. *The Sermons of John Donne*, eds George R. Potter and Evelyn M. Simpson. Berkeley: University of California Press, 1953–62.
—— *John Donne: The Complete English Poems*, ed. C.A. Patrides. London: Dent, 1985.
Milton, John. *Complete English Poems and Major Prose*, ed. Merritt Y. Hughes. New York: Odyssey, 1957.
—— *Complete Prose Works of John Milton*, 8 vols, eds Don M. Wolfe *et al*. New Haven: Yale University Press, 1953–82.
Pseudo-Dionysius: The Complete Works. New York: Paulist Press, 1987, 82–3 (712C).

Secondary sources

Carey, John. *John Donne: Life, Mind, and Art*. New York: Oxford University Press, 1981.
Certeau, Michel de. *The Mystic Fable*, trans. Michael B. Smith. Chicago: University of Chicago Press, 1992.
Clements, Arthur. *Poetry of Contemplation: John Donne, George Herbert, Henry Vaughan, and the Modern Period*. Albany: SUNY Press, 1990.
Collinson, Patrick. *The Religion of Protestants: The Church in English Society, 1559–1625*. Oxford: Clarendon Press, 1982.
Duffy, Eamon. *The Stripping of the Altars: Traditional Religion in England, c. 1400–c. 1580*. New Haven: Yale University Press, 1992.
Frontain, Raymond-Jean and Francis M. Malpezzi. *John Donne's Religious Imagination*. Conway: University of Central Arkansas Press, 1995.
Guibbory, Achsah. *Ceremony and Community from Herbert to Milton*. Cambridge: Cambridge University Press, 1998.
Herbert, George. *The Works of George Herbert*, ed. F.E. Hutchinson. Oxford: Clarendon Press [1941], 1964.
King, John N. *English Reformation Literature: The Tudor Origins of the Protestant Tradition*. Princeton: Princeton University Press, 1982.
Lewalski, Barbara Kiefer. *Protestant Poetics and the Seventeenth-century Religious Lyric*. Princeton: Princeton University Press, 1979.
Lieb, Michael. *Theological Milton: Deity, Discourse and Heresy in the Miltonic Canon*. Pittsburgh: Duquesne University Press, 2006.
Low, Anthony, *Love's Architecture: Devotional Modes in Seventeenth-century English Poetry*. New York: New York University Press, 1978.
Lubac, Henri de. *Corpus Mysticum*. Paris: Aubier, 1944.

McGinn, Bernard. *The Presence of God: A History of Western Christian Mysticism*, 4 vols (New York: Crossroads, 1991–).

McNees, Eleanor. *Eucharistic Poetry: The Search for Presence in the Writings of John Donne, Gerard Manley Hopkins, Dylan Thomas, and Geoffrey Hill*. Lewisburg: Bucknell University Press, 1992.

Marshall, Peter, ed. *The Impact of the English Reformation, 1500–1640*. New York: St Martin's Press, 1997.

Martz, Louis. *The Poetry of Meditation: A Study in English Religious Literature of the Seventeenth Century*. New Haven: Yale University Press, 1954.

Schwartz, Regina. *Remembering and Repeating: On Milton's Theology and Poetics*. Chicago: University of Chicago Press, 1990.

—— *When God Left the World: Sacramental Poetics at the Dawn of Secularism*. Stanford: Stanford University Press, 2006.

Strier, Richard. *Love Known: Theology and Experience in George Herbert's Poetry*. Chicago: University of Chicago Press, 1983.

Summers, Claude J. and Ted-Larry Pebworth, eds. *Renaissance Discourses of Desire*. Columbia: University of Missouri Press, 1993.

Targoff, Ramie. *Common Prayer: The Language of Public Devotion in Early Modern England*. Chicago: University of Chicago Press, 2001.

Wandel, Lee Palmer. *The Eucharist in the Reformation: Incarnation and Liturgy*. Cambridge: Cambridge University Press, 2006.

Young, R. V. *Doctrine and Devotion in Seventeenth-century Poetry: Studies in Donne, Herbert, Crashaw, and Vaughan*. Rochester, N.Y.: D. S. Brewer, 2000.

PART VII

A NEW ORDER OF KNOWLEDGE

CHAPTER THIRTY-FOUR

THE SUN AT THE CENTER OF THE WORLD

Paula Findlen

Around 1514 a small pamphlet began to circulate in manuscript among scholars and clerics in northern Europe. Entitled the *Little Commentary* and written by a Polish church canon from Frombork, who studied the heavens when he was not otherwise occupied with ecclesiastical finances and bureaucracy, it proposed nothing less than a wholesale rethinking of the premise of Aristotelian physics and Ptolemaic astronomy, both of which had firmly placed the earth at the center of the universe. Instead, the author informed his readers that this idea was a product of a long-standing misperception of the structure of the cosmos. Based on careful examination of the best planetary data available at the beginning of the sixteenth century, Nicolaus Copernicus (1473–1543) came to the following conclusion: "All the spheres revolve about the sun as their mid-point, and therefore the sun is the center of the universe."[1] Some 30 years later he would develop this idea more fully in *On the Revolutions of the Heavenly Spheres*, published as he lay dying in 1543.

The idea of heliocentrism has been so scientifically important and so culturally mythologized since the seventeenth century that it is hard for us to envision the many centuries in which people did not agree with Copernicus. Placing the sun at the center of the universe did indeed alter the human understanding of the cosmos. It collapsed the absolute distinction between the celestial and terrestrial worlds that had been an essential component of Aristotelian physics, transforming the earth from the unique physical center of the universe into just another planet. It offered a mathematical explanation for the observed order of the planets, leading other astronomers to scrutinize the heavens in order to find evidence that might confirm or deny this opinion. Observational astronomy became a more instrumental science because of Copernicus; as a result, within the next few generations the heavens were populated with many new phenomena that had previously gone undetected. The scientific community produced numerous revisions of the traditional portrait of the heavens in response to this fruitful combination of theory and practice. Quite unintentionally, Copernicus encouraged more radical philosophers to imagine an infinite universe with no center at all. By the end of the seventeenth century the controversial idea of a Polish canon would become the cornerstone of a new astronomy, an essential component of Isaac Newton's explanation of gravity as a physical force affecting both the heavens and the earth.

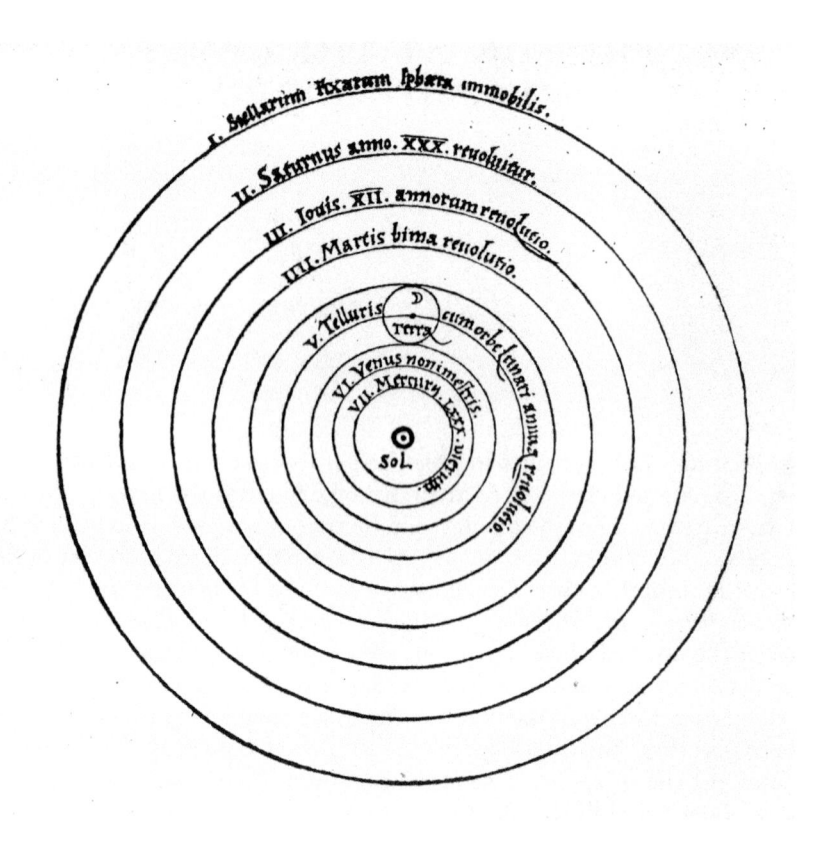

Figure 34.1 The heliocentric universe, from Copernicus, *De revolutionibus orbium coelestium* (Nuremburg, 1543). Select/Art Resource NY.

The essential features of Copernican astronomy can be summarized as follows: His universe was heliostatic, since the sun was not its mathematical but its physical center (Figure 34.1). Six planets – Mercury, Venus, Earth, Mars, Jupiter, and Saturn – moved around it in circles, while the moon, which had previously been the first planet of a geocentric system, was now the earth's satellite. Above the planets lay a sphere of fixed stars, an important feature of traditional astronomy, though Copernicus had considerably enlarged its size to reflect the new dimensions of his universe. Arguing for the harmony and unity of celestial motions, Copernicus provided a qualitative rationale for the position of the inferior and superior planets, explaining the perceived differences in their motions "around" the earth as an effect of the earth's new position in a solar system. He described the earth as having three principal motions: its daily eastward rotation on its axis, its annual westward rotation around the sun, and the conical rotation of its axis at the poles.

To accommodate the persistent eccentricity of planetary motions that resulted in trying to explain the circularity of what we now know to be elliptical orbits, Copernicus retained two key elements of Ptolemaic astronomy: the epicycle, a small circle on which each planet revolved as it followed its ideal circular orbit, and the eccentric, a mathematical point diverging from the exact center of the circular orbit in order to complete the process of transforming elliptical into circular motion. His astronomy rejected a third Ptolemaic device – the equant – whose angle helped to resolve the perceived speeding up and slowing down of the planets as they seemingly circled the earth. In a Copernican cosmos, everything moved with pleasing uniformity and regularity.

Copernicus was not the first astronomer to propose a heliocentric cosmology. A handful of ancient astronomers, mathematicians, and philosophers had entertained this idea since the fifth century BC, while some medieval Islamic astronomers had critiqued Ptolemaic astronomy for failing to represent the true nature of the heavens. According to Aristotle, the Pythagoreans believed that a great fire existed at the center of the universe and the earth orbited around it. This qualitative displacement of the earth from the center found a more detailed exposition in the calculations of Aristarchus of Samos (310–230 BC), whose lost work on heliocentrism was known to Copernicus only indirectly in brief accounts by other ancients such as Plutarch (*c.* AD 46–119). Aristarchus apparently had begun to explore the mathematical dimensions of a universe whose dimensions were much larger than those previously considered. Using the data of ancient astronomy, he raised some of the preliminary questions that would animate Copernicus' own inquiry into the state of the heavens; he may have begun to construct a heliocentric account of planetary motions. Yet since Greek astronomers and philosophers did not pursue this hypothesis further – finding it unconvincing – and since Aristarchus' own research on this subject did not survive, only the idea of heliocentrism could be considered truly ancient. Not until the appearance of Copernicus' *On the Revolutions* in 1543 did anyone offer a detailed exposition of how this theory might work in practice.

The early sixteenth century was a particularly auspicious moment for rethinking astronomy. The preceding half-century had seen a significant resurgence of interest in reforming this body of knowledge. The celestial observations and mathematical calculations of Georg Peuerbach (1423–61), professor at the University of Vienna, and his pupil Johannes Regiomontanus (1436–76), resulted in a critical revision of earlier editions of Ptolemy's *Almagest*. Their *Epitome of the Almagest*, completed by Regiomontanus in 1463 and first published in 1496, in conjunction with his printed edition of Peuerbach's influential textbook the *New Theorics of the Planets* in 1472, exemplified the revisions of ancient and medieval Ptolemaic astronomy then underway, even prior to the introduction of a new all-encompassing theory of planetary motion. Both astronomers emphasized the importance of instrumental observation and mathematical precision and uniformity to astronomy. They worried about the inability of many of their contemporaries to examine Ptolemy's work in its original language, Greek, and participated in the humanistic search for new exemplars that might generate fresh readings of the text. They sought to compare its data and conclusions with the content of medieval astronomical textbooks and tables calculating planetary positions. Regiomontanus, for example, was highly attentive to emerging discrepancies between new data and old theory. "I cannot but wonder at the indolence of the common astronomers of our age," he lamented in 1464, "who, just as credulous women, receive as something divine and immutable whatever they come upon in books either of tables or their canons, for they believe in writers and make no effort to find the truth."[2] He encouraged other astronomers to examine these errors, paving the way for a more rigorous re-evaluation of traditional astronomy.

The appearance of Copernicus' slim pamphlet also occurred at a critical moment in the history of the Roman Catholic Church's interest in a new astronomy. Calendar reform had preoccupied various Church officials and scholars since at least the middle of the fifteenth century. In 1470, for example, the learned Cardinal Bessarion suggested to Pope Paul II that it might be time to confront the discrepancies that had crept into the liturgical calendar. In an unpublished treatise Regiomontanus had discussed the growing gap between the official dating of Easter and the natural length of the year. The question of calendar reform resurfaced during the Fifth Lateran Council (1512–17), resulting in a papal commission of 1515 overseen by Paul of Middleburg, bishop of Fossombrone, who invited experts throughout the Catholic world to offer solutions to the imprecision of the calendar. While Copernicus' *Little Commentary* seems to have been written prior to these events, his magnificent *On the Revolutions* emerged as a product of careful reflection on the practical problems of astronomy for astronomers and churchmen alike at the height of the Renaissance. Both communities had a stake in the reinvention of the heavens.

PRACTICING ASTRONOMY IN THE RENAISSANCE

By the time Copernicus sketched the outline of his new theory he had absorbed many of the lessons of his predecessors engaged in the task of reforming the heavens. Starting in 1491, his youthful studies at the Kraków Academy exposed him to the astronomy of Peuerbach and Regiomontanus, perhaps at the hands of its distinguished astronomy professor, Albert Brudzewski (1445–97). When Copernicus' powerful uncle, Lucas Watzenrode, bishop of Warmia, sent him to Italy to study canon law at the University of Bologna, he continued to pursue his scientific interests. There the mathematics professor Domenico Maria Novara (1454–1504), a self-professed disciple of Regiomontanus with an increasingly critical view of Ptolemaic astronomy, became his mentor. Copernicus lived in Novara's house, attended his lectures, and made his first recorded observation – of a star eclipsed by the moon – with Novara on March 9, 1497.

During this important period of his intellectual formation Copernicus might have come across a section of Peuerbach and Regiomontanus' newly published *Epitome of the Almagest* that asked the following hypothetical question: "Does the earth move or remain at rest?"[3] While Peuerbach posed this question as an intellectual exercise in scholastic disputation in 1460, without ever suggesting any dissatisfaction with geocentrism, it took on new meaning several decades later in the hands of a critical and inquiring reader like Copernicus. Similarly, neo-Platonic writings by humanists such as Marsilio Ficino (1433–99) did not advocate heliocentrism but celebrated the symbolic importance of the sun in their Christian theology and revival of Platonic philosophy. "The sun can signify God himself to you, and who shall say that the sun is false," wrote Ficino in *The Book of the Sun* in 1494.[4] In all likelihood Copernicus did not become a heliocentrist in the late 1490s but honed his skills as a reader, observer, and calculator, all of which provided him with the tools to address one of the most critical scientific problems of his age.

The Italian peninsula, filled with scholars, manuscripts, great universities, a lively court culture, and a nascent printing industry, must have been an exhilarating place for a young northern European scholar eager to soak up learning. Copernicus stayed in Italy long enough to join the crowds of pilgrims flocking to Rome during the Jubilee of 1500, where he observed a lunar eclipse. After a brief trip to see his bishop-uncle, Copernicus received permission to return to Padua and pursue a second course of studies in the medical faculty, since it was this faculty in which such subjects as astronomy, astrology, and mathematics were taught. The opportunity to study in the Venetian Republic, one of the great centers for Greek learning in western Europe, gave Copernicus a chance to develop a facility with this language that would allow him to benefit from the first printing of the Greek original of Ptolemy's *Almagest* in 1538, while he was finalizing *On the Revolutions*. He was fully a product of the humanistic as well as scientific learning of the Renaissance.

Copernicus' astronomical activities excited considerable curiosity among astronomers, mathematicians, and clerics in the decade prior to the appearance of *On the Revolutions*. News of his activities traveled as far south as Rome. In 1533 Pope Clement VII presented the papal secretary Johann Albrecht Widmanstetter with a Greek manuscript after hearing his description of heliocentrism in the gardens of the Vatican. Widmanstetter subsequently became secretary to Nicholas Schönberg, cardinal of Capua, who wrote Copernicus on November 1, 1536 to congratulate him on formulating "a new cosmology." Schönberg urged the 63-year-old astronomer "to communicate this discovery of yours to scholars," and dispatched someone to copy Copernicus' treatise in Frombork and deliver it to him in Rome.[5] Did this happen? Possibly. Did the pope see the manuscript? Perhaps, though there is no documentation confirming that Clement ever saw a written account of the intriguing theory he had heard about a few years earlier. All we can say with any certainty is that two influential clerics – Schönberg and Tiedemann Giese, bishop of Chelmo – supported his work, and Copernicus did not neglect to mention them in the preface to his book.

They were not alone in their enthusiasm for Copernicus' new theory. In 1539, as news of his activities percolated through the lively German community of astronomers and mathematicians, a young German scholar, Georg Joachim Rheticus (1514–74), left the city of Wittenberg to travel to Frombork. His goal was to meet the man who was quietly reforming astronomy. He came laden with gifts designed to assure Copernicus of his good intentions. Upon his arrival, Rheticus presented Copernicus with three bound volumes containing five titles of special interest to a mathematical astronomer: the 1533 Greek edition of Euclid's *Geometry* bound with Regiomontanus' book on triangles, a 1534 trigonometry book by the distinguished Ingolstadt mathematician Petrus Apianus filled with sine tables, a 1535 edition of the thirteenth-century scholar Erazmus Witelo's *Optics*, and the 1538 Greek edition of Ptolemy.

At the moment of Rheticus' arrival, Copernicus had a complete draft of his book in hand. Rheticus became its first reader and Copernicus' only bona fide disciple. Rheticus was so enthralled with what he found that he composed a letter to the

Nuremberg astronomer and cartographer Johannes Schöner on September 23, 1539 before he had even completed reading the book in its entirety. The publication of Rheticus' *First Report* in 1540 conveyed his excitement about the possibilities of a new theory of the heavens: "I have mastered the first three books, grasped the general idea of the fourth, and begun to conceive the hypotheses of the rest," he wrote. Praising the "remarkable symmetry and interconnections of the motions and spheres," Rheticus celebrated heliocentrism on theological, astrological, and numerological grounds.[6] A heliocentric system revealed God the clockmaker who set the universe in motion, surrounded himself with exactly six planets, and revealed the vicissitudes of fortune according to the movement of the sun's eccentric, which Rheticus – not Copernicus – believed to be the arc by which such events as the rise and fall of empires, indeed the entire history of the world, could be traced.

When Rheticus returned to Wittenberg in December 1540 he was able to report in greater detail about the content of *On the Revolutions* to the distinguished group of astronomers and mathematicians in this city. The mathematics professor Erasmus Reinhold (1511–53) was so intrigued by what he heard that he inserted a reference to Copernicus in his *Commentary on Peurbach's New Theorics of the Planets* (1542): "He has raised a lively expectancy in everybody. One hopes that he will restore astronomy."[7] Rheticus generated enough interest to produce a second edition of his *First Narration* in 1541, as he returned to Frombork to persuade Copernicus to part with the manuscript. Within the year, he passed through Wittenberg again, now carrying his precious cargo to Nuremberg where Johannes Petreius would publish it with his assistance.

Upon hearing that he had been awarded a professorship at the University of Leipzig, Rheticus was forced to abandon his job as Copernicus' editor to take up his teaching. Between September 1542 and May 1543 the final preparation of the book was left in the hands of a Lutheran theologian, Andreas Osiander (1498–1552). In addition to having a personal relationship with the printer Petreius, who was also his publisher, Osiander had his own reasons to be interested in new developments in astronomy. He was in correspondence with many astronomers, among them Copernicus, about their work. Like his Catholic counterparts, he understood the significance of a more accurate account of the heavens to calendar reform. He may also have agreed with Rheticus about the apocalyptic relevance of a new astronomy in the age of the Reformation, since it would allow better predictions about such crucial subjects as the end of days.

Osiander completed the editing of *On the Revolutions*. His final contribution to the project was the insertion of an anonymous preface, "To the Reader Concerning the Hypothesis of This Work," appearing just after the title page and before Copernicus' own dedication to Pope Paul III. Osiander's preface presented heliocentrism as nothing more than a hypothesis in the sixteenth-century sense: a pleasing fiction that need not correspond in any way to physical reality but provided a new method for computing planetary positions and motions. "So far as hypotheses are concerned, let no one expect anything certain from astronomy, which cannot furnish it, lest he accept as the truth ideas conceived for another purpose, and depart from this study a greater fool than when he entered it."[8] Heliocentrism need not be true or even probable as long as it provided a sound basis for calculation.

Was this what Copernicus had intended? In correspondence with him during 1540 and 1541, Osiander had cautioned his Polish colleague against proclaiming heliocentrism to be the truth rather than a hypothesis. Since Copernicus' side of the correspondence is lost, we do not know how he responded to Osiander's suggestion that he address these issues in the preface. All we can say is that in his dedication to the pope, Copernicus defined the philosopher's task as a quest "to seek the truth in all things, to the extent permitted by human reason to God." He highlighted his hesitation to publish as not due to lack of confidence in his own conclusions but to concern over how they might be received by less knowledgeable readers. He expressed frustration over the lack of certainty in the cosmology of his idea, famously describing the Aristotelian-Ptolemaic cosmos as "a monster rather than a man."[9] Copernicus argued quite strongly that a deformed and poorly understood universe did little honor to the divine artisanship of God. Such statements led a number of readers, among them Johannes Kepler (1571–1630) and Galileo Galilei (1564–1642), to conclude that Copernicus did not share Osiander's views.

Copernicus' first editor, Rheticus, was so incensed when he saw what Osiander had done to his recently deceased master's work that he angrily obliterated this addition in red crayon. He, too, did not believe that it reflected Copernicus' opinion – and we should recall that he, after all, had worked closely with Copernicus for two years on the project, though not in the year of its completion. At least one important patron of *On the Revolutions* shared Rheticus' outrage. On July 26, 1543 Bishop Tiedemann Giese wrote to Rheticus to commiserate about "the wickedness of Petreius" in allowing Osiander to determine the final shape of the book. He invited Rheticus to take their complaints to the Nuremberg city council, re-edit the manuscript, and append to it Rheticus' own treatise, "in which you entirely correctly defend the earth's motion from being in conflict with the Holy Scripture."[10] They were firmly committed to upholding the truth of heliocentrism in the name of the originator of this idea.

THE GRADUAL ACCEPTANCE OF A THEORY

Neither Rheticus nor Giese were in the majority, however. Between 1543 and 1596 – the year in which Kepler published his overtly Copernican *Cosmographic Mystery* – no astronomy book declared strongly and unequivocally in print that heliocentrism was a true account of the cosmos. At the same time, astronomers, mathematicians, and natural philosophers did not ignore the appearance of *On the Revolutions*. They read and annotated it carefully, mining the densely mathematical sections that followed the prefatory matter and Book I for material that could improve the accuracy of astronomy. They also puzzled over its seeming contradictions – not only the mystery of the two prefaces but the paradoxes of a new astronomy that was still as technically elaborate as the Ptolemaic system, full of epicycles and eccentrics and therefore not truly a simplification of the system, and was also neglectful of the physical consequences of heliocentrism for Aristotelian natural philosophy. The great astrologer-physician Girolamo Cardano (1501–76) observed in 1547: "Indeed, the opinions of Copernicus are not yet well understood, for he barely seems to say what he wants."[11]

Nonetheless, gradually and with little fanfare, heliocentrism entered the curriculum of many European universities. In 1545 Reinhold's *Commentary* became the standard astronomy textbook at the University of Wittenberg. Around 1560 Wittenberg students would learn astronomy by reading Ptolemy's *Almagest* with Copernicus' *On the Revolutions*. In 1561 the statutes of the University of Salamanca allowed students to vote on whether they would like to devote their second year to reading Euclid, Ptolemy, or Copernicus. By 1594 Salamanca would simply require *On the Revolutions*. Heliocentrism was successfully taught by the mid-sixteenth century – not as an idea that vanquished geocentrism but as an alternative that enriched the calculating skills of astronomers without any explicit consideration of its physical and cosmological implications. It was possible to read Copernicus as a manual rather than a manifesto. Osiander's preface had helped to defuse the more controversial aspects of Copernicanism for all but a handful of true believers who could not stomach any effort to dilute its truth. He would have been pleased with the results.

The seeds of controversy that erupted in full force in the early seventeenth century, culminating in the Roman Catholic Church's decision to put *On the Revolutions* on the Index of Prohibited Books in 1616 and to try to condemn Galileo for advocating heliocentrism in 1633, were of course there from the start. As Copernicus himself recognized, there might be Scriptural objections to heliocentrism. "Perhaps there will be babblers who claim to be judges of astronomy although completely ignorant of the subject and, badly distorting some passages of Scripture to their purpose, will dare to find fault with my undertaking and censure it." He strongly cautioned them against pursuing this line of inquiry by invoking the specialized and arcane nature of his subject. "Astronomy is written for astronomers."[12] Nonetheless, the worry remained and this may have been one of the reasons why neither Rheticus nor Osiander, both Lutherans, were named in a text dedicated to a pope.

During the 1540s a few learned scholars and clerics, both Protestant and Catholic, attempted to define the relationship between heliocentrism and biblical cosmology; in particular, its description of the sun's and earth's movement. Bishop Giese, who encouraged Rheticus to publish his own treatise on this subject, seems to have composed a now lost treatise defending heliocentrism on biblical grounds. Rheticus' own work, probably written between 1541 and 1543, eventually resurfaced as an uncredited *Letter of a Certain Anonymous Author on the Motion of the Earth* in an obscure Utrecht publication of 1651. Highlighting the instances in which Aristotelian natural philosophy contradicted Scripture – for example, in its argument for the eternity of the world – Rheticus sought to demonstrate how current scientific teachings did not universally uphold faith. He argued passionately that "the Holy Spirit has not wished to compose a course of Physics, but rather a rule of life." Accordingly, the Bible cannot be read "as if Scripture were a philosophical textbook."[13] At the same time and without recognizing the potential contradiction, Rheticus eagerly sought to demonstrate that key biblical passages did indeed demonstrate the truth of heliocentrism in a more allegorical fashion. His goals were twofold: to defend heliocentrism's compatibility with Christianity while maintaining a distinction between theology and science as diverse but complementary realms of expertise that looked differently at the natural world.

The collaboration between a Catholic bishop and a Protestant mathematician in the defense of Copernicus in the 1540s might strike us as odd unto itself. Yet Giese's and Rheticus' shared interests reveal the ways in which the idea of heliocentrism became entangled with active efforts to reunify Christianity, or at the very least create the means for productive dialogue across sectarian divisions. Heliocentrism was a test case for the idea of philosophizing freely, a legacy of a world shaped by open-minded humanists such as Desiderius Erasmus (d. 1536) who believed that ideas could not diminish faith.

Yet this ecumenical view of the relationship between knowledge and faith was already under strain in the 1540s, as the failure of the Diet of Regensberg (1541) to reconcile Lutherans and Catholics signaled an end to the first stages of the Reformation. Had it not been for a providential death in the Apostolic Palace, Copernicus' *On the Revolutions* might well have been condemned by the Roman Catholic Church shortly after its appearance rather than in 1616. It was rumored in Rome that the Master of the Sacred Palace Bartolomeo Spina (d. 1546), the pope's theologian and later the official in charge of approving all book publications, planned to condemn *On the Revolutions*. Our evidence for this controversy comes from the pen of Spina's close associate, a Florentine Dominican named Giovanni Maria Tolosani (c. 1471–1549), who had also responded to the 1515 commission for the reform of the calendar with a short treatise on this subject. In 1544 he completed a new work entitled *On the Truth of Holy Scripture*. Subsequently he decided to add several appendices, including one dealing with *Heaven and the Elements* that discussed Copernicus' idea.

While praising Copernicus' skills as an astronomer and mathematician, Tolosani found fault with his work on other grounds. He critiqued his understanding of physics and logic, suggesting, not unreasonably in fact, that Copernicus had failed to develop the argument for heliocentrism on these grounds. "For Copernicus puts the indestructible sun in a place subject to destruction," he observed, invoking Aristotle's description of the Pythagorean fire at the center of the world. Tolosani further wondered what would happen to the Empyrean Heaven, the eighth and final crystalline sphere housing God in the traditional cosmology, when the heavens were no longer literally above the earth. He did not believe that even Copernicus himself considered heliocentrism to be true and invoked Osiander's letter as proof that *On the Revolutions* was a book filled with deliberately false hypotheses.

Most devastatingly, Tolosani highlighted the contradictions between the new astronomy and Scripture. In a form of deliberate understatement, he attributed these problems to Copernicus' lack of understanding of the Bible. "Pythagoreanism could easily give rise to quarrels between Catholic expounders of Holy Writ and those persons who might wish to adhere to this false belief. I have written this little work for the purpose of avoiding this scandal."[14] He reminded his readers that his friend Spina had planned to condemn the book. Since neither Rheticus nor Tolosani published their interpretations of the relationship between the Bible and the new astronomy, the extent to which heliocentrism might be theologically unsound doctrine did not become an immediate topic of public discussion. Instead, the most pressing issues for Copernicanism in the late sixteenth century were technical. Did this theory really improve Ptolemaic astronomy and offer astronomers, astrologers, and navigators a more accurate predictive science?

The great Flemish cartographer Gerard Mercator (1512–94) felt that it did. In 1551 he created the first celestial globe based on Copernicus' data. The man who produced the first map identifying North America by name and who invented an entirely new form of mathematical projection to depict the three-dimensional space of the globe on a two-dimensional surface was perhaps more open to revising the heavens because of his intimate knowledge of the dramatic changes in geography underway in an age of global exploration and conquest. Like his mentor Gemma Frisius (1508–55), who publicly praised Copernicus in 1555 for his fruitful combination of observation and geometric demonstration, Mercator valued techniques to improve the accuracy of scientific information. His decision to produce a Copernican globe coincided with increasingly favorable statements about the quality of this new data by noteworthy mathematicians such as the English magus John Dee (1527–1608), who studied with Mercator in the period when he was creating his celestial globe. While Dee himself never became a heliocentrist, he approached Copernicus in the manner of the Wittenberg circle that had incorporated the canon's findings into traditional astronomy.

Scattered references to heliocentrism abound during the 1550s, not only in the specialized works of astronomers and mathematicians but in vernacular publications designed to reach a broader audience. The Pléiade poet and bishop Pontus de Tyard (c. 1521–1605) offered a French summary and partial translation in his *The Universe or Discourse on the Parts of the World* (1552). Two years later an account of Copernicus' work appeared in a Spanish commentary on Plato's *Timaeus*. The mathematician Robert Recorde (c. 1510–58) presented the first description of heliocentrism in English in his *Castle of Knowledge* (1556). Slowly news of this interesting scientific theory traveled. It not only transformed the way astronomy was taught in the mid-sixteenth century but increasingly led perceptive observers and participants in these debates to demand some criteria by which one might ascertain how exactly the heavens moved. In 1565 the great French educational reformer Petrus Ramus (1515–72) offered to endow a chair in astronomy for anyone who could explain astronomy without hypotheses. Kepler later would joke in his *New Astronomy* (1609) that he had won this prize by making heliocentrism a physical fact.

In 1572 astronomers throughout Europe observed the appearance of a nova. It excited considerable curiosity and increased speculation about the problems of an Aristotelian account of the heavens, which were allegedly perfect, incorruptible, and eternal in contrast to the dynamic, changing earth. Even the Jesuit astronomer Christopher Clavius (1538–1612), a committed geocentrist, was forced to concede that the nova was supralunar. After observing the nova, the Elizabethan mathematician Thomas Digges (c. 1546–95) called for more extensive examination of Copernicus' idea. He became increasingly convinced of the fact of heliocentrism as the only plausible mathematical explanation of the harmonious ordering of the planets, writing on his own copy of *On the Revolutions* that geocentrism was simply a vulgar error. In his *Perfit Description of the Caelestial Orbes* of 1576, Digges famously modified Copernicus' own account of the universe by eliminating the sphere of fixed stars. Instead Digges imagined an infinite world, unending space populated by stars with the system of planets at its center.

Another observer of the 1572 nova, the Danish nobleman Tycho Brahe (1546–1601), also began to think more carefully about the implications of heliocentrism in the 1570s. In a public lecture at the University of Copenhagen in September 1574 he praised Copernicus for his observations and for the elimination of the Ptolemaic equant from astronomy, but nonetheless remained firmly opposed to heliocentrism. King Frederick II's munificent bequest of the island of Hven in 1576 provided Tycho with a unique opportunity to advance the cause of astronomy by creating Uraniborg, where he built an elaborate observatory, hired artisans to create bigger and better instruments, and employed assistants to aid him in the observation of the heavens. Rather than observing celestial phenomena periodically, Tycho sought to observe them continuously. His data revealed previously undetectable discrepancies in the perceived motions of the planets, further destabilizing traditional cosmology.

Tycho vastly increased the Ptolemaic star catalogue. He spent over two months observing the next important heavenly phenomenon: the comet of 1577. His record of its path further convinced him that the Aristotelian distinction between the celestial and terrestrial realms did not exist in nature: the comet clearly was high above the moon, where it should not be. He wondered how it might reveal the relations among all the different bodies in the heavens. Since the comet's tail pointed away from the sun, Tycho reasonably concluded that its orbit was heliocentric. This ought to have made him a Copernican, by our count, but Tycho was not yet prepared to throw out the baby with the bath water. He simply could not imagine a moving earth and he increasingly found error with Copernicus' observations as the instruments and observers at Uraniborg generated new and better results. At the same time, subsequent observations – for example, the orbits of Mars and Venus during the 1580s – convinced him that elements of heliocentrism were true. An opportunity to view another comet in 1585 further cemented his opinion that the crystalline spheres did not exist. Finally he was ready to announce to the public his conclusions about the actual shape of the cosmos. In 1588 he published *Concerning the New Phenomena in the Ethereal World*, announcing a third alternative to geocentrism and heliocentrism: a geoheliocentric system that maintained the earth at its center, with the sun and moon orbiting around it, while placing all other planets in motion around the sun.

Tycho's compromise may strike us as unsatisfying, a transparent attempt to preserve the core principle of an ancient idea while accommodating new observations and conclusions. The artificiality of this system, as much as the debates over novas and comets, spurred a handful of astronomers committed to the physical dimensions of heliocentrism to declare themselves wholeheartedly in favor of Copernicus – among them the Hessian court astronomer Christoph Rothmann (1550–c.1650), who visited Tycho at Uraniborg in 1590 to debate these points of astronomy. Rothmann increasingly felt that efforts to diminish the cosmological aspects of Copernicus' theory reduced it to nothing more than a convenient calculating device rather than a reasoned exploration of the true nature of the heavens. The young Kepler, who began his study of astronomy with Michael Maestlin (1550–1631) at Tübingen in

1589, was equally dissatisfied with the idea of astronomy as a speculative fiction without teeth. His highly theological conception of science as a higher calling necessitated the creation of an astronomy concerned with truth as well as accuracy. His explanations in the *Cosmographic Mystery* were "physical, or rather metaphysical" in contrast with the arguments of Copernicus who was satisfied, much to Kepler's dismay, vaguely to place the sun *near* but not *at* the center of the universe.[15]

Others, such as the Jesuit Clavius, who was increasingly critical of Copernicus in print between the 1570s and 1610s, found the Tychonic system an appealing alternative. "The earth ought to stand firm at the center of the whole world," he affirmed repeatedly in his influential textbook.[16] Clavius understood the value of Copernicus' contribution to mathematical astronomy but could not satisfactorily resolve its violation of the tenets of Aristotelian physics and its contradictions with Scripture. Yet he also belonged to a generation that finally addressed the question that had initiated Copernicus' own research. He participated in the final calendar commission, whose 1580 report to Pope Gregory XIII resulted in the loss of ten days for Roman Catholics, as the Gregorian calendar leapt forward from October 4 to October 15, 1582 to synchronize Church time with the celestial clock. The Dominican mathematician Egnazio Danti (1536–86) played a crucial role in this endeavor by demonstrating the ten-day gap using a meridian he constructed in the Tower of Winds at the Vatican. Copernican data and methods of calculation contributed to the success of this project, but no official endorsement of the theory was forthcoming.

By the 1590s a strictly Aristotelian-Ptolemaic system seemed increasingly untenable. Even astronomers unwilling to commit to heliocentrism agreed on this fact, especially once Galileo transformed their science by observing the heavens with a telescope in 1609 and 1610.[17] His observations of the moon made it more earth-like – full of mountains, valleys, and craters, and other physical irregularities that further weakened the Aristotelian explanation of planets as exemplars of celestial perfection. Galileo also put to rest a key criticism of Copernican astronomy, which queried why only the earth would have a satellite. Between January and March 1610 he observed several mysterious planetary bodies circling Jupiter and came to the conclusion that they were its four "moons." Aware of the significance of his discovery, Galileo rushed his findings into print, publishing his *Sidereal Messenger* (1610) so quickly that he was still completing his observations while the first pages rolled off the press.

Leading astronomers, among them Clavius and Kepler, confirmed Galileo's findings. Subsequent telescopic observations revealed the phases of Venus – impossible to imagine in a strictly geocentric system where Venus would always be fully visible as it circled the earth – and the presence of sunspots at or near the sun's surface. Like Tycho before them, the seventeenth-century astronomers who participated in the identification of these new celestial phenomena without wanting to commit to Copernicanism had to find a resolution to the growing rift between theory and observation. In 1620 the Society of Jesus, whose order produced many of the best Catholic astronomers of the late sixteenth and seventeenth centuries, officially adopted the cosmology of the Danish Lutheran Tycho. When the Jesuit astronomer Giovanni Battista Riccioli (1598–1671) published his *New Almagest* (1651), he

Figure 34.2 G. B. Riccioli. *Almagestum novum astronomiam veterem novamque complectens* (Bologna, 1651). Scala Archives.

allegorized the demise of the Ptolemaic system by depicting the astronomical muse Urania weighing the value of competing cosmologies (Figure 34.2). Ptolemy's system lay discarded on the ground while Riccioli's own modified Tychonic system – in which only Mercury, Venus, and Mars orbited the sun while Jupiter and Saturn retained the earth as their central reference point – outweighed heliocentrism in its virtues. Geoheliocentrism had finally arrived.

COMMITTING TO HELIOCENTRISM

In *The Ash Wednesday Supper* of 1584, the ex-Dominican Giordano Bruno (1548–1600) passionately embraced Copernicanism as an article of faith. His book presented Copernicus as a harbinger of an even deeper truth – the idea of an unbounded cosmos, an animistic, magical, and pluralistic universe with multiple solar systems and deities – that only Bruno could reveal. Bruno felt that Copernicus' mathematical outlook limited his understanding of the true nature of heliocentrism which was, for Bruno and no one else, a physics of infinity. The sun could not be *the* center of the universe, though Bruno was quite certain it was the center of our solar system, because "no body can simply be in the middle of the universe or at its periphery or anywhere between these two limits."[18] Crafting a natural philosophy in support of his heretical theology, Bruno considered heliocentrism to be an important point of departure for even more radical ideas about the role of science in transforming faith.

Like Rheticus, Bruno did not reflect general opinion. At the dawn of the seventeenth century many prominent scientific figures were reluctant to give their assent to the idea of heliocentrism. Francis Bacon (1561–1626) allowed for its possibility in *The Advancement of Learning* (1605) before determining that it had been insufficiently proven. The French encyclopedist Jean Bodin (1530–96) – no friend of Aristotle in other respects – was quite sure of its absurdity since he felt that cosmology was more a question of physics than of mathematics. "No one in his senses, or imbued with the slightest knowledge of physics, will ever think that the earth, heavy and unwieldy from its own weight and mass, staggers up and down around its own center and that of the sun," he responded tartly in 1596.[19] Bodin did not live long enough to incorporate a new vision of astronomy created by Kepler, which addressed these criticisms by developing specific physical arguments in support of heliocentrism. While Rheticus, Digges, and Rothmann all agreed that Copernican astronomy was more than just an interesting hypothesis, Kepler sought to prove that heliocentrism could indeed be a simpler, more powerful, and unifying account of God's creation.

Kepler's *Cosmographic Mystery* inaugurated this project by defining the heliocentric ordering of the planets in relation to the nesting of the five Platonic solids. He argued that there was a divinely inscribed geometry of the universe that did not permit random reordering. After sending Galileo two copies of his book, Kepler received an encouraging letter in return from the Tuscan mathematics professor who was then living in Padua. Galileo wrote on August 4, 1597 that he had secretly been a Copernican for many years but had not published on the subject, "intimidated by the fortune of our teacher Copernicus, who though he will be of immortal fame to some, is yet by an infinite number (for such is the multiplicity of fools) laughed at and rejected." Kepler responded two months later, urging Galileo to defend Copernicus publicly: "so great is the power of truth."[20]

The truth of Copernicanism was increasingly on the minds of astronomers and natural philosophers. The English physician William Gilbert's (1544–1603) treatise *On the Loadstone* (1600) reflected the emerging consensus that Copernicus had argued "not with mere probability but with certainty" that the earth revolved daily around its axis. Gilbert offered a novel explanation of the physical basis for the earth's motion by describing it as a product of the sun's influence conjoined with the "astral magnetic mind" of the earth that drew it physically into an orbit around the sun. Describing the sun as "chief inciter of action in nature," he hypothesized magnetism as a specific physical cause for the earth's rotation.[21] Kepler would find this idea very appealing since it helped to explain why the earth must rotate the sun. "In the center of the world is the sun, heart of the universe, fountain of light, source of heat, origin of life and cosmic motion," he proclaimed in his *Conversation with the Sidereal Messenger* (1610), written immediately upon hearing news of Galileo's spectacular discoveries with the telescope.[22]

Between 1596 and 1619 Kepler built his case for heliocentrism, in part, by rejecting key assumptions of Copernican astronomy. By the time he published his *New Astronomy* (1609) he no longer believed that planets moved in perfect circles. He presented readers with a breathtaking account of his first two laws, arguing (1) that planets moved elliptically with the sun as one of their two foci, and (2) that they did so by covering equal areas in equal times. These findings addressed several problems of Copernican astronomy. They made the mathematical account of planetary motion a direct reflection of its physical appearance, eliminating the artifice of both the Ptolemaic and Copernican systems while reintroducing the equant as a device that helped to measure the otherwise erratic progression of planets in time and space. He subsequently presented his third or harmonic law – a constant in which the square of periodic times of the planets' orbits equals the cube of their mean distances – in *The Harmony of the World* (1619). This insight revealed the great architecture of the cosmos that Kepler had been searching for since his early exposure to heliocentrism with Maestlin in Tübingen.

Kepler, who had worked as an assistant to Tycho Brahe in Prague (in 1600–1), could not have performed this feat without access to Tycho's splendid data. His famous obsession with accuracy, which led him to calculate and recalculate the orbit of Mars for eight years until he diminished the degree of error, was a critical factor in his willingness to rethink the cosmos. But we should also credit his splendid imagination, which allowed him to deform the circle in order to create a different shape that conformed to his data, to select the best mathematical tools to describe what he saw, and to offer creative solutions to the problems of a new astronomy. It was in the *New Astronomy* that Kepler not only declared "the truth of the Copernican hypothesis" on his own grounds but finally unmasked in print what many scholars had privately suspected: that Osiander rather than Copernicus was the author of the anonymous letter that opened *On the Revolutions*.[23] His *Epitome of Copernican Astronomy* (1618–21) elaborated the workings of a science that no longer had its origins in antiquity but had begun in 1543.

Kepler believed astronomers to be priests of nature, compelled to illuminate its sacred truths. He argued, for example, that the sunspots observed in the years 1611 to 1613 by astronomers such as the Jesuits Christoph Scheiner and his rival Galileo indicated the presence of a soul within the sun. When he republished his *Cosmographic Mystery* in 1621, he recalled how critics of his astronomy had tried to suppress its publication and successfully attacked his Scriptural defense of heliocentrism in such works as the *Epitome*. He warned his adversaries "not to twist the tongue of God so that it refutes the finger of God in nature."[24] By the time he wrote these words, Galileo had been privately warned by the pope's theologian, cardinal Robert Bellarmine (1542–1621), in February 1616 to abandon heliocentrism; he had been told by the Cardinal Inquisitor Michelangelo Segizzi "henceforth not to hold, teach, or defend it in any way whatever, either orally or in writing." On March 5, 1616 the Roman Catholic Church placed *On the Revolutions* on the Index of Prohibited Books, in conformance with the Roman Inquisition's decree that the idea of a motionless sun at the center of the universe was "foolish and absurd in philosophy and formally heretical." Similarly, the 11 consultants asked to judge this book declared the idea of a moving earth to be equally preposterous on philosophical grounds but merely "erroneous in faith."[25] They advised the Congregation of the Index to draw up a plan to edit the book since it was considered critical to the new science of the calendar. "If certain passages on the motion are not hypothetical, make them hypothetical; then they will not be against . . . the truth of the Holy Writ."[26] The Lutheran Kepler publicly lamented this turn of events and found his *Epitome* on the Index in 1619.

Throughout the 1610s, as Galileo inaugurated a new age of instruments and observations and Kepler proclaimed a new astronomy, theologians, astronomers, and natural philosophers working within the Roman Catholic Church grew increasingly concerned about the problem of reconciling heliocentrism with Scripture. Emboldened by his discoveries, Galileo accepted Kepler's challenge to defend Copernicus' idea. While his *Sidereal Messenger* was tacitly Copernican, his *Letters on Sunspots* (1613) left no doubt where his sympathies lay. "An understanding of what Copernicus wrote in his *Revolutions* suffices for the most expert astronomers to ascertain that Venus revolves about the Sun, as well as to verify the rest of his system."[27]

Then in his unpublished "Considerations on the Copernican Opinion," written in 1615 shortly before the condemnation of Copernicus, Galileo argued that "there is more value in the authority of a single person who follows the Copernican opinion than in that of one hundred others who hold the contrary, since those who are persuaded of the truth of the Copernican system were in the beginning all very opposed."[28] Pressured from many directions about the theological consequences of heliocentrism and concerned about the hardening of attitudes in Rome, he composed his famous *Letter to the Grand Duchess Christina* in 1615, though it remained unpublished until 1636. This manifesto on the relationship between science and Scripture argued passionately for the unity of truth, knowing that the fate of a scientific theory hung in the balance. Galileo uncontroversially argued that scientific truth and the Bible could not contradict each other. However, he began to tread on dangerous ground when he not only interpreted key Scriptural passages in favor of heliocentrism – a theologian's job – but argued that Scripture ought to be illuminated by science, at least in matters concerning the natural world.[29] Indirectly, Galileo received a warning from his patron and friend, Cardinal Maffeo Barberini (1568–1644) in February 1615, cautioning him "to limit his arguments to mathematics and physics without getting into the theology of the matter."[30] As Bellarmine also reminded him, many people did not yet believe that the Copernicans had proved their case definitively and quite a few felt that astronomy could never be more than a hypothetical science.

Galileo disagreed but he did so quietly after 1616. He did not want to be associated with the public infamy of the Carmelite friar Paolo Antonio Foscarini's *Letter on the Pythagorean and Copernican Opinion of the Earth's Motion and Sun's Rest and the New Pythagorean World System* (1615), which had received far harsher treatment than either Copernicus' book or the Augustian theologian Diego de Zuñiga's pro-Copernican *Commentary of Job* (1584), both suspended until corrected; instead it had been "completely prohibited and condemned" by the consultants to the Holy Office.[31] He also kept his distance from one of his most enthusiastic supporters, the controversial Dominican Tommaso Campanella (1568–1639), whose *Defense of Galileo* was written from a Neapolitan prison, shortly before or after the 1616 decree and subsequently published in Protestant Frankfurt in 1622. One year later Campanella published his utopian *City of the Sun*, describing an ideal society of Solarians who admired Copernicus without absolutely subscribing to his ideas because they, in the tradition of Bruno, had their own "new astronomy."

Galileo dutifully complied with the corrections to Copernicus mandated by the Congregation of the Index in 1620. He revised his own copy of *On the Revolutions* to expunge any statements of the fact of heliocentrism – just like the Jesuits who brought two censored copies of the book on their 1618 mission to China to show Beijing the best fruits of European astronomy. Galileo began to outline what he believed to be compelling physical evidence that might disabuse even Bellarmine of his position: his ultimately flawed theory of the tides that became the centerpiece of arguments in favor of Copernicanism in his controversial *Dialogue Concerning the Two Chief World Systems* (1632) (Figure 34.3).[32]

The election of his fellow Florentine Barberini as Pope Urban VIII in 1623 gave Galileo new hope for a public airing of these issues. He renewed his attacks on opponents and returned to a project that he described to readers of his *Sidereal Messenger* as the *System of the World*. As the title suggests, Galileo's original idea had been to write a treatise on *the* system of the world, which was evidently Copernican. The events of 1616 modified these plans. He instead crafted a dialogue with three participants: the witty Copernican Salviati, his Venetian friend Sagredo whose job was to arbitrate the discussion, and the dull-witted defender of the Aristotelian-Ptolemaic view aptly named Simplicio. In contrast to Copernicus, whose frontispiece proclaimed in Greek, "Let no one untrained in geometry enter here," Galileo's *Dialogue* was written in an elegant Tuscan style and eschewed dense mathematical and physical proofs in favor of arguments drawing upon common knowledge and experience. He deliberately made its content accessible to generally literate readers and did everything possible to encourage them to laugh at the folly and stupidity of those stubborn minds that would not change with the times. Even the allegedly

Figure 34.3 Frontispiece from Galileo, *Dialogo sopra i due massimi sistemi del mondo* (Florence, 1632). The British Library.

impartial Sagredo concluded after four days of conversation that "we have, then, strong evidences in favor of the Copernican system." Galileo overtly expressed his contempt for geocentrism. "Utterly childish reasons suffice to keep imbeciles believing in the fixity of the earth," he printed in the margin next to a speech by Simplicio.[33] He wrote that if Aristotle were alive in 1632 even he would change his mind. He blatantly allowed no room for geoheliocentrism, deriding the Tychonic compromise in no uncertain terms at the end of the book. There were only *two* systems of the world to debate in his analysis, and only one was right.

Galileo hoped that the hypothetical nature of a dialogue might conform to the guidelines imposed in 1616, especially when they were liberally interpreted by a more lenient papacy. Events proved him wrong. Galileo published the *Dialogue* in February 1632; by the summer it had been confiscated by the Holy Office and an irate pope had appointed a special commission to review its content. In September 1632 the commission determined that Galileo had indeed violated the 1616 decree, and the Inquisition summoned him to Rome. After delaying as long as possible, Galileo reluctantly complied. Between April and June 1633, the Inquisition examined the aging mathematician four times. The sentence of June 22, 1633 declared Galileo "vehemently suspected of heresy," prohibited the *Dialogue*, and invited him publicly to recant his belief in heliocentrism.[34] After formally abjuring in Rome, Galileo spent the remainder of his life under house arrest in Arcetri, in the hills just outside Florence.

At Arcetri Galileo continued to meditate on the consequences of the Roman Catholic Church's decision to declare heliocentrism a heresy. On his own copy of the *Dialogue*, he scribbled the following observation:

> Take note, theologians, that in your desire to make matters of faith out of propositions relating to the fixity of the sun and the earth you run the risk of eventually having to condemn as heretics those who would declare the earth to stand still and the sun to change position – eventually, I say, at such a time as it might be physically or logically proved that the earth moves and the sun stands still.[35]

At what point was heliocentrism scientifically proven? The 1616 decree had not prohibited discussion of this idea by any means. It specifically banned any declaration of it as a proven truth. While the popular view of the trial and condemnation of Galileo has presented it as the end of scientific inquiry in the Catholic world, this was far from the case. Many of the best astronomers and mathematicians of the late seventeenth and eighteenth centuries did their work in the universities, academies, and religious orders of the Italian peninsula. They continued to discuss Copernicus' theory, albeit only in hypothetical terms.

When the Jesuit Riccioli published his *New Almagest* in 1651 he still considered arguments for heliocentrism to be insufficient. Many Jesuits in the mid-seventeenth century felt compelled, whether out of obedience or personal conviction, publicly to reject Copernicanism in print. Other Catholic scholars such as René Descartes (1596–1650) responded to the events of 1632–3 by revising their own philosophies of nature, delaying publication of anything controversial to avoid the fate of Galileo. Bolder souls, among them Gottfried Wilhelm Leibniz (1646–1716) at the end of the century, worked to convince the papacy that it had all been a colossal mistake. "For this hypothesis is now confirmed by so many reasons, taken from new discoveries," wrote the Protestant Leibniz in 1688, "that the greatest astronomers hardly doubt it any longer."[36] Writing one year after the appearance of Isaac Newton's

(1642–1727) *Mathematical Principles of Natural Philosophy* (1687), Leibniz referred not specifically to this important work but more generally to the effect of several decades of further observations and calculations, done on behalf of new institutions such as the Royal Society of London (founded 1660), the Royal Observatory at Greenwich (founded 1675), and the Paris Academy of Sciences (founded 1666), with greatly improved instruments such as Newton's reflecting telescope. On several occasions during the 1690s and early 1700s, he sought to rectify what he considered to be a grave injustice. Privately, many Catholic astronomers agreed with him.

While the Congregation of the Index did not remove its ban on Copernican books until 1758, Copernicus' arguments, made some 200 years earlier, had, through the observations and practices of several generations of astronomers and humanists, gained the upper hand well before the papacy gave its official nod to heliocentrism. Galileo's marginalia in his own copy of the *Dialogue* proved prophetic. Indeed, to a majority of astronomers and theologians it was clear by the end of the seventeenth century – well before the Church acted – that the sun, not the earth, stood at the center of the universe. Building on methods developed by Renaissance humanists and astronomers, Copernicus, Kepler, Brahe, and Galileo had gradually eroded and then eventually overthrown a cosmology that had put humankind at the center of creation for the previous millennium.

NOTES

1 Nicolaus Copernicus, *Commentariolus* (c. 1514), in *Three Copernican Treatises*, 2nd edn, ed. Edward Rosen (New York: Dover, 1959), p. 58. Some readings date it as early as 1507 and as late as 1515. This edition dates it *c.* 1512, but I am using the most recent dating by Owen Gingerich.
2 Noel Swerdlow, "Regiomontanus on the Critical Problems of Astronomy," in *Nature, Experiment, and the Sciences: Essays on Galileo and the History of Science in Honour of Stillman Drake* (Dordrecht: Kluwer, 1990), pp. 170–1 (Johannes Regiomontanus to Giovanni Bianchini, undated letter written after February 11, 1464).
3 As quoted in E. J. Aiton, "Peuerbach's Theoricae novae planetarum: A Translation with Commentary," *Osiris* 2nd ser., 3 (1987): 8.
4 As quoted in Thomas Kuhn, *The Copernican Revolution* (Cambridge, Mass.: Harvard University Press, 1957), p. 130.
5 Nicolaus Copernicus, *On the Revolutions*, ed. and trans. Edward Rosen, 2nd edn (Baltimore: Johns Hopkins University Press, 1992), p. xxi.
6 Georg Joachim Rheticus, *Narratio prima* (1540), in Rosen, *Three Copernican Treatises*, pp. 110, 145.
7 Erasmus Rheinhold, *Theoricae novae planetarum Georgii Purbacchij Germani ab Erasmo Reinholdo Salueldensi pluribus figuris auctae, & illustratae scholiis, quibus studiosi praeparentur, ac inuitentur ad lectionem ipsius Ptolemaei* (Wittenberg, 1542), in Kenneth J. Howell, *God's Two Books: Copernican Cosmology and Biblical Interpretation in Early Modern Science* (Notre Dame, Ind.: University of Notre Dame Press, 2002), p. 67.
8 Copernicus, *On the Revolutions*, p. xx.
9 Copernicus, *On the Revolutions*, pp. 3–4.
10 Copernicus, *On the Revolutions*, p. 339.
11 Girolamo Cardano, *Apohrismata astronomica* (Nuremberg, 1547), aphorism 69, as quoted

in Owen Gingerich, *The Book Nobody Read: Chasing the Revolutions of Nicolaus Copernicus* (New York: Walker & Company, 2004), p. 181.
12. Copernicus, *On the Revolutions*, p. 5.
13. While the authorship of this text remains uncertain, I am inclined to agree with scholars who have attributed it to Rheticus based on internal evidence. R. Hookyaas, ed. and trans., *G. J. Rheticus' Treatise on the Holy Scripture and the Motion of the Earth* (Amsterdam: North-Holland Publishing Company, 1984), pp. 93, 71.
14. Giovanni Maria Tolosani, *De coele supreme immobili et terra infirma stabili, coterisque coelis et elementis intermediis mobilibus*, appendix to *De veritate sacrae scripturae* (1544), as quoted in Edward Rosen, "Was Copernicus' *Revolutions* Approved by the Pope?" *Journal of the History of Ideas* 36 (1975): 536, 538.
15. Johannes Kepler, *Mysterium Cosmographicum: The Secret of the Universe*, trans. A. M. Duncan, ed. E. J. Aiton (New York: Abaris, 1981), p. 63.
16. Christopher Clavius, *Commentary on the Sphere of Sacrobosco*, as quoted in James M. Lattis, *Between Copernicus and Galileo: Christoph Clavius and the Collapse of Ptolemaic Cosmology* (Chicago: University of Chicago Press, 1994), p. 117.
17. Galileo's English contemporary Thomas Harriot also designed a telescope independently in 1609 and used it to observe the moon and later sunspots. However, since he did not publish his findings they did not have the impact of Galileo's spectacularly public discoveries.
18. Giordano Bruno, *The Ash Wednesday Supper*, 2nd edn, ed. and trans. Edward A. Gosselin and Lawrence S. Lerner (Toronto: University of Toronto Press, 1995), p. 152.
19. Jean Bodin, *Univerae naturae theatrum* (1596), as quoted in Dorothy Stimson, *The Gradual Acceptance of the Copernican Theory of the Universe*, 2nd edn (Gloucester, Mass.: Peter Smith, 1972).
20. Galileo quoted in Stillman Drake, *Galileo at Work: His Scientific Biography* (Chicago: University of Chicago Press, 1978), p. 41; Kepler quoted in Hans Blumberg, *The Genesis of the Copernican World*, trans. Robert M. Wallace (Cambridge, Mass.: MIT Press, 1987), p. 387.
21. William Gilbert, *De magnete*, trans. Father Fleury Mottelay (New York: Dover, 1958), pp. 327, 333, 344.
22. Edward Rosen, ed. and trans., *Kepler's Conversation with Galileo's Sidereal Messenger* (New York: Johnson Reprint Corporation, 1965), p. 45.
23. Johannes Kepler, *New Astronomy*, trans. William H. Donahue (Cambridge: Cambridge University Press, 1992), p. 66.
24. Kepler, *Mysterium Cosmographicum*, p. 85.
25. Maurice A. Finocchiaro, ed. and trans., *The Galileo Affair: A Documentary History* (Berkeley: University of California Press, 1989), pp. 146–7.
26. Anon., *On the Emendation of the Six Books of Nicholas Copernicus' De revolutionibus* (Biblioteca Apostolica Vaticana, Cod. Barb. XXXIX.55), as quoted in Owen Gingerich, *The Eye of Heaven: Ptolemy, Copernicus, Kepler* (New York: American Institute of Physics, 1993), p. 276.
27. Stillman Drake, ed. and trans., *Discoveries and Opinions of Galileo* (Garden City, N.J.: Doubleday Anchor, 1957), p. 130.
28. Finocchiaro, *Galileo Affair*, p. 72.
29. The biblical passages relevant to the debate about heliocentrism included Genesis 1: 14, Joshua 10: 12, Job 9: 6 and 26: 7, Ecclesiastes 1: 4–5, Proverbs 30: 3, and Psalm 104: 5.
30. Howell, *God's Two Books*, p. 188 (Giovanni Ciampoli to Galileo, February 27, 1615).
31. Finocchiaro, *Galileo Affair*, p. 149.

32 Galileo argued that the earth's motion around the sun produced the tides, eschewing earlier explanations that they were a product of lunar influence because he believed this idea to be too occult. He ignored discrepancies in his own data to argue this point forcefully. By contrast, Kepler's ability to imagine the role of unseen physical forces in nature reinforced the idea of lunar attraction, which Newton would later describe as the effect of gravitation.
33 Copernicus, *On the Revolutions*, p. xix; Galileo Galilei, *Dialogue Concerning the Two Chief World Systems*, 2nd edn, ed. and trans. Stillman Drake (New York: Modern Library, 2001), pp. 380, 536.
34 Finocchiaro, *The Galileo Affair*, p. 291.
35 Howell, *God's Two Books*, p. 195.
36 Maurice A. Finocchiaro, *Retrying Galileo 1633–1992* (Berkeley: University of California Press, 2005), p. 102.

SUGGESTIONS FOR FURTHER READING

Barker, Peter. "Constructing Copernicus." *Perspectives on Science* 10 (2002): 208–27.
Biagioli, Mario. *Galileo, Courtier: The Practice of Science in an Age of Absolutism*. Chicago: University of Chicago Press, 1993.
Blackwell, Richard. *Galileo, Bellarmine, and the Bible*. Notre Dame, Ind.: University of Notre Dame Press, 1991.
Blair, Ann. "Tycho Brahe's Critique of Copernicus and the Copernican System." *Journal of the History of Ideas* 51 (1990): 355–77.
Blumenberg, Hans. *The Genesis of the Copernican World*, trans. Robert M. Wallace. Cambridge, Mass.: MIT Press, 1987.
Fantoli, Annibale. *Galileo: For Copernicanism and the Church*. Rome: Vatican Observatory Publications, 1994.
Feldhay, Rivka. *Galileo and the Church: Political Inquisition or Critical Dialogue?* Cambridge: Cambridge University Press, 1995.
Finocchiaro, Maurice. *Retrying Galileo 1633–1992*. Berkeley: University of California Press, 2005.
Gatti, Hilary. *Giordano Bruno and Renaissance Science*. Ithaca, N.Y.: Cornell University Press, 1999.
Gingerich, Owen and Robert S. Westman. *The Wittich Connection: Conflict and Priority in Late Sixteenth-century Science*. Transactions of the American Philosophical Society, vol. 78, part 7. Philadelphia, 1988.
—— *The Eye of Heaven: Ptolemy, Copernicus, Kepler*. New York: American Institute of Physics, 1993.
—— *The Book That Nobody Read: Chasing the Revolutions of Nicolaus Copernicus*. New York: Walker & Company, 2004.
Heilbron, John L. *The Sun in the Church: Cathedrals as Solar Observatories*. Cambridge, Mass.: Harvard University Press, 1999.
Hellyer, Marcus. *Catholic Physics: Jesuit Natural Philosophy in Early Modern Germany*. Notre Dame, Ind.: University of Notre Dame Press, 2005.
Howell, Kenneth J. *God's Two Books: Copernican Cosmology and Biblical Interpretation in Early Modern Science*. Notre Dame, Ind.: University of Notre Dame Press, 2002.
Johnson, Francis R. "The Influence of Thomas Digges on the Progress of Modern Astronomy in Sixteenth-Century England." *Osiris* 1 (1936): 390–410.

Kozhamthadam, Job, S.J. *The Discovery of Kepler's Laws: The Interaction of Science, Philosophy, and Religion*. Notre Dame, Ind.: University of Notre Dame Press, 1994.

Kuhn, Thomas S. *The Copernican Revolution: Planetary Astronomy in the Development of Western Thought*. Cambridge, Mass.: Harvard University Press, 1957.

Lattis, James. *Between Copernicus and Galileo: Christoph Clavius and the Collapse of Ptolemaic Astronomy*. Chicago: University of Chicago Press, 1994.

Lindberg, David C. and Ronald L. Numbers, eds. *God and Nature: Historical Essays on the Encounter between Christianity and Science*. Berkeley: University of California Press, 1986.

Metheun, Charlotte. "Maestlin's Teaching of Copernicus: The Evidence of His University Textbook and Disputations." *Isis* 87 (1996): 230–47.

Moran, Bruce T. "Christoph Rothmann, the Copernican Theory, and Institutional and Technical Influences on the Criticism of Aristotelian Cosmology." *Sixteenth Century Journal* 13 (1982): 85–108.

Navarro Brotons, Victor. "The Reception of Copernicus in Sixteenth-century Spain: The Case of Diego de Zúñiga." *Isis* 86 (1995): 52–78.

Rosen, Edward. "Was Copernicus' *Revolutions* Approved by the Pope?" *Journal of the History of Ideas* 36 (1975): 531–42.

Schofield, Christine Jones. *Tychonic and Semi-Tychonic World Systems*. New York: Abaris, 1981.

Shea, William. "Galileo's Copernicanism: The Science and the Rhetoric," in Peter Machamar, ed., *The Cambridge Companion to Galileo*. Cambridge: Cambridge University Press, 1998, 211–43.

Stevenson, Bruce. *Kepler's Physical Astronomy*. Princeton: Princeton University Press, 1994.

Stimson, Dorothy. *The Gradual Acceptance of the Copernican Theory of the Universe*, 2nd edn. Gloucester, Mass.: Peter Smith, 1972.

Westman, Robert S. "The Melachthon Circle, Rheticus and the Wittenberg Interpretation of the Copernican Theory." *Isis* 85 (1974): 79–115.

—— "The Astronomer's Role in the Sixteenth Century: A Preliminary Study." *History of Science* 18 (1980): 105–47.

—— "Proof, Poetics, and Patronage: Copernicus' Preface to *De revolutionibus*," in David C. Lindberg and Robert S. Westman, eds, *Reappraisals of the Scientific Revolution*. Cambridge: Cambridge University Press, 1990, 167–205.

—— ed. *The Copernican Achievement*. Berkeley: University of California Press, 1975.

INDEX

Note: page references in *italics* indicate illustrations

academies 197
Accademia degli Elevati 487
Acosta, Christobal *see* Costa, Cristóvão da
Acosta, José de (1540–1600) 10–11, 166–88; on Indian society and culture 179–81; on language 174–5; on native religion 181–3, 184–5; on natural history 166–7, 183–4; on origins of native peoples 177–8; on writing systems 175–7; *Natural and Moral History of the Indies* 166–88; *On Winning Salvation for the Indians* 178
Actopan, convent of 124
Adriani, Marcello Virgilio 263
Africa 10, 126, 168; on maps 146, 147, 154; Portuguese and 118, 120, 132, 144; slave trade 119, 120, 321, 561, 635
Age of Religious War 369, 375–7, 378
Agramont, Jacme d' 74
agriculture 89–90, 92, 143, 144, 193, 272, 273
Agustín, Antonio (1517–86) 244, *245*, 246, 247, 248, 249–50, 251, 252, 255, 256–9
ahidnames 351, 352, 353, 356
Aix-en-Provence 115
Alamos de Barrientes, Baltasar 319
Alberti, Leandro 227
Alberti, Leon Battista (1404–72) 23, 35, 372, 550; on cities 105, 107; on fatherhood 383; illegitimacy 486; on perspective (in *On Painting*) 7, 8, 53–6, 57, 63; study of Roman buildings 180
Albrecht Hohenzollern, duke of Prussia 210–11
album amicorum 204
Alcalá, University of 250–1, 253, 254, 255, 322, 582, 594
alchemy 195, 424–5, 488
Aldus Manutius (Aldo Manuzio) (c.1450–1515) 193, 203, 244, 572
Aleksander Jagiełło, king of Poland 560
Alemán, Mateo (1547–1610 or 1620) 200
Aleppo 88, 356, 357
Alexander VI, Pope (Rodrigo Borgia) (c.1431–1503) 39–41, 42, 46, 310–11
Alhazen (c.965–1039) 54
Allegrini, Romolo 400
Allori, Alessandro (1535–1607) 490, 492, *493*
alphabets 144
altarpieces 196, 296
Althusius, Johannes 159
Altona 565
alumbrados 607
Álvarez, Francisco 135–6
Alypius 536–7, 538, 541
ambassadors 199, 200, 355–6, 359–60, 560
Amberger, Christoph 462
Amboise, Edict of 562
Americas *see* New World
Amsterdam 102, 108, 114, 142, 198, 460;

Index

prints of 197; religious minorities 564, 569
Amyot, Jacques (1513–93) 193
Anabaptists 556, 558, 559, 564, 574, 600, 601–2
anamorphosis 61–2
anatomy 415, 616
Anchieta, José de (1534–97) 133, 621, 626
Anguissola, Sofisniba 387
animals, attitude to 470; *see also* apes
Annius of Viterbo 171, 246
antiquarianism: Spanish 242–61
antitrinitarianism 556, 564, 567
Antwerp: building 108; cartography 154, 155, 162; festivals 155, 157; foreigners in 115, 202; growth 102; publishing 154, 192; traffic jams 105
apes and aping 415–34
apprenticeships 113–14
Aquinas, St Thomas (1225–74) 578
Arabic language 132
Aragon 244, 246, 315, 316, 321
architecture: circulation of knowledge 198; and city planning 340; harmony 107; Manueline style 124; military 122; in new territories 122–6; pattern books 196; Plateresque style 123; publications 58; *see also* buildings
Arditi, Bastiano 485
Aretino, Pietro (1492–1557) 20, 232; and food 501–16; portrait 512, *513*; *The Courtesan* 504–5, 511; *Dialogues* 505–9; *The Hypocrite* 501–2; *Letters* 510–14
Arezzo 333, *334*
Argyropoulos, John (1416–*c*.1486) 548
Ariosto, Ludovico (1474–1533) 442–4, 446, 448; *Five Cantos* 442–3; *Orlando Furioso* 134, 442
Aristarchus of Samos (310–230 BC) 657
Aristotle (384–22 BC) 22, 45, 616; Acosta on 166, 168, 169, 173; and astronomy 655, 657, 661, 662, 663, 664, 665, 666; Dante and 436–7; and mimesis 446, 447; and Platonism 547, 548, 550; scholasticism and 578, 595; Sepúlveda as scholar of 248, 254; *Poetics* 446, 448; *Politics* 158, 193
Armada, Spanish 320, 376
Armazém da Guiné 146
Armenians 88, 556, 565

armies: ex-soldiers 398–9; papal 406–7; private 408; Spanish 320
arms: manufacture 89, 92; *see also* firearms
arquebus, wheel-lock 400–9
art: and allegory 235; apes in 426–7; battle scenes 333–4; bifocalism 57; circulation of 195–7, 198; collections 98, 196, 482, 488–94, 495–6; decorative arts 126–7, 481–2; drawings 196; Ficino's conception of the *idea* 551; hybridism 125–6; as illusion 236; investment in 95, 97; Madonna in 387–9, 392; mannerism 232, 236; monastic 293; Montaigne on 234–9; narrative cycles 336–8; in new territories 124, 125–7; and princely power 292–306; prints 196–7; Rape of Europa theme 155; realism and naturalism 64, 65, 287–8, 471–4; religious 336, 343; St Augustine in 535, *536*, 538–44, *539, 540, 541, 542, 543* 545–6, 548, 550, 551; skull symbolism 61; still life 61; triumphalism in 326–46; trophy art 334–40; window as metaphor 63; *see also* perspective; portraiture; sculpture
artisans 109, 114
Artois 292, 298
Asia: and European expansion 119–20, 126–7; geographical study of 129; on maps 154; Piccolomini on 141; political writers on 158; trade with 88
associations 109–10
astrology 172, 616, 617
astronomy 22–3, 118–19, 128–9, 167, 617, 657; comets 665; equant 657, 669; Galileo's observations 666, 670; heliocentrism (Copernicus and followers) 655–77; Kepler's system 669–70; *nova* 664; Uraniborg observatory 665
Atlantic Ocean 119, *125*, 320
Augsburg 109, 566; Confession 586
Augsburg, Peace of (1555) 566
Augustine of Hippo, St (354–430) 20, 23, 31, 535–54, 606; Acosta on 168–9, 173; conversion 536–8, 541–6, 551; depictions of 11, 20, 535, *536*, 538–44, *539, 540, 541, 542, 543* 545–6, 548, 550, 551; Ficino and 546, 548–9; influence on More 274, 280; letters

falsely attributed to (Pseudo-Augustine) 535–6, 545; on music 546–7, 550; and Neoplatonism 546, 547, 548–52; as student and teacher 544; theory of seeing and illumination 546–7, 549; *City of God* 47, 274, 280, 538; *Confessions* 536–7, 538, 541, 544; *Soliloquies* 549
Augustinian Hermits, Order of the 538, 544
Augustinians 124, 125, 589, 590, 591
Aurispa, Giovanni 192, 202
Austria 558, 561, 601
authorship and readership, theories of 19, 435–51; Ariosto 442–4, 446, 448; Cervantes 449–50; Dante and Petrarch 436–40, 445, 446, 447, 448, 449; dramatists 518; Erasmus 579, 595; Machiavelli 440–1; Montaigne 443, 445–6, 449; Rabelais 443–5, 446; St Augustine 544–5; Tasso 446–9
Avignon: Black Death 73–4; papacy in 31, 32, 557, 590
Azpilcueta, João de 624, 625
Aztecs 10–11, 170, 174, 178, 180, 181, 195, 316

Bacon, Francis (1561–1626) 166, 668
Bagnaia: Villa Lante 237
Bajazet II, Sultan (1447–1512) 42
Balkans 556, 557
ballads, popular 408
bandits (*banniti/banditi*) 17, 399–400, 402–4, 406, 407, 408
banishment 399
baptism 598, 600–1, 624, 633
Barberini, Anna *see* Colonna Barberini, Anna
Barbarini, Maffeo (Taddeo's son) 390, 392
Barbarini, Maffeo (Taddeo's uncle) *see* Urban VIII
Barbarini, Taddeo 389, 390–2
Barbarini family 390, 391, 392
Barbaro, Daniele (1513–70) 58–9
Barbaro, Marcantonio 359–60
Barbarossa, Chaireddin (d.1546) 316
Barbosa, Luísa 628–9
Barcelona 69, 79, 105, 192–3, 610
Baron, Hans 371, 440
Baronio, Cesare 323

Barros, João de (1496–1570) 200
Basle (Basel) 202, 203, 562; Basle, Council of 372, 561, 564, 585, 589
Baudouin, François 171, 175
Baxandall, Michael 64–5
Beatus Rhenanus (1485–1547) 192, 203, 246, 572
Becanus, Ioannes Goropius 171
Bechefer, François de 460
Bellarmine, Roberto (1542–1621) 194, 670, 671
Bellini, Gentile (*c*.1429–1507) 202
Bellori, Giovanni Pietro 427, *428*
Belon, Pierre (1517–64) 199, 200
Bembo, Pietro (1470–1547) 579
Bendysh, Thomas 357, 358, 360
Benedetto da Ravenna 122
Benzoni, Girolamo 135
Berger, Harry 455
Bertelli, Pietro 468, *469*
Bessarion, Johannes (d.1472) 548, 549, 551, 658
Bible: on baptism 601; censorship of vernacular versions 615; complexities and ambiguities 602; Complutensian Polyglot 253, 580, 594; Council of Trent and 606, 616; depicted in art 336; Erasmus and 21, 23, 169, 572, 580, 582, 594, 595, 597; and heliocentrism 662–4, 670–1; humanists and 580, 582–3, 584, 594; importance in Lutheranism 373–4, 375, 378, 421–2, 580, 582, 583, 596, 597, 598; literary writers and 442–5, 446–7; Reformation and 592, 595; translations 194, 572; and writing 365, 367; Zwingli and 597
biography 198, 262; portrait-books 467–70; Petrarch's *Lives* 307, 308; Vasari's *Lives* 326, 452, 470; *see also* prosopography
Biondo, Flavio (1392–1463) 173, 310, 343
Birckman, Arnaldo 318
bishops 607, 608
Black Death 8, 69–83, 140, 501; contagion 72–3, 75; contemporary attitudes to 74–6; contrasted to bubonic plague 70, 72–4; decline 80; development of immunity 73–4, 75, 80; effect on economy 91–2, 102; geographical

extent 69–70, 71; mortality rates 69, 73–4; and revolts 76–80; seasonal patterns 73; signs and symptoms 70, 72
Black Sea 88, 349
Blastenbrei, Peter 400
blindness 471–2, 473, 474
Boccaccio, Giovanni (1313–75) 141, 199, 438; simian metaphors in 418–19, 424; *Decameron* 70
Bocchi, Francesco 471
Bodin, Jean (1530–96) 136, 171, 172, 173, 175, 183, 185, 668
Bohemia 298, 315; religion 556, 557, 559, 563–4, 566, 567, 576, 584
Bohemian Brethren 563–4, 567
Boldroni, Niccolò 426, 427
Bologna: autonomy of 309; Carracci Academy 424; conquest by Julius II 45, 311; Dürer in 57–8; female labor 94; Protomedicato tribunal 613, 614; religious reforms 474; revolts 76, 78, 79; textile industry 88, 93
Bologna, University of 198, 202, 616, 658; Spanish College 248, 249, 253
bookkeeping 144
books: circulation of 191–5; on geometry 58; how-to books 505; illustrations 196–7; portrait-books 467–70; scarcity of 255; translations 193–5; travel 171, 194–5, 197, 227–31; *see also* censorship; Index of Prohibited Books; manuscripts; publishing
Books of Hours 296
Bordeaux 108, 616
Borgia, Cesare (1475–1507) 40, 41, 271, 311
Borgia, Lucrezia (1480–1519) 35, 40
Borgia, Rodrigo *see* Alexander VI
Borgia family 486
botany 130–2, 166–7, 616
Botero, Giovanni 101, 129–30, 136, 194, 315, 359
boti 457–9
Botticelli, Sandro (1444–1510) 487, 489, 545–6
Botticini, Francesco 545
Boudin, Michel 460
Brabant 298, 299, 301
Brahe, Tycho (1546–1601) 202, 665, 666, 669, 672–3

Bramante of Urbino, Donato (1444–1514) 43–4, 47, 310
Brandt, Sebastian 420
Brazil 120, 146, 319–20; Christianity in 621–36; creation myths 632; disease 626, 628, 631; language 132–3; *mamelucos* 630–1, 634; mission villages (*aldeias*) 626, 628, 631, 634; music and songs 624, 625; natural history 132; ransoming (*resgate*) 627; resistance 626, 631–2; Santidade de Jaguaripe (and "the pope" Antonio) 621, 623, 624, 629–35; schools 628, 629; shamanism 624–6; slavery 321, 626–8, 630, 634, 635; tobacco 625, 629, 632; wandering prophets (*santidades*) 625, 626–7, 628–9
Brescia and the Bresciano 92, 94, 96
brewing 106
Broederlam, Melchior (*fl.*1381–1409) 298
Brötli, Johannes 601
Brown, Patricia Fortini 97
Bruges 298, 304
Brunelleschi, Filippo (1377–1446) 180; and perspective 7, 53, 54, 55, 58, 343
Bruni, Leonardo (1369–1444) 307, 399, 548
Bruno, Giordano (1548–1600) 48, 199, 204, 668, 671
Brussels 157; Coudenberg Palace 291
Bry, Theodore de 195, 197
Bucer, Martin (1491–1551) 574, 585
Budé, Guillaume (1467–1540) 173, 192, 580–1
buildings and building programs: of New World native peoples 179–80; preserve of elites 96, 97; in Rome 33, 34, 35–6, 37, 38–9, 40–1, 43–5, 47, 102, 310, 311–12; urban 105–6; *see also* architecture
Bulhões, Cristóvão de 630, 631
Bünting, Heinrich 150
Buonaccorsi, Filippo *see* Callimachus
Buontalenti, Bernardo (*c.*1536–1608) 486, 488
Burckhardt, Jacob (1818–97) 270, 326, 342, 349, 365, 398, 440, 454, 482
burghers 111, 114
Burgundy: court and portraiture 13, 288–306; map 289; poverty 90
Burnet, Macfarlane 72

Byzantine Empire 33, 88, 136, 145

Cabral, Pedro Alvares (c.1467–c.1520) 319, 320
Caesar, Gaius Julius (c.100–44 BC) 307–9, 311, *317*; *Commentaries* 308
calendar reform 47, 566, 658, 663, 666
Calixtus III, Pope (1378–1458) 39
Callimachus 209
Calvi, Giulia 382, 384
Calvin, John (1509–64) 193, 374, 375, 560, 598
Calvinism 202, 377, 556, 557, 558, 562, 564, 565, 566, 567, 585
Camões (Camoens), Luis de (1524–80) 200, 203; *Lusiads* 157, 200
Campanella, Tommaso (1568–1639) 133, 671
Campion, Edmund (1540–81) 194
cannibalism 134, 627, 639
Cantino Map 146
Capestrano 483, 484
Cappello, Bianca (1548–87) 482–5, 487–8, 490, 491–2, 494, 495
Cappello family 491–2
Caravaggio, Michelangelo Merisi da (1573–1610) 551
Caravia, Alessandro 203
Carcassonne: revolts 77
Cardano, Girolamo (1501–76) 172, 184, 452, 661–2
Cardim, Fernão 132, 632
Caribbean 119, 321
Carpaccio, Vittore (c.1455–1522): Zanetti on 4, 24; *St Augustine in His Study* 11, 20, 535, *536*, 545, 546–7, 548, 550, 551; *Scenes from the Life of Saint Ursula* 3–6, *4–5*, 7, *9*, *12*, *15*, *17*, 17, *18*, 19, 24, *25*, 426, *426*
Carracci, Agostino (1557–1602): portrait of Gabrielli 452, *453*, 455, 457
Carracci, Annibale (1540–1609) 455; *Portrait of a Blind Woman* 471, *473*, 474
cartography 10, 24, 128–9, 196–7, 664; of Europe 145–56, 161–2
Casa, Giovanni della (1503–56) 506
Casali, Battista 45
Casino, Florence 482, 486–7, 488–94, 495–6
Cassirer, Ernst (1874–1945) 65

Castell Sant'Angelo, Rome 33, 35, 38
Castiglione, Baldassare (1478–1529): *The Courtier* 193, 199, 204, 231, 232, 234, 290, 502, 503, 504, 505, 508, 509; *see also* Górnicki, Łukasz: *The Polish Courtier*
Castile 242–3, 249, 316–17, 559
Cateau-Cambrésis, Treaty of (1559) 160, 225–6, 398–9, 555
Catherine of Siena, St (1347–80) 31–2, *41*
Catholics: as minority communities 556, 557, 558, 559, 560, 562–3, 565, 567; *see also* Church; Counter-Reformation; papacy
Cattanei, Vannozza (1442–1518) 39
Cazalla, Agustín de 255
Cellini, Benvenuto (1500–71) 198, 401–2, 487
Celtis, Konrad (Conrad) 104, 202, 209, 465
Cennini, Cennino 459
censorship 171, 194, 195; *see also* Index of Prohibited Books
Cervantes Saavedra, Miguel de (1547–1616) 200, 443; *Don Quixote* 157–8, 253, 449–50
Ceylon 120, 126
Chacón, Alonso 251
Charles IV (of Luxembourg), Holy Roman Emperor (1316–78) 293, 298, 299
Charles V, Holy Roman Emperor (1500–58): abdication 157; Aretino and 503; as Charles I, king of Spain 13; death 319; depictions of 147, 150, 157; extent of empire 312, *314*, 315–18, 319, 322; as financial patron of Rome 312; military architecture 122; and *moriscos* 561; palace 321; and Reformation 597; rise to power 160; sacks Rome 47, 160, 248, 307, 486; Sépulveda as chronicler to 248–9; triumphal processions 330; visits Antwerp 155; wars 159
Charles V, king of France (1338–80) 295, 299, 303, 304–5
Charles VIII, king of France (1470–98) 3
Charles IX, king of France (1550–74) 104
Charles I, king of Great Britain (1600–49) 304, 357–8
Charles the Bold, duke of Burgundy (1433–77) 288, 290–1, 293, *301*, 304

– Index –

Chigi, Agostino (1466–1520) 36, 42–3, 45
childbirth 575
children: contribution to economy 93, 94; custody cases 384–7
China 119, 120, 134, 147, 178, 200, 671; decorative arts 126, 127, 203; influence of European art 197, 198; writing 177
Chinucci, Tommaso 237
Chios 350, 351, 352, 353
Christ: authority of 373, 374; Erasmus on 169; and Madonna 387–9; as pelican 444
Christendom: as term 141, 143
Christianity: beliefs 20–2; in Brazil 621–36; communion 637–51; diversity within 21–2, 575–8; early writings 20, 21; and European expansion 119, 120, 132, 170–1, 197; humanist movement for unity in 572–88; importance to Rome 31, 33, 35, 48; and Platonism 548–52; scholasticism and 578–9, 580; world-view of 145, 146, 154, 168–9; *see also* Bible; Church; clergy; Counter-Reformation; papacy; Protestantism; Reformation; religion
Chronicles of Gargantua 443–4
Chroniques de Hainault 295, 295–6
Church: administrative fragmentation 585–7; calls for reform of 589–604; complexity of 593; consumption by 95; contradictions in 590–1; courts 386, 387; distinction between sacramental and judicial power 376; effect of printing and literacy 14–15; feast days 290; female institutions 112; and heliocentrism 662–4, 670–3; medieval 366–8, 372; property 104; revolts against 78–9, 555, 559; role in Europe 144; and scholarship 248, 249; Thomas More on 280; and trade 39; and triumphal art 343; and women 381; *see also* Bible; Catholics; Christianity; clergy; Counter-Reformation; Orthodox Church; papacy; Protestantism; Reformation; religion
churches: shared 567
Cicero, Marcus Tullius (106–43 BC) 192, 211, 217, 218, 220, 238, 271, 309, 537; definition of "author" 436; imitations of 419–21, 422–3; on love and fear 275; on oratory 417–18; on simians 416–17; on virtue 370
Ciompi, Revolt of the 78, 79
Cipolla, Carlo 91, 94, 96
Cisneros *see* Jiménez de Cisneros, Francisco
cities and towns 9, 101–17; architecture and planning 107–8, 340–2; citadel towns 102–3; cultures 108–10; economies 92, 93; elites 107–8, 111; fortifications and gates 103–4, 106, 122; growth 101–8; impact of migration 113–15; labor 94, 108–9; militia 111; neighbourhoods and parishes 110–13; in new territories 122–3, 124–5; as nodes of communication 200–3; plans and views 197; social status in 110–11; spatial organization 104–5; squares 107–8, 122; suburbs 105–6; zoning (lateral and vertical) 105
Civitates orbis terrarum 197
class difference 87, 89–90, 91, 96; in cities 105, 106, 110–11; *see also* elites
classical heritage (influence of): art 33, 55; cartography 161; circulation of manuscripts 191–2; cosmography and geography 127, 128, 129; historiography 166–7, 168, 169, 172–4, 182; humanists and 192, 193, 318, 371, 547–8, 578; language 144, 370–1; Polish scholars and 211; printing and 193; religion 182, 370–2; sculpture 195; translations 193; writers 7, 23, 191–2, 193, 211, 370; *see also* coins, ancient; Greek culture; Roman Empire; *and individual classical writers*
Clavius, Christoph (1538–1612) 47, 664, 666
Clement VII, Pope (1478–1534) 248, 264, 338, 490, 659
Clement VIII, Pope (1536–1605) 48, 559
Clenardus, Nicholas 199, 200
clergy: calls for reform of 589–90; and firearms 407–8; German 372; and healing rituals 611–12; influence of classical antiquity on 370; marriage 567; medieval 365–6; often uneducated 575; relationship with laity 372; and religious minorities 563, 567, 568; and spread of literacy 368, 369, 370, 371–2

climate, study of 172
clocks and clockmaking 89, 109, 175, 401
clothing 90, 92, 94, 97, 162; costume books (*Trachtenbuch*) 461, 462
Clouet, Albert 427, *428*
Clusius, Carolus (1525–1609) 131
coal 110
coca 179
codes of honour 408
codices 126, 170, 175–7, 195
Coimbra, University of 323, 616
coins, ancient: influence on art 33, 195, 335; study of 244, 250, 251–2, 257, 258
Colet, John (*c*.1467–1519) 192, 203, 589, 590, 591
Collaert, Adriaen, II 154
College of Cardinals 38
colleges: Jesuit 47, 169, 199, 563, 616; New World 119, 120; professional 110
Colocci, Angelo 247, 248
Cologne 158–9, 193, 558, 562
Cologne, University of 594
Colonna, Francesco 157
Colonna, Vittoria (*c*.1490–1547) 35
Colonna Barberini, Anna (1601–58) 389–93
Colonna family 32, 322, 389, 390, 391
Columbus, Christopher (1451–1506) 24, 119, 146, 194–5, 316
Comenius, Jan Amos (1592–1670) 159
Commandino, Federigo (1509–75) 59
Commynes, Philippe de 141
compass 167–8, 175
conciliar movement 372, 577
Condulmer, Elisabetta 462
confessionalization 21, 585–7, 605
Congregations 608, 609, 615
Constance, Council of (1414–18) 372, 576, 585
Constantine, Emperor (*c*.274–337) 322–3, 338, 601
Constantinople: fall of (1453) 33, 36, 349, 351, 548, 579; foreigners in 14, 199, 202, 353, 355–6, 357, 358; population 102; Venetian attack on 88
consumption 87, 89–90, 95–8, 481; of food (Aretino) 502–14
Continents, Four 145, 153, 154, 157–8, 160, 161

Contrario, Andrea 420
convents 112
conversion 536–8, 541–6, 551–2, 560, 561
Copernicus, Nicolaus (1473–1543) 22, 209, 655–77; censorship of 662, 670; dedication and preface to *On the Revolutions* 660–1, 662, 663, 669; diagram of heliocentric universe *656*; early support for 659–60, 661; education 658–9; later acceptance of theories 661–74
Coptic Church 135–6
copyists 255
Correia, Pedro 621, *622*, 623–4, 625, 635
Corselli, Margherita 385
Cortés, Hernando (1485–1547) 119, 123, 134, 195, 316, 317
Cortesi, Paolo 419–20
cosmography 129, 169
cosmology 22, 662, 663
Costa, Cristóvão da 131
cotton industry 92
Counter-Reformation 375–6, 446, 606–8, 612, 613, 615–16; *see also* Trent, Council of
court culture: Aretino on 502, 505, 506, 509–10, 512; Burgundy 13, 288–306; development from late Middle Ages 287–8; *see also* Castiglione, Baldassare: *The Courtier*; Górnicki, Łukasz: *The Polish Courtier*
Courtrai 298, 299
courts: church 386, 387; secular 609
Couvin, Simon de 74
Covarrubias, Diego de (1512–77) 250, 251–2
Cracow 202, 208, 209–10, 565; academy 658
Cracow, University of 209, 210
Cremona 88, 92, 93
Cristina of Lorraine 484, 485, 492
Cromberger family 199
Crow, Sackville 357–8, 360
Crucé, Emeric 159
crusades 36, 37, 88, 141, 377, 558
Cuauhtinchan, Mexico 125
Cuernavaca, Mexico 123
Curia 37, 38, 39, 43
Cusa, Nicholas 147

Daniel, Samuel (1562–1619) 199
Dante Alighieri (1265–1321) 23, 141; on authorship 436–8, 439–40, 442, 443, 445, 446, 447, 448, 449; *Convivio* 436–7, 447; *Divine Comedy* 437–8; *Vita Nuova* 447
Danti, Egnazio (1536–86) 58, 59, *313*, 666
Dantiscus, Johannes 199
Day of Judgment 633–4
death masks 455–60
Dee, John (1527–1608) 155, 664
Delfini, Gentile 247, 249
Desargues, Girard (1591–1661) 59
Descartes, René (1596–1650) 63, 67, 427, 428, 673
devil 610
Días, Bartolomeu (c.1450–1500) 320
Dias, Bras 631, 632–3
Dias, Diogo 633
Dias, Paulos 631, 632
Digges, Thomas (c.1546–95) 664–5
Dijon 102, 111
Dionysius the Areopagite 549, 643
diplomacy, new 349–50, 355, 356, 361
Diu, India 122
doctors 74–5, 512, 613, 614, 616
documents, identification 460–1
Dominicans 249, 612
Donatello (1386–1466) 53, 333
Donation of Constantine 169, 338
Donne, John (c.1572–1631) 22, 158, 198, 641–5, 647
Doria family 322
Douai 69, 70, 75
dowry system 382–3
drama 157–8, 310, 452; Elizabethan 24, 348, 361; Europa as theme 155, 157; stage sets 58, 107; *see also* Aretino, Pietro; Shakespeare, William
Dürer, Albrecht (1471–1528): collections of work 196, 489; and perspective 7, 8, 57, 59–61; visits to Italy 57; *Draughtsmen with Lute* 52–3, *53*; *Great Triumphal Chariot* 328, *329*; *Kaiser Maximilian I* 292; *The Martyrdom of the Ten Thousand* 465, 466; *Melencholia 1* 59–61, *60*, 465–6; *Portrait of Hieronymus Holzschuher* 463, *464*; *Rape of Europe* 155; *Self-Portrait* (Erlangen) 465, 465–6; *Self-Portrait* (Prado) 466
Dutch East India Company 135
Dutch language 171
Dutch Reformed Church 562
Dutch Revolt 159
dwarves 490
Dyck, Anthony van (1599–1641) 304
dyeing 94, 106

Eastern Europe 88, 161–2, 194, 199, 556; *see also* Hungary; Poland
Eck, Johannes (1486–1543) 591, 595, 598
economy 89, 91–5, 96, 101; *see also* consumption; production; trade
education 144; humanist 169–70, 578–9, 580–2, 593–5; Jesuit 47, 169–70, 199, 563, 616; medieval 368; in the New World 119, 120, 170, 628; and printing 581; scholasticism 578–9, 580, 581–2, 592, 593–5
Edward IV, king of England (1442–83) 279, 304
effigies, funeral 459–60
Egypt 41, 47, 88
Eighty Years War 159
Eitzinger, Michael 150, 155, *156*
Eleanora of Toledo 487, 492
electors 315
elites 95, 96–8, 107–8, 111; and firearms 407; merchants as 110; *see also* nobility
Elizabeth I, queen of England (1533–1603) 154, 155, 304, 334, 560
Emmanuel Filibert, duke of Savoy (1528–80) 108, 555
emperors 309, 315
England: agriculture 272, 273; Black Death 69, 79; Catholics 560, 562, 563, 585; Church 280; and concept of Europe 142, 143; funeral effigies 459; Lollards 556, 576–7; and Ottoman Empire 356–8, 360, 361; poets 22, 637–51; politics and monarchy 269, 270–1, 280; revolts 79; trade 88
English Civil War 357–8, 376
English Levant Company 356, 358
engravings 196–7
Enlightenment 23, 80, 428
Ennius, Quintus (c.239–169 BC) 416, 423–4

entrelacement 442
Epicureanism 274
epigraphy 251
equator 166, 168
Erasmus, Desiderius (1466–1536) 572–4, 576, 578, 583, 587, 591, 593, 663; and the Bible 21, 23, 169, 572, 580, 582, 594, 595, 597; on Christendom and Europe 141, 158, 159; compared to Luther 596–7; depictions of 266, *573*; followers harassed 607; Góis and 135, 136; Górnicki and 213; on Julius II 45, 331; letters 192, 572, 581; More and 203, 268; and Pseudo-Augustine 535; Thirty-Nine Articles 586; translated 193–4; translation of *logos* 578; *Adages* 421, 572; *Ciceronianus* 46, 416, 418, 420–1; *Colloquies* 572, 581, 594; *Enchiridion militis christiani* 582, 594; *Hyperaspistes* 572; *The Praise of Folly* 274, 278, 572, 579, 594; *Querela Pacis* 158
Ercilla, Alonso de (1553–*c*.1595) 200
Escorial, El 162, 256, 321
Este, Francesco d' 290, 300, *302*
Este, Ippolito d' 442, 481
Este family 196, 487
Ethiopia 120, 135–6, 168
ethnography 128, 131
Etzlaub, Erhard 147
Eucharist 637–51
Euclid 52, 59, 128, 659, 662; *On Sight* 55
Eugenius IV, Pope (1383–1447) 33, 310
Eurocentrism 347
Europa, Rape of 155, 157
Europa Virgo Crowned (Queen Europe) 145, 150, *152*, 153, 154–5, 160–1
Europe, conception of 140–65; arts 155–8; cartography 145–56, 161–2; culture 144–5; geography 143–4, 161; numerology 160; politics 158–61; representations 145–61; temporal and spatial limits 140–5; usage of terms "Europe" and "European" 141–3
Europe, early modern: map 16
European Union 162–3
Eusebius of Caesarea (*c*.264–340) 322
ex votos 457–9, 462
exile 399; see also *fuorusciti*
expansion, European 10, 118–39, 141, 262, 347–8; accounts and chronicles 127–8, 130, 133; criticisms of 134–5; cultural exchange 122–7; Genoa 95, 144, 315; impact on knowledge 127–37; maps *121*, *125*; Portugal 10, 118–20, 122, 124–5, 126–8, 134, 135–7, 144, 319–20, 621–36; Spain 10, 119, 122–4, 125, 128, 135, 160, 312–20; Venice 88, 315, 349
experience: and truth 127–8
experiments 483, 488
extraterritoriality 355
Eyck, Jan van (d.1441) 291, 303; self-portrait 466; *Leal Sovvenir* 455, *456*, 460

fallimagini 457
families 112, 391; see also motherhood
famine 69, 96, 273, 501
Fawkes, Guy (1570–1606) 269
federalism 159
Ferdinand of Aragon (1452–1516), king of Spain and Naples 3, 288, 310, 316, 564–5
Fernandes, Gonçalo 632, 634
Ferrara 202, 558
Ferrara-Florence, Council of (1438–45) 144, 372
festivals 141–2, 155, 157, 290
feudalism 400, 408
Ficino, Marsilio (1433–99) 23, 193, 209, 213, 546, 548–51; *The Book of the Sun* 658
Field of the Cloth of Gold 340
Filarete, Antonio (*c*.1400–*c*.1469) 33, 34, 107, 341
Findlen, Paula 98
fire 106
firearms 17, 400–9; see also arms
Fisher, John (1469–1535) 591, 595
flagellation 76, 80
Flanders: art 196; dukes of Burgundy and 292; dynastic change 298; genealogical portraits 296, *297*, 298, *299*; revolts 76, 77, 78, 290; tapestries 114, 339–40; see also Low Countries
flintlock 401, 408
flood control 277
Florence: architecture 107; Bianchi faction 399; Black Death 69, 73, 74, 102;

686

Casino 482, 486–7, 488–94, 495–6; civic improvement 340, 341; compared to Rome 33; depictions of Four Continents 157; Duomo 333; economy 95, 102; entertainment 482, 486; *ex votos* (*boti*) 457; female labor 94; fortifications 104, 122; ghetto 565; Greco-Roman influence 55; Machiavelli and 263, 264, 268, 270, 271, 274, 277; Medici family 482–96; Michelangelo and 336; motherhood 382–4; Neoplatonism 548; as node of communication 202, 203; perspective in art of 53, 54, 64–5; republican tradition 307, 308–9; revolts 76, 78, 79; silk industry 93; Uffizi 490, 491, 495; wages 501
Fludd, Robert (1574–1637) 424–5, *425*
Fontana, Domenico (1543–1607) 47, 157
Fonte, Moderata 381–2, 389, *390*, 483
food 20, 88, 89–90, 96, 127, 501–16
fortifications 103–4, 106, 122, 136
Foscarini, Paolo Antonio 671
fountains 44, 48, 237, 489
France: Black Death 69, 76; and concept of Europe 142–3; and Italy 3, 45, 159, 349–50, 555; Machiavelli on 158; and navigation 135; propaganda 304–5; religion 558, 559, 561–2, 563, 565, 566, 584; revolts 76, 77–8, 290; succession crisis 298; wars 77, 78, 103, 159, 160, 376
Francis I, king of France (1494–1547) 192, 195, 196, 198, 340, 503
Francken, Franz 157
Franco, Juan Fernández 251
Franco, Veronica 231–3, 238
Frankfurt Fair 200
frescoes 124, *125*, 337–8
friars 373
Frisius, Gemma (1508–55) 664
Friuli 608, 609
Froben, Johann (1460–1527) 203, 572
Fugger, Johann Jakob (1459–1525) 43
fuorusciti 399, 400
furniture 90

Gabrielli, Giovanni (*c*.1555–1612) 452, *453*, 455, 457
Gaismair, Michael 600

Galata 353
Galen (*c*.130–*c*.201) 195, 415, 416, 428
Galileo Galilei (1564–1642) 22–3, 26, 194, 488, 661, 662, 666, 668–9, 670–3; *Dialogo dei massimi sistemi* 671–3, *672*, 674
Galle, Philip 154
galleys (*galeotti*) 399–400, 406
Gallipoli 355
Galluzzi, Riguccio 485
Gama, Vasco da (*c*.1469–1525) 119, 146, 320
Garzoni, Tommaso 107
Gąsiorek, Stanisław 208
Gauricus, Pomponius 459
Gemistus, Georgius *see* Pletho
genealogies, pictorial 296–9
Genoa: expansion and empire 95, 144, 315, 349, 350; migrants from 115; poverty 89; revolts 79; silk boom 96; trade 88, 143
Gentileschi, Artemisia (1590–*c*.1642) 387, *388*, 389
geography, study of 128, 129–30, 172, 664; *see also* cartography
geography of Europe 143–4, 145–56; and circulation of knowledge 191–207; historical 161–3
geometry 58, 59, 64–5, 128; *see also* Euclid; optics; perspective
George of Trebizond 548
Germany: Charles V and 315; imports from Venice 88; Peasants War 376, 461, 598–600, 601; religion 558, 562–3, 564, 566, 567, 583, 584–5, 586, 595–6, 597, 601; textiles 92; writing 372
Ghent 76, 299, 304
ghettos 564–5
Ghirlandaio, Domenico (1449–94) 545, 550; *The Adoration of the Shepherds* 463–4, *466*
Ghirlandaio, Ridolfo (1483–1561) 267, *267*
Giambologna (Giovanni da Bologna) 489
Giese, Tiedemann 659, 661, 662, 663
Gilbert, William (1544–1603) 669
Giles of Viterbo 550, 551, 589–90, 591, 592
Gilles de Laveux 80

Giovanna of Austria 482, 483, 485, 490, 492
Giovio, Paolo 136, 467–8
glass 488
globalization 87–8
Goa 120, 124–5, 127, 130–1, 136–7, 203
God: as author 436, 446; Word of 599–600
gods, departure of 647
Góis, Damião de (1502–74) 135–6, 199
Golden Fleece, Order of the 292, 293, 295
Goldthwaite, Richard 95, 97, 98, 501
Gombrich, E.H. (1909–2001) 64
Gómez de Castro, Alvar (1515–80) 251, 258
Gonçalves, João 628
Gonzaga family 55, 196, 290, 322
González de Mendoza, Juan 194
Górnicki, Łukasz 208, 209–10, 211, 212, 213, 221–2; *The Polish Courtier* 208, 210, 213–14, 218–19, 220, 221, 222
Goślicki, Wawrzyniec 212
gossip 112–13
Gozzoli, Benozzo (c.1420–97): *Conversion of St Augustine* 542, 543, 544
Graf, Urs (1485–1527): *Battlescene* 334, 335
graffiti 195
grain 88; prices 96
Granada 321, 555–6, 557, 559, 561
Grebel, Conrad 600, 601
Greco, El (1541–1614) 198, 200
Greek culture 33, 45, 182, 195, 548; *see also* classical heritage; Orthodox Church; *and individual writers*
Greek language 132, 582, 583, 594
Gregory XIII, Pope (1502–85) 47, 225, 308, 487
Gregory XIV, Pope (1535–91) 323
Griffoli, Agnese, of Montepulciano 386
Grimani, Domenico 196
Groebner, Valentin 461, 462
Grotius, Hugo (1583–1645) 135, 204
Gryphius, Sebastian (1493–1556) 199
Guarani peoples 621, 623, 624, 625, 633, 635
Guariento di Arpo 541, 541
Guevara, Felipe and Diego de 251
Guicciardini, Francesco (1483–1540) 193, 308–9, 315

guidebooks 227–8
Guidobaldo del Monte (1545–1607) 59
guilds 94, 106, 108, 109–10, 563
guns *see* firearms
Gypsies 607

Habsburgs 144–5, 150, 155, 159, 160–1, 162, 181, 220–1, 290, 291–2, 331, 398, 558, 564
Hainault 292, 295, 298
Hakluyt, Richard (c.1552–1616) 195, 199
Harvey, Gabriel (c.1550–1630) 422–3
Hasselt, Jan van 296–8
Hebrew language 572, 580, 583, 594
Heidegger, Martin (1889–76) 63, 65
Heidelberg, University of 202
Heidelberg Confession 586
Helena of Russia 560
Hellius Hessus 344
Hendrix, Scott 584
Henri III, king of France and Poland (1551–89) 212, 233, 491
Henri IV, king of France (1553–1610) 107, 159, 460, 486, 491, 565
Henriques, Henrique 132
Henry VII, king of England (1457–1509) 459
Henry VIII, king of England (1491–1547) 263, 264–5, 271, 278, 280, 288, 293, 304, 323, 340, 585
Hentzer, Paul 227
Heraclitus 550
Herbert, George (1593–1633) 22, 642, 645–6, 647
heresy 368, 377, 555–71, 576, 668, 673; *see also* Inquisition
Hergot, Hans 600
Hernández, Francisco 131–2, 166
Herodotus (c.485–425) 172–3, 193
heroes: leaders depicted as 330–40
Het Spaens Europa 153, *153*
Hirschvogel, Augustin (1503–53) 58
history, study of: by Acosta 170–6; distinguished from biography 262; by humanists 371; influence of Roman writers 318–19; by Spanish scholars 242–61
Hoffman, Melchior 601
Holbein, Hans, the Younger (1497/8–1543) 202, 265–6, 293;

Erasmus 573; *The French Ambassadors* 61–2, *62*; *Portrait of Sir Thomas More* 265–6, *266*
Holy Spirit 599–600, 601
Holzschuher, Hieronymus 463, *464*
homosexuality 548
Hondius, Henricius 154
Horace (65–8 BC) 217; *Ars poetica* 56
host-box 126
household economy 94
housing 90, 105, 106–7; interior decoration 97; New World 123
Hubmaier, Balthasar 601
Huguenots 559, 561–2, 566
human exceptionalism *see* apes
humanism and humanists: and the Bible 580, 582–3, 584, 594; and cartography 24, 145; centers of activity *201*; and Christian unity 21, 572–88, 593–4; and church reform 372; and classical writers 192, 193, 318, 371, 547–8, 578; and concept of Europe 141, 159; and education 169–70, 578–9, 580–2, 593–5; importance of eloquence 417–18; influence 585; and language 370–1, 572, 578–9, 580, 582–3, 593–5; and new territories 135; and Ottoman Empire 359, 361; papal attitudes to 38; Polish 208–24; political theory 320; and printing 581; and the Reformation 572–4, 576, 577–8, 580, 583–7; in Rome 310; and simian metaphors 416, *417*; Spanish 224–61, 317–18, 607; tension between sincerity and prudence 219, 220; and travel and communications networks 199, 202, 203, 204; in universities 581, 582, 583, 592; *see also* Acosta, José de; Erasmus, Desiderius; Julius II
Hundred Years War 77, 78, 103
Hungary 195, 556, 558, 559, 564, 567
hunger 501; *see also* famine
Hurtado de Mendoza, Don Diego 250, 251, 255, 257, 462
Huss, Jan (*c.*1369–1415) 372, 556, 584
Hussites 557, 558, 559, 564, 566, 567, 576–7
Hut, Hans 601
Hutter, Jacob, and Hutterites 556, 601

iconography 293–6, 338, 459, 462
ideas, movement of 11–13
identities 17–20
idolatry 643–4
Ignatius Loyola, St (1491–1556) 157, 169, 607, 621
Ilhéus, Brazil 628, 631
illegitimacy 485–6, 490, 494
illumination, divine 546–7, 549
Imitation of Christ, The 193, 592
imperialism 13–14, 307–25, 347–8; *see also* expansion, European
Incas 123, 170, 174, 178, 179–80, 316
Index of Prohibited Books 194, 608, 614–18; and Copernicus 662, 670, 671, 674
India: architecture 126; art 126; bubonic plague 72–3; in cartography 146; decorative arts 126–7; fortifications 122; language 132; Portuguese and 120, 126; slave trade 561; Tamil language 132; towns 124–5
Indian Ocean 119, 130, 136–7, 320
indulgences 43, 575, 576, 598
industry 89, 91–5
inheritance 385–6; *see also* wills
Innocent VIII, Pope (1432–92) 39
Innocent X, Pope (1574–1655) 48, 141–2, *142*
Inquisition 134, 254, 255, 321, 449, 558, 559, 565, 605, 606, 607–11, 613, 614–18; and Brazil 623, 630, 634; Galileo and 673; in Rome 608–11; Spanish 607–8, 609–11, 616–18
iron industry 96
Isabella of Castile, queen of Spain (1451–1504) 3, 288, 316, 564–5
Isidore of Seville, St (*c.*560–636) 145, 416
Islam: astronomy 657; attitude to foreigners 351; in Europe 555, 556, 557, 558, 559, 561, 564, 565, 567, 568; law 352, 353; and portraiture 467–8
Istanbul *see* Constantinople
Italian Wars 103
Italy: cities 101–2, 103, 340–2; consumption 95–8; diplomacy 349–50; economy 91–5, 605; foreign students 560–1; France and 3, 45, 159, 349–50, 555; guidebooks 227–8; Jews 88, 558–9; motherhood 382–93; and

Ottoman Empire 349, 351–2, 355–6, 358–61; Protestants 608; Protomedicato tribunals 613–14; revolts 76–7, 78–9; Spain and 322, 408; territorial systems 359; trade 87–90; violence 398–41; Waldenses 555, 556, 559; writing 370; *see also specific cities and regions*
Ius Gentium 135
Ivan III, Tsar (1440–1505) 198, 560
ivory goods 126
Ixmiquilpan, Mexico 125
Izmir 352, 353, 355, 356, 357–8

Jacquerie 76, 77
Jamnitzer, Wenzel (1508–85) 58
Japan 119, 120, 147, 203; language 133
Jardine, Lisa 95, 98
Jerome, St (*c*.342–420) 545, 582
Jerusalem 355, 575
Jesuits: and astronomy 666–7, 671, 673; in Brazil 621–36; colleges 47, 169, 199, 563, 616; and historiography 157, 169–70, 172–3, 175–7, 181; and humanism 595; martyrs 621, *622*; missionary work 39; scholarship 192, 583; and slavery 627–8; and travel 199, 203; *see also* Acosta, José de
jewelry 126, 127, 335
Jews 376, 556–7, 561, 564, 565, 568, 580; burning of 76, 80; conversion 560, 561; distinguishing clothes and marks 558, 563; expulsions 558–9, 565; ghettos and charters 483, 565; home worship 562; in Italy 88, 558–9; in Ottoman Empire 352, 353, 355, 357, 559, 566
Jiménez de Cisneros, Francisco (1436–1517) 253, 580, 594
Jode, Gerardus and Cornelis de 162
John VIII Palaiologos, Byzantine emperor (1390–1449) 33, 36
Jones, Inigo (1573–1652) 107, 198, 199
journeymen 109
Julius II, Pope (1443–1513) 39, 41–5, 46, 47, 48, 311, 322, 486, 550, 589; portrait 331, *332*
justification, doctrine of 575, 598
Justinian Plague 70

Kappel, Second Peace of 565–6

Karlstadt, Andreas Bodenstein von (1480–1541) 598, 600
Karlstein castle, Bohemia 298, 299
Keere, Pieter van den 154
Kempis, Thomas à (1379–1471) 193
Kepler, Johannes (1571–1630) 22, 661, 664, 665–6, 668–70
Klapisch-Zuber, Christiane 382
Kleryka *see* Gąsiorek, Stanislaw
knowledge, circulation of 191–207; circles and sociability 203–5; images 195–7; people 197–200; routes and nodes 200–3; *see also* books; manuscripts
Koberger, Anton 193
Kochanowski, Andrzej 208–9
Kochanowski, Jan (1530–84) 23–4, 208–9, 210–13, 214, 218–19, 220–1; *Treny* 214, *215*, 216–18, 219–20, 221, 222
Kochanowski, Mikolaj 208–9
Komenský, Jan *see* Comenius, Jan Amos
Königsberg 210, 213
Kosovo 557, 567–8
Kraków *see* Cracow
Kristeller, Paul Oskar 371, 549
Kromer, Marcin 213, 221
Kryski, Wojciech 210
Kuehn, Thomas 383, 387

La Boétie, Étienne de 225, 226, 231, 233
la Tour, Georges de (1593–1652) 551
La Villa, Baths of 226, 227
Labé, Louise (*c*.1520–66) 204
labor 92, 106, 108–9; wages 94, 96, 501; women and children 93–5; wool-workers 75, 76, 78, 79, 94, 96
Laguna, Andrés: *Europa* 158–9
Laínez, Diego 628
language(s): and the Bible 194, 572, 615; diversity 144; grammar 371; humanists and 370–1, 572, 578–9, 580, 582–3, 593–5; and missionary work 623, 624; non-European 119, 120, 132–3, 174–5; Petrarch on 371; Reformed poets and 646; study of 253; translations of texts 193–5, 211, 549; *see also individual languages*
Lapps 135, 136
las Casas, Bartolomé de (1474–1566) 10, 134–5, 184, 248, 249, 321
Laski, Jan (*c*.1499–1560) 574

Lateran Council: Fourth (1215) 377; Fifth (1512–17) 45, 46, 551, 589–90, 591, 639–40, 658
Latin language 119, 132, 175, 192, 193, 194; humanists and 572, 579, 580, 593, 594
Lausanne 563
law: canon 593; humanist study of 249; international 135; Islamic 352, 353; knowledge of 387; More and 279; women and 112, 384–7
le Baker, Geoffrey 70
Le Roy, Louis 193
leather workers 115
Lefèvre d'Étaples, Jacques (1455–1536) 580, 594
Leibniz, Gottfried Wilhelm (1646–1716) 673–4
Leipzig 193; disputation 598
Leipzig, University of 660
Lencker, Hans (1523–85) 58
Leo X, Pope (1513–21) 45–6, 196, 505, 596
Leonardo da Vinci (1452–1519) 107, 196, 198, 203, 235, 277, 489; bronze horse 333; city plans 341; and notion of experience 127; and Pacioli 58; and perspective 51, 54, 56–7, 61; on portraiture 462, 463; on vision 56
Lepanto, battle of (1571) 320
Léry, Jean de 625
letters 192, 194–5, 231–3, 310, 384, 483, 581; of Anna Colonna Barberini 389–93; of Aretino 510–14; of Erasmus 192, 572, 581; of Spanish scholars 247, 251, 253–9
Levant 88, 90
libraries 44, 213, 250, 255, 256, 257, 548; Vatican 33–4, 38, 39, 44, 45
Liège 80
light 547, 551–2
Ligozzi, Jacopo 484, 492
Lima 119, 124, 132
Linacre, Thomas (1460–1524) 203
Linschoten, Jan Huygen van (1563–1611) 136–7
Lipsius, Justus (1547–1606) 192, 204
Lisbon 157, 561
literacy 14–15, 144, 368–72, 591, 595; medieval 365–8

literature: influence of European expansion 133–4; theme of Europa 157–9; triumphalism in 343; *see also* books; manuscripts
Lithuania 208, 210, 211, 212, 558, 560, 567
living standards 89–90, 95
Livorno 565
Livy (59 BC–17 AD) 318
Lodi 92, 93; Peace of 159, 399, 548
Lollards 556, 576–7
Lomazzo, Giovanni Paolo (1538–1600) 61, 424, 452, 471
Lombardy: manufacturing 92, 93, 95
London 102, 105, 106, 107–8, 111, 114, 142, 202; guilds and associations 109, 110; and Ottoman Empire 357; Thomas More and 269, 271–2
Lopez, Robert 91–2
Lorenzetti, Ambrogio (c.1300–c.1348) 341
Lorenzetti, Pietro (c.1306–45): *Birth of the Virgin* 57
Loreto 227
Lotto, Lorenzo (c.1480–1556) 203, 462–3
Louis XI, king of France (1423–83) 288
Louis XIII, king of France (1601–43) 143, 491
Louis XIV, king of France (1638–1715) 143, 304
Louis (II) de Male, count of Flanders (1330–84) 76, 296–7, 298
Louvain, University of 594
love 551, 643, 645–6
Low Countries: art 288; cities 291; dynastic change 298; Habsburgs and 290, 291; religion 601; *see also* Brabant; Burgundy; Flanders; Netherlands
Lübeck 110, 114
Lucca 78, 614
Lucian 421
Lucretius 273–4
Luther, Martin (1483–1546) 46, 226, 262, 268, 315, 372–5, 572, 574, 575, 591, 594, 596–8, 602, 607; attitude to lay authorities 598, 602; and the Bible 580, 582, 583, 597, 598; differences with other new doctrines 597–8, 599, 600, 601; and prints 196; translations of 193, 194; use of simian metaphor 421–2

691

Lutheranism 202, 210, 264, 377, 556, 557, 558, 562, 563, 564, 565, 566, 567, 586
Luxemburg, House of 298–9
luxury goods 88, 89, 97, 114, 144
Lyon 199, 200, 202, 204

Macao 120, 203
Machiavelli, Niccolò (1469–1527) 13, 23, 173, 193, 262–84, 310, 311, 342; attitude to authorship 440–1, 449; career 263, 271; character 268; death and burial 268, 270; depictions of 267, 267, 268; education 263; on the Ottoman Empire 359; and religion 269–70, 274; writings 264, 271, 273–4, 441; *The Prince* 158, 271, 274–7, 279–80, 281, 440–1
Maciejowski, Samuel 209–10
Macrobius, Ambrosio 145
Madeira 118, 120, 319, 561
Magalhães Gândavo, Pero de 132
Magellan, Straits of 178
magic 610–13, 616, 624–5
Magistrato dei Pupilli 384–5
Magli, Giovanni Gualberto 487
Maiorino, Giancarlo 236
maize 88, 90, 92, 95
Malatesta, Sigismondo Pandolfo (1417–68) 36
Malta 558, 561
Mander, Karel van (1548–1606) 196
Manetti, Antonio (1423–97) 54
mannerism 232, 236
Mantegna, Andrea (1431–1506); *Dead Christ* 61; *Triumph of Caesar* 317
Mantz, Felix 600, 601
manufacturing 89, 92–5
manuscripts: art 335; circulation of 191–2, 195; copies 255, 296; frontispieces 295–6; *see also* books
maps *see* cartography
Marburg, Colloquy of (1529) 597
Margaret of Navarre 204
Margarit i Pau, Joan (*d.*1484) 244, 246
Maria Maddalena of Austria 485, 492, 495
Mariana, Juan de (1536–1624) 557–8
Marlowe, Christopher (1564–93) 348, 361, 510
Marot, Clément (1497–1544) 199, 204

marriage 112, 113, 114–15, 155, 299, 386; dowry system 382–4; mixed 560, 563
Marseilles 70, 72
Martin V, Pope (1366–1431) 32, 35
Martin, John 455
Martines, Lauro 97
Martir de Anglería, Pedro 131
Mary, Virgin 387–9, 392, 459, 575
Masaccio (1401–28) 53, 54
masnadieri 398–9, 400
Mass, Roman 596, 597
matchlock 401, 407
mathematics 61, 64, 66, 616; Arabic influence 128, 143–4; and perspective 56, 57–9, 64, 65
Maus, Katharine 455
Maximilian I, Holy Roman Emperor (1459–1519) 291–2, 292, 296, 404; tomb 300, 301; triumphal woodcuts 327–30
Maximilian II, Holy Roman Emperor (1527–76) 561
Mazagan, Morocco 122
medals 335–6, 463, 467, 468
Medici, Alessandro de' 401–2
Medici, Antonio de' (1576–1621) 19–20, 482–500; background and life 482–6, 488, 494; children 495; collection of art and objects 482, 488–94, 495–6; death and burial 494–5; documents 488; experiments 488; heraldic device 494; as impresario 482, 486–7, 494; as Knight of Jerusalem 494, 495; portraits of 490, 492, 493, 493–4, 495; reputation 495
Medici, Bianca de' *see* Cappello, Bianca
Medici, Carlo de', Cardinal 495
Medici, Catherine de', queen of France (1519–89) 333, 491
Medici, Cosimo I de' (1519–74) 565
Medici, Cosimo II de' (1590–1621) 484, 485, 492
Medici, Cosimo III de' (1642–1723) 142
Medici, Cristina de' *see* Cristina of Lorraine
Medici, Ferdinando I de' (1549–1609) 484–5, 486, 488, 489, 490, 565
Medici, Ferdinando II de' (1610–70) 485
Medici, Filippo de' (1577–82) 482, 484, 490

Index

Medici, Francesco I de' (1541–87), 482–4, 486, 488, 490, 491, 494, 495
Medici, Giovanna de' *see* Giovanna of Austria
Medici, Giovanni de' *see* Leo X
Medici, Giuliano de' 457, 468
Medici, Giulio de' *see* Clement VII
Medici, Lorenzo de' (1449–92) 45–6, 457–8, *458*, 489
Medici, Maria (Marie) de' (1575–1642) 486, 491, 492
Medici family 270, 336, 482–96; portraits 490–4, 495; statues 234
medicine 88, 172; anatomy 415, 616; and censorship 617; new plants 130–2, 167, 489; superstitious healing and Protomedicato 605, 610, 611–14; surgeons 110; *see also* Black Death; doctors
Mediterranean 320, 348, 349, 561
Mehmet II, Sultan 33, 36, 351, 467–8, *469*
Mela, Pomponius 253, 254
Melanchthon, Philip (1497–1560) 210, 574, 579, 585
Melozzo da Forlì (1438–94) 39, *40*
Mennonites 556, 565
Mercator, Gerard (1512–94) 147, 150, 664
merchants 106, 111, 114, 144, 203, 272; associations 110; foreign 115; literacy 368; in Ottoman Empire 352, 357; and religion 561, 564
metallurgy 92, 93, 94, 488
Mexico 119, 134, 170, 178, 199, 312, 321; art 125; botanical gardens 132–3; language 132; map *313*; mines 320; writing systems 175–7; *see also* Aztecs
Mexico City 119, 122, 123–4
Michelangelo (1475–1564) 198, 234, 333, 344; and Capitoline Hill 312; portrayed by Raphael 550; Sistine Chapel paintings 43, 44, 311, 550–1; *David* 336, *337*
Middle Ages: cartography 145–6; education 578; interest in Roman writers 23; Marian devotion 389, 392; perception of apes 416; princely power 287–8; religion 365–9, 372, 568, 575, 581
midwives 575

migration, urban 113–15
Milan 69, 88, 92, 93, 321, 614
millenarian movements 633–4
Milton, John (1608–74) 22; *De doctrina christiana* 637; *Paradise Lost* 637–9, 642, 646–7
mining 92, 93, 94, 180, 181, 320, 488
Moctezuma 180, 181
Modrzewski, Andrzej Frycz (1503–72) 202, 212
Monardes, Nicolas 131
Monau, Jakob 198
monks and monasteries 293, 373, 590, 594
monopoly/monopsony 272–3
Montaigne, Michel (1533–92) 13, 23–4, 158, 163, 225–41; on animals 422, 423–4, 427, 428; attitude to authorship 443, 445–6; on Italian art 234–9; language abilities 229–31; on New World peoples 134; and Veronica Franco 231–3, 238; *Apology for Raymond Sebond* 423–4; *Essays* 19, 225, 226, 229, 230, 231, 234, 236, 238; *Journal de Voyage* 227–31, 234, 238–9; "Of Cruelty" 424; " Of Experience" 424; "Of Physiognomy" 470–1
Montalboddo, Francesco da 133
Montpellier 104, 616
Morales, Ambrosio de (1513–91) 242–4, *243*, 246, 247, 249, 250–2, 256, 258, 318
Moravia 556, 557, 558, 564, 601
More, Thomas (1478–1535) 13, 23, 192, 203, 262–84, 545, 582; career 263–4, 271–2, 278–9; character 268; depictions of 265–6, *266*, 269; education 263, 264; fall and death 264–5, 268, 269; sainthood 268, 269; writings 265, 272; *History of King Richard the Third* 270; *Treatise upon the Passion* 272–3; *Utopia* 133, 134, 141, 271–2, 273, 274, 277–81
moriscos 558, 559, 560, 561, 564, 607
Morocco 122, 134
Moroni, Giovanni Battista (1525–78): *The Woman in Red* 471, *472*, 274
Mosellanus, Petrus 579
motherhood 15, 381–97; breastfeeding and wet nurses 382, 390–1; case study 389–93; extent of involvement with

children 382–4; in religious art 387–9, 392; in Shakespeare 524–5; single mothers 113; Tuscan custody cases 384–7
Münster 561, 563, 567, 601
Münster, Sebastian (1489–1552) 147, 153, 227
Müntzer, Thomas (c.1489–1525) 599, 600, 601
Muscovy 173, 198
music 93, 175, 486, 487, 489, 546–7, 550, 624
Myszkowski, Piotr 211

Nadal, Jeronimo 197
Nanni, Giovanni *see* Annius of Viterbo
Nantes, Edict of (1598) 562, 566
Naples: Charles V and 315; depictions of Europe 157; festivals 142; manufacturers 92; as node of communication 202, 204; religious minorities 608; slaves 561; Spanish Quarter 108
Naples, University of 616
natural history 130–2, 166–7, 183–4, 424–5
natural philosophy 615–16, 617
naturalism *see* realism
navies: Italian 399–400; Spanish 320
navigation: charts 146; freedom of 135; instruments 118, 129, 167–8
Nebrija, Antonio de (*d*.1522) 244, 246–7, 248, 252, 253, 318
Nelli, Ottaviano: mural cycle 541, *542*, 544
Neri, Antonio 488
Netherlands: art 198, 291, 292, 296, 303; albums amicorum 204; governors 321; religion 558, 562, 563, 564; sculptors 195–6; tapestries 339–40; *see also* Low Countries
networks 114, 203–5
New World: Acosta on 166–88; architecture 122–4; art 124–6; in cartography 147, 153–4; Charles V and 312, 313, 315, 316–17; cultural changes 119, 120; food 88, 90; gold 39; language 132–3, 174–5; native peoples 10–11, 119, 120, 124, 125–6, 128, 134, 170–1, 174–85, 197, 621–36; natural history 131–2, 166–7, 183–4; Philip II and 319–20; religion 119, 170, 171, 181–3, 184–5, 321, 621–36; towns 122–3; writing systems 175–7; *see also* Brazil; expansion, European; Mexico; Peru
Newcastle-upon-Tyne 109, 110
newsletters 195
Newton, Isaac (1642–1727) 655, 673–4
Niceron, Jean-François 61
Nicholas V, Pope (1397–1455) 33–6, 43, 193, 310, 341
Nidecki, Andrzej Patrycz 211, 221
nobility 563–4; *see also* elites
Nobre, Domingos Fernandes 631, 633
Nóbrega, Manuel de (1517–70) 624, 625, 626, 628
North, Thomas (c.1535–c.1600) 193
Nova Europae descriptio 162
Novara, Domenico Maria (1454–1504) 658
numerology 160
numismatics 244, 250, 251–2, 257, 258
Nunes, Leonardo 624
Núñez de Guzmán, Hernán *see* Pinciano, El
Nuremberg: astronomy 660, 661; defences 104; humanism 581, 582; publishing 58, 193; religion 564, 582; shrine to St Sebald 344; silver bowl 150; triumphs 328; wheel-lock 401
Nuremberg Chronicle 146, 147

Observantine movement 590, 591, 592, 594, 596
Ocampo, Florián de 254, 256, 318
On the New Transformation of the Christian Life (*attrib*. Hergot) 600
Onegardo, Polo 170
opera 486
optics (and vision) 51, 52, 53, 54, 55, 56, 59, 63, 64–5; *see also* perspective
oral communication 175, 176, 191, 197–8, 365
oratory 231–2, 417–18
Oratory of Divine Love 592
Orsini, Fulvio 249
Orsini family 32
Orsino, Camilla da Lamentana 468–9
Orta, Garcia d' 130–1
Ortelius, Abraham (1527–98) 153–5, 204;

Parergon maps 161–2; *Theatrum Orbis Terrarum* 147, 150, *151*, 196–7
Orthodox Church 350, 351, 556, 557, 560, 561, 565, 567, 579
Orzechowski, Stanislaw 213, 221
Osiander, Andreas (1498–1552) 660–1, 662, 663, 669
Otto III, Holy Roman Emperor (980–1002) 293, *294*
Ottoman Empire 14, 41, 141, 144, 159, 221, 343, 347–63; Charles V and 315, 316; Constantinople falls to (1453) 33, 36, 349, 351, 548, 579; England and 356–8, 360, 361; European diplomats in 355–6, 357, 359; factionalism 360; Italy and 349, 351–2, 355–6, 358–61; Machiavelli on 158; perception of 347–9; religious minorities 350, 351, 353, 355, 556, 557, 559, 566; sultans' portraits 467–8, *469*; taxes 350, 352, 353; trade 356–7; treatment of foreigners in 350–6
outlaws *see* bandits
Ovid 125, 155, 157, 228
Oviedo, Gonzalo Fernández de (1478–1557) 128, 131
Oxford, University of 582, 594

Pacheco Pereira, Duarte (*c.*1460–1533) 127–8
Pacific Ocean 119, 120, 147, 320
pacifism 159, 601
Pacioli, Luca (1445–1517) 57–8
Padua 202, 203, 208, 333; Eremitani paintings *541*, 541 Poles in 210, 211
Padua, University 198, 203, 211, 561, 659
Páez de Castro, Juan (*c.*1520–70) 255–6, 257
palaces 291, 320–1, 341–2
Paleotti, Gabrielle 452, 471, 474
Palermo 102, 561
Palladio, Andrea (1508–80) 194, 308
Pallavicino, Ferrante 232
Panofsky, Erwin (1892–1968) 65, 303, 460
Paolo da San Leocadio 198
papacy: and censorship 614–15; centralized administration 608; and church reform 372, 373–4, 376, 377–8; encouragement of anatomy 616; instigates revival of Rome 35–60, 309, 310–12; Lutheran attitude to 596; medieval 367, 368, 369; patronage by 7; picked from obscure families 35, 39; relationship with emperors 312; and religious minorities 558–9, 565, 584–5; return to Rome 32–5; revolts against 79; schism 31, 32, 140, 577, 590, 593; scripture used to challenge 602; secularism 590; Suarez on 323; Swiss Guard 45; universities 44–5, 616; weakness 593; *see also* Vatican; *and individual popes*
Papal States: violence 398–9, 403–4, 405–6, 407, 408
paper 93, 368
Paracelsus (1493–1541) 202, 203, 488
paradises, earthly 162
Paris: the Marais 104, 108, 111; Medical Faculty 74; merchants 111; as node of communication 202; population 102; publishing 192; revolts 78; squares 107–8; spatial organization 104, *105*; university 582, 594
Parmigianino (1503–40): self-portrait 466–7
passports 460–1
Patrizi, Francesco 171, 173–4
patronage 7, 199, 326–7, 344, 440, 483
Paul II, Pope (1417–71) 37–8, 310, 658
Paul III, Pope (1468–1549) 47, 311–12, 660
Paul IV, Pope (1476–1559) 614–15
Pavia: relics and *arca* of St Augustine 538, *540*, 540–1
Pazzi conspiracy (1478) 270
Peasants War 376, 461, 598–600, 601
peddlers 91, 108
Pedro de Toledo 108
Pelagianism/Semipelagianism 575–6
Pélerin, Jean *see* Viator
pepper 90
Pérez de Oliva, Fernán (*c.*1494–1533) 250
perspective 7, 51–68, 343, 344; history 53–9; legacy of 63–6; as self-critiquing art 59–62; and stage sets 107
Peru 119, 123, 124, 312, 321, 489; Acosta and 170; buildings 179–80; language 132; mines 180, 181, 320; Montaigne on 134; religion 181–2; *see also* Incas

Perugia 45, 78; violence 400–1, 403–4, 405
Perugino, Pietro (c.1450–1523): *Giving of the Keys to St Peter* 41, *42*
Petrarch (1304–74) 23, 169, 199, 213, 512, 545, 582; on apes 19, 418; attitude to authorship and readership 417, 438–40, 445; influenced by Cicero 370; and Latin 32; on language 371; on Plato 547–8; and Rome 6, 24, 31–2, 242; and St Augustine 20, 23, 538, 547–8; on triumphs of the virtues 327, 343; *The Lives of Illustrious Men* 307, 308; *On His Own Ignorance and That of Many Others* 26, 578; *Secretum* 20
Petreius, Johannes 660, 661
Peuerbach, Georg (1423–61) 657, 658
Philip II, king of Spain (1527–98) 131, 153, 157, 160, 162, 176, 196, 318, 487, 558, 608, 616; imperial ambitions 319–20, 323; and Spanish scholarship 248–9, 254, 255, 256, 318
Philip IV, king of Spain (1605–65) 160, 320–1
Philip the Bold, duke of Burgundy (1363–1404) 288, 298
Philip the Good, duke of Burgundy (1419–67) 288, 290–1, *295*, 295–6, 298, 299, *300*, 304
Philippines 119, 319
philosophy: human exceptionalism 427–9; moral 371; natural 615–16, 617
physiognomy 470
Piccolomini, Aeneas Silvius *see* Pius II
Pienza 37, *37*, 103
Piero della Francesca (c.1420–92) 56, 58; *Battle of Heraclius* 333, *334*
pilgrimages 575
Pinciano, El (c.1473–1553) 252–5, 256
Pinturicchio, Bernardino (1454–1513) *41*, 41
Pinzio, Paolo 470
pirates, Barbary 315–16
Pirckheimer, Willibald 581
Pires, António 624–5
Pires, Tomé 130
Pisa 74, 565
Pius II, Pope (Piccolomini) (1405–64) 36–7, 103, 310, 372; on Europe 141; *Historia rerum ubique gestarum* 129, 130

Pius V, Pope (1504–72) 47, 48, 559
Pizarro, Francisco (c.1478–1541) 119, 134, 316
plague *see* Black Death
Plancius, Peter 154
plasterers 115
Platina, Bartolommeo (1421–81) 38
Plato (c.428–c.348 BC) 23, 45, 167, 193, 647; on art 236, 237–8; and astronomy 658, 668; Ficino and 548–51; Neoplatonism 546, 547, 548–52; St Augustine and 546, 547–52
Pletho 548, 549
Pliny the Elder (23–79) 168, 169, 173, 181, 183; on apes 416; on painting 235; Spanish scholars and 242, 253, 254
Plotinus (c.205–270) 546, 547, 548, 549, 551
Plutarch (c.46–119) 159, 193, 209, 251, 262, 657
Podlodowski, Stanislaw Lupa 210, 212
poetry 56, 195, 199, 310, 371, 550; English 22, 637–51; Petrarch on 440; Polish 212–13, 214–22; Tasso on 446, 447, 448
Poggio, Gian Francesco Bracciolini (1380–1459) 192
Poland 12–13, 161–2, 195, 202, 208–24; language 211; political thinkers 202; religion 556, 557, 559, 564, 565, 567, 574; royal court 211–12, 213, 214; Union of Lublin 212; women 213–14, 220
police 404, 406
political theory 135–6, 158–60, 173–4
Poliziano, Angelo 419–20, 457
Polybius (c.205–c.123 BC) 173, 251
population: and Black Death 69–70, 92; New World 119; urban 102, 103, 105, 340
porcelain 127, 203, 488–9
Porta, Giovanbattista della (1543–1615) 467
portraiture 19, 291–306, 452–80; artifice *v.* naturalism debate 470–4; of blind people 471–2, *473*, *474*; Casino collection 490; death masks and effigies 455–60; double-sided 300–3, *462*, *463*; evolution 452–4; as expression of power

291–306, 330–1; as identification 460–2; "independent" or miniature 299–303; as indicator of character 467–70; interiority problem 454–5, 474–5; medals 335–6, 463, 467, 468; move from likeness to representation 454, 459–60; panels 299–303, 462–3; parodied 427; pictorial genealogies 296–9; political context 303–5; portrait-books 467–70; reproduction 459–60; self-portraits 463–7; use of covers 462–3
ports 89, 561, 565
Portugal: expansion and empire 10, 118–20, 122, 124–5, 126–8, 134, 135–7, 144, 319–20, 621–36; Jews in 556, 558; military architecture 122; nautical charts 146
Portuguese language 132
Possevino, Antonio 172–3, 175, 192, 199, 567
postcolonialism 347–8
Postel, Guillaume 199
Potosí, Peru 180, 181, 320
poverty 89–90, 96; urban 106
power 13–17, 96, 348; relationship with art 287–306, 326–7; *see also* triumphalism
Prague 202, 342, 564, 566
Prague, University of 576
prices 96, 97
Primaticcio, Francesco (c.1504–70) 195, 198
printing 14–15, 89, 119, 120, 141, 157, 192–3, 194, 199, 200, 202, 368, 369, 572, 581, 591
prints 196–7
production 91–5
propaganda 304–5
property 91, 92, 104; and religious minorities 561, 600, 601
prosopography 154, 200, 203
prostitution 231, 232–3, 505–8
Protestantism 556, 557, 558, 559, 560, 561, 564, 565, 566, 567, 574, 583, 584, 606; and censorship 614; Inquisition and 607, 608–9; *see also* Calvin, John; Calvinism; Luther, Martin; Lutheranism; Reformation; Zwingli, Huldrych

Protomedicato tribunals 606, 613–14, 617–18
Ptolemy (c.90–168) 10, 22, 58, 59, 150, 168, 242, 255; and heliocentrism 655, 656–7, 661, 668; *Almagest* 657, 659, 662; *Geographia* 145–6, 147, 193, 196
publishing 119, 131, 155, 213; *see also* books
punishment 122, 399–400, 404, 406, 407; Inquisition 605, 606, 607, 609, 618
Purgatory 575, 576
Putsch, Johann: *Europa Virgo Crowned* 150, *152*
Pythagoras 145, 657, 663

Quad, Mathias 150, 153

Rabelais, François (c.1494–c.1553) 199, 204, 238; attitude to authorship 443–5, 446; *Pantagrel* 133, 157, 443–5
Ramus, Petrus (1515–72) 664
Ramusio, Giovanni Battista 195
Rangone, Ludovico 511
ransoming 627
Raphael (1483–1520) 43, 196, 236, 311, 489; Vatican fresco cycles 337–8; *Donation of Constantine* 338, *339*; *Pope Julius II* 331, *332*; *School of Athens* 45, 46, 550
raw materials 88, 96
Raymundus Chalmelli 73–4
readership *see* authorship and readership
realism 64, 65, 287–8, 471–4
reason 547
Recorde, Robert (c.1510–58) 664
Reformation 21–2, 46–7, 369, 372–5, 378, 560, 589–604; confessionalization 21, 585–7, 605; contrasting doctrines and movements 596–603; humanism and 572–4, 576, 577–8, 580, 583–7; and natural philosophy 615–16; *see also* Protestantism
refugees 197
Regensberg, Diet of (1541) 663
Regiomontanus, Johannes (1436–76) 657–8
Reichenau Gospels 293, *294*
Reinhold, Erasmus 660, 662
religion: authority and governance 364–80; conversion 536–8, 541–6, 551–2, 560,

561; cooperation 567–9; dissemination of texts 193, 194; and European travel 199; foreign diplomats 355; freedom of worship 364–5, 376–8, 555, 561–2, 563–4, 565–7; Greco-Roman 182; guilds and 109; house churches 562; medieval 365–9; millenarian movements 633–4; minorities and confessionalization 21, 555–71, 585–7, 605, 607; and motherhood 387–9; in new territories 119, 120, 170, 171, 181–3, 184–5; and Ottoman Empire 350, 351, 353, 355; and pacifism 159; persecution 114; pilgrimages 575; popular 591, 592, 606, 611–13, 618; pre-Reformation divisions 144; revolts 78–9, 555, 559; sacraments 575, 596, 597, 600, 606; segregation 564–6; transubstantiation 597, 637–41, 646–8; urban conflict 111; wars 375–7, 378; *see also* Bible; Christianity; Church; Counter-Reformation; Protestantism; Reformation

Renaissance, significance of 23–6
rents 96
republicanism 307, 308
Retiro Palace 320–1
Reublin, Wilhelm 601
Reuchlin, Johannes (1455–1522) 580
revolts 76–80, 290, 555, 559; *see also* Peasants' War
Rheticus, Georg Joachim (1514–74) 659–60, 661, 662–3
rhetoric 279, 371
rhumb lines 150
Riall, Lucy 93
Ricci, Matteo (1552–1610) 147, 197, 199, 203
Riccio, Il (1470–1532) 155
Riccioli, Giovanni Battista 666–8, 667, 673
rice 88, 92, 95
Richelieu, Cardinal (1585–1642) 103
Rigaud, Jean-Antoine 227
Rinuccini, Ottavio (1562–1621): *Euridice* 486
Ripa, Cesare 154, 196
Rodrigues, Álvaro 634
Rodrigues, Luísa 634
Roman Empire, influence of 6–7, 13–14, 23; antiquarianism 242–50, 257; art 333; building techniques 180; cityscapes 340; historiography 318–19; imperialism 307–25; maps 161; palaces 341; religion 182; statues 195; *see also* classical heritage; coins; *and individual Roman writers*

Rome, city of 31–50; academy 310; aqueducts and sewers 44, 47; Baroque 47–8; buildings, architecture and planning 33, 34, 35–6, 37, 38–9, 40–1, 43–5, 47, 102, 310, 311–12; *bulli* 408; Capitoline Hill 311–12; condition around 1400 31–2, 309; conflict with rural hinterlands 398–9; corrupt image 46; education 47, 616; effect of Reformation 47; finances 36; firearms 404, 405, 406, 407–8; fountains 44, 48; graffiti 195; Index of Prohibited Books 614–15; Inquisition 608–11; inseparability of past and present 38; Jubilees 35–6, 48, 659; Montaigne and 225–6, 227, 234–5; motherhood 384; murder rate 400; as New Athens 33; as node of communication 200, 203; processions 141–2, *142*, 341; return of the papacy 32–5; roads 43, 44, 47; sack of (1527) 47, 160, 248, 307, 486; St Augustine in 544; social mobility 9, 35; Spanish influence 310–11, 312; statues 195; university 44–5; women 35; *see also* St Peter's basilica; Vatican
rosary 612
Rossellino, Bernardo (1409–64) 37, *37*
Rossi, Bernardo de' 462–3
Rothman, Christoph (1550–*c*.1650) 665
Rouen: revolts 76, 77, 78
Rovere, Felice della 481, 486
Rovere, Giuliano della *see* Julius II
Rovere Colonna, Lucrezia della 389
Rudolf II, Holy Roman Emperor (1552–1612) 150, 202, 564
rural economy 92, 93, 96, 101

Sá, Mem de 626
Sabinus, Georgius 210
sacramentals 575, 611–12
sacraments 575, 596, 597, 600, 606; *see also* transubstantiation
Saint-Germain, Edict of (1562) 561–2

St Peter's basilica, Rome 33, *34*, 35, 43, 44, 45, 48, 310, 311, 312, 322
saints 21, 31, 608
Salamanca, University of 135, 252, 253, 255, 322, 582, 662
salt 90; cellars 126
Salutati, Coluccio (1331–1406) 307, 419
Salvador da Bahia 621, 626, 628, 629
salvation 575–6
Sambucus, Johannes 198-8, 202
San Gimignano 542–4
Sangallo, Antonio da (1485–1546) 122
Sano di Pietro 545
Sansovino, Francesco 468–9, 483
Santa Maria Maggiore, Rome 39
Santidade de Jaguaripe 621, 623, 624, 629–35
São Vicente, Brazil 623, 625, 626, 627
satire 514
Savonarola, Girolamo (1452–98) 3, 263, 270, 591
Savoy, Duchy of 555
Sayce, Richard A. 236
Scève, Maurice 199, 204
Schedel, Hartmann 146, *146*
Schleitheim Articles (1527) 601
Schmalkaldic League 376, 585
Schoenbeke, Gilbert van 108
scholasticism 578–9, 580, 581–2, 592, 593–5
Schon, Erhard (1491–1542) 61
Schönberg, Nicholas 659
Schwarz, Matthias 461, *461*, 462
sculpture and statues 195–6, 287, 336, 489–90; equestrian 331–3
Scupoli, Lorenzo 194
Sebastian, king of Portugal (1554–78) 319, 627–8
Sella, Domenico 93, 94, 95
Seneca 211, 217, 221, 235, 253, 550
Sepúlveda, Juan Ginés de (1490–1574) 248–50, 253–4 Serlio, Sebastiano (1475–1554) 58, 107, 196, 203, 204
sermons 197–8
Seville 102, 193, 194, 199
sex: in Donne's poetry 641–4; and food 502–3, 504, 507–9, 511; Inquisition and 609
Sextus Empiricus 424
Sforza, Bona 209

Sforza, Caterina (*c.*1463–1509) 35
Sforza family 341
Shakespeare, William (1564–1616) 157, 348, 517–32; *alazon* figures in 524, 527, 529; collaborations with Fletcher 517; father and daughter theme 521–5, 527, 528, 529; history plays 157, 525; lost son motif 525–6, 528, 530; marriage and children 523, 525–6, 528; wives and mothers theme 520, 524–5, 526–8, 530; *As You Like It* 520, 525; *Cymbeline* 519, 524–5, 528; *Hamlet* 26, 520–1; *King Lear* 519, 521–2, 525, 530; *Macbeth* 470; *A Midsummer Night's Dream* 519, 520, 527; *Much Ado About Nothing* 520, 525; *Othello* 361, 519, 521, 525, 530; *Pericles* 519, 523–4, 525, 527; *Romeo and Juliet* 460, 520; *The Tempest* 20, 517–20, 521, 522–3, 525, 526, 527, 528–30; *Twelfth Night* 525–6, 528; *The Winter's Tale* 519, 525, 526–8, 529, 530
shamanism 624–6
shoemakers 109, 115
Siberch, Johan 199
Sicily 69, 76, 88, 90, 102, 315, 321, 561
Siena 74, 76, 78, 96, 103, 340–1, 565, 614
signings 611–12
sight: spiritual 546; *see also* optics
Sigismund I, king of Poland (1466–1548) 209
Sigismund II Augustus, king of Poland (1520–72) 208, 211–12, 213
Sigonio, Carlo 211, 244, 249 silk industry 92, 93, 94, 96
Simplicianus 541–2
Sistine Chapel 38–9, 41–2, 43, 44, 311, 550–1
Sivello, Il *see* Gabrielli, Giovanni
Sixtus IV, Pope (1418–84) 38–9, *40*, 42, 44, 310
Sixtus V, Pope (1521–90) 47, 483, 608
slavery 10, 119, 120, 319, 321, 561; in Brazil 626–8, 630, 634, 635
Smyrna *see* Izmir
soap 94
Soares de Sousa, Gabriel 132
Society of Jesus *see* Jesuits
Socinians 556
Socrates (469–399 BC) 232

Soderini, Piero 263, 264
soul, immortality of 551
Sousa, João de 621, *622*
Sousa, Tomé de 623, 625
Spain: antiquarianism 242–61, 317–19; censorship 617; expansion and empire 10, 119, 122–4, 125, 128, 135, 160, 312–20; Inquisition 607–8, 609–11, 616–18; and Italy 322, 408; Jews and *Judaizers* in 556, 558, 564–5, 607; monarchy 320–3; *moriscos* in 558, 559, 560, 561, 564, 607; Muslims in 555–6, 557, 559, 564–5; navy 320; Protomedicato tribunals 613–14; religious orders 321; and Rome 310–11, 312; royal institutions 321; struggle for dominance in Europe 159–60; universities 250–4
speech 19, 417–18, 422
Speyer, Johann and Wendelin von 199
spices 88, 90, 130, 320
spies 195
Spina, Bartolomeo (d.1546) 663
Spranger, Bartholomeus (1546–1611) 196, 198, 202
Sri Lanka *see* Ceylon
states 14, 270–1, 330
statues *see* sculpture and statues
Stefan Batory, king of Poland 213, 220, 221
Stock, Brian 544–5
Stoer, Lorenz (1540–1620) 58
Strambi, Domenico 544
Strasbourg 202, 557, 563, 590–1
Strozzi, Alessandra 384
Suarez, Francisco (1548–1617) 323
Suetonius 318
sugar 120, 319, 627, 628
Sully, Maximilien de Béthune, Duke of (1560–1641) 159
Summers, David 452, 454
superstition 605, 606, 609–13
Sutton, Christopher 640
Swiss Brethren 601
Swiss Confederation 565–6, 582, 597

tableware 127
Tacitus (*c*.55–120) 171, 173, 318, 319
taifes 350, 351
tailors 115

Talavera la Vieja 251
tapestries 338–40
Tarragona 257, 258
Tasso, Torquato (1544–95) 446–9, 483
taverns: Aretino on 504–5, 511
taxes: elites and 96; hearth 106; in Ottoman Empire 350, 352, 353; revolts against 77, 78, 79; rises 79, 96
technology 89
Tempietto, Rome 310
Ter Duinen, abbey of 298, 299
textile industry 76, 77, 92, 93, 94, 96, 271; employment 106; technology 89; trade 88; *see also* wool industry
Thevet, André 128, 195
Thirty Years War 145, 159, 160, 376
Thucydides (*c*.460–*c*.400 BC) 173, 193
Ticci (Tizio), Sigismondo 48
Titian (*c*.1488–1576) 155, 195, 198, 331, 333, 426, 462, 510; *Portrait of Pietro Aretino* 512, *513*
Tivoli: Villa d'Este 237
tobacco 625, 629, 632
Toledo 123, 251, 608
Tolosani, Giovanni Maria (*c*.1471–1549) 663
Tomaso da Modena 7
Torda, Diet of 567
Tornabuoni, Maddalena Nerli 383
Torrigiano, Pietro 459
torture 609
Toulmin, Stephen 428
Tournai 69, 75, 77
Tovar, Juan de 170, 176–7
towns *see* cities and towns trade 8, 39, 87–8, 89–90, 143–4; and Ottoman Empire 356–7; routes 91, 200–3
transport 200
transubstantiation 61, 597, 637–41, 646–8
Transylvania 556, 567
travel, European 198–200; books 171, 194–5, 197, 227–31; dangers of 402, 408; routes 200–3, 266–7
Trent, Council of (1545–63) 47, 127, 250, 375–6, 386, 448, 449, 471, 586, 591, 606–7, 608, 616; and censorship 614, 615
Treschel, Johann 199
Treviso 79, 612
triumphalism: in art 14, 326–46;

processions 311, 316, 334–5, 340, 341; reasons for 342–4
Tuchins 77
Tunis 316
Tupi peoples 623, 624, 625, 627, 632, 633, 635
Turin 108, 109, 114
Tuscany: child custody cases 384–9; metallurgy 93; Pius II and 36, 37; religious minorities 565
Tyard, Pontus de (c.1521–1605) 664
Tyrol 599, 600

United Provinces 143; religion 557, 562; see also Netherlands
universities 144, 197, 198, 202, 581, 582, 583, 592; and languages 594; medical faculties 613, 659; and natural philosophy 616; New World 119; papacy and 44–5, 616; and religion 560–1, 576; Spanish 250–4; see also individual universities
Urban VIII, Pope (1568–1644) 671, 672, 389–90
urbanisation see cities and towns
Ursula, St 34, 158–9, 214, 629; Scenes from the Life of (Carpaccio) 3–6, 4–5, 7, 9, 12, 15, 17, 17, 18, 19, 24, 25, 426, 426
utopian genre 133
Utrecht, Union of (1579) 562

Valdés, Juan de (1500–41) 204
Valencia 198, 555, 559
Valla, Lorenzo (c.1405–57) 169, 175, 199
Valladolid 106, 252, 255
Valois dynasty 160, 212; dukes of Burgundy 290, 291, 293, 298
Vasari, Giorgio (1511–74): on casting 459; as painter 333; on portraiture 452, 454, 457, 466, 546; Lives of the Most Eminent Italian Architects, Painters and Sculptors ... 326, 452, 470
Vatican: improvements to 36, 37–9, 40–1, 43, 44, 311, 333, 341; library 33–4, 38, 39, 44, 45; museums 44, 48; Reformation and 47; stanze 337–8; Tower of Winds 666; see also Sistine Chapel
Veneto 90, 92, 93, 103
Venice: in 1490s 3; bull-running 111;

Cappello family 491–2; censorship 614; consumption 95–6, 97–8, 102; court 502; defences 104; diet 88; elites 111; expansion and empire 88, 315, 349; firearms 404, 406; ghetto 565; health concerns 105; industry 92, 93, 95; Inquisition 608–9; Julius II and 45; labor 94; library 548; luxury goods 97–8; merchants 110, 115; Montaigne and 226, 231–2; as node of communication 202, 203; and Ottoman Empire 359–60; Patriarchal Court (and mothers' rights) 386, 387; Piazza San Marco 107; poverty 89, 90; prints of 197; prostitution 231, 232–3; publishing 192, 193, 194, 199; religious minorities 556, 560, 561, 565, 569, 608–9; republican tradition 307; and St Ursula 4; slaves 561; statues 333; street names 105; surgeons 110; trade 87–8, 90, 143; women 94, 97
Vergara, Juan de 253, 254
Vesalius, Andreas (1514–64) 23, 415–16, 428
Vespucci, Giorgio Antonio (1434–1514) 545–6
Viator (c.1435–1524) 57
Vienna 202, 213, 559
Vignola, Jacopo Barozzi da (1507–73) 58, 59
Villani, Filippo 419
Villani, Matteo 60, 70, 75
villas 237
violence 109, 111, 398–411; domestic 112
Virgil (70–19 BC) 23, 309, 437, 442; Aeneid 193, 209
Vischer, Nicolaes 154, 155 Visconti, Domenico 487
Visconti, Filippo Maria, duke of Milan (1392–1447) 296, 304
Visigoths 257
vision see optics
visitation records 586
Vitruvius 57, 107, 193
Vives, Juan Luis (1492–1540) 141, 580

wages 94, 96, 501
Waldenses 555, 556, 558, 559, 560
Waldseemüller, Martin (c.1480–c.1521) 147, 148, 149

warfare: arms 89, 92, 406–7; and concept of Europe 159; economic burden 96; just-war doctrine 627; religious 369, 375–8, 559; Spanish resources 320; techniques and ideology 144
Warsaw 212, 564
weapons *see* arms; firearms
weavers: Flanders 76, 77
Wenceslas IV, king of Bohemia (1361–1419) 298–9
Westphalia, Peace of (1648) 369, 376, 377
Weyden, Rogier van der (d.1464) 196, 291, *295*, 300, *302*
wheel-lock 400–9
Widmanstetter, Johann Albrecht 659
widows 112, 382–3, 384, 385, 392
Wieland, Johann 557
William of Orange (1650–1702) 143
wills 75–6, 90, 112, 383
Wills, Garry 537–8
witchcraft 610, 612–13, 614
Wittenberg 202, 599, 660
Wittenberg, University of 583, 598, 662
Wolsey, Thomas (*c.*1475–1530) 263, 264
women: in art 333–4; contribution to economy 91, 93–5; Donne on 644–5; education 580; elite 97, 112; and European expansion 119, 120; and gossip 112–13; growing autonomy of 17; as healers 611; illegitimate 486; and law 112; literacy 595; Polish attitudes to 213–14, 220; in Rome 35; and social networks 204; urban 97, 111–13; *see also* motherhood; widows
woodcuts: German 327–30, 333
wool industry: in England 272; workers 75, 76, 78, 79, 94, 96
world, center of 147
"world picture" concept 63, 65
writing: alphabets 144; Chinese 177; copyists 255; New World 175–7; and religious authority 365–9, 372
Wycliffe, John (*c.*1329–84) 556, 576, 592

Ximénes de Cisneros *see* Jiménez de Cisneros, Francisco

Yates, Frances 204
Yersin, Alexandre (1863–1943) 70

Zacatecas, Mexico 320
Zamoyski, Jan 213
Zanetti, Anton Maria 4, 24
zimmis 350, 353
Zsámboky, János *see* Sambucus, Johannes
Zuñiga, Diego de 671
Zurich 597, 600, 601
Zurita, Jerónimo (1512–80) 246, 247, 249–50, 251–2, 253, 254–9
Zwickau prophets 599, 600
Zwinger, Theodor 171, 227
Zwingli, Huldrych (1484–1531) 375, 556, 582, 585, 597–8, 599, 600, 601, 602

eBooks – at www.eBookstore.tandf.co.uk

A library at your fingertips!

eBooks are electronic versions of printed books. You can store them on your PC/laptop or browse them online.

They have advantages for anyone needing rapid access to a wide variety of published, copyright information.

eBooks can help your research by enabling you to bookmark chapters, annotate text and use instant searches to find specific words or phrases. Several eBook files would fit on even a small laptop or PDA.

NEW: Save money by eSubscribing: cheap, online access to any eBook for as long as you need it.

Annual subscription packages

We now offer special low-cost bulk subscriptions to packages of eBooks in certain subject areas. These are available to libraries or to individuals.

For more information please contact webmaster.ebooks@tandf.co.uk

We're continually developing the eBook concept, so keep up to date by visiting the website.

www.eBookstore.tandf.co.uk

9780415455114